FISKE GUIDE TO COLLEGES

2018

FISKE GUIDE TO COLLEGES 2018

EDWARD B. FISKE

former Education Editor of
the *New York Times*

with Michelle Lecuyer
and
the *Fiske Guide to Colleges* staff

 sourcebooks

Published by Sourcebooks, Inc.
P.O. Box 4410
Naperville, Illinois 60567-4410
(630) 961-3900
Fax: (630) 961-2168
www.sourcebooks.com

Thirty-Fourth Edition

**Your comments and corrections
are welcome. Please send them to:**

Fiske Guide to Colleges
Email: editor@fiskeguide.com

Printed and bound in the United States of America.

DR 10 9 8 7 6 5 4 3 2 1

To Sunny

Contents

Index by State and Country

The colleges in this guide are listed alphabetically and cross-referenced for your convenience. Below is a list of the selected colleges grouped by state. Following this listing, you will find additional listings that categorize the colleges by their yearly costs of attendance and by the average debt accrued by students during their tenure at each school.

University of North Carolina
  Wilmington, 524
North Carolina State University, 527
Wake Forest University, 769
Warren Wilson College, 772

OHIO
Case Western Reserve, 128
University of Cincinnati, 147
University of Dayton, 209
Denison University, 217
Hiram College, 331
Kenyon College, 417
Miami University, 471
Oberlin College, 538
Ohio State University, 546
Ohio University, 549
Ohio Wesleyan University, 551
Wittenberg University, 819
The College of Wooster, 824

OKLAHOMA
University of Oklahoma, 553
University of Tulsa, 742

OREGON
Lewis & Clark College, 432
University of Oregon, 559
Oregon State University, 562
Reed College, 603
Willamette University, 809

PENNSYLVANIA
Allegheny College, 13
Bryn Mawr College, 86
Bucknell University, 88
Carnegie Mellon University, 125
Dickinson College, 227
Drexel University, 232
Franklin and Marshall College, 272
Gettysburg College, 290
Haverford College, 323
Juniata College, 406
Lafayette College, 422
Lehigh University, 429
Muhlenberg College, 499
University of Pennsylvania, 566
Pennsylvania State University, 569
University of Pittsburgh, 574
Susquehanna University, 707
Swarthmore College, 709

Ursinus College, 747
Villanova University, 760
Washington and Jefferson College, 777

RHODE ISLAND
Brown University, 82
Providence College, 588
University of Rhode Island, 608
Rhode Island School of Design, 610

SOUTH CAROLINA
College of Charleston, 140
Clemson University, 167
Furman University, 274
Presbyterian College, 577
University of South Carolina, 672
Wofford College, 822

TENNESSEE
Rhodes College, 613
University of the South (Sewanee),
  670
University of Tennessee Knoxville,
  715
Vanderbilt University, 752

TEXAS
Austin College, 43
Baylor University, 56
University of Dallas, 201
Rice University, 615
Southern Methodist University, 677
Southwestern University, 680
University of Texas at Austin, 717
University of Texas at Dallas, 720
Texas A&M University, 722
Texas Christian University, 725
Texas Tech University, 727
Trinity University, 732

UTAH
Brigham Young University, 79
University of Utah, 749

VERMONT
Bennington College, 61
Champlain College, 135
Marlboro College, 451
Middlebury College, 479
Saint Michael's College, 648
University of Vermont, 757

VIRGINIA
George Mason University, 277
Hampden–Sydney College, 311
Hollins University, 338
James Madison University, 401
University of Mary Washington, 456
Randolph College, 598
University of Richmond, 617
University of Virginia, 762
Virginia Tech, 765
Washington and Lee University, 780
College of William and Mary, 811

WASHINGTON
The Evergreen State College, 255
Gonzaga University, 292
University of Puget Sound, 591
Seattle University, 662
University of Washington, 775
Whitman College, 804

WASHINGTON, D.C. (SEE DISTRICT OF COLUMBIA)

WEST VIRGINIA
West Virginia University, 797

WISCONSIN
Alverno College, 18
Beloit College, 59
Lawrence University, 426
Marquette University, 453
Ripon College, 620
University of Wisconsin–Madison,
  817

CANADA
University of British Columbia, 366
McGill University, 369
Queen's University, 371
University of Toronto, 373

GREAT BRITAIN AND IRELAND
University of Aberdeen, 378
University of Edinburgh, 381
University of Glasgow, 384
University of St Andrews, 387
Trinity College Dublin, 390

Index by Price

	PUBLIC	PRIVATE
$$$$	More than $13,500	More than $50,000
$$$	$11,001–$13,500	$46,001–50,000
$$	$9,500–$11,000	$41,000–$46,000
$	Less than $9,500	Less than $41,000

Price categories are based on current tuition and fees and do not include room, board, transportation, and other expenses.

PUBLIC COLLEGES AND UNIVERSITIES

PRIVATE COLLEGES AND UNIVERSITIES

* These colleges are public institutions, but Americans and other non-Europeans
  should compare them in cost and academic quality to top U.S. privates.

Index by Average Debt

$$$$	More than $32,500
$$$	$27,001–$32,500
$$	$22,500–$27,000
$	Less than $22,500

Debt categories are based on the average cumulative amount of principal borrowed per undergraduate at each college or university during their tenure as a student. Public and private institutions have been rated using the same criteria. Institutions for which data on average borrowing was unavailable have been omitted.

LOW AVERAGE DEBT—$

Amherst College, 23
Barnard College, 51
Bates College, 54
Birmingham–Southern College, 66
Boston College, 69
Bowdoin College, 74
Brigham Young University, 79
Brown University, 82
UC–Berkeley, 96
UC–Davis, 99
UC–Irvine, 102
UC–Los Angeles, 104
UC–Riverside, 106
UC–San Diego, 109
UC–Santa Barbara, 111
California Institute of Technology, 116
Carleton College, 122
University of Chicago, 143
Colgate University, 171
Colorado College, 177
The Cooper Union, 192
Dartmouth College, 203
Davidson College, 207
Deep Springs College, 212
Duke University, 235
Emerson College, 247
The Evergreen State College, 255
University of Florida, 260
University of Georgia, 285
Grinnell College, 301
Hamilton College, 308
Harvard University, 319
Haverford College, 323
Loyola University Maryland, 436
Macalester College, 444
University of Mary Washington, 456
University of Miami (FL), 469

Middlebury College, 479
New College of Florida, 504
University of North Carolina at Chapel Hill, 521
North Carolina State University, 527
Olin College of Engineering, 556
Pitzer College, 155
Pomona College, 157
Princeton University, 582
Principia College, 586
Reed College, 603
St. Mary's College of Maryland, 645
Sarah Lawrence College, 660
Scripps College, 159
Smith College, 667
University of the South (Sewanee), 670
Stanford University, 683
SUNY–College at Geneseo, 695
Swarthmore College, 709
University of Texas at Dallas, 720
University of Utah, 749
Vanderbilt University, 752
Vassar College, 755
Warren Wilson College, 772
University of Washington, 775
Washington and Lee University, 780
Wellesley College, 788
Whitman College, 804
Williams College, 814
Xavier University of Louisiana, 829
Yale University, 832

MODERATE AVERAGE DEBT—$$

University of Arizona, 25
Arizona State University, 28
University of Arkansas, 31
College of the Atlantic, 39

Bryn Mawr College, 86
Bucknell University, 88
UC–Santa Cruz, 114
College of Charleston, 140
Claremont McKenna College, 150
Colby College, 169
University of Colorado–Boulder, 174
Colorado State University, 181
University of Connecticut, 187
Cornell University, 197
DePauw University, 225
Drew University, 230
Earlham College, 239
Emory University, 249
Eugene Lang College–The New School for Liberal Arts, 252
Florida State University, 268
Fordham University, 270
Franklin & Marshall College, 272
Georgetown University, 282
Georgia Institute of Technology, 287
Guilford College, 303
Hampshire College, 313
University of Hawaii–Manoa, 326
College of the Holy Cross, 341
Howard University, 350
University of Illinois at Urbana–Champaign, 355
James Madison University, 401
The Johns Hopkins University, 403
Kenyon College, 417
Lewis & Clark College, 432
Louisiana State University, 434
University of Maryland, 458
University of Maryland Baltimore County, 460
Massachusetts Institute of Technology, 465

The Best Buys of 2018

Following is a list of 38 colleges and universities that qualify as Best Buys based on the quality of their academic offerings in relation to the cost of attendance.
(See page xxi for an explanation of how Best Buys were identified.)

Public

Arizona State University
The Evergreen State College
University of Florida
University of Iowa
University of Maryland
University of Missouri
University of Nebraska–Lincoln
New College of Florida
University of North Carolina Asheville
University of North Carolina at Chapel Hill
North Carolina State University
University of Oregon
SUNY–Binghamton University
SUNY–University at Buffalo
SUNY–College at Geneseo
Texas A&M University
Truman State University
University of Utah
University of Washington
University of Wisconsin–Madison

Private

Brigham Young University
Centre College
The Cooper Union
Earlham College
Florida Southern College
Guilford College
McGill University*
Mount Holyoke College
Oglethorpe University
Olin College of Engineering
Principia College
Rice University
University of St Andrews*
St. Olaf College
University of the South (Sewanee)
Warren Wilson College
Wheaton College (IL)
Xavier University of Louisiana

*These colleges are public institutions, but Americans and other non-Europeans should compare them in cost and academic quality to top U.S. privates.

Introduction

FISKE GUIDE TO COLLEGES—AND HOW TO USE IT

The 2018 edition of the *Fiske Guide to Colleges* is a revised and updated version of a book that has been a bestseller since it first appeared over three decades ago and is universally regarded as the definitive college guide of its type. Features of the new edition include:

- Updated write-ups on more than 300 of the country's best and most interesting colleges and universities

- An index that categorizes the colleges according to how much debt, on average, students accumulate during their tenure at each school

- A list of schools that no longer require the SAT or ACT of all applicants

- A "Sizing-Yourself-Up" questionnaire that will help you figure out what kind of school is best for you

- "A Guide for Preprofessionals," which lists colleges and universities strong in nine preprofessional areas

- A list of schools with strong programs for students with learning disabilities

- Designation of the 38 schools that constitute this year's Best Buys

- Statistical summaries that give you the numbers you need, but spare you those that you do not

- Authoritative rankings of each institution by academics, social life, and quality of life

- The unique "If You Apply To" feature, which summarizes vital information about each college's admission policies—including deadlines and required components

- A section on top Canadian, British, and Irish universities that offer first-rate academics and are easily the equivalent of the flagship public institutions and elite privates in the U.S.—but much less expensive than the latter

Picking the right college—one that will coincide with your particular needs, goals, interests, talents, and personality—is one of the most important decisions any young person will ever make. It is also a major investment. Tuition and fees alone now run at least $9,500 per year at a typical public university and close to $41,000 per year at a typical private college, and the overall tab at the most selective and expensive schools tops $60,000 per year. Obviously, a major investment like that should be approached with as much information as possible.

That's where the *Fiske Guide to Colleges* fits in. It is a tool to help you make the most intelligent educational investment you can.

WHAT IS THE *FISKE GUIDE TO COLLEGES?*

Fiske Guide to Colleges mirrors a process familiar to any college-bound student and his or her family. If you are wondering whether to consider a particular college, it is logical to seek out friends or acquaintances who go there and ask them to tell you about their experiences. We have done exactly that—but on a far broader and more systematic basis than any individual or family could do alone.

In using the *Fiske Guide*, you should keep some special features in mind:

- The guide is **selective**. We have not tried to cover all four-year colleges and universities. Rather, we have taken more than 300 of the best and most interesting institutions in the nation—the ones that students most want to know about—and written descriptive essays of 1,000 to 2,500 words about each of them.

- Since choosing a college is a matter of making a calculated and informed judgment, this guide is also **subjective**. It makes judgments about the strengths and weaknesses of each institution, and it contains a unique set of ratings of each college or university on the basis of academic strength, social life, and overall quality of life. No institution is a good fit for every student. The underlying assumption of the *Fiske Guide* is that each of the colleges chosen for inclusion is the right place for some students but not a good bet for others. Like finding the right husband or wife, college admissions is a matching process. You know your own interests and needs; the *Fiske Guide* will tell you something about those needs that each college seems to serve best.

- Finally, the *Fiske Guide* is **systematic**. Each write-up is carefully constructed to cover specific topics—from the academic climate and the makeup of the student body to the social scene—in a systematic order. This means that you can easily take a specific topic, such as the level of academic pressure or the role of fraternities and sororities on campus, and trace it through all of the colleges that interest you.

HOW THE COLLEGES WERE SELECTED

How do you single out "the best and most interesting" of the more than 2,200 four-year colleges in the United States? Obviously, many fine institutions are not included. Space limitations simply require that some hard decisions be made.

The selection was done with several broad principles in mind, beginning with academic quality. Depending on how you define the term, there are about 200 "selective" colleges and universities in the nation, and by and large these constitute the best institutions academically. All of these are included in the *Fiske Guide*. In addition, an effort was made to achieve geographic diversity and a balance of public and private schools. Special efforts were made to include a good selection of four types of institutions that seem to be enjoying special popularity at present: engineering and technical schools, those with a religious emphasis, those with an environmental focus, and those located along the Sunbelt, where the cost of education is considerably less than at their Northern counterparts.

Finally, in a few cases, we exercised the journalist's prerogative of writing about schools that are simply interesting. The tiny College of the Atlantic, for example, would hardly qualify on the basis of a superior academic program or national significance, but it offers an unusual and fascinating brand of liberal arts within the context of environmental studies. Likewise, Deep Springs College, the only two-year school in the *Fiske Guide*, is a unique institution of intrinsic interest.

HOW THE *FISKE GUIDE* WAS COMPILED

Each college or university selected for inclusion in the *Fiske Guide to Colleges* was sent a questionnaire to be filled out and returned online. This questionnaire covered topics ranging from their perception of the institution's mission to the demographics of the student body. Administrators were also asked to recruit a cross section of students to complete another electronic questionnaire with questions relating to what it is like to be a student at their particular college or university.

The questions for students, all open-ended and requiring short essays as responses, covered a series of topics ranging from the accessibility of professors and the quality of housing and dining facilities to the type of nightlife and weekend entertainment available in the area. By and large, students responded enthusiastically to the challenge we offered them. The quality of the information in the write-ups is a tribute to their diligence and openness. American college students, we learned, are a candid lot. They are proud of their institutions, but also critical—in the positive sense of the word.

Other sources of information were also employed. Administrators were invited to send us any in-house research or other documents that would contribute to an understanding of the institution, and they were invited to comment on their write-up in the last edition. Also, staff members have visited many of the colleges, and in some cases, additional information was solicited through published materials, such as the Common Data Set, telephone interviews, and other contacts with students and administrators.

The information from these various questionnaires was then incorporated into write-ups by staff members under the editorial direction of Edward B. Fiske, former education editor of the *New York Times*.

THE FORMAT

Each essay covers certain broad subjects in roughly the same order. They are as follows:

Campus setting	**Housing**
Academics	**Food**
Student body	**Social life**
Financial aid	**Extracurricular activities**

Certain topics are covered in all of the essays. The sections on academics, for example, always discuss the departments (or, in the case of large universities, schools) that are particularly strong or weak, while the sections on housing contain information on whether the dorms are co-ed or single sex and how students get the rooms they want. Other topics, however, such as class size, the need for a car, or the number of volumes in the library, are mentioned only if they constitute a particular strength or weakness at that institution.

We paid particular attention to the effect of the 21-year-old drinking age on campus life and efforts by colleges to deal with growing concerns about sexual assault. Also, we noted efforts that schools' administrations have been making to change or improve the social and residential life on campuses through such measures as creating learning communities, restricting fraternities, and constructing new recreational facilities.

BEST BUYS

One of the lesser-known facts of life about higher education in the U.S. is that price and quality do not always go hand in hand. The college or university with the jumbo price tag may or may not offer a better education than the institution across town with much lower tuition. The relationship between the cost paid by the consumer and the quality of the education is affected by factors ranging from the size of an institution's endowment to calculations by college officials about what the market will bear.

In the face of today's skyrocketing tuition rates, students and families in all economic circumstances are looking for ways to get the best value for their education dollar. To help out, the *Fiske Guide* has an "Index by Price" that groups public and private institutions into four price categories, from inexpensive to very expensive, as well as an "Index by Average Debt." We also suggest a number of schools that offer outstanding academics at relatively modest costs and where students graduate with relatively low student debt. This year we have designated 38 such institutions—20 public and 18 private—as Best Buys. Look for the Best Buy graphic next to the college name. (A list of all 2018 Best Buys appears on page xviii.)

Most of our Best Buys fall into the inexpensive or moderate price category, and many have four- or five-star academic ratings. But there are bargains to be found among all levels and types of institutions. For example, some of the best values in American higher education are public liberal arts colleges and universities that offer the smaller classes and personalized approach to academics that are typically found only in expensive private liberal arts colleges. Several of these are included as Best Buys.

STATISTICS

At the beginning of each write-up are basic statistics about the college or university—the ones that are relevant to applicants. These include the address, type of location (urban, small town, rural, etc.), enrollment, male/female ratio, SAT or ACT score ranges of the middle 50 percent of the students, percentage of students receiving financial aid, relative cost, percentage of students eligible for Pell Grants, percentage of students who procure loans, average debt incurred by students, whether or not the institution has a chapter of Phi Beta Kappa, the number of students who apply and the percentage of those who are accepted, the percentage of accepted students who enroll, the percentage of freshmen who graduate within six years, and the percentage of freshmen who return for their sophomore year. For convenience, we include the telephone number of the admissions office, the school's website, and email and mailing addresses.

Unlike some guides, we have intentionally not published figures on the student/faculty ratio because colleges use different—and often self-serving—methods to calculate the ratio, thus making this particular statistic virtually meaningless.

Within the statistics, you will sometimes encounter the letters "N/A." In most cases, this means that the statistic was not available. In other cases, however, such as schools that do not require standardized tests, it means "not applicable." The write-up should make it clear which meaning is the relevant one.

We have included information on whether the school has a chapter of Phi Beta Kappa because this academic honorary society is a sign of broad intellectual distinction. Keep in mind, though, that even the very best engineering schools, because of their relatively narrow focus, do not usually qualify under the society's standards.

Tuition and fees are constantly increasing at American colleges, but for the most part, the cost of various institutions in relation to one another does not change. Rather than put in specific cost figures that would immediately become out of date, we have classified colleges into four groups ranging from inexpensive ($) to very expensive ($$$$) based on estimated costs of tuition and fees for the 2017–2018 academic year. The results for each college can be found in the "Index by Price" on pages xii–xiv. Separate scales were used for public and private institutions, and the ratings for the public institutions are based on the cost for residents of the state; out-of-staters should expect to pay more. If a public institution has a particularly low or high surcharge for out-of-staters, this is noted in the essay. The categories are defined as follows:

	PUBLIC	PRIVATE
$$$$	More than $13,500	More than $50,000
$$$	$11,001–$13,500	$46,001–$50,000
$$	$9,500–$11,000	$41,000–$46,000
$	Less than $9,500	Less than $41,000

In assessing the relative costs of various colleges and universities, it is important to keep in mind that the posted charges for tuitions and fees are, in effect, "sticker prices." Every American consumer who has ever walked into an automobile showroom knows that the price on the car window is not necessarily the amount he or she will end up paying, but rather the starting point for negotiations over matters such as trade-ins, financing terms, and so forth. The same rule applies to posted tuition and fee levels, especially at private colleges. Some wealthy students will pay the full sticker price, but many others—often a substantial majority of others—will receive "discounts" in the form of merit- or need-based scholarships, loans, and other concessions. It all depends on (1) your personal financial situation and (2) how much the school wants you to enroll and is thus willing to sweeten your financial aid package. Bottom line: don't write off a school that you really like simply because the sticker price looks too expensive.

SAT AND ACT SCORES

A special word needs to be said about standardized test scores. Some publications follow the practice of giving the median or average score registered by entering freshmen. Such figures, however, are easily misinterpreted as thresholds rather than averages. Many applicants forget that if a school reports average SAT–Critical Reading scores of 500, this means that, by definition, about half of the students scored below this number and half scored above. An applicant with a 480 would still have lots of company.

To avoid such confusion, we report the range of scores of the middle half of freshmen—or, to put it another way, the scores achieved by those in the 25th and 75th percentiles. For example, that college where the SAT–Critical Reading average was 500 might have a range of 440 to 560. So if you scored within this range, you would have joined the middle 50 percent of last year's freshmen. If your score was above 560, you would have been in the top quarter and could probably look forward to a relatively easy time; if it was below 440, you would have been struggling along with the bottom quarter of students.

Keep in mind that score ranges (and averages, for that matter) are misleading at the growing number of colleges that no longer require test scores from all applicants (see the section on SAT and ACT Optional Schools on pages xxxviii–xxxix). The ranges given for these colleges typically represent the range of scores of students who choose to submit their test scores, despite not being required to do so.

Unfortunately, another problem that arises with SAT and ACT scores is that, in their zeal to make themselves look good in a competitive market, some colleges and universities have been known to be less than honest in the numbers they release. They inflate their scores by not counting certain categories of students at the low end of the scale, such as athletes, certain types of transfer students, or students admitted under affirmative action programs. Some colleges have gone to such extremes as reporting the relatively high math scores of foreign students, but not their relatively low verbal scores. Aside from the sheer dishonesty of such practices, they can also be misleading. A student whose own scores are below the 25th percentile of a particular institution needs to know whether his profile matches that of the lower quarter of the student body as a whole, or whether there is an unreported pool of students with lower scores.

Even when dealing with a range rather than a single score, keep in mind that standardized tests are an imprecise measure of academic ability, and comparisons of scores that differ by less than 50 or 60 points on a scale of 200 to 800 have little meaning. According to the laws of statistics, there is one chance in three that the 550 that arrived in the little envelope from ETS should really be at least 580 or no more than 520. On the other hand, median scores offer some indication of your chances to get into a particular institution and the intellectual level of the company you will be keeping—or, if you prefer, competing against. Remember, too, that the most competitive schools have the largest and most sophisticated admissions staffs and are well aware of the limitations of standardized tests. A strong high school average or achievement in a field such as music will usually counteract the negative effects of modest SAT or ACT scores.

Note that the College Board launched a new, revised SAT exam in March 2016. As of this writing, most colleges and universities are accepting scores from both the "old" and "new" versions of the exam, and have not yet released data regarding applicant scores on the "new" version. Thus, the SAT scores published in this 2018 edition of the *Fiske Guide* represent scores that applicants achieved on the "old" version of the exam.

SCHOLARSHIP INFORMATION

Since the first edition of the *Fiske Guide to Colleges* appeared, the problems of financing college have become increasingly critical, mainly because of the rising cost of education and a shift from grants to loans in financial aid packages.

In response to these developments, many colleges and universities have begun to devise their own plans to help students pay for college. These range from subsidized loan programs to merit scholarships that are awarded without reference to financial need. Most of these programs are aimed at retaining the middle class. The last year or so has seen a number of both public and private universities substituting grants for loans and even eliminating tuition for low- and many middle-income students. The "Financial Aid" statistic in this book refers to the proportion of enrolled students receiving financial aid.

Some colleges advertise that they are "need-blind" in their admissions, meaning that they accept or reject applicants without reference to their financial situation and then guarantee to meet the "demonstrated need" of all students whom they accept. Others say they are need-blind in their admissions decisions, but do not guarantee to provide the financial aid required of all those who are accepted. Still others agree to meet the demonstrated need of all students, but they package their offers so that students they really want receive a higher percentage of their aid in the form of outright grants and a lower proportion in repayable loans.

"Demonstrated need" is itself a slippery term. In theory, the figure is determined when students and families fill out a needs-analysis form, which leads to an estimate of how much the family can afford to pay. Demonstrated need is then calculated by subtracting that figure from the cost at a particular institution. In practice, however, various colleges make their own adjustments to the standard figure.

Students and parents should not assume that their family's six-figure annual income automatically disqualifies them from some kind of subsidized financial aid. In cases of doubt, they should fill out a needs-analysis form to determine their eligibility. Whether they qualify or not, they are also eligible for a variety of awards made without regard to financial need.

Inasmuch as need-based awards are universal at the colleges in this guide, the awards generally singled out for special mention in the write-ups in the *Fiske Guide to Colleges* are the merit scholarships. We have not mentioned awards of a purely local nature—restricted to residents of a particular county, for example—but college applicants should search out these awards through their guidance offices and the bulletins of the colleges that are of interest to them. Similarly, we have not duplicated the information on federally guaranteed loan programs that is readily available through both high school and college counseling offices, but we cite novel and often less expensive variants of the federal loan programs that are offered by individual colleges.

For more information on the ever-changing financial aid scene, we suggest that you consult the companion book to this guide, the *Fiske Guide to Getting Into the Right College*.

STUDENT LOANS AND AVERAGE DEBT RATING

In today's academic climate, it is common for students and/or their families to borrow funds to assist with paying tuition and other college expenses. Therefore, a potentially useful piece of information is the proportion of students at each school who find it necessary to procure loans to finance their education. The student loan percentage considers any loan program used by students at any time during their tenure at an institution. Included are institutional, state, Federal Perkins, Federal Direct Subsidized and Unsubsidized student loans, Federal Family Education Loans, and private loans certified by an institution, excluding parent loans. To ensure the most accurate information, schools submitted this data for students comprising their last graduating class. When available, this data was confirmed using the Common Data Set.

For a variety of reasons, the average debt carried by graduating seniors varies greatly from college to college as well as from student to student. Nevertheless, when considering a particular school, many prospective students will find it useful to know how much debt is typically incurred by students at that school. Thus the 2018 *Fiske Guide* lists the Average Debt Rating (ADR) for each school as reported in each institution's Common Data Set. The ADR is based on the average cumulative amount of principal borrowed per undergraduate at each college or university during their tenure as a student. Using $27,000 as the median, we have organized the schools into four categories from low average debt ($) to very high average debt ($$$$). Both public and private institutions were rated using the same criteria.

DEBT RATING	AVERAGE PER UNDERGRADUATE CUMULATIVE PRINCIPAL BORROWED
$$$$	More than $32,500
$$$	$27,001–$32,500
$$	$22,500–$27,000
$	Less than $22,500

As previously noted at the end of the discussion of college costs on page xxii, it is important when thinking about the cost of college to keep in mind your particular financial situation. Even if a school has high average debt levels, students who qualify for substantial financial aid packages may end up with little or no debt.

RATINGS

Much of the fierce controversy that greeted the first edition of the *Fiske Guide to Colleges* more than three decades ago revolved around its unique system of rating colleges in three areas: academics, social life, and quality of life. In each case, the ratings are done on a system of one to five, with three considered normal for colleges included in the *Fiske Guide*. If a college receives a rating higher or lower than three in any category, the reasons should be apparent from the narrative description of that college.

Students and parents should keep in mind that these ratings are obviously general in nature and inherently subjective. No complex institution can be described in terms of a single number or other symbol, and different people will have different views of how various institutions should be rated in the three categories. They should not be viewed as either precise or infallible judgments about any given college. On the other hand, the ratings are a helpful tool in using this book. The core of the *Fiske Guide* is the essays on each of the colleges, and the ratings represent a summary—an index, if you will—of these write-ups. Our hope is that each student, having decided on the kind of configuration that suits his or her needs, will then thumb through the book looking for other institutions with a similar set of ratings. The three categories, defined as follows, are academics, social life, and quality of life.

Academics ✍

This is a judgment about the overall academic climate of the institution, including its reputation in the academic world, the quality of the faculty, the level of teaching and research, the academic ability of students, the quality of libraries and other facilities, and the level of academic seriousness among students and faculty members.

Although the same basic criteria have been applied to all institutions, it should be evident that an outstanding small liberal arts college will by definition differ significantly from an outstanding major public university. No one would expect the former to have massive library facilities, but one would look for a high-quality faculty that combines research with a good deal of attention to the individual needs of students. Likewise, public universities, because of their implicit commitment to serving a broad cross section of society, might have a broader range of curriculum offerings but somewhat lower average SAT scores than a large private counterpart. Readers may find the ratings most useful when comparing colleges and universities of the same type.

In general, an academics rating of three pens suggests that the institution is a solid one that easily meets the criteria for inclusion in a guide devoted to the top 10 percent of colleges and universities in the nation.

An academics rating of four pens suggests that the institution is above average even by these standards and that it has some particularly distinguishing academic feature, such as especially rich course offerings or an especially serious academic atmosphere.

A rating of five pens for academics indicates that the college or university is among the handful of top institutions of its type in the nation on a broad variety of criteria. Those in the private sector will normally attract students with combined SAT scores of at least 1300 on Critical Reading and Math, and those in the public sector are invariably magnets for the top students in their states. All can be assumed to have outstanding faculties and other academic resources.

In response to the suggestion that the range of colleges within a single category has been too broad, we have introduced some half-steps into the ratings.

Social Life ☎

This is primarily a judgment about the amount of social life that is readily available. A rating of three telephones suggests a typical college social life, while four telephones means that students devote an above-average amount of time to socializing. It can be assumed that a college with a rating of five is something of a party school, which may or may not detract from the academic quality. Colleges with a rating below three have some impediment to a strong social life, such as geographic isolation, a high percentage of commuting students, or a disproportionate number of nerds who never leave the library. Once again, the reason should be evident from the write-up.

Quality of Life ★

This category grew out of the fact that schools with good academic credentials and plenty of social life may not, for one reason or another, be particularly wholesome places to spend four years. The term "quality of life" is one that has gained currency in social science circles, and, in most cases, the rating for a particular college will be similar to the academic and/or social ratings. The reader, though, should be alert to exceptions to this pattern. A liberal arts college, for example, might attract bright students who study hard during the week and party hard on weekends, and thus earn high ratings for academics and social life. If the academic pressure is cutthroat rather than constructive, though, and the social system is manipulative of women, this college might get an apparently anomalous two stars for quality of life. By contrast, a small college with modest academic programs and relatively few organized social opportunities might have developed a strong sense of supportive community, have a beautiful campus, and be located near a wonderful city—and thus be rated four stars for quality of life. As in the other categories, the reason can be found in the essay to which the ratings point.

OVERLAPS

Most colleges and universities operate within fairly defined "niche markets." That is, they compete for students against other institutions with whom they share important characteristics, such as academic quality, size, geographic location, and the overall tone and style of campus life. Not surprisingly, students who apply to College X also tend to apply to the other institutions in its particular niche. For example, "alternative" colleges such as Bard, Bennington, Hampshire, Marlboro, Oberlin, Reed, and Sarah Lawrence share many common applications, as do those with an evangelical flavor, such as Calvin, Gordon, and Wheaton (IL).

As a service to readers, we ask each school to give us the names of the eight colleges with which they share the most common applications, and these are listed in the "Overlaps" section at the end of each write-up. We encourage students who know they are interested in a particular institution to check out the schools with which it competes—and perhaps then check out the "overlaps of the overlaps." This method of systematic browsing should yield a list of 15 or 20 schools that, based on the behavior of thousands of past applicants, would constitute a good starting point for the college search.

IF YOU APPLY TO

An extremely helpful feature is the "If You Apply To" section at the end of each write-up. This is designed for students who become seriously interested in a particular college and want to know more specifics about what it takes to get in.

This section begins with the deadlines for early admissions or early decision (if the college has such a program), regular decision, financial aid, and housing. If the college operates on a rolling-admissions basis—making decisions as the applications are received—this is indicated.

Many colleges require a fee in order to apply to their institution. This section includes any application fees that may be required. If there is no application fee, or if a school offers a discounted fee for online applications, this information is indicated as well.

Colleges have widely varying policies regarding interviews, both on campus and with alumni, so we indicate whether each of these is required, recommended, or optional. We also indicate whether reports from the person doing the interview are used in evaluating students or whether, as in many cases, the interview is seen only as a means of conveying information about the institution and answering applicants' questions. You are within your rights to ask the admissions office to explain how they view interviews.

This section also describes what standardized tests—SAT, ACT, or Subject—are required, and whether applicants are asked to provide letters of recommendation and/or write one or more essays.

CONSORTIA

Many colleges expand the range of their offerings by banding together with other institutions to offer unusual programs that they could not support on their own. These options range from foreign study programs around the world to semesters at sea, and keeping such arrangements in mind is a way of expanding the list of institutions that might meet your particular interests and needs. The final section of the *Fiske Guide* describes 12 of these consortia and lists the member institutions.

MOVING FORWARD

Students will find the *Fiske Guide* useful at various points in the college selection process—from deciding whether to visit a particular campus to selecting among institutions that have accepted them. To make it easy to find a particular college, the write-ups are arranged in alphabetical order in the indexes. An "Index by State and Country," the "Index by Price," and the "Index by Average Debt" can be found on pages ix, xii, and xv, respectively.

While most people are not likely to start reading at Adelphi and keep going until they reach Yale (though some tell us they do), we encourage you to browse. This country has an enormously rich and varied network of colleges and universities, and there are dozens of institutions out there that can meet the needs of any particular student. Too many students approach the college selection process wearing blinders, limiting their sights to local institutions, the pet schools of their parents or guidance counselors, or ones they know only by possibly outdated reputations.

But applicants need not be bound by such limitations. Once you have decided on the type of school you think you want—a small liberal arts college, an engineering school, or whatever—we hope you will thumb through the book looking for similar institutions that might not have occurred to you. As already noted, one way to do this is to look at the overlaps of schools you like and then check out those schools' overlaps. Many students have found this worthwhile, and quite frankly, we view the widening of students' horizons about American higher education as one of the most important purposes of this book. Perhaps the most gratifying remark we hear comes when a student tells us, as many have, that she is attending a school that she first heard about while browsing through the *Fiske Guide to Colleges*.

Picking a college is a tricky business. But given the current buyer's market, there is no reason why you should not be able to find the right one. That's what the *Fiske Guide to Colleges* is designed to help you do. Happy college hunting.

Sizing Yourself Up

The college search is a game of matchmaking. You have interests and needs; the colleges have programs to meet those needs. If all goes according to plan, you'll find the right one and live happily ever after——or at least for four years. It ought to be simple, but today's admissions process resembles a high-stakes obstacle course.

Many colleges are more interested in making a sale than they are in making a match. Under intense competitive pressure, many won't hesitate to sell you a bill of goods if they can get their hands on your tuition dollars. Guidance counselors generally mean well, but they are often under duress from principals and trustees to steer students toward prestigious schools regardless of whether the fit is right. Your friends won't be shy with advice on where to go, but their knowledge is generally limited to a small group of hot colleges that everyone is talking about. National publications rake in millions by playing on the public's fascination with rankings, but a close look at their criteria reveals distinctions without a difference.

Before you find yourself spinning headlong on this merry-go-round, take a step back. This is your life and your college career. What are you looking for in a college? Think hard and don't answer right away. Before you throw yourself and your life history on the mercy of college admissions officers, you need to take some time to objectively and honestly evaluate your needs, likes and dislikes, strengths and weaknesses. What do you have to offer a college? What can a college do for you? Unlike the high school selection process, which is usually predetermined by your parents' property lines, income level, or religious affiliation, picking a college isn't a procedure you can brush off on dear ol' Mom and Dad. You have to take some initiative. You're the best judge of how well each school fits your personal needs and academic goals.

We encourage you to view the college selection process as the first semester in your higher education. Life's transitions often call for extra energy and focus. The college search is no exception. For the first time, you'll be contemplating a life away from home that can unfold in any direction you choose. Visions of majors and careers will dance in your head as you sample various institutions of higher learning, each with hundreds of millions of dollars in academic resources; it is hard to imagine a better hands-on seminar in research and matchmaking than the college search. The main impact, however, will be measured by what you learn about yourself. Piqued by new worlds of learning and tested by the competition of the admissions process, you'll be pushed as never before to show your accomplishments, clarify your interests, and chart a course for the future. More than one parent has watched in amazement as an erstwhile teenager suddenly emerged as an adult during the course of a college tour. Be ready when your time comes.

DEVELOP YOUR CRITERIA

One strategy is to begin the search with a personal inventory of your own strengths and weaknesses and your "wish list" for a college. This method tends to work well for compulsive list-makers and other highly organized people. What sorts of things are you especially good at? Do you have a list of skills or interests that you would like to explore further? What sort of personality are you looking for in a college? Mainstream? Conservative? Offbeat? What about extracurriculars? If you are really into riding horses, you might include a strong equestrian program in your criteria. The main problem won't be thinking of qualities to look for—you could probably name dozens—but rather figuring out what criteria should play a defining role in your search. Serious students should think carefully about the intellectual climate they are seeking. At some schools, students routinely stay up until 3:00 a.m. talking about topics like the value of deconstructing literary texts or the pros and cons of free trade. These same students would be viewed as geeks or weirdos on less cosmopolitan campuses. Athletes should take a hard look at whether they really want to play college ball and, if so, whether they want to go for an athletic scholarship or play at the less-pressured Division III level. Either way, intercollegiate sports require a huge time commitment.

Young women have an opportunity all to themselves—the chance to study at a women's college. The *Fiske Guide* profiles 11 such campuses, a vastly underappreciated resource on today's higher education scene. With small classes and strong encouragement from faculty, students at women's colleges move on to graduate study in significantly higher numbers than their counterparts at co-ed schools, especially in the natural sciences. Males seeking an all-male experience will find four options in the *Fiske Guide*.

Students with a firm career goal will want to look for a course of study that matches their needs. If you want to major in aerospace engineering, your search will be limited to schools that have the program. Outside of specialized areas like this, many applicants overestimate the importance of their anticipated major in choosing a college. If you're interested in a liberal arts field, your expected major should probably have little to do with your college selection. A big purpose of college is to develop interests and set goals. Most students change their intentions regarding a major at least two or three times before graduation, and once out in the working world, they often end up in jobs bearing no relation to their academic specialty. Even those with a firm career goal may not need as much specialization as they think at the undergraduate level. If you want to be a lawyer, don't worry yourself looking for something labeled "prelaw." Follow your interests, get the best liberal arts education available, and then apply to law school.

Naturally, it is never a bad idea to check out the department(s) of any likely major, and occasionally your choice of major will suggest a direction for your search. If you're really into national politics, it may make sense to look at some schools in or near Washington, D.C. If you think you're interested in a relatively specialized field, say, oceanography, then be sure to look for some colleges that are a good match for you and also have programs in oceanography. But for the most part, rumors about top-ranked departments in this or that should be no more than a tie-breaker between schools you like for more important reasons. There are good professors (and bad ones) in any department. You'll have plenty of time to figure out who is who once you've enrolled. Being undecided about your career path as a senior in high school is often a sign of intelligence. Don't feel bad if you have absolutely no idea what you're going to do when you "grow up." One of the reasons you'll be paying megabucks to the college of your choice is the prospect that it will open some new doors for you and expand your horizons. Instead of worrying about particular departments, try to keep the focus on big-picture items, such as: What's the academic climate? How big are the freshman classes? Do I like it here? and Are these my kind of people?

KEEP AN OPEN MIND

The biggest mistake of beginning applicants is hyperchoosiness. At the extreme is the "perfect-school syndrome," which comes in two basic forms.

In one category are the applicants who refuse to consider any school that doesn't have every little thing they want in a college. If you're one who begins the process with a detailed picture of Perfect U. in mind, you may want to remember the oft-quoted advice, "Two out of three ain't bad." If a college seems to have most of the qualities you seek, give it a chance. You may come to realize that some things you thought were absolutely essential are really not that crucial after all.

The other strain of perfect-school syndrome is the applicant who gets stuck on a "dream" school at the beginning and then won't look anywhere else. With those 2,200 four-year colleges out there (not counting those in Canada and Great Britain), it is just a bit silly to insist that only one will meet your needs. Having a first choice is OK, but the whole purpose of the search is to consider new options and uncover new possibilities. A student who has only one dream school—especially if it is a highly selective one—could be headed for disappointment.

As you begin the college search, don't expect any quick revelations. The answers will unfold in due time. Our advice? Be patient. Set priorities. Keep an open mind. Reexamine priorities. Again, be patient.

To get the ball rolling, move on to the Sizing-Yourself-Up Survey.

FISKE'S SIZING-YOURSELF-UP SURVEY

With apologies to Socrates, knowing thyself is easier said than done. Most high school students can analyze a differential equation or a Shakespearean play with the greatest of ease, but when it comes to cataloging their own strengths, weaknesses, likes, and dislikes, many draw a blank. But self-knowledge is crucial to the matching process at the heart of a successful college search. The 30-item survey on page xxix offers a simple way to get a handle on some crucial issues in college selection—and what sort of college may fit your preferences.

In the space beside each statement, rate your feelings on a scale of 1 to 10, with 10 = Strongly Agree, 1 = Strongly Disagree, and 5 = Not Sure/Don't Have Strong Feelings. (For instance, a rating of 7 would mean that you agree with the statement, but that the issue is a lower priority than those you rated 8, 9, or 10.) After you're done, read on to "Grading Yourself" to find out what it all means.

FISKE'S SIZING-YOURSELF-UP SURVEY

Size

_____ 1. I enjoy participating in many activities.

_____ 2. I would like to have a prominent place in my community.

_____ 3. Individual attention from teachers is important to me.

_____ 4. I learn best when I can speak out in class and ask questions.

_____ 5. I am undecided about what I will study.

_____ 6. I want to earn a Ph.D. in my chosen field of study.

_____ 7. I learn best by listening and writing down what I hear.

_____ 8. I would like to be in a place where I can be anonymous if I choose.

_____ 9. I prefer devoting my time to one or two activities rather than many.

_____ 10. I want to attend a college that most people have heard of.

_____ 11. I am interested in a career-oriented major.

_____ 12. I like to be on my own.

Location

_____ 13. I prefer a college in a warm or hot climate.

_____ 14. I prefer a college in a cool or cold climate.

_____ 15. I want to be near the mountains.

_____ 16. I want to be near a lake or ocean.

_____ 17. I prefer to attend a college in a particular state or region.

_____ 18. I prefer to attend a college near my family.

_____ 19. I want city life within walking distance of my campus.

_____ 20. I want city life within driving distance of my campus.

_____ 21. I want my campus to be surrounded by natural beauty.

Academics and Extracurriculars

_____ 22. I like to be surrounded by people who are freethinkers and nonconformists.

_____ 23. I like the idea of joining a fraternity or sorority.

_____ 24. I like rubbing shoulders with people who are bright and talented.

_____ 25. I like being one of the smartest people in my class.

_____ 26. I want to go to a prestigious college.

_____ 27. I want to go to a college where I can get an excellent education.

_____ 28. I want to try for an academic scholarship.

_____ 29. I want a diverse college.

_____ 30. I want a college where the students are serious about ideas.

Grading Yourself

Picking a college is not an exact science. People who are total opposites can be equally happy at the same college. Nevertheless, particular types tend to do better at some colleges than others. Each item in the survey is designed to test your feelings on an important issue related to college selection. "Sizing Up the Survey" (below) offers commentary on each item.

Taken together, your responses may help you construct a tentative blueprint for your college search. Statements 1–12 deal with the issue of size. Would you be happier at a large university or a small college? Here's the trick: Add the sum of your responses to questions 1–6. Then make a second tally of your responses to 7–12. If the sum of 1–6 is larger, you may want to consider a small college. If 7–12 is greater, then perhaps a big school would be more to your liking. If the totals are roughly equal, you should probably consider colleges of various sizes.

Statements 13–21 deal with location. The key in this section is the intensity of your feeling. If you replied to number 13 with a 10, does that mean you are going to look only at schools in warm climates? Think hard. If you consider only schools within a certain region or state, you'll be eliminating hundreds of possibilities. By examining your most intense responses—the 1s, 2s, 9s, and 10s—you'll be able to create a geographic profile of likely options.

Statements 22–30 deal with big-picture issues related to the character and personality of the college that may be in your future. As before, pay attention to your most intense responses. Read on for a look at the significance of each question.

SIZING UP THE SURVEY

1. **I enjoy participating in many activities.** Students at small colleges tend to have more opportunities to be involved in many activities. Fewer students means less competition for spots.

2. **I would like to have a prominent place in my community.** Student-council presidents and other would-be leaders take note: it is easier to be a big fish if you're swimming in a small pond.

3. **Individual attention from teachers is important to me.** Small colleges generally offer more one-on-one with faculty in both the classroom and the laboratory.

4. **I learn best when I can speak out in class and ask questions.** Students who learn from interaction and participation would be well-advised to consider a small college.

5. **I am undecided about what I will study.** Small colleges generally offer more guidance and support to students who are undecided. The exception: students who are considering a preprofessional or highly specialized major.

6. **I want to earn a Ph.D. in my chosen field of study.** A higher percentage of students at selective small colleges earn a Ph.D. than those who attend large institutions of similar quality.

7. **I learn best by listening and writing down what I hear.** Students who prefer lecture courses will find more of them at large institutions.

8. **I would like to be in a place where I can be anonymous if I choose.** At a large university, the supply of new faces is never-ending. Students who have the initiative can always reinvent themselves.

9. **I prefer devoting my time to one or two activities rather than many.** Students who are passionate about one activity—say, writing for the college newspaper—will often find higher quality at a bigger school.

10. **I want to attend a college that most people have heard of.** Big schools have more name recognition because they're bigger and have Division I athletic programs. Even the finest small colleges are relatively anonymous among the general public.

11. **I am interested in a career-oriented major.** More large institutions offer business, engineering, nursing, etc., though some excellent small institutions do so as well (depending on the field).

12. **I like to be on my own.** A higher percentage of students live off campus at large schools, which are more likely to be in urban areas than their smaller counterparts.

13. **I prefer a college in a warm or hot climate.** Keep in mind that the Southeast and the Southwest have far different personalities (not to mention humidity levels).

14. **I prefer a college in a cool or cold climate.** Consider the Midwest, where there are many fine schools that are notably less selective than those in the Northeast.

15. **I want to be near the mountains.** You're probably thinking Colorado or Vermont, but don't zero in too quickly. States from Maine to Georgia and Arkansas to Arizona have easy access to mountains.

16. **I want to be near a lake or ocean.** Oceans are only on the coasts, but keep in mind the Great Lakes, the Finger Lakes, etc. Think about whether you want to be on the water or, say, within a two-hour drive.

17. **I prefer to attend a college in a particular state or region.** Geographical blinders limit options. Even if you think you want a certain area of the country, consider at least one college located elsewhere just to be sure.

18. **I prefer to attend a college near my family.** Unless you're planning to live with Mom and Dad, it may not matter whether your college is a two-hour drive or a two-hour plane ride.

19. **I want city life within walking distance of my campus.** Check out the neighborhood(s) surrounding your campus. Urban campuses—even in the same city—can be wildly different.

20. **I want city life within driving distance of my campus.** Unless you're a hard-core urban dweller, a suburban perch near a city may beat living in the thick of one. Does public transportation or a campus shuttle help students get around?

21. **I want my campus to be surrounded by natural beauty.** A college viewbook will take you only so far. To really know if you'll fall in love with the campus, visiting is a must.

22. **I like to be surrounded by people who are freethinkers and nonconformists.** Plenty of schools cater specifically to students who buck the mainstream. Talk to your counselor or browse the *Fiske Guide to Colleges* to find some.

23. **I like the idea of joining a fraternity or sorority.** Greek life is strongest at mainstream and conservative-leaning schools. Find out if there is a split between Greeks and non-Greeks.

24. **I like rubbing shoulders with people who are bright and talented.** This is perhaps the best reason to aim for a highly selective institution, especially if you're the type who rises to the level of the competition.

25. **I like being one of the smartest people in my class.** If so, maybe you should skip the highly selective rat race. Star students get the best a college has to offer.

26. **I want to go to a prestigious college.** There is nothing wrong with wanting prestige. Think honestly about how badly you want a big-name school and act accordingly.

27. **I want to go to a college where I can get an excellent education.** Throw out the *U.S. News* rankings and think about which colleges will best meet your needs as a student.

28. **I want to try for an academic scholarship.** Students in this category should consider less-selective alternatives. Scholarships are more likely if you rank high in the applicant pool.

29. **I want a diverse college.** All colleges pay lip service to diversity. To get the truth, see the campus for yourself and take a hard look at the student-body statistics in the *Fiske Guide*'s write-ups.

30. **I want a college where students are serious about ideas.** Don't assume that a college necessarily attracts true intellectuals merely because it is highly selective. Some top schools are known for their intellectual climate—and others for their lack of it.

A Guide for Preprofessionals

The lists that follow include colleges and universities with unusual strength in each of nine preprofessional areas: architecture, art/design, business, communications/journalism, engineering, film/television, dance, drama, and music. We also offer lists covering two of today's hottest interdisciplinary majors: environmental studies and international studies. In compiling the lists, we drew on data from the thousands of surveys used to compile the *Fiske Guide*. We examined the strongest majors at each college as reported in student and administrative questionnaires, and then weighed these against the selectivity and overall academic quality of each institution. After compiling tentative lists in each subject, we queried our counselors advisory group, listed on page 846, for additional suggestions and feedback. To make the lists as useful as possible, we have included some schools that do not receive full-length write-ups in the *Fiske Guide*. Moreover, while the lists are suggestive, they are by no means all-inclusive, and there are other institutions in the *Fiske Guide* that offer fine programs in these areas. Nevertheless, we hope the lists will be a starting place for students interested in these fields.

If you are planning a career in one of the subjects below, your college search may focus largely on finding the best programs for you in that particular area. But we also recommend that you shop for a school that will give you an adequate dose of liberal arts. For that matter, you might consider a double major (or minor) in a liberal arts field to complement your area of technical expertise. If you allow yourself to get too specialized too soon, you may end up as tomorrow's equivalent of the typewriter repairman. In a rapidly changing job market, nothing is so practical as the ability to read, write, and think.

ARCHITECTURE
Private Universities Strong in Architecture
Carnegie Mellon University
The Catholic University of America
Columbia University
The Cooper Union
Cornell University
Drexel University
Hobart and William Smith Colleges
Howard University
Lehigh University
Massachusetts Institute of Technology
University of Miami (FL)
Northeastern University
University of Notre Dame
Princeton University
Rensselaer Polytechnic Institute
Rice University
University of Southern California
Syracuse University
Temple University
Tuskegee University
Tulane University
Washington University in St. Louis

Public Universities Strong in Architecture
University of Arizona
UC–Berkeley
University of Cincinnati
Clemson University
University of Florida
Georgia Institute of Technology
University of Illinois at Urbana–Champaign
University of Kansas
Kansas State University
University of Maryland
Miami University (OH)
University of Michigan
University of Nebraska–Lincoln
New Jersey Institute of Technology
University of Oregon
Pennsylvania State University
SUNY–University at Buffalo
University of Texas at Austin
Texas A&M University
Virginia Tech
University of Washington

A Few Arts-Oriented Architecture Programs
Barnard College
Bennington College
Pratt Institute
Rhode Island School of Design
Savannah School of Art and Design
Wellesley College
Yale University

ART/DESIGN
Top Schools of Art and Design
Art Center College of Design
School of the Art Institute of Chicago
California College of the Arts
California Institute of the Arts
The Cooper Union
Kansas City Art Institute
Maryland Institute, College of Art
Massachusetts College of Art
Moore College of Art and Design
School of the Museum of Fine Arts (MA)
North Carolina School of the Arts
Otis Institute of Art and Design
Parsons School of Design
Pratt Institute
Rhode Island School of Design
Ringling School of Art and Design
San Francisco Art Institute
Savannah College of Art and Design
School of Visual Arts (NY)

Major Universities Strong in Art or Design

American University
University of the Arts (PA)
Boston College
Boston University
Carnegie Mellon University
University of Cincinnati
Cornell University
Drexel University
Harvard University
University of Michigan
New York University
University of Pennsylvania
Syracuse University
University of Washington
Washington University in St. Louis
Yale University

Small Colleges and Universities Strong in Art or Design

Alfred University
Bard College
Brown University
Centre College
Champlain College
Cornell College
Dartmouth College
Furman University
Hollins University
Kenyon College
Lake Forest College
Lewis & Clark College
Manhattanville College
Mills College
Randolph College
Sarah Lawrence College
Scripps College
Skidmore College
Smith College
Southwestern University
SUNY–Purchase College
Vassar College
Wheaton College (MA)
Willamette University
Williams College

BUSINESS
Major Private Universities Strong in Business

American University
Baylor University
Boston College
Boston University
Carnegie Mellon University
Case Western Reserve
University of Dayton
Emory University
Fordham University
Georgetown University
Howard University
Ithaca College
Lehigh University
Massachusetts Institute of Technology
New York University
University of Notre Dame
University of Pennsylvania
Pepperdine University
Rensselaer Polytechnic Institute
University of San Francisco
Santa Clara University
University of Southern California
Southern Methodist University
Syracuse University
Texas Christian University
Tulane University
Villanova University
Wake Forest University
Washington University in St. Louis

Public Universities Strong in Business

University of Arizona
UC–Berkeley
University of Cincinnati
University of Connecticut
University of Florida
University of Georgia
University of Illinois at Urbana–Champaign
Indiana University
James Madison University
University of Kansas
University of Maryland
University of Massachusetts Amherst
Miami University (OH)
University of Michigan
University of Minnesota
University of Missouri
University of North Carolina at Chapel Hill
Ohio State University
Ohio University
University of Oregon

Pennsylvania State University
University of Pittsburgh
Rutgers–The State University of New Jersey
University of South Carolina
SUNY–University at Albany
SUNY–Binghamton University
SUNY–University at Buffalo
SUNY–College at Geneseo
University of Tennessee Knoxville
University of Texas at Austin
Texas A&M University
University of Vermont
University of Virginia
University of Washington
College of William and Mary
University of Wisconsin–Madison

Small Colleges and Universities Strong in Business

Agnes Scott College
Babson College
Bentley University
Bucknell University
Butler University
Calvin College
Claremont McKenna College
Clarkson University
Eckerd College
Fairfield University
Franklin & Marshall College
Furman University
Gettysburg College
Guilford College
Hendrix College
Lafayette College
Lake Forest College
Lewis & Clark College
Millsaps College
Morehouse College
Muhlenberg College
Oglethorpe University
Ohio Wesleyan University
Presbyterian College
Rhodes College
University of Richmond
Ripon College
Skidmore College
Southwestern University
Stetson University
Susquehanna University
Trinity University (TX)

Washington and Jefferson College
Washington and Lee University
Whittier College
Wofford College
Worcester Polytechnic Institute
Xavier University of Louisiana

COMMUNICATIONS/ JOURNALISM
Colleges and Universities Strong in Communications/Journalism
American University
Arizona State University
Boston University
UC–Los Angeles
UC–San Diego
University of Florida
University of Georgia
University of Illinois at Urbana–Champaign
Indiana University
Ithaca College
University of Kansas
University of Maryland
University of Michigan
University of Missouri
University of Nebraska–Lincoln
University of North Carolina at Chapel Hill
Northwestern University
Ohio University
University of Oregon
Pepperdine University
St. Lawrence University
University of San Francisco
University of Southern California
Stanford University
Syracuse University
Texas Christian University
University of Utah
University of Wisconsin–Madison

ENGINEERING
Top Technical Institutes
California Institute of Technology
California Polytechnic State University–San Luis Obispo
Colorado School of Mines
The Cooper Union
Florida Institute of Technology
Georgia Institute of Technology

Harvey Mudd College
Illinois Institute of Technology
Massachusetts Institute of Technology
Michigan Technological University
New Jersey Institute of Technology
New Mexico Institute of Mining and Technology
Rensselaer Polytechnic Institute
Rochester Institute of Technology
Rose–Hulman Institute of Technology
Stevens Institute of Technology
Worcester Polytechnic Institute

Major Private Universities Strong in Engineering
Boston University
Brigham Young University
Brown University
Carnegie Mellon University
Case Western Reserve
The Catholic University of America
Columbia University
Cornell University
Drexel University
Duke University
The George Washington University
The Johns Hopkins University
Northeastern University
Northwestern University
University of Notre Dame
University of Pennsylvania
Princeton University
University of Rochester
Santa Clara University
University of Southern California
Southern Methodist University
Stanford University
Syracuse University
Tufts University
Tulane University
University of Tulsa
Vanderbilt University
Villanova University
Washington University in St. Louis

Public Universities Strong in Engineering
University of Arizona
UC–Berkeley
UC–Davis
UC–Los Angeles
UC–San Diego

University of Cincinnati
Clemson University
University of Connecticut
University of Delaware
University of Florida
University of Illinois at Urbana–Champaign
Iowa State University
University of Kansas
University of Maryland
University of Massachusetts Amherst
McGill University
University of Michigan
Michigan State University
University of Missouri–Rolla
University of New Hampshire
The College of New Jersey
North Carolina State University
Ohio State University
Oregon State University
Pennsylvania State University
Purdue University
Queen's University (Can)
University of Rhode Island
Rutgers–The State University of New Jersey
SUNY–Binghamton University
SUNY–University at Buffalo
University of Texas at Austin
Texas A&M University
Texas Tech University
University of Toronto (Can)
University of Virginia
Virginia Tech
University of Washington
University of Wisconsin–Madison

Small Colleges and Universities Strong in Engineering
Alfred University
Bradley University
Bucknell University
Butler University
Calvin College
Clarkson University
Dartmouth College
Lafayette College
Lehigh University
Loyola University Maryland
Olin College of Engineering
University of the Pacific
Rice University

Smith College
Spelman College
Swarthmore College
Trinity College (CT)
Trinity University (TX)
Tuskegee University
Union College

FILM/TELEVISION
Major Universities Strong in Film/Television
Arizona State University
Boston University
UC–Los Angeles
University of Cincinnati
DePaul University
Drexel University
University of Florida
Ithaca College
University of Kansas
Memphis State University
University of Michigan
New York University
Northwestern University
Pennsylvania State University
Quinnipiac University
University of Southern
  California
Syracuse University
University of Texas at Austin
Wayne State University

Small Colleges and Universities Strong in Film/Television
Bard College
Beloit College
Brown University
California Institute of the Arts
Champlain College
Columbia College (CA)
Columbia College (IL)
Emerson College
The Evergreen State College
Hampshire College
Hofstra University
Hollins University
Occidental College
Pitzer College
Pomona College
Sarah Lawrence College
SUNY–Purchase College
Wesleyan University

PERFORMING ARTS—DANCE
Major Universities Strong in Dance
Arizona State University
UC–Irvine
UC–Los Angeles
UC–Riverside
Case Western Reserve
Florida State University
The George Washington University
Howard University
Indiana University
University of Iowa
University of Minnesota
New York University
Ohio University
Southern Methodist University
University of Texas at Austin
Texas Christian University
University of Utah
Washington University in St. Louis

Small Colleges and Universities Strong in Dance
Amherst College
Barnard College
Bennington College
Butler University
Connecticut College
Goucher College
Hollins University
Juilliard School
Kenyon College
Middlebury College
Mills College
Muhlenberg College
North Carolina School of the Arts
Princeton University
Sarah Lawrence College
Smith College
SUNY–Purchase College

PERFORMING ARTS—DRAMA
Major Universities Strong in Drama
Boston College
Boston University
UC–Los Angeles
Carnegie Mellon University
The Catholic University of America
University of Chicago
DePaul University

Florida State University
Fordham University
Indiana University
University of Iowa
University of Minnesota
New York University
University of North Carolina at
  Chapel Hill
Northwestern University
University of Southern California
Southern Methodist University
Syracuse University
Texas Christian University
University of Washington
Yale University

Small Colleges and Universities Strong in Drama
Beloit College
Bennington College
Butler University
Centre College
Colorado College
Columbia College (IL)
Connecticut College
Drew University
Emerson College
Ithaca College
Juilliard School
Kenyon College
Lawrence University
Macalester College
Middlebury College
Muhlenberg College
Occidental College
Otterbein University
Princeton University
Rollins College
Sarah Lawrence College
Skidmore College
SUNY–Purchase College
Vassar College
Whitman College
Wittenberg University

PERFORMING ARTS—MUSIC
Top Music Conservatories
Berklee College of Music
Boston Conservatory
California Institute of the Arts
Cleveland Institute of Music
Curtis Institute of Music

Eastman School of Music
Juilliard School
Manhattan School of Music
New England Conservatory
  of Music
North Carolina School of the Arts
Peabody Conservatory of Music
San Francisco Conservatory of Music

Major Universities Strong in Music

Baylor University
Boston College
Boston University
UC–Los Angeles
Carnegie Mellon University
Case Western Reserve
University of Cincinnati
University of Colorado–Boulder
University of Denver
DePaul University
Florida State University
Harvard University
Indiana University
University of Miami (FL)
Miami University (OH)
University of Michigan
University of Nebraska–Lincoln
New York University
University of North Texas
Northwestern University
University of Oklahoma
University of Southern California
Southern Methodist University
Vanderbilt University
Yale University

Small Colleges and Universities Strong in Music

Bard College
Bennington College
Bucknell University
Butler University
DePauw University
Furman University
Gordon College
Illinois Wesleyan University
Ithaca College
Knox College
Lawrence University*
Loyola University New Orleans
Manhattanville College

Mills College
Oberlin College*
University of the Pacific
Rice University
St. Mary's College of Maryland
St. Olaf College
Sarah Lawrence College
Skidmore College
Smith College
SUNY–College at Geneseo
SUNY–Purchase College
Stetson University
Wesleyan University
Wheaton College (IL)

* These two schools are unusual
  because they combine a world-
  class conservatory with a top-notch
  liberal arts college.

ENVIRONMENTAL STUDIES

Allegheny College
College of the Atlantic
Bowdoin College
UC–Davis
UC–Santa Barbara
University of Chicago
Clark University
Colby College
University of Colorado–Boulder
Dartmouth College
Deep Springs College
Eckerd College
The Evergreen State College
Hampshire College
Hiram College
Hobart and William Smith
  Colleges
McGill University (Can)
Middlebury College
University of New Hampshire
University of New Mexico
University of North Carolina
  Asheville
Oberlin College
Prescott College
St. Lawrence University
Tulane University
University of Vermont
University of Washington
Williams College
University of Wisconsin–Madison

INTERNATIONAL STUDIES

American University
Austin College
Brandeis University
University of British Columbia (Can)
Brown University
Bucknell University
University of Chicago
Claremont McKenna College
Clark University
Colby College
Connecticut College
Dartmouth College
Davidson College
Denison University
University of Denver
Dickinson College
Earlham College
Eckerd College
The George Washington University
Georgetown University
Goucher College
Hiram College
The Johns Hopkins University
Kalamazoo College
Lewis & Clark College
University of Mary Washington
University of Massachusetts Amherst
Middlebury College
Mount Holyoke College
Occidental College
University of the Pacific
University of Pittsburgh
Pomona College
Princeton University
University of Puget Sound
Randolph College
Reed College
Rhodes College
University of Richmond
St. Olaf College
Scripps College
University of South Carolina
Tufts University
Wesleyan University
College of William and Mary

Learning Disabilities

Accommodation for students with learning disabilities is one of the fastest-growing academic areas in higher education. Colleges and universities recognize that a significant segment of the population may suffer problems that qualify as learning disabilities, and the range of support services offered to such students is increasing. Assistance ranges from counseling services to accommodations such as tapes of lectures or extended time on exams.

Following are two lists—the first of major universities, the second of smaller colleges—that offer particularly strong services for LD students. If you qualify for such support, you should be diligent in checking out the services at each college on your list. If possible, pay a visit to the LD support office or have a phone conversation with one of the administrators. Since many such programs depend on the expertise of one or two people, the quality of the services can change abruptly with changes in staff.

Keep in mind also that many colleges are becoming increasingly skeptical of requests for LD services, especially when the initial diagnosis is made on the eve of the college search.

STRONG SUPPORT FOR STUDENTS WITH LEARNING DISABILITIES

Major Universities

American University
University of Arizona
Clark University
University of Colorado–Boulder
University of Connecticut
University of Denver
DePaul University
Fairleigh Dickinson University
University of Georgia
Hofstra University
Northeastern University
Purdue University
Rochester Institute of Technology
Syracuse University
University of Vermont

Small Colleges

Bard College
Beacon College
Curry College
Landmark College
Lesley University
Loras College
Lynn University
Manhattanville College
Marist College
Marymount Manhattan College
Mercyhurst College
Mitchell College
Muskingum College
New England College
University of New England
St. Thomas Aquinas College (NY)
West Virginia Wesleyan College
Westminster College (MO)

SAT and ACT Optional Schools

Many years ago a small number of pioneering U.S. colleges and universities, most notably Bates and Bowdoin, decided that they would no longer require all applicants to submit SAT or ACT scores. They reasoned that there is a significant pool of bright students who can do quality academic work but who for one reason or another do not test well. A "test-optional" policy would allow schools to tap into this market.

Over the years the number of "test-optional" or, in some cases, "test-flexible" schools has grown dramatically. The National Center for Fair and Open Testing (FairTest), a Cambridge, Massachusetts–based advocacy organization that is critical of standardized testing in general, has tracked this growth, and at press time its website (www.fairtest.org) listed more than 900 such colleges and universities. Reasons for this growing aversion to college admissions tests are many. The early test-optional schools have been happy with the way the policy has worked out. The SAT has been a focus of repeated controversy, especially around incidents of scoring errors. In a parallel development, a number of schools and a national commission headed by William Fitzsimmons, the dean of admission and financial aid at Harvard University, have begun to argue that SAT Subject Tests, AP exams, and International Baccalaureate exams—tests that are closely tied to curriculum—are more useful than regular SAT and ACT scores. And perhaps most importantly, the whole field of "test prep" has spiraled out of control. Students and parents alike are tired of the anxiety surrounding prep courses—not to mention the financial cost of helping bolster the coffers of Kaplan or Princeton Review.

Until recently there was not much that students could do—especially if they hoped to be able to choose among a range of quality colleges. Over the last few years, however, a critical mass has emerged of quality liberal arts colleges and major state universities that are test-optional or test-flexible in the sense that they offer applicants a range of options for the tests they take. There are now 100 such institutions covered in the *Fiske Guide*. For the first time, students who wish to avoid getting involved in the admissions-test rat race can do so while still enjoying a range of colleges and universities from which to choose.

Accordingly, we now publish a list of those colleges and universities in the guide that are test-optional. We are not recommending that any particular student eschew college admissions tests and apply only to these schools. As a resource designed to help students and parents, we are simply pointing out that applicants now have that option.

In looking over the list below of test-optional or test-flexible colleges and universities described in the *Fiske Guide*, please keep a couple of things in mind. First, most of the schools are large state universities or small liberal arts colleges. You won't find many other types, including the Ivies or flagship publics. Second, keep in mind that there are different ways of being test-optional or test-flexible. Some schools, for example, only exempt students who meet certain GPA or class-rank criteria, while others on the list still require other types of tests. Qualifications are noted in the footnotes. Finally, the test-optional field is changing daily, so go to www.fairtest.org for updated information and, above all, confirm current policy with any school to which you are thinking of applying.

Agnes Scott College
Allegheny College
American University
University of Arizona
Arizona State University
College of the Atlantic
Austin College
Bard College
Bates College
Beloit College
Bennington College
Birmingham–Southern College (5)
Bowdoin College

Brandeis University
Bryn Mawr College
The Catholic University of America
Clark University
Colby College (5)
Colorado College (5)
Connecticut College
Cornell College (5)
Denison University
DePaul University
Dickinson College
Drew University
Drexel University (5)

Earlham College
Eugene Lang College–The New School
  for Liberal Arts
Fairfield University
Franklin & Marshall College
Furman University
George Mason University
The George Washington University
Gettysburg College
Goucher College
Guilford College (5)
Gustavus Adolphus College
Hamilton College

Hampshire College
Hartwick College (4)
Hiram College
Hobart and William Smith Colleges
Hofstra University (4)
College of the Holy Cross
Hood College (3)
The College of Idaho
Ithaca College
Juniata College
Kalamazoo College
Knox College
Lake Forest College
Lawrence University
Lewis & Clark College (5)
Loyola University Maryland
Manhattanville College
Marlboro College
University of Mary Washington (3)
Middlebury College (5)

Mills College
Mount Holyoke College
Muhlenberg College
New York University (5)
Ohio Wesleyan University (3)
Pitzer College
Presbyterian College (3)
Providence College
University of Puget Sound
Quinnipiac University (4)
Ripon College
University of Rochester (5)
Rollins College
St. John's College
St. Lawrence University
Saint Michael's College
Sarah Lawrence College
Skidmore College
Smith College
University of the South (Sewanee)

Stetson University
Stevens Institute of Technology (5)
Susquehanna University
Trinity College (CT)
Union College (4)
Ursinus College
Wake Forest University
Warren Wilson College
Washington and Jefferson College
Washington College
Wells College
Wesleyan University
Wheaton College (MA)
Whitman College
Whittier College (3)
Willamette University
Wittenberg University
Worcester Polytechnic Institute

KEY

1 = SAT/ACT used only for placement and/or academic advising

2 = SAT/ACT required only from out-of-state applicants

3 = SAT/ACT may be required but considered only when minimum GPA and/or class rank is not met

4 = SAT/ACT required for some programs

5 = Test Flexible: SAT/ACT not required if other college level exams specified by school, such as SAT Subject Test, Advanced Placement, or Int'l Baccalaureate, submitted—contact school for details

6 = Placement test or school-specific admissions exam score required if not submitting SAT/ACT

7 = Admissions/Eligibility Index calculated with 3.5 GPA and combined SAT Critical Reading plus Math score of 400

A Note to the Reader

It seems like only yesterday that a small band of journalists gathered each evening in the back of the newsroom of the *New York Times*—where I was the Education Editor—to create the first edition of the *Fiske Guide to Colleges*. Now we've been in publication for more than 30 years!

The higher education scene was quite different in the early 1980s. Tuition and room and board averaged only $3,200 at public universities and $7,000 at private institutions. Stanford had just emerged as a national university, and hardly anyone outside the South had heard of Duke. AP exams and the Common Application were in their infancy, and Columbia still had not gotten around to admitting women. Division I university presidents still had some control over their athletic directors, and *U.S.News & World Report* was little more than a mediocre newsweekly.

But important changes were on the way. By the early 1980s the last of the baby boomers had worked their way through college. Admissions directors were losing sleep over whether they could fill their classrooms, so they responded with aggressive marketing campaigns. The methods they used seem quaint by current standards: telephone calls, videotapes (remember them?), and lavish four-color brochures that overflowed the mailboxes of any students whose ACT scores were larger than their shoe size.

The aggressive marketing of colleges produced a backlash—and an opportunity. Someone needed to wade in on the side of students and parents and cut through all the hype that was coming from the colleges. Thus was born the *Fiske Guide to Colleges*. Our vision was to use basic journalistic techniques to create a college guide that would provide reliable information on what it was like to be a student at the "best and most interesting" colleges and universities in the country. Since then we have done just that for millions of students, parents, and school counselors.

Consistent with changes in the culture of higher education over the last three decades, the content of the school profiles in the *Fiske Guide* has evolved. Given the impact of globalization, we have documented the proliferation of study abroad programs, and we have added write-ups on universities in Canada, Britain, Scotland, and Ireland. The write-ups reflect colleges' increased sensitivity to issues of campus safety, alcohol and drug abuse, and, more recently, to challenges surrounding sexual assault. Colleges today talk more about racial, ethnic, and socioeconomic diversity than they did in the early 1980s, although the numbers do not always show much progress. Many large universities have created "living/learning" communities in order to offer more intense learning environments within the context of a large institution. Perhaps most importantly, colleges, for better or worse, have seen it to be in their competitive interest to invest huge amounts of resources in student centers, fitness facilities, and other amenities designed to make the undergraduate experience more comfortable.

But one thing that has not changed over the last three decades is the importance of institutional cultures. When we started out to create the *Fiske Guide*, the big editorial risk was: Will numerous descriptions of small liberal arts colleges where "the faculty often invite students to their homes for dinner," make all liberal arts schools begin to sound alike—creating a pretty dull reading experience? But it turned out not to be a problem. The schools in the *Fiske Guide* are just as diverse as the students who apply to them. Even schools that look the same on paper have their own distinctive institutional cultures and personalities. The task of the *Fiske Guide* has been to capture those cultures and personalities of the "best and most interesting" colleges in the country. Students can then decide which schools are the best match for their own interests and learning styles.

In the age of the Internet, information is abundant and cheap. Endless facts and opinions about any particular college or university are just a few clicks away, but to know everything is to know nothing. The real challenge for college-bound students—the same challenge that faced an earlier generation in the early 1980s—is to cut through the mass of information that is being thrown at them and figure out what is really important. That's what the *Fiske Guide to Colleges* has been doing with authority for more than three decades. That's what we pledge to continue to do in the decades to come.

Edward B. Fiske
Durham, NC

University of Aberdeen: See page 378.

Adelphi University

One South Avenue, Garden City, NY 11530

Situated in a comfortable Long Island suburb within shouting distance of Manhattan, Adelphi lets you taste urban life without being overwhelmed. Long established as an innovator in public health and the arts. The last 15 years have brought lots of new buildings, faculty, and professional programs grounded in the liberal arts. Almost all undergrads are New Yorkers, two-thirds are women, and almost everyone gets some financial aid. The campus clears out on the weekends. Compare to Fairfield and Quinnipiac.

Think of Adelphi as a Gen Y of higher education. After going through a tumultuous time in the late 1990s when its president and most of the board were summarily fired, Adelphi began coming of age in 2002 thanks to new leadership and a revamped mission. The campus has seen more than $250 million of new construction and the renovation of 500,000 square feet of facilities. Enrollment has grown by nearly 65 percent, and 300 new faculty have been hired. Student financial aid has been expanded, and Adelphi has a policy of keeping tuition lower than peer institutions. Students say that, as a result, there is a palpable sense of energy among students and faculty.

Founded in 1863 as a prep school in Brooklyn, Adelphi morphed into a coeducational college and in 1928 moved to Garden City, where it occupies 75 acres in an attractive residential suburb replete with Gothic cathedrals and stately homes. The campus is recognized as an arboretum. New buildings on campus include centers for recreation, sports, and the performing arts that qualify as LEED certified.

General education requirements include a 24-credit distribution in several areas (arts, humanities and languages, natural sciences and mathematics, and social sciences) as well as courses in composition and English, a foreign language, statistics, computer programming, critical thinking, or public speaking. Freshmen take part in an orientation course and a three-credit freshman seminar that introduces students to life at Adelphi. Seniors complete a capstone course. Adelphi's most popular majors have a decidedly preprofessional bent: nursing, various health sciences, psychology, business, sport management, and social work. Physics and the fine and performing arts are also strong. Adelphi University's Robert B. Willumstad School of Business has earned accreditation from the Association to Advance Collegiate Schools of Business, joining an elite group of fewer than 10 percent of the world's business schools. The notable theater program draws creative students not inclined to stray far from home. Joint degree programs have been established in a number of disciplines, including physics, dentistry, law, and physical therapy. The combined degree program in engineering with Columbia allows students to earn a B.S. in physics from Adelphi and a B.S. in engineering from Columbia in five years, or an undergraduate and graduate degree in six years.

> **"It is a relaxed but still serious environment."**

A communications major says of the academic climate, "It is a relaxed but still serious environment. The students are generally working hard, but it never feels too intense." Fifty-one percent of all classes have fewer than 20 students, and professors are commended for their accessibility and knowledge. "Most professors are very

Website: www.adelphi.edu
Location: Suburban
Private
Total Enrollment: 5,660
Undergraduates: 4,400
Male/Female: 32/68
SAT Ranges: CR 500–600, M 510–620
ACT Ranges: 19–25
Financial Aid: 96%
Pell Grant: 37%
Expense: Pr $
Student Loans: 68%
Average Debt: $ $ $ $
Phi Beta Kappa: No
Applicants: 9,367
Accepted: 72%
Enrolled: 13%
Grad in 6 Years: 67%
Returning Freshmen: 84%
Academics: ✍ ✍ ✍
Social: ☎ ☎
Q of L: ★ ★ ★
Admissions: (516) 877-3050
Email Address: admissions@adelphi.edu

Strong Programs:
Nursing
Health Sciences
Psychology
Business
Sport Management
Social Work
Physics
Fine and Performing Arts

available outside of class time and are always willing to assist with classwork and material that might go beyond the course syllabus," says one English literature major.

Adelphi prides itself on its strong retention and graduation rates, which may reflect its emphasis on experiential learning and student engagement. The new Levermore Global Scholars program, open to students in all majors, takes an interdisciplinary approach to addressing global issues through special seminars, as well as cultural excursions, activities at the U.N. headquarters in New York City, and opportunities for internships, study abroad, and service projects. Overall, 20 percent of students study abroad. The recently expanded Honors College offers a rigorous liberal arts program for exceptional students, and Adelphi also has a well-staffed program for students with learning disabilities.

"We recently started a huge ongoing project called Racial Justice Matters."

The Levermore Global Scholars program addresses global issues through special seminars, cultural excursions, and activities at the U.N.

"The majority of students are white females from Long Island and New York City, but there are significant groups of students from all backgrounds and identities," says one student. Eighty-nine percent of undergraduates hail from New York, while 4 percent arrive from foreign countries. Minority enrollment is consistent with the university's proximity to the Big Apple: 9 percent of students are African American, 15 percent are Hispanic, and 9 percent are Asian American. Political activism doesn't dominate the campus, but students are aware of current issues. "We recently started a huge ongoing project called Racial Justice Matters that engages students with discussions, panels, and talks about race, racism, and violence," says a studio art major. Thirty-seven percent of current freshmen qualify for Pell Grants. Adelphi offers merit scholarships, worth an average of $13,839 each, to qualified students. More than 250 athletic scholarships are available in 23 sports.

Despite "comfortable and well-maintained" residence halls, Adelphi remains primarily a suitcase school. Seventy-six percent of students live off campus, "even if they live close to school," says one student. "The housing on campus is pretty plentiful, especially because Adelphi just built another new dorm building," says a business management major. Campus dining is a frequent complaint among students. "The quality of the food definitely does not match its price," grumbles one student. A senior says, "Campus security is very helpful. I have never felt unsafe on campus." The university is expanding its mandatory Title IX training programs to reach the entire student body.

"This is a commuter college," a nursing student explains. "The weekdays are great. The weekends are quiet." A senior adds, "I would definitely not call Adelphi a party school." The school sponsors 70 clubs and organizations, including 11 sororities and fraternities that attract 8 percent of the women and 10 percent of the men, respectively. "While there are a lot of people in Greek life, you definitely don't feel excluded if you're not a part of it," says one senior. Adelphi is a dry campus, and students say that the policy is strictly enforced. In the fall, students look forward to Family Weekend and to Ephemeral, a large art festival with a theme that changes every year. One student describes Garden City as "a very safe, low-key residential neighborhood," if not a college town. A senior says, "Manhattan is just a few stops away and you can see a Broadway show, go to a museum, or just walk around for fun. Our Center for Student Involvement also offers discounted show tickets as well as discounted movie tickets for local theaters."

"This is a commuter college. The weekdays are great. The weekends are quiet."

In the fall, students look forward to Ephemeral, a large art festival with a theme that changes every year.

Adelphi fields several competitive Division II teams (the Panthers), including men's and women's basketball and lacrosse, and women's soccer, tennis, volleyball, and softball. Indeed, the men's basketball team is a perennial tournament competitor, and women's lacrosse is a powerhouse, having won national titles in 2014 and 2015. In addition, the university has won the coveted Northeast-10 Conference President's Cup, awarded to the most outstanding program, for three of the last four years. More than a dozen intramural sports are available, as are 13 club sports.

At Adelphi, signs of rebirth and renewal are everywhere, from the campus facilities to the burgeoning enrollment. Although the university's commuter heritage can leave some wanting for more social opportunities, most welcome the chance to play an active role in shaping not just their education, but the community as a whole. Says a senior, "I really feel that all of our departments, as well as our students, work together to collaborate on new ideas, classes, events, and opportunities for the campus community."

If You Apply To ➤ **Adelphi:** Rolling admissions. (Priority deadline: Mar. 1.) Early action: Dec. 1. Financial aid: Mar. 1. Application fee: $40. Campus interviews: recommended, evaluative. No alumni interviews. SATs or ACTs: required. Subject Tests: optional. Letters of recommendation: required. Essay: required. Accepts the Common Application with supplement.

Agnes Scott College

141 East College Avenue, Decatur, GA 30030

Combines the tree-lined seclusion of Decatur with the bustle of Atlanta. More money in the bank per student than most Ivy League schools, and enrollment is up. Recent physical plant additions give ASC exceptional facilities for a college of its size. Small classes, sisterhood, and a more exciting location than some of its cohorts. Big emphasis on leadership and global learning.

Agnes Scott College, founded in 1889, offers a small-town campus atmosphere and provides women with an intellectually challenging institution—absent the distractions of men. The college is known for its science and math programs, but it also produces skilled writers and artists and continues to be one of the South's leading women's schools. It has become increasingly focused in recent years on designing a curriculum that cultivates globally aware women leaders. ASC's climate as a small, single-sex institution leads to close relationships with the faculty and very involved students—both academically and socially. "We believe in the power of women, of deep thinking, of honor, of social justice, of learning for the sake of learning," asserts one senior.

The Agnes Scott campus sits on 100 acres in the historic district of Decatur, just outside of Atlanta. The well-maintained Gothic and Victorian buildings are surrounded by gardens filled with rare shrubs, bushes, and trees—all evidence of thriving alumnae support. The $36.5 million Bullock Science Center includes an X-ray spectrometer, nuclear magnetic resonance imaging equipment, and a scanning tunneling microscope. The school's Delafield Planetarium has a computer-controlled Zeiss projector, one of only 10 in the United States. The Campbell Hall Living and Learning Center was recently renovated to house more than 80 beds and semi-suite style rooms, along with two learning centers; it received LEED Gold certification in 2015.

"We believe in the power of women."

In addition to outstanding instruction in the sciences, Agnes Scott provides students with solid grounding in the liberal arts. General education requirements have been reduced in order to encourage interdisciplinary majors and immersive experiences such as internships and mentored research, and a new Summit requirement

Website: www.agnesscott.edu
Location: City Center
Private
Total Enrollment: 838
Undergraduates: 838
Male/Female: 0/100
SAT Ranges: CR 550–690, M 510–640
ACT Ranges: 24–29
Financial Aid: 100%
Pell Grant: 47%
Expense: Pr $
Student Loans: 76%
Average Debt: $ $ $ $
Phi Beta Kappa: Yes
Applicants: 1,461
Accepted: 62%
Enrolled: 30%
Grad in 6 Years: 68%
Returning Freshmen: 87%
Academics: ✍ ✍ ✍
Social: ☎ ☎
Q of L: ★ ★ ★ ★

(continued)

Admissions: (404) 471-6285
Email Address: admission@
agnesscott.edu

Strong Programs:
Psychology
Public Health
English Literature
Neuroscience
Astrophysics
Mathematics
German Studies

As part of Summit, each student assembles her own board of advisors and documents her progress with a digital portfolio.

Diversity initiatives include the Transgender 101 Workshop and Diversity and Racial Justice programs.

has been added to encourage leadership skills in a context of global learning. As part of Summit, first-year students participate in a leadership immersion experience prior to arriving on campus in the fall, and then in the spring semester embark on a weeklong faculty-led study tour to places like Trinidad and Tobago, Cuba, and Bolivia. Each student also assembles her own board of advisors with faculty and staff members, a peer advisor, and a career mentor, and documents her progress throughout her four years with a digital portfolio. A junior praises Summit for introducing students to "a group of people totally committed to making sure you get where you want to be."

Academically, Agnes Scott delivers strong programs in biology, math, and astrophysics. The school also offers a top-notch German program, a rarity these days in U.S. higher education. Popular majors include psychology, English literature, and neuroscience. Engineers may complete their degrees through a 3–2 program with Georgia Tech. As a member of the Atlanta Regional Council for Higher Education*, Agnes Scott shares facilities and resources with 19 other schools in the area through a cross-registration program. New offerings include majors and minors in business management and public health.

The overall academic climate at ASC is rigorous but collaborative, and students are focused on learning first. "We are encouraged to find our own paths instead of competing for the same one," says a public health major. Adds a senior, "In every course, there is a cross-curricular approach. You will, at the end of your four years, be an excellent writer, speaker, and critical thinker." An honor system, enforced by a student judiciary, allows for self-scheduled and unproctored exams. The average first-year class size is 22 students, which encourages close student/faculty interactions in the classroom. "The professors provide fantastic assistance both in and out of the classroom and are unbelievably committed to their students," says one sophomore. "I cannot emphasize enough how invested Agnes Scott professors are in their students."

For those students wishing to leave Agnes Scott's idyllic campus behind for a time, there are study abroad options available at more than 150 universities in more

"We are encouraged to find our own paths instead of competing for the same one."

than 50 countries, including China, Germany, Korea, Poland, and Spain. The Hubert Scholars Program combines experiential learning with humanitarian service either at home or abroad. Past Hubert scholars have conducted HIV/AIDS research in South Africa and developed gender-equality education programs in Bangladesh. Seventy percent of students participate in research and may attend or present results at an annual conference held in the spring.

"Students who attend Agnes come from all over the globe," a sophomore says, and they "recognize the value of two very simple things: the value of diversity and the value of a women's education." The ASC student body hails mainly from the Southeast, and 55 percent are Georgia natives. Despite the school's small size, its denizens are quite diverse; 34 percent of the student body is African American, 10 percent Hispanic, and 6 percent Asian American. International students make up another 8 percent. The school has made socioeconomic diversity a priority as well—an impressive 47 percent of current freshmen are eligible for Pell Grants. Ample support is available for students of diverse backgrounds, and the school has implemented initiatives like the Transgender 101 Workshop and Diversity and Racial Justice programs to educate the campus community. "Because of the diversity I have in every one of my classes," says a business management major, "I am challenged every day to think about the world from perspectives that I could never think about myself." Scotties are generally liberal-leaning, and national issues of human rights, immigration, and refugee services have attracted attention on campus recently. Agnes Scott awards merit scholarships averaging $24,476 annually, based on academic performance, leadership, or musical ability.

Eighty-seven percent of students live in Agnes Scott's six dorms, which are linked by tree-lined brick walks. "The residence halls are pretty nice. They have walk-in closets, lots of storage, and all but two of them have air-conditioning," says a student. Another notes that living on campus is "essential to our campus culture, and I would feel quite distant from the school if I was not constantly in the midst of whatever is going on." Juniors and seniors can live in Avery Glen, the college-owned apartment complex, while incoming students are assigned to one of two first-year dorms. Two living/learning communities are available, one for first-year students interested in STEM, and the other for sophomores and juniors studying business. Students say that dining services staff is friendly and receptive to student feedback, and the food is usually good. They report feeling safe on campus too: "Campus security is very tight. There are always officers around keeping watch."

Living/learning communities are available for first-years interested in STEM and for sophomores and juniors studying business.

As for the ASC social scene, there are no sororities, but the college itself is a close-knit sisterhood. The programming group on campus (ProBo) always provides students with something to do. "Most social life takes place off campus at the neighboring colleges and universities," one junior says. "We have events here throughout the week, but the weekends are pretty quiet," adds a sophomore. Convenient public transportation serves cultural landmarks and provides access to the social scene in nearby Atlanta. Enforcement of drinking policies falls under the honor code. One student says the restrictions work well, and 21-year-olds

"I am challenged every day to think about the world from perspectives that I could never think about myself."

can enjoy alcohol in their dorms and at certain functions. Every October, students celebrate Black Cat week, during which classes compete in various activities and students attend a formal dance. Other quaint traditions survive too, such as throwing recently engaged classmates into the alumnae pond. And seniors who get into grad school or find jobs go to the top of the college bell tower, ringing the bell to share the good news.

Decatur itself is not really a college town, but there are some attractions for Agnes Scott students. "There are nice little venues and coffee shops; very hip and fun," a student says. Many ASC students get involved with community service both on and off campus, with Habitat for Humanity, the DeKalb Rape Crisis Center, Girl Scouts, Hands Across Atlanta, and Best Buddies. Popular road trips include Stone Mountain and Six Flags, or New Orleans for Mardi Gras.

Agnes Scott is a member of the USA South Athletic Conference, and the most competitive teams include tennis, soccer, and softball. The Scottie tennis team won the conference championship in 2015 for a seventh consecutive year, and the softball team brought home conference titles in 2014 and 2016. About 13 percent of students participate in intramural activities, which include the standard roundup of sports plus a few more exotic options, such as Zumba and scavenger hunts.

Small but mighty, ASC stands out for the little touches that make students feel they're part of an intimate community, starting with pine-scented brochures sent to accepted applicants. One Scottie Sister reflects, "Agnes Scott builds women who are fearless, who change the world, who question things and inspire others."

Overlaps

Georgia State, Spelman, Emory, University of Georgia, Kennesaw State, Oglethorpe, Mercer, Howard

If You Apply To ➤ **Agnes Scott:** Early decision: Nov. 1. Early action I: Nov. 15. Early action II: Jan. 15. Regular decision: Mar. 15. Financial aid: Feb. 15. Housing: May 1. No application fee. Campus interviews: optional, evaluative. No alumni interviews. SATs or ACTs: optional (required for homeschooled applicants). No Subject Tests. Letters of recommendation: required. Essay: required. Accepts the Common Application.

University of Alabama

Box 870132, Tuscaloosa, AL 35487

"Roll, tide, roll" still says a lot—but not everything—about Alabama, which is the fastest-growing public flagship in the country. Passion for the Crimson Tide is as strong as ever, but also look for strong honors programs, emphasis on undergraduate research, and pockets of professional excellence. Though its football team is back among the nation's elite, 'Bama still pales academically in comparison with rivals University of Georgia and University of Florida.

Although the University of Alabama earned its national reputation on the gridiron, the state's first university is committed to making an academic name for itself as well. In an effort to attract the South's best and brightest, UA has increased its emphasis on global perspectives, computer-based technologies, freshman learning communities, and undergraduate research and adopted a generous policy of merit scholarships.

'Bama's thousand-acre campus combines pristine brick, classical, revival-style buildings (several of which survived the Civil War) with modern structures. One of the most stunning in the South, the campus boasts an expansive lawn and majestic trees and wraps around a shaded quadrangle, the home of the main library and "Denny Chimes," a campanile carillon that rings the Westminster Chimes on the quarter hour. A student activity center and several Greek chapter houses have been completed recently.

The only course Alabama requires students to take during their first year on campus is a two-term English composition sequence. Before graduation, students must also complete courses in writing, natural sciences, math, humanities, and social sciences, and either two semesters of a foreign language or one of computer science. About 20 percent of 'Bama freshmen take part in the Arts and Sciences Mentoring Program, which pairs them with faculty mentors who ease the adjustment to college through informal counseling and enrichment activities such as concerts, movies, or lectures. The Freshman Learning Communities allow students to take two or three academic courses together, and a seminar taught by a full professor. The one-credit FLC seminar topic ties the academic courses together. All students may also enroll in the two-credit Academic Potential Seminar, which covers skills like self-assessment, personal responsibility, time management, note-taking, and test preparation. Incoming freshmen who are at the low end of UA's admissions requirements may participate in the Crimson Edge Program, which limits their first semester to 12 to 14 credit hours, requires an academic support class such as a Freshman Compass course, and includes specialized academic advising.

The university is organized into eight undergraduate colleges and schools, which together offer more than 80 undergraduate degree programs. The Culverhouse College of Commerce offers strong programs in marketing and management information systems. The College of Communication and Information Sciences is one of the country's top communication schools, while respected programs in the College of Human Environmental Sciences include food and nutrition and athletic training. The

"The classes are pretty tough because the teachers require your best and nothing less."

School of Music is a regional standout, attracting guest artists such as Itzhak Perlman and Wynton Marsalis. New College allows students to work with faculty to design their own interdisciplinary major. The most popular majors include business, communication studies, journalism, health professions, and engineering. UA's core

Website: www.ua.edu
Location: City Center
Public
Total Enrollment: 31,763
Undergraduates: 28,447
Male/Female: 45/55
SAT Ranges: CR 490–600, M 490–610
ACT Ranges: 22–31
Financial Aid: 42%
Pell Grant: 20%
Expense: Pub $ $
Student Loans: 46%
Average Debt: $ $ $
Phi Beta Kappa: Yes
Applicants: 36,203
Accepted: 54%
Enrolled: 37%
Grad in 6 Years: 67%
Returning Freshmen: 86%
Academics: ✑ ✑ ✑
Social: ☎ ☎ ☎
Q of L: ★ ★ ★
Admissions: (205) 348-5666
Email Address: admissions@ua.edu

Strong Programs:
Business
Communication Studies
Journalism
Health Professions
Engineering
Marketing
Management Information Systems
Food and Nutrition

curriculum is no cakewalk, students say. Says one senior, "The classes are pretty tough because the teachers require your best and nothing less." Professors teach lectures and many seminar courses, including some classes for freshmen. "Most of my teachers have been outstanding," a junior reports, "but I have had a teacher or two who just wasn't approachable or didn't cover their material very well."

The Honors College, established in 2003, now serves 6,500 students; it houses the three university-wide honors programs: computer-based honors, international honors, and university honors. Honors programs feature smaller classes, early registration privileges, and the opportunity to write a senior thesis. The University Scholars Program provides gifted undergraduates whose objectives include master's or doctoral degrees an opportunity to begin graduate work during their senior year and become eligible for graduate fellowships and scholarships. About 2,000 undergraduates conduct research each year, and other offerings include study abroad options (including more than 50 faculty-led and 27 reciprocal exchange programs around the world) and the innovative May interim term, when students spend three weeks focusing on one course in depth.

Freshman Learning Communities allow students to take two or three academic courses together, and a seminar taught by a full professor.

Just 46 percent of 'Bama's undergraduates are Alabama natives, and 3 percent are international students representing more than 60 countries. UA students are "smart, hardworking individuals who also have a good time when not studying," says a finance major. Eleven percent of UA students are African American, 1 percent are Asian American, and 4 percent are Hispanic. The biggest social and political issues on campus include free speech and diversity. 'Bama awards 259 athletic scholarships in 21 sports and has expanded the number of merit scholarships in the hopes of increasing enrollment; merit scholarships now average $13,514. Consistent with its efforts to lure strong students from outside of Alabama, the school spends more than $100 million on merit aid—more than twice what it allocates to students with financial need.

Although UA requires freshmen to reside on campus, most Alabama students live in off-campus apartments in the Tuscaloosa area; only 26 percent remain in campus residence halls, where options range from private rooms and suites to apartment-style living. "Most of the dorms have suites that house one to four people, though there are cheaper double-occupancy dorms as well," notes one student. "Most of the dorms are co-ed." A freshman gives high marks to the living/learning communities, some of which, like the Blount Scholars Program, are for first-year students; others bring together students from a particular school or college. Students report that campus dining options are edible, diverse, and expensive.

"[UA students are] smart, hardworking individuals who also have a good time when not studying."

Much of 'Bama's social life revolves around the Greek system and athletic events. Twenty-six percent of men pledge fraternities and 39 percent of women join sororities, and they may live in chapter houses. "The social life ranges from Greek life to campuswide activities to departmental events," says one student. Partying has remained a staple of the social scene in recent years, despite administrators' efforts to weaken it by prohibiting fraternities and sororities from having parties on campus. Regarding alcohol policies, "Unless someone is walking around, noticeably drunk, underage offenders don't get caught. If someone is going to drink, they'll find a way to do it." Those who don't go Greek, or who don't wish to drink, will find everything from the Society for Creative Anachronism (medievalists) to Bible study groups. A modern trolley service connects the 'Bama campus to the city's thriving downtown. Tuscaloosa is described as "an awesome college town," that is "mostly centered around the university." Road trips to New Orleans (for Mardi Gras and Greek weekend formals), Atlanta, Nashville, Birmingham, and the Gulf Coast and Florida beaches are popular, but "many people never leave UA!" says a sophomore.

The Honors College, established in 2003, now serves 6,500 students.

'Bama football remains the cornerstone of the university's competitive Division I athletic programs and is a perennial powerhouse. The annual Auburn–Alabama game—the Iron Bowl, one of the most intense rivalries in the nation—is the highlight of the school year. "Any Alabama football game is a festival," a sophomore says. Although the football program reported a $33 million operating surplus in 2014, the university supports a relatively modest 21 varsity teams. Men's golf has won two national championships in the last five years, and recent Southeastern Conference title winners include football and women's gymnastics, golf, softball, and tennis. 'Bama sports a number of solid nonathletic teams as well, including the Alabama Forensic Council, which has won 19 national speech and debate championships. Intramurals draw 30 percent of students.

> **"Any Alabama football game is a festival."**

Although sports are still an integral part of the UA experience, the university's emphasis is now on technology, merit scholarships, global perspectives, and undergraduate research. It seems students have taken notice: "We are more academically based," observes one senior, "and we have better programs and facilities."

If You Apply To ➤

Alabama: Rolling admissions. (Priority deadline: Feb. 1.) Financial aid: Mar. 1. Housing: May 1. Application fee: $40. Campus and alumni interviews: optional, evaluative. SATs or ACTs: required. Subject Tests: optional. Letters of recommendation: recommended. Essay: recommended.

Albion College

Albion, MI 49224

Nestled between evangelical Hope and Calvin and out-there Kalamazoo, Albion is Michigan's middle-of-the-road liberal arts college. Think Gerald Ford, the moderate Republican president who is the namesake of Albion's signature institute for public service. Future doctors, lawyers, and businesspeople are well served.

Albion is a small, private college in Michigan that emphasizes the importance of combining learning with hands-on experience, particularly when it comes to citizenship and service. Albion helps students achieve their goals "through classes, internships, projects, and a strong alumni network," says a senior. And when the work is through, students here enjoy a close-knit social life. "Albion is where I have built lifetime friendships," says a student.

Founded in 1835 by the Methodist Church, Albion is located near the banks of the Kalamazoo River. In addition to its newer Georgian-style architecture, the college has retained and restored several of its 19th-century buildings. The campus is spacious, with statuesque oaks and a beautiful nature center. Robinson Hall, the campus centerpiece, houses myriad departments, including the Gerald R. Ford Institute for Leadership in Public Policy and Service, the Carl A. Gerstacker Institute for Business and Management, and the Shaw Women's Center. The college is also home to the largest collegiate indoor riding arena in the United States, which is being expanded to host regional and national equestrian events. Renovations to the Davis Athletic Complex and a new living/learning center are also underway.

> **"Because of the small-school setting, it is easy to talk to anyone in my class."**

Albion has a rich academic history and was the first private college in Michigan

Website: www.albion.edu
Location: Small Town
Private
Total Enrollment: 1,354
Undergraduates: 1,354
Male/Female: 50/50
SAT Ranges: CR 500–590, M 420–570
ACT Ranges: 22–27
Financial Aid: 99%
Pell Grant: 36%
Expense: Pr $ $
Student Loans: 68%
Average Debt: $ $ $ $
Phi Beta Kappa: Yes
Applicants: 2,803
Accepted: 80%
Enrolled: 20%

to have a Phi Beta Kappa chapter (1940). Students are required to take core courses distributed among humanities, natural sciences, social sciences, fine arts, and math. They must also satisfy requirements in environmental science and gender and ethnicity studies. Freshmen take first-year seminars designed to provide a "stimulating learning environment" in a small-class setting, while seniors participate in a capstone experience.

The Ford Institute takes a unique approach for future civic leaders. Students participate in a simulation of city government in which they play the roles of community leaders. Visiting speakers include senators and congresspeople, governors and state legislators, and interest-group representatives. The premed and prelaw programs draw dedicated undergrads, and the English and economics and management departments are well respected. Other popular majors include biology, psychology, business, and accounting. New offerings include a major in physics with an astronomy emphasis, and minors in accounting and finance.

The academic climate at Albion is described as competitive in certain departments, but not cutthroat. One student says, "Because of the small-school setting, it is easy to talk to anyone in my class to work together or ask questions," and professors "get to know you really well." Top-notch academic and career counseling and low student/faculty ratios keep students on track and motivated. Class size varies, but 63 percent of classes have fewer than 20 students. Professors are interested in students' academic performance and their emotional well-being. "They have additional office hours on Sundays, come in for review sessions at 10 o'clock at night, and give out their personal phone numbers for questions," according to a junior. Teaching assistants are used for tutoring, not teaching.

For those looking to expand their educational experience, Albion offers roughly 120 study abroad programs in 40 countries, as well as an honors program for highly motivated students. The Foundation for Undergraduate Research, Scholarship, and Creative Activity, which pairs students from

"The food is relatively healthy, but usually hit or miss."

all disciplines with faculty mentors, is highly praised by students. One participant, a biochemistry major, says, "My professor walked me through new and old techniques individually, so I feel much more independent in the lab than most."

Albion attracts an ambitious, involved group of students. "I feel that surrounding myself with genuine, intelligent, passionate, athletic, and hardworking people has pushed me to become a better version of myself," says a business management major. Michigan residents make up 86 percent of the student population, and just 2 percent hail from abroad. Six percent are African American, 5 percent are Hispanic, and 2 percent are Asian American. Up to now, there has been little deviation from the white, upper-middle-class norm. In an effort to change this, a host-family program matches minority students with families from within the community. Additionally, 36 percent of accepted freshmen are now Pell-eligible. A senior describes the student body as "very social and friendly, and concerned about current issues"; recent issues drawing attention on campus include immigration, women's rights, and minority rights. There are a number of merit scholarships available, averaging $19,522, but no athletic scholarships.

Ninety percent of Albion students call the co-ed residence halls home, although the housing system draws complaints from students. "We overpay for old rooms," says one senior, and another adds, "Albion needs to allow students to live off campus for financial reasons." The majority of the freshman class inhabits Wesley Hall. During their sophomore year, many students move to the suite-style rooms in Whitehouse Hall or Mitchell Towers; seniors occupy apartment-style housing called The Mae. Other housing options include apartment annexes and fraternity houses. Sororities do not have houses; they hold their meetings in lodges. Campus residents

(continued)

Grad in 6 Years: 72%
Returning Freshmen: 80%
Academics: ✍ ✍ ✍
Social: ☎ ☎
Q of L: ★ ★ ★
Admissions: (800) 858-6770
Email Address: admission@albion.edu

Strong Programs:
Biology
Premed
Psychology
Economics and Management
Business
Accounting
Communication Studies
English

Students in the Ford Institute participate in a simulation of city government in which they play the roles of community leaders.

enjoy many made-to-order menu items at the centrally located dining hall, which was renovated in 2013. "The food is relatively healthy, but usually hit or miss," according to a junior. As for safety, one student reports, "Albion has a great campus security staff," although others note that sexual assault is increasingly becoming an issue on campus. While the school has developed several education programs and student organizations to help prevent sexual assaults, students agree that it could better handle incidents once they've occurred. "Punishments should be stronger for students convicted of sexual assault," says a communication studies and English major. But students do rate campus counseling services very highly.

Fifty-three percent of Albion men and 43 percent of the women belong to one of the school's six national fraternities and seven sororities. Greek parties draw large crowds, composed of Greeks and non-Greeks, making them a primary part of many students' social lives. "Greek organizations do tend to set the tone for social life, because most parties happen at the frats," says one student. A well-run union board organizes all sorts of activities—films, lectures, plays, comedians, and concerts—to keep students occupied in their spare time. Several students report that, although there is not much to do in the town of Albion,

"Albion is the support system that I did not know I needed."

its Festival of the Forks is an annual favorite, and the movie theater offers "free movies if you show a valid student ID!" Students 21 and older may consume alcohol in certain campus residence areas, and Cascarelli's is a popular bar in town. Road trips are a big part of weekends for many students; Ann Arbor and East Lansing are frequent destinations.

"The town of Albion needs improvements," says a junior, but some new developments are in progress in the downtown area. Students focus some of their energy by working for groups supported by the Student Volunteer Bureau; in fact, half of the students volunteer in the community on a regular basis, participating in "city cleanup day, Habitat for Humanity, and volunteering at nursing homes and schools." Some traditional events that offer a nice break from academics are the Briton Bash, a fair that familiarizes students with clubs and organizations, and the Day of Woden, which is a picnic held in the spring on the last day of class.

The Britons football team competes in the Division III Michigan Intercollegiate Athletic Association and has won 36 conference championships—the most in MIAA history. Other recent conference champs include men's and women's lacrosse, men's and women's tennis, and women's soccer. Hope College is a bitter rival, as is Alma College. Recreational and intramural sports attract 32 percent of students, and some of the most popular include canoeing, disc golf, basketball, volleyball, and indoor soccer.

"Albion is the support system that I did not know I needed," muses one student. Professors are accessible and interested, and academics are challenging without being overwhelming. Students appreciate the appeal of a "small campus with friendly students, caring faculty, and kind staff members."

If You Apply To ➤ | **Albion:** Rolling admissions. Early action: Dec. 1. Financial aid: Feb. 15. No application fee. Campus and alumni interviews: optional, evaluative. SATs or ACTs: required. Subject Tests: optional. Letters of recommendation: required. Essay: required. Accepts the Common Application with supplement.

Alfred University

Alumni Hall, Saxon Drive, Alfred, NY 14802

Talk about an unusual combination: Alfred combines a nationally renowned college of ceramics, a school of art and design, an engineering program, and a business school wrapped up in a university of just over 1,700 undergraduates. The Finger Lakes is a region full of natural beauty, but it takes elbow grease to pry coastal types to the hinterlands of western New York.

With 1,700 undergraduate students, Alfred University isn't a bustling academic factory; it's a quiet, cloistered, self-described "educational village" in a tiny town wholly dedicated to the "industry of learning." The university boasts highly respected programs in art and design, as well as ceramic engineering. Innovation not only shapes the curriculum, but also has a profound effect on campus life. Small classes and friendly competition support this diversity while encouraging individuals to succeed. Along with being able to handle the academic rigors of the college, students also have to weather brutal winters that dump snow by the foot on the region.

Alfred's campus consists of a charming, close-knit group of modern and Georgian brick buildings, along with a stone castle. The Kanakadea Creek runs right through campus, and the town of Alfred consists of two colleges (the other is Alfred State College) and a main street with one stoplight. There are a few shops and restaurants, but certainly no malls, parking lots, or tall buildings. Recent additions to campus include a health and wellness center, a center for academic success, and the Alfred Ceramic Art Museum.

The university and its students share a no-nonsense approach to education. Although prospective students apply directly to one of four colleges and declare a tentative major, half of all requirements for a bachelor's degree are earned in the liberal arts college. Requirements are quite different in each school. However, the mix usually includes coursework in oral and written communication, foreign language and culture, social sciences, history, literature, philosophy, and religion.

Alfred, though private, is actually the "host" school for the New York State College of Ceramics, which is a unit of the state university system and comes with a public university price tag. Ceramic engineering (the development and refinement of ceramic materials) is the academic cornerstone and the program that brings Alfred international recognition. All engineering programs are found within the School of Engineering, and there is a degree in renewable energy engineering. The School of Art and Design's art department, with its programs in ceramics, glass, printmaking, sculpture, video, and teacher certification, is also highly regarded. The business administration school also gets good reviews from students and provides undergraduates with work experience through a small business institute where students have real clients. Art and design, psychology, mechanical engineering, business, and marketing are the most popular majors. The major in foreign language and culture sponsors trips abroad, and faculty-led study abroad programs are offered during the May term and spring break, in addition to hundreds of exchange and affiliate programs around the globe. The Track II program enables students to design their own interdisciplinary majors with personal guidance from top faculty members.

"I would say that Alfred is pretty competitive," says a junior. "The studio courses are challenging," adds a sophomore. Whatever their major, all students enjoy small classes, and the quality of teaching is reported as high. "The teachers are very accessible and more than willing to help students with anything they need," says a freshman. Most classes are taught by full professors, with graduate students and teaching

Website: www.alfred.edu
Location: Rural
Private
Total Enrollment: 1,923
Undergraduates: 1,730
Male/Female: 50/50
SAT Ranges: CR 450–570, M 470–580
ACT Ranges: 21–28
Financial Aid: 99%
Pell Grant: 44%
Expense: Pr $
Student Loans: 83%
Average Debt: $ $ $
Phi Beta Kappa: Yes
Applicants: 3,640
Accepted: 68%
Enrolled: 18%
Grad in 6 Years: 60%
Returning Freshmen: 75%
Academics: ✍ ✍ ✍
Social: ☎ ☎ ☎
Q of L: ★ ★ ★
Admissions: (800) 541-9229
Email Address: admissions@alfred.edu

Strong Programs:
Ceramic Engineering
Art and Design
Psychology
Mechanical Engineering
Business Administration
Marketing
Glass Engineering Science
Accounting

assistants helping out only in lab sessions. The university stresses its commitment to helping undergrads plan their future, and the academic advising and career planning services are strong enough for Alfred to deliver on its promise. Students say faculty members really want to see them succeed, both in class and in the real world. "Most teachers have high expectations, resulting in greater student performance," says one junior.

Alfred students are "creative and like to be challenged," says a business administration major. Seventy-seven percent of the students at Alfred are from New York State, and 3 percent are international. African Americans comprise 9 percent of the student body, Hispanics 7 percent, and Asian Americans 2 percent. Forty-four percent of freshmen are Pell-eligible, a notable number for a school of Alfred's size. Outstanding students can apply for many merit scholarships, averaging $10,616. There are no athletic scholarships.

No one seems to mind the two-year on-campus residency requirement because the rooms are large and comfortable, and the dorms are equipped with lounges,

"Most teachers have high expectations, resulting in greater student performance."

kitchens, and laundry facilities. Upperclassmen have a choice of dorms that are co-ed by floor with single rooms, suites, or apartments. Freshmen enjoy their own housing divided into doubles. Seventy-six percent of all students choose to live on campus, but some juniors and about half of the seniors opt to live off campus. The school has two dining halls, and students say the offerings include plenty of selections for vegetarians and vegans. "The dining facilities are very nice and well equipped, and the food is both diverse and edible," says a junior. Campus security is good, according to most students. "There are blue lights all over campus, and AU security will provide rides or walking escorts if you feel unsafe walking alone," a biology major says.

Alfred's location in the Finger Lakes region, almost two hours from Buffalo and an hour and a half from Rochester, is isolated. The other chief complaint is the chilly, snowy weather. Social life is difficult due to the rural atmosphere and lack of Greek organizations, but the Student Activities Board brings many events to campus, including musicians, comedians, lecturers, and movies. Alfred is a dry campus, and students say the alcohol policy is largely respected, and enforced in the dorms. "Alfred doesn't have too many problems with drinking that I have heard of," a student says. Because Alfred shares the town with Alfred State College, the dominant student population makes Alfred a good college town. "It is a small town, and a very close community," observes a biology major. About a quarter of Alfred students volunteer in the community. The downtown scene provides students with an adequate number of movie theaters and eateries. Every spring brings the annual Hot Dog Weekend, a big carnival-like event that fills Main Street with game booths, bands, and lots of hot dog stands.

Alfred's Division III Saxons are ominous opponents on the football, soccer, and lacrosse fields, and the football and softball teams each won their respective conference championships in 2015. The equestrian team is competitive too. Many Alfred students are skiing, hunting, camping, and rock-climbing enthusiasts, and favorite road trips include Letchworth and Stony Brook state parks, as well as Ithaca, Rochester, Buffalo, and Toronto. Intramurals draw 28 percent of students, with volleyball, soccer, and basketball being most popular, and friendly games of Frisbee and other sports can often be found on campus.

"[Students are] creative and like to be challenged."

Overlaps

Rochester Institute of Technology, SUNY–Buffalo, Clarkson, SUNY–Binghamton, SUNY–Brockport, SUNY–Cortland, Alfred State

"Alfred University will prepare you to go into the real world," says a freshman. Although small and somewhat secluded, Alfred University is a good choice for those students who want to concentrate on the ABCs of arts, business, and ceramic engineering—just be sure to bundle up for the long, snowy winters.

Allegheny College

520 North Main Street, Meadville, PA 16335

An unpretentious cousin to more well-heeled places like Dickinson and Bucknell. Draws heavily from the Buffalo-Cleveland-Pittsburgh area. The college's powerhouse athletic teams feast on Division III competition. A robust Greek system gives Allegheny a strong traditional college life. If you've ever wondered what lake-effect snow is, you'll find out here.

Allegheny College is a down-to-earth Eastern liberal arts school boasting a rich history of academic excellence in an intimate setting. Administrators here understand the importance of providing students with real-world experience to complement their classroom work and place a special emphasis on the development of oral communication skills. The school's innovative May term offers time for internships or other off-campus work and study, and a commitment to civic responsibility has spurred several new programs. Allegheny's small size means students don't suffer from lack of attention, and despite the heavy workload, anyone struggling academically will get help before the situation becomes dire. "The education you will receive at Allegheny is priceless," says one senior.

Allegheny's 79-acre campus is tucked away in Meadville, Pennsylvania, 90 miles north of Pittsburgh. Founded in 1815 and nestled in the Norman Rockwell–esque rolling hills of northwestern Pennsylvania, the campus is home to traditional architecture and redbrick streets, as well as new additions such as apartment-style housing for upperclassmen. A nationally acclaimed science complex supports already strong programs, and students who wish to break a sweat can do so at the Wise Sports and Fitness Center. The college also owns a 123-acre outdoor recreational complex, a 283-acre research reserve, and an 80-acre protected forest. The 40,000 square-foot Vukovich Center for Communication Arts is home to rehearsal and instructional areas, video production facilities, and a large performance space.

Allegheny offers more than 30 majors and 40 minors, and all students are required to complete at least one minor in addition to their major. The college operates on two 15-week semesters each year, and each features an Academic Programming Day: classes do not meet and students are able to participate in a number of college-sponsored programs, including open houses, advising and career counseling workshops, and other campus events. Allegheny's newly revised curriculum requires all students to complete at least one course in each of eight distribution areas: civic learning; human experience; international and intercultural perspectives; modes of expression; power, privilege, and difference; quantitative reasoning; scientific process and knowledge; and social behavior and institutions. Freshmen take two first-year seminars that help them transition to college-level work and develop writing and speaking skills. Sophomores take a communication-focused seminar, juniors take a seminar in their major field, and seniors complete an intensive capstone project in their major, where they are required to orally defend a work of independent research.

Website: www.allegheny.edu
Location: Small City
Private
Total Enrollment: 1,882
Undergraduates: 1,882
Male/Female: 46/54
SAT Ranges: CR 503–630, M 510–620
ACT Ranges: 22–29
Financial Aid: 99%
Pell Grant: 31%
Expense: Pr $ $
Student Loans: N/A
Average Debt: N/A
Phi Beta Kappa: Yes
Applicants: 4,324
Accepted: 68%
Enrolled: 17%
Grad in 6 Years: 75%
Returning Freshmen: 83%
Academics: ✍ ✍ ✍
Social: ☎ ☎ ☎
Q of L: ★ ★ ★
Admissions: (800) 521-5293
Email Address: admissions@allegheny.edu

Strong Programs:
Environmental Science
Economics
International Studies
Psychology
Biology
English
Physical Sciences

Students at Allegheny typically work hard and do well. "The school is definitely competitive," says a sophomore. The school's strongest programs include environmental science, economics, physical and biological sciences, and international studies (which offers tracks in Middle Eastern and North African studies). Psychology, biology, economics, and English enroll the most students. There is a major in biochemistry, a chemistry curriculum, and a track for students interested in entrepreneurial and managerial economics. Co-op programs include a 3–2, 3–3, or 3–4 option leading to degrees in engineering, public policy and management, nursing, and allied health. Additionally, Allegheny is a member of the Great Lakes Colleges Association*.

"Students at Allegheny are not only very friendly, but very willing to learn and to take chances."

Students praise Allegheny's faculty for their passion, knowledge, and accessibility. "The quality of instruction is outstanding. If I have questions, professors will always sit down with me and work through a problem or concept until I understand it. They're very patient," a junior says. You won't find a TA at the lectern in any Allegheny classroom, and sixty-eight percent of courses have fewer than 20 students. The college's honor code allows students to take unproctored exams.

All students are required to complete at least one minor in addition to their major.

The Allegheny Gateway is a clearinghouse for internship opportunities, service learning, and overseas study. Off campus, Allegheny offers study in several U.S. cities and 16 countries, and semester internships or job shadowing experience. Twenty-eight percent of students partake in some form of study abroad. There's also an on-campus independent study option, and a three- or four-week Experiential Learning term following spring semester that allows students to pursue study abroad programs and internships that aren't available during the year. More than 100 students receive funding each summer to participate in faculty-guided research. Although Allegheny does not have an honors program, there are 15 national honor society chapters on campus.

Fifty-one percent of Allegheny's students hail from Pennsylvania, and sizable contingents come from nearby Ohio, New York, and New England. Three percent of students are international. "Students at Allegheny are not only very friendly, but very willing to learn and to take chances," says one senior. African Americans make up 6 percent of the student population, Hispanics 7 percent, and Asian Americans 2 percent. "Students are very aware politically," claims one sophomore. The college's Center for Political Participation engages students by fostering an appreciation for the vital link between an engaged, active citizenry and a healthy democracy. Merit scholarships averaging $17,480 are available but there are no athletic awards. Thirty-one percent of the most recent freshman class was eligible for Pell Grants, highest among the Western Pennsylvania liberal arts schools.

Seniors complete an intensive capstone project in their major, where they are required to orally defend a work of independent research.

Housing is guaranteed for four years, and residence halls and houses accommodate 92 percent of the student body in relative style and comfort, offering TV and study rooms. "We need more apartment-style residence halls, and older residence halls need to be renovated," says one student. Options include all-freshman dorms; co-ed and single-sex halls; small houses; and single, double, and triple rooms and suites. Students are happy with their on-campus food choices and "security is all right," says a student. "It's a small town and nothing really happens, however like any campus there are sexual assaults and thefts. The school recently revamped its sexual assault protocol." That protocol includes a sexual assault victim bill of rights and a "no-tolerance" stance on campus violence.

"Greek life is very big here."

Greek organizations draw 28 percent of the men and 29 percent of the women, and provide a great deal of nightlife. "Greek life is very big here," confirms a history major. There are two campus theater series, free movies in the quad, and comedians, ventriloquists, and live bands provided by the Office of Student Involvement.

Large-scale philanthropic events like Make a Difference Day and the Month of Service, in March, are also popular. "Social life at Allegheny takes place predominantly on campus, as Meadville is a small town without many recreational accommodations," says one student. College policy states that students must be 21 to have or consume alcohol on campus, but according to one student, "The social scene doesn't revolve around alcohol." Homecoming, Greek Sing, Wingfest in the fall (featuring free wings), Springfest (a day full of bands, activities, and food), and Winterfest break up the monotony of studying, and midnight breakfasts served by faculty help ease end-of-semester stress. As for Allegheny traditions, there's the somewhat suspect "13th Plank" ritual, which states that all freshman women must be kissed on the 13th plank of the campus bridge by an upperclassman, in order to be considered "true Allegheny co-eds." Of course, a group of freshman men steal the plank every year at the beginning of the first semester to prevent that from happening.

Students contribute more than 60,000 hours of community service each year.

Downtown Meadville, lovingly referred to as Mudville, is a 10-minute walk from campus and worlds away from a college town. It has several community playhouses, as well as schools, hospitals, children's homes, animal shelters, and other organizations that benefit from the more than 60,000 hours of service students contribute each year. "We've really gotten to know the local businesses and take pride in supporting our local community," says an English major. When more time in Meadville is too much to bear, students hit the road, venturing to factory outlets in nearby Grove City, Pennsylvania, or heading toward the bright lights of Pittsburgh, Buffalo, or Cleveland. "What's nice is that even though Meadville is small, larger cities are close by so you can get away if need be," a senior says. Nearby state parks, Conneaut Lake, and Lake Erie offer waterskiing and boating in warm weather and cross-country skiing in the winter.

> **"We've really gotten to know the local businesses and take pride in supporting our local community."**

Athletics play a big role in Allegheny life, and the sports and fitness complex gives students reason to cheer. Twenty-five percent of Allegheny students compete in Division III athletics, and the Gators field 19 varsity teams. Women's soccer has won multiple conference championships in recent years, and men's and women's cross-country and golf have enjoyed tournament success. Thirty percent of students participate in club, recreational, and intramural sports, with basketball, soccer, and volleyball drawing the most interest.

Allegheny College boasts a rich history of academic excellence in an intimate setting, augmented by a new emphasis on extracurricular experiences designed to produce well-rounded alumni. The campus's natural beauty and the genuine affection students feel for it and for each other remain unchanged. What's more, students appreciate the value placed on individuality and involvement. "Students are encouraged to explore their unusual combinations of interests, skills, and talents," says one junior. "The word 'no' is not often used here."

Overlaps

Washington and Jefferson, University of Pittsburgh, Penn State, College of Wooster, Westminster College (PA), Denison, Duquesne, Juniata

If You Apply To ➤

Allegheny: Early decision I: Nov. 1. Early action: Dec. 1. Early decision II: Feb. 1. Regular decision and financial aid: Feb. 15. No application fee. Campus interviews: recommended, informational. Alumni interviews: optional, informational. SATs or ACTs: optional. Subject Tests: optional. Letters of recommendation: required. Essay: required. Accepts the Common Application with supplement.

The college that put the "Alma" back in "alma mater." As friendly a campus as you'll find, Alma savors its Scottish heritage and combines the liberal arts with distinctive offerings in health and preprofessional fields. Students are socioeconomically diverse, but few out-of-staters enroll. If central Michigan eventually makes you stir-crazy, join the hordes who go abroad. Bring your bagpipes.

A tiny gem on Michigan's lower peninsula, Alma College was founded in 1886 by Presbyterians with an ambitious fourfold mission: "To prepare graduates who think critically, serve generously, lead purposefully, and live responsibly as stewards of the world they bequeath to future generations." Located in the city dubbed "Scotland, USA," the college puts its strong Scottish heritage on display. "Every spring, the city of Alma holds an annual Highland Festival that draws participants from all over the world," explains an environmental health major. "Our marching band also wears traditional Scottish kilts to every football game." Alma has a wide array of choices for its undergraduates, including distinctive offerings in health and preprofessional fields, as well as the opportunity to learn abroad.

Alma's campus features 27 Prairie-style buildings of redbrick and limestone surrounding a scenic central mall. Although Alma was founded more than 130 years ago, most of the buildings have been built or renovated in recent years. There are lots of trees and open places to sit, at least in the warmer months.

The Alma experience begins with Orientation Week, a freshmen-only week of activities that help students get to know each other and ease the transition into college; students also begin their First-Year Seminar classes during this week. A peer-mentoring program places successful upper-class students in contact with new students to help them adapt to the opportunities and expectations of an engaged college community. Trustee Honors Scholarship recipients are invited to attend a two-credit Freshman Honors Seminar during their first year. To graduate, students must satisfy general education requirements, including the first-year seminar and 12 credits in each of three divisions: humanities, social sciences, and natural sciences. Students must also demonstrate proficiency in a second language or international awareness.

> **"Our marching band…wears traditional Scottish kilts to every football game."**

The college offers 47 majors, of which public health, communication, and environmental studies are some of the strongest. Alma's most popular majors, per student enrollment, are business administration, integrative physiology and health science, psychology, English, and biology. Biology and psychology prepare students for work with wellness intervention programs and public health agencies, or graduate study in medicine, nursing, or physical therapy. A new major in neuroscience was recently added. "The academic climate of Alma College is competitive, but there is support to help students who might be struggling," says one student. Another adds, "The Counseling and Wellness Center at Alma is a great resource for anyone who may need extra support, especially in times of stress." Students interested in the Scottish arts find a range of opportunities to work with nationally known instructors of bagpipe and Highland dance, or join in seminars offered by award-winning Scottish authors. Alma's professors garner plenty of praise. "The professors here want to see you succeed and will guide and assist you," says a freshman. Sixty-eight percent of undergraduate classes have fewer than 20 students. Undergraduate research is big at Alma, and 42 percent of students pursue an independent project under a professor's guidance or join shared faculty projects.

Website: www.alma.edu
Location: Small City
Private
Total Enrollment: 1,329
Undergraduates: 1,329
Male/Female: 43/57
SAT Ranges: CR 518–650, M 510–670
ACT Ranges: 21–27
Financial Aid: 98%
Pell Grant: 29%
Expense: Pr $
Student Loans: 75%
Average Debt: $ $ $ $
Phi Beta Kappa: Yes
Applicants: 2,479
Accepted: 68%
Enrolled: 20%
Grad in 6 Years: 61%
Returning Freshmen: 84%
Academics: ✐ ✐ ✐
Social: ☎ ☎ ☎
Q of L: ★ ★ ★
Admissions: (800) 321-2562
Email Address: admissions@alma.edu

Strong Programs:
Public Health
Communication
Environmental Studies
Business Administration
Integrative Physiology and Health Science
Psychology
English
Biology

Alma's student-centered philosophy is exemplified by the Alma Commitment, which offers a four-year graduation promise and a pledge that each interested student can participate in an experiential learning opportunity, such as an internship, research fellowship, or study abroad. Participating students receive $2,500 in Alma Venture funding. Despite Alma's small size and rural surroundings, the terms "provincial" and "insular" just don't apply here. In fact, one of the college's selling points is its wide variety of study abroad opportunities, in which 38 percent of students participate. During the one-month spring term, students enroll in a single intensive course, many of which involve off-campus study; in recent courses, students have studied social change in China, explored marine organisms in Hawaii, and volunteered in schools and hospitals in Peru. Alma offers a study abroad program with the University of Aberdeen in Scotland, along with opportunities in 13 other countries, such as Austria, India, Italy, and New Zealand. "I went to London for a Shakespeare course and it was incredible," cheers one religious studies major. "We saw more than 15 plays and lived in flats in the city." Additionally, the Posey Global Leadership Initiative provides opportunities for students to participate in international internship, research, and leadership experiences. The college's Service Learning Program gives students academic credit for work with nonprofit economic development organizations or educational, environmental, and social service agencies.

The Alma Commitment offers a four-year graduation promise and a pledge that each interested student can participate in an experiential learning opportunity.

"Alma students are extremely involved, hardworking, dedicated to helping others, and caring," says one junior. The campus is largely homogeneous, with 91 percent of the student population coming from Michigan and 2 percent from abroad. African Americans account for 4 percent, Asian Americans 1 percent, and Hispanics 4 percent of the student population. There is more to be said for socioeconomic diversity; 29 percent of students are eligible for Pell Grants. While not an overly political campus, Alma does have its fair share of activists; personal rights and diversity concerns top the list of hot issues. Brainy types can vie for merit scholarships worth an average of $19,258; there are no athletic scholarships.

"The professors here want to see you succeed and will guide and assist you."

Eighty-eight percent of Alma's students reside on campus. "Residence halls are a bit outdated, but at the same time, livable," says one first-year student. Freshmen are assigned rooms in co-ed halls, while upperclassmen play the lottery and usually get suites. Other options include an international house, a Model UN house, and a Women's Resource Center. Everyone buys 14 or 19 meals a week, and gets his or her grub on at the all-you-can-eat Commons or at Joe's Place, a snack bar. Students say they feel safe on campus thanks to the presence of patrolling security guards. Still, "Sexual assault has been an issue on campus, especially this year," says one freshman. "The school is responding by educating students more on this topic."

When it comes time to socialize, says a student, the Alma College Union Board provides plenty of on-campus fun. "We offer music performances, movie nights, speakers, student panels, and tons of events in the dorms," says a senior. "Greek life and athletics are the main extracurricular activities that students are involved in," adds another student. Twenty-four percent of the men and 25 percent of the women go Greek. Alcohol plays a part in the social scene, but most students tend to agree that drinking is not a big problem on campus. "We are not a dry campus so there are parties on weekends for those that choose to go," explains a sophomore. Underage students caught imbibing are written up and fined. "There is no stigma for people who don't drink," reassures one student.

Alma's Model United Nations teams have received top recognition for a record 20 consecutive years.

Town/gown relations at Alma are strong, with the vast majority of students volunteering, taking part-time jobs, and otherwise getting involved in the community.

"There is a movie theater and a few restaurants," one student says. "Alma is a very small city, and does not offer too much to do outside of campus," adds another. The annual Highland Festival features bagpipers and Scottish dancing; for members of the Alma marching band, who strut in kilts stitched from the college's own registered Alma College tartan, every performance might as well be a festival. Students with wheels will find diversions within easy reach, as Mount Pleasant, Saginaw, and the East Lansing campus of Michigan State are less than an hour away, and ski slopes are just a bit farther. In the warmer months, the beaches of two Great Lakes, Huron and Michigan, are also two hours away.

> **"The overall atmosphere at Alma is warm and inviting."**

The Alma Scots compete at the Division III level as a member of the Michigan Intercollegiate Athletic Association, the oldest existing athletic conference in the nation. Alma offers 24 varsity sports—12 for the women and 12 for the men—and the most popular include football, wrestling, women's soccer, and softball. The softball team advanced to the national championship finals in 2015. For nonvarsity types, there is an active intramural program—more than half of the students participate. Alma's Model United Nations teams have received top recognition at the world's largest and most prestigious collegiate Model UN conference for a record 20 consecutive years (1997 through 2016), the longest streak of any college or university.

"The overall atmosphere at Alma is warm and inviting," says one satisfied student. "The friendships that students make during their time at Alma are ones that will last a lifetime." Helpful advisors and caring faculty members help Alma students chart a course on campus and in the broader world, allowing them to leave well prepared for today's competitive job market. Michigan natives and newcomers alike are sure to find a warm welcome and friendly faces at Alma.

Overlaps

Grand Valley State, Michigan State, Central Michigan, Albion, University of Michigan, Hope, Western Michigan, Saginaw Valley State

If You Apply To >

Alma: Rolling admissions. Financial aid: Mar. 1. Housing: May 1. Application fee: $25 (paper), free (online). Campus interviews: optional, evaluative. No alumni interviews. SATs or ACTs: required. Subject Tests: optional. Letters of recommendation: optional. Essay: required. Accepts the Common Application with Alma supplement.

Alverno College

3401 South 39th Street, P.O. Box 343922, Milwaukee, WI 53215

At last, a college that evaluates students on what they can do rather than how well they can memorize. Forget oval-blackening; students here show mastery in their chosen fields. Practical and hands-on, Alverno gives its students the real-life experience necessary to succeed beyond graduation.

Website: www.alverno.edu
Location: City Outskirts
Private
Total Enrollment: 1,583
Undergraduates: 1,178
Male/Female: 0/100
SAT Ranges: N/A
ACT Ranges: 16–22

If you're the type of student who obsesses over your GPA, take heed: at Alverno College, you can forget about earning an A. That's because this Roman Catholic, women's liberal arts college emphasizes ability-based learning instead of letter grades. While its roots go back to 1887, Alverno came into its own in the 1970s with its distinctive approach to learning and, unlike other educational innovations of that era, has found a continuing niche. The student body is diverse—in age, ethnic background, and religion—and the learning environment is highly collaborative, though the ability-based method can "create a lot of work requiring much thought," says a professional communication major.

Alverno is located in a quiet residential area. The parklike 46-acre campus is just 15 minutes from downtown Milwaukee and a 10-minute walk from shops and restaurants. The Sister Joel Read Center houses 73,000 square feet of science labs, multimedia production space, and computer facilities. Alexia Hall, the newest addition to campus, features a high-tech nursing simulation center, art and dance studios, classrooms, private study rooms, and a student commons area.

Alverno students are required to show mastery in eight key abilities: communication, analysis, problem solving, values in decision making, social interaction, global perspectives, effective citizenship, and aesthetic engagement. Students move through interdisciplinary progressive levels toward a degree by being "validated" in these areas. For example, a course in sociology might contribute to validation in communication and social interaction, as well as in making independent value judgments. The college offers detailed feedback rather than traditional letter grades, and administrators find innovative, "real-life" ways to assess students' mastery of subject matter and specific abilities. First-year students take an orientation seminar and introductory courses in the arts and humanities, science, psychology and social science, communication, and math. Religious studies aren't required, but for those who seek it, a Catholic liturgy is available. Students are also required to participate in off-campus, credit-bearing internships through one of the country's longest-standing, highly acclaimed internship programs.

"The level of professionalism that Alverno students have compared to those at other colleges or universities is amazing," one junior says. Alverno's business and management program is well established and among the most popular majors, along with nursing, psychology, and biology. Students praise the professional communication and teacher education programs as well. Many professors at Alverno teach all levels of classes, so the quality of teaching is consistent throughout a student's college career. "The faculty and staff really care whether you are successful," says a social science major. "They want to see you achieve and are willing to go [above] and beyond to make sure you do." Academic counseling and individual attention run throughout students' academic careers to keep them on track. With an average class size of under 20 students and a low student/faculty ratio, students have easy access to faculty. Alverno also boasts a dedicated Career Education Center that provides career planning and job search assistance to students and alumnae, including regular networking and on-campus recruiting events with employers. "We couldn't have more help," one junior says. Fourteen percent of Alverno students study abroad each year, often heading out on short, 10- to 14-day trips that complement a semester-long course.

"Students are extraordinarily driven, and they know what it takes to succeed in the real world," says a junior. Ninety-five percent of Alverno students hail from Wisconsin; there are no international students. Even so, Alverno is one of the most inclusive and diverse colleges in the state, particularly socioeconomically: sixty-four percent of freshmen are eligible for Pell Grants. African Americans comprise 15 percent of the student body, Hispanics 23 percent, and Asian Americans 5 percent. Students and faculty often engage in roundtable discussions to look at political or social issues, according to a sophomore. Merit scholarships are awarded based on a personal evaluation of each incoming student.

A three-day orientation program serves freshmen, transfer, resident, and commuter students. The majority of students are commuters, though dorm rooms house 15 percent of students, who say the residence halls offer clean, spacious rooms with fully equipped lounges, laundry, and cooking facilities available on each floor. "Dorms are comfortable and well maintained every day, including weekends," says

"The level of professionalism that Alverno students have compared to those at other colleges or universities is amazing."

(continued)

Financial Aid: 98%
Pell Grant: 64%
Expense: Pr $
Student Loans: 84%
Average Debt: $ $ $ $
Phi Beta Kappa: No
Applicants: 613
Accepted: 77%
Enrolled: 48%
Grad in 6 Years: 42%
Returning Freshmen: 69%
Academics: ✍ ✍ ✍
Social: ☎
Q of L: ★ ★ ★ ★
Admissions: (414) 382-6101
Email Address: admissions@ alverno.edu

Strong Programs:
Business and Management
Nursing
Psychology
Biology
Professional Communication
Education

Students are required to participate in off-campus, credit-bearing internships.

The majority of students are commuters, though dorm rooms house 15 percent of students.

one junior. Male visitors are allowed, but they must sign in and be out by midnight on weekdays and 2:00 a.m. on weekends.

Dozens of student groups and cultural groups are active on campus, but most of the social life takes place off campus at local clubs, bars, restaurants, coffee shops, and nearby colleges. The campus also has an on-site childcare center and a fitness center, and it sponsors dance and theater groups. "Milwaukee is a thriving city of the arts—visual, theatrical, and performance—not to mention the festivals that go on every year," says one art education major. There are also parks and shopping centers, a Performing Arts Center, professional sports teams, ethnic festivals, and free outdoor concerts. Students look forward to the annual Rotunda Ball, homecoming festivities, and Community Day, which allows students and faculty to participate in an annual day of service.

> **"The faculty and staff really care whether you are successful."**

Alverno competes in Division III athletics, including basketball, cross-country, golf, soccer, softball, tennis, and volleyball. The Inferno tennis and basketball teams have been the most successful programs, having set school records for wins. The college has just recently developed a formal intramural sports program, in which 20 percent of students participate.

Attending a school like Alverno promises an experience far afield in some ways from the traditional college world. The emphasis on real-world applications builds confidence in one's actual ability to perform, rather than the ability to score an A. Students and faculty are often on a first-name basis from the start and build relationships that help students find their "own unique style of learning," one senior says. It's a method that obviously works.

Overlaps

University of Wisconsin–Milwaukee, Mount Mary University, Carroll University, Cardinal Stritch

---

If You Apply To ➤

Alverno: Rolling admissions. No application fee. Campus interviews: optional, evaluative. No alumnae interviews. ACTs: required. No Subject Tests. No letters of recommendation. Essay: optional.

American University

4400 Massachusetts Avenue NW, Washington, D.C. 20016-8001

If the odds are against you at Georgetown and you can't see yourself on GW's ultra-urban campus, welcome to American University. The allure of AU is simple: Washington, D.C. American has a nice campus in a nice neighborhood with easy access to the Metro. American is about a third smaller—and now more selective—than GW.

Website: www.american.edu
Location: City Outskirts
Private
Total Enrollment: 9,952
Undergraduates: 7,039
Male/Female: 37/63
SAT Ranges: CR 590–690, M 560–650
ACT Ranges: 26–30

Located just a few miles from our country's seat of power, American University is a breeding ground for the next generation of reporters, diplomats, lobbyists, and political leaders who will shape domestic and international policy. Alongside these eager buzzhounds is a host of students who take advantage of AU's strong programs in the arts and sciences and business, and who recognize that Boston and New York City are not the only good urban destinations for college students. "American University is a diverse, pulsing, and dynamic school driven by some of the best faculty, staff, scholars, and students in the world," a senior says. Thanks to phenomenal internships, a comfortable location, and a strong international focus, AU continues to attract students from around the world.

AU's 84-acre residential campus is located in the northwest corner of Washington, D.C., in an upscale (and safe) area that's just minutes from downtown; free shuttle buses transport students to the nearby Metro (subway) station. There's a mix of classical and modern architecture and flower gardens alongside the parking lots. The quad has numerous sitting areas for reflection and study, and the campus is totally wireless. The 70,000-square-foot, environmentally friendly School of International Service building is LEED Gold–certified and features the first LED-lit parking garage in Washington, D.C. New construction includes a science and technology building and new residence halls.

"AU is a very international campus."

All AU undergraduates must demonstrate competency in writing and English, either through two courses or an exam; for math or statistics, it's one semester of class or placing out through a test. The general education program requires 30 credit hours from five areas: the creative arts, traditions that shape the Western world, global and multicultural perspectives, social institutions and behavior, and the natural sciences. The requirements are typically completed during the first two years so that upperclassmen can study abroad—choosing from more than 150 programs in more than 40 nations—or participate in an internship or co-op, thanks to the school's relationships with hundreds of private, nonprofit, and government institutions. The school also uses these connections in its Washington Semester* program, which attracts a wide range of majors. Fifty-five percent of students study abroad and 86 percent complete internships each year.

In the classroom, AU has outstanding programs in political science and government, international studies, business, and communication. In all, students may choose from more than 70 programs and have the option to design their own interdisciplinary major. Three-year bachelor's degree programs are available in international studies, public health, and politics, policy, and law. New undergraduate programs include majors in public health, Arabic studies, and neuroscience. An honors program offers a select group of about 25 entering students small seminars, special sections of many courses, and designated floors in the residence halls, plus specialized work in their major and a senior capstone experience.

"Students are friendly and intelligent in the classroom, as are the professors. The courses are challenging but are not extremely hard," says one senior. "There is definitely a belief that one's own success does not have to come at the expense of our classmates' success," adds another. Nearly half of all classes taken by undergraduates have fewer than 20 students, nearly all professors hold the highest degree in their fields, and TAs do not teach classes. "Professors are more than willing to help you and are open to questions and available for office hours," cheers one sophomore.

"Students at AU are smart, compassionate, politically aware, and driven to make the world a better place," a senior observes. AU prides itself on drawing students from every state and approximately 130 foreign countries: 81 percent are from states outside D.C. and another 7 percent are international. "AU is a very international campus," observes one senior. Seven percent of undergraduates are African American, 12 percent are Hispanic, and 7 percent are Asian American. A relatively high proportion—nearly two-thirds—are women.

"What really sets AU apart from other schools is that when AU students are unhappy they do something about it."

Not surprisingly, AU is politically active—after all, this is Washington, D.C. "What really sets AU apart from other schools is that when AU students are unhappy they do something about it," a student says. The school offers hundreds of merit scholarships averaging $14,788 and has reallocated much of its financial aid to assist more financially needy students. A slew of athletic scholarships are available as well.

(continued)

Financial Aid: 73%
Pell Grant: 19%
Expense: Pr $ $
Student Loans: 65%
Average Debt: $ $ $
Phi Beta Kappa: Yes
Applicants: 16,735
Accepted: 35%
Enrolled: 31%
Grad in 6 Years: 81%
Returning Freshmen: 88%
Academics: ✍ ✍ ✍ ½
Social: ☎ ☎ ☎
Q of L: ★ ★ ★
Admissions: (202) 885-6000
Email Address: admissions@ american.edu

Strong Programs:
International Studies
Business Administration
Political Science
Communication Studies
Economics
Art

Fifty-five percent of students study abroad and 86 percent complete internships each year.

More than two-thirds of AU students, mostly freshmen and sophomores, live on campus. "The housing options are not great," complains one student. "The rooms are pretty small, and there are many, many forced triples. Lots of students have trouble getting a room, even though the school says they're guaranteed housing." Living/learning options are available for first-years, including the Community-Based Research Scholars program, which involves opportunities for service-oriented research. Campus dining receives good reviews for its taste and variety. "It's really easy to eat healthy here," reports one student. "Campus police are present, friendly, productive, and trustworthy," a journalism major says.

A good deal of the social life at AU revolves around campus-related functions. A student says, "On campus, American University Student Government holds events. From political speakers to comedy groups and musical performances, students can always find something to do." Six percent of the men and 9 percent of the women go Greek, and the women lament that the skewed male/female ratio is "a little ridiculous." The AU campus is officially dry, and most students take that seriously. The immediate area around AU has restaurants and shops, but you need to get a bit farther away for true nightlife over in Dupont Circle and in Georgetown. While greater D.C. certainly has its share of clubs and bars, they're largely off-limits to students under 21. Happily, D.C. offers ample alternatives for entertainment, and much of it free—the art house movie theaters, gallery openings, pro soccer games, museums and monuments, and funky live music. "You just jump on the Metro to get anywhere in the city," says a communication major. Each year, Family Weekend brings games, rides, and popular bands to campus, along with a carnival on the quad. Homecoming and Founder's Week are also campus favorites. Popular road trips include Baltimore, Annapolis, Williamsburg, Richmond, the Ocean City shore, and nearby amusement parks and outlets.

"It's really easy to eat healthy here."

Although there's no football, the American University Eagles compete in Division I athletics. Students are particularly enthusiastic about the men's basketball team, which has won the Patriot League conference championship multiple times, as has women's volleyball and basketball. Games against Bucknell, Holy Cross, and the Naval Academy highlight the schedule. Roughly 28 percent of students take part in 20 intramural and 25 club sports, ranging from flag football and badminton to field hockey and sailing, which are divided into different levels of competitiveness.

AU is heaven on earth for C-SPAN junkies. But even if you are not addicted to following current events, AU and Washington, D.C. are still a top combo for a rich college life. The opportunities for real-world experience—in fields ranging from business to international studies to political science—are outstanding. But AU is small enough to keep students from feeling lost in the fast-paced world inside the Beltway. As a junior explains, "We are a small campus, which gives the feeling of being out of the city, but yet the city is at our fingertips."

Overlaps

Boston College, Boston University, George Washington, Georgetown, Johns Hopkins, Northeastern, Syracuse, Fordham

If You Apply To >

American: Early decision I: Nov. 10. Early decision II, regular decision, and financial aid: Jan. 10. Housing: May 1. Application fee: $70. No campus or alumni interviews. SATs or ACTs: optional. No Subject Tests. Letters of recommendation: required. Essay: required. Accepts the Common Application.

Amherst College

Amherst, MA 01002-5000

Original home to the well-rounded, superachieving, gentle-person jock. Compare to Williams, Middlebury, and Colby. Not Swarthmore, not Wesleyan. Amherst has always been the king in its category—in part because there are four other major institutions in easy reach to add diversity and depth. Among the few liberal arts colleges with as many men as women.

Amherst offers a dynamic curriculum in the traditional academic disciplines and in numerous interdisciplinary fields. There are no core curriculum or distribution requirements, so students choose their program based on their own individual interests and plans for the future. Indeed, students' focus isn't on racking up high grade point averages, but rather on becoming people who base their thinking on a strong foundation in the liberal arts. Emphasizing "freedom to explore," the spotlight here is on learning. "If your education is really your first priority," says a sophomore, "then I don't think there's a better school."

Amherst's 1,000 acres overlook the picturesque town of Amherst and the Pioneer Valley and offer a panoramic view of the Holyoke Range and the Pelham Hills. On campus, a plot of open land housing a wildlife sanctuary and a forest shares space with academic and residential buildings, athletic fields, and facilities. While Amherst's predominant architectural style remains 19th-century academia—redbrick is key—everything from a "pale yellow octagonal structure to a garish, modern new dorm" can be found here. Amherst looks like a college is supposed to look, with trees and paths winding through the buildings to offer long, contemplative walks. The new Greenway Residence Halls opened in 2016.

To graduate, students must take a first-year seminar, declare a major at the end of sophomore year, fulfill departmental program requirements, pass the requisite number of electives, and perform satisfactorily on comprehensive exams in their major field. First-year seminars, each of which are taught by two or more professors and limited to 15 students, help foster interdisciplinary approaches across topics and are offered in several subject areas.

The most popular majors include economics, psychology, history, and biology. Students may mix and match among these subjects to form dual-degree programs. About 40 percent of students pursue double majors, and a few overachievers even triple major. Students may create their own courses

> **"Amherst professors are what gives this place its life."**

of study from Special Topics classes if the subject of their interest is not available. Amherst's unique Law, Jurisprudence, and Social Thought program is not a prelaw major; instead, it's an interdisciplinary study of the law, drawing on fields as diverse as psychology, history, philosophy, and literature, with a strong theoretical focus. New majors include film and media studies, biochemistry and biophysics, and architectural studies. Amherst's membership in the Five College Consortium* means that students can also take courses from partner schools Hampshire, Mount Holyoke, the University of Massachusetts Amherst, and Smith, a benefit that significantly expands students' options. The consortium's joint dance department, for instance, is a popular choice among Amherst students.

The academic climate at Amherst is intense, but a senior advises, "It's a matter of balancing your time and identifying how much you'd like to challenge yourself." Amherst is home to a rich intellectual environment that centers on a wealth of acclaimed instructors, and on such a small campus with no graduate students,

Website: www.amherst.edu
Location: Small Town
Private
Total Enrollment: 1,795
Undergraduates: 1,795
Male/Female: 50/50
SAT Ranges: CR 680–780, M 680–780
ACT Ranges: 31–34
Financial Aid: 58%
Pell Grant: 21%
Expense: Pr $ $ $ $
Student Loans: 25%
Average Debt: $
Phi Beta Kappa: No
Applicants: 8,568
Accepted: 14%
Enrolled: 39%
Grad in 6 Years: 94%
Returning Freshmen: 98%
Academics: ✎ ✎ ✎ ✎ ✎
Social: ☎ ☎ ☎
Q of L: ★ ★ ★ ★
Admissions: (413) 542-2328
Email Address: admission@amherst.edu

Strong Programs:
Economics
Psychology
History
Biology
English
Dance
Law, Jurisprudence, and Social Thought

interaction with professors is encouraged. "Amherst professors are what gives this place its life," says a computer science and environmental studies major. "They will play a huge part in your time here." Students also praise the college's robust career services. "The career center has a program where you can be mentored by Amherst alumni who are experts and well-respected in their respective industries," says an economics major.

In addition to being part of the Five College Consortium*, Amherst also belongs to the Maritime Studies Program* and the Twelve College Exchange*. Each year, more than 40 percent of the junior class spends a semester or year abroad; recent students have chosen from 250 programs in dozens of countries, ranging from a computer science program in Budapest to a human rights program in Buenos Aires. Amherst also has a sister university in Göttingen, Germany, and another in Kyoto, Japan, where one of the college's colonial-style buildings has been duplicated.

As one junior explains, "Amherst College is populated by nearly every sort of person. Whether you are a geek, jock, hippie, or any other hard-to-define type of human being, you will find kindred spirits." Only 13 percent of Amherst students hail from Massachusetts, and 10 percent are international. Eighty-six percent were in the top 10th of their high school class. The student body is unusually diverse; 14 percent are Asian American, 13 percent are Hispanic, and 12 percent are African American. The school has made a concerted effort to enroll students eligible for Pell Grants, and 21 percent of freshmen qualify for the award. Amherst's campus is generally liberal, and students are politically active. "The Amherst Uprising student movement for students of color was a particularly high-profile event that occurred this past year and worked to unify and impact the campus in many ways," says a political science and sociology major. Admissions is need-blind, and all financial aid is awarded based on need. While there are no merit or athletic scholarships, Amherst guarantees to meet 100 percent of admitted students' demonstrated financial need, and all financial aid packages are loan-free, which helps attract a substantial number of low-income students. Financial aid extends to study abroad programs as well.

Housing at Amherst is guaranteed for four years, and 98 percent of students live on campus. "The rooms are huge with lots of storage space," raves a student. Those who feel shafted by the room draw can participate in a lip-synch competition; the winner receives the top room pick for his or her class. Everyone who lives on campus, and anyone else who wants to, eats in Valentine Hall, which includes a buffet-style central serving station and five dining rooms. Much of the produce comes from Book and Plow, the on-campus farm. "Amherst has been in the news more than most schools for issues of sexual assault," according to one junior, who explains that the college has overhauled how it handles the issue by implementing a number of initiatives, including a Consentfest event, which has helped "destigmatize and normalize talking about consent and sexual respect." A senior notes that students generally feel safe "not only because the peer culture is respectful, but also because the police presence on campus is constant without being overbearing."

Although frats are nothing more than a faint memory, social activities are conducted almost entirely on campus. They range from dorm study breaks to social clubs to campuswide parties. Students report a sizable rift in the social landscape: "We have a pretty notorious athlete/nonathlete divide on campus that does have an effect on the social scene here," says a history major. "The sports teams set the tone for party culture on campus," agrees one student, but another adds, "There is no pressure to drink." Students also take advantage of the Five Colleges* membership for social life and cultural events. The Powerhouse, a building that originally served as a campus

> There are no core curriculum or distribution requirements.

> Amherst's membership in the Five College Consortium* significantly expands students' options.

"The sports teams set the tone for party culture on campus."

"People carry themselves very seriously here, and that in itself creates a culture of pressure."

steam plant at the turn of the century, was recently converted into a nightlife venue with live performances and also offers movie screenings, art exhibits, pub nights, and other activities. Although some students bemoan the lack of campus traditions, festivals including Spring Weekend and Farm Fest are popular events.

The town of Amherst is "small but charming, and has everything students need," says a sophomore. The nearby city of Northampton offers more options for restaurants, concerts, and nightlife. Students take part in community service projects, including "Big Brothers Big Sisters and Habitat for Humanity, just to name a few," says a freshman, and the college funds roughly 150 summer public service internships every year. For the many outdoorsy types, good skiing in Vermont is not far, and Boston (an hour and a half) and New York (a little over three hours) are close enough to be convenient road-trip destinations.

Sports are taken seriously, both varsity and intramurals, and "impact" athletes get favored treatment from the admissions office. The school recently voted to remove its century-old unofficial mascot, "Lord Jeff," due to controversy surrounding its historical associations. Amherst competes in Division III, but the strong baseball team takes on Division I opponents as well. Men's soccer won the Division III championship for the first time in 2015, and men's tennis and men's basketball are also recent national champs. Women's basketball and tennis are strong as well, along with football and men's and women's ice hockey, lacrosse, and swimming. Any showdown with archrival Williams is inevitably the biggest game of the season, drawing fans from all corners of campus. Amherst's intramural and club programs attract 80 percent of the student body.

"People carry themselves very seriously here, and that in itself creates a culture of pressure to succeed and achieve," remarks one sophomore. Yet the lack of restrictive requirements, a cadre of professors who are focused on teaching, and a devoted alumni network make it clear why most students love their institution. Says a junior, "The Amherst community goes far beyond your years on campus."

Amherst guarantees to meet 100 percent of admitted students' demonstrated financial need, and all financial aid packages are loan-free.

Overlaps

Brown, Yale, Harvard, Princeton, Stanford, Columbia, Dartmouth, University of Pennsylvania

If You Apply To ➢ **Amherst:** Early decision: Nov. 15. Regular decision: Jan. 1. Financial aid: Feb. 15. Application fee: $60. No campus or alumni interviews. SATs and two Subject Tests or ACTs: required (SAT essay or ACT writing test recommended). Letters of recommendation: required. Essay: required. Accepts the Common Application with supplement.

University of Arizona

Robert L. Nugent Building, Tucson, AZ 85721

Tucson is an increasingly popular destination, and it isn't just because of the UA basketball team. A well-devoted honors program attracts top students, as do excellent programs in the sciences and engineering. Generally viewed as a cut above ASU in academic quality. Now offering tuition discounts to out-of-staters. Bring plenty of shorts and sunscreen.

With a campus that's encircled by mountain ranges and the beautiful Sonoran Desert, lined with palm trees and cacti, and set against a backdrop of stunning Tucson sunsets, it's no surprise that students at the University of Arizona love to hang out at the mall. Not the shopping center, mind you—but a huge grassy area in the middle of campus where 36,000 Wildcats gather between classes. Judging by numbers alone, that's enough people to fill a medium-sized town. But students are

Website: www.arizona.edu
Location: Small City
Public
Total Enrollment: 36,633
Undergraduates: 29,652

The astronomy department boasts a 176-inch telescope operated jointly by the university and the Smithsonian.

quick to point out that UA has a strong sense of community and offers a genuinely friendly campus. "Nobody else has a huge central meeting place like we do," says a senior. "I always see familiar and friendly faces around the mall area." With all the natural beauty that surrounds them, many Wildcats simply purr through four satisfying years.

Architecturally, the UA campus distinguishes itself from the city's regiment of adobe buildings with a design that seems a study in the versatility of redbrick. Old Main, the university's first building, is into its second century, but others verge on high-tech science facilities. The Student Recreation Center boasts state-of-the-art exercise equipment, a computer lab, student-tutoring center, and a healthy organic food restaurant. It is also LEED certified. A recent expansion to Arizona Stadium (home of the Wildcats football team) was completed to the tune of $72 million.

UA has 20 colleges and more than 160 degree programs. Under the core curriculum, students take 10 general education courses in common. They fall under the broad categories of arts, humanities, traditions and cultures, natural sciences, and individuals and societies. In addition, almost everyone gets a healthy dose of freshman composition, math, and foreign language. Sciences are unquestionably

> **"Professors and advisors urge us to…get as many experiences as we possibly can under our belts."**

the school's forte—the astronomy department is among the nation's best, helped by those clear night skies. Students have access not only to leading astronomers, but also to the most up-to-date equipment, including a huge 176-inch telescope operated jointly by the university and the Smithsonian. A $28 million aerospace and mechanical engineering building has a state-of-the-art subsonic wind tunnel and rocket-combustion test facility. The small and rigorous College of Architecture, Planning, and Landscape Architecture is a national leader in sustainable planning for arid regions. The history and English departments are standouts, as are several of the social science programs. Eager shutterbugs can pore through photographer Ansel Adams's personal collection, and the Center for Creative Photography offers one of the leading photographic collections in the world. Students in the popular business and public administration school can pick racetrack management as their area of expertise, while interested anthropology students can delve into garbage research. Programs in biomedical engineering, optical sciences, entrepreneurship, and retailing and consumer science are also well regarded.

Academic competition, according to most students, is left up to both the individual and the specific course or area of study. "Students are taught early on the value of being able to work not only with other students, but also with teaching assistants and professors," says a criminal justice and economics double major. "This creates an environment where very intense and challenging work becomes a little more relaxed and a little less stressful." Teaching is well regarded, with some freshman courses taught by graduate students and 40 percent of all classes enrolling fewer than 20 students. "The quality of teaching has been mostly positive," says one student. "Most of my professors are very well versed in their fields and continue to do research." Students also praise the student-staffed Think Tank tutoring program that operates out of several academic buildings and dorms for additional academic support.

UA's new 100 Percent Engagement initiative provides every interested student the opportunity to have a significant real-world learning experience, whether through courses that involve experiential learning components or through out-of-classroom opportunities like internships, field work, and research or service projects. Participants receive special "engaged learning experience" notations on their academic transcripts. The University Honors Center offers one of the nation's largest and most selective honors programs (students must maintain a grade point average of 3.5 to remain in the program). In addition to offering 200 honors courses per year, the center features smaller classes, personalized advising, special library privileges, and great research opportunities. The Undergraduate Biology Research Program also has a national reputation. For those seeking new vistas, there are study abroad programs available in more than 60 countries.

"We have well-rounded students who like to have a fun college experience, but also work hard," says one senior. Despite tougher admissions standards, the administration cites a sharp increase in freshman applications over the past few years, especially from out-of-staters, who constitute 37 percent of the undergraduate student body, including 6 percent who hail from foreign countries. Hispanics

> **"We have well-rounded students who like to have a fun college experience, but also work hard."**

account for 25 percent, African Americans 4 percent, and Asian Americans 6 percent. A diversity action council, a student minority advisory committee, and cultural resource centers help promote positive race relations. Thirty-two percent of students qualify for Pell Grants. Various merit and athletic scholarships are available to qualified students.

A junior says dorm quality is "all over the board" but all are well maintained: "Dorms range from brand new with every amenity to a 1920s women-only dorm with sleeping porches that's a historical landmark." Only 20 percent of undergraduates live in the dorms; some freshmen and most upperclassmen flock to the abundant and inexpensive apartments near the school. Students say the best way to enjoy the excellent food service at the student union's seven restaurants and other dining spots around campus is to use the university-issued CatCard, which frees them from carrying cash. The UAPD, a division of the Tucson police department, helps students feel safe on campus, and regarding campus sexual assault, a senior notes, "Our school has responded with increased security and services on campus, as well as educational programs to promote students making better choices when in a social environment."

The student-staffed Think Tank tutoring program operates out of several academic buildings and dorms.

Despite the high percentage of off-campus residents, students stream back onto campus on weekends for parties, sports, and cultural events. Five percent of the men belong to fraternities, and 10 percent of the women join sororities. The campus is technically alcohol-free, though some question whether the frats have realized that yet. "There are opportunities on campus to socialize, but at

> **"Tucson is a hippie town and offers a different local vibe and a fun atmosphere for a college town."**

night, most social life is done off campus," explains a junior. "Tucson is a hippie town and offers a different local vibe and a fun atmosphere for a college town." Students enjoy Tucson's shops, restaurants, bars, and various dance clubs, some of which have after-hours for underage people. Those who feel they must go elsewhere need only head to the Mexican town of Nogales (one hour away), where there is no drinking age. One of UA's most time-honored traditions is Spring Fling, said to be the largest student-run carnival in the country. On Dead Day, the day before final exams begin, seniors jump into the Old Main fountain after midnight and splash around—a ritual that may or may not be related to preceding hours of drinking.

The university is home to 500 athletes who compete in 20 sports as a member of the Division I Pac-12 conference. Over the years, UA warriors have won dozens of national team championships and more than 100 conference titles. The Wildcats basketball teams have been among the nation's leaders in recent years. Football and baseball enjoy national prominence, generate lots of money for other men's

The 100 Percent Engagement initiative provides every student the opportunity to have a significant real-world learning experience.

and women's sports teams, and provide great weekend entertainment, especially when the opposing team is big-time rival Arizona State. UA's battle cry, "Bear Down!"—frequently heard at sporting events—dates back to 1926, when a campus football hero, fatally injured in a car crash, whispered his last message to his teammates: "Tell them, tell them to bear down." Ninety years later, the enigmatic slogan still appears on T-shirts and in a gym on the central campus.

The University of Arizona offers a wide variety of academic opportunities along with spectacular weather. Prospective students are warned to honestly

> **"Most of my professors are very well versed in their fields and continue to do research."**

evaluate how that will affect their ability to concentrate. "Professors and advisors urge us to get involved in any way possible and get as many experiences as we possibly can under our belts before we finish our four years," says a marketing major. Indeed, UA is a place to go in pursuit of knowledge, experience, and a good tan.

Overlaps

Arizona State, Northern Arizona, University of Colorado–Boulder, Grand Canyon, University of Oregon, Cal Poly–San Luis Obispo, San Diego State

If You Apply To ➤ **Arizona:** Rolling admissions: May 1. Financial aid: Mar. 1. Housing: May 1. Application fee: $50 (Arizona residents), $75 (nonresidents). No campus or alumni interviews. SATs or ACTs: recommended (required to be considered for scholarships and admission to Honors College). Subject Tests: optional. No letters of recommendation. Essay: optional.

Arizona State University

Box 870112, Tempe, AZ 85287

ASU is the largest university in the nation—with ambitions to grow even larger. Big push underway to enhance interdisciplinary applied research and increase socioeconomic diversity in student body. Location in the Valley of the Sun attracts plenty of Northerners who like the idea of seeing the sun every day. Administration's relentless emphasis on growth rather than increased academic quality makes the professional schools and Barrett Honors College the best bets. Strong student support services. Compare to George Mason.

Website: www.asu.edu
Location: City Center
Public
Total Enrollment: 45,375
Undergraduates: 37,753
Male/Female: 57/43
SAT Ranges: CR 510–630, M 520–640
ACT Ranges: 23–28
Financial Aid: 84%
Pell Grant: 28%
Expense: Pub $ $
Student Loans: 55%
Average Debt: $ $
Phi Beta Kappa: Yes
Applicants: 25,380
Accepted: 83%

Arizona State University has transformed itself over the last decade into the nation's largest public university. With no pretense of modesty, this mega-university, situated in a desert oasis that is one of the nation's fastest-growing metro areas, describes itself as the model for a New American University—one where "massive innovation" is the norm and where an interdisciplinary culture is seen as the best means of developing "world-changing ideas." ASU's stated goal is to serve any Arizona student qualified for college-level work and, in the process, it has become a national model of how to deal with the emerging demographics of U.S. higher education. Research spending is up, as are student retention and graduation rates. Not surprisingly, ASU can seem overcrowded and overwhelming at times—you will have 11,000 fellow freshmen—but it provides motivated students who can find a manageable niche with countless opportunities for work and play.

The most populous of ASU's four locations, the Tempe campus offers a beautiful blend of palm-lined walkways and contemporary urban architecture. It is home to the College of Liberal Arts and Sciences and engineering. Fifteen minutes by light rail brings you to the Downtown Phoenix campus, which looks like it sounds. It houses journalism, nursing, and more engineering and has a young professionals feel. The Polytechnic campus, a converted Air Force base, specializes in science and technology and boasts a desert arboretum, while West campus has the feel of a traditional liberal arts learning community complete with an Oxford-style courtyard. The 3,430-square-foot Pat Tillman Veterans Center is located on the lower level of the Memorial Union and brings together a number of academic and student support services that serve the university's continually growing enrollment of veterans and their dependents—currently more than 5,600 undergraduate and graduate students. A new $40 million Student Pavilion, featuring performance space for student productions, guest lecturers, and other events, as well as offices for student organizations, is set to open on the Tempe campus in 2017.

The academic star at ASU is Barrett, the Honors College, a selective school-within-a-school that serves more than 6,000 students spread across all four campuses. The overwhelming majority reside in a cloistered facility on the Tempe campus that was designed by students, faculty, and staff working with nationally renowned architects

"There are a few great professors who want to educate and help students."

and features multiuse classrooms and meeting spaces, a dining hall, a fitness center, numerous unique outdoor courtyards, and a central amphitheater. The nation's first four-year residential honors college within a major public university, Barrett has 42 dedicated faculty members who oversee students pursuing ambitious honors projects.

ASU has 16 undergraduate schools and has added more than 40 new undergraduate programs since 2015. Regardless of major, all students must fulfill distribution requirements that include courses in three awareness areas: global, historical, and U.S. cultural diversity. The most popular majors are in business, management, marketing, biological and biomedical sciences, social sciences, and engineering. The School of Sustainability emphasizes the study of land use and planning models that minimize environmental harm. The Walter Cronkite School of Journalism and Mass Communication enjoys state-of-the-art facilities and a growing national reputation, while the Herberger Institute for Design and the Arts features an innovative child drama program and nationally recognized majors in art, music, and dance. The sciences (including biochemistry, chemistry, geology, and biology) and social sciences boast first-class facilities, notably the largest university-owned meteorite collection in the world. The School of Earth and Space Exploration is a leading center for research in astronomy and astrophysics. Anthropology benefits from its association with the Institute of Human Origins' Donald C. Johanson, who discovered the 3.2-million-year-old fossil skeleton named Lucy. ASU also offers the largest teacher preparation program of any university in the nation.

Engineering programs, especially microelectronics, robotics, and computer-assisted manufacturing, are sure bets; the facility for high-resolution microscopy allows students to get a uniquely close-up view of atomic structures. The Ira A. Fulton Schools of Engineering, composed of six discipline-specific schools, has a presence on the Tempe and Polytechnic campuses and offers a traditional engineering education with an emphasis on designing and creating innovative and entrepreneurial solutions. Future engineers can opt for a B.S. degree or, for those with broader interests, a

"It is mostly freshmen who choose to live on campus, but our dorms are so nice!"

B.A. The B.S.E. in construction engineering focuses on a combination of design and management topics; other degrees include a B.S.E. in engineering management and a B.S. in human systems engineering. The Fulton Undergraduate Research Initiative is designed to enhance and enrich a student's engineering education by providing hands-on lab experience, independent and thesis-based research guided by faculty mentors, and travel to national conferences.

(continued)

Enrolled: 39%
Grad in 6 Years: 63%
Returning Freshmen: 86%
Academics: ✎ ✎ ✎
Social: ☎ ☎ ☎ ☎ ☎
Q of L: ★ ★ ★ ★ ★
Admissions: (480) 965-7788
Email Address: admissions@asu.edu

Strong Programs:
Business
Management
Marketing
Biological and Biomedical Sciences
Social Sciences
Engineering
Sustainability
Fine Arts

The Pat Tillman Veterans Center serves the university's continually growing enrollment of veterans—currently more than 5,600 students.

Faculty members are expected to do both teaching and research, preferably with a practical emphasis. As one administrator explains, "We don't do 30-year longitudinal studies." Students say the university's emphasis on research can have a negative impact on the classroom experience. "There are a few great professors who want to educate and help students," says one student. "However, this is often overshadowed by terrible professors who mainly want to focus on research." Another adds that the academic climate presents a "huge amount of stress because of the workload, difficulty, and focus on GPA." Still, the university has made serious efforts to provide students with strong support services. The First-Year Success Center connects new students with upperclassmen and graduate students for weekly coaching sessions on topics like time management, finances, and health and wellness. Incoming freshmen who are undecided on a major participate in the Major and Career Exploration program, which involves seven-week courses offering individual attention and opportunities for hands-on career exploration. ASU has drawn national attention for its innovative eAdvisor system that keeps students on track to meet degree requirements and is backed up by a corps of full-time professional advisors. It also guarantees that students will find a place in any required course. Those wishing to study abroad have access to more than 250 programs in more than 55 countries.

"ASU has an incredible amount of school spirit."

Barrett, the Honors College, is the nation's first four-year residential honors college within a major public university.

Sixty-seven percent of ASU students are Arizona natives, while 12 percent come from abroad. Nineteen percent of the undergraduate student body is Hispanic; African Americans contribute 4 percent and Asian Americans 7 percent. Students say a big issue on campus is the "walk-only zones" that prevent students from using bikes (of which there are 14,000), skateboards, or other modes of transportation in certain high-traffic areas. "It certainly isn't making campus travel easier or safer," says a student. "I've seen many petitions to remove the walk-only zone, but the university insists on its existence." ASU offers merit scholarships averaging $8,237 to qualified students and awards 353 athletic scholarships annually to athletes in 23 sports. It guarantees to meet the demonstrated need of any student from Arizona. Twenty-eight percent of incoming students qualify for the Pell Grant.

"ASU has gotten away from its party school reputation in recent years."

Only 22 percent of ASU students live in the co-ed dorms. "It is mostly freshmen who choose to live on campus, but our dorms are so nice! I've visited several other schools, and ASU has some of the largest rooms. The furniture in them is also replaced every five years, so nothing is old or broken," says one junior. No matter where they live, students don't have to buy a meal plan, which is a good thing according to one student. "Dining is subpar with the exception being the honors dining hall and that is still only average." Students say campus security is sufficient: "I have never felt unsafe on campus in my four years as an ASU student," says an English literature major.

The First-Year Success Center connects new students with upperclassmen and graduate students for weekly coaching sessions.

"Sometimes I feel there is so much stuff going on that I have to pick between two or three things on a day or night or weekend," says one junior. "But, hey, that's a good problem to have!" ASU's Greek system attracts only 8 percent of the men and 16 percent of the women, and "small kick-backs in dorms are just as common as huge house parties," says a sophomore. The campus is officially dry, and those under the legal drinking age are also warned against drinking in student housing. Perhaps that's why students head off campus on weekends—often far off campus. Many have cars, giving them access to the mountains of Northern Arizona, the lakes on the outskirts of town, and the natural beauty of the Grand Canyon. Tempe gets generally positive reviews from students. "It has great restaurants nearby, different shopping centers, and a street called Mill Ave that has stores, food, and bars/nightclubs for the 21-and-over set," says a communication major. Devils in Disguise, an annual, student-run day of service, sends students out to complete various volunteer projects in the community.

"ASU has an incredible amount of school spirit," says a junior. Arizona State's Division I athletics department—supported by a fee required of all students—is consistently ranked among the nation's best, and the Sun Devil Fitness Center is first-rate. ASU women's basketball, soccer, and softball recently reached their respective national tournaments. Baseball has racked up 53 straight 30-win seasons, and women's golf is also a top performer. Teams are known as the Sun Devils after a meteorological phenomenon, and the biggest rival is the University of Arizona, normally referred to simply as "that school down south."

Arizona State may seem like an overwhelmingly big school with a reputation for rowdiness, but that's not the full story. "ASU has gotten away from its party school reputation in recent years," says a senior. To its credit, ASU likes to pride itself on how many students it accepts, not how many it turns away, and on its strong student support services. Despite common college complaints ("Parking, parking, parking!"), the university gives students much to appreciate. For those not frightened away by its sheer immensity, ASU may be a good place to earn a degree while enjoying a four-year relationship with the sun.

If You Apply To ➤ | **Arizona State:** Rolling admissions. (Priority deadline: Feb. 1.) Priority financial aid: Jan. 1. Housing: May 1. Application fee: $50 (Arizona residents), $70 (nonresidents). Campus interviews: optional, informational. No alumni interviews. SATs or ACTs: recommended. Subject Tests: required for some programs. Letters of recommendation: required for some programs. No essay.

University of Arkansas

200 Hunt Hall, Fayetteville, AR 72701

University of Arkansas rates in the second tier of Southern public universities alongside Alabama, LSU, and Ole Miss. Though conservative by national standards, Fayetteville is progressive by those of Arkansas. With traditional strength in agriculture, U of A has also developed programs in business, engineering, and other professional fields. Its most popular program takes the field on Saturday afternoons in the fall.

The flagship public institution for the state of Arkansas, the University of Arkansas is a nationally competitive, student-centered research institution. Freshman class enrollment has increased more than 63 percent since 2008, and the university has grown to keep pace. A $300 million cash gift from the family of Walmart founder Sam Walton—one of the largest ever made to an American public university—created the undergraduate Honors College, which frequently produces Marshall, Truman, and other national scholarship winners, and it also endowed the graduate school.

The Arkansas campus is nestled among the mountains, lakes, and streams of the Ozarks, in the extreme northwest corner of the state. "Come to a Razorback game in the fall when the leaves are changing," says one student, "and you will be totally won over." The community is friendly and safe, and the moderate climate means recreational opportunities abound. Architectural styles range from modern concrete to buildings that date from the Depression. The center of campus is the

Website: www.uark.edu
Location: Small City
Public
Total Enrollment: 21,220
Undergraduates: 19,426
Male/Female: 47/53
SAT Ranges: CR 500–600, M 510–620
ACT Ranges: 23–28
Financial Aid: 41%
Pell Grant: 19%
Expense: Pub $
Student Loans: 48%

(continued)

Average Debt: $ $
Phi Beta Kappa: Yes
Applicants: 20,542
Accepted: 60%
Enrolled: 40%
Grad in 6 Years: 62%
Returning Freshmen: 82%
Academics: ✐ ✐ ✐
Social: ☎ ☎ ☎ ☎
Q of L: ★ ★ ★
Admissions: (479) 575-5346
Email Address:
    uofa@uark.edu

Strong Programs:
Management
Marketing
Engineering
Health Professions
Social Sciences
English
Poultry Science
Architecture

The 3,000 undergrads who join the Honors College are required to complete research or creative work culminating in an honors thesis.

stately brick Old Main, which once housed the entire university. Recent construction includes Champions Hall, housing math and biology labs and classrooms, and the Jones Family Student-Athlete Success Center.

Established as a land grant institution in 1871, with agricultural and mechanical roots, U of A serves more than 19,000 undergraduates and includes 10 colleges, as well as 54 research and outreach centers. U of A's core requirements include six credits in English; three credits each in history, math, humanities, and fine arts; eight in science; and nine in social sciences. The 3,000 undergrads who join the Honors College are required to complete research or creative work culminating in an honors thesis. The Sam M. Walton College of Business offers two of the most popular majors on campus: management and marketing. Other popular disciplines here include engineering, health professions, social sciences, and English, particularly creative writing. The Dale Bumpers College of Agricultural, Food, and Life Sciences includes the Center of Excellence for Poultry Science, a national leader in research on poultry epidemiology. The Fay Jones School of Architecture and Design's architecture program is also notable.

Students are quick to point out that U of A's academic climate is "laid back, but still demanding a high standard of excellence," says a senior. To help ease into the college transition, a junior recommends ROCK Camp, an optional summer orientation weekend: "It is a great way to meet new students, get on email lists, and start making connections." While there is a healthy portion of large, TA-taught lecture classes, 48 percent of classes enroll fewer than 20 students. Students say professors are knowledgeable and particularly helpful when it comes to research opportunities. Says a biology major, "Getting involved in campus research is very easy and often just requires talking to an enthusiastic professor with room in their lab." Undergraduates in all disciplines are encouraged to conduct research, and about a third do so, often with generous funding. U of A also offers study abroad programs in 50 countries across six continents; 14 percent participate.

> **"Getting involved in campus research is very easy and often just requires talking to an enthusiastic professor with room in their lab."**

U of A students "have high aspirations and work as hard as they can every day to accomplish their goals," says one senior. Fifty-four percent of U of A freshmen are Arkansas residents, and the vast majority attended public high schools; 3 percent are international. African Americans make up 5 percent of the student body, Hispanics 8 percent, and Asian Americans 2 percent. Students tend to lean right, and although there are pockets of politically engaged students, a senior remarks, "Partying takes precedence over activism most of the time." Arkansas awards thousands of merit scholarships each year, averaging $4,945. There are also 378 athletic scholarships, representing all of U of A's 19 varsity sports teams. Additionally, the New Arkansan Non-Resident Tuition Award gives scholarships to students from neighboring states with GPAs of 3.20 or higher and ACT scores of at least 24.

Roughly one-quarter of all undergrads at Arkansas live in the residence halls; most move off campus after their first year to save money. "On-campus housing is generally expensive, but is very convenient, and it is usually easy to get a room if you desire one," says a senior. About 250 students participate in the nine living/learning community options. Campus dining is described as adequate, and a variety of dietary accommodations are available. Campus police are said to be effective, and a presence at Greek parties. With regard to sexual assault on campus, one student notes, "Much of the coordination and conversation around this issue actually comes from the student government and Greek life."

Arkansas's Greek chapters attract 22 percent of the men and 37 percent of the women. Aside from the annual Springtime of Youth music festival and the revelry that accompanies Razorback football and basketball, students say Greek parties are pretty much the only game in town on weekends. Dickson Street, the main drag in the town of Fayetteville (population 79,000), is full of restaurants and bars that are popular with upperclassmen; the town also offers drive-in movies, live music at local clubs, and touring Broadway shows at the Walton Arts Center. U of A students log more than 120,000 hours of community service each year, through programs like Full Circle Campus Food Pantry, Make a Difference Day, and Hogs Care Week. Those with cars will find Dallas, Tulsa, Oklahoma City, Memphis, and St. Louis all within a six-hour drive.

The New Arkansan Non-Resident Tuition Award gives scholarships to students from neighboring states.

Varsity teams are the Razorbacks (wild hogs), and the beloved Hog Call "Woooooo! Pig sooie!" rings out during football and basketball weekends, although according to one senior, "No matter the time, place, or situation, it is always considered appropriate to call the hogs." Red Razorback logos are all over town—on T-shirts, napkins, book covers, license plates, and on game day,

"No matter the time, place, or situation, it is always considered appropriate to call the hogs."

the cheeks of ecstatic fans. Powerhouse teams include men's and women's track and field and basketball, men's baseball, and women's gymnastics, golf, and volleyball. Recreational sports are hugely popular and include everything from flag football and sand volleyball to ballroom dance and shotgun sports.

The University of Arkansas boasts "genuinely friendly" students, says a senior. "If they encounter someone who needs help, they help." This kind of Southern hospitality means poultry science students aren't the only ones flocking to Arkansas for a solid education at a bargain price. Northerners may feel out of their element, and those who dislike football should keep their feelings to themselves. But all students here look forward to graduation day, when their names will join forever those of 175,000 other alumni, etched into the five-mile network of sidewalks on campus.

Overlaps

Texas A&M, Texas Tech, University of Oklahoma, University of Texas at Austin, Baylor, Oklahoma State, Texas State, Texas Christian

If You Apply To ➤   **Arkansas:** Rolling admissions: Aug. 1. (Priority deadline: Nov. 1.) Priority financial aid: Mar. 1. Application fee: $40. No campus or alumni interviews. SATs or ACTs: required. No Subject Tests. Letters of recommendation: optional. Essay: optional.

Atlanta University Center

Atlanta is viewed as the preeminent city in the country for bright, talented, and successful African Americans. It became the capital of the civil rights movement in the 1960s—a town described by its leaders as "too busy to hate."

At the heart of this extraordinary culture is the Atlanta University Center, the largest African American educational complex in the world, replete with its own central library and computing center. The four component institutions have educated generations of African American leaders. The Reverend Martin Luther King Jr. went to Morehouse College; his grandmother, mother, sister, and daughter went to Spelman College. Graduates spread across the country in a pattern that developed when these were among the best of the few colleges to which talented African Americans could aspire. Even now, when the options are almost limitless, alumni continue to send their children back for more.

The center consists of two undergraduate colleges (Morehouse and Spelman) and two offering graduate degrees (Clark Atlanta University and the Morehouse College of Medicine) on adjoining campuses in the center of Atlanta, three miles from downtown. Two other institutions, Morris Brown College and the Interdenominational Theological Center, are no longer members. Students at the affiliated schools can enjoy the quiet pace of their beautiful magnolia-studded campuses or plunge into all the culture and excitement of this most dynamic of Deep South cities. The six original schools—all but the medical school—became affiliated in 1929 using the model of California's Claremont Colleges, but the remaining members are fiercely independent. Each has its own administration, board of trustees, and academic specialties, and each maintains its own dorms, cafeterias, and other facilities. There is cross-registration among the institutions (Morehouse students, for example, go to Spelman for drama and art courses) and with Georgia State and Emory University as well. The governing body of the consortium, the Atlanta University Center, Inc., administers a centerwide dual-degree program in engineering in conjunction with Georgia Tech—and it runs campus security, a student crisis center, and a joint institute of science research. There is also a centerwide service of career planning and placement, where recruiters may come and interview students from all four institutions.

Dating and social life at the coeducational institutions tend to take place within the individual schools, though Morehouse, a men's college, and Spelman, a women's college, maintain a close academic and social relationship. The Morehouse–Spelman Glee Club takes its abundance of talent around the nation, and its annual Christmas concert on the Spelman campus is a standing-room-only event.

Morehouse and Spelman (see full write-ups) constitute the Ivy League of historically African American colleges. The following is a sketch of the other institution offering undergraduate degrees.

CLARK ATLANTA UNIVERSITY (WWW.CAU.EDU)

Formed by the consolidation of Clark College, a four-year liberal arts institution, and Atlanta University, which offered only graduate degrees, CAU is a comprehensive coeducational institution that offers undergraduate, graduate, and professional degrees. The university draws on the former strengths of both schools, offering quality programs in the health professions, public policy, and mass communications (including print journalism, radio and television production, and filmmaking). Graduate and professional programs include education, business, library information studies, social work, and arts and sciences. Undergraduate enrollment: 2,700.

830 Westview Drive SW, Atlanta, GA 30314

Along with sister school Spelman, Morehouse is the most selective of the historically black schools. Alumni list reads like a *Who's Who* of African American leaders. Best known for business and popular 3–2 engineering program with Georgia Tech. Built on a Civil War battlefield, Morehouse is a symbol of the new South.

Founded in 1867, Morehouse College has the distinction of being the nation's only historically African American, four-year liberal arts college for men. Top students come to Morehouse because they want an institution with a strong academic program and a supportive atmosphere in which to cultivate their success orientation and leadership skills without facing the additional barriers they might encounter at a predominantly white institution. "Morehouse is a college of young, assertive, ambitious black men," says a psychology major. Notable alumni include the Reverend Martin Luther King Jr., Samuel L. Jackson, Spike Lee, and Dr. Louis Sullivan, president emeritus of the Morehouse School of Medicine and former U.S. Secretary of Health and Human Services.

Located near downtown Atlanta, the 61-acre Morehouse campus is home to 35 buildings, including the Martin Luther King Jr. International Chapel. Over the last decade, the college has enriched its academic program, conducted a successful multimillion-dollar national fund-raising campaign, increased student scholarships and faculty salaries, doubled its endowment, improved its physical plant, and acquired additional acres of land.

The general education program includes not only 53 semester hours in four major disciplines (humanities, natural sciences, math, and social sciences), but also the study of "the unique African and African American heritage on which so much of our modern American culture is built." "Many students are here to get a greater understanding of their heritage and to promote it," attests one student. As part of their general education requirements, students also need to pass freshman, sophomore, and junior year assemblies which "celebrate Morehouse heritage and traditions." The academic climate at the House can get intense, with students studying and challenging themselves for the sake of learning and not just to bust a curve. "Morehouse offers an academic structure that is both competitive and rigorous," states a freshman. Counseling, including career counseling, is considered quite strong, although students caution applicants to expect bureaucratic red tape as they navigate Morehouse student life.

> **"Morehouse is a college of young, assertive, ambitious black men."**

Undergraduate programs include the traditional liberal arts majors in the humanities and social and natural sciences, but as a rule of thumb, the more preprofessional your plan, the better Morehouse fits. While the sciences have been traditionally strong at Morehouse, business courses have risen in prominence and business administration is now the most popular major. Current students in this field are linked to graduates who serve as mentors in the ways of the business world. Engineering, another popular choice, is actually a 3–2 program in conjunction with Georgia Tech and other larger universities. The school also runs a program with NASA that allows students to engage in independent research. Many students major in economics, biology, political science, and psychology. Programs that receive less favorable reviews from students are English, art, and drama, and the administration admits that physical education and some of the humanities offerings could use some strengthening. Study abroad options include programs

Website: www.morehouse.edu
Location: City Center
Private
Total Enrollment: 2,066
Undergraduates: 2,066
Male/Female: 100/0
SAT Ranges: CR 440–550, M 430–550
ACT Ranges: 18–23
Financial Aid: 97%
Pell Grant: 50%
Expense: Pr $
Student Loans: 80%
Average Debt: $ $ $ $
Phi Beta Kappa: Yes
Applicants: 2,288
Accepted: 76%
Enrolled: 34%
Grad in 6 Years: 53%
Returning Freshmen: 83%
Academics: ✐ ✐ ✐
Social: ☎ ☎ ☎ ☎
Q of L: ★ ★ ★ ★
Admissions: (404) 215-2632
Email Address: admissions@morehouse.edu

Strong Programs:
Business
Engineering
Economics
Biology
Political Science
Psychology

offered through the Associated Colleges of the South* consortium. The school also offers courses and additional resources as a member of the Atlanta Regional Council for Higher Education*.

Sixty-eight percent of Morehouse students come from outside the state, with a sizable number from the Southeast and the Mid-Atlantic; 3 percent hail from other nations. Ninety-five percent are African American and 1 percent are Hispanic; half are eligible for the Pell Grant. Merit scholarships averaging $18,154 are available, in addition to roughly 120 scholarships for athletes.

Housing is somewhat limited, leaving about one-third of the student body (mostly upperclassmen) to find their own off-campus accommodations. Those who do get campus housing sometimes wish they hadn't. Complaints range from "too small" to "not well maintained." For freshmen, students recommend Graves Hall, the college's oldest building, constructed in 1889. The meal plan at Morehouse is mandatory for students living on campus and draws its share of complaints as well.

> **"Many students are here to get a greater understanding of their heritage."**

Morehouse's homecoming is a joint effort between Morehouse and Spelman. The queen elected by Morehouse men has traditionally been a Spelman woman, as are the cheerleaders and majorettes, who have been known to quip, "You can always tell a Morehouse man, but you can't tell him much." The four fraternities, which sign up just 3 percent of the students, hold parties, though "drinking is not a big deal here," most students concur. Going out on the town in Atlanta is a popular evening activity, and on-campus football games, concerts, movies, and religious programs all draw crowds.

In its early years, Morehouse left much to be desired in the area of varsity sports, but the Maroon Tigers now compete well in Division II. Track, cross-country, tennis, basketball, and football are all strong, but it is the intramural program that allows students a chance to become the superstars they know are lurking within them. During football season, Morehouse men road-trip to follow the games at Howard, Hampton, and Tuskegee universities.

Morehouse is well equipped to serve the modern heirs of a distinguished tradition. Morehouse students don't just attend Morehouse. They become part of what amounts to a network of "Morehouse Men" who share the bonds of having had the Morehouse experience, and graduates find that alumni stand ready and willing to help them with jobs and other opportunities.

Overlaps
Clark Atlanta, Georgia Tech, Hampton, Howard

If You Apply To ➤

Morehouse: Early decision and early action: Nov. 1. Regular decision: Feb. 1. Financial aid: Feb. 15. Application fee: $50. Campus and alumni interviews: required, evaluative. SATs or ACTs: required (SAT essay or ACT writing recommended). Subject Tests: recommended. Letters of recommendation: required. Essay: required. Accepts the Common Application.

Spelman College

350 Spelman Lane SW, Atlanta, GA 30314

The Wellesley of the black college world, Spelman's reputation draws students from all corners of the country. Unusually strong in the sciences with particular emphasis on undergraduate research. Wooded 42-acre Atlanta campus offers easy access to urban attractions. Significantly more selective than brother school Morehouse. Has scrapped varsity sports to emphasize lifelong physical fitness.

As one of only two surviving African American women's colleges in the United States (the other is Bennett), Spelman College holds a special appeal for African American women seeking to become leaders in fields ranging from science to the arts. Students flock here for that something special that the predominantly Caucasian schools lack: an environment with first-rate academics where African American women can develop self-confidence and leadership skills before venturing into a world where they will once again be in the minority.

Founded in 1881 by two white women from New England (it was named after John D. Rockefeller's in-laws, Mr. and Mrs. Harvey Buel Spelman), the school was traditionally the starting point for teachers, nurses, and other African American female leaders. Today's emphasis is on getting Spelman grads into the courtrooms, boardrooms, and engineering labs. Honing women for leadership is the main mission, and that nurturing takes place on a classic collegiate-green campus with a $367 million endowment.

These are heady times for Spelman. Although it finds itself competing head-on with the Seven Sisters and other prestigious and predominantly Caucasian institutions that are eager to recruit talented African American women, the college is holding its own. Spelman offers a well-rounded liberal arts curriculum that emphasizes the importance of critical and analytical thinking and problem solving. Usually, by the end of sophomore year, students are expected to complete 34 credit hours of core requirements, including English composition, foreign language, health and physical education, mathematics, African diaspora and the world, African American women's studies, and computer literacy. In addition, freshmen are required to take First-Year Orientation, and sophomores must take Sophomore Assembly. Spelman's liberal arts program introduces students to the principal branches of learning, specifically languages, literature, English, the natural sciences, humanities, social sciences, and fine arts.

Spelman's established strengths lie in the natural sciences (especially biology) and the humanities, both of which have outstanding faculties. Biology is among the most popular majors, as are English, psychology, and social sciences. Over the last decade, the college has greatly strengthened its offerings in math and the natural sciences; extensive undergraduate research programs provide students with publishing opportunities, and many end up attending grad school to become researchers. Students have moved beyond the popular majors of the early '70s—education and the fine arts—in favor of premed and prelaw programs, and these programs remain strong. The dual-degree program in engineering (in cooperation with Georgia Tech) is also a standout. The Women's Research and Resource Center specializes in women's studies and community outreach to women.

"The academic climate is very competitive," says an English major. "The school is made up of the top students from around the country, and the courses are designed to be a challenge for the best of the best." Individual attention is the hallmark of a Spelman education. About 70 percent of the faculty have doctorates, and many are African American and/or female—and thus, excellent role models, ones the students find very accessible. Except for some of the required courses, classes are small; two-thirds have fewer than 20 students. Through the Spelman MILE (My Integrated Learning Experience), all students complete internships or undergraduate research projects in their majors. Students who want to spread their wings can venture abroad through a variety of programs, or try one of the domestic exchange arrangements with Wellesley, Mount Holyoke, Vassar, or Mills. The school also offers courses and additional resources as a member of the Atlanta Regional Council for Higher Education*.

> "Courses are designed to be a challenge for the best of the best."

Website: www.spelman.edu
Location: City Center
Private
Total Enrollment: 2,072
Undergraduates: 2,072
Male/Female: 0/100
SAT Ranges: CR 460–560, M 440–540
ACT Ranges: 19–24
Financial Aid: 89%
Pell Grant: 48%
Expense: Pr $
Student Loans: 56%
Average Debt: $ $
Phi Beta Kappa: Yes
Applicants: 4,324
Accepted: 54%
Enrolled: 24%
Grad in 6 Years: 74%
Returning Freshmen: 89%
Academics: ✍ ✍ ✍
Social: ☎ ☎ ☎ ☎
Q of L: ★ ★ ★ ★ ★
Admissions: (800) 982-2411
Email Address: admissions@spelman.edu

Strong Programs:
Biology
English
Psychology
Social Sciences
Engineering
Premed
Prelaw
African Diaspora and the World

Spelman's reputation continues to attract African American women from all over the country, including a high proportion of alumnae children. Students represented here include high achievers looking for a supportive environment and those women with high potential who performed relatively poorly in high school. Twenty-six percent of the students come from Georgia, and 1 percent come from abroad. Eighty-seven percent of the student body is African American, while Hispanics and Asian Americans each account for less than 1 percent. Spelman does not guarantee to meet the financial need of all those admitted, but it does offer merit scholarships, and 48 percent of students receive Pell Grants. There are no athletic scholarships.

Sixty-nine percent of students live on campus, and housing is "dated," reports a biology major. "We have little to no air-conditioning." Still, the older dorms certainly can add to the school's historical charm, and students report having little trouble in getting a room. There are 11 dorms, and students recommend that freshmen check out the Howard Harreld dorm. The meal plan is mandatory for campus-dwellers and food is described as "edible," if not diverse.

> **"If there is any place that a student can be academically enriched, it is [Atlanta]."**

Largely because of the Atlanta University Center, students also have plenty of chances for social interaction with other nearby colleges. "Students mingle in the student centers of all four schools all the time, especially on Fridays," a veteran explains. "Atlanta is a great college town!" gushes one junior. "If there is any place that a student can be academically enriched, it is here." Spelmanites do take advantage of the big-city nightlife; they attend plays, symphonies, and the hot Atlanta nightclubs such as Ethiopian Vibrations. Lenox Square is popular for shopping. Sororities are present but only in small numbers—just 1 percent of the students go Greek. The attitude on drinking leans toward the conservative. Says one student, "No alcohol on campus—period." The most anticipated annual events include sisterhood initiation ceremonies and the Founders Day celebration. Varsity sports, never all that important, have now been scrapped for a general fitness and nutrition program, with an extensive list of physical activities such as running and yoga. The college also introduced a new intramural program in 2016 that includes basketball, flag football, soccer, and volleyball.

Spelman College has spent more than 135 years furthering the education and opportunities of African American women. It has adapted its curriculum to meet the career aspirations of today's youth, built up its bankroll, and successfully met the challenge posed by affirmative action in other universities. Still an elite institution in African American society, Spelman is staking its future on its ability to provide a unique kind of education that allows its graduates to compete with anyone.

If You Apply To ➤

Spelman: Early decision: Nov. 1. Regular decision and financial aid: Feb. 1. Application fee: $35. No campus or alumnae interviews. SATs or ACTs: required. Subject Tests: optional. Letters of recommendation: required. Essay: required. Accepts the Common Application. Seeks women who are active in school, church, or community.

College of the Atlantic

105 Eden Street, Bar Harbor, ME 04609

In today's practical world, COA is as out-there as it gets—a haven for communal, earthy, vegetarian types who would rather save the world than make a buck. Lacks many of the usual trappings of college life, such as varsity teams and Greek life. With 325 undergrads, it makes smallness an academic and social virtue. Students have a big voice in running the school.

The College of the Atlantic attracts rugged individualists troubled by the world's most pressing issues, notably pollution, environmental damage, and troubled inner cities around the globe. The college's curriculum is focused on human ecology—the study of the relationship between humans and their natural, social, and built environments—which is the only major offered. COA bucks the national obsession with growth—seeing smallness as the key to education that cuts across disciplines, eschews academic conventions, and takes a personalized approach to teaching and learning. "I chose COA because I found no other school that gave me as much freedom to create my own educational path," says one sophomore.

The 35-acre campus, covered in lush flowers, vegetable gardens, and lawns, sits on the island of Mount Desert, along the shoreline of Frenchman Bay and adjacent to the magnificent Acadia National Park. In addition, the college has acquired two offshore island research centers and two agricultural properties, and has opened wood-pellet-heated "green" dorms and an oceanside campus center. COA is serious about its mission, and this is reflected in the facilities: sustainability is prized, and the college uses environmentally responsible materials as much as possible. "We believe the most sustainable building is that which isn't built," says an administrator. COA's organic vegetable operation, Beech Hill Farm, has recently completed construction on additional housing where student-workers live during the summer season, as well as a greenhouse and a solar-powered electric vehicle charging station.

Most courses focus on a single aspect of humans' relationships with the world. Instead of traditional academic departments, the school has three broad resource areas: environmental science, arts and design, and applied human studies. Many students choose to concentrate on more narrowly defined topics within human ecology, such as climate change and energy, environmental law and politics, farming and food systems, culture and place, or educational studies. With advisors and resource specialists, each student designs an individual course of study. The natural sciences are stellar, with excellent instruction in marine science, field ecology and natural history, and zoology. The arts are catching up, with a more formal video and performance art program, run by a Guggenheim recipient, created in recent years. Geology has recently been added to the curriculum, and the school has expanded its offerings in anthropology and ethnography. Allied Whale, the school's marine mammal laboratory founded in 1972, offers excellent opportunities for hands-on field research. In response to some entrepreneurially minded graduates who wished that they had learned some business skills, COA has established the Hatchery, a program that encourages students to come up with ideas and gives them 10 weeks to build a prototype. The emphasis is on interdisciplinary exploration, and the most compelling ideas get a $5,000 grant from the college.

Student life at COA is intense and semicommunal, beginning with an optional, rugged five-day wilderness orientation preceding the first trimester. Before graduating,

> **"I found no other school that gave me as much freedom to create my own educational path."**

Website: www.coa.edu
Location: Small Town
Private
Total Enrollment: 334
Undergraduates: 325
Male/Female: 29/71
SAT Ranges: CR 590–680, M 540–630
ACT Ranges: 28–32
Financial Aid: 96%
Pell Grant: 28%
Expense: Pr $ $
Student Loans: 57%
Average Debt: $ $
Phi Beta Kappa: No
Applicants: 400
Accepted: 75%
Enrolled: 27%
Grad in 6 Years: 70%
Returning Freshmen: 80%
Academics: ✍ ✍ ✍
Social: ☎ ☎
Q of L: ★ ★ ★
Admissions: (800) 528-0025
Email Address:
  inquiry@coa.edu

Strong Programs:
Human Ecology
Marine Science
Field Ecology and Natural History
Zoology
Visual Arts and Design
Environmental Law and Politics
Farming and Food Systems
Culture and Place

students must also complete a 10-week off-campus internship and 10-week final project. Other requirements are few: freshmen must take the human ecology core course, and two courses are required in environmental sciences, human studies, and arts and design. Sophomores must submit a writing portfolio for evaluation. All students incorporate research into their studies, whether it is a development impact study for the local government or a study on the aggression of fire ants for Acadia National Park.

"The college encourages small classes to increase the dialogue between students and offer more opportunities for group work," observes one student. Some areas only have a professor or two, and 94 percent of all classes have fewer than 20 students. Since the student body is so small, scholars can become close to faculty members. "All of the professors I have encountered have been very enthusiastic and easy to talk to, offering easy office hours and responding to emails," says one student. In lieu of grades, students receive in-depth written evaluations of their work, although they may request grades as well. They must reciprocate with a self-evaluation of their performance.

> **"The college encourages small classes to increase the dialogue between students."**

COA offers regular study abroad programs in Mexico's Yucatán Peninsula, in Guatemala, and in Vichy, France. Each program includes a strong language immersion component. In Guatemala and the Yucatán, students do ethnographic, agricultural, or scientific research of their own choosing. In France, they take literature, philosophy, and/or art classes, along with intensive language studies. "I am very impressed by the level of fluency students obtain after the program, and for most it is the crowning experience of their time at COA," says one senior. COA also supports student participation in other study abroad programs through partner institutions such as the EcoLeague consortium and SEA Semester*. Sixty percent of students go abroad during their time at COA.

"People outside of the college would characterize the students as 'hippies,' but this is only the case for a small minority of students. Most are hardworking, passionate, and environmentally conscious," says one student. Many traveled the world before beginning school and move on to the Peace Corps or AmeriCorps after. Seventeen percent of students are native to Maine, and 16 percent are international. The student body is 1 percent African American, 3 percent Asian American, and 5 percent Hispanic. Twenty-eight percent are Pell-eligible. "Most students get along very well and there is a huge diversity of cultures, religions, countries, beliefs, financial statuses, and thoughts," says a freshman. The college's governance system gives students and administrators almost equal voices in how it's run; anyone may voice concerns or vote on policy-change proposals or the hiring of new faculty at the All College Meeting. Students aren't shy about also speaking out on more worldly issues, "from 'students for a free Tibet,' to antiwar protests, to environmental justice, to the global AIDS campaign," says a sophomore. A limited number of merit scholarships, worth an average of $11,149, are available to top achievers.

> **"[Bar Harbor] nearly shuts down in the winter."**

Thanks to the college's green waterfront housing village, half of the students live on campus, while the balance find cozy, inexpensive apartments or houses in the nearby town of Bar Harbor. "The dorms are super comfortable, from the new, spacious Blair/Tyson, to the eccentric, ocean-view, bay-windowed Sea Fox. Peach House houses only eight people—it's a little cabin in the woods," a junior says. Dining fare is "like home-cooked meals but with more options," according to one student. Another says COA "is a safe campus situated in a safe town in one of the safest states in the U.S."

Bar Harbor is a tourist community that "nearly shuts down in the winter," according to one student. A sophomore adds, "Bar Harbor is nice, but the whole island is one of the best places to go to school in the world." Students get to know the townspeople through the required 40 hours of community service. "The winter can be lonely, but the college does its best to offer activities and programs to keep students occupied and social. Many will form close bonds with their housemates that will remain through their four years and after graduation," a human ecology major says. There are no fraternities or sororities, and students kick back at off-campus house parties, which are generally alcohol-free. Drinking on campus is not allowed, and it's tough for underage students to get served in town. There are no varsity sports, but many students sign up for the intramural program, which offers sports such as soccer and volleyball. Outdoor programs, which take students hiking, cross-country skiing, and rock climbing in the wilds of Maine, are very active.

College of the Atlantic is a place where Earth Day really is cause for celebration, where students have been known to ride nude through the cafeteria and on nearby streets during Bike Week, and where everyone, from students to trustees, jumps into frigid Frenchman Bay on the first Friday of the fall term to try to swim from the school's docks to Bar Island and back. Says one happy junior, "This is a place for people who might feel boxed in by the traditional four-year institutions with baseline requirements."

Overlaps

Bennington, Hampshire, Warren Wilson, University of New England, University of Maine–Orono, Evergreen, Eckerd, Lewis & Clark

If You Apply To ➤ **COA:** Early decision I: Dec. 1. Early decision II: Jan. 15. Regular decision and financial aid: Feb. 1. Housing: May 1. Application fee: $50. Campus and alumni interviews: recommended, evaluative. SATs or ACTs: optional. Subject Tests: optional. Letters of recommendation: required. Essay: required. Accepts the Common Application with supplement.

Auburn University

202 Mary Martin Hall, Auburn, AL 36849

Sweet Home Alabama, where the skies are so blue and the spirit of football lasts year-round. Auburn was once called Alabama Polytechnic, and today AU's programs in engineering, agriculture, and the health fields are still among its best. AU's down-home, small-town atmosphere may feel claustrophobic to those from outside the Deep South. As for the role of football, the $14 million scoreboard says it all.

Founded in 1856, Auburn University is a public land grant university that excels in professional and technical fields such as architecture, engineering, and agriculture. But the school also welcomes students with frenzied athletics, warm and cozy hospitality, and Southern charm. "It truly is a family atmosphere. We are here to learn and help each other," says one happy Tiger. "That is what makes us such a great university."

The town of Auburn, which grew up amid miles of forest and farmland largely to serve the university, is called the "loveliest village of the plain," a moniker taken from a line in an Oliver Goldsmith poem that depicts the town. The campus stretches for nearly 2,000 acres, graced by mossy trees, lush lawns, and majestic colonnades. Most buildings are redbrick and Georgian in style, with some more modern facilities grouped in a compact central location. The Auburn Recreation and Wellness Center is a 240,000-square-foot facility containing an indoor track, a virtual golf simulator, three rock-climbing walls, eight basketball courts, a weight room, and an outdoor leisure pool.

Auburn's core curriculum includes courses in the humanities, natural science

Website: www.auburn.edu
Location: Small City
Public
Total Enrollment: 22,802
Undergraduates: 19,625
Male/Female: 50/50
SAT Ranges: CR 530–630, M 540–650
ACT Ranges: 24–30
Financial Aid: 57%
Pell Grant: 14%
Expense: Pub $ $
Student Loans: 41%
Average Debt: $ $ $

(continued)

Phi Beta Kappa: No
Applicants: 19,414
Accepted: 78%
Enrolled: 33%
Grad in 6 Years: 73%
Returning Freshmen: 90%
Academics: ✍ ✍
Social: ☎ ☎ ☎
Q of L: ★ ★ ★
Admissions: (334) 844-6425
Email Address: admissions@
   auburn.edu

Strong Programs:
Biomedical Sciences
Accounting
Mechanical Engineering
Finance
Architecture
Agriculture
Pharmacy
Wireless Engineering

and mathematics, social sciences, and fine arts; all core curriculum courses are aligned with one or more of the 10 general education student learning outcomes that all Auburn students are expected to attain by the time they graduate. Auburn has implemented a writing-in-the-disciplines program that bolsters every major with significant writing instruction. To ease the transition into college life, freshmen undergo the two-day "Camp War Eagle" session. The academic climate varies by department, and students say classroom competition is rare. "I have found that rather than students competing with each other for higher grades, they are more willing to help their classmates through tutoring or group study sessions," says a senior. Regardless of the rigor, students say professors generally go the extra mile for them. "Although I have not liked every teacher I've had, every teacher has taught me something new and useful," a junior says.

The engineering, architecture, agriculture, and pharmacy programs are stellar. Auburn has established a first-of-its-kind program in wireless engineering for students who want to design network hardware or software for cell phones and other mobile devices. The Samuel Ginn College of Engineering has an aerospace engineering department and has produced six NASA astronauts. The most popular majors include biomedical sciences, accounting, mechanical engineering, and finance. The Accelerated Bachelor's/Master's Plan allows eligible students to count approved graduate hours toward both a bachelor's and a master's degree, with the goal of completing both degrees in as little as five years. A new major in rehabilitation and disability studies has been added, as has a minor in sustainability studies.

Many Auburn students are eager to get started on their careers, so the co-op program, which provides pay and credit in several professional fields, is increasingly popular. Five areas identified as "strategic research clusters" compete for millions of dollars in special funding, which means more opportunities for undergrads to assist faculty with research in areas including health disparities, pharmaceutical engineering, climate and earth systems science, omics and informatics, and scalable energy conversion science and technology. Highly motivated freshmen may apply to the Honors College, and through the Auburn Abroad Experience, about 20 percent of all students study abroad in programs that include more than 50 faculty-led expeditions. Closer to home, the Rural Studio program sends students in the College of Architecture, Design, and Construction to live in economically underserved Hale County, Alabama, to design and build innovative community buildings and homes for local residents.

> **"[Students are] willing to help their classmates through tutoring or group study sessions."**

Auburn students are "mostly Southern people who are from Alabama and who have family that went to Auburn," says a junior. Indeed, 65 percent of Auburn students are Alabama natives, and many are second- or third-generation legacies. African Americans account for 7 percent of the largely homogenous student body, Hispanics add 3 percent, and 3 percent are Asian American; 1 percent hail from foreign countries. The conservative tone of this Bible Belt campus makes it hospitable for many Christian groups, and Auburn is home to one of the largest chapters in the United States of the Campus Crusade for Christ. "Half of Auburn students love politics and enjoy the political process, while the other half wouldn't know where their polling place was if you gave them a map," quips one senior. Each year, the university awards merit scholarships averaging $6,903. Gifted athletes vie for 267 athletic scholarships in 21 sports.

The majority of Auburn's 31 residence halls are co-ed by floor, but there are several single-sex halls; 21 percent of undergrads live on campus. First-year students compete for rooms on a first-come, first-served basis with returning students, and the dorms fill up fast. "Get on a waiting list ASAP," advises a junior.

Auburn has established a first-of-its-kind program in wireless engineering.

Twenty percent of Auburn men join fraternities, and 39 percent of women join sororities, perhaps because chapters get space in the best dorms. Students grumble about the mandatory—and pricey—meal plan, but say the dining has improved considerably in recent years. "The food continues to diversify and get healthier," confirms a student.

Aside from varsity sporting events and fraternity parties, Auburn sponsors concerts, free movies, and plenty of intramural leagues. "Social life is great whether you are Greek or not," says a freshman. "The university holds several events throughout the year that are fun," adds a senior, "but most of the social scene is off campus at apartments or fraternity houses." The campus is officially dry, except on game days, and students say the alcohol policy is enforced. Long-standing traditions include Hey Day, when everyone wears a nametag and walks around saying, "Hey!" Seventy percent of students participate in a variety of community service programs.

Auburn is a football powerhouse with pockets as deep as its location in the South and values to match. The school paid $11 million to a fired football coach and his staff, and there is a $14 million video scoreboard hailed by the athletic director as "a great asset, not only for our fans but also our students

The Rural Studio program sends students to live in Hale County, Alabama, to design and build homes for local residents.

"Social life is great whether you are Greek or not."

and our prospective student-athletes." On fall Saturdays, nearly 90,000 screaming fans turn the campus into Alabama's fourth-largest city. The rallying cry "Warrrrr Eagle!" rocks the place each time an Auburn back runs to daylight; the football team brought home a Southeastern Conference title in 2014. The annual Iron Bowl pits Auburn against archrival Alabama. In 2016 the equestrian team won its fourth national title, and Aubie, the official tiger mascot, won its record-setting ninth (yes, mascots compete in national championships too) at the UCA Cheer and Dance competition. Other solid Tigers teams include men's swimming and diving and women's golf and track and field. The McWhorter Center for Women's Athletics is one of the finest gymnastics training facilities in the country.

Auburn is working hard to increase the caliber of its students and academic programs, and especially to achieve a top 20 national ranking for its college of engineering. "Auburn has become more focused on the future," one senior says. But students agree that certain key characteristics have stayed the same—and that's a good thing. Says one student, "We just keep getting cooler."

Overlaps

University of Georgia, University of Alabama, Georgia Tech, University of Florida, University of Tennessee Knoxville, Clemson

If You Apply To ➤ | **Auburn:** Rolling admissions: Jan. 15. Financial aid: Mar. 1. Application fee: $50. Campus and alumni interviews: optional, informational. SATs or ACTs: required. Subject Tests: optional. No letters of recommendation. Essay: required. Out-of-state enrollment is capped on a year-to-year basis; there are no set limits.

Austin College

900 N. Grand Avenue, Sherman, TX 75090

The second most famous institution in Texas with Austin in its name. Half the size of Trinity (TX), runs neck and neck with Southwestern to be the leading Texas college with fewer than 1,500 students. Combines the liberal arts with strong programs in business, education, science, and health, including premed. Don't look for the 'Roos on a map of the city of Austin. The college is actually near Dallas.

Website: www.austincollege
.edu

Location: Small City

Private

Total Enrollment: 1,259

Undergraduates: 1,242

Male/Female: 48/52

SAT Ranges: CR 540–650,
M 540–640

ACT Ranges: 22–28

Financial Aid: 93%

Pell Grant: 30%

Expense: Pr $

Student Loans: 75%

Average Debt: N/A

Phi Beta Kappa: Yes

Applicants: 3,357

Accepted: 54%

Enrolled: 20%

Grad in 6 Years: 77%

Returning Freshmen: 83%

Academics: ✑ ✑ ✑

Social: ☎ ☎ ☎

Q of L: ★ ★ ★

Admissions: (903) 813-3000

Email Address: admission@
austincollege.edu

Strong Programs:
Business
Biology
Psychology
Foreign Languages
Premed
Predentistry
Prelaw
Education

The Global Outreach fellowship program gives 10 to 15 students the chance to volunteer in educational programs around the world.

For historical reasons over which reasonable persons can and do disagree, the Kangaroo has become the symbol of all things Austin College. All freshmen receive 'Roo Crew T-shirts at orientation, students hold a trick-or-treat alternative known as 'Roo Boo for local children, and the online career management system is known as 'Roo Connect. AC's preprofessional programs, most notably premed, are among the strongest in the state. Professors here even serve students breakfast at 10 p.m. the night before finals. It's just another example of the personal style that is typical of this charming Southern institution. "You feel comfortable and safe at Austin College," says a sophomore. "It becomes your second home."

Austin College's 85-acre campus is in a residential area in the city of Sherman. The campus is designed in the traditional quadrangle style and comprises beige sandstone buildings, tree-lined plazas, decorative fountains, and an impressive 70-ton sculptured solstice calendar. Dorms are conveniently located approximately 200 yards from most classrooms, which eases the pain of first-period classes. The 103,000-square-foot IDEA Center for hands-on, experiential learning in the sciences features laboratory classrooms, lecture rooms, and a 108-seat auditorium, as well as a $1 million, 24-inch telescope and astronomical image camera in the building's domed observatory.

The core curriculum begins with a freshman seminar called Communication/Inquiry. Each professor who teaches the course becomes the mentor for the 20 freshmen in his or her class. Then students select from courses in three categories in humanities, social sciences, and natural sciences. Students can combine three of the school's majors into an interdisciplinary degree, and all must complete one major and a minor or a double major to graduate. During the January term, students can focus on just one course, and many use that time to study abroad or undertake off-campus internships.

When it comes time to apply to grad school, premed and predentistry students at this little college have one of the highest acceptance rates of any Texas school, and aspiring lawyers also do well. AC's teaching program grants students both a bachelor's and a master's degree. Science and education receive high marks from students, and business, biology, psychology, and foreign languages are the most popular majors. The Jordan Family

"The mentor program really helps when it comes to… looking for summer research programs or internships."

Language House is home to 48 students studying Chinese, French, German, Japanese, and Spanish, along with a native speaker of each language, and students have to speak the language in all common areas. A cooperative engineering program links the college with other schools. New programs include majors in global management, business finance, and public health and minors in accounting and education.

Of the academic climate, a chemistry major says, "It is competitive enough to push you to do the best work you can, yet very collaborative through working with peers on group projects, lab assignments, research experiences, and other tasks." Sixty-seven percent of all classes have fewer than 20 students. "Teachers always make time for students, they're approachable, and the mentor program really helps when it comes to registering for classes and looking for summer research programs or internships," says a student. The college also offers independent study and departmental honors programs. The Posey Leadership Institute offers seminars and courses, and a minor in leadership studies is available. AC also provides five research areas in Grayson County. Thirty-three percent of students conduct undergraduate research and 60 percent study abroad each year. The Global Outreach fellowship program gives 10 to 15 students the chance to volunteer in educational programs around the world.

Eighty-nine percent of AC students hail from the Lone Star State, and 2 percent come from abroad. Hispanics and African Americans comprise 19 and 7 percent of the student body, respectively, and Asian Americans make up 13 percent. "Everyone is intelligent in a deep and insightful way," says a senior. "They enjoy the little things in life and welcome new ideas and experiences." Students also say there is a wide range of political views on campus. The college was founded by a Presbyterian missionary in 1849, and its continuous ties to the Presbyterian Church (USA) can be seen in the emphasis on values in the core courses, high participation in service activities, and limited residence-hall visitation hours—a chief complaint of students. AC offers merit scholarships worth an average of $19,794, and 30 percent of freshmen qualify for the Pell Grant.

"All of the housing on campus is extremely comfortable."

Eighty-two percent of undergraduates live on campus, and they are required to do so for their first three years. "All of the housing on campus is extremely comfortable," a biology major says. Dorms are co-ed, except for one all-female and one all-male dorm. Juniors and seniors choose from suites, flats, and cottages. Dean is a popular choice for freshmen, despite (or perhaps because of) its reputation as being loud and social. As for campus dining, "The staff here is amazing," cheers one student. "They always have smiles on their faces and aren't afraid to save you an extra cookie." The Pouch Club, an on-campus joint, serves pizza and burgers, as well as beer and wine for those students 21 and over. Students report feeling safe on campus thanks to a thorough campus security program. A senior says, "Everyone is required to take sexual assault training before the school year begins, and I have never heard of any offenses."

Most of the social life is either on or near campus. "There is always something to do on campus, from smaller activities and club meetings to big dinners and guest speakers," a junior says. Twenty-five percent of the men and 18 percent of the women belong to local fraternities and sororities, respectively, but the Greeks are not school-funded and are not allowed to advertise off-campus parties without the college's permission. Students get an eyeful during the Baker Bun Run, in which the men of Baker Hall strip to their boxers and cavort around the campus on the Monday night before finals. Mega Texas is a campus carnival in the fall, and Kangapalooza brings a big-name musician to campus in the spring. Students can have alcohol in dorm rooms only if they are 21 or older, and school policy prohibits booze at campus events. Popular weekend excursions are a drive to Dallas or to the college's 28-acre recreational spot on Lake Texoma (a half hour north). Sherman is "quaint" and "historic," and is becoming a better college town, students say. "There are lots of restaurants," a junior says, "but for the most part there is nothing to do late at night."

"Austin College cares for each student, and no one falls through the cracks."

Mega Texas is a campus carnival in the fall, and Kangapalooza brings a big-name musician to campus in the spring.

Even without athletic scholarships, varsity sports are generating increasing support. The Kangaroos compete in Division III, and solid teams include men's and women's basketball, soccer, and tennis, along with volleyball. The Mason Athletic/Recreation Complex provides facilities for athletes and the fitness-conscious. There's also a recreational sports program, with basketball, softball, flag football, and lacrosse proving popular; 20 percent of undergrads participate.

At this college with roots in the Presbyterian Church, students praise the preprofessional programs and the intimate, supportive environment. "Austin College cares for each student, and no one falls through the cracks," says a senior. "If you need help, often before you need it, people are reaching out to provide it to you." And while Sherman may seem to be a sleepy little place, Austin College is definitely hoppin'.

Overlaps
Baylor, University of Texas at Austin, University of Texas at Dallas, Texas A&M, Trinity University (TX), Texas Christian, Southwestern, Southern Methodist

Babson College

Babson Park, MA 02457-0310

The only college in the *Fiske Guide* devoted entirely to business. Babson is the birthplace of entrepreneurial studies—which continue to define the campus ethos. Only 14 miles from College Student Mecca, a.k.a. Boston, and tougher to get into than ever. Has about half as many undergraduates as Bentley, its closest competitor. The one college in Massachusetts where it is possible to be a Republican with head held high.

Website: www.babson.edu
Location: Suburban
Private
Total Enrollment: 2,568
Undergraduates: 2,141
Male/Female: 52/48
SAT Ranges: CR 580–720, M 620–720
ACT Ranges: 27–30
Financial Aid: 44%
Pell Grant: 17%
Expense: Pr $ $ $
Student Loans: 42%
Average Debt: $ $ $ $
Phi Beta Kappa: No
Applicants: 7,516
Accepted: 26%
Enrolled: 27%
Grad in 6 Years: 91%
Returning Freshmen: 96%
Academics: ✍ ✍ ✍
Social: ☎ ☎
Q of L: ★ ★ ★
Admissions: (781) 239-5522
Email Address:
ugradadmission@babson.edu

Strong Programs:
Business
Entrepreneurship
Finance
Economics
Marketing

Babson is a preeminent training ground for budding entrepreneurs and corporate bigwigs. The college is a pioneer in the study of entrepreneurship, dating to the 1970s—a time when people thought it couldn't be taught. Here, hands-on experience is the norm; students get school funding to start businesses during their first year and may hone their stock-picking skills by managing part of the college's endowment. Always the foremost business college in the Boston area, Babson attracts budding tycoons and entrepreneurs from around the globe.

Founded in 1919, the college sits on 370 acres near the sedate Boston suburb of Wellesley. The tract features open green spaces, gently rolling hills, and heavily wooded areas. Buildings are gently shaded and parking lots (filled with expensive foreign cars) are relatively hidden. Architecturally, the campus is mainly neo-Georgian and modern. Park Manor West, the newest addition to campus, doubles as a first-year residence hall and the home of the Schlesinger Innovation Center, offering an amphitheater, classrooms, and collaboration spaces.

Although Babson is a business school, about half of students' classes are in the liberal arts. General education requirements emphasize rhetoric (public speaking); ethics and social responsibility; international and multicultural perspectives; and leadership, teamwork, and creativity. In the Foundations of Management and Entrepreneurship course, first-year students are split into groups to develop business plans; each group gets up to $3,000 in seed money from the college to get their concept up and running. At the end of the year, the business is liquidated and profits go to charity. Former FME groups have developed Babsonopoly (a Babson-themed version of Monopoly), opened a Krispy Kreme Doughnuts franchise, and organized a 5K to raise money for suicide awareness organizations.

> **"It is very easy to build relationships with your professors."**

All Babson students major in business and then select a concentration, such as management or business analytics—or even identity and diversity studies or literary and visual arts. (The Sorenson Visual Arts Center has painting, ceramics, and sculpture studios; labs for photography and digital art; a student art gallery; and workspace for artists-in-residence.) Finance, economics, marketing, and entrepreneurship are the most popular concentrations, and the entrepreneurship program is one of Babson's strongest, bringing in venture capitalists and executives from such companies as Dunkin' Donuts and Jiffy Lube for how-to lectures. Courses are rigorous, and although just 21 percent of classes have fewer than 20 students, most others are still relatively small. "Each student finds his or her own way during the four years here, and everyone is able to support one another as well," says a senior.

In the classroom, Babson relies on the case-study approach more typically employed by M.B.A. programs. Students break into groups or act as officers of pseudo-corporations to address specific business situations and solve marketplace problems. "It is very easy to build relationships with your professors, and they are always excited to see you and hear about how you are doing," says one student. Accounting students may take graduate classes at Babson in the summer and fall after finishing their bachelor's degrees, letting them sit for the CPA exam about one year earlier than most other programs. The Management Consulting Field Experience program places students in consultant roles with Boston-area organizations, giving them real-world experience in addressing business challenges. Babson offers more than 100 study abroad programs in 38 countries, and students in the Honors Program are required to study abroad. Students can go away for an entire semester or school breaks, and not all programs are business focused; the London Theatre Program, for example, focuses on arts appreciation.

First-year students are split into groups and given up to $3,000 in seed money to get their business concept up and running.

"Babson students are driven, passionate, and entrepreneurial. We enjoy comparing how full our Google calendars are, leading a group, and promoting positive social change," says one senior. Although Babson welcomes 10 Posse scholars annually from urban public high schools, the campus remains largely white and wealthy, with African Americans making up 5 percent of the undergraduate student body, Hispanics 10 percent, and Asian Americans 12 percent. Foreign students comprise 26 percent, while 27 percent are Massachusetts natives. "One could say that Babson is very prep," admits a student. "No one blinks an eye when a student is walking around campus in a suit and many consider it a faux pas to be wearing anything less than dark jeans to class." No one seems to care much about politics. Merit scholarships averaging $20,880 are available; there are no athletic scholarships.

The Management Consulting Field Experience program places students in consultant roles with Boston-area organizations.

Babson guarantees housing for four years, and 78 percent of undergraduates live on campus, resulting in high demand for singles and suites. "The suite-style living is awesome," says a freshman. "It allows you to live with a bunch of your best friends but still have separate singles to sleep in." Dorms are air-conditioned and carpeted, and most upper-class rooms have their own bathrooms. After the first year, the large rooms are assigned by lottery, with standing based on credits earned. At the main dining hall, you'll find sushi, make-your-own stir-fry, and vegan stations; every Wednesday is gourmet night, and the menu may include fresh lobster, Italian specialties, or turkey with all the trimmings. Security gets high marks: "Babson has a police force of trained first responders that provide the campus with safety and security," explains one student. The student-led ASAP (Alliance for Sexual Assault Prevention) organization is active in raising awareness about campus sexual assault.

"We enjoy comparing how full our Google calendars are, leading a group, and promoting positive social change."

According to one senior, "Babson students create their own social experiences." Social life is centered on campus during the first two years; after that, most students are 21 and have cars, so they head to the clubs and bars of Boston proper, about 20 minutes away. "Because Babson is so close to Boston, many students partake in nightlife activities in the city," confirms one student. For those who aren't of age, or who lack wheels, the Campus Activities Board brings in comedians and organizes parties, as do Greek organizations, which attract 14 percent of the men and 27 percent of the women. Underage drinking on campus is treated with a three-strike policy, and the third offense gets violators kicked out of the dorms. Popular road trips include the beaches of Cape Cod and Martha's Vineyard, the ski slopes of Vermont and New Hampshire, and the bright lights of New York City and Montreal.

Foreign students comprise 26 percent of the undergraduate student body.

The "very affluent" town of Wellesley has shops and restaurants, and there is a subway stop. Students can take the T's Green Line into the city to explore Quincy Market or the campuses of Harvard, Northeastern, Emerson, and Boston Universities.

"No one blinks an eye when a student is walking around campus in a suit."

The school sponsors trips to Celtics and Red Sox games. Wellesley is also home to Wellesley College, and it's not unheard of for Babson students to socialize with Wellesley women; Babson also offers cross-registration at Wellesley, and the Olin College of Engineering. Favorite campus festivals include homecoming (great networking opportunities), Oktoberfest, and Spring Weekend, when bands come to play and parties are thrown. Students also contribute more than 30,000 volunteer hours annually through the Office of Faith and Service.

While making money may be the most popular "sport" at Babson, students recognize the importance of keeping their bodies in competitive condition too. Popular intramural sports include volleyball, rugby, and ice hockey, and on the varsity level, the Beavers play in Division III. Any match against archrival Bentley and soccer games against Brandeis and Colby draw crowds. The men's ice hockey team is a powerhouse, and men's and women's basketball have won their respective conference championships, with the men recently advancing to the NCAA Final Four.

At Babson, "There are a million resources," cheers one finance major. Students embrace entrepreneurship as an ethos and are willing to work hard for what they want. After all, learning how to balance work with everything else that's important in life is a prerequisite to climbing the corporate ladder. And thanks to small classes, a laser-like focus on all things financial, and plenty of hands-on experience, students leave Babson well equipped to begin scampering up those rungs.

Overlaps

Bentley, Northeastern, Boston University, Boston College, NYU, University of Pennsylvania, Cornell University, University of Massachusetts Amherst

If You Apply To ➤

Babson: Early decision and early action: Nov. 1. Regular decision: Jan. 3. Financial aid: Feb. 15. Housing: May 1. Application fee: $75. Campus and alumni interviews: optional, evaluative. SATs or ACTs: required. Subject Tests: optional. Letters of recommendation: required. Essay: required. Accepts the Common Application with supplement.

Bard College

Annandale-on-Hudson, NY 12504

Bard is a dominant presence in the world of nontraditional liberal arts colleges. Like Reed on the West Coast, combines unabashed individuality with rigorous traditional academics. Long-standing president Leon Botstein, a polymath known simply as "Leon," is an iconic educator who has championed the liberal arts in countries around the world.

Website: www.bard.edu
Location: Small Town
Private
Total Enrollment: 2,140
Undergraduates: 1,919
Male/Female: 45/55
SAT Ranges: CR 590–690, M 570–680

Bard College has come a long way since its 1860 founding by 12 men studying to enter the seminaries of the Episcopal Church. Those pioneers would no doubt be surprised at the eclectic mix of students now running around Annandale-on-Hudson in an ethos described by the *New Yorker* as one of "quixotic unworldliness." But the idea that Bard is strictly a school for artists and social studies majors has largely disappeared, and the result is a school with lots of intellectual depth. Having expanded its mission beyond undergraduate and graduate education to also encompass support for the arts, secondary education reform, and the development of partnerships that bring education to underserved areas around the globe, Bard has earned a well-deserved national profile. To succeed in such a dynamic environment, one student advises, "You don't need perfect grades. You just need an adventurous spirit, an ambitious attitude toward self-improvement, and an ability to evaluate your experiences and capabilities."

Bard's campus occupies 1,000 well-landscaped acres in New York's Washington Irving country, on the shores of the Hudson River. Consistent with everything else at Bard, there's no prevailing architectural theme, so each ivy-covered brick building stands out—especially the dorms, which range from cottages in the woods to Russian Colonial in style. Renowned architect Frank Gehry designed the stunning, $62 million Fisher Center for the Performing Arts, which provides teaching and performance space for everything from opera to improvisation. The Center for Science and Computation, designed by Rafael Vinoly, promotes collaborative, hands-on science. In 2016, Bard acquired Montgomery Place, a 380-acre estate and National Historic Landmark adjacent to the main campus, which provides additional space and facilities for programs in the arts, humanities, and environmental sciences.

Despite Bard's reputation for nonconformism, the list of requirements is extensive, including nine distribution requirements. Classes are small and seminar style, and freshmen show up three weeks before classes start for the Workshop in Language and Thinking, where they read extensively in several genres and meet in small groups to discuss reading and writing. (A literature major calls L&T "the best three weeks of my life.") The First-Year Seminar introduces the intellectual, artistic, and cultural ideas at the core of a liberal arts education. Citizen Science, another three-week workshop in January, examines topics not normally covered in the traditional science curriculum, such as infectious disease; organized into teams, the entire first-year class then teaches science lessons in the local public schools. In the spring of the second year, students declare a major through Moderation, a midway review of performance and proposed study plans discussed with a board of professors in the relevant area. In the junior year preparation for the Senior Project begins. Students create original work as evidence of mastery in their field or fields. The Senior Project is also discussed with a faculty board.

With authors such as Neil Gaimon, Francine Prose, and Dinaw Mengestu teaching at Bard, literature and written arts are among the school's best programs. Bard was one of the first to grant a B.A. in visual and performing arts and boasts one of the finest studio programs in the country; photography

"Professors value the students as individuals first."

is one of the toughest majors to get into. Bard established what administrators believe is the first collegiate program in human rights. There is also a five-year, dual-degree conservatory program for music students, and although Bard is far from pre-professional, it does offer combined programs of its own and with other schools in sustainability, finance, engineering, public health, and a number of other fields.

Bard's academic climate is "intellectual and consistently challenging," says a senior, but students agree that the atmosphere is collaborative. "Students are more eager to engage in discussions about what they just learned in class than they are likely to discuss what grades they received on the most recent exam," says a sociology and human rights major. Seventy-seven percent of classes have fewer than 20 students, and if students want more individual attention, they can devise a syllabus for their own tutorial and find a professor to sponsor it. There are no teaching assistants here, and professors receive outstanding reviews, both for their expertise and their personal approach. "Professors value the students as individuals first," says a senior.

Bard and the Rockefeller University have collaborated to provide students the opportunity to study topics in biology and medicine for a semester in New York City, and spots are reserved for Bard students as Summer Undergraduate Research Fellows. Also located in New York City, Bard's Globalization and International

(continued)

ACT Ranges: N/A
Financial Aid: 66%
Pell Grant: 25%
Expense: Pr $ $ $ $
Student Loans: 54%
Average Debt: $ $ $
Phi Beta Kappa: No
Applicants: 7,044
Accepted: 32%
Enrolled: 20%
Grad in 6 Years: 75%
Returning Freshmen: 85%
Academics: ✍ ✍ ✍ ✍
Social: ☎ ☎ ☎
Q of L: ★ ★ ★ ★
Admissions: (845) 758-7472
Email Address: admission@bard.edu

Strong Programs:
Languages and Literatures
Visual and Performing Arts
Photography
Human Rights
Social Studies
Biology
Computer Science

Students declare a major through Moderation, a midway review of performance and proposed study plans.

Affairs program merges advanced coursework in global affairs with internships at leading public, private, and nonprofit agencies. Study abroad is available in far-flung locales around the globe; 50 percent of students take part. The Trustee Leader Scholar program provides grants and support for student-run community service projects. In an effort to expand liberal arts instruction overseas and to help nurture emerging democratic societies, Bard has developed partnerships with educational institutions in locations as diverse as Lithuania, South Africa, the West Bank, and Kyrgyzstan, as well as among prison inmates in the U.S.

Bard established what administrators believe is the first collegiate program in human rights.

Bard students tended to march to their own drummer in high school. "Many struggle their first year, when they realize everyone is just as unique as they are," says one senior. But Bardians take pride in diversity, whether racial, geographical (66 percent are from out of state, with 56 countries represented), or ideological, though they admit the latter can be lacking. "If you're a Republican or conservative, please come and add some dimension to our conversation," implores one student. "I'm sick of agreeing with everyone." While Bard has its share of extremely wealthy children of media moguls and Hollywood actors, 25 percent of current freshmen qualify for Pell Grants. African Americans make up 8 percent of the student body, Asian Americans 6 percent, and Hispanics 1 percent. Bard offers academic scholarships based on need but no athletic awards. Under the Excellence and Equal Cost program, qualified high school students may apply to attend Bard for the price of a public-school education in their home state. Bard offers a unique early-decision application option in which students can take the Bard Entrance Examination, demonstrating their academic ability by submitting four 2,500-word essays on a range of scholarly topics that are graded by professors.

"If you're a Republican or conservative, please come and add some dimension to our conversation."

Seventy-three percent of Bard students live on campus, and freshmen are required to do so. Residence halls vary in style, explains one student: "Some are old Victorian mansions, some are new modern buildings that are eco-friendly, one looks like a castle, and others are big cement monsters from the 1950s." Juniors and seniors are not guaranteed beds on campus, and many upperclassmen move off campus. To help ease their commute, Bard runs a shuttle to the nearby towns of Red Hook and Tivoli, which are home to a variety of restaurants, bars, and other conveniences. Campus dining is described as "decent, but not amazing," but students appreciate that all dietary needs are easily accommodated, and much of the fresh produce comes from Bard's own student-operated farm. Students say they feel safe on their rural campus, but sexual assault has become a point of student activism. A senior notes, "The general sentiment is that the administration has not done enough to prevent or handle sexual assault on campus."

All Bard students are automatically made members of the student government, and cocurricular life is run by students.

All Bard students are automatically made members of the student government, and cocurricular life is run by students; there are more than 120 different clubs. The school offers cultural shows and performances, concerts, and movies, with indie films and alternative rock and hip-hop particularly popular. The Student Activities Board plans Urban Cowboy Night, Welcome Back Weekend, Midnight Breakfast complete with karaoke, the ever-popular Thursday Night Live, and Spring Fling. There are no fraternities or sororities, and when it comes to alcohol, policies are focused on safety and respect, although underage drinking in the dorms is taken seriously. Bard's hometown of Annandale-on-Hudson is 20 miles from the crafts and antiques meccas of Woodstock and Rhinebeck, and not much farther from the ski slopes of the Catskills and the Berkshires. Having a car helps to prevent occasional attacks of claustrophobia, and New York City is just 100 minutes away by train.

"The one real thing that unites Bard is an ability to be self-driven and independent."

The Raptors compete in 18 Division III sports and are members of a number of conferences, including the Eastern College Athletic Conference, the Liberty League, and the College Squash Association. Bard is virtually devoid of dedicated jocks, but one student notes, "There are plenty of pseudo jocks and intellectuals in good shape." Thirty-five percent of the students get involved in intramurals, such as basketball, floor hockey, and bowling, which emphasize participation and fun. Across campus, miles of trails stretch through the woods along the Hudson, perfect for everything from raspberry picking to jogging and hiking. "If you like the woods, it's amazing," sighs an anthropology major. "If you like the city, you'll go stir-crazy."

Thanks to the iconoclastic vision of President Leon Botstein, also conductor of the American Symphony Orchestra, Bard offers strong programs that reach far beyond the arts. Come prepared to work hard and have your mind opened. "The Bard culture is a weird mixture of apathy and activism, arts and sciences, quirkiness and coolness," says a senior. "However, the one real thing that unites Bard is an ability to be self-driven and independent. Bard students are not followers, but establish their own paths."

If You Apply To > **Bard:** Early decision and early action: Nov. 1. Regular decision: Jan. 1. Financial aid: Feb. 15. Application fee: $50. Campus interviews: optional, evaluative. No alumni interviews. SATs or ACTs: optional. Subject Tests: optional. Letters of recommendation: required. Essay: required. Accepts the Common Application with supplement.

Barnard College

New York, NY 10027

With more applicants than any other women's college, Barnard is academically right up there with Wellesley. Step outside and you're on Broadway; across the street lies Columbia College, whose academic riches are yours for the taking. Barnard women are a little more artsy and a bit more city-ish than their female counterparts at Columbia.

Barnard students get the best of both worlds—the small, close-knit atmosphere of a liberal arts school along with the limitless opportunities of Columbia College, the Ivy League undergraduate research institution just across the street. Whether they are passionate about art and music or urban studies and politics, women seeking a high-energy, empowering environment with top-notch academics are likely to find a niche here. "Barnard is a rigorous yet nurturing environment," says a senior. "Barnard students are firm believers in women's education."

Barnard's campus is on the Upper West Side of Manhattan, in the Morningside Heights neighborhood. It's just blocks from Riverside Drive, which has a lovely path parallel to the Hudson River for running, biking, or rollerblading. Trees and other greenery shade grand prewar apartment buildings, and grassy medians break up the wide expanse of Broadway itself. Barnard's architecturally diverse buildings are more modern than Columbia's, and in recent years, the college has invested to upgrade labs, classrooms, and the residence halls. A new, 128,000-square-foot teaching and learning center, slated to open in fall 2018, will include a state-of-the-art library featuring interactive technologies and learning spaces.

Website: www.barnard.edu
Location: City Center
Private
Total Enrollment: 2,510
Undergraduates: 2,510
Male/Female: 0/100
SAT Ranges: CR 640–730, M 620–720
ACT Ranges: 29–32
Financial Aid: 41%
Pell Grant: 19%
Expense: Pr $ $ $ $
Student Loans: 44%
Average Debt: $
Phi Beta Kappa: Yes
Applicants: 6,655

(continued)

Accepted: 20%

Enrolled: 48%

Grad in 6 Years: 89%

Returning Freshmen: 95%

Academics: ✍ ✍ ✍ ✍

Social: ☎ ☎ ☎

Q of L: ★ ★ ★

Admissions: (212) 854-2014

Email Address: admissions@
barnard.edu

Strong Programs:

Psychology

English

Biology

Visual and Performing Arts

Architecture

Women's Studies

Education

Students must fulfill requirements in areas such as Thinking Technologically and Digitally, Thinking Locally, and Thinking about Social Difference.

Barnard competes head-to-head with Columbia in admissions, an interesting dilemma because Barnard is an affiliate college of Columbia University, similar to the engineering school, the medical school, the business school, and, of course, Columbia College. In general, women looking for a more traditional "rah-rah" experience may prefer Columbia. Some students apply to Barnard as a back door to Columbia, which is harder for women to get into, but Barnard's admissions officers have become adept at sniffing out Columbia wannabes.

"All Barnard professors care deeply about mentoring their students and specifically about educating women."

Those who opt for Barnard like the fact that advising and housing are better on their side of Broadway and value its distinctive approach to educating women. Once enrolled, Barnard students share a first-year orientation program with Columbia, where they mix together in small groups and take tours of the campus and city. Students can also take part in a preorientation urban volunteer program.

Barnard's new Foundations curriculum, launched in fall 2016, is designed to enable students to gain general knowledge in a range of academic disciplines, develop critical thinking and communication skills, and spend more of their time exploring other areas of interest or pursuing cocurricular opportunities that enhance their major. First-year students must take a writing course, a first-year seminar, and a physical education course. In addition to taking two courses each in the languages, arts and humanities, social sciences, and sciences, students must fulfill Modes of Thinking requirements in six areas, such as Thinking Technologically and Digitally, Thinking Locally, and Thinking about Social Difference. A senior project or thesis ensures academic depth within the major.

Barnard's most popular majors are psychology, English, biology (there's a healthy contingent of premeds), and visual and performing arts. Architecture is also well regarded. "Many students double major or take additional courses in departments other than their own," offers one student. Barnard boasts strong support for budding writers and is a hotbed of new talent. Women's studies and education draw praise, though students in these programs must also choose another major. The Athena Center for Leadership Studies offers workshops, mentoring programs, internships, guest speakers, and other special features. Barnard students may cross-register at Columbia if they find more courses of interest there, or enroll in graduate courses in a number of Columbia's schools. A dual-degree program is available with the Jewish Theological Seminary, and music students may apply to take classes at Juilliard and the Manhattan School of Music. Roughly 200 students study abroad in more than 52 countries, including Argentina, Australia, China, India, Morocco, and Spain.

"The academic climate of Barnard is exhilaratingly rigorous. Students are deeply committed to their studies and their intellectual pursuits," says one senior. Many students come to Barnard because of its low student/faculty ratio. Seventy percent of classes have fewer than 20 students. Another plus: Barnard has no graduate teaching

"From research in labs to internships at the Met, there is no shortage of amazing opportunities."

assistants. In fact, Barnard professors enjoy Columbia's proximity almost as much as undergraduates, and each year one-third of the full-time faculty teaches in graduate departments throughout the university. Still, faculty members focus on their teaching responsibilities to undergraduates first. "All Barnard professors care deeply about mentoring their students and specifically about educating women," says a cell and molecular biology major. Undergraduate research is also a priority at Barnard, especially in the sciences. Guided internships, colloquia, and seminar courses often provide the structure for such research and, in most cases, coursework fulfills major requirements. "From research in labs to internships at the Met, there is no shortage of amazing opportunities outside of the classroom for Barnard students in New York City," cheers a junior.

"We are a diverse group of smart, ambitious, and talented women," says a junior. Twenty-six percent of Barnard students are New York natives, including a sizable contingent from the East Side of Manhattan, and 8 percent are international. Asian Americans make up 14 percent of the student body, African Americans 7 percent, and Hispanics 12 percent. The campus leans left politically and according to a history major, "Hot-button topics range from struggles of first-generation students to gender expression to divesting from fossil fuels." Barnard does not offer merit or athletic scholarships, but it does meet the full demonstrated financial need of admitted students.

Ninety-one percent of Barnard students live in the dorms, which have come a long way since the college's beginning as a commuter school: there's an 18-story Barnard dormitory tower, plus one dorm complex and seven off-campus apartment buildings; nonresidents must be signed in by a resident, and entries are always guarded, so students say they feel safe. In addition, Barnard shares two co-ed dorms with Columbia. "The dorms and housing at Barnard are amazing," says one senior. "They are clean, comfortable, spacious (mostly!), and very well maintained." Barnard guarantees four years of housing to enrolling first-years, which one student says is "a relief considering how difficult and expensive it can be to find an apartment in New York City." Seniors get the best rooms through a lottery system. Dorm-dwellers must buy a meal plan, which may also be used at Columbia's John Jay cafeteria, though students say Barnard's food is better. "The college has created a Step Up program that teaches students how to recognize what sexual assault is and how to handle it both as a potential victim and as a passerby," explains a junior.

"This is not a school where students go out every night. Maybe once a weekend, or every other weekend."

When it comes to social life, students tend to divide their time between on campus and off. "Most of the social life takes place around campus," a junior says, "but you obviously have all of New York City to explore." Traditions on campus include Midnight Breakfast the night before finals begin, when deans and administrators serve up eggs and waffles in the student center. Women in the arts are celebrated in the annual Winterfest. Alcohol is prohibited in first-year dorms, and students seeking parties head next door to Columbia or bars in Morningside Heights, but an English major notes, "This is not a school where students go out every night. Maybe once a weekend, or every other weekend." Many of the city's offerings are free to students with their school ID. Road trips are infrequent, as not many students have cars, but when they happen, destinations range from Washington, D.C., to Boston, easily reached by train and plane, to skiing and snowboarding in Vermont, or spring break on the beaches of South Carolina.

Barnard athletes compete in the Division I Ivy League conference alongside their peers enrolled at Columbia, and basketball, tennis, soccer, swimming, track, volleyball, and field hockey are popular and competitive. The fencing team is also strong. Columbia's marvelous gym and co-ed intramurals are also available to Barnard women, but many of them prefer to exercise their minds.

Students see Barnard as having "the supportive community of a small liberal arts women's college, the resources of a large research institution through Columbia, and the infinite opportunities of New York City right outside the gates," in the words of one proud Barnard woman. It's a winning combination that turns out well-rounded students ready to leap toward the future. "If you want to learn how to be a leader while also getting a holistic education, you should choose Barnard," advises one happy student.

Overlaps

Columbia, NYU, Princeton, Brown, University of Chicago, Wellesley, Northwestern, University of California

Bates College

23 Campus Avenue, Lewiston, ME 04240

Bowdoin got rid of its frats; Bates never had them, and therein hangs a tale. With its long-held tradition of egalitarianism and sense of community, Bates is a kindred spirit to Quaker institutions such as Haverford and Swarthmore. A month-long spring term helps make Bates a leader in studying abroad. Blue-collar Lewiston is not a draw, but New England countryside is within arm's reach.

Website: www.bates.edu
Location: Small City
Private
Total Enrollment: 1,792
Undergraduates: 1,792
Male/Female: 49/51
SAT Ranges: CR 590–713, M 600–703
ACT Ranges: 28–32
Financial Aid: 44%
Pell Grant: 10%
Expense: Pr $ $ $ $
Student Loans: 39%
Average Debt: $
Phi Beta Kappa: Yes
Applicants: 5,651
Accepted: 22%
Enrolled: 42%
Grad in 6 Years: 89%
Returning Freshmen: 95%
Academics: ✍ ✍ ✍ ✍ ½
Social: ☎ ☎ ☎
Q of L: ★ ★ ★
Admissions: (855) 228-3755
Email Address: admission@bates.edu

Strong Programs:
Economics
Psychology
Politics
History
Environmental Studies

Founded by abolitionists in 1855, Bates College takes pride in its heritage as a haven for seekers of guidance, freedom, and justice. Its 4–4–1 calendar offers ample opportunity for study abroad, even for just one month at year's end. The school's small size also means student/faculty interaction is plentiful, and close friendships are easily formed.

The Bates campus features a mix of Georgian and Federal buildings and Victorian homes spread out over the grassy lawns of Lewiston. The comprehensive Campus Facilities Master Plan, undertaken over several years, has given Bates a new campus core in terms of facilities: Bates has transformed two former student residence halls into key academic buildings, converted a historic Victorian home into a new student residence, and dramatically renovated one of the country's earliest college football fields into a multisport turf field.

Bates emphasizes a broad-based education in the liberal arts that encompasses the humanities, sciences and mathematics, social sciences, and the arts. Although there are no core course requirements, students are expected to select a major and two thematic concentrations, each consisting of four interrelated courses structured on the basis of a central organizing principle. These concentrations may fall within one department or program, or may focus on a particular topic or area of inquiry designed by faculty from different disciplines. "One unique part of Bates is that just about all seniors write a thesis," says a chemistry major. "Some are semester-long, while others are yearlong, depending on the department and what you want to do." The Ladd Library is often crowded with the 97 percent of students who write a thesis or produce an equivalent research, service, performance, or studio project. Ladd has almost 600,000 printed volumes, plus an all-night study room, computer labs, and a music composition work station.

While Bates was a pioneer in not requiring standardized tests for admission, don't expect to coast through. "The academic climate at Bates is extremely rigorous," says one junior. "The academic standard for an institution such as Bates is high, and students are held to that standard in all aspects across all major and minor disciplines." The most popular majors include economics, psychology, politics, history, and environmental studies, and these are also among Bates's best. The music and art departments benefit from the Olin Arts Center, which houses a performance hall, gallery, recording studio, art studios, and practice rooms. Interdisciplinary programs at Bates include American cultural studies, neuroscience, and women and gender studies. Professors teach all courses, including lab and discussion sections, and 67 percent of classes enroll fewer than 20 students. "The professors are always so accessible and make a real effort to get to know their students on a personal basis," one senior states.

For those whose horizons extend beyond the charms of Lewiston, Bates offers study abroad opportunities in more than 80 foreign locations, such as China, Russia, Croatia, Chile, and Austria, and more than two-thirds of students take advantage of them. The school also participates in the Washington Semester of American University* and the American Maritime Studies Program* at Mystic Seaport—both attractive options for students seeking real-world experience. Bates's 4–4–1 calendar allows for a five-week short term at the end of the academic year, and students may use this term to focus on a single subject of interest, frequently off campus. Recent examples include marine biological studies at stations on the coast of Maine; art, theater, and music studies in New York City and Europe; and field projects in economics, sociology, and psychology.

> "One unique part of Bates is that just about all seniors write a thesis."

Ten percent of Bates students come from Maine, 7 percent arrive from foreign countries, and many others hail from Massachusetts, Connecticut, and New York. "Students at Bates are intelligent, quirky, and eager to try new things," a student says. While the administration is trying to make Bates more diverse, minorities remain a fragment of the student population, with African Americans accounting for 5 percent, Hispanics 8 percent, and Asian Americans 4 percent. Socioeconomically, a mere 10 percent of students qualify for Pell Grants, a number notably lower than at close competitor Bowdoin. Students are drawn to social and political causes, and "Diversity is the biggest social issue on campus," reports a French major. There are no merit or athletic scholarships available, although the college does guarantee to meet the demonstrated need of all students.

Virtually all Bates students live on campus, as housing is guaranteed for four years and singles, doubles, triples, quads, and suites are available. "Housing is great here," a student raves. Students report that the campus dining hall offers tasty fare. "We have a vegan bar, a pasta bar, a brick-oven pizza station, a grill station, a Euro station, soup, salad, and sandwich stations, as well as a toaster station for bagels and toast," reports one politics major. "We also have over sixty cereals in circulation in the dining hall." Students say campus security is visible and more than adequate. "Given the nature of a small campus, students know a majority of the officers' names and do not feel intimidated to approach them about a problem," explains a history major.

> "The professors are always so accessible and make a real effort to get to know their students on a personal basis."

Since there's not much to do in Lewiston, weekend diversions mostly occur on campus. "Whether it is parties, comedians, movies, or bands, there is always something to do for everyone on campus," a freshman says. The Chase Hall Committee, run by students, plans many of the social events, including an annual gala. Without a Greek system, college alcohol policies are fairly loose, a student says, and a ban on hard liquor is often ignored. Barbecues and clambakes are big when the weather is nice, and the annual Winter Carnival includes an Iron Chef competition, ice skating, and the Puddle Jump, where a hole is cut in the ice on Lake Andrews and students plunge in. Students with cars can easily road-trip to the outlet stores in Freeport and Kittery, Maine. Other popular destinations include Bar Harbor in Acadia National Park, or "Portland, for great food," says a senior. Montreal and Boston are not far, and neither are the ski slopes of Vermont and New Hampshire. The Outing Club hosts weekend trips into the great Maine outdoors.

Bates offers study abroad opportunities in more than 80 foreign locations, and more than two-thirds of students take part.

Bates is home of the famed undergraduate debate organization the Brooks Quimby Debate Council.

Bates's 31 varsity Bobcat teams compete in Division III, except for the ski team, which is Division I. Everyone gets excited for matches against Bowdoin and Colby, especially when it comes to basketball, football, and lacrosse. The women's rowing team is a recent national champion. The intramural program, organized by the students, is "strong and spirited" and attracts a large number of participants, with softball, ultimate Frisbee, soccer, and basketball being some of the favorites. Bates is home of the famed undergraduate debate organization the Brooks Quimby Debate Council. Founded in the 1800s when completing a public debate was a graduation requirement at Bates, the team was one of the first in the nation to go co-ed and to include African American students. Bates was also the first American institution to debate with foreign universities and recently secured its first national championship in British parliamentary-style debate.

"Students at Bates are intelligent, quirky, and eager to try new things."

If you can stand the cold and the silent, starry nights, Bates may be a good choice. With caring professors, a small student body, and a focus on the liberal arts, students quickly become big fans. "I came to Bates for the people," says a sophomore. "The friends you make here will remain your friends well beyond your final days at Bates."

Overlaps

Bowdoin, Middlebury, Colby, Dartmouth, Wesleyan

If You Apply To >

Bates: Early decision I: Nov. 15. Early decision II, regular decision, and financial aid: Jan. 1. Housing: May 1. Application fee: $60. Campus and alumni interviews: optional, evaluative. SATs or ACTs: optional. Subject Tests: optional. Letters of recommendation: required. Essay: required. Accepts the Common Application.

Baylor University

Waco, TX 76798

The largest and best–endowed Baptist university anywhere, Baylor has set its sights on becoming a leading research university. Atmosphere is avowedly Christian, but pious image has been blurred by charges that administrators failed to comply with the Title IX gender-equity law or to respond properly to incidents of sexual violence, especially by football players.

Website: www.baylor.edu
Location: City Center
Private
Total Enrollment: 16,787
Undergraduates: 14,189
Male/Female: 42/58
SAT Ranges: CR 560–650, M 580–670
ACT Ranges: 25–30
Financial Aid: 94%
Pell Grant: 25%
Expense: Pr $ $
Student Loans: N/A
Average Debt: N/A

Baylor University offers students a solid Christian-influenced education at a bargain price. The university's Baptist tradition fosters a strong sense of community among students and faculty, and the school's vision plan promises a slew of strategic changes, such as lowering the student/teacher ratio and building new residence halls. The university aspires to become a top-tier research university while enhancing its Christian identity. "Baylor's commitment to academic excellence and an incredible alumni network ensures a great education and a chance to get a job," says a junior.

The 1,000-acre Baylor campus, nicknamed Jerusalem on the Brazos, abuts the historic Brazos River near downtown Waco, Texas (population 130,000). The architectural style emphasizes the gracious tradition of the Old South, and the central part of campus, the quadrangle, was built when Baylor moved from Independence, Texas, in 1886. The campus has been witness to a number of renovations and new construction, including the Foster Campus for Business and Innovation and an athletic nutrition center.

Students pursue their major in arts and sciences or one of Baylor's five other schools: business, education, engineering and computer sciences, music, and nursing. Core requirements include four English courses and four semesters of human performance. All students also take two religion courses and two semesters of Chapel Forum, a series of lectures and meetings on various issues or Christian testimonies. Freshmen take a New Student Experience course in the fall. The Honors College oversees the honors program (which offers opportunities for course integration and independent research) and the University Scholars Program (which waives most distribution requirements).

Popular majors include biology, nursing, finance, accounting, and marketing. More unusual options include church-state studies, institutes focusing on environmental studies and childhood learning disorders, and a major and minor in Great Texts, an interdisciplinary program exploring "the richness and diversity of the Western intellectual heritage." The archaeology and geology departments benefit from fossil- and mineral-rich Texas prairies. An increasing number of Baylor students are traveling on study abroad programs, which send them packing to dozens of countries, including China, Spain, Honduras, and Malawi. About 20 percent of undergrads get involved in research.

Students say that one of Baylor's greatest strengths is the sense of campus community, fostered by the emphasis on Christianity and by the administration's efforts to focus faculty members on teaching, rather than on research and other activities. Baylor also strives to keep classes small—54 percent have fewer than 20 students. The university's endowment is hefty and the largest among the nation's Baptist-affiliated schools. "Most of my prerequisite classes tended to be more collaborative and relaxed, but once I started taking the upper-level business courses, the atmosphere became much more competitive," says a senior. Full professors often teach freshman courses. "The professors are engaging and encouraging," says one sophomore.

"The students at Baylor tend to be kind, involved, and driven," says a finance and economics major. "They differ from some of our closest rivals mainly because of the spiritual influence that many students tend to have and seek out." Seventy percent of undergraduates are Texans and 3 percent

> **"The students at Baylor tend to be kind, involved, and driven."**

are international. African Americans account for 7 percent of the student body, Hispanics 14 percent, and Asian Americans 6 percent. The university has launched several new initiatives to increase and support diversity on campus, including cultural competence training for students, faculty, and staff. Twenty-five percent of freshmen are Pell-eligible. Students vie for numerous academic scholarships, averaging $13,546, and 369 athletic scholarships in 15 sports.

As might be expected on such a conservative and religious campus, dorms are single sex and have restrictive visitation privileges, which is a big complaint among the 36 percent of students who call them home. "There has been a lot of money invested into remodeling and building new student housing, so the quality is definitely improving," says one senior. Upperclassmen look off campus for cheaper housing with private rooms and fewer rules, but there is a push for more students to stay on campus with the construction of a newer residence hall with apartment-style rooms. Students say they feel safe, provided they stay on campus. "There are lights everywhere on campus and police cars constantly patrolling the grounds," one student explains. Moreover, "there are people on watch at all times, especially at night." Baylor recently enacted sweeping changes in the management of its athletic program following reports that it had mishandled and covered up reports of sexual assaults on campus. President Ken Starr (of Whitewater fame) and the football coach lost their jobs in the process. Campuswide sexual assault training and prevention

(continued)

Phi Beta Kappa: Yes
Applicants: 32,136
Accepted: 44%
Enrolled: 24%
Grad in 6 Years: 72%
Returning Freshmen: 89%
Academics: ✍ ✍ ✍
Social: ☎ ☎ ☎
Q of L: ★ ★ ★
Admissions: (254) 710-3435
Email Address: admissions@baylor.edu

Strong Programs:
Biology
Accounting
Nursing
Finance
Marketing
Computer Science
Engineering
Communication Sciences and Disorders

Most of Baylor's 330 student organizations involve a community service requirement.

programs are being implemented, but continuing publicity about the university's flawed handling of sexual assault cases has damaged its national reputation.

Fifteen percent of Baylor's men and 28 percent of the women belong to a fraternity or sorority, and students may also choose from more than 330 other student organizations, most of which involve a community service requirement. With so many students residing off campus, the social life is decent but not a party atmosphere. "Alcohol is much less prevalent at Baylor than at most schools," says a senior. It isn't served on campus or at campus-sponsored events. "Common Grounds, an on-campus coffee shop, hosts concerts most weekends," says one student. "The movies are popular (a ticket costs $5 with a student ID)." Easy road trips include Dallas, Austin, San Antonio, Bryan/College Station, and beaches at Galveston, South Padre Island, and Corpus Christi. Most destinations are within a two-and-a-half-hour drive, students say, making a set of wheels a big help, if not a necessity.

Baylor has the largest collegiate homecoming parade in the nation.

Highlights of Baylor's social calendar include the weekly Dr Pepper Hour with free soda floats and the Dia del Oso (Day of the Bear), when classes are canceled for a day in April in favor of a campuswide carnival. Christmas on 5th Street, organized by Student Life, gives students an opportunity to enjoy the annual Christmas tree lighting, concert, and other holiday festivities. The school also has the largest collegiate homecoming parade in the nation.

When it comes to football, remember: you're in Texas. The Division I Baylor Bears play in the new $266 million McLane Stadium. Freshmen wear team jerseys to games and take the field before the players, then sit together as a pack. "It's a very awesome part of the freshman experience," one student says. The team won the Big 12 championship in 2013 and 2014. The women's basketball team claimed its sixth straight conference title in 2016, while the acrobatics and tumbling team repeated as national champions. Other recent conference champs include men's and women's tennis and women's golf. For weekend warriors, the McLane Student Life Center offers the tallest rock-climbing wall in Texas. The university maintains a small marina for swimming and paddleboating, and several lakes with good beaches are nearby. Popular intramural sports include flag football, indoor volleyball, and the country's largest collegiate dodgeball tournament.

"Baylor is a Baptist institution that has been 100 percent commissioned to do God's work in education."

"Baylor is a Baptist institution that has been 100 percent commissioned to do God's work in education," states one student. "Its faculty and staff reflect this faith." Students here focus less on finding the right party than on academics, spiritual nourishment, community involvement, and discovering their vocational calling. One content junior reflects, "I will always proudly say that my decision to come to Baylor is one of the best life decisions I have ever made."

Overlaps

Texas A&M, University of Texas at Austin, Texas Tech, Texas Christian, Texas State, University of Texas at San Antonio, University of North Texas, University of Oklahoma

If You Apply To ➢

Baylor: Early action: Nov. 1. Regular decision and financial aid: Feb. 1. Application fee: $50. No campus or alumni interviews. SATs or ACTs: required. No Subject Tests. Letters of recommendation: recommended. Essay: recommended. Accepts the Common Application with supplement.

Beloit College

700 College Street, Beloit, WI 53511

A small Midwestern college known for freethinking students and international focus, Beloit has steered back toward the mainstream after its heyday as an alternative school in the '60s and '70s. Wisconsin location makes Beloit easier to get into than comparable schools in sexier places. Well-known anthropology program is among the best in the nation.

Beloit College remains dedicated to the liberal arts and sciences, but encourages students to "practice the liberal arts by integrating knowledge with hands-on experience." Known for attracting liberal freethinkers in the 1960s and '70s, the school has steered back toward the mainstream. What hasn't changed is its emphasis on tolerance, understanding, and the world beyond the United States. "To really enjoy Beloit, you should be open to new ideas, concepts, and people," advises an education and youth studies major. "You will learn how to think critically about your positions and beliefs and work to have a deeper understanding of the world as a whole."

Beloit's 40-acre campus is a Northeastern-style oasis an hour's drive from Madison and Milwaukee and nearly two hours from Chicago. Academic and administrative buildings sit on one side, with residence halls on the other. Two architectural themes dominate, says one student: "1850s colonial and obtuse 1930s." In the last few years, the World Affairs Center, dedicated as a Carnegie library in 1905, has been renovated, as has the historic Emerson residence hall. The college's Turtle Creek Bookstore, located three blocks away in downtown Beloit, offers a cozy coffee bar and a patio for relaxing, reading, or studying.

Beloit does not have core requirements. Instead, students complete a required "beyond the classroom" Liberal Arts in Practice experience, three writing-intensive courses, a quantitative reasoning class, one intercultural literacy course, and a capstone experience. In addition to an Initiatives orientation and discovery course in their first semester, Beloiters tackle classes on Big Questions and Transformational Works while earning five credits across five domains that focus on systems, arts, behavior, the universe, and texts.

Anthropology is a signature program at Beloit, and the health and society, psychology, economics, and international relations programs are also well regarded; these are also among the most popular majors. Among the more unusual options are a museum studies minor, enhanced by hands-on experience in the college's Wright Museum of Art and Logan Museum of Anthropology, which was established in 1894. The health and society major encourages students to take an interdisciplinary look at health and medical care in the U.S. and around the world. Cross-registration is available with the University of Wisconsin–Madison, as is a 3–2 engineering degree with nine institutions. Beloit is also a member of the Associated Colleges of the Midwest* consortium, further increasing students' choices.

The academic milieu is described as challenging but not competitive. "Students are expected to do significant work—papers, research, symposiums—but there is also an atmosphere of meaningful collaboration," says one student. Teaching is the faculty's first priority, and 69 percent of classes have fewer than 20 students. "I have always felt that faculty have worked with me to achieve my own goals and have opened themselves to their classes entirely," says an international relations and French double major. "They learn with us much of the time, as opposed to being a font of knowledge—the learning goes both ways."

Website: www.beloit.edu
Location: Small City
Private
Total Enrollment: 1,266
Undergraduates: 1,266
Male/Female: 45/55
SAT Ranges: CR 540–695, M 540–645
ACT Ranges: 24–30
Financial Aid: 97%
Pell Grant: 21%
Expense: Pr $ $ $
Student Loans: 70%
Average Debt: $ $ $
Phi Beta Kappa: Yes
Applicants: 3,552
Accepted: 69%
Enrolled: 16%
Grad in 6 Years: 82%
Returning Freshmen: 88%
Academics: ✑ ✑ ✑
Social: ☏ ☏ ☏
Q of L: ★ ★ ★ ★
Admissions: (608) 363-2500
Email Address: admiss@beloit.edu

Strong Programs:
Anthropology
Health and Society
Psychology
Economics
International Relations
Foreign Languages
Physical Sciences
English

To satisfy Beloit's experiential learning and global diversity requirements, students may apply for summer Venture Grants, which offer up to $2,000 for "entrepreneurial, self-testing, or intellectually challenging" activities that engage with outside communities; recent awardees have volunteered with an organic farming and reforesting initiative on the Galapagos Islands and studied women's health issues at tea plantations in Sri Lanka. The Sanger Summer Scholars program provides full funding for students to work directly with a faculty member on a research project, and students may also conduct biological and biomedical research at Northwestern and Rush Universities in Chicago. The Center for Entrepreneurship in Liberal Education at Beloit enables students from any major to plan and execute original entrepreneurial projects. Roughly 45 percent of Beloit's students study or do research abroad and may choose from programs in 38 countries.

> **"[Professors] learn with us much of the time, as opposed to being a font of knowledge—the learning goes both ways."**

The museum studies minor is enhanced by hands-on experience in the college's Logan Museum of Anthropology.

"Anyone who has gone to Beloit will tell you that it is exceptionally difficult to characterize a Beloiter, given that the small campus is host to so many strong individual personalities and opinions," says a senior. Seventy-five percent of students hail from out of state, and 9 percent from abroad. Hispanics comprise 9 percent of the total, African Americans 5 percent, and Asian Americans 3 percent. "Our Sustained Dialogue program mixes faculty, staff, and students each week to talk about issues surrounding topics like race, gender, sexual orientation, harassment, inequality, and other forms of identity," says a student. Merit scholarships averaging $20,149 are available, although there are no athletic scholarships. Twenty-one percent of students are Pell-eligible.

Eighty-seven percent of Beloit students live in the 37 on-campus housing facilities, where they're required to remain for three years. "The dorms at Beloit will never win an award for beauty, but the rooms are large and comfortable," according to one student. Fraternities attract 19 percent of the men, and sororities draw 20 percent of the women; members may live in their chapter houses. Numerous special-interest houses cater to those interested in foreign languages, music, anthropology, and other disciplines, as well as to student organizations. Food in the Commons dining hall is described as hit-or-miss at best, but options in D.K.'s Café and Java Joint are better received. "Our campus security and resident assistants do a great job of keeping an eye out for our campus community," says a business economics and psychology double major.

> **"It is exceptionally difficult to characterize a Beloiter."**

Social life is almost entirely campus-based. "On the weekends there are always events going on such as lectures, music groups, movie showings, theater productions, dance shows, and parties," says one junior. Two all-campus festivals liven up the calendar: the Folk and Blues Fall Music Festival brings jazz, reggae, folk, and blues bands to campus, while on Spring Day classes give way to a carnival and everyone kicks back to enjoy the (finally!) warmer weather. Students describe the party scene as very low key, and Greek organizations often team up with special-interest houses and other student clubs to throw parties. The school's alcohol policy is lax, students say. "We have an alcohol philosophy," says a sociology major. "Beloit would never go so far as to say 'policy.'"

Summer Venture Grants offer up to $2,000 for activities that engage with outside communities.

"The town of Beloit is in the midst of a change. It was previously in fairly poor economic shape; however the downtown is making a comeback," a student says. Several new restaurants have popped up in the last few years, as has a Saturday farmers market, and the city also offers a few local bars, a bowling alley, a movie theater, and a Walmart. "Groups such as Habitat for Humanity, Beloit Interaction Committee, and the Outreach Center work hard to integrate students into the community," says a sophomore. When in need of a change of scenery, Beloiters take off for Chicago or the college town of Madison, easily reached through a cheap local bus service. For the outdoors-minded, the nearby Dells offer camping and water parks.

Sports at Beloit are played more for fun than glory. Among the school's 19 Division III Buccaneers squads, standouts include baseball, men's and women's track and field, and men's basketball, lacrosse, and football, especially against rival Ripon College. The baseball team took home the Midwest Conference champion- ship in 2016. Intramural ultimate Frisbee typically draws hundreds of players and spectators, and more than one-third of students participate in the intramural pro- gram, with basketball, volleyball, and soccer also popular.

> **"We have an alcohol philosophy. Beloit would never go so far as to say 'policy.'"**

Beloit is a bundle of contradictions: a small liberal arts college in the heart of Big Ten state university country, and an academic program that has an East Coast rigor but a laid-back classroom vibe reflective of the friendly spirit of the Midwest. Although the school continues to evolve, "the essential core of Beloit has stayed the same," says a senior. "It is still a campus full of artistic creators, unabashed activ- ists, and people who love making dorm-room forts. We're still weird, and we like it that way."

Overlaps

Carleton, Grinnell, Lawrence, Knox, Macalester, St. Olaf, Kalamazoo, Kenyon

---

If You Apply To ➤

Beloit: Early decision I and early action I: Nov. 1. Early action II: Dec. 1. Early decision II and regular decision: Jan. 15. Financial aid: Mar. 1. No application fee. Campus and alumni interviews: optional, evaluative. SATs or ACTs: optional. No Subject Tests. Letters of recommendation: required. Essay: required. Accepts the Common Application with supplement.

Bennington College

Bennington, VT 05201-6003

Known for top-notch performing arts and lavish attention on every student. Arts programs rely heavily on faculty who are practitioners in their field. Less competitive than Bard and Sarah Lawrence, comparable to Hampshire. With fewer than 700 undergraduates, Bennington is one-third the size of most liberal arts colleges. New leadership is revitalizing the Bennington brand and reversing recent enrollment slump.

Bennington College is a school where architects are teachers, biologists sculpt, and a sociologist might work on Wall Street or in graphic design. It's no wonder they strive to abandon the theory of regimented knowledge. Bennington's focus is on learning by doing. The emphasis on self-direction, fieldwork, and personal relationships with professors sets it apart even from other liberal arts colleges of similar (small) size. Says one junior, "If you want an education you can shape yourself and you want that education to transcend your homework and the classroom, this is a great place to go to school."

Bennington sits on 470 acres at the foot of Vermont's Green Mountains. The campus was once an active dairy farm, and a converted barn houses the main classroom and administrative spaces. But don't let the quaint New England setting fool you. The Dickinson Science Building offers high-tech equipment for aspiring chemists, biologists, environmental scientists, and geneticists. A 14,000-square-foot student center offers students a snack bar, grill, convenience store, and multi- purpose spaces.

Website: www.bennington.edu
Location: Small Town
Private
Total Enrollment: 776
Undergraduates: 680
Male/Female: 35/65
SAT Ranges: CR 590–730, M 550–670
ACT Ranges: 26–31
Financial Aid: 83%
Pell Grant: 22%
Expense: Pr $ $ $ $
Student Loans: 74%
Average Debt: $ $ $

(continued)

Phi Beta Kappa: No
Applicants: 1,099
Accepted: 62%
Enrolled: 32%
Grad in 6 Years: 68%
Returning Freshmen: 82%
Academics: ✍ ✍ ✍
Social: ☎ ☎ ☎
Q of L: ★ ★ ★ ★
Admissions: (800) 833-6845
Email Address: admissions@
   bennington.edu

Strong Programs:
Visual and Performing Arts
Social Sciences
Languages
Literature
Anthropology
Computer Science
Mathematics
Advancement of Public Action

Each student completes a seven-week internship each January and February in a field of interest and a location of the student's choice.

Thanks to its focus on John Dewey–style experiential learning, Bennington's academic structure differs from that of a typical college or university. Each student designs a major, although there are some academic requirements, including a seven-week internship each January and February in a field of interest and a location of the student's choice. Students receive narrative evaluations instead of grades (although they do have the option to request grades in addition to the evaluations). Even Bennington's application process is nontraditional. In lieu of a standard application, prospective students may choose to submit a "dimensional application"—an open-form application that allows them to choose any materials, in any format, that they believe best convey why they are well suited to attend Bennington. Under this option, a transcript is not required (although submitting one could increase your chances of being admitted). This alternative application seems to have captured the attention of many students; it's just one of the moves the college's president has made to successfully turn around the declining applications and enrollment that she inherited when she stepped into the role in 2013.

> **"Half of the students here do work in the arts."**

"The academic climate is very collaborative, but challenging and intense," says one senior. Eighty-nine percent of classes enroll fewer than 20 students. Without academic departments, the faculty works to provide students with a well-rounded academic foundation. A psychology major says, "Teachers are very passionate about their field of study and teaching students. Most of them are very accessible and encourage students to meet with them often." The most popular area of study is visual and performing arts, followed by social sciences, languages, literature, and anthropology. Computer science and mathematics are strong too, although they attract a smaller number of students than many of the college's programs. "Half of the students here do work in the arts, whether it's theater or dance or studio art. Those are obviously well regarded," says a sophomore. Consistent with Bennington's judgment that traditional academics have become "insular and self-perpetuating," the Center for the Advancement of Public Action invites students to put the world's most pressing problems at the center of their education via hands-on, change-the-world workshops—known as Design Labs—and three-week modules aimed at developing capacities that may be applied in a broad array of disciplines. Closely related are the "pop-up courses" that faculty offer in response to unfolding events or current cultural phenomena. Recent topics of these three-week courses, often suggested by students, have included the European refugee crisis and the work of Gloria Steinem, the pioneering feminist who was an upcoming commencement speaker.

> **"Social and political issues are a big deal on campus."**

"Students here are passionate, often love to read, and like being engaged in their academics. The average student here tends to be more hippie-ish, maybe a little granola," says one junior. Just 2 percent are from Vermont and 13 percent are foreign nationals. Curiosity and excitement about exploration and experimentation will take you far here, and if you lean liberal in the voting booth, so much the better. "Social and political issues are a big deal on campus. Students are very involved in current events and politics," says a student. Diversity is a challenge: African Americans account for only 2 percent of the student body, Hispanics 6 percent, and Asian Americans 2 percent. Merit scholarships worth an average of $24,747 are awarded to qualified students; there are no athletic scholarships available. In addition, 22 percent of incoming students are eligible for Pell Grants.

As Bennington lacks traditional departments, requirements, and even faculty tenure, it's probably not surprising that the school also eschews traditional dorms. Ninety-seven percent of students live in one of the college's co-ed houses; 12 are white New England clapboard, and six are more modern. Each house holds 25 to 30 people with an appointed chair to govern house affairs. "Each house has a distinct history and personality," says a student, "and exists on a spectrum of social climate, from loud/quiet to party/study." The college food service provides plenty of options, from vegetarian and vegan choices to a salad bar, wok station, and pizza machine. "As far as college food goes," says one student, "we're lucky." A literature major states, "Students feel comfortable and safe on campus."

"The social life mostly takes place on campus. Bennington is fairly isolated, so we often live a bit in our own bubble," explains one junior. The alcohol policies on campus are fairly standard: no one under 21 is allowed to imbibe. "I think the high level of academic expectations here makes us self-regulate our drinking and partying habits," says a student. The annual theme parties always draw raves—themes have included Gatsby's Funeral and Mods vs. Rockers. Twice each year, the college turns part of its huge Visual and Performing Arts complex into an indoor roller rink for a Rollerama party: "We lower a disco ball in our auditorium, and the nearby roller skating rink comes and gives out all of their skates. Students dress up in wacky '70s garb and skate around to music until late into the night." For 12 hours one day each May, the campus celebrates spring with Sunfest, which includes bands, games, and other events. And during finals week each term, the blaring of fire-truck sirens tells weary students to head to the dining hall, where professors, staff, and the college president serve up French toast and other breakfast favorites.

Although the vibe on Bennington's campus is liberal, sophisticated, and cosmopolitan, the neighboring town of the same name—four miles away—is far more conservative, typical of rural New England. "The town is split up into Bennington and North Bennington," a junior explains. "North Bennington borders campus, and is a nice little village with good restaurants and a lake with a public beach. Bennington proper has the typical Walmart/fast food kind of area, but there is also the center of town, which has really nice coffee shops, galleries, and used bookstores." Students often find their way into the community through volunteer work in local schools and homeless shelters, though such programs can be tough because of the mandatory midyear internship term, which takes many students away from campus.

Sports aren't a big focus, but Bennington does compete in a co-ed soccer league that also includes other Northeastern colleges. The college has also partnered with Southern Vermont College and the NCAA to allow students to try out and compete with SVC's Division III athletic program. Available programs include men's and women's soccer, volleyball, basketball, and cross-country. The way one student sees it, "Bennington kids prefer going to a dance performance or poetry reading over playing sports." Given Bennington's rugged location, hiking, rock climbing, caving, camping, and canoeing keep students moving. Ski slopes beckon in the colder months.

As the first school in the nation to grant the arts equal status with other disciplines, Bennington offers a novel, participatory, and hands-on approach. Whether they're painters or writers, musicians or scientists, sculptors, dancers, or some combination thereof, what Bennington students have in common is self-motivation and a real thirst for knowledge. Bennington is likely a good fit for "students who are interested in an education that bridges academia and the 'real world' (or encourages students to not distinguish between the two)," says a senior. "Successful Bennington students have learned the ability to self-advocate," adds another. Crossing disciplines is encouraged, and forget about taking the road less traveled; each student here charts his or her own course.

Bennington lacks traditional departments, requirements, and even faculty tenure.

Twice each year, the college turns part of its huge Visual and Performing Arts complex into an indoor roller rink for a Rollerama party.

"Successful Bennington students have learned the ability to self-advocate."

Overlaps

Bard, Sarah Lawrence, Hampshire, NYU, Oberlin, University of Vermont, Skidmore, Reed

Bennington: Early decision I: Nov. 15. Early action: Dec. 1. Early decision II and regular decision: Jan. 15. Financial aid: Mar. 15. No application fee. Campus and alumni interviews: recommended, evaluative. SATs or ACTs: optional. Subject Tests: optional. Letters of recommendation: required. Essay: required. Accepts the Common Application. Applicants may submit an alternative "dimensional application" consisting of any materials they choose; under this option, transcripts are preferred but not required.

Bentley University

175 Forest Street, Waltham, MA 02452

Bentley means business—studying it, that is, in the context of strong liberal arts. Now competes on even footing with archrival Babson. Offers both B.A. and B.S. tracks and provides career-oriented internships to more than 90 percent of its students. Bentley's scenic colonial-style campus is at arm's length from Boston with shuttles to Harvard Square.

Website: www.bentley.edu
Location: Small City
Private
Total Enrollment: 4,840
Undergraduates: 4,076
Male/Female: 59/41
SAT Ranges: CR 540–640, M 600–690
ACT Ranges: 26–30
Financial Aid: 70%
Pell Grant: 12%
Expense: Pr $ $
Student Loans: 54%
Average Debt: $ $ $
Phi Beta Kappa: Yes
Applicants: 8,346
Accepted: 42%
Enrolled: 26%
Grad in 6 Years: 89%
Returning Freshmen: 95%
Academics: ✐ ✐ ✐
Social: 🏳 🏳 🏳
Q of L: ★ ★ ★
Admissions: (800) 523-2354
Email Address:
  ugadmission@bentley.edu

Strong Programs:
Finance
Economics
Marketing
Accounting
Liberal Studies
Business Studies

Formerly known as Bentley College, this small New England university excels at turning out men and women who are committed to taking their place among the ranks of future business leaders. "Bentley prepares its students for the workplace by giving them comparable experiences socially, academically, and—most importantly—professionally," says a sophomore. With the university's solid courses in business, state-of-the-art facilities, and a dedication to the liberal arts, students find much to admire. As one enthusiastic junior says, "Bentley is a school that will simulate the real world as much as possible so that its students graduate prepared!"

Bentley is situated on 163 acres in Waltham, Massachusetts, just minutes west of the hustle and bustle of Boston. The dominant architectural style is Georgian, and the majority of campus buildings are classically built in redbrick. The Bentley campus has three tiers. The upper campus revolves around academics and features a library, more than 70 "smart" classrooms, and high-tech labs and centers. Mid-campus centers on student life and is anchored by the 70,000-square-foot student center. Finally, the lower campus focuses on recreation and includes the Dana Athletic Center. Residential housing is spread throughout each tier of the campus. Recent construction includes an 11,250-square-foot addition to the student center.

Bentley has long been committed to producing "liberally educated business students," and this is reflected in the curriculum, which offers both B.A. and B.S. tracks. Every student must complete 47 credit hours of general education coursework, including courses in information technology, literature, mathematics, natural and behavioral sciences, economics, government, history, philosophy,

> **"Bentley is a school that will simulate the real world as much as possible so that its students graduate prepared!"**

and diversity. Students who choose to pursue a B.A. degree must also fulfill business core requirements, which consist of a sequence of five courses from the first two years of the general business core. Those pursuing B.S. degrees in business must complete a team project in partnership with an area business or nonprofit group. Freshmen take a mandatory First-Year Seminar that is designed to help them with their overall adjustment and decision-making abilities regarding their academic and social development. Their seminar instructor also serves as their academic advisor for the first three semesters. In addition, freshmen take a seven-week Career Development Introduction Seminar, cotaught by career services advisors and professionals from top companies like Fidelity and Liberty Mutual, to get on track early for internships and jobs.

Not surprisingly, Bentley's most popular majors are finance, economics, marketing, and accounting. Students seeking a bachelor of science degree may choose from more than a dozen disciplines, including new majors in creative industries and professional sales, while those pursuing bachelor of arts degrees have a slightly more limited selection that includes such fields as English, global studies, sustainability sciences, and health studies. Motivated students may pursue the liberal studies major (LSM), a highly integrated (and optional) second major that must be paired with a business or business-related major. Current LSM concentrations range from American studies to earth, environment, and global sustainability to quantitative perspectives.

"It is definitely not a 'dog-eat-dog' campus," a management major explains, "but there are some majors that tend to be more competitive." A freshman adds, "Courses at Bentley are challenging and encourage an exploration of the subject beyond what is taught in the classroom." Twenty-five percent of classes have fewer than 20 students, and adjunct professors and senior lecturers with professional expertise teach many of the courses, although with varying success. "There are a few professors who are so intelligent they have a hard time breaking down the material, slowing down the pace, and understanding their students' confusion," says one junior.

As befits the university's focus on the corporate world, approximately 90 percent of undergraduates participate in experiential learning via internships. In keeping with the university's mission to educate students to be active leaders in a global economy, the Cronin Office of International Education offers semester, summer, or week-long faculty-led programs and other experiences abroad. Each year more than 500 Bentley students participate. The top 10 percent of students in each entering class (about 90 students) are invited to participate in the honors program, which tackles a variety of topics—from the ethics of genetic research to analyzing complex financial crises—all in a seminar setting that is designed to promote discussion and debate.

Freshmen take a Career Development Introduction Seminar, cotaught by career services advisors and professionals from top companies.

"Bentley students are ambitious and very competitive."

"Bentley students are ambitious and very competitive," says one student. "The students are incredibly involved in a variety of activities that include cultural organizations, sports, Greek life, professional fraternities, and academic clubs." Although twice the size of rival Babson College, Bentley's student body is less diverse. Thirty-eight percent of Bentley undergraduates are from Massachusetts, and 14 percent are international. African Americans comprise 3 percent of the student body, Asian Americans 8 percent, and Hispanics 7 percent. Social and political issues generally take a backseat to studies, but diversity and equality are common concerns, according to students. Merit scholarships averaging $17,852 are doled out annually, and talented athletes vie for 80 athletic scholarships in 14 sports.

The university's student residences include apartments, suites, and traditional dormitories and house 79 percent of the student body. All rooms include wireless Internet access, cable TV, local telephone service, and air-conditioning. "Housing is good. I feel the conditions are livable and comforting," says one student. Sixty-one percent of students participate in living/learning communities, in which service learning is a big emphasis. The various dining facilities offer the usual college fare, and those on the meal plan are given unlimited meals at the main dining hall, although some say that's not really a perk. "Every student complains about the food, and it needs to be improved. Honestly, I've lost weight since coming to school because I refuse to eat many meals from the dining hall," grumbles one (presumably hungry) sophomore. Students report feeling safe on campus, thanks to an active police patrol, 24/7 safety escorts, and several new sexual assault prevention programs. "As a female, I have never felt nervous walking around campus by myself, regardless of the time," says a junior.

The liberal studies major is a highly integrated (and optional) second major that must be paired with a business or business-related major.

Students say the social scene begins on campus and spills out into the surrounding areas. "There is so much involvement in Bentley's 100-plus organizations," says one student. "A group is bound to have an event on any given day." Another adds, "Most social life happens off campus at Greek life houses or athletic houses, or in Boston or Harvard Square." Sponsored events include an annual Halloween Party, Hawaiian luaus, fashion shows, Latin dance night, a Boston scavenger hunt, "drive-in" movies on the quad, comedy nights, and Spring Day. Although Greeks attract 11 percent of the men and 11 percent of the women, they don't dominate the social scene. Students of legal age may have alcohol, but "peer pressure is not an issue" for those who choose not to imbibe, according to one accounting major.

Waltham may not have the cachet of nearby Boston, but students say it has the basic amenities every college student craves: restaurants, bars, shops, and salons. "Overall, Waltham does not play a huge role in a Bentley student's daily way of life." For those seeking a bit more action, the university provides a free shuttle into Harvard Square, where students can mix and mingle with peers from other local colleges and universities. Jaunts to the beaches of New Hampshire, the ski resorts of Vermont, and weekend trips to the Cape make for popular diversions as well.

"The academic support at Bentley is amazing."

Competition at Bentley is not confined to the classroom; the university also fields 22 men's and women's varsity teams at the Division II level and a competitive Division I ice hockey team. Solid Falcon teams include men's and women's basketball, men's cross-country and golf, and women's volleyball. The women's basketball team has competed in a record 32 NCAA tournaments and recently captured the national championship. Students get fired up anytime rivals Babson and Bryant take the field, and there is the predictable T-shirt reading, "Friends don't let friends go to Babson." Intramurals draw roughly 60 percent of students; popular activities include flag football, soccer, volleyball, and Ultimate Frisbee.

"The academic support at Bentley is amazing," cheers one junior. "A student can get a tutor for their business class, attend extra lectures, go to the center that focuses on that specific subject, and still be able to stop by their teacher's office for help." Like the university itself, Bentley students have a keen sense of who they are and where they're headed. For those students charting a course into the upper echelons of corporate America, Bentley may be the first step to a long and fruitful career.

Overlaps

Babson, Northeastern, Boston College, Bryant, Boston University, University of Massachusetts Amherst, University of Connecticut, Fordham

If You Apply To ➢

Bentley: Early decision: Nov. 15. Regular decision and financial aid: Jan. 7. Application fee: $50. Campus interviews: recommended, informational. No alumni interviews. SATs or ACTs: required. Subject Tests: optional. Letters of recommendation: required. Essay: required. Accepts the Common Application with supplement.

Birmingham–Southern College

Box 549008, 900 Arkakelphia Road, Birmingham, AL 35254

One of the Deep South's better liberal arts colleges, now fighting its way back from a management and financial crisis. With just over 1,300 students, BSC is smaller than Rhodes (Tennessee), larger than Millsaps (Mississippi). Its strong fraternity system is a throwback to the way college used to be. Relatively low tuition and plenty of scholarships.

Once an old-school conservative Southern institution, BSC is now striving to prepare students for all aspects of the modern world, with high-tech facilities and a more global curriculum. More than half the student body participates in community service through the Bunting Center for Engaged Study and Community Action, and attentive faculty add to a sense of commitment to both personal and community growth. A junior says BSC is a good choice for those students who "want to spend four years preparing, maturing, and challenging their minds so that they can make a difference in the world."

Known as the Hilltop for obvious topographical reasons, BSC is the result of the 1918 merger of two smaller colleges: Birmingham College and Southern University. The campus, a green and shady oasis in an urban neighborhood, contains a pleasing hodgepodge of traditional and modern architecture, all surrounded by a security fence for added safety. Two LEED-certified residence halls have recently been completed and provide suite-style living for 167 students. BSC has for several years been recovering from a major financial crisis, and with contributions and student enrollment back on the rise, the school is beginning to reestablish some programs that had been eliminated as part of drastic budget cuts.

The Explorations general education curriculum is designed to help students develop effective communication and problem-solving skills, connect with their social and political world, and direct their own learning. It comprises 32 units across several disciplines, including fine and performing arts, social sciences, natural sciences, and humanities, as well as three global and local citizenship courses. All freshmen take an introductory first-year seminar, and all seniors complete a capstone experience and a public presentation of their work. The Explorations term, a four-week term between the fall and spring semesters, allows students to explore new areas of study, from cooking lessons to travel in China.

> "[Professors] love to challenge our beliefs and ideas by making us defend what we think."

Business administration is the most popular major, followed by visual and performing arts, biology, education, and English. The many premed students cite biology and psychology as major drawing cards. The Stephens Science Center gives these programs, as well as the chemistry and physics departments, a further boost. The art, theater, and music programs are all among the best in the South, and the college offers a major in musical theater as well. Students stage several major productions each year, often including American and world premieres. Other notable majors include urban environmental studies and media and film studies. BSC is also a member of the Associated Colleges of the South* consortium.

The courses at BSC are "somewhat competitive" and "challenging but not impossible," according to one senior. Each student is assigned a faculty member who serves as his or her academic advisor from freshman convocation to graduation, an arrangement that students praise for its effectiveness. Equal praise goes out to faculty in the classrooms, where 65 percent of classes have fewer than 20 students. An education major says professors "love to challenge our beliefs and ideas by making us defend what we think." The honors program allows 25 exceptional first-year students to take small seminars with one or more professors. The Krulak Institute coordinates opportunities for experiential learning, such as service-learning projects, study abroad programs, and an entrepreneurial scholars program.

Forty-five percent of the students are homegrown Alabamians, and practically all the rest hail from Deep South states; many have family ties to BSC. Though moderate by Alabama standards, the student body is quite conservative. "The students are hardworking, liberal arts students," says one junior. "Most students at BSC

Website: www.bsc.edu
Location: City Outskirts
Private
Total Enrollment: 1,337
Undergraduates: 1,337
Male/Female: 50/50
SAT Ranges: CR 480–600,
   M 490–620
ACT Ranges: 21–28
Financial Aid: 92%
Pell Grant: N/A
Expense: Pr $
Student Loans: 49%
Average Debt: $
Phi Beta Kappa: Yes
Applicants: 3,638
Accepted: 54%
Enrolled: 24%
Grad in 6 Years: 61%
Returning Freshmen: 86%
Academics: ✐ ✐ ✐
Social: ☎ ☎ ☎
Q of L: ★ ★ ★
Admissions: (205) 226-4696
Email Address: admiss@
   bsc.edu

Strong Programs:
Business
Biology
Education
English
Psychology
Art
Theater

All seniors complete a capstone experience and a public presentation of their work.

Though moderate by Alabama standards, the student body is quite conservative.

tend to be overcommitted by most standards," adds a freshman. Eleven percent of BSC students are African American, 2 percent are Hispanic, and 5 percent are Asian American. "We have an expanding international student base and multicultural affairs and the beginning of some African American sororities. The college is taking steps to diversify," a student says. BSC offers various merit scholarships, with an average award of $20,252.

Eighty-seven percent of the students live on campus, including many whose families reside in Birmingham. Dorms are described as comfortable and convenient. "You can wake up 10 minutes before class, get ready, walk to class, and still have two or three minutes to spare," says a business administration major. More importantly, "The water pressure is great in the hall showers," cheers one picky student. Dining facilities get mixed reviews; students say the quality is decent and special tastes are accommodated, but the food can get repetitive. Campus security officials are said to be visible and effective.

Thirty-eight percent of the men and 52 percent of the women are members of Greek organizations, which means that much of the social activity at BSC revolves around the Greek system. "Social life is good on campus," says a student. "Many people are involved in Greek life, but there is no pressure for others to join or hang out with them. They are very open to having non-Greeks spend time with them and are not exclusive." As for alcohol, it's not allowed on the quad, and elsewhere it must be in an opaque container, a policy most students find reasonable, described by one senior as a "'don't see it, ignore it' policy." The biggest social event of the year is Soco, a two-day festival. Freshmen take part in a square dance during orientation. Other popular events include E-Fest and Halloween on the Hilltop, where students "dress up in costumes and the neighborhood kids go trick-or-treating." When social opportunities on campus dry up, many students take the shuttle to Birmingham for the city's nightlife. Road trips to Auburn, Nashville, and Atlanta are popular, and beaches and mountains are less than five hours away.

> **"Many people are involved in Greek life, but there is no pressure for others to join."**

BSC currently fields 20 varsity teams for men and women. The Panthers compete in the Division III Southern Athletic Association, and the baseball team has been champion multiple times. Seventy percent of students take part in the intramural program. Basketball, flag football, and soccer are popular, but less traditional sports, such as dodgeball and kickball, are also offered.

Students at BSC continue to focus on academics while balancing community service and an active social scene. Small classes, a caring faculty, and an expanding menu of academic offerings continue to draw attention to this close-knit liberal arts school.

Overlaps

University of Alabama, Auburn, University of Alabama at Birmingham, Rhodes, Millsaps, Samford, Berry

If You Apply To ➤

Birmingham–Southern: Early decision: Nov. 1. Early action: Nov. 15. Regular decision: Feb. 1. Financial aid: Mar. 1. Housing: May 1. Application fee: $50. Campus and alumni interviews: optional, evaluative. SATs or ACTs: optional (test-optional applicants must interview and submit academic portfolio). No Subject Tests. Letters of recommendation: required. Essay: required. Accepts the Common Application with supplement.

Boston College

140 Commonwealth Avenue, Devlin Hall, Room 208, Chestnut Hill, MA 02467

Many students clamoring for a spot at Boston College are surprised to learn that it is affiliated with the Roman Catholic Church. Set on a quiet hilltop at the end of a T (subway) line, BC's location is solid gold. A close second to Notre Dame in the pecking order among true-blue Catholics. About 70 percent of the students are Catholic, compared to Georgetown's 50 percent and Notre Dame's 80 percent.

Boston College is a study in contrasts. The academics and the athletic teams are both well respected. The environment is safely suburban, yet barely 20 minutes from Boston, the hub of the Eastern seaboard's college scene. The Jesuit influence on the college, one of the largest Roman Catholic schools in the country, provides a guiding spirit for campus life, but the social opportunities still seem endless. Despite the paradoxes (or perhaps because of them), students at BC enjoy a rich college experience.

Don't let the modest name fool you. Boston College is actually a research university with nine schools and colleges. It has three campuses: the main campus at Chestnut Hill, the Brighton campus across the street, and the Newton campus a mile and a half away. The dominant architecture of the main campus (known as "the Heights") is Gothic Revival, with modern additions over the past few years. There's lots of grass and trees, not to mention a large, peaceful reservoir (perfect to jog around) right in the front yard. The university is in the midst of a multi-year master plan that will double the size of the main campus. A new dorm recently opened, and construction is underway on a new gym.

Boston College was originally founded by the Jesuits to teach the sons of Irish immigrants. These days, the college's mission is to "educate skilled, knowledgeable, and responsible leaders within each new generation." To accomplish this goal, the Core Curriculum requires courses not only in literature, science, history, philosophy, social science, and theology, but also in writing, mathematics, the arts, and cultural diversity, in addition to specific requirements set by each undergraduate school. "Core Curriculum forces you to take classes you might not want to take but end up enjoying," says a senior. Students in arts and sciences must also show proficiency in a modern foreign language or classical language before graduation. Freshmen are required to take a writing workshop in which each student develops a portfolio of personal and academic writing and reads a wide range of texts. Seniors participate in the Capstone Program, choosing one of several seminars that aim to give a "big picture" perspective to the college experience and students' personal development.

> "Core Curriculum forces you to take classes you might not want to take but end up enjoying."

The schools of arts and sciences, management, nursing, and education award bachelor's degrees. Biology, communication, finance, and economics are the most popular majors. Programs in English, physics, chemistry, and theology are also well regarded. Outside the traditional classroom at the McMullen Museum of Art in Devlin Hall, students find exhibitions, lectures, and gallery tours. The Music Guild sponsors professional concerts throughout the year, and music students emphasizing performance can take advantage of facilities equipped with Steinways and Yamahas. Theater majors find a home in the 600-seat Robsham Theater Arts Center, which produces eight student-directed productions each year.

BC students are serious about their work, but not excessively so, helping to create a collaborative atmosphere. "If you are better at science than your roommate, you will help her out," states one senior, "and perhaps when it comes time to fulfill

Website: www.bc.edu
Location: Suburban
Private
Total Enrollment: 12,683
Undergraduates: 9,192
Male/Female: 47/53
SAT Ranges: CR 620–720, M 640–750
ACT Ranges: 30–33
Financial Aid: 67%
Pell Grant: 10%
Expense: Pr $ $ $ $
Student Loans: 49%
Average Debt: $
Phi Beta Kappa: Yes
Applicants: 29,486
Accepted: 29%
Enrolled: 26%
Grad in 6 Years: 92%
Returning Freshmen: 95%
Academics: ✍ ✍ ✍ ✍
Social: 🐦 🐦 🐦 🐦
Q of L: ★ ★ ★
Admissions: (617) 552-3100
Email Address: N/A

Strong Programs:
Biology
Communication
Finance
Economics
English
Physics
Chemistry
Theology

your philosophy core requirement, her love of Plato will get you through the class." Forty-nine percent of classes have fewer than 20 students, and professors are praised for their passion and knowledge, as well as their accessibility. "I have certainly been challenged by my professors but also supported, since they consistently make themselves available outside of the classroom through office hours or other appointments," says one history major. The Jesuits on BC's faculty (about 35 out of 800) exert an influence out of proportion to their numbers. "The philosophy, theology, and ethics departments are the most important in setting the tone of the campus, because they encourage the students to be open-minded," says a freshman.

The PULSE program provides opportunities to fulfill philosophy and theology requirements while engaging in social-service fieldwork.

Students searching for out-of-the-ordinary offerings will be happy at BC. The PULSE program provides participants with the opportunity to fulfill their philosophy and theology requirements while engaging in social-service fieldwork at any of about 35 Boston organizations. The program reinforces the Jesuit emphasis on community service and sometimes inspires students to major in those areas. A Freshman-Year Experience program offers seminars and services to help students adjust to college life and take advantage of the school and the city. Each undergraduate school offers its own

"I have certainly been challenged by my professors but also supported."

honors program, allowing students to work at a more intensive pace and undertake a senior thesis. Forty-nine percent of Boston College undergraduates engage in an international volunteer or academic experience by the time they graduate. BC offers nearly 60 academic programs in 30 countries around the world, as well as three-week summer study abroad programs. The Undergraduate Faculty Research Fellows Program requires participating students to spend an average of 100 hours per semester assisting faculty with serious research, for which they receive financial aid.

Twenty-four percent of BC undergraduates come from Massachusetts, and 6 percent come from abroad. Catholics comprise about 70 percent of the student body. African Americans constitute 4 percent, while Asian Americans make up 10 percent and Hispanics 10 percent. "The student body is a socially conscious, environmentally responsible, academically oriented group on the whole," offers one student. "There is a pervasive spirit of compassion that runs through the student body here." Indeed, the Jesuit appeal for tolerance means that students can find support and interaction even when approaching hot-button issues that orthodox Catholicism frowns upon, such as homosexuality. Nearly 300 athletic awards are doled out annually in 14 men's and women's sports; merit scholarships are worth an average of $20,200. BC observes need-blind admissions and meets the full demonstrated need of accepted students, but just 10 percent of incoming freshmen receive Pell Grants.

Spiritual retreats occur throughout the year at BC's own retreat center on the Charles River, 30 minutes from campus.

Eighty-four percent of BC students live on campus. When students are admitted, they are notified whether they will get on-campus housing for three or four years, and most juniors with three-year guarantees live off campus or study abroad in the fourth year. The city of Boston has a fairly reliable bus and subway system to bring distant residents to campus; the few students who drive to school are required to show that they need to park on campus. Another lottery system determines where on-campus residents hang their hats. "The dorms are comfortable and spacious," says an international studies major, "with the exception of forced triples for freshmen." Students pay in advance for a certain number of dining hall meals, served a la carte. "The food is expensive," a student says, "but it is great quality."

"The student body is a socially conscious, environmentally responsible, academically oriented group."

BC's reputation as a hard-core party school is diminishing, now that no kegs or cases of beer are allowed on campus grounds. Those of legal age can carry in only champagne on the lawn. The presentation of lanterns and class colors to incoming freshmen on Lantern Night, and regal pageants, such as Parade Night and Step-Sings, fill life with a Gothic sense of wonder and school spirit. Bryn Mawr is located on suburban Philly's wealthy Main Line (named after a railroad), and the campus is two blocks from the train station. A 20-minute train ride provides students with easy access to cultural attractions, as well as social and academic events at the nearby University of Pennsylvania. "I consider our social life to be hanging out with friends, poetry slams, and watching plays and cultural shows," muses a junior.

As for athletics, the Bryn Mawr Owls compete in the Division III Centennial Conference, and the indoor and outdoor track and field teams are standouts. Intramurals like rugby, cross-country, volleyball, and field hockey are also available, and club sports range from all-female teams to co-ed teams shared with Haverford, such as ultimate Frisbee and fencing. Students in computer science compete in a number of robot competitions, including the international Robocup, which pits colleges against each other in a robo-soccer match.

Bryn Mawr is a study in contrasts: the campus is in suburbia, but steps from a major city. Humanities programs are very strong, but science majors are also enormously popular. The students are independent but revel in college traditions. The result is overwhelmingly positive. Says a student, "The Bryn Mawr experience is one of complete freedom to explore one's interests and individuality without the fear of being ostracized."

Overlaps

Smith, Mount Holyoke, Wellesley, Barnard, Vassar, Grinnell, Brown, Haverford

If You Apply To ➤

Bryn Mawr: Early decision I: Nov. 15. Early decision II: Jan. 1. Regular decision: Jan. 15. Financial aid: Mar. 1. Housing: May 1. Application fee: $50 (paper), free (online). Campus and alumnae interviews: recommended, evaluative. SATs or ACTs: optional. Subject Tests: optional. Letters of recommendation: required. Essay: required. Accepts applications from all individuals who identify as women. Accepts the Common Application with supplement.

Bucknell University

Lewisburg, PA 17837

Bucknell, Colgate, Hamilton, Lafayette—all a little more conservative than the Ivy schools, and all just a little less selective. Bucknell is the biggest of this bunch and, like Lehigh, offers engineering. Bucknell's Greek system is strong, but students don't join until they are sophomores. The central Pennsylvania campus is remote but one of the most beautiful anywhere.

Website: www.bucknell.edu
Location: Small Town
Private
Total Enrollment: 3,556
Undergraduates: 3,513
Male/Female: 48/52
SAT Ranges: CR 590–680, M 620–710
ACT Ranges: 28–32
Financial Aid: 62%
Pell Grant: 11%
Expense: Pr $ $ $ $

The students at Bucknell University strike a healthy balance between hitting the books and hitting the bars or the frat houses of their pastoral central Pennsylvania campus. Yes, they tend to be preppy: "Bucknell students are mostly upper-middle-class, relatively conservative, and materially conscious. However, they are also highly motivated and eager to succeed," says one student. With small classes, engaging faculty, and not a subpar dorm to be found, it's no wonder that students like this junior complain, "Four years at Bucknell go by way too fast."

In addition to being comfortable and friendly, Bucknell is physically beautiful. Located on a hill just south of quaint Lewisburg, the campus overlooks the scenic Susquehanna River valley. Playing fields, shaded by leafy trees, are sprinkled among the Greek Revival buildings. While some structures date from the 19th century, lending a fairy-tale quality, others are far more modern, including an $8 million engineering building. Four new apartment-style residence halls enough beer for personal consumption. Bars and clubs in Boston ("the college town of all college towns," cheers a junior) are a big draw, along with Fenway Park. On weekends, especially in the winter, the mountains of Vermont and New Hampshire beckon outdoorsy types. The campus is replete with sporting events, movies, festivals, concerts, and plays. "Volunteer work is huge," says one student; three-quarters of the students get involved in community service. As at other Jesuit institutions, there is no Greek system at BC, and "the social life is much more inclusive" as a result, according to a senior. Spiritual retreats occur throughout the year at BC's own retreat center on the Charles River, 30 minutes from campus.

Division I athletic events, especially football games, become social events too, with frequent tailgate and victory parties. The annual football contest with Notre Dame is jokingly referred to as the "Holy War" and makes for a popular road trip. The Eagles football program has been recognized for achiev-

"[Boston is] the college town of all college towns."

ing the highest graduation rate in the NCAA, and the men's ice hockey team has brought home numerous national titles. Other solid teams include women's soccer, fencing, cross-country, golf, and basketball, and men's soccer, sailing, and fencing. The Conte Forum Sports Arena is well attended, and BC meets fierce competition from Atlantic Coast Conference rivals Duke, Miami, Florida State, Virginia Tech, and others. Students even get the day off from classes to line the edge of campus and cheer Boston Marathon runners up "Heartbreak Hill." Intramural sports are huge here. Roughly 4,000 students participate in more than 50 intramural, recreational, and club sports, from basketball and volleyball to skiing and golf.

Since its founding as a Jesuit institution, Boston College has been committed to "educating students who will use their knowledge, talents, and abilities in the service of others." BC students spend four years fine-tuning the art of the delicate balance, finding ways to make old-fashioned morals relevant to life in the 21st century, and finding time for fun while still tending to their academic performance.

Overlaps

Brown, University of Pennsylvania, Cornell University, Boston University, Northeastern, Villanova, Notre Dame, Georgetown

If You Apply To ➤

BC: Single choice early action: Nov. 1. Regular decision: Jan. 1. Financial aid: Feb. 1. Housing: May 1. Application fee: $75. No campus or alumni interviews. SATs or ACTs: required. Subject Tests: optional. Letters of recommendation: required. Essay: required. Accepts the Common Application with supplement. Apply to particular school or program.

Boston University

121 Bay State Road, Boston, MA 02215

One of the nation's largest private universities and namesake to a city that boasts 46 four-year colleges. Location adjacent to the Fenway is the promised land for hordes of students from all over the world seeking a funky, artsy, youth-oriented urban setting that is less in-your-face than New York City. More selective than in the past and comparable to NYU and George Washington.

Like The George Washington University and NYU, Boston University is an integral part of the city it calls home. The school's mammoth collection of nondescript highrises stretches 1.3 miles along bustling, six-lane Commonwealth Avenue—and so do thousands upon thousands of students. From aspiring actors, musicians, journalists, and filmmakers, to future doctors, dentists, and hotel managers, BU seems to offer something for everyone. "BU has endless opportunities in academics, research,

Website: www.bu.edu
Location: City Outskirts
Private
Total Enrollment: 20,402
Undergraduates: 16,082

The First-Year Student Outreach Project brings freshmen to campus a week early to do community service.

study abroad, and internship experiences," cheers one senior. A junior adds, "You definitely walk away from BU with a sense of accomplishment and individuality."

The BU campus is practically indistinguishable from the rest of the city that surrounds it. A measure of relief is available on the tree-lined side streets, which feature quaint Victorian brownstones. Facilities include the 35,000-square-foot Hillel House, a multilevel fitness center, and a hockey arena that doubles as a concert hall. Construction on a new Center for Integrated Life Sciences and Engineering, which will feature a cognitive neuroimaging center, a satellite vivarium, and six floors dedicated to faculty research, is scheduled for completion in 2017.

Each of BU's 10 undergraduate schools and colleges sets its own general education requirements, and together they offer more than 250 majors and minors. "All of the academic programs I've encountered have an accomplished faculty that bring 'real-world' experiences into the classroom," says a political science major. The College of Communication combines theory with hands-on training—some of it by adjunct professors with day jobs at major newspapers and TV networks. It also houses the nation's only center for the study of political disinformation. The School of Music benefits from its own concert hall and from faculty who also belong to the Boston Symphony Orchestra. The College of Arts and Sciences caters to the premed and prelaw students, and BU also offers highly competitive seven-year programs admitting qualified students simultaneously to the undergraduate program and the university's medical or dental school. Many students in the Sargent College of Health and Rehabilitation Sciences go on to earn graduate degrees from the college's highly ranked physical and occupational therapy programs.

> **"You definitely walk away from BU with a sense of accomplishment and individuality."**

The Questrom School of Business, one of BU's top programs and also its most popular, offers an honors program for sophomores and concentrations in such areas as law, health and life sciences, and entrepreneurship. Future employers of students in the School of Hospitality Administration offer paid internships in exotic locales such as Sydney and Shanghai. The College of Engineering boasts a robotics and biomedical engineering lab. Students in the School of Education can test their ideas for curricular reform in the public schools of nearby Chelsea, while those in the School of Visual Arts may show their work in one of three campus galleries. Fifty-eight percent of classes have fewer than 20 students, and students say the academic climate encourages both cooperation and competition. "While I am consistently challenged, I do not feel overwhelmed by the workload," says one senior. A new major has been added in philosophy and neuroscience, as has one in linguistics and speech, language, and hearing sciences.

Students rave about FYSOP, the First-Year Student Outreach Project, which brings freshmen to campus a week early to do community service. For a break from brutal Boston winters, BU offers more than 100 study abroad programs in 25 countries, including internships, field work, research, language study, and liberal arts programs; 38 percent of students participate. There's also a marine science program at the Woods Hole Institute and the Semester at Sea*. The Kilachand Honors College is a four-year undergraduate program that offers students the small classes, close interaction with faculty, and communal atmosphere of a small liberal arts college along with the resources of a major urban research university. Perhaps a further indicator of the university's elite status, BU has joined the exclusive and prestigious Association of American Universities.

"The students here are diverse," says a junior. "I feel like that is an overused word, especially when looking at colleges, but it's true. On my freshman floor of 40 girls, seven were from outside the country and 25 were from outside of Massachusetts." Indeed, 80 percent of BU undergrads are from outside the state and 21 percent are international. Asian Americans are the largest minority group on campus, at 14 percent of the total; Hispanics comprise 11 percent, and African Americans add 4 percent. "I would consider BU to be a very active and socially aware campus," a student reports. The university offers merit scholarships averaging $17,925 each year; there are also hundreds of athletic scholarships in 20 sports. Graduates of Boston public high schools receive no-loan financial aid packages that meet their full demonstrated financial need.

Seventy-five percent of BU students live in campus housing, which is guaranteed for four years. "Since we are on a lottery system, it is possible to get a not-so-great room," explains a psychology major. "Freshman/sophomore dorms are fairly typical, but housing gets better as you get to be a senior." Luxury apartments, known as 10 Buick Street, house 817 upperclassmen on 17 floors, in apartments with four single bedrooms each, plus a kitchen, living and dining area, and two full bathrooms. Meal plans are flexible, and one of the six dining halls on campus is kosher. "BU has great food!" cheers a senior. There's also a farmers market and a food court with national chains like Starbucks and Panda Express. Students say campus security is up to the task of keeping them safe: "For being in an urban area, I feel extremely safe on campus," reports one senior. The Sexual Assault Response and Prevention Center provides programming around awareness and prevention of sexual assault, as well as support and advocacy for those who have experienced it.

"We can just hop on our Boston trains and be anywhere in the city within minutes."

"The social scene at BU has a lot to offer," a student says. "We always have on-campus events every day of the week, including the weekends. If we don't feel like staying on campus, we can just hop on our Boston trains and be anywhere in the city within minutes." Five percent of the men and 15 percent of the women go Greek, and parties at neighboring schools are an option as well. Drinking is fairly common, though not in the dorms, because state laws are strictly enforced and violators may find themselves without university housing. Owing to Boston's heavily Irish heritage, St. Patrick's Day is an occasion for revelry. The Splash party in September, homecoming in October, and Culture Fest in March round out the social calendar. Possible road trips include Cape Cod, Cape Ann, and Providence, Rhode Island. Even better, "Fenway Park, downtown, Landsdowne Street, and Boston Common are all within walking distance," says a marine biology major.

BU doesn't field a football team, so hockey season is the athletic high point of the school year. All Terrier teams compete in Division I, and solid teams include men's hockey and basketball and women's softball, tennis, rowing, and track and field. BU has won 30 of 64 titles in the annual Beanpot men's ice hockey tournament, which pits BU against Harvard, Northeastern, and archrival Boston College. The Head of the Charles regatta, which starts at BU's crew house each fall, draws college crew teams from across the country. Of the dozen or so intramural sports offered, by far the most popular is broomball, which is like ice hockey on sneakers, with a ball instead of a puck and a broom instead of a stick; students may also compete in 34 club sports.

"You have to be proactive about finding out what's going on around campus."

BU has won 30 of 64 titles in the annual Beanpot men's ice hockey tournament.

Boston University shamelessly urges students to just "Be You" (ahem) and most are happy to do so, but they warn that being successful here requires a certain degree of initiative. The school is "a great place, with lots of academic and social opportunities, but it's not for the timid student," remarks a geophysics and planetary sciences major. "You have to be proactive about finding out what's going on around campus, so that you can find your niche."

Overlaps

Boston College, Northeastern, University of Southern California, NYU, Tufts, University of Massachusetts Amherst, George Washington, UCLA

BU: Early decision I: Nov. 1. Early decision II and regular decision: Jan. 3. Financial aid: Feb. 1. Housing: May 1. Application fee: $80. Campus interviews: recommended, informational. No alumni interviews. SATs or ACTs: required. Subject Tests: required for some (varies by program of study). Letters of recommendation: required. Essay: required. Accepts the Common Application. Apply to particular school or college. Applicants to fine arts programs must submit a portfolio or audition.

Bowdoin College

Brunswick, ME 04011

Rates with Amherst, Williams, and Wesleyan for liberal arts excellence and pioneered in not requiring the SAT. More selective than Bates and Colby. Bowdoin has strong science programs, and outdoor enthusiasts benefit from proximity to the Atlantic coast. Smaller than some of its competitors, with less overt competition among students.

Website: www.bowdoin.edu
Location: Small Town
Private
Total Enrollment: 1,793
Undergraduates: 1,793
Male/Female: 50/50
SAT Ranges: CR 690–765, M 685–770
ACT Ranges: 31–34
Financial Aid: 48%
Pell Grant: 14%
Expense: Pr $ $ $
Student Loans: 34%
Average Debt: $
Phi Beta Kappa: Yes
Applicants: 6,790
Accepted: 15%
Enrolled: 50%
Grad in 6 Years: 93%
Returning Freshmen: 97%
Academics: ✍ ✍ ✍ ✍ ✍
Social: 🎪 🎪 🎪
Q of L: ★ ★ ★
Admissions: (207) 725-3100
Email Address: admissions@ bowdoin.edu

Strong Programs:
Government
Economics
Mathematics
Environmental Studies
Neuroscience

For more than two centuries, Bowdoin College has sought to make nature, art, and friendship as integral to the student experience as the world of books. This is, after all, the alma mater of the great American poets Longfellow and Hawthorne. In fact, when they matriculate, new students sign their names in a book on Hawthorne's very desk. Though the New England winter can be brutal, students are quick to point out that good food and friendships that "transcend labels" help make the campus a warm and friendly place. Says one freshman, "If you're passionate about anything, Bowdoin provides you with the resources to explore those passions."

Bowdoin's 207-acre campus sits in Brunswick, Maine, the state's largest town. Hidden amid the pine groves and athletic fields are 119 buildings, in styles from German Romanesque, colonial, medieval, and neoclassical to neo-Georgian, modern, and postmodern. Former fraternity houses now serve as academic and administrative offices and social houses, since Greek groups were phased out. The college recently completed a careful renovation of the historic Harriet Beecher Stowe House, in which the famed author wrote *Uncle Tom's Cabin*, and which now houses faculty offices. Extensive renovations to Coles Tower, a 16-story residence hall, are slated for completion in 2017.

To graduate, Bowdoin students must complete 32 courses, including one each in natural sciences and math, social and behavioral sciences, and fine arts and humanities, in addition to a required course in the visual and performing arts. Distribution requirements emphasize issues vital to a liberal education in the 21st century and include courses within interdisciplinary areas such as International Perspectives and Exploring Social Differences. First-years also have their choice of seminars, capped at 16 students each, which emphasize reading and writing; recent topics have included The Art of the Deal: Commerce and Culture, Performance and Theory in James Bond, and Racism. "Freshman Seminars are immensely valuable," says one senior. "They can give you a good sense of what you really need to work on to succeed at Bowdoin."

Academic strengths include the sciences, particularly neuroscience, environmental studies, earth and oceanographic science, chemistry, and biology. Making a virtue out of climatic necessity, Bowdoin also offers a concentration in Arctic studies (its mascot is the polar bear), as well as opportunities for Arctic archaeological research in Labrador or ecological research at the Kent Island Scientific Station in Canada. The Coastal Studies Center, just 15 minutes away on Orr's

Island, provides additional research opportunities in marine science. Mathematics, Africana studies, and classics are also well regarded, and students say the popularity of government and economics—the majors with the highest enrollment—is well deserved. The Digital and Computational Studies Initiative "integrates new technologies, methodologies, and forms of knowledge production" into Bowdoin's curriculum. Dual-degree programs in engineering are available through Caltech, Columbia, Dartmouth, and the University of Maine, as is a 3–3 law degree with Columbia Law School.

(continued)

Earth and Oceanographic
    Science
Africana Studies
Classics

"Bowdoin is exceptionally collaborative," says one neuroscience major. "Group projects are a staple of almost any class, and people genuinely want each other to succeed." Adds a junior, "The workload is definitely intense, but we only take four classes and it is certainly manageable." Sixty-eight percent of classes have fewer than 20 students. Professors teach all Bowdoin classes—there are no graduate students here, and thus no TAs—and their skills in the classroom draw raves. "The professors are committed to their students and are always available to discuss class material," says a biochemistry major.

> **"Group projects are a staple of almost any class, and people genuinely want each other to succeed."**

Before school begins, the entire entering class takes preorientation hiking, canoeing, kayaking, or community service trips that teach them about the people and landscape of Maine; there's also a community service experience in Brunswick for students less interested in the outdoors. Indeed, service learning is increasingly an emphasis at Bowdoin; more than half of all students apply their classroom work to real-world problems faced by local community groups. Undergraduate research is a priority too, and it's common for juniors and seniors to conduct independent studies with faculty members, then publish their results in professional journals. Many seniors complete yearlong honors projects culminating in a written thesis, oral defense, or original creative piece. Fifty-three percent of students study abroad through more than 100 programs, covering six different continents.

The Coastal Studies Center, just 15 minutes away on Orr's Island, provides research opportunities in marine science.

Bowdoin students are "collaborative, funny, smart, engaged, political, respectful, and fun," according to one sophomore. Just 9 percent of students hail from Maine, and 7 percent are international. African Americans make up 5 percent of the student body, Hispanics 12 percent, and Asian Americans 7 percent. "Many are outdoorsy, athletic, a little preppy—but everyone has an interest and a passion that might surprise you," a mathematics major says, "and most people have friends from all different social groups on campus." Bowdoin was the first U.S. institution to make SAT I scores an optional part of the admissions process, shifting the emphasis to a student's whole body of work. Additionally, Bowdoin employs a need-blind admissions policy, meets the full demonstrated financial need of admitted students, and has eliminated loans from its financial aid packages, replacing them with grants.

> **"Most people have friends from all different social groups on campus."**

Ninety-one percent of Bowdoin students live on campus, where first-years start off in quads, with two double bedrooms and a shared common room, in renovated yet historic halls. After that, students try their luck with the lottery, although members of the social houses, which have replaced sororities and fraternities, can escape by living with these groups. Upper-class students may choose four-bedroom quads. Students give rave reviews to dining service workers and the food they serve. They particularly love the lobster bake that kicks off each school year, and vegans and vegetarians are happy with the options available to them. "Bowdoin's food is restaurant quality, and the menu is different every day," cheers a senior. Security is good too, according to students. "Campus security is incredible and protects students effectively," a senior says.

Bowdoin has eliminated loans from its financial aid packages, replacing them with grants.

Social life at Bowdoin centers around two groups: sports teams and social houses. "There are no Greek life organizations on campus," says one junior. "Rather, we have a system of eight College Houses that host all types of events—academic, cultural, and parties—that are open to all students at the college. This sense of inclusivity ensures that people do not feel the pressure to drink." Hard liquor is prohibited on campus. Students look forward to homecoming and Ivies Weekend, one last blast of fun before spring finals. The latter celebrates the fact that Bowdoin didn't join the Ivy League, with bands at Whittier Field.

Ivies Weekend celebrates the fact that Bowdoin didn't join the Ivy League.

One student says Brunswick (population 20,000) is "a great, quiet college town." Habitat for Humanity and various mentoring programs help build bridges between students and local residents. A car comes in handy for the 15-minute drive to the outlets of Freeport (including L.L. Bean's flagship 24/7 factory store) or a quick trip to Portland for a "real" night out. The bus, train, and a school shuttle take students to Boston, a little more than two hours away, and ski bums will find several resorts even closer.

While "the long winters are certainly not a favorite," according to a senior, they do bring out school spirit, and rooting for the ice hockey team is an important strategy for winter survival. Bowdoin's Polar Bears compete in the Division III New England Small College Athletic Conference, and students "get blacked out" to demonstrate support, wearing all black when they attend games. Any sporting event against Colby is exciting, and the annual hockey matchup draws crowds of alumni and Brunswick locals alike. Recent conference champions include men's soccer and women's basketball, tennis, and volleyball, and the men's tennis team brought home the national championship in 2016. The field hockey team is a perennial powerhouse as well. About 70 percent of students participate in club sports, intramurals, and recreational activities, including those organized by the student-run Bowdoin Outing Club, whose weekend jaunts range from rock climbing and white-water rafting to fireside knitting.

"Bowdoin's food is restaurant quality, and the menu is different every day."

Outdoorsy types and those who can brave the cold will find warm and inviting academics at Bowdoin, where close friendships with peers and professors are easily forged. "Bowdoin College is an incredibly special place," says one happy student, "and it's not just the resources, the food, or the surrounding area that makes it so great. Rather, it's the people that make it a beautiful community."

Overlaps

Yale, Brown, Harvard, Dartmouth, Stanford, Pomona, Princeton, Williams

If You Apply To ➤

Bowdoin: Early decision I: Nov. 15. Early decision II and regular decision: Jan. 1. Financial aid: Feb. 15. Application fee: $60. Campus and alumni interviews: optional, evaluative. SATs or ACTs: optional. Subject Tests: optional. Letters of recommendation: required. Essay: required. Accepts the Common Application with supplement.

Brandeis University

Waltham, MA 02453

Founded in 1948 by Jews who wanted an elite institution to call their own. Now down to 55 percent Jewish and seeking top students of all faiths. Academic specialties include the natural sciences, the Middle East, and Jewish studies. Has one of the top programs in neuroscience at a small university. Competes with Tufts in the Boston area.

Brandeis University, founded to provide educational opportunities to those facing discrimination, has always had a reputation for intense progressive thought. Now it's being recognized as a rising star among research institutions and is expanding its experiential learning offerings. The only nonsectarian Jewish-sponsored college in the nation, Brandeis continues its struggle to maintain its Jewish identity while attracting a well-rounded, eclectic group of students.

Set on a hilltop in a pleasant residential neighborhood nine miles west of Boston, Brandeis's attractively landscaped 235-acre campus boasts many distinctive buildings. The music building, for example, is shaped like a grand piano; the theater looks like a top hat. The 24-hour Carl and Ruth Shapiro Campus Center includes a student theater, electronic library, and bookstore. The Abraham Shapiro Academic Building houses a state-of-the-art distance-learning classroom; conference rooms; the International Center for Ethics, Justice, and Public Life; the Center for Middle Eastern Studies; the Mandel Center for Jewish Education; and faculty offices.

Undergraduates enter the College of Arts and Sciences, which offers more than 40 different majors and nearly 50 minors through its departments and interdepartmental programs. The Brandeis core curriculum is rooted in a commitment to developing strong writing, foreign language, and quantitative-reasoning skills and an interdisciplinary and cross-cultural perspective. Students complete courses in composition, foreign language, physical education, quantitative reasoning, and non-Western and comparative studies.

Neuroscience, biochemistry, chemistry, and physics are top-notch programs, while biology, psychology, economics, and business enroll the most students. Dedicated premeds are catered to hand and foot, with special advisors, internships, and their own premedical center with specialized laboratories for research opportunities. With the largest faculty in the field outside of Israel, the university is virtually unrivaled in Near Eastern and Judaic studies; Hebrew is a Brandeis specialty. A growing number of interdisciplinary programs are becoming increasingly popular, particularly the international and global studies major and the health: science, society, and policy major. Brandeis also maintains a commitment to the creative arts, with strong theater offerings and a theory-based music program founded by the late Leonard Bernstein. A new minor in architectural studies has recently been added.

"Brandeis takes its academic integrity seriously," says a creative writing and English major. There is an out for those in need of respite from the intense academic climate; the Flex 3 option allows students to take three classes one semester if an especially rough course is required, and five the next, to stay on track for four-year graduation. The Transitional Year Program is a one-year academic program for inner city and economically disadvantaged students that guarantees small classes, rigorous academics, and strong academic support. Sixty-one percent of all classes at Brandeis have fewer than 20 students, and professors are "engaging, incredibly smart, and, most of all, [they] care about their students," according to one English major.

Rising sophomores and juniors have the opportunity to earn credit through summer internships related to their studies. More than 300 off-campus programs are offered in 64 countries, including four university-run programs: an international justice and human rights program in The Hague;

"Brandeis takes its academic integrity seriously."

a science and math program in Bangalore, India; an economics program in Copenhagen; and a studio art and art history program in Siena, Italy. Forty percent of students study abroad. The Schiff Undergraduate Fellows Program enables 10 fellows each year to work with faculty mentors on research and teaching projects. The Justice Brandeis Semester allows groups of 10 to 15 students to earn credits while

Website: www.brandeis.edu
Location: Suburban
Private
Total Enrollment: 5,158
Undergraduates: 3,601
Male/Female: 43/57
SAT Ranges: CR 600–700, M 650–770
ACT Ranges: 29–32
Financial Aid: 55%
Pell Grant: 21%
Expense: Pr $ $ $ $
Student Loans: 58%
Average Debt: $ $ $
Phi Beta Kappa: Yes
Applicants: 10,528
Accepted: 34%
Enrolled: 22%
Grad in 6 Years: 87%
Returning Freshmen: 92%
Academics: ✍ ✍ ✍ ✍
Social: ☎ ☎ ☎
Q of L: ★ ★ ★
Admissions: (781) 736-3500
Email Address: admissions@brandeis.edu

Strong Programs:
Near Eastern and Judaic Studies
Neuroscience
Chemistry
Physics
Biology
Psychology
Economics
Business

focusing on topics of personal interest, such as bio-inspired design, ethnographic fieldwork, or mobile app and game development. The linked courses feature field-work, internships, or research under faculty supervision.

Twenty-six percent of the Brandeis student body is from Massachusetts, and the population is heavily bicoastal otherwise, with sizable numbers of New York, New Jersey, and California residents. Twenty percent hail from foreign nations. Though more than half the student body is Jewish, there are three chapels on campus—Roman Catholic, Jewish, and Protestant—placed so that the shadow of one never crosses the shadow of another. It's an architectural symbol that students say reflects the realities of the campus community. Muslim students, with an enrollment of more than 200, have their own dedicated prayer space. African Americans make up 5 percent of the student body, Hispanics 7 percent, and Asian Americans 13 percent. "Students who attend Brandeis are passionate, involved in student life, outgoing, friendly, think out of the box, and are intellectual," says a senior. Hot-button issues include the Israeli-Palestinian conflict and environmental concerns. Even with one of the highest tuition rates in the country, Brandeis does not guarantee to meet each student's full demonstrated financial need, but help is generally available to those who apply on time. The level of support remains fairly constant over four years, students report. Twenty-one percent of freshmen are Pell-eligible, and the university also offers merit scholarships averaging $17,416 to qualified students.

As befits its mold-breaking heritage, Brandeis is the only school in the nation where you can live in a replica of a Scottish castle with stairways leading to nowhere.

"Housing on campus improves as you get older."

More pedestrian housing options include traditional quadrangle dormitories, where freshmen and sophomores live in doubles, and juniors live in singles. The Foster Living Center, or the "Mods," are co-ed; university-owned townhouses are reserved for seniors. "Housing on campus improves as you get older," one student observes. Another option is the Village, which offers singles and doubles clustered around family-style kitchens, semiprivate bathrooms, and lounges. Freshmen and sophomores are guaranteed housing, while upperclassmen play the lottery each spring. Seventy-nine percent of students live on campus, and the rest find affordable off-campus housing nearby. Brandeis boasts the best college food in the Boston area, as well as the most appetizing set-ups, students say, thanks to a decision to outsource dining services. Campus meal tickets buy lunch or dinner in a fast-food joint, the pub, a country store, a kosher dining hall with vegetarian selections, or the Boulevard, a cafeteria where "the salad bars are huge." The university has implemented several initiatives, including opening a new campus rape crisis center and creating new prevention programming, to address sexual violence on campus.

"There is always something to do on campus," cheers one student, including "dances, movie showings, and gatherings on the Great Lawn." Brandeis also hosts more than 250 student clubs, ranging from volunteerism and activism to sports

"Brandeis is…an open, accepting place where anyone can feel at home."

and religion. Some of the largest include the Waltham Group (a community service organization), Student Events (the campus programming board), and Triskelion (an LGBTQ+ student social group). The unofficial fraternities and sororities that have colonized at Brandeis are clamoring for recognition from the school. Weekends begin on Thursday, with live entertainment at the on-campus Stein pub. Students can party at will in the dorms, provided they don't get too rambunctious, but suites are officially "dry" unless a majority of the residents are over 21. Major events on the campus calendar include a Tropics Night dance (where beachwear is required in February), the massive Bronstein Weekend festival just before spring finals, and

Dedicated premeds are catered to hand and foot, with special advisors, internships, and their own premedical center.

Though more than half the student body is Jewish, there are three chapels on campus—Roman Catholic, Jewish, and Protestant.

the Screw Your Roommate dance, where dormies set up their roommates on blind dates. Also well attended are the homecoming soccer match and the annual lacrosse tilt against crosstown rival Bentley University.

The possibilities for off-campus diversion are nearly infinite, thanks to the proximity of Boston and Cambridge, which are accessible by the free Brandeis shuttle bus or a nearby commuter train. (A car is more trouble than it's worth.) Brandeis's host town, Waltham, receives lukewarm reviews from students, but one global studies major asks, "Who needs Waltham for excitement when Boston is a short shuttle ride away?"

Though the school does not field a football team, the Judges athletic program gets a boost from its membership in the Division III University Athletic Association, a neo-Ivy League for high-powered academic institutions such as the University of Chicago, Emory, NYU, and Carnegie Mellon. Brandeis has developed strong men's and women's soccer squads, and the women's basketball and softball teams are recent Eastern College Athletic Conference champions. The men's soccer team has made three straight Sweet 16 appearances. An extensive intramural program draws 45 percent of students, and IM contests run nearly every day of the year thanks to the artificial turf and lights on the recently renovated Gordon Field, also home to the varsity soccer teams.

Few private universities have come as far as Brandeis so quickly, evolving from a bare 270-acre site with the leftovers of a failed veterinary school to a modern research university of more than 100 buildings, an $860 million endowment, and ever-evolving academic opportunities. Landscaping, residential and dining services, health services, and the campus computer network have all been dramatically improved in the past few years, students say, adding to their feelings of pride in the school. One student sums it up this way: "Brandeis is not only an awesome place to get an education, it's also an open, accepting place where anyone can feel at home."

Some of the largest student groups include the Waltham Group (a community service organization) and Triskelion (an LGBTQ+ social group).

Overlaps

Brown, Emory, University of Pennsylvania, Washington University in St. Louis, Yale, Harvard, NYU, Columbia

If You Apply To ➤

Brandeis: Early decision I: Nov. 1. Early decision II, regular decision, and financial aid: Jan. 1. Housing: May 1. Application fee: $80. Campus and alumni interviews: optional, evaluative. SATs or ACTs: optional. Subject Tests: optional. Letters of recommendation: required. Essay: required. Accepts the Common Application with supplement.

Brigham Young University

Provo, UT 84602

From the time they are knee high, Mormons all around the world dream about coming to BYU. Most men and some women do a two-year stint as a missionary. Strongest academic programs are all preprofessional. The atmosphere is generally mild-mannered and conservative, but BYU goes bonkers for its sports teams.

Brigham Young University's strong ties with the Church of Jesus Christ of Latter-day Saints means that "BYU has high morals and a wholesome environment, which makes students feel safe and comfortable," a senior says. A sense of spirituality pervades most everything at BYU, where faith and academia are intertwined and life is governed by a demanding code of ethics that has even led to the suspension of star athletes in mid-season. The strict Honor Code covers everything from dating practices to academic honesty; no-no's include men wearing beards; the

Website: www.byu.edu
Location: Small City
Private
Total Enrollment: 29,342
Undergraduates: 27,339
Male/Female: 53/47

(continued)

SAT Ranges: CR 570–680,
  M 580–680
ACT Ranges: 27–31
Financial Aid: 68%
Pell Grant: N/A
Expense: Pr $
Student Loans: 27%
Average Debt: $
Phi Beta Kappa: No
Applicants: 13,376
Accepted: 48%
Enrolled: 78%
Grad in 6 Years: 80%
Returning Freshmen: 86%
Academics: ✐ ✐ ✐
Social: ☎ ☎ ☎
Q of L: ★ ★ ★ ★
Admissions: (801) 422-2507
Email Address: admissions@
  byu.edu

Strong Programs:
Business
Accounting
Law
Engineering
Nursing
Exercise Science

consuming of drugs, alcohol, and caffeine; and entering the bedroom of a member of the opposite sex. While students elsewhere might find the code burdensome, at BYU it is a point of pride. Indeed, the school's commitment to church values is the reason most students choose it. "The students who attend BYU are unique," says a communications major. "Everyone is clean-cut, shaven, modestly dressed, and proper in their etiquette."

The church's values of prosperity, chastity, and obedience are strongly evident on BYU's 557-acre campus, where the utilitarian buildings, like everything else, are "clean, modern, and orderly." The campus lies on the western edge of the Rocky Mountains, 4,600 feet above sea level, between the shores of Utah Lake and Mount Timpanogos, offering breathtaking sunsets and easy access to magnificent skiing, camping, and hiking areas. Days begin early; church bells rouse students at 8 a.m. with the first four bars of the hymn "Come, Come Ye Saints." (The same bells also peal every hour throughout the day.)

The church's influence continues when students set their schedules; students must take one religion course per term to graduate, and offerings include, of course, the Book of Mormon. BYU requires students to demonstrate proficiency in math, writing (first-year and advanced), and advanced languages, a catch-all category that can be satisfied with coursework in a foreign language or in statistics, advanced math, or advanced music. Students must also complete an extensive liberal arts core, which includes work in civilization, American heritage, biology, physical sciences, and electives in the natural sciences, social and behavioral sciences, and arts and letters.

BYU's academic offerings run the gamut, from liberal arts and sciences to pre-professional programs in engineering, nursing, business, and law. Students say the strongest offerings include the J. Reuben Clark Law School and most departments in the Marriott School of Management, especially accounting. "One of the most popular

> **"[The honors program is] an excellent way to get more out of your college experience."**

programs has been exercise science," says a sophomore. There are also degrees in public health education, school health education, and ancient near Eastern studies. Brigham Young has campuses in Idaho and Hawaii, a center in Jerusalem, and boasts the 15th largest study abroad program in the nation—nearly 200 programs in more than 50 nations. Approximately 90 percent of the men and 20 percent of the women interrupt their studies—typically after the freshman year—to serve two years as a missionary.

Students agree that the academic climate is demanding. "It is competitive," a senior reports, and "some courses are known for being extremely difficult to pass, such as American Heritage or Econ 110." Freshmen are often taught by full-time professors, who generally get good marks. "Most professors have a passion for their subject and for teaching," says a student. General education courses can be quite large, although 56 percent have fewer than 20 students, and registration can be a chore. The honors program, open to highly motivated students, offers small seminars with more faculty interaction and is "an excellent way to get more out of your college experience," one participant says. The strength of the faculty is one reason BYU has more full-time students than any other church-sponsored university in the United States, almost all of them undergraduates.

Not surprisingly, the typical BYU student is conservative. "The students are very academically and spiritually minded," confides a junior, who further describes students as "intelligent, friendly, and honest." Thirty-one percent of BYU undergraduates are from Utah. Many others hail from California and Idaho, and 3 percent come from more than 100 other countries. Hispanic students contribute 6 percent to the student body, Asian Americans 2 percent, and African Americans less than

The strict Honor Code prohibits men wearing beards and the consuming of drugs, alcohol, and caffeine.

1 percent. Tuition for church members is lower than for nonmembers, because Latter-day Saint families contribute to BYU through their tithes. Academic scholarships averaging $4,113 are available, as are roughly 250 athletic scholarships in 21 sports.

Nineteen percent of BYU undergrads—primarily freshmen—live in the single-sex residence halls, where the "very valuable" Freshman Academy program allows them to take courses and eat meals with fellow dorm-dwellers and professors. "The dorms are small but comfortable and very clean," says a student. Upperclassmen typically opt for cheaper off-campus apartments, which are also single-sex (remember the Honor Code?). When it comes to food, the student dining outlets on campus are described as adequate. "The school provides decent, affordable on-campus meal plans," says a senior. Although it is widely assumed that, because of the Honor Code and the religious tone on campus, sexual violence is not much of a problem, BYU drew national attention in 2016 after female students and alumni spoke out against the school's practice of opening Honor Code investigations of students who report being assaulted. A new policy of immunity for such victims has now been instituted.

Brigham Young has campuses in Idaho and Hawaii, a center in Jerusalem, and boasts the 15th largest study abroad program in the nation.

Whether it's work with the homeless or disabled, dances, firesides, concerts, plays, sporting events, or special activities within the campus religious wards (small groups of about 100 students), most of BYU's social life is organized through or linked to the church. Community service is big, with students visiting patients at hospitals and care centers, performing at local festivals, and building and refurbishing houses. Social life is carried out within the church's bounds of propriety and is given a lighthearted feeling with groups that encourage "creative dating and lots of dating, period," says a senior. There are no fraternities or sororities to provide housing or parties, which is just fine with most students, since alcoholic drinks are banned. Road trips include Vegas or southern Utah and, with the mountains being so close, you'll find plenty of skiing and camping. Provo itself has plenty of places to eat and shop. "Provo wouldn't really exist without BYU," says a student, and "it's a good college town for people who don't like bustling metropolises."

"The students are very academically and spiritually minded."

Physical fitness is big here, and the intramural facilities are some of the country's best, with indoor and outdoor jogging tracks; courts for tennis, racquetball, and handball; and a pool. Also important are varsity sports. The church philosophy of discipline and obedience has worked wonders for Cougar teams, and the football rivalry against the University of Utah provides some serious end-of-season intensity—the ESPN television network has dubbed the BYU–Utah rivalry the "Holy War." One of the most popular courses offered at BYU is ballroom dancing, partly because many participants aspire to join BYU's award-winning dance team.

To most Americans, BYU probably seems old-fashioned or like a step back in time. But for young members of the Church of Jesus Christ of Latter-day Saints, that may be just what the elder ordered. "BYU's dedicated faculty, devout atmosphere, and beautiful, clean campus set it apart from all other universities," a satisfied senior says.

Overlaps

BYU–Hawaii, BYU–Idaho, University of Utah, Utah State, Utah Valley State

If You Apply To ➢

BYU: Rolling admissions: Feb. 1. (Priority deadline: Dec. 1.) Financial aid: Apr. 15. Priority housing: Dec. 1. Application fee: $35. Campus and alumni interviews: optional, informational. SATs or ACTs: required. No Subject Tests. No letters of recommendation. Essay: required. Ecclesiastical endorsement required.

Brown University

45 Prospect Street, Providence, RI 02912

To today's stressed-out students, the fantasy of taking every course pass/fail seems like a dream come true. Nobody at Brown actually does this, but the pass/fail option, combined with the school's notable lack of distribution requirements, gives it the freewheeling image that students love. In reality, doing well at Brown is just as tough as at other Ivies. Scorned by conservatives as a hotbed of political correctness.

Website: www.brown.edu
Location: Small City
Private
Total Enrollment: 8,873
Undergraduates: 6,302
Male/Female: 48/52
SAT Ranges: CR 680–780,
   M 690–780
ACT Ranges: 31–34
Financial Aid: 52%
Pell Grant: 13%
Expense: Pr $ $ $ $
Student Loans: 34%
Average Debt: $
Phi Beta Kappa: Yes
Applicants: 30,396
Accepted: 9%
Enrolled: 56%
Grad in 6 Years: 96%
Returning Freshmen: 98%
Academics: ✍ ✍ ✍ ✍ ✍
Social: ☎ ☎ ☎ ☎
Q of L: ★ ★ ★ ★ ★
Admissions: (401) 863-2378
Email Address: admission@
   brown.edu

Strong Programs:
Economics
Computer Science
Biology
Business, Entrepreneurship,
   and Organizations
Neuroscience
Classics
Applied Mathematics
Geology

Brown University is a perennial "hot college," with an overwhelming number of happy students and many more clamoring to join their ranks. Once here, students not only receive a prestigious and quality education, but also a chance to explore their creative sides at a liberal arts and sciences college that does not emphasize grades or preprofessionalism and shuns GPAs, required courses, and competitive attitudes among its undergraduates. Brown's environment and policies have drawn both praise and criticism over the years, but its students thrive on this discussion and lively debate. "Brown's open curriculum, though not for everyone, is incredibly liberating," says one student.

Founded in 1764 as the College in the English Colony of Rhode Island and Providence Plantations, Brown was renamed in 1804 after Nicholas Brown Jr., a major benefactor whose father—one of the school's founders—was a businessman with controversial ties to the slave trade. The school recently established a memorial to slaves at Brown and a Center for the Study of Slavery and Justice. The university sits atop College Hill on the east side of Providence, and its 140-acre campus affords an excellent view of downtown Providence. Campus architecture is a composite of old and new—plenty of grassy lawns surrounded by historic buildings that offer students refuge from the city streets beyond. The neighborhoods that surround the campus lie within a national historic district and boast beautiful tree-lined streets full of ethnic charm. Recent construction includes a new building for the School of Engineering that is devoted to undergraduate teaching and laboratory space.

Brown's faculty has successfully resisted the notion that somewhere in their collective wisdom and experience lies a core of knowledge that every educated person should possess. As a result, aside from completing courses in a major, the only university-wide requirements for graduation are to demonstrate writing competency and complete the 30-course minimum satisfactorily. (The assumption is that students will take four courses a term for a total of 32 in four years.) All students must demonstrate that they have worked at least twice on developing their writing (once during their first two years and again as upperclassmen), which they can do by taking approved English or writing-across-the-curriculum courses or by documenting their writing work in any other Brown course. Freshmen are normally required to carry a full courseload, but they do not have course distribution requirements. Students can take their classes one of two ways: for traditional marks of A, B, C, or No Credit; or for Satisfactory/No Credit. The NC is not recorded on the transcript, while the letter grade or Satisfactory can be supplemented by a written evaluation from the professor. A habit of NCs, however, lands students in academic hot water.

> **"Students are mostly only in classes that they really want to be in."**

The most popular majors (or concentrations, as they are called here) are economics, computer science, biology, and the multidisciplinary concentration in business, entrepreneurship, and organizations. Neuroscience, classics, applied mathematics, and geology are some of the university's best concentrations, and students also praise political science, religious studies, and history—although one says, "As far as I know, all our academic departments are super strong (like oxen or Heracles)." Other top-notch programs include comparative literature, modern languages, and the writing program in the English department. Among the sciences, engineering and the premed curriculum are standouts. Future doctors can try for a competitive eight-year liberal medical education program where students can earn an M.D. without having to sacrifice their humanity. Fields related to scientific technology have very good facilities, including an instructional technology center, while minority issues are studied at the Center for Race and Ethnicity. The School of Engineering has recently added a track in environmental engineering.

The only university-wide requirements are to demonstrate writing competency and complete the 30-course minimum satisfactorily.

Those with interests in interdisciplinary fields will enjoy Brown's wide range of concentrations that cross departmental lines and cover everything from cognitive science to public policy. Indeed, there are bona fide departments in cognitive and linguistic sciences and media and modern culture. Students can also create their own concentration from the array of goodies offered. Brown also offers group independent study projects, a popular alternative for students with the gumption to take a course they have to construct primarily by themselves, and a dual-degree program with the Rhode Island School of Design

"If Brown students share one attribute, it is open-mindedness."

(RISD), also located on College Hill. Students can cross-register for individual courses at RISD as well. The Starr Fellow program awards $4,000 for a summer project to 10 to 15 students, and there is the potential for an additional $2,000 award in the subsequent academic year. Particularly adventurous students can choose to spend time in one of Brown's more than 120 study abroad programs in 11 countries. In addition to the 35 percent of students who study abroad, others go overseas to complete research or internships during the summer.

"Although the coursework is definitely rigorous, students are mostly only in classes that they really want to be in, and therefore it leads to an enjoyable, relaxed climate," says a computer science major. Brown prides itself on undergraduate teaching and considers skill in the classroom as much as the usual scholarly credentials when making tenure decisions. A student says, "Faculty members are readily accessible, given that the majority of our classes are quite small, and every professor teaches undergraduates." The advising system reflects the administration's commitment to treating students as adults. It pairs each freshman with a professor and a peer advisor, and resident counselors in the dorms are also available to lend an ear. Sophomores utilize special advising resources, upperclassmen are assigned an advisor in their concentration, and a pool of interdisciplinary faculty counselors is on hand for general academic advising problems.

Future doctors can try for a competitive eight-year liberal medical education program.

Through the Curricular Advising Program, Brown offers nearly 90 special freshman seminars, capped at 20 students each, taught by faculty in all disciplines who also serve as academic advisors for their students' first year. Overall, 70 percent of undergraduate classes have fewer than 20 students. Even so, particularly popular courses are usually jammed

"Students take the initiative to create spaces for people of all identities."

with students, and often there aren't enough teaching assistants to staff them effectively. Some popular smaller courses, especially writing courses in the English department and studio art courses, can be nearly impossible to get into, although the administration claims that perseverance makes perfect—in other words, show up the first day and beg shamelessly.

"If Brown students share one attribute, it is open-mindedness," says one English major. With a mere 6 percent of undergraduates hailing from tiny Rhode Island, and 12 percent coming from foreign countries, geographical diversity is one of Brown's hallmarks. Consistent with its Rhode Island location and with the spirit of openness that persists to this day, Brown was the first Ivy League school to accept students from all religious affiliations. Today, Brown is one of the few remaining hot spots of student activism in the nation; nary a semester has passed without at least one demonstration about the issue of the day. African Americans comprise 7 percent of the student body, Hispanics 11 percent, and Asian Americans 13 percent. Minorities rarely miss an opportunity to speak out on issues of concern, and the LGBTQ community is also prominent. "Brown is one of the most conscious schools when it comes to identities, and students take the initiative to create spaces for people of all identities," observes a cognitive science major. Although Brown doesn't offer athletic or academic merit scholarships, it does guarantee to meet the full demonstrated need of everyone admitted. The university has also eliminated loans for families with incomes below $100,000 a year and eliminated the parent contribution toward tuition for those with incomes below $60,000 a year.

The university's nationally recognized public service center helps place students in a variety of volunteer positions.

About half the freshmen are assigned to one of eight co-ed Keeney Quad dorms, in "loud and rambunctious" units of 40 to 60 with several sophomore or junior dorm counselors. The other half live in the quieter Pembroke campus dorms or in a few other scattered locations. "Housing at Brown is wonderful," says a sophomore. "Freshman accommodations are by and large quite plush; the vast majority of freshman residence halls have been very recently and very handsomely renovated."

After their freshman year, students seeking on-campus housing enter a lottery based on seniority. There are many options from which to choose, including apartment-like suites with kitchens, special-interest houses, two social dorms, and Greek housing. Brown guarantees housing for all four years, and 76 percent of undergrads choose to stay on campus, but a significant number of upperclassmen get "off-campus permission." Apartments nearby are becoming more plentiful—and more expensive—as the area gentrifies. Campus meal plans range from seven to twenty meals a week, and although the food gets middling reviews, students appreciate the variety of accommodations offered at the two main dining halls and four smaller eateries, one of which is vegetarian only. "The campus tends to be pretty safe," says one senior, and another adds, "Brown is constantly reforming its policies on sexual assault, and students are constantly working to improve the environment for survivors of sexual assault."

"Freshman accommodations are by and large quite plush."

"The great thing about Brown's social life is the diversity of options," says one junior, ranging from "fraternity parties to off-campus sports parties, as well as concerts and club nights in downtown Providence." The few residential Greek organizations are generally considered much too un-mellow for Brown's taste (only 12 percent of the men and 9 percent of the women sign up), hence freshmen and sophomores are their chief clientele. The nonresidential multicultural fraternities and sororities serve a more comprehensive student-life function. Tighter drinking rules have curtailed campus drinking somewhat. The university sponsors frequent campuswide parties and plays, concerts, and special events. Funk Nite every Thursday night at the Underground, a campus pub, draws a mixed bag of dancing fools. The biggest annual bash of the year is Spring Weekend, which includes plenty of parties and a big-name band. More than a dozen a cappella groups, strong theater and dance programs, daily and weekly newspapers, a skydiving club, political organizations, and "even a Scrabble club and a successful croquet team" represent just a few of the ways Brown students manage to keep themselves entertained.

Brown boasts the fourth largest collegiate athletic program in the country, with roughly 900 athletes competing on 38 Division I varsity teams.

Providence, an old industrial city that has undergone a renaissance of sorts, is Rhode Island's capital, so many internship opportunities in state government are available, as are a few good music joints, lively bars, and several fine, inexpensive restaurants. The city is also home to a number of colleges and universities, which helps to liven up the social scene. Plenty of other good things are right in the neighborhood. "Students will often go to Thayer (a street with many restaurants kind of in the middle of campus), Wickenden (another street to the south), or down the hill into downtown Providence for food or nightlife," explains a junior. For those interested in community outreach—and many at Brown are—the university's nationally recognized public service center helps place students in a variety of volunteer positions. Brown Community Outreach is, in fact, the largest student organization on campus. For a change of scenery, many students head to Boston or the beaches of Newport, each an hour away.

Brown does not have a reputation as an especially sports-minded school, yet it boasts the fourth largest collegiate athletic program in the country, with roughly 900 athletes competing on 38 Division I varsity teams, many of which make regular appearances in NCAA tournament play. The Bears women's crew team has won several NCAA championships. Recent Ivy League Conference champions include men's soccer, baseball, lacrosse, tennis, water polo, crew, and football, along with women's basketball. Athletic facilities include an Olympic-sized swimming pool and an indoor athletic complex with everything from tennis courts to weight rooms. There's also a basketball arena for those trying to perfect their slam dunks. Thirty-three club sports, plus intramurals ranging from ice hockey and squash to cornhole and kickball tournaments, offer a good mix of competitiveness and fun.

> **"It's cool to be excited about anything here."**

Ever since the days of Roger Williams, Rhode Island has been known as a land of tolerance, and Brown certainly is a 21st-century embodiment of this tradition. "Brown students build themselves up by building others up," says a physics and philosophy double major. "It's cool to be excited about anything here, and Brown students celebrate the talents of all of their peers." The education offered at this university is decidedly different from that provided by the rest of the Ivy League, or for that matter, by other top universities. Brown is content to gather a talented bunch of students, offer a diverse and imaginative array of courses, and then let the undergraduates, with a little help, make sense of it all. It takes an enormous amount of initiative, maturity, and self-confidence to thrive at Brown, but most students feel they are up to the challenge.

Overlaps

Yale, Harvard, Cornell University, Columbia, University of Pennsylvania, Princeton, Stanford, Dartmouth

If You Apply To ➤ **Brown:** Early decision: Nov. 1. Regular decision: Jan. 1. Financial aid: Feb. 1. Application fee: $75. No campus interviews. Alumni interviews: optional, evaluative. SATs and two Subject Tests or ACTs (with writing recommended): required. Letters of recommendation: required. Essay: required. Accepts the Common Application with supplement. Certain programs require supplemental admissions essays.

Bryn Mawr College

101 North Merton Avenue, Bryn Mawr, PA 19010-2899

BMC has the most brainpower per capita of the elite women's colleges. Politics range from liberal to radical, and the honor code shapes the campus culture. Bryn Mawrtyrs may take themselves a bit too seriously. The college still benefits from ties to nearby Haverford, though the relationship is not as close as in the days when Haverford was all male. A train station just off campus offers easy access to Philadelphia.

Website: www.brynmawr.edu
Location: City Outskirts
Private
Total Enrollment: 1,611
Undergraduates: 1,327
Male/Female: 0/100
SAT Ranges: CR 620–730,
 M 620–730
ACT Ranges: 28–32
Financial Aid: 75%
Pell Grant: 12%
Expense: Pr $ $ $
Student Loans: 60%
Average Debt: $ $
Phi Beta Kappa: No
Applicants: 2,890
Accepted: 39%
Enrolled: 35%
Grad in 6 Years: 85%
Returning Freshmen: 94%
Academics: ✍ ✍ ✍ ✍ ✍
Social: ☎ ☎ ☎
Q of L: ★ ★ ★
Admissions: (610) 526-5152
Email Address: admissions@
 brynmawr.edu

Strong Programs:
Psychology
Biology
Mathematics
English
Growth and Structure of Cities
Chemistry
Classics
Art History

Leafy suburban enclaves are a dime a dozen around Philadelphia, but only one is home to Bryn Mawr College, a top-notch liberal arts school that happens to be all female. On this campus, students find a range of academic pursuits from archaeology to film studies to physics, and a diverse yet community-oriented student body. Founded in 1885, Bryn Mawr has evolved into a hotbed of intellectualism that prepares students for life and work in a global environment. Although students here abide by a strict academic honor code and participate in a host of long-standing campus traditions, they remain doggedly individualistic. "We are social-justice minded, fiercely independent trailblazers who do not take no for an answer," asserts one sophomore. "I am absolutely certain that we will run the world someday."

Bryn Mawr's lovely campus is a path-laced oasis set among trees (many carefully labeled with Latin and English names) and lush green hills, perfect for an afternoon walk, bike ride, or jog. Just a 20-minute train ride from downtown Philadelphia, Bryn Mawr provides a country setting with a vital and exciting city nearby. The predominant architecture is collegiate Gothic, a combination of the Gothic architecture of Oxford and Cambridge Universities and the local landscape—a style that Bryn Mawr introduced to the United States. Ten of Bryn Mawr's buildings are listed in the National Register of Historic Places. The M. Carey Thomas Library, which was named after the school's first dean and second president, a pioneer in women's education, is also a National Historic Landmark. Variations on the collegiate Gothic theme include a sprinkling of modern buildings, such as Louis Kahn's slate-and-concrete residence hall and Bryn Mawr's newest residence hall, which provides housing for 130 students.

The general education requirements include one semester of "quantitative" work; one semester in each of four "approaches to inquiry" (scientific investigation, critical interpretation, cross-cultural analysis, and inquiry into the past); an intermediate level of competency in a foreign language; and the requirements of a major. Students are also required to take eight half-semesters of physical education and must pass a swimming test. In addition, all freshmen are required to take a college seminar to develop their critical thinking, writing, and discussion skills.

> **"I am absolutely certain that we will run the world someday."**

Most departments are strong, especially the sciences, classics, archaeology, art history, and the foreign languages, including Russian and French. The growth and structure of cities major is a unique, interdisciplinary program that blends coursework in urban studies, architecture, history, economics, and sociology, among other subjects. Doing serious work in music, art, photography, or astronomy requires a hike over to Haverford College, Bryn Mawr's nearby partner in the bicollege system, which allows students at each institution to take courses, use the facilities, eat, and even live in the dormitories of the other. Approximately 550 Bryn Mawr students take courses at Haverford each semester. Bryn Mawr and Haverford students cooperate on a weekly newspaper, radio station, orchestra, and other clubs and sports, and a free shuttle bus connects the campuses. Students may also cross-register with Swarthmore and Penn. Programs offered in conjunction with Caltech and Penn allow participating students to earn degrees in engineering in just five years. The most popular majors at Bryn Mawr are psychology, biology, mathematics, and English; two new majors, biochemistry and health studies, have recently been introduced.

Out of respect for their academic honor code, students refrain from discussing their grades, but they freely admit that they work hard. "The academic climate of Bryn Mawr is competitive and intense," says one student. Freshmen and transfer students are initiated to the Bryn Mawr experience during Customs Week, which includes a variety of seminars and workshops, as well as a tour of the campus and town. The quality of teaching at Bryn Mawr is unquestionably high and, thanks in part to small class sizes, "faculty members are very accessible," according to a sociology major. "They all have office hours, and if you can't make office hours, you can make an appointment."

For those looking ahead to see what the college's steep tuition will buy in the long term, the campus has a career resource center that offers information on interviewing and building a résumé—and there is no lack at Bryn Mawr of special academic programs with which to fill those résumés. The 360-Degree program is an interdisciplinary experience that brings students from a variety of majors together to examine a central theme from multiple perspectives. Students take a cluster of two or

The growth and structure of cities major blends coursework in urban studies, architecture, history, economics, and sociology.

"A lot of people are talking about race at Bryn Mawr, and also transgender issues."

three courses in a single semester and also complete a hands-on component, such as travel, fieldwork, or lab research. Recent examples include Migrations and Borderlands, Contemplative Traditions, and Struggles for Global Health Equity. Thirty-eight percent of students study overseas during their time at Bryn Mawr; students choose from more than 70 programs in nearly 30 countries.

"Bryn Mawr tends to attract passionate, intelligent, kind, supportive, and involved individuals," says one student. The campus has a strong international flavor, with 24 percent of undergraduates hailing from abroad, and only 12 percent coming from Pennsylvania. African Americans make up 6 percent of the student body, Hispanics 9 percent, and Asian Americans 12 percent. Freshmen can take an intensive four-hour session during orientation on pluralism, which teaches students to examine assumptions about class, race, and sexual orientation. "A lot of people are talking about race at Bryn Mawr, and also transgender issues," says one student. There are no athletic scholarships, but merit scholarships averaging $12,405 are available, and the school does guarantee to meet the demonstrated financial need of everyone admitted.

Bryn Mawr and Haverford students cooperate on a weekly newspaper, radio station, orchestra, and other clubs and sports.

Ninety-three percent of the student body reside on campus. "Our residence halls are spectacular," says one sophomore. "Each dorm is unique, but they all are very comfortable, and every student is guaranteed housing for all four years." Dorm features include hardwood floors, window seats, and fireplaces. For good reason, the food service has received national recognition. Choices are plentiful and tasty, according to students. "We have a nutritionist available for stu-

"[Traditions] play a big role in uniting all four classes."

dents to consult should they have dietary restrictions," says a French major. Students generally report feeling safe on campus; says a classical culture and society major, "Public Safety seems to really care about students at Bryn Mawr and are there to help and keep students safe."

Traditions are a very important part of the campus social scene: "They play a big role in uniting all four classes and give students a role in the greater history of the college," says a student. The Elizabethan-style May Day festivities are held the Sunday after classes end in May. Everyone wears white, eats strawberries, and watches Greek plays. Students are known to skinny-dip in the fountains and drink

opened in 2015, providing 344 beds in 88 apartments. A new commons building includes meeting rooms, multipurpose spaces, a dining facility, and a convenience store.

Students in Bucknell's College of Arts and Sciences and School of Management must complete general education courses in three areas—Intellectual Skills (including a writing-intensive Foundation Seminar), Tools for Critical Engagement, and Disciplinary Perspectives—and must complete a capstone experience their senior year. In the College of Engineering, students take a common course their first semester that introduces them to all eight of the engineering degree programs, and they must take courses in mathematics, science, social sciences, and arts and humanities. All freshmen, regardless of discipline, participate in the First-Year Integration Series, a series of workshops designed to help them transition to college, featuring topics such as university resources, diverse perspectives, and lifelong learning. And along with major-related requirements, each student must demonstrate competence in writing in order to graduate.

While Bucknell is known for engineering, management, and the natural sciences, students say academics are strong across the curriculum and weaker programs are hard to find. The most popular majors are economics, political science, biology, and accounting and financial management. Other highlights include the animal

> **"I got to work one-on-one with a faculty mentor who truly viewed me as an equal."**

behavior program, which benefits from an outdoor naturalistic primate facility for teaching and research, and environmental studies, which includes not only science courses but also courses in the humanities, social policy, and civil engineering. Management 101 is a favorite course among business students, who create and sell a product and donate their profits to charity. Majors in elementary and secondary education were recently dropped, although students can still get certified in these areas, and new majors have been added in applied mathematical sciences and vocal performance.

"The academic climate is not competitive between students, but students are highly ambitious and competitive against their own personal standards," says a markets, innovation, and design major. Fifty-nine percent of courses have fewer than 20 students, and the emphasis is on discussion and group work. "Bucknell prides itself on impeccable teaching, and it truly succeeds," a mathematics major says. "Faculty members encourage students to engage with them outside of the classroom for extra help and are always available," adds a senior.

Forty-four percent of students study abroad. Semester-long, faculty-led programs take them to England, France, Ghana, Greece, Spain, and Washington, D.C. Relationships with other colleges and universities enable students to choose from more than 430 other programs worldwide. The College of Engineering has one of the highest study abroad participation rates for students in an engineering program, and it also offers a specialized three-week study abroad course, taught by Bucknell faculty at the end of the spring semester, that places engineering concepts into a real-world, global context. The Institute for Leadership in Technology and Management allows a select group of students to learn new ways to solve problems, while building their teamwork and communication skills. Department-specific honors programs attract top scholars, and twenty percent of all undergraduates—in all disciplines—participate in undergraduate research. A political science major points to research as a defining experience at Bucknell: "I got to work one-on-one with a faculty mentor who truly viewed me as an equal and valued my opinions and insights."

Bucknell students are "bright and highly social," says a senior. "Friday nights are generally not a time to be in the library," adds another. Twenty-two percent

(continued)

Student Loans: 54%
Average Debt: $ $
Phi Beta Kappa: Yes
Applicants: 10,967
Accepted: 25%
Enrolled: 35%
Grad in 6 Years: 90%
Returning Freshmen: 93%
Academics: ✍ ✍ ✍ ✍
Social: ☎ ☎ ☎ ☎
Q of L: ★ ★ ★
Admissions: (570) 577-3000
Email Address: admissions@bucknell.edu

Strong Programs:
Economics
Political Science
Biology
Accounting and Financial
    Management
Engineering
Animal Behavior
Environmental Studies

Bucknell has one of the highest study abroad participation rates for students in an engineering program.

are Pennsylvanians, and 64 percent went to public high school. Racial and cultural diversity have been slow in coming, and many students comment that self-segregation of different groups is noticeable on campus. Asian Americans account for 4 percent of the student body, African Americans 3 percent, and Hispanics 6 percent, while international students represent 5 percent of the student body. Students here traditionally don't get too vocal when it comes to social and political issues. Each year, Bucknell awards a small number of merit scholarships averaging $11,764, as well as 142 athletic scholarships in 14 sports.

More than a third of freshmen join the Residential Colleges, choosing from among eight themed living/learning communities.

Ninety-one percent of the student body live on campus and all first-years are required to do so. More than a third of each entering class joins the Residential Colleges (which a biomedical engineering major calls "fantastic for first-years"), choosing from among eight themed living/learning communities: Discovery, Arts, Humanities, Environmental, Global, Languages and Cultures, Social Justice, and Society and Technology. A senior notes, "For upperclassmen not in a residential college, on-campus housing can be tough," and the university limits the number of seniors allowed to move off campus. Students evaluate Bucknell dining as being better than your average institutional fare, if sometimes lacking in variety. Students report feeling safe on campus and well-informed when it comes to issues of sexual assault. "Our school has sexual assault awareness weeks and speakers, as well as groups like Speak Up who are constantly engaging the campus in conversations," explains a senior.

"Friday nights are generally not a time to be in the library."

"Greek organizations and sports teams tend to run the social scene," a senior reports. Indeed, Bucknell's robust Greek system draws 42 percent of the men and 49 percent of the women, though rush is delayed until the start of sophomore year. And while drinking at frat parties and the two bars close to campus is a weekly pastime for those of age, the university offers on-campus alternatives. Two student organizations arrange everything from carnivals to hypnotists to religious retreats, while the school-run Uptown nightclub offers bands, karaoke, pub nights, and other social events. Favorite traditions include Midnight Mania (the official start of the basketball season) and the formal Chrysalis Ball in the spring. Also special are the Candlelighting and Convocation ceremonies. "Convocation is an important tradition to Bucknell because you only pass through the Christy Mathewson gates twice in your life: on your first and last days as a student here," says a senior.

The Division I Bucknell Bison have captured the Patriot League Presidents' Cup 18 times in 26 years.

Lewisburg is small and rural, but Market Street has boutiques, restaurants, and an old-style movie theater that serves up first-run flicks. "Market Street is a great way to get off campus without having to get in a car to do so," says a senior. Through the Office of Civic Engagement, students have opportunities to volunteer and participate in service learning. When students get claustrophobic, New York, Philadelphia, and Washington/Baltimore are less than three hours away; the main campus of Penn State, in State College, Pennsylvania, is even closer. Bucknell also sponsors road trips to these communities for students who lack wheels.

The Division I Bucknell Bison have captured the Patriot League Presidents' Cup, for the league's all-sports champion, 18 times in 26 years and were runners-up for the 2015–16 season. Men's and women's cross-country and track and field are perennially strong, having combined for dozens of Patriot League championships; the women's teams in both sports were conference champions in 2015–16. Men's and women's basketball both claimed regular-season titles in 2016, and baseball, wrestling, and men's and women's soccer are also competitive. Basketball is a fan favorite, and Bucknell's biggest rivalries are with Lafayette and Lehigh, though these aren't a tremendous focus. Notably, Bucknell's athletic program consistently ranks among the

"Alumni want to give back."

top 10 Division I institutions in graduation rates and total number of Academic All-Americans. Intramural and club sports draw 37 percent of the students.

Bucknell students get the best of several worlds: excellence in engineering and the liberal arts, abundant research opportunities, and a healthy social life. "Undergraduates are the focus of all academics and the primary people to enjoy all of these great resources," cheers one economics major. Another perk: "Both students and alumni have a serious amount of pride for their school," says a senior, "and you find that alumni want to give back." The school's rural Pennsylvania location and the preponderance of preppies may seem stifling at times, but if you're seeking small classes and a supportive environment, Bucknell may be a good fit.

If You Apply To ➤

Bucknell: Early decision I: Nov. 15. Early decision II, regular decision, and financial aid: Jan 15. Application fee: $40. No campus or alumni interviews. SATs or ACTs: required. Subject Tests: optional. Letters of recommendation: required. Essay: required. Audition required for applicants to music program. Accepts the Common Application.

Butler University

Indianapolis, IN 46208

Small, private university with an attractive campus near Indianapolis and a relaxed Midwestern feel. Butler combines a strong liberal arts emphasis with practical learning. Strong in dance, theater, and international business. Classes are small with no TAs. Students are a homogeneous lot who share Indiana's trademark passion for basketball. Larger than DePauw, smaller than Northwestern.

College hoops fans may recognize Butler University as the unheralded outsider who fought its way to the final game of the NCAA Division I Basketball Championships not once but twice in recent years. But those who attend this small Midwestern university know that Bulldogs basketball is representative of the Butler way of life, which emphasizes teamwork, tenacity, and solid fundamentals. "Butler University offers quality education, friendly and approachable professors, plenty of opportunities for involvement, and an overall friendly atmosphere," says one student. Despite the sometimes claustrophobic atmosphere of the "Butler Bubble," most students find the school's cozy campus and solid academics to be a slam dunk.

Located five miles from downtown Indianapolis in the city's historic Butler-Tarkington neighborhood, Butler University's 295-acre campus is hailed as one of the most attractive in the Midwest for its parklike setting, which includes centuries-old trees, open landscaped malls, curving sidewalks, fountains, a nature preserve, a prairie, a historical canal, a formal botanical garden, an observatory, and jogging paths. The first building, Jordan Hall, features Gothic architecture and has set the tone for subsequent buildings. Butler's Hinkle Fieldhouse, which opened in 1928, has reigned as one of the nation's great sports arenas for more than eight decades. A 42,000-square-foot pharmacy building features large, tiered lecture rooms, a pharmacy lab, patient examination rooms, offices, and study spaces. The newest addition to campus is the Fairview House, a 633-bed, apartment-style residence facility.

As part of Butler's core curriculum, students enroll in two common elements: First-Year Seminar, a two-semester sequence in their first year, and Global and Historical Studies, a sophomore-year sequence of courses. They must also complete courses in six general areas of inquiry: analytic reasoning, the natural world,

Website: www.butler.edu
Location: Suburban
Private
Total Enrollment: 4,346
Undergraduates: 3,954
Male/Female: 40/60
SAT Ranges: CR 520–620, M 530–630
ACT Ranges: 25–30
Financial Aid: 94%
Pell Grant: 16%
Expense: Pr $
Student Loans: 65%
Average Debt: $ $ $ $
Phi Beta Kappa: No
Applicants: 9,943
Accepted: 70%
Enrolled: 15%
Grad in 6 Years: 78%
Returning Freshmen: 89%
Academics: ✏ ✏ ✏
Social: ☎ ☎ ☎
Q of L: ★ ★ ★ ★

(continued)

Admissions: (888) 940-8100
Email Address: admission@
butler.edu

Strong Programs:
Dance
Theater
International Business
Marketing
Biological Science
Elementary Education
Pharmacy
Physician Assistant Studies

Butler's Hinkle Fieldhouse has reigned as one of the nation's great sports arenas for more than eight decades.

The Indianapolis Community Requirement and the Butler Cultural Requirement are designed to connect students to the community.

perspectives in the creative arts, physical well-being, the social world, and texts and ideas. Butler students also complete writing across the curriculum and speaking across the curriculum requirements, as well as two experiences designed to connect them to the campus community: the Indianapolis Community Requirement and the Butler Cultural Requirement.

"Butler students are extremely competitive," says a strategic communication major. "Whether that be for who has the best presentation in a class, the highest grade on a test, and even for internships in the Indianapolis area—Butler students want to be the best and be recognized for that." The university's most popular programs are also among its best and include marketing, biological science, elementary education, and preprofessional tracks in pharmacy and physician assistant studies. Other solid offerings include dance, theater, international business, and English, especially the creative writing track. The risk management and insurance major focuses on teaching students how to mitigate and manage risks through a combination of insurance and noninsurance techniques; graduates of the program can work in the insurance and financial services industries. Fifty-two percent of classes have fewer than 20 students, and the majority of classes taken by freshmen are taught by full professors. "Every so often you get a professor that isn't that great, but never are they terrible," says a junior.

> **"Butler students want to be the best and be recognized for that."**

The Butler Honors program is designed to foster a diverse and challenging intellectual climate and features courses, events, independent study, and research opportunities. The competitive Undergraduate Student Research program invites up to four students annually to conduct research under the guidance of a faculty mentor; participants also receive a stipend. For those who wish to travel to far-flung locales around the globe, Butler offers more than 110 study abroad programs in more than 40 countries, including Australia, Ireland, Germany, Ghana, and India. Roughly one-third of Butler students participate. "Study abroad programs are very important to students," a chemistry major confirms.

Forty-six percent of Butler students come from Indiana, and "most come from middle- to upper-class families and are very well put together," according to one student. "They are all very bright and very welcoming. The school isn't really cliquey," adds a freshman. Seventy-seven percent ranked in the top quarter of their high school class and eight out of 10 attended public high school. African Americans account for 4 percent of the student body, Hispanics 4 percent, and Asian Americans 3 percent; another 1 percent are international. Social and political issues elicit quiet shrugs from most: "I wouldn't say that there are any major social issues on campus," says one student. Still, Butler does receive its share of complaints, including the lack of parking and the cost to attend. Merit scholarships averaging $12,928 are available to qualified students, as are athletic awards.

> **"It feels good to know that our campus security, BUPD, is always there."**

Sixty-six percent of students live in university-sponsored housing, with all but seniors required to do so. "Students are given the opportunity to share very comfortable places with other roommates, either in the dormitories, houses, fraternity houses, or apartments—all with Wi-Fi access," says a senior. Another student grumbles, "As it is now, Butler doesn't have the space to put students, and with the school growing, these problems will continue." Students may dine in the student union or one of two campus dining halls. "The dining facilities are so-so. The food isn't really that great, but they make up for that by giving a wide variety of options," says a pharmacy major. And while Butler is "not in the best part of town," students report feeling safe on campus: "Butler is a very tight-knit community and we all look out for each other," says a junior, "but it feels good to know that our campus security, BUPD, is always there."

"Generally, Greek life is social life at Butler," says a student. Indeed, Greek life attracts 26 percent of the men and 40 percent of the women, and although the university is a wet campus, students say the social scene doesn't revolve around booze. "Butler students think they know how to party, but compared to state schools like IU and Purdue, that's laughable," remarks one senior. Students seeking a change of pace head off campus and into Indianapolis, where bars, restaurants, and cultural events are plentiful. "Students can attend performances by the Indianapolis Symphony Orchestra or a game by the Indiana Pacers, go to Circle Center Mall, or even visit the Indianapolis Children's Museum," says one adventurous sophomore. Volunteering is a favorite pastime, and traditions include homecoming week, "where students decorate the lawns of the Greek houses, participate in Yell Like Hell, and make a midnight snack run," according to a marketing and finance major.

Butler fields 18 Division I teams (the Bulldogs), and all but one compete in the Big East—the football team is a member of the Pioneer Football League. In addition to men's basketball, recent conference champs include women's soccer, softball, and men's and women's cross-country. Intramurals are popular, especially volleyball, five-on-five basketball, flag football, and soccer, and more serious students may also compete in 18 club sports.

Butler University desires to provide students with a strong undergraduate liberal arts experience and access to professional programs of "local impact and global reach." "Butler cares about its students as individuals," says one freshman, and students have taken note of the school's revamped programs, improved facilities, and focus on personal attention. Although the school's size can seem limiting ("It can sometimes feel like 'Butler High School,'" quips a student), most seem to value the small classes and close-knit campus vibe. "Butler truly becomes a community for our students," says a sophomore. "The students and faculty all work to make Butler life an enjoyable experience for all."

Butler offers more than 110 study abroad programs in more than 40 countries.

"Generally, Greek life is social life at Butler."

Overlaps
Indiana University, Purdue, Miami University (OH), Ball State, University of Dayton, DePauw, Marquette, IUPUI

If You Apply To ➤

Butler: Early action: Nov. 1. Regular decision: Feb. 1. Financial aid: Mar. 1. Housing: May 1. No application fee. No campus or alumni interviews. SATs or ACTs: required. No Subject Tests. Letters of recommendation: optional. Essay: required. Accepts the Common Application with supplement.

California Colleges and Universities

California's three-tiered system of colleges and universities has long been viewed as a model of excellence by other public higher education institutions around the world. The system offers a wealth of educational opportunities, including world-class research universities, more than 60 Nobel laureates, and courses on everything from film to viticulture. Underlying the creation of this remarkable system was a commitment to the notion that all qualified Californians, whatever their economic status, were entitled to the benefits of a college education.

Unfortunately, the well-publicized financial turmoil that has racked the State of California has jeopardized the ability of its public colleges and universities to fulfill their traditional egalitarian mission. The much-heralded 1960 Master Plan for Higher Education has not been updated to take note of the state's changing demographics and growing workforce needs; and while the state's financial situation has improved recently, increased spending has not returned funding to previous levels. Changed statewide priorities have led to expanded research capacity, to the detriment of investment in undergraduate education. For students, this means larger classes, reduced course offerings, and a big increase in student fees that pushes the published tuition costs for in-state residents to $13,500 a year. Individual campuses vary in the amount of fees they charge on top of tuition. To bring in more revenue, the UC system has increased its enrollment of out-of-state and international students, who pay more than triple the tuition rate: about $40,200 per year. The Los Angeles, Berkeley, and San Diego campuses now enroll almost 30 percent of their students from out of state. Paradoxically, large numbers of California residents are heading to places like Arizona State.

The California public higher education system is composed of the 10 combined research and teaching units of the University of California (UC), 23 state universities (CSU) that focus primarily on undergraduate teaching, and 112 two-year community colleges that offer both terminal Associate's degrees and the possibility of transferring into four-year institutions. While most of the community colleges are campus-based, some are partially or completely online. Community colleges are open to virtually everyone with a high school diploma or its equivalent. High school students, active military members, and students who have already graduated from high school are also welcome to take classes at community colleges.

CALIFORNIA STATE UNIVERSITY SYSTEM (CSU)

The CSU system is totally separate from the University of California, and the two systems have historically competed for funds as well as students. The largest system of higher education in the nation, CSU focuses on undergraduate education. While its members can offer master's degrees, they can award doctorates only in collaboration with a UC institution. Research in the state university system is severely restricted, a blow to CSU's national prestige but a big plus for students. Unlike UC school professors who face the pressure to publish or perish, teachers in the state system are there to teach. CSU's biggest problem is the success of the UC system, and its frequent lament—"Anywhere else we'd be number one"—is not without justification.

The top third of California high school graduates (as measured by a combination of SAT scores and GPA) may enroll in at least one of the CSU campuses. Admission requirements include a standard set of 15 academic courses, including four years of English, three years of math, two years of a foreign language, two years of laboratory science, two years of humanities/social sciences, one in fine or performing arts, and one college preparatory elective. CSU campuses give priority to students from their surrounding counties, and some community colleges are part of a Guaranteed Admissions Program with a local CSU campus. Community college students may apply to transfer without SAT scores once prerequisites have been met.

The 23-campus CSU system caters to more than 447,000 students a year. And while most of the campuses serve mainly commuters, Cal State Chico, Humboldt, Monterey Bay, San Luis Obispo, and Sonoma State stand out as residential campuses. While a solid liberal arts education is offered, the stress is usually on career-oriented professional training, and the system produces large numbers of engineers, nurses, and teachers for California's workforce. Size varies dramatically, from more than 33,000 students at Cal State Fullerton and Cal State Northridge to more than 6,000 at branches like Cal State Channel Islands and Monterey Bay. Each campus has its own specific strengths, although in most cases a student's choice of school is dictated by location rather than by academic specialties. Engineering and business are highly competitive majors on all CSU campuses. For those with a wider choice, some of the more distinctive campuses are profiled below:

Cal State Chico (undergraduate enrollment 16,100), which is situated in the beautiful Sacramento Valley but draws heavily from outside a 100-mile radius, is highly selective in its admissions. The on-campus undergraduate life is strong and the social life great.

Cal State Bakersfield (8,000) and **Cal State San Bernardino** (17,700) boast residential villages along with more conventional dorms.

California Polytechnic–San Luis Obispo (20,400) is the most prestigious of the CSU units and thus the toughest one to get into. Strengths include applied branches of such fields as agriculture, architecture, business, and engineering.

Cal State Fresno (21,500), located in the verdant Central Valley, has the only viticulture school in the state outside of UC–Davis. Undergraduates can even do research and work in the school winery. Yosemite, Kings Canyon, and Sequoia national parks are nearby.

San Diego State University (29,300), the balmiest of the campuses, has become highly selective. With a more residential, outdoorsy, and campus-oriented social scene, it appeals more to traditional-age undergraduates. "You could go for the weather alone—some do," says one former student. Unlike other state schools, athletics are very important, and the academic offerings are almost as oriented to the liberal arts as at its neighbor UC–San Diego.

San Jose State University (26,800), strategically located in the heart of the Silicon Valley, boasts strong programs in computer science and engineering (including aerospace engineering) and offers amazing internship opportunities for students right in its backyard.

Another unique opportunity within the system is **Sonoma State**'s (8,600) Hutchins School of Liberal Studies, which allows students to complete their lower-division general education requirements in small seminar-style classes that emphasize critical examination and excellence in written communication.

Humboldt State (8,200) is perched at the top of the state near the Oregon border in the heart of the Redwoods. Its forestry and wildlife departments have national reputations, and the natural sciences are notably rigorous. Students have excellent laboratory facilities in Redwood National Park. In-state students come here to get away from Los Angeles and enjoy the rugged coastline north of San Francisco.

California Maritime Academy (1,100), located 30 miles northeast of San Francisco, specializes in marine transportation, engineering, and maritime technology, and it offers summer cruises on the T.S. Golden Bear.

Cal State Monterey Bay (5,800) is located one mile from the beach and offers an interdisciplinary focus with a global perspective, opportunities for internships, and a unique Capstone Festival featuring the culminating projects of graduating seniors.

UNIVERSITY OF CALIFORNIA (UC)

The UC system boasts 251,700 full-time students, 209,300 faculty and staff, and 1.7 million living alumni. Although one university system, the nine undergraduate UC campuses (UC San Francisco is for upper-division and graduate students) each offer a full range of academic programs and each has its own distinctive character. The most recent addition, UC Merced, opened in 2005 as the first American research university to be founded in the 21st century. While still in its infancy, Merced now has more than 6,800 undergraduates and 500 graduate students and is becoming a viable undergraduate option. Unfortunately, its remote location limits its appeal.

The UC system targets the top 12.5 percent of the state's high school graduates. In-state students graduating in the top 9 percent of their high school class who meet regular admissions standards will be guaranteed admission to the UC system, although not necessarily to the campus of their choice. The 9 percent provision is part of the Eligibility in the Local Context (ELC) plan designed to attract students who might not otherwise consider a UC school, including those who live far from any of the UC campuses. Out-of-state students continue to face very rigorous competition for a limited number of spots. Non-California residents, including international students, accounted for only 10 percent of enrollment in 2016.

In the past few decades, selection procedures for attending a UC school have moved from relying primarily on statistical academic information to a "comprehensive review" that takes into consideration not only coursework and test scores, but also leadership, special talent, and the educational opportunities available to each student. Although letters of recommendation are not required, some campuses are inviting selected students to submit one or two on an optional basis in an effort to better understand their strengths. Students must submit official standardized test scores from either the SAT or the ACT. Whichever the student chooses, scores from all "sittings" should be sent to UC by the testing agency. Admissions readers will then be able to determine the student's "best" scores on each individual section of the test. Subject Tests are no longer required; however, when applying to colleges or majors that are impacted, it can be to the student's benefit to submit Subject Test scores. For example, for engineering, it is highly recommended that students submit scores in Math 2, Chemistry, and/or Physics. Despite state laws that prohibit the university from considering race in admission, the system remains dedicated to achieving a diverse student body. The university offers a number of outreach programs, such as the Educational Opportunity Program, designed to assist low-income or educationally disadvantaged students who have promising academic potential with admissions and support services.

ADMISSIONS PROCEDURES

Applications for both UC and CSU schools must be filed between November 1 and November 30.

To apply to a California State University campus, complete the electronic application available at www.CSUMentor.edu. You choose one campus to complete the first application. Once this application is completed, the data will automatically transfer to each additional campus. The only screen that must be completed per campus is the Enrollment Information screen (the first screen of the application). Students who apply to Cal Poly San Luis Obispo, however, must choose a major and complete additional screening. There is a $55 application fee for each campus.

To apply for admission to the University of California, students complete the electronic application available at www.universityofcalifornia.edu/admissions. Prospective undergraduates may apply to each of the nine undergraduate UC campuses on the application, and students are encouraged to apply broadly to maximize their chances of gaining admission to at least one campus. Officials of each campus to which a student applies review the application using their own separate methodology and criteria. Decisions are thus campus-unique; applying to one school does not have any impact on admission probabilities for a different campus. Applicants are asked to choose "a major and alternate major," but most choose "undecided," especially if they are applying to the College of Letters and Sciences. Once enrolled, students are free to change their minds. These procedures differ from those of the CSU system, where students do apply to a major and must stick with it. There is a $70 application fee for each campus.

Following are profiles of the eight major UC universities.

UC–Berkeley

110 Sproul Hall #5800, Berkeley, CA 94720-5800

Like everything else at Berkeley, the academic offerings at this flagship of flagship universities can be overwhelming. With more than 25,000 undergraduate overachievers crammed into such a small space, it is no wonder that the world-class academic climate is about as intense as you can get at a public university. Don't expect to be on a first-name basis with your professor in Intro Bio.

Website: www.berkeley.edu
Location: City Center
Public
Total Enrollment: 35,960
Undergraduates: 26,622
Male/Female: 48/52
SAT Ranges: CR 610–730,
   M 640–770
ACT Ranges: 29–34
Financial Aid: N/A
Pell Grant: N/A
Expense: Pub $ $ $
Student Loans: 38%
Average Debt: $
Phi Beta Kappa: Yes
Applicants: 78,924
Accepted: 15%
Enrolled: 46%
Grad in 6 Years: 91%
Returning Freshmen: 97%
Academics: ✑ ✑ ✑ ✑ ✑
Social: ☎ ☎ ☎ ☎
Q of L: ★ ★ ★
Admissions: (510) 642-3175
Email Address: N/A

Strong Programs:
Engineering
Architecture

Berkeley. Mention the name, and even down-to-earth students get stars in their eyes. Students who come here want the biggest and best of everything, though sometimes that idealism runs headlong into budget cuts, tuition increases, and housing shortages. Never mind. Berkeley is where the action is. If you want a quick indicator of Berkeley's academic prowess, look no farther than the parking lot. The campus is dotted with spots marked "NL"—spots reserved for resident Nobel laureates. The last time anyone counted, Berkeley boasted 22 of them, more than 400 Guggenheim fellows, and a bevy of Pulitzer Prize recipients, MacArthur fellows, and Fulbright scholars. Is it any wonder that this radical institution of the '60s still maintains the kind of reputation that makes the top private universities take note? The social climate at this mother of UC schools is not as explosive as it once seemed to be, but don't expect anything tame on today's campus. Flower children and granola chompers still abound, as do fledgling Marxists, young Republicans, and body-pierced activists.

Spread across 1,200 scenic acres on a hill overlooking San Francisco Bay, the Berkeley campus is a parklike oasis in a small city. The startlingly wide variety of architectural styles ranges from the stunning classical amphitheater to the modern University Art Museum draped in neon sculpture. Large expanses of grass dot the campus and are just "perfect for playing Frisbee or lying in the sun." The oaks along Strawberry Creek and the eucalyptus grove date back to Berkeley's beginnings nearly 150 years ago. Sproul Plaza, in the heart of the campus, is one of the great people-watching sites of the world.

Of course, Berkeley is not only gorgeous; it's also academically intense. "Everyone was the top student in his or her high school class, so they can't settle for anything

> **"[The campus is] perfect for playing Frisbee or lying in the sun."**

less than number one," says one student. A classmate concedes that "it can be a stressful environment, especially during the first years," and another says bluntly, "Expect very little sleep." Although 60 percent of all undergraduate classes have fewer than 20 students, some introductory courses, particularly in the sciences, have as many as 800, and professors, who must publish or disengage from the university's highly competitive teaching ranks, devote a great deal of time to research. After all, Berkeley has made a large part of its reputation on its research and graduate programs, many of which rank among the best in the nation.

While the undergraduate education is excellent, students take a gamble with the trickle-down theory, which holds out the promise that the intellectual might of those in the ivory towers will drip down to them eventually. As a political science major explains, "This system has allowed me to hear outstanding lectures from amazing professors who write the books we read, while allowing far more personal attention from the graduate-student instructors." Another student opines, "It's better to stand 50 feet from brilliance than five feet from mediocrity." Evidence of such gravitational pull is seen in the promising curricula designed specifically for freshmen and sophomores that include interdisciplinary courses in writing, public speaking, and the history of civilization and an offering of small student seminars (enrollment is limited to 15) taught by regular faculty. Despite these attempts at catering to undergraduates, the sheer number of students at Berkeley makes it difficult to treat each student as an individual. As a result, such things as academic counseling suffer. "Advising? You mean to tell me they have advising here?" asks one student.

Each of Berkeley's six undergraduate colleges or schools has its own set of general education requirements, which are generally not extensive, and a set of breadth requirements, which expose students to disciplines outside of their major. All students, however, must take English composition and literature and one term each of American history and American institutions. Many of these requirements can be fulfilled through Advanced Placement exams in high school. Undergrads also have an American cultures requirement for graduation—an original approach (via courses offered in several departments) to comparative study of ethnic groups in the United States.

"Everyone was the top student in his or her high school class."

Most of the departments at Berkeley are noteworthy, and some are about the best anywhere (like engineering and architecture). Business, sociology, mathematics, physics, chemistry, history, economics, and English are just a handful of the truly dazzling departments. Berkeley offers seven departments and seven interdisciplinary programs in engineering, and the biological sciences department integrates several undergraduate majors in biochemistry, biophysics, botany, zoology, and others into more interdisciplinary programs such as integrative biology and molecular and cell biology. The College of Natural Resources has five departments and participates in five interdisciplinary research centers.

Special programs abound at Berkeley, though it's up to the student to find out about them. Students may study abroad on fellowships at one of 50 centers around the world, or spend time in various internships around the country. If all you want to do is study, the library system, with more than eight million volumes, is one of the largest in the nation and maintains open stacks. The system consists of the main library (Doe-Moffitt) and more than 20 branch libraries, including the Hargrove Music Library. The Coalition for Excellence and Diversity in Mathematics, Science, and Engineering, which provides women and minorities with undergraduate mentors in these fields, is highly regarded.

Although most Berkeley students are California natives, 15 percent come from out of state, and another 14 percent come from foreign nations. Thirty-five percent are Asian American, 2 percent are African American, and 14 percent are Hispanic. The university provides a variety of programs to promote diversity, including Project DARE (Diversity Awareness through Resources and Education), the Center for Racial Education, and a Sexual Harassment Peer Education Program. Despite Berkeley's

(continued)
Business
Sociology
Mathematics
Physics
Chemistry
History

Some introductory courses, particularly in the sciences, have as many as 800 students.

The Coalition for Excellence and Diversity in Mathematics, Science, and Engineering provides women and minorities with mentors.

liberal reputation, the recent trend is away from the legacy of the free speech movement. Business majors and fraternity members outnumber young Communists and peaceniks, though the school does produce a large number of Peace Corps volunteers. Merit scholarships averaging $5,637 are awarded to qualified students, and athletic scholarships are offered too. The Berkeley Middle Class Access Plan, a program for families whose gross income ranges from $80,000 to $150,000 annually, caps the contribution parents make toward the total annual cost of attendance at a maximum of 15 percent of their total income. The plan applies to California residents only.

Berkeley's highly prized residence halls have room for only 26 percent of the students, and new students receive housing priority. After that, the Cal Rentals is a good resource for finding an apartment in town. Many students live a couple of miles off campus, where "apartments are cheaper," says one student. A number of student-housing projects have opened in recent years, offering a variety of rooms in low-rise and high-rise settings. In the absence of a mandatory meal plan, everybody eats "wherever and whenever they wish," including in the residence halls.

> "This system has allowed me to hear outstanding lectures from amazing professors who write the books we read."

If the housing shortage gets you down, the beautiful California weather will probably take your mind off it, as will the never-ending social opportunities. "Social life at UC–Berkeley is killer!" exclaims one geography major. More than 1,200 student clubs and groups are registered on campus, which ensures that there is an outlet for just about any interest and that no one group will ever dominate campus life. Greek life has become more popular, with 10 percent of the men and 10 percent of the women in a fraternity or sorority. Weekends are generally spent in Berkeley, hanging out at the many bookstores, coffeehouses, and sidewalk cafés, heading to a fraternity or sorority party, or taking advantage of the many events right on campus. Berkeley is a quintessential college town ("kind of a crazy little town," says one anthropology major), and of course, there's always the people-watching; where else can an individual meet people trying to convert pedestrians to strange New Age religions or revolutionary political causes on every street corner? Nearby Telegraph Avenue is famous (notorious?) for such antics every weekend.

> *Despite Berkeley's liberal reputation, business majors and fraternity members outnumber young Communists and peaceniks.*

Many students use the weekend to catch up on studying, but when they want to get away, the BART public transportation system provides easy access to San Francisco, by far one of the most pleasant cities in the world and a cultural and countercultural mecca. The Bay Area boasts myriad professional sports teams, including the Golden State Warriors, the Oakland A's, the San Francisco 49ers, and the San Francisco Giants. From opera to camping, San Francisco has a wide variety of activities to offer. Get access to a car, and you can hike in Yosemite National Park, ski and gamble in Nevada, taste wine in the Napa Valley, or visit the aquarium at Monterey. But be advised that a car is only an asset when you want to go out of town—students warn that parking in Berkeley is difficult, to say the least.

> "At Berkeley, it is worse to be dull than odd."

Division I varsity athletics have always been important here, with strengths in the men's gymnastics and crew teams. A surge in popularity for the Golden Bears basketball team probably has to do with its great performance in the Pac-12. And just about everyone turns out for the football team's "Big Game," where the favorite activity on the home side of the bleachers is bad-mouthing the rival school to the south: Stanford. Intramurals are popular, and the personal fitness craze is fed by an extensive recreational facility and gorgeous weather year-round. Students are also reviving an old tradition whereby they hike up Charter Hill and paint the giant "C" their class color.

The common denominator in the Berkeley community is academic motivation, along with the self-reliance that emerges from trying to make your mark among

Overlaps

UC–Davis, UCLA, UC–San Diego, Harvard, Stanford

upward of 25,000 peers. Beyond that, the diversity of town and campus makes an extraordinarily free and exciting college environment for almost anyone. "It makes one feel free to dress, say, think, or do anything and not be chastised for being unorthodox," explains a student. "At Berkeley, it is worse to be dull than odd."

If You Apply To ➢   **Berkeley:** Regular decision: Nov. 30. Financial aid: Mar. 2. Housing: May 25. Application fee: $70. No campus or alumni interviews. SATs (with essay) or ACTs (with writing): required. Subject Tests: recommended for chemistry and engineering applicants. No letters of recommendation. Essay: required. Two pieces of writing limited to 1,000 words. Apply to a particular college, school, or program. Application includes optional question about gender/sexual identity.

UC–Davis

178 Mrak Hall, Davis, CA 95616

The closest thing to a cow college in the UC system, but with a cultured, upscale feel. Premed, prevet, food science—you name it. If the subject lives and breathes, you can study it here. A small-town alternative to the bright lights of UC–Berkeley and UCLA. As is often true at science-oriented schools, the work is hard.

At the University of California–Davis, environmental science and most everything that has to do with animals, agriculture, or biological science is noteworthy. The Aggies' cup truly runneth over. Originally developed as the University of California Farm, the campus maintains its sprawling, verdant beauty, replete with native and imported forestry, charming bike paths, and mooing cows. But lest you assume this environmentally oriented university is full of quaint country folk right out of *American Gothic*, think again. UC–Davis has become an international leader in the agricultural, biological, biotechnical, and veterinary sciences.

Located 20 miles west of Sacramento and 73 miles north of San Francisco, the 6,000-acre campus is located along the Capitol Corridor, skirting the Sacramento–San Joaquin Delta watershed. It features nearly 1,000 buildings with a blend of architectural styles, from traditional dairy barn to modern concrete. The hub of the university is a central area known as the Quad, one of many grassy open spaces on campus. Recent construction includes Tercero North, a LEED Platinum residence hall composed of seven buildings and a lecture hall.

> "[UC–Davis is] the number 1 choice for any prevet."

General education requirements stipulate that all students take courses in three broad areas: topical breadth, social-cultural diversity, and writing experience. These areas include courses in the arts and humanities, science and engineering, and the social sciences. Students may elect to take a general education theme option, sets of general education courses that share a common intellectual theme.

Biological sciences, economics, and psychology are among the campus's most popular majors. Animal science and engineering are strong departments, and the botany program is one of the best in the country. The school is "the number 1 choice for any prevet," and it's great for premeds too. The food science major is also stellar and not for the faint of heart or those afraid of chemistry. It was Davis food scientists who gave us the square tomato (better for packing into boxes), as well as more useful things such as the method for creating orange juice concentrate. UC–Davis recently launched a World Food Center dedicated to innovating food production methods for improved human health and environmental sustainability. Studio art, boasting several internationally known artists, is also among the top in

Website: www.ucdavis.edu
Location: Small City
Public
Total Enrollment: 34,430
Undergraduates: 27,825
Male/Female: 41/59
SAT Ranges: CR 510–630, M 560–710
ACT Ranges: 24–30
Financial Aid: 75%
Pell Grant: 34%
Expense: Pub $ $ $ $
Student Loans: 56%
Average Debt: $
Phi Beta Kappa: Yes
Applicants: 64,510
Accepted: 38%
Enrolled: 22%
Grad in 6 Years: 85%
Returning Freshmen: 92%
Academics: ✑ ✑ ✑ ✑
Social: ☎ ☎ ☎
Q of L: ★ ★ ★ ★
Admissions: (530) 752-2971
Email Address: undergraduate admissions@ucdavis.edu

Strong Programs:
Biological Sciences
Economics

the nation. The Interdisciplinary Electronics Arts Lab allows students to create electronically based productions by integrating photography, video, digital editing, and the Internet. Film studies and exercise biology have been dropped, while marine and coastal science, global disease biology, and sustainable environmental design have been added.

"Academics are fairly intense, yet the students are positive and collaborative," says an economics major. Many introductory courses are quite large, and 27 percent of all classes have more than 50 students, but UC–Davis also offers 40 small freshman seminars taught by the best instructors. The quality of teaching is generally high, according to students, and although some professors seem to prefer to prioritize their research, most make themselves available outside of class. "Most of the teachers I have had were very high quality. Many would come in on weekends to offer study sessions and review sessions, despite the fact that they were married and had children," says one junior.

Faculty members here are expected to do top-level research as well as teach, and the two missions are readily blended when undergraduate students contribute to first-class research groups as paid technicians or volunteer interns. The University Honors Program is for academically talented first-year and transfer students who want to enhance their education through special courses. Study abroad options include more than 150 host institutions in 35 countries. "You can study abroad essentially wherever your heart desires for as short as one month or upwards of a year," cheers one senior, and 18 percent of students do just that. UC–Davis also offers the innovative UC Center Sacramento and the Washington Program, which give undergraduates academic credits for courses and internships in state and federal governments, respectively.

> "Academics are fairly intense, yet the students are positive and collaborative."

"Our student body is made up of very sharp, driven, yet somehow still genuinely kind folks," observes one senior. Eighty-five percent of undergraduates hail from California, and 11 percent come from abroad. African Americans account for 2 percent of the students, Asian Americans 32 percent, and Hispanics 19 percent. Thirty-four percent of freshmen are eligible for Pell Grants. In its pledge to foster awareness of diversity issues, the university has an Office of Campus Diversity and a Cross-Cultural Center. Campus hot topics include fair labor practices and political correctness. Davis awards merit scholarships averaging $5,675 and there are 255 athletic awards in 23 sports.

UC–Davis recently launched a World Food Center dedicated to innovating food production methods.

Only 18 percent of undergraduates live on campus, although virtually all freshmen choose to do so. Campus housing is secure, well maintained, and includes a number of living/learning community options. "Dorms are really nice and new and air-conditioned. Housing is guaranteed the first two years," a student says. Six different meal plans for the dining halls are available, and one student says, "Healthy eating is very important, and they have a simple system to tell you if something is a good or bad choice. Each item's description is followed by anywhere between zero and four happy apple faces to tell you how good it is for you." A variety of nearby eating establishments serve the student clientele as well (no word on whether or not they also employ the "happy apple face" system).

> "You can study abroad essentially wherever your heart desires."

"There are many ways to be involved socially," says one student. "UC–Davis has a great mix of academics and social life." Active drama and music departments provide frequent entertainment, and there is plenty of room for homegrown talent in the Coffee House, which offers mellow live entertainment and poetry readings on a regular basis. The 1,800-seat Mondavi Center for the Performing Arts features international and local groups. There are more than 700 student clubs, and fraternities and sororities attract 7 percent of the men and 10 percent of the women. Alcohol is allowed in the dorms for those 21 and over; those too young to imbibe have trouble finding booze, unless it's supplied by peers. Major annual social events include the BUZZ (a welcome event for students); Picnic Day, in which alumni join current students in a massive outdoor shindig; nearly three months of cultural celebrations every spring; and the Whole Earth Festival, "an earthy, tie-dyed sort of event" in celebration of Mother Earth. Health and energy consciousness runs high here, and bicycles are the main form of transportation across the incredible 100 miles of bike paths that crisscross the campus and environs. "Bicycles are the norm at Davis. Don't come without one," advises one psych major. The university has encouraged environmental awareness by sponsoring solar energy projects and promoting such novelties as contests between residence halls for the lowest heating and electric bills.

Davis has encouraged environmental awareness by promoting contests between residence halls for the lowest heating and electric bills.

In between quizzes and cram sessions, the surrounding communities offer a welcome change of pace. With its tree-lined streets and quiet nights, the city of Davis itself is small but offers enough restaurants, activities, and entertainment to keep those who want to stay close to campus happy. The relationship between the college and town is one of unusual cooperation (partly because the students, who make up half the population, are a significant voting bloc in local elections). A car can come in handy if you are looking for an urban night out in Sacramento (20 minutes) or a big-name show in San Francisco (a little more than an hour). Undergrads who lack wheels of their own can get around town for free on the student-run Unitrans bus system. Beaches are a two-hour drive from the campus, and the ski slopes and hiking trails of Lake Tahoe and the Sierra Nevada mountains are a little closer.

"Bicycles are the norm at Davis. Don't come without one."

Several years ago, the university's varsity athletic teams, the UC–Davis Aggies, made the jump to Division I, where they compete in the Big West Conference along with fellow UC campuses Irvine, Riverside, and Santa Barbara. Women's swimming and diving and track and field are recent conference champions, and other solid teams include men's and women's basketball and golf, women's gymnastics, and men's tennis. The annual Causeway Classic football game against rival Sacramento State stirs passions, but UC–Davis students tend to prefer being participants rather than spectators; each year nearly 10,000 of them play in more than 70 club and intramural sports. Given the Mediterranean climate, outdoor activities are the most popular, and almost everyone does something athletic—jogging, softball, tennis, swimming, or Frisbee—if only to break up the monotony of their studies with a different kind of competition.

Each year nearly 10,000 students play in more than 70 club and intramural sports.

Proud of its small-town atmosphere, UC–Davis is not for the lazy or faint of heart. As one student says, "There's no free ride. You are going to have to work for everything you get." And most students get a lot out of their four or more years at UC–Davis. It's the ideal spot to combine high-powered work in science and agriculture with that famous easygoing California lifestyle.

Overlaps

UC–San Diego, UCLA, UC–Irvine, UC–Berkeley, UC–Santa Barbara, UC–Santa Cruz, UC–Riverside, UC–Merced

If You Apply To ➤ **Davis:** Regular decision: Nov. 30. Financial aid: Mar. 2. Application fee: $70. No campus or alumni interviews. SATs (with essay) or ACTs (with writing): required. Subject Tests: optional. No letters of recommendation. Essay: required. Apply to a particular college, school, or program. Application includes optional question about gender/sexual identity.

260 Aldrich Hall, Irvine, CA 92697

Irvine sits in the midst of one of the nation's biggest suburbs, combining funky, modern architecture with perhaps the most conservative student body in the UC system. Premed is the featured attraction, along with various other health-related offerings. Not quite as close to the beach as Santa Barbara—but close enough for students to go there often.

Website: www.uci.edu
Location: Small City
Public
Total Enrollment: 29,904
Undergraduates: 24,851
Male/Female: 46/54
SAT Ranges: CR 490–620,
  M 550–690
ACT Ranges: 21–27
Financial Aid: 76%
Pell Grant: N/A
Expense: Pub $ $ $ $
Student Loans: 59%
Average Debt: $
Phi Beta Kappa: Yes
Applicants: 71,768
Accepted: 39%
Enrolled: 21%
Grad in 6 Years: 87%
Returning Freshmen: 93%
Academics: ✑ ✑ ✑ ✑
Social: ☎ ☎
Q of L: ★ ★ ★
Admissions: (949) 824-6703
Email Address: admissions@
  uci.edu

Strong Programs:
Biological Sciences
Psychology and Social
  Behavior
Business Economics
Political Science
Visual and Performing Arts
Creative Writing
Nursing
Computer Game Science

On the surface, UC–Irvine's clean, contemporary campus appears to be home to students who study diligently in the busy library, wear sensible shoes to biology lab, and resist that double shot of espresso at the local coffeehouse. But that image starts to dissipate as soon as you hear that bizarre noise: "Zot! Zot! Zot!" Then a UCI student explains that "it's the sound that an anteater supposedly makes when it swipes an ant with its tongue." Hey, any school that has a marauding anteater as a mascot can't be completely straitlaced. The university is, however, serious about its reputation as a school with stellar programs in biology and creative writing.

Located in the heart of Orange County and founded in 1965, UCI is among the newest of the UC campuses. While enrollment is up and the administration anticipates further expansion, according to one English major, "It is the perfect size." UCI is liberally supplied with trees and shrubs from all over the world. Futuristic buildings are arranged in a circle around a 19-acre park, "giving it the appearance of a relaxed art school," says one observer. Undergraduates have long quipped that UCI stood for "Under Construction Indefinitely." The Mesa Court Towers, three new first-year residence halls housing 300 students apiece, opened in 2016.

UCI's general education requirements involve three courses each in writing, science and technology, social and behavioral sciences, and arts and humanities. Students also fulfill requirements in foreign language; quantitative, symbolic, and computational reasoning; multicultural studies; and international/global issues. Students may choose from more than 80 majors, and the Campuswide Honors Program is available for top students; several individual departments offer honors programs as well.

A "premed mentality" reigns at Irvine, since the School of Biological Sciences is the best and most competitive academic division; the engineering school is quite competitive too. The Center for Health Sciences focuses on five areas of research: neuroscience, genetics, cancer, infectious diseases, and aging. The university also houses the Reeve-Irvine Research Center, which supports the study of spinal cord trauma and disease with emphasis on finding a cure. After biology, the most popular majors are psychology and social behavior, business economics, and political science. The Claire Trevor School of Arts offers nationally ranked programs in dance, drama, music, studio art, and music theater, and the school's Beall Center for Art and Technology enables students to explore the relationship between digital technology and the arts and sciences. The popular, interdisciplinary School of Social Ecology offers courses combining criminology, environmental and legal studies, and psychology and social behavior, and strongly emphasizes faculty/student relationships. Languages are strong at UCI, and a fiction-writing program is gaining national recognition. Other programs of note include majors in nursing, computer game science, and pharmaceutical sciences.

> **"[Dorms are] exceptional compared to the high-rise dormitories of other institutions."**

Like most of the other UC campuses, UCI is on a 10-week quarter system, so the pace is fast and furious. "UCI is fairly competitive, and the courses are moderately rigorous," says a junior, but students are also said to be "surprisingly cooperative."

Getting into required classes can be difficult at times, and "Graduate students teach lower-division writing courses," says one student, adding that "most classes are overcrowded, leaving little room for personal attention." Even so, 58 percent of undergraduate classes enroll fewer than 20 students.

Eighty-one percent of undergraduates are in-staters, the majority from Southern California and many of those from wealthy Orange County—although an impressive 51 percent of incoming freshmen are first-generation college students. Sixteen percent hail from foreign countries. The students are in general "much more conservative than at the other UC campuses," says one applied math major. Minorities account for nearly two-thirds of the student body, with Asian Americans comprising 37 percent, African Americans 2 percent, and Hispanics 25 percent. One senior notes, "Cultural groups seem to segregate from each other," although several initiatives and events, including the Cross-Cultural Center, the Community Roots Festival, the Dr. Martin Luther King Jr. Symposium, and the Deconstruction Zone Series, are designed to educate and engage the campus community in diversity, social justice, and cultural wellness. Merit scholarships averaging $8,242 are awarded annually, as are 114 athletic awards.

An impressive 51 percent of incoming freshmen are first-generation college students.

Forty-one percent of undergraduates live on campus. Condominium-style dorms, both single sex and co-ed, are "exceptional compared to the high-rise dormitories of other institutions," says one senior. Others agree that the homey campus dwellings provide a good experience for freshmen, though finding a room can be a challenge. "If you really want on-campus housing," warns a student, "you need to make sure you meet the deadlines." Although freshmen are guaranteed on-campus housing for two years, 21 percent of them choose to live off campus, which can create a slight commuter-school atmosphere. Most upperclassmen opt for themed housing, fraternity and sorority houses, or off-campus dwellings, often on the beach.

UCI has launched an official eSports program for organized, multiplayer video game competitions, and its coaching staff is actively recruiting top gamers.

One student remarks, "You have to find the social life on this campus. It won't find you." Still, the Greek scene is vigorous, attracting 9 percent of UCI men and 9 percent of the women. There are 18 fraternities and 18 sororities, and each has something going on every weekend. UCI is a dry campus and students say finding a drink on campus without proper ID is difficult. The one event that brings everybody out is the daylong Wayzgoose, a student-run festival featuring live performances, free food, carnival games and rides, and a car show.

But if life on campus is slow, beyond it is not. That's because the campus is located just 50 miles from L.A., five miles from the beach, and a little more than an hour from the ski slopes. Catalina Island, with beaches and hiking trails, is a quick boat trip off Newport Harbor; Mexico is two hours away. While some students treasure the quiet setting of Irvine,

"You have to find the social life on this campus. It won't find you."

others lament its "lackluster, homogeneous communities." Notes one student, "UCI and the city of Irvine seem like completely different entities; the former is slightly liberal while the latter is ultraconservative."

UCI fields 20 Division I Anteater athletic teams. Tennis and cross-country are perennial Big West powerhouses, while men's volleyball and water polo are nationally ranked. There is no football team, but intramurals are extremely popular, as is the state-of-the-art campus recreation center. UCI has also launched an official eSports program—the first of its kind at a public research university—for organized, multiplayer video game competitions, and its coaching staff is actively recruiting top gamers.

What lures students to UCI is its top-name professors, innovative academic programs, and the chance to be a part of its cutting-edge research. For those who come here prepared to keep their heads buried in a book for a few years, the reward will be an exceptional education.

Overlaps

UC–Berkeley, UC–Davis, UC–Merced, UCLA, UC–Riverside, UC–San Diego, UC–Santa Barbara, UC–Santa Cruz

Irvine: Regular decision: Nov. 30. Financial aid: Mar. 2. Application fee: $70. No campus or alumni interviews. SATs (with essay) or ACTs (with writing): required. Subject Tests: recommended. No letters of recommendation. Essay: required. Apply to a particular college, school, or program. Music and dance applicants must audition. Application includes optional question about gender/sexual identity.

UC–Los Angeles

1147 Murphy Hall, Box 951436, Los Angeles, CA 90095

Tucked into exclusive Beverly Hills with the beach, the mountains, and chic Hollywood hangouts all within easy reach. The adjacent town of Westwood is an ideal student hangout. Practically everything is offered here, but the programs in arts and media are some of the best in the world. More conservative than Berkeley and nearly as difficult to get into.

Website: www.ucla.edu
Location: City Center
Public
Total Enrollment: 40,529
Undergraduates: 29,004
Male/Female: 44/56
SAT Ranges: CR 580–710, M 610–760
ACT Ranges: 25–33
Financial Aid: 55%
Pell Grant: 30%
Expense: Pub $ $ $
Student Loans: 46%
Average Debt: $
Phi Beta Kappa: No
Applicants: 92,728
Accepted: 17%
Enrolled: 35%
Grad in 6 Years: 91%
Returning Freshmen: 96%
Academics: ✍ ✍ ✍ ✍ ✍
Social: ☎ ☎ ☎
Q of L: ★ ★ ★
Admissions: (310) 825-3101
Email Address:
www.admissions.ucla.edu
/contactus.htm

Strong Programs:
Political Science
Psychology
Economics
Sociology
Engineering

With four Nobel Prizes awarded to alumni and faculty in the past six years, you might think UCLA is an intellectual brain trust. Or with a long list of well-known and highly accomplished alumni in the arts, film, and sports, maybe UCLA is some sort of incubator for truly talented and gifted people. Well, UCLA is all that and more. A superb faculty, a reputation for outstanding academics, and a powerful athletics program make this university the ultimate place to study.

UCLA's prime location—sandwiched between two glamorous neighborhoods (Beverly Hills and Bel Air) and a short drive from the beach, Hollywood, the Sunset Strip, and downtown Los Angeles—makes it appealing for students who want more from their college experience than going to class. The beautifully landscaped, 419-acre campus features a range of architectural styles, with Romanesque/Italian Renaissance as the dominant motif, providing only one of a number of reasons students enjoy staying on campus. A wealth of gardens—botanical, Japanese, and sculpture—add a touch of quiet elegance. The campus is philosophically divided into North and South. North attracts more liberal arts aficionados, while those in math and science tend to favor South. Newer construction includes a bevy of student housing options that offer a total of more than 1,800 beds.

First-year students are encouraged to participate in a three-day summer orientation that provides workshops, counseling, an introduction to the campus and community, and a chance to register for classes. In Fall Quarter, freshmen can begin a yearlong cluster of interdisciplinary courses on topics such as Environment and Sustainability or enroll in small-group seminars such as Student Activism from the Sixties to Present. To graduate, first-year students are required to take (or test out of) quantitative reasoning and English composition courses. Lab science and a language requirement are necessary for a liberal arts degree, and all students must take a course on diversity. Concerned that too many majors have been requiring too little from students, the university is now encouraging departments to require capstone projects in which students must use the methodological training of their discipline and integrate what they have learned across topics and fields.

Strong programs abound at UCLA, and many are considered among the best in the nation. UCLA is well established in the STEM fields; the Henry Samueli

> "We are spoiled by incredible faculty at UCLA—top researchers in their field and amazing lecturers."

School of Engineering and Applied Science is highly regarded and sets the tone on campus. The biological sciences are strong, and the math and chemistry departments boast a Fields medalist and a Nobel Prize winner among the faculty. The School of Theater, Film, and Television is first-rate, and its students have the opportunity to study in Verona, Italy, with the Theater Overseas program. The popular music school offers a course in jazz studies and has added legends Herbie Hancock and Wayne Shorter to its distinguished faculty. Political science, psychology, economics, and sociology enroll the most students. Research opportunities in the sciences are plentiful, and the university ranks seventh in the nation in federal funding for research. UCLA's Ocean Discovery Center on the Santa Monica Pier is an innovative, hands-on ocean classroom for both students and the public.

(continued)

Biological Sciences
Theater
Music

UCLA gets more applications than any other college in the country, and the academic environment is extremely intense and competitive. Although 51 percent of undergraduate classes have fewer than 20 students, required core classes, usually taken in the first two years, can be as large as 300 to 400 people, with smaller sections. Savvy students come to UCLA with advanced courses from high school and test out of intro courses. The faculty is impressive, but students warn that some are more interested in their research. Still, a political science major says, "We are spoiled by incredible faculty at UCLA—top researchers in their field and amazing lecturers." Faculty-led study abroad programs are popular, and "financial aid travels with you," according to a junior.

The campus is philosophically divided into North (liberal arts) and South (math and science).

"UCLA is a school of leaders and optimists—people who truly believe they can, and will, change the world," says a global studies major. Seventy-seven percent of undergraduates are California residents, and 12 percent are international. Asian Americans account for 29 percent of UCLA's student population, Hispanics 21 percent, and African Americans 3 percent. UCLA is one of the few universities in the nation with a gay fraternity and a lesbian sorority, and students

"UCLA is a school of leaders and optimists—people who truly believe they can, and will, change the world."

are active in advocating for social justice issues. Among major research universities, UCLA has the highest number of students receiving federal financial aid. Thirty percent of freshmen qualify for Pell Grants. Merit scholarships are also available, averaging more than $4,500 each, as well as athletic scholarships in 21 sports.

Forty-five percent of undergraduates, and almost all freshmen, live on campus in the residential area known as "the Hill"; freshmen are guaranteed three consecutive years of university housing. "The dorms are a fun place to make friends and go to campus-sponsored events," a student says. Residential learning communities with a faculty member in residence are an option for those who wish to bond with classmates over shared interests. Fifteen dining halls, restaurants, and snack bars serve meals that students rave about. "I have friends who attend other universities who will visit me just so they can eat UCLA's food," says a senior. UCLA has its own police department that keeps the campus safe, and a junior says, "Our Title IX officer is actively working to spread awareness [of sexual assault] and connect those affected with the right resources."

UCLA gets more applications than any other college in the country.

Consistent with the gargantuan size of UCLA, there is no shortage of social options on campus. "Social life is bustling," cheers a junior. "What I love about UCLA is that a lot of social things happen on campus—you always feel like you are a part of something greater because so many students participate in activities going on." Fifteen percent of men and fifteen percent of women join one of UCLA's nearly 60 fraternities and sororities, and a senior says Greek life "is a fun way to get involved and meet people, but it does not monopolize social life." The university's alcohol policy is similar to that of other UC schools—open consumption is a no-no. Top-name entertainers, political figures, and speakers of all kinds come to the campus; film and theater presentations are frequent, and the air is thick with live music. Spring Sing, a campuswide student talent show presided over by celebrity judges, is a favorite tradition. Volunteer Day is a big deal here too, and attracts more than 8,000 student volunteers annually.

With all the attractions of the City of Angels at its doorstep, the campus tends to empty out on the weekends (except when the Bruins football team has a home game). The hopping Westwood neighborhood, which borders the university, has at least 15 movie theaters and scores of restaurants, but the shops cater to the upper class. "There's nowhere to dance and only two bars, but a lot of coffee and cheap food," a junior says. The beach is five miles away, and the mountains are only a short drive. Although public transportation is cheap, it's also relatively inconvenient (although new bus routes have eased this somewhat). The easiest solution is to live close to campus and ride a bike.

UCLA has won a staggering number of collegiate championships, including more than 110 NCAA Division I team championships and more than 130 total national championships. The most recent championships include men's water polo, baseball, and women's soccer and tennis. UCLA has won more than 260 Olympic medals and has won a gold medal in every Olympics

"You always feel like you are a part of something greater because so many students participate in activities."

in which the U.S. has competed since 1932. The men's football and basketball teams are the undeniable crowd pleasers, although beating crosstown rival USC is the name of the game in any sport. UCLA fans regard their intra-city rivalry with enthusiasm. Beat USC Week, the week leading up to the football game between the two, is an event in itself, featuring a bonfire, concert, and blood drive. About a third of students compete in club and intramural sports.

"Although everyone is striving for excellence, UCLA allows everyone to experience *life*," muses a junior. "That means taking time to prepare for exams and do it well, while also making time to play beach volleyball at Sunset Rec with all of your friends." A leading research center, 200 fields of study, distinguished faculty members, and outstanding athletics make UCLA one of the most prestigious universities in the nation. And despite the large size, students still feel they are part of a tight-knit community bubbling with Bruin pride.

Overlaps

UC–Berkeley, UC–San Diego, Stanford, University of Southern California, UC–Irvine, UC–Davis, UC–Santa Barbara, Harvard

If You Apply To ➤ **UCLA:** Regular decision: Nov. 30. Financial aid: Mar. 2. Application fee: $70. No campus or alumni interviews. SATs (with essay) or ACTs (with writing): required. Subject Tests: optional. No letters of recommendation. Essay: required. Two pieces of writing limited to 1,000 words. Apply to a particular college, school, or program. Application includes optional question about gender/sexual identity.

UC–Riverside

Riverside, CA 92521

Most diverse UC school and the easiest to get into. Social life is relatively tame, since so many of the students commute. While some complain of a lack of nightlife in Riverside, they readily agree that activities on campus make up for it. Returning students are welcomed back every year with a campuswide block party, and Spring Splash and HEAT concerts bring in hot bands.

Lacking the big-name reputation and booming athletic programs of the other UC schools, UC–Riverside has chosen to place its emphasis on something that not all schools consider to be an important priority: the student. Riverside offers one of the lowest student/faculty ratios in the UC system, strong programs with personalized attention, and a diverse academic community that seems to have been forgotten at other UC schools. "Students are well taken care of and get personal attention," says one satisfied senior. Though part of the UC system, UC–Riverside is a breed apart.

Located 60 miles east of Los Angeles, UCR is surrounded by mountains on the outskirts of the city of Riverside. The beautifully landscaped, 1,200-acre campus consists of mainly modern architecture, with a 160-foot bell tower (with a 48-bell carillon) marking its center. Wide lawns and clusters of oaks create "a veritable botanical garden," where students and faculty enjoy relaxing between classes. Acres of citrus groves form a half-circle on the outer edges of campus and perfume the air. Additional facilities include a 77,000-square-foot materials science and engineering building and the School of Medicine Research Building.

All students are required to meet extensive "breadth requirements" that include courses in English composition, natural sciences and math, humanities, and social sciences. Some majors include a foreign language requirement. The campus libraries have an impressive 2.5 million volumes, an interlibrary loan system within the UC system, and vast electronic databases. A specialized research collection in science fiction is world-class. UCR's California Museum of Photography, located in downtown Riverside and available on the Web, has grown in stature.

Decades ago, researchers at the Citrus Experiment Station in Riverside perfected the growing methods for the imported navel orange, making discoveries to protect the fruit from disease and pests and saving California's citrus industry. Riverside continues to excel in plant biology and entomology. But the campus has grown since its founding in 1954 to include excellent programs in engineering, natural sciences, social sciences, humanities, the arts,

> **"Students are well taken care of and get personal attention."**

business, and education. The biomedical sciences program is UCR's most prestigious and demanding course of study, and its most successful students can earn a B.S./M.D. in partnership with the medical school at UCLA. The engineering program is also quite selective, more so than the campus as a whole, which generally accepts students who are ranked in the top 12 percent of the state's high school graduates. One of the few undergraduate environmental engineering programs is at UCR, as is an undergraduate program in creative writing.

Students say the academic climate is cooperative rather than competitive. "Instead of being super competitive," says a student, "I see more students working together to get the job done." State funding woes have not gone unnoticed on campus. "We've lost a lot of core classes and financial aid does not offer as much," grumbles one student. Budget cuts have caused class sizes to rise over the years as well, and 34 percent of undergraduate classes have more than 50 students. Research is an institutional priority for faculty, so the quality of instruction can vary dramatically from "awful to fantastic," according to one sophomore. Still, UCR has a tradition of undergraduate and faculty interaction, with a wide range of undergraduate research grants available during the academic year. This may be why one in six graduates goes on to get a Ph.D. The University Honors Program offers exceptional students further academic challenges, in addition to extracurricular activities and special seminars for freshmen. Talented student singers, dancers, and actors can earn stipends for performing in the community through an arts outreach program funded by the Maxwell H. Gluck Foundation. Short-term, faculty-led, summer study abroad options are popular, and through the UC system, students have access to more than 120 international programs.

Website: www.ucr.edu
Location: Small City
Public
Total Enrollment: 21,171
Undergraduates: 18,269
Male/Female: 47/53
SAT Ranges: CR 500–600, M 520–650
ACT Ranges: 22–28
Financial Aid: 81%
Pell Grant: 53%
Expense: Pub $ $ $ $
Student Loans: 69%
Average Debt: $
Phi Beta Kappa: Yes
Applicants: 38,505
Accepted: 56%
Enrolled: 19%
Grad in 6 Years: 69%
Returning Freshmen: 91%
Academics: ✐ ✐ ✐ ½
Social: ☎ ☎
Q of L: ★ ★ ★
Admissions: (951) 827-3411
Email Address: admissions@ucr.edu

Strong Programs:
Biomedical Sciences
Engineering
Plant Biology
Entomology
Business Administration
Psychology
Sociology
Environmental Engineering

A hefty 53 percent of first-time freshmen receive Pell Grants.

Ninety-four percent of UCR undergraduates are from California, mainly L.A., Riverside, San Bernardino, and Orange County; 3 percent are international.

"Instead of being super competitive, I see more students working together to get the job done."

"UCR is one of the most diverse universities in the nation," a political science major says. "Because of this, there is a wide range of students at UCR that make a blended environment of different cultures, nationalities, and social statuses." Indeed, Asian Americans account for 36 percent of the students, Hispanics 38 percent, and African Americans 4 percent. A hefty 53 percent of first-time freshmen receive Pell Grants. As part of the UC commitment to diversity, Riverside supports centers for various ethnicities, for women, and for LGBTQ students. Numerous merit scholarships averaging $4,903 are doled out every year, as well as athletic scholarships.

Housing is relatively easy to obtain, but the quality varies greatly. "While West Lothian looks like a prison, Pentland Hills is like a resort," says one student. Thirty-five percent of the students live in the dorms, where freshmen are guaranteed a spot. Campus dining is generally described as adequate. "I could eat their tater tots forever," gushes one student. Students say they feel safe on campus; security measures include an escort service and patrolling security officers.

Fraternities and sororities attract 6 percent of the men and 10 percent of the women. The groups usually hold campuswide parties once a quarter. "There is always something going on, whether it be a concert, lecture, or sorority/fraternity party," one sophomore says. Campus hangouts, including the Barn, have live bands and comedy nights, and a cultural arts program brings professional shows to campus. Every Wednesday the campus can enjoy a "nooner," where live bands play during lunch. University Village is a commercial center offering a movie theater, restaurants, and an arcade right on the edge of campus. Riverside weather is temperate except during the summer months, when the heat and haze combine to make a trip to the ocean look really inviting. The coast is only about 45 minutes by freeway and the desert is an hour east. Big Bear and numerous ski resorts are also within an hour's drive.

"UCR has grown immensely over the past few years."

The Riverside Highlanders compete in Division I, and men's and women's cross-country, track and field, men's soccer, and women's basketball are especially competitive. A recreational program in men's and women's karate has turned out national champions. A student recreation center offers a health-club atmosphere with sand volleyball, weight and workout machines, and intramural leagues.

All in all, Riverside is growing and improving, albeit not without some growing pains, including rising tuition and living costs. Although smaller than some sister UC campuses, it offers more personal attention to its students. UCR is fast becoming a nationally recognized research institution, from which students surely will benefit. "UCR has grown immensely over the past few years," one sophomore says. "The emphasis for the future is to establish a name for UCR, to let the nation know what a wonderful university this is."

Every Wednesday the campus can enjoy a "nooner," where live bands play during lunch.

Overlaps

UC–Berkeley, UC–Davis, UC–Irvine, UCLA, UC–San Diego, UC–Santa Barbara, UC–Santa Cruz, California State University–Long Beach

If You Apply To ➤ **Riverside:** Regular decision: Nov. 30. Financial aid: Mar. 2. Application fee: $70. No campus or alumni interviews. SATs (with essay) or ACTs (with writing): required. Subject Tests: optional. No letters of recommendation. Essay: required. Apply to a particular college, school, or program. Application includes optional question about gender/sexual identity.

9500 Gilman Drive, MC 0021, La Jolla, CA 92093

Applications have doubled in the past 10 years at this seaside paradise. UC–San Diego now rivals better-known Berkeley and UCLA as the Cal campus of choice for top students. Six undergraduate colleges break the university down to a more manageable size. Best known for science, engineering, and the famed Scripps Institution of Oceanography.

Some say that looking good is better than feeling good, but at UC–San Diego, they're doing a lot of both. Set against the serene beauty of La Jolla's beaches, students catch as much relaxation time as they do study time. But it's not all fun and games around this campus. The research star of the UC system, San Diego's faculty rates high nationally among public institutions in science productivity. And within each of the six undergraduate colleges, a system that offers undergraduates more intimate settings, students are honing their minds with the classics and the cutting edge in academics. Sure, San Diegans tend to be more mellow than the average Southern Californian, and the students here follow suit. But beneath the tanned foreheads and bright smiles, UC–San Diego is bubbling with intellectual energy and the healthy desire to be at the top of the UC system.

San Diego's tree-lined campus sits high on a bluff overlooking the Pacific in the seaside resort of La Jolla. The predominant architectural theme is contemporary, with a few out-of-the-ordinary structures, including a library that looks like an inverted pyramid. Another tinge of the postmodern is the nation's largest neon sculpture, which wraps around one of the high-rise academic buildings and consists of seven-foot-tall letters that spell out the seven virtues superimposed over the seven vices.

Prospective freshmen apply to UC–San Diego—the admissions requirements are identical for each college—but students must indicate their college preference. UC–San Diego's six undergraduate colleges have their own sets of general education requirements, their own personalities, and differing ideals on which they are based. Revelle College, the oldest, is the most rigorous and mandates that students become equally acquainted with a certain level of coursework in the humanities, sciences, and social sciences, as well as fulfill a language requirement. Muir allows more flexibility in the distribution of requirements. Thurgood Marshall College was founded to emphasize and encourage social awareness. Like

> "You end up teaching a lot of the material to yourself."

Revelle, it places equal weight on sciences, social sciences, and humanities, but it also stresses a liberal arts education based on "an examination of the human condition in a multicultural society." Warren has developed a highly organized internship program that gives its undergraduates more practical experience than the others do. Eleanor Roosevelt College devotes its curriculum to international and cross-cultural studies. Sixth College focuses on art, culture, and technology. Its goal is to graduate multicultural students who can work collaboratively and enjoy working in their communities.

UC–San Diego's programs in science, engineering, and computer science have global reputations and are "not for the faint of heart," says one student. Engineering is particularly competitive, and a limit to the number of students who can declare this major means acceptance into the major usually requires an A average and top test scores in entry-level courses. The Scripps Institution of Oceanography is also excellent, due to the university's advantageous location. Biology, human biology,

Website: www.ucsd.edu
Location: Suburban
Public
Total Enrollment: 31,615
Undergraduates: 26,195
Male/Female: 52/48
SAT Ranges: CR 580–680, M 630–770
ACT Ranges: 27–32
Financial Aid: 85%
Pell Grant: N/A
Expense: Pub $ $ $ $
Student Loans: 60%
Average Debt: $
Phi Beta Kappa: Yes
Applicants: 78,056
Accepted: 34%
Enrolled: 20%
Grad in 6 Years: 86%
Returning Freshmen: 95%
Academics: 🐜 🐜 🐜 🐜 🐜
Social: ☎ ☎ ☎
Q of L: ★ ★ ★ ★
Admissions: (858) 534-4831
Email Address: admissionsreply@ucsd.edu

Strong Programs:
Engineering
Computer Science
Marine Biology
Human Biology
Chemistry
Economics
Psychology
Political Science

and chemistry are also strengths, but you really can't go wrong in any of the hard sciences. Although the humanities and social sciences are not as solid in comparison, economics, psychology, and political science are among the most popular majors. Imaginative interdisciplinary offerings include computer music, urban planning, ethnic studies, and a psychology/computer science program in artificial intelligence, as well as majors devised by students themselves. Study abroad programs are popular, with 32 percent of students participating.

The research star of the UC system, San Diego's faculty rates high nationally among public institutions in science productivity.

San Diego operates on the quarter system, which means students cram 3 or 4 courses into 10 weeks. Science students in particular find the workload intense. "Courses are competitive, especially in biology courses since it's the most popular major," says one senior. The quality of research done by the faculty, half a dozen of whom are Nobel laureates, is extremely high, and students have ample opportunities to assist with research, sometimes as early as freshman year. Students say the typical scenario of research over teaching seen at most large research universities is not as common at UC–San Diego. Even so, given the large class sizes—37 percent of undergraduate courses enroll more than 50 students—"you end up teaching a lot of the material to yourself," according to an anthropology major.

A theater major notes that the university's academic intensity "does not mean that all the students here are nerdy. We enjoy athletics and extracurricular activities, but academic excellence is our priority." A short walk to the beach, however, reveals the student body's wild and crazy half-surfers and their fans, who celebrate the "kick back." Students jumping curbs on skateboards are common on this campus. Yet these beach babies are no scholastic slouches. The average student pulls a 3.0 GPA while at UC–San Diego. Many students here choose to take five years to graduate in order to gain a higher GPA, and San Diego ranks highly among public colleges and universities in the percentage of graduates who go on to earn a Ph.D. and in the percentage of students accepted to medical school. Only 5 percent of undergraduates are from states outside of California, although 18 percent are international. Minority representation is high, with 34 percent of the student body Asian American, 15 percent Hispanic, and 2 percent African American. Diversity education includes a Cross-Cultural Center for students, faculty, and staff that provides activities, brown-bag luncheons, and programs on race relations. Merit scholarships are doled out to eligible undergraduates, but budding athletic superstars must look elsewhere for financial awards, as there are currently no athletic scholarships.

> "We enjoy athletics and extracurricular activities, but academic excellence is our priority."

The biggest annual event pays tribute to a hideously loud and colorful statue of the Sun God, which is the unofficial mascot.

Each of the university's colleges has its own housing complex, with either dorms or apartments. Most freshmen live on campus and are guaranteed housing for their first two years. "The residence halls are very nice, with all the amenities," says an animal physiology major. Dorm residents are required to buy a meal plan, and their Dining Dollars are good at any of the campus's 13 eateries. Overall, 43 percent of undergraduates live on campus; by junior year, students usually decide to take up residence in La Jolla proper or nearby Del Mar, often in beachside apartments. But that can be costly: the price ends up being inversely proportional to proximity to the beach. If you are willing to relinquish the luxury of a five-minute walk to the beach, a short commute will bring you relatively affordable housing.

> "Most students hang out at the dance clubs, jazz bars, and great restaurants in the Gaslamp Quarter."

UC–San Diego's immediate surroundings, however, are definitely not affordable. "La Jolla is a rich, conservative, retired, white, snobbish community," one sophomore says. "Not a college town!" Cars are, of course, an inescapable part of

Southern California life, and owning one—many people do—makes off-campus living even more pleasant. "No car equals no fun," one international studies major says. Unfortunately, trying to park on campus can be difficult. Mexico is a half-hour drive (even nearer than the desert, where many students go hiking), and the two-hour trip to Los Angeles makes for a nice weekend jaunt.

For those looking to stay closer to campus, the Pacific Beach and downtown San Diego, with its zoo, Sea World, and Balboa Park, are all only 12 miles away. Torrey Pines State Natural Reserve is great for outdoor enthusiasts. "Most students hang out at the dance clubs, jazz bars, and great restaurants in the Gaslamp Quarter," says a senior. The university offers more than 600 student-run groups, and 10 percent of the men and 10 percent of the women join a fraternity or sorority. The campus is dry, but some students claim that lax RAs and good fake IDs make for easy underage drinking. Although campus life is relatively tame, everyone looks forward to university-sponsored festivals, including the Open House, UnOlympics, and the Reggae Festival. The biggest annual event pays tribute to a hideously loud and colorful statue of the Sun God, which is the unofficial mascot for this sun-streaked student body. The Sun God Festival draws such big-name performers as Drake and Wiz Khalifa.

Students recently voted to compete at the Division I level.

Although San Diego will never be mistaken for a sports-crazed school (à la USC), its students recently voted to compete at the Division I level, and the university has begun to make that transition. For now, the Triton volleyball, water polo, and basketball teams do well in Division II competition, and the women's volleyball and tennis teams have won numerous national championships. For weekend warriors, classes are available in windsurfing, sailing, scuba diving, and kayaking at the nearby Mission Bay Aquatic Center. Most students participate in one intramural league or another, and according to one, if you're not on a team, "you're not a true UC–San Diego student."

"[We have] a beautiful beachfront environment that eases a life of academic rigor."

The students at UC–San Diego are exceptionally serious and out for an excellent education. But the pace (study, party, relax, study more) and the props (sun, sand, Frisbees, and flip-flops) give the rigorous curriculum an inimitable flavor that undergraduates would not change. Indeed, many believe they have the best setup in higher education: "a beautiful beachfront environment that eases a life of academic rigor."

Overlaps

UCLA, UC–Berkeley, UC–Irvine, UC–Santa Barbara, UC–Davis, University of Southern California, California State, San Diego State

If You Apply To ➤ **San Diego:** Regular decision: Nov. 30. Financial aid: Mar. 2. Application fee: $70. No campus or alumni interviews. SATs (with essay) or ACTs (with writing): required. Subject Tests: recommended for engineering and science students. No letters of recommendation. Essay: required. Apply to a particular college, school, or program. Application includes optional question about gender/sexual identity.

UC–Santa Barbara

Santa Barbara, CA 93106

Willpower is the word at UC–Santa Barbara. On a beautiful day with the sound of waves crashing in the distance, that's what it takes to hang in there with pen, paper, laptop, or book. Fairly or not, Santa Barbara is known as the party animal of the UC system. In the classroom, science is the best bet. Free spirits should check out the unusual College for Creative Studies.

Website: www.ucsb.edu

Location: Small City

Public

Total Enrollment: 23,128

Undergraduates: 20,242

Male/Female: 47/53

SAT Ranges: CR 550–670,
  M 580–700

ACT Ranges: 24–30

Financial Aid: 59%

Pell Grant: 40%

Expense: Pub $ $ $ $

Student Loans: 56%

Average Debt: $

Phi Beta Kappa: Yes

Applicants: 70,444

Accepted: 33%

Enrolled: 19%

Grad in 6 Years: 81%

Returning Freshmen: 93%

Academics: ✎ ✎ ✎ ✎

Social: ☎ ☎ ☎ ☎

Q of L: ★ ★ ★ ★

Admissions: (805) 893-2881

Email Address: admissions@
  sa.ucsb.edu

Strong Programs:

Biological Sciences

Psychology

Economics

Communication

Marine Biology

Chemical Engineering

Physics

Chemistry

The Bren School of Environmental Science and Management boasts six Nobel Prize winners in economics, chemistry, and physics.

For students at UC–Santa Barbara, California's famed beaches serve as both classroom and playground. On weekends, sun-worshipping students grab surfboards and don bikinis and head to the water for some serious fun. During the week, those same students can likely be found studying technology rather than tan lines. UCSB provides a comfortable mixture of work and play that is unique to the UC system and draws praise from its students. "On a nice sunny day, the beaches and grassy areas will be flooded with students," says a freshman, "but most of them are there with a book."

Located just a stone's throw from the beach, UC–Santa Barbara's 1,000-acre campus is bordered on two sides by the Pacific Ocean, with a clear view of the Channel Islands. On the landward side are a nature preserve and the predominantly student community of Isla Vista, and five miles to the north lie the Santa Ynez Mountains. The campus itself features mainly 1950s Southern California architecture with a Southern California atmosphere to match. A new biomedical engineering building opened in 2016; the 48,000-square-foot facility houses offices, research labs, and a 100-seat auditorium.

UCSB's general education program requires all students to fulfill four subject areas: writing, non-Western cultures, quantitative relationships, and ethnicity. In order to graduate, all students must take courses in English reading and composition, must fulfill a unit requirement, and must also meet the requirements of their individual majors. Other required courses include science, math, and technology; foreign language; civilizations; social sciences; arts; and literature.

Not surprisingly, the marine biology department capitalizes on the school's aquatic resources and stands out among the university's best; chemical engineering, physics, and chemistry are also well regarded. The most popular majors include biological sciences, psychology, economics, and communication. "The academic climate of UC–Santa Barbara is very collaborative," says one sophomore, but "the workload is definitely strenuous at times." The accounting program is strong, and the courses are geared toward taking and passing the CPA exam, so graduation is usually followed by a mass recruitment by California's big accounting firms. The College of Creative Studies offers an unstructured curriculum to about 400 self-starters ready for advanced and independent work in the arts, math, or the sciences. An interdisciplinary program called the Global Peace and Security Program combines aspects of physics, anthropology, and military science. The National Science Foundation provides funding for the National Center for Geographic Information and Analysis program. The Bren School of Environmental Science and Management is home to world-renowned faculty—the college boasts six Nobel Prize winners in economics, chemistry, and physics.

"Our on-campus housing is amazing, right in front of the beach."

Still, teaching is a hit-or-miss affair, according to one junior: "Many of the professors are more interested in their research than teaching a class." On the flip side, many opportunities are available for undergrads to assist professors, and 60 percent of students get involved in undergraduate research. For those who seek time away, Santa Barbara is the headquarters of the UC system's Education Abroad Program, which sends students to any of 100 host universities worldwide; 17 percent of UCSB students study abroad.

UCSB students, 88 percent of whom are California residents, are traditionally public-spirited and laid-back. "There are some who aren't the most academically focused, but for the most part I'd say the students are great at balancing their academic and social lives while getting involved in helping the community," says one mechanical engineering major. Asian Americans comprise 20 percent of the student body, African Americans make up 2 percent, and Hispanics account for 26 percent; 7 percent are international. The campus vibe is decidedly liberal. "Some of the biggest political issues on campus have to do with the environment. As a coastal area, UCSB is very susceptible to pollution," says one student. Merit scholarships averaging $12,981 and 100 athletic scholarships in 10 sports are available for those who qualify. Forty percent of students are Pell-eligible.

University housing, which includes both dorms and privately run residence halls, is comfortable, well maintained, and much sought after. "Our on-campus housing is amazing, right in front of the beach," a junior says. "They come fully furnished, with high-speed Internet, cable, telephone lines, and a great atmosphere." Unfortunately, there is a waiting list to get into the dorms—even with the latest student housing addition, Manzanita Village. Only 39 percent of students, most of whom are freshmen, snag on-campus housing. Meals in the dorms are available to residents and nonresidents alike, and are, according to most students, more than simply edible. "Great food and tons of it!" cheers one student. While all students say they feel extremely safe on campus, one frequently used motto is "four years, four bikes," because of the frequency of bicycle thefts. Regarding campus sexual assault, "The school has provided as many resources as it can, really," says a chemical engineering major, and it "does its best to prevent it."

"It is really easy to get involved and make friends through campus activities," says a sophomore. "Additionally, the social scene off campus is really thriving in the community of Isla Vista." Neighboring Isla Vista has welcomed its student population—after all, most of its population is UCSB students. As a result, students are very active in the community. The fraternities and sororities, which attract 8 percent of men and 13 percent of women, are known for their philanthropy. Alcohol isn't allowed on campus, and one student says, "Drinking alcohol on campus is pretty well regulated and not easy to do." Movies and concerts are also available, and the mountains, Los Padres National Forest, and L.A. are all an easy drive away. The annual Extravaganza is an all-day, free concert, and students are known to go wild on Halloween and dress up for the entire weekend. "Halloween is our claim to fame," boasts one student.

All of UCSB's varsity teams (the Gauchos) compete in Division I, and the most successful include soccer, water polo, baseball, volleyball, swimming, and basketball. A never-ending rotation of intramurals is available on and off the beach, and approximately 25 percent of the student body participate. Ultimate Frisbee is also quite popular, as well as nationally competitive.

Sure, UCSB students love to play, but that's not why most come to this coastal institution. "If there was anything that I would like to improve, it would be the lingering reputation UCSB has as a party school," observes one student. "This reputation is more of a relic from times past." Students rave about their professors and the academic challenges they face. But they also know a good thing when they see it: not everyone gets to spend four years on the beach and come away with a degree.

UCSB is the headquarters of the UC system's Education Abroad Program, which sends students to any of 100 host universities worldwide.

"Drinking alcohol on campus is pretty well regulated and not easy to do."

There is a waiting list to get into the dorms.

Overlaps

UCLA, UC–Berkeley, UC–San Diego, UC–Irvine, UC–Davis

If You Apply To ➤ **Santa Barbara:** Regular decision: Nov. 30. Financial aid: Mar. 2. Application fee: $70. No campus or alumni interviews. SATs (with essay) or ACTs (with writing): required. Subject Tests: recommended. No letters of recommendation. Essay: required. Two pieces of writing limited to 1,000 words. Apply to a particular college, school, or program. Application includes optional question about gender/sexual identity.

1156 High Street, Santa Cruz, CA 95064

From its flower-child beginnings, UC–Santa Cruz has wandered back toward the mainstream. The yoga mats and surfboards still abound and Sammy the banana slug is still the mascot. But the students are a lot more conventional than in its earlier incarnation, and UCSC is not quite the intellectual powerhouse of yore. Santa Cruz's relatively small size and residential college system give it a homey feel.

Website: www.ucsc.edu
Location: Small Town
Public
Total Enrollment: 17,391
Undergraduates: 15,823
Male/Female: 47/53
SAT Ranges: CR 520–640,
    M 550–670
ACT Ranges: 23–29
Financial Aid: 65%
Pell Grant: 35%
Expense: Pub $ $ $ $
Student Loans: 64%
Average Debt: $ $
Phi Beta Kappa: Yes
Applicants: 44,871
Accepted: 51%
Enrolled: 16%
Grad in 6 Years: 78%
Returning Freshmen: 88%
Academics: ✍ ✍ ✍ ✍
Social: ☎ ☎ ☎
Q of L: ★ ★ ★ ★ ★
Admissions: (831) 459-4008
Email Address: admissions@ ucsc.edu

Strong Programs:
Psychology
Biology
Sociology
Business Management
    Economics
Marine Sciences
Technology and Information
    Management
Computer Game Design
Environmental Studies

UC–Santa Cruz, still a baby in the UC system, was born during the radical '60s when it reigned as the ultimate alternative school. The founding vision of an integrated learning environment remains to this day, and every undergraduate affiliates with one of the residential colleges. Progressive thought continues to flourish, as does a strong academic program that strives to focus on undergraduate education. Students still come to UCSC to do their own thing.

The campus, among the most beautiful in the nation, is set on a 2,000-acre expanse of meadowland and redwood forest overlooking Monterey Bay. Bike paths and hiking trails wind throughout the redwood-tree-filled campus, and the beach is a quick drive away—or a spectacular bike ride or scenic hike. The buildings range from 1860 Cowell Ranch farm structures to the multi-award-winning modern colleges, whose styles range from Mediterranean to Japanese to sleek concrete block. Thanks to a unique building code, nothing may be built taller than two-thirds the height of the nearest redwood tree. Designed by Bohlin Cywinski Jackson—the same architectural firm that created Pixar Studios—the 26,000-square-foot Digital Arts Research Center serves as a social and intellectual hub for UCSC's Arts Division. The main library, McHenry, houses more than 1.5 million books and 25,000 periodicals, and students have access to books at other UC campuses through an online catalog system and interlibrary loans. The science library houses an additional 300,000 volumes.

Santa Cruz's academic offerings range as widely as its architecture and feature both traditional and innovative programs, but overall, the emphasis is on the liberal arts, and students will find few programs with a vocational emphasis. A majority of the students eventually go on to graduate study. To meet the general education requirements, students must complete courses in cross-cultural analysis, ethnicity and race, interpreting arts and media, mathematical and formal reasoning, scientific inquiry, statistical reasoning, and textual analysis and interpretation. In addition, students must choose one of three "perspectives" courses focused on environmental awareness, human behavior, or technology and society, and they must select a course on creative process, collaborative endeavor, or service learning. All seniors complete a capstone experience.

> **"I've been very impressed with how accessible professors are."**

Led by marine sciences and biology, the sciences are Santa Cruz's strongest suit and frequently give students the opportunity to coauthor published research with their professors. Science facilities include state-of-the-art laboratories; the Institute of Marine Sciences, which boasts one of the largest groups of experts on marine mammals in the nation; and the nearby Lick Observatory for budding stargazers. UCSC also includes the Jack Baskin School of Engineering, which was developed to accommodate the growing needs of engineering students. Programs in technology and information management and computer engineering are strong, and the computer game design B.S. is noteworthy as the first such major in the UC system and for its interdisciplinary approach that teaches both the technical aspects of computer game engineering and the artistic, narrative, and dramatic elements of game design. In fact, UCSC boasts more than the average number of interdisciplinary programs, including environmental, community, feminist, and Latin American/Latino studies; bioinformatics; and a new offering, critical race and ethnic studies. The most popular majors are psychology; molecular, cell, and developmental biology; sociology; and business management economics. While most students pursue traditional majors, the possibility is still there for eclectically minded students to pursue "history of consciousness" or just about anything else they can get a faculty member to OK. Nearly two-thirds of students engage in undergraduate research, and 13 percent study abroad; field study and internships are also encouraged.

"Courses are very rigorous, in my experience," warns one undergrad. Though the curriculum is demanding and the quarter system keeps the academic pace fast, the atmosphere is emphatically noncompetitive. Such competition as there is tends to be internalized. Classes can be large, with 25 percent enrolling more than 50 students. All UC campuses insist on faculty research, but most Santa Cruz professors are there to teach. "I've been very impressed with how accessible professors are," says a sophomore. "Whether it's via email or regular office hours, I feel very comfortable approaching and talking to all of my professors."

Eclectically minded students may pursue "history of consciousness" or just about anything else they can get a faculty member to OK.

"Before I came here I was told that UCSC was a 'hippie-dippie' college," says one student, "but it's not true at all." Even so, Santa Cruz remains the most liberal of the UC campuses, and, according to one student, is "still a school with a social conscience." Ninety-four percent of undergraduates are Californians, though Santa Cruz always manages to lure a few Easterners; 3 percent are international. Asian Americans account for 21 percent, Hispanics 31 percent, and African Americans 2 percent. "Racial, ethnic, and cultural diversity is celebrated and strongly encouraged by the majority of the students here," reports a politics major. Thirty-five percent of incoming freshmen qualify for Pell Grants. Merit scholarships, which average $5,095 each, are available, but there are no athletic scholarships.

"[Santa Cruz is] still a school with a social conscience."

In an effort to become what one official calls a "near-perfect hybrid" between the large university and the small college, campus life revolves around the residential colleges. Fifty-three percent of the undergraduate population lives in university-sponsored housing. Freshmen and transfer students are guaranteed on-campus housing for two years, while upperclassmen can take their chances in the lottery or move off campus. Some dorms have their own dining halls with reasonably good food; students may also opt to join a food co-op. The newly established CARE (Campus Advocacy, Resources, and Education) office provides education on issues of sexual assault and support to survivors.

In an effort to become a hybrid between the large university and the small college, campus life revolves around the residential colleges.

A dozen fraternities and sororities attract 5 percent of the men and 7 percent of the women, respectively. Students 21 and over are allowed to drink alcohol on campus, although not in public areas, and parties must be registered. More than 150 student organizations on campus—including major-focused clubs, ethnic and cultural groups, hobby clubs, and honor societies such as the Tau Beta Pi engineering honor society and Golden Key International Honor Society—cover a wide range of interests. The beach and resort town of Santa Cruz, with its boardwalk and amusement park, are only 10 minutes away from campus by bike, although pedaling back up the hill takes much longer. Those looking for city lights can take the windy, mountainous highway to San Jose (35 miles away) or the slow, scenic coastal highway to San Francisco (75 miles), or ride a bus to either city. If you have a car, destinations such as Monterey, Big Sur, the Napa Valley, and the Sierras are easily accessible.

"Racial, ethnic, and cultural diversity is celebrated and strongly encouraged."

Although Santa Cruz fields only a few varsity teams, which compete in Division III, students love their school mascot, Sammy the banana slug. Men's tennis is strong and makes regular appearances in the NCAA Tournament; women's tennis, cross-country, and men's and women's volleyball have also performed well in recent years. Participation in intramurals ("Friendship through Competition" is the motto) and club sports is widespread, with rugby in particular growing in popularity. Sailing and scuba diving are among the many physical education classes offered, and the student recreation department sponsors everything from white-water rafting to cooking classes.

Santa Cruz is a progressive school with a gorgeous campus and innovative academic programs, where the main priority is the education of undergraduates. Many students are concerned that UCSC is growing too fast, and an ambitious proposal for future expansion has threatened its heretofore cozy relationship with local citizens. Still, as long as UCSC retains its belief in "to each his or her own," it will remain uniquely Santa Cruz.

If You Apply To ➤

Santa Cruz: Regular decision: Nov. 30. Financial aid: Mar. 2. Housing: May 1. Application fee: $70. No campus or alumni interviews. SATs (with essay) or ACTs (with writing): required. No Subject Tests. No letters of recommendation. Essay: required. Two pieces of writing limited to 1,000 words. Apply to a particular college, school, or program. Application includes optional question about gender/sexual identity.

California Institute of Technology

1200 East California Boulevard, Pasadena, CA 91125

If you're armed with a near-perfect SAT score; a burning desire to study math, science, or engineering; and some independent research or published papers already under your belt, maybe you'll have a fighting chance of getting into and out of the California Institute of Technology. Caltech is best experienced with grit, a propensity for pranks, and wide-ranging intellectual curiosity.

Website: www.caltech.edu
Location: Small City
Private
Total Enrollment: 2,255
Undergraduates: 1,001
Male/Female: 61/39
SAT Ranges: CR 730–800, M 770–800
ACT Ranges: 34–35
Financial Aid: 50%
Pell Grant: 13%
Expense: Pr $ $ $
Student Loans: 39%
Average Debt: $
Phi Beta Kappa: No
Applicants: 6,507
Accepted: 9%
Enrolled: 42%
Grad in 6 Years: 92%
Returning Freshmen: 97%

The California Institute of Technology counts 34 Nobel Prize winners among its faculty and alumni, and with administrators' permission—which is easy to obtain—students may tap into that brilliance by taking as many classes as they can cram in each semester. Expectations are high; "Techers" are fond of saying that "the admissions office doesn't make mistakes," and it's fairly common to take time off to deal with stress and avoid burnout. "The atmosphere promotes a love of science, learning, and discovery that is truly exhilarating," says a biology major. No doubt about it—if you prefer particle physics to partying, Caltech is the place to be.

Caltech's 124-acre campus is located in Pasadena, "a wealthy suburban town about 15 miles outside Los Angeles," says a senior. "It's not a college town at all." The distance from downtown means the school is relatively isolated from the glitz, glamour, and good times that many people associate with "La La Land." Outside the classroom, at least, tranquility prevails, with olive trees, lily ponds, and plenty of flowers breaking up clusters of older Spanish mission-style buildings. Leafy courtyards and arcades link these with the more modern, "block institutional" structures. The Beckman Auditorium (affectionately dubbed "The Wedding Cake" due to its round shape and conical roof) features spaces for performing arts, lectures, films, classes, and entertainment events.

Caltech's mission, one official says, is "to train the creative type of scientist or engineer urgently needed in our educational, governmental, and industrial development." After all, it was here that Albert Einstein abandoned his concept of a static cosmos and endorsed the expanding-universe model. This is also where physicist Carl Anderson discovered the positron. With these luminaries as their models, students plunge right into the demanding general requirements, which include three terms each of math and physics, three terms of chemistry, one term of biology, one term of science communication, two introductory lab terms, and 12 terms in the humanities and social sciences to round things out. Students complain about these, "and usually take no more than absolutely required," says a biology major. Still, they can be tough to get into come registration time, says a computer science major, since enrollment is limited "to allow for discussion among a small group." The pass/fail grading system in the freshman year goes a long way toward easing the acclimation period for new arrivals. And the honor system, which mandates that "no one shall take unfair advantage of any other member of the Caltech community," helps discourage competition for grades. Professors give take-home exams, and if violations of the honor code are suspected, "students decide if a violation was indeed made," one student explains.

> "The atmosphere promotes a love of science, learning, and discovery that is truly exhilarating."

Caltech made its name in physics, and students say that program remains strong. A junior says, "I love mechanical engineering. The profs are great, the subject is fun, and you get to do fun contests." Regardless of major, Caltech students benefit from state-of-the-art facilities, including the Beckman Institute, a center for fundamental research in biology and chemistry, and the Keck telescope, the largest optical telescope in the world. The Moore Laboratory has 90,000 square feet of the latest equipment for engineering and communications majors studying fiber optics and the like, and the university's endowment is the largest of the nation's engineering schools. Summer Undergraduate Research Fellowships give 80 percent of undergraduates the chance to get a head start on their own discoveries, with help from a faculty sponsor. Some 20 percent of these students publish results from their endeavors in scientific journals.

Despite Caltech's reputation for brilliance, students say the quality of teaching is hit or miss. "At times, you get lucky and get amazing professors," says a computer science major. "Other times, you get professors who either don't care about the class they teach, or are so advanced in their field that they are unable to convey 'simple' concepts." A senior reasons, "The quality of teaching improves as you get into your major." Here, the student adds, professors in the humanities and social sciences really shine, since they actually want to teach, rather than hole up in a lab with mass spectrometers and computer simulations of atomic fission. Another student describes the academic climate as "collaborative, intense, and busy." While teaching assistants do lead some recitation sections affiliated with large lectures, it's not uncommon for professors to lead them too—even for freshmen.

The pass/fail grading system in the freshman year goes a long way toward easing the acclimation period for new arrivals.

Twenty-nine percent of Techers come from California, and 8 percent hail from foreign nations. Forty-five percent are Asian American; other minorities are less well represented, with Hispanics making up 12 percent of the student body and African Americans just 1 percent. Ninety-nine percent of students graduated in the top 10th of their high school class. Men outnumber women, which has inspired the bittersweet observation among distaff Techers that "the odds are good, but the goods are odd." Social and political issues are generally not a big deal on campus. "People live in a Tech bubble, where they care about nothing more than 50 meters from campus," says a sophomore. All financial aid is awarded based on need—meaning no merit or athletic scholarships—and Caltech guarantees to meet the full demonstrated need of all admitted domestic students.

> "The housing system [offers] social support in an academically intense environment."

(continued)

Academics: ✍ ✍ ✍ ✍ ✍
Social: ☎
Q of L: ★ ★ ★
Admissions: (626) 395-2645
Email Address:
  ugadmissions@caltech.edu

Strong Programs:
Engineering
Physics
Applied Sciences

Caltech also guarantees on-campus or school-affiliated housing for all four years, and 86 percent of students live in the "comfortable and convenient" dorms.

"Ask any local bartender for a Caltech Cocktail and you will get three ounces of straight water."

"The housing system is great," cheers one student, who describes residence life as "social support in an academically intense environment." While there are no fraternities or sororities, the eight co-ed on-campus houses inspire a loyalty worthy of the Greeks. The four older houses, which have been renovated, offer mostly single rooms, while the three newer dorms have doubles. Freshmen select their house during Rotation Week, after spending an evening of partying at each one, and indicating at week's end the four they like the most. Resident upperclassmen take it from there in a professional-sports-type draft, which places each new student in one of his or her top choices. Business-minded types, for example, may choose Avery House, which focuses on entrepreneurship. Each dorm has a dining hall, and those who live on campus must buy a meal plan, which a junior calls "quite expensive for the quality of food." A vegetarian calls the food "awful," and says that "by the end of the week, I am often wondering if we're being served the same spinach for five days in a row." Among Caltech's efforts to address issues of sexual misconduct on campus is an annual, student-led Title IX Summit, in which students plan solutions and strategies to prevent sexual violence.

Summer Undergraduate Research Fellowships give 80 percent of undergraduates the chance to get a head start on their own discoveries.

The houses are the emotional center of Caltech life, and the scene of innumerable practical jokes. On Ditch Day, seniors barricade their dorm rooms using everything from steel bars to electronic codes, leave clues as to how to overcome the obstacles, and disappear from campus. Underclassmen spend the day figuring out how to break in, using "cleverness, brute force, and finesse," to claim a reward inside, which can range from the edible to, well, anything is possible. Perhaps the best student prank occurred during the 1984 Rose Bowl game, when crosstown rival UCLA played Illinois. A group of Caltech whiz kids spent months devising a radio-control device that would allow them to take control of the scoreboard in the second half, to gain national exposure for Caltech by flashing pictures of their school's mascot, the beaver, and a new version of the score that had Caltech trouncing MIT.

While drinking might seem a reasonable escape from the pressure of all the hard work, Caltech requires any organization hosting a party to hire a professional bartender—"and they card," says a senior. "Ask any local bartender for a Caltech Cocktail and you will get three ounces of straight water," quips a sophomore. Social life at Caltech "is horrible," agrees a junior. "There are occasional parties, but the administration does not allow students from other colleges to attend, unless accompanied by a Caltech student." So students head off campus—to Old Pasadena, nearby schools like USC, Occidental, and the Claremont Colleges, or to downtown L.A., now easily reachable on the Metro's gold line. Disneyland and Hollywood are always options, and road trips to the beach, mountains, or desert—or south of the border, to Mexico—are options for those with cars. But some Caltech students still prefer to make their own fun. The annual Pumpkin Drop (on Halloween, of course) involves immersing a gourd in liquid nitrogen, and then dropping it from the library roof, so that it shatters into a zillion frozen shards. During finals week, stereos blast "The Ride of the Valkyries" at seven o'clock each morning, just the thing to get you going after that all-nighter.

"I call almost all of [my professors] by their first names."

During finals week, stereos blast "The Ride of the Valkyries" at seven o'clock each morning.

Caltech fields 19 Division III teams, and the most popular include men's soccer, men's and women's track and field, and men's cross-country. The Beavers' men's basketball team became campus heroes in March 2011 when they ended a conference losing streak that dated back to 1985. The school also offers more unusual sports, such as water polo and fencing. Perhaps more popular than varsity competition, though, are the intramural matches between the houses, in nine sports every year. Also popular is the annual design competition that's the culmination of Mechanical Engineering 72; it helped inspire the TV shows *Battle Bots* and *Robot Wars*. The city of Pasadena is home to the granddaddy of postseason college football competition—the storied Rose Bowl.

Caltech students must learn to thrive under intense pressure, thanks to the school's tremendous workload and lackluster social life. But students say they appreciate the freedom to think and explore—and the trust administrators place in them through the honor code. "The unique student body, how available professors are (I call almost all of them by their first names), and how much we learn make Caltech a special place," says a sophomore.

If You Apply To ➤ **Caltech:** Early action: Nov. 1. Regular decision: Jan. 3. Financial aid: Mar. 2. Application fee: $75. No campus or alumni interviews. SATs (with essay) or ACTs (with writing): required. Subject Tests: required (math level 2 and either physics, biology, or chemistry). Letters of recommendation: required. Essay: required. Students have the option of submitting published scientific research papers and letters from research mentors. Accepts the Common Application with supplement.

Calvin College

3201 Burton Street, Grand Rapids, MI 49546

An evangelical Christian institution that ranks high on the private college affordability list. Nearly half the students are members of the Christian Reformed Church. Archrival of Michigan neighbor Hope and Illinois cousin Wheaton. Best known in the humanities and as one of the few Christian colleges with engineering.

Calvin College takes seriously its mission to equip students to "think deeply, to act justly, and to live wholeheartedly as Christ's agents of renewal in the world." Along with Wheaton College in Illinois, it is regarded as one of the country's top evangelical colleges. Though no one is required to attend the school's daily chapel services, classes stop when worship starts, and most students view Christian values as central to the academic experience. "Calvin students seek to be enriched by culture, education, and faith," says one junior.

Calvin was founded in 1876, as the educational wing of the Christian Reformed Church in North America. After outgrowing one of its first homes, the college bought a tract of land on the edge of Grand Rapids and built its present campus. Calvin spreads out over 400 beautifully landscaped acres, including playing fields and three ponds. The campus also includes a 90-acre woodland and wetland ecosystem preserve used for classes, research, and recreation. Most facilities are less than 50 years old and were designed by a student of famed architect Frank Lloyd Wright. The east campus includes the Prince Conference Center, DeVos Communication Center, Gainey Athletic Facility, and the award-winning Bunker Interpretive Center, powered primarily by student-designed solar energy technology. The Covenant Fine Arts Center includes space for offices, classrooms, a 1,100-seat auditorium, a 3,800-square-foot art gallery, and a student lounge.

Calvin's core curriculum has four components: core gateway, studies, competencies, and senior capstone courses. All first-year students must take the two linked gateway courses, First-Year Seminar and Developing a Christian Mind. Students then tackle the liberal arts core, An Engagement with God's World, which challenges them to develop knowledge, skills, and Christian character. Studies courses include

Website: www.calvin.edu
Location: Suburban
Private
Total Enrollment: 3,742
Undergraduates: 3,699
Male/Female: 44/56
SAT Ranges: CR 520–670, M 530–670
ACT Ranges: 23–30
Financial Aid: 95%
Pell Grant: 27%
Expense: Pr $
Student Loans: 62%
Average Debt: $ $ $
Phi Beta Kappa: No
Applicants: 3,824
Accepted: 74%
Enrolled: 33%
Grad in 6 Years: 74%
Returning Freshmen: 86%
Academics: ✐ ✐ ✐
Social: ☎ ☎ ☎
Q of L: ★ ★ ★ ★

(continued)

Admissions: (800) 688-0122

Email Address: admissions@
calvin.edu

Strong Programs:
Business Administration
Engineering
Education
Nursing
Psychology
English
Philosophy
Asian Studies

Calvin is the only Christian college in the U.S. to offer a comprehensive Asian studies program.

the Physical World, Societal Structures in North America, and Biblical Foundations. Competencies courses cover foreign languages and Rhetoric in Culture.

Preprofessional programs, such as business, engineering, education, and nursing, tend to be Calvin's best bets, students say—perhaps that's why those programs,

> **"The support services at Calvin have helped me in tremendous ways with grace, patience, and authentic kindness."**

along with psychology and English, are the college's most popular majors. Biology, chemistry, philosophy, and religion are also regarded as strong, though faculty members in those departments are said to be tough. Calvin is the only Christian college in the U.S. to offer a comprehensive Asian studies program, which includes courses in Chinese, Japanese, and Korean language, history, and culture. In addition, Calvin has expanded its speech pathology and audiology undergraduate program to add a five-year bachelor-to-master's program, and has added a new major in public health.

Academically, Calvin's atmosphere is tough but collaborative. "Calvin can sometimes be daunting to students, especially in their first year," says a senior. The school is founded on the belief that every subject—even the sciences or mass media and popular culture—can be approached from a Christian perspective, and faculty members work hard to integrate faith and learning. An international development major says, "The faculty will challenge students in their intellectual pursuits as well as encourage them in their personal lives." Thirty-six percent of classes at Calvin have fewer than 20 students and only a few have more than 50; a social work major says, "Class sizes are small enough that professors will get to know our name, but big enough to offer a variety of opinions in discussions." Faculty members must be committed to Christian teachings, and in the absence of teaching assistants, professors are expected to reserve about 10 hours per week for advising and assisting students outside of class. Students also give high ratings to peer tutoring and personal counseling services. "The support services at Calvin have helped me in tremendous ways with grace, patience, and authentic kindness," says a senior.

Learning also takes place outside of the classroom through internships and practicums, and 80 percent of students complete at least one internship before they graduate. Twenty percent collaborate with faculty on research projects. Calvin offers more than 40 faculty-led off-campus programs in such locales as Britain, China, Ghana, Honduras, and Washington, D.C. Students also study abroad in programs offered in conjunction with other colleges and universities. "Study abroad programs are an essential part of the Calvin experience," says a psychology major. Seventy-eight percent of students participate in study abroad, and the college is among the top in the nation for the number of students who do so.

Though Calvin still has a strongly Dutch heritage, students who are members of the Christian Reformed Church now account for less than half of the student body.

> **"Students here create a community that is positive, inviting, inquisitive, and comfortable."**

"Students here create a community that is positive, inviting, inquisitive, and comfortable," says an engineering major. Fifty-one percent are Michigan natives, and 11 percent are international. African Americans constitute 3 percent of the total, Hispanics 4 percent, and Asian Americans 4 percent. Overall, Calvin students are politically aware and committed to serving others. "Calvin is constantly hosting forums and panels about issues that students want to engage with," says a senior, citing racial violence, same-sex relationships, and gender equality as prominent topics of discussion. Eligible Calvin students receive scholarships based on academic merit, worth an average of $8,547 annually; there are no athletic awards. Twenty-seven percent of incoming students receive Pell Grants.

Fifty-nine percent of Calvin students live on campus in the single-sex dorms. Freshmen and sophomores bunk in suites with two bedrooms, connected by a bathroom, while juniors and seniors move off campus or into the on-campus apartments. "The residence halls are awesome. They focus on positive community building, giving a safe place for students to live, study, have fun, and grow," cheers one nursing student. Each residence hall and two of the apartment buildings have computer rooms in the basement, along with free washers and dryers. Calvin offers three intentional living/learning floors—Creation Care (recreational pursuits/environmental stewardship and sustainability), Grassroots (exploring race and identity in North America), and Honors. Campus dining receives fair reviews, but students note that they can usually count on a variety of options and accommodations. "Campus safety is top-notch," says a sophomore. "These people work hard, 24/7, to keep everyone on campus feeling safe."

Calvin has no Greek system, and—owing to its religious emphasis—the campus is officially dry. That's no great loss, students say, because there is so much to do on campus, including movies, speakers, concerts, and dances. "The social life at Calvin is great," says one student. "Most of it takes place on campus, but the Grand Rapids area is also a great way to bond with friends." Indeed, downtown Grand Rapids offers restaurants, coffee shops, minor-league sports, galleries, and the annual ArtPrize festival and competition. A popular annual event is Chaos Day, which brings the dorms together for a day of athletic contests. The Airband lip-synch competition each February is also a favorite, as are athletic contests versus Hope College. Road trips include the beaches of Lake Michigan (a one-hour drive) or Chicago (three hours distant). Spring break trips see a number of students traveling to places like Mississippi and Louisiana to complete service projects.

> **"Drinking and party culture is hard to find on campus."**

Calvin fields a robust Division III athletic program that competes in the Michigan Intercollegiate Athletic Association (MIAA). The women's volleyball team is a recent national champion, and other particularly competitive Knights teams include men's and women's cross-country and soccer, men's golf and basketball, and women's volleyball. Calvin's competition with Hope is one of the great rivalries in Division III athletics, and current students and alumni alike rally together for the annual basketball game. "Any game against Hope always turns into a big deal," says a speech pathology major. The college's intramural program offers leagues and tournaments in sports from dodgeball to ultimate Frisbee and fantasy football. Half of all undergraduates participate.

"Drinking and party culture is hard to find on campus," says one student. Indeed, those who come to Calvin College are looking to build community with friends and faculty members who share their already-strong Christian faith. Says one senior, Calvin is a place where "people are intentionally seeking connection with one another, in pursuit of a community where people are welcomed and embraced."

Spring break trips see a number of students traveling to places like Mississippi and Louisiana to complete service projects.

Overlaps

Hope, Grand Valley State, University of Michigan, Michigan State, Wheaton (IL), Cornerstone, Trinity Christian (IL), Taylor

If You Apply To ➤ **Calvin:** Rolling admissions: Aug. 15. (Priority deadline: Nov. 15.) Application fee: $35. No campus or alumni interviews. SATs or ACTs: required. No Subject Tests. Letters of recommendation: required. Essay: required. Accepts the Common Application with supplement.

Carleton College

Northfield, MN 55057

Less selective than Amherst, Williams, and Swarthmore, mainly because of its out-of-the-way Minnesota location. Yet Carleton retains its position as the premier liberal arts college in the upper Midwest. Predominantly liberal, but not to the extremes of its more antiestablishment cousins, students at Carleton excel at making their own fun. Turns out lots of students who go on to get Ph.D.s.

Website: www.carleton.edu
Location: Small Town
Private
Total Enrollment: 2,014
Undergraduates: 2,014
Male/Female: 48/52
SAT Ranges: CR 660–750, M 660–770
ACT Ranges: 29–33
Financial Aid: 82%
Pell Grant: 13%
Expense: Pr $ $ $ $
Student Loans: 41%
Average Debt: $
Phi Beta Kappa: Yes
Applicants: 6,722
Accepted: 21%
Enrolled: 35%
Grad in 6 Years: 93%
Returning Freshmen: 96%
Academics: ✍ ✍ ✍ ✍ ✍
Social: ☎ ☎ ☎
Q of L: ★ ★ ★
Admissions: (800) 995-2275
Email Address: admissions@carleton.edu

Strong Programs:
Biology
Chemistry
Computer Science
Geology
Economics
Psychology
History
Visual and Performing Arts

Minnesota is many things: the land of 10,000 lakes, home to the massive Mall of America, birthplace of lore from Hiawatha to Paul Bunyan, and proud parent of the Mississippi River. Beyond all that history-book stuff, tucked into a small town in the southeastern corner of the state is Carleton College, arguably the best liberal arts school in the expansive Midwest. Add to this a midwinter carnival complete with human bowling, badminton competitions that raise money to fight cancer, and an expulsion of Coca-Cola from campus for human rights violations, and you have the makings of an engaged, unique institution. "Students at Carleton love learning," says one junior. "They love immersing themselves in their work and applying what they learn to other classes and to their life in general."

Surrounded by rolling farmland, Carleton's 955-acre campus is in the small town of Northfield, whose one-time status as the center of the Holstein cattle industry brought it the motto "The City of Cows, Colleges, and Contentment." Lakes, woods, and streams abound, and you can traverse them on 12 miles of hiking and cross-country skiing trails. The city boasts of fragrant lilacs in spring, rich summer greens, red maples in the fall, and a glistening blanket of white in winter. There's even an 800-acre arboretum. Carleton's architectural style is somewhat eclectic, with everything from Victorian to contemporary, but mostly redbrick.

Carleton's top-notch academic programs are no less varied: the sciences—biology, physics, astronomy, chemistry, geology, and computer science—are among the best anywhere, and scores of Carleton graduates go on to earn Ph.D.s in these areas. Of all the liberal arts schools in the country, Carleton's undergrads were recently awarded the highest number of National Science Foundation fellowships for graduate studies. Economics, psychology, and history are other popular majors. Engineers can opt for a 3–2 program with Columbia University or Washington University in St. Louis, and for geologists seeking fieldwork—and maybe wanting to thaw out after a long Minnesota winter—Carleton sponsors a program in Death Valley. Closer to home at the "arb," as the arboretum is affectionately known, environmental studies majors have their own wilderness field station, which includes a prairie-restoration site. At the opposite end of the academic spectrum, the arts also flourish. Music and studio art majors routinely get into top graduate programs, and may take advantage of expanded offerings in dance and theater. Carleton offers interdisciplinary programs in Asian, Jewish, urban, African and African American, and women's studies. A concentration in cross-cultural studies brings in foreign students to discuss global issues and dynamics with their American counterparts. Seventy percent of students spend at least one term abroad, and many take advantage of programs available through numerous organizations, including Carleton and the Associated Colleges of the Midwest*.

> "The academic climate at Carleton is intense, but in the most fulfilling way possible."

Distribution requirements ensure that a Carleton education exposes students not only to rigor and depth in their chosen field, but also to "a wide range of subjects and methods of studying them," administrators say. All students must show proficiency in English composition and a foreign language while fulfilling requirements in the areas of humanistic and social inquiry, literary/artistic analysis, the arts, science, and formal or statistical reasoning. There's also a Global Citizenship requirement, under which students must take at least one course dealing with a non-Western culture, and a first-year Argument and Inquiry Seminar. In their final year, all students complete a senior comprehensive project (known around campus as "Comps").

With highly motivated students and a heavy workload, Carleton isn't your typical mellow Midwestern liberal arts college. The trimester calendar means finals may be just three months apart and almost everyone feels the pressure. The six-week Christmas vacation is Carleton's way of dealing with the cold winters. "The academic climate at Carleton is intense, but in the most fulfilling way possible," says a junior. "Everyone is really working diligently, but this breeds a climate of solidarity." Seventy-one percent of classes have fewer than 20 students, so Carls are expected to participate actively. Carleton's faculty members are accessible and committed. A freshman cheers, "The professors are very knowledgeable in their area of expertise, and are also very excited about teaching."

> **"Even though there are diversity talks throughout the year, there is still obvious segregation on campus."**

"Carleton students are incredibly kind, laid-back, and fascinated by the world around them," says a biology major. "They are always asking questions." Not to be confused with the typically Midwestern students across town at St. Olaf, just 17 percent of Carleton students are Minnesota natives, and 11 percent are international. More than half of the out-of-staters are from outside the Midwest, with both coasts heavily represented. African Americans account for 4 percent of the student body, Hispanics 7 percent, and Asian Americans 9 percent. "Diversity and racial issues are big on campus," observes a freshman. "Even though there are diversity talks throughout the year, there is still obvious segregation on campus." The Carleton campus is left of center, concerned with issues including the environment, multiculturalism, LGBTQ rights, and Title IX. Carleton meets the full demonstrated financial need of all enrolled students; the only merit-based awards are granted to National Merit, Achievement, and Hispanic Scholars, and there are no athletic scholarships.

Ninety-six percent of Carleton students live on campus, and housing is guaranteed for all four years; those who wish to live off campus must receive approval to do so. Campus accommodations range from comfortable old houses to modern hotel-like residence halls. "Housing accommodations are generally excellent; even the worst dorms are totally livable and spacious compared to those of friends that I have from other colleges," says a junior. Dorms are co-ed by room, but there are two halls with single-sex floors. Ten college-owned off-campus "theme" houses focus on special interests such as foreign languages, the outdoors, or nuclear power issues. With the exception of the Farm House, an environmental studies house sitting on the edge of the arb, all the theme houses are situated in an attractive residential section of town close to campus. All campus residents must submit to a meal plan, to the chagrin of many. "The meals are usually the same, and bland. There are options for vegan, vegetarian, gluten-free, and lactose intolerance," says a freshman. Students also report being "unsatisfied with the structure in place to deal with" sexual assaults on campus, although one notes, "The school is trying to listen to all of the students' concerns."

> **"Housing accommodations are generally excellent; even the worst dorms are totally livable and spacious."**

Absent a Greek system, Carleton's social life tends to be relaxed and informal. "The social life is vibrant on Fridays and Saturdays, with almost all parties happening

Carleton's undergrads were recently awarded the highest number of National Science Foundation fellowships for graduate studies.

The trimester calendar means finals may be just three months apart and almost everyone feels the pressure.

on campus and in the dorms," says one student. A group called Co-op sponsors dances and Wednesday socials every two weeks, free movies, and special events like Comedy Night. Students say there is no pressure to drink on campus. A sophomore says, "If you don't want to drink and are not looking for parties, you may never see any alcohol on campus at all." Popular annual events include the Winter Carnival, the Spring Concert, and Mai-Fete, a gala celebrated on an island in one of the two lakes on campus. Traditions include the weeklong freshman orientation program, where, during opening convocation, students bombard professors with bubbles as the faculty members process. Another distinctive Carleton tradition is the regular liberation and dramatic reappearance—such as dangling from a helicopter over homecoming football games—of a plaster bust of Friedrich Schiller, the Romantic philosopher and buddy of Goethe.

Northfield itself is a history-filled town with a population of about 20,000. A favorite town event is the annual reenactment of Jesse James's failed bank robbery

"Carleton is quirky,
and we're not afraid
to embrace our quirk."

in 1876. There are old-style shops and a beautiful old hotel. "Northfield is quaint, but there's not much to do," a sophomore says. Students often frequent the St. Olaf College campus and a nightspot known as the Reub'n'Stein. Minneapolis-St. Paul, 35 miles to the north, is a popular road-trip destination. Since students aren't allowed to have cars on campus, Carleton charters buses on weekends.

The Knights compete in Division III athletics; about a third of the students play on varsity teams. Men's and women's soccer have won multiple Minnesota Intercollegiate Athletic Conference titles in recent years, and women's tennis, swimming and diving, and golf and men's tennis are also competitive. The school's ultimate Frisbee club teams have won multiple national championships. Roughly 80 percent of students compete in intramural and recreational sports, including Rotblatt, which is "the world's longest intramural sport," according to one junior. "Played once each spring, this marathon softball game begins at sunrise and lasts one inning for each year of Carleton's existence. It is Rotblatt tradition for players to both bat and field with a beverage of their choice in one hand."

"Carleton is quirky, and we're not afraid to embrace our quirk. In fact, we revel in it," says a biology major. It can be cold in Minnesota, in a face-stinging, bone-chilling kind of way. And the classes are far from easy. But Carleton is a warm campus where students toe the line between individuality and community. At Carleton, says one student, "It isn't about getting the degree; it's about having an impactful experience where students learn more about themselves and the world they live in."

Carnegie Mellon University

5000 Forbes Avenue, Pittsburgh, PA 15213-3890

Carnegie Mellon University is the only premier university equally strong in technology and the arts. Applications have nearly doubled in the past 10 years, so it must be doing something right. Shares its urban neighborhood with a variety of cultural and academic institutions, including the University of Pittsburgh.

Students at Carnegie Mellon don't have to choose between soaking up the high drama of Shakespeare and plunging into the fast-paced dot-com world. The university is known for both its science offerings and strong drama and music programs. But scholars can't just focus on their own course of study—Carnegie Mellon continues to strive to offer both its technical and liberal arts students a well-rounded education that requires a lot of hard work but promises great results. "CMU is filled with passionate students who push themselves to participate in as much as they can," says one information systems major.

Carnegie Mellon was formed by the merger of Carnegie Institute of Technology and the Mellon Institute in 1967, resulting in a self-contained, 150-acre campus attractively situated in Pittsburgh's affluent Oakland section. Next door is the city's largest park and its major museum, named after—you guessed it—Andrew Carnegie. Henry Hornbostel won a competition in 1904 to design the Carnegie Technical Schools, now Carnegie Mellon University. Hornbostel, who attended the École des Beaux-Arts in the 1890s, created a campus plan that is a modification of the Jefferson plan for the University of Virginia, with the Beaux-Arts device of creating primary and secondary axes and grouping buildings around significant open spaces. Buildings are designed in a Renaissance style, with buff-colored brick arches and piers, tile roofs, and terra cotta and granite details.

Carnegie Mellon has seven constituent colleges—H. John Heinz III College, offering graduate degrees in public policy, management, and information systems—and six others that offer undergraduate and graduate courses: the College of Fine Arts, the Dietrich College of Humanities and Social Sciences, the College of Engineering, the Mellon College of Science, the School of Computer Science, and the Tepper School of Business. Each college has its own distinct character and admissions requirements. All the colleges, however, share the university's commitment to what it calls a "liberal-professional" education, which shows the relevance of the liberal arts while stressing courses that develop technical skills and good job prospects. Humanities and social science types can major in applied history, professional writing, or information systems, for example, instead of traditional disciplinary concentrations. Each college requires core work from freshmen; in the Dietrich College of Humanities and Social Sciences, students are introduced to computers in a required first-year philosophy course, using the machines to work on problems of logic.

Most departments at Carnegie Mellon are strong, but exceptional ones include engineering, computer science, and drama. The most popular majors are computer science, electrical and computer engineering, mechanical engineering, and information systems, and students generally agree that Carnegie Mellon is more of a science-oriented school. The Science and Humanities Scholars program allows talented undergrads to develop their own course of study. In addition, the Fifth-Year Scholars program provides full tuition for outstanding students who want to remain at Carnegie Mellon for an additional year to pursue more studies that interest them.

Courses are "extremely rigorous with many hours expected outside of the classroom," says one student. "Students are always competing to see who can have the

Website: www.cmu.edu
Location: City Center
Private
Total Enrollment: 12,422
Undergraduates: 6,232
Male/Female: 54/46
SAT Ranges: CR 650–740,
  M 710–800
ACT Ranges: 31–34
Financial Aid: 52%
Pell Grant: 12%
Expense: Pr $ $ $ $
Student Loans: 54%
Average Debt: $ $ $
Phi Beta Kappa: Yes
Applicants: 20,547
Accepted: 24%
Enrolled: 32%
Grad in 6 Years: 88%
Returning Freshmen: 98%
Academics: ✍ ✍ ✍ ✍
Social: ☎ ☎ ☎
Q of L: ★ ★ ★
Admissions: (412) 268-2082
Email Address:
  undergraduate-admissions@
  andrew.cmu.edu

Strong Programs:
Computer Science
Electrical and Computer
  Engineering
Mechanical Engineering
Information Systems
Drama
Music

most classes, activities, or projects," adds another. Students at Carnegie Mellon work hard, no doubt about it, and many complain that the academic environment encourages a serious culture of stress, but the university has taken steps to try to counteract that. Every day includes a designated "meeting-free" time for students, allowing them time to study or participate in student activities. A mechanical and biomedical engineering double major notes that there is a "mindfulness room" that serves as "a space for students to relax and take a break from schoolwork" (and get weekly visits from trained therapy dogs), and that students are encouraged to use campus counseling services "even if it is just to discuss stress and how to manage a new environment." Nearly all the classes are small, with average class sizes of 25 to 35 students, and professors rate highly with most students. "Professors are usually happy to spend time outside of class with us and really go the extra mile, often engaging us with events outside of the campus bubble and helping us with projects independent of classes," says a junior.

Students looking to hone their professional skills will find ample opportunities. A number of five-year, dual-degree options exist, including a joint B.S./M.S. or an industrial internship co-op program in materials science and engineering, which places students in the industrial environment. Research opportunities are available for every field of study, as are several types of grants and fellowships to fund them. Those interested in service learning can get involved with the university's extensive outreach efforts to improve youth STEM education in the local area. Study abroad options are plentiful, including the university's established campus in the Arabian Gulf nation of Qatar and other degree-granting and exchange programs worldwide, but participation tends to be low, as students often have difficulty fitting study abroad into their rigorous schedules.

> The Fifth-Year Scholars program provides full tuition for outstanding students who want to pursue more studies that interest them.

> "Students are always competing to see who can have the most classes, activities, or projects."

Despite the university's core emphasis on interdisciplinary, well-rounded education, Carnegie Mellon remains one of the most fragmented campuses in the nation. Students divide themselves between actors, dancers, and other artsy types and engineers, scientists, and architects. "CMU is for people who know what they want to do," asserts one student. In any case, students here are all high achievers—78 percent of freshmen graduated in the top 10th of their high school class—and are united in their quest for a good job after graduation. "Everyone is dedicated, respectful, and proud to be at Carnegie Mellon," says a French major.

> Students divide themselves between actors, dancers, and other artsy types and engineers, scientists, and architects.

Once a largely regional institution, drawing mostly Pennsylvania residents, Carnegie Mellon now counts 84 percent of its undergraduate students from out of state, including 22 percent from foreign countries. More than one-third are from minority groups, including 27 percent Asian American, 4 percent African American, and 8 percent Hispanic. Students report that campus politics lean liberal, but many students don't get actively involved in social or political matters. The university says it remains committed to need-blind admissions, but it provides larger proportions of outright grants in financial aid packages to "academic superstars." Carnegie Mellon guarantees to meet the full demonstrated financial need of students admitted under early decision, and has stopped guaranteeing to meet full financial need of all regular decision students, but it does offer an early evaluation of financial aid eligibility for interested prospective students.

> "Professors are...often engaging us with events outside of the campus bubble and helping us with projects."

Housing is guaranteed for undergraduates all four years if they stay in the university housing system, and 61 percent do so. Upperclassmen get first pick, so the popular university-owned apartments fill up fast, and freshman assignments are made from a lottery of the remaining options. The best dorms for freshmen are

Stever House—the first LEED-certified residence hall in the U.S.—Donner, Resnik, and Morewood Gardens. "The dorms are generally very comfortable and well maintained, with ample living space," says one student. The Carnegie Mellon Café was the first cafeteria in the nation to earn LEED certification and offers students a state-of-the-art dining space. Still, one student advises, "Don't come to CMU for the food. Just don't." Students report feeling safe on campus, thanks to a comprehensive security program, and note that the school has numerous programs to deal with sexual assault.

Spring Carnival is a festival where students set up booths and race in buggies designed by engineering majors.

With all the academic pressure at Carnegie Mellon, it's a good thing there are so many opportunities to unwind, especially with the entire city of Pittsburgh close at hand. "The social life takes place mostly off campus, though there are late-night events and concerts on campus," says a student. The Greek system provides the most visible form of on-campus social life, with 17 percent of men joining fraternities and 14 percent of women joining sororities. Those of age who want to imbibe should know that "drinking takes place mostly off campus, because it is not allowed in dorms," according to one student. Nearby Oakland has coffeehouses, inexpensive films, dances, and concerts, and downtown Pittsburgh (just 20 minutes away by bus) offers a rich social scene, with opera, ballet, symphony, concerts, and sporting events.

One event that brings everyone together is the Spring Carnival, a four-day weekend festival. Students set up booths with electronic games, and student groups race in buggies made of lightweight alloys designed by engineering majors. Drama students put on original "Scotch 'n' Soda" presentations, two of which—*Pippin* and *Godspell*—have gone on to become Broadway

"Everyone is dedicated, respectful, and proud to be at Carnegie Mellon."

hits. "There are lots of social groups like the CIA, the KGB, and Fringe, which participate along with Greek organizations in the yearly Carnival celebrations," says one student. "These groups are a great way to meet upperclassmen and get involved with people outside of your program."

As for sports, the Carnegie Mellon Tartans compete in Division III. The women's soccer team won its conference championship in 2015, and both women's and men's soccer have made multiple appearances in the national championship tournament. Men's and women's tennis and swimming, men's cross-country, and volleyball are also strong. Students also participate in two dozen intramural sports.

Carnegie Mellon appeals just as much to those yearning for the bright lights of Broadway as it does to those pursuing the glowing computer screens of the scientific and business worlds. And with a broad range of liberal arts and technical courses not only available, but required, there's no doubt students leave with a well-rounded education—and an impressive diploma. Students more interested in specializing in one field than gaining exposure to many may fare better elsewhere, but most agree that the demanding environment is well worth it. As one recent graduate attests, Carnegie Mellon "shaped not only my education, but also my personality, and helped me formulate my post-graduate plans."

Overlaps

Cornell University, MIT, Princeton, UC–Berkeley, Stanford, Brown, Columbia, Johns Hopkins

If You Apply To > **Carnegie Mellon:** Early decision: Nov. 1. Regular decision: Jan. 1. Priority financial aid: Feb. 15. Housing: May 1. Application fee: $75. Campus and alumni interviews: recommended, evaluative. SATs or ACTs: required (SAT essay and ACT writing recommended). Subject Tests: required (varies by program). Letters of recommendation: required. Essay: required. Accepts the Common Application.

Case Western Reserve

103 Tomlinson Hall, 10900 Euclid Ave, Cleveland, OH 44106

CWRU has most of the offerings available at Carnegie Mellon or Washington U, but it has never found a niche in the national consciousness. Students in the know sing its praises, especially since CWRU is less difficult to get into than other institutions of comparable quality. Students get an outstanding technical education with solid offerings in other areas.

Website: www.case.edu

Location: City Center

Private

Total Enrollment: 10,140

Undergraduates: 4,996

Male/Female: 55/45

SAT Ranges: CR 620–720, M 680–770

ACT Ranges: 30–33

Financial Aid: 83%

Pell Grant: 15%

Expense: Pr $ $ $

Student Loans: 57%

Average Debt: $ $ $

Phi Beta Kappa: Yes

Applicants: 22,807

Accepted: 36%

Enrolled: 15%

Grad in 6 Years: 81%

Returning Freshmen: 94%

Academics: ✎ ✎ ✎ ✎

Social: ☎ ☎

Q of L: ★ ★ ★

Admissions: (216) 368-4450

Email Address: admission@case.edu

Strong Programs:
Biomedical Engineering
Mechanical Engineering
Nursing
Music
Anthropology
Biology
Psychology
Business Management

Cleveland's Case Western Reserve has much in common with Pittsburgh's Carnegie Mellon. Both are the product of mergers between a technical college, known for excellence in engineering, and a more traditional university, focused on the arts and sciences. Both are located in aging Rust Belt cities, which have struggled to reinvent themselves. And both tend to attract brainy students more concerned with studying than socializing. CWRU has increased its investment in the arts, humanities, and social sciences, with an aim toward helping students connect these disciplines with their technical studies. Indeed, the school's mission remains unchanged and emphasizes a commitment to "improving people's lives through preeminent research, education, and creative endeavor."

CWRU is located on the eastern edge of Cleveland, at University Circle. This 550-acre area of parks and gardens is home to more than 40 cultural, educational, medical, and research institutions, including the city's museums of art and natural history, its botanical gardens, and Severance Hall, home of the Cleveland Orchestra. Campus buildings are an eclectic mix of architectural styles, and several are listed on the National Register of Historic Places. The Lewis Building, designed by Frank Gehry, is home of the Weatherhead School of Management. It features undulating walls similar to those of Gehry's Guggenheim Museum in Bilbao, Spain, along with offices, classrooms, and meeting rooms on every floor, to encourage informal student/faculty interaction. The newest addition to campus, the 82,000-square-foot Tinkham Veale University Center ("the Tink") meets LEED Silver standards and serves as a hub for campus dining, special events, and more than 160 student organizations.

The product of the 1967 marriage between Case Institute of Technology and Western Reserve University, CWRU has four undergraduate schools: the College of Arts and Sciences, the Case School of Engineering, the Frances Payne Bolton School of Nursing, and the aforementioned Weatherhead School; all also offer graduate programs. All CWRU students participate in a general education program known as

> **"CWRU is a collaborative environment that allows students to excel in their own way."**

SAGES—the Seminar Approach to General Education and Scholarship. Emphasizing small seminars, critical thinking, and writing, the program requires four seminars, a writing portfolio, and a senior capstone experience that can be an individual or group effort. According to a biomedical engineering major, "CWRU is a collaborative environment that allows students to excel in their own way."

CWRU's strongest programs include engineering, especially biomedical and mechanical engineering, and nursing. The school's polymer science major is one of the few such undergraduate programs in the country. Strengths in the College of Arts and Sciences include music (a joint program with the nearby Cleveland Institute of Music), anthropology (especially medical anthropology), biology, and psychology. Business management is also strong. Combined bachelor's and master's programs are popular, as is the Preprofessional Scholars program, which gives top freshmen conditional acceptance to CWRU's law, social work, medical, or dental schools, assuming satisfactory progress through prerequisite courses. Fifty-nine percent of classes enroll fewer than 20 students, and a biochemistry major says, "While you may run across some professors who are difficult to learn from, there are far more professors who care a great deal about the students." Undergraduate research is highly encouraged, and 77 percent of students conduct research as part of senior capstone projects or independent studies. Roughly 45 percent of students take part in study abroad; locales include El Salvador, Israel, Cameroon, and the Netherlands.

An engineering major describes her peers like this: "It's like you took the nerds from high school and put them together, so they reorganized into 'popular,' 'stoner,' 'student government,' and 'nerd.'" Twenty-nine percent of CWRU's students are Ohio natives, and 71 percent graduated in the top 10th of their high school class. International students represent a strong contingent at 11 percent. African Americans make up 5 percent of the student body, Asian Americans 20 percent, and Hispanics 6 percent. Diversity 360 is a new campuswide training program, launched in response to student recommendations, designed to increase knowledge and awareness about diversity issues. Students say conservatives and liberals are well represented on campus. Eligible students receive scholarships based on academic merit, but there are no athletic awards.

> **"If a party takes place, it can get pretty wild."**

> *CWRU's polymer science major is one of the few such undergraduate programs in the country.*

Students are required to live on campus for their first two years, and eighty percent of all undergrads stay on campus. "Housing at CWRU is great," says a sophomore. "The residence halls become a student's home away from home." Each first-year student participates in one of four residential colleges, with themes focusing on growth through the arts, knowledge through multiculturalism, engagement through sustainability, and leadership through service. Upperclassmen rave about the amenities in the university's apartment-style suites, which also feature music practice rooms, a fitness center, and a cyber café. Another choice for upperclassmen is off-campus housing, where there are many desirable apartments within walking distance of campus. Dining-hall fare is "not Mom's cooking every night, but it's not bad," reasons one student, adding, "Students can also eat in Uptown and Little Italy, which are nearby campus." Campus police are "extremely friendly and they love to talk to students about campus life and other happenings around campus," according to a biology major. To more effectively respond to and prevent issues of campus sexual assault, the university recently created a new Office of Title IX and comprehensive educational programming.

> *Diversity 360 is a new campuswide training program, launched in response to student recommendations.*

On campus, there are dances and fraternity parties (Greek groups draw 34 percent of the men and 39 percent of the women). "The social life on campus at CWRU is very limited, as students are highly focused on academics. But if a party takes place, it can get pretty wild," one mechanical engineering major says. Community service projects are also big in the Greek community. Popular campus traditions are Greek Week, which includes nearly everyone on campus; the Springfest carnival to celebrate the end of classes; and "Study Overs," where students gather during finals week for free food, massages, study groups, and more. The annual sci-fi movie marathon is a rite of passage, while Engineering Week features a fuel-cell-powered car competition.

> **"[Cleveland is] very budget-friendly."**

CWRU is located five miles from downtown Cleveland. "It's very budget-friendly," notes one senior. Another says, "Cleveland is more than just Case, and I wouldn't have it any other way." The city features the Rock and Roll Hall of Fame, and—in the warmer months—Cleveland Indians games at Progressive Field. Students can make their way around with unlimited bus service for about $25 a semester, but having a car is helpful, especially for road trips to nearby cities in Ohio, or for longer jaunts to Chicago or Windsor, Ontario, where students under 21 are free to drink and gamble.

Although sports are not a major focus on campus, the Tartans versus Spartans football game against Carnegie Mellon is big. Men's and women's cross-country and tennis, men's baseball and swimming and diving, and women's volleyball all competed in their respective Division III national championship tournaments in the 2015–16 season. About 85 percent of students participate in at least one of the 20 intramural and 15 club sports available, ranging from flag football and soccer to crew and kendo. The 26-mile Hudson Relay, held the last week of the spring semester to commemorate CWRU's relocation from Hudson to Cleveland, pits teams of runners from the four classes against one another, with each person running a half mile.

Although a rigorous, science- and engineering-oriented research university, CWRU devotes noteworthy attention to the student experience. "CWRU is home. There is a home for everyone," says a sophomore. "And our campus focuses on building that relationship, that community, so all students fit in and feel safe and welcomed." And with challenging academics, preprofessional programs, and research opportunities across all disciplines, students are also well-equipped to excel in their future careers.

If You Apply To ➤

Case: Early decision I and early action: Nov. 1. Early decision II and regular decision: Jan. 15. Financial aid: Feb. 15. Housing: May 1. No application fee. Campus and alumni interviews: optional, evaluative. SATs or ACTs: required (SAT essay and ACT writing optional). Subject Tests: optional. Letters of recommendation: required. Essay: required. Accepts the Common Application. Audition required for artists and musicians.

The Catholic University of America

Washington, D.C. 20064

There are other Roman Catholic–affiliated universities, but this is THE Catholic University. Catholics make up nearly 80 percent of the undergraduate student body here (versus roughly half at nearby Georgetown). If you can't be in Rome, there is no better place than D.C. to work and play. CUA even has a Metrorail stop right next to campus. Academic freedom is the norm except in theology.

Founded in 1887 under a charter from Pope Leo XIII, The Catholic University of America was the brainchild of U.S. bishops who wanted to provide an American institution where the curriculum was guided by the tenets of Christian thought. Over time, the university has garnered a reputation as a research-oriented school that also provides a strong undergraduate, preprofessional education, and an appreciation for the arts. However, the university's new strategic plan calls for an emphasis on the humanities, less large-scale research, and a return to single-sex residence halls. The changes have ruffled a few feathers; the school pulled out of the Association of American Universities, a group composed of 62 elite research institutions, citing differences in mission.

Catholic University's campus comprises 176 tree-lined acres, an impressive layout for an urban university. Buildings range from ivy-covered limestone and brick to ultramodern, giving the place a true collegiate feel. The campus has undergone a spate of renovations, including updates to many of the residence halls, and has made way for an open green space.

CUA is one of the few colleges in the country that began as a graduate institution (others are Clark University and The Johns Hopkins University), and grad students still account for a respectable portion of the student population. Ten of its 12 schools now admit undergrads. Students need at least 40 courses in order to graduate. In the School of Arts and Sciences, approximately 25 of these must be from a core curriculum spread across the humanities, social and behavioral sciences, philosophy, theology and religious studies, math and natural sciences, and languages and literature. English composition is also required.

Students have excellent options in almost any department at CUA. In addition to politics, which sets the tone on campus, the psychology, business, and physics departments are very strong. The School of Nursing is one of the best in the nation, and engineering and architecture are highly regarded. Architecture and physics have outstanding facilities, the latter enjoying a modern vitreous-state lab, a boon for both research and hands-on undergraduate instruction.

> **"The courses are challenging and require a commitment to studying and learning the material in order to be successful."**

CUA's Benjamin T. Rome School of Music offers several bachelor of music degrees, such as composition, music education, organ, and piano pedagogy, as well as a B.A. in music. The National Catholic School of Social Service offers a bachelor of social work degree.

"The courses are challenging and require a commitment to studying and learning the material in order to be successful," a senior says. Fifty-seven percent of classes have fewer than 20 students, which means special attention from faculty members. It also means that there's no place to hide. "One of the things I really love about Catholic is the professors," says one sophomore. "They all teach with passion, and it is apparent that they love what they do." Clergy are at the helm of the school of theology and religious studies and the school of canon law, but most schools and departments have a primarily lay faculty; religious faculty make up about 7 percent of the teaching posts for the entire university. Its chancellor is the archbishop of Washington, and Catholic churches across the country donate a fraction of their annual collections to the university. One downside of being the only Catholic school with a papal charter is that officials in Rome, who do not always warm up to American traditions of academic freedom, keep a sharp eye on who teaches in the theology school and what they write and say.

Top students can enroll in the University Honors Program, which offers course sequences in philosophy, theology, humanities, social science, and environmental studies. The university offers a wide variety of semester, academic year, summer, and short-term education abroad programs, as well as international internships, through its CUAbroad

> **"[Professors] teach with passion, and it is apparent that they love what they do. "**

office, and several scholarships are available to support these ventures. Currently, there are more than 75 semester-long and nearly 50 summer options available in countries around the globe, in which 31 percent of students participate. The flagship Rome Center, jointly operated by CUA and the Australian Catholic University, emphasizes experiential, on-site learning, with programs for both liberal arts and architecture students, as well as a new summer program for the First-Year Experience. CUA is also part of the 14-member Consortium of Universities of the Washington Metropolitan Area and the Oak Ridge Associated Universities Consortium; the latter gives students access to federal research facilities and scientists through the Oak Ridge National Laboratory.

Catholicism is clearly the tie that binds the student body. Sunday Masses are so well attended that extra services are offered in the dorms. Ninety-seven percent of undergraduates are from outside D.C., including 5 percent from foreign countries

(continued)

Phi Beta Kappa: Yes
Applicants: 5,991
Accepted: 79%
Enrolled: 19%
Grad in 6 Years: 69%
Returning Freshmen: 86%
Academics: ✍ ✍ ✍
Social: ☎ ☎ ☎
Q of L: ★ ★ ★
Admissions: (202) 319-5305
Email Address:
  cua-admissions@cua.edu

Strong Programs:
Political Science
Nursing
Engineering
Architecture
Psychology
Business
Physics
Music

The School of Nursing is one of the best in the nation.

and most of the rest from the Northeast. Five percent are African American, 13 percent are Hispanic, and 3 percent are Asian American. A big issue on campus is the pro-life movement. Catholic University maintains a need-blind admissions policy but does not guarantee to meet the full demonstrated need of all admitted students. "For most students, CUA is a large financial sacrifice," says one student. "I think in a lot of ways it drives them to do well and succeed at whatever they're pursuing." All applicants are considered for merit scholarships, which average $16,734, and five full-tuition scholarships are offered to each entering class. No athletic scholarships are offered.

Sunday Masses are so well attended that extra services are offered in the dorms.

Fifty-seven percent of undergraduates live in the single-sex residence halls, which are intended to foster an environment of virtuous living. All first-year students are assigned to interest communities organized around shared academic or personal interests. On-campus housing offers a variety of options ranging from the traditional (a shared double or triple room with a shared bathroom down the hall) to suites (multiple rooms sharing a bathroom) and apartments. "The newer dorms are more comfortable than the older dorms, but Catholic is very good about revamping and reconstructing older dorms," according to one student. Campus fare is a mixed blessing: "The dining is unlimited, which is awesome for big appetites," says one student. "The problem is that it's overpriced and bland." Emergency phones, shuttle buses, and escort services are provided as part of campus security, and students agree that they feel safe on campus. The Peer Educators Empowering Respectful Students (PEERS) group helps to raise awareness about sexual assault prevention.

"Catholic is very good about revamping and reconstructing older dorms."

All first-year students are assigned to interest communities organized around shared academic or personal interests.

When students want to explore the city, they need only walk to the Brookland-CUA Metrorail stop adjacent to campus and then enjoy the ride. Capitol Hill is 15 minutes away; the stylish Georgetown area, with its chic restaurants and nightspots, is only a half hour away. No one under 21 can drink on campus, and most students agree that this policy is effective in curbing underage drinking. Also, alcohol "abuse" has been added as an offense, in addition to unlawful use, possession, and distribution. Campus Ministry offers students numerous opportunities to engage in faith and service through regular community service events, student retreats, summer mission trips, and other events. Annual activities on campus include a weeklong homecoming celebration, Light the Season, Mistletoe Ball, Mr. CUA, Founder's Ball, and Luaupalooza, a popular celebration of the end of the academic year.

Sports on campus include varsity and intramural competition. CUA's Cardinals compete in Division III. Women's lacrosse has won seven Landmark Conference championships in the last eight years, and other recent winners include women's basketball, field hockey, and soccer and men's basketball, baseball, and lacrosse. Intramurals and recreational programs attract plenty of activity too; popular programs include basketball, indoor soccer, and flag football.

When discussions first raised the idea of a Catholic university, the man who would become the university's first rector, Bishop John Joseph Keane, argued for an institution that would "exercise a dominant influence in the world's future" with a superior intellectual foundation. Now, 130 years later, CUA offers students a wealth of preprofessional courses spanning the arts and sciences. The founders' quest for "a higher synthesis of knowledge" is constantly being realized at Catholic University, a unique university and a capital destination.

Overlaps

Saint Joseph's University, Loyola University Maryland, University of Maryland, Villanova, Penn State, University of Delaware, Fordham, American University

Centre College

600 West Walnut, Danville, KY 40422

Centre may not be the most famous institution of higher learning in Kentucky, but it is certainly the best. Centre offers college the way it used to be—football games, Greek row, and a decades-old tradition that obliges students to run through campus (in the nude). There is also the unparalleled closeness between students and faculty that comes with a student body of close to 1,400. Compare to Sewanee, Rhodes, and Davidson.

Centre College, the only independent school in Kentucky with a Phi Beta Kappa chapter, has produced two-thirds of the state's Rhodes scholars over the last 40 years. But the school is not all work and no play. It's also a throwback to the way college used to be, with Friday night parties on Greek row and Saturday afternoon football games. Centre's small size offers an intimate classroom environment. And its liberal arts focus means that despite Centre's southern location, students are progressive, intellectual, and perhaps more well-rounded than their peers at neighboring schools. "We have an amazing balance of 'Northern academics' paired with 'Southern hospitalities,'" says a sophomore.

Located in the heart of Kentucky Bluegrass country, Centre's campus is a mix of old Greek Revival and attractive modern buildings. More than 14 of them are listed on the National Registry of Historic Places, a fact that's less surprising when you know that Centre is the 48th oldest college in the United States. The college is home to four LEED-certified buildings, including two at the Gold level. Recent construction projects include a new soccer facility and a renovation and expansion of the Parsons Student Health Center.

General education requirements include basic skills in expository writing, math, and foreign language and two courses in four contexts—aesthetic, social, scientific, and fundamental questions. Students must also take a computer seminar. Required first-year seminar courses are offered during the three-week January "CentreTerm." Capped at 15 students each, they offer a chance to explore off-beat topics such as cloning, baseball in American politics, and coffee-shop culture.

Centre's most popular majors are economics and finance, biology, history, and international studies. Behavioral neuroscience is emerging as a popular major as well, and other strong programs include mathematics, computer science, and English. Art is solid too, and glassblowing enthusiasts will find one of the few fully equipped undergraduate facilities for their pursuit in the nation. A 3–2 program sends aspiring engineers on to one of four major universities, including Columbia and Vanderbilt. Centre also belongs to the Associated Colleges of the South*. "Centre College fosters a learning environment in which the boundaries of everyone's academic limits are pushed while maintaining a sense of camaraderie between classmates," says a math major. Sixty percent of classes have fewer than 20 students. "My professors

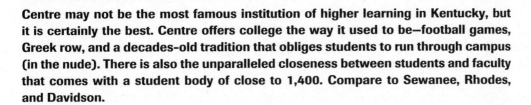

"We have an amazing balance of 'Northern academics' paired with 'Southern hospitalities.'"

Website: www.centre.edu
Location: Small Town
Private
Total Enrollment: 1,351
Undergraduates: 1,351
Male/Female: 50/50
SAT Ranges: CR 540–660, M 570–740
ACT Ranges: 26–31
Financial Aid: 95%
Pell Grant: 18%
Expense: Pr $
Student Loans: 55%
Average Debt: $ $ $
Phi Beta Kappa: Yes
Applicants: 2,716
Accepted: 71%
Enrolled: 19%
Grad in 6 Years: 86%
Returning Freshmen: 89%
Academics: ✿ ✿ ✿ ½
Social: ☎ ☎ ☎
Q of L: ★ ★ ★
Admissions: (859) 238-5350
Email Address: admission@centre.edu

Strong Programs:
Economics and Finance
Biology
History
International Studies
Behavioral Neuroscience

took the time to really get to know me and my learning style and how I understood the material being taught," says a politics major. "Our small class sizes allow professors to really feed off of the energy and needs of the class and make it a more personal environment."

The Centre Commitment guarantees students an internship or research experience, study abroad, and a degree in four years. Eighty-five percent of any given class takes advantage of Centre's extensive study abroad programs. Centre runs regular semester-long programs for students in all majors in China, England, France, Japan, Mexico, Northern Ireland, Scotland, and Spain, in addition to several others offered during the January term. Study-away semesters in Washington, D.C., and Chicago combine coursework with internships. Approximately 82 percent of students engage in an internship or perform collaborative research with faculty.

> "My professors took the time to really get to know me and my learning style."

The Centre Commitment guarantees students an internship or research experience, study abroad, and a degree in four years.

"We all have personal leadership goals we want to pursue and are ready to make what we want happen," says a sophomore. "We are willing to do the hard work." Fifty-three percent of Centre students hail from Kentucky, and 7 percent arrive from foreign nations. African Americans comprise 5 percent of the student body, Asian Americans 4 percent, and Hispanics 3 percent. Students say the campus leans left politically, but all viewpoints are represented and respected. "Whatever is in the national spotlight definitely gets discussed over dinner or in class," says a senior. Centre offers hundreds of merit scholarships averaging $19,657. Through the Grissom Scholars Program, 10 incoming first-generation students are awarded full-tuition scholarships plus $5,000 to support study abroad, research, or an internship.

Ninety-eight percent of students live on campus, and students say the four-year residential requirement makes for a strong sense of community. "While the dorms aren't the Ritz, they make a pretty nice home away from home," says a junior. Suite- and townhouse-style accommodations are available for upperclassmen, but the lottery system means not everyone gets their top choices. Forty percent of men and 41 percent of women go Greek and may bunk in fraternity or sorority houses, respectively. Students dine in one main dining hall, Cowan, and two café-style eateries. "Cowan has done a great job increasing the diversity of food options and the number of locally sourced food options," explains a junior. "We have a strong Title IX team as well as a developing student advisory board to help advise and give student input regarding sexual assault," reports a sophomore.

> "There are no barriers to success at Centre, only opportunities for students to take advantage of."

Through the Grissom Scholars Program, 10 incoming first-generation students are awarded full-tuition scholarships.

Greek life is the center of the social scene, and their parties are open to all. "Alcohol is a large part of the weekend social life here for many students," says a senior. The Student Activity Council sponsors a variety of alternatives, such as free midnight movies at the local theater and events like comedians, karaoke, and laser tag. Students also get free admission to Centre's separately endowed Norton Center for the Arts, which brings touring musicals, plays, and other performances to campus. Homecoming in the fall and Carnival in the spring are major annual events. Campus superstitions involve placing pennies on the toe of the Abraham Lincoln statue for good luck on exams, and not stepping on the Centre Seal to avoid failing them. But Centre's most hallowed tradition is "Running the Flame," which has students dashing from their residence halls to a large sculpture of a flame in the center of campus, circling it three times, and running back—"naked, of course." Eighty percent of the student body does community service through the Greek system, Habitat for Humanity, or other organizations. The small town of Danville doesn't have much to offer, but Lexington and Louisville are within an hour's drive, and it's easy to get to the countryside for camping, fishing, and other outdoor pursuits.

Centre's football team has been around for more than a century, and while it now competes against regional opponents in Division III, that wasn't always the case. In 1921 the Colonels beat then-powerhouse Harvard, six to zero, a triumph that has been called the greatest sports upset in the first half of the 20th century. Nowadays, Centre's archrival is nearby Transylvania University. "We are better than them in every way and that's that," declares a senior. The women's soccer team advanced to the Final Four in the 2015 national tournament, and the football team claimed the conference title that same year. Men's basketball, men's and women's golf, and men's cross-country are also competitive. Sixty percent of the student body regularly play in the intramural program, with flag football, softball, and basketball drawing the most players.

What Centre College lacks in size, it more than makes up for in quality. With a safe, bucolic campus, an emphasis on academic excellence, and faculty and students who care about forming lasting friendships with each other, this undiscovered gem may be worth a look. Says one satisfied senior, "There are no barriers to success at Centre, only opportunities for students to take advantage of."

If You Apply To ➤

Centre: Early decision: Nov. 15. Early action: Dec. 1. Regular decision and financial aid: Jan. 15. No application fee. Campus interviews: recommended, evaluative. No alumni interviews. SATs or ACTs: required. No Subject Tests. Letters of recommendation: required. Essay: required. Accepts the Common Application.

Champlain College

251 South Willard Street, Burlington, VT 05401

A small college with a unique "upside-down" approach to blending professional education and the liberal arts. Champlain's major academic strengths are game design, whose students shape the campus culture, as well as business and international studies. A good fit for students eager to get started in a career but not a great place to explore options and find yourself. Social life revolves around student-friendly Burlington, and Vermont's nearby ski slopes beckon. Low graduation rate is an issue.

Champlain is an up-and-coming small college, situated on a hill overlooking Vermont's scenic Lake Champlain, that has set out to reinvent the relationship between professional studies and the liberal arts through its so-called "upside-down" curriculum. Instead of following the traditional academic path—two years of general education courses followed by two years of in-depth study in a major—students at Champlain immediately pursue both their major and a highly structured liberal arts curriculum simultaneously for all four years. This approach appeals to career-minded students who still appreciate the value of a strong dose of the liberal arts.

The college sits on 22 acres in the historic Hill Section of Burlington, adjacent to the University of Vermont. The core academic campus consists of a mix of lovely restored Victorian mansions and complimentary modern structures of brick with slate roofs and green trim. The adjacent "lakeside" campus houses the Leahy Center for Digital Investigation and a variety of administrative facilities, while a "downtown" campus, connected to the academic core by shuttle buses, offers housing and dining for 300 upperclassmen. Computer labs and phone charging stations abound on campus. A new Center for Communication and Creative Media,

Website: www.champlain.edu
Location: Small City
Private
Total Enrollment: 2,908
Undergraduates: 2,159
Male/Female: 62/38
SAT Ranges: CR 520–630, M 510–630
ACT Ranges: 23–29
Financial Aid: 98%
Pell Grant: 23%
Expense: Pr $
Student Loans: 73%
Average Debt: $ $ $ $
Phi Beta Kappa: No

(continued)

Applicants: 5,587
Accepted: 66%
Enrolled: 15%
Grad in 6 Years: 58%
Returning Freshmen: 79%
Academics: ✍ ✍ ✍
Social: ☎ ☎ ☎
Q of L: ★ ★ ★
Admissions: (802) 860-2727
Email Address: admission@
  champlain.edu

Strong Programs:
Game Design
Game Art and Animation
Business Administration
Communication
Graphic Design and Digital
  Media
Psychology
Computer and Digital
  Forensics
Computer Networking and
  Cybersecurity

Students at Champlain immediately pursue both their major and a highly structured liberal arts curriculum simultaneously for all four years.

a 75,000-square-foot facility with game and audio labs, studio spaces, and a traditional and digital photo lab, recently opened.

Champlain's distinctive curriculum is built around three legs ("Education in 3D," to use the local lingo), starting with professional programs. Students apply to one of four academic divisions—Stiller School of Business; Communication and Creative Media (CCM); Education and Human Studies; or Information Technology and Sciences—and then select a major in that division. For example, CCM, the largest division, offers nine choices, with broadcast media production, creative media, filmmaking, game art and animation, and professional writing among them. Students disillusioned by their initial choices can transfer to another major within their division, but switching to another division can be difficult. The second leg, the liberal arts component, is a highly structured set of Core courses taught on an interdisciplinary basis by professors from all departments. Students pursue a series of courses over three years that focus in progressive fashion on the nature of the self, concepts of a just and sustainable community in the West, and global themes, such as human rights. Seniors complete a capstone experience that integrates learning from their professional, liberal arts, and out-of-classroom experiences. The school argues that four years of working simultaneously in a professional field and the liberal arts gives students the broad thinking and learning skills that will serve them well beyond their first jobs. The third and final piece of the curricular pie is the Life Experience and Action Dimension, or LEAD. This is a set of mandatory noncredit workshops extending over four years and dealing with life skills, such as how to manage personal finances, how to manage a career, and the value of community service. "Champlain puts a lot of effort into the thought of 'after college,'" says a junior. LEAD also provides first-year students with an older peer advisor.

> **"Champlain puts a lot of effort into the thought of 'after college.'"**

Professors bring "a great deal of passion, dedication, and experience that the students can tap into to expand their own knowledge," says one student. Sixty-eight percent of classes at Champlain have fewer than 20 students, and all are taught on an inquiry basis by professors or adjuncts, with no teaching assistants. A senior says, "The academic climate is extremely collaborative. From your Core classes to your major-specific classes, you will be engaged in discussions and group projects almost every day." Game design is a particularly popular field, and seniors in game-development-related majors often compete against one another to complete projects for school-sponsored events. The most popular majors are business administration, communication, graphic design and digital media, and psychology. Computer and digital forensics and computer networking and cybersecurity are also highly regarded, and the new CCM building promises to offer a big boost to writing and the arts. Many students also take minors in areas such as global studies. A new major in data analytics is now available.

> **"You will be engaged in discussions and group projects almost every day."**

Virtually all students participate in some sort of internship at some point. Study abroad, which draws about half of the students, plays an important role at Champlain, and the college offers free passports to students who do not already have them. The college maintains satellite campuses in Dublin, Ireland, from which students have easy access to the rest of Europe, and Montreal, a major global center for the game industry. Still dozens of other students go abroad through the school's internship sites in Shanghai or through Champlain's service-learning program. There are no honors programs or undergraduate research opportunities, and most graduates—education majors are an exception—head for the job market rather than graduate or professional schools.

"Champlain students are focused, driven, and passionate," says a social work and psychology major—and they arrive with a career choice in mind. Twenty-two percent of students are native Vermonters, with the rest hailing mainly from the East Coast and Midwest. Champlain students are a fairly homogenous crowd, with African Americans accounting for 2 percent of the total, Hispanics 4 percent, Asian Americans 2 percent, and international students only 1 percent. Largely because of the nature of the curriculum, men outnumber women by a ratio of three to two. "Most of the campus is comprised of geeks and gamers," says a student. "There are many skiers and snowboarders, of course, and a great deal of people who care about the environment or social issues." Twenty-three percent of freshmen qualify for Pell Grants, and the school awards merit scholarships averaging $9,893.

"The housing at Champlain is such a neat experience," cheers one junior. "They are old Victorian mansions, and you will most likely become a family with everyone living in your house." Sophomores and upperclassmen can choose among well-maintained traditional dorms, some quite new, that feature tuning and repair facilities for bikes, skis, and skateboards, or they can live in an off-

> **"Hard-core party folks go to our neighbors, UVM."**

campus apartment hall or find their own off-campus digs. Overall, 64 percent of undergrads reside in college-owned housing. Students take their meals at a single dining hall where, this being Vermont, the emphasis is on fresh, local, and healthy foods. Food is available on an all-you-can-eat basis, but there are no trays, and paper plates or plastic utensils are definite no-nos. One student reports, "Our school's Public Safety department is incredibly friendly to students and always shows up quickly (even if you just locked yourself out of your room)."

"Because our campus is so small, most of the social life is off campus," says a marketing major, "whether it's downtown on Church Street, by the lake, a friend's apartment, or a concert." The campus is dry and policies are enforced; in the absence of fraternities and sororities, says a sophomore, "hard-core party folks go to our neighbors, UVM." The college organizes a range of activities on and off campus, from hiking and bowling to club sports. A small city of 43,000 residents, Burlington is near the top of everyone's list of best college towns. "Burlington is a very artistic and bustling community," says one student. The Church Street pedestrian mall, just below the campus, offers an array of cafés and shops for all tastes, as well as abundant nightlife, and there is a park and bike path that runs along the lake's waterfront.

No one seems to mind that Champlain has no intercollegiate sports (though it does have a mascot named Chauncey T. Beaver). But there are plenty of intramural options, including soccer, basketball, and dodgeball, as well as rugby and coed hockey clubs that compete against other schools; roughly 20 percent of Champlain students

> **"The gaming culture might be a deterrent to those who aren't interested in video games."**

participate. Not surprisingly for a school full of gamers, Quidditch and Humans vs. Zombies are popular. "Even people who work out in the gym go with novelty tees or spend time there talking about video games," explains a sophomore. Annual traditions include the Spring Meltdown, a carnival just before final exams, and the One World Festival featuring food and music from various countries. The end of the year brings the Game Development Senior Show, where graduating seniors show off their projects to the college community, family members, and company recruiters.

Administrators at Champlain are sensitive about the fact that only 57 percent of entering students graduate within six years. One contributing factor, students suggest, is the need to plunge immediately into a professional field that may not be a good fit. "Students end up switching out of the program or out of the school, especially if they have trouble deciding what major they want," says a sophomore. Other students point to the heavy workload in some majors and the lack of cultural diversity as possible factors. "People interested in Greek life and sports fans might not feel comfortable here," says a game art and animation major. "The gaming culture

The college maintains satellite campuses in Dublin, Ireland, and Montreal, a major global center for the game industry.

Champlain has no intercollegiate sports (though it does have a mascot named Chauncey T. Beaver).

Overlaps

University of Vermont, Rochester Institute of Technology, University of New Hampshire, University of Maine–Orono, University of Connecticut, Ithaca, University of Massachusetts Amherst

might be a deterrent to those who aren't interested in video games." In fact, gaming is so ingrained in the culture here that even one of the college's training programs on sexual assault prevention is delivered through a faculty-developed video game, called *Make a Change.*

For gaming enthusiasts, techies, creatives, and other career-oriented students who don't mind a hearty helping of quirky gaming culture, Champlain is a small school with a big vision of how to refashion the relationship between professional training and the liberal arts. It offers a unique option for students who have a strong, focused interest in its professional majors and who are eager to "press start" on their careers.

Chapman University

One University Drive, Orange, CA 92866

Chapman sits at the hub of Orange County and a stone's throw away from L.A. Has parlayed its O.C. location into burgeoning popularity in film, television, and the performing arts. Those without showbiz aspirations can opt for strong programs in business, communication studies, or biology. Disneyland is in the neighborhood, but you need a car to get there.

Website: www.chapman.edu
Location: Suburban
Private
Total Enrollment: 7,478
Undergraduates: 6,056
Male/Female: 39/61
SAT Ranges: CR 550–640, M 550–650
ACT Ranges: 25–30
Financial Aid: 89%
Pell Grant: 18%
Expense: Pr $ $ $
Student Loans: 61%
Average Debt: $ $ $
Phi Beta Kappa: Yes
Applicants: 13,670
Accepted: 48%
Enrolled: 22%
Grad in 6 Years: 79%
Returning Freshmen: 90%
Academics: ✍ ✍ ✍
Social: ☏ ☏ ☏
Q of L: ★ ★ ★

Although best known as a Southern Californian mecca for budding filmmakers to hone their craft, Chapman University continues to stake its claim as a comprehensive institution that happens to offer one of the nation's best film programs—rather than a film school that also happens to offer other majors. Chapman boasts stellar programs in business and has increased its emphasis on health sciences, technology, and physics. It also facilitates countless internships to send its students out into the workforce with real-world experience. A junior says, "A Chapman student is a leader, someone who wants to be actively involved in their community and consciously making a difference."

Founded in 1861, Chapman University is one of the oldest private universities in California. Originally called Hesperian College, the school later merged with California Christian College in Los Angeles. In 1934 the institution was renamed in honor of C. C. Chapman, an Orange County entrepreneur and benefactor of the school. In 1991 the college became Chapman University, reflecting its evolution into a comprehensive institution of higher learning. The beautiful residential campus, situated on 80 tree-lined acres, features a mixture of landmark historic buildings and state-of-the-art facilities. It is located in the historic Old Towne district of Orange, near outstanding beaches, Disneyland, and the world-class cultural offerings of Orange County and Los Angeles. Recent construction includes the new, 140,000-square-foot Center for Science and Technology, scheduled to open in 2018.

Regardless of major, all students complete a four-part general education program: a First-Year Foundations Course (FFC); six inquiry categories (natural science, quantitative reasoning, writing, social sciences, values and ethics, and artistic studies); a Global Citizen cluster (two courses in global studies, one in civic issues, and a language course); and a mini-minor, minor, or second major. All first-year students complete the FFC seminar in fall term. More than 50 wide-ranging topics are offered, all supporting the goal of engaging students in critically analyzing and communicating complex issues and ideas.

The most popular majors are business administration, film production, communication studies, and psychology. The Dodge College of Film and Media Arts is a comprehensive, production-based school that offers such majors as creative production, news/broadcast journalism and documentary, screenwriting, and public relations and advertising, as well as internships and other active learning opportunities. Emerging entrepreneurs can take advantage of a well-stocked portfolio of business programs through the Argyros School of Business and Economics. The Economic Science Institute allows for the study of experimental economics under the direction of Nobel laureate Dr. Vernon Smith and encompasses fields as diverse as finance, engineering, neuroscience, computer science, and philosophy, among others. The strong communication department expanded to become the new School of Communication in 2016. Notable programs in music, theatre, and dance involve frequent national and international performance components. Additionally, accelerated degree programs that allow students to earn a bachelor's and a master's in five years are available in several disciplines.

> **"I always feel supported and like I have a multitude of resources."**

"Every classroom environment that I was a part of was inclusive, collaborative, and welcoming. I always felt like I had a place and that my input was valued," reflects a senior health sciences major. Forty-five percent of classes have fewer than 20 students. Freshmen are taught by professors—there are no TAs—and professors are praised for being accessible and "genuinely interested in their students," says a senior. "I always feel supported and like I have a multitude of resources for class help, as well as career-planning and mentoring," adds a junior. Students interested in conducting faculty-mentored research can apply to the SURF (Summer Undergraduate Research Fellowship) program, which awards up to $3,000 in funding to selected fellows. Those seeking a global learning experience can choose from more than 90 preapproved study abroad programs; only 17 percent of students study abroad, although administrators say the university is committed to significantly increasing that number.

Chapman attracts a friendly, largely affluent student body. "Everyone is self-motivated and determined to get involved outside of the classroom in any way possible," says a student. Just over two-thirds of students hail from California, and 5 percent are international. African Americans comprise 1 percent of the population, Asian Americans 10 percent, and Hispanics 14 per-

> **"Everyone is self-motivated and determined to get involved outside of the classroom in any way possible."**

cent. "I think there are many students who are vocal about both sides of issues in regards to social justice, immigration, and marriage equality, among other topics," reports a creative production major. Eligible undergraduates receive merit scholarships worth an average of $16,640, but since Chapman is a Division III school, there are no athletic scholarships.

Thirty-four percent of Chapman students reside on campus. First-years are housed in residence halls based on their chosen academic program; one student explains, "This allows for students to know their peers on day one of classes and always have a study partner throughout the semester." The Randall Dining Commons was fully renovated in 2016, and meals are described as tasty and diverse. Chapman's public safety department receives positive reviews, and the CARES (Creating a Rape-Free Environment for Students) student organization is active in raising awareness about campus sexual assault.

Twenty-two percent of the men join fraternities, and sororities attract 40 percent of the women; all members of the Greek community are required to perform

(continued)

Admissions: (888) CU-APPLY
Email Address:
admit@chapman.edu

Strong Programs:
Business Administration
Film Production
Communication Studies
Psychology
Biology
Health Sciences
Economics
Performing Arts

All students complete a mini-minor, minor, or second major.

The Economic Science Institute allows for the study of experimental economics under the direction of a Nobel laureate.

community service, and Greek life doesn't dominate the social scene. A junior describes Chapman's off-campus party culture as "intimate," adding, "Students prefer to keep it to a lower scale, mostly due to the lack of a Greek row." Students also enjoy a plenitude of school-sponsored events. "Our University Program Board hosts hundreds of events throughout the year, including movie screenings; Midnight Breakfast; weekend excursions to the beach, museums, and hiking trails; dances; and many other events," cheers one senior. Every year, students flock to the homecoming celebration, WinterFest, and the Greek Week festival.

The city of Orange (population 140,000) is a college town only in the technical sense of the term. "It's actually a very quiet city," says a junior. The Old Towne district is well known as "the Antique Capital of California," although several trendy restaurants, brew pubs, and boutiques have opened their doors in the last few years. When students grow weary of the area, they take advantage of

"Students…know their peers on day one of classes and always have a study partner throughout the semester."

the pristine Southern California weather to explore the great outdoors or take trips to "Mexico, Disneyland, Knott's Berry Farm, the mall, and L.A.," according to a film major.

The Chapman Panthers compete in Division III, and football and men's and women's basketball are recent Southern California Intercollegiate Athletic Conference (SCIAC) champs. Women's tennis and volleyball advanced to national tournament play in recent years, and baseball and women's lacrosse are also competitive. The Chapman Dance Team has brought home eight consecutive national championships. Intramurals draw a quarter of the student body.

Students at Chapman are not only expected to hit the books, but also to actively express their creativity through hands-on learning and forays into the real world. In return, they are rewarded with an exceedingly supportive environment that both nurtures and challenges them every step of the way. "Chapman students love where they are," says a junior, "and take the time to add to the community as much as they can."

Overlaps

University of Southern California, UCLA, Loyola Marymount, Cal Poly–San Luis Obispo, NYU, Santa Clara, UC–Santa Barbara, University of San Diego

If You Apply To ➢

Chapman: Early action: Nov. 1. Regular decision: Jan. 15. Financial aid: Mar. 2. Housing: May 1. Application fee: $70. Campus and alumni interviews: optional, evaluative. SATs or ACTs (with writing): required. Subject Tests: recommended. Letters of recommendation: required. Essay: required. Talent-based programs require submission of a creative supplement. Accepts the Common Application with supplement.

College of Charleston

Charleston, SC 29424

A public school about half the size of the University of South Carolina that offers business, education, and the liberal arts and sciences. Location a feast for history buffs. College of Charleston compares to William and Mary in both scale and historic surroundings but is far less rigorous academically. Addressing its housing crunch to help it reach the next level.

Website: www.cofc.edu
Location: City Center
Public
Total Enrollment: 9,878

Whether sampling the traditional Lowcountry cuisine or delving into the wide range of courses offered at this strong liberal arts and sciences institution, students at the College of Charleston know they are getting a solid education based on creative expression and intellectual freedom. Founded in 1770 as Colonial South Carolina's first college, CofC's original commitment to the liberal arts and sciences and to the citizens of the region has helped it become a well-respected institution throughout the Southeast. And the location only adds to the experience, providing opportunities for volunteering and interning, and a robust social scene.

The 13th oldest college in the country, CofC was founded as a private college and, after a number of identity changes, became a state university exactly 200 years later. Located in Charleston's famous Historic District, the campus features many of the city's most historic and venerable buildings. More than 80 of its buildings are former private residences, ranging from the typical Charleston "single" house to the Victorian, and the clap-clap of horse-drawn carriages bearing tourists is a routine sight. The wooded area in front of Randolph Hall, known as the Cistern Yard, is a student gathering point and the site of graduation ceremonies. The campus has received countless awards for its design and has been designated a national arboretum and a National Historic Landmark. The Jewish Studies Center has been expanded to make way for a vegan/kosher kitchen and dining hall.

"I feel surrounded by students, staff, and professors who push me to succeed."

CofC has a core curriculum rooted strongly in the liberal arts, sciences, and professional programs. The focus is on the development of writing, computing, language acquisition, and thinking skills. Each student is required to complete six hours in English, history, mathematics or logic, and social science; eight hours in natural sciences; and 12 hours in humanities. Students must also show proficiency in a foreign language. All new students attend Convocation, where they are introduced to the college's academic traditions, and freshman minority students can participate in several support programs designed to ensure their successful transition to college. Freshmen take part in the First-Year Experience and choose between seminar and learning community options; sample seminars include Charleston and the Civil Rights Movement, Viruses and the Coming Apocalypse, and Hemingway in the Hispanic World. Cougar Excursion is offered through the Higdon Student Leadership Center and is an optional three-day summer leadership retreat in which about 100 participants meet other incoming freshmen, student leaders, and administrators.

"The academic climate at College of Charleston is very collaborative. I feel surrounded by students, staff, and professors who push me to succeed," a senior says. Biology and chemistry are two of the strongest programs; many of the graduates end up at the Medical University of South Carolina a few blocks down the street. Several programs have been awarded with Commendations of Excellence, including all those in the School of Sciences and Mathematics. Majors in astronomy and astrophysics are available, while data science (formerly discovery informatics)— an interdisciplinary program that integrates sta-

"Living on campus after freshman year is considered a little uncool."

tistics, social sciences, math, computer science, learning theory, logic, information theory, and artificial intelligence—is one of only a handful of degrees of its type in the country. The most popular majors are communication, psychology, biology, political science, and business administration. Thirty-seven percent of all classes enroll fewer than 20 students, and a senior says, "It isn't uncommon for a full professor to teach an introductory level course to freshmen."

Those in the honors college are given a more demanding workload, including a culminating Bachelor's Essay that is undertaken with the support of a faculty mentor. The Undergraduate Research and Creative Activities program awards competitive grants to fund student/faculty research projects. CofC sponsors more than 30 faculty-led study abroad programs, including semester-long and summer programs, as well as several weeklong spring break trips that are tied to First-Year Seminar courses. Students may also choose from hundreds of additional options

(continued)

Undergraduates: 9,494
Male/Female: 36/64
SAT Ranges: CR 520–610, M 510–600
ACT Ranges: 23–28
Financial Aid: 47%
Pell Grant: 24%
Expense: Pub $ $ $
Student Loans: 51%
Average Debt: $ $
Phi Beta Kappa: No
Applicants: 11,722
Accepted: 77%
Enrolled: 25%
Grad in 6 Years: 68%
Returning Freshmen: 79%
Academics: ✍ ✍ ✍
Social: ☎ ☎ ☎ ☎
Q of L: ★ ★ ★ ★
Admissions: (843) 953-5670
Email Address: admissions@ cofc.edu

Strong Programs:
Communication
Psychology
Biology
Political Science
Business Administration
Chemistry
Data Science

The campus has been designated a national arboretum and a National Historic Landmark.

through partnerships with the Semester at Sea* and other preapproved providers. Many performing arts majors take advantage of internship opportunities with Spoleto Festival USA, Charleston's annual arts festival.

According to one public health major, CofC has "a very open-minded and liberal student body." Forty percent of students hail from out of state, and another 1 percent from foreign countries. African Americans account for 7 percent of the student body, Asian Americans 2 percent, and Hispanics 5 percent. "While no one issue has been primary on campus, we have clubs that push their own issues," says a student. "College Democrats, College Republicans, and the Political Science Club all raise awareness." Twenty-four percent of freshmen qualify for the Pell Grant. The college offers merit scholarships averaging $11,350 and 118 athletic scholarships in 15 sports.

CofC sponsors several study abroad trips during spring break that are tied to First-Year Seminar courses.

"On-campus housing at CofC is very nice, with choices between dormitories, apartments, or historic houses," says a student. "Living on campus after freshman year is considered a little uncool," admits one junior, "which is kind of a nuisance because to find somewhere that's comparable in price and services, you need to go a little farther from campus and find roommates." The percentage of students living on campus has slowly increased to 31 percent. Parking is limited but food is plentiful; there are options for all types of eaters, including "homestyle, grill, deli, salad bar, Greek, dessert, and cereal bar" selections, as well as vegetarian and kosher fare. "Being in the heart of a city can sometimes be overwhelming, but generally, campus feels safe," says one student.

Students party off campus in local clubs and apartments as well as on campus, where 19 percent of the men and 24 percent of the women belong to fraternities and sororities, respectively. "Campus clubs ensure there is always an event for on-campus fun," explains a junior. Due to a well-enforced policy on drinking, students report that it is difficult to be served on campus if you are not 21, but off campus it is not a problem. Women far outnumber men, but females looking to beat the odds can always go to the Medical University of

"The city is a social playground for college students."

South Carolina or The Citadel Military College, both in Charleston. Students enjoy Charleston, with its sporting events, concerts, and festivals. As one student puts it, "The city is a social playground for college students. There are tons of restaurants, events to attend, and beautiful architecture to enjoy." On weekends, students can head to beaches such as Folly Beach, Sullivan's Island, and Isle of Palms, which are merely minutes away. For those who don't mind a drive, there's "the Grand Strand," Myrtle Beach, 90 miles north, Savannah and Hilton Head to the south, and Atlanta and Clemson University to the west.

The absence of a football team is a common gripe among students, but other athletics are relatively popular. The College of Charleston is a Division I school, and several Cougar teams have claimed recent conference championships, including volleyball, men's tennis, co-ed and women's sailing, and men's and women's golf. The intramural program offers eight team sports throughout the year, and basketball and soccer are the most popular, both in terms of participation and competitive fervor; 25 club sports are also available.

The College of Charleston has become the finest public liberal arts and sciences institution in South Carolina, propelled by an honors college, opportunities for internships and study abroad, and a healthy social life. "Here, you will find faculty and staff who care for your success and great friends who come from all different backgrounds," a senior says. "Plus, if you decide to come here, your parents will have an excuse to visit one of the best cities in the world!"

Overlaps

University of South Carolina, Clemson, Elon, James Madison, University of Delaware, Coastal Carolina, University of Georgia, Winthrop

University of Chicago

Rosenwald Hall, 1101 East 58th Street, Chicago, IL 60637

Traditionally known as a haven for true intellectuals who enjoy nothing more than the chance to debate a fresh idea. The Common Core remains the intellectual heart of the school, but Chicago is working to shed its traditional sense of institutional modesty along with its reputation as the place where "fun comes to die." Recent investments in dormitory life, the arts, and athletic facilities—coupled with more aggressive recruiting—have helped attract a growing number of Ivy-caliber applicants, including first-generation undergrads. Quarter system can be stressful.

The University of Chicago attracts students eager to move beyond the cliquishness of high school and the superficial trappings of Ivy League prestige—the kids more concerned about learning for learning's sake than about getting a job after graduation, though they're certainly capable of the latter. "'Life of the Mind' is taken very seriously," says a student. "The academic atmosphere extends beyond the classroom, and most people like it that way." Still, administrators have realized that in the 21st century, even the best schools cannot survive on intellectual might alone. To make UChicago more attractive, they've made the core curriculum less restrictive, expanded study abroad programs and career advising, and completed a bevy of new facilities. The result? A surge in applications and enrollment. Says a freshman, "The fact that college here is a good time just makes us that much happier."

The university's 217-acre, tree-lined campus is in Hyde Park, an eclectic community on Chicago's South Side, surrounded by neighborhoods on three sides and Lake Michigan on the other. One of 77 city neighborhoods, Hyde Park "is pretty intellectual," says one student, noting that "two-thirds of our faculty live here." Streets are lined with brownstones, rowhouses, and townhouses, giving way to luxury high-rises with beautiful views as you get closer to the lake; the city's Museum of Science and Industry is within spitting distance. The campus itself is self-contained and architecturally magnificent. The main quads are steel-gray Gothic—gargoyles and all—and other buildings were designed by the likes of Frank Lloyd Wright, Eero Saarinen, Mies van der Rohe, and Edward Durrell Stone. The Regenstein Library (known as "the Reg") is a national treasure, symbolically located in the heart of the campus. Next to the Reg is the Mansueto Library, a geodesic dome featuring millions of books stored underground and retrieved by a 50-foot robotic arm. The new 277,000-square-foot Eckhardt Research Center includes conference rooms, labs, and offices, and houses the university's new molecular engineering program.

Historically, UChicago has drawn praise for its graduate programs, but in recent years administrators have realized that they must pay attention to undergraduates as well if UChicago is to compete successfully with the likes of Stanford, Harvard, and Princeton. To that end, the university remains unequivocally committed to the view that a solid foundation in the liberal arts is the best preparation for future study or

> **"The academic atmosphere extends beyond the classroom, and most people like it that way."**

Website: www.uchicago.edu
Location: City Outskirts
Private
Total Enrollment: 9,764
Undergraduates: 5,783
Male/Female: 52/48
SAT Ranges: CR 720–800, M 720–800
ACT Ranges: 32–35
Financial Aid: 62%
Pell Grant: 12%
Expense: Pr $ $ $ $
Student Loans: 34%
Average Debt: $
Phi Beta Kappa: Yes
Applicants: 30,069
Accepted: 8%
Enrolled: 61%
Grad in 6 Years: 92%
Returning Freshmen: 100%
Academics: ✍ ✍ ✍ ✍ ✍
Social: ☎ ☎ ☎
Q of L: ★ ★ ★ ★
Admissions: (773) 702-8650
Email Address: collegeadmissions@uchicago.edu

Strong Programs:
Economics
Biological Sciences
Mathematics

work and, moreover, that theory is better than practice. Thus, music students study musicology, but also learn calculus, along with everyone else. Regardless of major, 15 to 18 of a student's 42 courses fall under general education requirements called the Common Core, which is one of the most comprehensive sets of distribution requirements anywhere. (The precise number of courses in the core depends on how much foreign language instruction a student needs to reach proficiency.)

Other core requirements include courses in the sciences and math, humanities, social sciences, and a sequence of study in a specific civilization. There is a required writing tutorial as well. Sound intense? Well, yes, students say it is, especially because UChicago pioneered the quarter system, whereby class material is presented over 10-week periods, with the first term starting in late September and ending in mid-December. In practice, this means virtually unin-

"With an intense workload, it is important to practice time management."

terrupted work through the year, punctuated by a long summer vacation and three exam weeks. A senior says, "With an intense workload, it is important to practice time management in order to succeed. Once you get into the swing of things, however, everything is manageable (though still intense)." Seniors are also encouraged to do final-year projects. Classes are intimate, with 78 percent enrolling fewer than 20 students, and led by brilliant and distinguished faculty members who've won Nobel Prizes, Guggenheims, and other prestigious awards. Professors "expect your work to be completed at a very high level, which causes some assignments to take longer than they would somewhere else," says one mathematics major.

The economics department, a bastion of neoliberal or New Right thinkers, is UChicago's main academic claim to fame. Popular majors include economics, biological sciences, mathematics, political science, and English. The university also prides itself on interdisciplinary and area studies programs, such as those focusing on East Asia, South Asia, the Middle East, and the Slavic countries. Undergrads can engage with any of the university's graduate and professional schools—law, divinity, social service, public policy, humanities, social sciences, biological and physical sciences, and business. In the spirit of alumni such as Mike Nichols and Elaine May, a major in theater and performance studies is available. The Accelerated Medical Scholars Program allows exceptional undergrads to begin medical school during their fourth year. The new, cross-subject molecular engineering major—the university's first ever undergraduate degree in engineering—focuses on "solving societal problems at the molecular level"; students delve into such topics as water conservation, quantum computing, efforts to improve nanotechnology, and advances in biological immuno-engineering.

The new, cross-subject molecular engineering major is the university's first ever undergraduate degree in engineering.

Students enjoy an abundance of research assistantships and opportunities for publication, even before they graduate. Through the Jeff Metcalfe Internship Program, students have access to more than 1,700 fully funded internships that are offered exclusively to UChicago students. Established internships are available at the Argonne National Laboratory and Fermilab, both located in nearby suburbs and operated by UChicago in conjunction with the U.S. Department of Energy, and at the UChicago-affiliated Marine Biological

"Hyde Park has tons of really cute, cheap apartments."

Laboratory in Woods Hole, Massachusetts. When Chicago gets too cold and snowy, students may take advantage of study abroad programs, which reach most corners of the globe and include study at the university's centers in Hong Kong, Beijing, Delhi, and Paris. Financial aid applies to study abroad programs, and 45 percent of students take part.

"The students at UChicago are intellectual, passionate, and incredibly diverse in their interests," says a junior. "What brings together the student body is a love for learning and maybe just a bit of geekiness, whether that comes from a love of Plato or an obsession with Big Bang Theory." Seventy-four percent of undergraduates come from out of state, including many East Coasters with academic parents; another 11 percent are international. Asian Americans represent 17 percent of the total, Hispanics 9 percent, and African Americans 5 percent. Students are quick to give voice to opinions and political allegiances. "It would be nice if there was a less hostile political climate on campus," laments one student. In a sign of UChicago's educational philosophy that attracted national attention in the fall of 2016, incoming freshmen received a letter informing them that the university rejects "trigger warnings" about unsettling course material, "safe spaces" for the hypersensitive, and cancellations of invitations to controversial speakers. Admissions at UChicago are need-blind, and the university meets 100 percent of students' demonstrated financial need. The No Barriers program eliminates loans from financial aid packages, replacing them with grants, and waives the application fee for students who request financial aid.

UChicago guarantees on-campus housing for four years, and 52 percent of all undergrads live in the dorms. "Every incoming first-year has to live in a House," explains a student. "Houses here are like Hogwarts in the sense that students form very intense loyalty towards their House and therefore there is competition between Houses." All halls are co-ed, though some offer single-sex floors, and each dorm is different—some house fewer than 100 people in traditional, shared double rooms without kitchens, while another has 700 beds organized into colorful suites. The newly constructed Campus North Residential Commons, complete

"The city of Chicago is the backyard for UChicago, and students are always exploring it."

with a dining commons, replaced a number of off-campus apartment buildings that were scattered throughout the neighborhood. It is part of a long-term campaign to provide more on-campus housing. Still, "Hyde Park has tons of really cute, cheap apartments," reports one student, so many of the more "independent-minded" students move off campus. "The campus feels very safe," says one student. "Not only does UChicago employ its own police force, but security guards are stationed around the neighborhood to help increase the safety." Through the Sexual Assault Dean-on-Call program, students who have experienced assault can reach a trained campus official who is available 24/7 to offer immediate crisis assistance and continued support.

The UChicago social scene is varied, according to a senior. "There is always some sort of event going on around campus, be it a theater performance or an a capella show, but the city of Chicago is the backyard for UChicago, and students are always exploring it." Indeed, the city offers museums galore; world-class symphony, opera, and dance; the Second City comedy improv troupe (invented by University of Chicago undergrads); professional spectator sports; and plenty of clubs and bars. The university provides students with free, unlimited access to all parts of the city via public transportation, and Arts Pass offers free or discounted student admission to city art, theater, and cultural events. Cars are a nice luxury (if you can find a parking place). Road trips are infrequent, but one popular destination is Ann Arbor, about five hours away, for concerts and more traditional collegiate fun at the University of Michigan. Greek life has a small presence on campus, with 8 percent of the men and 12 percent of the women joining local fraternities and sororities.

Tradition is a hallmark at UChicago. Students have fond memories of freshman orientation, known as O-Week, an event administrators claim was invented at the university in 1934. In the winter, students head for the outdoor skating rink on the Midway, site of the 1893 World's Fair, for broomball. Students also celebrate the festival of Kuviasungnerk/Kangeiko ("Kuvia" for short), a week of early morning calisthenics and other activities, culminating in a Friday morning yoga session by Lake Michigan and a Polar Bear Run, where naked or seminaked co-eds dash across the academic quad. Each spring, students look forward to Scavenger Hunt ("Scav"), "a pumped-up version of a regular scavenger hunt, with a list of 300 bizarre items," says a sociology major. Come summer, students can be found "doing Jell-O wrestling and other carnival activities" as part of Summer Breeze, which also includes a concert. And one game in particular captures students' attention year-round: "Humans vs. Zombies is a quarterly campus-wide game that involves people running around pretending to be either zombies or humans until there is one human standing," one student explains.

UChicago's Maroons compete in Division III, and the school belongs to the University Athletic Association, where rivals include Emory and Washington University in St. Louis. Aside from hitting the gridiron or the basketball court, "even the varsity athletes are Phi Beta Kappa (that is, very smart) and involved with university theater," a junior marvels. In fact, athletes here have a higher overall GPA than the student body as a whole. To everyone's surprise, the football team has had a couple of winning seasons. Consistently solid programs include men's and women's tennis; women's basketball, cross-country, and volleyball; and men's soccer and wrestling. When it comes to intramurals, 70 percent of undergraduates compete on their house teams in sports ranging from the traditional (football, soccer, and volleyball) to the offbeat (inner-tube water polo, broomball, and archery).

"Even the varsity athletes are Phi Beta Kappa (that is, very smart)."

"Students at UChicago are so extremely passionate about ideas and learning. People love to teach one another and learn from one another and be challenged by one another's ideas," says one biochemistry major. Although T-shirts lovingly mock the university's rigor ("Where Fun Comes to Die"), the University of Chicago has moved well beyond the Spartan attitudes of former president Robert Maynard Hutchins, who led UChicago from 1929 to 1951 and once told members of the football team that was about to be abolished, "When I feel like exercising, I just lie down until the feeling goes away." A major national force for the liberal arts, he also once declared, "My idea of education is to unsettle the minds of the young and inflame their intellects." UChicago continues to open its doors to more of the sort of bright overachievers who have learned to work the system and make it into the Ivies and other elite schools. Chicago undergraduates probably are having more fun and engaging in more extracurricular activities than their predecessors. The question is whether, in the process, Chicago may be slowly losing the quirky intellectual edge that has defined its special niche in U.S. higher education.

Overlaps

Columbia, Harvard, Yale, University of Pennsylvania, Northwestern

If You Apply To ➤ **UChicago:** Early decision I and early action: Nov. 1. Early decision II and regular decision: Jan. 1. Financial aid: Feb. 15. Housing: May 1. Application fee: $75. Campus and alumni interviews: optional, evaluative. SATs or ACTs: required. Subject Tests: optional. Letters of recommendation: required. Essay: required. Accepts the Common Application with supplement.

University of Cincinnati

P.O. Box 210091, Cincinnati, OH 45220

In most states, UC would be a big enchilada. But with Ohio State two hours up the road and Miami U even closer, Cincinnati has to hustle to get its name out there. The inventor of co-op education, it offers quality programs in everything from engineering to art—and a competitive men's basketball team to boot.

Many first-time visitors to Cincinnati are surprised to find an attractive and very livable city. As they traverse the city's hilly roads, they are in for another surprise—its university. Not only has the University of Cincinnati made its mark with its extensive research programs, but its cooperative education program is also the largest of any public college or university in the country.

The compact campus is a mile uphill from Cincinnati's downtown area. Ultramodern buildings rise up next to traditional ivy-covered Georgian halls. The university undertook a major $233 million construction project to create a "Main Street" in the center of campus and consolidate all student activities. A renovation of the historic Nippert Stadium was recently completed, and students may also take advantage of the $113 million campus recreation center.

Research has been a UC specialty. Campus scientists have given the world anti-knock gasoline, the electronic organ, antihistamines, and the U.S. Weather Bureau. UC is also the place where, in 1906, cooperative education was born, allowing students to earn while they learn. More than 40 programs across the Cincinnati curriculum offer the popular five-year professional-practice option, and more than 3,000 students take advantage of it. UC has taken steps to improve the quality of the undergraduate education by strengthening its general education requirements to focus on critical thinking and expression and by expanding its honors program. Freshmen must take English and math as well as a contemporary issues class; other requirements vary by college. All students are required to complete a capstone experience as well.

The colleges of engineering; business administration; and design, architecture, art, and planning (the schools with the most co-op students) are the best bets at UC. The university's music conservatory, one of the best programs in the field, also offers electronic media and broadcasting training. The schools of nursing and pharmacy are well known and benefit from UC's health center and graduate medical school. The most popular majors fall under the fields of business administration and marketing, health professions, engineering, and

> **"We are your traditional hardworking college students."**

visual and performing arts. Education students earn two bachelor's degrees: one in education and one in a liberal arts subject. Additional initiatives include a culinary arts and science degree program offered jointly with Cincinnati State, and the state's first baccalaureate program in facilities and hospitality management. UC also sponsors a language-immersion house, a freestanding residence where students are required to live, work, study, and play 24/7 in another language. Six percent of students choose to study abroad in programs in more than 60 countries.

The academic rigor is determined largely by the major. Fields such as engineering, business, and nursing require a substantially larger academic commitment. "I would say that the most rigorous courses are those that are nontraditional," offers one student, citing "study abroad, capstones, projects with corporate partners, and advanced topics classes." Some courses end up being quite large (in popular design courses, two people to a desk is not unusual); 41 percent of classes have fewer than

Website: www.uc.edu
Location: Small City
Public
Total Enrollment: 26,263
Undergraduates: 21,060
Male/Female: 53/47
SAT Ranges: CR 510–630, M 530–660
ACT Ranges: 23–28
Financial Aid: 53%
Pell Grant: 23%
Expense: Pub $ $
Student Loans: 67%
Average Debt: $ $ $
Phi Beta Kappa: Yes
Applicants: 15,286
Accepted: 86%
Enrolled: 15%
Grad in 6 Years: 65%
Returning Freshmen: 88%
Academics: ✍ ✍
Social: ☎ ☎ ☎
Q of L: ★ ★ ★
Admissions: (513) 556-1100
Email Address: admissions@uc.edu

Strong Programs:
Business Administration
Marketing
Health Professions
Engineering
Visual and Performing Arts
Architecture and Design
Nursing
Music

20 students. A third of the faculty members hold outside jobs, bringing fresh, practical experience to the classroom. "Most of my professors are accessible because they offer office hours, however I have run into difficulty from time to time receiving answers to my emails," says one student.

"We are your traditional hardworking college students," says a sophomore of UC's largely homogenous student body. Eighty-six percent of undergraduates are native Ohioans, and 5 percent come from abroad. African Americans, Asian Americans, and Hispanics comprise a mere 7, 3, and 3 percent of the student body, respectively. Diversity, feminist issues, campus construction, and rising tuition are the hot topics on campus. The school offers merit scholarships averaging $4,841 and 176 athletic scholarships for men and women. Twenty-three percent of incoming students receive Pell Grants.

Twenty percent of UC students live on campus. Many upperclassmen consider off-campus living far better than dorm life, and inexpensive apartments can usually be found. A student says, "The Clifton area is in the process of developing and building several new complexes that offer apartments for students." A senior says, "Campus has three dining facilities, multiple fast food restaurants in the university center, and a few cafés located in certain buildings." A marketing major adds, "Living in an urban environment means there are extra safety precautions that keep students safe. Never have I felt unsafe on campus."

"Living in an urban environment means there are extra safety precautions that keep students safe."

Merchants have turned the area surrounding UC, called Clifton, into a mini college town with plenty to do. Although not a major metropolis like Chicago or Boston, the "Queen City" of Cincinnati does offer an urban feel. Nine nearby bus lines take undergraduates into the heart of the city in minutes; there, they find museums, ballet, professional sports teams, parks, rivers, hills, and as many large and small shops as anyone could want. On-campus activities include 450 student clubs, with everything from mountaineering to clubs in various majors. Fraternities and sororities attract less than 10 percent of the men and women, but are still the most active places to party on campus, usually opening their functions to everyone. "There is a party culture present at the university, but it is by no means dominant," says one senior. The university sponsors some events, such as WorldFest and Greek Week. The most popular road trips are to the city of Cleveland and white-water rafting in West Virginia.

In sports, men's and women's basketball are solid, and 17 Bearcat teams compete in the Division I American Athletic Conference. The men's basketball team is highly competitive, as is football and women's basketball and volleyball. Everyone mentions the football rivalry with Miami (of Ohio) as a game you won't want to miss, and the same holds true when the men's basketball squad takes on Xavier University. Weekend athletes also take advantage of UC's first-rate sports center.

UC offers students a lively social scene, both on campus and minutes away in downtown Cincinnati. But cooperative education is the name of the game at this Ohio school, where the co-op program allows students to take their degrees out for a test drive before graduation and have a head start on their peers after it.

Overlaps

Ohio State, Miami University (OH), Ohio University, Bowling Green State, Wright State, Xavier University (OH)

If You Apply To ➤

UC: Rolling admissions: Mar. 1. Early action and financial aid: Dec. 1. Housing: May 1. Application fee: $50. No campus or alumni interviews. SATs or ACTs: required. No Subject Tests. Letters of recommendation: optional. Essay: required. Apply to particular program. Accepts the Common Application.

Claremont Colleges

In 1925, James A. Blaisdell had the vision to create a group of colleges patterned after Oxford and Cambridge in England—an "Oxford of the Orange Groves," as he elegantly put it. Nearly a century later, the five schools that comprise the Claremont Colleges thrive as a consortium of separate and distinct undergraduate colleges with two adjoining graduate institutions, a theological seminary, and botanical gardens. Like families, the colleges coexist, interact, and experience their share of both cooperation and tension. Ultimately, however, the Claremont Colleges consortium forms a mutually beneficial partnership that offers its students the vast resources and facilities one might only expect to find at a large university.

The colleges are located 35 miles east of Los Angeles on 317 acres in the suburb of Claremont, a peaceful, tree-lined neighborhood at the foot of the San Gabriel Mountains. The picture-perfect California weather has some-times been marred by smog, courtesy of the neighbors in nearby L.A., but the smog level has declined dramatically in the past few years.

Of the five undergraduate colleges that make up the Claremont Colleges—Claremont McKenna, Harvey Mudd, Pitzer, Pomona, and Scripps—Pomona is the largest, with 1,640 students. Each school retains its own institutional identity, with its own faculty, administration, admissions, and curriculum, although the boundar-ies of both academic work and extracurricular activities are somewhat flexible. Each of the schools also tends to specialize in a particular area that complements the offerings of all the others. Claremont McKenna, which caters mainly to students planning careers in economics, business, law, or government, has 10 research institutes located on its campus, while Harvey Mudd is a liberal arts college specializing in engineering, science, and math. Pitzer, a classical liberal arts institution and the most socially progressive of the five, excels in environmental and sustain-ability studies, and at the all-women Scripps, the top majors include the social sciences, biology, and visual and performing arts. The oldest of the five colleges, Pomona ranks as one of the top liberal arts colleges anywhere and is strong across the board.

Collectively, the colleges share many services and facilities, including a student newspaper, a biological field station, a student health center, auditoriums, a 2,500-seat concert hall, a 350-seat theater, bookstores, a main-tenance department, a business office, and a shared campus safety force. The Queer Resource Center, housed at Pomona but serving the whole community, is a model of collaboration, and the newly established EmPOWER Center provides the community with comprehensive support and educational resources on sexual assault, dating and domestic violence, and stalking. The Claremont library system makes more than 1.9 million volumes available to all students. Faculties and administrations are free to arrange joint programs or classes between all or just some of the schools. Courses are open to students from the other colleges (approximately 1,200 courses in all), but each college sets limits on the number of classes that can be taken elsewhere. Perhaps the best example of academic cooperation is the team-taught interdisciplinary courses, which are organized by instructors from the different schools and appeal to a mix of different academic interests.

The Claremont Colleges draw large numbers of students from within California, although their national repu-tation is growing. These days, about half the students hail from other Western and non-Western states, with a sizable contingent from the East Coast. The tone at the Claremont Colleges is decidedly intellectual, and graduate programs in the arts and sciences are more common goals than business or law school. Anyone who is bright and hardworking can find a niche at one of the five schools.

"The town of Claremont provides great dining options, although it is a small and quiet town," says a biol-ogy major. Indeed, the local community ("the Village") has its share of senior citizens, but it also offers a flavor reminiscent of Ann Arbor (home to the University of Michigan), with quirky boutiques, coffee shops, truly remark-able candy stores, and eateries ranging from fine dining to diners and specialty bagel shops. There are even ice cream shops that freeze your ice cream with liquid nitrogen before your eyes—and it's all an easy walk or bike ride from any campus. Students report that the endless list of social activities offered at the colleges make up for anything Claremont might lack. For hot times, Hollywood's glamour and downtown are within sniffing distance. The availability of shared Zip Cars and a nearby Metro line make these and other locations easy to access. Nearby mountains and the fabled surfing beaches make this collegiate paradise's backyard complete. Mount Baldy ski lifts, for instance, are only 15 miles away, and you'll reach Laguna Beach before the end of your favorite album. For spring break, Mexico is cheap and a great change of pace.

On campus, extracurricular life maintains a balance between cooperation and independence. The five colleges dance team is highly popular. Claremont McKenna, Harvey Mudd, and Scripps field joint athletic teams, and the men's teams especially are Division III powers, due to the exploits of CMC athletes. Pomona and Pitzer also compete together with particular strength in cross-country, water polo, and men's soccer. Each of the five colleges has its own dorms, and since off-campus housing is limited in Claremont proper, the social life of students revolves around their dorms. Large five-school parties are regular Thursday, Friday, and Saturday night fare. "In my opinion, Mudd's parties are the best because they always have themes," says a physics major. Claremont McKenna is said to have the most raucous party scene, while Pitzer hosts multiple music festivals throughout the year. There are no fraternities, except for three local ones at Pomona, where joining is far from de rigueur. All cafeterias are open to all students, and most big events—films, concerts, etc.—are advertised throughout each campus. Day-to-day social interaction among students at different schools, be it for meals or dates, is not what it might be. Occasional political squabbles break out between liberal faculty and students at Pitzer and their conservative counterparts at Claremont McKenna. For the most part, students benefit not only from the nurturing and support within their own schools, each of which has its own academic or extracurricular emphasis, but also from the abundant resources the Claremont Colleges consortium offers as a whole.

Claremont McKenna College

890 Columbia Avenue, Claremont, CA 91711

Make way, Pomona—this up-and-comer is no longer content with being a social sciences specialty school. CMC is half the size of a typical liberal arts college and smaller than Pomona by about 300 students. CMC continues to develop its national reputation, and Californians now make up less than half the student body.

Website: www.cmc.edu
Location: Suburban
Private
Total Enrollment: 1,344
Undergraduates: 1,323
Male/Female: 51/49
SAT Ranges: CR 670–750, M 670–780
ACT Ranges: 29–33
Financial Aid: 40%
Pell Grant: 16%
Expense: Pr $ $ $ $
Student Loans: 22%
Average Debt: $ $
Phi Beta Kappa: Yes
Applicants: 7,156
Accepted: 11%
Enrolled: 44%
Grad in 6 Years: 90%
Returning Freshmen: 95%
Academics: ✎ ✎ ✎ ✎ ½
Social: ☎ ☎ ☎
Q of L: ★ ★ ★
Admissions: (909) 621-8088

Claremont McKenna College's special niche in the Claremont College pantheon is top programs in government, economics, and international relations. In addition, CMC has 10 research institutes located on campus, which offer its undergraduates ample opportunities to study everything from political demographics to the environment. The arts and humanities are also available, but Claremont McKenna is better suited to those with high ambitions in business leadership and public affairs. "CMC provides students with a pragmatic liberal arts education that will prepare them for grad school and a career," a senior says. "It is a great place to spend four years."

The 69-acre campus is mostly "California modern" in its architecture, with lots of Spanish tile roofs and picture windows that look out on the San Gabriel Mountains. Described by one student as "more functional than aesthetic," the physical layout fits right in with the school's practical attitude. Kravis Center is a state-of-the-art academic center that houses classrooms, seminar rooms, a computer laboratory, and faculty offices. The new Roberts Pavilion, which opened in 2016, serves as an athletic, fitness, and events center.

CMC's extensive general education requirements include two semesters in the humanities; three in the social sciences; one each in the natural sciences and mathematics; and a senior thesis. All first-years take a Freshman Writing Seminar and a Freshman Humanities Seminar. Claremont McKenna offers top programs in economics and government, but the international relations, psychology, and history programs are also considered strong. A few programs combine these strengths into interdisciplinary majors, such as the environment, economics, and politics major. The biology, chemistry, and physics departments are greatly enhanced through the use of Keck Science Center,

"CMC provides students with a pragmatic liberal arts education."

an outstanding facility providing students with hands-on access to a variety of equipment. In addition, the 85-acre Bernard Biological Field Station is located just north of the CMC campus and is available to students for field work. The college offers popular 3–2 programs in management and engineering and economics and engineering, a four-year B.A./M.A. program, and a 4–1 M.B.A. program in conjunction with the Claremont Graduate University.

The academic climate is fairly strenuous at Claremont McKenna, but not overwhelming. "There are very difficult courses that will push you to the brink of your comfort zone in every major," a junior says. Eighty-three percent of classes have fewer than 20 students ("one of the perks of a small college," says a neuroscience major), and professors are praised for their accessibility. "I have met some of the most incredible teachers at CMC who are both brilliant and devoted to their students," an economics major says. All freshmen take part in a five-day orientation program that includes a Wilderness Orientation Adventure (WOA!) trip and a reception with the president and department chairs. More than 40 percent of Claremont McKenna students take advantage of study abroad programs in 56 countries, including Australia, Brazil, Costa Rica, and Japan. CMC also offers active campus exchange programs with Haverford, Colby, Spelman, and Morehouse. Another popular program is the Washington Semester program, in which students can intern with the Sierra Club, the State Department, the White House, and lobbying groups.

"Basketball games rock this campus."

A senior describes CMC students as "career-oriented, ambitious, and serious about their classes." The CMC student body is 38 percent Californian, with many other domestic students coming from the East Coast, and 18 percent of students coming from other countries. Seventy-three percent graduated in the top 10th of their high school class. Asian Americans comprise 10 percent of the student body, Hispanics 14 percent, and African Americans 4 percent. Although CMC is the most conservative of the five Claremont schools, one student notes, "There is a good mix of liberals, conservatives, and libertarians." The school accepts applicants on a need-blind basis and guarantees to meet the demonstrated need of all admitted students. It also awards merit scholarships, averaging $16,059, to a limited number of eligible students.

Ninety-seven percent of CMC students live on campus "because of the social life." The housekeeping service probably doesn't hurt. "They dust and vacuum our rooms and clean our bathrooms! We do nothing (except study, of course)!" declares a happy resident. All the residence halls are co-ed; freshmen are guaranteed a room. Stark Hall, a substance-free dorm, gives students more living options. A cluster of on-campus apartments equipped with kitchen facilities is a popular option for upperclassmen. Dorm food is said to be quite good, and students can eat in dining halls at any of the other four colleges, though the best bet may be CMC's Collins Dining Hall. "They have a large spread with lots of different options," says one student, including vegetarian, vegan, and organic fare. CMC has recently expanded its staff dedicated to assisting the campus community with issues related to discrimination, harassment, and sexual misconduct.

"Leadership pervades almost everything that goes on here."

Most students agree that the social life at CMC is more than adequate, thanks to the five-college system. "There are always parties, club events, barbecues, movie screenings, and other events," says a junior. CMC has a reputation for raucous partying, at least in comparison to its other Claremont counterparts, and is said to have something of a "bro culture" around drinking—an atmosphere that appeals to some students, but keeps others away. Aside from that party scene, a calendar full of annual bashes features Monte Carlo Night, Disco Inferno, Oktoberfest, and Chez Hub. Ponding, another unusual CMC tradition, involves being thrown into one of

(continued)

Email Address: admission@
cmc.edu

Strong Programs:
Economics
Government
International Relations
Psychology
History
Management and Engineering
Economics and Engineering

Through the Washington Semester program, students can intern with the State Department, the White House, and lobbying groups.

CMC is the most
conservative of
the five Claremont
schools.

the two campus fountains on one's birthday. The college sponsors an outstanding lecture series at the Cook Athenaeum on Monday through Thursday nights each week. Before each lecture, students and faculty can enjoy a formal gourmet dinner together and engage in intellectual debates. Students also highly recommend road trips to Joshua Tree, San Francisco, Las Vegas, and Mount Baldy.

Division III athletics are an important part of life at Claremont McKenna, and the school has an overstuffed trophy case to prove it. The men's golf team won its first national championship in 2016, and the men's tennis team brought home the national title in 2015. Other competitive men's teams (the Stags) include basketball, cross-country, and track and field; solid women's teams (the Athenas) include cross-country, track and field, and soccer. A third of the students play varsity sports, and CMC students tend to dominate the teams jointly fielded with Harvey Mudd and Scripps. Top rivalries include Pomona–Pitzer, both in athletics and academics, one student claims. "Basketball games rock this campus," another student says. The Claremont Colleges Debate Union has brought home three national debate championships and has placed in the top 10 nationally for 18 years.

CMC has embraced its mission to produce great leaders by providing students with ample opportunities for research and study abroad, as well as top-notch programs in government and economics. "Leadership pervades almost everything that goes on here," says a junior. "Claremont McKenna builds character, fosters a sense of ambition among its students, and drives them to set their sights high."

Overlaps

**UC–Berkeley,
UCLA, Pomona,
University of
Southern California,
Stanford**

If You Apply To ➤ **Claremont McKenna:** Early decision I: Nov. 1. Early decision II, regular decision, and financial aid: Jan. 1. Housing: Jul. 1. Application fee: $70. Campus and alumni interviews: recommended, evaluative. SATs (with essay) or ACTs (with writing): required. Subject Tests: optional (required for homeschooled students). Letters of recommendation: required. Essay: required. Accepts the Common Application.

Harvey Mudd College

301 Platt Blvd, Claremont, CA 91711

Renowned for encouraging women to go into engineering and other STEM fields, Harvey Mudd may rank as the finest institution that few people outside of these areas have ever heard of. Future Ph.D.s graduate from here in greater percentages than at any other school in the nation. HMC rivals Caltech for sheer brainpower and tops it in access to outstanding faculty. Offers more exposure to the liberal arts than most science- and technology-oriented schools.

Website: www.hmc.edu
Location: Suburban
Private
Total Enrollment: 812
Undergraduates: 812
Male/Female: 53/47
SAT Ranges: CR 670–760,
   M 730–800
ACT Ranges: 33–35
Financial Aid: 72%
Pell Grant: 11%

A top-ranked liberal arts college with a technical bent, Harvey Mudd College strives to give its students a sense of academic balance. Although it's a leading provider of high-quality programs in science and engineering (Where else can you take a freshman seminar in integrated-circuit chip design?), it also emphasizes a well-rounded education with knowledge in the humanities. "We're characterized as the nerd school of the five Claremonts because the classes are hardest and, yes, we talk about science and math over dinner sometimes. Mudders definitely know how to balance working and having fun, though," says a junior.

HMC's mid-'50s vintage campus of cinder-block buildings even "looks like an engineering college; it's very symmetrical and there's no romance." In addition, the buildings have little splotches all over their surfaces that students have dubbed "warts"—not a very attractive picture. As part of a massive building campaign, however, the college recently completed a new, 131-bed residence hall and the Shanahan Center for Teaching and Learning, which features technology-rich classrooms, a 300-seat auditorium, and an art gallery.

While most technology schools tend to have a narrow focus, HMC has come up with the novel idea that even scientists and engineers "need to know and appreciate poetry, philosophy, and non-Western thought," says an administrator. The Common Core includes three semesters of mathematics; two and a half semesters of physics and an associated laboratory; one and a half semesters of chemistry and an associated laboratory; an interdisciplinary Core lab; one course each in biology, computer science, and engineering; a half-semester of college writing; and a course in critical inquiry in the humanities, social sciences, and the arts. Students report that classes are formidable, and the heavy workload is a common complaint. "The incredibly intense workload becomes manageable because all of my classmates are happy to help. We will stay up for each other into the wee hours of the morning to make sure that we're all finished with our homework," says one student. The small class sizes and absence of graduate programs means that undergraduates get uncommon amounts of attention, even from top faculty. "Instruction here is excellent, and professors have a really wonderful open-door policy," says a physics major.

"The incredibly intense workload becomes manageable because all of my classmates are happy to help."

Of the nine on-campus majors, engineering ranks as the most popular by enrollment, followed by computer science, physics, mathematics, and chemistry. HMC has one of the nation's top computer science programs and an award-winning math department, and a combined major in computer science and mathematics is also very popular. Students rave about the Clinic Program, which plops real-life math, science, and engineering tasks (sponsored by major corporations and government agencies to the tune of more than $40,000 per project) into the laps of students. Recent sponsors have included Elon Musk's SpaceX, as well as Intel, Amazon, and Yelp. All students must either participate in the Clinic Program or complete original thesis-driven research in order to graduate. About 200 students stay on campus in the summer for 10-week research experiences, and a sophomore says, "In research positions, students are working one-on-one with the professors—they aren't washing beakers." Sixteen percent of students pack their bags each year for study abroad programs in more than 20 countries.

These budding technology leaders are also top achievers: 93 percent graduated in the top 10 percent of their high school class. "We love to learn, and we love to have fun," says a sophomore. "We take pride in the esoteric and the weird." For a technically oriented school, Mudd boasts a relatively high proportion of female students, at 47 percent, and it is also one of the few colleges strong in engineering and science that has a woman president. Forty-six percent of the students are homegrown Californians, and 13 percent are international. African Americans represent 2 percent of the student body, Hispanics 13 percent, and Asian Americans 20 percent. A senior notes that while students are often too "wrapped up in schoolwork" to get involved in social and political issues, the recent formation of two student groups, FEM Union (Female Empowerment at Mudd) and BLAM (Black Lives and Allies at Mudd) "have created spaces for discussions about issues of diversity and privilege." Merit scholarships averaging $11,332 help some with the hefty tuition bill, but as a Division III college, Mudd offers no athletic scholarships. It does, however, honor a policy of covering 100 percent of students' demonstrated need with its financial aid packages.

"In research positions, students are working one-on-one with the professors—they aren't washing beakers."

(continued)

Expense: Pr $ $ $ $
Student Loans: 47%
Average Debt: $ $ $
Phi Beta Kappa: No
Applicants: 4,119
Accepted: 13%
Enrolled: 40%
Grad in 6 Years: 90%
Returning Freshmen: 96%
Academics: ✐ ✐ ✐ ✐ ½
Social: ☎ ☎ ☎
Q of L: ★ ★ ★
Admissions: (909) 621-8011
Email Address: admission@ hmc.edu

Strong Programs:
Engineering
Computer Science
Physics
Mathematics
Chemistry

Recent sponsors of Mudd's Clinic Program have included Elon Musk's SpaceX, as well as Intel, Amazon, and Yelp.

Ninety-nine percent of undergrads live on campus, and students speak of a strong "dorm culture" on campus. "Each dorm has a proctor (think: the 'mom' or 'dad' of the dorm, usually a senior) as well as several mentors (the 'older siblings' of the dorm, who are mostly there for freshmen)," explains a computer science major. "The proctor-mentor team helps keep the dorm community strong and safe." Mudd's dining options are said to be average, and students appreciate their access to dining facilities at the other Claremont Colleges, which vastly expands their options; many Mudders eat at Scripps in particular. Students describe the party scene as one where classmates look out for each other and respect individuals' decisions to consume alcohol or stay sober ("If anything, there is peer pressure *not* to peer pressure!"), and regarding sexual assault, one student says, "This has not been an issue on my campus, but Mudd has made sure the resources are available to us in case it ever becomes one."

Despite their heavy workload, most HMC students find abundant social outlets, even if it's just joining the parade of unicycles that has overrun the campus—not to mention skateboards, longboards, scooters, and rollers attached to shoes. A student describes the town of Claremont as "a wonderful place if you're married or about to die," so most social life takes place in and around the dorms, where there are parties every weekend. "We have a party called Wild Wild West, where we fill a dorm courtyard with peanut shells and get a mechanical bull," says a physics major. Students also frequent the other Claremont campuses to socialize, but it's Mudd's many traditions that really get them going. In the annual turkey trot, students run a 4K while "enjoying" a complete Thanksgiving dinner. Also, at the end of each semester, Noisy Minutes provides breaks from long hours of studying with loud music, snacks, and activities like a bouncy ball drop, non-Newtonian fluid racing, and battle tie-dye. There is also an annual Five Class competition among the four classes and alumni, complete with an amoeba race, backwards unicycling, and a five-way tug of war. Engineering pranks are popular but must be reversible within 24 hours.

> "The proctor-mentor team helps keep the dorm community strong and safe."

Mudd fields varsity sports teams together with Claremont McKenna and Scripps, and the teams do extremely well. In 2014–15, a dozen Claremont–Mudd–Scripps teams made appearances in their respective NCAA Championships, and the men's tennis and golf teams brought home national titles in 2015 and 2016, respectively. Intramurals, also in conjunction with Claremont McKenna and Scripps, are even more popular. King among these is inner-tube water polo, which draws huge cheering crowds and, most importantly, removes the most difficult aspect of the sport—treading water.

A common student refrain is "too much work," and students might welcome more time to reflect on what they are learning, but the work tends to pay off in grad school and in the job world. HMC is right on the heels of Caltech as the best technically oriented school in the West. The college offers a gem of a technical education perfectly blended with a dash of humanities and social sciences, and a welcoming attitude toward women. As one student asserts, "Mudd is the college for students to be challenged like they never have been before and have the support to go through it."

Pitzer College

1050 North Mills Avenue, Claremont, CA 91711

Offers a haven for the otherwise-minded without the hard edge of nonconformity at places like Bard and Evergreen. Traditional strengths lie in the social and behavioral sciences. Far more selective than it was 10 years ago. A national leader in turning out Fulbright Scholars.

As the most laid-back of the Claremont Colleges, Pitzer College offers students a creative milieu, abundant opportunities for intellectual exploration, and a sense of fierce individualism. Founded in the '60s, this small school has changed with the times but continues its emphasis on progressive thought, social responsibility, and open social attitude. In the last 15 years, Pitzer students and alums have won more than 80 Fulbright fellowships, and the school continues to attract top talent from around the world.

Even Pitzer's campus is, well, different. The classroom buildings are modernistic octagons, and the grass-covered "mounds" that distinguish the grounds "are perfect for sunbathing and Frisbee," says one student, and for lounging in Adirondack chairs beneath the palm trees. Drought-tolerant landscaping pervades the campus, and there is an organic garden. One interesting campus curiosity is Grove House, a California craftsman-style house students saved from the wrecking ball nearly two decades ago and moved to campus. It houses a dining room, study areas, and art exhibits. Additional facilities include LEED-certified, environmentally friendly dorms and an expanded Benson Auditorium. Renovations to the athletic facilities in the Gold Student Center have recently been completed.

In keeping with Pitzer's philosophy of student autonomy, each student has the maximum freedom to choose which classes to take, and students are encouraged to design their own majors. Instead of traditional academic departments, Pitzer has "field groups," which, as a political studies and Spanish double major explains, "allow for students to major in one subject area, yet receive a holistic education." All students must take two courses in Interdisciplinary and Intercultural Exploration and two courses in Social Responsibility. A lively freshman seminar program sharpens students' learning skills, especially writing. Students select from more than 40 majors in the sciences, humanities, arts, and social sciences. Almost anything in the social and behavioral sciences is a sure bet, especially psychology (one of the most popular majors). Environmental analysis, political studies, media studies, English and world literature, and sociology are other strong and popular programs. Pitzer is the first college in the country to offer a program in secular studies, with courses such as God, Darwin, and Design in America. Most courses in Pitzer's weaker areas can be picked up at one of the other Claremont schools; on average, Pitzer students take 30 percent of their courses at the other colleges.

The academic climate is "relaxed, interdisciplinary, collaborative, and very discussion-based," according to a sociology major. Class size is generally small, with 73 percent of classes enrolling fewer than 20 students, which promotes close interaction between students and faculty. "The professors I have had are very down-to-earth and incredibly knowledgeable in their fields," says a sociology and gender/feminist studies major. Students play a large role in Pitzer's community government and sit on all policy committees, including those on curriculum and faculty promotion. The Firestone Center for Restoration Ecology in Costa Rica is home to

> **"Pitzer people are genuinely socially conscious and academically adventurous."**

Website: www.pitzer.edu
Location: Suburban
Private
Total Enrollment: 1,036
Undergraduates: 1,036
Male/Female: 43/57
SAT Ranges: CR 620–720, M 630–720
ACT Ranges: 29–32
Financial Aid: 42%
Pell Grant: 14%
Expense: Pr $ $ $ $
Student Loans: 37%
Average Debt: $
Phi Beta Kappa: No
Applicants: 4,149
Accepted: 14%
Enrolled: 48%
Grad in 6 Years: 84%
Returning Freshmen: 93%
Academics: ✎ ✎ ✎
Social: ☎ ☎ ☎
Q of L: ★ ★ ★
Admissions: (909) 621-8129
Email Address: admission@pitzer.edu

Strong Programs:
Psychology
Environmental Analysis
Political Studies
Media Studies
English and World Literature
Sociology

Instead of traditional academic departments, Pitzer has "field groups."

programs in science, language, and international studies and provides opportunities for research. Pitzer also runs its own study abroad programs in Botswana, Ecuador, Italy, and Nepal and offers students access to 48 exchange programs; in all, 51 percent of Pitzer students participate in study abroad programs.

Individualism is a prized characteristic among Pitzer students, but one junior says the oft-bandied "hippie" label is unfair: "Pitzer people are genuinely socially conscious and academically adventurous, but do go on to good jobs." Forty-seven percent of students are from California, and 8 percent are from foreign nations. Many come from wealthy backgrounds. African Americans comprise 5 percent of the student body, Hispanics 15 percent, and Asian Americans 9 percent. Students cite "racism on campus, labor rights, immigration reform, environmental issues, and police brutality" as hot-button social and political issues. All financial aid at Pitzer is need-based, and the school is committed to meeting 100 percent of enrolled students' demonstrated need, but it is not need-blind in its admissions.

Seventy-six percent of students live on campus and many find themselves in the new, environmentally friendly dorms; the remainder hang their hats in "old but spacious" rooms. Boarders can choose from a variety of meal plans, and the foot gets rave reviews, especially the fresh salad, sandwich, and fruit juice bars in the main dining hall. "The food is awesome: locally sourced, excellent variety, easy to be vegetarian," says a senior. Pitzer recently hired a Title IX coordinator to handle issues of sexual assault, and students say the Pitzer Advocates for Survivors of Sexual Assault student group has been a helpful resource.

"The food is awesome: locally sourced, excellent variety, easy to be vegetarian."

As for the social scene, "Most students stay on campus to attend events or go to parties," says a senior. Pitzer has no Greek organizations, nor does it want any, and social life tends to be fairly low-key. Kohoutek, an alternative music festival, is the big annual event, featuring bands, food, and a "whole week of hoopla"; there are reggae and rockabilly festivals as well. "There is very heavy alcohol and weed usage on campus," says a junior. All parties that serve alcohol must be registered. As much as students enjoy the campus scene, some warn that without a car, things can get claustrophobic.

The Pomona–Pitzer football team—the Sagehens—has had winning seasons, and the school fields a variety of competitive teams within the Southern California Intercollegiate Athletic Conference. The women's water polo team has won several national championships recently, and women's tennis, lacrosse, soccer, and swimming and diving are also strong. Competitive men's teams include soccer, tennis, and cross-country. The annual Humans vs. Zombies game is hugely popular, drawing 500 participants across campus.

Pitzer attracts open-minded students looking for the freedom to go their own ways. "Pitzer people are really caring and often fight for what they believe in. It is a really loving place," muses one student, "a place that values the silly and the weird parts of yourself."

If You Apply To ➤ **Pitzer:** Early decision I: Nov. 15. Early decision II, regular decision, and financial aid: Jan. 1. Housing: May 1. Application fee: $70. Campus interviews: optional, evaluative. No alumni interviews. SATs or ACTs: optional. Subject Tests: optional. Letters of recommendation: required. Essay: required. Accepts the Common Application with supplement. Application includes optional question on gender identity.

Pomona College

333 North College Way, Claremont, CA 91711

The great Eastern-style liberal arts college of the West, and one of the few that Easterners will travel west to attend. Offers twice the resources of stand-alone competitors with access to the other Claremonts. A haven for the otherwise-minded, though not to the same extent as nonconformist neighbor Pitzer. Strong across the academic spectrum.

Pomona College, located just 35 miles east of the glitz and glamour of Hollywood, is the undisputed star of the Claremont Colleges and one of the top small liberal arts colleges anywhere. This small, elite institution is the best liberal arts college in the West. But the school's prestigious reputation doesn't go to the heads of Pomona's friendly students. "Students here are very open about different types of people—[Pomona] prides itself on its diverse community," chirps one Sagehen (the school's mascot).

The architecture is variously described as Spanish Mediterranean, pseudo-Italian, or, as a sophomore puts it, "a perfect mix of Northeastern Ivy and Southern California modern." The administration building, Alexander Hall, is described as "postmodern with Mediterranean influences," and one notices more than one stucco building topped with a red tile roof on campus, as well as eucalyptus trees, canyon live oaks, and an occasional "secretive courtyard lined with flowers." The numerous open courtyards and gardens are popular study spots. By virtue of its location and beauty, Pomona's campus has served as the quintessential collegiate milieu in various Hollywood movies. Recent campus projects include a $29 million studio art facility and the 75,000-square-foot Millikan Laboratory and Andrew Science Hall. The latter features a host of cutting-edge spaces and equipment, including a digital planetarium.

In order to graduate, students must take at least one course in each of five areas: creative expression; social institutions and human behavior; history, values, ethics, and cultural studies; physical and biological sciences; and mathematical reasoning. The required Critical Inquiry seminar empha-
sizes thoughtful reading, logical reasoning, and graceful writing; students choose from more than two dozen offerings, with subjects such as First Person America and Living with Our Genes. Students must also complete foreign language and physical education requirements, as well as a senior exercise in their final year. A five-day freshman orientation program divides the new arrivals into groups of six to 12 students headed by a sophomore. "We provide a great deal of support in acclimating students to a college environment," says a senior. Economics, mathematics, computer science, neuroscience, and biology are the most popular majors.

> **"[Campus is] a perfect mix of Northeastern Ivy and Southern California modern."**

Classes at Pomona are challenging. "Although classes can be difficult, students help each other out and the classroom environment is an enjoyable one," offers one economics major. Students often form study groups in an effort to help one another through the demanding curriculum. One undergrad estimates the average student spends 20 to 30 hours a week studying outside the classroom. Classes are small—68 percent have fewer than 20 students—and the faculty makes a point of being accessible. It's not uncommon for professors to hold study sessions at their homes. "Pomona professors are bright, enthusiastic, and highly respected leaders in their respective fields," a student says. An ever-popular take-a-professor-to-lunch

Website: www.pomona.edu
Location: Suburban
Private
Total Enrollment: 1,640
Undergraduates: 1,640
Male/Female: 50/50
SAT Ranges: CR 670–760, M 690–770
ACT Ranges: 30–34
Financial Aid: 74%
Pell Grant: 18%
Expense: Pr $ $ $
Student Loans: 39%
Average Debt: $
Phi Beta Kappa: Yes
Applicants: 8,099
Accepted: 10%
Enrolled: 48%
Grad in 6 Years: 93%
Returning Freshmen: 97%
Academics: ✍ ✍ ✍ ✍ ✍
Social: ☎ ☎ ☎
Q of L: ★ ★ ★ ★
Admissions: (909) 621-8134
Email Address: admissions@pomona.edu

Strong Programs:
Economics
Mathematics
Computer Science
Neuroscience
Biology

program gives students free meals when they arrive with a faculty member in tow. Better still, "We do not have graduate students or TAs teaching class," says a senior. "Thus, students do not have to wait until they are upperclassmen to enjoy the benefits of working with and learning from brilliant professors."

Educational enrichment opportunities abound at Pomona. Students can spend a semester at Colby or Swarthmore, pursue a 3–2 engineering plan with the

California Institute of Technology, or spend a semester in Washington, D.C., working for a congressperson. Roughly half of the students take advantage of 57 study abroad programs offered in 34 countries. More than half of the students also conduct research mentored by a faculty member, and the Summer Undergraduate Research Program provides funding to more than 200 students to pursue such opportunities each summer.

Pomona students "tend to be high-achieving, confident, verbal students with a fairly liberal political ideology," says a senior. "Students are laid-back in a very Southern California kind of way," adds another. Twenty-seven percent are Californians, and a growing percentage venture from the East Coast; 10 percent come from abroad. Pomona is proud of its diverse student body: 7 percent are African American, 15 percent are Hispanic, and 14 percent are Asian American. There is a healthy mix of liberals and conservatives on campus, though the leftists, especially the feminist wing, are much more vocal. One interesting way students voice their issues is by painting the Walker Wall. Anyone is allowed to paint any message they want on the wall, and the school will even provide groups with the paint. The student government is active, and the administration is credited with respecting students' opinions. Pomona is need-blind in admissions and meets the full demonstrated financial need of all those who attend. Although there are no merit or athletic awards, the college has replaced loans with grants in an effort to reduce the debt burden for families. The college also participates in the QuestBridge and Posse programs.

Virtually all Pomona students (98 percent) live on campus all four years. The dorms are co-ed, student-governed, and divided into two distinct groups. Those

on South campus are family-like and fairly quiet, offer spacious rooms, and house freshmen and sophomores, while those on the North end have smaller rooms with a livelier social scene and house juniors and seniors. "Pomona's dorms are like palaces," says a student. The two newest residence halls, Dialynas and Sontag, are LEED Platinum and feature suite-style apartments for upperclassmen. Oldenborg Center is a language dorm with wings for speakers of Mandarin Chinese, French, German, Japanese, Spanish, and Russian, and Pomona also has established language tables at lunch. A handful of students isolate themselves in Claremont proper, where apartments are scarce and expensive. Boarders must buy at least partial meal plans. The food is good, with seafood certified by the Marine Stewardship Council, humanely raised beef and cage-free eggs, and ice cream for dessert every day. Students generally feel safe on campus. "The worst that usually happens are bike thefts," says a junior. "We're in a pretty nice suburb, so there really aren't many problems with crime."

Social life begins in the dorms, where barbecues, parties, and study breaks are organized. There are movies several nights a week, and students also enjoy just tossing a Frisbee on the lawn. One student wanted to be sure that incoming freshmen and transfers knew of the Coop's (student union) "best milkshakes west of the Mississippi," pool tables, and large-screen TV and gaming system. Students

An ever-popular take-a-professor-to-lunch program gives students free meals when they arrive with a faculty member in tow.

The college has replaced loans with grants in an effort to reduce the debt burden for families.

at often spend Friday afternoons relaxing with friends over a brew at the Greek Theater. Pomona is unique among the Claremont Colleges in that it has three nonnational fraternities (two co-ed; there are no sororities). There is "no peer pressure to join frats," and no fraternity rivalry. As for booze, "I haven't noticed any pressure to drink here," reports one student, but "alcohol is definitely present in the social scene."

"I appreciate the diversity and depth that the five-college community brings to the social life," says a student. "You are guaranteed to meet new and interesting people whenever you step off campus." Five-college parties happen nearly every weekend. During midterms and finals, however, the campus is a "social ghost town." Harwood dorm throws the five-college costume party every Halloween. Freshman orientation gets interesting too. "First-years have to run through the gates of Pomona with blue and white carnations while upperclassmen throw water balloons and shoot water at them," says a student. It helps to have a set of wheels here because "it's virtually impossible to get around in Southern California without a car," according to one student. Every February or March, hundreds of students spend the morning at a nearby ski resort, then head to a local beach to swim, and end the day with an oceanside cookout.

> *Every February or March, hundreds of students spend the morning at a nearby ski resort, then head to a local beach to swim.*

There once was a time when the Pomona Sagehens were an athletic powerhouse; the football team even knocked off mighty USC on Thanksgiving Day back in 1899. Currently, men's and women's soccer and water polo, men's basketball and baseball, and women's swimming and tennis are strong programs. Intense rivalry exists between the Claremont Colleges; basketball games between

> **"I appreciate the diversity and depth that the five-college community brings to the social life."**

Pomona–Pitzer and CMS (Claremont–Mudd–Scripps) are "particularly heated." Intramurals, including hotly contested inner-tube water polo matches, attract many participants, and Pomona's $14 million athletic complex makes its facilities the best of the Claremonts.

"Pomona offers a unique and desirable juxtaposition of rigorous academics and a comfortable social atmosphere," says a student. Another says, "Once you take advantage of the five-college system, you realize how cool it is." The strongest link in an extremely attractive chain, Pomona continues to symbolize the rising status of the Claremont Colleges—and the West in general—in the world of higher education. There are few regrets about coming to Pomona. Says a senior, "We're in California. The sun is always shining. What's the problem?"

Overlaps

Stanford, Yale, Brown, Harvard, Dartmouth, University of Southern California, UC–Berkeley, UCLA

If You Apply To > **Pomona:** Early decision I: Nov. 1. Early decision II and regular decision: Jan. 1. Financial aid: Mar. 1. Housing: May 1. Application fee: $70. Campus and alumni interviews: recommended, evaluative. SATs or ACTs: required (SAT essay or ACT writing recommended). Subject Tests: optional. Letters of recommendation: required. Essay: required. Accepts the Common Application with supplement.

Scripps College

1030 Columbia Avenue, Claremont, CA 91711

Scripps is easily the premier women's college on the West Coast, offering a commitment to women's education while interacting with co-ed institutions that are literally next door. Attracts more well-rounded women than either Pomona or Pitzer. Innovative Core Curriculum takes an interdisciplinary approach to learning.

*First-year students
are assigned to Peer
Mentor Teams,
consisting of six to
eight classmates and
an older peer mentor.*

Scripps College offers the best of both worlds—a close-knit women's college, where traditions include weekly tea and fresh-baked cookies, and the size and scope of a major research institution, thanks to its membership in the Claremont Colleges. Founded in 1926 by newspaper publisher Ellen Browning Scripps, the college continues to pursue her mission: "To educate women by developing their intellects and talents through active participation in a community of scholars." Students tend to be outgoing, articulate, and serious about their studies, though they still know how to have fun. "The atmosphere is helpful, not competitive and scary," says one student. "It is impossible to be depressed in this beautiful place."

Indeed, Scripps's scenic 30-acre campus, listed on the National Register of Historic Places, offers a tranquil, safe, and comfortable environment. The architecture is Spanish and Mediterranean, with tiled roofs and elegant landscaping. A performing arts center provides permanent space for the Claremont Concert Orchestra and Concert Choir. In addition to a 700-seat theater, the center offers a music library, recital hall, practice rooms, faculty offices, and classrooms. The Lincoln Ceramic Art Building offers more than 5,000 square feet of work area and kiln yards.

Everyone at Scripps takes the Core Curriculum in interdisciplinary humanities, focusing on ideas about the world and the methods used to generate them. Other requirements include courses in fine arts, letters, natural and social sciences, women's studies, race and ethnic studies, foreign language, and math. All students also complete a senior thesis or project. First-year students are assigned to Peer Mentor Teams, consisting of six to eight classmates and an older peer mentor, to help ease the transition to college. Mentoring programs specifically for Jewish, Asian American, African American, Latina, international, and LGBTQ students are also available.

"Scripps is a very supportive community."

Popular and well-regarded majors at Scripps include social sciences, biological/ life sciences, psychology, and visual and performing arts. The Sheets Art Center offers a state-of-the-art studio and freestanding museum-quality gallery for aspiring painters and sculptors. Premeds benefit from the Keck Science Center, a joint facility for students at Scripps, Claremont McKenna, and Pitzer. Programs in area and ethnic studies, such as Middle East and North Africa studies and Chicana/Latino studies, are strong, and the feminist, gender, and sexuality studies major is also popular. The Scripps Humanities Institute offers seminars and lectures open to the general public, along with fellowships for juniors; recently, the institute explored the problem of raced, gendered, and classed violence in America. Scripps students can also take coursework at the other Claremont Colleges.

The academic experience at Scripps emphasizes cooperation. "Scripps is a very supportive community," a junior says. "It is a place where professors encourage you to work in groups because more brains [are] always better." Eighty-three percent of classes have fewer than 20 students. "I feel like my professors are my mentors and teachers, as well as my friends," says one student. "They are always up for a discussion, always willing to answer questions (even difficult ones), and always up to chat about how their day is going." When they're ready to branch out, typically in the junior year, more than 60 percent of Scripps students study abroad, choosing from more than 120 program options in 47 different countries.

Forty-three percent of Scripps women are from California, and 4 percent come from other countries. African Americans account for 4 percent of the student body, Hispanics 11 percent, and Asian Americans 16 percent. "The students here are diligent, thoughtful, and really down-to-earth," observes one politics major. "They are usually privileged and have had the opportunity to have really impressive experiences." SCORE, the Scripps Communities of Resources and Empowerment, provides support and funding to student organizations that promote inclusion and social justice. Scripps meets 100 percent of admitted students' demonstrated financial need and has made more grant money available for students with the most need. The college also awards merit scholarships averaging $16,927 to top achievers, although there are no athletic scholarships.

Ninety-nine percent of Scripps students live in one of the eight "spectacular" dorms, where options range "from singles to seven-person suites, apartment-style living arrangements, and charming Spanish Mediterranean residence halls built in the 1920s." A student says, "The dorms are gorgeous. They are well maintained and have lots of charm with French doors, balconies, or the occasional fireplace." Freshmen live in the same halls as sophomores, juniors, and seniors. The cafeteria garners rave reviews as well: "This is not traditional college food," says a bioethics major. "The salad bar is gourmet, the bread comes from a local bakery, and the pizza is made in a wood-fired brick oven. Don't get me started about the hot cookies!"

> **"[Students] are usually privileged and have had the opportunity to have really impressive experiences."**

Social life at Scripps centers on the residence halls, which take turns throwing parties. "Our social life is very much based on campus," explains a chemistry major. "With five undergraduate universities literally across the street from each other, it is challenging not to have something to do—from movie screenings, art exhibits, concerts, special events like a carnival or the International Festival, and parties." The school's alcohol policy complies with state law but also specifies that if an underage student is drunk at a party, she will be helped and kept safe, rather than written up and punished. Traditions are important at Scripps, including the Matriculation Ceremony at the start of each year, and the signing of the "graffiti wall" by each class before graduation. The town of Claremont offers a farmers market on Sundays, with fresh fruit, flowers, and gifts. For students with cars, popular road trips include Pasadena, Mount Baldy, San Diego, and even Las Vegas and Mexico; students without wheels can hop on the MetroLink commuter train and get to and from Los Angeles for 10 dollars on weekends.

> *The Scripps Humanities Institute offers seminars and lectures open to the general public, along with fellowships for juniors.*

Athletic rivalries aren't the focus here, but Scripps does field joint teams with Claremont McKenna and Harvey Mudd, and when those teams face off against Pomona and Pitzer, students pay attention. All of the Stag (men's) and Athena (women's) teams compete in Division III, and 11 teams brought home SCIAC championships in 2014–15. In addition, the Claremont Colleges Ballroom Dance Company has won multiple national collegiate championships. Intramural sports are also played jointly, and popular options include inner-tube water polo, soccer, flag football, volleyball, rugby, and lacrosse.

> **"Don't get me started about the hot cookies!"**

Scripps offers a winning combination of outstanding academics and personal attention, with a cooperative, nonthreatening feel. Scripps students want to achieve great things, but not if that requires stepping on their classmates' toes. And should the women-only environment begin to feel claustrophobic, the other Claremont Colleges beckon, with parties, intramural sports, and cross-registration privileges for a comprehensive college experience.

> ## Overlaps
> **Pomona, UC–Berkeley, UCLA, University of Southern California, Wellesley**

If You Apply To >

Scripps: Early decision I: Nov. 15. Early decision II and regular decision: Jan. 1. Financial aid: Feb. 1. Application fee: $60. Campus and alumnae interviews: optional, evaluative. SATs or ACTs: required. No Subject Tests. Letters of recommendation: required. Essay: required. Accepts the Common Application. Applicants must also submit a graded analytical paper from junior or senior year of high school.

950 Main Street, Worcester, MA 01610-1477

If Clark were located an hour to the east, it would have become the hottest thing since Harvard. Worcester is not Boston, but Clarkies bring a sense of mission to their relationship with this old industrial town. Clark is liberal, tolerant, and world-renowned in psychology and geography. Has a less national student body than some institutions of comparable quality.

Website: www.clarku.edu
Location: Small City
Private
Total Enrollment: 3,144
Undergraduates: 2,301
Male/Female: 39/61
SAT Ranges: CR 560–670,
   M 560–670
ACT Ranges: 26–30
Financial Aid: 90%
Pell Grant: 23%
Expense: Pr $ $
Student Loans: 94%
Average Debt: $ $ $
Phi Beta Kappa: Yes
Applicants: 8,045
Accepted: 55%
Enrolled: 15%
Grad in 6 Years: 83%
Returning Freshmen: 87%
Academics: ✍ ✍ ✍ ✍
Social: ☎ ☎ ☎
Q of L: ★ ★ ★
Admissions: (508) 793-7431
Email Address: admissions@
   clarku.edu

Strong Programs:
Psychology
Geography
International Development and
   Social Change
Environmental Science
Political Science
Biology
Economics

Clark University started in 1887 as an all-graduate school on a German model, excelling in disciplines including psychology and geography, and now welcomes undergraduates of all backgrounds and interests with small classes and no shortage of faculty attention. Clark's Liberal Education and Effective Practice (LEEP) educational model is designed to prepare students for success after college by combining a liberal arts curriculum with "intensive world, workplace, and personal experiences."

Clark's compact, 50-acre campus has "enough ivy, tall maples, and collegiate brick buildings to make a traditionalist happy," even though it's located in the rather gritty Main South section of Worcester. Buildings range from remodeled Victorian-era residences—former homes of prosperous merchants—to the award-winning Robert Hutchings Goddard Library. Clark is always renovating something, and careful restoration has brought a renewed sense of history to the area. Clark is the only American university where famed psychoanalyst Sigmund Freud lectured, and his statue adorns the spot in the center of campus where he spoke. The new, four-story Alumni and Student Engagement Center opened in 2016, serving as a home to the LEEP Center as well as a venue for lectures, panel discussions, and other events.

While Clark now serves primarily undergraduates, its history of graduate education is evident in its classrooms. Most courses are seminars and 55 percent have fewer than 20 students. First-Year Intensives, part of the LEEP model and required of all students, are limited to a small number of students (usually no more than 16) to help introduce them to the intellectual, social, and emotional growth they will experience in college. In most cases, the faculty member teaching the course acts as an academic advisor until students declare a major. "It is a nice way to immediately meet people and continue having contact with them throughout the semester, and your advisor gets to know you better," a junior says.

Clark's Program of Liberal Studies promotes the habits, skills, and perspectives essential to lifelong learning. In addition to fulfilling requirements for their major, each student must complete eight courses: one in verbal expression, one in formal analysis, and six in perspectives—aesthetic, global comparative, historical, language, scientific, and values. Many of Clark's course offerings are practice-based, tying in hands-on experiences outside the classroom. Before graduating, all students must also complete a LEEP Culminating Capstone demonstrating the knowledge and capabilities they have honed during their four years. Seniors who finish with a grade point average of 3.4 or better may take a fifth year tuition-free to obtain a master's degree.

"The academic climate at Clark is a cooperative and friendly one."

Clark's historically strong psychology and geography departments continue to burnish their national reputations, the latter having churned out more Ph.D.s in the field than any other school in the nation, plus five members of the National Academy of Sciences (the most of any geography program). Clark is the birthplace of the American Psychological Association and the concept of adolescence as being distinct from childhood. International development and social change is another traditional strength, as is environmental science, and the most popular majors include psychology, political science, biology, and economics. A new major in media, culture, and the arts has recently been added, as has a concentration in Africana studies.

While courses at Clark are challenging, students say the atmosphere is fairly relaxed. "The academic climate at Clark is a cooperative and friendly one. Students tend to work in groups and are always willing to help one another with course material," says a geography major. The quality of teaching is said to be "exceptional" and a junior comments, "Not only do I feel like my professors are invested in my learning, but many of them are also interested in getting to know me as a person." Nearly one-third of Clark students spend at least one semester studying abroad, usually during their junior year, at one of more than 50 programs in more than 30 countries. Sixty-four percent of students participate in undergraduate research, either assisting with faculty projects or pursuing their own as an independent study.

Many of Clark's course offerings are practice-based, tying in hands-on experiences outside the classroom.

"Clark students care about each other, the community, and the world around them," says one student. Thirty-two percent of Clark students hail from Massachusetts, and international students from about 65 countries make up another 15 percent. African Americans account for 4 percent of the student body, Hispanics 7 percent, and Asian Americans 7 percent. The political climate on campus is liberal, and "Students tend to involve

"Clark students care about each other, the community, and the world around them."

themselves in issues such as the environment, LGBTQ rights, politics, social justice, racial equality, etc.," says a junior. The Presidential LEEP Scholarship, awarded to highly motivated students with exceptional academic records, includes full tuition, room, and board for four years. Other merit and non-need-based awards are also available, but athletic scholarships are not. Twenty-three percent of freshmen qualify for Pell Grants.

First-year students and sophomores at Clark are required to live in the residence halls, and all except one are co-ed by floor or wing. In all, 70 percent of the student body live on campus in accommodations that are described as clean, comfortable, and "surprisingly big." Some upperclassmen find apartments and group houses nearby. Campus dwellers must buy the meal plan, and "There will always be a vegan station, gluten-free, and kosher station," a student explains. "Students can even submit their own recipes." Students report that the Clark Anti-Violence Education Program has been effective at educating students on sexual assault prevention, and a sophomore adds, "We have members of the local Worcester police who are stationed on campus and act as university police."

Clark's geography department has churned out more Ph.D.s in the field than any other school in the nation.

Clark has no Greek life, but more than 120 student-run organizations offer "a ton of concerts, bands, comedians" and other programs, says a student. Most students get involved with multiple clubs, and social life tends to be centered on campus. First-year dorms are dry, but alcohol may be consumed in other dorms by those who are of age, and students say that alcohol policies emphasize safety over punishment. Coping with the frigid New England winters includes quaffing cups of hot chocolate and dreaming about Spree Day, when classes are canceled and students enjoy live music, food trucks, face-painting, rock-climbing walls, mechanical bulls, and other festivities. And according to a geography major, "The newest tradition is

"Main South Worcester… [has] flavor and spice, and you'll either love it or hate it."

Elephant Thursday," in which, every Thursday, a student donning an elephant hat spreads cheer by giving "elephant tickets" to anyone wearing gray; students then redeem their tickets at the end of the year for an elephant-themed prize. "Why, you might ask? No one truly knows, but it is truly magical."

Worcester and the vicinity host 12 colleges, and Worcester itself is described as "a city of hidden gems," according to one student, offering movie theaters, restaurants with every conceivable type of cuisine, small clubs with live music, and the DCU Center, a 13,000-seat arena. "Main South Worcester is not the prettiest, quietest locale for a college, but it's got flavor and spice, and you'll either love it or hate it," a biology major says. Students mix with neighborhood residents through extensive volunteer programs coordinated by the Community Engagement and Volunteering Center. To get away, Clarkies head to the larger cities of Boston and Providence, or the rural wilds of Vermont, New Hampshire, and Maine—all easily reachable by car or public transit.

The Clark Cougars compete in the Division III New England Women's and Men's Athletic Conference (NEWMAC), and the university fields 17 intercollegiate teams. Solid teams include baseball, men's and women's basketball, men's and women's soccer, field hockey, and volleyball. About half of the students participate in intramural sports, the most popular of which are soccer, basketball, and softball.

Along with Johns Hopkins and Catholic University, Clark started out serving only graduate students but now offers a dynamic, undergraduate-focused educational environment. Clark continues to challenge convention, pioneering new teaching methods, pursuing new fields of knowledge, and finding new ways to connect thinking and doing. Through all this, community has remained a constant. Says a junior, "Clark is a warm and accepting place with students who hold the door open for others for just a little too long."

If You Apply To ➤ **Clark:** Early decision and early action: Nov. 1. Regular decision and financial aid: Jan. 15. Housing: May 1. Application fee: $60. Campus and alumni interviews: recommended, informational. SATs or ACTs: optional. Subject Tests: optional. Letters of recommendation: required. Essay: required. Application includes optional gender identity field. Accepts the Common Application.

Clarkson University

Holcroft House, Box 5605, Potsdam, NY 13699

You know you're in the North Country when the nearest major city is Montreal. Clarkson lies over the river and through the woods. With an informal and close-knit atmosphere, Clarkson is one of the few small, undergraduate-oriented technological universities in the nation. Compare to Lehigh, Bucknell, and Union. Out-of-the-way location makes Clarkson easier to get into, but doing well is no easy task.

At Clarkson University, engineering and ice hockey reign supreme. About half of the student body is enrolled in the engineering program, and the hockey teams are a perennial contender for top honors. Students here get a quality technical education in a small-town environment that offers plenty to do, especially during the sled-dog days of winter. "There are students who are the CEOs of their own companies, designing and creating new ideas and inventions, and uncovering new research," marvels one junior. "The academics challenge students to learn and grow every day."

The village of Potsdam, New York, is cloistered away between the Adirondacks and the St. Lawrence River. The campus relies mainly on modern architecture and lots of woods and wildlife. The Clarkson Institute for a Sustainable Environment is home to Clarkson's extensive environmental activities associated with research, interdisciplinary graduate and undergraduate degree programs, and outreach programs. Renovations to residential and athletic facilities are ongoing, and the university recently broke ground on the new Damon Hall Business Incubator.

As part of the university's general education requirements (Clarkson Common Experience), all students are required to complete a set of courses and a professional experience. The program emphasizes four components: learning to communicate effectively; developing an appreciation for diversity in both living and working environments; recognizing the importance of personal, societal, and professional ethics; and understanding how technology can be used to serve humanity. All freshmen take a first-year seminar designed to help them adjust to college life.

Engineering isn't the only academic offering at Clarkson, but it certainly gets top billing, and it includes four of the top five most popular majors. The combined programs in electrical/computer engineering and mechanical/aeronautical engineering earn the highest marks from students. In the natural sciences, biology and biomolecular science are the strongest offerings. Clarkson's School of Business is highly praised too and offers several majors, including distinctive programs in global supply chain management and engineering and management. What's more, all business students must have an international study experience in order to graduate, and first-year students actually start and run a business.

"We are encouraged to work together to solve problems."

Clarkson prides itself on intimacy and personalized instruction; 42 percent of classes have fewer than 20 students, and nearly 200 students conduct research with a faculty mentor each year. "The faculty are extremely accessible, friendly, and deeply invested in the academic and professional success of the students, and they do all this while also being experts in their fields and conducting innovative research," says one student. Some students say Clarkson isn't the academic pressure cooker that many technical institutes can be. "The heavy and sometimes daunting workload is counteracted by the supportive nature of the students and faculty members," says an environmental engineering major. "We are encouraged to work together to solve problems." The bottom line of a Clarkson education is getting a job after graduation, and students uniformly praise the career counseling office for contributing to the university's high job-placement rate. "They do a great job of helping us to get internships, co-ops, and research opportunities, because it is required for us to graduate," explains a junior.

Study abroad opportunities are available at 47 different schools in 24 countries, including Australia, Croatia, France, South Korea, and Sweden. The honors program offers an intensive four-year curriculum to roughly 150 students each year. Several hundred students from all majors join teams in Clarkson's Student Projects for Engineering Experience and Design program; most compete in collegiate engineering design competitions, but others engage in outreach efforts, such as Clarkson's Engineers Without Borders, which recently researched infrastructure improvements in remote locations in Uganda. For women on this male-dominated campus who are interested in STEM fields, the unique Women in Science and Engineering program enrolls 40 first-year students into a living/learning residential program that emphasizes engineering, science, and math.

"The food is very edible. Even professors eat it."

"Students at Clarkson are the most down-to-earth, fun, and hardworking individuals I have ever met," says an engineering and management major. Seventy-two percent of the student body is native to New York. Clarkson has trouble luring minorities to its remote locale, although efforts to change that are underway; African Americans, Hispanics, and Asian Americans combine for 9 percent of the student population, and international students add another 3 percent. Socioeconomically, the school is more diverse, with 24 percent of freshmen eligible for Pell Grants. Students agree that the campus doesn't usually get too riled up about national politics or issues. Clarkson awards a handful of merit scholarships each year averaging $21,047. Forty-four athletic scholarships are offered, but only ice hockey players need apply (it's Clarkson's only Division I sport).

(continued)

Average Debt: $ $ $
Phi Beta Kappa: No
Applicants: 6,906
Accepted: 68%
Enrolled: 17%
Grad in 6 Years: 73%
Returning Freshmen: 90%
Academics: ✍ ✍ ✍
Social: ☎ ☎
Q of L: ★ ★ ★
Admissions: (315) 268-6480
Email Address: admission@ clarkson.edu

Strong Programs:
Mechanical Engineering
Engineering and Management
Civil Engineering
Chemical Engineering
Global Supply Chain
    Management
Environmental Science and
    Policy
Biology
Biomolecular Science

The combined programs in electrical/ computer engineering and mechanical/ aeronautical engineering earn the highest marks from students.

Eighty-four percent of students live in campus housing. Students are required to reside on campus all four years, unless exempted to live in a Greek house. All freshmen are housed with students in their major areas of study and in some instances in their department, giving them the chance to study and learn together. "Housing is good. It is centrally located, so it's a maximum 15-minute walk to class, and that is across campus," says a civil engineering major. Many underclassmen are housed in conventional dorms, but university-owned townhouse apartments offer more gracious living. The dining facilities get average marks for variety and taste. "The food is very edible," says a student. "Even professors eat it."

In keeping with Clarkson's "come-as-you-are" atmosphere, the social scene is low-key. "On campus, the residence dorms, classes, and clubs and activities are good avenues for socializing with others," offers one senior. "Off campus, Clarkson's close proximity to three other colleges (SUNY–Potsdam, St. Lawrence, and SUNY–Canton) allows for socializing with students from other institutions." Ten percent of the men and 12 percent of the women join the Greek system. Drinking is permitted on campus for those of age, and those not into the Greek scene can head to the handful of bars in downtown Potsdam, which one student describes as having "small-town charm

"Our motto is to 'defy convention,' and we take that to heart in all that we do."

with an Adirondack twist." The extended snowy winters are great for snowboarders and ice climbers, and many students join the popular Outing Club to enjoy such outdoor adventures year-round. "In the fall and spring students can be found working toward their '46,' or summiting all 46 high peaks in the Adirondack State Park," according to a senior. For those who crave the bustle of city nightlife, Ottawa and Montreal are each about an hour and a half away by car.

When it comes to sports, hockey is first and foremost in the hearts of Clarkson students. The Golden Knight women's hockey team claimed the Division I championship title in 2014. The men's and women's teams have been ECAC champs in recent years and contend for the national championship with other blue-chip teams like archrivals St. Lawrence and Cornell. "The game between Clarkson and St. Lawrence is one of the most popular rivalries in the area. Cheel Arena is filled hours before the game begins," says one senior. Clarkson also offers 17 Division III sports. Women's volleyball has brought home four consecutive Liberty League tournament championships, and men's and women's basketball are on the rise. About 80 percent of students take advantage of the intramural program, with soccer, broomball, and volleyball proving to be favorites.

While other majors are offered, Clarkson's bread and butter is its technological programs, particularly its slew of engineering majors. Students here gain ample exposure to the ever-growing variety of specialties in the field. "Our motto is to 'defy convention,'" says one student, "and we take that to heart in all that we do, whether it be how we look at creating the latest technologies, solving the ever-changing problems of our world, or how we treat each other as individuals."

If You Apply To ➤

Clarkson: Early decision: Dec. 1. Regular decision: Jan. 15. Financial aid: Feb. 15. Application fee: $50 (paper), free (online). Campus and alumni interviews: recommended, informational. SATs or ACTs: required. Subject Tests: recommended. Letters of recommendation: required. Essay: required. Accepts the Common Application with supplement. Application includes optional field for gender identity.

Clemson University

Clemson, SC 29634

Clemson is a technically oriented public university in the mold of Georgia Tech, North Carolina State, and Virginia Tech. Smaller than the latter two and more focused on undergraduates than Georgia Tech, Clemson serves up its education with ample helpings of school spirit and orange paint. Small-town location makes for a tight-knit campus, though also a hayseed image next to more sophisticated locales such as Columbia and Chapel Hill.

Nestled in the foothills of the Blue Ridge Mountains, Clemson University is a place where traditional Southern spirit continues to flourish alongside modern academics, big-time athletics, and state-of-the-art facilities. This public university has the ring of a private institution and features quality academics in technical and scientific areas such as engineering and biology. Tiger spirit is as strong as ever, as evidenced by the ubiquitous orange tiger paws that decorate the campus, and students here are happy to make tracks of their own.

CU's 1,400-acre campus is situated on what was once Fort Hill Plantation, the homestead of Thomas Green Clemson. The campus is surrounded by 17,000 acres of university farms and woodlands and offers a spectacular view of the nearby lake and mountains. Architectural styles are an eclectic mix of modern and 19th-century collegiate. Clemson Bottoms, half a mile down the road from the 80,000-seat football stadium, is home to the Calhoun Field Laboratory, a pastoral site dedicated to agricultural research that features a large, student-run organic garden. A fantastic resource for science enthusiasts and history buffs is the library's collection of first editions of the scientific works of Galileo and Newton. Several construction projects are underway, including a new residential village.

General education requirements include courses in advanced writing; oral communications; mathematical, scientific, and technological literacy; social sciences; arts and humanities; cross-cultural awareness; and science and technology in society. An electronic portfolio pilot allows freshmen to build their portfolio, demonstrating changes in competencies throughout their experiences at Clemson. Electrical engineering is Clemson's largest department, and computer engineering is among the nation's best in research on large-scale integrated computer circuitry and robotics. The College of Architecture, one of the school's most selective programs, offers intensive semesters at the Overseas Center for Building Research and Urban Study in Genoa, Italy. Biological sciences, management, engineering, and parks, recreation, and tourism management are the most popular majors, and the agriculture and nursing programs are also well regarded. Undergraduate teaching has always been one of Clemson's strong points, and for students interested in pursuing a liberal arts curriculum, the school has degrees in fine arts, philosophy, and languages and enjoys a strong regional reputation for its history program. Because of the prevailing technical emphasis, however, most students interested in the liberal arts head "down country" to the University of South Carolina.

Academically, the level of difficulty varies. "Classes are very competitive," says one junior. "While challenging at times, the coursework is stimulating and applicable." Professors run the gamut from average to stellar, with most receiving high marks from students. "Professors not only teach the classes but also make themselves available for tons of extra hours outside of the classroom," says a psychology major. Fifty-three percent of classes have fewer than 20 students. Students report some problems finishing a degree in four years, and class registration can be a hassle.

Website: www.clemson.edu
Location: Suburban
Public
Total Enrollment: 20,046
Undergraduates: 17,175
Male/Female: 53/47
SAT Ranges: CR 560–660, M 590–690
ACT Ranges: 27–31
Financial Aid: 38%
Pell Grant: N/A
Expense: Pub $ $ $ $
Student Loans: 49%
Average Debt: $ $ $
Phi Beta Kappa: Yes
Applicants: 22,396
Accepted: 51%
Enrolled: 30%
Grad in 6 Years: 81%
Returning Freshmen: 93%
Academics: ✍ ✍ ✍
Social: ☎ ☎ ☎ ☎
Q of L: ★ ★ ★ ★
Admissions: (864) 656-3311
Email Address: cuadmissions@clemson.edu

Strong Programs:
Engineering
Architecture
Agriculture
Nursing
History
Biological Sciences
Management
Parks, Recreation, and Tourism Management

Highly motivated students should consider Calhoun Honors College—the oldest honors program in South Carolina—open to freshmen who scored at least 1380 on their SATs or 30 on their ACTs. Clemson also offers exchange programs in venues from Mexico to Australia, and one-third of students study abroad.

"Students are friendly, kind, academically driven, and are a part of a true family on our campus," cheers one elementary education major. Clemson's student body has a decidedly Southern air, as 64 percent of undergrads hail from South Carolina, with most of the rest from neighboring states; 1 percent come from foreign countries. African Americans make up 7 percent of the student body, Hispanics 3 percent, and Asian Americans 2 percent. The average Clemson student is friendly and conservative, and though, as a public institution, the school isn't affiliated with any church, there is a strong Southern Baptist presence on campus. The university offers thousands of merit scholarships averaging $5,216 and hundreds of athletic scholarships.

Housing gets positive reviews, and 41 percent of the students live on campus, usually during their first two years. Most of the dorms are single sex, though co-ed, university-owned apartment complexes are also an option. "Apartment housing is competitive, but rooms on campus are usually available," says a student. Clemson House and Calhoun Courts, the co-ed halls, are considered the best places to be. "The west campus highrise dorms are awesome," raves a junior. The dining facilities have been improving, according to students. "They have specials and even ask students to contribute recipes," explains one student. Upperclassmen can cook for themselves, and each dorm has kitchen facilities. Students say they feel safe on campus, thanks to a robust security program. "We have three separate police forces that work on campus at all times, and they truly take care of the students," says a junior.

"While challenging at times, the coursework is stimulating and applicable."

"At Clemson, the fun is mostly right outside our windows," says one student. "Whether it's a football game, a pep rally, an RHA program, or one of our U-Nites Friday night activities, students always find something to do." Aside from the sports teams, fraternities and sororities provide most of the social life. Eighteen percent of Clemson men and 32 percent of women go Greek, and the college has threatened actions to curb hazing, alcohol abuse, and other problems related to the Greek scene. Stay tuned for further developments. The town of Clemson is pretty small, with a few bars and movie theaters, but some students love it. After class, many students hop on their bikes and head to nearby Lake Hartwell. The beautiful Blue Ridge mountain range is also close by for hiking and camping, and beaches and ski slopes are both within driving distance. Atlanta and Charlotte are only two hours away by car, and Charleston is four hours away on the coast.

Clemson has a high-powered sports scene and fields a number of competitive teams in the Division I Atlantic Coast Conference. The football team upset Alabama to become national champions in 2016, after finishing as runners-up for the title the previous year. On weekends when the Tiger teams are playing, there are pep rallies, cookouts, dances, and parties for the mobs of excited fans. Football fever starts with the annual First Friday Parade, held before the first home game, and on every game day the campus dissolves into a sea of Tiger orange. The roads leading to campus are painted with large orange pawprints. So, too, are half the fans, making the stands in "Death Valley" look like an orange grove. Tiger fans are especially rowdy when the reviled University of South Carolina Gamecocks are in town. The annual South Carolina game, which has been played for more than a century, has now been named the Palmetto Bowl. Other very competitive athletic teams include basketball, baseball, men's track and field, and men's and women's soccer.

"At Clemson, the fun is mostly right outside our windows."

Overlaps

Winthrop, College of Charleston, UNC at Chapel Hill, Duke, University of Georgia, North Carolina State, Georgia Tech, University of South Carolina

Clemson is best at serving those whose interests lie in technical fields. School spirit is contagious, fueled by a love of big-time college sports, and becomes lifelong for many Clemson students. Everyone can become part of the Clemson family, from Southern belle to Northern Yankee, as long as they're friendly, easygoing, and enthusiastic about life in general and the Tigers in particular.

If You Apply To ➤

Clemson: Rolling admissions: May 1. (Priority deadline: Dec. 1.) Financial aid: Mar. 1. Housing: May 1. Application fee: $70. No campus or alumni interviews. SATs or ACTs: required. Subject Tests: optional. Letters of recommendation: optional. Essay: optional. Music and theater applicants must audition.

Colby College

Waterville, ME 04901

The northernmost venue for high-quality, private higher education in New England. Colby's picturesque setting is a short hop from the sea coast or the Maine wilderness. No frats since the college abolished them more than 30 years ago. A well-toned, outdoorsy student body in the mold of Middlebury and Dartmouth, and more buttoned-up than Bates or Bowdoin. Invented the month-long January term. Still requires SAT or ACT, or two SAT subject tests.

Colby College draws students who like to push themselves, whether in the classroom or on the ski slopes. The nearby city of Waterville, Maine (population 16,000), offers few distractions, and close friendships with peers and professors help ward off the winter chill. Colby's top study abroad program offers students an opportunity to explore the world, and even those who don't spend a semester or year away can get a taste during the month of January, when Jan-Plan trips send Colby students far and wide. "Colby students seem to feel at home here," muses one freshman, "based on the immensely friendly population and community feeling that comes across on campus."

Colby sits high on Mayflower Hill, with beautiful views of the surrounding city and countryside. Its 714 acres include a wildlife preserve, miles of cross-country trails, and a pond used in winter as an ice-skating rink. Georgian architecture predominates, and the oldest buildings are redbrick with white trim, ivy, and brass nameplates above their hunter green doors. The more contemporary buildings lend a touch of modernity. One of the most iconic Colby buildings is the library tower, which is topped with a blue light. The student center features a 7,000-square-foot pavilion with a snack bar, coffee shop, and lounge areas. Recent construction includes new baseball and softball fields.

As a small college with a history of innovation and educational excellence, Colby encourages students to learn for learning's sake rather than for a good grade. Students must complete distribution requirements in English composition, foreign language, "areas" (one course each in arts, historical studies, literature, quantitative reasoning, and social sciences, and two courses in natural sciences), diversity (two courses focusing on how diversity has contributed to the human experience), and wellness (five supper seminars over the first two semesters). Colby was the first men's college in New England to admit women, and also the first to establish a special January term. Students must take three such terms for credit to graduate, but almost all take four. Motivated students might

Website: www.colby.edu
Location: Small Town
Private
Total Enrollment: 1,857
Undergraduates: 1,857
Male/Female: 48/52
SAT Ranges: CR 630–720, M 640–740
ACT Ranges: 29–32
Financial Aid: 46%
Pell Grant: 8%
Expense: Pr $ $ $ $
Student Loans: 32%
Average Debt: $ $
Phi Beta Kappa: Yes
Applicants: 7,593
Accepted: 23%
Enrolled: 30%
Grad in 6 Years: 94%
Returning Freshmen: 93%
Academics: ✎ ✎ ✎ ✎ ½
Social: ☎ ☎ ☎
Q of L: ★ ★ ★ ★
Admissions: (800) 723-3032
Email Address: admissions@colby.edu

(continued)

Strong Programs:
Biology
Economics
Government
English
Psychology

Half of the school's majors have an international component, and 55 percent of Colby students spend some time abroad.

use the month off to serve an internship, study abroad, or prepare an in-depth research report.

In all, Colby offers more than 50 majors. Popular and well-regarded programs include biology, economics, and government, followed closely by English and psychology. Students study oceanography through Colby's partnership with the Bigelow Laboratory for Ocean Sciences in East Boothbay, Maine. For would-be engineers, there is a joint 3–2 program with Dartmouth and a 4–2 program with Columbia, and others may take exchange programs with the Claremont Colleges and Howard. New majors in educational studies and astrophysics have recently been added. One student describes Colby as "an intensely collaborative work environment," and Colby's faculty is unusually devoted to undergraduate teaching. "The professors believe that if you are having difficulty, they aren't doing their job correctly for you and want to fix that in any way possible," a computer science major says. Seventy-two percent of all classes have fewer than 20 students, allowing those highly lauded profs to spend more time with each student.

> **"The professors believe that if you are having difficulty, they aren't doing their job correctly."**

Study abroad is a serious emphasis at Colby, and the opportunities to do so begin early. Freshmen can apply to the Global Entry Semester program, whisking off to France or Spain and delaying on-campus enrollment until the second semester. The school also sponsors Jan-Plan trips to everywhere from India and Belize to Bermuda (for biology). Half of the school's majors have an international component, and 55 percent of Colby students spend some time abroad, taking advantage of more than 200 approved international programs. A high proportion of graduates enter the Peace Corps and the Foreign Service. Those who stay on campus during the summer as research assistants for faculty are rewarded with a two-day Summer Research Retreat in Forks, Maine, dedicated to short talks, presentations, and white-water rafting or hiking adventures.

"The typical Colby student is the well-rounded student," says a freshman, "someone involved in everything from academics to athletics to community service, and an open member of a welcoming community." Only 12 percent of Colby students are Mainers; the rest learn to act like natives during the COOT program (Colby Outdoor Orientation Trips). These four-day excursions by bicycle, canoe, or foot introduce them to the beauty of the Maine wilderness or to service or theater experiences. African Americans account for 3 percent of the student body, Hispanics 6 percent, and Asian Americans 6 percent. Twelve percent are international. "The biggest social and political issues on campus are racism and LGBTQ awareness," says a junior. All financial aid at Colby is need-based, the college meets 100 percent of students' demonstrated need, and it has replaced student loans with grants in all its financial aid packages. Despite those generous aid packages, a mere 8 percent of students qualify for the Pell Grant.

> **"The three dining halls do a wonderful job of providing delicious food and unique atmospheres."**

Students who work as summer research assistants for faculty are rewarded with a two-day Summer Research Retreat.

Ninety-four percent of Colby students live on campus, where residence halls have live-in faculty members. "The residence halls are great. Some are better than others, of course, but none are like the stereotypical crappy dorm rooms that you see in movies or on TV," says one student. About 100 seniors live off campus each year in apartment-style buildings. Dining halls cater to various tastes, lifestyles, religions, and even holidays throughout the year, including a weekend omelette bar. "The three dining halls do a wonderful job of providing delicious food and unique atmospheres. Students are free to eat at whichever one they want," states a senior. Comprehensive initiatives to prevent campus sexual assault include various peer-to-peer training and support programs.

When the weekend comes, you'll find most Colby students staying close to campus, though some do make supply runs into Waterville. "There's everything you might need in Waterville (grocery stores, pharmacies, movie theaters, every fast food chain you could ever want, decent restaurants, and cafés)," says one student. "Colby

"Colby does not have Greek life, which definitely sets a more inclusive tone on campus."

does not have Greek life, which definitely sets a more inclusive tone on campus," adds a senior. "While there is a drinking culture, I don't think there is pressure to drink." Popular road trips include Augusta and Freeport, Maine (home to the L.L. Bean factory and store). Also easy to reach are the bright lights of Boston and Montreal and the slopes of Sugarloaf, Maine.

The Colby administration likes to share two "big secrets" about Maine winters: they're beautiful, and they're a lot harsher in the telling than in the living. Everyone looks forward to football, basketball, lacrosse, and hockey games, as well as the annual winter carnival and snow-sculpture contest. The Colby Mules have come a long way since the first intercollegiate croquet game, played at Colby in 1860. Sports are Division III, except for squash and skiing, which are Division I, and solid programs include women's lacrosse and men's cross-country. Nonvarsity athletes are eager participants in 10 club teams and six intramural sports.

Colby's traditional New England liberal arts college vibe and increasingly global focus extend far beyond its small-city setting and historic, ivy-covered buildings. They permeate the air, punctuated by the long-standing traditions, abundant school spirit, and caring faculty members who focus on developing their students' minds.

Overlaps

Bowdoin, Middlebury, Brown, Bates, Williams, Hamilton, Dartmouth, Amherst

If You Apply To ➤ **Colby:** Early decision I: Nov. 15. Early decision II and regular decision: Jan. 1. Financial aid: Feb. 1. No application fee. Campus interviews: recommended, evaluative. Alumni interviews: optional, evaluative. SATs or ACTs or two Subject Tests: required (SAT essay or ACT writing recommended). Letters of recommendation: required. Essay: required. Accepts the Common Application with supplement.

Colgate University

13 Oak Drive, Hamilton, NY 13346

With fewer than 3,000 students, Colgate is smaller than Bucknell and Dartmouth but bigger than Hamilton and Williams. Like the other four, it offers small-town living and close interaction between students and faculty. Greek organizations and jocks are still well entrenched despite administration's perennial efforts to neutralize their influence.

While you may see the same North Face or Patagonia fleece coming and going (and coming and going) as you stroll across Colgate University's campus, students here aren't all spun from the same cloth. "Most students at Colgate are freethinkers and open to new ideas," says a sophomore. From the herbarium to the Devonian fossils to the plethora of interdisciplinary courses, it's clear that Colgate has more to offer than just its picture-postcard setting. "I think Colgate draws students who want a high level of academic rigor and a top-tier liberal arts education," says one student, "without the competitive air that usually accompanies these."

Colgate's 13 founders started the school with 13 prayers and 13 dollars. Their prayers were answered in 1880, when toothpaste mogul William Colgate gave $50,000 to the fledgling university, enough to get the name changed from Madison

Website: www.colgate.edu
Location: Small Town
Private
Total Enrollment: 2,837
Undergraduates: 2,834
Male/Female: 45/55
SAT Ranges: CR 620–720, M 630–730
ACT Ranges: 30–33
Financial Aid: 47%

(continued)

Pell Grant: 14%

Expense: Pr $ $ $ $

Student Loans: 34%

Average Debt: $

Phi Beta Kappa: Yes

Applicants: 8,724

Accepted: 27%

Enrolled: 32%

Grad in 6 Years: 90%

Returning Freshmen: 95%

Academics: ✍ ✍ ✍ ✍ ½

Social: ☎ ☎ ☎

Q of L: ★ ★ ★

Admissions: (315) 228-7401

Email Address: admission@ colgate.edu

Strong Programs:
Economics
Political Science
History
English
Environmental Studies
International Relations

Interdisciplinary study has been a foundation of Colgate's curriculum since 1928.

to his own (and less than the current annual cost to attend!). Today, the 575-acre campus sits on a hillside in rural New York, overlooking the village of Hamilton. Ivy-covered limestone buildings peek out from tree-lined drives; lush green spaces are perfect for rugby, Frisbee, or other outdoor diversions, at least in the warmer months. Rolling hills and farmland surround the campus, making for stunning vistas during the snowy season, which stretches from mid-October to mid-March. A new ice hockey rink opened in 2016.

Aside from blazing a trail to rural New York, Colgate has led its peers in emphasizing interdisciplinary study. The faculty first established an interdisciplinary core program in 1928, and it's been a foundation of the curriculum ever since. Even now, all freshmen take a first-year seminar that introduces liberal arts topics, skills, resources, and ways of learning. The seminars are capped at 18 students each, and there are more than 40 topics, ranging from the history of rock and roll to the advent of the atomic bomb. Seminar instructors double as academic advisors, since students don't declare majors until the sophomore year. Students also complete two courses from each of Colgate's three academic divisions: natural sciences and math, social sciences, and arts and humanities. Five courses in the liberal arts core—on legacies of the ancient world, challenges of modernity, communities and identities, scientific perspectives, and global engagements—round out the requirements and equip students to contemplate the issues they will face throughout their lives. Aside from a major (or two), Colgate also mandates foreign language proficiency and two physical education classes.

> **"Colgate draws students who want a high level of academic rigor and a top-tier liberal arts education."**

Students give high marks to Colgate's natural and social sciences programs, and economics, political science, history, and English are the most popular majors. Befitting Colgate's rugged location, there are five majors within the environmental studies program: environmental studies, environmental biology, environmental geography, environmental geology, and environmental economics. New minors have recently been added in mathematical systems biology and museum studies. Classes at Colgate are small, and 71 percent have fewer than 20 students. A computer science major says, "Colgate students always receive a very personalized education. Professors are always accessible in office hours, but they often take their commitment to their students a step further by taking them to coffee or inviting them over to their house for dinner."

Classrooms and labs devoted to foreign language study help students gain comfort with another tongue—a good thing, since 61 percent of students study abroad. In addition to 20 semester-long, faculty-led off-campus study programs, Colgate offers seven "extended-study" travel programs that serve as three-week extensions of regular on-campus courses. More than 100 other preapproved study abroad programs offer additional options, as do the Maritime Studies Program* and the SEA Semester*. The Sophomore Residential Seminars program enables selected students to live together in the same residence hall and take a semester-long course that is capped off with a weeklong trip during winter break; recent participants have traveled to such locales as San Francisco for a course on immigrant and sexual cultures and to India for an art and architecture course. Each summer approximately 200 students work under faculty members as paid research assistants. When graduation arrives, students who go straight into the workforce benefit from the help of Colgate's strong and loyal alumni network.

> **"Colgate students always receive a very personalized education."**

"We are an incredibly ambitious group, so this drives the average Colgate student to work very hard in academics, but one's academics don't limit one's ability to get involved in extracurriculars on campus or in the community," says a junior.

Students are mostly white graduates of public high schools, and 25 percent are New Yorkers. African Americans account for 4 percent of the population, Hispanics 9 percent, and Asian Americans 4 percent; 9 percent of students are international. Students credit the ALANA Cultural Center with "fostering a comfortable and friendly environment" and describe a mix of political views on campus. A physics major reports, "Several discussion points on campus have been about general inclusivity, the influence of Greek life on campus, and gender and safety issues." Although there are no merit scholarships, Colgate's need-based financial aid program meets 100 percent of enrolled students' demonstrated financial need, and Colgate grants usually represent the largest portion of a typical financial aid award. Additionally, 257 athletic scholarships are available in 13 sports.

The Sophomore Residential Seminars program involves a semester-long course that is capped off with a weeklong trip during winter break.

Ninety percent of Colgate students live in the dorms, which range from traditional buildings with fireplaces to newer facilities that seem more like hotels. "While first-year students begin their housing experience next to the academic buildings, students will continue to move away from the academic quad every year, creating a new, independent experience for upperclassmen," explains a senior. About 250 upperclassmen are allowed to live off campus each year. Two dining halls provide students with a wide choice of victuals, including salad and sandwich bars, soup, cereal, and bagels. Take-out food is provided at the campus center, known as the Coop. Campus security officers are said to be well respected, but administrative handling of campus sexual assaults has incited protests from students. "The difference between Colgate and other schools is that Colgate listened to its students and in response is making some really important and powerful changes to protocol," comments an economics major.

"We are an incredibly ambitious group."

"Colgate has more than 190 clubs and organizations on campus, so there is no end to the opportunities students can have to pursue their interests," says a junior. Adds another, "Greek life and sports teams will hold large events, but clubs and smaller student groups provide a social scene too." Eleven percent of the men and 21 percent of the women join the Greek system. In an effort to cut down on alcohol consumption, hazing, and other problems that regularly get out of hand, the administration forced fraternities and sororities to sell their off-campus houses to the university. Everyone looks forward to ALANApalooza, Dancefest, and Spring Party Weekend, a last blast before finals, which celebrates the thaw with barbecues, fireworks, and multiple bands. Given the significance of the number 13 to the school's founding, every Friday the 13th is dubbed Colgate Day, a time to show off school spirit and pride. On the eve of graduation, seniors light torches and form a circle around Lake Taylor, where they sing their alma mater and throw their torches into a bonfire.

Given the significance of the number 13 to the school's founding, every Friday the 13th is dubbed Colgate Day.

In addition to a required four-day orientation program, freshmen may also participate in Wilderness Adventure, where groups of six to eight canoe and hike in the Adirondacks, or in Outreach, which involves three days of community service in the surrounding area. "Community service is quite popular," confirms a senior. Hamilton is within walking distance of campus, but there's also a free bus that cycles through every half hour, especially nice in the dead of winter. Students enjoy free "Take Two" movies on Friday and Saturday nights and open-mic nights at Donovan's Pub or the Saxbys at the Barge coffee shop downtown. The Palace draws

"Colgate...is making some really important and powerful changes to [sexual assault] protocol."

crowds with music, dancing, a bar, and a Mexican restaurant. For those with wheels, skiing is 45 minutes away in Toggenburg, and the malls and city lights of Syracuse and Utica are roughly the same distance.

While many Colgate students enjoy facing off in 12 intramural competitions and 40 club sports, their most fervent cheers are reserved for Division I football against Bucknell and men's lacrosse and ice hockey against Cornell. The Raiders football and men's lacrosse teams are recent conference champions, and men's and women's soccer, men's basketball, and women's ice hockey and volleyball are also strong. Even weekend warriors may take advantage of facilities like the Sanford Field House, the Lineberry natatorium, and the Seven Oaks golf course, which is ranked among the top five collegiate courses nationally.

Colgate led the way in interdisciplinary work and continues to do so now. What else has remained constant? A senior offers this assessment: "I think Colgate has embraced its identity as different from other liberal arts colleges in that we are not a crunchy granola hippy school and we are not a socially progressive bastion of forward thinking. Colgate is what it is: a hidden gem in the Chenango Valley."

Overlaps

Cornell University, Dartmouth, Middlebury, Boston College, Bowdoin, Tufts, Brown, Colby

If You Apply To ➤ **Colgate:** Early decision I: Nov. 15. Early decision II, regular decision, and financial aid: Jan. 15. Housing: May 1. Application fee: $60. Campus and alumni interviews: optional, informational. SATs or ACTs: required. No Subject Tests. Letters of recommendation: required. Essay: required. Accepts the Common Application with supplement.

University of Colorado–Boulder

Office of Admissions, 552 UCB, Boulder, CO 80309

Boulder is a legendary place that draws everyone from East Coast ski bums to California refugees. The scenery is breathtaking and the science programs are first-rate. The University of Arizona is the only public university of similar stature in the Mountain West. Check out the "academic neighborhoods" and other residential academic programs.

Website: www.colorado.edu
Location: Small City
Public
Total Enrollment: 27,210
Undergraduates: 24,808
Male/Female: 55/45
SAT Ranges: CR 530–640, M 540–660
ACT Ranges: 24–30
Financial Aid: 58%
Pell Grant: 30%
Expense: Pub $ $ $
Student Loans: 44%
Average Debt: $ $
Phi Beta Kappa: Yes
Applicants: 31,326
Accepted: 80%
Enrolled: 25%
Grad in 6 Years: 71%
Returning Freshmen: 86%
Academics: ✐ ✐ ✐ ✐
Social: 🏛 🏛 🏛 🏛 🏛

Wild buffalo may be all but extinct on America's Great Plains, but they're in boisterous residence, proudly wearing gold and black, at the University of Colorado–Boulder. A bevy of scholars' programs, learning communities, and academic neighborhoods give the campus a community feel, and students choose from a solid menu of academic programs, including research experience, study abroad, service learning, and honors classes and programs. "There are so many ways to be active and engaged in your learning at Boulder," cheers a sophomore. And with more than 300 days of sunshine a year, is it any wonder students here are a contented lot?

Tree-shaded walkways, winding bike paths, open spaces, and an incredible view of the dramatic Flatirons rock formation make CU's 600-acre Boulder campus a haven for students from both coasts and for Colorado residents eager to pursue knowledge in a snowy paradise. The campus includes about 200 classic rural Italian-style buildings and complexes built of Colorado sandstone with red tile roofs. The 45,000-square-foot Discovery Learning Center houses 11 labs in which engineering students tackle society's challenges using video-conferencing and other high-tech capabilities. The Sierra Club has named CU–Boulder as a top public university for its efforts to protect the environment. City bus passes are included in the cost of tuition and fees, the campus Environmental Center facilitates sustainable culture and practices, and ongoing residence hall renovations and other construction projects embody its commitment to sustainability and energy efficiency.

Entering freshmen and transfer students at CU–Boulder choose from four colleges, one program, and one school: the College of Arts and Sciences (which enrolls

70 percent of the students); the College of Music; the College of Engineering and Applied Science (the hardest to enter, students say); the new College of Media, Communication, and Information; the Program in Environmental Design; and the Leeds School of Business. Each has different entrance standards and requirements. General education requirements cover four skills acquisition areas—writing, quantitative reasoning and math, critical thinking, and foreign language—and seven content areas: historical context, culture and gender diversity, U.S. context, natural sciences, contemporary societies, literature and the arts, and ideals and values.

"Unlike other highly competitive universities, there is a high level of collaboration," says an applied mathematics major. "Your classmates won't refuse to work with you, and you are always comfortable asking questions and asking for help." CU–Boulder offers more than 3,600 courses each year in approximately 150 areas of study; integrative physiology, psychology, economics, and communication are among the most popular majors. Outstanding programs include aerospace engineering, physics, chemical and biological engineering, music, astrophysics and planetary sciences, biochemistry, and business entrepreneurship. CU–Boulder is consistently among the top universities in the country to receive NASA funding, leading to unparalleled opportunities for the design, construction, and flight of model spacecraft—and to 18 CU–Boulder alumni having worked as astronauts. Concurrent, five-year bachelor's/master's degree programs are available in dozens of fields. Forty-seven percent of undergraduate classes enroll fewer than 20 students, and a freshman says, "In my experience, professors and graduate student instructors alike have taken a keen interest in students' progress, success, and learning."

> **"There are so many ways to be active and engaged in your learning at Boulder."**

CU–Boulder has tried to make its large campus seem smaller through "academic neighborhoods" (specialized living and learning environments) focusing on topics such as leadership; diversity; natural or social sciences; international studies; engineering; sustainability and innovation; music; and history, culture, and society. In these programs, students take one or two courses, each limited to 25 students, in their residence halls. "The Residential Academic Program for freshmen is essential for gaining a well-rounded experience at CU," advises a senior. The Presidents Leadership Class is a four-year scholarship program that exposes the most promising students to political, business, and community leaders through seminars, work and study trips, and site visits. "All 50 students are incredible people who are inspiring to be around," says one recent participant. The top 10 percent of each incoming class is invited to join the Honors Program, which offers more than 80 honors courses per year. About a third of students undertake undergraduate research, and a quarter of students pack their bags for 300 university-sponsored study abroad programs in more than 65 countries around the world.

"Students are relaxed and explorative, curious and inquisitive, fun-loving and good-natured, focused and committed," says one Buffalo. Sixty-one percent of CU–Boulder's undergraduates come from Colorado, and 6 percent come from abroad. Hispanics comprise 10 percent of the undergraduate population, Asian Americans 5 percent, and African Americans 2 percent. Hot topics include "wealth,

> **"The Residential Academic Program for freshmen is essential for gaining a well-rounded experience at CU."**

liberalism, and inequality," according to one student. Qualified undergrads receive merit scholarships worth an average of $8,758, and 276 athletes receive scholarships as well. Additional programs provide debt-free financial incentives for qualified students whose family income is at or below the federal poverty line. Thirty percent of entering students are eligible for Pell Grants. The university now offers a four-year tuition guarantee for all of its undergraduates.

(continued)

Q of L: ★ ★ ★
Admissions: (303) 492-6301
Email Address: apply@ colorado.edu

Strong Programs:
Integrative Physiology
Psychology
Economics
Communication
Aerospace Engineering
Physics
Chemical and Biological
  Engineering
Music

NASA funding has led to unparalleled opportunities for the design, construction, and flight of model spacecraft.

First-year students are required to live on campus, and 29 percent of undergraduates stay in university housing. "The older dorms are still in pretty good shape but aren't as nice as the newer dorms," a sophomore reports. Most sophomores, juniors, and seniors find off-campus digs in Boulder, and those who want to stay on campus are advised to make early reservations for Farrand, Sewall, or Kittredge halls. An alternative to the four dining halls and nine cafés is the student-run Alferd Packer Restaurant & Grill, which takes its name from a controversial 19th-century folk figure known as the "Colorado Cannibal." *Bon appétit.* Generally, students say campus is safe, helped by emergency telephones in strategic locations. CU–Boulder also offers walking and riding escorts at night via a service called CU NightRide.

For the culturally minded, the university and the city of Boulder offer films and plays, the renowned Colorado Shakespeare Festival, art galleries and museums, and concerts by top rock bands. Denver is only 30 miles southeast, reachable by a free bus service. Most students get involved in community service, and the new CU Engage center coordinates service-learning courses and community-based research opportunities. Ten percent of CU–Boulder men and 19 percent of women go Greek, though fraternity and sorority parties have changed dramatically since CU–Boulder's sorority chapters became the first in the nation to voluntarily make their houses dry. On campus, the ban on alcohol is taken seriously, and dorms are officially substance-free. Still, "The party scene is fairly large and has a lot going on most weekends," says a political science major. "CU is considered a top party school and people do live up to that expectation." Day trips to ski resorts like Breckenridge and Vail largely replace weekend getaways here, but for those who've got to get out of the cold, Las Vegas isn't so far, says one student.

Physical exercise is a popular extracurricular activity at CU–Boulder. The massive Student Recreation Center features four pools, an ice rink, a climbing gym,

> **"CU is considered a top party school and people do live up to that expectation."**

several multipurpose courts, and 30,000 square feet of strength and cardio space, among other facilities. Varsity teams compete in the Division I Pac-12 Conference, and the Buffaloes have won numerous championships, including the 2014 NCAA national title for men's cross-country and the school's 20th championship in skiing in 2015. Men's and women's basketball are also strong, as are women's soccer and lacrosse. Each year, football fans flock to Denver for the game against Colorado State. Ralphie, the live buffalo who acts as CU–Boulder's mascot, doesn't miss a game—and neither do many students. Club sports are highly competitive, winning more than 60 national championships in the last 20 years in sports ranging from cycling and ice hockey to snowboarding and ultimate Frisbee. Intramurals sign up 15,000 students each year.

If you want to flex your muscles as well as your mind, look beyond the ivy-covered bricks and gray city skies endemic to so many Eastern institutions, and consider going West instead. "The amount of resources students can utilize to further their education or gain experience in their field at CU and in the city of Boulder is immense and overwhelming," says one student. "Don't be too intimidated, though, as CU attracts the most friendly and adventurous people I've ever met."

Overlaps

Colorado State, University of Denver, University of Arizona, Cal Poly–San Luis Obispo, University of Oregon, Indiana University, Penn State, Purdue

If You Apply To ➤

CU–Boulder: Early action: Nov. 15. Regular decision: Jan. 15. Financial aid: Feb. 15. Housing: May 1. Application fee: $50. No campus or alumni interviews. SATs or ACTs: required. No Subject Tests. Letters of recommendation: required. Essay: required. Accepts the Common Application with supplement. Music applicants must audition.

Colorado College

14 East Cache La Poudre Street, Colorado Springs, CO 80903

The Block Plan is CC's claim to fame. It is great for in-depth study and field trips but less suited to projects that take an extended period of time. Colorado Springs is an ideal location at the base of the Rockies, which draw outdoor enthusiasts and East Coasters who want to ski. CC is the only top liberal arts college between Iowa and the Pacific.

Colorado College is one of the few U.S. schools offering one-course-at-a-time block scheduling, also known as the Block Plan. For more than a century, CC's focus on creative approaches to academics and its breathtaking location at the edge of the Rocky Mountains have drawn bright, independent liberal arts enthusiasts who also like to go out and play. "People don't come to CC because they want to make a ton of money or maintain the status quo," asserts a senior. "They come because they want to change the world, help others, and have a little fun."

Founded in 1874, the college campus lies at the foot of Pike's Peak, in the town of Colorado Springs. Many homes in the surrounding neighborhood are on the National Register of Historic Places, as are many CC buildings, including its first, Cutler Hall, and Palmer Hall, named after town founder William J. Palmer, a major force behind the establishment of the college. The prevailing architectural styles are Romanesque and English Gothic, with some more modern structures thrown in. The Cornerstone Arts Center includes a 433-seat auditorium, a black-box performance venue, a sound stage, a 108-seat film-screening room, the IDEA (Interdisciplinary Experimental Arts) Space, and additional multipurpose space.

CC requires students to take 32 courses, at least 18 outside their major department. Within those 32 courses, one course (for two units) must focus on the Western tradition; one course must focus primarily on the study of non-Western societies; another must focus primarily on issues of inequality—with respect to nationality, race, ethnicity, gender, class, and/or sexuality; two units must focus on the natural sciences, including lab or field study; and one must focus on quantitative reasoning. Foreign language proficiency is also required. What really defines the academic climate, though, is the block schedule (see also Cornell College in Iowa). Students take eight courses between early September and mid-May, but focus on each one, in turn, for three and a half weeks. Some courses, such as neuroscience or those involving longer-term projects, are two blocks long. Four-and-a-half-day breaks separate the terms. The plan helps students stay focused, eliminating the temptation to let one course slide so that they can catch up in another. But there are trade-offs. Students say it can be hard to integrate material from courses taken one at a time. There's also the danger of burnout, because so much material is crammed into such a short span.

> "[People] come [to CC] because they want to change the world, help others, and have a little fun."

The First-Year Experience program, with a student mentor and two advisors, helps students adjust to college-level academics and the fast pace of the Block Plan. "CC is extremely collaborative," notes an environmental policy major, "However, it's extremely intense." Seventy-one percent of classes have fewer than 20 students, and required courses aren't hard to get into, since spots are secured with an auction system. At the beginning of each year, students get 80 points to "bid" on the classes they want. Those who bid the most for a particular class get a seat. And if you're going to take only one class at a time, it helps to like the teacher. Students say that's

Website:
   www.coloradocollege.edu
Location: City Center
Private
Total Enrollment: 2,107
Undergraduates: 2,096
Male/Female: 46/54
SAT Ranges: CR 630–710,
   M 620–710
ACT Ranges: 28–32
Financial Aid: 45%
Pell Grant: 13%
Expense: Pr $ $ $ $
Student Loans: 37%
Average Debt: $
Phi Beta Kappa: Yes
Applicants: 8,062
Accepted: 17%
Enrolled: 42%
Grad in 6 Years: 87%
Returning Freshmen: 96%
Academics: ✍ ✍ ✍ ✍
Social: ☎ ☎ ☎ ☎
Q of L: ★ ★ ★ ★
Admissions: (800) 542-7214
Email Address: admission@
   coloradocollege.edu

Strong Programs:
Economics
Sociology
Political Science
Environmental Science
Geology
Southwest Studies

no problem here. "The professors are very accessible, and it is easy to have a good working relationship," says a history and political science major.

The most popular majors at Colorado include economics, sociology, political science, and environmental science. Students say that the sciences in general, and particularly geology, are strengths. The block schedule permits some classes at unique times and in unique places—for instance, astronomy at midnight, or coral biology work in the Caribbean. The college's popular major in Southwest studies includes time at its Baca campus, 175 miles away in the historic San Luis Valley. Other interesting interdisciplinary programs include Asian studies; race, ethnicity, and migration studies; and organismal biology and ecology. In addition to giving students the option to pick semester- and yearlong abroad programs in more than 60 countries, Colorado College faculty also teach about 25 off-campus blocks, both domestically and internationally, during the school year and summer session. Still more options are available through the Associated Colleges of the Midwest*. More than 80 percent of students study off campus at least once during their time at Colorado.

Just 16 percent of Colorado College students are in-staters, 8 percent are international, and the rest are from all over the United States. "The students are laid-back, nature-loving hippies," says a student. CC is less diverse than its closest peer, Cornell College, particularly socioeconomically—13 percent of Colorado freshmen qualify for the Pell Grant. Three percent of undergrads are African American, 9 percent Hispanic, and 5 percent Asian American—and the school is trying to attract more diversity. Groups like the Queer Straight Alliance, the Feminist Collective, the Jewish Chaverim, and the Black Student Union provide support to students of varied backgrounds and viewpoints. "The general political orientation is extremely liberal," says a senior. The college meets 100 percent of admitted students' demonstrated financial need, and a limited number of merit scholarships, averaging $9,360, and athletic scholarships are available to eligible students.

> "There is a very large drug and alcohol presence on campus, though it absolutely is not mandatory."

Seventy-five percent of the students call campus housing home, and only seniors are permitted to live off campus. "The underclassmen dorms range from brand-new, almost luxury suites, to pretty old but full of character," says a senior. Six living/learning communities are also available: Sense of Place, CARE (Community in Action through Reflection and Engagement), Enclave, Outdoor Education, PRIDE, and Revitalizing Nations. The "exceptional" dining facilities include a traditional, all-you-can-eat dining hall; a grill with American, Mexican, and sushi options; and an all-natural café and convenience store.

When the weekend comes, students unwind at parties in friends' rooms or seniors' off-campus houses. "There is a very large drug and alcohol presence on campus," reports a senior, "though it absolutely is not mandatory." The "low-key" Greek system attracts 11 percent of the men and 11 percent of the women. Favorite traditions include the annual Llamapalooza and Blues & Shoes (bluegrass and horseshoes) music festivals, and the monthly Full Moon Cruisers, where "students gather at 10 p.m. decked out in crazy outfits to ride their bikes downtown and party under the full moon," explains a student. For those seeking a bit of urban culture, Denver and Boulder are a short drive away. Most CC students love heading off campus to ski or hike, either at nearby resorts or in Utah, New Mexico, or the Grand Canyon area. Freshman outdoor orientation trips help newcomers sort out the options, from backpacking and hiking to rafting, bicycling, and windsurfing. Students can even reserve a college-owned mountainside cabin. Service trips are sponsored during

> "The intensive and demanding nature of the Block Plan calls for deep but quick thinkers."

Students take eight courses between early September and mid-May, but focus on each one, in turn, for three and a half weeks.

CC faculty teach about 25 off-campus blocks during the school year and summer session.

block breaks, and the majority of students do some type of community service during their time at CC.

The Colorado College Tigers compete in two Division I sports—men's ice hockey and women's soccer—as well as 15 Division III sports. Men's and women's soccer, lacrosse, swimming, and cross-country and women's volleyball all have made national tournament appearances in recent years. The hockey rivalry with the University of Denver is huge. Nearly 70 percent of students partake in 15 intramural sports, and 15 club sports are also available.

The Block Plan made Colorado College what it is today, and the school continues to build on this reputation. As one senior underscores, "The intensive and demanding nature of the Block Plan calls for deep but quick thinkers [and] hard but patient workers." For those who are up to the challenge, CC offers a supportive environment, with a healthy dose of fun, where they can thrive.

Overlaps

University of Denver, University of Colorado–Boulder, University of Vermont, Lewis & Clark, Whitman, University of Southern California, Tulane, Reed

If You Apply To ➤

Colorado College: Early decision I and early action: Nov. 10. Early decision II, regular decision, and financial aid: Jan. 15. Application fee: $60. Campus interviews: recommended, evaluative. Alumni interviews: optional, evaluative. SATs or ACTs or three exams from a list of approved category options that includes Subject Tests: required. Letters of recommendation: required. Essay: required. Accepts the Common Application with supplement.

Colorado School of Mines

1812 Illinois Street, Golden, CO 80401

Mines is the preeminent technical institute in the Mountain West. Getting in is not hard; graduating is another story. One-sixth the size of Texas Tech and best known for mining-related fields but strong in many areas of engineering. Men outnumber women 3 to 1, and Golden provides little other than a nice view of the mountains.

If you're a bit of a geek whose only dilemma is what type of engineer to become, and you want to spend your scarce free time hiking, biking, and skiing with friends, then Colorado School of Mines may be the place for you. This public school's small size and rugged location endear it to the mostly male students who shoulder heavy workloads to earn their degrees. "There are often fun and entertaining conversations that could only be possible with the types of students here," says a mechanical engineering major. Just down the road from Coors Brewing Co., which taps the Rockies for its legendary brews, students at Mines learn to tap the same mountains for coal, oil, and other natural resources.

CSM's 373-acre campus sits in the shadow of the spectacular Rocky Mountains in tiny Golden, Colorado. Architectural styles range from turn-of-the-century gold dome to present-day modern, and native trees and greenery punctuate lush lawns. Construction on the new, $50 million CoorsTek Center for Applied Science and Engineering is set for completion in fall 2017.

CSM's academics are rigorous. All freshmen take the same first-year program, which includes chemistry, calculus, physics, design, earth and environmental systems, quantitative chemical measurement, nature and human values, physical education, and the Freshman Success Seminar, an advising and mentoring course designed to increase retention. The required two-semester EPICS program—the acronym stands for Engineering Practices Introductory Course Sequence—helps develop communication, teamwork, and problem-solving skills with weekly presentations and written reports. Because of CSM's narrow focus, the undergraduate majors—or

Website: www.mines.edu
Location: Small City
Public
Total Enrollment: 5,438
Undergraduates: 4,334
Male/Female: 72/28
SAT Ranges: CR 600–690, M 650–730
ACT Ranges: 28–32
Financial Aid: 77%
Pell Grant: 14%
Expense: Pub $ $ $ $
Student Loans: 60%
Average Debt: $ $ $ $
Phi Beta Kappa: Yes
Applicants: 11,752
Accepted: 38%
Enrolled: 23%
Grad in 6 Years: 77%
Returning Freshmen: 94%
Academics: ✍ ✍ ✍ ½

(continued)

Social: ☎ ☎ ☎
Q of L: ★ ★
Admissions: (303) 273-3220
Email Address: admissions@
  mines.edu

Strong Programs:
Mechanical Engineering
Petroleum Engineering
Chemical and Biological
  Engineering
Electrical Engineering
Computer Science
Metallurgical and Materials
  Engineering
Geophysical Engineering
Engineering Physics

"options," as they're called—are quite good. There's plenty of variety, as long as you are into engineering; programs range from geophysical, metallurgical, and petroleum to chemical, electrical, and mechanical. Computer science is another popular choice, and the school's fastest-growing program. Mines offers the only B.S. degree in economics in Colorado, and the school has been investing more in humanities and social sciences, offering several minors in these areas. Courses in a student's option start in the second semester of sophomore year, after yet more calculus, physics, and differential equations, and as seniors, all students complete a capstone requirement.

Pass/fail grading is unheard of at Mines, but failing grades are not. "The courses are hard," says a junior, "but good time management and friends" help ease the angst. "We are all working together," another adds. Professors are qualified and helpful, and adjunct professors, who work in the fields they teach, draw raves for their practical knowledge. "Most of the teachers have industry experience and bring that into the classroom," a chemistry major says. Twenty-five percent of undergraduate classes have fewer than 20 students.

> "Most of the teachers have industry experience and bring that into the classroom."

CSM supplements coursework with a required six-week summer field session, enabling students to gain hands-on experience. About 100 undergraduates participate in the McBride Honors Program in Public Affairs, which includes seminars and off-campus activities that encourage them to think differently about the implications of technology. The WISEM program provides training, mentoring, and other support for women in science, engineering, and math. CSM also offers the opportunity to live and study at more than 50 universities in Europe, Australia, Latin America, Asia, and the Middle East, but only 7 to 10 percent of students take part. Each year, 100 to 120 undergraduates participate in research with faculty members or on their own.

Mines is a state school, making it a good deal for homegrown students, who comprise 59 percent of the undergraduate student body. Six percent hail from foreign nations. "Most of the students would be considered nerds or geeks at other schools," a civil engineering major explains, "but almost everyone fits in here." Hispanics comprise 7 percent of the student body, Asian Americans 5 percent, and African Americans 1 percent. Students are generally too wrapped up in academics to pay attention to political issues, according to a physics major. Merit scholarships averaging $7,997 are available to qualified students, and athletes may vie for roughly 160 athletic scholarships.

The required two-semester EPICS program helps develop communication, teamwork, and problem-solving skills.

Thirty-six percent of CSM students—mostly freshmen—live in the residence halls. Most buildings are co-ed, though the preponderance of men results in a few single-sex dorms. "All the residence halls have been refurbished and are looking better than ever," a sophomore says. Most upperclassmen move to fraternity or sorority housing, college-owned apartments, or off-campus condos and houses. There's only one cafeteria, and a junior says, "The vegetarian options are not very good unless you really like cereal and salad" (presumably not during the same meal).

There is life outside of the computer labs here. On campus, a junior says, "There is always a club putting together an event or just students throwing parties." CU–Boulder offers more partying 20 minutes away. Mines also has an active Greek system, with fraternities and sororities attracting 12 percent of the men and 21 percent of the women. Still, rush is dry, and, owing to Mines's small size, those serving the alcohol almost always know the age of those trying to obtain it, making it tough for the underaged to imbibe. Social life also includes comedy shows, homecoming, and Engineering Days (E-Days)—a three-day party with fireworks, a pig roast, tricycle races, taco-eating contests, and cheap beers. New student orientation includes the M-climb, in which freshmen hike up

> "There is always a club putting together an event."

Mount Zion lugging a 10-pound rock, "and whitewash it, and each other," says one participant. The rock is added to an M formation atop the mountain, then "seniors return to take down a rock, completing the cycle."

CSM's location at the base of the Rockies means gorgeous Colorado weather (make sure to bring sunscreen) and easy access to skiing, hiking, mountain climbing, and biking. Denver is also nearby, and aside from its museums, concerts, and sports teams, the city is home to many government agencies and businesses involved in natural resources, computers, and technology, including the regional offices of the U.S. Geological Survey and Bureau of Mines. Golden hosts the National Earthquake Center, the National Renewable Energy Laboratory, and, of course, the Coors Brewery. (The 3,000-foot pipeline that runs from the Coors plant to campus is there to convert excess steam from the brewery into heat for the school—not to supply the frats with the foamy stuff.) The biggest complaints are too much homework and (among guys) not enough women. Road trips to Las Vegas or Texas provide some respite.

CSM fields 16 Division II varsity teams, which is more varsity teams than any other college or university in the state. The men's cross-country team brought home the school's first ever team national champi-onship in 2015. Other competitive Oredigger teams include men's and women's soccer, men's track and field, and women's basketball and volleyball, all of which are recent conference champs. The intramural and club sports programs have grown dramati-cally, with 70 percent of students now participating.

"When you leave here, you're prepared for anything."

While time spent in the classroom at Mines may not be fun, for those who are focused on engineering, educational options don't get much better than those offered here. "Lots of companies recruit our students," says one senior, thanks to a stellar reputation in the fields of mining and engineering. A junior adds, "When you leave here, you're prepared for anything." Especially if you are an engineer.

If You Apply To ➤	**CSM:** Rolling admissions. (Priority deadline: Nov. 15.) Financial aid: Mar. 1. Housing: May 31. Application fee: $45 (paper), free (online). No campus or alumni interviews. SATs or ACTs: required (SAT essay or ACT writing recommended). No Subject Tests. Letters of recommendation: optional. Essay: optional.

Colorado State University

Fort Collins, CO 80524

It lacks Boulder's glitz and glamour, but Colorado State offers a more complete slice of the Rocky Mountain West. Known throughout the region for its prevet program, CSU turns out more STEM (science, technology, engineering, and math) graduates than any other Colorado campus. Has a traditional college feel with a first-rate student center and strong ties to the local community.

Founded in 1870 as the Colorado Agricultural College, Colorado State University began with five students, two faculty members, and a mission "to serve society through teaching, research, and outreach." Today, the university boasts approxi-mately 1,400 faculty across eight colleges and 52 academic departments, as well as more than 116,000 living alumni, including state governors, heads of corpora-tions, Olympic gold medalists, teachers, researchers, and artists. Students here enjoy ample research opportunities, a slew of solid academic programs, and an unbeatable

(continued)

SAT Ranges: CR 520–620,
   M 520–630
ACT Ranges: 22–28
Financial Aid: 45%
Pell Grant: 20%
Expense: Pub $ $ $
Student Loans: 57%
Average Debt: $ $
Phi Beta Kappa: Yes
Applicants: 18,556
Accepted: 81%
Enrolled: 31%
Grad in 6 Years: 67%
Returning Freshmen: 87%
Academics: ✍ ✍ ✍
Social: ☎ ☎ ☎ ☎
Q of L: ★ ★ ★ ★
Admissions: (970) 491-6909
Email Address: admissions@
   colostate.edu

Strong Programs:
Business Administration
Mechanical Engineering
Biological Sciences
Psychology
Health and Exercise Science
Veterinary Medicine
Biomedical Engineering
Fermentation Science and
   Technology

Freshmen may participate in a midsummer orientation, a variety of first-year seminars, and living/learning communities.

location, so it's little wonder they take pride in calling CSU home. "CSU has a great community and a wonderful friendliness about it," says one happy Ram. "It really is a fun and comfortable place to be."

Situated at the foot of the spectacular Rocky Mountains, CSU gives students easy access to abundant natural resources. The open space on the main campus reflects the university's heritage as a land grant institution. The Oval, a wide expanse of lawn encircled by towering elm trees, anchors the northwest corner of campus. Architectural styles range from Beaux-Arts to Renaissance Revival, and the campus features a spacious outdoor plaza, 32 acres of recreation fields, and stunning views of Long's Peak. The South Campus is the site of the Veterinary Teaching Hospital and Natural Resource Research Center, the Foothills Campus is home to facilities specializing in everything from equine science to disease control, and the Pingree Park Campus is an ideal location for field research in the heart of the Rockies.

All CSU students complete a university-wide core curriculum that includes 31 credit hours of coursework in written communication, mathematics, oral communi-

> **"It really is a fun and comfortable place to be."**

cation, biological and physical sciences, arts and humanities, social and behavioral sciences, historical perspectives, and global and cultural awareness. CSU offers more than 71 undergraduate majors, the most popular of which include business administration, mechanical engineering, biological sciences, psychology, and health and exercise science. "Our science programs are really strong," a sophomore says, and the prevet program is also distinguished. The performing arts have received a boost thanks to improved facilities, but the humanities are not as solid as other departments. Other notable undergraduate majors are available in biomedical engineering and fermentation science and technology, as are concentrations in horticulture therapy, viticulture and enology, and conservation biology.

The academic climate is competitive—especially in the preprofessional programs—and students say classes can be difficult. "The courses are hard, but manageable," a junior says. Thirty-eight percent of classes have fewer than 20 students, and "professors are very knowledgeable," according to one student. Another says, "If you express an interest in their area of study, they may invite you to do research in their lab, write a paper and be published in a major journal, or help you with graduate school applications—who knows!" Freshmen may participate in a midsummer orientation, a variety of first-year seminars, and living/learning communities designed to ease the transition from high school to college. "The number one program that students should know about is the Key Communities," says one sophomore. "As a Key student you take three classes with a cluster of 19 people who you meet before classes start. This is so nice because you immediately have friends and people you know who also live in Braiden Hall and can help you study." Qualified students can opt for the honors program or take part in the Honors Undergraduate Research Scholars program, which allows students to conduct long-term research alongside a faculty mentor. Additional hands-on learning opportunities include a four-week geology field camp, a watershed management field camp, hundreds of study abroad programs, and an undergraduate research symposium.

"The students at CSU are friendly and accepting," says a junior. "Students who attend this university are passionate about what they study and want to change the world." Seventy-five percent of CSU students are from Colorado, and 4 percent are international. African Americans account for 2 percent of the student body, Asian Americans 2 percent, and Hispanics 11 percent. CSU is a politically active campus, and liberal and conservative viewpoints are both well represented. "The biggest issues on campus are probably environmental issues," says a student, "due mainly to our proximity to the Rocky Mountains." Thousands of merit scholarships averaging

$4,158 are handed out each year, and athletes vie for more than 150 scholarships in 16 men's and women's sports.

Twenty-seven percent of all CSU students live on campus in residence halls and campus apartments. "All freshmen are required to live in the dorms," a sophomore reports, "but most move off campus after their first year." Another student adds, "Of the residence halls, 75 percent have been renovated or built within the past five years, so they are in great condition and more like a resort than the dorms we all picture from movies." Campus residents may choose from among six meal plans, and the residence hall dining center provides an all-you-can-eat option. "The food is awesome," a student says. "I think it is as good as any restaurant in town." Students also report feeling safe on campus; security measures include a "safe walk" escort program, emergency phones, and an active security staff.

"The number one program that students should know about is the Key Communities."

Although the Greek scene attracts 9 percent of the men and 12 percent of the women, students say social life is divided between on-campus activities (including art exhibits, picnics, and comedians) and off-campus fun. "Campus activities, such as free movies or concerts, draw a large crowd," says one student, "while parties and other gatherings off campus do the same." The Lory Student Center hosts events on a regular basis, and "there are over 300 clubs, which many students use as a social outlet," a junior explains. The CSU campus is dry and "there is no tolerance for alcohol in the residence halls," one biochemistry major says. "The policies are enforced."

Fort Collins is "a fun city that revolves around the school," says one junior. "There is a definite sense of community and support for CSU in the town," a senior adds. Students not only frequent the downtown bars, shops, and eateries, but also can be found performing volunteer work or community service alongside the locals. Popular road trips include quick getaways to nearby ski resorts and hiking trails, and longer treks to Utah and Nevada. Back on campus, students enjoy a number of traditions: "We have a huge homecoming," says one student, "with a bonfire, lighting of the 'A,' parade, and football game."

"There is a definite sense of community and support for CSU in the town."

The CSU Rams compete in Division I as members of the Mountain West Conference, and the most competitive teams include football, volleyball, men's golf, women's cross-country, and women's swimming. Women's volleyball has made 22 consecutive trips to the NCAA tournament. The University of Colorado is the hated rival—especially in football—and "the Rocky Mountain Showdown is probably the biggest event of the year," says a family and consumer sciences major. Intramurals attract roughly 16 percent of the student body, and "some of the most popular are soccer, flag football, and basketball," a senior says. The Student Recreation Center features an indoor track, basketball and volleyball courts, cardio machines and free weights, and a host of other facilities for students who want to stay in shape.

Despite ubiquitous complaints about limited parking, rising tuition, and the need for more bike racks, students at Colorado State are quick to say why they appreciate their alma mater: "Because CSU rocks! It is an awesome school to go to and has lots to offer students of all ages and backgrounds," cheers a student. What's more, it's a "fun and beautiful place to be," says a junior, "and you know that your degree will mean something."

Hands-on learning opportunities include a four-week geology field camp and a watershed management field camp.

Overlaps

University of Colorado–Boulder, University of Denver, University of Northern Colorado, Cal Poly–San Luis Obispo, University of Arizona, University of Oregon, Colorado School of Mines

Columbia University

212 Hamilton Hall, New York, NY 10027

Once an Ivy League afterthought, Columbia now rivals the Ivy League's big three in selectivity. Applications have doubled in the past 10 years for one simple reason: Manhattan trumps New Haven, Providence, Ithaca, and every other Ivy League city, with the possible exception of Boston. The often overlooked engineering program is among the best in the nation for undergraduates. The heart of Columbia is still its Core Curriculum.

Website: www.columbia.edu
Location: City Center
Private
Total Enrollment: 23,465
Undergraduates: 6,102
Male/Female: 52/48
SAT Ranges: CR 700–790,
  M 700–800
ACT Ranges: 32–35
Financial Aid: 60%
Pell Grant: 17%
Expense: Pr $ $ $ $
Student Loans: N/A
Average Debt: N/A
Phi Beta Kappa: Yes
Applicants: 36,250
Accepted: 6%
Enrolled: 63%
Grad in 6 Years: 96%
Returning Freshmen: 99%
Academics: ✑ ✑ ✑ ✑ ✑
Social: ☎ ☎ ☎
Q of L: ★ ★ ★ ★
Admissions: (212) 854-2522
Email Address: ugrad-ask@
  columbia.edu

Strong Programs:
Social Sciences
Engineering
Biological and Biomedical
  Sciences
English

Though students entering Columbia will, of course, expect the rigorous academic program they'll encounter at this Ivy League school, they must also be streetwise, urbane, and together enough to handle one of the most cosmopolitan cities in the world. Columbia lets its students experience life in the Big Apple, but serves as a refuge when it becomes necessary to escape from New York, allowing students to immerse themselves in the best academia has to offer. "Columbia students all share at least two reasons for coming to this university," says a freshman. "The Core Curriculum and New York City. This means the students here want a classical liberal arts education but do not want to live in a college bubble." Famous alums can be found in the highest echelons of their chosen professions, whether it be politics, literature, sports, or entertainment. Think Barack Obama.

With a total university-wide enrollment of more than 23,000 students, says one of them, "It's easy to feel lost." Columbia's 6,100 undergraduates are split into two divisions: the flagship Columbia College and the Fu Foundation School of Engineering and Applied Science. (Sister school Barnard College, affiliated with Columbia but governed by its own board of trustees, has an additional 2,500 students.) Columbia's campus has a large central quadrangle in front of Butler Library and at the foot of the steps leading past the statue of Alma Mater to Low Library, which is now the administration building. The redbrick, copper-roofed neoclassical buildings are "stunning," and the layout, says an undergrad, "is well thought out and manages to provide a beautiful setting with an economy of space."

The undergraduate experience at Columbia centers on its renowned Core Curriculum. While these courses occupy up to a third of the first two years and can become laborious, students generally praise them as worthwhile and enriching. "The Core truly unifies the school in a way that transcends most social limitations and gives us all a great basis for further pursuits of knowledge," says a freshman. As it has since World War I, the college remains committed to the Core while at the same time expanding the diversity of the canon and requiring Core classes on non-Western cultures. According to a junior, some students find that the Core can "spark some interest in a subject they had never thought of before."

Two of the most demanding introductory courses in the Ivy League—Contemporary Civilization (CC) and Literature Humanities—form the basis of the

> **"Students here want a classical liberal arts education but do not want to live in a college bubble."**

Core. Both are yearlong and taught in small sections, generally by full profs. LitHum (as it is affectionately called) covers about 26 masterpieces of literature from Homer to Dostoyevsky, usually with some Sappho, Jane Austen, and Virginia Woolf thrown in for alternative perspectives. CC examines political and moral philosophy from Plato to Camus, though professors have some leeway in choosing 20th-century selections. One semester each of art and humanities is required and, while they are not given the same reverence as their literary counterparts, they are eye-opening all the same. Foreign language proficiency is required, as are two semesters of science; two semesters of "global Core," classes dealing in cultures not covered in the other Core requirements; two semesters of phys ed; and University Writing. Students at the School of Engineering and Applied Science complete approximately half of the Core Curriculum.

(continued)

History
Psychology
Chemistry
Foreign Languages

Columbia is an intellectual school, not a preprofessional one, and even though a large percentage of students aspire to law or medical school, "we are mostly content to be liberal artists for as long as possible," says an English major. Even students in the School of Engineering and Applied Science pursue "technical education" with a liberal arts base. Almost all departments that offer undergraduate majors are strong, notably English, history, political science, and psychology. Chemistry and biology are among the best of Columbia's high-quality science offerings. The earth and environmental science department owns 200 acres in Rockland County, home to many rocks and much seismographic equipment. The fine arts are improving, thanks to departmental reorganization, new facilities, and joint offerings with schools such as the Juilliard School of Music. Columbia offers many challenging combined majors such as philosophy/economics and biology/psychology. There are 50 offerings in foreign languages, ranging from Czech to Persian to Urdu, and the East Asian languages and cultures department is one of the best anywhere. There is also an African American studies major, and a women's studies major that delves into topics ranging from the Asian woman's perspective to the lesbian experience in literature. Columbia students can take classes at Barnard and graduate-level courses in several departments, notably political science, gaining access to the resources of the School of International and Public Affairs and its multitude of regional institutes.

> **"Many Core classes are taught by grad students."**

Columbia is tough; the workload is often stressful and classmates can be competitive, but some say that's not necessarily a bad thing. "The academic climate at Columbia has taught me invaluable skills in managing my time, saying no to tasks I don't want to do, and navigating group dynamics that aren't always cooperative," remarks an earth and environmental engineering major. Student/faculty interaction is supported by one of the smallest student-to-faculty ratios in the country, with 83 percent of classes having fewer than 20 students. "Some of the professors are real leaders in their fields and you can learn from them," says a philosophy major, who cautions, "Many Core classes are taught by grad students, which has led to some less than ideal experiences for me." Additional interaction stems from professorial involvement in campus politics and forums and from the faculty-in-residence program, which houses professors and their families in spruced-up apartments in several of the residence halls. First-year students are assigned an academic advisor whom they work with all four years, and they receive a departmental faculty advisor when they declare a major at the end of sophomore year. For students wishing to spend time away from New York, Columbia offers credit through more than 150 programs in more than 100 cities around the world; 28 percent of students go abroad. Research is big here too, and the university conducts $1 billion of research annually in the sciences, humanities, and social sciences; hundreds of undergraduates participate.

Contemporary Civilization and Literature Humanities are two of the most demanding introductory courses in the Ivy League.

A sophomore says that Columbia is attended by "smart, diverse, individualistic, driven students who tend to contemplate the organization of society and the meaning of life pretty frequently." Twenty-three percent of undergraduates come from New York, and 14 percent come from abroad. Columbia has the largest percentage of students of color in the Ivy League: 12 percent are African American, 12 percent are Hispanic, and 22 percent are Asian American. Columbia remains one of the nation's most liberal campuses, but a computer science major cautions against generalizing: "We are not all raging liberals that protest on campus daily." The university awards financial aid based on need, meeting the full demonstrated need of all students with grants instead of loans. Students coming from families with annual incomes below $60,000 are not expected to contribute to the cost of tuition, fees, room, or board; the family contribution is reduced for those with incomes between $60,000 and $100,000.

> "[Students] tend to contemplate the organization of society and the meaning of life pretty frequently."

With the New York housing market out of control, 94 percent of Columbia students live in university housing, which is guaranteed for four years. "The spaces are kind of small, but that's university housing for you," says one student. "It's much cheaper than living in apartments around the city." Many rooms are singles, and it is possible to go all four years without a roommate. Carman Hall is one of three exclusively first-year dorms, and "the fact that you get to meet your classmates compensates for the noise and hideous cinderblock walls," says a music major. First-year students are automatically placed on a 19-meal-a-week plan and take most of those meals at John Jay, where a junior says, "People complain about the meals, but it's buffet style, and I think there are a good variety of options. Many options are healthy, and special dietary needs are met." After the first year, many scale down their meal plans or convert to a buy-what-you-want point system. Several dorms have kitchens, allowing students to do their own cooking.

> "I love that no one activity dominates the social scene."

"Columbia's Public Safety makes sure that students feel safe and supported on campus and the surrounding neighborhood at all times of the day," a senior says. "Columbia has taken a lot of heat for the way it handles sexual assault on campus," adds another, although the university has introduced several initiatives, including a comprehensive new gender-based misconduct policy, the opening of an additional sexual violence support center, and expanded mandatory programming.

The social scene starts on the Columbia campus and spills over into the bustling streets of New York City. "We have the best of both worlds, because Columbia students can be a part of the vibrant on-campus community but also take part in New York's eclectic environment!" cheers one student. The challenge, others say, is finding time to relax and enjoy all the city has to offer. Rarely are there big all-inclusive bashes, the exception being spring's Bacchanal concert. Orgo Night, when the marching band takes over Butler Library the night before the first final (usually organic chemistry) "in an attempt to lower the curve," is a favorite tradition. Eight percent of the men and 10 percent of the women go Greek, and the advent of co-ed houses has raised interest in Greek life, as has the arrival of sororities open to both Columbia and Barnard women. But Columbia is hardly a Hellenocentric campus. "I love that no one activity dominates the social scene," says a freshman. "You do not have to attend the basketball and football games to be 'in,' nor do you have to pledge fraternities and sororities." The Community Impact organization coordinates 27 local community service programs, in which nearly 1,000 students participate. "Columbia has an excellent relationship with its Morningside Heights neighborhood," explains a freshman.

Columbia has the largest percentage of students of color in the Ivy League.

On Orgo Night, the marching band takes over Butler Library the night before the first final (usually organic chemistry).

Columbia athletics don't inspire rabid loyalty. "Columbia students are individualists," according to one sophomore. "This is not a school that rallies together at football games." Still, the Lions field 31 Division I teams. The fencing and women's archery teams are recent national champions, while baseball and men's tennis have claimed Ivy League conference titles. As an urban school, Columbia lacks team field facilities on campus; however, 100 blocks to the north is the modern Baker Field, home of the football stadium, the soccer fields, an Olympic track, and the crew boathouse. On campus, the Dodge Gymnasium, an underground facility, houses four levels of basketball courts, swimming pools, weight rooms, and exercise equipment. More than 80 intramural and club sports are available; men's and women's ultimate Frisbee are both nationally competitive.

> "Columbia is definitely not a stress-free, friendly community, but it has its own charm."

"Columbia is definitely not a stress-free, friendly community, but it has its own charm," explains a senior. "The university is quintessentially New York: as a student, there are so many experiences to be had, but you really have to engage in the community and seek them out." Columbians are proud to attend college in New York City, and most would have it no other way.

Overlaps

Harvard, Yale, Stanford, Princeton, University of Pennsylvania, MIT, Brown, University of Chicago

If You Apply To ➢

Columbia: Early decision: Nov. 1. Regular decision: Jan. 1. Financial aid: Feb. 15. Application fee: $85. No campus interviews. Alumni interviews: optional, evaluative. SATs or ACTs: required. Subject Tests: optional. Letters of recommendation: required. Essay: required. Accepts the Common Application with supplement.

University of Connecticut

Tasker Building, 2131 Hillside, Storrs, CT 06269

Squeezed in among the likes of Brown, UMass, Trinity, Wesleyan, and Yale—all within a two-hour drive—UConn could be forgiven for having an inferiority complex. But applications have been soaring, with championship basketball teams, both men's and women's, helping to ignite Husky pride and boost selectivity. One of the highest retention and graduation rates among public universities. Storrs is nobody's idea of an exciting destination, but it does offer easy access to beautiful countryside.

The top public university in New England and highly regarded nationally, the University of Connecticut has recently seen billions of dollars poured into new facilities and into expanding educational opportunities and research in STEM disciplines. Couple these initiatives with the glow of two championship basketball teams, a wealth of research opportunities, and more than 600 clubs and organizations, and it's clear why UConn has moved well beyond its erstwhile "cow college" image. "I'm incredibly proud to be a UConn student," says a senior. UConn is also the only public university in New England with its own law school, medical school, dental school, and school of social work—and undergraduates benefit greatly from these resources. What's more, it's one of the few major public universities that continues to significantly expand their faculty ranks, adding nearly 300 tenure-track positions in recent years.

UConn's 4,000-acre campus is about 23 miles northeast of Hartford. Building styles range from collegiate Gothic and neoclassical to half-century-old redbrick. Dense woods surround the campus, which also boasts two lakes, Swan and Mirror. Ongoing renovations are the norm, sparking jokes about the "University

Website: www.uconn.edu
Location: Rural
Public
Total Enrollment: 23,718
Undergraduates: 18,131
Male/Female: 50/50
SAT Ranges: CR 550–650, M 580–690
ACT Ranges: 26–31
Financial Aid: 86%
Pell Grant: N/A
Expense: Pub $ $ $ $
Student Loans: 64%
Average Debt: $ $

UConn is the only public university in New England with its own law school, medical school, dental school, and school of social work.

of Construction," but the results are impressive. The 212,000-square-foot NextGen residence hall houses more than 700 students in several living/learning communities and features an innovative makerspace. The five-story, $95 million Engineering and Science Building is set to open in 2017, as is the first building in UConn's new Technology Park, intended to foster research and commercialization of technology through industry partnerships.

Students say UConn's strongest offerings are preprofessional, including business, engineering, education, pharmacy, and allied health, including nursing and physical therapy. The school's historic focus on agriculture is giving way to an emphasis on environment and ecology. Also notable are basic sciences, history, linguistics, psychology, and, of course, agriculture. (UConn was founded more than a century ago as a farm school; it's where America learned to get more eggs per chicken by leaving the lights on in the coops.) In addition to new buildings, UConn continues to add new curricula, including electrical engineering, materials science and engineering, and mechanical engineering. There are also notable programs in biomolecular engineering, neuroscience, cognitive science, coastal studies, and human rights. Engineering is demanding, and, as at many schools, it has a relatively high attrition rate, with many students switching to the less rigorous major in management information systems. A special program in medicine and dentistry allows students to earn bachelor's degrees in any of UConn's more than 100 disciplines, and guarantees admission to the School of Medicine or Dental Medicine if they meet all criteria.

"The academic climate here is quite rigorous."

UConn's academic atmosphere is described as moderately competitive and challenging, depending on a student's course of study. "The academic climate here is quite rigorous," says a molecular cell biology major. UConn's core requirements include courses in four basic areas: arts and humanities, social sciences, diversity/multiculturalism, and science and technology. Also required are two foreign language courses, waived if a student has studied three years of a single language in high school, and competency in computer technology and information literacy. Seminar-style writing classes are available to all freshmen, and 75 percent also take one or more First-Year Experience courses that guide them through the transition to college. The Academic Center for Exploratory Students helps freshmen and sophomores who still need to decide on a major. Students generally applaud the enthusiasm of their professors—and the graduate teaching assistants who administer tests, collect assignments, and run labs and discussion groups—but note that some seem more interested in research than teaching. "Some lack the ability to connect with students and the skills to teach students effectively," grumbles one senior.

UConn's engineering, business, pharmacy, and honors students are required to undertake research projects, and each year two teams of finance majors run the $1 million student-managed investment fund. Students who aspire to graduate school in academic fields, rather than professional certification, may win grants to work independently under faculty members through the undergraduate summer research program. The 8 percent of students who qualify for the honors program gain access to special floors and dorms; several programs for disadvantaged students are also available. In addition, 15 percent of students participate in the study abroad program, which offers 275 programs in more than 60 countries.

"Students are very much concerned with what is going on today in our world."

UConn students are "hardworking, responsible, intelligent, passionate, and inspirational," according to one psychology major. Roughly three-quarters of UConn undergraduates are from Connecticut, and 5 percent are international. Many students choose to transfer to the Storrs campus after beginning coursework in their chosen major and earning 54 credits at one of UConn's four regional campuses. Six percent of undergrads are African American, 9 percent are Hispanic, and 10 percent are Asian American. There are cultural centers for African American, Asian American, Latin American, and Puerto Rican students, as well as the Rainbow Center, a resource for LGBTQ students. "Students are very much concerned with what is going on today in our world," a student says. Eligible UConn students receive merit scholarships averaging $7,246, and hundreds of athletic scholarships are available in 18 sports. Persistence rates are high, with 92 percent of freshmen returning for their sophomore year and a graduation rate of 83 percent.

Seventy percent of the students live in university housing, which is available to all undergraduates. "All the dorms are very well maintained," says a senior. Dorms are all co-ed, and the entire campus, including outdoor areas, is equipped with Wi-Fi. Eight dining halls offer plenty of choices, even for vegetarians and vegans, though many students would just as soon visit the snack bar for some ice cream, freshly made with help from the cows grazing nearby. "The food at UConn each night is diverse, and a student can always find something he or she wants," one student says. A group of students are selected to live on a sustainable farm just off campus where they raise foods that are served in the dining halls. Students report feeling safe on campus. "There are blue lights everywhere, crime is so low we think it doesn't exist, the police don't bother anyone unless they have to, and we have a great system of security alerts," says a junior.

> **"The food at UConn each night is diverse."**

"Social life is the best part of college life and includes clubs, frats, sports, and so much more," says one student. "As you get involved, you will be wicked busy!" Students 21 and over are allowed to possess no more than a six-pack of beer, one bottle of wine, or a small bottle of liquor. Students under 21 who are caught with booze may be evicted from campus housing. Late-night activities at the student union and other campus events provide a lot of alternatives to alcohol use. Fraternities attract 10 percent of the men, and sororities claim 15 percent of the women; members can live in chapter housing at the Husky Village. On weekends, there are buses to Hartford (only 30 minutes away), Boston, New Haven, New York, and Providence. Cape Cod and the Vermont ski slopes are within weekend driving distance. Favorite annual campus events include the mud volleyball tournament, carnival-style UConn Late Nights, midnight breakfasts during finals, homecoming, Winter Weekend, and Midnight Madness—the first official day of basketball practice. In addition to cheering for the Huskies, "it is good luck to rub the nose of the bronze statue of our mascot, Jonathan," says a sophomore.

The town of Storrs "is basically UConn," says one student. A recent downtown Storrs initiative offers shops, restaurants, and a town green, as well as additional living options available to students. The university provides transportation for students who volunteer in area schools and hospitals. Legend holds that UConn also offers one diversion most other colleges can't: cow tipping—that is, sneaking up on unsuspecting cows, which sleep standing up, and tipping them over. The administration contends that this is a myth, though students always claim to "know someone who did it."

> **"As you get involved, you will be wicked busy!"**

UConn's teams are known as the Huskies (UConn. Yukon. Get it?), and in a state without any major league professional sports teams, the UConn women's basketball team routinely sells out the XL Center. Men's basketball won the national Division I title in 2014, while in 2016 the women's team brought home its 11th—and fourth-straight—national championship. Other championships have been racked up in men's soccer, women's water polo, and field hockey. Intramurals are offered at three levels, from recreational to competitive. Popular offerings range from underwater hockey and inner-tube water polo to basketball, volleyball, and flag football.

UConn's engineering, business, pharmacy, and honors students are required to undertake research projects.

In 2016 the women's basketball team brought home its 11th—and fourth-straight—national championship.

Overlaps

University of Massachusetts Amherst, Boston University, Northeastern, University of Delaware, Quinnipiac, Syracuse, University of Rhode Island, Penn State

UConn continues to build on its agricultural roots and adapt them to the 21st century. Those seeking greener pastures will be hard-pressed to find a more dynamic public institution. "We are a well-rounded campus with students from every background," a junior pharmacy student says. And with the campus undergoing a complete face-lift, it's a good time to be at UConn.

If You Apply To ➢   **UConn:** Regular decision: Jan. 15. (Priority deadline: Dec. 1.) Financial aid: Mar. 1. Housing: May 1. Application fee: $80. No campus or alumni interviews. SATs or ACTs: required. No Subject Tests. Letters of recommendation: recommended. Essay: required. Accepts the Common Application with supplement. Most fine arts programs require a portfolio, audition, or interview.

Connecticut College

270 Mohegan Avenue, New London, CT 06320

Like Skidmore and Vassar, Connecticut College made a successful transition from women's college to co-ed. That means a slightly more progressive campus tenor than at, say, Hamilton or Trinity. The college is strong in the humanities, especially dance and drama, and renowned for its study abroad programs. New London does not offer much, but at least it is on the ocean.

Website: www.conncoll.edu
Location: Small City
Private
Total Enrollment: 1,922
Undergraduates: 1,852
Male/Female: 37/63
SAT Ranges: CR 610–700, M 610–700
ACT Ranges: 28–31
Financial Aid: 55%
Pell Grant: 14%
Expense: Pr $ $ $ $
Student Loans: 47%
Average Debt: $ $ $ $
Phi Beta Kappa: Yes
Applicants: 5,182
Accepted: 40%
Enrolled: 23%
Grad in 6 Years: 83%
Returning Freshmen: 90%
Academics: ✑ ✑ ✑ ✑
Social: ☎ ☎ ☎
Q of L: ★ ★ ★ ★
Admissions: (860) 439-2200
Email Address: admission@conncoll.edu

Strong Programs:
Economics

Students at Connecticut College follow the example of their mascot, the camel—they take pride in drinking up and storing knowledge. The student-run honor code means finals are not proctored; they're even self-scheduled, whenever students prefer, during a 10-day window. "The honor code gives the freedom for the student to be responsible for their actions academically and socially," says an economics major. "It creates a respectful and trustful relationship between professors and students."

Placed majestically atop a hill, the Conn College campus sits within a 750-acre arboretum with a pond, wetlands, wooded areas, and hiking trails. It offers beautiful views of the Thames River (pronounced the way it looks, not like the "Temz" that Wordsworth so dearly loved) on one side and Long Island Sound on the other. The granite campus buildings are a mixture of modern and collegiate Gothic in style, with some neo-Gothic and neoclassical architecture thrown in for good measure. The library has undergone a $10 million renovation and recently reopened as a fully updated space for research, group and individual study, and public talks and meetings.

Conn was founded in 1911 as a women's college but went co-ed in 1969. The general education program, now called Connections, has been revamped to span all four years of a student's undergraduate experience. Coursework includes two semesters of foundational courses, including a first-year seminar and an interdisciplinary 100-level

> "Professors at Conn take great personal responsibility in their teaching styles."

ConnCourse, followed by a series of thematically linked courses called an "Integrative Pathway." The senior year culminates with an integrative project. Academics are definitely the focus here. "I'd consider the academic climate at Conn to be rigorous and intense, but supportive all the same," says a film studies major. Much of that support comes from professors, who are lauded for their accessibility and thoughtfulness. "I've found that a majority of professors at Conn take great personal responsibility in their teaching styles and try to cater to students' needs as much as possible," observes a psychology major.

Conn's dance and drama departments are superb, and it's not uncommon for dancers to take time off to study with professional companies. Aspiring actors, directors, and stagehands may work with the Eugene O'Neill Theater Institute, named for New London's best-known literary son. Chemistry majors may use high-tech gas chromatograms and mass spectrometers from their very first day, and students say Conn also offers excellent programs in biology and physics. Four interdisciplinary centers, to which students can apply as sophomores, administer certificate programs in international studies, arts and technology, community action and public policy, and environmental studies. The most popular majors are economics, psychology, biological sciences, government, international relations, and English. New programs include a global Islamic studies major and a linguistics minor.

(continued)

Psychology
Biological Sciences
Government
International Relations
English
Dance
Drama

To escape Conn's small size and occasionally claustrophobic feel, the Study Away/Teach Away (SATA) initiative allows groups of about a dozen Conn students and two faculty members to spend a semester living and working together at an overseas university, in locations as far-flung as Egypt, Ghana, Peru, and Vietnam. In fact, more than half of Connecticut College juniors study in 50 countries around the world through SATA and other college-approved study abroad programs. Conn also participates in the Twelve College Exchange Program*. A gift from Conn helps students secure extraordinary summer internships; everyone who participates in a set of workshops is guaranteed one $3,000 grant during his or her four years to help cover housing or other costs incurred while gaining real-world work experience. Opportunities for funded summer research with professors are also available.

> **"Students can make requests to dining staff by writing their thoughts on a 'napkin note.'"**

Everyone who participates in a set of workshops is guaranteed one $3,000 grant to pursue an internship.

"Connecticut College has a reputation for being a 'preppy' school; many of the students are very well-off," says a computer science major. Only 17 percent of Conn College students come from Connecticut, and 6 percent come from abroad. African Americans and Asian Americans each make up 4 percent of the student body, and Hispanic students add 9 percent. Freshmen must attend a session on issues of race, class, and gender, run by a panel of diverse peers. Students say there is a growing interest in activism on campus, and the political atmosphere is largely liberal. There are no merit or athletic scholarships, but the college meets students' full demonstrated financial need. Loan reduction is available for students of highest need.

Ninety-nine percent of students live on campus and, "The housing is nothing special, but definitely livable," according to a freshman. Dorms house students of all ages, and are run by seniors who apply to be "house fellows." Among the seven specialty houses are Earth House (environmental awareness), the Abbey House co-op (where students cook their own meals), and houses dedicated to substance-free living, quiet lifestyles, and international languages. "There is a great sense of house pride on campus," says one student. "There is even an entire weekend devoted to honoring your house." The campus boasts five dining halls that receive generally good reviews; Freeman is devoted exclusively to vegan and vegetarian fare. "Students can make requests to dining staff by writing their thoughts on a 'napkin note' and pinning it to a provided bulletin board," notes a senior. A junior says that life on campus feel safe: "Campus safety officers patrol campus constantly." Another adds, "Conn has a local Green Dot program, which is really successful in educating the community about consent and destigmatizing discussions about sexual assault."

> **"The a cappella groups are the closest thing Conn has to Greek life."**

Dorms house students of all ages, and are run by seniors who apply to be "house fellows."

Students keep busy with parties, movie nights, comedy shows, student productions, and dances—sometimes with out-of-town bands and DJs. "The a cappella groups are the closest thing Conn has to Greek life, the only major difference being their preference for practicing complex vocal arrangements over playing mindless

drinking games," quips a sophomore. Students say the absence of Greek groups creates a more inclusive community. The alcohol policy falls under the honor code, so those under 21 can't imbibe at the campus bar, and students take that prohibition seriously. Camelympics, when houses compete against each other in a Conn-style Olympics, is a favorite tradition, as is the Festivus holiday celebration. Students also anticipate the annual Floralia festival in the spring, when "students camp out in tents, eat lots of free food, and dance to music," says a junior. Many students volunteer at the local schools, aquarium, youth community center, and women's center; a college van makes it easy to get to and from work sites. When students get the urge to roam, the beaches of Mystic and other shore towns are 20 minutes from campus, and the Mohegan Sun casino is also very close. Trains go to Providence, Rhode Island, New York City, or Boston, while Vermont and upstate New York offer camping, hiking, and skiing.

> *Camelympics, when houses compete against each other in a Conn-style Olympics, is a favorite tradition.*

The Conn Camels compete in Division III, and men's ice hockey games against NESCAC rival Wesleyan draw crowds. Women's soccer brought home a conference title in 2014, and men's swimming is also strong. More than 700 students participate in intramural and club sports, the most popular of which are ultimate Frisbee and broomball. Between classes or at the end of the day, all students may use the natatorium's pool and fitness center and the rowing tanks and climbing walls at the field house.

On its friendly campus, Conn College fosters strong student/faculty bonds and takes pride in its ability to challenge—and trust—students, both in and out of the classroom. "Connecticut College promotes a sense of self-awareness and being able to be yourself in an environment that fosters creativity, acceptance, and community," reasons one junior. A classmate asks, "Who else has a dromedary camel as the mascot?!"

Overlaps

Colby, Bates, Hamilton, Tufts, Wesleyan, Boston College, Northeastern, Bowdoin

If You Apply To ➤ **Conn College:** Early decision I: Nov. 15. Early decision II and regular decision: Jan. 1. Financial aid: Feb. 1. Housing: May 1. Application fee: $60. Campus interviews: recommended, evaluative. Alumni interviews: optional, evaluative. SATs or two SAT Subject Tests or ACTs: optional. Letters of recommendation: required. Essay: required. Accepts the Common Application with supplement.

The Cooper Union

30 Cooper Square, New York, NY 10003

As college costs skyrocket, so does the popularity of The Cooper Union's low-cost education in art, architecture, and engineering. Expect Ivy-level competition for a place in the class here. Instead of a conventional campus, The Cooper Union has the East Village—which is quite a deal. But be prepared to spend your nights hitting the books rather than the cafés.

Website: www.cooper.edu
Location: City Center
Private
Total Enrollment: 870
Undergraduates: 815
Male/Female: 67/33
SAT Ranges: CR 610–720, M 630–790

Tuition is no longer free at The Cooper Union for the Advancement of Science and Art, and the school has been going through considerable administrative turmoil. But if you manage to get accepted into this technical institute, you get a half-tuition scholarship (and additional aid to those who demonstrate need) and some of the nation's finest academic offerings in architecture, engineering, and art. With cool and funky East Village in the background and rigorous studying in the forefront, college life at The Cooper Union may seem to be faster than a New York minute. Whatever the pace, though, no one can deny that a CU education is one of the best bargains around—probably the best anywhere. The only complication is that the number of applicants is booming, and its acceptance rate is comparable to the Ivies.

The school was founded in 1859 by entrepreneur Peter Cooper, who believed that education should be "as free as water and air." With hefty contributions from J. P. Morgan, Frederick Vanderbilt, Andrew Carnegie, and various other fellow robber barons, the school was able to stay afloat in order to recruit poor students of "strong moral character." Trustees ended the famous tuition-free policy in 2013, citing dire financial straits.

In place of a traditional collegiate setting are two academic buildings and one dorm plunked down in one of New York's most eclectic and exciting neighborhoods. The stately brick art and architecture building is a beautiful historic landmark. Built of brick and topped by a classic water tower, the dorm blends right in with the neighborhood. The Great Hall was the site of Lincoln's "Right Makes Might" speech and the birthplace of the NAACP, the American Red Cross, and the national women's suffrage movement. Wedged between two busy avenues in the East Village, Cooper offers an environment for survivors. A LEED-certified academic building opened in late 2009—the first academic building in New York City to achieve LEED Platinum status, the highest and most rigorous level of certification.

> **"[Students] range from being complete geeks who love math, science, and gaming to artsy and out-of-this-world."**

CU's curriculum is highly structured, and all students must take a sequence of required courses in the humanities and social sciences. The first year is devoted to language and literature and the second to the making of the modern world. In some special circumstances, students are allowed to take courses at nearby New York University and the New School for Social Research. The nationally renowned engineering school offers both bachelor's and master's degrees in chemical, electrical, mechanical, and civil engineering, as well as a bachelor of science in general engineering studies. The architecture school is "phenomenal—even unparalleled," in the words of one pleased participant. "Architecture and engineering are the most acclaimed, but then, these occupations are more mainstream, and graduates get big money and success," reflects an art major. "It's harder to measure success in the art school." The art school, rather than offering individual majors, awards a bachelor of fine arts degree that encompasses a broad-based generalist curriculum in graphic design, drawing, painting, sculpture, photography, printmaking, film, and video. All students must fulfill a capstone requirement: engineers complete a senior project, architects a yearlong senior thesis, and artists a senior show.

The academic climate is intense. "Although the courses are difficult and the coursework is challenging, the students are more than willing to cooperate with one another and collaborate when studying," says one freshman. Academic counseling is available, but the school's rigorously structured academic programs largely determine which classes the students take, eliminating a lot of confusion or decision making. Classes are small—70 percent enroll fewer than 20 students—and, with a little persistence, not too difficult to get into. Students "tend to talk to other students, recommending or insulting various classes and profs around registration time," notes a senior. While some say the teaching quality is hit or miss, students report that professors are generally engaging.

> **"We are a racially mixed student body that stays mixed."**

"I've received excellent teaching," a chemical engineering major says. Despite their full schedules and the stimulation of the city, 20 percent of students find time to take their education global, through a variety of study abroad programs. About a quarter get involved in undergraduate research.

(continued)

ACT Ranges: 30–34
Financial Aid: 100%
Pell Grant: 25%
Expense: Pr $ $
Student Loans: 34%
Average Debt: $
Phi Beta Kappa: No
Applicants: 3,258
Accepted: 13%
Enrolled: 55%
Grad in 6 Years: 81%
Returning Freshmen: 96%
Academics: ✐ ✐ ✐ ½
Social: ☎
Q of L: ★ ★ ★
Admissions: (212) 353-4120
Email Address: admissions@cooper.edu

Strong Programs:
Fine Arts
Architecture
Engineering

The Great Hall was the site of Lincoln's "Right Makes Might" speech and the birthplace of the NAACP.

Strong moral character is no longer a prerequisite for admission, but an outstanding high school academic record most certainly is; 85 percent of students graduated in the top 10th of their high school class. CU students "range from being complete geeks who love math, science, and gaming to artsy and out-of-this-world," one student says. Forty-seven percent of undergraduates are from New York State, and most of them grew up in the city. Many are the first in their family to attend college; 25 percent qualify for Pell Grants. Eleven percent of students are international. Asian Americans account for 18 percent of the student population, 3 percent are African American, and 9 percent are Hispanic. The campus is politically liberal, and one student attests that diversity is not an issue: "We are a racially mixed student body that stays mixed. There's no overt hostility and rare self-segregation." The campus is home to ethnically based student clubs, but, according to one student, membership is not exclusive: "In other words, you can be white and be a member of Onyx—a student group promoting black awareness."

Students love the dorm, a 15-story residence hall that saves many students from commuting into the Village or cramming themselves into expensive apartments. It is noteworthy that housing here is guaranteed only to freshmen, thus only 30 percent of the student body reside on campus. The facility is composed of furnished apartments with kitchenettes and bathrooms complete with showers or tubs and is "in great condition and well maintained," states one resident. A less enraptured dweller notes, "Rooms are barely big enough to fit a bed, a table, and a clothes cabinet." Still, each apartment does have enough space for a stove, microwave, and refrigerator. So you can cook for yourself, eat at the unexciting but affordable school cafeteria, or head for one of the myriad nearby delis and coffee bars.

> **"The workload, living alone in New York, and the administrative policies force you to act like an adult."**

"The social life here is centered around the many clubs and activities offered on campus," says one student. "This is where most people find their crowd." More than 30 percent of students belong to professional societies, such as the American Society of Civil Engineers. Drinking on campus is allowed during school-sponsored parties for students over 21—otherwise, no alcohol on campus. But as one student puts it, "This is New York; one can be served anywhere." McSorley's bar is right around the corner, the Grassroots Tavern is just down the block, and nearby Chinatown and Little Italy are also popular destinations. The heart of the Village, with its abundance of theaters, art galleries, and cafés, is just a few blocks to the west. The Bowery and SoHo's galleries and restaurants are due south; all of midtown Manhattan spreads to the northern horizon. Students are mindful of potential safety concerns, given the urban campus, and Cooper is expanding its education and training programs aimed at preventing sexual assault.

Cooper teams (the Pioneers) compete in the Division III Hudson Valley Athletic Conference, and the most competitive teams include men's and women's tennis, basketball, soccer, and cross-country. The intramural sports program is held in several different facilities in the city and attracts 35 percent of students. Students organize clubs and outings around interests such as skiing, fencing, table tennis, ballroom dancing, classical music, religion, and drama.

Getting into The Cooper Union is tough, and once admitted, students find that dealing with the onslaught of city and school is plenty tough as well. But most students like the challenge. "The workload, living alone in New York, and the administrative policies force you to act like an adult and take care of yourself," explains a senior. Surviving the school's academic rigors requires talent, self-sufficiency, and a clear sense of one's career objectives. Students who don't have it all can be sure that there are six or seven people in line ready to take their places. That's quite an incentive to succeed.

The art school, rather than offering individual majors, awards a B.F.A. degree that encompasses a broad-based generalist curriculum.

Eighty-five percent of students graduated in the top 10th of their high school class.

Overlaps

Cornell University, NYU, Columbia, Carnegie Mellon, SUNY–Stony Brook, Rensselaer Polytechnic, Pratt Institute, Macaulay Honors College at CUNY

The Cooper Union: Early decision: Dec. 1. Regular decision: Jan. 9. Financial aid: Jun. 1. Housing: May 1. Application fee: $75. Campus interviews: optional, evaluative. No alumni interviews. SATs or ACTs: required (SAT essay or ACT writing recommended). Subject Tests: required for engineering (math and physics or chemistry). Letters of recommendation: required. Essay: required. Accepts the Common Application with supplement. Apply to a particular program. Architecture and art applicants must complete take-home test. Art applicants must submit portfolio.

Cornell College

600 First Street Southwest, Mount Vernon, IA 52314-1098

The One Course At A Time model is Cornell's calling card. The main challenge: trying to lure top students to rural Iowa. Encourages students to do off-campus study in distant corners of the world. With a student body of about 1,000, Cornell showers its students with personal attention. More accessible and diverse than Colorado College. Though primarily a liberal arts institution, Cornell has programs in business, engineering sciences, and education.

Cornell College attracts the type of student who seeks an intense yet flexible, self-designed program and a liberal, progressive atmosphere in which to solidify strict habits and routines. It suits those who aren't satisfied with easy answers, don't mind heading to the rural Midwest, and do want loads of personal attention while focusing on one class. "If you want a normal college experience, don't pick Cornell," warns one student, but "if you want to pour yourself into a class for three and a half straight weeks and feel exhausted but accomplished," Cornell may be just the right fit.

Aside from its distinctive schedule (shared by only one other school, Colorado College), Cornell has one of only two U.S. college or university campuses listed in its entirety on the National Register of Historic Places. The majestic bell tower of King Chapel offers an unparalleled view of the Cedar River valley. A pedestrian mall runs through campus, and other campus facilities include suite-style residence halls for 96 upper-class students. The school's Cole Library is also the town of Mount Vernon's public library, one of only two such libraries in the country. Cornell's student center, Thomas Commons, recently underwent a complete interior renovation, including a redesigned dining hall, the Hilltop Café; a new entryway and grand foyer; an indoor-outdoor fireplace; new classrooms, meeting spaces, and study rooms; and a new glass-enclosed dining room with panoramic views of campus.

Current general education requirements include two humanities courses, one math, one science, one social science, and one fine arts, as well as at least 124 semester hours to graduate. Freshmen must take a first-year seminar and a writing-intensive course, and all students complete a capstone project. Block scheduling makes it easier for some students to graduate early; others use the flexibility to finish with a double major. A sophomore explains, "At Cornell, a semester's worth of work is completed in a month. This makes for a fast-paced class that is normally composed of a couple papers, maybe some annotations, a midterm, a final, and a final project." A biology and Spanish double major adds, "Each class is pretty intense." If that sounds intimidating, it can be. But administrators say it also improves the quality of Cornell's liberal arts education by helping students acclimate to the business world, where "what needs to be done needs to be done quickly and done well." The One Course method also helps in academic advising—with grades every four weeks, signs of trouble are quickly apparent.

Website: www.cornellcollege.edu
Location: Small Town
Private
Total Enrollment: 1,033
Undergraduates: 1,033
Male/Female: 49/51
SAT Ranges: CR 510–660, M 500–640
ACT Ranges: 23–29
Financial Aid: 98%
Pell Grant: 26%
Expense: Pr $
Student Loans: 74%
Average Debt: $ $ $
Phi Beta Kappa: Yes
Applicants: 1,934
Accepted: 71%
Enrolled: 20%
Grad in 6 Years: 68%
Returning Freshmen: 82%
Academics: ✑ ✑ ✑
Social: ☎ ☎ ☎
Q of L: ★ ★ ★
Admissions: (800) 747-1112
Email Address: admission@cornellcollege.edu

Strong Programs:
Psychology
Kinesiology
Biochemistry
Economics and Business

Cornell awards bachelor of arts (B.A.) degrees in nearly 40 academic majors, as well as an extensive group of preprofessional programs. The college also offers the bachelor of special studies, pursued by 5 percent of students, which administrators describe as "an opportunity which permits students to combine courses in an individualized fashion and to broaden or deepen their studies beyond the traditional framework of the bachelor of arts." Among the most popular programs are psychology, kinesiology, biochemistry, economics and business, and biology; other strong options include English and creative writing and theater. "Most of the courses at Cornell are extremely challenging and require a lot of focus and studying to be successful," observes one sophomore. The Berry Center for Economics, Business, and Public Policy provides academic enrichment programs for undergraduates in applied economics and public policy. The college also offers preprofessional centers for health sciences, law and society, and literary arts. Newer programs include finance, analytics, and engineering sciences. "Cornell emphasizes the importance of full professors teaching, and the students really do appreciate it," says one student. Classes are intimate, with 85 percent enrolling fewer than 20 students, and professors are described as dedicated and highly accessible through office hours. Says a senior, "The professors do a great job of teaching practical, hands-on knowledge."

> **"At Cornell, a semester's worth of work is completed in a month. This makes for a fast-paced class."**

Forty percent of Cornell students study off campus. Cornell faculty teach between 20 and 24 courses off campus each year; recent international courses have included Geology of New Zealand, Medieval Literature in Florence, Women and Politics in India, and an International Economics Seminar in Shanghai. Students can also spend a semester at sea or in one of nearly 40 countries through the Associated Colleges of the Midwest* consortium. During the short breaks between courses, students can take advantage of symposia, carnivals, and athletic events. The Student-Faculty Collaborative Summer Research Program offers a 10-week stipend for summer research projects.

Cornell offers preprofessional centers for health sciences, law and society, and literary arts.

"'Cornell weird' is a phrase that gets thrown around a lot and it's accurate," says one student. "With the block plan and a variety of interests to offer to students, there is no singular way to describe a Cornellian other than *unique*." Only 17 percent of students are homegrown. African Americans represent 5 percent of the student population, Hispanics 13 percent, and Asian Americans 3 percent. Three percent hail from other nations, and 26 percent qualify for Pell Grants. "Cornell starts with one huge disadvantage in terms of diversity: it's in the middle of a relatively small town in Iowa," admits one student. Politically, Cornell leans liberal. Merit scholarships averaging $19,519 are offered to qualified students, although there are no athletic awards.

Ninety-three percent of students live on campus, and first-years enjoy completely renovated residence halls. Twenty percent of students participate in living/learning communities. Everyone eats together in Thomas Commons. Bon Appétit runs the kitchen, and the food is "usually good," a junior says. Vegetarian options are always available.

> **"'Cornell weird' is a phrase that gets thrown around a lot and it's accurate."**

Student safety is taken seriously, students say, and, "Campus Security is very accessible on campus, with an officer on call and on campus 24/7." The school has enacted a number of policy changes and programs to deal with sexual assault, including bystander intervention training and risk education.

"Most of the social life happens on campus," says a psychology major. "Because everyone lives on campus, there is a lot of effort to make sure that there is always a lot to do and nobody has time to be bored." Fraternities draw 16 percent of the men and sororities sign up 22 percent of the women, though they are not associated with national Greek systems. "Some are completely dry or emphasize their commitment to service and having dry events," explains one student, "while others are notorious for parties and jungle juice (never, *ever* drink jungle juice). The Greek orgs and other social groups set the tone of social life only for those involved." The Performing Arts and Activities Council (PAAC) is in charge of bringing entertainment to campus, which includes bands, comedians, speakers, musicians, and hypnotists. Mount Vernon itself is "small, but very welcoming," says a physical education major. Students either love the town's idyllic pace—a few local bars; an acclaimed restaurant; some funky shops; and a lot of peace, quiet, and safety—or long for more excitement. The latter is available in Cedar Rapids (home of archrival Coe College) or Iowa City (home to the University of Iowa), each less than half an hour away. Chicago is less than four hours away.

On the field or on the court, Cornell's competition with Coe "is intense, and the entire student body is involved," says one student, especially when it comes to Rams football or basketball. "'Beat Coe' and 'Coe Sucks' have been emblazoned on Cornell fanwear since the 1920s," says one student. "We have the archival records to back that up." Cornell teams compete in the Division III Midwest Conference and

> "'Beat Coe' and 'Coe Sucks' have been emblazoned on Cornell fanwear since the 1920s."

competitive teams include volleyball (recent back-to-back conference champs), softball, baseball, wrestling, and women's basketball. One-third of the students, and some faculty and staff, participate in intramural sports.

"Everyone is involved in something, and that's not an overstatement," says one former student. Indeed, Cornell offers plenty of opportunities, a top-notch education, and a supportive community. And while the curriculum requires students to focus on just one course at a time, "it is the most practical and interesting way to learn," declares a senior. A junior adds, "We are very much a nurturing, happy microcosm that is turning out great things and wonderful, socially conscious people."

The Student-Faculty Collaborative Summer Research Program offers a 10-week stipend for summer research projects.

Overlaps

Beloit, Coe, Grinnell, Knox, University of Illinois at Chicago

If You Apply To >

Cornell College: Rolling admissions. Early decision I: Nov. 1. Early action: Dec. 1. Early decision II and regular decision: Feb. 1. Financial aid: Mar. 1. Housing: May 1. Application fee: $30 (paper), free (online). Campus interviews: recommended, informational. No alumni interviews. SATs or ACTs: optional (test-optional applicants must submit portfolio and respond to two short-answer questions). Subject Tests: optional. Letters of recommendation: recommended. Essay: required. Accepts the Common Application.

Cornell University

Ithaca, NY 14850

Cornell University's reputation as a pressure cooker comes from its preprofessional attitude and a "we try harder" mentality. Spans seven undergraduate colleges—four private and three public—and tuition varies accordingly. Strong in engineering and architecture, world famous in hotel administration. Easiest Ivy to get into, and also the farthest from an urban center. Ithaca is a great college town.

Cornell University has a long tradition of being the lone wolf among the Ivy League universities. So it should come as no surprise that Cornell took another huge step away from its Ivy League counterparts by aspiring to become the finest research university for undergraduate education in the nation. The mixture within one institution of private and state-funded colleges and schools, preprofessional programs,

Website: www.cornell.edu
Location: Rural
Private
Total Enrollment: 21,717

(continued)

Undergraduates: 14,226
Male/Female: 49/51
SAT Ranges: CR 650–750,
M 680–780
ACT Ranges: 30–34
Financial Aid: 46%
Pell Grant: 15%
Expense: Pr $ $ $ $
Student Loans: 43%
Average Debt: $ $
Phi Beta Kappa: Yes
Applicants: 41,900
Accepted: 15%
Enrolled: 50%
Grad in 6 Years: 94%
Returning Freshmen: 97%
Academics: ✍ ✍ ✍ ✍ ✍
Social: ☎ ☎ ☎ ☎
Q of L: ★ ★ ★
Admissions: (607) 255-5241
Email Address: admissions@
cornell.edu

Strong Programs:
Biology
Industrial and Labor Relations
Agricultural Economics
Hotel Administration
Engineering Physics
Mathematics
Architecture
Asian Studies

and liberal arts results in, as one student says, "a diversity of opportunities in and outside of the classroom."

Perched atop a hill that commands a view of both the city of Ithaca and Cayuga Lake, Cornell is breathtakingly scenic, with ravines, waterfalls, and parks bordering all sides of the campus. (As the saying goes, "Ithaca is gorges.") The Cornell Botanic Gardens, more than 3,500 acres of woodlands, natural trails, streams, and gorges, provide space for walking, picnicking, or contemplation. Cornell students have access to more than eight million volumes, 63,000 journals, and 1,000 networked resources in the 20 libraries comprising Cornell's superb library system. The beautiful underground Carl A. Kroch Library features sky-lit atriums, the renowned Fiske Icelandic Collection, and the Echols Collection, one of the finest Cambodian collections on display. The Johnson Museum of Art, designed by I. M. Pei, has been rated as one of the 10 best university museums in America, and the Schwartz Center for the Performing Arts attracts more than 20,000 patrons each year. The 101,000-square-foot Bill and Melinda Gates Hall houses the Faculty of Computing and Information Sciences. The LEED Gold–certified building features open, collaborative spaces and research and teaching labs, including specialized labs for human-computer interaction, robotics, computational sustainability, systems and networking, graphics, and computer vision. Opened in 2016, the LEED Platinum–certified Klarman Hall is dedicated to teaching, research, and education in the humanities.

At the undergraduate level, the university has four privately endowed colleges: architecture, art, and planning; arts and sciences; engineering; and hotel administration. Cornell is also New York State's land grant university, and as such operates three other colleges under contract with the state: agriculture and life sciences, human ecology, and the school of industrial and labor relations. New York residents at these "contract colleges" pick up their Ivy League degrees at an almost-public price (as tuition at these schools is slightly steeper than SUNY rates). The new Cornell College of Business, formed in 2016, houses two undergraduate schools (the privately endowed School of Hotel Administration and the Dyson School of Applied Economics, which it shares with the agriculture college) and one graduate school. Prospective students apply to one of the seven colleges or schools through the central admissions office, and admissions standards vary by school.

Cornell offers more than 4,000 courses in more than 100 fields of study. Cornell's College of Arts and Sciences boasts considerable strength in history, government, and just about all the natural and physical sciences. The English program has turned out a number of celebrated writers, including Toni Morrison, Thomas Pynchon, and Kurt Vonnegut. Foreign languages, required for all arts and sciences students, are strong (try taking Tamil, Zulu, or Nepali), and the performing arts, mathematics, and social science departments are considered good. Cornell was early among universities to add women's studies to the curriculum and continues to be an innovator, with programs in China and Asia-Pacific studies (which requires a semester in China and another in Washington, D.C.) and by offering its students programs like SEA Semester*. The College of Agriculture and Life Sciences is highly ranked and a good bet for anyone hoping to make it into a veterinary school (Cornell's graduate College of Veterinary Medicine is among the best), while the School of Industrial and Labor Relations is the preeminent school of its kind. The College of Business offers more than a dozen concentrations, including agribusiness management; finance, accounting, and real estate; and business analytics.

> **"The majority of professors are regarded as experts in their respective fields."**

"The quality of teaching is top-notch because the majority of professors are regarded as experts in their respective fields," says one student. "Some of the educators struggle to communicate their knowledge, but the professors have great command of their subject matter." First-year courses in the sciences and social sciences are generally large lectures, though many are taught by "charismatic profs" who try to remain accessible. Overall, 57 percent of classes have fewer than 20 students. "Freshman year it was difficult to build personal relationships with faculty because the classes are so large," a senior observes, "but as the years pass, classes become smaller and more intimate, which is a big advantage from a student perspective."

Cornell academics are demanding and foster an intensity found on few campuses. "There is a competitive atmosphere, as students who attend Cornell are ambitious and passionate. However, this is a positive and motivating force," says one sophomore. Eighty-nine percent of Cornell students ranked in the top 10th of their high school class, so those who were the class genius in high school should be prepared for a struggle to rise to the top. After a number of well-publicized suicide incidents several years ago, Cornell has greatly strengthened its mental health support program. To cope with the anxieties that the high-powered atmosphere creates, the university has one of the best psychological counseling networks in the nation, including an alcohol-awareness program, peer sex counselors, personal-growth workshops, and EARS (Empathy, Assistance, and Referral Service).

The English program has turned out celebrated writers, including Toni Morrison, Thomas Pynchon, and Kurt Vonnegut.

A co-op program is available to engineering students, and Cornell-in-Washington is popular among students from all seven undergraduate colleges. Students looking to study abroad can choose from more than 200 programs and universities throughout the world, including those in Indonesia, Belgium, Ireland, and Nepal; 37 percent of students participate. "Studying abroad is a celebrated opportunity at Cornell," says a sophomore. "The number of quality programs seems inexhaustible." The College of Human Ecology offers exchange programs with Hong Kong Polytechnic University and the University of New South Wales. Nearly 50 percent of undergraduates participate in a mentored research experience with Cornell faculty during their four years; popular options include the Human Ecology Urban Semester Program and the student project teams in the College of Engineering. About half of the students engage in community service opportunities coordinated by the Public Service Center.

"Studying abroad is a celebrated opportunity at Cornell."

Cornell students are "friendly, fun, and balanced," says a sophomore. "We are cooler than the nerdy kids, and nerdier than the cool kids," quips one senior. "We don't quite fit in anywhere else. We by and large didn't get into other Ivies, so compared to those students we feel a need to validate and distinguish ourselves through hard work and a more robust social life." Thirty-two percent of Cornell's undergraduates hail from New York; another 10 percent are international. African Americans constitute 6 percent of the student body, Hispanics account for 12 percent, and Asian Americans comprise 18 percent. Cornell offers many diversity workshops and discussion groups aimed at increasing dialogue and engagement. Upon graduation, nearly one-third of Cornell students attend graduate and professional schools.

Cornell is need-blind in admissions and meets the demonstrated need of all accepted applicants, but the proportion of outright grants—as opposed to loans that must be repaid—in the financial aid package varies based on income. Cornell eliminates the parental contribution for students from families with incomes below $60,000 and assets below $100,000 and caps need-based student loans at varying amounts for students whose families have annual incomes between $60,000 and $120,000. The Cornell Installment Plan allows students or their parents to pay a year's or semester's tuition in monthly interest-free installments. The university does not award merit or athletic scholarships.

Nearly 50 percent of undergraduates participate in a mentored research experience with Cornell faculty.

Just over half of Cornell's students live in university housing; many try their luck off campus in Collegetown, where demand has kept the housing market tight and rents high, although options are increasing. "Housing was one of the main reasons I chose Cornell," says one junior. "I was able to essentially guarantee myself a single room even freshman year. My room was huge, and my dorm was quiet." North Campus residence halls are the home of all freshmen, and about 2,000 students (mostly sophomores) live in the West Campus House System, in five living/learning "houses" with professors in residence, house chefs, and creative programming. There are dorms devoted to everything from ecology to music, and cultural houses include the International Living Center, Latino Living Center, Ujamaa Residential College, and Akwe:kon, a program house focusing on American Indian culture (the only facility of its kind in the U.S.). Cornell's food service is reputedly among the best in the nation, with eight residential meal plan dining halls that function independently; one student enthuses, "The food is very diverse and super tasty!"

> *About 2,000 students live in five living/ learning "houses" with professors in residence, house chefs, and creative programming.*

Despite the intense academic atmosphere—or maybe because of it—Cornell social life beats most of the other Ivies hands down. Once the weekend arrives, local parties, state parks, and ski slopes are filled with Cornell students seeking a balance between study and play. With 33 percent of men and 34 percent of women pledging fraternities and sororities, these groups play a significant role in the social scene. "Social life at Cornell is really built around Greek life, especially for those under 21. Students who go Greek tend to have busy social schedules, and those who don't really need to find an organization they are passionate about," advises one student. Students have their pick of roughly 1,000 student organizations—including clubs for Japanese drumming and Bhangra dancing—and there are innumerable concerts and sporting events throughout the year. Alcohol is part of the social scene, but one student says the university is "cracking down" on underage and high-risk drinking. Freshmen are not allowed to attend fraternity parties during the fall semester, and after freshmen receive a bid to a house in the spring, there is an eight-week dry period. Big events include Fun in the Sun (a day of friendly athletic competition), Dragon Day (architecture students build a dragon and parade it through campus), and Springfest (a gathering on Ho Plaza). Students celebrate the last day of classes—Slope Day—with a concert on Libe Slope.

"We are cooler than the nerdy kids, and nerdier than the cool kids."

Cornell has won several Ivy League team titles during the last decade, along with individual NCAA championships and a slew of high-profile Division I national championship appearances. In recent years, wrestling has had multiple top-five finishes, women's ice hockey has appeared in the Frozen Four, men's lacrosse has advanced to the Final Four four times, and men's basketball has reached the Sweet Sixteen. But men's ice hockey is unquestionably the dominant sport on campus (its chief goal being to defeat Harvard), and camping out for season tickets is an annual ritual. Lightweight rowing has brought home six Intercollegiate Rowing Association titles. Cornell boasts the largest intramural program in the Ivy League, with more than a dozen sports, including 100 hockey teams. The "four seasons of Ithaca" can make walking to class across the vast and hilly campus challenging, but with the first snow of the winter, "traying" down Libe Slope becomes the sport of choice for hordes of fun-loving Cornellians. Ithaca has "wonderful outdoor enthusiast stores," says one student. Students head to Greek Peak Mountain for skiing, Cayuga Lake for boating and swimming, and countless places for hiking and watching the clouds roll by.

> *Cornell boasts the largest intramural program in the Ivy League, with more than a dozen sports, including 100 hockey teams.*

"Social life at Cornell is really built around Greek life, especially for those under 21."

One junior sums up the Cornell experience like this: "The people are passionate, the academics are rigorous, and the extracurricular activities are empowering." Like most other Ivy League universities, Cornell is a premier research institution with a

> ### Overlaps
> **Harvard, University of Pennsylvania, Princeton, Stanford, Yale**

distinguished faculty and outstanding academics. What sets it apart is the diversity of opportunities and a student body willing to work hard to achieve their goals while remaining grounded in an active social life.

If You Apply To ➤

Cornell University: Early decision: Nov. 1. Regular decision: Jan. 2. Financial aid: Feb. 15. Application fee: $80. No campus interviews. Alumni interviews: recommended, informational (varies by program). SATs or ACTs: required. Subject Tests: required (varies by program). Letters of recommendation: required. Essay: required. Accepts the Common Application with supplement. Apply to individual programs or schools.

University of Dallas

Irving, TX 75062

Bulwark of academic traditionalism in Big D. Despite being a "university," UD has fewer than 1,400 undergraduates. The curriculum is exclusively liberal arts. The only outpost of Roman Catholic education between Loyola of New Orleans and University of San Diego. A big drawing card is the university's program in Rome, pursued by most sophomores.

While many universities around the nation have reexamined their Eurocentric core curriculums, the University of Dallas—the best Roman Catholic college south of Washington, D.C.—remains proudly dedicated to fostering students in the study of great deeds and works of Western civilization. Conservative traditions guide the tenor of campus life, but a senior says, "You will get a very good education here and also have a lot of fun."

UD's 744-acre campus occupies a pastoral home in a Dallas suburb on top of "the closest thing this region has to a hill." A major portion of the campus is situated around the Braniff Mall, a landscaped and lighted gathering place near the Braniff Memorial Tower, the school's landmark. The primary tone of the buildings is brown, and the architecture, as described by one student, is "post-1950s, done in brick, typical Catholic—institutional." While it may not be a picture-perfect school, it does have a beautiful chapel and a state-of-the-art science building. The Art Village has five buildings, and each art major has private studio space. SB Hall, the $16 million home of the Gupta College of Business, opened in 2016 and features a financial markets lab, a production studio, faculty offices, and study lounges.

Appropriately for a Roman Catholic school, most eyes at UD look to Rome, where 80 percent of the sophomore class treks every year. The unique and intense Rome Program focuses on the art and architecture of Rome, the philosophy of man, classical literature, Italian, and the development of Western civilization. The Rome

> **"The University of Dallas is very much like a coffeehouse. It is laid-back, but intellectual."**

semester is part of UD's four-semester Western civilization core curriculum. "The study abroad program is an integral part of the University of Dallas," confirms a psychology major. Included in the core are philosophy, English, math, fine arts, science, American civilization, Western civilization, politics, and economics, as well as a serious foreign language requirement. Two theology courses (including Scripture and Western Theological Tradition) are also required of all students.

Students choose from 29 majors and 32 concentrations. The social sciences are popular, as are business, English, biology, history, and psychology. The business program draws on the learning opportunities in the Dallas Metroplex to develop

Website: www.udallas.edu
Location: Suburban
Private
Total Enrollment: 1,641
Undergraduates: 1,315
Male/Female: 44/56
SAT Ranges: CR 540–690, M 540–650
ACT Ranges: 24–30
Financial Aid: 95%
Pell Grant: N/A
Expense: Pr $
Student Loans: 58%
Average Debt: $ $ $ $
Phi Beta Kappa: Yes
Applicants: 2,228
Accepted: 65%
Enrolled: 27%
Grad in 6 Years: 70%
Returning Freshmen: 81%
Academics: ✍ ✍ ✍
Social: ☎ ☎
Q of L: ★ ★ ★
Admissions: (800) 628-6999
Email Address: crusader@udallas.edu

Strong Programs:
Social Sciences
Business

responsible and competent managers through classroom and industry experiences. Political philosophy is also a popular major, although students claim that most courses tend to be slanted toward the conservative side. Premed students are well served by the biology and chemistry programs, and 80 percent of UD graduates plan to go on to grad school. Those inclined toward the sciences may take advantage of the O'Hara Chemical Science Institute, which offers a hands-on, eight-week summer program to prepare new students for independent research and earns them eight credits in chemistry.

"The University of Dallas is very much like a coffeehouse," says one junior. "It is laid-back, but intellectual, it is fun, and all your friends are there with you." The university uses no teaching assistants, and professors are easy to get to know, especially since 66 percent of classes enroll fewer than 20 students. "The professors are brilliant and have chosen to teach at UD because they understand the education the core entails," says a theology major.

The Rome semester is part of UD's four-semester Western civilization core curriculum.

"The students are fun, friendly, caring, dedicated, smart, and spiritual," one student says. "They study hard but know when to stop and have fun." Eighty-two percent of UD students are Roman Catholic, and many of them choose this school because of its religious affiliation. Forty-six percent of undergraduates are home-grown, and 3 percent are international. Twenty-one percent are Hispanic, 5 percent are Asian American, and 2 percent are African American. A senior points out, "We are a Catholic institution and most students are conservative," and topics such as abortion and homosexuality tend to lead political discussions. UD offers various merit scholarships averaging $18,397 but no athletic awards.

Sixty-eight percent of students live on campus, where tradition and religion govern conduct. Students under 21 who don't reside at home with their parents must live on campus in single-sex dorms, "where visitation regulations are relatively strict," one student reports. "The dorms are like living at a summer camp," a junior says. "You do have to make a few sacrifices, but honestly it is a blast!" The most popular dorms are, paradoxically, Jerome (all-female) and Madonna (all-male). At Gregory, the dorm reserved for those who like to party, the goings-on are less than saintly. In addition to a spacious and comfortable dining hall with a wonderful view of north Dallas, there is the Rathskeller, which serves snacks and fast food (and great conversation). "We have a personal chef who always makes sure everything is fresh and keeps the menu changing at all times," a junior explains.

"The Office of Student Life runs a tight ship regarding alcohol."

Eighty-two percent of UD students are Roman Catholic, and many of them choose this school because of its religious affiliation.

With no fraternities or sororities at UD, the student government sponsors most on-campus entertainment. Three free movies a week, dances, and visiting speakers are usually on the agenda. Church-related and religious activities provide fulfilling social outlets for a good number of students. Annual events include Mallapalooza, a spring music festival, and Groundhog, a party on Groundhog Day weekend. During Charity Week in the fall, the junior class plans a week's worth of fund-raising events. Each year, students dread Sadie Hawkins Day and the annual Revenge of the Roommate dance—dark nights of the soul, each. The university can be vigorous in enforcing restrictive drinking rules and, as a result, it is difficult for a minor to drink at campus events. "The Office of Student Life runs a tight ship regarding alcohol," a student warns. Students describe Irving (population 225,000) as "a suburb just like any other," but the Metroplex offers almost unlimited possibilities, including a full agenda for bar-hopping on Lower Greenville Avenue, about 15 minutes away. The West End and Deep Ellum offer a taste of shopping and Dallas's alternative music scene. And for the more adventurous, Austin and San Antonio aren't too far away.

The University of Dallas is unusual for a Texas school in that its entire population does not salivate at the sight of a football or basketball. But baseball and men's basketball are competitive, as is women's soccer, which has reached the Division III tournament multiple times. Intramural sports are well organized and very popular, with volleyball attracting the most players. Chess is also a favored activity.

UD appeals to those students who pride themselves on being the "philosopher kings of the 21st century," but whose roots go back to the Roman thinkers of an earlier era. The mix of religion and liberal arts can serve a certain breed of students well. In the words of one senior, "Come here to have fun, build sincere friendships, work hard, and graduate with a deep sense of your place in the Western cultural tradition."

If You Apply To ➤
Dallas: Early action I: Nov. 1. Early action II: Dec. 1. Regular decision and financial aid: Mar. 1. Application fee: $50. Campus interviews: optional, informational. No alumni interviews. SATs or ACTs (with writing): required. Subject Tests: optional. Letters of recommendation: optional. Essay: required. Accepts the Common Application.

Dartmouth College

6016 McNutt Hall, Hanover, NH 03755

The smallest Ivy and the one with the strongest emphasis on undergraduates. Traditionally the most conservative member of the Ivy League, it has steered toward more student diversity and more serious scholars, but long-standing party culture persists. Ivy ties notwithstanding, Dartmouth has more in common with places like Colgate, Middlebury, and Williams. Great for those who like the outdoors.

While tradition is revered at Dartmouth, the school also continues to grow, change, and evolve. Former president Jim Yong Kim was the first physician to serve in that role, and he came to Dartmouth after founding Partners in Health and leading the HIV/AIDS Department at the World Health Organization. Dr. Kim honored Dartmouth's long-standing tradition of taking on the "world's troubles" by establishing new innovations like the Center for Health Care Delivery Science (a collaboration of Dartmouth's schools of engineering, business, and medicine). The school still attracts plenty of hiking and skiing enthusiasts, and the most popular extracurricular organization is the Dartmouth Outing Club, the oldest collegiate outdoors club in the nation. But these days, students are just as likely to join a hip-hop dance group called Sheba, or to spend a vacation doing Dartmouth-sponsored community service in South America.

Unlike the other seven members of the Ivy League, which trace their roots to Puritan New Englanders or progressive Quaker colonists, Dartmouth College was founded in 1769 to educate Native Americans. The student body has always been the smallest in the Ancient Eight, and the school's focus on undergraduate education differentiates Dartmouth from its peers, though the college does offer graduate programs in engineering, business, and medicine. Dartmouth's campus is probably the most remote of the Ivies, and its winters may be the coldest, with the possible exception of those at Cornell. The Big Green compensates with warmth of community, keeping sophomores on campus for the summer to build closeness, and using intensive language training and study abroad to emphasize the importance of global ties.

Set in the "small, Norman Rockwell town" of Hanover, New Hampshire, which is bisected by the Appalachian Trail, Dartmouth's picturesque campus is arranged around a traditional New England green. It's bounded by the impressive library at one end

Website: www.dartmouth.edu
Location: Small Town
Private
Total Enrollment: 6,236
Undergraduates: 4,267
Male/Female: 51/49
SAT Ranges: CR 660–780, M 670–780
ACT Ranges: 30–34
Financial Aid: 50%
Pell Grant: 14%
Expense: Pr $ $ $ $
Student Loans: 43%
Average Debt: $
Phi Beta Kappa: Yes
Applicants: 20,507
Accepted: 11%
Enrolled: 50%
Grad in 6 Years: 95%
Returning Freshmen: 97%
Academics: ✎ ✎ ✎ ✎ ✎
Social: ☏ ☏ ☏ ☏ ☏
Q of L: ★ ★ ★
Admissions: (603) 646-2875

(continued)

Email Address: admissions
.office@dartmouth.edu

Strong Programs:
Economics
Government
History
Psychology
English
Engineering
Biological Sciences
Computer Science

The Women in Science Project encourages female students to pursue courses and careers in science, math, and engineering.

and by the college-owned Hanover Inn at the other. Architectural styles range from Romanesque to postmodern, but the dominant theme is copper-topped colonial frame. The nearest big city, Boston, is two hours away, but major artists like Itzhak Perlman routinely visit Dartmouth's Hopkins Center for the Arts, adding a touch of culture.

Dartmouth's status as a member of the Ivy League means academic excellence is a given. But that doesn't mean students have complete freedom when it comes to choosing courses. First-years must take a seminar that involves both independent research and small-group discussion; about 75 are offered each year. The seminars "ensure that every student's writing is up to par," while supplementing the usual introductory survey courses available in most disciplines and offering a glimpse of the self-directed scholarship expected at the college level. Students must also demonstrate proficiency in at least one foreign language. And they must take three world culture courses (one non-Western, one Western, and one Culture and Identity), and 10 courses from various distribution areas: the arts; literature; systems and traditions of thought, meaning, and value; international or comparative studies; social analysis; quantitative or deductive science; natural and physical science; and technology or applied science. In addition, Dartmouth has a senior culminating activity—a thesis, public report, exhibition, seminar, production, or demonstration—that allows students to pull together work done in their major with a creative and intellectual twist of their own. "For a relatively small college, the class options are astounding," says one sophomore.

> **"For a relatively small college, the class options are astounding."**

Though Dartmouth students work hard, the climate is far from cutthroat. "The academic climate at Dartmouth is challenging but supportive. The courses increase in difficulty as you advance in the department," says one junior. Popular majors include economics, government, history, psychology, and English. Programs in engineering and biological sciences are strong, and the languages are also well regarded; students benefit from the Intensive Language Model developed by Professor John Rassias. Computer science offerings are among the best in the nation, thanks in no small part to the late John Kemeny, the former Dartmouth president who coinvented time-sharing and the BASIC language. Indeed, computing is a way of life here; well before the Internet, all of Dartmouth's dorm rooms were networked, and students would "Blitzmail" each other to set up meetings, discussions, or meals. A Voice-over-Internet Protocol phone system also lets students use their laptops as telephones, which means long-distance calls home are free.

Professors get high marks at Dartmouth, perhaps because of the school's focus on undergraduates. The isolated location also helps; faculty make a conscious choice to teach here, leaving behind some of the distractions afflicting their peers at more urban schools. "If you come to Dartmouth for only one thing, it would be the faculty," says an economics major.

> **"If you come to Dartmouth for only one thing, it would be the faculty."**

"The professors are truly the best out there for undergraduates." Sixty-four percent of undergraduate classes have fewer than 20 students, and more than 60 percent of undergrads take advantage of abundant research opportunities. The Presidential Scholars Program offers one-on-one research assistantships with faculty, and the Senior Fellowship Program enables 10 to 12 students a year to pursue interdisciplinary research projects and to pay no tuition for their final term. The Policy Research Shop helps undergraduate public policy students write policy briefs for state legislators and government agencies in New Hampshire and Vermont. The Women in Science Project encourages female students to pursue courses and careers in science, math, and engineering with mentors, speakers, and even research positions for first-years. The Montgomery Fellowships bring well-known politicians, writers, and others to campus for periods ranging from a few days to several months, while the

Visionary in Residence program invites notable thinkers to campus to share their talents and insights.

The school's most notable eccentricity is the Dartmouth Plan, or "D-Plan"—four 10-week terms a year, including one during the summer. Students must be on campus for three terms during the freshman and senior years, and also during the summer after the sophomore year, but otherwise, as long as they're on track to graduate, they can take off whenever they wish. More than half of the students use terms away for one of Dartmouth's nearly 43 faculty-led study abroad programs, where they may focus on the classics in Greece or the environment in Zimbabwe; other students pursue part-time jobs, internships, or independent travel. The college also participates in the Twelve College Exchange Program* and the Maritime Studies Program*.

Eighty-eight percent of undergraduates hail from states outside of New Hampshire, and 9 percent come from other countries. Dartmouth went co-ed in 1972, and women now make up half of the student body. Minorities also comprise a substantial portion, with African Americans making up 7 percent, Asian Americans 15 percent, and Hispanics 8 percent. Consistent with its historical roots, Dartmouth continues to have a strong interest in recruiting and supporting Native American students, who currently represent 2 percent of the undergraduate student body. Students

> "[Students have] a passion for learning not simply for the grade but for the experience."

here have a "true, true love for this school and a passion for learning not simply for the grade but for the experience," says a senior. Students retain that passion after graduation, as Dartmouth has the most elaborate network of alumni organizations of any college in the country. Admissions are need-blind, even for students who get in off the waitlist, and the school meets the full demonstrated need of all admits. It also offers free tuition and no loans to students from families with incomes below $100,000 a year. No merit or athletic scholarships are awarded; the Ivy League prohibits the latter.

Eighty-seven percent of Dartmouth students live on campus in one of more than 30 dorms, which have been grouped into 11 clusters to help create a sense of community. "The dorms are spacious and comfortable and very well maintained," says an environmental studies major. "You can live in a single, double, triple, or quad, with anywhere from one to three rooms of different shapes and sizes." Beginning in their freshman year, students can apply to live in one of five living/learning communities: East Wheelock, Global Village, Triangle House, Gender Neutral Program Floor, and DEN (Dartmouth Entrepreneurial Network) in Residence. Sophomores may get squeezed during the housing lottery, but because of the D-Plan, people are always coming and going; it may be easier to find a new room or roommate than at schools on the semester system. Seniors may move off campus into group houses, and many choose to do so. Dining facilities are open until 2:30 a.m. for those needing sustenance during late-night study sessions. Safety is not a big concern here, and students say the university is assertive in dealing with potential issues, including sexual assault. "The Dartmouth Bystander Initiative is a program geared toward educating students about how to intervene in risky situations," explains one psychology major.

"Social life at Dartmouth takes place through many of the organizations and groups that exist on campus," says a geography major. "Almost all of it takes place on campus at fraternities or sororities." Dartmouth's Greek system attracts 46 percent of the men and 46 percent of the women. "What's really unique about our Greek system is that it's open to the

> "Almost all [social life] takes place on campus at fraternities or sororities."

entire campus—if you have a Dartmouth ID card, you cannot be denied entry." The Greeks have become less of a force in campus social life because of the Student Life Initiative, a steering committee that developed more rigorous behavior standards. In an effort to reduce binge drinking and other alcohol-soaked misbehavior, the college has banned hard liquor on campus. Parties and kegs must also be registered, and the houses where they're being held are subject to walk-throughs by college safety and security personnel. Alcohol policies are aimed at keeping booze away from those under 21 and reducing the number of students who end up in the emergency room. Indeed, recognizing that the nickname of its hometown has long been "Hangover," Dartmouth was one of the first schools to develop a counseling and educational program to combat alcohol abuse. Good road trips, although relatively infrequent, include Montreal or Boston, for a dose of bright lights and the big city, or the White Mountains for camping. Dartmouth has a 27,000-acre land grant in the northeast corner of New Hampshire where cabins may be rented for five dollars a night.

Dartmouth is striving for 100 percent participation in community service by graduation.

"I was sold on Dartmouth because it is steeped in tradition," says one senior. Weekends include traditions such as a 75-foot-tall bonfire at homecoming, and Winter Carnival, which includes ski racing at the college's skiway, 20 minutes away, as well as snow-sculpture contests and partiers from all over the Eastern seaboard. Spring brings mud as the snow slowly melts, and also Green Key weekend, which one student calls "an excuse to drink under the guise of community service." The school is striving for 100 percent participation in community service by graduation, "and we're close," says one student. "I've traveled twice to rural Nicaragua on a Dartmouth-sponsored, student-organized, cross-cultural education and service program; we provide medical assistance to villagers and construct clinics, compostable latrines, and organic farms."

Love of the outdoors at Dartmouth extends to varsity athletics. Dartmouth offers 35 Division I varsity sports. Big Green football and women's basketball teams have each won the most championships in Ivy League history. In recent years, Dartmouth has captured league crowns in men's soccer, football, women's cross-country, and volleyball, as well as a division title in baseball. The school's sports facility boasts a 2,100-seat arena, a 4,000-square-foot fitness center, and the only permanent three-glass-wall squash court in North America. Dartmouth offers 33 club sports including nationally competitive teams in sailing, skiing, figure skating, and men's rugby. There are also 24 intramural sports. Nonathletes beware: Dartmouth does have a nontimed swimming test and a physical education requirement for graduation; you can fulfill the latter with classes such as fencing or ballet, or with participation in a club or intramural sport.

"Dartmouth is really a place for a go-getter."

"Dartmouth is really a place for a go-getter," advises one student. The college attracts outdoorsy, down-to-earth students who develop extremely strong ties to the school—and each other—during four years together in the hinterlands. It seems as if every other grad has a title like deputy assistant class secretary, and many return to Hanover when they retire, further cementing their bonds with the college, and driving local real estate prices beyond the reach of most faculty members. You'll have to be made of hardy stock to survive the harsh New Hampshire winters. But once you defrost, you'll be rewarded with lifelong friends and a solid grounding in the liberal arts, sciences, and technology.

Overlaps

Harvard, Cornell University, Yale, Brown, University of Pennsylvania, Columbia, Princeton, Duke

If You Apply To ➤

Dartmouth: Early decision: Nov. 1. Regular decision: Jan. 1. Financial aid: Feb. 1. Application fee: $80. No campus interviews. Alumni interviews: optional, evaluative. SATs (with essay) or ACTs (with writing): required. Subject Tests: recommended (any two). Letters of recommendation: required. Essay: required. Accepts the Common Application with supplement. Submission of a peer recommendation is strongly recommended. Applicants may submit optional arts supplement. Application includes an optional question on gender identity.

Davidson College

P.O. Box 7156, Davidson, NC 28035

Has always been styled as the "Dartmouth of the South." Goes head-to-head with Washington and Lee (VA) as the top liberal arts college below the Mason-Dixon Line. An early leader in the trend to replace loans with grants, it boasts a strong honor system that sets the campus tone. Small-town location is a stone's throw from Charlotte and near prime vacation spots.

Davidson College boasts the Southern tradition and gentility of neighbors like Rhodes and Sewanee, with the academic prowess more common to Northern liberal arts powerhouses such as Dartmouth and Middlebury. It turns out more than its share of the region's political, education, legal, and other leaders. Often overlooked because of its small size and Carolina location, Davidson offers students strong interdisciplinary, international, and preprofessional programs, as well as a thriving social scene. As a senior economics major puts it, "Davidson offers one of the best undergraduate experiences and is the liberal arts school of the South."

Located in a beautiful stretch of the North Carolina Piedmont, Davidson's wooded campus features Georgian and Greek Revival architecture. The central campus is designated as a national arboretum, and college staff lovingly maintain a collection of the woody plants that thrive in the area. Davidson retains its original quadrangle, which dates from 1837, plus literary society halls built in the 1850s. Recent construction includes a new academic building and an addition to the athletics center.

Core requirements at Davidson include one course each in historical thought; literary studies, creative writing, and rhetoric; mathematical and quantitative thought; natural science; philosophical and religious perspectives; social-scientific thought; visual and performing arts; and liberal studies. Students must also take a class in a foreign language, cultural diversity, and first-year writing. Four physical education classes are required, including Davidson 101, two lifetime activities, and a team sport. The most popular majors are political science, economics, biology, psychology, and English. For those whose academic interests lie outside the mainstream, Davidson's Center for Interdisciplinary Studies allows students to develop and design their own majors with faculty or on their own. The interdisciplinary health and human values minor explores the role ethical values play in defining problems as "medical" and worthy of scientific study. A 3–2 engineering program is available with five larger universities.

Davidson's academic climate is rigorous but not grueling. "There are times when I find myself staying up several nights during the week to finish up papers, projects, and tests," says a sophomore. Seventy-three percent of classes have fewer than 20 students. Davidson's Honor Code allows students to take exams independently and to feel comfortable leaving doors unlocked. "Because of an Honor Code that works, Davidson students are able to walk around campus feeling safe and can leave their belongings anywhere without worrying that they will be stolen," says a senior. Every entering freshman agrees to abide by the code, and all work submitted to professors is signed with the word "pledged." Professors are highly lauded for being friendly and accessible, and with no graduate students around, opportunities to work with faculty members on research projects abound.

> **"Davidson offers one of the best undergraduate experiences and is the liberal arts school of the South."**

Website: www.davidson.edu
Location: Small Town
Private
Total Enrollment: 1,779
Undergraduates: 1,779
Male/Female: 50/50
SAT Ranges: CR 630–720, M 630–720
ACT Ranges: 29–32
Financial Aid: 51%
Pell Grant: 15%
Expense: Pr $ $ $
Student Loans: 27%
Average Debt: $
Phi Beta Kappa: Yes
Applicants: 5,382
Accepted: 22%
Enrolled: 43%
Grad in 6 Years: 93%
Returning Freshmen: 96%
Academics: ✍ ✍ ✍ ✍ ½
Social: ☎ ☎ ☎
Q of L: ★ ★ ★ ★ ★
Admissions: (800) 768-0380
Email Address: admission@ davidson.edu

Strong Programs:
Political Science
Economics
Biology
Psychology
English
Health and Human Values

The Sustainability Scholars Summer Program provides students with real-world summer projects that emphasize sustainability issues; students can be found in locations ranging from skyscrapers to community gardens. Environmental studies majors may apply to the School for Field Studies to spend a month or a semester studying environmental issues in other countries or to work and conduct research at Biosphere 2. Study abroad programs, including 10 faculty-led programs and more than 100 partner programs, are available in countries from France, Germany, and England to Cyprus and Zambia, and 75 percent of the students graduate with some foreign experience, whether it's coursework, service learning, research, or an internship.

"The Honor Code is a cornerstone not just for academics, but for all aspects of life at Davidson."

Four physical education classes are required, including Davidson 101, two lifetime activities, and a team sport.

While the school embraces its Presbyterian heritage, Davidson "is alive with an ecumenical spirit, so all students of all religious backgrounds feel comfortable while here," a political science major explains. Another student adds, "The Honor Code is a cornerstone not just for academics, but for all aspects of life at Davidson," which means that student attitudes and behaviors are shaped by their respect for the code. Twenty-two percent of Davidson students come from North Carolina and 7 percent from abroad. African Americans comprise 7 percent of the student body, Hispanics 8 percent, and Asian Americans 5 percent. Seventy-four percent of freshmen graduated in the top 10th of their high school class. Davidson lures top students with generous merit scholarships averaging $21,091, and under its highly touted Davidson Trust, the college guarantees to meet 100 percent of admitted students' demonstrated need through grants and student employment—eliminating loans from all financial aid packages. Additionally, 185 athletic scholarships are available.

Ninety-four percent of Davidson's students live on campus in co-ed or single-sex dorms. "The dorms are generally nice and centrally located," a sophomore says. Freshmen are housed together and eat in Vail Commons, where the "food is great—all you can eat, and lots of options, though it's hard to be a vegan at Davidson." Upperclassmen may live in the dorms or off campus with permission of the residence life office. Seniors get apartment-style housing with private bedrooms. Most upperclassmen take meals at one of the fraternity or eating houses. These groups have their own cooks and serve meals family style.

"Because we are such a small school, it's not uncommon [to] meet someone in a class, on a team, or at a service project and end up hanging out with them and being great friends," says a student. The Alvarez College Union provides a main gathering place, but Davidson's eight fraternities, two sororities, and four all-female eating houses are the real center of social life on campus. All but one are in Patterson Court, which freshmen are not allowed to enter for the first three weeks of school. The dues charged by these clubs cover meals, as well as parties and other campuswide events. The fraternities claim 39 percent of the men, and the sororities and eating houses attract 70 percent of the women. The eating houses, each of which supports a different philanthropic cause, such as cancer and autism research, are not much different from Greek life. Freshmen women simply sign up for the eating house they want to join on Self-Selection Night, with no "rushing" allowed. And even if you don't join up, don't despair; Davidson requires that most parties—"at least two per weekend" at the eating houses—be open to the entire community. Alcohol policies comply with North Carolina law; officially, no one under 21 can be served. "Policies are tied into the Honor Code, so they are enforced," a student says.

"It's not uncommon [to] meet someone in a class, on a team, or at a service project and end up…being great friends."

Davidson's eight fraternities, two sororities, and four all-female eating houses are the real center of social life on campus.

Davidson's five-day freshman orientation includes the Cake Race, which provides runners with about 200 cakes they select based on order of finish. Orientation also introduces students to the cozy town of Davidson, which has coffee shops and cafés, and to the college's 100-acre Lake Norman campus, which provides for sailing, swimming, and waterskiing. "Davidson is a great college town," a chemistry major says. The equally quaint town of Cornelius is adjacent to Davidson, so it's a common destination for dinner and a movie or a relaxed night out. When those diversions grow old, North Carolina's largest city, Charlotte, is just 20 miles away with clubs and other attractions. A car definitely helps here, as Myrtle Beach and skiing are several hours from Davidson, in different directions. Students without wheels of their own can rent a car through the college's We Car program.

Davidson fields 18 varsity teams (the Wildcats) that compete in the Division I Atlantic 10 Conference, as well as a nonscholarship football team that competes in the Division I Pioneer Football League. About 20 percent of students are varsity athletes. Basketball, soccer, and wrestling are the most competitive programs. Intramural and club sports are also varied and popular.

Despite its North Carolina location, Davidson has the look and feel of a New England liberal arts college and continues to attract top students to its charming neck of the woods. "So many factors contribute to Davidson being such a great place," says a junior. "If it's the right college for you, you can probably tell from the moment you step on campus." From study abroad and independent research to a strawberries-and-champagne reception with the college president for graduating seniors, students here combine tradition with forward thinking to make great memories, friends, and intellectual strides.

> *The college's 100-acre Lake Norman campus provides for sailing, swimming, and waterskiing.*

Overlaps

UNC at Chapel Hill, University of Virginia, Duke, Vanderbilt, Georgetown, Princeton, Wake Forest, Harvard

If You Apply To ➤ | **Davidson:** Early decision I: Nov. 15. Early decision II and regular decision: Jan. 2. Financial aid: Feb. 15. Application fee: $50. Campus and alumni interviews: optional, evaluative. SATs or ACTs: required (SAT essay or ACT writing recommended). Subject Tests: recommended. Letters of recommendation: required. Essay: required. Accepts the Common Application with supplement.

University of Dayton

Dayton, OH 45469

Part of a cohort of Roman Catholic institutions in the Midwest that includes DePaul, Duquesne, Loyola of Chicago, Saint Louis University, and Xavier (OH). Drawing cards include engineering, business, education, and the social sciences, as well as a pioneering program in human rights. Medium-size school with larger feel. The city of Dayton, home to the Wright Brothers, is enjoying a resurgence. UD's appeal is largely regional.

Anyone who thinks college students of today subscribe to postmodern cynicism ought to take a peek at Dayton, where optimism and Christian charity are alive and well. Although its name suggests that it is a public university, Dayton was founded by the Society of Mary (Marianists) and continues to emphasize that order's devotion to service. The majority of UD students volunteer their time in 30 different public service areas. "If you used one word to describe UD students, it would be 'friendly,'" a senior says. "Everyone on campus is very welcoming. We smile and say 'hi' to people we don't know and hold the doors open for each other." There's good reason for the cheery disposition: applications are at an all-time high and selectivity continues to increase.

Website: www.udayton.edu
Location: City Outskirts
Private
Total Enrollment: 9,286
Undergraduates: 8,189
Male/Female: 53/47
SAT Ranges: CR 510–620, M 520–630
ACT Ranges: 24–29

(continued)

Financial Aid: 96%

Pell Grant: 10%

Expense: Pr $

Student Loans: 62%

Average Debt: $ $ $ $

Phi Beta Kappa: No

Applicants: 16,968

Accepted: 58%

Enrolled: 22%

Grad in 6 Years: 76%

Returning Freshmen: 91%

Academics: ✑ ✑ ✑

Social: 🐎 🐎 🐎 🐎

Q of L: ★ ★ ★

Admissions: (937) 229-4411

Email Address: admission@
   udayton.edu

Strong Programs:
Engineering
Entrepreneurship
Marketing
Biology
Communication
Accounting
Early Childhood Education
Human Rights Studies

The majority of UD students volunteer their time in 30 different public service areas.

Located two miles from downtown Dayton, the 388-acre parklike campus with a riverfront vista is bordered by a quiet suburban neighborhood. The more historic buildings make up the central core of the campus and blend architectural charm with modern technological conveniences. The university has been making substantial investments in student housing, including ArtStreet, an arts-centered living/learning complex, and renovation of all existing residential facilities. The $51 million EPIS Center boasts labs where UD researchers and students work side by side with GE Aviation scientists and engineers to create advanced electrical power technologies. The new, $35 million Helix Innovation Center offers opportunities for students to explore advanced technology for HVAC systems.

> **"Students work in a comfortable environment where they shouldn't feel pressured."**

The new undergraduate curriculum, the Common Academic Program, is designed to equip students with the skills and experience to participate in a complex global society. All students are required to have a notebook computer upon entering UD. The first-year experience course helps entering students prepare for their academic careers and explore various majors, and all students complete a capstone experience their senior year. UD students take full advantage of the strong offerings found in engineering (mechanical, chemical, civil, and electrical), entrepreneurship, marketing, biology, communication, accounting, and early childhood education—the most popular majors. Consistent with its religious mission, Dayton offers a major in human rights, the first of its kind, and has launched a new Human Rights Center. The Hanley Sustainability Institute is creating new kinds of experiential learning in sustainability, and students in any major can earn a minor in sustainability, energy, and the environment. The entrepreneurship program dispenses $35,000 loans to participating sophomores to start their own businesses, with any profits going to charity, as well as mentorship from local entrepreneurs. Finance students manage $20 million of the university's endowment.

"Our faculty expects the best from our students, yet with the spirit of collaboration and support, students work in a comfortable environment where they shouldn't feel pressured," says a premed major. Thirty-one percent of classes have fewer than 20 students. Students speak highly of the quality of teaching and professors' enthusiasm about their courses. "Professors are clearly interested in my growth and are extremely accessible and helpful," a civil engineering major says. Career services are described as dynamic and effective in making sure students are well-networked upon graduation. "Career services offers mock interviews, résumé building, and LinkedIn workshops that I believe have been incredibly helpful," says a senior.

> **"Career services offers mock interviews, résumé building, and LinkedIn workshops that I believe have been incredibly helpful."**

Qualified freshmen may join the University Honors Program, which features special activities and opportunities for fellowships and research. The University of Dayton Research Institute also offers students a chance to gain hands-on experience. Study abroad programs are popular tickets to the world's most exciting cities and include study at the University of Dayton China Institute in the Suzhou Industrial Park or at universities in Ireland and Spain, for the same cost as a semester on campus. "Campus ministry provides opportunities for retreats, service-learning trips, cultural immersion, and outreach," adds a senior.

"Students at UD love one word above all," says a sophomore: "community." Forty-five percent of Dayton's undergraduates are from Ohio, while 11 percent come from abroad. The school is becoming more selective, but the minority population is still small: 3 percent are African American, 3 percent are Hispanic, and 1 percent are Asian American. While students are interested in social justice, they say overt political activism is not common on campus. "Students are more concerned with building and fostering relationships with people on campus, rather than finding political differences," observes a mechanical engineering major. Dayton's 185 athletic scholarships go to athletes in 14 sports, and merit-based academic awards average $14,541. An innovative tuition plan eliminates fees, offers free books, and guarantees that tuition will not increase over four years.

Seventy-two percent of undergraduates are campus residents; those who live off campus generally live adjacent to it. First-year students live in one of four traditional residence halls, many of them opting to join living/learning communities with their classmates, while sophomores select suites or apartments. Upperclassmen take up quarters in the 400 university-owned houses, apartments, and townhouses that comprise the student neighborhood, which a senior says is "nice because the university will come and fix any broken things in your house, shovel driveways, and cut grass."

An innovative tuition plan eliminates fees, offers free books, and guarantees that tuition will not increase over four years.

"Students at UD love one word above all: community."

Dining facilities in first- and second-year residence halls have been renovated, with new full-service, casual restaurant-style menu selections. Other dining facilities are centrally located with a variety of cafés, delis, and convenience stores spread throughout the campus. "UD prides itself on being a very safe campus, and in my experience I definitely feel safe," says one senior. The Women's Center, which offers support for students, faculty, and staff, is a resource for social and gender justice, and the university has a comprehensive policy on sexual harassment.

"Students love to stay on campus for the weekends or even for some of our shorter breaks," says a student. The student neighborhood serves as a sort of continuous social center. A lit porch light beckons party-seeking students to join the weekend festivities, and students say the party culture is safe and inclusive and the alcohol policies are effective. A 24-hour campus police department keeps watch over the area. St. Patrick's Day celebrations are a major event each year. Greek organizations draw 16 percent of UD men and 22 percent of the women, with all chapters playing an active role in community service and social life. Christmas on Campus, when UD students "adopt" local elementary students for a night of crafts, games, and a visit with Santa, is one of the most student-involved activities. "We bring in about 1,000 inner-city Dayton school kids and walk them around campus, which has been transformed into a winter wonderland," says one student.

Upperclassmen take up quarters in the 400 university-owned houses, apartments, and townhouses that comprise the student neighborhood.

The university is part of Dayton's bike share program, which has five stations on campus and is popular with students. Just a short ride away by bike, bus, or car are attractions like the Dayton Dragons minor-league baseball team, the Dayton Art Institute, the U.S. Air Force's museums, and a symphony or opera in

"UD prides itself on being a very safe campus."

the Schuster Performing Arts Center. Three large shopping malls are also easily accessible. Weekend excursions take aim at cities ranging from Louisville to Chicago to Indianapolis, as well as the restaurants, shops, and sports arenas in Cincinnati. But the best road trip is the Dayton-to-Daytona trip after spring finals, a 17-hour trek that draws loads of students each year.

The Dayton Flyers field 14 Division I men's and women's teams, and sports play a big role in campus life. Football competes in the Pioneer League, and other sports, with the exception of women's golf, play in the Atlantic 10 Conference. Both the men's and women's basketball teams have reached the Elite 8 in recent years, and the Red Scare student cheering section loves to intimidate opponents. Men's soccer, baseball, and cross-country and women's soccer, volleyball, and track and field are also competitive. About half of students participate in one of the many intramural programs, and 36 club sports teams are available; the men's club lacrosse team is a recent national champion.

"UD's community is a great place to form lifelong friendships and prepare yourself for your future career," cheers one senior. The success of Dayton's attempts to provide its students with a high quality of life and a sense of cohesiveness is reflected in the strong social life and family-like atmosphere among both students and faculty. As a midsize university where the undergraduates come first, Dayton has managed to maintain an exciting balance of personal attention, academic challenge, and all-American fun.

If You Apply To ➤	**Dayton:** Early action: Nov. 1. Regular decision: Feb. 1. Financial aid: Mar. 1. Housing: May 1. No application fee. No campus or alumni interviews. SATs or ACTs: required. No Subject Tests. Letters of recommendation: required. Essay: required. Accepts the Common Application with supplement.

Deep Springs College

Deep Springs Ranch Road, Highway 168, Big Pine, CA 93513

Picture 26 Ivy League–caliber men living and learning on a working ranch in a remote desert outpost—that's Deep Springs. DS is the most elite two-year institution in the nation, and also the most unusual—and not just because of its free tuition. Occupies a handful of ranch-style buildings set on 50,000 acres on the arid border of Nevada and California. Students transfer to highly selective colleges after two years. The college hopes to go co-ed.

Website: www.deepsprings.edu
Location: Rural
Private
Total Enrollment: 26
Undergraduates: 26
Male/Female: 100/0
SAT Ranges: CR 670–770, M 650–740
ACT Ranges: 31–34
Financial Aid: 100%
Pell Grant: N/A
Expense: Pr $
Student Loans: N/A
Average Debt: $
Phi Beta Kappa: No
Applicants: 203
Accepted: 10%
Enrolled: 75%
Grad in 6 Years: 100%
Returning Freshmen: 90%
Academics: ✍ ✍ ✍ ✍ ½
Social: ☎
Q of L: ★ ★ ★
Admissions: (760) 872-2000

If the thought of spending countless hours under the fluorescent lights of the classroom makes you grimace, you may consider getting your hands dirty at Deep Springs College. This two-year institution doubles as a working ranch. Bonding is easy here, and students enjoy a demanding and individualized education supplemented by the challenges and lessons of ranch life. Both, it seems, demand the same things: hard work, commitment, and pride in a job well done. Deep Springs College students are also rewarded for their efforts in other ways: tuition is free and so is room and board. Students pay only for books, travel, health insurance, and personal items; the average cost of one year at Deep Springs is about $2,500. Still, students do have a few complaints: loneliness, saddle-chafing, and no female students (so far). Many of the men who work, study, and live at this college have shunned acceptance at Ivy League schools to embrace the rigors of a truly unique approach to learning. Deep Springs students tend to be of the academic Renaissance-man variety with wide-ranging interests in many fields. Almost all transfer to the Ivies or other prestigious universities after their two-year program, and 70 percent eventually earn a Ph.D. or law degree. Efforts to go co-ed have thus far been blocked by the courts.

California's White Mountains provide a stunning backdrop for the Deep Springs campus, set on a barren plain 5,200 feet above sea level, near the only water supply for miles around. The campus is an oasis-like cluster of trees and a lawn with eight ranch-style buildings that were built from scratch by the class of 1917. Deep Springs is 28 miles from the nearest town, a thriving metropolis known as Big Pine, population 1,756. The focal point of campus is the Main Building, a venerable ranch-style building with wide eaves that includes a computer room and offices. Faculty houses and the dining facilities are grouped around the circular lawn a few yards away from the sole dorm, and the trappings of farm life surround the tiny settlement. The college has 170 acres under cultivation, mostly with alfalfa, and an assortment of barnyard animals. A solar array produces twice as much energy as the college requires—except during peak summer times when the alfalfa needs irrigating—and is the most efficient array in North America.

Founded in 1917 by an industrialist who made a fortune in the electric-power industry, Deep Springs today remains true to its charter to combine taxing practical work, rigorous academics, and genuine self-government—the three pillars of the school. Ideals of self-government, reflectiveness, frugality, and community activity have weathered nearly 100 years of a grueling academic climate. "Deep Springers tend to think of academics as part of our community life," says one student. "The courses are challenging," says another. Students are also required to perform 20 hours per week of labor, which can include everything from harvesting alfalfa to branding and herding cattle to cooking dinner.

> **"Deep Springers tend to think of academics as part of our community life."**

Students' input carries a lot of weight at this school. The student body committees are an essential part of the self-governance pillar at DS. There are four committees: the student-run Applications Committee, which is made up of eight students, a faculty member, and a staff member; the Curriculum Committee; the Review and Reinvitations Committee; and the Communications Committee. They help choose the college's faculty and even elect two of their own to be full-voting members on the board of trustees. They play a determining role in admissions and curricular decisions. And they abide by a Spartan community code that bans all drugs, including alcohol, and forbids anyone to leave Deep Springs Valley (the 50 square miles of desert surrounding the campus) while classes are in session, except for medical visits and college business. There are no phones and no Internet in the dorm, although there is limited Wi-Fi in all the other buildings on campus, including classrooms and the library. Lest these rules sound unnecessarily strict, keep in mind that these are all decided on and enforced by the student body, not the administration.

Like almost everything else about it, Deep Springs has an unorthodox academic schedule: two summer terms of seven weeks each, and a fall and spring semester of 14 weeks each. Between 7 and 10 classes are offered every term. Upon arriving at Deep Springs, all new students complete an intensive summer seminar with some of their older peers. The seminar, often taught by an interdisciplinary team of professors, focuses on issues of ethics and governance and prepares students to read and write effectively for the fall. Currently, the only required courses are public speaking and composition. The students control the academic program and quickly replace courses—and faculty—that do not work out. Students say the humanities, especially literature and philosophy, tend to set the academic tone.

> **"Faculty are generally accessible most hours of the day or night—as long as their porch lights are on."**

The faculty consists of three "permanent" professors—the humanities chair, the social sciences chair, and the natural sciences chair—who sign on for two years but can stay for up to six. Other courses are taught by the dean, the president, and visiting professors who stay for a single semester or summer term. The quality of particular academic areas varies as professors come and go, but generally, a student says, professors have "a deep respect for students as intellectual equals." With class sizes ranging from two to 14, there is ample opportunity for close student/faculty interaction—and students must be prepared to discuss their ideas. Close living arrangements have fostered a kind of kinship between faculty and students, who routinely continue class discussions over meals. "Faculty are generally accessible most hours of the day or night—as long as their porch lights are on, students can stop by to talk about papers, books they are reading outside of class, or for life advice," says a student.

(continued)

Email Address: apcom@
deepsprings.edu

Strong Programs:
Humanities
Environmental Studies
Philosophy
Literature

Taxing practical work, rigorous academics, and genuine self-government are the three pillars of Deep Springs.

The humanities, especially literature and philosophy, tend to set the academic tone.

Deep Springers can truly boast of being handpicked to attend; of the approximately 200 applications received each year, only a handful of students are accepted. Most DS students are from upper-middle-class families and typically rank in the top 3 percent of their high school class. "Students tend to be highly academic, curious about a number of disciplines, and excited about learning," a student says. With only 26 students enrolled, demographics can fluctuate from year to year. Many Deep Springers are transplanted urbanites; the rest hail from points scattered across the nation or across the seas. Political leanings run the gamut, and there is diversity even among this small population, although that may only translate to a few students of color here.

Rooms in the dorm are said to be spacious and comfortable, and a student explains, "The dorm includes a lovely common room with a library and a fire (the 'rumpus room'), as well as a gym, meditation room, multiple porches, and a backyard (with a tree-house!)." Room selection and dorm maintenance is entirely the responsibility of the students, who also pitch in with preparing the meals, from butchering the meat to milking the cows to washing the dishes. "The food is usually five stars," boasts a student. "Vegetarians are usually provided for, but we are a cattle ranch." And what about security? "Unless a tractor runs over you, you're fine," says a freshman. A classmate adds, "Sometimes the bulls get loose."

> **"Vegetarians are usually provided for, but we are a cattle ranch."**

Social life can be a challenge, and loneliness can be an issue. Still, one student says, "Movies, board games, dance parties, and hangouts are the regular staples of student life and are integral in keeping the community close." When the moon is full, students go out en masse in the middle of the night to frolic in the 700-foot-high Eureka Sand Dunes with Frisbees and skis. "We slide down the Eureka Valley sand dunes au naturel," says one student. Perhaps the most popular social activity on campus is conversation over a cup of coffee in the Boarding House (Deep Springs's dining hall), where the chatter is usually lively until the wee hours of the morning. Other common activities include pick-up soccer games, hikes in the nearby mountains, horseback riding, and competitive gopher-trapping in the winter months. The Turkey Bowl football game, the potato harvest, and Sludgefest (an annual event involving cleaning out the reservoir) are only some of the time-honored Deep Springs traditions.

> *Common activities include hikes in the nearby mountains, horseback riding, and competitive gopher-trapping in the winter months.*

Critics of Deep Springs charge that DS cultivates arrogance and social backwardness among students who were too intellectual to be in the social mainstream during high school. They argue that students who come here are doomed to be misfits for life. While that charge is debatable, even supporters of Deep Springs confess to a love-hate relationship with the college. Although the interpretations may vary, one common thread winds through the DS mission from application to graduation: training for a life of service to humanity.

> **"We are oriented toward serving humanity."**

Perhaps more than any other school in the nation, Deep Springs is a community where students and faculty interact day-to-day on an intensely personal level. Though the financial commitment is small, the school demands an intense level of personal commitment. All must quickly learn how to get along in a community where the actions of each person affect everyone. "We are oriented toward serving humanity," says a freshman, "and we try to understand what service means in a nuanced and original way." Urban cowboys who dream of riding into the sunset are in for a rude awakening. For a select few, however, the camaraderie and soul-searching fostered in this tight-knit community can be mighty tempting.

> ## Overlaps
>
> **Brown, Cornell University, Yale, University of Chicago, Harvard, Columbia, Stanford, Princeton**

University of Delaware

116 Hullihen Hall, Newark, DE 19716

Plenty of students dream of someday becoming Nittany Lions or Cavaliers—even Terrapins—but not many aspire to be Blue Hens. The challenge for UD is how to win its share of students without the name recognition that comes from big-time sports. The state of Delaware is tiny, and less than half the students are in-staters. Check out the variety of residential learning options.

The University of Delaware is a public gem that boasts solid academic programs, from engineering to nursing. Though lacking a big-time sports program, UD has been gradually attracting more and more students who are looking for strong academics and hands-on experiences. It all adds up to "the small-school feel with the opportunities of a larger university," as one junior says.

Delaware's 970-acre Newark campus has an attractive mix of colonial and modern geometric buildings, set among flowering and native plantings. The hub of the campus is a grassy green mall, flanked by classic Georgian buildings. Mechanical Hall is a climate-controlled art gallery and home to the Paul R. Jones collection. Hotel and restaurant management students benefit from classes in a fine dining restaurant and a Courtyard by Marriott right on campus, which doubles as a learning and research facility. The new Caesar Rodney Complex opened in 2015, featuring a 400-bed residence hall for first-year students and a 55,000-square-foot dining facility.

As UD has grown in popularity, academic standards have become more rigorous. To graduate, students must pass freshman English (critical reading and writing) and earn at least three credits of discovery-based or experiential learning, such as an internship, research, or study abroad. All incoming freshmen begin with a First-Year Seminar course, and a capstone experience is required during the senior year; other requirements vary by college.

Delaware's academic menu includes 139 majors, ranging from the liberal arts and sciences to more professional programs such as apparel design and fashion merchandising. Finance and nursing are the most popular majors, followed by marketing, exercise science, and biological sciences. Engineering, especially chemical engineering, is one of UD's specialties, and the school benefits from the close proximity of DuPont, the chemical giant that has been a major benefactor of the university. The music department is another attraction, with a 300-member marching band and several faculty members holding impressive professional performance credits.

> "They really want us…to experience everything that we might encounter in the real world before we get there."

Success at UD requires "a great deal of time management and a desire to learn," according to one senior, but another adds, "Professors stress the importance of collaboration and working together to succeed in classes." Classes tend to be larger, although 31 percent enroll fewer than 20 students. "The vast majority of professors

Website: www.udel.edu
Location: Small City
Public
Total Enrollment: 19,792
Undergraduates: 16,789
Male/Female: 42/58
SAT Ranges: CR 550–650, M 560–660
ACT Ranges: 25–29
Financial Aid: 50%
Pell Grant: N/A
Expense: Pub $ $ $
Student Loans: 61%
Average Debt: $ $ $ $
Phi Beta Kappa: Yes
Applicants: 24,881
Accepted: 63%
Enrolled: 26%
Grad in 6 Years: 81%
Returning Freshmen: 92%
Academics: ✐ ✐ ✐
Social: ☎ ☎ ☎ ☎ ☎
Q of L: ★ ★ ★
Admissions: (302) 831-8123
Email Address: admissions@ udel.edu

Strong Programs:
Finance
Nursing
Marketing
Exercise Science
Biological Sciences
Chemical Engineering
Music

go the extra mile to make sure their students understand the subject and that the material is presented in an engaging fashion," says a criminal justice major. Students say that career preparation here is hands-on and useful. "Career Services is excellent at UD," says a biochemistry major. "I love how they really want us as students to experience everything that we might encounter in the real world before we get there."

UD created the nation's first study abroad program in 1923, and today one-third of students travel to more than 70 study abroad programs on all seven continents, mostly for short-term, faculty-led programs during the month-long winter session or summer break. Each year, about 400 UD students receive stipends to do summer research with faculty members. Those wishing to spend their summers serving the local community may apply for the Service Learning Scholars Program, a 10-week immersion program. Overall, 62 percent of students get involved in some form of community service during their time at UD. About 500 new students enter the University Honors Program each year, which offers interdisciplinary colloquia, priority seating in honors sections of regular courses, personal attention, and extracurricular and residence hall programming.

Only thirty-nine percent of undergraduates at Delaware hail from the First State; many of the rest are from the Northeast. Minority enrollment continues to increase; 5 percent are African American, 7 percent are Hispanic, and 5 percent are Asian American. International students, at 4 percent, provide a strong presence on campus, and the majority come from China. The campus attracts a mix of liberal and conservative students, and a senior reports that "the racial climate at UD" has been a prominent topic of discussion of late. Merit and athletic scholarships are offered. The Commitment to Delawareans initiative is designed to meet the full demonstrated need of state residents.

> **"There is a big party culture on campus, but it is not controlled by Greek life."**

Forty-three percent of students live on campus, including all freshmen not commuting from home. After that, dorm housing is guaranteed and awarded by lottery, though many juniors and seniors move into off-campus apartments. Honors students live together in designated residence halls, and certain academic departments require first-year students to reside in living/learning communities. A variety of optional special-interest communities are available as well. Students in traditional residence halls must buy the meal plan; one student advises, "The food courts are excellent and have a range of options for different dietary needs, but the dining halls could be improved." Campus safety is said to be good, and UD began overhauling its handling of campus sexual assault in 2015, with new personnel, new investigative procedures, and ongoing development of training programs.

"Most of the social life takes place on and around campus. Many students are involved in student organizations, which tend to host events," says a freshman. A classmate adds, "There is a big party culture on campus, but it is not controlled by Greek life." Fraternities attract 19 percent of the men and sororities 23 percent of the women. Aside from parties, common diversions range from concerts and plays on campus to casual gatherings in friends' rooms. Hen Fest welcomes students back to campus every fall, and Resapalooza is the annual spring bacchanal, bringing music and a carnival to the central campus green. Juniors mark their progress in the fall with the Halfway There party, featuring half-legged races, half-lemonade/half-iced-tea Arnold Palmers, and a DJ who plays popular songs—but only halfway through.

Main Street, the heart of downtown Newark, "practically runs right through campus," one student says. "It's easy walking distance from anywhere, and there are tons of coffee shops, pizza places, restaurants, a movie theater, bookstores, and shops—anything you could possibly want." For those seeking further excitement,

UD benefits from the close proximity of DuPont, the chemical giant that has been a major benefactor of the university.

Certain academic departments require first-year students to reside in living/ learning communities.

New York, the Washington/Baltimore area, and Philadelphia are all within a two-hour drive. When the weather is warm, the beaches of Rehoboth and Dewey beckon, and in chilly months, the Pennsylvania ski slopes aren't too far.

Delaware's Division I Blue Hens are becoming more competitive, and on Saturdays in the fall, watch out. "Football is big," says one student. Tailgate picnics are popular before and after the game. In 2014, the men's basketball team won the Colonial Athletic Association championship and advanced to the NCAA tournament. That followed a 2013 CAA championship and a run to the NCAA regional semifinals by the women's basketball team. Recreational sports are popular; students have their pick of more than 30 club sports and 30 intramural programs.

"From our music department to engineering, I have met students from across the board who have had internships, jobs, research opportunities, and other experiences that are very unique and enriching," says a student. Indeed, with UD's traditional emphasis on out-of-classroom experiences, stimulating academic environment, and up-and-coming athletic teams, Blue Hens need never put all their eggs in one basket. "There is too much to do on this campus," sighs a senior. "I feel sad I will never get the opportunity to do it all."

If You Apply To ➤ **Delaware:** Regular decision and financial aid: Jan. 15. Housing: May 1. Application fee: $75. Campus and alumni interviews: optional, evaluative. SATs (with essay) or ACTs (with writing): required. Subject Tests: recommended. Letters of recommendation: required. Essay: required. Accepts the Common Application with supplement.

Denison University

Granville, OH 43023

Nearly as selective as Kenyon, Denison draws more Easterners than cohorts such as Wittenberg and Ohio Wesleyan, and it fashions itself as a sort of Midwestern Haverford. Denison has a middle-of-the-road to conservative student body, fewer preppies than in years past, and one of the most beautiful campuses anywhere. Increasing selectivity has helped create a more serious student body.

Denison University, tucked into the "quaint, small, and beautiful" hamlet of Granville, draws "unabashedly curious, down-to-earth, straightforward, and accepting" men and women from diverse backgrounds, according to one happy student. Thanks to Denison's small size, there's ample opportunity to interact (and do research with) professors and to form close relationships with peers as everyone focuses on the liberal arts. "At Denison, there are very high expectations about academics," explains a junior. "Students are expected to engage in learning both inside and outside the classroom."

Denison's campus is set atop rolling hills in central Ohio. Huge maples shade the sloping walkways, which offer a panoramic view of the surrounding valley. Denison retained park architect Frederick Law Olmsted (designer of New York City's Central Park) for its first master plan back in the early 1900s. The Georgian style of many buildings—redbrick with white columns—also evokes shades of New England and its private liberal arts colleges. A $38.5 million construction project has resulted in the renovation and expansion of Mitchell Center, a centerpiece of the university's athletics and recreation facilities. The space includes new classrooms, gathering areas, the Trumbull Aquatics Center, and the Crown Fitness Center.

Website: www.denison.edu
Location: Small Town
Private
Total Enrollment: 2,253
Undergraduates: 2,253
Male/Female: 43/57
SAT Ranges: CR 580–680, M 590–690
ACT Ranges: 26–31
Financial Aid: 99%
Pell Grant: 22%
Expense: Pr $ $ $
Student Loans: 50%
Average Debt: $ $ $
Phi Beta Kappa: Yes
Applicants: 6,110

(continued)

Accepted: 48%

Enrolled: 22%

Grad in 6 Years: 82%

Returning Freshmen: 87%

Academics: ✍ ✍ ✍ ½

Social: 🍷 🍷 🍷 🍷 🍷

Q of L: ★ ★ ★

Admissions: (740) 587-6276

Email Address: admissions@
denison.edu

Strong Programs:
Economics
Communication
Biology
Psychology
Mathematics
Music
Philosophy, Politics, and
   Economics

Denison's general education requirements are comprehensive. Students take two first-year seminars, and then during their four years, two courses each in the fine arts, the sciences (one with lab), the social sciences, the humanities, and a foreign language. Some courses may be double-counted to fulfill oral communication and quantitative reasoning requirements. Students must also complete an "interdivisional requirement" by selecting a course from one of seven interdisciplinary programs, such as international studies or queer studies. The Power and Justice requirement seeks to give students the ability to question their own place in the structures of power and privilege that constitute human societies.

Students say that some of the best majors are distinctive to Denison. The PPE major is effectively a triple major in philosophy, politics, and economics. Economics, communication, biology, and psychology enroll the most students. Denison's 350-acre biological reserve is a boon for biology and environmental studies majors. The mathematics department is strong, and the music department features a concentration in bluegrass designed by a faculty member who is an accomplished fiddler. New majors in data analytics and global commerce have been added, as has a concentration in narrative nonfiction writing. Courses are rigorous, but a junior says, "While students care about their own academic success, they also care about each other's, and you can always find students in the library studying together." Classes are small—88 percent have fewer than 20 students—and individual attention is the norm. "I can't put into words how selfless, committed, and passionate the Denison faculty are," one student says.

> **"[Students are] unabashedly curious, down-to-earth, straightforward, and accepting."**

Denison's signature Summer Scholar Program provides scholarships for more than 150 students to stay on campus during the summer, earning a stipend to complete 10 weeks of full-time research in collaboration with faculty members. Typically, more than half of the summer scholars are science students. Those with wanderlust can sign up for internships and off-campus studies through the Great Lakes Colleges Association* and the Associated Colleges of the Midwest*—45 percent do so. Students rave about the Denison Seminars, small, interdisciplinary classes that are team-taught by two professors and involve a travel component. "I've taken two Denison Seminars," says a history major, "and they were defining classes of my time at Denison." The school has also placed an increasing emphasis on career preparation, and the Denison Internship Program offers students a selection of more than 250 internships around the country. Those considering a run for office may be interested in the Richard G. Lugar Program in American Politics and Public Service, which includes political science courses on campus and culminates in a House or Senate internship in Washington. (The former senator happens to be a Denison grad.)

> *Denison's 350-acre biological reserve is a boon for biology and environmental studies majors.*

Twenty-five percent of Denison's population is homegrown, and 8 percent come from abroad. African Americans now constitute 7 percent of the student body, Hispanics 10 percent, and Asian Americans 4 percent. Students are engaged in social and political issues, according to a biology and Spanish double major: "Every week there are multiple events going on, whether it's LGBTQ rights, women's and minority rights, and many others." Admissions are need-blind, and 22 percent of freshmen qualify for Pell Grants. The average merit-based financial aid award is $20,089, and there are no athletic scholarships. The school also funds 80 full-tuition scholarships each academic year for student leaders from Chicago and Boston public high schools.

> **"While students care about their own academic success, they also care about each other's."**

Ninety-nine percent of Denison students live on campus; the only ones allowed to live elsewhere are those commuting from home. (One exception is the dozen

Homesteaders, who live in three student-built solar-paneled cabins on a sustainable farm less than a mile away, and grow much of their own food.) One student says the school's residential focus "creates a great sense of community, which is so important." Housing options range from singles to apartments with kitchens. Students also say dining options are improving, but still grumble about the cost. Safety is considered a given here: "Granville is a *very* safe town," says a senior. "Parents can feel comfortable sending their kids to this school." A junior adds, "The administration is very transparent and receptive to student input regarding ways to prevent sexual assault at Denison."

"Almost all social life takes place on campus. Dorm parties and the like are the norm," says a student. The school runs trips to the Easton Town Center, an outdoor shopping and dining mecca in nearby Columbus, the state capital and fifteenth-largest city in the U.S., and the student government has even been known to hold fireworks shows. Alcohol policies are less punitive and more focused on ensuring **"Granville is a *very* safe town."** safety. Though the Greek system is nonresidential and does not dominate the social scene, 21 percent of the men and 34 percent of the women still join up. Students look forward to three all-campus parties each year—D-Day, Culture Jam, and Aestavalia. There's also "Naked Week" in February, which affords concerned students a chance to run naked through campus to promote healthy body image and acceptance.

One student describes the town of Granville this way: "If you held up each month of a Norman Rockwell calendar while looking at the village for the respective months, you might think you were looking at the same thing!" There are four churches on the corners of the town's main intersection, along with "two bars, a coffee shop, a bank, a greasy spoon restaurant, a library, and gift shops," says another student. Most stores and restaurants close by 8 p.m., though students appreciate the feeling of safety and security that results. The Denison Community Association frequently sends students into Granville and nearby Newark to provide tutoring, mentoring, and other volunteer services. Popular road trips include Ohio University, Ohio State, and Miami University in Oxford, Ohio. Pittsburgh, Cleveland, Cincinnati, and Dayton are also close by.

Denison students are enthusiastic supporters of the Big Red, and Division III football and lacrosse games against Ohio Wesleyan always draw large crowds. The university has won the North Coast Athletic Conference All-Sports Trophy a record 15 times. The men's swimming and diving team claimed the national championship in 2016, taking down longtime rival Kenyon College, while men's and women's basket- **"Denison does a great job of crossing over and piecing together academic interests."** ball and lacrosse and women's soccer, tennis, and swimming and diving all advanced to their respective national tournaments. Intramurals and club sports remain popular too, drawing roughly 45 percent of students to a variety of pursuits, ranging from rugby and crew to flag football and sand volleyball.

Denison University aims to graduate independent thinkers who become active citizens of a democratic society. The school continues to value tradition— woe to the student who steps on the school seal in front of the chapel, for doing so will cause him to fail all his finals—while growing and evolving to emphasize academics and the life of the mind. Throw in a vibrant social scene and you've found a recipe for a dynamic college experience. A recent graduate says, "Denison does a great job of crossing over and piecing together academic interests, and they have tons of connections in the world to help you succeed after you graduate."

Overlaps

Miami University (OH), Kenyon, Bucknell, Carleton, Oberlin, Grinnell, Bates, Franklin & Marshall

Denison: Early decision I: Nov. 15. Early decision II and regular decision: Jan. 15. Financial aid: Feb. 1. Housing: May 1. No application fee. Campus interviews: recommended, evaluative. No alumni interviews. SATs or ACTs: optional. Subject Tests: optional. Letters of recommendation: required. Essay: required. Accepts the Common Application.

University of Denver

2199 South University Boulevard, Denver, CO 80208

The only major midsized private university between Tulsa and the West Coast. DU's campus in residential Denver is pleasant, and brochures tout Rocky Mountain landscapes and healthy lifestyles. A haven for skiing enthusiasts and business majors, DU has gotten more selective in recent years.

Website: www.du.edu
Location: City Center
Private
Total Enrollment: 8,617
Undergraduates: 5,437
Male/Female: 46/54
SAT Ranges: CR 550–660, M 560–660
ACT Ranges: 23–30
Financial Aid: 86%
Pell Grant: 18%
Expense: Pr $ $ $
Student Loans: 45%
Average Debt: $ $ $
Phi Beta Kappa: Yes
Applicants: 15,036
Accepted: 73%
Enrolled: 13%
Grad in 6 Years: 76%
Returning Freshmen: 86%
Academics: ✍ ✍ ✍
Social: ☎ ☎ ☎ ☎
Q of L: ★ ★ ★ ★
Admissions: (303) 871-2036
Email Address: admission@du.edu

Strong Programs:
Finance
Psychology
International Studies
Marketing
Hospitality Management
Music
Political Science
Chemistry

The oldest private university in the Rocky Mountain region, the University of Denver is where former secretary of state Condoleezza Rice earned her B.A. in political science at age 19 and later returned for a Ph.D. in international studies. Her mentor was Soviet specialist Joseph Korbel, father of former secretary of state Madeline Albright. Thus, it's not surprising that DU boasts strong programs in political science, international studies, and public affairs. Many students, however, opt for DU's business program, and the campus location offers ample opportunities for networking, skiing, and taking in the beautiful Colorado landscape. "Students bring their exploration of the world into the classroom by being inquisitive and curious about their chosen fields," observes a senior.

DU's 125-acre main campus is located in a comfortable residential neighborhood only eight miles from downtown Denver and an hour east of major ski areas. Architectural styles vary and materials include brick, limestone, Colorado sandstone, and copper. Nearby Mount Evans (14,264 feet) is home to the world's loftiest observatory, a DU facility available to both professors and students. A new facility for the Ritchie School of Engineering and Computer Science recently opened, serving as a hub for interdisciplinary, STEM-related research and scholarship.

Under the general education requirements, undergraduate students choose from a series of courses from the Common Curriculum that emphasize writing and rhetoric, language, analytical inquiry, and scientific inquiry. "At first I thought, 'Who wants to take these science, art, and English classes?'" explains a business major. "But now that I've completed the core, I feel better about myself and my world knowledge." University rules stipulate that all core courses must be taught by senior faculty. Core courses are supplemented by a first-year seminar (limited to 15 students) and an advanced seminar, which serves as a capstone to the curriculum model. As part of their orientation, freshmen spend 10 hours with a small group of students and a professor discussing a collection of essays by prominent writers.

> **"I personally enjoy how rigorous the quarter system can be, because you are constantly learning something new."**

DU is known for its business school—especially the Fritz Knoebel School of Hospitality Management. Preprofessional programs are feeders for graduate schools in business, international studies, engineering, and the arts, and undergrads can opt for a five-year program toward a master's degree in business, international studies, or law. Finance, psychology, international studies, and marketing are the most popular majors, and music, chemistry, and computer science have solid reputations. A new major in business analytics was added recently, as was an entrepreneurship minor.

Since DU operates on a quarter system, classes move quickly and the workload can get intense. "I personally enjoy how rigorous the quarter system can be, because you are constantly learning something new," says an art history major. Students say small class sizes—53 percent have fewer than 20 students—make for a collaborative environment with plenty of support from professors. "Professors desire to become more like mentors to their students, rather than 'that one professor who taught that one class,'" says an accounting major. DU is also recognized for its strong academic support services. "I am in the Learning Effectiveness Program, which is for students with learning disabilities," says a psychology major. "They have been amazing and given me the accommodations and resources I need to succeed."

"DU fosters a global perspective."

DU's honors program draws more than 400 students; in the past few years, the university has produced Rhodes, Marshall, Goldwater, Truman, and Fulbright scholars. All juniors and seniors have the chance to study abroad at no extra cost; 65 percent of students go abroad, and they say the 150 available programs are an integral part of the DU experience. "DU fosters a global perspective in which students understand their role in and responsibility to the global community," says a psychology major.

University rules stipulate that all core courses must be taught by senior faculty.

"We have a funky mix of really preppy East Coasters and Midwesterners mixed in with all the laid-back outdoorsy people," says one student. Thirty-two percent of the students are from Colorado, and 9 percent arrive from overseas. African Americans account for 2 percent of the student body, Asian Americans 4 percent, and Hispanics 10 percent. "We definitely have groups on both ends of the political spectrum," says a junior, and students cite the environment and social justice as issues of particular concern. As one of the few private colleges in the West, DU is also among the most expensive in the region. There are hundreds of merit scholarships averaging $15,253 and 206 athletic scholarships.

Students are required to spend their first two years on campus in the residence halls. "Housing is simple to deal with and is a lot of fun," says a marketing major. A classmate adds, "Each residence hall has a leadership development team that plans programming events just for that residence." The Johnson-McFarlane hall ("J-Mac") is supposed to be the best place for freshmen, though another student says that the Towers are a much quieter option. Students praise the five living/learning communities open to first-years: "Being able to come onto campus and already have a structured and supportive group of people who shared a similar interest was incredibly helpful," a senior recalls. Overall, 44 percent of undergrads reside on campus; most juniors and seniors opt for the decent quarters found within walking distance. Campus dining receives mixed reviews; while it can be repetitive and occasionally unappealing, a junior says, "There is always a vegetarian option, always a vegan option, as well gluten-free toasters and allergen-free fridges." Campus police "are quick to communicate with the entire campus if there is anything fishy going on," according to one student, and another adds, "During my four years at DU I have seen a definite change and push in terms of education and advocacy regarding sexual assault."

"There is more of a bar scene around DU than a party scene, I have found."

DU is recognized for its strong academic support services.

Social life is divided between on-campus activities and off-campus diversions. Twenty-seven percent of the men and 29 percent of the women belong to a fraternity or sorority, respectively. "While Greek organizations offer opportunities to party, they certainly do not set the tone of social life on campus and do not dictate what is deemed socially acceptable and cool," says an international studies major. A classmate adds, "There is more of a bar scene around DU than a party scene, I have found." Students make regular trips into the city, made easy by free access to the nearby light rail. One student cheers, "Campus is minutes from downtown Denver, where there is great shopping, festivals, events, concerts, phenomenal restaurants, and, for students over 21, one of the best microbrewery scenes." With consistently beautiful, sunny weather and great skiing, hiking, and camping less than an hour away in the Rockies, many DU students head for the hills on weekends, often on trips organized by the Alpine Club. Besides various ski areas, one can explore Estes Park, Mount Evans, and Echo Lake. Additionally, DU is not far from Moab, Albuquerque, and Las Vegas.

The students unite when the DU hockey team, a national powerhouse, skates out onto the ice, especially against archrival Colorado College. The Pioneers co-ed ski team has won five national championships in the last 10 years, while men's lacrosse brought home a national title in 2015. Other competitive Division I programs include men's soccer, men's and women's swimming and tennis, and women's golf and volleyball. Intramural and club sports are varied and popular; more than a quarter of students take part. Each January, academics are put aside for the three-day Winter Carnival. Top administrators, professors, and students all pack off to Steamboat Springs, Crested Butte, or another ski area to catch some fresh powder and see who can ski the fastest, skate the best, or build the most artistic ice sculptures.

Students like the University of Denver for its modest size, its friendly atmosphere, and the flexibility afforded by the (sometimes stressful) quarter system. As the school pushes for a more ethnically diverse student body and improves its curriculum and facilities, the University of Denver is striving to become better known for its intellectual rigor than for its gorgeous setting in the Rocky Mountains.

Overlaps

University of Colorado–Boulder, Colorado State, University of Puget Sound, University of Vermont, George Washington, Colorado College, University of Michigan, University of Minnesota

If You Apply To ➤

DU: Early decision I and early action: Nov. 1. Early decision II and regular decision: Jan. 15. Financial aid: Feb. 1. Housing: May 1. Application fee: $65. No campus or alumni interviews. SATs or ACTs: required. No Subject Tests. Letters of recommendation: required. Essay: required. Accepts the Common Application.

DePaul University

Chicago, IL 60604

Few universities have come so far, so fast. DePaul gets the nod over Loyola as the best Roman Catholic university in Chicago. Its Lincoln Park setting is like a Midwestern version of New York's Greenwich Village or Upper West Side. About one-third of all undergraduate students are Catholic. Especially strong in business, film, and the performing arts.

Website: www.depaul.edu
Location: City Center
Private
Total Enrollment: 18,630
Undergraduates: 13,594
Male/Female: 47/53
SAT Ranges: CR 520–620, M 490–610

There is no refuting that DePaul is the largest Roman Catholic university in the nation, and students claim its diversity and politically liberal leanings set it apart from rival institutions. Based in the heart of the city, DePaul is a feeder to Chicago's business community. A spate of campus construction has transformed it from the "little school under the tracks" to Chicago's version of NYU.

DePaul, which was founded by Vincentian fathers in 1898 and is named after the 17th-century French priest Vincent de Paul, has two residential campuses. The Lincoln Park campus, with its state-of-the-art library and new student center, is home to the College of Liberal Arts and Sciences, the College of Education, the

Theatre School, the School of Music, and the College of Science and Health, as well as residence halls and academic and recreational facilities. Lincoln Park itself is a fashionable Chicago neighborhood with century-old brownstone homes, theaters, cafés, parks, and shops. The Loop, or "vertical" campus, 20 minutes away by elevated train in downtown Chicago, houses the College of Law, the School for New Learning, the Driehaus College of Business, the College of Communication, and the College of Computing and Digital Media. The DePaul Center, a $70 million teaching, learning, and research complex, is the cornerstone of this campus.

All freshmen take a course called Discover Chicago or its alternative, Explore Chicago. "This class is one of the best things about DePaul. It's really fun and valuable," says a senior. Other common core courses include composition and rhetoric as well as quantitative reasoning for freshmen, a sophomore seminar on multiculturalism in the United States, and a junior-year program in experiential learning. Students also take foreign language courses and complete a series of "learning domains," consisting of arts and literature, philosophical inquiry, religious dimensions, scientific inquiry, social science, and history.

> "[The Discover Chicago] class is one of the best things about DePaul."

DePaul's name is closely associated with Midwestern business and law, and undergraduates can find internships with local legal and commercial institutions. The most popular majors include public relations and advertising, finance, accounting, and psychology. The School of Accountancy and MIS is reported to be the most challenging department in the Driehaus College of Business. The College of Communication offers majors in journalism, public relations and advertising, communication and media, and others. The College of Science and Health encompasses programs in biology, chemistry, physics, nursing, psychology, environmental science, math, and statistics. The college also includes the health sciences program, which prepares students for a variety of health care professions by "combining biomedical instruction and preparation for medical practice with an understanding of how societal factors impact health." The School of Cinematic Arts has teamed up with Cinespace Chicago, the city's premier movie studio, to create a learning environment that provides students with film and television production experience in the midst of a working studio.

"The courseload is rigorous at times, but if a student is dedicated to their studies, it is nothing that can't be handled," says a senior. Classes are often small, with 35 percent enrolling fewer than 20 students, and professors teach at all levels. The administration appoints student representatives from each school and college to faculty promotion and tenure committees. "DePaul professors are respectful, intelligent, and don't put up with nonsense," says one senior. The highly selective honors program includes interdisciplinary courses, a modern language requirement, and a senior thesis. Seventeen percent of students participate in study abroad programs that take them to more than 40 locations around the world, including Paris, Nairobi, Istanbul, and Buenos Aires.

> "DePaul professors are respectful, intelligent, and don't put up with nonsense."

DePaul's president is a priest, and clerics teach some courses and celebrate (voluntary) mass every day. In addition, the University Ministry hosts other religious services and leads programs to teach students about other faiths. Seventy-six percent of DePaul undergraduates hail from Illinois, and less than 1 percent come from foreign countries. Hispanics represent 18 percent of the student body, African Americans 8 percent, and Asian Americans 8 percent. DePaul hopes to boost those figures by reaching out to disadvantaged inner-city students with high academic potential. Thirty-three percent of current students are eligible for Pell Grants. "The students

The School of Cinematic Arts has teamed up with Cinespace Chicago to provide students with experience in a working studio.

(continued)

ACT Ranges: 22–28
Financial Aid: 67%
Pell Grant: 33%
Expense: Pr $
Student Loans: 68%
Average Debt: $ $ $
Phi Beta Kappa: Yes
Applicants: 19,628
Accepted: 72%
Enrolled: 18%
Grad in 6 Years: 73%
Returning Freshmen: 84%
Academics: ✍ ✍ ✍
Social: ☎ ☎
Q of L: ★ ★ ★
Admissions: (312) 362-8300
Email Address: admission@depaul.edu

Strong Programs:
Public Relations and
    Advertising
Finance
Accounting
Psychology
Health Sciences
Film and Television
Performing Arts

at DePaul are very diverse," says a sophomore. "There are student organizations to represent all different faiths, ethnicities, and backgrounds." DePaul has a reputation for being politically liberal, and "it has become more liberal in recent years," says a junior. In addition to academic merit scholarships, DePaul also awards scholarships to students who have artistic talent or strong leadership skills or those who participate in community service; such awards average $12,944 per year. Scholarships for athletes are available too.

One student complains, "Weekends can be boring because many students go home." Traditionally, DePaul has been a commuter school, but 20 percent of undergraduates live in university housing. Students find the dorms comfortable and well maintained, but they advise applying early to secure a bed, especially after sophomore year. "Housing is in high demand around here," says a junior. The Lincoln Park campus includes eight modern co-ed dorms, several townhouses, and apartments. At the Loop campus, a 1,700-student residence hall includes a rooftop garden, fitness center, and music, art, and study rooms. Although students like campus housing, some find the food overpriced and limited. "I'm a vegan, and there is not a large or good variety," says a junior. While Chicago may have a high-crime reputation, students say campus security is visible, with officers patrolling in cars and on foot, emergency blue lights on campus, and dorms requiring students to swipe ID cards at two or three places before allowing entrance.

Fraternities and sororities draw just 3 percent of DePaul men and 6 percent of the women, respectively. Not surprisingly, with the school's proximity to Chicago's clubs (especially on Rush Street), sporting events, and bars, most social life occurs off campus. A music major says of the city, "There is everything to do here." In the warmer months, the beaches of Lake Michigan beckon downtown students, while the college's huge annual outdoor Fest concert attracts large crowds from both campuses. Alcohol policies forbid beer for underage students, but students say that enforcement doesn't always work.

> **"Weekends can be boring because many students go home."**

DePaul is a member of the Big East Conference, and the Blue Demons compete in Division I in 13 sports. Men's basketball is the headline story, beginning with the Midnight Madness of each fall's first practice in October. The game against Notre Dame always draws a capacity crowd, though Loyola is DePaul's oldest rival. Women's basketball, tennis, soccer, and softball have won Big East championships recently. Intramurals and club sports are big draws, and the Campus Recreation department offers a 123,000-square-foot fitness and recreation facility, which includes a four-court gymnasium, a pool, a 200-meter track, and more than 100 pieces of cardio and selectorized equipment.

DePaul's student body has become more diverse while increasing in size, an admirable achievement. The administration credits the school's "increased academic reputation" for growth, but students say DePaul's popularity is due as much to the special bonds they feel with fellow Blue Demons. "DePaul University provides students a unique atmosphere in which to learn and grow," says a sophomore. "The campus and its students are friendly, open, and always inviting."

Overlaps

University of Illinois at Chicago, Loyola University Chicago, University of Illinois at Urbana–Champaign, Columbia College Chicago, Illinois State, Northwestern, University of Chicago, Northern Illinois

If You Apply To ➤ **DePaul:** Early action: Nov. 15. Regular decision: Feb. 1. Financial aid: Nov. 15. No application fee. No campus or alumni interviews. SATs or ACTs: optional (test-optional applicants must respond to additional short essay questions). Subject Tests: optional. Letters of recommendation: required. Essay: required. Accepts the Common Application with supplement.

DePauw University

315 South Locust Street, P.O. Box 37, Greencastle, IN 46135

DePauw is a solid Midwestern liberal arts institution in the mold of Denison, Dickinson, Illinois Wesleyan, and Ohio Wesleyan. Its Greek system is among the strongest in the nation and full of students destined for Indiana's business and government elite. DePauw's center for management and entrepreneurship is a major draw for career-oriented students.

DePauw University offers a liberal arts education with an orientation toward experiential learning. The economics and management, natural sciences, and arts departments are solid, and the university produces a high number of Fulbright Scholars. Students here are career-oriented and happy to take advantage of the rigorous classwork and ample real-world experiences. And with an undergraduate population of just over 2,200 students, close ties to classmates and faculty are a given.

Founded in 1837 and named after the first American bishop of the Methodist Church, DePauw is set amid the gently rolling hills of west-central Indiana. The lush green campus has a mix of older buildings and more modern redbrick structures, centered on a well-kept, 520-acre park with nature trails. Notable facilities include the Prindle Institute for Ethics, the Green Center for the Performing Arts, and the Percy L. Julian Science and Mathematics Center, named after the DePauw alumnus and famous African American chemist. DePauw has significantly upgraded its physical campus in recent years in accordance with a master plan that includes renovation of the library and student union and redesign of the East College Lawn as a center of community life.

DePauw's first-year program helps students transition into college by combining academically challenging coursework with cocurricular activities and programs. Before they arrive, students are assigned to mentor-groups with 10 to 12 peers, plus an upperclassman advisor and a faculty member who will teach their first-year seminar and serve as their academic advisor until they declare a major. By graduation, students must demonstrate competence in writing, quantitative reasoning, and oral communication; fulfill a Power, Privilege, and Diversity requirement; and complete an international experience. Additionally, students must complete two Extended Study experiences, which may include courses taken during the month-long Winter or May terms, independent study or research, off-campus study, service-learning projects, or internships.

> "[Class discussions] more closely model academic conversations than traditional lectures."

Academically, the DePauw student body is as career-oriented as they come in a liberal arts college. Aspiring business leaders benefit from courses, speakers, and internships offered through the McDermond Center for Management and Entrepreneurship. Future reporters, editors, anchors, and producers will find a home in the Pulliam Center for Contemporary Media, which supplements DePauw's strong student-run newspaper, TV station, and radio stations. DePauw's School of Music is also worth a mention, offering a five-year dual-degree program in music performance/liberal arts, as well as opportunities for all students to take lessons, join ensembles, and perform, in genres from orchestra to jazz to opera. The most popular majors include biology, biochemistry, communication and theatre, creative writing, economics, political science, and psychology, and students may also design their own majors. Students say that the classes are rigorous but well supported. "The classroom environment is highly collaborative and encouraging,"

Website: www.depauw.edu
Location: Small Town
Private
Total Enrollment: 2,220
Undergraduates: 2,220
Male/Female: 46/54
SAT Ranges: CR 510–620, M 550–670
ACT Ranges: 25–29
Financial Aid: 98%
Pell Grant: 21%
Expense: Pr $ $ $
Student Loans: 49%
Average Debt: $ $
Phi Beta Kappa: Yes
Applicants: 5,182
Accepted: 65%
Enrolled: 18%
Grad in 6 Years: 80%
Returning Freshmen: 94%
Academics: ✍ ✍ ✍ ½
Social: ☎ ☎ ☎
Q of L: ★ ★
Admissions: (765) 658-4006
Email Address: admission@depauw.edu

Strong Programs:
Biology
Biochemistry
Communication and Theatre
Creative Writing
Economics
Political Science
Psychology
Music

says one sophomore, "and in many courses the students and professors engage in class discussions that more closely model academic conversations than traditional lectures." Another student adds, "I have been lucky to have professors that care about my education."

For exceptionally motivated students, four Fellows programs offer the chance to focus on an area of interest: media, management, scientific research, or the environment. Each involves a semester-long internship or research experience and opportunities to interact with top scholars and industry leaders both on and off campus. Participants in the Honor Scholars Program embark on interdisciplinary study and complete a capstone thesis. Approximately 40 percent of DePauw students study off campus for a semester or year, and many more participate in shorter, faculty-led programs during the Winter and May terms. The school's membership in the Great Lakes Colleges Association* expands students' study abroad options.

One student describes her peers at DePauw as "intellectually curious, philanthropically minded, and socially active." Sixty-three percent of students are from out of state, and 8 percent are international. The minority presence has grown, thanks in part to recruitment of Posse Foundation students from New York and Chicago. African Americans now account for 5 percent of the student body, Hispanics 4 percent, and Asian Americans 4 percent. Twenty-one percent of incoming freshmen receive Pell Grants. Merit scholarships averaging $16,483 are available, although there are no athletic scholarships. Three-quarters of DePauw students volunteer with area churches and social service agencies, which can also help them qualify for scholarships.

Ninety-seven percent of DePauw students live in university housing, which is guaranteed for four years. Options include residence halls, suites, apartments, and college-owned houses, as well as Greek chapter houses. The homey buildings have computer labs, common areas, and TV lounges; students recommend Humbert Hall for freshmen because of its hotel-like atmosphere. A whopping 79 percent of DePauw's men and 67 percent of the women go Greek. That's not surprising: the first modern-day sorority, Kappa Alpha Theta, began here in 1870, and the university is home to the longest continually running fraternity anywhere.

> "[Students are] intellectually curious, philanthropically minded, and socially active."

"Students love being at DePauw on the weekends," says a student. Perhaps because of the prevalence of Greeks on campus, and spurred by the disciplining several years ago of a sorority accused of purging its overweight members, Greek groups have worked hard to change the stereotypes of fraternities and sororities. They've devised a risk-management policy and instituted a community council to review conduct violations. In addition, rush is delayed until second semester so freshmen can first get their feet on the ground academically. Fraternities still maintain the old custom of having "house moms." Still, students say it's easy for underage drinkers to imbibe, especially at fraternity parties. Off campus, however, fake IDs "get confiscated quicker than you can take them out," one student warns.

The town of Greencastle has a movie theater, a bowling alley, and several pizza places and restaurants, but it "lacks an atmosphere," says a student. "It is fine for sustaining day-to-day living, but doesn't offer many alternatives to the university." In good weather, several state parks offer hiking trails and a lake for the sailing club. Indianapolis is only a 45-minute drive, and St. Louis, Chicago, and Cincinnati make for good road trips. A cherished tradition is a takeoff on Indiana University's famed Little 500 bike race, itself a takeoff on the Indianapolis 500 auto race—teams of cyclists compete on a course that circles the heart of the DePauw campus.

Everyone gets excited about varsity athletics, especially the annual football game against Wabash College, derisively dubbed the "Wallies." The Wabash–DePauw

Fellows programs in media, management, scientific research, and the environment involve a semester-long internship or research experience.

A whopping 79 percent of DePauw's men and 67 percent of the women go Greek.

rivalry is the oldest west of the Alleghenies, and the winner of each year's contest gets the much-cherished Monon Bell, hence the popular T-shirt: "Beat the bell out of Wabash." Women's basketball has brought home the Division III national championship twice in the last several years. Other competitive Tigers teams include men's and women's cross-country, tennis, and golf and women's soccer. Intramural sports are popular, and students stay fit in the new, two-story Welch Fitness Center.

For a small school, DePauw offers a multitude of opportunities, balancing strong academics with a healthy dose of school spirit and a wealth of opportunities to lead—whether in one of the abundant extracurricular activities or by blazing a trail through study abroad.

If You Apply To ➤

DePauw: Early decision: Nov. 1. Early action: Dec. 1. Regular decision and financial aid: Feb. 1. No application fee. Campus interviews: recommended, evaluative. Alumni interviews: optional, evaluative. SATs or ACTs: required. Subject Tests: optional. Letters of recommendation: required. Essay: required. Accepts the Common Application.

Dickinson College

P.O. Box 1773, Carlisle, PA 17013

With traditions dating to the 18th century, Dickinson occupies a historic setting in the foothills of central Pennsylvania. "Engage the World" model emphasizes international studies, foreign languages, and study abroad, while student-run organic farm signals push for sustainable development. With underrepresented minorities, international students, and hippies now more numerous, Dickinson is shedding its image as a preppy haven. Competes head to head with nearby Gettysburg.

Dickinson College won its charter just six days after the Treaty of Paris recognized the United States as a sovereign nation in 1783, and this small liberal arts school has been blazing trails ever since. The moving force behind it was Dr. Benjamin Rush, the famous physician and signer of the Declaration of Independence who convinced John Dickinson, the then governor of Pennsylvania, to lend his name to the new school. Now, administrators are focused on diversity, global education, and attracting the best and brightest academic talent. "Dickinson is such a perfect school for students who are looking to find their passion," offers one junior.

Almost all of Dickinson's Georgian buildings are carved from gray limestone from the college's own quarry, which lends a certain architectural consistency. The campus is part of the historic district of Carlisle, an economically prosperous central Pennsylvania county seat nestled in a fertile valley. The newest addition to campus is the 29,000-square-foot Kline Squash Court and Fitness Center.

To help students understand how the liberal arts fit into the broader world, Dickinson requires distribution courses in the arts and humanities; social sciences and laboratory sciences; writing; quantitative reasoning; sustainability; and physical education. Required cross-cultural studies courses include comparative civilizations, United States diversity, and a foreign language. The required First-Year Seminar introduces new students to college-level writing and critical thinking, with interdisciplinary courses such as Digital Culture, Food Justice, and Molecules of Madness. Eighty-five percent of students also complete a capstone program.

> **"Dickinson is such a perfect school for students who are looking to find their passion."**

Website: www.dickinson.edu
Location: Small Town
Private
Total Enrollment: 2,370
Undergraduates: 2,370
Male/Female: 42/58
SAT Ranges: CR 590–680, M 600–700
ACT Ranges: 27–30
Financial Aid: 76%
Pell Grant: 10%
Expense: Pr $ $ $ $
Student Loans: 55%
Average Debt: $ $ $
Phi Beta Kappa: Yes
Applicants: 6,031
Accepted: 47%
Enrolled: 26%
Grad in 6 Years: 85%
Returning Freshmen: 92%
Academics: 🖉 🖉 🖉 🖉
Social: ☎ ☎ ☎

Dickinson is best known for its workshop approach to science education, for its outstanding and comprehensive international education program, and for the depth of its foreign language program, with more than a dozen languages offered, including Arabic, Chinese, Japanese, Hebrew, Italian, and Portuguese. International business and management, Dickinson's most popular major, includes coursework in economics, history, and financial analysis, as well as internships and overseas education. Other popular majors include psychology, economics, and biology.

Students can affect global change in social justice and cultural understanding through women's, gender, and sexuality studies, and they gain a hands-on understanding of human culture and behavior by studying archaeology in an on-campus simulation lab and through off-campus fieldwork in locations such as Mycenae, Greece. They bring their work to life by staging productions at Dickinson's own Mathers Theatre or curating an art exhibition at the Trout Gallery. Several interdisciplinary programs, such as neuroscience and workshop physics, incorporate opportunities to conduct research with faculty, and a number of certificate programs are available too, focusing on urgent and emerging issues, including security studies, health studies, and social innovation and entrepreneurship. A 3–3 program with Penn State's Dickinson School of Law allows students to obtain undergraduate and J.D. degrees in six years.

Academics are demanding and can get competitive in some majors. "The academic climate can become intense during the midterms and finals week. Especially during those times, students come together to support one another," says one junior.

"Most professors that I have had are experts in their fields and are passionate about the academic growth of their students."

Seventy-five percent of classes have fewer than 20 students, allowing freshmen easy access to their professors. A psychology and biology double major says, "Most professors that I have had are experts in their fields and are passionate about the academic growth of their students. Full professors commonly teach introductory level classes." Career services get less enthusiastic reviews, and a psychology major comments, "The Career Center is helpful for some individuals and not others, and heavily helps out majors that the college is interested in promoting."

Dickinson sponsors more than 40 study abroad programs, many of them faculty-directed, in 24 countries on six continents; 56 percent of students participate. Options include academic year programs, semester programs, summer programs, Globally Integrated courses that include a January international field experience, and specialized programs such as the Mosaic Program, which combines domestic study with international study. About half of all students complete internships, where they may learn about stock trading at a brokerage firm, assist a judge in a common pleas court, or work with the editorial staff of a magazine. Undergraduate research involves 34 percent of students, typically as part of a senior project or an independent study.

Dickinson is known for the depth of its foreign language program, offering more than a dozen languages.

"Students at Dickinson are highly competitive and very hard workers," says a sophomore. Twenty percent of the student body hails from the Keystone State. African Americans account for 4 percent of the student population, Asian Americans 3 percent, and Hispanics 6 percent; international students comprise 10 percent. Dickinson has been enrolling a growing number of minority and international students, especially through partnerships with New York's Posse Foundation and the Philadelphia Futures Foundation, and with schools and foundations abroad, but some students note that the atmosphere on campus does not feel as much like an integrated community as they would like. Dickinson awards three types of merit scholarships but does not offer athletic scholarships.

Given that only seniors are allowed to live off campus and Dickinson guarantees four years of housing, 94 percent of students remain in the dorms. "Freshman dorms have small rooms but they can be made quite comfortable," says a freshman.

Additional housing options include small houses and apartments, as well as a formerly abandoned factory that the college transformed into a combination of art studios and loft-style apartments for upperclassmen. About half of freshmen choose to participate in living/learning communities, as extensions of the First-Year Seminar program. The college farm manages 50 acres and supplies produce to the dining halls and a local food bank. It also serves as a classroom and work-study opportunity for students interested in sustainable development. "Dining services has a rotating menu so that the options always change," says one junior, and aside from the main cafeteria, there are café and snack-bar options. Students report feeling safe on campus, and the Prevention, Education, and Advocacy Center (PEAC) offers comprehensive education and training related to sexual assault.

"Whether it is a club, a sport, or a floor in your dorm, you must get involved in something to have a good social life," advises a political science major. Fraternities and sororities attract 14 percent of the men and 26 percent of the women, and they throw open parties in houses that are owned and maintained by the college. Monitors check IDs at parties, kegs aren't permitted in any college housing, and four underage drinking incidents will get you suspended. "Drinking and parties are a large part of the social culture on campus, especially on the weekends," says a student. At the Quarry, a former frat house, you can grab a cup of coffee, play some video games, or show your moves on the dance floor. In addition to one big concert per semester, each fall brings an arts festival, and a spring carnival gives students one last blast before finals.

> **"You must get involved in something to have a good social life."**

Carlisle is 20 miles from the Pennsylvania state capital of Harrisburg, and has plenty of "cool little shops that you wouldn't find in big cities," says a student. "It's a fun place to be," adds a senior. Big Brothers Big Sisters, the Alpha Phi Omega community service fraternity, and other programs help bring the school and community together. In the spring and early fall, Maryland and Delaware beaches beckon; they're just a two- to three-hour drive. Come winter, good skiing is half an hour away. Nature lovers will enjoy hiking the nearby Appalachian Trail. For those craving urban stimulation, the best road trips are to Philadelphia, New York, and Washington, D.C. All are accessible by bus or train—a good thing, since first-years can't have cars.

Dickinson students get riled up for any match against top rival Franklin & Marshall; the schools battle it out each year for the Conestoga Wagon trophy. The Red Devils also square off with Gettysburg College each year for the Little Brown Bucket. Men's basketball won the Centennial Conference championship in 2015, and football, women's basketball, and men's and women's cross-country are also competitive. About 16 percent of students take part in intramurals, where floor hockey, basketball, and soccer are most popular. Students may also organize club teams to compete with other schools in sports like ice hockey and ultimate Frisbee.

Although Dickinson was founded more than two centuries ago, some things remain the same. Seniors still share a champagne toast before graduation. And the steps of Old West, the first college building, are still used only twice a year—in the fall, at the convocation ceremony that welcomes new students, and in the spring, for commencement. Dickinson continues to honor Rush's global vision, with its wealth of study abroad options and its demand that students cross the traditional borders of academic disciplines to grasp the interrelated nature of knowledge.

A number of certificate programs focus on urgent and emerging issues, including security studies and health studies.

The college farm serves as a classroom and work-study opportunity for students interested in sustainable development.

Overlaps

Franklin & Marshall, Gettysburg, Lafayette, College of William and Mary, Bucknell, Skidmore, Connecticut College, University of Richmond

If You Apply To ➤

Dickinson: Early decision I: Nov. 15. Early action: Dec. 1. Early decision II: Jan. 15. Regular decision and financial aid: Feb. 1. Application fee: $65. Campus interviews: recommended, evaluative. Alumni interviews: optional, evaluative. SATs or ACTs: optional. Subject Tests: optional. Letters of recommendation: required. Essay: optional. Accepts the Common Application with supplement.

Madison, NJ 07940

From Drew's wooded perch in suburban Jersey, Manhattan is only a 30-minute train ride away. That means Wall Street and the UN are both easy destinations for Drew interns. Drew is New Jersey's only prominent liberal arts college and one of the few in the greater New York City area. More than 60 percent of the students are from Jersey, and Drew is still struggling to find a national identity.

Website: www.drew.edu
Location: Suburban
Private
Total Enrollment: 1,609
Undergraduates: 1,330
Male/Female: 38/62
SAT Ranges: CR 500–620,
    M 490–620
ACT Ranges: 22–29
Financial Aid: 96%
Pell Grant: 36%
Expense: Pr $ $ $
Student Loans: 69%
Average Debt: $ $
Phi Beta Kappa: Yes
Applicants: 3,025
Accepted: 70%
Enrolled: 17%
Grad in 6 Years: 67%
Returning Freshmen: 85%
Academics: ✎ ✎ ✎
Social: ☎ ☎ ☎
Q of L: ★ ★ ★
Admissions: (973) 408-3739
Email Address:
    cadm@drew.edu

Strong Programs:
Political Science
Economics
Psychology
Business
Theatre Arts
International Relations
English
Neuroscience

Founded more than a century ago as a Methodist university, Drew University has grown into a place where an emphasis on hands-on learning, research, independent studies, and internships is just as important as performance in the classroom. The university sends its students abroad for month-long educational ventures, promotes internships on Wall Street, and encourages theater and the arts to thrive. The university has also recently reinforced its commitment to global education and has sought to bring a much larger number of international students to campus.

The school occupies 186 acres of peaceful woodland in the upscale New York City suburb of Madison and is known as the "University in the Forest." Fifty-six campus buildings peek through splendid oak trees and boast classic and contemporary styles, a physical reflection of Drew's respect for both scholarly traditions and progressive education. The Hall of Sciences recently reopened after extensive renovations and includes a research annex, renovated biology wing, and new labs and equipment.

Drew's general education requirements include coursework in six areas: depth of study (courses within the student's chosen major); breadth of knowledge; proficiencies (writing, quantitative literacy, foreign language, and information literacy); local and global citizenship; an off-campus experience; and a first-year experience dubbed the DREW Seminar. Freshman seminar teachers escort their students on a day-long, course-related field trip to Manhattan. All students also complete a senior capstone experience. The university's commitment to liberal arts education includes the lofty goal of universal computer literacy.

Political science is Drew's strongest undergraduate department, and future politicos can take advantage of off-campus opportunities in Washington, D.C., in London, and at the United Nations in New York City. Other popular majors include economics, psychology, business, and theatre arts; programs in international relations, English, and neuroscience are also well regarded. "The courses are competitive and collaborative," observes a senior. "Professors bring in experience and new perspectives and expect students to challenge themselves." Future financiers can follow in the footsteps of the school's founder, Daniel Drew, a financier and railroad tycoon, and take advantage of the Wall Street Semester, an on-site study of the national and international finance communities. The theatre arts department works closely with the Playwrights Theatre of New Jersey to produce plays that are written, directed, and designed by students. Aspiring doctors can earn a B.A. and M.D. from Drew and the Rutgers New Jersey Medical School in seven years, and dual-degree programs are available in several other fields as well, including a newly added law program with Seton Hall.

> **"[Professors] expect students to challenge themselves."**

The Dana Research Institute for Scientists Emeriti offers opportunities for students to do research with distinguished retired industrial scientists, including William Campbell, who shared the 2015 Nobel Prize for Medicine. About 70 percent of Drew undergraduates in all fields undertake research. The Baldwin Honors program includes master classes with elite speakers, special trips, and exclusive activities. Drew's Center for Civic Engagement supports teaching, research, scholarship, art, and other university-based activities that benefit communities. Drew has long been a proponent of study abroad programs, including the Drew International Seminar program, where students study another culture in-depth on campus, then spend three to four weeks in that country. "These seminars are a great way of learning firsthand about a country and experiencing a once-in-a-lifetime chance to put your education into practice," says one student. Roughly half of all undergrads participate in a study abroad experience.

"The identity of the Drew student is difficult to pin down. We're all very different in our interests, but we're largely hardworking students, and we're very accepting of each other's interests," says one junior. Sixty-four percent of students are from New Jersey and most attended public high schools; 5 percent are international. The school continues to work on increasing its racial diversity, which has been the topic of many student-led discussions as of late; 10 percent of students are African American, 10 percent are Hispanic, and 6 percent are Asian American. "My favorite thing about Drew is that although people are politically and socially active, they are more interested in listening to what others have to say than in projecting their own opinions," says a senior. Thirty-six percent of freshmen are eligible for Pell Grants. Merit awards average $16,720, although there are no athletic scholarships available.

"[Students] are more interested in listening to what others have to say than in projecting their own opinions."

Seventy-six percent of the students live in university housing, which includes both single-sex and co-ed dorms, theme houses, and, for upperclassmen, townhouses. "The rooms are extremely nice for college dorms and I've never had a problem getting a room," says a student. A lottery gives housing preference to seniors and juniors, and most freshmen reside in dorms situated at the back of campus. All first-years take part in living/learning communities. Drew's dining options receive modest reviews, but one student points out that a "massive renovation" to The Commons "promises that dining will substantially improve." The university recently hired a Title IX coordinator to handle sexual assault on campus, and students take a Drew the Right Thing training program that involves a pledge to stand up against sexual assault.

With no Greek life, a sophomore explains, "The athletic teams and theatre groups hold the most vibrant parties on campus," and for those who don't care to party, "Our Office of Student Activities supplements student-run programming by bringing in comedians, musicians, slam poets, and other performers every Thursday to engage the community." There is a 21-and-over pub on campus, as well as two coffeehouses. New York City's Pennsylvania Station is less than an hour away by commuter train, and Philadelphia, the Jersey shore, and the Delaware River are close by. The Shakespeare Theatre of New Jersey is in residence on campus part of every year and offers both performances and internships. The First Annual Picnic, held on the last day of classes and numbered like Super Bowls (spring 2017 marked FAP XLIV), provides an opportunity to enjoy live music and food. On Multicultural Awareness Day, students are excused from one day of classes to celebrate cultural diversity by attending lectures, workshops, and social events.

"The athletic teams and theatre groups hold the most vibrant parties on campus."

Approximately 50 percent of students volunteer in local and international activities such as Mentors at Drew and the Honduras Project, in which a group of Drew students travel to Honduras to help at an orphanage. The commuter town of Madison doesn't have the amenities of larger metropolitan areas, of course, but there are several unique shops and restaurants within walking distance of campus. One student says the town "is a nice college town according to my parents, but not to students. Everything closes up pretty early." Nearby Morristown is more of a college place.

Interest in the school's 20 Division III varsity teams has grown as the Rangers have become more successful. Men's tennis won 13 consecutive conference titles from 2000 through 2013. Women's lacrosse and men's and women's soccer are also strong, and the competitive men's and women's fencing teams beat and parry with the likes of Duke and Cornell. Intramural and club sports range from flag football and basketball to belly dancing and rugby, and special recreation events like Hunger Games Dodgeball and the Rock Paper Scissors Tournament are student favorites.

At Drew, "It's easy to get involved, make friends, and feel like you make a difference," says a senior. Indeed, Drew offers its small body of students a wide range of opportunities and plenty of personal attention in a classic liberal arts structure. Above all, says one international relations major, "A culture of understanding, open-mindedness, and accepting others is *the* Drew culture." Not too bad for a school in the forest.

If You Apply To ➤

Drew: Early decision I: Nov. 15. Early decision II: Jan. 15. Regular decision: Feb. 1. Financial aid: Feb. 15. Housing: Jun. 1. Application fee: $60. Campus and alumni interviews: optional, evaluative. SATs or ACTs: optional. No Subject Tests. Letters of recommendation: required. Essay: required. Accepts the Common Application.

Drexel University

3141 Chestnut Street, Philadelphia, PA 19104

Drexel is a streetwise, no-nonsense technical university in the heart of Philadelphia. Like Lehigh, Drexel also offers programs in business and arts and sciences, and its most distinctive offering is the Westphal College of Media Arts and Design. A financial bargain compared to other leading technical schools, Drexel has abandoned its aggressive expansion plans and in-your-face recruitment style of recent years in order to increase yield and graduation rates. Check out the co-op program.

Website: www.drexel.edu
Location: City Center
Private
Total Enrollment: 18,677
Undergraduates: 14,060
Male/Female: 57/43
SAT Ranges: CR 530–630, M 565–680
ACT Ranges: 25–30
Financial Aid: 87%
Pell Grant: 26%
Expense: Pr $ $ $ $
Student Loans: 60%
Average Debt: N/A
Phi Beta Kappa: Yes
Applicants: 28,758
Accepted: 75%

For career-minded students who want to bypass the soul-searching of their liberal arts counterparts, Drexel University offers both solid academics and an innovative co-op education that combines high-tech academics with paying job opportunities—a mix that's particularly appealing in today's economic reality. "If you want a good job, you go to Drexel and you do co-op," asserts a student.

"Drexel's campus is impressive for its downtown Philadelphia location, with gardens and greenery on every block," says a student, "but the campus is woven tightly into the fabric of the city." Drexel's 123-acre campus, which is adjacent to the University of Pennsylvania, is condensed into about a 20-block radius. It lies in a formerly crime-ridden neighborhood that is now one of the most desirable parts of Philadelphia, with plenty of restaurants and stores. A neighborhood remake will include a $3.5 billion "Innovation Neighborhood" along the Schuylkill River rail yards that will house new research facilities and incubator space. The campus's older buildings are simple and made of brick; most are modern and in good condition. Additional facilities include the Center City campus for the College of Nursing and Health Professions.

Cooperative education is the hallmark of Drexel's curriculum, which alternates periods of full-time study and full-time employment for four or five years, providing students with six to 18 months of job experience before they graduate. The co-op possibilities, which 91 percent of undergraduates take advantage of, are unlimited: students can co-op virtually anywhere in the country or in 45 international locations. Freshman and senior years of the five-year programs are spent on campus, and the three intervening years (sophomore, prejunior, and junior) usually consist of six months of work and six months of school. A 10-week preparatory course covers such topics as skills assessment, ethics in the workplace, résumé writing, interviewing skills, and stress management. Most co-ops are paid, and the median six-month salary for co-op students is just over $17,000. And although some students complain that jobs can turn out to be six months of busywork, most enjoy making important contacts in their potential fields and learning while earning.

To accommodate the co-op students, Drexel operates year-round. "I would describe the climate as intense but manageable," says one senior. "Being on a quarter system is rigorous at times." Flexibility in requirements varies by college, but in the first year everyone must take freshman seminar, English composition, mathematics, and Cooperative Education 101.

"The campus is woven tightly into the fabric of the city."

Engineering majors must also complete the Drexel Engineering Curriculum, which integrates math, physics, chemistry, and engineering to make sure that even techies enter the workforce well rounded and able to write as well as they can compute and design. Students enjoy the 700,000-volume library, which offers good hours and lots of room for studying. What's more, each entering freshman is assigned a "personal librarian" charged with helping them make the best use of library facilities. Professors receive high praise from most, and are noted for their accessibility and warmth. Says one student, "The only things that teaching assistants run are labs and study sessions." Fifty-eight percent of classes have fewer than 20 students.

The most popular majors are mechanical engineering, computer science, finance, and biological sciences. Drexel's greatest strength is its engineering college, which churns out more than 1 percent of all the nation's engineering graduates, B.S. through Ph.D. The materials science, electrical, and architectural engineering pro-

"It's hard to get people involved because of the amount of schoolwork and co-ops."

grams are particular standouts. Game design and production, business analytics, and nursing are other noteworthy programs, and the College of Arts and Sciences is well recognized for theoretical and atmospheric physics. Recent academic changes include a new Department of Biodiversity, Earth, and Environmental Science.

Drexel is shedding its long-standing reputation as an easy-admission commuter college. Forty-two percent of freshmen graduated in the top 10th of their high school class. According to one sophomore, Drexel students are "not afraid of hard work because we do it all the time, even when we're exhausted." The undergraduate student body is 39 percent Pennsylvanian, with another large chunk of students from adjacent New Jersey. The international student population is 15 percent. Asian Americans comprise 14 percent, African Americans 6 percent, and Hispanics 6 percent. The student body tends to lean right politically, and one student says, "This is a science and technology school full of conservative students who don't really have the time to worry about liberal issues." Twenty-six percent of freshmen are Pell-eligible. In addition to need-based financial aid, merit scholarships averaging $14,589 and 161 athletic scholarships are awarded to qualified students.

Freshmen live in one of nine co-ed residence halls, including a luxurious highrise, but many upperclassmen reside in nearby apartments or the fraternities, which are frequently cheaper and more private than university housing. Overall, 26 percent

(continued)

Enrolled: 13%
Grad in 6 Years: 67%
Returning Freshmen: 85%
Academics: ✍ ✍ ✍
Social: ☎ ☎
Q of L: ★ ★ ★
Admissions: (800) 2-DREXEL
Email Address:
  enroll@drexel.edu

Strong Programs:
Engineering
Computer Science
Finance
Biological Sciences
Game Design and Production
Business Analytics
Nursing
Physics

Ninety-one percent of undergraduates complete co-ops, and can do so virtually anywhere in the country or in 45 international locations.

of the students live in the dorms; another third commute to campus from home. Students say the cafeteria offers a variety of "adequate" food, but it's far away from the dorms. Another dining center opened in 2015. While on-campus freshmen are forced to sign up for a meal plan, most upperclassmen make their own meals; the dorms have cooking facilities on each floor. If all else fails, nomadic food trucks park around campus, providing quick lunches. Students are encouraged to use a shuttle bus between the library and dorms at night, and access to dorms, the library, and the physical education center is restricted to students with IDs, so most say they feel safe on campus.

With so many students living off campus and the city of Philadelphia at their disposal, Drexel tends to be a bit deserted on weekends. A student notes, "In a single weekend, I may play paintball in the Poconos, swim at the Jersey shore, see an opera in Philadelphia, and go mountain biking in nearby Wissahickon Park." Friday-night flicks on campus are cheap and popular with those who stay around, and dorms sponsor floor parties. The dozen or so fraternities, which recruit 12 percent of the men, also contribute to the party scene, especially freshman year,

> **"Drexel graduates are surely among the most capable and motivated individuals I have ever met."**

but the handful of smaller sororities, which attract 11 percent of the women, has little impact. "Greek life is relatively small, so there are plenty of other ways to be involved socially," a senior says. "There's no pressure to drink," says a communication major, and campus policies are strict; dorms require those of age to sign in alcohol and limit the quantities they may bring in.

Drexel's co-op program often undermines any sense of class unity and can strain personal relationships. Activities that depend on some continuity of enrollment for success—music, drama, student government, athletics—suffer most. "It's hard to get people involved because of the amount of schoolwork and co-ops," says one student. Even so, the university sponsors 18 Division I teams, competing in the Colonial Athletic Association. There is no football team, but the Dragons men's and women's basketball, crew, and soccer teams are strong. "Our biggest rivalry is our feud with Delaware," admits one frenzied student. "We delight in sacrificing blue plastic chickens!"—Delaware's mascot. An extensive intramural program serves all students, and joggers can head for the steps of the Philadelphia Art Museum, just as Rocky did in the movies. Students take full advantage of their urban location by frequenting clubs, restaurants, cultural attractions, and shopping malls in Philadelphia, easily accessible by public transportation.

Aspiring poets, musicians, and historians may find Drexel a bit confusing. But for future computer scientists, engineers, and other technically oriented minds, the university's unique approach to learning inside and outside the classroom could give your career a fantastic jump-start. As one satisfied student explains, "The terms are intense, the activities unlimited, but Drexel graduates are surely among the most capable and motivated individuals I have ever met. When I graduate, I will be prepared and proud of it."

Overlaps

Penn State, Syracuse, University of Pittsburgh, George Washington, Temple, Rochester Institute of Technology

If You Apply To ➤ **Drexel:** Early decision and early action: Nov. 1. Regular decision: Jan. 15. Financial aid: Feb. 15. Housing: May 1. Application fee: $50. Campus interviews: optional, evaluative. No alumni interviews. SATs or ACTs or two Subject Tests or two AP Exams or two IB Higher Level Exams: required. Letters of recommendation: required. Essay: required. Accepts the Common Application. Apply to particular school or program.

Duke University

2138 Campus Drive, Durham, NC 27708

What fun to be at Duke—face painted blue, rocking Cameron Indoor Stadium as the Blue Devils win again. Duke is the most prestigious private university in the South— more selective than Rice and Vanderbilt, and academically competitive with the Ivies and Stanford. Strong in engineering as well as the humanities, it offers public policy and economics rather than business. Big emphasis on community service and study across disciplines. Serious efforts to attract more first-gen students.

Duke University is one of the few elite U.S. colleges where strong academics and championship-caliber sports teams manage to coexist. It might be south of the Mason-Dixon Line, and may seem a bit wet behind the ears compared to those ancient and prestigious Northeastern schools known for the erstwhile foliage on their walls, but Duke competes with them and wins its fair share of intellectually serious super-achievers, as well as lots of top athletes. One senior says Duke offers plenty to cheer about, including "a diverse student body, challenging academics, world-renowned professors, research opportunities, and an immense amount of school spirit."

Founded in 1838 as the Union Institute (later Trinity College), Duke University is young for a school of its stature. It sprouted up in 1924, thanks to a stack of tobacco-stained dollars called the Duke Endowment. Duke's campus in the lush forest of the North Carolina Piedmont is divided into two main sections, West and East. With 8,300 acres of adjacent forest, it offers enough open space to satisfy even the most diehard outdoors enthusiast. West Campus, the hub of the university, is laid out in spacious quadrangles and dominated by the impressive Gothic chapel, a symbol of the university's Methodist tradition. Constructed in the 1930s, West includes collegiate Gothic residential and classroom quads, the administration building, Perkins Library (with almost six million volumes, nearly 18 million manuscripts, and two million public documents), and the student union. East Campus, built in the 1920s, consists primarily of Georgian redbrick buildings. East and West are connected by shuttle buses, though many students enjoy the mile-or-so walk or bike ride between them along wooded Campus Drive. With the recent recession over, the campus is now a massive construction site.

Students opt for one of two undergraduate schools: the Pratt School of Engineering and Trinity College of Arts & Sciences (the latter resulted from a merger in the 1970s of the previously separate men's and women's liberal arts colleges). The school's engineering programs—particularly electrical and biomedical—are national standouts. Natural sciences, most notably ecology, biology, and neuroscience, are also first-rate. The proximity of the Medical Center enhances study in biochemistry and pharmacology. Public policy attracts the most majors, followed by economics, biology, and biomedical engineering.

Duke's Sanford School of Public Policy offers an interdisciplinary major—unusual at the undergraduate level—that trains aspiring public servants in the machinations of the media, nonprofit organizations, government agencies, and other bodies that govern public life. Internships and apprenticeships are a big part of the program. Duke's dance program is notable, but students say the language offerings can be weak. Duke has more than 60 interdisciplinary centers, including the Duke Global Health Institute, the Nicholas Institute for Environmental Policy Solutions, and the John Hope Franklin Humanities Institute.

Trinity College's curriculum, part of the traditional undergraduate coursework known as Program I, requires courses in five general areas of knowledge: arts,

Website: www.duke.edu
Location: Small City
Private
Total Enrollment: 14,950
Undergraduates: 6,485
Male/Female: 51/49
SAT Ranges: CR 670–760, M 690–790
ACT Ranges: 31–34
Financial Aid: 43%
Pell Grant: 12%
Expense: Pr $ $ $ $
Student Loans: 35%
Average Debt: $
Phi Beta Kappa: Yes
Applicants: 30,112
Accepted: 12%
Enrolled: 49%
Grad in 6 Years: 95%
Returning Freshmen: 97%
Academics: ✍ ✍ ✍ ✍ ✍
Social: ☎ ☎ ☎ ☎
Q of L: ★ ★ ★ ★
Admissions: (919) 684-3214
Email Address: undergrad-admissions@duke.edu

Strong Programs:
Public Policy
Economics
Biology
Biomedical Engineering
Electrical Engineering
Ecology
Neuroscience
Dance

literature, and performance; civilizations; social sciences; natural sciences; and quantitative studies. Students must also fulfill requirements in six modes of inquiry, including foreign language, writing, research, and ethical inquiry. All students must also complete three Small Group Learning Experiences: one seminar course during the freshman year—offered in topics such as Imagining Dinosaurs and The Psychology of Social Influence—and two more as upperclassmen. Students must finish 34 courses to graduate; those who wish to explore subjects outside and between usual majors and minors may choose Program II, to which they are admitted after proposing a topic, question, or theme for which they plan an individualized curriculum with faculty advisors and deans.

When college counselors say Duke is hot, they're not referring to the boiling temperatures in the South. Duke competes with the Ivies and a select few other colleges for top-notch students. Courses here are rigorous, and the academic atmosphere has become more intense, particularly in the sciences and engineering. "The workload is heavy, but, because of the highly collaborative environment, it is manageable," says a public policy major. Seventy-three percent of classes have fewer than 20 students, and the university focuses resources on undergraduate education and having senior professors teach more classes. "My professors have been engaged, excited about the material, and focused on the student, not just their research," says a sophomore. A senior adds, "Faculty members are accessible, especially through a program called FLUNCH, where you are able to have a meal with a faculty member on Duke's dime." Duke's former president, lured from Yale, made the expansion of interdisciplinary work—already part of the Duke culture—a priority for faculty and students alike. The FOCUS program offers first-year students groups of seminars with 15 or fewer students clustered around a single broad, interdisciplinary theme, such as biotechnology and social change or humanitarian challenges at home and abroad; participants also live together in the same residence hall. It is "an incredible opportunity to engage with the university's top professors," a senior says. The Bass Connections program gives undergraduates a chance to work with faculty and graduate students in interdisciplinary, research-based project teams in five thematic areas: brain and society; information, society, and culture; global health; education and human development; and energy.

> "Faculty members are accessible, especially through a program called FLUNCH."

The Bass Connections program gives undergraduates a chance to work with faculty and grad students in interdisciplinary, research-based project teams.

Fifty-one percent of Duke's students study abroad, and there are ample opportunities for those who want a break from campus life without leaving the country. DukeEngage, an ambitious and innovative program backed by a $30 million endowment, makes civic engagement an integral part of the undergraduate experience. It supports students willing to spend summers working on projects ranging from building schools in Kenya to working with Gulf Coast flood victims. One-quarter of all undergrads participate in the program; it has become a centerpiece of the school's commitment to "knowledge in service to society."

"Students tend to be extremely driven, upper middle class, and focused on succeeding far after college," says one public policy studies major. Thirteen percent of Duke students are from North Carolina, and the Northeastern corridor sends a fair-sized contingent, as does California. Ten percent of undergraduates now hail from overseas. Duke's Southern gentility is reflected in campus attire, which is generally neatly pressed on guys and maybe a bit outfit-y on women, in contrast to the thrown-together antistatus uniform of jeans and sweats that dominates on some other campuses. Undergraduate women sometimes complain that they feel pressured to be "perfect" in all respects, from appearance to achievement. Despite the unmistakable air of wealth on campus, 60 percent come from public high schools. Ten percent of students are African American, 7 percent are Hispanic, and the growing Asian

American contingent has reached 22 percent. Students of different ethnicities and races tend to "self-segregate," students say, producing little tension but also little interaction. Overcoming these self-imposed barriers has been an ongoing quest for administrators and students who created a Center for Race Relations, which seeks to evaluate and improve the way Duke educates its students about diversity and conflict resolution. Also noteworthy: Duke was among the first universities to include in their admissions application an optional short essay question in which applicants can discuss their sexual, gender, or other identities.

Duke admits students without regard to financial need and meets 100 percent of their demonstrated need. The university has eliminated loans from financial aid packages for families with incomes below $40,000 a year, and families with incomes below $60,000 a year are not expected to contribute to the cost of tuition. Like other Division I universities, Duke hands out lots of athletic scholarships. Duke offers a small number of merit scholarships, including full-tuition scholarships offered through the Washington Duke Scholars Program, established in 2016 for high-achieving, first-generation students from low-income backgrounds. Incoming Washington Duke Scholars participate in a six-week summer academic program, receive personal mentoring from top faculty, and take special seminars during the academic year.

The Washington Duke Scholars Program offers full-tuition scholarships to first-generation students from low-income backgrounds.

Duke undergrads are required to live on campus for three years; overall, 82 percent stay in university-owned housing. Students live in residence halls or quads that house both independent students and members of selective living groups such as fraternities. Freshmen all reside in dorms on the East Campus led by a faculty member and his or her family. The decision to have all freshmen live on the East Campus was aimed at making it easier to adjust to academic life and insulating them from the wilder aspects of Duke's vigorous social scene. "The dorms look like castles on the outside and feel like *Harry Potter*," says a junior, who adds that the new dorms "are like five-star hotels." Sophomores move to West Campus, where there are also special-interest dorms focused on themes such as women's studies, the arts, languages, and community service. Seniors can move off campus, but "the apartments vary in quality." One student says, "Campus security is nice and makes me feel safe for the most part."

"The dorms look like castles on the outside and feel like *Harry Potter*."

Duke has been engaged in a massive physical expansion over the last few years aimed at enhancing students' creature comforts, including a 70,000-square-foot, state-of-the-art Health and Wellness Center. The glass-fronted West Union, recently reopened after a three-year renovation funded by an $80 million grant, is home to an over-the-top collection of dining options operated by local chefs and restaurateurs that, consistent with Durham's reputation as a foodie destination, the university trumpets as offering the most lavish (and, students say, costly) dining on any college campus. Off-campus restaurants—many of which will deliver—are linked to the Duke meal plan. A percentage of unused "money" from prepaid meal cards is refunded at the end of the semester, a rare and much-appreciated policy.

"There is a strong drinking and party culture on campus, though students are not pressured to participate."

"Duke students are the type who will start a club if they are interested in something that nobody else is doing, work hard on a paper late into the night, and then go out Thursday, Friday, and Saturday," says a public policy major. Students agree that most social life takes place on campus or in surrounding houses and apartments. Although it has been pushed away from the center of campus, "the Greek scene dominates," says a history major. Fraternities and sororities attract 29 percent of the men and 42 percent of the women, respectively. Fraternity parties are open to everyone, and the free shuttle bus service that connects the school's various dorm and apartment complexes runs until 4 a.m., making it easy to socialize in rooms or suites. There are three tightly regulated bars on campus, including the Washington Duke Inn, for students who are of age to drink. "There is a strong drinking and party culture on campus, though students are not pressured to participate," one sophomore reports.

Duke is also a culturally active campus; theater groups thrive, and the relatively new Nasher Museum of Art, with its world-class exhibits by Picasso, Calder, and El Greco, among others, has become a popular social hub. During the summer, Duke plays host to the splendid American Dance Festival. The popular Springternational festival brings in live bands and vendors peddling local crafts and exotic foods each spring, and the traditional Joe College Day has been revived as a daylong fall affair filled with food, arts and crafts, and music. Popular road trips include Franklin Street in nearby Chapel Hill, home of archrival UNC, and Raleigh, the state capital and home of North Carolina State University. In warm weather, the broad beaches on North Carolina's outer banks are two to three hours away, while winter ski slopes are three to four hours distant.

Durham is a small, working-class city that has had its share of racial tensions but also boasts a vibrant African American middle class and good political leadership. The contrast between Duke's wealth and the economic depression afflicting some of Durham's residents is obvious. But Duke as an institution has been active in the community, especially in public schools, and hundreds of undergrads are involved in service learning, tutoring, and related activities. "Everyone is involved in volunteer work," says one student. Downtown Durham is undergoing a revival, with old tobacco warehouses being converted into restaurants, stores, offices, and apartments. The *New York Times* frequently writes up Durham as a foodie destination. Students have access to discounted tickets to traveling Broadway shows at the state's largest performing arts center. During the basketball season, men's games sell out, and the town is proud of its Durham Bulls, the local minor-league baseball team, which coined the term "bullpen." No one misses the irony of the fact that Durham, once known as the "City of Tobacco," now bills itself as the "City of Medicine." Durham includes most of the Research Triangle Park, the largest research center of its kind in the world. Duke, North Carolina State, and the University of North Carolina at Chapel Hill created the park for nonprofit, scientific, and sociological research. Many Silicon Valley technology companies have East Coast outposts in the park, which has helped make the Raleigh-Durham area one of the most productive regions in the nation, with the highest percentage of Ph.D.s per capita in the United States.

Duke's official motto is *Eruditio et Religio* only to a few straitlaced administrators; everyone else knows it as *Eruditio et Basketballio*, which translates more or less as "Go to hell, Carolina"—meaning UNC at Chapel Hill, Duke's archrival in the rough-and-tough Atlantic Coast Conference. At games, students transform into the legendary Cameron Crazies and get the best courtside seats, where they make life miserable for the visiting team. Their efforts paid off in 2015 when the Blue Devils won the national Division I men's basketball championship for the fifth time under fabled coach Mike Krzyzewski. Sports-crazed Blue Devils erect a temporary tent city—dubbed "Krzyzewskiville"—to vie for the best seats. This is far from "roughing it"—students form groups to hold their places so that some fraction can go to class and keep their peers on track academically while those who hold down the fort check their email through wireless connections. "There is something magical about Duke basketball, and the feeling of being in the student section with the Cameron Crazies

West Union is home to a collection of dining options operated by local chefs and restaurateurs, offering the most lavish dining on any college campus.

"Everyone is involved in volunteer work."

Intramurals are big, with roughly 950 teams, and operate on two levels, one for competitive types and one for strictly weekend athletes.

during the Duke–UNC game is something that can't be captured in words. Revered by fans and hated by our rivals, the devotion of the Duke students is impressive and incredible," gushes one fan. The women's basketball team has been strong in its own right. The lacrosse team, a national powerhouse that is trying to forget the scandal of a few years ago resulting from off-the-field behavior by some its members, bounced back to win the national championship in 2013 and 2014. Football has undergone a renaissance under coach David Cutcliffe. The team, which now plays in a renovated stadium complete with luxury boxes for Iron Duke supporters, makes regular bowl bids. The Duke debate team is stellar too, and brought home the national title recently. Intramurals are big, with roughly 950 teams, and operate on two levels, one for competitive types and one for strictly weekend athletes.

"There is something magical about Duke basketball."

Meandering around Duke's up-to-date campus, you can see the latest technology, but you can also hear the whisper of the Old South through those big old trees. "If you come here, there isn't a chance in the world that you won't fall in love with it, with its possibilities and opportunities and people and beauty," one student says. In addition to blending old and new, Duke also does an amazing job combining sports and academia, producing students who almost define the term "well-rounded." But this may be changing. Says a junior, "It's attracting better students, shifting the focus away from basketball and fraternities, and trying to create a more intellectual environment on campus."

> ### Overlaps
> **University of Pennsylvania, Harvard, Cornell University, Vanderbilt, Columbia, Yale, Brown, Princeton**

If You Apply To ➤

Duke: Early decision: Nov. 1. Regular decision: Jan. 3. Financial aid: Feb. 1. Application fee: $85. No campus interviews. Alumni interviews: optional, evaluative. SATs (with essay) or ACTs (with writing): required. Subject Tests: recommended (any two). Letters of recommendation: required. Essay: required. Accepts the Common Application with supplement. Additional optional essay invites applicants to share a perspective or experience related to a community, family, culture, sexual orientation, or gender identity.

Earlham College

Richmond, IN 47374

Earlham is a member of the proud circle of liberal colleges in the Midwest that includes Beloit, Grinnell, Kenyon, and Oberlin, to name just a few. Less than half the size of Oberlin and comparable to the other three, but manages to attract a more diverse student body, despite its conservative southern Indiana location. Earlham is distinctive for its Quaker orientation, welcoming environment, and international perspective.

Earlham is a study in contradictions—a top-notch liberal arts college in a relatively conservative city that few could place on a map, and an institution that in the 21st century remains true to the traditions of community, peace, and justice that are hallmarks of its Quaker heritage. Earlham's curriculum and programs engage students with the world by exposing them to classmates from approximately 70 nations and offering more than 200 academic courses that incorporate an international perspective. A variety of study abroad programs offers close faculty involvement and a thoughtful focus on cross-cultural perspectives.

Earlham's 800-acre campus sits in the small, quintessentially Midwestern city of Richmond, just a short distance from Cincinnati and Indianapolis. Georgian-style buildings dominate, surrounded by mature trees and plantings, while the Japanese gardens symbolize the college's long friendship and closeness with Japan.

> **Website**: www.earlham.edu
> **Location**: Small City
> **Private**
> **Total Enrollment**: 978
> **Undergraduates**: 930
> **Male/Female**: 43/57
> **SAT Ranges**: CR 550–700, M 560–690
> **ACT Ranges**: 25–31
> **Financial Aid**: 94%
> **Pell Grant**: 27%

(continued)

Earlham offers more than 200 academic courses that incorporate an international perspective.

Fine arts students benefit from the Center for the Visual and Performing Arts, and math and science students from the new Center for Science and Technology, opened in 2015.

To graduate, students must complete general education requirements in the arts, analytical reasoning, wellness, scientific inquiry, foreign language, and, not surprisingly, diversity. All students take a first-year seminar and complete a capstone experience. Biology is the most popular major, followed by psychology, English, art, business, and politics. A wide range of interdisciplinary offerings includes such programs as peace and global studies, Quaker studies, environmental studies, human development and social relations, and Japanese studies, a field in which Earlham is a national leader. "The Japanese program has high national standing," says one student, "and the sciences have high placement for graduate studies and jobs post-graduation." Earlham has significantly invested in its Center for Integrated Learning, providing domestic and international internships, preprofessional preparation, and integrated learning programs in such areas as health professions, business, and sustainability. The business and nonprofit management major emphasizes experiential learning while preparing students to work in a global economy.

> "[The academic climate is] very collaborative, but still leaves room for individual critical thinking."

Challenged to think and meet high academic expectations, students see themselves as capable and eager to learn. An international studies major says the academic climate is "very collaborative, but still leaves room for individual critical thinking." Discussion rather than lecture is the predominant learning style here, facilitated by small classes—79 percent have fewer than 20 students. Earlham faculty members are selected for their excellence in teaching and their ability to cross disciplinary lines. "Faculty members are extremely accessible, and most students form close relationships with their professors," says a student. Another explains that, as a matter of Quaker principle, faculty, staff, and students are never addressed by honorifics or social titles like Dr. or Ms., but by their first names: "It's an equality thing."

About three-quarters of students eventually pursue postgraduate study, often after taking some time off for a job or to participate in volunteer or service programs.

> "Earlhamites are very concerned with social justice and human rights."

During their undergrad years, 65 percent of Earlham students participate in at least one off-campus study experience. Earlham offers study abroad programs in more than two dozen countries, including Ecuador, Germany, Japan, Jordan, and New Zealand. Most programs are managed by the college and most have an on-site director; students receive preparation for a multicultural experience before embarking on their destinations. In a Border Studies program, students live with families in Tucson, Arizona, and take courses focusing on United States–Mexico border issues. The popular May Term courses send students off campus with faculty for one-month intensive courses in various locations around the world. "One of my friends, only a rising sophomore, is spending several weeks in Germany with a professor studying ancient fossils in one of the most advanced DNA analysis labs in the world," says one sophomore. "His story is not an uncommon one for freshmen and this speaks to the unique availability of great opportunities here."

"Students at Earlham are generally critical thinkers, intellectually curious, open-minded, and very comfortable in their own skin," says a junior. Only 18 percent of the students are Hoosiers; 21 percent hail from abroad. Twelve percent are African American, with Hispanics adding 6 percent and Asian American students contributing 5 percent. The political climate is generally liberal, and a student reports, "Earlhamites are very concerned with social justice and human rights." Twenty-seven percent of students are Pell-eligible. Merit scholarships averaging $17,222 are available for qualified students; there are no athletic scholarships.

Ninety-six percent of Earlham students live on campus in nine residence halls, all of which have been renovated within the last six years. Single, double, and triple rooms are available in the two older dorms, which connect with the suite-style accommodations of the newer Mills Hall. Dorm space is reserved for first-years, and upperclassmen enter a lottery for the remaining rooms or petition to live together in small houses. Most students eat in the college dining hall, and although there have been complaints about the new service provider, a junior says, "They have been taking our feedback and slowly implementing changes." A senior says safety officers are helpful in all situations: "Once, I had a conversation with a campus security officer about the best places to hide on campus in case of a zombie attack." Some note that the administration has been slow to respond to the issue of campus sexual assault, but that it's making strides in the right direction.

As a matter of Quaker principle, faculty, staff, and students are never addressed by social titles like Dr. or Ms., but by their first names.

There are no fraternities or sororities at Earlham, but on-campus activities abound. "Most everything happens on campus, which is great because everything is more open and accessible," a student says. Students enjoy improv comedy, a cappella music, equestrian programs, a lip-synch competition, fall and spring festivals, concerts, and sports. Student groups include numerous religious, ethnic, and cultural organizations, some of which also take the lead on throwing campus parties. Students 21 and over can consume alcohol, although only in their residence hall rooms. Day trips to Cincinnati, Indianapolis, or Columbus and weekend visits to other nearby universities are also popular diversions.

"The city of Richmond is not your typical college town and, while it has some gems, is a little limited at times," a neuroscience major says. Still, the city does offer standard American and a variety of ethnic restaurants, as well as movie theaters, bowling alleys, golf, and a popular biking and running trail. Students fan out into the city, racking up more than 25,000 hours of volunteer service a

"Most everything happens on campus, which is great because everything is more open and accessible."

year. "Volunteerism is an important value of many Earlham students, and despite classwork and other commitments, many students still make time to volunteer," says a first-year.

Earlham's 18 varsity teams (the Quakers) attract nearly a third of the student body and compete in Division III sports. Baseball and men's and women's tennis and soccer are among the school's strongest squads, with women's basketball on the rise. Men's and women's lacrosse and golf teams have recently been added. Half of the students play intramural sports, and soccer, basketball, and kickball are the most popular.

Earlham students graduate ready to take on the world, thanks to the school's cooperative, can-do spirit, international perspective, and caring student/faculty community—and its commitment to an educational process that it calls "becoming fully present." Says one student, "Earlham allows an individual to pursue many areas of interest, and the people you meet will be friends for a lifetime."

Overlaps

Beloit, Oberlin, Kenyon, College of Wooster, Kalamazoo, Grinnell, Haverford, Lawrence

If You Apply To ⮞

Earlham: Early decision I: Nov. 15. Early action I: Dec. 1. Early decision II and early action II: Jan. 15. Regular decision: Feb. 15. Financial aid: Mar. 1. No application fee. Campus and alumni interviews: recommended, evaluative. SATs or ACTs: optional. Subject Tests: optional. Letters of recommendation: required. Essay: required. Accepts the Common Application.

Eckerd College

4200 54th Avenue South, St. Petersburg, FL 33711

There are worse places to attend than a college with its own stretch of beach on the shores of Tampa Bay. Eckerd's only direct competitor in Florida is Rollins, which has a business school but is otherwise similar. Marine science, environmental studies, and international studies are among Eckerd's biggest draws. The student body is mainly from out of state, with an abundance of Yankee accents.

Website: www.eckerd.edu
Location: City Outskirts
Private
Total Enrollment: 1,738
Undergraduates: 1,738
Male/Female: 38/62
SAT Ranges: CR 500–610, M 500–600
ACT Ranges: 23–28
Financial Aid: 95%
Pell Grant: N/A
Expense: Pr $ $
Student Loans: 60%
Average Debt: $ $ $
Phi Beta Kappa: Yes
Applicants: 4,135
Accepted: 73%
Enrolled: 16%
Grad in 6 Years: 64%
Returning Freshmen: 81%
Academics: ✍ ✍ ✍
Social: ☎ ☎ ☎
Q of L: ★ ★ ★ ★ ★
Admissions: (727) 864-8331
Email Address: admissions@eckerd.edu

Strong Programs:
Marine Science
Environmental Studies
International Business
Biology
Psychology
Communication

It's not unusual to spot dolphins frolicking in the adjacent waters.

Attending Eckerd College demands a special sort of willpower. Why? In the words of an international business major: "We are right on the water, and it is like going to college in a resort." With free canoes, kayaks, boats, coolers, and tents always available for student use, it's a wonder anyone finds time to study. But study they do, as administrators continue to lure capable students to Eckerd with small classes, skilled professors, and a thriving social scene. "Few schools are located right on the beach," says a sophomore. "It's Eckerd's paradise-like setting that seals the deal for most prospective students."

Founded in 1958 as Florida Presbyterian College and renamed 12 years later after a generous benefactor (of drugstore fame), Eckerd considers itself nonsectarian. Still, the school maintains a formal "covenant" with the major Presbyterian denomination, from which it receives some funds. The lush, grassy campus is on the tip of a peninsula bounded by the Gulf of Mexico and Tampa Bay, with plenty of flowering bushes, trees, and small ponds—it's not unusual to spot dolphins frolicking in the adjacent waters. Campus buildings are modern, and none are taller than three stories. The GO Pavilion takes advantage of Florida's year-round outdoor living climate and offers nearly 10,000 square feet of open-air space for sports, concerts, and other events. The $25 million, LEED Platinum–rated James Center for Molecular and Life Sciences houses the biology, chemistry, and biochemistry programs.

Autumn Term, Eckerd's version of freshman orientation, is a three-week term before the regular fall semester that introduces new students to the academic expectations and social responsibilities of the Eckerd community. First-years also take a yearlong course called Human Experience, which focuses on topics like justice, power, freedom, and global citizenship, and all students must meet composition, foreign language, information technology, oral communication, and quantitative skills requirements. Also required are one course in each of the four academic areas—arts, humanities, natural sciences, and social sciences—plus one course each in environmental and global perspectives. The capstone senior seminar, organized around the theme "Imagining Justice," asks students to draw on what they've learned during college to find solutions to important issues. Seniors present their capstone work at a festival in the spring. All students are also expected to complete at least 40 hours of community service before graduation; service opportunities are built into reflective service-learning courses that are offered in every major.

> **"We are right on the water, and it is like going to college in a resort."**

"Although the classes are intellectually stimulating, engaging, and challenging, there is not too much competition among the students," one junior observes. Popular majors include marine science, environmental studies, international business, biology, psychology, and communication. Wet subjects are especially strong. "Eckerd College is renowned for its marine science program," says a student. "The close proximity to the ocean gives [students in] this major a great amount of hands-on, close-up experience." Eckerd was a pioneer of the 4–1–4 term schedule, in which students work on a single project for credit each January. Every student has a faculty mentor, and there are no graduate assistants; 52 percent of classes have fewer than 20 students. "The faculty here is amazing," says a psychology major. "They are here for us and they want us to do well."

Each year, 20 to 25 top incoming freshmen are selected to participate in freshman research associateships, receiving stipends of up to $1,000 to work side by side with leading professors on active research projects. A four-year honors program is also available. While St. Petersburg isn't exactly a college town (a freshman says it is "more a vacationing spot"), a side benefit to the school's location is the Academy of Senior Professionals, a group of senior citizens who mentor undergrads. Academy members, who come from all walks of life, take classes with students, work with professors on curriculum development, help students with career choices, and lead workshops in their areas of expertise. A whopping 85 percent of Eckerd's students study abroad in more than 300 destinations, including the school's study centers in London, Latin America, and China. Marine science programs include a SEA Semester* and the Eckerd College Search and Rescue, which performs more than 500 marine rescues annually and inspires a popular campus T-shirt that tells students to "GET LOST! Support Eckerd Search and Rescue."

Eckerd's president once referred to students as "intellectuals in sandals," says a junior. "I like the quote, and it really works." Another student says Eckerd attracts "friendly, liberal, free-spirited, and intelligent" students who enjoy the great outdoors. Seventy-three percent of the student

"[Students are] friendly, liberal, free-spirited, and intelligent."

body hails from out of state, with a large contingent coming from the Northeast; another 5 percent are foreign. Hispanics account for 9 percent of the student body, African Americans 3 percent, and Asian Americans 2 percent. Merit scholarships averaging $15,393 and athletic awards are available to qualified students.

"The dorms at Eckerd vary greatly," reports one student. "The traditional dorms are basic and unsightly, while the newer dorms are fantastic and aesthetically pleasing." Eighty-seven percent of students live in the housing quads, separated from the rest of campus by the imaginatively named Dorm Drive. Rooms are fairly large and air-conditioned, and waterfront views and beach access are a given—and free. Two trendy townhouse- and apartment-style residence halls provide suite living, and other dorms have been renovated to add computer labs and kitchens in lounges. "There is usually no problem getting a room," says a senior. And how about the food? "Dining is superior," says one student, "with a variety of food choices ranging from traditional hamburgers and pizza, to a lively and diverse vegetarian and global selection."

There are no Greek organizations at Eckerd, and a strict alcohol policy—no kegs on campus, no alcohol at university events—means wristbands at campus parties, even for those over 21. The policy has been relaxed a bit to allow students of drinking age to imbibe at the campus bar, the Triton Pub, and to drink in public areas of the dorms. Students say those who are underage still manage to get booze and consume it in their rooms, away from prying eyes. "Most students learn how to stay out of trouble and play by the rules," says a sophomore. Off campus, it's next to impossible for underage students to be served at bars and restaurants, students say—though they do enjoy St. Petersburg, about 10 minutes from campus.

"Social life is primarily on campus, and it really is what you make it," a junior states. Students can partake in concerts, lectures, shows, and games arranged by the student activity board. The Kappa Karnival offers rides and games galore. Off campus, students can take in the nightclubs and bars of Latin-flavored Ybor City, about 30 minutes away. Tampa and St. Pete also offer a Salvador Dalí museum—which Eckerd students get into for free—and professional baseball, football, hockey,

All students are expected to complete at least 40 hours of community service; service-learning courses are offered in every major.

Twenty to 25 top incoming freshmen are selected to participate in freshman research associateships, receiving stipends of up to $1,000.

and soccer teams. Tempting road trips include Orlando's Walt Disney World and Islands of Adventure theme parks, Miami's South Beach, and that hub of debauchery on the delta, New Orleans.

Varsity teams (the Tritons) compete in Division II, and the Sunshine State Conference, which is known as the "Conference of National Champions." "Men's basketball is the only sport that attracts lots of fans and spectators," a senior says, and it's well deserved—the team claimed the conference title in 2016. A night of Midnight Madness helps kick off the season. The co-ed sailing team has claimed several recent divisional and regional championships. Eckerd doesn't have a football team, but popular intramurals include flag football, soccer, softball, and the assassin game, in which students try to shoot their peers with dart guns.

Eckerd is striving to add "experiential, service, and international learning" to the traditional classroom experience and attract a higher caliber of students. That mission, combined with new facilities and the fun to be had in the Florida sun, gives Eckerd its distinctive flavor.

> "[Dining offers] a lively and diverse vegetarian and global selection."

If You Apply To ➤

Eckerd: Rolling admissions. Early action: Nov. 15. Priority financial aid: Feb. 1. Application fee: $40. Campus interviews: optional, evaluative. No alumni interviews. SATs or ACTs: required. Subject Tests: optional. Letters of recommendation: required. Essay: required. Accepts the Common Application.

University of Edinburgh: See page 381.

Elon University

Elon, NC 27244

One of the leading liberal arts colleges in the Southeast and an emerging name nationally, Elon boasts a welcoming environment and a nurturing faculty. Once known for turning on average students to the life of the mind, has become increasingly selective but seemingly at the cost of socioeconomic diversity. Strong emphasis on global perspectives and active, experiential learning. Classic-looking campus adds to the appeal.

Elon University derives its name from the Hebrew word for "oak," which is fitting when you consider the ways in which the school is growing. At each year's opening convocation, entering students are given an acorn. Four years later, they are presented with an oak sapling at commencement. It's a charming tradition and a reminder of how things grow and change. With an emphasis on undergraduate research, internships, service learning, study abroad, and leadership—the five Elon Experiences—the university also provides its students with plenty of opportunities to grow, intellectually and socially. "All schools want students to grow holistically, but Elon is the only one I've heard of that actively pursues that goal on many levels," says a senior.

Elon was founded in 1889 and occupies a 636-acre campus in North Carolina's Piedmont region. With apologies to Colby and Miami (OH), it is arguably the most architecturally consistent campus in the nation. Buildings are Georgian-style brick with white trim, and newer buildings have been adapted to modern architectural lines while maintaining this classic collegiate feel. On the north end of campus is Lake Mary Nell, home to an abundance of geese and ducks. Academic buildings are organized in three clusters: a historic quad near a fountain in the older section of the campus; the Academic Village, complete with an amphitheater; and business and science centers in close proximity to the student center. A new fitness center opened in 2015, and new facilities housing the School of Communications were completed in 2016.

To graduate, students must complete a core curriculum that includes English, mathematics, eight courses in liberal arts and sciences, three courses at the advanced level, two experiential learning components, a world language component, and an interdisciplinary capstone seminar. The university offers more than 60 undergraduate degrees; business, communications, psychology, and exercise science are the most popular majors. Programs in the performing arts and education are also strong. The School of Communications is nationally recognized and benefits from two ultramodern digital television studios. New majors in cinema and television arts, media analytics, and communication design were recently added, as were new minors in wellness and health education, poverty and social justice, and teaching and learning.

Elon has an elaborate support system designed to ensure that first-year students don't fall through the cracks. Students begin general studies with a first-year course called The Global Experience, a seminar-style interdisciplinary class that investigates challenges facing the world. An optional experiential learning summer program partners more than 120 freshmen with returning students for activities ranging from white-water rafting to volunteer work. "Are You Ready?" is a new series of live webcasts and chats offered the summer before students enroll. Elon 101 serves as an academic orientation for all first-years; students meet weekly in small groups with an academic advisor and an upper-level student.

Students agree that the academic climate is rigorous. "We are a small school of incredibly talented students, so it's easy to start feeling pressured to do your best work in order to stay on top," says one junior. Fifty-one percent of classes have fewer than 20 students, and, although there is the occasional less-than-stellar instructor, professors generally receive kudos. "Many of the faculty members have been successful in professional positions before entering academia, giving them a variety of real-world experiences to share with their students," says a junior. A senior adds, "Professors are readily accessible and love to meet with students outside of class to discuss anything and everything."

"Elon students are kind, engaged in their respective activities, and contributors to the greater university community."

The university places a big emphasis on undergraduate research. Approximately one in four undergrads are engaged in research with faculty and present their work at a research forum in the spring. Seventy-two percent study abroad, thanks to the 4–1–4 academic calendar and more than 100 study abroad programs. Elon's six Fellows Programs, to which prospective students can apply alongside their admissions applications, are designed for exceptionally motivated students. They offer faculty support, scholarships, and peer networks, and current participants highly recommend them as being "profoundly impactful."

"Elon students are kind, engaged in their respective activities, and contributors to the greater university community," says an anthropology major. Of Elon's predominately female student body, 28 percent come from North Carolina, and

The emphasis is on the five Elon Experiences— undergraduate research, internships, service learning, study abroad, and leadership.

(continued)

Expense: Pr $
Student Loans: 43%
Average Debt: $ $ $
Phi Beta Kappa: Yes
Applicants: 10,256
Accepted: 57%
Enrolled: 26%
Grad in 6 Years: 83%
Returning Freshmen: 90%
Academics: ✍ ✍ ✍
Social: ☎ ☎ ☎ ☎
Q of L: ★ ★ ★ ★ ★
Admissions: (800) 334-8448
Email Address: admissions@ elon.edu

Strong Programs:
Business
Communications
Psychology
Exercise Science
Performing Arts
Education

most of the rest hail from the Northeast. Six percent are African American, 5 percent Hispanic, 2 percent Asian American, and 2 percent international. Somewhat surprisingly for a school that was once a top choice for first-generation college students, only 7 percent of undergraduates qualify for Pell Grants. Lack of diversity is a common complaint, but students note that the administration is making efforts to diversify the "fairly rich, white, and preppy campus." And while, according to a senior, "both conservative and liberal niches exist on campus," the student body as a whole tends not to get too involved in social and political issues. The top 15 percent of admitted applicants are automatically awarded the Presidential Scholarship. Students can also vie for merit scholarships averaging $7,162, and there are 294 athletic scholarships available.

Sixty-two percent of students reside on campus and are required to for their first two years, and afterward many students choose to live off campus to save money. "Housing is a little bit of a hassle at Elon. There isn't enough for the amount of students admitted," says one junior. Options include traditional residence halls, university-owned apartments, and the Global and Colonnades neighborhoods, which feature more than 20 living/learning communities, such as Art and Culture Shop, La Casa de Español, Gender and Sexuality, and ELONCH-Entrepreneurship.

"Service is one of the bigger components of life as an Elon student."

Designed to bridge classroom learning with social experiences, these communities also serve to bring together diverse groups of students with common interests in a safe space; many participants in the gender and sexuality community, for instance, identify as LGBTQIA. Campus dining gets good reviews: "The food is excellent, with three dining halls and almost 20 retail locations and lots of options for kosher, vegetarian, gluten-free, etc.," says one student. Campus security programs are said to be effective and include "a Live Safe app to help students who are walking home alone from parties, and we also have escort services and Safe Rides, which are really essential services," according to a public health studies major.

When it's time to let off steam, students generally turn to the active Greek scene—which attracts 18 percent of the men and 39 percent of the women—or countless activities on campus. "There are many events hosted on campus during the weekends," states one student. "The Oak House is another great social setting and somewhere to grab a casual drink with friends or faculty members." Despite the presence of alcohol and the dominant Greek life, "You are not pressured to drink here, and there are many students that do not and are still engaged in social life," a psychology major reports. Road trips to the beach (three hours), the mountains (one hour), and Chapel Hill or Raleigh-Durham (less than an hour) are popular diversions.

The tiny town of Elon is virtually indistinguishable from the university, and students take an active role in the community through volunteer projects. Eighty-eight percent of students participate in community service, both domestically and abroad, and one student confirms, "Service is one of the bigger components of life as an Elon student." The well-known Elon University Poll, which the school runs as a public service, tracks political and public policy issues. Favorite campus traditions include a weekly College Coffee, where students and faculty mingle over free breakfast and coffee—a tradition since 1984. An exercise science major says, "We have a Festival of Lights before winter break, and a holiday party at our president's house is a hallmark of the holiday season."

"The opportunities to work in a hands-on environment are never-ending."

Elon joined the Colonial Athletic Association in 2014 and offers ten Division I women's sports and seven for men. Women's track and field won a conference title

Overlaps

UNC at Chapel Hill, Wake Forest, Boston College, Bucknell, College of William and Mary, University of Richmond, University of Maryland, University of Virginia in 2015. Women's and men's tennis, basketball, softball, football, and baseball are also strong. There's also an intramural program covering more than 20 sports, in which 30 percent of students take part, and a successful club sports program that lets students compete with those at other schools.

"Elon's best asset is honestly its commitment to engaged learning," says one student. By steadily ramping up its educational offerings, growing and improving its facilities, and becoming more selective, this liberal arts university is quickly outgrowing its local reputation. "It's a welcoming university," says one happy senior, "and the opportunities to work in a hands-on environment are never-ending."

If You Apply To ➤ | **Elon:** Early decision: Nov. 1. Early action: Nov. 10. Regular decision: Jan. 10. Application fee: $50. No campus or alumni interviews. SATs or ACTs (with writing): required. No Subject Tests. Letters of recommendation: optional. Essay: required. Application includes optional field for students who identify as part of the LGBTQIA community.

Emerson College

120 Boylston Street, Boston, MA 02116

Emerson is strategically located on Boston Common in the heart of Boston's Theater District and within walking distance of many of the city's major attractions. Specializes in communication and the arts. With roughly 3,700 undergraduates, Emerson is a smaller alternative to neighboring giants Boston U and Northeastern. Like most Beantown institutions, it is far more selective than it once was.

Those who aspire to a career in film, television, or marketing may want to start with a four-year stint in Boston. There they will find Emerson College, a small liberal arts school that offers strong programs in communication and the arts, as well as top-notch performance and production facilities. At Emerson, students take notes from professors who also happen to be working directors, producers, actors, editors, and writers. It's an approach that helps talented, city-savvy students find their voices. "If you are serious about surrounding yourself with creative people during your college years," says a journalism major, "this is the school for you." Prospective students take note: getting into Emerson requires more than dreams. You'll need solid test scores and plenty of talent too.

Founded in 1880, Emerson is located by Boston Common in the middle of the city's Theater District, and much of the surrounding city is accessible by foot. The campus features a mix of traditional and modern high-rise buildings. Nearly half of the facilities have been refurbished or newly built since 2002. The historic 1,200-seat Cutler Majestic Theatre, the anchor of Emerson's urban campus, has been restored to its original 1903 appearance. The 11-story Tufte Performance and Production Center features rehearsal spaces, a theater design/technology center, a costume shop, a makeup lab, and television studios. Students here also have access to professional-grade equipment and digital labs, audio postproduction suites, sound-mix studios, radio stations (Emerson is home to the oldest noncommercial radio station in Boston), a multimedia newsroom, and a marketing research suite featuring eye-tracking technology and a two-way mirror for conducting focus groups.

Core requirements at Emerson consist of a combination of traditional courses and interdisciplinary seminars. All students must take courses in three areas: Foundations, which includes courses in writing, oral communication, and quantitative reasoning;

Website: www.emerson.edu
Location: City Center
Private
Total Enrollment: 4,329
Undergraduates: 3,733
Male/Female: 40/60
SAT Ranges: CR 560–670, M 540–640
ACT Ranges: 25–29
Financial Aid: 61%
Pell Grant: 16%
Expense: Pr $ $
Student Loans: 74%
Average Debt: $
Phi Beta Kappa: Yes
Applicants: 8,618
Accepted: 49%
Enrolled: 22%
Grad in 6 Years: 80%
Returning Freshmen: 87%
Academics: ✍ ✍ ✍
Social: ☎ ☎
Q of L: ★ ★ ★
Admissions: (617) 824-8600

(continued)

Email Address: admission@
emerson.edu

Strong Programs:
Performing Arts
Visual and Media Arts
Writing, Literature, and
    Publishing
Marketing Communication
Film Production
Journalism

*Emerson students have
access to professional-
grade equipment
and digital labs.*

*Students in the
semester-long program
at Kasteel Well (in
the Netherlands) are
housed in a restored,
college-owned, 14th-
century castle.*

Perspectives, which includes courses in aesthetics, ethics and values, history, literature, and scientific, social, and psychological perspectives; and U.S. and Global Diversity. Freshmen take a required, interdisciplinary First-Year Seminar.

Undergraduates may choose from 19 majors in communication and the arts, ranging from stage and screen design technology and business of creative enterprises to communication disorders and journalism. The Interdisciplinary Studies program allows students to design their own major. Performance-related majors, such as acting and musical theatre, tend to be the most popular, along with visual and media arts; writing, literature, and publishing; and marketing communication. An entrepreneurship minor features a business plan competition known as the Entrepreneurship Exposition; students vie for thousands of dollars in start-up funds.

> **"There is a high amount of collaboration at the college across all majors."**

"There is a high amount of collaboration at the college across all majors," explains a sophomore. "For example, if a student is working on a film, they will recruit classmates and friends from different majors to do everything from acting to filming to editing to marketing, and so on." Sixty-seven percent of all classes have fewer than 20 students, and a political communication major says professors "give us real-world perspective and also always have an ear to the ground for those of us looking for internships." For even more course options, students may cross-register with the ProArts Consortium, which consists of six area arts colleges, including the Berklee College of Music and the School of the Museum of Fine Arts.

For those seeking a spotlight and stage in a different setting, Emerson offers several global study options, including a semester-long program at Kasteel Well (in the Netherlands), where students are housed in a restored, college-owned, 14th-century castle complete with moats, gardens, and a gatehouse. Each year about 200 students spend a semester at Emerson's recently built Los Angeles Center on Sunset Boulevard in Hollywood, where they can participate in internships with companies such as Interscope Records, CNN, Warner Bros., Dreamworks, and NBC. Another semester-long program sends participants to Washington, D.C., for classes and internships. "Above all, cocurriculars are the backbone of an Emerson education," a film production major says. "Classes are thought-provoking, but nothing prepares you for the real world better than actually getting out into the field to practice as much as possible."

"The students at Emerson are artistic, passionate, and career-focused," says a student. Adds another, "We have a very large 'hipster' presence at our school."

> **"Above all, cocurriculars are the backbone of an Emerson education."**

Nineteen percent of undergraduates hail from Massachusetts, and most come from public high schools. Seven percent are international. African Americans account for 3 percent of the student body, Hispanics 11 percent, and Asian Americans 4 percent. Despite a noticeable lack of socioeconomic and ethnic diversity, "Emerson is known for being extremely LGBT friendly," says one senior. "Students are always championing for liberal social causes." Emerson offers merit scholarships to qualified applicants, as well as scholarships to support underrepresented students. There are no athletic scholarships.

Fifty-seven percent of students live on campus. Freshmen and sophomores are guaranteed college-provided housing. "A lot of students take it as a rite of passage to move off campus for their last two years," says a junior. Several living/learning communities are available, including Community Outreach, Digital Culture, and Writers' Block, among others. A senior says campus fare passes muster: "The food is fine, but definitely not a highlight." Each building requires an ID to enter, and public safety officers regularly patrol the streets outside the buildings. According to a marketing communication major, Emerson has taken several positive measures to better address its handling of sexual assault cases. "The Office of Violence Prevention and Response is incredibly active, especially during orientation events, in order to bring this tough issue to students' attention."

"While there is no shortage of on-campus events like comedy shows, performances, and club meetings, a lot of the traditional college nightlife tends to happen in the city or at someone's off-campus apartment," says one sophomore. More than 90 student organizations offer ample opportunity for involvement, including two radio stations, six humor and literary journals, 10 performance troupes, and six production organizations. "I have never met a busier student body in my life," says one student. "Each student is involved in a million different things." Greek life, which attracts 2 percent of Emerson men and 3 percent of the women, is not a major influence on the social scene. Though the campus is considered "dry," a sophomore reasons, "Drugs and alcohol are as easy to find as they are to avoid, and it is up to the students' discretion to be responsible." Popular annual festivities include the EVVY Awards, the largest student-run awards show in the country. When students tire of on-campus events, they can step off campus into Boston. A student says, "Emerson students live, study, work, and volunteer in

The EVVY Awards is the largest student-run awards show in the country.

"We have a very large 'hipster' presence at our school."

almost every major neighborhood and area of the city." There are plenty of diversions, including museums, the Franklin Park Zoo, the Boston Public Garden, the Freedom Trail, the Boston Symphony Orchestra, and major league baseball at Fenway Park.

Emerson fields 14 Division III athletic teams, and the Lions compete as a member of the Eastern College Athletic Conference and the New England Women's and Men's Athletic Conference. Solid teams include baseball, softball, basketball, cross-country, lacrosse, and soccer. Students also enjoy an active intramural program and take advantage of the 10,000-square-foot fitness center featuring state-of-the-art equipment, classes, and wellness workshops.

"Emerson prepares creative thinkers to get out into the workforce and make a difference," says one senior. While you are not guaranteed to become the next Oscar-winning director, the possibility is not out of the question at Emerson. And even if a lifestyle of fame is not for you, the excellent education, small classes, and attentive professors may teach you how to be the "star" of your own life story.

Overlaps

NYU, Boston University, Ithaca, Northeastern, University of Southern California, Syracuse, Fordham, American University

If You Apply To ➤

Emerson: Early action: Nov. 1. Regular decision: Jan. 15. Financial aid: Feb. 1. Housing: May 1. Application fee: $65. Campus interviews: recommended, evaluative. No alumni interviews. SATs (with essay) or ACTs (with writing): required. Subject Tests: optional. Letters of recommendation: required. Essay: required. Accepts the Common Application with supplement. Additional materials required for applicants to performing arts, media production, comedic arts, and honors programs.

Emory University

200 Boisfeuillet Jones Center, Atlanta, GA 30322

Often compared to Duke and Vanderbilt, Emory may be most similar to Washington University in St. Louis. Both are in major cities and both tout business and premeds as major draws. Emory's suburban Atlanta location is tough to beat. Attracts a larger contingent from the Northeast than more Southern competitors such as Vanderbilt. Also consider Oxford College, Emory's two-year, small-town liberal arts campus.

Website: www.emory.edu

Location: City Center

Private

Total Enrollment: 12,286

Undergraduates: 6,688

Male/Female: 42/58

SAT Ranges: CR 620–720,
    M 650–770

ACT Ranges: 29–33

Financial Aid: 43%

Pell Grant: 19%

Expense: Pr $ $ $

Student Loans: 41%

Average Debt: $ $

Phi Beta Kappa: Yes

Applicants: 20,492

Accepted: 24%

Enrolled: 28%

Grad in 6 Years: 89%

Returning Freshmen: 94%

Academics: ✍ ✍ ✍ ✍

Social: ☎ ☎ ☎

Q of L: ★ ★ ★ ★

Admissions: (404) 727-6036

Email Address:
    admiss@emory.edu

Strong Programs:

Business Administration

Biology

Economics

Nursing

Psychology

Neuroscience

English and Creative Writing

Irish Studies

All freshmen participate in PACE, which brings together faculty, staff, and student leaders to mentor first-year students.

Emory University may lack the liberal arts prowess of the Northeastern schools with which it competes, but it's a favorite of preprofessional students from both U.S. coasts. They come for its size (big, but not too big), location, and national reputation. Though most students are clean-cut and career-oriented, a freshman says the population ranges "from preppy, to Northeast and very designer-oriented, to hippie, and everything in between." Regardless of how they're dressed, students are challenged, not coddled, in the classroom; they form study groups and work together to succeed. An atmosphere of friendliness and Southern hospitality enhances the vibrant campus life.

Set on 631 acres of woods and rolling hills in the Druid Hills suburb of Atlanta, Emory's campus spreads out from an academic quad of marble-covered, red-roofed buildings. Contemporary structures dot the periphery of the lush, green grounds. In recent years, Emory has expanded science and math research facilities, constructed an apartment-style living complex for upper-class students, added a performing arts center and a psychology building, and opened freshman residence halls, which make up a freshman quad. "I enjoy our location because it offers a homey, 'neighborhood' feel, while providing the optimal location just 15 minutes from downtown Atlanta," says one senior.

Emory University offers applicants the choice between two different undergraduate experiences at two distinct campuses: Emory College in Atlanta, GA, and Oxford College in Oxford, GA. Emory College may be best for students who seek a four-year undergraduate experience at a research institution that values academic independence and intellectual engagement. Oxford College is suited for students who seek a small liberal arts college experience and early opportunities for leadership; it is also easier to get into. Following two years of study at Oxford, all students continue as juniors at Emory's Atlanta campus. Emory's distribution requirements aim to develop competence in writing, quantitative methods, a second language, and physical education, and include exposure to the humanities, social sciences, and natural sciences. Other required coursework helps broaden students' perspectives on national, regional, and global history and culture. Finally, students take two seminars—one as freshmen (50 to 60 are available each term, limited to 15 students each) and one at an upper level. All freshmen participate in PACE (Pre-Major Advising Connections at Emory). The program brings together faculty, staff, and student leaders to mentor first-year students on the aspects of college life.

> **"Faculty members make teaching a priority and set aside a significant amount of time for mentoring."**

"Though Emory is definitely not an easy school, and you have to work hard to earn your grades, overall, everyone manages to find a good balance between classwork, extracurriculars, and socializing," according to one senior. Sixty-one percent of classes have fewer than 20 students. Just as Emory has invested in its physical plant, the school has spent lavishly in the past to add star faculty members to key departments, such as Archbishop Desmond Tutu in the school of theology, the Dalai Lama, and Salman Rushdie. "Faculty members make teaching a priority and set aside a significant amount of time for mentoring and helping students with both the course material and with life in general," says one student. Opportunities for mentored research are available in all fields.

The most popular majors include business administration, biology, economics, nursing, psychology, and neuroscience. Biology and chemistry benefit from physical proximity to the federal Centers for Disease Control, while many political science professors have ties to the Carter Center (named for the former president, who holds a town hall meeting on campus each year) and serve as regular guests on nearby CNN. The English and creative writing program is strong too. Emory has received a significant portion of Nobel laureate Seamus Heaney's archive, and its

Irish studies program is said to rival those of Notre Dame and Boston College. A 3–2 dual-degree program allows students to earn a bachelor's degree at Emory and a bachelor's degree in engineering at Georgia Tech. Emory belongs to the Atlanta Regional Council for Higher Education*, which lets students take courses at other area schools. The Center for International Programs Abroad offers more than 100 study programs on six continents. The 36 percent of students who participate earn Emory credit and Emory grades, and they can receive Emory financial aid, scholarships, and grants.

Twenty-two percent of Emory undergraduates are from Georgia, and 17 percent are international. New York, New Jersey, California, and Florida are also well represented. African Americans make up 9 percent of the student body, Asian Americans 19 percent, and Hispanics 8 percent. Politically, the campus is less conservative than many Southern institutions. "Perhaps it's because of our history or our location in the birthplace of the Civil Rights Movement, but social issues seem to hold a place of importance on campus," a student says. Merit scholarships worth an average of $28,745 are awarded annually; there are no athletic scholarships. Under the Loan Cap Program, the university caps loans at $15,000 over four years for families with incomes between $50,000 and $100,000.

Sixty-four percent of Emory students live on campus; freshmen and sophomores are required to do so, and housing is guaranteed for two years. Students can request to live in a building that is co-ed by floor, co-ed by room, or single sex and can also request a specific roommate. "I lived in the oldest, smallest freshman hall (Dobbs) during my first year at Emory, but I loved it," a student says. "The sense of community was stronger than in any other dorm." Lucky juniors and seniors may hang their hats in the one- to four-bedroom Clairmont Campus apartments, which boast private bedrooms with full-size beds, kitchens, and baths, and a washer-dryer in each unit. Clairmont residents also get an activity center with basketball, volleyball, and tennis courts; a heated, outdoor, Olympic-sized pool; and weight-training facilities. In addition to the dining halls, there are small cafés, grills, and a food court on campus, each providing tasty fare. "The food is pretty good," says a freshman.

"Most social life takes place on campus, but we are so close to Atlanta nightlife that many students choose to explore the area," says a student. Fraternities and sororities attract 26 percent of Emory's men and 31 percent of the women so, of course, Greek parties are prevalent. Other options include college nights at local dance clubs and concerts organized by the Student Programming Committee. "You'll see talent sprinkled everywhere from breathtaking Theater Emory shows to First Fridays (a cappella concerts that draw crowds on the first Friday of every month)," says a senior. Alcohol isn't allowed in the freshman dorms, and "anyone caught will definitely suffer consequences," a freshman says. A very popular highlight of the social calendar is Dooley's Week, a spring festival in honor of the "Spirit of Emory" (the school's unofficial mascot), Dooley, a skeleton who reportedly escaped from the biology lab more than 100 years ago. If Dooley walks into your class, the class is dismissed, and the week culminates with a costume ball in his honor. Freshman halls also have Songfest, a competition where residents make up spirit-filled song-and-dance routines.

Atlanta offers a multitude of diversions, from Braves baseball and Hawks basketball to plays at the Fox Theatre, exhibits at the High Museum of Art, marine wildlife at the Georgia Aquarium, and shopping at Underground Atlanta or the Lenox Square, to which Emory provides a free shuttle every Saturday. Upperclassmen enjoy the Atlanta bar scene. Popular road trips include Stone Mountain, Athens, Savannah, and the beaches of Florida and the Carolinas.

Many political science professors have ties to the Carter Center (named for the former president) and serve as regular guests on nearby CNN.

"Social issues seem to hold a place of importance on campus."

Dooley's Week is a spring festival in honor of the unofficial mascot, Dooley, a skeleton who reportedly escaped from the biology lab more than 100 years ago.

Emory doesn't field a varsity football team, but the Eagles have produced a number of Division III national champs, including women's swimming and diving and men's tennis. Emory competes against such academic powerhouses as the University of Chicago and Carnegie Mellon in the University Athletic Association conference, and recent conference winners include men's basketball, baseball, and softball, and men's and women's tennis and swimming and diving. Many students join at least one intramural sports team at either a competitive or a recreational level. Popular intramurals include flag football, volleyball, soccer, basketball, water polo, and ultimate Frisbee.

"We are so close to Atlanta nightlife that many students choose to explore the area."

While many Southern schools suffer from a regional provincialism, that isn't true at Emory, which blends a focus on teaching and research to nurture creativity and turn out leaders who are highly sought after in the working world—and by postgraduate law, medical, and business programs. "The combination of stellar academics, countless extracurricular activities, the beautiful campus, and people who genuinely care about each other makes Emory a special place to be," says a senior.

Overlaps

Duke, Georgetown, University of Pennsylvania, Vanderbilt, Washington University in St. Louis

If You Apply To ➤

Emory: Early decision I: Nov. 1. Early decision II and regular decision: Jan. 1. Financial aid: Mar. 1. Housing: May 1. Application fee: $75. No campus interviews. Alumni interviews: optional, evaluative. SATs or ACTs: required. Subject Tests: optional. Letters of recommendation: required. Essay: required. Accepts the Common Application.

Eugene Lang College–The New School for Liberal Arts

65 West 11th Street, New York, NY 10011

Home to more than 1,400 street-savvy, freethinking urbanites, Eugene Lang College is becoming increasingly popular as an alternative to much larger neighbor NYU in Manhattan's chic Greenwich Village. Emphasis on progressive critical inquiry pursued in seminar settings. With the city as its campus, Lang offers little sense of community. Student body more than 70 percent female. Long-standing international perspective and strength in arts and humanities still predominate.

Website: www.newschool.edu
Location: City Center
Private
Total Enrollment: 1,465
Undergraduates: 1,465
Male/Female: 26/74
SAT Ranges: CR 500–620, M 500–630
ACT Ranges: 22–27
Financial Aid: 69%
Pell Grant: 58%
Expense: Pr $ $
Student Loans: 69%
Average Debt: $ $
Phi Beta Kappa: No

Students seeking a typical college experience—large lectures, rowdy football games, and rigid academic requirements—would do well to steer clear of Eugene Lang College. That's because Lang has seminars instead of traditional lectures, minimal required coursework, and not a single varsity sport. Instead, this small, urban liberal arts college offers individualized academic programs, small classes, and a campus that reflects the quirky and kinetic atmosphere of Greenwich Village. "We don't want to become business leaders, but instead teachers, community organizers, thinkers, professors, and writers," a junior says. "Students here want to change the world."

Lang fits right in amid the brownstones and trendy boutiques of one of New York's most vibrant neighborhoods. The majority of Lang's classrooms and facilities are in a single five-story building between Fifth and Sixth avenues on West 11th Street, although The New School occupies 16 buildings along Fifth Avenue. The New School's library is small, but students have access to the massive Bobst Library at nearby NYU, which is just a few blocks away, as is the excitement of Greenwich Village and Washington Square Park. The new 16-story University Center offers state-of-the-art facilities, including fully wired "smart" classrooms, design studios, a residence hall, and an auditorium.

The New School was founded in 1919 by a band of progressive scholars that included John Dewey, Charles Beard, and Thorstein Veblen. A decade and a half later, it became a haven for European intellectuals fleeing Nazi persecution, and over the years it has been the teaching home of many notable thinkers, including Buckminster Fuller and Hannah Arendt. Created in 1978, the undergraduate college was renamed in the late '80s for Eugene Lang, a philanthropist who made a significant donation to the school. In addition to Eugene Lang College, today's New School includes a graduate program in social research, a school of management, and various arts programs, most notably Parsons School of Design. At night, the Schools of Public Engagement are host to a huge assortment of lectures and continuing education courses.

The two most distinctive features of Lang College are the small classes—88 percent have fewer than 20 students—and undergraduates pursuing their own path of study with minimal general education requirements. As freshmen, students choose one required first-year seminar from a broad-based menu, such as Music and Politics and Beyond the Human Being, in addition to taking workshops on nonacademic concerns and study skills and one year of writing. As sophomores, they begin to focus on their chosen major. In their final year, students take on a senior capstone, through a seminar or independent project, that synthesizes their educational experience.

> "I appreciate the way that class discussions are so well planned and thought out."

Lang's most popular majors include culture and media, literary studies, the arts, and liberal arts; economics, journalism and design, and politics are other strengths. Its city location enhances the urban studies program. The writing concentration is highly praised, and the arts programs are generally strong. While introductory language courses are plentiful, upper-level language offerings are limited. The college has, however, beefed up its offerings on the history and literature of Third World and minority peoples, which were already better than those at most colleges. More than a dozen joint B.A./M.A. and B.S./M.S. programs are available, including media studies, international affairs, nonprofit management, psychology, and philosophy. Cooperation, not competition, is the norm at Lang. "The coursework and expectations are demanding," a senior says, but the focus is on "communal and collaborative learning." Professors are well versed and engaging, according to many students. "I appreciate the way that class discussions are so well planned and thought out," says one student.

The main academic complaint is the limited range of seminars, but outside programs and partnerships offer more variety. After their first year, students may enroll in a limited number of approved classes in other divisions of The New School. Exchange programs with Sarah Lawrence College, American University of Paris, and John Cabot University (among others) provide motivated students with additional academic opportunities. Lang's Civic Liberal Arts program offers courses that are cotaught by faculty and visiting fellows from community partners, the likes of which have included the *New York Times*,

> "We are nontraditional college students who relish in this difference."

the Whitney Museum of American Art, and Brooklyn Grange; one student in each course is selected to be a student fellow, receiving a stipend to take on various teaching assistant tasks, such as research or technical assistance. Twenty-three percent of students study abroad, and Lang has designed a new program that gives incoming freshmen a chance to spend their first year abroad, undertaking coursework, fieldwork, research, and an internship focused on issues of development, social justice, and sustainability.

(continued)

Applicants: 3,449
Accepted: 71%
Enrolled: 17%
Grad in 6 Years: 53%
Returning Freshmen: 74%
Academics: ✑ ✑ ✑
Social: ☎
Q of L: ★ ★ ★
Admissions: (212) 229-5665
Email Address:
   lang@newschool.edu

Strong Programs:
Culture and Media
Literary Studies
The Arts
Liberal Arts
Economics
Journalism and Design
Politics
Urban Studies

Lang's Civic Liberal Arts program offers courses cotaught by visiting fellows from community partners, such as the New York Times.

Lang attracts a disparate group of undergraduates, but most of them can be described as idealistic and independent. "We are nontraditional college students who relish in this difference and exciting uniqueness that sets us apart from conforming NYU students," a junior says. Some are slightly older than conventional college age and are used to looking after themselves. Twenty-eight percent of Lang's students are from New York, and 8 percent come from abroad. Eight percent are African American, 17 percent are Hispanic, and 5 percent are Asian American. Lang admits students regardless of their finances and strives to meet the demonstrated need of those enrolled, although it does not guarantee to do so. An impressive 58 percent of freshmen qualify for Pell Grants. A deferred-payment plan allows students to pay tuition in 10 installments, and there are various loan programs available. A handful of merit scholarships averaging $8,824 are offered, but no varsity teams means no athletic awards.

Roughly one-third of the students sign up for dorm life at Lang, and the rooms are reported to be in good shape. Stuyvesant Park and University Center are the newest dorms; Stuy Park caters predominantly to first-year students. Off-campus dwellers live in apartments in the Village (if they can afford it) or in Brooklyn (if they can afford it), or elsewhere in the New York City area. A meal plan is available, but most students opt for the hundreds of delis, coffee shops, and restaurants that line Sixth Avenue.

> **"Our lack of campus kind of makes all activity 'off campus.'"**

Indeed, many students cite the school's location as one of its best features. "Whatever is desired can be found somewhere in New York City," says a junior. "It's a nice place to be if you want to party or be a stone-cold intellectual." The social network at Lang is quite small and, like many things, is left up to the student. "Our lack of campus kind of makes all activity 'off campus,' though we do have dances and club activities within the school facilities themselves," a junior says. The social activities found on campus tend to involve intellectual pursuits such as poetry readings and open-mic nights, as well as typical college activities like the student newspaper and the literary magazine. Students generally avoid drinking on campus, and when they do imbibe, alcohol is "far from the central focus of activity," says a junior. Sixty percent of students get involved in community service. Athletics barely register here, although the school does field three teams: men's basketball, and men's and women's cross-country.

Despite the seeming lack of tradition and sense of community, Eugene Lang College's stock continues to rise. Students relish the freedom and independence they have here. For a student who yearns for four years of "traditional" college experiences, Lang would likely be a disappointment. But for those desiring an intimate education in America's cultural capital, Lang offers all the stimulation of the city it calls home.

Overlaps

Fashion Institute of Technology, Pratt Institute, School of Visual Arts, NYU, Berklee College of Music, Manhattan School of Music, Columbia

If You Apply To >

Eugene Lang: Early action: Nov. 1. Regular decision: Jan. 15. Financial aid: Feb. 1. Application fee: $50. Campus and alumni interviews: optional, evaluative. SATs or ACTs: optional. Subject Tests: optional. Letters of recommendation: required. Essay: required. Accepts the Common Application.

The Evergreen State College

Olympia, WA 98505

There's no mistaking Evergreen for a typical public college. Never mind its unconventional students; Evergreen's interdisciplinary, team-taught curriculum is unique. To find anything remotely like Evergreen, you'll need to go private and travel east to places like Hampshire or Sarah Lawrence. Evergreen is no longer as selective as it once was, and its graduation rate has suffered accordingly.

In "La Vie Bohème," the anthem of Jonathan Larson's rock opera *Rent*, one of the characters asks, "Anyone out of the mainstream / Is anyone in the mainstream?" At The Evergreen State College, the answer has always been a vehement "No!" The school's unofficial motto is *Omnia Extares*, Latin for "Let it all hang out." Founded in 1967 as Washington State's experimental college, Evergreen has narrative evaluations instead of grades and lacks formal majors, and even departments. This system may sound strange, but it works for those seeking the freedom to chart their own course. "The character of the school is openly artistic, earth-friendly, musically open, and a place to truly be an individual," says a freshman. Where else do you find a criminologist and a theater professor teaching a class together?

Evergreen lies in a fir forest at the edge of the 90-mile-long Puget Sound. The peaceful, 1,000-acre campus includes an organic plant and animal farm, as well as 3,300 feet of saltwater beach. Most of Evergreen's buildings are boxy concrete-and-steel creations, though the Longhouse Education and Cultural Center is designed in the Native American style typical of the Pacific Northwest. In keeping with Evergreen's progressive nature, all new building projects strive to comply with LEED standards. Recent additions include an agriculture laboratory, a Native American carving studio, and major renovations of the media and performing arts, lecture hall, and science laboratory buildings.

At first glance, Evergreen's wide-open curriculum looks like Easy Street: it's based on nine "planning units"—Native programs; critical and creative practices; culture, text, and language; environmental studies; expressive arts; sustainability and justice; scientific inquiry; consciousness studies; and society, politics, behavior, and change.

> **"[Evergreen] gives space for both self-directed learning and small learning communities."**

The structure of learning is different as well. Instead of signing up for unrelated courses to fulfill distribution requirements, students enroll in a coordinated full-time "program" spanning several disciplines, often team-taught by multiple professors. Recent offerings include Earth Dynamics: Climate, People, and History; Visualizing Microbial Seascapes: An Introduction to Animation and Marine Biology; and Business: Innovation, Stewardship, and Change. Still, there is some structure at the college, which operates on 10-week quarters. In addition to professor and self-evaluations, students must write an annual Academic Statement, reflecting on their academic experiences and goals. Many freshmen select an interdisciplinary core program tailored for first-year students, while upperclassmen can concentrate in more specialized areas (though still usually with an interdisciplinary lens), often completing some form of capstone experience, writing a thesis, or fulfilling an Individual Learning Contract developed in partnership with a faculty sponsor.

Students praise Evergreen's environmental studies offerings, which span ornithology, marine science, and wetlands studies, among others. To supplement their coursework, environmental scientists may also study marine animals while sailing in Puget Sound, spend seven weeks at a bird sanctuary in Oregon, or trek to the

Website: www.evergreen.edu
Location: Small City
Public
Total Enrollment: 3,791
Undergraduates: 3,582
Male/Female: 45/55
SAT Ranges: CR 490–630,
   M 450–560
ACT Ranges: 20–26
Financial Aid: 66%
Pell Grant: 34%
Expense: Pub $
Student Loans: 56%
Average Debt: $
Phi Beta Kappa: No
Applicants: 1,744
Accepted: 98%
Enrolled: 34%
Grad in 6 Years: 57%
Returning Freshmen: 66%
Academics: ✍ ✍ ✍
Social: ☎ ☎ ☎
Q of L: ★ ★ ★ ★
Admissions: (360) 867-6170
Email Address: admissions@
   evergreen.edu

Strong Programs:
Environmental Studies
Native American and
   Indigenous Studies
Visual and Media Arts
Social Sciences
Humanities
Physical and Natural Sciences
Languages
Computer Science

Grand Canyon or the tropical rainforests of Costa Rica. The Native American and indigenous studies program is notable, and various arts programs—dance, writing, visual arts, and media arts—also get high marks. And regardless of what they study, students warn that while the integrated approach to learning may improve comprehension and deepen understanding, it likewise means a lot of work. "The academic climate at Evergreen is robust, collaborative, and engaging," says a junior. "It gives space for both self-directed learning and small learning communities." Many academic programs include a service-learning component, and several faculty-led study abroad programs are available; 18 percent of undergrads study abroad.

Because Evergreen attracts many nontraditional students and students who are older than the typical college freshman, administrators take advising and career counseling seriously. They've also asked faculty members to do more to help students adjust to life on campus. "A goal of the faculty here is to get to know each student personally and to understand their interests and goals well enough to make class personally engaging and relevant to them," explains a political economy student. Another bonus: because Evergreen doesn't award formal tenure, there's less pressure for professors to conduct research and publish their findings—and less to distract them from teaching undergraduates. Professors who do engage in research often involve students in their work, and students may apply for competitive Summer Undergraduate Research Fellowship stipends.

"Greeners want to be open-minded, intelligent, and actually meaningful to the world in which they live," says a student. Seventy-four percent of Evergreen's students are Washington residents, and just 1 percent come from foreign countries. African Americans account for 5 percent of the student body, Hispanics 10 percent, and Asian Americans 3 percent. Twenty-eight percent of students self-identify as LGBTQ, and 39 percent are of a nontraditional age. "For the most part people are very liberal and tend to be very involved in organizing around an issue they feel is important," a senior says. Students for Justice in Palestine, Feminists in Solidarity Together, Food Not Bombs, T-Rex (a transgender group), and Black Cottonwood Collective (an anarchist group) represent just a small sampling of the student activist groups on campus. An impressive number of incoming freshmen (34 percent) are eligible for the Pell Grant. A limited number of merit scholarships averaging $5,330 are available for qualified students, as are 23 athletic scholarships in 5 sports.

Twenty-three percent of Evergreen students, mostly freshmen and sophomores, live on campus. Students appreciate the amenities in the school's apartment complexes but say the dorms need sprucing up. "Housing is a really fun time for first-year students excited to become a part of the Evergreen community, but it is expensive and only really makes sense for the first year," reasons a junior. There's an efficient bus system to get nonresidents to class on time, though it helps to have a car. Evergreen's food service offers a wide variety of dishes. "We have the amazing student-run café, the Flaming Eggplant. They serve delicious, locally sourced food that caters to special diets," cheers one student. Students say campus security is good and instances of sexual assault are uncommon, but one student says that when it does happen, "Evergreen needs to work on reconciling its progressive, liberal image with the way that assaults are actually handled."

Given the pervasive individualism that flavors Evergreen, it's little surprise that the college lacks a Greek system. Still, the housing and student activities offices organize plenty of events—including open-mic nights, soccer and other field games, and parties. Student musicians are often at the center of the social scene, hosting

Evergreen has narrative evaluations instead of grades and lacks formal majors.

"We are in a marijuana-legal state, but you cannot have pot on campus. As you can imagine, this is the most violated rule."

Twenty-eight percent of students self-identify as LGBTQ, and 39 percent are of a nontraditional age.

"There is no box at Evergreen; there's just the experience of being here."

on-campus performances or playing popular "house shows" off campus. "We are in a marijuana-legal state, but you cannot have pot on campus. As you can imagine, this is the most violated rule on campus," quips a religious studies student. The fall Harvest Festival on the college's organic farm is a favorite annual event.

Olympia (the state capital) doesn't really qualify as a college town, but it is progressive and open-minded, with art walks through local galleries, coffee shops, clothing stores, co-ops, and a thriving music scene. "It's a rad little town with its own personality," says a junior. The college's outdoor program organizes mountaineering, backpacking, and rock-climbing trips and offers a wide range of gear for rent. Seattle (just over an hour away) and Portland and the rugged Oregon coast (two to three hours) provide changes of scenery; everything is kept green and lush by the (interminable) rain, which stops in time for summer break and resumes by November.

You may chuckle at Evergreen's mascot, an eight-foot clam named "Speedy" (a nod to the large geoduck clams found in Puget Sound), but the school has an active intercollegiate athletics program. Its basketball, soccer, track and field, and women's volleyball teams compete in the NAIA Division II Cascade Conference. While the Geoduck squads haven't brought home any titles recently, Evergreen has produced All-American athletes. About 10 percent of students choose to participate in recreational or intramural sports.

Evergreen remains one of the best choices for students who see traditional academic structures as too restrictive. Freed from requirements and grades, Greeners delight in exploring the connections between disparate disciplines at their own pace. It's a challenging task that requires an incredible ability to focus, but for Greeners, the rewards lie in an education that is personally meaningful and that allows them to develop and express their own identities. "Here you can truly be whoever you want to be," says a junior. "There's really nothing to fit into. There is no box at Evergreen; there's just the experience of being here."

The college's outdoor program organizes mountaineering, backpacking, and rock-climbing trips.

Overlaps

Western Washington, University of Washington, UC–Santa Cruz, Lewis & Clark, Washington State, Hampshire, Portland State, University of Puget Sound

If You Apply To ≫ **Evergreen:** Rolling admissions. (Priority deadline: Feb. 1.) Financial aid: Mar. 1. Housing: Jul. 14. Application fee: $50. Campus interviews: optional, evaluative. No alumni interviews. SATs or ACTs: required. No Subject Tests. Letters of recommendation: optional. Essay: recommended.

Fairfield University

Fairfield, CT 06824

Strategically located on Long Island Sound near New York City, Fairfield offers a classic Jesuit-style Roman Catholic education. Nursing and business are the biggest academic draws. Lack of big-time sports keeps Fairfield from enjoying the visibility of Boston College or Holy Cross. Lack of diversity, socioeconomic and otherwise, is both a problem and an issue on campus. Explosive party scene.

Fairfield University is trying to move into the same class as older, more revered East Coast Jesuit institutions such as Boston College to the north and Georgetown to the south. It offers a dynamic living and learning environment that combines solid academics, real-world opportunities in and outside of the classroom, and an abundance of community service projects. Priests and lay faculty alike promote the traditional religious and humanistic values of the Society of Jesus. Most students hail from privileged backgrounds, and the lack of Greek organizations is never an obstacle to

Website: www.fairfield.edu
Location: Suburban
Private
Total Enrollment: 4,214
Undergraduates: 3,702
Male/Female: 40/60

Students in the JUHAN club organize campus events raising awareness for humanitarian issues and serve as delegates to the U.N. Youth Summit.

organizing a good party. At Fairfield, one senior says, "the main goal of everyone is to make sure that every student is successful."

The physical beauty of the university's scenic, tree-lined campus just 60 minutes from Manhattan is a source of pride. The administration takes pains to preserve a lush atmosphere of sprawling lawns, ponds, and natural woodlands. Buildings are a blend of collegiate Gothic, Norman chateau, English manor, and modern. Students enjoy a 24-hour computer lab and a Geographic Information Systems lab. A new 3,000-seat stadium was recently completed.

Students may have difficulty finding time to savor the beautiful facilities. A demanding class schedule requires everyone to complete the liberal arts core curriculum over four years, with two to five courses from each of five areas: math and natural sciences; history and social and behavioral sciences; philosophy, religious studies, and applied ethics; English and visual and performing arts; and modern and classical languages. The core constitutes almost half of a student's total courseload. Freshmen are introduced to Fairfield with a thorough orientation program that includes a series of seminars and events. A formal academic convocation in the first week of classes includes a speaker chosen to reflect the school's Jesuit values.

Fairfield's main academic strengths—and most popular majors—are nursing, business (finance, management, and accounting), communication, and psychology.

"The main goal of everyone is to make sure that every student is successful."

Students enrolled in the Dolan School of Business have access to a state-of-the-art, multi-purpose financial markets classroom known as the Business Experiential, Simulation, and Trading Floor classroom. Irish studies has strong ties to the University of Galway, and Italian studies features links to the Florence University of the Arts. Four new undergraduate degrees have been added recently: bioengineering, environmental studies, digital journalism, and public relations. A new minor in humanitarian action was created in 2016, as an outgrowth of Fairfield's involvement as a founding member, along with Fordham and Georgetown, of the Jesuit Universities Humanitarian Action Network (JUHAN). Students can also join the JUHAN club to organize campus events raising awareness for humanitarian issues, participate in alternative spring breaks, and serve as delegates to the U.N. Youth Summit.

"The academic climate is definitely collaborative. I have never felt as though I am competing against my classmates," says a politics and communication double major. There are no teaching assistants at Fairfield, and 43 percent of classes have fewer than 20 students. Students report that the quality of teaching varies. "For every great professor, there was a terrible counterpart," says a biology and psychology double major. "That being said, the good professors I had were wonderful and helped me shape my future and change my life."

Thirty-four percent of students study abroad each year, through their choice of more than 80 programs. Students looking to travel without committing to a full semester can take a trip with one of several professors who lead educational tours for credit during the winter intercession, spring break, and the summer. Since 1993, 65 Fairfield students have been awarded Fulbright scholarships for studies abroad. Eight percent of students join the four-year honors program, and while participants give it mixed reviews, most agree that its best quality is the team-teaching from professors across departments, which lends an interdisciplinary perspective that "challenges you to think critically," according to a senior. Fifteen percent carry out undergraduate research projects, and qualified students in biology, chemistry, and physics are guaranteed the opportunity to do so.

Twenty-five percent of Fairfield undergraduates are from Connecticut, and 2 percent come from abroad. African Americans constitute 2 percent of the student body,

Hispanics 7 percent, and Asian Americans 2 percent. The vast majority of students come from conservative, relatively wealthy Roman Catholic families, and a senior says, "Any students of diversity have a hard time." Race and diversity became a topic of reflection on campus in 2016 after students held an off-campus "ghetto"-themed party that attracted the attention of the *New York Times* and went viral on social media. According to a junior, "there is a high level of entitlement," and others note that a predominant spending culture can make it difficult for students from lower-income backgrounds to fit in. To help students with Fairfield's price tag, the school offers merit scholarships annually, averaging $13,527, as well as athletic scholarships in 20 sports.

Qualified students in biology, chemistry, and physics are guaranteed the opportunity to carry out undergraduate research projects.

Fairfield's residence halls house 75 percent of the student body, and housing is guaranteed for all four years. Several living/learning communities are available for undergrads of all levels and come highly recommended. "Living in a tight-knit community and making wonderful friends while having important discussions about the state of the world and giving back to the community was very rewarding," says a junior. Seniors can apply to live off campus, and among the most popular options are the privately owned beach houses and apartments on Long Island Sound made available to students off-season. Meal plan options are available to all students, but many say the menu is middling at best. "The food is not impressive, but it is palatable," says a junior.

"The good professors I had were wonderful and helped me shape my future and change my life."

The social life at Fairfield revolves mainly around partying. "At night, you will be partying on campus or at the bar," says a senior, adding, "I would classify Fairfield as a party school." The university has built more dorms in recent years, in an effort to enhance the residential nature of the school and at the same time reduce the number of students living along the Sound, where partying was becoming boisterous, prompting complaints from beach residents. The move seems to have had the effect, however, of importing the party culture to campus, and students agree that alcohol policies the administration has implemented in response are ineffective. "The university has strict security and policies on alcohol, which encourages binge drinking," explains a junior. "People drink quickly and drink hard liquor to get drunk quick and avoid being caught. It is not a healthy party culture." Despite increased educational programming aimed at preventing sexual assault, students indicate that reported cases are not always taken seriously and "have not been dealt with as effectively as they could have been." Counseling services in general receive mixed reviews.

Clam Jam is an annual beach party with live music, kegs, and food trucks.

Party culture notwithstanding, students find plenty of on-campus activity to keep them busy, including a growing number of student organizations to meet just about any interest. Sponsored events range from dances to hanging out at the campus coffeehouse to concerts. Harvest Weekend at the end of October and Dogwoods Weekend at the end of April provide relief from the stress of studying, and Clam Jam is an annual beach party with live music, kegs, and food trucks. The Campus Ministry draws a large following, with daily masses, retreats, and regular community service work, including two weeks of programs in the Caribbean and Latin America.

"There is a high level of entitlement."

As for the surrounding area, some students say the quaint, wealthy Fairfield area can feel a bit "snobby," and though they enjoy frequenting the many shopping centers, boutiques, and restaurants, relations with local residents are sometimes strained. "Community members are not often comfortable participating in university events and vice versa," a student says. Even so, volunteerism abounds, with three-quarters of the student body performing community service, often in the troubled nearby city of Bridgeport. "The influence of Bridgeport on my Fairfield experience has been profound," says a student. Road trips to New York (an hour by train) and Boston (two hours away) are popular.

The Stags compete in Division I, and women's lacrosse, softball, field hockey, and volleyball were all Metro Atlantic Athletic Conference champions in 2015.

"I would classify Fairfield as a party school."

Men's lacrosse and baseball are also competitive. Men's and women's basketball both draw crowds, and the boisterous home-court fans, who come to games in full Fairfield regalia, have been dubbed the "Red Sea." Living up to the Jesuit commitment to sound mind and body, 39 percent of the students play on one of 18 intramural and 24 club sports teams. The school also takes pride in its high graduation rate for athletes, regularly one of the highest rates in the country.

Although Fairfield University is wrestling with issues of diversity and is reflecting seriously on how to create a safe, inclusive social atmosphere on campus, it remains committed to its Jesuit ideals and to offering an undergraduate experience defined by close bonds with faculty, challenging academics, an emphasis on community involvement, and the holistic development of each student. "Fairfield seeks to help people realize that there is more to life than your marketing degree," one satisfied student says. "Students are taught to open their eyes and see the real world."

Overlaps

Providence, Loyola University Maryland, Boston College, Villanova, Fordham, Quinnipiac, Bentley, College of the Holy Cross

If You Apply To >

Fairfield: Early action: Nov. 1. Early decision I: Nov. 15. Early decision II, regular decision, and financial aid: Jan. 15. Housing: May 1. Application fee: $00. Campus and alumni interviews: optional, evaluative, SATs or ACTs: optional (interviews are recommended for test-optional applicants). No Subject Tests. Letters of recommendation: required. Essay: required. Accepts the Common Application with supplement.

University of Florida

Gainesville, FL 32611

It should come as no surprise that UF is a world leader in citrus science. Add communications, engineering, and Latin American studies to the list of renowned programs. Among Deep South public universities, only the University of Georgia rivals UF in overall quality. None rivals it in alcohol consumption. Top-shelf varsity sports teams are a year-round draw.

Website: www.ufl.edu
Location: Small City
Public
Total Enrollment: 42,903
Undergraduates: 30,594
Male/Female: 44/56
SAT Ranges: CR 580–670, M 590–680
ACT Ranges: 27–31
Financial Aid: 93%
Pell Grant: 27%
Expense: Pub $
Student Loans: 43%
Average Debt: $

Set on 2,000 acres of rolling, heavily forested terrain in north-central Florida, the University of Florida is an athletic powerhouse, and administrators are working hard to gain the same level of national recognition for their academic offerings as well. With roughly 30,000 undergraduates, the school is already massive and continues to become more so as it adds scores of new faculty in areas such as food security, big data, drug discovery, and neuroscience. While some students certainly get lost in the shuffle, those who can navigate the bureaucratic red tape will find ample resources at their fingertips, including the world's largest collection of butterflies and moths, an $85 million Cancer and Genetics Research Complex, and extensive facilities for agriculture education. The state's flagship university has become more selective in its admissions and continues to wage an aggressive campaign against its long-standing tradition of free-flowing alcohol.

UF's campus has more than 20 buildings on the National Register of Historic Places. Most are collegiate Gothic in style—redbrick with white trim. They're augmented by more modern facilities, including a 173,000-square-foot complex for nursing, pharmacy, and the health professions, and an honors dorm complex. UF's research capabilities and equipment are likewise impressive, and a boon to aspiring physicians. The school has one of the nation's few self-contained intensive care hyperbaric chambers for treatment of near-drowning victims, and a world-class, federally funded brain institute. Two new residence halls have recently been completed, including one of only five in the nation designed specifically to accommodate students with severe physical impairments.

Academically, UF's strongest programs are those with a preprofessional bent, including engineering, accounting, and pharmacy. Popular majors include social sciences, engineering, business management, and the biological and biomedical sciences. Students also give high marks to the College of Journalism and Communications, which boasts the lavish Innovation News Center that houses the college's news, weather, and sports operations. The Bob Graham Center for Public Service trains students in languages, culture, and other skills vital to careers in public service. Students admitted to UF's freshman class with super-high GPAs and test scores are invited into the Honors Program, where most classes are limited to 25 students. The program offers honors sections in standard academic subjects, and interdisciplinary courses such as American Civil War and Pop Culture and Environmental Issues in Water Resources. Additionally, honors students are invited to live in the Honors Residential College at Hume Hall and are members of the Student Honors Organization. The Innovation Academy offers another distinct living/learning opportunity for undergraduates with a spring-summer schedule, offering options for internships and research in the fall. It draws students from more than 30 majors with one common minor: innovation. About 1,700 students study abroad each year through more than 60 university-sponsored programs, more than 80 exchange programs, and a wide variety of independent non-UF programs.

"Around football season, campus tends to be more relaxed."

To balance students' preprofessional coursework, UF's general education program requires credits in composition, math, humanities, social and behavioral sciences, and physical and biological sciences. Students must also take six credits in the humanities or social or physical sciences that focus on themes of internationalism or diversity, as well as nine credits of multidisciplinary courses focused on topics of current importance. "Prospective students should definitely look into a course called First Year Florida," one student suggests. "It is equivalent to a semester-long orientation to our university."

UF's academic climate is intense and collaborative. "Closer to midterms and final exams, campus feels constricted and very tense, with everyone huddled in libraries. However, around football season, campus tends to be more relaxed," says one political science major. While UF offers programs in every conceivable discipline, like many supersized schools, it also forces students to climb a mountain of bureaucracy to get the courses and credits they need. Occasionally, for example, lectures in the Warrington College of Business Administration are recorded and posted online so that everyone can see them. Still, administrators are working to fix these problems. Professors often have deep professional experience and bring enthusiasm to their work, though students often find TAs behind the lectern. A senior says, "I have yet to encounter a professor that is not absolutely passionate about the subject they are teaching."

"The University of Florida enrolls some of the most innovative and driven students in the nation," says a senior. UF is Florida's flagship university, and 94 percent of students here hail from the Sunshine State, while 1 percent come from overseas. Despite the geographical homogeneity, they're an ethnically diverse bunch, with African Americans adding 6 percent of the student body, Asian Americans 8 percent,

(continued)

Phi Beta Kappa: Yes
Applicants: 29,837
Accepted: 48%
Enrolled: 50%
Grad in 6 Years: 87%
Returning Freshmen: 96%
Academics: ✍ ✍ ✍ ✍
Social: 🍷 🍷 🍷 🍷 🍷
Q of L: ★ ★ ★ ★
Admissions: (352) 392-1365
Email Address: webrequests@
    admissions.ufl.edu

Strong Programs:
Social Sciences
Engineering
Business Management
Biology
Accounting
Pharmacy
Journalism
Citrus Science

UF boasts one of only five residence halls in the nation designed specifically to accommodate students with severe physical impairments.

and Hispanics 21 percent. Politically, the campus leans liberal, although conservative students are active too; a political science major cites "racism and LGBTQ+ affairs (all-gender restrooms on campus)" as hot-button issues. UF offers more than 480 athletic scholarships, as well as thousands of merit scholarships averaging $2,468. UF has also raised special funds for financial aid for students from low-income families; 27 percent of students are Pell-eligible.

Undergrads typically live on campus during their freshman year but then move out after that, largely because of lack of space; overall, 24 percent of students stay on campus. Dorms are described as comfortable, and a senior advises, "It is great to live on campus for at least one year to really immerse oneself in the UF experience and for simple convenience." Dining halls get mixed reviews, but students agree that suitable provisions are made for vegetarians and vegans. Campus security draws praise, thanks to a robust police presence and a late-night "Later Gator" transportation system. "While there have been no large-scale issues on campus, you would be hard-pressed to find a student who was unaware of UF's efforts to combat and educate students on sexual assault," says a student.

> **"Gainesville is an awesome, young town that is perfectly suited for college students."**

Students at UF have more than 1,000 student organizations to choose from, making it easier to find a social niche. Twenty percent of UF's men and 24 percent of the women go Greek; rush is held before classes start in the fall and again in the spring. UF students have a reputation for knowing how to party, but the binge-drinking rate has fallen sharply as a result of tough enforcement of zero-tolerance campus policies, including a ban on drinking games. Freshmen must pass a 90-minute online alcohol education course in order to register for their spring semester. "Fraternity row is generally hopping every Friday and Saturday night, but off-campus parties are certainly a fixture as well. Midtown, located right across from the stadium, is the typical place for students to find nightlife," a senior reports.

Gainesville, a city of about 127,000 between the Atlantic Ocean and the Gulf of Mexico, largely revolves around the university. "Gainesville is an awesome, young town that is perfectly suited for college students who wish to relax and unwind," a student says. There are plenty of stores, restaurants, and bars, as well as a sports arena and the Center for Performing Arts, which brings in world-class symphony orchestras, Broadway plays, opera, and large-scale ballet productions. The university owns a nearby lake, which is "great for lazy Sundays" and more vigorous water sports, and there's a plethora of parks, forests, rivers, and streams for backpacking, camping, and canoeing. Beaches and Orlando are also popular destinations.

Sports are a year-round obsession here, and the students go wild anytime the Division I Gators take to the court or the gridiron, especially when they're squaring off against rivals Florida State or the University of Georgia. The annual homecoming extravaganza, known as "Gator Growl," is billed as the biggest student-run pep rally in the country. Other sports are not forgotten, though; the university has one

> **"UF challenges all of its students to tap their inner strengths and talents and apply what they learn."**

of the top intercollegiate programs in the nation, with varsity competition (in the ferocious Southeastern Conference) for men and women in 16 sports, including powerhouse teams in baseball, track and field, lacrosse, tennis, swimming and diving, volleyball, and soccer. Women's gymnastics and softball are both recent national champions. Intramural sports are popular (27 percent of students participate), and for those who don't want to join a team, the 60,000-square-foot fitness park offers aerobics classes, martial arts, strength training equipment, and squash and racquetball courts.

The Innovation Academy offers a living/learning opportunity and a minor in innovation.

The annual homecoming extravaganza, known as "Gator Growl," is billed as the biggest student-run pep rally in the country.

Overlaps

Florida State, University of Central Florida, University of South Florida, University of Miami (FL), Florida International, Florida Atlantic, Florida Gulf Coast, University of North Florida

For some students, Florida's sheer size is overwhelming. For others, it's a drawing card. Combine great weather with nationally recognized programs in engineering and business, and nationally ranked athletic teams, and it's easy to see why Sunshine State natives clamor to study here. Says an agricultural education and communication major, "UF challenges all of its students to tap their inner strengths and talents and apply what they learn so that they may leave a positive mark on their communities and society."

If You Apply To >

Florida: Regular decision: Nov. 1. Financial aid: Dec. 15. Application fee: $30. No campus or alumni interviews. SATs or ACTs: required. No Subject Tests. No letters of recommendation. Essay: required. Students apply to a particular school within UF.

Florida Institute of Technology

Melbourne, FL 32901

FIT is practically a branch of the nearby Kennedy Space Center, so aeronautics and aviation are popular specialties. The Atlantic Ocean is close at hand, making the school an ideal spot for marine biology. Only drawback to otherwise ideal location is the occasional early-fall hurricane evacuation. FIT is the smallest of the major technical institutions in the Southeast.

Students at the Florida Institute of Technology can explore the endless depths of the ocean or shoot for the stars. Located just 40 minutes from one of NASA's primary launch pads, Florida Tech is a child of the nation's space program and the only independent technological university in the Southeast. The school's subtropical setting is perfect for scientific research and study in oceanography, meteorology, marine biology, and environmental science. It comes as no surprise that some of the most cutting-edge work in space and water-related sciences happens here. The combination of academic excellence and a convenient central Florida location—just an hour from the dizzying bustle of Walt Disney World—draws students to this high-flying and innovative school.

Founded in 1958 to meet the academic needs of engineers and scientists working at what is now the Kennedy Space Center, Florida Tech's 130-acre contemporary campus features a botanical garden, an aquatic center, and a textile art museum. Campus architecture ranges from modern to Georgian Gothic. The university has opened a number of new facilities in recent years, including the Harris Student Design Center, also referred to as "the PantherWorks," a high-tech maker space exclusively for student use.

If you're considering Florida Tech, make sure you have a strong background in math and science, especially chemistry and physics. Few students major in the less practical sciences. Though many students grouse that Florida Tech is too expensive for their tastes, those who plan their education well are able to get high-paying technical jobs as soon as they graduate. Everyone must take courses in communication, physical or life science, mathematics, humanities, and social sciences, and demonstrate proficiency in the technologies pertinent to their chosen major. All majors include hands-on projects and capstone requirements. Incoming freshmen are welcomed with a weeklong

"Florida Tech is very competitive because of the nature of the majors."

Website: www.fit.edu
Location: Small City
Private
Total Enrollment: 4,703
Undergraduates: 3,188
Male/Female: 71/29
SAT Ranges: CR 520–620, M 560–670
ACT Ranges: 24–29
Financial Aid: 85%
Pell Grant: 22%
Expense: Pr $
Student Loans: 51%
Average Debt: $ $ $ $
Phi Beta Kappa: No
Applicants: 9,303
Accepted: 57%
Enrolled: 12%
Grad in 6 Years: 55%
Returning Freshmen: 79%
Academics: ✍ ✍ ✍
Social: ☎ ☎ ☎
Q of L: ★ ★ ★
Admissions: (800) 888-4348
Email Address: admission@fit.edu

orientation program highlighted by trips to Disney World and the beach, just three miles away. Almost all freshmen take part in the University Experience course, which helps them adapt to college life. Prospective aviation students can major in aviation management, aviation meteorology, or aviation computer science, as well as aeronautics with or without a flight option. The flight school has a modern fleet of 30 airplanes and three flight-training devices. The most popular majors are mechanical engineering, electrical engineering, aviation management, aerospace engineering, and marine biology. New degree programs in human factors and safety (with a flight option), entrepreneurship, and biomedical engineering have recently been added.

The academic climate at FIT is challenging. "Florida Tech is very competitive because of the nature of the majors," says one junior. Forty-nine percent of classes have fewer than 20 students, and the majority are taught by full professors. All majors offer co-op programs and senior independent research at the Indian River Lagoon or on the *RV Delphinus*, a 60-foot research boat the school owns. Marine research has included manatee preservation, beach erosion, and sea turtle studies. The ProTrack cooperative education program allows students in the College of Engineering to complete three semester-long paid work experiences. Students graduate with their employers' names on their final transcripts. Study abroad options are available in Oxford, England, and other locales, although only 3 percent of undergrads study internationally while at FIT.

Fifty-one percent of Florida Tech students are Florida natives, while 34 percent hail from outside the country. "It is a microcosm of intelligent people representing 100 countries," says a sophomore. "It's like traveling the world in four years." African Americans comprise 6 percent of the student body, Asian Americans 2 percent, and Hispanics 7 percent. The proportion of women is low even by techie school standards. Florida Tech offers merit scholarships averaging $14,838 and 153 athletic scholarships in 22 sports; 22 percent of freshmen qualify for the Pell Grant.

There is a growing selection of dorms at Florida Tech, and they are modern and well maintained. Forty-two percent of students make their home on campus. "Residence Life takes a holistic approach to making every resident feel right at home," says a junior. Freshmen are required to live on campus in large double rooms. Four-student apartments are available to a small percentage of qualifying upperclassmen by lottery. Students who live off campus are drawn by cheap rent and not much else, because Melbourne is "quiet and is not a typical college town," reports an aerospace engineering major. The meal plan is an open, unlimited arrangement, and students report the food is fair to middling. FIT's thorough Title IX program includes the Stop It Before It Starts campaign, developed by students as a senior design project.

Watching space shots from campus with a trained eye and a cold brew is a treasured pastime. The campus bar, the Rat, is a popular hangout, and there are more than 100 active clubs and organizations on campus; performance-oriented groups such as Pep Band and the College Players are student favorites. Fraternities and sororities are becoming more popular at Florida Tech, claiming 3 percent of the men and 5 percent of the women, respectively. While the campus is officially dry, every frat party has beer that the underage eagerly guzzle, students say. Besides partying, students spend their downtime surfing, fishing, sailing, hanging out at the beach, shopping, or going for a "Sunday drive" (in the sky) with a flight school student. Most Florida Tech students who don't have cars choose bikes and skateboards as their favorite mode of transportation; dining halls and other common areas are equipped with skateboard racks. "If you don't have a car of your own, it may be hard because public transportation is limited," cautions one student. Diversions can

The flight school has a modern fleet of 30 airplanes and three flight-training devices.

Thirty-four percent of undergrads hail from outside the country, but the proportion of women is low even by techie school standards.

"Residence Life takes a holistic approach to making every resident feel right at home."

be found in Orlando (with Epcot, Disney Hollywood Studios, and Animal Kingdom abutting Disney World) or at the Kennedy Space Center, each within an hour's drive. Students also hit the road for other Sunshine State cities, including Tampa, Key West, Miami, Daytona, and St. Augustine. Every April, students brace for the invasion of other collegians on spring break.

The Florida Tech Panthers field 22 varsity teams that compete in Division II. Men's rowing captured back-to-back championship titles in the Dad Vail Regatta in 2015 and 2016, while softball won the NCAA South Region II championship. Baseball, men's swimming, women's basketball and track and field, and men's and women's golf have also been successful. The university's Precision Flight Team, the Falcons, regularly wins awards at National Intercollegiate Flying Association conferences. About a third of students participate in the expanding intramural program in sports like soccer, volleyball, flag football, and cricket.

Whether it's surveying the sky 30,000 feet above or marine coral 50 feet below the sea, students at Florida Tech get hands-on experience that serves to sharpen the school's already specialized, high-quality academics. The administration continues to focus on capital improvements, sponsor cutting-edge research, and embrace diversity. And with beaches and amusements close at hand, students can have some real fun in the sun while they prepare for high-flying or low-lying careers.

> **Overlaps**
>
> **Embry-Riddle Aeronautical, University of Central Florida, University of Florida, Penn State, Purdue, Rochester Institute of Technology, Drexel, Virginia Tech**

> **If You Apply To ➤**
>
> **Florida Tech:** Rolling admissions. (Priority deadline: Feb. 1.) Financial aid: Mar. 1. Housing: May 1. No application fee. Campus interviews: recommended, evaluative. Alumni interviews: optional, informational. SATs or ACTs: required. Subject Tests: optional. Letters of recommendation: required. Essay: required. Accepts the Common Application with supplement.

Florida Southern College

BEST BUY

111 Lake Hollingsworth Drive, Lakeland, FL 33801

FSC combines top-ranked Division II athletics, strong career-oriented programs, an active Greek system, and a picturesque campus that doubles as a Frank Lloyd Wright museum. Located between Tampa and Orlando. Competes with Rollins and Eckerd, but its reputation is more regional and its student body more conservative.

Founded in 1883, Florida Southern College remains committed to providing students with a solid liberal arts foundation and exceptional signature programs. Students enjoy a bevy of academic choices, including outstanding preprofessional programs, extensive internship opportunities, and a vigorous study abroad program. They also appreciate the college's United Methodist affiliation and its mission to develop well-rounded graduates.

Situated on more than 100 sloping acres overlooking pristine Lake Hollingsworth, Florida Southern encompasses one of the world's largest concentrations of buildings designed by famed architect Frank Lloyd Wright. The campus features 12 original Wright structures, as well as the Usonian Faculty House, which the college constructed based on one of Wright's 1938 Usonian home designs to serve as a museum and welcome center for the college's architectural tourism. Wright's Annie Pfeiffer Chapel is a popular meeting and performance venue. The campus is also home to several buildings designed by Robert A. M. Stern, dean of the Yale School of Architecture, including the new Becker Business Building, completed in 2015, which houses a large simulated trading floor with a 153-square-foot video wall, among other high-tech resources.

Website: www.flsouthern.edu
Location: Small City
Private
Total Enrollment: 2,450
Undergraduates: 2,260
Male/Female: 37/63
SAT Ranges: CR 520–620, M 530–610
ACT Ranges: 24–29
Financial Aid: 99%
Pell Grant: 25%
Expense: Pr $
Student Loans: 73%
Average Debt: $ $ $
Phi Beta Kappa: No

(continued)

Applicants: 6,190
Accepted: 45%
Enrolled: 25%
Grad in 6 Years: 57%
Returning Freshmen: 80%
Academics: ✍ ✍ ✍
Social: ☎ ☎ ☎
Q of L: ★ ★ ★
Admissions: (863) 680-4131
Email Address: fscadm@
  flsouthern.edu

Strong Programs:
Business Administration
Biology
Nursing
Psychology
Education
Premed

The campus features 12 original buildings designed by famed architect Frank Lloyd Wright.

The Junior Journey program guarantees all full-time undergrads a short-term travel-study experience.

Florida Southern's core curriculum is based on student learning outcomes in the following eight areas: critical and creative thinking, quantitative reasoning, effective oral and written communication, personal and social responsibility, meaning and value, knowledge of the social world, knowledge of the natural world, and artistic interpretation and expression. Most classes meet for four hours a week, with at least one of those hours fully devoted to engaged learning techniques such as debate, small-group discussions, case studies, and research. First-year students are assigned a faculty mentor who meets with them on a regular basis, and they take part in Up Next, a course that teaches time-management, critical-thinking, money-management, and organizational skills. Students also attend the annual Convocation Series, where they hear from notable figures spanning a spectrum of disciplines.

In all, FSC students may choose from more than 50 undergraduate majors and 40 minors. The most popular majors include business administration, biology, nursing, psychology, and education, and these are among the college's strongest programs. The premed program boasts an exceptional placement rate in medical, dental, and pharmacy programs nationwide. Dual-degree programs are available in preengineering with Washington University in St. Louis and in pre-pharmacy with Lake Erie College of Osteopathic Medicine. New and fast-growing majors include marine biology, musical theatre, dance, and biotechnology.

> **"FSC is a huge advocate for engaged learning."**

"We have a very relaxed academic climate," says a senior. "FSC is a huge advocate for engaged learning, so we always end up working in groups, creating a very collaborative culture." Fifty-nine percent of classes enroll fewer than 20 students. "From the time I was a freshman, I have had extraordinary professors who do their best to cover their material in depth and who genuinely want to see their students succeed," a psychology major says. Students rave about FSC's career services. Says an interpersonal and organizational communication major, "The Career Center is the *best* resource on campus. They offer resume building, 'Moc' interviews, and many more things to help you with your future career."

All students are guaranteed an internship in their fields of study. Students have interned with Charles Schwab, KPMG, the Kennedy Center, OPEC, Fox News, Lockheed Martin, the Walt Disney Company, NASA, and scores of other organizations. The Junior Journey program guarantees all full-time undergraduates a short-term travel-study experience, often at no additional cost. Students may embark on faculty-led trips during May term or summer, fall, and spring breaks to domestic and international locales such as Alaska, the Bahamas, Spain, and Japan. Traditional study abroad options are available as well through preapproved partner programs. Qualified students may enroll in the highly selective honors core, which offers specialized courses in cultural, environmental, artistic, and social heritage. Thirty-seven percent of students carry out undergraduate research projects during their time at FSC.

> **"The Career Center is the *best* resource on campus."**

Florida Southern students are "very down-to-earth and easy to get along with," says one student. Sixty percent of the student body hail from Florida, and 79 percent attended public high schools; 4 percent of students are international. African Americans account for 5 percent of the population, Asian Americans 2 percent, and Hispanics 11 percent. "People are not really concerned with political issues," reports one student. "They tend to mind their own business and have fun with their friends." The college awards merit scholarships, as well as 258 athletic awards in 19 sports. Twenty-five percent of students qualify for Pell Grants.

Eighty-six percent of FSC students reside in student housing. First-year students hang their hats in one of five residence halls, some of which offer stunning lake views, while upperclassmen may choose from a variety of single and double living arrangements, as well as apartment-style housing within walking distance of the campus. The cafeteria serves up "OK" fare, including special options for vegetarians. "Since my freshman year, the food has improved dramatically because of student feedback and suggestions," says a senior. Students report feeling safe on campus, thanks to an active security program. "The campus has a phenomenal program for working with Title IX and has been doing a great job educating students on the issue," say a psychology and criminology major.

The social scene is active on campus. "The college sponsors a myriad of social programs, such as cookouts, concerts, and sporting events, that allow students to stay entertained on campus if they lack transportation," says one student. "In addition, the school also sponsors various bimonthly wellness trips that vary from paintball to snorkeling with manatees." Thirty-four percent of the men and 35 percent of the women go Greek, but Greek life doesn't dominate the social scene. Alcohol is prohibited on campus, and "Greek life is not supposed to have parties," says a senior, adding that alcohol policies "are not always obeyed but are enforced." In addition to the nearly 90 student clubs and organizations, FSC offers a number of traditions, including the annual Christmas tree lighting, the Fair-Well Festival, Southern's Got Talent, Flapjack Fling during finals week, and the Winter Festival (complete with temporary Florida-style snow).

"People are not really concerned with political issues."

A junior describes Lakeland as "a quaint town with a thriving indie art and music scene." The town offers several eateries, malls, movie theaters, and an old downtown district with unique shops and attractions. Many students venture out into the local community to volunteer, often through Greek life programs, or to take part in off-campus church services. For those with access to wheels, popular road trips include excursions to Tampa's sandy beaches, Orlando's famed theme parks, or the Florida Keys.

The dominant Florida Southern Moccasins ("Mocs") field 20 varsity teams that compete in Division II as a member of the Sunshine State Conference. Women's lacrosse won the national championship title in 2016, as did men's basketball in 2015. Other competitive teams include men's and women's swimming, women's basketball, and men's golf and cross-country. "Our athletes dominate Division II sports every year," boasts one student, and the University of Tampa is the Mocs' chief rival. Intramural sports and activities attract 39 percent of undergraduates; the most popular activities include volleyball, flag football, basketball, and soccer. Students also take advantage of a variety of fitness and recreational programs, as well as a 12,000-square-foot wellness center.

Florida Southern College has a lot going for it. Despite the ubiquitous college student laments of limited parking and so-so food, most are quick to point out that they have access to strong academic programs, championship athletics, and all the sun and fun a person could want. "Florida Southern College is a great community where students can grow academically, socially, and emotionally," says one senior. "It truly becomes your home away from home."

Thirty-four percent of the men and 35 percent of the women go Greek, but it doesn't dominate the social scene.

Overlaps

University of South Florida, University of Central Florida, University of Florida, University of Tampa, Stetson, Rollins, Florida State, Eckerd

If You Apply To > **Florida Southern:** Rolling admissions. Early decision: Dec. 1. Priority admissions and financial aid: Mar. 1. Application fee: $30 (paper), free (online). Campus interviews: optional, evaluative. Alumni interviews: optional, informational. SATs or ACTs: required. No Subject Tests. Letters of recommendation: required. Essay: required. Accepts the Common Application with supplement.

A2500 University Center, Tallahassee, FL 32306

Located in Florida's down-home panhandle, FSU is far from the glitz of South Beach or Daytona. The motion picture school is among the best around, and business and the arts are also strong. Notable programs include several living/learning options for freshmen.

Website: www.fsu.edu
Location: Small City
Public
Total Enrollment: 35,129
Undergraduates: 29,185
Male/Female: 44/56
SAT Ranges: CR 560–640, M 560–640
ACT Ranges: 25–29
Financial Aid: 90%
Pell Grant: 24%
Expense: Pub $
Student Loans: 52%
Average Debt: $ $
Phi Beta Kappa: Yes
Applicants: 29,828
Accepted: 56%
Enrolled: 37%
Grad in 6 Years: 79%
Returning Freshmen: 93%
Academics: ✍ ✍ ✍
Social: ☎ ☎ ☎
Q of L: ★ ★ ★ ★ ★
Admissions: (850) 644-6200
Email Address: admissions@ admin.fsu.edu

Strong Programs:
Motion Picture Arts
Psychology
Criminology
English
Finance
Music
Natural Sciences
Engineering

At Florida State University, you could have a Nobel laureate for a professor, study in one of the finest science facilities in the Southeast, or network at the state capitol. The choices are plentiful here, and the pace of life makes it possible to taste a little of everything: a wide array of solid academic choices, blistering Florida sunshine, and plenty to do, from football to Tallahassee hangouts.

FSU is located in the "Other Florida": the one with rolling hills, flowering azaleas and dogwoods, and a canopy of moss-draped oaks. Glistening Gulf of Mexico waters are only half an hour away. The main campus features collegiate Jacobean structures surrounded by plenty of shade trees, with some modern facilities sprinkled in. Situated on 450 compact acres, the campus is the smallest in the state university system—it's just a 10-minute walk from the main gate on the east side to the science complex on the west side. Bicycling and skating are popular forms of transportation, and a free shuttle bus circles campus for those without wheels. Construction is under way on a 130,000-square-foot building that will house research labs, classrooms, and offices for the earth, ocean, and atmospheric science department.

FSU offers nearly 200 undergraduate degrees, the most popular of which are psychology, criminology, English, and finance. Outstanding programs include music, drama, art, and dance, and engineering and the sciences are solid, particularly biology, ecology and evolutionary biology, and physics. Communication, statistics, and business (especially accounting) have strong reputations in the Southeast. The English department and the School of Motion Picture, Television, and Recording Arts have consistently won national and international awards. The economics department has been controversial because of funding it received from the Koch brothers. Most of the more than 80 honors courses offered each academic year have fewer than 25 students, giving gifted students the opportunity to rub shoulders with top faculty. Certain students can even earn their degrees in three years. Directed individual study courses offer undergraduates the chance to participate in independent research projects with faculty direction. Internships and political jobs abound for tomorrow's politicians, since the state capitol and Supreme Court are nearby.

> "The quality of teaching is excellent."

Students report the academic climate is somewhat laid-back but that "the courses are rigorous." Within FSU's liberal studies program, students must complete six hours of multicultural understanding coursework focusing on diversity within the Western experience and cross-cultural studies. Freshmen must take math and English, and may find a TA at the helm in these courses. Thirty-three percent of undergraduate classes have fewer than 20 students, and a senior says, "The quality of teaching is excellent." Freshmen can take advantage of living/learning communities (where students with similar interests or majors live together in the same residence hall and freshman interest groups (clusters of high-demand freshman courses that have been linked by a theme or academic program). About a quarter of undergrads conduct out-of-class research. For those with wanderlust, FSU offers extensive study abroad programs, in which 20 percent of students take part. Options include time at branch campuses in England, Italy, Spain, and Panama and faculty-led programs in 13 other countries. The university is making strides in the world of distance learning: eight undergraduate degrees and a variety of certificates and specialty programs may be completed online.

Perhaps not surprisingly, FSU's student body has a distinctly Floridian flavor: in-staters comprise 90 percent of the group and international students just 1 percent. Eight percent of undergraduates are African American, 2 percent are Asian American, and 19 percent are Hispanic. There's little evidence of racial tension on the diverse campus. Seminoles are a mixture of friendly small-towners and city dwellers, and political tastes tend toward the conservative. Hot topics include voter registration, the environment, and student government concerns. Merit scholarships averaging $3,292 are available to qualified scholars, and athletes vie for 246 scholarships in 20 sports. Twenty-four percent of current freshmen qualify for Pell Grants.

"It is a place I can consider almost like my home."

Nineteen percent of FSU's freshmen live in the university dorms, all of which have been recently renovated. The dorms get mixed reviews from students, and the number who can live in them is limited, so rooms are assigned on a first-come, first-served basis. Upperclassmen generally forsake the housing rat race and move into nearby apartments, houses, or trailers, where they take advantage of the city and campus bus systems to get to school. The dorms are equipped with kitchens; meal plans that offer "good but expensive" food are also available.

When they're not studying, FSU students keep busy with plays, films, concerts, and dorm parties. "The social life is fine," a freshman says. Those with a valid ID can head for one of Tallahassee's bars or restaurants, which fall somewhere between "college hangout" and "real world." Generally, though, students give the area a thumbs-up. As for Greek life, 19 percent of the men and 25 percent of the women join fraternities and sororities, respectively, which constitute another important segment of the social scene.

The Seminoles compete in the Division I Atlantic Coast Conference. The football team won two national titles in the '90s and another in 2013. It attracted national attention in 2016 when it settled a lawsuit alleging sexual assault by a star quarterback. FSU's baseball team also draws an enthusiastic following, as do men's and women's basketball and women's soccer, volleyball, and softball. Nearly 70 percent of students participate in recreational activities, including more than 40 intramural sports and nearly 50 sports clubs.

Florida State remains a solid choice for those seeking knowledge under the blazing Florida sun. FSU students take pride in their school and what it has to offer. "It is a place I can consider almost like my home," says a business major.

Freshmen can take advantage of living/ learning communities and freshman interest groups.

Study abroad options include time at branch campuses in England, Italy, Spain, and Panama.

Overlaps

University of Florida, University of Central Florida, University of South Florida, Florida International, University of Miami (FL), Florida Atlantic, University of North Florida, University of West Florida

If You Apply To ➢

Florida State: Regular decision: Jan. 18. Housing: May 1. Application fee: $30. No campus or alumni interviews. SATs or ACTs: required. No Subject Tests. Letters of recommendation: optional. Essay: strongly recommended.

Rose Hill Campus: 441 East Fordham Road, Bronx, NY 10458
Lincoln Center Campus: 113 West 60th Street, New York, NY 10023

New York City's Fordham is riding the wave of euphoria for colleges in New York. Though still an underdog to places like NYU and Boston College, Fordham is coming on strong. There is no better location than Lincoln Center in Manhattan, where the performing arts programs are housed. The Bronx location is less appealing but adjacent to the New York Botanical Garden and Bronx Zoo.

Website: www.fordham.edu
Location: City Center
Private
Total Enrollment: 12,364
Undergraduates: 8,286
Male/Female: 44/56
SAT Ranges: CR 580–670, M 590–680
ACT Ranges: 27–31
Financial Aid: 84%
Pell Grant: 18%
Expense: Pr $ $ $
Student Loans: 60%
Average Debt: $ $
Phi Beta Kappa: Yes
Applicants: 42,811
Accepted: 48%
Enrolled: 11%
Grad in 6 Years: 81%
Returning Freshmen: 91%
Academics: ✍ ✍ ✍
Social: ☎ ☎ ☎
Q of L: ★ ★ ★
Admissions: (718) 817-4000
Email Address: enroll@fordham.edu

Strong Programs:
Business
Social Sciences
Communication and Media Studies
Psychology
Biological Sciences
Dance
Theatre
Global Business

At Fordham University, the Jesuit tradition pervades all aspects of life, from the quality of teaching, to the emphasis on personal relationships, to the pursuit of both "wisdom and learning," which also happens to be the school's motto. Students benefit from two campuses: the gated Bronx community of Rose Hill and the Lincoln Center facility, just a short subway ride away from the heart of midtown Manhattan. Small classes offer individual attention, and though nearly half of the student population is from New York, there's plenty of variation in ethnic background and in students' political and social views. Fordham is "more diverse than Boston College, less funky than NYU," says a German and English double major.

The 85-acre Rose Hill campus is an oasis of trees, grass, and Gothic architecture; it's close to the New York Botanical Garden and Yankee Stadium and had cameo appearances in films such as *A Beautiful Mind*. Rose Hill is home to Fordham College at Rose Hill, the largest liberal arts school at the university, as well as the primary programs of the Gabelli School of Business. The Lincoln Center campus benefits from its proximity to the Juilliard School, to the CBS and ABC television studios between Tenth and Eleventh Avenues, and to Lincoln Center itself, Manhattan's performing arts hub. In addition to its own liberal arts college, the campus also houses Fordham's law school and three other graduate schools. A newly renovated, 130,000-square-foot space opened in 2016 to support the business school's programs on the Lincoln Center campus. Shuttles run between the two campuses.

Undergraduate requirements include coursework in English, social and natural sciences, philosophy, theology, history, math/computer science, fine arts, and foreign languages. Students also complete four *Eloquentia Perfecta* seminars, including a capstone senior seminar on values. No matter where at Fordham you study, humanities are a good choice. Strengths at Rose Hill include history, philosophy, psychology, and economics, while at Lincoln Center theatre, English, and communication shine. The most popular majors across the university are those that fall within the fields of business, social sciences, communication and media studies, psychology, and biological sciences. The B.F.A. in dance is offered along with the Alvin Ailey American Dance Theater; students must be accepted both by Fordham and by the Ailey audition panel. Fordham's public radio station, WFUV, offers hands-on experience for aspiring deejays and radio journalists, and there is a TV production studio in Rose Hill. The global business program at Lincoln Center engages students in courses about the global dimensions of business and requires a study abroad experience. Both colleges offer 3–2 engineering programs with Columbia and Case Western Reserve, a 3–3 program with Fordham Law School, and a teacher-certification program. A new interdisciplinary major in math and computer and information sciences has recently been added.

> **"Every department has tutors at no cost to the students."**

"The academic climate is competitive in the sense that each student works hard to do the best they can. However, between students, there is no pressure," reports a junior.

Forty-eight percent of classes have fewer than 20 students, and professors are lauded for their abilities behind the lectern. "They share their experiences in academia, the professional sphere, and life. I consider some of my professors mentors," says one student. What's more, "Every department has tutors at no cost to the students," says a sociology and urban studies major. Helped by alumni connections, business students often obtain internships on Wall Street or elsewhere in the Manhattan financial community. Thirty-six percent of undergrads study abroad in 52 countries, choosing from 134 programs, including those offered by the university's London Centre.

"Students who choose Fordham are motivated to learn and ultimately want to make a difference," says an English major. Forty-five percent hail from New York state, and many of the rest are Roman Catholics from elsewhere on the East Coast, even though the school is independent of the church. The atmosphere is less intellectual than at nearby Columbia and NYU, but "Fordham's core curriculum integrates courses in theology and philosophy, and I feel this results in greater understanding of different political and religious cultures," says a senior. Adds a sophomore, "The Campus Ministry recently facilitated an LGBTQ retreat that went superbly." African Americans comprise 4 percent of the student body, Asian Americans make up 10 percent, and Hispanics 14 percent; another 7 percent are international students. There are hundreds of merit scholarships, averaging $15,724, available to eligible students, and the university now awards scholarships to those who demonstrate athletic gifts.

> "The Campus Ministry recently facilitated an LGBTQ retreat that went superbly."

Fifty-five percent of Fordham students live in the dorms, and they are guaranteed university housing for four years. Those lucky enough to snag rooms in the two high-rise residence halls near Lincoln Center are saved from the borough's unscrupulous brokers and unconscionable rents. At Rose Hill, "dorms are spacious, and community bathrooms are cleaned daily," says a senior. Both campuses offer living/learning communities; all Lincoln Center freshmen participate in the first-year experience integrated learning community, and first-years at Rose Hill can apply for the Manresa Scholars Program, which offers access to academic live-in tutors and a Jesuit priest-in-residence. Campus dining has received consistent complaints, but a marketing major says that "an improvement in quality is coming," as the university has changed food service providers. Despite its Bronx location, the Rose Hill campus is safe, students say. "The entire campus is gated, with security guards at each entrance," notes one junior.

Fordham's Campus Activities Board sponsors events like movies, concerts, and dances on both campuses; there is no Greek system. Off-campus parties provide an opportunity to imbibe, if students are interested, but "parties with alcohol are practically unheard of on campus," says one student. The Rose Hill campus backs up against the Bronx Zoo and it's around the corner from Arthur Avenue, the Little Italy of the Bronx. Both provide welcome weekend diversions. Students look forward to homecoming, Spring Weekend, and Senior Week. "Students also love to attend events and festivals in Manhattan, which is pretty much like a second campus," says a communication major. Fordham's Dorothy Day Center for Service and Justice helps connect students with local community service opportunities.

> "Manhattan…is pretty much like a second campus."

The Fordham Rams compete in Division I and the Atlantic 10 Conference (and the Patriot League for football), and its location near the Hudson River has also helped to produce the women's rowing Metropolitan champs. The football team advanced to its third straight NCAA FCS championship tournament in 2015. Women's softball has brought home four consecutive conference titles. The Lombardi Memorial Athletic Center (named for Vince, an alumnus) supports

The B.F.A. in dance is offered along with the Alvin Ailey American Dance Theater.

The Dorothy Day Center for Service and Justice helps connect students with local community service opportunities.

club sports and intramurals. Perhaps Fordham's most unusual athletic endeavor is Riding the Ram. "Students are expected to climb on the granite blocks and sit on the bronze statue of the Fordham Ram at least once in their time here," explains a computer science major. "However, ride the Ram at your own risk, as you will be reprimanded if caught in the act."

Consistent with its Jesuit tradition, Fordham fancies itself a family. Some things are changing—including its admissions and academic standards, which are inching up, and its national profile, which is also far higher than in years past. What hasn't changed is the idea that diversity and community can coexist, instilling confidence and pride in Fordham students and loyalty in the expanding alumni base. "Fordham University is the Jesuit university of New York," asserts one student. "The bustle of New York City is unlike anywhere else on the planet, and our students graduate as experts of the city and have their Jesuit ideals to guide them for the rest of their lives."

If You Apply To ➤ **Fordham:** Early decision and early action: Nov. 1. Regular decision: Jan. 1. Financial aid: Feb. 10. Housing: May 1. Application fee: $70. No campus or alumni interviews. SATs or ACTs (with writing): required. Subject Tests: optional. Letters of recommendation: required. Essay: required. Apply to particular school or program. Theatre and dance applicants must audition. Accepts the Common Application with supplement.

Franklin & Marshall College

637 College Avenue, Lancaster, PA 17604

F&M is known for churning out hardworking preprofessional students. Faces tough competition from the likes of Bucknell, Dickinson, Gettysburg, and Lafayette for Pennsylvania-bound students. Known for natural sciences, business, and internships on Capitol Hill. Bases all financial aid on need and meets the demonstrated need of every student.

At Franklin & Marshall College, set in the serene hills of Pennsylvania's Amish country, you might come nose-to-nose with a horse and buggy, but you can still enjoy the perks of being in one of the country's 50 largest metro areas. While the city has modernized beautifully, parts of this historic town look much the same as they did when two acclaimed but struggling colleges decided to pool their resources. Marshall College (named for Chief Justice John Marshall) merged with Franklin College (started with a donation of 200 English pounds from Ben himself) in Lancaster. These days, F&M is trying to modernize too, particularly by bringing a more international bent to the curriculum. "At F&M you have the chance to really explore and find yourself," says a junior.

F&M's 125-acre campus is surrounded by a quiet residential neighborhood shaded by majestic maple and oak trees. The campus itself is an arboretum and boasts 47 buildings of Gothic and colonial architecture. The College Square complex appeals to students seeking a study respite. Other notable facilities include the Life Sciences and Philosophy Building, the Brooks Tennis Center, and a 400-bed residential facility. As part of a decade-long urban renewal project, the college has developed 28 acres of land that was once home to aged industrial buildings and rail yards into a new North Campus for athletic fields and facilities. North Campus's first building, Shadek

> "At F&M you have the chance to really explore and find yourself."

Website: www.fandm.edu
Location: Small City
Private
Total Enrollment: 2,213
Undergraduates: 2,213
Male/Female: 48/52
SAT Ranges: CR 580–670, M 630–730
ACT Ranges: 28–31
Financial Aid: 53%
Pell Grant: 18%
Expense: Pr $ $ $ $
Student Loans: 51%
Average Debt: $ $
Phi Beta Kappa: Yes
Applicants: 7,146
Accepted: 32%
Enrolled: 26%
Grad in 6 Years: 87%

Stadium, will host the school's football and lacrosse teams and is scheduled to open in 2017.

First-year students are introduced to F&M's academic community through two required Connections seminars, intimate courses that teach the skills of critical analysis, research, writing, and civil debate. First-years also live together in seminar-based living/learning communities. Additional general education requirements include writing and language requirements and distribution requirements in the arts, humanities, social sciences, natural sciences, and non-Western cultures. Collaborations are optional opportunities to get course credit for an experience that includes working with others. F&M has long been known for being strong in the natural sciences, and the school is now placing more emphasis on courses with a service-learning component. A preprofessional college in line with Lafayette and Bucknell, F&M has an excellent reputation for preparing undergrads for medical school, law school, and other careers. The business, organizations, and society major is the most popular, followed by government, economics, and psychology. F&M offers cross-registration with two other small Pennsylvania colleges—Dickinson and Gettysburg—and several cooperative-degree and domestic-exchange programs, including the Sea Semester*.

> "[Professors] make Franklin & Marshall an exciting and comfortable place to learn."

(continued)

Returning Freshmen: 92%
Academics: ✍ ✍ ✍ ✍
Social: ☎ ☎ ☎
Q of L: ★ ★ ★
Admissions: (877) 678-9111
Email Address: admission@ fandm.edu

Strong Programs:
Natural Sciences
Business, Organizations, and Society
Government
Economics
Psychology

Students uniformly describe the coursework as strenuous and demanding, but say the environment remains more cooperative than competitive. "The courses are challenging, as professors aim to push students to new levels," a senior says. Still, "people are happy for each other if they do well," says a junior. Students say teaching is outstanding, and the relatively small student body and intimate class sizes help create a strong sense of community between students and professors. "Professors care about their students both inside and outside of the classroom," says a business major, "and make Franklin & Marshall an exciting and comfortable place to learn." Nearly 50 percent of F&M students engage in directed research under the guidance of faculty, including students in the Hackman Summer Research Scholars program. In the summer, the college sends students to countries such as Japan and Russia, and approximately half study in locations around the world during their time at F&M.

"Students here are open-minded and very free-spirited," says a sophomore. Twenty-three percent hail from Pennsylvania, and 15 percent come from foreign nations. African Americans comprise 6 percent of the student body, Hispanics 8 percent, and Asian Americans 5 percent. An occasional political debate may waft through the murmurs of light social exchanges during dinner, but "intense political debate is uncommon," according to a senior. Fummers do, however, take an interest when it comes to extracurricular activities and social opportunities. The 100-plus clubs on campus attest to that, as does an unusually high level of participation in community service activities. The school has eliminated merit scholarships and redirected the funds toward need-based financial aid, guaranteeing to meet 100 percent of admitted students' demonstrated need. There are no athletic scholarships.

The college requires students to live in college-operated housing all four years, and housing options include dorms, special-interest housing, suites, and apartments. A faculty-led College House system is designed to increase the quality of the residential experience. "The dorms are very cozy and clean," says a junior, "and there is never any trouble getting a room." Boarders eat most of their meals in the campus cafeteria under a flexible meal plan, but students are issued debit cards that they may use at a number of different food stops on campus. Campus security is described as "efficient and friendly," and students report feeling safe on campus.

As part of an urban renewal project, the college has developed 28 acres of land into a new North Campus for athletic fields and facilities.

Collaborations are optional opportunities to get course credit for an experience that includes working with others.

Seven fraternities attract 20 percent of the men, and five sororities attract 30 percent of the women. They are integral to much of the nightlife, although the residence halls and special-interest groups offer a range of alternatives, including concerts and comedians. Ben's Underground, a popular student-run nightclub, and Hildy's, a tiny local bar, are favorite meeting places. "Off-campus parties dominate the lives of students on the weekends," one student says. "Aside from the mall and the movies, frat houses are the only places to go for fun." In recent years, the student-run and college-funded College Entertainment Committee has brought a number of popular musicians and bands to the campus. The biggest annual event is Spring Arts, held the weekend before finals, which includes student air-band contests, live concerts, art exhibits, games, booths, and barbecues. Other highlights include the Flapjack Fest, when professors serve pancakes to students, and Fum Follies, a faculty-produced play.

Lancaster is a historical and well-to-do city located in a larger metro area of more than 400,000. Lancaster offers a 16-screen cinema, scores of shops, a farmers market, brick-and-cobblestone streets, and a plethora of quaint restaurants and cafés. Students have a measured, realistic appreciation of its urban amenities and rural ambiance. "Lancaster is a lot of fun," says one student. "There are great restaurants and bars." The Amish culture draws the interest of some students, although "the city is not full of Amish like many people expect," says a senior. Those with a hankering for contemporary action take road trips to Philly, Baltimore, Washington, D.C., and New York City.

"Intense political debate is uncommon."

With the exception of wrestling, which is Division I, F&M teams compete in Division III. The college boasts recent Centennial Conference championships in women's lacrosse, volleyball, and men's golf. Varsity squads are called the Diplomats, a moniker that gained currency in 1935 when the football team nearly upset national powerhouse Fordham. The annual football game against Dickinson for the Conestoga Wagon trophy is always a crowd pleaser. The college also offers a selection of five co-ed intramural sports and 13 club sports, such as cycling, rugby, and ultimate Frisbee.

Franklin & Marshall's illustrious namesakes would no doubt be proud of the institution that bears their names. "We have a stellar reputation and the best faculty," says one happy senior. "An F&M education will prep you for any job, and alumni jump at the chance to help."

Overlaps

Dickinson, Lafayette, Villanova, Gettysburg, Bucknell, University of Maryland, Colgate, Hamilton

If You Apply To ➤ **F&M:** Early decision I: Nov. 15. Early decision II and regular decision: Jan. 15. Financial aid: Feb. 1. Application fee: $60. Campus and alumni interviews: optional, evaluative. SATs or ACTs: optional (test-optional applicants must submit two graded writing samples). Subject Tests: optional. Letters of recommendation: required. Essay: required. Accepts the Common Application with supplement.

Furman University

3300 Poinsett Highway, Greenville, SC 29613

Furman's campus is one of the most gorgeous anywhere, with the swans a particularly nice touch. At just under 2,700 total enrollment, Furman is larger than Davidson and half the size of Wake Forest. Academic programs include a strong emphasis on student research. As befits its Baptist heritage, Furman is a conservative place and still a largely regional institution.

Furman University has been called the "Country Club of the South." And if you're Southern, white, Christian, and conservative, you're likely to feel like a member. Beyond the country club vibe, though, students find small classes led by caring faculty and plenty of opportunities for independent research. Prominent alums include Nobel Prize–winning physicist Charles Townes and Keith Lockhart, director of the Boston Pops Orchestra.

Furman's 750-acre campus is one of the country's most beautiful, with tree-lined malls, fountains, a formal rose garden and Japanese garden, and a 30-acre lake filled with swans and ducks. Flowering shrubs dot the well-kept lawns, which surround buildings in the classical revival, Colonial Williamsburg, and modern architectural styles. Many have porches, pediments, and other Southern touches, such as handmade Virginia brick. Recent campus projects include a new soccer field house and a renovation of the Lakeside Housing complex.

Furman operates under the "semester-plus" system. The school year begins in late August, and the first semester ends prior to the December holiday break. Students begin the second semester in January and then have the option of attending a three-week "Maymester" in (you guessed it) May. General education requirements include a first-year seminar and a series of core requirements that fulfill the following "ways of knowing": empirical studies; human cultures; mathematical and formal reasoning; foreign language; ultimate questions; and body and mind. Finally, students must fulfill global awareness requirements. The most popular majors include health sciences, business administration, political science, and communication studies. Chemistry and psychology are strong too. Students in the health sciences program have access to the innovative international health and nutrition program as well as a human performance laboratory.

Furman's academic climate is challenging. "Furman students all understand that the courses are difficult and seem to commiserate with one another," says one junior. Fifty-seven percent of classes taken by freshmen have fewer than 20 students, helping students get to know faculty members well. "I think the quality of teaching is exceptional," says one senior. "All classes are taught by professors, and only a handful of labs are taught by teachers' assistants." The Furman Advantage program helps fund research fellowships and internships for more than 350 students each year. Furman also typically sends one of the largest student delegations to the annual National Conference of Undergraduate Research. Forty-nine percent of students study abroad each year through one of two dozen Furman-sponsored programs on five continents, including programs in Iceland, Japan, Jordan, Belize, and Botswana. Furman also belongs to the Associated Colleges of the South*. Entering freshmen have the opportunity to travel in small groups to an island off the coast of Charleston, the mountains of North Carolina, or even China during the summer before they enroll.

Furman broke with the South Carolina Baptist Convention in 1992, but it remains in South Carolina, where religion ranks second only to football. Students are mostly white, upper-middle-class Southerners; 22 percent are native South Carolinians. A political science major says, "Students here tend to be sheltered and ignorant of real-world issues. They are very image-conscious and our gym stays busier than most others." Another student adds, "Bow ties and button-downs are expected for guys on game day at tailgates, and girls wouldn't be caught dead without their Longchamp totes and Tory Burch flats." The administration has committed to diversifying the school, but those efforts have been slow to bear fruit. African Americans make up 6 percent of the student body, Hispanics 4 percent, and Asian Americans 2 percent; another 6 percent are international. Every year, Furman awards a number of merit scholarships averaging $18,725, plus 242 athletic scholarships in 18 sports.

> "Students here tend to be sheltered and ignorant of real-world issues."

Website: www.furman.edu
Location: Suburban
Private
Total Enrollment: 2,657
Undergraduates: 2,615
Male/Female: 43/57
SAT Ranges: CR 550–660, M 550–660
ACT Ranges: 25–30
Financial Aid: 95%
Pell Grant: 13%
Expense: Pr $ $ $
Student Loans: 37%
Average Debt: $ $ $ $
Phi Beta Kappa: Yes
Applicants: 5,043
Accepted: 65%
Enrolled: 21%
Grad in 6 Years: 83%
Returning Freshmen: 89%
Academics: ✐ ✐ ✐ ½
Social: ☎ ☎ ☎
Q of L: ★ ★ ★
Admissions: (864) 294-2034
Email Address: admission@furman.edu

Strong Programs:
Health Sciences
Business Administration
Political Science
Communication Studies
Chemistry
Psychology

The Furman Advantage program helps fund research fellowships and internships for more than 350 students each year.

Ninety-six percent of students live on campus, as Furman has a four-year residency requirement. "The residence halls undergo cyclical renovations such that no one dorm is in disrepair," says a junior. Furman is no longer a completely dry campus, although the policy is strictly enforced in freshman and sophomore dorms, where underage students shouldn't be imbibing anyway. The atmosphere is more relaxed for students of legal drinking age, who may consume alcohol in North Village, a newer, university-owned apartment complex of 10 buildings for juniors and seniors. All dorms are equipped with telephone, cable TV, and Internet access, and students enjoy the camaraderie that results from a residential campus. Meal plan credits can be used in the dining hall or food court, which always offers student favorites like hamburgers and hot dogs. Overall, students say campus fare is tasty and diverse. Campus security helps provide a relatively safe environment. "Furman has its own police force," notes a senior.

"Greek life does tend to dominate life on Furman's campus," reports one student. "As someone who is not a part of Greek life, I've had to seek out activities on my own. There are a lot of interesting cultural and religious programs on campus, and great outdoor/sporting facilities." When the weekend comes, Furman's Student Activities Board sponsors "free movies, weekend trips, restaurant deals, huge concerts, and [there is] basically always something to do," says a communication major. Fraternities claim 33 percent of the men and sororities 58 percent of the women, and off-campus Greek parties draw crowds. "Greenville is a great city that is seeing a large amount of growth," says a senior. "The downtown is booming and is a really fun place to visit."

"Greenville is a great city that is seeing a large amount of growth."

The Peace Center for the Performing Arts, located downtown, brings in touring casts of Broadway shows and other top-rated acts. Seventy percent of Furman's students devote spare time to the Heller Service Corps, which provides volunteers to more than 50 community agencies and organizes the annual Exceptional Adults Valentine's Day Dance for special-needs adults. However, one freshman remarks, "A good amount of students volunteer, yes, but most are content to simply live out their privileged lives in the peace of the Furman bubble." The best road trips are to the mountains of Asheville (only 45 minutes away), Atlanta (for the big city and shopping, about two hours), and Charleston or Myrtle Beach (four hours).

Furman's athletic teams are the Paladins (after the toughest warrior in Charlemagne's court), and they compete in the Division I Southern Conference. Six teams brought home conference titles in 2015, including men's and women's soccer and cross-country, and women's volleyball and tennis, with women's tennis repeating as champs in 2016. Students happily yell out the school's tongue-in-cheek cheer ("F.U. one time, F.U. two times, F.U. three times, F.U. all the time!") during football games against archrivals Wofford and Georgia Southern. More than 70 percent of the student body competes for the coveted All Sports Trophy by participating in intramurals, which range from flag football to bowling. Furman's debate and mock trial teams are both nationally ranked and regularly compete in intercollegiate tournaments.

Two decades after severing its religious ties, Furman continues to evolve. It may call itself a university, but its educational approach is closer to that of a liberal arts college, emphasizing problem solving and experience-based learning. Says a junior, "Furman is a place marked by excellence, and its special programs are what set it apart from peer institutions."

If You Apply To ➢

Furman: Early decision and early action: Nov. 1. Regular decision: Jan. 15. Financial aid: Mar. 1. Application fee: $50. Campus interviews: optional, evaluative. Alumni interviews: optional, informational. SATs or ACTs: optional. No Subject Tests. Letters of recommendation: optional. Essay: required. Accepts the Common Application.

George Mason University

4400 University Drive, Fairfax, VA 22030

The largest public university in Virginia, George Mason is the antithesis of UVA—a place where traditions are still in their infancy and inclusive growth is a dominant value. A bastion of conservative political and economic thought and recipient of considerable Koch brothers largesse, GMU takes full advantage of location in job- and internship-rich northern Virginia. Big focus on overall student well-being. Half of current graduates started out in community colleges. Compare to Arizona State.

Located in the middle of greater Washington, D.C.'s budding high-tech corridor, George Mason University features an urban campus and symbiotic relationship with the surrounding region that contrasts starkly with Virginia's two other major universities, which have held classes for many years in the relative isolation of Charlottesville and Blacksburg. Well-established as a center of conservative thinking on social issues, GMU has grown by leaps and bounds for most of the past two decades, largely because of its commitment to extend the benefits of higher education to as many Virginians as possible. As one sophomore put it, "The university's biggest drives are for diversity and innovation."

Founded in 1957 as a sleepy outpost of the University of Virginia, GMU became independent in 1972. It sits on a 677-acre wooded campus 20 miles from Washington, D.C., in suburban Fairfax, Virginia. Campus architecture is modern and homogeneous, with lots of brick, glass, and metal, and just about everything is within a 15-minute walk. The campus observatory is second in the area only to that of NASA. GMU's 100,000-seat Eagle Bank Arena hosts both sporting and entertainment events. And although GMU's campus doesn't have the colonial ambiance or tradition of William and Mary or UVA, its namesake does have the same Old Virginia credentials. George Mason drafted Virginia's influential Declaration of Rights in 1776, and he later opposed ratification of the federal Constitution because there was no Bill of Rights attached.

Though it is growing up fast, Mason's youth shows in a number of ways. First, programs taken for granted at more established universities are just hitting their stride here. GMU's physical plant is expanding, thanks largely to a small but growing endowment, funding from the State of Virginia, and some public-private partnerships. One notable addition will be the Health and Human Services building, set to open in 2017. Through the library, which is also growing, students have access to more than 800 electronic databases, more than a million electronic monographs and journals, and borrowing privileges of the Washington Research Library Consortium.

> **"The university's biggest drives are for diversity and innovation."**

Mason has standard general education requirements, but students who prefer to find their own way can design a major under the bachelor's in integrative studies, which teams small groups of faculty and undergraduates on projects that can be easily connected to the world outside GMU. Nontraditional students who enter Mason have the option of creating their own degree in the Bachelor of Individualized Studies program. All students must complete a synthesis course in their major to reflect critically on what they have learned. GMU recently earned Carnegie Classification recognition as a top research university, and it has had two Nobel Prize laureates in its libertarian-oriented economics department, which is probably its strongest. Not surprisingly, given the school's location, the Schar School of Policy and Government also receives accolades. Psychology tops the list of popular majors,

Website: www.gmu.edu

Location: Suburban

Public

Total Enrollment: 22,236

Undergraduates: 18,226

Male/Female: 48/52

SAT Ranges: CR 520–620, M 520–630

ACT Ranges: 23–29

Financial Aid: 49%

Pell Grant: 27%

Expense: Pub $ $ $

Student Loans: 58%

Average Debt: $ $ $

Phi Beta Kappa: No

Applicants: 21,981

Accepted: 69%

Enrolled: 21%

Grad in 6 Years: 69%

Returning Freshmen: 87%

Academics: ✍ ✍ ✍

Social: ☎ ☎

Q of L: ★ ★

Admissions: (703) 993-2400

Email Address: admissions@gmu.edu

Strong Programs:
Economics
Psychology
Criminology
Biology
Information Technology
Conflict Analysis and Resolution
Computer Game Design
Computer Science

followed by criminology, law, and society; biology; and information technology. Other notable majors include the nation's first conflict analysis and resolution major, a fast-growing computer game design major, and computer science. Newly added programs include kinesiology, atmospheric science, cyber security engineering, mechanical engineering, and human development and family science.

"The climate at George Mason is not competitive," says a community health major. "I have never felt extrinsically pressured to be better than anyone else." All faculty members are required to teach, although some do better than others. "I have had some professors that have been great, accessible, and excited about their classes," says one student. "However, some professors just like to hear themselves talk and don't want to help anyone." GMU's Center for the Advancement of Well-Being is a national leader in encouraging students, faculty, and staff members to live more mindful and meaningful lives.

GMU's career-focused students seem to like learning on the job: 70 percent enter the working world after graduation and just 20 percent proceed to graduate and professional schools, although GMU does offer its undergrads 50 accelerated master's degree programs. The Smithsonian Semester allows students to live on-site at the Conservation and Research Center of the Smithsonian's National Zoo and study global conservation issues and civic concerns. Twenty-one percent of students conduct undergraduate research, and an Honors College is available to top achievers. For those seeking adventure in faraway places—as about 9 percent of undergraduates do—the Center for Global Education offers more than 75 different study abroad programs in more than 40 sites around the world, including Mason's new campus in South Korea.

> **"I have never felt extrinsically pressured to be better than anyone else."**

"Our student body is greatly made up of commuters," says one student, and "a great deal of our students are older in age, work full time, and attend classes in the evening." Eighty-eight percent of Mason undergraduates are from Virginia, and 5 percent are international; the university boasts students from all 50 states and more than 130 countries. Half of current students started out at Northern Virginia Community College or other two-year institutions. African Americans account for 11 percent of the student population, Hispanics 12 percent, and Asian Americans 19 percent. Twenty-seven percent of freshmen are Pell-eligible. "The diversity of Mason has certainly enriched my academic experience. It has opened my eyes to other cultures," says one senior. Students are politically aware and tend to lean rightward. Merit scholarships averaging $4,370 are available to those who qualify, as are 150 athletic scholarships in 22 sports.

George Mason's status as a commuter school is changing. On-campus housing is guaranteed for the first two years; 26 percent of students live on campus or around campus in university-sponsored housing, including 69 percent of first-time freshmen. "Housing is competitive but the residence halls are generally nice," says a global affairs major. Those who want an active campus social life should definitely consider a stint in the dorms, but freshman dorms are dry, and you can get the boot if you're caught having a party with alcohol. Freshmen live together in Presidents Park, while other students get rooms on a first-come, first-served basis prioritized by class status. Fourteen academic- and lifestyle-focused living/learning communities are available for those seeking tighter-knit relationships with their classmates. Campus dining facilities are plentiful and operate around the clock, but students complain about a lack of variety. "GMU has a police station located on campus and also many different security officers patrolling the area at all times,"

> **"Due to the fact that the majority of our students are commuters, weekends are pretty dead."**

says an English major, and students agree that the university responds quickly and effectively to incidents of campus sexual assault.

"If you become involved at the university, it will not be difficult to build a social life," advises one senior. A junior adds, "Due to the fact that the majority of our students are commuters, weekends are pretty dead." Mason's Johnson Center, with its food court, movie theater, library, classrooms, computer labs, student support offices, and study areas, is the center of on-campus social life. Two student unions, the Student Union Building and the HUB, offer additional options for socializing and studying. Six percent of the men and 9 percent of the women go Greek. On the weekends, students find a predictable assortment of malls and shopping centers in Fairfax, just southwest of D.C., but off-campus parties and the sights and sounds of downtown Washington, Georgetown, and Old Town Alexandria beckon when the sun goes down. Best of all, these are only a short commute away via a free shuttle bus to the Metro. Those searching for alternative collegiate scenes take road trips to other local schools, including James Madison and UVA.

Students are proud of the colorful pep band, known as the Green Machine and directed by a tuba professor known as Doc Nix.

With barely a generation of history under its belt, Mason is notably lacking in traditions and annual events: "Come here and invent one!" a student urges. Patriots Day, Gold Rush, and Mason Day are major bashes, in addition to homecoming and International Week. GMU competes in Division I, and the basketball team is the marquee program—any game against Virginia Commonwealth University draws a big crowd. Students are proud of the colorful pep band, known as the Green Machine and directed by a tuba professor known as Doc Nix. Other Patriots teams that regularly bring home Atlantic 10 conference championships include men's and women's soccer, track and field, and volleyball, women's lacrosse, and baseball. Club sports and intramurals are also growing in popularity, with 13 percent of students participating.

"Nearly every aspect of Mason is developing at breakneck speed."

"Nearly every aspect of Mason is developing at breakneck speed. We haven't hit our best yet," says one student. The name of George Mason may not have the cachet of George Washington, James Madison, or the other luminaries of Virginia history who have had universities named for them, but with improving academics, an ever-expanding physical campus, and the rich cultural and economic resources of Washington, D.C., Mason's namesake may be set to follow in their footsteps.

Overlaps
Virginia Commonwealth, James Madison, Virginia Tech, Old Dominion, University of Virginia, University of Maryland, Penn State

If You Apply To ➢

Mason: Early action: Nov. 1. Regular decision: Jan. 15. Financial aid: Mar. 1. Housing: May 1. Application fee: $70. No campus or alumni interviews. SATs or ACTs: required (optional for students who meet certain requirements). No Subject Tests. Letters of recommendation: recommended. Essay: recommended. Additional materials required for applicants to dance, music, art and visual technology, computer game design, and theater programs.

The George Washington University

Washington, D.C. 20052

Not so long ago, GW was a backup school with an almost 80 percent acceptance rate and maligned for its lack of identity. But the allure of Washington, D.C., coupled with ambitious leadership and an intellectually stimulating educational environment, has made it increasingly selective. Located steps away from the White House. One of the most expensive private schools in the country, it is also the nation's leader in internships per capita.

Website: www.gwu.edu
Location: City Center
Private
Total Enrollment: 17,580
Undergraduates: 10,078
Male/Female: 43/57
SAT Ranges: CR 590–690,
M 600–700
ACT Ranges: 27–31
Financial Aid: 66%
Pell Grant: 14%
Expense: Pr $ $ $ $
Student Loans: 51%
Average Debt: $ $ $ $
Phi Beta Kappa: Yes
Applicants: 19,837
Accepted: 46%
Enrolled: 28%
Grad in 6 Years: 83%
Returning Freshmen: 94%
Academics: ✐ ✐ ✐ ½
Social: ☎ ☎ ☎
Q of L: ★ ★ ★
Admissions: (202) 994-6040
Email Address: gwadm@
gwu.edu

Strong Programs:
International Affairs
Finance
Economics
Psychology
Political Communication
Geography
Biological Anthropology
Archaeology

The Center for Career Services connects students with more than 12,000 internship opportunities.

Like Washington, D.C., itself, the George Washington University draws students from all over America—and 130 countries around the world. Upon arrival, they find a bustling campus in the heart of D.C., enriched with cultural and intellectual opportunities. Students often have rare access behind the scenes of the Smithsonian Institution museums, the U.S. Capitol, the Library of Congress, and other national treasures. GW offers a front-row seat to history as top political officials and influential leaders serve as frequent guest speakers and visiting professors—and it is the only school in the country to hold its commencement on the National Mall. "We are the students who will make change in the world and we are at the center of the important things that are going on right now," says one confident junior.

"We are the students who will make change in the world."

GW was established in 1821 by an act of Congress as a testament to George Washington's dream of a national institution of higher learning in D.C. Today, undergraduates experience life at GW on primarily two campuses—the Foggy Bottom campus on Pennsylvania Avenue near the White House and the Mount Vernon campus, three miles away in the Foxhall neighborhood. (A few other satellite campuses in the area serve mostly graduate students, though some undergrads can take classes or conduct research at them.) The Foggy Bottom campus has a mix of renovated federal row houses and modern buildings and is virtually indistinguishable from the rest of the neighborhood, while the wooded Mount Vernon campus spans 23 bucolic acres near Georgetown and includes athletic fields, tennis courts, and an outdoor pool. Students live and take classes on both campuses and travel between the two on the "Vern Express," a shuttle that runs 24/7 during the academic year. A spate of new construction includes the 500,000-square-foot, LEED-certified Science and Engineering Hall and the 880-bed District House residence hall.

Freshmen may enroll in the School of Engineering and Applied Science, the School of Business, the Elliott School of International Affairs, the Milken Institute School of Public Health, and the largest undergraduate division, the Columbian College of Arts and Sciences (which also houses the School of Media and Public Affairs and the Corcoran School of the Arts and Design). During freshman year, all undergraduates take a University Writing course. As part of the university's strategic plan (dubbed "Vision 2021"), a new set of general education requirements have been implemented. All undergraduates are now required to complete a 19-credit core curriculum in the following areas: writing, natural or physical science, mathematics or statistics, social science and the humanities, plus two writing-in-the-disciplines courses. The most popular majors are international affairs, finance, economics, and psychology. GW's political communication major, which combines political science, journalism, and communication technologies, is one of the few undergraduate programs of its kind and benefits from its Washington location. Programs in geography, biological anthropology, and archaeology are also well regarded. A number of combined undergraduate/graduate degree programs are available. Students warn that recent budget cuts have impacted several humanities and arts programs, including women's studies, music, and dance.

"Students intern at Capitol Hill (we call it hill-terning because of how common it is)."

The workload at GW tends to be heavy, and a human services and social justice major says the climate is "less competitive than you would expect, with definite space for collaboration (at least in liberal arts classes)." Fifty-three percent of the classes taken by undergraduates have fewer than 20 students; professors handle lectures and seminars, and TAs facilitate discussions or labs. Almost half of GW's faculty members divide their time between the halls of academia and real-world positions, many of them governmental, but the quality of teaching is said to be "hit or miss."

For highly motivated and capable students in all majors, the University Honors Program offers special seminars, independent study, and a university symposium on both campuses. Forty percent of students study abroad in more than 300 programs in more than 50 countries, including GW-run programs in England, France, Spain, and Chile. The Center for Career Services connects students with more than 12,000 internship opportunities. "Students intern at Capitol Hill (we call it hill-terning because of how common it is), the Kennedy Center, the Smithsonian, and many other local organizations," says a junior.

"Students who go to GW are driven by success," says an economics major. "They know what they want and they will go after it." Ninety-eight percent of undergraduates come from outside D.C., including 10 percent who hail from foreign countries. Six percent are African American, 8 percent are Hispanic, and 10 percent are Asian American. Students say most of their classmates come from wealthy families and don't mind spending money on frequent nights out on the town, and a senior comments that the campus "remains fairly segregated according to race and cultural background." As you might expect, political issues are important here and the biggest concerns include "anything and everything," according to a criminal justice major. A fixed-rate plan guarantees that tuition will not increase for up to five years of full-time undergraduate study. Merit scholarships are available, averaging $19,541, and athletes vie for 175 awards in 27 sports. GW is need-aware, not need-blind, in its admissions, and is now test-optional.

"[The campus] remains fairly segregated according to race and cultural background."

Sixty-two percent of GW undergrads live in campus housing and are required to do so for the first three years. "The conditions and popularity of the dorms are varied," reports one junior, and another adds that the quality generally improves as you get older. Those who move off campus typically find group houses in Foggy Bottom or go to fashionable nearby neighborhoods like Dupont Circle and Georgetown, just a short walk from campus. GW's meal plans allow students to dine at on-campus cafés or at more than 100 off-campus vendors, which means there are a "variety of options ranging from fast food, to food truck, to nice sit-down dinners at fancier restaurants," according to one sophomore. Given GW's open, urban campus, safety can be a concern, but one student says, "There are many services to ensure security." A junior adds, "Student organizations like Students Against Sexual Assault (SASA), Allied in Pride, the Feminist Student Union, and others work very diligently to increase awareness of sexual assault and provide students with the tools to protect themselves and others."

"If you're bored at GW, you're doing something wrong," states one business administration major. "Whether it's on campus or off campus, there's always something to do." Twenty-three percent of GW men and 27 percent of the women go Greek, and there are more than 450 student organizations on campus. The campus is technically dry, and a D.C. police crackdown has made it extremely difficult for those under 21 to be served at off-campus restaurants and pubs. Major annual events include the Fall Fest and Spring Fling carnivals, with free food and nationally known musical performers. And every four years, GW celebrates the beginning of the new U.S. presidential term with a formal Inaugural Ball of its own in January. Popular road trips include the beaches of Ocean City, Maryland, and Virginia Beach, Virginia. Philadelphia and New York City are easily accessible by bus or train, a boon because most GW students don't have cars.

"If you're bored at GW, you're doing something wrong."

GW doesn't field a football team, but its 27 varsity teams (the Colonials) are competitive in Division I Atlantic 10 Conference play. Men's and women's basketball make regular NCAA tournament appearances, and women's basketball, men's and women's tennis, and men's soccer have all won recent conference championships. Gymnastics, sailing, women's rowing, and men's and women's squash are also competitive. Approximately 25 percent of undergraduates participate in the recreational sports program, which offers 15 intramural leagues throughout the year, in addition to 34 club sport options. And while the school's official mascot resembles a certain U.S. president, its quirky, unofficial one is the hippopotamus.

Perhaps it's fitting that a university located in the nation's seat of government would generate complaints about red tape: "Stop with the bureaucracy," grumbles one student. "The simplest of problems for students could be fixed if we didn't have to go through so many hoops to just get an answer." Still, despite the bureaucratic annoyances, GW continues to build its reputation by putting its location to good use. "The opportunities are endless," says a student. "Picking and choosing what you want to do is the hardest part." For students interested in urban living in the heart of the nation's political establishment, GW may fit the bill. But that bill will be hefty.

If You Apply To ➤

GW: Early decision I: Nov. 1. Early decision II, regular decision, and financial aid: Jan. 1. Housing: May 1. Application fee: $75. Campus and alumni interviews: optional, evaluative. SATs or ACTs: optional. Subject Tests: optional. Letters of recommendation: required. Essay: required. Accepts the Common Application. Art and design applicants must submit portfolio.

Georgetown University

37th and O Streets NW, Washington, D.C. 20057

For anyone who wants to be a master of the political universe, this is the place. Strong international and multicultural environment. In the excitement of studying in D.C., students may pay little attention to the Jesuit affiliation, which adds a conservative tinge to the campus. Getting in is also easier if you're Roman Catholic. Occupies a tree-lined neighborhood that is home to many of the nation's most powerful people.

Website: www.georgetown.edu
Location: City Center
Private
Total Enrollment: 14,393
Undergraduates: 6,954
Male/Female: 45/55
SAT Ranges: CR 660–750, M 660–750
ACT Ranges: 30–34
Financial Aid: 56%
Pell Grant: 14%
Expense: Pr $ $ $ $
Student Loans: 38%
Average Debt: $ $
Phi Beta Kappa: Yes
Applicants: 19,478
Accepted: 17%
Enrolled: 47%

As the oldest and most selective of the nation's Roman Catholic schools, Georgetown University offers students unparalleled access to Washington, D.C.'s corridors of power. Aspiring politicos benefit from the university's emphasis on public policy, international business, and foreign service. The national spotlight shines brightly on this elite institution, drawing dynamic students and athletes from around the world. A senior says, "Georgetown balances academics, social life, and faith in an all-encompassing college experience based on 'care of the whole person.'"

From its scenic location just blocks from the Potomac River, Georgetown affords its students an excellent vantage point from which to survey the world. The 104-acre campus reflects the history and growth of the nation's oldest Jesuit university. The Federal style of Old North, which once housed guests such as George Washington and Lafayette and is now home to the McCourt School of Public Policy, contrasts with the towers of the Flemish Romanesque-style Healy Hall, a post-Civil War landmark on the National Register of Historic Places.

Although Georgetown is a Catholic university (founded in 1789 by the Society of Jesus), the religious atmosphere is by no means heavy-handed, and the student body tends to be liberal. Just over half of the undergraduates are Catholic, but all major faiths are respected and practiced on campus. That's partially due to the pronounced international influence here. The school's hefty endowment is the largest among the nation's Jesuit colleges and universities. Georgetown has worked to atone for its historical ties to slavery by offering preferential admissions status to descendants of 272 slaves who were sold in 1838 to keep its doors open. In addition to offering a formal apology, it will create an institute for the study of slavery and erect a public memorial to the slaves whose labor benefited the institution.

Through its broad liberal arts curriculum, GU focuses on developing the intellectual prowess and moral rigor its students will need in future national and international leadership roles. The curriculum has a strong multidisciplinary and intercultural slant. Would-be Hoyas may apply to one of four undergraduate schools: Georgetown College for liberal arts, the School of Nursing and Health Studies, McDonough School of Business, and the Walsh School of Foreign Service, which gives future diplomats, journalists, and others a strong grounding in the social sciences. Prospective freshmen must declare intended majors on their applications, and their secondary school records are judged accordingly. This means, among other things, intense competition within the college for the limited number of spaces in Georgetown's popular premed program. All students must complete requirements in humanities and writing, philosophy, and theology; other requirements are specific to each school. First-years read the same novel during the summer, and the author visits campus during the first few weeks for a day-long seminar. There are no special academic requirements for the freshman year, but about 30 Georgetown College freshmen are accepted annually into the liberal arts colloquium.

> "Georgetown balances academics, social life, and faith in an all-encompassing college experience."

International affairs, diplomatic history, international economics, and regional and comparative studies are among the hottest programs, as evidenced by former secretary of state Madeleine Albright's return to the Walsh School of Foreign Service (SFS). SFS offers several five-year undergraduate and graduate degree programs in conjunction with the Graduate School of Arts and Sciences. The most popular majors include international affairs, government, international politics, finance, and nursing. Of course, the theology department is also strong. The business school balances liberal arts with professional training, which translates into strong offerings in international and intercultural business as well as an emphasis on ethical and public policy issues. Curiously, given its location in D.C., Georgetown does not offer an undergraduate public policy major. The School of Nursing and Health Studies runs an integrated program combining the liberal arts and humanities with professional nursing theory and practice, and offers majors in nursing and health studies. The Faculty of Languages and Linguistics, the only undergraduate program of its kind nationwide, grants degrees in nine languages, as well as degrees in linguistics and comparative literature.

> "The professors are outstanding and the teaching is first-rate."

"Students take their coursework very seriously," says a senior. "The courses are challenging, but it certainly isn't impossible to do well." Sixty percent of classes have fewer than 20 students. Georgetown likes to boast about its faculty, and well it should. "The professors are outstanding and the teaching is first-rate," says an American studies major, and TAs are used only to lead discussion sections and recitations. That GU views most subjects through an international lens is evidenced by the 57 percent of students who study abroad. The Office of Global Education offers more than 120 programs in 40 countries.

A senior says GU students are not the stereotypical "pastel polo and pearl-clad preppies from Long Island." Almost half of the undergraduates come from private or parochial schools. Eighty-eight percent come from states outside D.C., and another 12 percent are international. African Americans make up 6 percent of undergrads,

(continued)

Grad in 6 Years: 95%
Returning Freshmen: 96%
Academics: ✏️ ✏️ ✏️ ✏️ ½
Social: 🍺 🍺 🍺 🍺
Q of L: ★ ★ ★ ★
Admissions: (202) 687-3600
Email Address: guadmiss@ georgetown.edu

Strong Programs:
International Affairs
Government
International Politics
Finance
Nursing
Diplomatic History
International Economics
Theology

The school's hefty endowment is the largest among the nation's Jesuit colleges and universities.

International affairs is among the hottest programs, as evidenced by former secretary of state Madeleine Albright's return to the school.

Hispanics 8 percent, and Asian Americans 10 percent. A student committee works with the vice president for student affairs to improve race relations and develop strategies for improving inclusiveness and sensitivity to issues of multiculturalism. Georgetown offers no academic merit scholarships, but it does guarantee to meet the full demonstrated need of every admit, and more than 120 athletic scholarships draw male and female athletes of all stripes. The Georgetown Scholarship Program offers additional financial incentives and academic support to eligible students.

University-owned dorms, townhouses, and apartments accommodate some 65 percent of undergrads, and "housing is extremely nice," says a senior. All dorms are co-ed, and some have more activities and community than others. Two dining halls serve "steadily improving" but expensive fare. GU students feel relatively safe on campus, thanks to the school's ever-present Department of Public Safety and its walking and riding after-dark escort services.

> **"Social life is a major part of campus."**

Jesuits frown upon fraternities and sororities at their colleges, so there are none at Georgetown, although that doesn't mean there aren't secret societies to be found. The university's strict enforcement of the 21-year-old drinking age has led to a somewhat decentralized social life, which is not necessarily a bad thing. Alcohol is forbidden in undergrad dorms, and all parties must be registered. The dozens of bars, nightclubs, and restaurants in Georgetown—Martin's Tavern and the Tombs are always popular—are a big draw for students who are legal, but they can get pricey. Bulldog Tavern, a campus pub in the spectacular student activity center, is a more affordable alternative. Popular annual formals such as the Diplomatic and the Blue/Gray Ball force students to dress up and pair off. "Social life is a major part of campus," says a student. "Kids can easily find their niche." Georgetown has a reputation as a gay-friendly campus, and regular events include Gay Pride Month and a popular drag ball called Genderfunk.

There are no fraternities or sororities at Georgetown, although that doesn't mean there aren't secret societies to be found.

Washington offers unsurpassed cultural resources, ranging from the museums of the Smithsonian to the Kennedy Center. "Washington is an ideal place to spend your college years," says a student. "The city has everything students could want, including culture, shopping, museums, monuments, social life, and the clean and convenient Metro for transportation." Given the absence of on-campus parking, a car is probably more trouble than it's worth. Road trips are said to be infrequent.

> **"Washington is an ideal place to spend your college years."**

Should you notice the hills begin to tremble with a deep, resounding, primitive chant—"Hoya Saxa Hoya Saxa"—don't worry; it's probably just another Georgetown basketball game. Hoya is derived from the Greek and Latin phrase *hoya saxa*, which means "What rocks!" Some say it originated in a cheer referring to the stones that formed the school's outer walls. The Hoya men's basketball team has a long history of prominence. The Hoyas are also competitive in Division I men's and women's lacrosse and sailing; the women's lacrosse team has won numerous Big East championships. The thrill of victory in intramural competition at the superb underground Yates Memorial Field House is not to be missed, either.

For anyone interested in discovering the world, Georgetown offers an outstanding menu of choices in one of the nation's most dynamic cities. Professors truly pay attention to their undergrads and the diverse students, who are "hardworking, diligent, caring individuals," says one sophomore. "Georgetown is a place where students of all backgrounds, all traditions, and all faiths come together for a common purpose of educating each other and making an impact on the world."

Overlaps

Boston College, University of Chicago, Duke, NYU, Northwestern, Notre Dame, University of Pennsylvania, University of Virginia

University of Georgia

212 Terrell Hall, Athens, GA 30602-1633

What a difference (nearly) free tuition makes. Top Georgia students now choose UGA over highly selective private institutions. Business and social and natural sciences head the list of strong and sought-after programs. The college town of Athens boasts a great nightlife and is within easy reach of Atlanta. The university's Center for Undergraduate Research offers rich opportunities.

College-aged Georgians hit the jackpot when the state began using lottery receipts to fund the HOPE Scholarship program. The program covers 90 percent of tuition at the University of Georgia for all four years for students who finish high school in the state with a B average and maintain that average in college. In fact, the scholarship has made it much tougher to get into UGA, which not long ago was known mostly for its dynamite football team and raucous parties. In the last decade, UGA students have received nearly 60 major scholarships from Rhodes and Truman to Marshall. "Georgia offers the most complete 'Southern college experience' in the South," says a senior.

Founded in 1785, Georgia was the nation's first state-chartered university (UNC was chartered later but wins bragging rights as the first public university to open its doors). Its attractive 706-acre campus is dotted with greenery and wooded walks. The older north campus houses administrative offices and the law school, and features 19th-century architecture and landscaping. The southern end of campus has more modern buildings and residence halls. The new $48 million Science Learning Center, which features 122,500 square feet of lecture halls, classrooms, and labs for undergraduates, opened in 2016.

UGA's core curriculum includes one course in life sciences and one in physical sciences, as well as courses in world languages and culture, humanities, and the arts. Computing, calculus, engineering, and statistics courses are also emphasized. Before the semester starts, freshmen may spend a month on campus to learn their way around, meet new friends, and even earn six hours of credit. Don't want to stay for an entire month? Choose the Dawg Camp weekend retreat, which promotes networking and leadership skills and includes programs on time and stress management, diversity, and "What It Means to Be a Georgia Bulldog." During the year, freshman seminars allow first-year students to study under a senior faculty member in a small, personalized setting while earning an hour of academic credit. The new Experiential Learning Initiative requires students to take part in hands-on learning opportunities, such as research, study abroad, service learning, and internships. UGA's Grady School of Journalism is home to the prestigious Peabody Awards, and the Terry College of Business is also noteworthy. Education, agricultural sciences, and public and international affairs are also strengths, and the university's health-related programs are rapidly expanding. The most popular majors are psychology, finance, biology, and marketing.

> **"I love that I have the same professors multiple times in my college."**

Website: www.uga.edu
Location: Small City
Public
Total Enrollment: 32,333
Undergraduates: 25,734
Male/Female: 43/57
SAT Ranges: CR 570–660, M 580–670
ACT Ranges: 26–31
Financial Aid: 43%
Pell Grant: 19%
Expense: Pub $ $ $
Student Loans: 48%
Average Debt: $
Phi Beta Kappa: Yes
Applicants: 21,945
Accepted: 53%
Enrolled: 45%
Grad in 6 Years: 85%
Returning Freshmen: 95%
Academics: ✍ ✍ ✍
Social: ☎ ☎ ☎ ☎ ☎
Q of L: ★ ★ ★
Admissions: (706) 542-8776
Email Address: adm-info@uga.edu

Strong Programs:
Psychology
Finance
Biology
Marketing
Journalism
Education

(continued)

Agricultural Sciences
Public and International Affairs

Students say that academic rigor varies by major but generally agree that the atmosphere is more collaborative than competitive. An online registration system helps students sign up for courses; first pick usually goes to the 2,500 honors students and to UGA's varsity athletes, with everyone else prioritized by class standing. As you might expect, large lecture classes are common, but students do have the opportunity for more intimate learning environments in upper-level courses within their individual majors. "I love that I have the same professors multiple times in my college," says a human development and family science major. "That way, I am able to build a relationship with them and establish deeper networks." Students find ample assistance with securing internships and jobs from the hands-on counselors in the Career Center. "My counselor walked me through the internship process every step of the way. She was not only encouraging, but she went above and beyond to make sure I felt prepared for the interview process as well," cheers a marketing and public relations major.

> **"The dorms aren't the Ritz, but freshman year is so much fun you never notice."**

The Center for Undergraduate Research Opportunities allows students to conduct a research or service project, write a thesis, or develop a creative work with close faculty supervision. The University of Georgia ranks among the top 10 research universities in the number of students who study abroad each year (20 percent). In addition to offering study abroad opportunities at its campuses in Oxford, Italy, and Costa Rica, UGA offers over more than 100 faculty-led study abroad trips to dozens of countries, exchange programs with partner universities, and independent research and internship opportunities.

The new Experiential Learning Initiative requires students to take part in hands-on learning opportunities.

Eighty-seven percent of UGA students are Georgian, and 5 percent are international. Ninety-three percent graduated in the top quarter of their high school class. African Americans account for 8 percent of the student body, Asian Americans 10 percent, and Hispanics 6 percent. Politically, the school tends to lean right, and LGBTQ issues and immigration laws have drawn attention recently. Merit scholarships are available, and UGA also doles out 454 athletic scholarships in 12 sports. As many as 100 top undergraduates are named Foundation Fellows, netting a full scholarship plus stipends for international travel and research.

Thirty-three percent of Bulldogs live in the dorms, and freshmen are required to do so. "The dorms aren't the Ritz, but freshman year is so much fun you never notice," says a political science and speech communication major. Most keep their meal cards even after moving off campus. There are four campus dining halls—each with its own specialty cuisine—and a snack bar, and the excellence of UGA's food service program has been recognized with the Ivy Award. When the weekend comes, students know how to have a good time. "The party scene is alive and well with house parties, frat parties, and downtown Athens," says a senior. Fraternities and sororities attract 22 percent of the men and 31 percent of the women, respectively. Alcohol is prohibited in the dorms, but as at most schools, the determined manage to imbibe anyway. There are also more than 500 student organizations for students to choose from.

> **"Students are very involved in the Athens community."**

The Georgia–Florida rivalry—billed as the "World's Largest Cocktail Party"—is particularly notable.

The funky mix of shops, restaurants, clubs, and various cultural events found in downtown Athens is only a 10-minute walk from most residence halls. A senior explains that Athens is "far enough away from Atlanta to maintain the college community, yet close enough to provide an escape." Many clubs in Athens cater to UGA students and admit those under 21, who get hand stamps indicating that they can't drink. "Students are very involved in the Athens community, especially through mentorship and volunteer programs with the Athens public schools," says a senior, and philanthropic organizations like UGA Miracle, UGA HEROs, and CURE are some of the largest student groups on campus. Popular road trips include the Florida and Carolina beaches, and anywhere the Bulldogs are playing on a fall Saturday.

It's no stretch to claim that Athens residents worship UGA's perennially fierce football team. The Georgia–Florida rivalry—billed as the "World's Largest Cocktail Party"—is particularly notable: "The game takes place on neutral ground in Jacksonville, and since it coincides with fall break, 90 percent of the students go," says an accounting major. Teams compete in the tough Southeastern Conference, and men's and women's tennis, women's gymnastics, and the equestrian team are especially competitive. Women's swimming and diving won its seventh national championship in 2016, and Georgia's Debate Union enjoys consistent national success as well. Recreational sports are taken seriously too, with 45 clubs and 24 intramural sports available for students to compete in.

UGA's sheer size means you could coast through four years here as nothing more than a number. But with a little effort, that doesn't have to happen. Freshman seminars, research projects, study abroad, and honors courses offer the opportunity to graduate with a solid background in any number of areas and fond memories of Saturdays spent cheering on the Bulldogs—along with 92,000 of your closest friends. "There's a lot of pride at my school," confirms a senior. "Even the city of Athens brags on the Bulldawgs, and we all feel a part of something special."

If You Apply To > **Georgia:** Early action: Oct. 15. Regular decision: Jan. 15. Financial aid: Mar. 15. Housing: May 15. Application fee: $60. No campus or alumni interviews. SATs or ACTs: required. Subject Tests: recommended. Letters of recommendation: required. Essay: required.

Georgia Institute of Technology

Atlanta, GA 30332

As the South's premier technically oriented university, Ma Tech does not coddle her young. Students must survive the sometimes mean streets of downtown Atlanta and fight through a wall of graduate students to talk with their professors. Architecture and big-time sports supplement the engineering focus. Tech's 64/36 male/female ratio is offset by women from all-female Agnes Scott.

If you're looking for lazy days on the college green and hard-partying weekends, look elsewhere. You won't find those at Georgia Institute of Technology, the South's premier tech university, and a relatively new member of the elite Association of American Universities. What you will find are challenging courses that prepare you for a high-paying job as an engineer, architect, or computer scientist. "Tech is tough," reasons one student. "You have to want to be here." Even those who want to be there are happy to finally arrive at graduation day. What makes Tech a special place? "The fact that I survived it and got out with a degree," says a computer science major, only partially joking. As part of its efforts to become a top technological research university globally, Tech has developed an extensive offering of Massive Open Online Courses (MOOCs), available for free to the general public.

Located just off the interstate in Georgia's capital city, Tech's 450-acre campus embraces 42 residence halls, an aquatic center, a sports performance complex, and an amphitheater. Reflective of the history of Georgia Tech, the building styles include the Georgian Revival and Collegiate Gothic of the historic Hill District (listed on the

Website: www.gatech.edu
Location: City Center
Public
Total Enrollment: 19,422
Undergraduates: 13,572
Male/Female: 64/36
SAT Ranges: CR 630–730, M 680–770
ACT Ranges: 30–33
Financial Aid: 62%
Pell Grant: 17%
Expense: Pub $ $ $
Student Loans: 40%
Average Debt: $ $

(continued)

Phi Beta Kappa: No
Applicants: 27,277
Accepted: 32%
Enrolled: 35%
Grad in 6 Years: 85%
Returning Freshmen: 97%
Academics: ✐ ✐ ✐ ✐ ✐
Social: ☎ ☎
Q of L: ★ ★
Admissions: (404) 894-4154
Email Address: admission@gatech.edu

Strong Programs:
Industrial Engineering
Biomedical Engineering
Aerospace Engineering
Civil Engineering
Mechanical Engineering
Computer Science
Mathematics
Architecture

National Register of Historic Places) and surrounding area, the International Style buildings constructed from the 1940s into the 1960s, the modernist structures of the 1970s and '80s, the postmodern facilities of the '90s, and the newly built high-tech facilities. All these styles coexist comfortably on a tree-filled and landscaped campus that serves as a green oasis in the midst of a dense urban environment. The ambitious Campus Master Plan resulted in the opening of more than two million square feet of new and renovated space at a cost of nearly $500 million.

Regardless of major, students must complete nine semester hours of social sciences, eight hours of science, six hours each of English and humanities, four hours of math, three hours of U.S. or Georgia history, U.S. Perspectives Overlay, a global perspectives course, and two hours of wellness. Strong programs include math and computer science, as well as most types of engineering, especially industrial, biomedical, aerospace, and civil. Tech also offers electrical, environmental, mechanical, computer, materials, and nuclear engineering. Students in several disciplines complete a Capstone Design course, in which they work in teams to design, build, and test prototypes of products with real-world applications. Aside from the technical fare, Tech's business college is increasingly popular, and its school of architecture has done pioneering work in historic preservation and energy conservation. Among the architecture program's alumni is Michael Arad, whose winning design for the September 11 memorial in lower Manhattan was selected from a field of more than 5,200. The prelaw certificate is a boon to aspiring patent attorneys, as is the minor in law, science, and technology. Tech has plenty of liberal arts courses, but students say history, philosophy, and English aren't the reasons why most students enroll.

> **"Tech is tough. You have to want to be here."**

Courses at Tech are "extremely rigorous," says a senior, at least in the sciences and engineering. "Grading on a curve creates hypercompetitive situations because your absolute grade is largely irrelevant—you just have to do better than most of the others." Classes tend to be big—26 percent of those taken by undergraduates have more than 50 students—and a computer science major warns that Tech is "absolutely horrible for things like freshman math classes. You're typically taught by TAs. Things get better as you progress and get to know professors." Faculty members have real-world experience; some are Nobel Prize winners and former NASA astronauts.

> **"There are a lot of left-brain types here—high on the introspection and thinking, low on the social skills."**

Tech's demanding workload means it's common to spend five years getting your degree. Students say the course selection process can be frustrating, and getting into required courses can be an issue. One positive factor contributing to delayed graduation dates is the popular co-op program, through which more than 4,000 students earn money for their education while gaining on-the-job experience. Tech offers more than 85 exchange programs and 40 faculty-led study abroad programs, sending more than 1,900 students abroad each year. More than 52 percent of students have some sort of international study or internship experience by the time they graduate. An honors program is available for the extremely motivated, and the Center for the Study of Women, Science, and Technology offers a living/learning community and research opportunities for women in STEM fields.

Tech's demanding workload means it's common to spend five years getting your degree.

Most Georgia Tech students are too focused on school or their co-op jobs to care about politics, causes, or any of the issues that get their peers riled up on nearby campuses. "There are a lot of left-brain types here—high on the introspection and thinking, low on the social skills," says a senior. And though they may be united in their pursuit of technical expertise, the campus is hardly homogenous: African Americans account for 7 percent of the student body, Hispanics 7 percent, and Asian

Americans 19 percent. To limit burgeoning enrollment, out-of-state applicants must meet somewhat higher criteria than their Georgia counterparts; 57 percent of undergraduates are in-staters and 11 percent are international. Thousands of merit scholarships averaging $8,546 are available, as are 325 athletic scholarships in 10 sports. In addition, Tech has eliminated loans for Georgia residents with family incomes below $33,300 a year.

Fifty-three percent of students live in the dorms, where freshmen are guaranteed a room. A senior says that the quality of residence halls varies widely. "Some dorms are new, apartment-style, and nice," the student says. "Others are foul dungeons." Many dorms have full kitchen facilities, though, and while most halls are single-sex, visitation rules are lenient. The campus dining halls offer "little variety and less quality," according to another student. Off-campus housing is generally comfortable, but parts of the surrounding neighborhood are unsavory. "Far too many cars are broken into or stolen," says one student. "There's usually a couple of armed robberies (at least) per semester." VOICE is a campuswide initiative working to address the issue of campus sexual assault.

Fortunately, even if mystery meat is on the day's menu at Tech, the school is smack-dab in the middle of "Hot-Lanta," with its endless supply of clubs, bars, movie theaters, restaurants, shopping, and museums, both in midtown Atlanta and the Buckhead district. "Atlanta is not a college town," reasons a computer science major. "However, it is the best

"Some dorms are new, apartment-style, and nice. Others are foul dungeons."

thing going in Georgia," with friendly, young residents, good cultural activities, beautiful green spaces, and a booming economy. The city also offers plenty of community service opportunities. Fraternities draw 25 percent of Tech's men and sororities attract 30 percent of the women, and members may live in their chapter houses. Alcohol flows freely at frat parties, but otherwise, students say, Tech's policies against open containers and underage drinking are strictly enforced. "There's not much in the way of social life here outside of the frats," says a senior. "You have your group of friends and you do your own thing." The best road trips include Florida's beaches, which are a half-day's drive, and Athens, Georgia, for basketball or football games against the University of Georgia.

Tech's Division I varsity sports teams (the Yellowjackets) have become as big-time as any in the South, and when the weekend comes, students throw off their lab coats and become wild members of the "Rambling Wreck from Georgia Tech." Men's swimming and track are recent national champions, and other solid teams include football, baseball, golf, and women's swimming, track, and tennis. About 40 percent of students participate in the university's 42 club and 20 intramural sports. Among Tech's many other traditions is "stealing the T," in which students try to remove the huge yellow letter T from the tower on the administration building and return it to the school by presenting it to a member of the faculty or administration. The addition of alarms, motion sensors, and heat sensors on the T has made the task more difficult, but "certainly not impossible for a Georgia Tech engineer," says an electrical engineering major. And then there's the Mini 500, a 15-lap tricycle race around a parking garage with three pit stops, a tire change, and a driver rotation.

Forget fitting the mold; the engineers of Georgia Tech are proud to say they make it. Self-direction, ambition, and motivation will take you far here, as will dexterity with a graphing calculator and a fondness for highly complex software algorithms. And despite their complaints about the workload, the social life (or lack thereof), the safety of their surrounding neighborhood, and the impact of budget cuts, Tech students do have a soft spot for their school. Says one student, "I love a good challenge, and Tech is perfect for that."

Gettysburg College

300 North Washington Street, Gettysburg, PA 17325

The college by the battlefield is strong in U.S. history—that's a given. The natural sciences and business are also popular, and political science majors enjoy good connections in D.C. and New York City. For a small school, participation in undergraduate research and study abroad is notably high.

Website: www.gettysburg.edu
Location: Suburban
Private
Total Enrollment: 2,430
Undergraduates: 2,430
Male/Female: 47/53
SAT Ranges: CR 600–670, M 610–680
ACT Ranges: 27–29
Financial Aid: 60%
Pell Grant: 14%
Expense: Pr $ $ $ $
Student Loans: 61%
Average Debt: $ $ $
Phi Beta Kappa: Yes
Applicants: 6,386
Accepted: 40%
Enrolled: 28%
Grad in 6 Years: 84%
Returning Freshmen: 91%
Academics: ✍ ✍ ✍ ½
Social: ☎ ☎ ☎
Q of L: ★ ★ ★
Admissions: (717) 337-6100
Email Address: admiss@ gettysburg.edu

Strong Programs:
English
Economics
Psychology
Organization and Management Studies
History
Political Science

Whether the reference is to the Pennsylvania town steeped in Civil War history or the small, high-caliber college located in the famed battlefield's backyard, a certain pride and reverence are immediately evident when the name "Gettysburg" is uttered. This feeling is not lost on students at Gettysburg College, who come to southeastern Pennsylvania to acquaint themselves with American history while gearing up for the future. "I have been afforded opportunities inside and outside the classroom that I could not have imagined," says one senior, "but here at Gettysburg, these types of joy are just everyday moments."

Situated in the midst of gently rolling hills, Gettysburg's 200-acre campus is "a historical treasure," an eclectic assemblage of Georgian, Greek, Romanesque, Gothic Revival, and modern architecture, plus several styles not easily categorized. One campus building—Penn Hall—was actually used as a hospital during the Battle of Gettysburg. Rumor has it that ghostly Civil War soldiers can still be seen walking the grounds.

General education requirements cover typical liberal arts disciplines and goals, and students in all majors must complete a capstone requirement. The English department, home of the *Gettysburg Review*, is among the strongest at Gettysburg, as are the natural sciences, which are well endowed with state-of-the-art equipment. The fine psychology department offers opportunities for students to participate in faculty research. Organization and management studies and economics are also popular, as is, of course, the excellent history department, which is bolstered by the school's nationally recognized and prestigious Civil War Institute. Students may choose from three degrees within the Sunderman Conservatory of Music, and cooperative dual-degree programs in engineering and forestry are available. Through the Central Pennsylvania Consortium, students may take courses at two nearby colleges—Dickinson and Franklin & Marshall. Recent additions to the curriculum include a major in cinema and media studies and a minor in public history.

> **"I have been afforded opportunities inside and outside the classroom that I could not have imagined."**

"I am surrounded by faculty and peers who strive for quality and excellence but understand the importance of supporting one another inside and outside of the classroom," says one senior. Two-thirds of classes enroll fewer than 20 students, and the small class sizes make for close student/faculty relationships; the academic honor code contributes to the atmosphere of community and mutual trust as well. "Faculty members are accessible, and all classes are taught by professors," says one junior. The popular first-year seminars explore topics such as Why Do People Dance?; participants live in the same residence hall and are in the same first-year residential college program. "First-Year orientation, seminars, the honor code, and the RISE program are important because they are all learning experiences," says one student. Another popular program is the Area Studies Symposium, which focuses each year on a different region of the world and offers lectures and films for the whole campus, in addition to academic credit for participating students.

Undergraduate research is a big emphasis at Gettysburg, with roughly 80 percent participating across all disciplines. The chemistry department offers a summer cooperative research program between students and professors in which they work on a joint publication. Outstanding seniors may participate in the Senior Scholars' Seminar, with independent study on a major contemporary issue, but all students have a chance to do independent work and/or design their own majors. Most departments offer structured internships, and Gettysburg sponsors a Washington semester with American University* and a United Nations semester through Drew University in New Jersey. Participation in study abroad programs is also high, with 60 percent of students traveling to more than 100 programs worldwide for the same price they pay for regular tuition at Gettysburg.

"A Gettysburg College student yearns for challenges and growth," says one student. The student body is mostly middle- to upper-middle-class. Just 26 percent are native Pennsylvanians, and 5 percent are international. African Americans represent 3 percent of the student body, Asian Americans 2 percent, and Hispanics 5 percent. Students are so interested in public service that the school set up a Center for Public Service to direct their community activities. No athletic scholarships are available, but academic scholarships average $12,016.

Campus housing at the 'Burg is guaranteed for all four years. "First-years live in traditional dorms, sophomores typically live in dorm or suite-style (bedroom with bathroom) buildings, juniors and seniors are typically in apartment-style housing." The top scholars in each class get first crack at the best rooms. Student rooms have been added in renovated historical properties on campus (some reputed to be haunted). Off-campus apartments lure 6 percent of the student body away, while freshmen are required to remain in the residence halls. There are a variety of dining options, including Servo and the Bullet Hole. Kitchens are also available in the residences for upperclassmen. "All of our food is prepared fresh with many healthy and delicious options," states a junior. Concerning safety, a senior says, "Campus security is very good and very visible."

"Most of the social life takes place on campus," says one student, and it mostly involves the Greek system and other student groups. Thirty-one percent of the men and 33 percent of the women go Greek. Greek parties are open and attract crowds eager to dance the night away, although students insist they're not the only source of fun on campus. The Campus Activities Board provides alternative social events, including concerts, comedians, bus trips to Georgetown, movies, and campus coffeehouses. Officially the campus is dry, but as on many such campuses, drinking can be done, albeit carefully, students report. The orchards and rolling countryside surrounding the campus are peaceful and scenic, and there is a small ski slope nearby. Students also get free passes to the historic attractions in town. Many participate in the November 19 Fortenbaugh Lecture by noted historians commemorating the Gettysburg Address and in the yearly wreath-laying ceremony in front of the Eisenhower Admissions Office to commemorate the general's birthday. Tourist season is a common complaint among students. But those who want to escape can do so—the campus is within an hour and a half of Washington, D.C., and considerably closer to Baltimore, where students enjoy the scenic Inner Harbor area.

(continued)
Biology
Civil War Era Studies

The history department is bolstered by the school's nationally recognized and prestigious Civil War Institute.

Undergraduate research is a big emphasis, with roughly 80 percent participating across all disciplines.

"A Gettysburg College student yearns for challenges and growth."

Student rooms have been added in renovated historical properties on campus (some reputed to be haunted).

Gettysburg sponsors 22 varsity sports—11 for men and 11 for women—that compete at the Division III level. The annual football game against Dickinson draws a good turnout, and the Little Brown Bucket, mahogany with silver handles, is passed to the team that wins. The college is a frequent winner of the President's Cup, awarded to the top overall athletic program in the Centennial Conference. Recent conference champs include men's and women's lacrosse and swimming, and women's golf. Ninety percent of students participate in intramural and club sports and recreational fitness programs. "Intramural sports are one of the most popular programs on campus," a senior confirms.

At Gettysburg, students stay true to their slogan: "Work Hard, Play Smart." A junior says, "Gettysburg students have a network of friends and faculty supporting their every decision." Students wanting personal attention from professors, solid academics, and an area rich with history might consider getting their education with a Gettysburg address.

Overlaps

Dickinson, University of Richmond, Franklin & Marshall, Lafayette, Bucknell, American University, College of William and Mary, Muhlenberg

If You Apply To ➤

Gettysburg: Early decision I: Nov. 15. Early decision II, regular decision, and financial aid: Jan. 15. Housing: May 1. Application fee: $60. Campus interviews: recommended, informational. No alumni interviews. SATs or ACTs: recommended (required for students applying for academic merit scholarships). Subject Tests: optional. Letters of recommendation: required. Essay: required. Accepts the Common Application.

University of Glasgow: See page 384.

Gonzaga University

502 East Boone Avenue, Spokane, WA 99258-0102

Best known outside the Northwest for its unlikely successes on the basketball court, Gonzaga is a medium-sized private university with a picturesque residential campus in an urban setting. Offers classic Jesuit education with rigorous core and emphasis on service, though only half of undergrads are Roman Catholic. Spokane is not as cosmopolitan as Seattle or San Francisco. Less selective than Santa Clara or USD, comparable to USF. Good bet for those who relish school spirit.

Website: www.gonzaga.edu
Location: Small City
Private
Total Enrollment: 6,776
Undergraduates: 4,910
Male/Female: 47/53
SAT Ranges: CR 540–640, M 560–650
ACT Ranges: 25–29
Financial Aid: 98%
Pell Grant: 17%
Expense: Pr $

Gonzaga University burst into the nation's frontal lobes in 1999 when its men's basketball team fought their way to the quarterfinals of the Division I tournament. Consistent success in the tournament since then has softened the Zag's image as a midsized David doing battle with Goliaths like UConn. What has lingered, though, is the image of a solid regional liberal arts university committed to the Jesuit ideal of educating the whole person: mind, body, and spirit. "Everyone brings their own experiences, ideas, and dreams," a biology major observes, "and it's amazing to go to a school where people try to foster growth in all aspects of life."

Founded in 1887 as a Jesuit mission, the school takes its name from St. Aloysius Gonzaga, a 16th-century Italian aristocrat who joined the Society of Jesus and was martyred while serving victims of an epidemic. The campus occupies 131 picturesque acres along the Spokane River, only a 15-minute walk from downtown. A 37-mile paved bike trail borders the campus and river. Architectural styles range from the Romanesque College Hall to the sleek PACCAR Center for Applied Science. The library's Crosby Collection contains recordings, photographs, and other memorabilia pertaining to Gonzaga's most famous alumnus, crooner Bing. The new Hemmingson Center boasts ample space for the student body association, student clubs and organizations, and the primary dining hall.

Consistent with its Jesuit liberal arts traditions, Gonzaga requires undergraduates to complete an extensive core curriculum, beginning with a first-year seminar and ending with a core integration seminar. Centered around the question of how students may "educate themselves to become women and men for a more just and humane global community," the core includes courses in English composition, speech communication, and critical reasoning, with doses of philosophy and religious studies, literature, and mathematics. Writing, social justice, and global studies are emphasized throughout students' four years. "Classes from our core curriculum tie into courses from our majors and minors, which is really fun," reports a business administration major. Although Gonzaga is a Jesuit school and offers 16 spiritual retreats annually, there are no requirements to attend mass or chapel.

Gonzaga offers 75 academic majors and programs in five undergraduate divisions: the College of Arts and Sciences and the schools of Business Administration, Education, Engineering and Applied Science, and Nursing and Human Physiology. Students say the strongest programs are engineering, nursing, and business, with accounting a particular strength. Biology majors have the option of adding a research concentration to their degree, while psych students may focus on specialized areas of interest such as child psychology and clinical research. Newly established programs include a major in computer science and computational thinking and minors in women's and gender studies and Native American studies. Additionally, the School of Business Administration recently opened its minor in entrepreneurship and innovation to all majors.

Students describe the academic climate as rigorous but mostly collaborative. "At times it may be competitive," says one junior, "but everyone works together." Students say professors are knowledgeable and ready to help, and most "practically beg their students to get to know them through visiting office hours and giving one-on-one attention in class," says a senior. No TAs or graduate assistants teach classes, and 35 percent of undergraduate classes have 20 or fewer students. Students also praise the school for offering a plethora of resources, including strong support for students with learning disabilities. A criminal justice and philosophy major says the career center has "helped me clean up my résumé, research internships, and given me the tips I needed to attend a career fair and not make a total fool of myself."

> "[Professors] practically beg their students to get to know them through visiting office hours."

The Freshman Retreat offers incoming students the chance to escape for a weekend and bond with classmates through games and other activities ("the best thing I did my freshman year"). Top students may apply for the honors program, and many students participate in Undergraduate Research Week, where they have a chance to show off their research projects. Depending on academic major, students may participate in a variety of capstone programs, including a Senior Design option for engineers. Other special offerings include the three-year Hogan Entrepreneurial Leadership Program, open to high-achieving freshmen seeking an entrepreneurial leadership concentration in addition to their regular majors, and the Comprehensive Leadership Program, which provides a concentration in leadership studies. Gonzaga's Army ROTC program (Bulldog Battalion) ranks as one of the best anywhere.

The centerpiece program for study abroad is Gonzaga-in-Florence, which offers students of any major, including engineering, the opportunity to study at Gonzaga's campus in Florence, Italy, without interrupting their four-year path to graduation.

(continued)

Student Loans: 65%
Average Debt: $ $ $
Phi Beta Kappa: Yes
Applicants: 6,729
Accepted: 73%
Enrolled: 27%
Grad in 6 Years: 83%
Returning Freshmen: 95%
Academics: ✐ ✐ ✐
Social: ☎ ☎ ☎ ☎
Q of L: ★ ★ ★
Admissions: (800) 322-2584
Email Address: admissions@ gonzaga.edu

Strong Programs:
Business
Accounting
Social Sciences
Engineering
Biology
Nursing
Communication Studies
Psychology

The Hogan Entrepreneurial Leadership Program offers high-achieving freshmen an entrepreneurial leadership concentration.

Overall, the university offers more than 60 programs, in which nearly half of students participate. "I studied in Paris the fall semester of my junior year and took classes at a French university with 10 other Gonzaga students," says a business administration major. "I received my Gonzaga scholarship while abroad, and all the credits that I took transferred easily."

"Gonzaga students are excited, passionate, service-driven, and open-minded," according to one history major. Two percent of Zags are from other countries, with the rest fairly equally divided between Washingtonians and out-of-staters. Ten percent are Hispanic, 5 percent are Asian American, and African Americans make up just 1 percent of the student body. Regarding diversity, an English major says, "We have awesome cultural clubs and movements toward gender equality, but there's still a lot to be done." Social activism on campus revolves around issues such as the lack of diversity on campus, women in the church, and abortion. The school offers merit scholarships averaging $14,545 and athletic scholarships in 16 sports. Gonzaga's Family Discount policy guarantees discounts to siblings attending GU at the same time.

Sixty percent of undergraduates reside in campus housing. Freshmen and sophomores are required to live on campus and purchase a meal plan, while juniors and seniors usually head elsewhere; students say that housing can become limited for upperclassmen. On-campus residence halls offer a variety of living styles, including both co-ed and single-sex corridors and floors, and several living/learning communities. A senior explains that residence halls "range in how old they are and how nice some of the facilities are. Regardless of this, you will find devout fans of each residence hall, no matter which one it is." The so-called Hotel Coughlin, the newest residence hall, offers living communities around themes such as cultural diversity, health and wellness, and leadership. Campus vittles are served in a new cafeteria, and students say the food is decent. They report feeling safe on campus, but note that sexual assault has been a growing issue that has resulted in the hiring of a new Title IX director and "a push for change in university policy," according to a junior.

There are no fraternities or sororities at Gonzaga, but students say that their absence has hardly put a damper on social life, either on or off campus. Students agree that while "there is a noticeable party scene off campus in the houses of upperclassmen," they don't feel pressured to drink on campus. Underage students found in possession of alcohol may be fined or required to take an alcohol awareness and safety program. The Hemmingson Center offers a variety of social activities, and a favorite event is "Spochella, which is a music festival similar to Coachella but for Gonzaga students," says a biology major. The festival features music, games, food, and a beer garden. With just over 200,000 residents, Spokane is the second-largest city in Washington but has the feel of a much smaller city. "People will go to downtown Spokane a lot because it's so close and has lots of food, a mall, and is a nice excuse to walk on Centennial Trail," says a senior.

The culture of Gonzaga places strong emphasis on issues of social justice and service. The school offers more than 40 service-learning courses, and 59 percent of undergraduates participate in some form of community service. "Being involved in the community is a specific Jesuit trait that we all try to live out," says one student. Each spring, more than 100 students travel to sites across the nation to participate in community service projects through Mission Possible, and the university ranks tops in alumni Peace Corps volunteers nationwide.

GU's intercollegiate teams, known as the Zags or Bulldogs, compete in the Division I West Coast Conference. In the absence of football (shut down in 1941

Gonzaga offers more than 40 service-learning courses.

"I received my Gonzaga scholarship while abroad, and all the credits that I took transferred easily."

An elaborate process for tickets to basketball games involves strategic tweeting and living in a tent city.

"You will find devout fans of each residence hall."

and never resurrected), basketball is both king and queen. Gonzaga's men's team reached the finals in 2017, and the women's team made it to the Sweet 16 in 2015. Other solid programs include men's and women's golf, women's rowing and volleyball, and men's baseball. The intramural program, mostly run by students themselves, is strong and attracts about 60 percent of undergraduates each year. The debate team is a powerhouse, having sent debaters to the national tournament for 18 consecutive years. Outdoorsy types can take advantage of four ski areas within a 90-mile radius, and GU Outdoors sponsors rafting, hiking, and skiing excursions, including trips to Montana and Canada.

> "At GU, community is almost a belief."

School spirit is a big deal at Gonzaga—mainly when it comes to sports and especially when the opponent is California-based St. Mary's. Since Gonzaga's mascot is the Bulldog, the student cheering section is naturally known as the Kennel. Students go through an elaborate process for tickets to big home basketball games that involves strategic tweeting and living in a tent city days before the opening tip. "It's insanity," confesses one sophomore, "but it's so much fun." A junior adds, "Every Zag should experience this at least once."

At Gonzaga, "spirit" takes on multiple meanings. Basketball may inspire the most vocal outpourings of school spirit, but students say that the religious and humanistic values to which the university has long been committed run deep. "Community is a word tossed around quite frequently at all college campuses," says a psych major, "but at GU, community is almost a belief."

Overlaps

University of Portland, University of Washington, Seattle, Santa Clara, Washington State, Western Washington, Whitworth, University of Oregon

If You Apply To ➤

Gonzaga: Early action: Nov. 15. Regular decision and financial aid: Feb. 1. Housing: May 1. Application fee: $50. Campus interviews: optional, evaluative. No alumni interviews. SATs or ACTs: required. No Subject Tests. Letters of recommendation: required. Essay: required. Accepts the Common Application.

Gordon College

255 Grapevine Road, Wenham, MA 01984

Gordon is the most prominent Christian college in New England and competes nationally with Wheaton (IL) and Messiah, though it lacks the prestige of the former. Not quite in Boston, but close enough to be within easy reach. Extensive core curriculum shapes the undergraduate experience. Emphasis on integrating faith and learning.

Evangelical Christian values are at the heart of almost all aspects of life at this New England college, where faith sets the tone for campus life inside and outside the classroom. Yet Gordon College is also unique in that it is the only Christian college of its type that has no formal denominational ties. Founded as a missionary training school "to prepare the people of God to do the work of God," the college now sees its mission as promoting intellectual maturity and Christian character. Always evolving, Gordon is sharpening its offerings across the board, from international affairs to music education to leadership programs, and looking to increase its diversity. The students revel in the atmosphere. "Gordon is a safe and comfortable place to wrestle with faith and expand our worldview," says a senior.

Gordon is located on Massachusetts's scenic North Shore, three miles from the Atlantic Coast and 25 miles from Boston. The campus sits on more than 450

Website: www.gordon.edu
Location: Suburban
Private
Total Enrollment: 1,718
Undergraduates: 1,627
Male/Female: 38/62
SAT Ranges: CR 480–620, M 470–610
ACT Ranges: 23–29
Financial Aid: 99%
Pell Grant: 25%

*Freshmen take The
Great Conversation,
a seminar on how
to integrate faith
into their academic
experience.*

forested acres, landscaped with flowers and boasting four large ponds. Most campus structures are Georgian-influenced traditional redbrick, except for the administration building, Frost Hall, an old stone structure modeled after a European castle that provides a stark contrast. The Ken Olsen Science Center, an 83,456-square-foot science and technology center at the heart of the campus, is home to a fabrication lab, a vivarium, an aquarium, a new human cadaver lab, and a new biology greenhouse space.

Religious commitment at Gordon is seen as the foundation of serious academic learning rather than a threat to free inquiry. Gordon's core curriculum includes 52 course hours of instruction distributed among Christian theology, the fine arts, humanities, social and behavioral sciences, natural sciences, math, and computer science. Freshmen also take The Great Conversation, a first-year seminar that helps them learn how to integrate faith into their academic experience, and complete an experiential outdoor education requirement. The most popular majors are business administration, psychology, biology, and English language and literature. Biblical studies, physics, theatre arts, and music are also strong programs, although they may draw fewer students. Finance is available as a major—a rarity at small Christian colleges—as is a 3–2 engineering program. The Pike Scholarship program allows high-achieving students to design their own majors.

> "Gordon is a safe and comfortable place to wrestle with faith and expand our worldview."

"The academic climate is rigorous, but not extremely competitive. There is plenty of room for collaboration," says a senior. "Open discussion is welcome, to allow all students to learn from each other and engage at a higher level of learning," adds an English major. Sixty percent of classes have fewer than 20 students, and students say professors are helpful. "If I ever don't understand something, I know that I can meet with my professor during office hours or even during lunch," says a student.

The Jerusalem and Athens Forum, a yearlong great books seminar, is Gordon's principal honors program, along with the Elijah Project, a yearlong program that explores the concept of personal vocation through two seminar courses, a living community, and a culminating internship experience. Off-campus opportunities include stints in Washington, D.C., for aspiring politicos, in Michigan for environmentalists, in Tennessee for contemporary music followers, and in Los Angeles for filmmakers, as well as trips abroad through the Christian College Consortium*. The college operates its own study abroad programs in several locations, including its signature program in Orvieto, Italy, and it partners with other programs to offer more than 40 approved study locations; 34 percent of students participate. Finance majors can take advantage of a Hong Kong seminar and internship program.

"Gordon students strive to be thoughtful and generous," says an English major. Gordon is one of two top Evangelical schools that requires applicants to describe how their faith impacts their lives and to affirm that they recognize the Bible as "the Word of God and hence fully authoritative in matters of faith and conduct" (see also Wheaton College in Illinois). The trustees recently reaffirmed Gordon's policy forbidding "homosexual practice." While observation of the Sabbath is expected, Gordon gives students a bit more latitude than some Christian colleges in determining how they will "separate themselves from worldliness." Thirty-two percent of students are native to Massachusetts, and 8 percent are international. Up to 4 percent of students are Roman Catholics. African Americans constitute 4 percent, Asian Americans 4 percent, and Hispanics 7 percent. Students say that LGBTQ issues, diversity, and social justice tend to get attention on campus, although one notes,

> "On weekends Gordon is a ghost town."

"Because it's a Christian school, even the liberals aren't too liberal." Institutional non-need-based scholarships and grants worth an average of $14,330 are offered to qualified undergrads, and 25 percent of incoming freshmen are eligible for the Pell Grant. Each year, the Clarendon Scholars program provides full-tuition scholarships, as well as mentoring and leadership training, to ten selected freshmen from urban areas.

Eighty-seven percent of Gordon students live in the co-ed residence halls, which are clustered either around the central quad or on an area of campus known as The Hill. "Even the oldest residence halls are nice and spacious," says a freshman. Men and women live in separate wings of the same buildings—separated by a lobby, a lounge, and a laundry room. Persons of the opposite sex may traverse these barriers only at specified times. Permission to move off campus may be granted by petition. Students say the main dining hall, which overlooks a pond and doubles as a study area at night, could offer more options but is "constantly improving to help students with special restrictions." The new Bistro Two Fifty-Five offers a grab-and-go menu that includes upscale salads, wraps, and sandwiches. "Our campus police are wonderful individuals that are dedicated to protecting our students," says a senior. The college has a newly revised sexual misconduct policy and has implemented training programs to educate the community on the issue of sexual assault.

Gordon's Campus Events Council organizes events like movie showings, dances, and coffeehouses held in Chester's Place, a student-run coffee shop with a pub atmosphere, named after a cat. But one freshman laments, "On weekends Gordon is a ghost town." A senior attributes this to the "lack of a pure

"Gordon takes volunteerism very, very seriously."

student center with activities or other things to help students congregate and enjoy each other's company." There is also no Greek system. Still, students highly anticipate annual events like the Winter Ball formal, the Last Blast spring party, and the Gordon Globes student film festival, during which students dress up and walk a red carpet. The "hilarious" Golden Goose talent show, which pits all four classes against each other, is another favorite tradition. Drinking and smoking are forbidden on campus (and may result in suspension or expulsion); those who are 21 or older may drink off campus, but are expected to do so responsibly. The town of Wenham offers "cute shops and restaurants along with other oddities—like used bookstores, jewelry shops, and fresh markets."

For those who love the outdoors, Gordon's setting on rugged Cape Ann is ideal, and it attracts its share of tourists. The campus has cross-country ski trails and ponds for swimming, canoeing, and skating. The ocean is a quick bike ride away, nice beaches are available on Cape Cod and in Maine, and students frequently ski New Hampshire's nearby White Mountains. Volunteering through a prison ministry and in soup kitchens and local churches is popular, and missions take students all around the world, including New York City, Haiti, and Mexico. "Gordon takes volunteerism very, very seriously," a sophomore reports. Boston is 25 miles away by a five-minute drive to the T, the city's public transit system, so access to weekend diversions (and excellent internship opportunities) is relatively easy. Gordon students enjoy free entry to the city's Museum of Fine Arts and can also attend Harvard lectures for free.

Gordon's Fighting Scots compete in Division III athletics, and "a good portion of the student body comes out to the games" when the opponent is rival Endicott College, says a history major. Popular and competitive sports include women's field hockey and men's and women's soccer. About one-third of the student body participates in intramural sports. Everyone looks forward to the annual Highland Games, a day of games and traditional Scottish competitions between dorms.

The Clarendon Scholars program provides full-tuition scholarships to ten freshmen from urban areas.

The Gordon Globes is a student film festival, during which students dress up and walk a red carpet.

Overlaps

Wheaton (IL), Messiah, Grove City, Calvin, Liberty, Eastern University, Biola, Houghton

For many students, Gordon's combination of Christian values, strong academics, and a relaxed setting is a winning one. Gordon wants to graduate men and women of academic excellence and high Christian character. Says one student, "Our school cultivates a great understanding between faculty and students. Gordon strives to keep this relationship at the forefront of everything, something I greatly appreciate."

If You Apply To >

Gordon: Early decision and early action I: Oct. 15. Early action II: Nov. 15. Regular decision I: Feb. 1. Regular decision II and financial aid: Mar. 1. Housing: May 1. Application fee: $50. Campus interviews: required, evaluative. No alumni interviews. SATs or ACTs (with writing): required. Subject Tests: optional. Letters of recommendation: required. Essay: required. Applicants to music or art programs must audition or submit portfolio.

Goucher College

Baltimore, MD 21204

Once a staid women's college, Goucher added men and a more progressive ambiance, making it similar to places like Vassar and Skidmore. Strategically located near Baltimore and not far from D.C., Goucher offers an excellent internship program. Unusual requirement that all students spend time studying or working abroad makes for a globally oriented community.

Website: www.goucher.edu
Location: Suburban
Private
Total Enrollment: 1,579
Undergraduates: 1,450
Male/Female: 32/68
SAT Ranges: CR 500–630, M 480–590
ACT Ranges: 23–28
Financial Aid: 94%
Pell Grant: 22%
Expense: Pr $ $
Student Loans: 65%
Average Debt: $ $ $
Phi Beta Kappa: Yes
Applicants: 3,577
Accepted: 77%
Enrolled: 14%
Grad in 6 Years: 64%
Returning Freshmen: 82%
Academics: ✑ ✑ ✑
Social: ☎ ☎ ☎
Q of L: ★ ★ ★
Admissions: (410) 337-6100
Email Address: admissions@goucher.edu

Goucher is the kind of place where quirky students take part in stellar programs ranging from the arts to public policy. There's a decidedly international bent to the Goucher experience, including a robust study abroad program that sends students packing for far-flung locales around the globe. The school's mission is to prepare students for a life of inquiry, creativity, and critical and analytical thinking. "Goucher provides students with a demanding yet manageable academic environment in which they can develop both an understanding of the material and how it applies to their own experiences in the outside world," says a first-year student.

A former women's college that went co-ed in 1987, Goucher has a long-standing history of excellence. Phi Beta Kappa established a chapter on campus only 20 years after the college was founded, and the college ranks among the nation's top 50 liberal arts colleges in turning out students destined for Ph.D.s in the sciences. Set on 287 landscaped acres in the suburbs of Baltimore, Goucher's wooded campus features lush lawns, stately fieldstone buildings (the fieldstone is mined from local quarries), and rare trees and shrubs from all corners of the globe. The Athenaeum is the central gathering place, housing the library, an open forum for performances, exercise spaces, a café, and other vital college facilities. Construction on two new residence halls, a new dining center, and a new equestrian center is underway.

> **"Everyone receives individualized suggestions and attention specific to [their] strengths and improvement points."**

Traditionally requiring a rigorous set of courses spanning the liberal arts and sciences, Goucher is rolling out a redesigned curriculum for fall 2017, centered around three core elements: relationships, resilience, and reflection. The new curriculum expands opportunities for first-year seminars and colloquia outside students' majors, and it introduces new capstone and portfolio requirements that encourage students to synthesize their educational experiences.

Of Goucher's offerings, the science departments (especially biology and chemistry) are arguably the strongest, bolstered by resources like a nuclear magnetic resonance spectrometer and an observatory with a six-inch refractor telescope. Mathematics and computer science are other traditional strengths, and the dance department is recognized as one of the best at a liberal arts school. The psychology, English, business management, and environmental studies majors draw the highest enrollment. A new minor in Arabic studies was recently added. Future engineers can take advantage of the 3–2 program offered in conjunction with the Whiting School of Engineering at The Johns Hopkins University. Goucher students may take courses at 11 smaller area colleges as well.

(continued)

Strong Programs:
Biology
Chemistry
Mathematics
Computer Science
Dance
Psychology
English
Business Management

"Goucher provides a unique academic climate in that it is geared toward self-actualization," says a psychology major. "It's about growth, meaning that everyone receives individualized suggestions and attention specific to [their] strengths and improvement points." Faculty members here devote most of their time and energy to undergraduate teaching and have a good rapport with students. "Goucher has taught me to stop looking at professors as superior beings with infinite knowledge, but instead to see them as fellow intellectuals that can facilitate classroom conversation," says a student. Each freshman has a faculty advisor to assist with the academic and overall adjustment to college life, which is made easier by Goucher's trademark small classes and individual instruction. Students roundly praise the Academic Center for Excellence (ACE), which offers academic support services from study-skills workshops and supplemental instruction to stress-reducing meditation sessions. Says a senior, "ACE contains some of the most calming, enlightened souls you'll encounter."

In addition to their academic work, some Goucher students are required to do a three-credit internship or off-campus experience related to their major. Popular choices include congressional offices, museums, law firms, and newspapers. The International Scholars Program is an honors series of three courses tracing the

"We are dining pretty lavishly here."

evolution of the Atlantic cultures and post-colonial globalization, taken alongside other classes over the fall, January, and spring terms. Goucher was the first college in the nation to require all of its undergraduates to study abroad at least once before graduation; more than 60 programs are available in 32 countries. Most students study abroad during their junior year, and the experience is expected to complement their major field of study. About half of students embark on semester- or year-long programs, while the other half engage in three-week intensive courses offered during January term or summer. The college provides a need-based grant ranging from $200 to $2,500 to offset the cost.

"The two words that best describe the student body at Goucher are 'quirky community,'" says a student. Twenty-seven percent of Goucher's students are homegrown, and most of the rest hail from Pennsylvania, New York, New Jersey, and California. African Americans make up 12 percent of the student body, Hispanics 9 percent, Asian Americans 4 percent, and international students 3 percent. The college established the Center for Race, Equity, and Identity in 2015 to support diverse populations on campus and create programming that encourages cross-cultural understanding. Students agree that social activism is prevalent on campus. "I always joke that while many schools bond over football or basketball, Goucher bonds over feminism and black activism," says a senior, adding, "It's nice though—it means our students really care." Goucher offers merit scholarships averaging $16,284 for those who are qualified but no athletic scholarships. Pell Grants are available to the 22 percent of incoming students who qualify.

Eighty-two percent of students live on campus, and freshmen double up in spacious rooms, while upperclassmen select housing through lotteries. The available

Goucher requires all of its undergrads to study abroad, and the experience is expected to complement their major field of study.

singles usually go to juniors and seniors, though a lucky sophomore may occasionally get one. "Housekeeping is friendly, and most students get the rooms that they want. It's a very family-like atmosphere," says a sophomore. Campus dining options, which include vegan and vegetarian fare, receive enthusiastic reviews. Says a senior, "We are dining pretty lavishly here." Students note that sexual assault on campus has been an issue in recent years, but, according to a sophomore, the school has been "working with the students to find out what we feel is necessary to avoid it being an issue in the future."

"The party scene is not particularly strong on campus, but there are plenty of students who get together in each other's rooms to kick back and relax on the weekends," an environmental studies major says. Goucher has no sororities or fraternities, but the close-knit housing units hold periodic events, and the college hosts weekend movies, concerts, and lectures. Alcohol is ever-present but not the hub of the social scene. Major annual social events include Get into Goucher Day, Winter Carnival, and Gala. "Get into Goucher Day is a huge festival held every spring that students look forward to. There are inflatables, great food, live music, and all kinds

"Goucher will force you to engage with challenging topics."

of other cool stuff," explains a senior. Students who are of age frequent restaurants and bars in Towson, the small but bustling college town a five-minute walk away, and a car is useful for visiting Baltimore's Inner Harbor for entertainment. Roughly 60 percent of students volunteer, many through community-based learning programs that tie hands-on service experience in the local area with academic coursework. Students get involved in local politics too, according to a senior: "The Goucher Poll is a pretty unique activity...which monitors public perception of social issues and decisions via telephone poll."

The Gophers field a number of competitive teams in the Division III Landmark Conference. As Goucher was a women's college for so long, women's athletics are more highly developed than those at many co-ed schools. The equestrian team is nationally competitive, winning its second consecutive IHSA Zone IV title in 2015 and earning its fifth consecutive top 10 national finish in 2016. Men's and women's lacrosse, men's soccer, and men's tennis are also highly competitive and frequent conference playoff contenders. Men's tennis took the Landmark Conference championship title in 2016. Students here can get creative with their recreational activities: the Humans vs. Zombies game originated at Goucher in 2005.

Goucher is far from a stagnant place. Indeed, it is constantly rethinking its mission and redirecting its resources to broaden student experiences in a hands-on, global way. "Goucher will force you to engage with challenging topics like sexism, racism, and classism," says a senior, but in a close-knit, supportive environment focused on personal growth for all kinds of learners. A sophomore says it succinctly: "We're a family."

If You Apply To ➤ **Goucher:** Early decision: Nov. 15. Early action: Dec. 1. Regular decision: Feb. 1. Financial aid: Feb. 15. Housing: Apr. 1. Application fee: $55. Campus interviews: recommended, informational. Alumni interviews: optional, informational. SATs or ACTs: optional. No Subject Tests. Letters of recommendation: required. Essay: required. Accepts the Common Application. Applicants may choose the alternative Goucher Video Application option.

Iowa cornfields provide a surreal backdrop for Grinnell's funky, progressive, and talented student body. With about 1,600 students, Grinnell's population is 1,200 less than Oberlin's. That translates into tiny classes and tutorials. Second only to Carleton as the best liberal arts college in the Midwest. Grinnell's biggest challenge is simply getting prospective students to the campus. The cornfields make for a tight-knit campus community. Turns out lots of future Ph.D.s.

"Go West, young man, go West," Horace Greeley said to Josiah B. Grinnell in 1846. The result of Grinnell's wanderings into the rural cornfields, about an hour from Des Moines and Iowa City, is the remarkable college that bears his name. Despite its physical isolation, Grinnell is a powerhouse on the national scene. Ever progressive, it was the first college west of the Mississippi to admit African Americans and women, and the first in the country to establish an undergraduate political science department. It was once a stop on the Underground Railroad, and its graduates include Harry Hopkins, architect of the New Deal, and Robert Noyce, inventor of the integrated circuit, two people who did as much as anyone to change the face of American society in the 20th century. The school's 120-acre campus is an attractive blend of collegiate Gothic and modern Bauhaus academic buildings and Prairie-style houses. (Architecture buffs should take note of the dazzling Louis Sullivan bank facade just off campus.)

True to its liberal arts focus, Grinnell mandates a first-semester writing tutorial, modeled after Oxford University's program, but doesn't require anything else. The more than 35 tutorials, limited to about 12 students each, help enhance critical thinking, research, writing, and discussion skills, and allow first-year students to work individually with professors. Recent offerings include Archaeoastronomy, Icelandic Sagas, and Human Rights in the Modern World. "Tutorials are fun, interesting, and a great introduction to the academic possibilities that Grinnell has to offer," one student says. When it comes to declaring a major, students determine their own course of study with help from faculty. Departments in the social and natural sciences are strong, the latter bolstered by an influx of research grants, including one from the National Science Foundation. "Due to the college's enormous endowment, the sciences are top-notch," offers one student. "With the best equipment and graduate-level research at the undergraduate level, Grinnell's science division is a popular choice." Psychology and foreign languages, including German and Russian, are popular too.

> **"With the best equipment and graduate-level research at the undergraduate level, Grinnell's science division is a popular choice."**

Grinnell's admissions standards are high—81 percent of students were in the top 10th of their high school class—and nearly one-third of graduates move on directly to graduate and professional schools. Students who don't mind studying, even on weekends, will be happiest here. "The academic climate is fairly intense," says one junior, "but not competitive." Sixty-nine percent of classes have fewer than 20 students. During finals, perhaps to help ease the stress, costumed superheroes run around the library giving out candy, according to a sociology major. Teaching is the top priority for Grinnell faculty members, and because the college awards no graduate degrees, there are no teaching assistants. "In general, profs are here to teach and have generous office hours," a sophomore says. Academic advising is also highly regarded, as students are assisted by the professor who

Website: www.grinnell.edu
Location: Small Town
Private
Total Enrollment: 1,665
Undergraduates: 1,665
Male/Female: 45/55
SAT Ranges: CR 640–740, M 660–770
ACT Ranges: 30–33
Financial Aid: 87%
Pell Grant: 19%
Expense: Pr $ $ $
Student Loans: 59%
Average Debt: $
Phi Beta Kappa: Yes
Applicants: 6,414
Accepted: 25%
Enrolled: 28%
Grad in 6 Years: 89%
Returning Freshmen: 94%
Academics: ✍ ✍ ✍ ✍ ½
Social: ☎ ☎
Q of L: ★ ★ ★
Admissions: (641) 269-3600
Email Address: admission@grinnell.edu

Strong Programs:
Social Sciences
Biological and Life Sciences
Foreign Languages
Literature
Linguistics

leads their first-year tutorial, and then choose another faculty member in their major discipline.

When the urge to travel arises, students may study abroad in more than 100 locations through the Associated Colleges of the Midwest* consortium and Grinnell-in-London. Fifty-five percent of students spend some time away from campus, and financial aid extends to study abroad. The Grinnell-in-Washington program combines coursework with an internship in the nation's capital. Forty-five percent of students participate in undergraduate research, including the Mentored Advanced Project program, which enables them to work closely with a faculty member on scholarly research or the creation of a work of art. Co-ops in architecture, business, law, medicine, and 3–2 engineering programs are also available.

Grinnell is a bit of Greenwich Village in corn country. Despite the rural environment, the college attracts an urban clientele, especially from the Chicago area.

"Profs are here to teach and have generous office hours."

Only 8 percent of Grinnell students are from Iowa, and 16 percent are international. "We're quirky, often hippie and liberal, though increasingly diverse," a student observes. The student body is 7 percent Hispanic, 8 percent Asian American, and 6 percent African American. Women's rights, gay rights, labor rights, human rights, globalization, the environment, and groups such as the Politically Active Feminist Alliance, Grinnell Escalating AIDS Response, and Fearless (formed to combat gender-based violence) set the tone. Admissions are need-blind, and the college meets 100 percent of admitted students' demonstrated financial need. Merit awards averaging $17,533 are handed out annually, but there are no athletic awards. Grinnell has a policy that at least 15 percent of every freshman class will be students whose parents did not go to college.

The college guarantees four years of campus housing, and 88 percent of students take advantage of the dorms, each of which has kitchen facilities, cable television, and a computer room. All but two dorms are co-ed, and after freshman year, students participate in a room draw, which can be stressful but usually works out. "The dorms are good," a student says, "with no ridiculously small rooms." Despite being located in the middle of Iowa, students say they are glad to have campus security available.

With no fraternities or sororities, all-campus parties and intramurals revolve mainly around the dorms. "I liken the experience to that of a cruise ship," says one student, "in that the students all stay in one place and entertainment is brought to campus." Each dorm periodically sponsors a party using wordplay from its name in the title. For instance, James Hall puts on the Mary-Be-James party, for which everyone comes in drag. As for alcohol, a senior reports, "Grinnell is not a dry campus, but there are no bars on campus and there is no peer pressure to drink or culture of problematic drinking." Grinnell's social groups and activities range from the Society for Creative Anachronism and the Black Cultural Center to improvisational work-

"We're quirky, often hippie and liberal, though increasingly diverse."

shops, poetry readings, symposia, concerts, and movies. Highlights of the campus calendar include semiformal Winter and Spring Waltzes, where "most people wear formals and look very nice, not a common occurrence at a school where comfort is the usual standard and women rarely wear makeup," notes one student. At Disco, "everyone dresses up in clothes from the '70s and dances all night." Other noteworthy events include Titular Head (a festival of five-minute student films) and Pipe Cleaner Day (which brings upwards of 20,000 of the sculptable wires to campus for students to play with and de-stress before finals).

Grinnell (population 9,200), is "a small farming community with a nice downtown." The college's Service Learning and Civic Engagement Program works to bridge the town-gown gap by connecting students with more than 50 area non-profit and community partners for service opportunities. Nearby Rock Creek State Park lends itself to biking, running, camping, kayaking, and cross-country skiing, and the Grinnell Outdoor Recreation Program sponsors a variety of pursuits, including off-campus trips and open rock-climbing sessions for both beginning and experienced participants. There are a few bars and pizza joints downtown, but for those craving bright lights, Iowa City and Des Moines are within an hour's drive, and the college runs a shuttle service to them. Chicago and Minneapolis are each about four hours distant.

The Grinnell Pioneers compete in Division III athletics, and the men's basketball team has won national attention for an unusual run-and-gun offense that uses waves of five players like hockey shifts in an effort to wear down opponents. Recent conference champions include men's and women's tennis, swimming and diving, and cross-country, women's golf, and baseball. As for recreational sports, one psychology major explains, "Because almost 40 percent of the student body participates in intercollegiate athletics, the intramural program isn't as extensive as it would be in a larger school."

Grinnell wouldn't put a grin on every prospective college student's face. "Most of us don't apologize for what at first turns people off about Grinnell," explains a senior. "We like being in the middle of Iowa, we like that you've probably never heard of us, we love that you won't come here because you want a big name." But there's no denying that Grinnell—a first-rate liberal arts college in the cornfields—is a real gem of a school, and one that is still relatively accessible.

James Hall puts on the Mary-Be-James party, for which everyone comes in drag.

Overlaps

Carleton, Macalester, Oberlin, St. Olaf, Vassar

If You Apply To ➤ **Grinnell:** Early decision I: Nov. 15. Early decision II: Jan. 1. Regular decision and financial aid: Jan. 15. No application fee. Campus and alumni interviews: recommended, evaluative. SATs or ACTs: required. No Subject Tests. Letters of recommendation: required. Essay: required. Accepts the Common Application.

Guilford College

5800 West Friendly Avenue, Greensboro, NC 27410

One of the few schools of Quaker heritage in the South, Guilford emphasizes a collaborative approach and is among the most liberal institutions below the Mason-Dixon line. A kindred spirit to Earlham in Indiana. With a notably high African American population, Guilford's signature program is justice and policy studies. Substantial number of older students enriches the campus culture.

If your idea of a rousing road trip is protesting in Washington, D.C., you'll likely find plenty of like-minded compatriots at Guilford College. Founded in 1837 by the Religious Society of Friends (Quakers), this generally left-leaning campus loves to debate just about any issue and get involved in the world around it. There's none of that college "bubble" that envelops many other schools. Instead, enrollment numbers are going up and the student body is becoming more diverse.

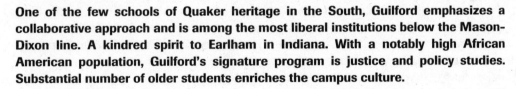

"Be prepared to learn as well as to work hard."

"The students are extremely open to different ideas," says a senior. Campus inclusiveness is enhanced by an ambitious adult education program. More than one-third of full-time undergraduates are 23 or older and benefit from a large selection of evening classes and their own orientation and counseling services.

Website: www.guilford.edu
Location: Small City
Private
Total Enrollment: 1,554
Undergraduates: 1,554
Male/Female: 48/52
SAT Ranges: CR 450–600, M 460–570
ACT Ranges: 18–22
Financial Aid: 91%

(continued)

Pell Grant: 37%
Expense: Pr $
Student Loans: 88%
Average Debt: $ $
Phi Beta Kappa: No
Applicants: 2,775
Accepted: 63%
Enrolled: 18%
Grad in 6 Years: 61%
Returning Freshmen: 67%
Academics: ✐ ✐ ✐
Social: ☎ ☎
Q of L: ★ ★ ★ ★
Admissions: (800) 992-7759
Email Address: admission@
  guilford.edu

Strong Programs:
Community and Justice
  Studies
Criminal Justice
Business Administration
Religious Studies
Accounting
Political Science

Guilford was an embarkation point on the Underground Railroad.

Located on 340 wooded acres in northwest Greensboro, Guilford's redbrick buildings are mainly in the Georgian style. The school is the only liberal arts college in the Southeast with Quaker roots, as well as the oldest coeducational institution in the South and the third oldest in the nation. During the Civil War, Guilford was one of a few Southern colleges that remained open—perhaps because it was also an embarkation point on the Underground Railroad. All of the residence halls have recently been renovated.

Students fulfill general education requirements in three areas: Foundations, Explorations, and Interdisciplinary Studies Capstone. As part of the Foundations component, students take a First-Year Seminar and coursework in writing and historical perspectives; they also demonstrate proficiency in a foreign language and quantitative literacy. For Explorations, students take one course in each of five divisions—arts, business and policy studies, humanities, natural sciences and math, and social sciences—in addition to three Critical Perspectives courses that cover intercultural issues, social justice/environmental responsibility, and U.S. diversity. During the senior year, students take an interdisciplinary capstone course.

"As a student coming to Guilford, one should be prepared to learn as well as to work hard in order to achieve excellence," says a senior. "The college is centered on the Quaker values of community, diversity, equality, excellence, integrity, justice, and stewardship." Students say Guilford's most popular programs are also its best: justice and policy studies, business administration, religious studies, accounting, and political science. The justice and policy studies department offers majors in community and justice studies and criminal justice, as well as minors in interpersonal communications and organizational communications. Classes at Guilford are small, with 67 percent enrolling fewer than 20 students, helping to create a more personal environment. A student says, "As long as students are willing to be challenged and not avoid more advanced classes, they will be forming strong student and professor relationships."

> **"Guilford students are known to unify and protest or advocate aspects of local, national, or international importance."**

Guilford believes that experiential learning adds immeasurably to classroom work, so faculty-mentored research and travel are important emphases. Science majors conduct research in areas ranging from molecular genetics and computer modeling to Barrier Island geomorphology and astrophysics. In addition to standard laboratory equipment, students have access to a wide range of resources, including a lake, organic farm, and 220 acres of woodland property on campus, which provide a rich resource for field studies related to diversity and sustainability. Guilford has several endowed funds that support student scientific research and travel, including an award for Women in Physical Science. The college offers study abroad in dozens of nations; 30 percent of students participate. In the summer, students may participate in a five-week seminar that includes hiking, camping, and geological and biological research in the Grand Canyon, or in a seminar on the East African rift, which includes a three-week trip to Africa.

Guilford students come from across the globe and a range of socioeconomic backgrounds; most are liberal. "Guilford students are known to unify and protest or advocate aspects of local, national, or international importance," says a student. Fifty-seven percent of students are in-staters, and 1 percent are international. African Americans comprise 21 percent of the student body, Hispanics 6 percent, and Asian Americans 4 percent; 37 percent are eligible for Pell Grants. Qualified Guilford students receive merit scholarships, which average $14,697 apiece, but there are no athletic scholarships.

Seventy-four percent of Guilford students live in the dorms. "Housing is very comfortable," says one student. "The cleaning staff is so helpful." On-campus apartments for juniors and seniors are comparable in price to off-campus digs—a good thing, since getting permission to move off campus is tough. Bryan is the party dorm, and English (for men) and Shore (for women) are the single-sex quiet dorms. The female residents of Mary Hobbs, a co-op dorm built in 1907, do their own housekeeping in exchange for cheaper rent. The college is also piloting a "Community Agreements" project to strengthen community life in a first- and second-year residence hall. "The dining options on campus are fantastic and the food is wonderful. At every meal there are vegetarian, vegan, gluten-free, and dairy-free options for students with dietary restrictions," explains a student. Students say incidences of sexual assault have raised some concerns. "There were times when I did not feel safe on campus, especially after midnight," says one psychology major. "But generally speaking, campus is a safer space than the public space."

Guilford's social life revolves around various clubs and organizations. "There is a large social life on campus. When the weather is nice, a lot of events happen outside, and it is easy to find people just lounging in the grass or down by the lake," says one student. No alcohol is allowed at college functions, but it remains fairly easy for underage students to drink—despite efforts to impose fines on those who are caught. Serendipity, a celebration of spring with games, mud wrestling, streakers, big-name musicians, and "a sense of mass disorientation," is a cherished tradition. Beyond the campus gates, students find all of the essentials—Target, some clubs in downtown Greensboro (only 10 minutes away), the ethnic restaurants of Tate Street, the college's Quaker Village, a pool hall, and a Starbucks. Popular road trips include UNC at Chapel Hill (one hour), Asheville and the mountains (three and a half hours), and the famous Outer Banks beaches (four and a half hours).

"It is easy to find people just lounging in the grass or down by the lake."

Guilford's Division III athletic teams compete as the Fighting Quakers, and students love the oxymoron, as in their cheer: "Fight, fight, inner light! Kill, Quakers, kill!" Students root for the football team in the annual Soup Bowl against Greensboro College, while the men's golf team has brought home a slew of conference titles in recent years. The women's basketball team and the women's lacrosse team are strong too. Intramurals draw 40 percent of the students. Because of Guilford's emphasis on developing the whole person, physically, mentally, and spiritually, students are encouraged to participate in school-sponsored outdoor adventures, such as a ropes course, sailing, and white-water rafting.

A popular Guilford mantra is: "How are you going to change the world?" And with students who'd rather get involved than sit back and watch, you can expect some pretty passionate answers to that question. It all goes back to Guilford's traditional Quaker goal of "educating individuals not only to live, but to live well." As one student explains it, the college "supports me while allowing me to grow as a person," adding, in typical Guilford-speak: "It gives me the tools I need to make a change in the world when I leave."

Overlaps

UNC Greensboro, UNC at Chapel Hill, Earlham, Appalachian State, UNC Asheville, Elon, High Point, Haverford

If You Apply To ➢ **Guilford:** Rolling admissions. Early decision: Nov. 1. Early action: Dec. 1. Financial aid: Feb. 15. No application fee. No campus or alumni interviews. SATs or ACTs: optional (academic portfolio with two writing samples may be substituted). No Subject Tests. Letters of recommendation: required. Essay: required. Accepts the Common Application.

Gustavus Adolphus College

800 West College Avenue, St. Peter, MN 56082

A touch of Scandinavia in southern Minnesota, GA is a guardian of the tried and true in Lutheran education. With Minnesotans comprising three-quarters of the students, GA is less national than cross-state rival St. Olaf. Extensive distribution requirements include exploring values and moral reasoning. Minnesota location makes for a homogeneous student body.

Website: www.gustavus.edu
Location: Small Town
Private
Total Enrollment: 2,342
Undergraduates: 2,342
Male/Female: 47/53
SAT Ranges: CR 550–620, M 530–675
ACT Ranges: 24–30
Financial Aid: 98%
Pell Grant: 26%
Expense: Pr $ $
Student Loans: 81%
Average Debt: $ $ $ $
Phi Beta Kappa: Yes
Applicants: 4,657
Accepted: 67%
Enrolled: 20%
Grad in 6 Years: 81%
Returning Freshmen: 89%
Academics: ✍ ✍ ✍
Social: ☎ ☎ ☎
Q of L: ★ ★ ★
Admissions:
    1-800-GUSTAVUS
Email Address: admission@gustavus.edu

Strong Programs:
Biology
Economics
Management
Psychology
Education
Physics
Classics
Music

Gustavus Adolphus College is named for Sweden's King Gustav II Adolph (1594–1632), who is credited with making Sweden a major European power and defending Lutheranism against the Roman Catholics. While the king's battle victories earned him the title Lion of the North, he was also an advocate of education and culture. Save for the women now attending classes, King Gustav would probably feel at home at the college that bears his name, where a not-so-subtle Swedish influence pervades everything from the buildings to the curriculum. Gustavus is the "epitome of Minnesota nice," says one sophomore.

The 340-acre GA campus is about 65 miles southwest of the Twin Cities. Not surprisingly, the prevailing architectural theme is Scandinavian, with mostly modern and semimodern brown brick buildings. Highlights include the 134-year-old Old Main and the centrally located Christ Chapel, with spires and shafts resembling a crown. Thirty bronze works by sculptor-in-residence Paul Granlund are strategically placed, and the 135-acre Linnaeus Arboretum and Interpretive Center offers plant study and retreats. The sidewalk running through the middle of campus is nicknamed the Hello Walk, because it's a tradition for students to greet one another as they pass—whether they know each other or not. The $30 million Beck Academic Hall earned LEED Platinum certification from the U.S. Green Building Council and includes state-of-the-art tools and technologies.

To fulfill core requirements, Gustavus students have two options. Curriculum I includes 12 courses from seven areas of knowledge, plus a first-term seminar covering critical thinking, writing, speaking, and recognizing and exploring values. Curriculum II is an integrated 12-course sequence focused on related classic works from various disciplines. Sixty students may select this option on a first-come, first-served basis. In addition to the core courses, students must satisfy a writing-across-the-curriculum requirement, with three courses that have a substantial amount of writing, and the first-term Values in Writing seminar, which explores questions of value while emphasizing critical thinking, writing, and speaking.

> **"Professors expect you to give your best every day and in return they give you their best."**

In the classroom, students find an academic smorgasbord, as GA aims to offer an education both "interdisciplinary and international in perspective." There are interdisciplinary programs in Scandinavian studies, environmental studies, women's studies, and materials science, and if neither those nor traditional departments suffice, students may design their own courses of study. While biology, economics, management, psychology, and education are among the most popular majors, physics and classics are also strengths, and students give high marks to GA's premed advising program and its offerings in music. For the professionally minded, Gustavus offers 3–2 engineering programs with the University of Minnesota and Minnesota State in Mankato. Overall, academics at Gustavus are rigorous, but study groups are common, and students don't compete for grades. "The courses require a lot of work both inside and outside the classroom," says one junior. "Professors expect you to give your best every day and in return they give you their best." Students find faculty members knowledgeable and friendly. One student says, "Professors go the extra step to make sure students are learning in a positive environment." Profs even serve up a free meal for students during Midnight Express, which precedes final exams.

During the January term, when winter winds force almost everyone indoors, Gustavus students (appropriately known as Gusties) may take concentrated courses on campus or pursue travel and co-op opportunities. The school sponsors study abroad programs at five colleges and universities in—surprise, surprise—Sweden, as well as in non-Scandinavian haunts such as India, Malaysia, Australia, Russia, and Scotland, and about half of the students participate. Learning opportunities also come from several internationally renowned meetings, such as the Nobel Conference, which brings Nobel laureates and other experts to campus for two days each October. Undergraduate research is a hallmark, and Gustavus Adolphus consistently ranks in the top 10 for papers presented at the National Conference on Undergraduate Research.

"The dorms...stay full on the weekends and are well maintained."

"Students are very involved," says one biology major, and they "shuffle about campus from classes, music ensembles, sports practices, interest groups, and community service." For all its good points, though, this liberal arts college is hardly a model of diversity. In fact, the population is more reminiscent of Garrison Keillor's Lake Wobegon: 82 percent of students are Caucasian, 78 percent are Minnesotan, and more than half are Lutheran. African Americans account for 2 percent of the student body, Hispanics 4 percent, and Asian Americans 4 percent; international students add another 4 percent. The school is working hard to increase diversity, but finding students who are not blond and blue-eyed in Minnesota can be a challenge. Politically, the campus has its fair share of both conservatives and liberals, and students debate everything from campus issues to topics of global concern. The merit-based President's Scholarship program offers top students awards of up to $26,000 annually; the only renewability requirement is a 3.25 GPA. Dean's Scholarships ranging from $13,000 to $23,000 are also available for qualified students. There are no athletic scholarships. Twenty-six percent of incoming students receive Pell Grants.

Eighty-eight percent of Gusties live in the dorms, and why not? Housing is guaranteed for four years, and one student says, "The dorms are wonderful. They stay full on the weekends and are well maintained." Substance-free floors are available, as is the Crossroads International House, for students interested in languages and contemporary global issues. Norelius is exclusively for freshmen and sophomores, which helps students form friendships by encouraging group activities. Two dorms with single rooms and apartment-style suites, and some college-owned houses, are exclusively for upperclassmen, who get priority at room draw. Juniors and seniors (and all students over 21) may also request permission to live off campus. Students rave about the a la carte meal plan, and especially about the Marketplace dining hall. In response to recommendations from a student task force, the administration has recently revised its sexual misconduct policies.

"Any time, any sport—if St. Olaf is in town, the event is packed."

Sixteen percent of the men and 18 percent of the women go Greek, and GA's social life does not revolve around fraternities and sororities. In fact, service projects are far more important, with about two-thirds of students participating and giving 15,000 hours of service each semester. Projects include working with children, the elderly, and the local animal shelter, as well as with Habitat for Humanity. "From concerts, to sporting events, to movies and dances, there is never a shortage of things to do on the weekends," says one senior. Because students 21 and older may drink in their rooms—with the door closed—underage students can get alcohol if they want it, but students say drinking isn't a popular pastime here. GA's many musical ensembles all perform together at the Christmas in Christ Chapel concert. The chapel holds 1,500 people and performances usually sell out. The town of St. Peter has coffee shops and bowling, and the college offers periodic trips to Mankato, 10 miles away, and to the Twin Cities, for "real" shopping at the Mall of America or for a professional baseball, basketball, or hockey game.

When it comes to athletics, "Any time, any sport—if St. Olaf is in town, the event is packed," says a lusty Gustie fan. GA competes in Division III, and the men's and women's tennis teams are perennial contenders for the national championship title. Men's and women's golf, soccer, and ice hockey have also been successful in Minnesota Intercollegiate Athletic Conference play. The college's forensics team is nationally competitive as well. The fitness center features treadmills, stair-climbers, Nautilus equipment, and a pristine weight room. Approximately 75 percent of Gusties participate in intramurals.

The Gustavus Adolphus campus may be gorgeous in the spring and fall and too cold in the winter, but it's warmhearted all year long. Small classes, one-on-one academic attention, a plethora of research opportunities, and an active campus social life go a long way toward making St. Peter, Minnesota, seem a lot less isolated. Says one senior, "Our core values of community, service, faith, justice, and excellence prevail both in and out of the classroom, and students commit themselves and their time here to such values."

Overlaps

St. Olaf, University of Minnesota, University of St. Thomas, Luther, College of St. Benedict and St. John's University, Minnesota State, Carleton

If You Apply To ➤

Gustavus Adolphus: Rolling admissions. Early action: Nov. 1. Priority financial aid: Mar. 15. Housing: May 1. No application fee. Campus interviews: recommended, evaluative. Alumni interviews: optional, informational. SATs or ACTs: optional. No Subject Tests. Letters of recommendation: optional. Essay: required. Accepts the Common Application with supplement.

Hamilton College

198 College Hill Road, Clinton, NY 13323

Hamilton is part of the network of elite, rural, Northeastern liberal arts colleges that extends from Colby in Maine through Middlebury and Williams to Colgate, about half an hour's drive to Hamilton's south. Hamilton is on the small side of this group and emphasizes close contact with faculty and a senior project requirement.

Website: www.hamilton.edu
Location: Small Town
Private
Total Enrollment: 1,861
Undergraduates: 1,861
Male/Female: 49/51
SAT Ranges: CR 650–740, M 650–730
ACT Ranges: 31–33
Financial Aid: 48%
Pell Grant: 17%

Founded in 1793, Hamilton College took its name from Alexander Hamilton, who was an early trustee, and for much of its early life offered its male students a staunchly traditional education rooted in a classical curriculum. In 1978 Hamilton merged with Kirkland College, the artsy, experimental women's college founded under its auspices a decade before. Given the notable differences in institutional cultures, the coeducational liaison took some getting used to, but today Hamilton is marked by its close sense of community and its commitment to the liberal arts. Particularly dedicated to transforming students into excellent communicators, the college is also gradually increasing opportunities for experiential learning and internships. "Come to Hamilton because you will learn much more than simple facts and data," says an economics major. "You will learn how to think critically, communicate clearly, and lead effectively."

The old Hamilton campus features collegiate Victorian architecture rendered in rich, warm brownstone. In fact, the only facility interrupting the rhythmic beauty of campus is the eyesore that houses the library. By contrast, the adjacent Kirkland campus consists mostly of boxy concrete structures of a 1960s "brutalist" vintage, otherwise described as "faux I. M. Pei." Straddling the ravine that divides the campuses and joining them literally and figuratively is a student activities building with a diner, lounges, and areas for student and faculty relaxation. Surrounding the campuses are more than 1,000 college-owned acres of woodlands, open fields, and glens, with trails for hiking or cross-country skiing. The college has invested nearly $250 million over the past decade in new and renovated facilities; the most recent campus addition is an apartment-style residence hall housing 52 students.

In the classroom, Hamilton is pure liberal arts. The general education curriculum has no distribution requirements, but all students must pass at least three writing-intensive courses and a quantitative and symbolic reasoning course. The development of writing skills is a key area of focus in all majors, and more than 100 courses each year require oral presentations. In an effort to reinforce its commitment to inclusion, the faculty has adopted a new curriculum requirement that all majors feature relevant, mandatory coursework on diversity. First-years may participate in an optional series of proseminars—classes of no more than 16 that require intensive interaction—that emphasize writing, speaking, and discussion. Hamilton also requires all students to undertake a senior program in their area of concentration, which may take the form of a research project, a seminar with a presentation and research paper component, or a comprehensive exam.

"You will learn how to think critically, communicate clearly, and lead effectively."

Economics, mathematics, government, and psychology are the most popular majors. Hamilton's Arthur Levitt Public Affairs Center, named for the former New York State comptroller, is a working think tank where students focus on social innovation, public scholarship, leadership, and citizenship. The natural sciences are strong, bolstered by a $56 million science center, and the college recently added a major in cinema and media studies. Students say that courses are rigorous and the emphasis is on performance. "A lot of students strive to get the best grades they can possibly get, regardless of how other students are doing," says a philosophy major. "Most students on our campus are in constant competition with themselves and therefore strive to work smarter and harder each semester." You'll always find a professor, not a teaching assistant, at the lectern. Says one government and Chinese double major: "I think Hamilton's faculty is overwhelmingly made up of brilliant, caring, and beyond competent professors. However, I have had issues with a couple of visiting professors." Even with the intimate size of most classes—76 percent enroll fewer than 20 students—students report few problems getting needed courses, once they declare a major.

Each year, up to seven academically outstanding juniors are designated as Senior Fellows and allowed to eschew the conventional curriculum in favor of courses or projects that are relevant to their educational goals. At the close of the fellowship year, they submit a written thesis and deliver a public lecture. Stipends are awarded to 155 students each year for summer research, and another 65 students receive stipends to pursue unpaid summer internships. When the town of Clinton gets claustrophobic, students can spend a semester or a year in France, China, Spain, or India, or study off campus for a term in Washington, D.C., New York City, or the Adirondacks; 61 percent of undergraduates study off campus.

"It's cool to be passionate about things here," says a psychology major. "Students are so involved in a range of different activities; it's kind of lame if you only go to class and don't have a whole bunch of extracurriculars." Thirty percent of Hamilton

(continued)

Expense: Pr $ $ $ $
Student Loans: 39%
Average Debt: $
Phi Beta Kappa: Yes
Applicants: 5,434
Accepted: 25%
Enrolled: 35%
Grad in 6 Years: 92%
Returning Freshmen: 93%
Academics: ✐ ✐ ✐ ✐ ½
Social: 🏮 🏮 🏮 🏮
Q of L: ★ ★ ★
Admissions: (315) 859-4421
Email Address: admission@hamilton.edu

Strong Programs:
Economics
Mathematics
Government
Psychology
Public Policy
Natural Sciences

The development of writing skills is a key area of focus in all majors, and more than 100 courses each year require oral presentations.

students are New York residents, and 77 percent were in the top 10th of their high school class. African Americans constitute 5 percent of the student body, Hispanics 7 percent, and Asian Americans 7 percent; 6 percent are international. Although the campus is no political hotbed, students report that current issues (both global and local) receive ample attention from student activists. There are no merit or athletic scholarships, but the college has a need-blind admissions policy and guarantees to meet 100 percent of admitted domestic students' demonstrated financial need.

All students reside on campus. Options range from old fraternity houses renovated and turned into dorms to stately mansions with posh amenities, and newer apartments that accommodate three to four students each. "It's possible to get decent housing even as a rising sophomore," says a student. The Hamilton side of campus is the place for party animals; Dunham gets cheers for being social, but some students liken it to a "dungeon." The Kirkland dorms have a more mellow reputation. Students may also choose to live in a co-ed cooperative house, or in residences that are substance-free or quiet.

> "Most students…are in constant competition with themselves and therefore strive to work smarter and harder each semester."

"The food is surprisingly good for college food," one senior acknowledges. Students say campus security is effective: "Campus Safety is always patrolling the grounds," says one junior. "I have always felt safe on campus."

Social life at Hamilton ranges from the campus pub, which occupies an old barn, to programming arranged by the campus activities board, such as comedy shows, a casino night, an award-winning acoustic coffeehouse series, and concerts. "Campus parties tend to be dominated by underclassmen. The upperclassmen attend them occasionally, but they generally make their own parties in the suites or the quads or they go downtown to the two bars," one student says. There's also the Greek system, which draws 28 percent of the men and 21 percent of the women. Much of the social life does revolve around alcohol, one student says, although stiff punishments are meted out to underage imbibers.

Clinton itself is "a picturesque village good for pizza and coffee," says a sophomore. The nearest small city, Utica, is only 10 minutes away by car. The college maintains a jitney service and sponsors two Zipcars for student transportation. "On the weekend, people will sometimes go to the Adirondacks because they are so close and beautiful," a student reports. "This can be a great way to get back in touch with nature and also have a fun weekend excursion." Given the long, snowy winters, such excursions are often best enjoyed by skiers and other winter-sports enthusiasts. Other popular road trips include Syracuse and New York City, while Boston, Toronto, and Montreal are each less than five hours away.

> "People will sometimes go to the Adirondacks because they are so close and beautiful."

In athletics, Hamilton (the Continentals) offers varsity sports and is a member of the highbrow New England Small College Athletic Conference. The women's lacrosse team has brought home a national title and multiple conference titles, and women's rowing placed fourth in the nation in 2015. Men's basketball and golf have also competed in NCAA championships in recent years, as have men's and women's cross-country, track and field, soccer, and swimming and diving. Sixty percent of students compete in the extensive intramurals program. Even some school traditions are athletically minded. Class & Charter Day marks the last day of classes in the spring with ceremonies, a picnic, a concert, and even a triathlon the week before. "Many students believe this day is better than Christmas," says an economics major.

Hamilton students are, by necessity, hearty. They're used to the cold and the snow—and some may say that's what leads to the strong sense of community evident

Overlaps

Colgate, Middlebury, Bowdoin, Williams, Dartmouth, Amherst

on campus. But for most, it's the dedicated faculty who foster community spirit as they teach students how to think critically and express themselves effectively. Says a senior, "The professors at Hamilton, from my experience at least, picked Hamilton because they wanted to be closer to students—to watch them grow and to help them grow both inside of the classroom and outside of it."

<table>
<tr><td>

If You Apply To ➤

</td><td>

Hamilton: Early decision I: Nov. 15. Early decision II and regular decision: Jan. 1. Financial aid: Feb. 15. Application fee: $50. Campus and alumni interviews: recommended, evaluative. SATs or ACTs: recommended. Subject Tests: recommended. (Students may also substitute three AP or IB exams, including one English, one quantitative, and one other.) Letters of recommendation: required. Essay: required. Accepts the Common Application.

</td></tr>
</table>

Hampden–Sydney College

P.O. Box 667, Hampden–Sydney, VA 23943

The last bastion of the Southern gentleman and one of two all-male colleges in the nation. Feeder school to the economic establishment in Richmond. Picturesque rural setting evokes the old South. While some would argue that it is out of step with today's world, H–SC holds to its mission of asking what it means to be a "good man" in today's society. Somewhat less selective than neighboring (and co-ed) Washington and Lee.

Hampden–Sydney College was founded by Scotch-Irish Presbyterians in 1775 with the University of Edinburgh as its model and was named after two 17th-century English patriots (John Hampden and Algernon Sydney). Perhaps a bit of an anachronism in a society increasingly focused on diversity, the all-male school still aims to expose its small student body to a broad liberal arts education, which is entirely focused on undergraduate success. H–SC is one of only two all-male colleges in the nation without a coordinate women's college (see Wabash). The environment supports "a special sense of brotherhood and community," says one student. Tradition reigns here and students like to call themselves "Southern gentlemen." Of course, there's plenty of not-always-gentlemanly fun to be had when you have roughly 1,100 guys together.

Hampden–Sydney's 1,340-acre campus, surrounded by farmland and woods, features mainly redbrick buildings in the Federal style. Construction on a new student center is underway, slated for completion in the fall of 2017. The nearby town of Farmville, population 8,000 and home to Longwood University, offers restaurants, stores, and a movie theater; it's just five miles from H–SC, but one student describes the town as "a black hole inside a time warp."

To graduate, students must demonstrate proficiency in rhetoric and a foreign language, along with completing seven humanities courses, three in the social sciences, and four in the natural sciences and mathematics. All freshmen have a special advising program, and 21 percent take freshman seminars. The most popular department is economics and business, which may help explain why more than half of the school's alumni have pursued business careers. The department offers three majors: economics and business, general economics, and mathematical economics. Instruction is "intensive," a junior says. History, biology, government, and psychology are also popular. The Wilson Center for Leadership in the Public Interest puts a public service focus on the

> **"Professors encourage us to contact them whenever we have a question."**

Website: www.hsc.edu
Location: Rural
Private
Total Enrollment: 1,085
Undergraduates: 1,085
Male/Female: 100/0
SAT Ranges: CR 500–620, M 500–610
ACT Ranges: 21–27
Financial Aid: 64%
Pell Grant: 28%
Expense: Pr $ $
Student Loans: 65%
Average Debt: $ $ $ $
Phi Beta Kappa: Yes
Applicants: 3,683
Accepted: 55%
Enrolled: 15%
Grad in 6 Years: 63%
Returning Freshmen: 83%
Academics: ✎ ✎ ✎
Social: 🍷 🍷 🍷 🍷
Q of L: ★ ★ ★ ★
Admissions: (434) 223-6120
Email Address: admissions@hsc.edu

(continued)

Strong Programs:
Economics and Business
Economics
History
Biology
Political Science
Government
Psychology

study of political science, preparing students for government work and garnering high marks in return. The school's small size offers many opportunities to work closely with professors, but has some academic drawbacks, including limited resources in some departments and fewer than 30 majors.

Students at Hampden–Sydney say there are no free passes when it comes to classwork. "Even though academic competition is a very real part of the experience…that competition is more friendly than anything else," says a biology major. Classes are small; 73 percent have fewer than 20 students and none exceed 50. Most H–SC professors live on campus and make themselves very available to students. Some even make house calls to find out why a student missed class. "I have been invited to numerous dinners at professors' homes, and professors encourage us to contact them whenever we have a question, even if that means at nine o'clock on a Wednesday night," says a junior.

> **"The prototypical Hampden–Sydney student is a Southern, white, Christian gentleman with conservative political values."**

Additional educational opportunities include the honors program, the summer research program (which is particularly popular among students in the sciences), and the Tigerfund, which allows students to manage an equity fund. More than 100 study abroad options are available in 30 countries and revered institutions around the world, including Oxford, Cambridge, and the London School of Economics. Career services are said to be effective, particularly when it comes to connecting students with alumni for job opportunities.

"The prototypical Hampden–Sydney student is a Southern, white, Christian gentleman with conservative political values," says a junior. Seventy percent of students are state residents, and 1 percent come from foreign countries. African Americans make up 6 percent of the student body, Hispanics constitute 2 percent, and Asian Americans comprise 1 percent. The college has added a director of intercultural affairs to help increase tolerance for diversity, and students say diversity is among the hot-button political issues on campus. Efforts have also been made to enroll more students from low-income backgrounds, and 28 percent of freshmen are eligible for the Pell Grant. As a Division III school, Hampden–Sydney offers no athletic scholarships. There are, however, academic awards averaging $16,055 for qualified students.

H–SC is one of only two all-male colleges in the nation without a coordinate women's college.

Ninety-five percent of students live on campus, as housing is guaranteed for four years, and H–SC is renovating older residence halls with mostly single rooms to offer more apartment-style living. "Freshmen are usually grouped in the larger housing areas in order for them to get the college roommate experience," says one student, and a dozen living/learning communities are available to choose from as well. The spacious dining facilities supply hungry students with "decent," all-you-can-eat fare. Campus security includes seven full-time police officers who provide 24/7 coverage. Student support services receive good reviews, although one religion major notes, "There is a bit of a stigma [against] using the counseling service, as we all aim to be macho at this boys' school."

> **"The party culture is huge. Greek organizations absolutely set the tone."**

Students praise the close-knit atmosphere fostered by Hampden–Sydney's all-male status. "Our code of etiquette requires that we acknowledge people we pass on the sidewalk and reserve our phone calls and headphones for less populated areas, so we get to know each other on a personal level," explains a junior. Hampden–Sydney's social nexus is the Circle, the site of the school's fraternities, which claim 34 percent of the students. "The party culture is huge. Greek organizations absolutely set the tone for the vast majority of our social environment," says one student, who adds, "Alcohol policies are not effective." Students under 21 can't drink, but where there's a will, there's a way—although students say that campus security will crack down if students get wild. The annual spring Greek Week brings out the *Animal House* aspect of Hampden–Sydney's budding gentlemen. Student clubs offer another important outlet for socializing, and homecoming and various music festivals are also eagerly anticipated. Men seeking members of the opposite sex can find them at all-female schools nearby—Hollins, Sweet Briar, and Mary Baldwin.

Despite its lack of bright lights ("You come here for the school, not the town," one student points out), nearby Farmville does provide numerous community service and outreach opportunities. A campus volunteer group called Good Men, Good Citizens spearheads projects such as tutoring, highway cleanup, and Habitat for Humanity home-building; about two-thirds of students perform community service. When rural Virginia gets too insular, H–SC students can be found on road trips to the University of Virginia and James Madison University, Virginia's beaches, or Washington, D.C. The ski slopes of Wintergreen are within a two hours' drive.

Perhaps because of all that testosterone on campus, Hampden–Sydney men are competitive, and that spells excellence in athletics. Tiger football is big; students attend games in coat and tie, and alumni come out in droves for tailgating. H–SC's football rivalry with Randolph–Macon (not the former women's college!) is one of the oldest in the South. At the annual pregame bonfire, the college rallies to sing songs and hear student and faculty leaders vilify the enemy and extol "the garnet and gray." Basketball, golf, tennis, and baseball are also competitive, and wrestling was added in 2014. Three-quarters of the student body participates in intramural and recreational sports ranging from basketball and flag football to clay-target club and water polo.

Hampden–Sydney is the 10th-oldest college in the United States, so it's largely conservative and a bit homogeneous. Still, the school offers more than just a flat demographic profile. Two centuries of tradition and a tight-knit student body make for a rich undergraduate experience. One enthusiastic freshman sums up the rewards of the H–SC experience like this: "The small community at Hampden–Sydney allows me to participate in a huge variety of academic programs and learning opportunities that have enriched my experience and contributed to the full liberal arts education."

Career services are said to be effective, particularly when it comes to connecting students with alumni for job opportunities.

Overlaps

University of Virginia, UNC at Chapel Hill, Virginia Tech, James Madison

If You Apply To > **Hampden–Sydney:** Early decision I: Nov. 15. Early action I: Dec. 15. Early action II: Jan. 15. Regular decision and financial aid: Mar. 1. Housing: May 1. Application fee: $30 (paper), free (online). Campus interviews: recommended, evaluative. No alumni interviews. SATs or ACTs (with writing): required. No Subject Tests. Letters of recommendation: required. Essay: required. Accepts the Common Application with supplement.

Hampshire College

P.O. Box 5001, Amherst, MA 01002

Part of a posse of nonconformist colleges that includes Bard, Bennington, Eugene Lang, and Sarah Lawrence. Instead of conventional majors, students complete self-designed interdisciplinary concentrations and independent projects. Gains breadth and resources from the Five College Consortium*. Even the campus architecture is postmodern rather than traditional.

In the fourth year, students are asked to complete a sizable independent study project, much like a master's thesis.

Passion reigns at Hampshire College. It's found in just about everything students do—from devising their own courses to starting new clubs to debating the most current social issues. There's no one way to do things at Hampshire, and the students revel in the freedom they have to direct the path of their education. "We love what we are studying because we get to choose what we are studying," says a junior studying sustainable agricultural methods. Without the yoke of traditional majors and the nail-biting stress of regular grades, Hampshire offers a virtually boundary-free exercise in intellectual nirvana.

Located in the Pioneer Valley of western Massachusetts, Hampshire's 800-acre campus sits amid former orchards, farmland, and forest. Buildings are eclectic and contemporary, and the school is proud of its bio-shelter, arts village, and multisports and multimedia centers. Two nationally known museums—the National Yiddish Book Center and the Eric Carle Museum of Picturebook Art—are located right on campus. Opened in 2016, the innovative new Kern Center houses the admissions and financial aid offices, classrooms, social areas, and a café—and is a model of sustainable design. Built entirely with local and regional nontoxic materials, the 17,000-square-foot building generates its own electricity and collects its own water. It's the latest in a series of sustainability efforts that also include converting the campus to 100 percent solar electricity.

Hampshire was created in 1970 as an alternative college by four nearby colleges—Amherst, UMass, Mount Holyoke, and Smith—that now make up the Five College Consortium*. Instead of grades, Hampshire professors hand out "narrative evaluations," which consist of written evaluations and critiques. Degrees are obtained by passing a series of examinations—not tests, but portfolios of academic work, evaluations, and students' self-reflections on their academic development. The first milestone, known as Division I, begins with a course in each of five multidisciplinary schools: natural science; social science; cognitive science; interdisciplinary arts; humanities, arts, and cultural studies; and other coursework.

> "We love what we are studying because we get to choose what we are studying."

The second milestone, Division II, is each student's "concentration"—the rough equivalent of a major elsewhere. Unlike a major, the requirements of a concentration are unique to each student, emerging from regular discussions with two faculty members, and include courses, independent study, and fieldwork or internships. Division III, or "advanced study," begins in the fourth year. Students are asked to complete a sizable independent study project centered on a specific topic, question, or idea, much like a master's thesis. In recent years, students have created smartphone software to monitor blood sugar, studied monologues on mountaintop removal in Appalachia, explored how Aztec ants protect coffee, and suggested alternative microcredit models. The Campus Engaged Learning program requires all students to commit to 40 hours of service or a semester-long equivalent. Because of the division system, there are as many curricula at Hampshire as there are students; each individual must devise a viable, coherent program specific to himself or herself. The common denominator is a heavy workload, an emphasis on self-initiated study, close contact with faculty advisors, and the assumption that students will eventually function as do graduate students at other institutions. "The Hampshire College academic climate is not competitive because no two students study the exact same thing," says a student.

Given the emphasis on close working relationships with faculty and those "narrative evaluations," the importance of qualified, attentive faculty is not to be underestimated. Students at Hampshire heap praise on their professors. "Professors at Hampshire are truly invested in their students," one student says. The Hampshire academic year has fall and spring semesters, each four months long; an optional

January term; and internships and other real-world experience are encouraged during all three. Befitting Hampshire's entrepreneurial nature, when it comes time for "Div Free" (as students call life after Hampshire), a large percentage of grads do go on to graduate school, and many Hampshire students begin their own businesses.

Hampshire's flexibility is ideal for artists, and the departments of film and photography are dazzling, which is also the reason they are overcrowded. Communications, creative writing, and environmental studies are also good bets, and Hampshire was the first college in the nation to offer an undergraduate program in cognitive science. A popular program called Invention, Innovation, and Creativity exposes students to the independent reasoning and thinking essential to the process of inventing. The college is actively transforming itself into a "language learning community," thanks to a gift from the Andrew W. Mellon Foundation. The study of languages is integrated into topics and questions of interest to individual students.

> **"Professors at Hampshire are truly invested in their students."**

Hampshire students also have access to selected courses at sister schools in the Five College Consortium*. The school's library is a quiet and pleasant place to study, and if you count the library resources at all five institutions, students have ready access to more than eight million volumes. There is no extra cost to use the other schools' facilities or the buses that link them. And use them they do—Hampshire students take 1,200 classes per year at the other schools. Hampshire offers its own study abroad programs in China, Cuba, and Germany, and students may also participate in programs through more than 130 institutions in nearly 40 countries.

Hampshire draws students from across the country who tend to be "driven and passionate about their studies," says one sophomore. "We are not cookie-cutter students. We are students who passionately teach ourselves in a school that is deliberately unique and experimental." Just as Hampshire eschews letter grades, it also refuses to consider SAT or ACT scores in the admissions process. Fifteen percent of students come from Massachusetts, and 5 percent come from abroad. For a school that's so focused on social issues, the minority community is relatively small—4 percent of students are African American, 11 percent are Hispanic, and 2 percent are Asian American—and most students would like to see these numbers rise. Hampshire's LGBTQ community is visible and vocal. The school is "100 percent politicized in every way," says a philosophy major. "Political correctness doesn't even begin to describe it." Take as examples the school's gender-neutral bathrooms and identity-based housing, which allows members of historically marginalized groups to live together. Merit scholarships, worth an average of $11,010, are available to qualified students.

Eighty-two percent of undergraduates live on campus. First-year students live in co-ed dorms, about 25 percent in double rooms. Many single rooms are available for older students who may move to one of more than 100 "mods"—apartments in which groups of four to 10 students share the responsibility for cleaning, cooking, and maintaining their space. The dining options are diverse

> *Just as Hampshire eschews letter grades, it also refuses to consider SAT or ACT scores in the admissions process.*

> **"[Hampshire] is deliberately unique and experimental."**

and include "many great vegan and vegetarian options," says one nanotechnology major, and, of course, great ice cream from local cows. Food that is produced in the area is labeled as such, and a map features the various farms from which each item originates. Students can also get healthy options from Mixed Nuts, a student-run food co-op that is Hampshire's longest-running student group. Campus safety is good, students say, and sexual assault addressed up front. "We have a loud and well-known consent culture on campus," says one geology and sustainability major. "Students learn about appropriate consent during orientation and it is reinforced consistently throughout all four years."

Hampshire has no fraternities or sororities, and on weekends, some students head for Boston, New York, Hartford, or, in season, the ski trails of Vermont and New Hampshire. But there are plenty of cultural resources within the Five College area, and the free buses to Amherst, Northampton, and South Hadley (all within 10 miles) are always crowded. From edgy record stores to ethnic restaurants and boutiques, the area abounds with diversions. The annual Spring Jam brings live bands to campus, and throughout the year there's almost always a party going on, including the drag ball and the much-anticipated Halloween bash—an intense, all-campus blowout complete with fireworks. A tradition called "Div Free Bell" celebrates the completion of Division III requirements—and graduation—with soon-to-be alumni ringing a bell outside the library, surrounded by friends.

Hampshire is no place for competitive jocks, since many sports are co-ed and primarily for entertainment (there never was a football team here). Division III Hampshire is affiliated with the United States Collegiate Athletic Association and also is a member of the Yankee Small College Conference. Students organize their own sports clubs (men's and women's soccer, basketball, and fencing are the biggies, and there's also the competitive Red Scare Ultimate Frisbee Team) and intramural teams. The outdoors program offers mountain biking, cross-country skiing, and kayaking; equipment may be borrowed for free. The school also has its own climbing wall and cave, a gym with a solar-heated pool, and a co-ed sauna.

"Political correctness doesn't even begin to describe [Hampshire]."

Hampshire's six-year graduation rate is low in comparison to other pricey, private liberal arts colleges, though not necessarily for bad reasons. Some students find the culture of individual study unnerving or miss traditional college life more than they thought they would. Others, however, having taken full advantage of Hampshire's freedom to explore, discover a passion that might be their life's work and move on to pursue it at a larger school with more resources. Hampshire considers the latter situation a success story.

"If you're an independent student and like to think outside the box, then Hampshire is for you," says an animal behavior major. There's a niche for every type of student, and even those pigeonholes are blown apart quite regularly. When you can make up your own education, and do it with great faculty and the option of studying at several other top-notch schools, there's little Hampshire students can't accomplish.

Overlaps

Bard, Bennington, Mount Holyoke, NYU, Oberlin, Reed, Sarah Lawrence, Smith

If You Apply To >

Hampshire: Early decision I: Nov. 15. Early decision II: Jan. 1. Early action: Dec. 1. Regular decision and financial aid: Jan. 15. No application fee. Campus and alumni interviews: recommended, evaluative. SATs or ACTs: not accepted. No Subject Tests. Letters of recommendation: required. Essay: required. Accepts the Common Application with supplement. Applicants have the option of submitting project samples and/or video/media supplements.

Hartwick College

Oneonta, NY 13820

Hartwick is known for its cozy atmosphere and ability to take good care of students. Combines liberal arts education with experiential learning opportunities. A general education program emphasizes hands-on learning, and a Three-Year Bachelor's Degree Program is an option. Most strong students can get at least a small merit aid award.

In recent years, Hartwick College has transformed itself by choosing to better focus on its liberal arts profile. Hartwick emphasizes community-centered learning, crystallizing the school's philosophy that learning isn't about memorization, it's about creating experiential knowledge and developing skills. The students here take full advantage of what's offered and feel at home on this close-knit campus. Says one student, "When coming here, you will feel like you instantly become an active and important member of the community."

Hartwick's campus has a New England feel with its ivy-covered, redbrick buildings and white cupolas, gables, and trim. The campus setting on Oyaron Hill, overlooking the city of Oneonta and the Susquehanna Valley, provides a breathtaking view, though the steepness of the campus may have some wishing for the legs of a mountain goat. Facilities include a tissue culture lab, electron microscopes, a greenhouse, an herbarium, a cold room, a biotechnology "clean lab," and a graphics imaging lab. The Wright Observatory, LEED-certified Golisano Hall, and the recently completed, state-of-the-art Campbell Fitness Center are other notable campus features.

Hartwick's general education program is divided into seven areas and places emphasis on experiential and integrative learning. Among the requirements are courses in humanities, physical and life sciences, social and behavioral sciences, foreign language, writing competency, and quantitative/formal reasoning. In addition, students must complete a first-year seminar and a senior thesis. Each academic year, a different campus theme is chosen that serves as a foundation for special course offerings, guest speakers, student projects, and campuswide events throughout the year; recent themes have included Fabric of Change, Food and Community, and Exploration.

> **"You will feel like you instantly become an active and important member of the community."**

The most popular majors are nursing, business administration, biology, and psychology. The music and art programs receive high marks too. The course catalog is necessarily limited by Hartwick's small size, but the Individual Student Program (ISP) enables students to create their own major dealing with a particular interest, and several new majors have recently been introduced, including actuarial mathematics, criminal justice, and global studies. Students may also broaden their options by taking courses at the nearby State University College at Oneonta. The Three-Year Bachelor's Degree Program allows students to take on a larger courseload in order to earn a B.A. or B.S. within three years—and save significantly on the cost of earning a degree.

Hartwick's academic environment is described as collaborative and relaxed. "Not only are students encouraged to discuss ideas among each other and work together to learn, but students are also welcomed to work alongside their professors," explains a political science major. "It makes one feel like everyone is on the same team working toward the same goal." With 71 percent of classes enrolling fewer than 20 students, collaboration with professors, who win nearly universal praise, is the norm. "The teaching staff is remark-

> **"Everyone is on the same team working toward the same goal."**

able," says a nursing student. Private tutoring and help sessions are offered, along with an innovative freshman early-warning program that identifies struggling students early and offers counseling.

Hartwick's emphasis on learning through real-world experiences is evident in the wide-ranging activities its students have pursued, from working in a Jamaican hospital to interning with the Metropolitan Museum of Art. The honors program provides students with the opportunity to design and carry out a coherent program of study consisting of challenges exceeding those offered in typical coursework required for graduation. Fifteen percent of students take part in study abroad courses

Website: www.hartwick.edu

Location: Small Town

Private

Total Enrollment: 1,353

Undergraduates: 1,353

Male/Female: 40/60

SAT Ranges: CR 450–560, M 460–550

ACT Ranges: 21–26

Financial Aid: 87%

Pell Grant: 34%

Expense: Pr $ $

Student Loans: 71%

Average Debt: $ $ $

Phi Beta Kappa: No

Applicants: 2,692

Accepted: 81%

Enrolled: 14%

Grad in 6 Years: 56%

Returning Freshmen: 74%

Academics: ✍ ✍ ✍

Social: ☎ ☎ ☎ ☎

Q of L: ★ ★ ★

Admissions:
  (888)-HARTWICK

Email Address: admissions@ hartwick.edu

Strong Programs:
Nursing
Business Administration
Biology
Psychology
Music
Art

available in 25 nations around the globe. The four-week January term is a favorite time to explore the world beyond Oneonta.

Hartwick has traditionally attracted a somewhat less academically oriented student body than most of the colleges with which it competes, but it has improved its academic position in recent years, thanks to a focused recruitment program. "The students here are hardworking, well-rounded, driven, and accepting," says a junior. Seventy-five percent are from New York State, especially upstate, and most of the rest come from New England or the Mid-Atlantic states; 3 percent are international. African Americans make up 9 percent of the student body, Hispanics 7 percent, and Asian Americans 2 percent. Thirty-four percent of students are eligible for Pell Grants. Students tend to be liberal, but the majority are not particularly politically engaged. Hartwick College awards merit scholarships averaging nearly $20,000, as well as 25 athletic scholarships for its Division I men's soccer and women's water polo athletes.

Seventy-seven percent of the student body reside on campus, most in traditional dorms, although limited suite-style options are available. Says a sophomore, "The dorms are all a comfortable size and are maintained properly." Freshmen, sophomores, and juniors are required to live on campus, though the latter may move into one of the fraternity or special-interest houses. Upperclassmen covet a place in one of the four townhouses described by one as "the yuppie version of on-campus living." Hartwick's 256-acre Pine Lake Environmental Campus has cabins that are heated by pellet stoves and a lodge where environmentally inclined students can live in rustic style. On-campus dining receives high marks; a psychology major says the school offers a "huge variety of foods for any culture or diet." Campus safety officers are also praised; says one student, "It's obvious through their actions that they really care about the well-being of the students at this college."

> "[Campus safety officers] really care about the well-being of the students."

Hartwick's social scene is found both on and off campus, according to students, and tends to be as mellow or rowdy as one chooses. From campus it's only a short walk, bike ride, or bus ride downhill into the small city of Oneonta, with its tantalizing profusion of bars. But underage Hartwick students usually don't get past the front doors of these taverns, and the administration is tough about enforcement on campus. "There is not a lot of drinking on campus, but many people drink off campus," says a sophomore. The Greek system attracts only 5 percent of the men and 8 percent of the women. Other entertainment includes movies, comedians, and lecturers. Popular campuswide bashes include a Last Day of Classes party, the Holiday Ball, and Winter and Spring Weekends, the latter of which features the notorious "Wick Wars," a schoolwide sports competition. There's also the Breakfast of Champions before final exams, when professors and administrators serve students breakfast between 11 p.m. and 2 a.m. Walking to class each day provides great hill workouts for your ski legs, and skiing is popular throughout the region. Oneonta is a "quaint, peaceful town," according to one student. "There aren't very many things to do, but my friends and I haven't gotten bored yet."

Oneonta is big on sports, and Hartwick delivers. Hartwick is nationally ranked at the Division I level in men's soccer, and the team brought home Sun Belt Conference championships in 2014 and 2015. The women's Division I water polo team has claimed the CWPA Northern Division title six of the last nine years. The remainder of the teams compete in the Division III Empire 8 Conference; men's basketball were conference champs in 2014 and 2016. Intramurals are popular as well—31 percent of the student body take part.

Change is good, the sages say, and the folks at Hartwick would definitely agree. By focusing its efforts on recruiting strong students and emphasizing top-notch experiential learning, Hartwick is bolstering its image as a solid liberal arts college.

Overlaps

SUNY–Oneonta, SUNY–Plattsburgh, SUNY–Binghamton, Quinnipiac, SUNY–Stony Brook, SUNY–University at Albany, SUNY–Cortland, SUNY–Buffalo

Even some of the T-shirts sold on campus broadcast the students' attitudes about their education: one simply says "Smartwick."

Harvard University

86 Brattle Street, Cambridge, MA 02138

An acceptance here is the gold standard of American education. Gets periodic slings and arrows for not paying enough attention to undergraduates, some of which is carping from people who didn't get in. It takes moxie to keep your self-image under control in the midst of all those geniuses, but most Harvard students can do it. ("I go to school in Boston.")

Over the past 380 years, the name Harvard has become synonymous with excellence, prestige, and achievement. Harvard University, the nation's first institution of higher learning, is still the benchmark against which all other colleges are compared. Seeking to "educate citizens and citizen leaders," it attracts the best students, the most academically accomplished faculty, and the most lavish donors of any institution of higher education nationwide. Sure, some academic departments at Hah-vahd are smaller than others, but all have faculty members who have made a name for themselves, many of whom have written the standard texts in their fields. Olympic athletes, concert pianists, and Rhodes scholars blend in easily here, ready to embrace the challenges and rewards only Harvard's quintessential Ivy League milieu can offer.

Spiritually as well as geographically, the campus centers on the famed Harvard Yard, a classic quadrangle of Georgian brick buildings whose walls seem to echo with the voices of William James, Henry Adams, and other intellectual greats who trod its shaded paths in centuries past. Beyond the yard's wrought-iron gates, the campus is an architectural mix, ranging from the modern ziggurat of the science center to the white towers of college-owned houses along the Charles River. The Loker Commons student center provides a place for students to meet and philosophize over gourmet coffee or burritos of epic proportions. Harvard has broken ground on a huge, $1 billion science and engineering complex across the river in Allston.

> **"This is not a small liberal arts college where people will reach out to you."**

Harvard's state-of-the-art physical facilities are surpassed only by the unparalleled brilliance of its faculty. Under its "star" system, Harvard grants tenure only to scholars who have already made it—usually someplace else—and then gives them free rein for research. It seems like every time you turn around, a Harvard professor is winning a Nobel Prize or being interviewed on CNN; every four years, half the government and econ departments move to Washington to hash out national policy. But one of Harvard's finest qualities is also one of its biggest problems. "You can have unlimited contact with professors, but it must be on your initiative," notes a biology major. "This is not a small liberal arts college where people will reach out to you." That's not to say profs are uncaring. Most teach at least one undergraduate

Website: www.college
.harvard.edu
Location: City Center
Private
Total Enrollment: 19,492
Undergraduates: 6,637
Male/Female: 53/47
SAT Ranges: CR 700–800,
M 700–800
ACT Ranges: 32–35
Financial Aid: 70%
Pell Grant: 17%
Expense: Pr $ $ $
Student Loans: 24%
Average Debt: $
Phi Beta Kappa: Yes
Applicants: 37,307
Accepted: 6%
Enrolled: 80%
Grad in 6 Years: 98%
Returning Freshmen: 97%
Academics: ✍ ✍ ✍ ✍ ✍
Social: ☎ ☎ ☎
Q of L: ★ ★ ★ ★
Admissions: (617) 495-1551
Email Address: college@
fas.harvard.edu

Strong Programs:
Economics
Government

*The African and
African American
studies department
has assembled the
most high-powered
group of black
intellectuals in
American higher
education.*

course per year, and even the luminaries occasionally conduct small undergraduate seminars (including those reserved for freshmen, which can be taken pass/fail). Harvard also sponsors faculty dining programs, such as Professors & Pastries and Classroom to Table, encouraging professors to chew on ideas and éclairs with students at residential houses and local eateries.

Back in the mid-1970s, Harvard helped launch a major curriculum reform movement. Although it is currently being reevaluated, the core curriculum that emerged was for decades regarded as perhaps the most exciting collection of academic offerings in all of American higher education. The core requires students to complete one letter-graded course in each of eight categories: Aesthetic and Interpretive Understanding, Culture and Belief, Empirical and Mathematical Reasoning, Ethical Reasoning, Science of Living Systems, Science of the Physical Universe, Societies of the World, and United States in the World. One of these eight courses must also engage substantially with the Study of the Past.

Harvard's best-known departments tend to be its largest; economics, government, psychology, English, biological sciences, applied mathematics, and computer science account for a large chunk of majors. But many smaller departments are gems as well: East Asian studies is easily tops in the nation. And under the leadership of Henry Louis Gates, the African and African American studies department has assembled the most high-powered group of black intellectuals in American higher education. Smaller, interdisciplinary honors majors, to which students apply for admission, boast solid instruction and happy undergraduates too. These programs—social studies, history and science, history and literature, and folklore and mythology—are the only majors that require a senior thesis, although many students in other departments elect to do one. Harvard's visual and environmental studies major serves filmmakers, studio artists, and urban planners, and a new major in theater, dance, and media is quickly growing in popularity. Although Harvard does not offer a major in education, the new Harvard Teacher Fellows program provides select seniors with a pathway to become middle school or high school math, science, history, or English teachers. Students can also petition for individualized majors, typically during the sophomore year. And should you not find a class you are looking for, Harvard offers cross-registration with several of its graduate schools and the Massachusetts Institute of Technology.

Freshmen are encouraged to explore a range of disciplines during their first year on campus. Seventy-three percent of classes have fewer than 20 students, but students uniformly complain about the overuse of teaching fellows (graduate students) for introductory courses in mathematics and the languages. TFs aren't all bad, though, says a junior: "They can give good advice, having just been in our position." Besides, it's easier to ask "dumb questions" of mere mortals than of the demigod professors. For many students, the most rewarding form of instruction is the sophomore and junior tutorial, a small-group directed study in a student's field of concentration that is required in most departments within the humanities and social sciences. Teaching of the tutorials is split between professors and graduate students, and the weight of each party's responsibility varies with the subject and the professor. With more than 200 study abroad programs available to choose from, about 60 percent of students have some sort of international experience before they graduate.

"[Teaching fellows] can give good advice, having just been in our position."

The oft-made claim that "the hardest thing about Harvard is getting in" is right on target. Flunking out takes serious and sustained effort. Once on campus, the possibilities are endless for those who are motivated. Then again, Harvard can feel uncaring and antisocial. While it offers unparalleled resources—including fellow students—brilliant overachievers who desire the occasional ego stroke might be better off at a small liberal arts college. All incoming freshmen participate in a weeklong orientation, and optional pre-orientation groups, such as the urban, outdoor, and arts programs, help students acquaint themselves with one another and the Boston area. Although most students feel little competition, the academic climate is still intense. "The courses are difficult, particularly in the beginning as students make the transition from high school to college," says one student. "But it's definitely doable." Stressed-out students can count on help from a variety of quarters, including the various deans' offices, the Bureau of Study Counsel, the Office of Career Services ("dedicated to working with Harvard students and alums for the rest of their lives," claims a senior), and counselors associated with each residential house. Students can also take advantage of the Radcliffe Institute for Advanced Study's network of professional women, researchers, and alumnae, which has evolved from the former Radcliffe women's college. Sooner or later, all roads lead to Widener Library, where incredible facilities lie in wait (and where snow-covered steps make prime sledding runs in the winter).

"It's certainly normal to spend Friday and Saturday nights studying."

Harvard does have one thing its $37.6 billion endowment can't buy: a diverse, high-powered, ambitious, and exciting student body. You will meet smooth-talking government majors who appear to have begun their senatorial campaigns in kindergarten. You will meet flamboyant fine arts majors who have cultivated an affected accent all their own. You will sample the intensity of Harvard's extracurricular scene, where more than 6,600 of the world's sharpest undergrads compete for leadership positions in a luminous galaxy of extracurricular opportunities.

No one can tell you exactly what it takes to gain admission to Harvard (and if anyone tries, apply a large grain of salt), but here's a hint: 95 percent of incoming freshmen ranked in the top 10th of their high school class and most went to public high school. Though there are a few old-money types who probably spit up their baby food on a Harvard sweatshirt, their numbers are smaller than one might imagine on this liberal campus. (Many enter as sophomores when no one is looking.) Undergrads come from all 50 states—74 percent are out-of-staters—although the student body is weighted toward the Northeast. Twelve percent are international, representing 70 different countries. African Americans account for 7 percent of the student body, Hispanics 10 percent, and Asian Americans 20 percent. There are no merit or athletic scholarships to ease the pain of Harvard's hefty tuition, but the university does practice need-blind admissions and it meets the full demonstrated need of accepted students. In an effort to make the university affordable for students of all income levels, Harvard has eliminated the expected family contribution for students from families with incomes below $65,000 a year and limited the family contribution for families with incomes between $65,000 and $150,000 to fixed percentages of their incomes, ranging from 1 to 10 percent. No-loan financial aid packages are optional.

Students can take advantage of the Radcliffe Institute for Advanced Study's network of professional women, researchers, and alumnae.

"Cambridge's Harvard Square is the perfect college town."

Ninety-nine percent of undergraduates reside on campus, and every first-year class lives and eats as a single unit in Harvard Yard, a privilege made more enticing by recent upgrades to all the freshman dorms. The older dorms provide spacious wood-paneled rooms, working fireplaces, and the gentle reminders of Harvard's rich traditions. Freshmen eat in the beautifully renovated Annenberg Hall (formerly Memorial Hall). For their last three years, students live in one of 12 residential houses, built around their own courtyards with their own dining halls and libraries. Designed as learning communities, the co-ed houses, which hold between 300 and 500 students, come equipped with a complement of resident tutors, affiliated faculty members, and special facilities—from art studios to squash courts. Each house has a student council, which plans programs and parties and arranges the fielding of intramural teams. Students are randomly assigned (with up to 15 friends) to one of the houses, but some houses still retain a personality from the days of old when each stood for a particular ideology, interest, or economic class. "The housing is one of the best parts of Harvard!" raves one student. The nine houses along the Charles River feature suites of rooms, while the three houses at the Radcliffe Quad, a half mile away, offer a mixture of suites and single rooms. Some students value the greater privacy of the Quad houses' singles; others consider it equivalent to a Siberian exile, especially during harsh Cambridge winters—although a shuttle does run regularly to the main campus.

Socializing at Harvard tends to occur on campus and in small groups. "It's certainly normal to spend Friday and Saturday nights studying," says a philosophy major. With the exception of the annual all-school Freshman Mixer and the annual theme festivals each house throws, parties tend to be private affairs in individual dorm rooms. A student-run website provides information and commentary on parties for those in the dark, and Harvard does enforce the legal drinking age on campus. The most distinctive and increasingly controversial aspect of social life at Harvard is the role of the so-called "final clubs." These are exclusive and upscale social clubs that, while occupying their own buildings and in other ways completely separate from the university, play a significant role in the campus social life for the small minority of students who are "punched" for membership. Currently, there are six all-male and five all-female final clubs and two others that have succumbed to pressure to go co-ed. There are also five fraternities and four sororities. Over the years the all-male final clubs functioned, as the *New York Times* recently put it, as "centers for privacy and 'good-fellowship,' cut off from the hectic university by their locked front doors, their aura of secrecy, and a generally shared feeling of superiority." In recent years the Harvard administration, convinced that the exclusive values of final clubs are anachronistic and out of place on Harvard's increasingly diverse campus, has taken steps to weaken their influence, but the tug of war continues. For many, the key to happiness in Harvard's high-powered environment is finding a niche, a comfortable academic or extracurricular circle around which to build your life. Outside activities include about 80 plays performed annually, two newspapers and several journals, and plenty of community service projects coordinated through the Phillips Brooks House Association student group.

The possibilities of Harvard's social life are increased exponentially by Cambridge and Boston, where there are many places to have fun. Harvard Square itself is a legendary gathering place for tourists, shoppers, bearded intellectuals, and coffeehouse denizens. The American Repertory Theater, transplanted from Yale in the mid-1980s, offers a season of professional productions and nearly as many professional student shows. Cambridge also enjoys an exceptional selection of new and used bookstores, including the Starr Bookshop (behind the Lampoon building), McIntyre & Moore, Grolier Books, and, of course, the Harvard Bookstore and the mammoth Harvard Co-op, known universally as "the Coop." Boston itself features Faneuil Hall, the Red Sox, the Celtics, and 52 other colleges. "Cambridge's Harvard Square is the perfect college town," a student boasts. "There are tons of shops, restaurants, and bars."

Harvard has 41 varsity sports (21 men's, 20 women's), which is the most of any Division I school and the most women's sports. The athletic facilities are across the river from the campus, and their incredible offerings often go unnoticed by students buried in the books. Both the men's and women's squash and crew teams are perennial national powers, and men's ice hockey and women's lacrosse are

Harvard has limited the family contribution for families with incomes between $65,000 and $150,000 to fixed percentages of their incomes.

"I gauge myself by how many allusions in the *New Yorker* I understand."

The most distinctive and increasingly controversial aspect of social life at Harvard is the role of the exclusive and upscale "final clubs."

also strong. Men's basketball has prospered in recent years under coach Tommy Amaker, a former Duke star. As for football, the team has been doing better in recent years, but the season always boils down to the Yale game, memorable as much for the antics of the spectators and marching band as for the fumbles of the players. Intramural sports teams are divided up by house, and each fall, league champs play teams from Yale the weekend of the game. Another fall highlight is the annual Head of the Charles crew race, the largest event of its kind in the world, where as many as 200,000 people gather to watch the racing shells glide by.

Nowhere but Harvard does the identity of a school—its history, its presence, its pretense—intrude so much into the details of undergraduate life. Admission here opens the door to a world of intellectual wonder, academic challenges, and faculty minds unmatched in the United States—but then drops students on the threshold. "I have quickly gained exposure to major theories in literature, psychology, anthropology, social sciences, and evolutionary biology," says a junior. "I gauge myself by how many allusions in the *New Yorker* I understand." That's the way Harvard is; what other kind of place could produce statesmen John Quincy Adams and John F. Kennedy, pioneers W. E. B. DuBois and Helen Keller, and artists T. S. Eliot and Leonard Bernstein? Even its dropouts are movers and shakers (witness Bill Gates). But caveat emptor: it is only the most motivated and dedicated student who can take full advantage of the Harvard experience.

Overlaps

MIT, Princeton, Stanford, Yale

If You Apply To ➤

Harvard: Single choice early action: Nov. 1. Regular decision: Jan 1. Financial aid: Feb. 1. Application fee: $75. Campus and alumni interviews: optional, evaluative. SATs (with essay) or ACTs (with writing): required. Subject Tests: recommended (any two). Letters of recommendation: required. Essay: required. Accepts the Common Application with supplement.

Harvey Mudd College: See page 152.

Haverford College

Haverford, PA 19041

Quietly prestigious college of Quaker heritage. With an enrollment of about 1,200, Haverford is half the size of some competitors but benefits from its relationship with nearby Bryn Mawr. Close cousin to nearby Swarthmore but not as far left politically. Exceptionally strong sense of community, with parklike campus amid the bustle of suburban Philadelphia. Honor code drives campus culture. Your only option if you want to play varsity cricket.

An overarching honor code covering everything from the classroom to the dorm room defines student life at Haverford College. Students schedule their own final exams, take unproctored tests, and police underage drinking on their own. "The honor code, in some respects, is a self-selecting system which draws many students to Haverford. For this reason, nearly all students who come here share common values of trust, concern, and respect for others as well as academic integrity," says a junior econ major. Haverford may be smaller and less well-known than some of its peers, but it holds its own against the finest liberal arts colleges in the country, especially for students who are willing to work hard. "Haverford offers an opportunity

Website: www.haverford.edu
Location: Suburban
Private
Total Enrollment: 1,229
Undergraduates: 1,229
Male/Female: 49/51
SAT Ranges: CR 660–760, M 660–770

(continued)

ACT Ranges: 31–34

Financial Aid: 50%

Pell Grant: 15%

Expense: Pr $ $ $ $

Student Loans: 28%

Average Debt: $

Phi Beta Kappa: Yes

Applicants: 3,467

Accepted: 25%

Enrolled: 41%

Grad in 6 Years: 90%

Returning Freshmen: 97%

Academics: ✍ ✍ ✍ ✍ ✍

Social: ☎ ☎ ☎

Q of L: ★ ★ ★ ★ ★

Admissions: (610) 896-1335

Email Address: admission@
  haverford.edu

Strong Programs:

Psychology

English

Biology

Mathematics

Physics

Economics

About half of Haverford students take at least one course at Bryn Mawr.

to work hard, be trusted, and learn about issues, while still feeling comfortable," says a senior.

Founded under Quaker auspices in 1833, Haverford functions much like a family. The campus consists of 204 acres just off Philadelphia's Main Line railroad and resembles a peaceful, well-ordered summer camp. The densely wooded campus has an arboretum, duck pond, nature trails, and more than 400 species of shrubs and trees. Architectural styles range from 19th- and early 20th-century stone buildings to a sprinkling of modern structures here and there. The combination enhances the sense of a balanced community, bringing together two traditional Quaker philosophies: development of the intellect and appreciation of nature. The 188,000-square-foot, $50 million Koshland Center for Integrated Natural Sciences provides a place for interdisciplinary teaching, learning, and research.

Haverford's curriculum reflects commitment to the liberal arts. General education requirements call for taking three courses in each of the three divisions: social sciences, natural sciences, and humanities. One of these nine courses must fulfill a quantitative reasoning requirement, and every student must also study a foreign language for a year, pass a freshman writing seminar, and complete a capstone project in their major. Psychology, English, biology, and mathematics are among the most popular majors, and the physics and economics programs are also strong. There are more than a dozen areas of concentration—which are different from minors—that are attached to certain majors, including peace, justice, and human rights; biophysics; and mathematical economics.

> **"Students who come here share common values of trust, concern, and respect for others."**

The bicollege system with Bryn Mawr College, the nearby women's school, allows Haverford students to major in subjects such as art history, growth and structure of cities, and environmental studies. The unique relationship between Bryn Mawr and Haverford dates to the days when Haverford was all-male, and it enables students at each institution to take courses, use the facilities, eat, and even live in the dormitories of the other. Haverford and Bryn Mawr students cooperate on a weekly newspaper, radio station, orchestra, and other clubs and sports, and a free shuttle bus connects the campuses. About half of Haverford students take at least one course at Bryn Mawr. Cross-registration is also available at Swarthmore and the University of Pennsylvania, and joint degree programs are available with a number of institutions, including Penn, Caltech, Claremont McKenna, and Georgetown.

Perhaps because of the intense classroom interaction, the workload is sizable, although students say they don't worry about each other's grades and try to squeeze in nonscholarly pursuits too. "Haverford is very challenging," says one geology major. "As a student, you expect to put in a lot of work." Advising is ever-present: freshmen are matched with professors who work with them from their arrival until they declare majors two years later, while upper-class "Customs people" are resources and mentors for living/learning groups of 8 to 16 first-year students. Haverford's biggest strength may be its faculty members, who are said to be very accessible; 50 percent of them live on campus. Most classes are small, with 71 percent enrolling fewer than 20 students, but a junior political science student recalls that one professor personalized a 90-student class by dividing it up into groups of 10 and having each group over for a pre-exam dessert. "The professors are only here for us. They really enjoy teaching as well as involving us in research." Indeed, since there are no graduate students at Haverford, undergraduates often help professors with research, and several publish papers each year. Haverford's Center for Peace and Global Citizenship offers summer internships that emphasize the study and promotion of social justice and global issues. More than 150 study abroad programs around the globe attract 50 percent of students.

Haverford's distinctive honor code governs all aspects of campus life. "I can take my final exam at 3 a.m. on Founder's Green," offers a junior as an example. The code, administered by students and debated and reratified each year at a meeting called Plenary, helps instill the values of "integrity, honesty, and concern for others." In good Quaker tradition, decisions are made by consensus rather than formal voting, and students play a large role in college policy. While the social honor code encourages students to "voice virtually any opinion so long as it is expressed rationally," this can also mean self-censorship, says a philosophy major. "Sometimes you feel like you are walking on eggshells to avoid offending anyone."

Only 12 percent of Haverford's students hail from Pennsylvania, but many are East Coasters nonetheless; 10 percent are international. Ninety-six percent of freshmen graduated in the top 10th of their high school class. "Students are very academically motivated, but we have a good mix of partiers and shut-ins," a student explains. Ten percent of students are Asian American, 10 percent are Hispanic, and 7 percent are African American. Though the college is nonsectarian, the Quaker influence lives on in the form of an optional meeting each week. "Although students tend to be very well informed on political issues and have great concern about these issues, few are very involved in political activism," says a philosophy major. Haverford meets the full demonstrated financial need of every admitted student and, for students from families with annual incomes below $60,000, has replaced loans with grants in its financial aid packages. Merit-based academic and athletic scholarships are not available.

"Students are very academically motivated, but we have a good mix of partiers and shut-ins."

Haverford's residence halls are spacious and well maintained, and most rooms are singles—even for freshmen—so it's no surprise that 99 percent of all students live on campus. All dorms are co-ed, but students may request single-sex floors. The extremely popular, school-owned Haverford College Apartments sit on the edge of campus and feature one- and two-bedroom units, each with a living room, kitchen, and bathroom. "Some of the dorms are incredible. The apartments are the best freshman housing anywhere," says an economics major. Upperclassmen in the apartments may cook for themselves, but all others living on campus (and all freshmen regardless of where they live) must buy the meal plan, which includes weekend board. Crime is virtually nonexistent, owing to the school's location in the ritzy Philadelphia suburbs. "There is little to worry about coming from the surrounding area," one student says.

While the community spirit at Haverford works well for academics and personal development, it doesn't always carry over to the social scene. Without fraternities and sororities, Haverford and Bryn Mawr hold joint campus parties, but students say these affairs can get tiresome after freshman and sophomore years. The alcohol policy is connected to the honor code. For nondrinkers, there are frequently free movies, concerts, and other activities on campus. Other traditional events include the weekend-long pre-exams Haverfest—Haverford's approximation of Woodstock—as well as the winter Snowball dance and Taste the Rainbow drag ball. Life in the close-knit, introspective environment that is Haverford can get stifling, but there are easy escapes: downtown Philadelphia is 20 minutes away by train. New York City, Washington, D.C., the New Jersey beaches, Pocono ski areas, and Atlantic City are only a couple hours away by car or train. Many students participate in the Eighth Dimension, which coordinates volunteer opportunities.

"The apartments are the best freshman housing anywhere."

The "Ford's" rich athletic history dates back more than 100 years, when the soccer team played in its first intercollegiate game. A popular T-shirt boasts that the football team has been "Undefeated Since 1971"—a reference to the year the sport was abolished. The men's cross-country team is a perennial national contender and baseball, women's basketball, and softball each brought home Division III conference titles in recent years. "The Haverford–Swarthmore men's basketball and lacrosse games are the two biggest athletic events of the year," says one student. Haverford also boasts the number-one varsity college cricket team in the country because, well, it's the only school that has one! Intramural sports are popular, especially because participation counts toward the required six quarters of athletic credit. In spite of all the rivalries, these Quakers have struggled to reconcile their peace-loving heritage with the desire to bash opponents' brains out on the court or the field. For now, students root for their Black Squirrels and chant, "Fight, fight, inner light—kill, Quakers, kill!"

Haverford's student body may be beyond the norm in regards to personal values, but the downside of the honor code is that "students are challenged to meet an ideal set before them of creating the best community possible. For this reason, students are constantly criticizing themselves and the community as a whole to find ways of solving the problems facing them." See? Mom was right. With freedom comes responsibility.

Overlaps

Brown, University of Pennsylvania, Swarthmore, Dartmouth

If You Apply To ➢ **Haverford:** Early decision I: Nov. 15. Early decision II: Jan. 1. Regular decision: Jan. 15. Financial aid: Feb. 1. Application fee: $65. Campus and alumni interviews: recommended, evaluative. SATs or ACTs: required. Subject Tests: optional. Letters of recommendation: required. Essay: required. Accepts the Common Application with supplement.

University of Hawaii–Manoa

2600 Campus Road, Room 001, Honolulu, HI 96822

One of the most accessible of the public flagships in the U.S., Hawaii at Manoa pursues its research and teaching in a distinctly unique and culturally cosmopolitan setting. While you may be thinking about surfing as much as studying, don't be fooled: it will take more than a great tan and the ability to catch a wave to earn your degree here.

Website: www.manoa.hawaii.edu

Location: City Center

Public

Total Enrollment: 13,889

Undergraduates: 11,212

Male/Female: 45/55

SAT Ranges: CR 480–580, M 500–610

ACT Ranges: 21–26

Financial Aid: 57%

Pell Grant: 27%

Expense: Pub $ $ $

Student Loans: 47%

Average Debt: $ $

One of the goals of the University of Hawaii at Manoa is to "serve as a bridge between East and West." It is one of the few schools that are land, sea, and space grant institutions. Despite—or perhaps because of—the fact that two out of three students are in-staters, UHM has more Asian American students than almost any other school. But not everything at UHM is so sunny: the university is currently grappling with budget cuts triggered by the state's economic troubles, the results of which have been bulging classrooms and talk of merging programs and laying off faculty members. Students complain of outdated facilities in need of upgrades and repairs. Despite these challenges, a plant and environmental protection science major says, "Students, faculty, and community members are friendly and give off the Aloha Spirit."

The UHM campus occupies 300 acres in the Manoa Valley, a residential Honolulu neighborhood. The architecture is regionally eclectic, mirroring historical and modern Asian Pacific motifs, and is enhanced by extensive subtropical landscaping. The campus is also within a few miles of the state capital and the city's major business district, providing excellent opportunities for students to interact with thought leaders, including mentorships and internships.

Core requirements are extensive: all students must take a semester in expository writing and math, two courses in world civilization, two years of a foreign language or Hawaiian, and three courses each in the humanities, social sciences, and natural sciences. The First-Year program gathers diverse groups of first-year students with similar interests to work and study together in Freshman Seminars, limited to ten students, and in Access to College Excellence residential learning communities. Founded in 1987, the Manoa Writing Program is one of the oldest writing-across-the-curriculum programs in the country. Faculty from more than 70 departments teach writing intensive (W) courses that use a variety of writing-to-learn techniques to teach their disciplinary ways of thinking and knowing, with an emphasis on student/faculty interaction during the writing process. Students are required to take five W courses in order to graduate, but many take more.

> "Each professor has his or her own style and priorities, but every professor that I have had is knowledgeable."

UHM offers 97 bachelor's degrees, 85 master's degrees, and 57 doctoral degrees. Among the best are astronomy, Pacific and Asian area studies, languages and the arts, ethnomusicology, and tropical agriculture. Astronomy and astrophysics benefit from the clear Hawaiian skies. It should come as no surprise that ocean-, climate-, and environment-related programs are also first-rate, with world-class facilities. The university takes pride in its programs in engineering, geology and geophysics, international business, political science, and travel industry management. The most popular majors, by enrollment, are nursing, psychology, biology, and accounting. "The courses can be challenging based on what you take and the major you declare," says a senior. Fifty percent of undergraduate classes have fewer than 20 students. Desirable classes and times are said to be difficult for freshmen and sophomores to get into, although departmental academic advisors keep close tabs on whether students are on schedule to complete their degrees in four years. The Student Success Center offers academic referrals and support services. Professors receive generally favorable reviews. "Each professor has his or her own style and priorities, but every professor that I have had is knowledgeable," says a biology and music double major. "Most of them are thoughtful and interested in the success of their students."

The two-tier Honors Program offers qualified freshmen and sophomores the opportunity for general education courses in small, intensive classes, while upperclass honors students are guided by faculty through independent, sustained research or creative work and must complete a final Honors thesis. The Undergraduate Research Opportunity Program provides financial support for motivated students to work closely with faculty mentors on independent and collaborative research or creative projects across the disciplines. In addition to presenting their work at a semester-end symposium, students are encouraged to publish their work and present it at conferences. Students who tire of Hawaii's endless beaches and beatific sunsets can study abroad in locations around the world, including Asia, Europe, Latin America, and Russia.

> "Many students are very driven, but others are here to appreciate the island life."

"Many students are very driven, but others are here to appreciate the island life," says a student. Sixty-eight percent of undergraduates are in-staters, and 3 percent are from other countries. Hawaii stands out among major American universities in that 41 percent of its undergraduates are Asian American, and another 17 percent are of Native Hawaiian or other Pacific Islander descent. African Americans and Hispanics each represent 2 percent of the student body. "The climate and diversity in Hawaii allow for a greater and more open dialogue about race and culture," observes an English and history major. Political and social issues often take a backseat to academics and play, but among the more prominent concerns are the environment

(continued)

Phi Beta Kappa: No
Applicants: 7,658
Accepted: 81%
Enrolled: 31%
Grad in 6 Years: 57%
Returning Freshmen: 78%
Academics: ✐ ✐
Social: ☎ ☎ ☎
Q of L: ★ ★ ★
Admissions: (808) 956-8975
Email Address: uhmanoa
 .admissions@hawaii.edu

Strong Programs:
Nursing
Psychology
Biology
Accounting
Astronomy
Pacific and Asian Studies
Tropical Agriculture
Engineering

UHM's ocean-, climate-, and environment-related programs are first-rate.

Because many students are commuters, UHM is pretty sedate after dark, especially on weekends.

and Native Hawaiian rights. Twenty-seven percent of freshmen are Pell-eligible, and especially promising students can compete for merit scholarships, which average $10,447 annually. The UH–Manoa Service Scholarship offers financial aid to students willing to complete 125 hours of service to the community. The university also disburses 243 athletic scholarships in 21 sports.

Twenty-five percent of students live in campus housing, and those who apply by the May deadline are guaranteed a spot. Students recommend the four towers, Ilima, Lehua, Lokelani, and Mokihana; the rooms are small and the hallways are happening. If you're thinking about off-campus housing, take note: housing in Honolulu is scarce and expensive. Cafeterias are located throughout the campus and serve diverse and adequate fare. "The Department of Public Safety has advertised more campus apps to help with safety so students can avoid getting into vulnerable situations," reports a history and economics double major.

Because many students are commuters, UHM is pretty sedate after dark, especially on weekends. Most social activity revolves around student clubs and, as one student explains, "simply being around the Campus Center, where you can find many students studying, socializing, or hitting the gym." Only 1 percent of the men and 1 percent of the women join the tiny Greek system. Drinking is not allowed in the dorms. A couple of local hangouts provide an escape, and the campus pub, Manoa Garden, is also an option. Many students head off campus to enjoy "more beaches and hikes than one can handle," according to a sophomore. Lest anyone forget, some of the world's most beautiful resorts—Diamond Head and all the rest—are less than a 20-minute drive away. Waikiki Beach? Within two miles' reach. And round-trip airfare to the neighboring islands—including Maui, Kauai, and the Big Island—is not unreasonable. The homecoming dance is one of the most popular campus events of the year. But what students really look forward to is Kanikapila, a festival of Hawaiian music, dance, and culture.

> **"The climate and diversity in Hawaii allow for a greater and more open dialogue about race and culture."**

UHM's athletic teams compete in Division I; the men's teams are known as the Rainbow Warriors, while the women's teams are the Rainbow Wahine. Men's basketball, football, baseball, and swimming and women's volleyball are among the top draws. Intramural and recreational activities range from soccer and basketball to Tai Chi and snorkeling.

Students seeking warm weather and great surfing won't be disappointed, but mainlanders should think twice about making the leap to UHM unless they are set on one of the university's specialized programs. It's up to you, one student says, to get the best out of Hawaii. "The location allows mainland students to get a different cultural experience," adds another. "You're only young once—might as well be 20 in Hawaii."

Overlaps

UCLA, Hawaii Pacific, University of Hawaii at Hilo, University of Southern California, University of Washington

If You Apply To ➤ **UHM:** Rolling admissions: Mar. 1. (Priority deadline: Jan. 5.) Financial aid: Feb. 1. Housing: May 1. Application fee: $70. No campus or alumni interviews. SATs (with essay) or ACTs (with writing): required. No Subject Tests. Letters of recommendation: optional. Essay: optional.

Hendrix College

1600 Washington Avenue, Conway, AR 72032

Hendrix is in the same class of mid-South liberal arts colleges as Millsaps and Rhodes. The smallest and most progressive of the three, Hendrix has a strong emphasis on international awareness. Small-town Arkansas is a tough sell, and the college accepts the vast majority of students who apply. About half of Hendrix students are from Arkansas, and most of the rest are Southerners.

For a school in the heart of the Bible Belt and Walton-land, Hendrix College is surprisingly liberal. In fact, it's among the South's most progressive liberal arts colleges. Academics are demanding but students are laid-back—even radical—in their political and social views. Ironically, healthy dialogue about tough issues such as gay rights, the environment, and capital punishment draws students together. "People here are passionate, intelligent, and fun," says a freshman. "They really want to change the world."

Hendrix's compact and comfortable campus stretches for 180 acres between the Ouachita and the Ozark mountains. College land boasts more than 80 varieties of trees and shrubs, and more than 10,000 budding flowers each spring. The main campus—with its own lily pool, fountain, and gazebo—occupies about one-fourth of the total acreage. The redbrick buildings are a mix of old and new, and a pedestrian overpass connects the main campus to the college's athletic facilities and a wooded fitness trail. An 80,000-square-foot student life and technology center houses state-of-the-art educational technology space, as well as a coffee shop and dining facility. Hendrix has added a new student residential facility with 54 student beds.

Under Hendrix's general education program, known as Collegiate Center, freshmen take two required courses, The Engaged Citizen and Explorations: Liberal Arts for Life. The Capacities component involves requirements in writing, foreign language, quantitative skills, and physical activity, while the Learning Domains component requires coursework in seven broad liberal arts areas. The Odyssey Program requires students to complete three experiences—which may be coursework, internships, or independent projects—selected from six categories: artistic creativity, global awareness, professional and leadership development, service to the world, special projects, and undergraduate research. Seniors in all majors must complete a capstone experience. Hendrix freshmen also participate in a weeklong orientation program, which includes a two-day, off-campus trip emphasizing outdoor experiences, urban exposure, or volunteer service.

> "Most students are liberal and eclectic."

Hendrix is strong in many areas, but natural and social sciences are definitely the school's forte. Popular majors include psychology, biochemistry/molecular biology, economics and business, and biology. The chemistry, politics, and international relations programs are also notable, and a new major in neuroscience is now available. Doing well at Hendrix means keeping up with the workload. "The workload is intense," says a sociology major. Thankfully, engaging professors are available to help students navigate the coursework. "There are very few bad faculty, and those are usually in temporary positions and are soon weeded out," a senior says. Seventy-three percent of classes have fewer than 20 students, so personal attention is the norm. The school is also a member of the Associated Colleges of the South* consortium, and it offers five-year programs with Columbia, Vanderbilt, and Washington University in St. Louis for aspiring engineers.

Website: www.hendrix.edu
Location: Suburban
Private
Total Enrollment: 1,310
Undergraduates: 1,299
Male/Female: 47/53
SAT Ranges: CR 540–680, M 580–660
ACT Ranges: 25–32
Financial Aid: 100%
Pell Grant: 26%
Expense: Pr $ $
Student Loans: 47%
Average Debt: $ $ $
Phi Beta Kappa: Yes
Applicants: 1,714
Accepted: 82%
Enrolled: 30%
Grad in 6 Years: 72%
Returning Freshmen: 79%
Academics: ✐ ✐ ✐
Social: ☎ ☎ ☎ ☎
Q of L: ★ ★ ★ ★
Admissions: (501) 450-1362
Email Address: adm@hendrix.edu

Strong Programs:
Psychology
Biochemistry/Molecular Biology
Economics and Business
Biology
Chemistry
Politics
International Relations

At Hendrix, undergraduate research takes priority, especially within the sciences, and students get the chance to present original papers at regional and national symposia. Many students get course credit for internships at U.S. embassies and organizations such as the National Institutes of Health and the U.S. Agency for International Development. Hendrix offers nationally recognized international programs, in which 34 percent of students participate, that provide opportunities for students to work, study, and serve abroad. Accademia dell'Arte in Arezzo, Italy, allows participants to experience Italian culture while gaining insight and experience in the world of European theater, vocal arts, and dance. In China, the Heilongjiang program focuses on Mandarin Chinese and Chinese culture, while the Shanghai program caters to business and economics majors. Hendrix also sponsors programs in Austria, England, Costa Rica, Spain, France, and Belgium, and students have access to more than 150 other partner exchange programs as well.

"Most students are liberal and eclectic, but all are respectful of political and social beliefs," says one student. "Hendrix students are almost always overinvolved. It seems like everyone is involved in at least something, whether it be athletics, Student Senate, or the informal Dungeons and Dragons club." Forty-seven percent of Hendrix students are from Arkansas, and 5 percent come from abroad. African Americans represent 5 percent of the student body, Hispanics 5 percent, and Asian Americans 4 percent. Twenty-six percent of freshmen are eligible for the Pell Grant. Hendrix offers a variety of merit scholarships, averaging $25,724, to academically qualified students, but there are no athletic scholarships. Through the new Arkansas Advantage Program, the college guarantees to meet the full demonstrated financial need of Arkansas residents who meet certain academic requirements.

All but one of Hendrix's dorms are single-sex, and freshmen are required to live on campus, which students say adds to the sense of community. Ninety-two percent of students live on campus, which has led to some overcrowding as of late. Still, "Hendrix housing is diverse and outstanding," says one student. Sophomores may take advantage of living/learning programs, including Global Issues, Social Justice, Artistic Creativity, and Sustainability. Students generally praise the dining options and report that plenty of choices are available for those with special dietary needs.

"Hendrix housing is diverse and outstanding."

"Our food rocks!" cheers one student. Students also report feeling safe on campus, due in part to a visible security program and the close-knit nature of the campus. Every member of the Hendrix community is required to complete two comprehensive seminars on issues related to gender, relationship violence, and sexual assault.

"Hendrix has such a vibrant social life that students hardly ever leave the campus to party," a junior explains. Greek life—a staple of most Southern schools—is conspicuously absent at Hendrix. Students are proud of their independence; the annual Hendrix Olympics allows them to celebrate the absence of Alphas, Betas, and Gammas from campus. Other major affairs include the Toga Party, Oktoberfest, and Beach Bash, as well as the annual Toad Suck Daze, a rollicking carnival in downtown Conway that features bluegrass music. Last but not least is the Shirttail Serenade, in which first-year men and women from each dorm croon out a song-and-dance routine in their shirts, ties, shoes, and socks for classmates. Judges rate each performance on the basis of singing, creativity, legs, and so on.

Despite being home to three colleges, Conway is essentially a "ghost town" for those seeking typical college-town activities. There are a number of shops and restaurants, but the 30-minute ride to Little Rock is the preferred destination. Faulkner County, where the school is located, is officially dry, so students must travel to buy booze—or find older peers to help out. School policies prohibit underage drinking, but "the alcohol policies could use some work," says one student. Popular road trips

Freshmen take two required courses, The Engaged Citizen and Explorations: Liberal Arts for Life.

The college guarantees to meet the full demonstrated financial need of Arkansas residents who meet certain academic requirements.

During the Shirttail Serenade, first-year men and women croon out a song-and-dance routine for classmates.

are Memphis (two hours by car) and Dallas and Oklahoma City (each a five-hour drive) for concerts and the like. For those who stay in town, the Volunteer Action Center coordinates participation in projects on Service Saturdays.

The Division III Hendrix Warriors field a number of competitive teams, and recent Southern Athletic Association conference champions include football, men's basketball, and volleyball; the volleyball team advanced to the NCAA Final Four in 2015. Rhodes College is the chief rival. For outdoor buffs, the college sponsors trips around Arkansas for canoeing, biking, rock climbing, and spelunking. Most students also compete in intramural or club sports, with sand volleyball, indoor soccer, basketball, and ultimate Frisbee proving the most popular.

> "Hendrix is tight-knit with a place for everyone."

"Hendrix is tight-knit with a place for everyone," says one student. Musician Jimi Hendrix—whose mug inevitably adorns a new campus T-shirt each year—once asked listeners, "Are you experienced?" After four years at Hendrix College, with small classes, an emphasis on research, and a laid-back atmosphere in which to test their beliefs and boundaries, students here can likely answer, "Yes!"

If You Apply To ➤ **Hendrix:** Rolling admissions. Early action I: Nov. 15. Early action II: Feb. 1. Financial aid: Mar. 1. Housing: May 1. Application fee: $40 (paper) free (online). Campus interviews: optional, informational. No alumni interviews. SATs or ACTs: required. No Subject Tests. Letters of recommendation: required. Essay: required. Accepts the Common Application with supplement.

Hiram College

P.O. Box 96, Hiram, OH 44234

The smallest of the prominent Ohio liberal arts colleges. Less nationally known than Denison or Wooster, Hiram draws the vast majority of its students from in state—and sends them around the globe. Lots of classes are taught in seminar format, and an extensive core curriculum ensures a broad education and undergraduate research opportunities.

Hiram College offers students a solid liberal arts education and plenty of opportunities to travel the globe. In fact, more than half study abroad in exotic locales ranging from Europe to Australia to Costa Rica. But no matter where they hang their hats, students here take advantage of ample research opportunities and a close-knit environment that ensures every Hiram Dawg has his or her day. "Because of its small size, students get noticed, not lost in the shuffle," one junior says.

Set on a charming hilltop campus that occupies the second-highest spot in Ohio, Hiram is blessed with an abundance of flowers and trees as well as a nice view of the valley below. The prevailing architectural motif is New England brick, and many Hiram buildings are restored 19th-century homes. The Coleman Sports, Recreation, and Fitness Center

> "Because of [Hiram's] small size, students get noticed, not lost in the shuffle."

houses a competition gymnasium; two multipurpose field houses; a pool; an indoor track; and facilities for fitness training. Hiram's biology and environmental studies majors, as well as other students, frequently work, study, and conduct research at the college-owned, 500-acre ecology field study station a mile away. Recent construction includes the new Teaching, Research, and Environmental Engagement House (home to the environmental studies department) and the renovated student center.

Website: www.hiram.edu
Location: Rural
Private
Total Enrollment: 918
Undergraduates: 905
Male/Female: 50/50
SAT Ranges: CR 450–590, M 430–578
ACT Ranges: 20–27
Financial Aid: 99%
Pell Grant: 42%
Expense: Pr $
Student Loans: 42%
Average Debt: $ $ $
Phi Beta Kappa: Yes
Applicants: 1,864
Accepted: 58%

(continued)

Enrolled: 15%

Grad in 6 Years: 60%

Returning Freshmen: 66%

Academics: ✍ ✍ ✍

Social: ☎ ☎ ☎

Q of L: ★ ★ ★

Admissions: (800) 362-5280

Email Address: admission@
    hiram.edu

Strong Programs:

Accounting and Financial
    Management

Business Management

Nursing

Biology

Chemistry

Creative Writing

Biomedical Humanities

Public Leadership

*Hiram's Intercultural
Forum club is one of
the largest and most
active on campus.*

The Hiram Plan allows students to cover a breadth of material in three courses during each semester's longer 12-week session and to focus on a seminar-style class during the additional three-week term. Hiram's core curriculum is extensive. Students are required to select courses from at least six different academic disciplines that fall under two categories, Ways of Knowing and Ways of Developing Responsible Citizenship. Through their studies, students learn various methods for acquiring knowledge while exploring what it means to be socially responsible citizens. In addition, Hiram requires the First-Year Colloquium, a writing and speaking skills seminar, an upper-division interdisciplinary course, an experiential learning (research, internship, or study abroad) component, and a senior capstone project.

**"Professors are involved
and are fun to talk with."**

The sciences, especially chemistry, are strong, as is the creative writing program. Hiram has the longest-standing biomedical humanities major in the country, and the Garfield Institute, named after the Hiram principal who went on to become the 20th U.S. president, offers a notable minor in public leadership. The most popular majors include accounting and financial management, business management, nursing, and biology. The music program has been bolstered by the addition of a student-created marching band, and Hiram has recently added a major in integrative exercise science.

Though the academic climate can be challenging, "there are a lot of resources to help students on campus," says a freshman, including tutors, the writing center, and help from peers or profs. Classes are small, with 68 percent enrolling fewer than 20 students, which allows for an impressive degree of faculty accessibility. "Professors are involved and are fun to talk with," says a freshman.

Hiram goes to great lengths to offer outstanding travel abroad programs. Trips led by professors make it to all corners of the globe, and all participating students get academic credit. Students can also study at Hiram's Rome affiliate, John Cabot International University, and transfer their credits. Hiram's unique academic calendar allows ample opportunity for off-campus endeavors of all types, including the Washington Semester at American University*, which Hiram helped found. Hiram offers several unusual summer opportunities as well, most notably the Northwoods Station up in the wilds of northern Michigan, where students choose courses ranging from photography and botany to geology and writing. And Hiram is the lone affiliate college of the Shoals Marine Lab, run by Cornell University and the University of New Hampshire, which offers summer study in marine science, ecology, coastal and oceanic law, and underwater archaeology. Hiram students can also participate in special interdisciplinary programs without leaving campus through the seven Centers of Distinction. Among others, these include the Center for Literature and Medicine, the Center for Global Interaction, and the Center for Integrated Entrepreneurship. Each center offers courses, workshops, guest lecturers, internships, and special seminars throughout the year. A four-year honors program has recently been established as well.

Seventy-eight percent of Hiram students are in-staters, and many of the rest hail from New York and Pennsylvania, though the administration is working aggressively to recruit more students from other states. International students represent 3 percent of the student body. African Americans constitute 17 percent, Asian Americans 1 percent, and Hispanics 4 percent. Hiram's Intercultural Forum club is one of the largest and most active on campus, and the Office for Diversity and Inclusion offers peer mentoring and tutoring programs for first-generation students, among other services. A large 42 percent of freshmen qualify for Pell Grants. In addition to need-based financial aid, Hiram awards merit scholarships, luring good students with irresistible financial aid. "My financial aid package at Hiram is unbelievable," says a junior. "After applying to larger, cheaper public universities, I came to realize it would actually cost me less to attend Hiram."

Most Hiram students—79 percent—live on campus, and everyone who wants a room gets one. "Ours are much better than some I have seen at other schools," says a junior. Most halls are co-ed, and upperclassmen who like their location can stay in the same room year after year. Most students live in two-person suites; the popular (and larger) triple and quad suites, and the townhouse apartments, are scarcer and usually claimed by upper-class students. The college has implemented several new policies and training programs to address campus sexual assault.

When the weekend rolls around, don't expect to find all Hiram students gathered around a keg; the college has cracked down on underage drinking. Hiram is a bit isolated, and there are few distractions in town, so students must make their own fun. Typically, that means hanging out in each other's rooms, at the tavern or the pizza place in town, or at other places in Garrettsville, just three miles away. "We always have tons of things happening on campus," says one student. Four percent of the men and 9 percent of the women go Greek. Every spring on Sugar Day, classes are canceled and the entire student body participates in a day

Every spring on Sugar Day, classes are canceled and the entire student body participates in a day of community service.

"My financial aid package at Hiram is unbelievable."

of community service at local nonprofit organizations. Sometimes the college offers free tickets to concerts, plays, and ballets in town. Cleveland's Progressive Field is a short road trip away, and the city's Rock and Roll Hall of Fame can get students rockin' all year-round. Other diversions include an excellent golf course three miles away, a college-owned cross-country ski trail, and good downhill slopes about an hour distant.

Hiram is hardly a mecca for budding athletic superstars, but it does have a decent Division III sports program, including a volleyball team that has gone to the NCAA Tournament in recent years. Other competitive Terriers teams include softball, football, and men's soccer. Approximately 25 percent of undergraduates play in intramurals, including basketball, volleyball, kickball, and many others.

Those looking for a school where anonymity will be ensured need not apply. People here are so close that they share an equivalent of a not-so-secret handshake. "Everyone smiles at you as you pass—faculty, staff, a senior football player, a freshman chemistry major, the lady that vacuums in the morning, the gardener," says a junior. Indeed, those seeking a friendly, all-American institution with a touch of internationalism might want to give Hiram a look.

Overlaps

Baldwin Wallace, College of Wooster, John Carroll, Kent State, Ohio Wesleyan

If You Apply To ➤ **Hiram:** Rolling admissions. Early action I: Oct. 1. Early action II: Dec. 1. Regular decision: Apr. 1. (Priority deadline: Feb. 1.) Financial aid: Feb. 15. Housing: May 1. Application fee: $25. Campus interviews: recommended, evaluative. No alumni interviews. SATs or ACTs: required (optional for applicants who meet certain requirements). No Subject Tests. Letters of recommendation: required. Essay: required. Accepts the Common Application with supplement. Submission of a graded writing sample or essay is recommended.

Hobart and William Smith Colleges

Geneva, NY 14456

Two independent, single-sex liberal arts colleges operating under a coordinate college system, overlooking one of New York's picturesque Finger Lakes. Two-college system makes for somewhat more traditional relations between the sexes, though most dorms are co-ed. Most social life takes place on campus, especially in the fraternities, but skiing and other outdoor activities beckon. HWS takes pride in personal attention from full professors and a culture of community service.

Website: www.hws.edu
Location: Small City
Private
Total Enrollment: 2,254
Undergraduates: 2,247
Male/Female: 49/51
SAT Ranges: CR 570–670,
  M 600–670
ACT Ranges: 26–30
Financial Aid: 83%
Pell Grant: 17%
Expense: Pr $ $ $ $
Student Loans: 61%
Average Debt: $ $ $ $
Phi Beta Kappa: Yes
Applicants: 4,488
Accepted: 57%
Enrolled: 25%
Grad in 6 Years: 79%
Returning Freshmen: 86%
Academics: ✐ ✐ ✐
Social: ☎ ☎ ☎
Q of L: ★ ★ ★
Admissions: (800) 852-2256
Email Address: admissions@
  hws.edu

Strong Programs:
Economics
Media and Society
Biology
Psychology
Architectural Studies
Geoscience
Environmental Studies
Political Science

*Students must
complete a major
and minor or a
double major.*

If you're unsure about a single-sex institution, the Hobart and William Smith "coordinate system" may offer the best of both worlds. Students eat together, study together, and even live together in co-ed residence halls, but also take advantage of unique traditions and programs generally reserved for single-sex establishments. If you can tolerate the frigid winters of upstate New York, you'll be rewarded with small classes, caring faculty, and a place where tradition still matters. "HWS is the place for you if you want to be inspired by your peers and graduate with so much more than just a degree," says one junior.

Hobart College was founded in 1822 by Episcopal Bishop John Henry Hobart, who conceived it to be an outpost for civilized and learned behavior. In 1908 William Smith College opened. The college bears the name of a wealthy businessman and philanthropist who wanted to introduce women to opportunities that were largely unrecognized at the time. The HWS campus stretches for 325 tree-lined acres and includes a forest, farmland, and a wildlife preserve. Architectural styles range from colonial to postmodern, with stately Greek Revival mansions and ivy-clad brick residences and classrooms. The nationally ranked sailing team enjoys a boathouse on the shores of Seneca Lake. The 65,000-square-foot Gearan Center for the Performing Arts opened in 2016, as did the Perkin Observatory.

The innovative HWS curriculum has no distribution requirements. Instead, students take an interdisciplinary seminar in the first year, constructed around a different interest; recent seminar offerings include Encountering Difference, Fracking?, The History of Everything, and *Paris Je T'Aime*. Students must also complete a

> **"The professors here treat serious students as colleagues rather than their students."**

major and minor or a double major, and all students conduct a senior capstone experience. Popular majors include economics, media and society, biology, and psychology, and the long list of minors includes entrepreneurial studies, sustainable community development, child advocacy, and aesthetics. Other solid programs include architectural studies, geoscience, environmental studies, and political science. Service-learning courses incorporate community service so that, as a senior puts it, "you are applying what you learn in class to the real world."

"I would not describe the academic climate as competitive at all, but that's not to say the workload is not intense," says one student. "Students work together for the sake of learning, and no one compares grades or GPAs," adds a junior. Small classes are the norm here: 65 percent have fewer than 20 students. Professors are praised for being accessible and engaging. "The professors here treat serious students as colleagues rather than their students," says a sociology and public policy major.

The Finger Lakes Institute gives students wide opportunities to work in various fields of scientific inquiry, as well as public policy. HWS students may take a term away from campus, and 60 percent do so, studying abroad on six continents in nearly 50 programs, all of which are faculty led. Each year, about 40 seniors elect to "do Honors," producing a research or critical paper or an equivalent creative work and then taking written and oral exams on their projects. The Senior Symposium offers seniors an opportunity to present research findings, discuss theory, display and discuss creative works, or present other significant scholarly activities. Students of good academic and social standing (and who successfully complete the HWS career preparation program) will experience at least one internship or research opportunity. "One of the most underrated programs on campus is the Centennial Center for Leadership," says one student. "The CCL runs multiple programs and workshops during the school year to promote leadership and entrepreneurship."

At HWS, "Students are largely incredibly passionate about what they're studying," says a student. "They continue their interests in academics beyond the classroom," adds a senior. New Yorkers make up 42 percent of the HWS student body and international students 6 percent. African Americans account for 5 percent of undergraduates, Hispanics 6 percent, and Asian Americans 3 percent. Politically, the Colleges lean liberal, but one student says, "everyone is respectful of each other's opinions." According to a senior, "Currently issues of inclusion as well as social justice are the most pertinent." Merit scholarships averaging $15,304 are awarded to qualified students; there are no athletic scholarships.

Ninety percent of HWS students live in campus housing, which includes nine lakefront residences. Housing is guaranteed for four years, and only seniors are allowed to live off campus, though few choose to do so. Twenty-two percent of first-years opt to participate in living/learning communities, and theme houses are popular too. When it comes to campus dining, the food receives mixed reviews, but one student cheers, "The staff are some of the most beloved on campus! They make a point to get to know students' names, and always have a smile for us on early morning coffee runs or late-night snack binges." Students say they feel safe on campus: "Campus security is very efficient and helpful at all times," says a sophomore. And despite the negative press that HWS received regarding sexual assault on campus, students report that the Colleges have taken steps to address the situation, including "increased bystander intervention training and resources for students who have been sexually assaulted," says a student. HWS is currently revising its sexual misconduct policy and has begun a Culture of Respect initiative that aims to "address the root issues of violence."

"One of the most underrated programs on campus is the Centennial Center for Leadership."

"Students rarely leave campus on the weekends, and if they do, it is to go skiing with friends or to go into New York City or Boston," says one art history major. Seven Hobart fraternities claim 18 percent of the men, who aren't permitted to pledge until sophomore year, but there are no sororities at William Smith. Much of the social life involves Greek parties and bashes at off-campus houses, but the Campus Activities Board also plans movies, concerts, dances, plays, and other events each weekend. There's a zero-tolerance policy for underage drinking, and students caught with booze must attend alcohol awareness classes and may face social probation. William Smith has retained a number of traditions typical of women's colleges, such as Moving Up Day, in which seniors symbolically hand over their leadership role to juniors. (Hobart, not to be left out, has a similar event called Charter Day.) A history major comments that community service is "a huge component of student life, whether it be semester-long volunteering with the Boys and Girls Club or one-day opportunities like Day of Service." All students participate in local community service activities, contributing more than 80,000 hours of service.

Since students are so involved with service activities in Geneva, an English and political science major says, "Geneva is more than just a place but a community intimately tied with HWS." The old industrial city has been revitalized in recent years and offers many amenities for students out on the town, including restaurants, bars, shops, concerts, and the Smith Opera House. Popular road trips include Rochester, Ithaca, and Syracuse, all about 45 minutes away. Seneca Falls, birthplace of the suffrage movement, is also nearby.

"Geneva is more than just a place but a community intimately tied with HWS."

Sports are the most popular diversion from studying here, whether you're a spectator or participant. HWS teams compete in Division III, except for men's lacrosse, which won 16 straight Division II and Division III championships before joining Division I in 1995. Hobart lacrosse, rowing, and ice hockey and William Smith lacrosse and rowing were all conference champions in 2016. Both

Overlaps

St. Lawrence,
University of
Vermont, Union,
Hamilton,
Gettysburg,
Franklin &
Marshall, Skidmore,
SUNY–Geneseo

of the Colleges' sailing teams are excellent, and Hobart football and basketball and William Smith field hockey and soccer are also perennially competitive. The HWS Debate Team, only a decade old, has had much success as well. Thirty-six percent of students participate in intramural and club sports.

At HWS, "The opportunities that students have to engage with each other, with Geneva, and with any field of interest are incredible," says a student. While some may shy away from the coordinate college system, those who come here for the intimate classes, robust service opportunities, and enduring traditions recognize that HWS is a community like no other. Says a senior, "I came here because of how genuine people are and for the ability to have a true sense of place."

If You Apply To ➤ **HWS:** Early decision I: Nov. 15. Early decision II: Jan. 15. Regular decision and financial aid: Feb. 1. Housing: May 1. Application fee: $45 (paper), free (online). Campus and alumni interviews: recommended, evaluative. SATs or ACTs: optional. Subject Tests: optional. Letters of recommendation: required. Essay: required. Accepts the Common Application.

Hofstra University

Hempstead, NY 11549

Boasts a combination of suburban setting with ready access to the Big Apple. Hofstra has outgrown its commuter-school origins and offers a broad range of preprofessional and other academic programs. Well known as a lacrosse powerhouse. Has become more selective in recent years, but for many it is still a backup to urban schools like BU and Northeastern.

Website: www.hofstra.edu
Location: Suburban
Private
Total Enrollment: 9,219
Undergraduates: 6,365
Male/Female: 45/55
SAT Ranges: CR 540–620, M 550–640
ACT Ranges: 24–29
Financial Aid: 68%
Pell Grant: 23%
Expense: Pr $ $
Student Loans: 70%
Average Debt: N/A
Phi Beta Kappa: Yes
Applicants: 27,991
Accepted: 61%
Enrolled: 10%
Grad in 6 Years: 60%
Returning Freshmen: 80%
Academics: ✎ ✎ ✎
Social: ☎ ☎ ☎

Although it sits within easy striking distance of Manhattan, Hofstra University occupies one of the loveliest campuses you'll find anywhere. Its bucolic setting is home not only to an accredited art museum and a nationally recognized arboretum, but also to the school's blossoming preprofessional offerings. Whatever their field, Hofstra students enjoy special learning communities, research opportunities, and first-year programs that help harried freshmen get off to a good start. "It's a friendly environment that allows you to find your special niches, without forcing anything upon you," reflects an accounting and political science major.

Founded in 1935 with one building—the Dutch colonial mansion left in trust by Kate and William Hofstra on their 15-acre estate—the campus is now home to 115 buildings on 240 acres. The suburban campus offers a parklike environment with a variety of architecture, from ivy-covered stone buildings to modern facilities with sleek angles and electronic signage, which surround open green quads. The campus is especially beautiful in the spring, when its 100,000 tulips, a tribute to the Dutch heritage of Hofstra's founders, are in bloom. Several major renovation projects are underway, and a new interactive lab called the ideaHUb opened in 2016 in Axinn Library, housing the new Center for Entrepreneurship.

> "It's a friendly environment that allows you to find your special niches."

With more than 140 academic programs for undergraduates, Hofstra offers students plenty of career paths. Regardless of what major they choose, all undergrad students must complete distribution requirements, including coursework in humanities, natural sciences and mathematics/computer science, social sciences, cross-cultural studies, and interdisciplinary studies. Students must also pass the English Proficiency Exam.

With the recent establishment of a School of Engineering and Applied Science and a School of Government, Public Policy, and International Affairs, as well as joint undergraduate programs with its medical school, Hofstra seeks to model itself on much larger and better-known Northeastern universities like NYU and Syracuse. Traditional areas of strength include business, communication, and engineering. Accounting, journalism, and radio production and studies are especially strong, and other popular majors include psychology, education, biology, and finance. Students in the Zarb School of Business benefit from one of the largest simulated trading rooms in the New York area. A spate of new dual-degree programs have been introduced (bringing the overall count to more than 150) that pair undergraduate degrees with corresponding master's degrees in such areas as physician assistant studies, linguistics, information systems, labor studies, and others. New majors in mathematical finance and public policy and public service have also been added.

"The workload that I have experienced has been mostly collaborative, not in the sense that we are working in groups most of the time, but because there is a conversation with the professors," explains a senior. Students agree that the academic climate is more supportive than it is competitive. Half of undergraduate classes have fewer than 20 students, giving them plenty of access to professors. "I've always felt that my professors are here to teach me and that they want me to succeed," says a biomedical engineering major. Adds a sophomore, "You can walk into any faculty's office at any time, and they will be more than happy to help you." Support services for students with learning disabilities are particularly strong at Hofstra and include accommodations as well as skill-development and coaching programs.

The First-Year Connections program offers new students a combined social and academic experience centered on small seminars (limited to 20 students) taught by senior faculty; recent seminars include Why Chimps Don't Drive Ferraris, CSI: Psychology (or, What Psychologists Could Teach Lawyers), and Art Is Really Dangerous. Freshmen may also enroll in clusters of thematically related courses, and several seminars and clusters also have living/learning community options associated with them. The Honors College offers approximately 325 qualified entering students a multidisciplinary program that allows them to graduate with both a bachelor's degree and Honors College designation. They may also take advantage of faculty mentors and special housing. Students with wanderlust can take advantage of study abroad options around the world, including programs in Cuba, India, Italy, and Japan, although only 10 percent of undergrads participate.

"I wanted to make sure I wound up at a school where everyone loved different things and brought something different to the table, and I definitely found it here," says a journalism major. Sixty percent of undergraduates hail from New York, and 5 percent come from abroad. African Americans account for 8 percent of the student body, Hispanics 14 percent, and Asian Americans 9 percent. "Politically it is a socially liberal school where acceptance is emphasized," reports a sophomore. The university offers merit scholarships worth an average of $15,009 and 145 athletic scholarships in 17 men's and women's sports. Twenty-three percent of freshmen are eligible for Pell Grants.

Sixty-nine percent of first-year students live in university housing. "Dorm rooms are pretty big," one student says, and another adds that every student who needs

"I've always felt that my professors are here to teach me."

"Our cultural diversity and proximity to the city provide for opportunities that some schools can't offer."

A spate of new dual-degree programs have been introduced, bringing the overall count to more than 150.

(continued)

Q of L: ★ ★ ★
Admissions: (516) 463-6700
Email Address: admission@ hofstra.edu

Strong Programs:
Engineering
Accounting
Journalism
Radio Production and Studies
Psychology
Education
Biology
Finance

campus housing will be able to find it. Dining options receive high marks. "Hofstra has it all. No matter what dietary restriction you have, they will accommodate. There are 20 different places to eat on campus," says one student. A junior reports, "The school takes safety very seriously, which is why we have five shuttle systems, including a night shuttle, a blue-light system for emergencies, and an emergency public safety line."

"Being involved is absolutely crucial to having a social life on campus," says a sophomore. "This is where Hofstra excels, though, offering an incredible number of clubs, in-dorm activities, and departmental organizations." Eight percent of the men and 9 percent of the women go Greek, but they don't dominate the social landscape. Alcohol policies include severe consequences for underage drinkers. "There are always people who want to go out and party, but if you aren't a big drinker there are plenty of things to do on campus that are alcohol-free," says a sophomore. Festivals include Greek Week, and "the Irish, Italian, and Dutch festivals are really fun events," a student says. Another adds, "Since we are right outside New York City, there are always fun opportunities to have day trips into the city or even take the bus down to the Long Island beaches in the summer." Hofstra also organizes Explore Next Door events that take students into the city to visit various neighborhoods and museums and to attend shows, sporting events, and other activities.

The Hofstra Pride compete in Division I and play an important role in shaping campus culture. Traditionally, men's and women's basketball, lacrosse, and soccer, along with softball and men's wrestling, have been the most competitive. Recently, softball, men's soccer, and volleyball have won Colonial Athletic Association championships. The nationally ranked dance team won a national championship in 2016, and the forensics team achieved national success in 2016 as well. Approximately 27 percent of undergrads participate in the university's 29 club sports and 25 intramural leagues and special events.

"I believe our cultural diversity and proximity to the city provide for opportunities that some schools can't offer," observes one senior. Indeed, opportunities abound at Hofstra, and the university continues to add resources—both curricular and extracurricular. Best of all, says one student, "Even with such a large student body, you get to know so many people." By offering solid academics and a bevy of programs aimed at first-years, the university seeks to put its students in a New York state of mind.

If You Apply To ➤ **Hofstra:** Rolling admissions. Early action I: Nov. 15. Early action II: Dec. 15. Financial aid: Feb. 15. Housing: May 1. Application fee: $70 (paper), $60 (online). Campus and alumni interviews: optional, evaluative. SATs or ACTs: optional (required for some programs; SAT essay and ACT writing recommended). Subject Tests: optional. Letters of recommendation: required. Essay: required. Accepts the Common Application with supplement.

Hollins University

(formerly Hollins College), P.O. Box 9707, Roanoke, VA 24020

One of the country's leading women's colleges, Hollins is on the edge of Roanoke, the biggest city in southwest Virginia. Hollins has long been noted for creative writing and its equestrian program. Social life often involves road trips to Virginia Tech and Washington and Lee, both about an hour's drive.

Traditions rule at Hollins University, a private, single-sex college on a lush 475-acre campus in the Virginia mountains. Each fall, students and staff hike up Tinker Mountain for skits, a picnic lunch, and a bird's-eye view of the changing foliage. A secret society known as Freya welcomes new students each year by walking across campus at night, hooded in black robes and holding candles symbolizing hope. A few male students can even be found on campus, since Hollins offers eight co-ed graduate programs. "A student should only attend Hollins if they want to be a part of a close-knit community that fosters creative minds and ambitious spirits," says a senior.

Described by the *New York Times* as "achingly picturesque," the neoclassical redbrick buildings at Hollins date back to the mid-19th century. There are some modern structures too, such as the Wetherill Visual Arts Center. Several buildings have been renovated in recent years, including Hollins Theatre, Turner Hall, Presser Hall, and Bradley Hall, which is now home to the university's Batten Leadership Institute.

General education requirements (known as Education through Skills and Perspective) stress breadth and depth across the curriculum. The skills component teaches students to write successfully, reason quantitatively, express themselves effectively, research astutely, and be adept technologically. The perspectives component includes seven areas of knowledge that help to explain how people view and understand the world: aesthetic analysis, creative expression, premodern worlds, modern and contemporary worlds, scientific inquiry, social and cultural diversities, and global systems and languages. Two terms of physical education are also mandatory, and those looking to take advantage of Hollins's acclaimed equestrian program can earn PE credits with riding lessons. All freshmen take a required first-year seminar and participate in Orientation Week, which includes academic programming, a day of community service, and plenty of time to form friendships with new classmates.

> "I have never been in doubt of my professors' intelligence, and their...ability to pass on their knowledge is excellent."

Academics are a top priority at Hollins, and students say the workload is demanding but doable. "I have been challenged by most of my classes here, but the workload has been manageable enough that I have been able to do a bunch of extracurriculars too," says one senior. English, biology, business, and psychology are the most popular majors. An environmental science major was added recently, as were concentrations in applied economics and data analytics. Students concentrating or minoring in creative writing benefit from the nationally recognized Jackson Center for Creative Writing. Classes are small, with 89 percent enrolling fewer than 20 students and none exceeding 50, and professors are well regarded. "I have never been in doubt of my professors' intelligence, and their collective passion for and ability to pass on their knowledge is excellent," says one student. Motivated students are encouraged to design their majors or apply to the honors program, which involves interdisciplinary projects carried out through a four-semester sequence of two-credit seminars. Additionally, because Hollins belongs to the Seven-College Exchange*, its students may cross-register for courses at any of the other six participating institutions.

The shorter January term offers a break for on-campus projects, travel, or internships, with the latter often being facilitated by loyal alumnae. Artists benefit from extensive internship opportunities at Christie's, Sotheby's, and various parts of the Smithsonian Institution, while the Hollins Repertory Dance Company, closely affiliated with the American Dance Festival, has been selected to perform at the Kennedy Center and at Aaron Davis Hall, Harlem's premier performing arts center. The annual Science Seminar features undergrad research, while the Batten Leadership Institute

Website: www.hollins.edu
Location: Suburban
Private
Total Enrollment: 665
Undergraduates: 617
Male/Female: 0/100
SAT Ranges: CR 520–630, M 470–580
ACT Ranges: 21–30
Financial Aid: 82%
Pell Grant: 43%
Expense: Pr $
Student Loans: 76%
Average Debt: $ $ $ $
Phi Beta Kappa: Yes
Applicants: 2,233
Accepted: 59%
Enrolled: 14%
Grad in 6 Years: 57%
Returning Freshmen: 81%
Academics: ✐ ✐ ✐
Social: ☎ ☎ ☎
Q of L: ★ ★ ★
Admissions: (800) 456-9595
Email Address: huadm@hollins.edu

Strong Programs:
English and Creative Writing
Biology
Business
Psychology
Environmental Science
Dance
Theatre

is the only college program in the nation that promotes personal and professional growth with videotaped performance reviews, senior mentoring, intensive communication skills groups, and experience in board governance. In addition to Hollins Abroad programs in Paris and London, students may study abroad through affiliated programs in 20 countries around the world; 48 percent of students choose to do so.

"In general, Hollins women are independent, ambitious, and passionate," a senior says. "There are some significant cliques, but for the most part everyone gets along." Forty-eight percent of undergrads are Virginians, and 5 percent hail from foreign countries. African Americans make up 12 percent of the total, while Asian Americans and Hispanics add 3 and 7 percent, respectively. "We have a very active gay and lesbian club called Outloud, and also an active women's studies department that puts together a lot of rallies and events," says a freshman. "Our campus has a definite liberal leaning, although there is a small, committed Republican group." The university has made socioeconomic diversity a priority, with 43 percent of freshmen qualifying for the Pell Grant. Hollins also hands out merit scholarships averaging $24,189, but no athletic scholarships.

Eighty-two percent of Hollins students live in the dorms; they have to, unless they're married, older than 23, or living at home in Roanoke with their parents.

> **"Hollins is a great school that empowers women. It has made me independent."**

"Most of the dorms are beautiful historic buildings full of character and comfort," says a student. Freshmen live in Randolph and Tinker; singles are only available to upperclassmen, and there is a fee. Upperclassmen make their homes in Main, West, and East, which have 10-foot ceilings and hardwood floors, and some rooms also boast brass doorknobs, walk-in closets, and even fireplaces. Students chow down in Moody or at the campus coffee shop, which is open late; the meal plan is mandatory, and some complain that it is overpriced. While the adjacent Roanoke neighborhood has its rough spots, "the campus is very safe," says one student.

"Most of Hollins's social life occurs on campus," says a student. "There are lots of events and programs to attend each week, with occasional off-campus offerings that are also very popular." Hollins shuns sororities, and sporadic student efforts to bring them to campus draw lively debate. To fill the gap, the school organizes mixers, concerts, dances, and second-run movies each weekend. There's also a free shuttle to help students get around Roanoke, a city with "malls, shopping centers, and movie and live theaters," says a freshman. "It has a nice historic downtown with an organic farmers market, but it is not densely urban like New York or Washington, D.C." As a result, road-tripping remains the preferred social option—to Hampden–Sydney College, Virginia Tech, the University of Virginia, or Washington and Lee.

Hollins's on-campus stable, in which students can board their own horses, complements the school's top-notch equestrian program, which has brought home the Old Dominion Athletic Conference championship multiple times in recent years. Women's tennis is also a recent conference champion, and the swim team has won national Division III championships. Although there are no intramural sports, the popular Hollins Outdoor Program offers hiking, spelunking, and other activities in the beautiful Shenandoah Valley and Blue Ridge Mountains.

"Hollins provides a tight-knit community of students, professors, and administration," says a senior. As the number of women's colleges continues to dwindle, Hollins remains committed to offering single-sex education. Students leave with confidence, critical-thinking skills, and intellectual depth, thanks to a solid grounding in the liberal arts. And the school's Southern heritage doesn't hurt, either. "Hollins is a great school that empowers women," says one senior. "It has made me independent."

Those looking to take advantage of Hollins's acclaimed equestrian program can earn PE credits with riding lessons.

Artists benefit from extensive internship opportunities at Christie's, Sotheby's, and various parts of the Smithsonian Institution.

Overlaps

North Carolina State, Sweet Briar, James Madison, Roanoke, Mount Holyoke

Hollins: Rolling admissions. (Priority deadline: Feb. 1.) Early decision: Nov. 1. Early action: Nov. 15. Financial aid: Feb. 15. Application fee: $40 (paper), free (online). Campus interviews: optional, evaluative. No alumnae interviews. SATs or ACTs: required. Subject Tests: optional. Letters of recommendation: required. Essay: required. Accepts the Common Application with supplement.

College of the Holy Cross

Worcester, MA 01610

A tight-knit Roman Catholic community steeped in church and tradition, much more so than relatively secularized Boston College. Many students are the second or third generation to attend. Set high on a hill above an evolving Worcester, an hour from Boston. Sports teams compete with (and occasionally beat) schools 10 times HC's size.

Students at Holy Cross, a Roman Catholic college in the heart of New England, are devoted to the Jesuit tradition of becoming "men and women for and with others." Students on "the hill" are driven to do something for their college or community, whether it's a football player becoming a Big Brother or an upperclassman interning at City Hall. Peers and professors alike offer support and spiritual guidance, and more than 90 community-based learning courses incorporate service opportunities. The classroom focus is critical thinking and writing, but the school's proximity to nine other colleges in the Boston area means Crusaders can focus on their social lives as well.

Located on one of the seven hills overlooking the industrial city of Worcester, the 174-acre Holy Cross campus is a registered arboretum. The school's landscaping has won national awards, including two first-place prizes as the best-designed and best-planted campus in the nation. Architectural styles range from classical to modern. A $90 million renovation and expansion of the Hart Recreation Center will be completed in 2018.

Holy Cross's general education requirements comprise 12 courses in 10 areas spanning the liberal arts and sciences. Ideas and thinking are the focus, rather than preparation for a specific vocation. All first-year students participate in Montserrat, a comprehensive program designed to enhance the academic and campus experience by integrating living and learning. The program features small, full-year seminars that facilitate collaboration among students and professors. The seminars are organized into six clusters, each devoted to a specific theme: contemporary challenge, the divine, the self, the natural world, global society, and core human questions. Students also live in the same residence hall and participate in cluster activities. "It was an eye-opening experience for me, and the friendships I made in my Montserrat class lasted throughout my entire four years," reflects a psychology major.

> **"The friendships I made in my Montserrat class lasted throughout my entire four years."**

HC's premed program boasts that it has twice the number of students accepted to medical school as the national average. Students also give high marks to the English, history, economics, psychology, and political science programs, and one notes that the classics department is one of the best-kept secrets on campus. As might be expected, philosophy and religious studies are strong, and concentrations in Latin American studies and peace and conflict studies are popular, as these are the disciplines central to Jesuit missionary work. Holy Cross is also part of the Higher

Website: www.holycross.edu
Location: City Outskirts
Private
Total Enrollment: 2,885
Undergraduates: 2,885
Male/Female: 50/50
SAT Ranges: CR 600–690, M 620–690
ACT Ranges: 28–31
Financial Aid: 51%
Pell Grant: 16%
Expense: Pr $ $ $
Student Loans: 59%
Average Debt: $ $
Phi Beta Kappa: Yes
Applicants: 6,595
Accepted: 37%
Enrolled: 30%
Grad in 6 Years: 92%
Returning Freshmen: 96%
Academics: ✍ ✍ ✍ ✍
Social: ☎ ☎ ☎ ☎
Q of L: ★ ★ ★ ★
Admissions: (508) 793-2443
Email Address: admissions@holycross.edu

Strong Programs:
English
History
Economics
Psychology
Political Science
Premed

(continued)

Philosophy
Religious Studies

Education Consortium of Central Massachusetts, which offers registration privileges at the region's most prestigious colleges and universities.

Classes are small—66 percent have fewer than 20 students—which helps faculty members keep in touch with undergraduates. Courses are demanding and intense, but according to an architectural studies major, "The atmosphere is one of collaboration and self-competition, in which students want to improve themselves but work together to meet common goals." Professors are praised for being accessible and willing to help. "There really is a partnership between professors and students here at HC," says a political science and Spanish double major. And students say the support they receive from each other is exceptional. One senior shares, "I have found notes in the Dinand Library with a positive quote or an encouraging message for the next student who sits there. Someone even attached a honey stick from Cool Beans, our campus coffee shop, to a note that I found!"

More than 90 community-based learning courses incorporate service opportunities.

Community-based learning courses include two to two and a half hours of weekly service with local volunteer, education, or health organizations, in addition to time in the classroom; some courses focus on research that benefits local organizations. HC's honors program enables a small number of juniors and seniors to enroll in exclusive courses and thesis-writing seminars, while the Fenwick Scholar program helps students design and carry out independent projects. Each April, approximately 300 Holy Cross students participate in a four-day conference and present the results of their independent work. Other opportunities include academic internships in the community, 26 study abroad programs in 16 nations, and the Washington Semester*.

"Students are supportive, hardworking, [and] focused both on their studies and on the well-being of one another," according to one student. The religious influence

> **"There really is a partnership between professors and students here at HC."**

at Holy Cross is somewhat greater than at other Jesuit schools—most students are Catholic—but students of all faiths are welcomed, and daily mass is not required. The chaplain's office offers numerous types of retreats for all faiths and reflective practices. It also offers an optional five-day silent retreat four times a year, in which student volunteers follow the spiritual exercises of Jesuit founder St. Ignatius Loyola. Thirty-seven percent of students are in-staters, and 2 percent are international. African Americans make up 4 percent of the student body, Asian Americans comprise 5 percent, and Hispanics account for 10 percent. "Widely speaking, I think there is an apathy toward politics. Social justice, on the other hand, is something talked about a lot on campus," notes one student. Admission is need-blind, and HC guarantees to meet accepted students' full demonstrated financial need. Merit scholarships are awarded annually, with an average payout of $37,530. Student-athletes may vie for 111 athletic scholarships in 14 sports.

All first-year students participate in Montserrat, a comprehensive program that integrates living and learning.

Ninety-one percent of Holy Cross students live in the residence halls, where freshmen and sophomores have double rooms, and juniors and seniors may opt for two- and three-bedroom suites—with living rooms, bathrooms, and kitchens. Floors are single-sex; buildings are co-ed. Most first-years live on "Easy Street," in Hanselman, Clark, and Mulledy (on the college's central hill next to the Hogan Campus Center) or in Wheeler (lower campus). Figge, Loyola, Alumni, and Carlin house mostly upperclassmen. Dorms receive good reviews, especially for their size and storage space. Dining options include several campus eateries and the main dining hall; students report the food to be tasty and plentiful. Students feel safe, according to one senior. "We are more or less a closed campus and have an official Holy Cross police department which routinely patrols the entire campus."

Because there are no Greek organizations, dorm life takes center stage. Each dorm has its own T-shirt, and they compete against each other for prizes in athletic and other contests. The Campus Activities Board hosts a variety of events, including karaoke, comedians, casino nights, and movie nights. Underage students caught with alcohol are put on probation and parents are notified. Still, as with most schools, students who seek to imbibe can find alcohol, regardless of their age. "On the weekends there are always loads of parties going on, which are generally very accessible to all students from all classes," a student says. Tradition is big at Holy Cross, from Reunion to homecoming to Purple Pride Day. Midnight breakfasts provide sustenance as students cram for finals, while the 100 Days weekend begins the senior class countdown to graduation. Spring Weekend brings well-known performers. And of course, given the high percentage of Irish Catholic students, St. Patrick's Day is an occasion for celebration.

"Volunteering is one way students live out the Holy Cross mission," a student says, and 45 percent of students get involved in community service. The SPUD (Student Programs for Urban Development) student organization is particularly popular and active in underserved areas of Worcester, which is an underrated college town gradually making a comeback from tough economic times. "Worcester has a lot of really fun things to do" and "so much

"Social justice…is something talked about a lot on campus."

to explore," says a senior. A school shuttle service takes students to the orchestra, the Worcester Centrum for athletic events and rock concerts, and the town's museum. Students are discouraged from having cars, but the college organizes trips to New York City and Providence, Rhode Island.

Holy Cross's Crusaders compete in Division I athletics. Men's basketball won the 2016 Patriot League championship, and women's ice hockey captured the 2016 New England Hockey Conference championship. Holy Cross's moot court team, which simulates Supreme Court arguments, won a national title for their written legal brief at the American Collegiate Moot Court Association's championship tournament in 2016. About half of HC students participate in intramural sports.

Holy Cross is keeping the faith—its emphasis on Catholicism and the Jesuit tradition, that is—even as administrators place a renewed focus on academics and small classes. "Holy Cross has prepared me to think critically, challenge the status quo, ask questions, and step outside my comfort zone to make changes in our world," cheers one senior. Indeed, the close-knit atmosphere offers students a multitude of opportunities to grow, serve others, and create lasting friendships.

HC's premed program boasts twice the number of students accepted to medical school as the national average.

Overlaps
Boston College, Villanova, Providence, Fordham, Notre Dame, University of Massachusetts Amherst, Fairfield, Georgetown

If You Apply To ➤ **Holy Cross:** Early decision: Dec. 15. Regular decision: Jan. 15. Financial aid: Feb. 1. Housing: May 1. Application fee: $60. Campus interviews: recommended, evaluative. Alumni interviews: optional, evaluative. SATs or ACTs: optional. Subject Tests: optional. Letters of recommendation: required. Essay: required. Accepts the Common Application.

Hood College

401 Rosemont Avenue, Frederick, MD 21701

With more than a decade of coeducation under its belt, Hood has made noteworthy strides toward building a fully co-ed environment. Male enrollment is now nearly 40 percent. A major asset: Hood's strategic location, one hour from D.C. and Baltimore. Hood's distinctive core curriculum stresses thematic study. Science is a specialty.

Website: www.hood.edu
Location: Small City
Private
Total Enrollment: 1,335
Undergraduates: 1,171
Male/Female: 38/62
SAT Ranges: CR 470–600,
    M 470–600
ACT Ranges: 19–27
Financial Aid: 97%
Pell Grant: 30%
Expense: Pr $
Student Loans: 88%
Average Debt: $ $ $
Phi Beta Kappa: No
Applicants: 1,636
Accepted: 79%
Enrolled: 20%
Grad in 6 Years: 71%
Returning Freshmen: 75%
Academics: ✐ ✐ ✐
Social: ☎ ☎ ☎
Q of L: ★ ★ ★
Admissions: (800) 922-1599
Email Address: admission@
    hood.edu

Strong Programs:
Biology
Business Administration
Computer Science
Psychology
English
Elementary/Special Education
History
Communication

The four-year honors program features a senior seminar for which students choose both the topic and the professor.

Founded as a women's college in 1893, Hood College undertook a bold reinvention of itself in 2003. That's the year it began admitting men as regular residential students (males had been commuting students since 1971). Now members of both sexes have the opportunity to partake of Hood's traditional mix of professional and liberal arts offerings on a campus strategically located in a historic Civil War setting. Students see their school's biggest strength in its people: students, staff, and faculty. "There are so many cultures and ethnicities and traditions to be shared," says one junior. "I love living here. I'm having the time of my life."

Hood's strikingly beautiful 50-acre campus features redbrick buildings and lush, tree-shaded lawns. Situated in the Civil War town of Frederick, Hood is within an hour and a half of nearly 30 colleges and within minutes of a major National Cancer Institute research complex, high-tech firms, small and large businesses, and both Washington, D.C., and Baltimore. On campus, technology programs, which are already important, get a further boost thanks to the Hodson Science and Technology Center. Hood recently opened a state-of-the-art trading room, in which students practice using technology and analytical tools similar to what is used on Wall Street.

Hood's required core curriculum, designed to expose students to different modes of thinking and critical reflection on global issues, is comprised of two parts, Foundations and Methods of Inquiry. Foundation courses include English composition, quantitative literacy, foreign language, and health and wellness. Methods of Inquiry requires coursework in seven areas: literary analysis, visual and performing arts, scientific thought, historical analysis, social and behavioral analysis, philosophical inquiry, and global perspectives. First-year students participate in Hood's First-Year Read program and in a small, writing-intensive First-Year Seminar, and they can opt to join living/learning communities; these programs are designed to provide the kinds of structured classroom environments and informal learning opportunities that help build academic skills, confidence, and a sense of belonging.

> **"Hood is not extraordinarily competitive, although hard work is required to do well."**

"Hood is not extraordinarily competitive," says a sophomore, "although hard work is required to do well." Hood's major strength lies in the sciences, especially the biology department, with its special emphases on molecular biology, marine biology, and environmental science and policy. A semester-long coastal studies program takes students along the East Coast on a biological educational mission. Education, especially early childhood, is a program of note, as are business administration and computer science. The most popular majors are psychology, English, elementary/special education, history, and communication. New offerings include global studies and law and criminal justice. Only labs are taught by graduate assistants, and 75 percent of classes have fewer than 20 students. "The professors here are extremely intelligent with excellent credentials," raves one student. A math major adds, "The teachers want their students to succeed and are very accessible when students need help."

If you really want to stimulate the brain cells, the four-year honors program features team-taught courses, a sophomore-year seminar on global issues that involves a community service project, and a senior seminar for which students choose both the topic and the professor—not to mention an annual $2,000 scholarship. Ten percent of students complete internships that include overseas jobs for language and business majors and legislative and cultural positions in Washington, D.C. Study abroad destinations, to which 13 percent of students take flight, include Ireland, Cyprus, Costa Rica, Morocco, and South Korea. With the outstanding resources of the Shouse Career Center (including a national electronic listing for résumés), students have a leg up on their next step in life, whether it be their career or graduate school.

In general, Hood students are "interested in their education and are serious and hardworking," says a sophomore. Nearly three-quarters of undergraduates call Maryland home, while 3 percent come to Hood from other countries. Twelve percent are African American, 9 percent are Hispanic, and 3 percent are Asian American. Students say the campus leans slightly left, politically speaking, and key issues include the environment and fiscal concerns. Hood provides merit scholarships worth an average of $15,609, and 30 percent of students qualify for the Pell Grant.

Hood's residence halls are well liked, with good-sized, air-conditioned rooms. Most dorms are co-ed by room or by floor, but Shriner Hall is all-female. The lottery system is based on seniority, and 55 percent of students live on campus. Freshmen can expect to be assigned to doubles (seniors and juniors can compete for singles), and language majors may choose to live in French-, Spanish-, or German-language houses. First-year students can also elect to live in themed living/learning communities within the residence halls. Campus dining options aren't stellar, students say, but campus security receives praise. "I feel very safe on our small, homey campus with lots of lights at night and plenty of officers walking or driving around at all times," says one student.

Each dorm has its own personality as well as its own house council, rules, and social activities.

Social life among the students is centered on the dorms, as each has its own personality as well as its own house council, rules, and social activities. Students report that there are parties every weekend, along with movies, dances, or other forms of entertainment. The Whitaker Campus Center, with its pool tables, snack bar, bookstore, and meeting rooms, offers a great gathering place for residents and commuters 24 hours a day. Campus alcohol policies have been tightened and follow state law, but drinking is generally not a big deal at Hood. "At parties and events, you have to show ID to get alcohol," one senior says. "However, in the dorms at other times, it is possible for underage students to get alcohol from those 'of age.'" "If you don't like to stay on campus, there are restaurants, bars, clubs, malls, and coffeehouses within 10 minutes of the college by car," explains an English major. Scenic Frederick is described as small, safe, and beautiful. "Downtown Frederick is a very up-and-coming, artsy town," reports one student. A one-hour car ride delivers students to the multiple diversions in Baltimore and Washington, D.C.

"I feel very safe on our small, homey campus."

With over a century of history, Hood is rife with traditions. Some of the most important ones include the Class Ring dinner and formal, a performance of Handel's *Messiah*, and Spring Parties, a weekend of carnival activities and dances. The Blazers compete in Division III, and competitive teams include men's and women's swimming, men's and women's track, and men's basketball. Recreational and intramural sports attract 20 percent of undergraduates; popular activities include soccer, touch football, kickball, basketball, and volleyball.

While Hood has undergone the major change from a women's college to a co-ed institution, its mission remains the same: to prepare students to face the challenges of a fast-changing society and professional environment. "The traditions are amazing," boasts a sophomore, "topped only by professors who care and friends you'll have forever."

Overlaps

Towson, University of Maryland, Stevenson, University of Maryland Baltimore County, McDaniel, Frostburg, Salisbury, Susquehanna

If You Apply To ➤

Hood: Rolling admissions. (Priority deadline: Mar. 1.) Financial aid: Feb. 15. Housing: May 1. No application fee. Campus interviews: recommended, evaluative (required for some). No alumni interviews. SATs or ACTs: required (optional for those with qualifying GPA). Subject Tests: optional. Letters of recommendation: required. Essay: required. Accepts the Common Application.

P.O. Box 9000, Holland, MI 49422

Hope has an in-between size—bigger than most small colleges but smaller than a university. It is evangelical in orientation, but less than a quarter of the students are members of the Reformed Church in America. In addition to the liberal arts, Hope offers education, engineering, and nursing, and makes undergraduate research a priority.

Website: www.hope.edu
Location: Small City
Private
Total Enrollment: 3,208
Undergraduates: 3,208
Male/Female: 40/60
SAT Ranges: CR 540–650, M 550–670
ACT Ranges: 24–29
Financial Aid: 85%
Pell Grant: 18%
Expense: Pr $
Student Loans: 64%
Average Debt: $ $ $
Phi Beta Kappa: Yes
Applicants: 4,420
Accepted: 72%
Enrolled: 25%
Grad in 6 Years: 80%
Returning Freshmen: 86%
Academics: ✍ ✍ ✍
Social: ☎ ☎ ☎
Q of L: ★ ★ ★
Admissions: (616) 395-7850
Email Address: admissions@hope.edu

Strong Programs:
Biology
Chemistry
Nursing
Engineering
Communication
Political Science
Dance
Business Administration

Each fall since 1897, Hope College freshmen have spent three grueling hours engaged in "the Pull," an epic tug-of-war against the sophomores, who stand assembled on the opposite end of a 650-pound rope across the 250-foot-wide Black River. This well-known annual tradition evokes the daily struggle Hope students face: maintaining their faith in a world eager to challenge it at every turn. The heritage of Hope's Dutch founders remains strong and visible on campus. "The academic programs, particularly the research and collaboration opportunities, far surpass those of Hope's rivals," opines a sophomore.

Hope was founded in 1866 with the biblical (Book of Hebrews) mission of becoming an "anchor of hope" for the Dutch church in the West. It is situated on six blocks near downtown Holland, the tulip capital of the nation, and a short bike ride from the shores of Lake Michigan. There's a lush pine grove in the center of campus, which features an eclectic array of buildings in architectural styles ranging from 19th-century Flemish to modern. The college has undergone a bit of a building boom, opening $70 million in facilities in the last few years, including an art museum, center for musical arts, and dining hall renovation.

Among Hope's academic offerings, the sciences (especially biology and chemistry) stand out, with excellent laboratory facilities and faculty who are eager to involve students in their funded research. During the school year, undergraduates often conduct advanced experiments and even publish papers; come summer, about 200 geology, chemistry, mathematics, computer science, physics, and engineering majors participate in research full time. Not surprisingly, many science majors go on to medical and engineering schools and Ph.D. programs. For those otherwise inclined, Hope's offerings in political science, psychology, dance, English, and business administration are solid too. Hope's communication department is one of the Speech Communication Association's two nationwide Programs of Excellence. One student says, "The sciences get lauded most often, but all four art departments (visual, theatre, dance, and music) are powerhouses in their own right." The modern and classical language departments offer students proficient in a second language the chance to use their skills in volunteer work and research with faculty members, while the Visiting Writers Series gives students an opportunity to interact with noteworthy authors.

> **"The sciences get lauded most often."**

The academic climate is demanding yet supportive. "The climate is competitive," says a junior, but "if you're struggling it's not looked down upon to get assistance." Most Hope students select a major from one of the college's fields, but the truly adventurous may design their own composite major. Hope's general education program, designed around the themes "knowing how" and "knowing about," includes a first-year seminar, which provides "an intellectual transition into Hope." Courses in expository writing, health dynamics, math and natural science, foreign language, religious studies, social sciences, the arts, and cultural heritage are also required; some must have a focus on cultural diversity. Students also complete a two-credit freshman seminar linked with academic advising and a senior seminar. "The faculty is very personable," says one student. "They love engaging students." Hope offers off-campus programs through the Great Lakes Colleges Association*, including semesters at other U.S. colleges and options combining classes and internships. Students may study abroad in more than 70 countries; 35 percent do so.

Students at Hope "tend to be very involved in academics, extracurriculars, athletics, and social events," says a junior. Adds another, "Our students are well-rounded individuals. They know how to be successful in and out of the classroom." The friendly student body is a rather homogenous lot,

"The faculty is very personable. They love engaging students."

with 67 percent hailing from Michigan and 3 percent coming from overseas. African Americans account for 3 percent of the student body, Hispanics 8 percent, and Asian Americans 2 percent. Within the college's prevailing Christian atmosphere, most students say there is room for other voices and viewpoints. "Currently, the biggest social issue on campus is the college's position on homosexuality," reports one student. Merit scholarships averaging $8,160 are available to qualified students, but there are no athletic scholarships.

Seventy-seven percent of Hope students live in university-sponsored housing. Traditional dorms are arranged in freshman clusters by gender or co-ed by suite. "Dorms are fine, and I enjoyed them as a freshman, but most students opt for the college-owned apartment complexes and cottages surrounding the campus area. They're much nicer and better-kept, though it can be difficult to secure one until you're a junior," says a student. On-campus students eat in one of two large dining halls where the fare—especially homemade bread and desserts—is tasty. The campus security staff is generally commended for their ability to handle campus issues. "They are there when you need them and they provide you with the assistance that you need in case of any emergency," says a student.

"The weekends are full and busy. The Student Activities Committee is the organization that makes the social life at Hope College thrive," says one student. The committee brings in comedians, bands, and hypnotists, shows movies in campus auditoriums, and plans the Spring Festival carnival and Winter Fantasia dance. Seven fraternities and eight sororities, all local organiza-

"The Student Activities Committee is the organization that makes the social life at Hope College thrive."

tions, claim 10 percent of the men and 10 percent of the women, respectively. "There are so many other activities that students can engage in that do not involve drinking," says a student, and those caught drinking must perform community service. Among the 80 student organizations are a variety of active religious life organizations, including the Fellowship of Christian Athletes, Hope for the Nations (ministry), and InterVarsity Christian Fellowship. There are a slew of unique student clubs, including Silent Praise, which seeks to praise God through American Sign Language (ASL) and worship music.

Holland (population 33,000) is the site of spring's Tulip Time, one of the largest U.S. flower festivals. When Hope's cozy campus and the quaint town of Holland get too close for comfort, students find relief at the beaches of Lake Michigan or drive 30 minutes to Grand Rapids, which offers some large-city amenities and good weekend rental deals at the ski slopes. Chicago and Detroit are other typical destinations for those trying to hit the road.

On the field and on the court, Hope's Flying Dutchmen are fearless and talented Division III competitors. Hope teams are frequent conference champions; solid programs include men's and women's golf and basketball, as well as women's tennis, volleyball, and cross-country. The college has also won the

Come summer, about 200 science and engineering majors participate in research full time.

Active religious life organizations include Silent Praise, which seeks to praise God through American Sign Language (ASL) and worship music.

Commissioner's Cup of the Michigan Intercollegiate Athletic Association multiple times; the trophy recognizes the conference's best cumulative sports program for men and women. Especially important are any competitions against Calvin (a century-old rivalry) and football versus Albion and Kalamazoo. Just over half of the students take part in 19 intramural sports, which range from soccer and softball to inner-tube water polo.

Hope's mission is "to educate students for lives of leadership and service in a global society." For those seeking an institution with traditional Christian roots and an emphasis on undergraduates, Hope may be worth a look. "Hope is a place where students are challenged to become better students," says one senior, "but, more important, better people."

If You Apply To ➤ **Hope:** Rolling admissions. (Priority deadline: Nov. 1.) Financial aid: Mar. 1. Housing: May 1. Application fee: $35. Campus interviews: recommended, informational. No alumni interviews. SATs or ACTs: required. No Subject Tests. Letters of recommendation: required. Essay: required. Accepts the Common Application.

Houghton College

Houghton, NY 14744

The mid-Atlantic's leading evangelical Christian college. Women outnumber men nearly 2 to 1. All students are required to take Biblical literature and Introduction to Christianity, and most go to chapel three times a week. Perks include a 386-acre horseback-riding facility. When rural New York gets claustrophobic, the college offers a variety of possibilities for a semester away.

Website: www.houghton.edu
Location: Rural
Private
Total Enrollment: 999
Undergraduates: 990
Male/Female: 36/64
SAT Ranges: CR 500–630, M 490–620
ACT Ranges: 21–29
Financial Aid: 96%
Pell Grant: 46%
Expense: Pr $
Student Loans: 82%
Average Debt: $ $ $
Phi Beta Kappa: No
Applicants: 737
Accepted: 94%
Enrolled: 35%
Grad in 6 Years: 71%
Returning Freshmen: 84%
Academics: ✍ ✍ ✍
Social: ☎ ☎ ☎

Located in the bucolic New York town that shares its name, Houghton College offers a solid, growing academic program and strong athletic teams, while remaining committed to its core mission as a Christian liberal arts school. Sponsored by the Wesleyan Church, Houghton celebrates its Christian heritage and encourages students to do the same. Applicants must explain in their essays why they desire to be a part of a Christian academic community, and current students are expected to attend a set amount of chapel services throughout the semester. These expectations help create true community on campus. One junior says, "Houghton combines academic rigor, athletic excellence, and intentional spiritual formation in a fun-loving and Christ-centered community."

Houghton's scenic hilltop campus covers 1,300 acres of rural beauty, surrounded by vast expanses of western New York countryside. The academic buildings are a mix of area fieldstone and brick. Recent construction includes a 115,000-square-foot athletic complex.

Houghton students must complete general education requirements known as Integrative Studies, designed to provide a context and framework for the entire educational program. Freshmen must take Biblical Literature, Writing in the Liberal Arts, and a course titled Transitions, aimed at easing the transition to college. The school's most popular programs include business, education, biology, and visual and performing arts, particularly music. The premed and theology programs are also strong, and according to a sophomore, "Communication is the fastest-growing department, with fantastic faculty and classes." Houghton is known for its programs in equestrian studies—which take advantage of the college's 386-acre riding facility. Other options include a 3–2 engineering program with Clarkson University (NY), a 3+4 Pharm.D. program with the University of Buffalo, and a medical early-acceptance program with the Lake Erie College of Osteopathic Medicine. In addition to a new major in sport, recreation, and wellness management, Houghton has implemented new degrees in data science and music industry.

Houghton's academic climate is rigorous, but not overwhelmingly so. "Houghton is a place where 'iron sharpens iron.' Walking into class, I know I will be challenged by faculty and fellow students to become better at what I do," says a student. Sixty-nine percent of classes have fewer than 20 students, and most courses are taught by senior faculty, who students say do an outstanding job of fostering a sense of community. "At Houghton I have coffee with my professors and real conversations. I see them at church and in the dining hall, and I've gotten to know their kids," says an intercultural studies major.

> **"At Houghton I have coffee with my professors and real conversations."**

Houghton offers three honors programs for incoming freshmen: London Honors, East Meets West, and Science Honors. The London Honors and East Meets West programs offer qualified students an intensive, hands-on experience in the humanities, along with study abroad experiences in the United Kingdom and the eastern Mediterranean, respectively. The Science Honors program allows select students to engage a significant scientific question in a research-oriented environment. Houghton's Summer Research Institute, designed for students in math and the sciences, is also well regarded. Thirty-eight percent of all students take advantage of off-campus study in a variety of programs throughout the year, including four-week Mayterm programs in Costa Rica, Ecuador, Sierra Leone, and Honduras. Students who want to get away within the U.S. can spend a semester at any Christian College Consortium* member school or participate in the American Studies program in Washington, D.C., sponsored by the Council for Christian Colleges and Universities*.

Sixty-four percent of those who enroll at Houghton are from New York, and 5 percent are international. "Students are generally dedicated and involved," says a senior. African Americans account for 3 percent of the student body, Hispanics 2 percent, and Asian Americans 2 percent. "The most noticed and discussed issues are those of race, sexual orientation, and often moral character. As Houghton College is a Christian liberal arts college, these issues are often addressed from a Christian perspective, but all views are welcome," a sophomore says. Qualified undergrads receive merit scholarships averaging $13,386, and an impressive 46 percent of students are eligible for Pell Grants.

> **"I joke that Houghton is a Christian campus with Amish reinforcements."**

Houghton's single-sex dorms, townhouses, and apartments house 81 percent of students. "Housing is fairly limited in terms of options, but all students are guaranteed a spot on campus," says one student. Students are required to live in the residence halls as freshmen and sophomores. After their first two years, some move off campus, but many opt for college-approved townhouses where regulations are less strict. "The food is pretty good, overall," says a senior, and options include "stations where you can cook your own omelets and even make stir-fry! Everyone loves that." Students report that they feel safe on campus and that training programs on sexual assault have been effective.

"Most social interaction happens right on campus, but it isn't rare for students to travel together and do something fun off campus. The surrounding area of Houghton is beautiful," cheers one communication major. "There is always lots of student programming available from the Campus Activities Board and other student programs," says an art major, and dorm-identity events, film festivals, and concerts are popular. The college even has its own ski trails. Students are involved in service projects such as Big Brothers Big Sisters and nursing home

---

(continued)

Q of L: ★ ★ ★ ★
Admissions: (585) 567-9353
Email Address: admission@ houghton.edu

Strong Programs:
Business
Education
Biology
Visual and Performing Arts
Premed
Communication
Equestrian Studies
Theology

Programs in equestrian studies take advantage of the college's 386-acre riding facility.

Houghton offers three honors programs for incoming freshmen: London Honors, East Meets West, and Science Honors.

visitation; the area surrounding the college is one of the poorest in New York State. The town of Houghton is dry, and the college's community covenant forbids alcohol. "I joke that Houghton is a Christian campus with Amish reinforcements. While I am not naive enough to suggest that no drinking takes place, if you want alcohol, you'll have to intentionally seek it out," says a junior. Students eagerly anticipate annual celebrations for homecoming, Christian Life Emphasis Week, and the annual Christmas Prism.

Houghton was approved for full Division III membership in 2016, and a $24 million field house accommodates the college's expanding athletic teams. Competitive Highlanders teams include men's and women's soccer, women's volleyball, and men's tennis. Nearly two-thirds of students participate in intramural sports, with volleyball and basketball being the most popular.

Students don't come to Houghton for the surrounding town, which is 30 minutes by car from the nearest mall, or for the weather, which can be tough once winter sets in. But they do come, and for good reason: there's little to distract them from their studies, their campus's natural beauty, and their connection to God. As one junior observes, "There are few schools that will work so closely with their students, through setting academic goals, [helping them pursue] internships, listening to their passions, and equipping them to work where their deep gladness and the world's deep hunger meet."

If You Apply To ➤

Houghton: Rolling admissions. (Priority deadline: Oct. 15.) Financial aid: Mar. 1. Housing: May 1. Application fee: $40. Campus interviews: recommended, evaluative. Alumni interviews: optional, evaluative. SATs or ACTs: required. No Subject Tests. Letters of recommendation: required. Essay: required. Music majors apply directly to music program. Accepts the Common Application with supplement.

Howard University

2400 Sixth Street NW, Washington, D.C. 20059

The flagship university of black America and the first to integrate the black experience into all areas of study. Strategically located in D.C., Howard depends on Congress for much of its funding. Preprofessional programs such as nursing, business, and architecture are strong. Only 11 percent of students are an ethnicity other than African American.

Website: www.howard.edu
Location: City Center
Private
Total Enrollment: 9,000
Undergraduates: 6,386
Male/Female: 32/68
SAT Ranges: CR 500–610, M 490–610
ACT Ranges: 21–27
Financial Aid: 82%
Pell Grant: 60%
Expense: Pr $
Student Loans: 81%

Contrary to the advice of early black leaders such as Booker T. Washington, who argued in favor of technical training, Howard has promoted the liberal arts since its inception. This focus has served the school well; Howard's law school counts the late Supreme Court Justice Thurgood Marshall among its alumni, and Nobel Prize–winning author Toni Morrison went here too. In recent years, Howard has strengthened its financial position and has begun implementing a strategic plan structured around "Leadership for America and the Global Community." The four-part plan focuses on strengthening academic programs and services, promoting excellence in teaching and research, increasing private support, and enhancing national and community service.

Founded in 1866 by General Oliver Howard primarily to educate freed slaves, the university now operates five campuses and serves roughly 9,000 students. Interestingly, Howard is one of a handful of universities in the nation supported partly by federal subsidies; these days, the school gets about 55 percent of its budget from Congress. The 89-acre main campus houses most classrooms, dorms, and administrative offices, as well as the university center, the Founders, and undergraduate, medical, and dental libraries. The Howard Law Center is on the west campus near Rock Creek Park; the Divinity School is on a 22-acre site in northeast Washington; and there's also a 108-acre campus in suburban Beltsville, Maryland, and a campus in Silver Spring. Architecturally, the main campus is a blend of old and new, with numerous sculptures and murals created by Jacob Lawrence, Richard Hunt, Elizabeth Catlett, and the late Romare Bearden. The state-of-the-art, 82,000-square-foot Interdisciplinary Research Building opened in 2016.

All students must complete general education requirements, which vary by school or college but uniformly encompass 18 credits in science, social sciences, humanities, computer literacy, math, languages, and one Afro American studies course. Freshman seminars and various other special programs for first-year students are available in the undergraduate schools, such as communication, engineering, and arts and sciences. Seniors in arts and sciences must weather a comprehensive exam to graduate.

"Some courses are more rigorous than others. But overall this school is tough."

The school has excellent programs in business, computer science, and psychology, and it has intensified offerings in Africana and diaspora studies. Other intriguing academic options are jazz studies, architecture, engineering (especially electrical engineering), and accelerated programs for a B.S. on the way to a medical or dental degree. The most popular majors are in the areas of business/marketing, communication, physical sciences, and social sciences. The Howard University Science, Engineering, and Mathematics Program is a multidisciplinary program involving nine departments in the College of Engineering and Architecture and the College of Arts and Sciences designed to support underrepresented minorities pursuing degrees in STEM disciplines. Howard students can cross-register for courses at 13 other area schools, including (among others) American University, Catholic University, Georgetown, George Washington, and Corcoran School of the Arts and Design.

In general, students say that the workload at Howard is demanding. "Some courses are more rigorous than others. But overall this school is tough," says a junior. Another student adds, "Come to Howard ready to study." Twenty-eight percent of classes have fewer than 20 students. Most students agree that professors are ready and willing to help when asked, though academic advising is not Howard's strength. "Sometimes you may get professors who do not know how to break down anything," explains a psychology major. "Then it is your job to speak up and ask questions. You must ask questions because a closed mouth does not get fed!" Howard's prime D.C. location means internship, co-op, and service-learning opportunities with all manner of government organizations, nonprofits, and corporations are practically limitless. Qualified students can apply for the Junior Experiential Learning Program, which helps them secure internships and other practical work experiences. The program also assigns each participant an alumni career mentor with experience in their field of interest who can assist with networking and career advice. About 1 percent of students study abroad at one of the more than 200 institutions in 36 countries where Howard grants credit.

Ninety-one percent of Howard undergraduates hail from outside of the District of Columbia, and another 5 percent are international. African Americans comprise 89 percent of the student body, while Hispanics and Asian Americans each add 1 percent. Many come from decidedly middle-class backgrounds, although 60 percent of students qualify for Pell Grants. Howard seems to be a very cohesive community, but career-minded and highly motivated men and women fit in best, students say, and most are politically liberal. "It's a very competitive school, from grades to

(continued)

Average Debt: $ $
Phi Beta Kappa: Yes
Applicants: 15,163
Accepted: 49%
Enrolled: 23%
Grad in 6 Years: 60%
Returning Freshmen: 89%
Academics: ✐ ✐
Social: ☎ ☎ ☎
Q of L: ★ ★ ★
Admissions: (202) 806-2755
Email Address: admission@ howard.edu

Strong Programs:
Business/Marketing
Communication
Physical Sciences
Social Sciences
Afro American Studies
Nursing
Architecture
Computer Science

The Howard University Science, Engineering, and Mathematics Program is designed to support underrepresented minorities pursuing degrees in STEM disciplines.

fashion," says a junior. A range of renewable merit scholarships are available on a first-come, first-served basis to freshman applicants based on their standardized test scores and GPA, and these awards average $25,040 per year. Transfer students are eligible for a separate pool of merit scholarships, and Howard also awards a limited number of athletic scholarships. A deferred-payment plan allows families to pay each semester's tuition in three installments.

Fifty-seven percent of Howard's students are accommodated on campus, and facilities receive lukewarm reviews. "Housing at Howard is average in regards to availability, maintenance, and comfort," says one student. Freshmen get room assignments, while upperclassmen take their chances in a lottery. "It is quite difficult to get a room at times," says a sophomore economics major. Many students live off campus purely to avoid the mandatory meal plan.

Weekends bring an assortment of social happenings to campus, many of which take place in the student center. On-campus parties and sports events are always big draws, but the restaurants and clubs in the nearby U Street corridor, the bars of Georgetown and Adams Morgan, and the Verizon Center arena (home to the NBA's Wizards and the NHL's Capitals)—most accessible by public transit—also beckon.

"It's a very competitive school, from grades to fashion."

Fraternities and sororities do not have their own housing or dining facilities, and only 5 percent of the men and 6 percent of the women go Greek. Though small in numbers, one student says the Greeks are "an integral part of the university."

Athletics are also an important presence on campus, particularly Division I Bison basketball, soccer, football, and swimming and diving. Women's soccer and volleyball are recent conference champs. The highlight of the season is always the grudge match with Hampton University to decide which school is the "true HU." Howard's homecoming is one of the best annual events, along with various Greekfests, concerts, and talent shows that alumni, current students, and members of the community enjoy together. Intramurals and club sports attract plenty of students, especially flag football, soccer, basketball, and baseball.

Among America's historically black colleges and universities, Howard stands out as the standard-bearer, a longtime center of excellence and leadership. Its scholarship and collections of artworks, rare books, manuscripts, and photographs are a repository of the African American experience, informing students' intellectual and personal growth. And with an increased focus on providing opportunities for real-world experience and service, Howard is sure to continue its long tradition of turning out African American leaders in all areas of society.

If You Apply To ➤

Howard: Early action: Nov. 1. Regular decision and financial aid: Feb. 15. Housing: Jul. 28. Application fee: $45. No campus or alumni interviews. SATs or ACTs: required (SAT essay or ACT writing recommended). Subject Tests: optional. Letters of recommendation: recommended. Essay: required. Accepts the Common Application with supplement.

The College of Idaho

(formerly Albertson College), Caldwell, ID 83605

Got a map? You'll need a sharp eye to spot C of I, the *Fiske Guide*'s only liberal arts school between the Rocky Mountains and the West Coast. Innovative programs include the PEAK curriculum and leadership studies. More than two-thirds of students are from Idaho. Diverse alumni roster includes seven Rhodes scholars, three state governors, and four NFL players.

With an emphasis on education and experiential learning, The College of Idaho (formerly Albertson College), the state's oldest four-year university, offers students an opportunity to earn a solid liberal arts education through small classes in a small town. Outside class, the school's scenic environment allows sports and nature enthusiasts to explore freely before heading back into the classrooms. At C of I, you'll be exposed to "hard work, great opportunities, and a healthy amount of fun," says a freshman.

The college is in the small town of Caldwell, where the atmosphere is calm and serene. For those looking for a little excitement, the state capital of Boise is a short drive from campus. Also nearby are some of Idaho's most scenic locations, such as beautiful mountains, deserts, and white-water rivers. The school, originally a Presbyterian college, first planted roots in downtown Caldwell in 1891 and then moved to its present site in 1910, where its 22 buildings now inhabit 43 acres. A 60,000-square-foot, state-of-the-art library is currently under construction.

The school's academic schedule is composed of 12-week semesters, spring and fall, separated by a four-week winter session, during which students can assist professors with research, take an internship, volunteer, or travel abroad. The college's distinctive PEAK program combines a liberal arts education with specialization in multiple fields. Over four years, students earn a major and three minors spread across four knowledge "peaks"—the humanities, social sciences, natural sciences, and a professional field. Students choose among 26 majors and 58 minors. Freshmen go through a first-year program that involves a common reading book, a junior or senior mentor, a team of advisors, and a weeklong orientation that includes an off-campus overnight stay. First-year students demonstrating leadership potential are invited to a series of seminars to draw them into the leadership studies program, a business minor.

> "The professors are masters of their craft."

"The workload can be relaxed or intense depending upon a student's desire for success," says one senior. Business, psychology, health sciences, biology, and environmental studies are among the majors recommended by students, and pre-professional programs, such as premed, prenursing, and prelaw are also popular and strong. Fifty-eight percent of all classes at C of I have fewer than 20 students, and faculty are praised for their knowledge and accessibility. "The professors are masters of their craft," a senior says. The school's small size also allows students to skip the registration hassles that plague larger institutions. The college cooperates with the University of Idaho to offer a five-year course of study in engineering. Undergraduate research opportunities are available in all fields, and students present their findings at state and regional conferences. The Center for Experiential Learning coordinates out-of-classroom experiences, such as international education and service learning. For those who want to venture abroad (physically or mentally), the college offers several options, including attending a foreign university, traveling overseas during the summer and winter breaks, and taking international

Website: www.collegeofidaho.edu

Location: Suburban

Private

Total Enrollment: 1,027

Undergraduates: 1,007

Male/Female: 50/50

SAT Ranges: CR 460–590, M 470–600

ACT Ranges: 20–26

Financial Aid: 70%

Pell Grant: 29%

Expense: Pr $

Student Loans: 70%

Average Debt: $ $ $

Phi Beta Kappa: No

Applicants: 955

Accepted: 90%

Enrolled: 23%

Grad in 6 Years: 68%

Returning Freshmen: 82%

Academics: ✍ ✍ ✍

Social: ☎ ☎ ☎

Q of L: ★ ★ ★

Admissions: (208) 459-5305

Email Address: admission@collegeofidaho.edu

Strong Programs:
Business
Psychology
Health Sciences
Biology
Environmental Studies
Leadership Studies
Premed
Prelaw

studies on campus. Travel has really taken off, with study abroad opportunities in nearly 60 countries around the world.

"Everyone seems like some kind of repressed genius trying to figure out their own existence, pursue stability, and create something meaningful," muses one student. "There are also those who are more career-minded." Seventy percent of the students are from Idaho and 7 percent come from 46 foreign countries. Fourteen percent are Hispanic, 2 percent are African American, and Asian Americans add another 2 percent. Political issues receive plenty of attention on campus, and debates about the school's honor code are not uncommon among students. Of the most recent freshman class, 29 percent qualify for the Pell Grant. The college offers merit scholarships averaging $15,635, as well as roughly 200 athletic scholarships. Not surprisingly, some of those dollars are set aside for skiers.

Fifty-nine percent of students live on campus. "Residences are great, easy to decorate, and relatively big," says one student. Other options include five traditional residence halls, two suite-style apartment buildings, and more than 20 rental houses. For those looking to get their food on, C of I provides "a grill, deli, salad bar, pizza, and vegetarian options" that are "to die for," according to one student. "Campus safety gets a 10 out of 10," says a junior. "There is an officer on duty 24/7 even over breaks and summer vacation."

> "Intramurals are huge at our school."

Seventeen percent of men and 18 percent of women participate in the Greek system, which dominates campus social life. Annual social highlights include Winterfest, Spring Fling, and homecoming week. Games against rival Northwest Nazarene also attract attention. "We have a fantastic social scene. We host events almost nightly," a student reports. Undergraduates can choose among more than 50 student clubs, and the arts are strong. Students of all majors participate in a wide range of instrumental and choral music, theater, visual arts, and other activities, and the choir has performed at Carnegie Hall and other venues around the country. "Finals breakfasts" offer something for bleary-eyed students to look forward to during finals week; at midnight on Tuesday, faculty and staff cook breakfast for students. Outdoor enthusiasts relish the fact that the C of I campus is just minutes away from world-class opportunities for skiing, hiking, camping, fishing, and white-water rafting. The student-run Outdoor Program offers trips, classes, and equipment rentals. Caldwell, with 50,000 people, is not a great spot for college students, but students get involved by helping out the local school district. Nearby Boise is a popular destination for shopping, dining, and cultural events, including a symphony orchestra, art museum, zoo, professional baseball and hockey, and the must-see World Center for Birds of Prey. Many students hit the road during a weeklong break taken every six weeks.

More than a third of students play for one of the college's 20 varsity teams, which compete in NAIA Division II. The "Yotes" (translation: "We are the Coyotes") have earned individual national titles in skiing, snowboarding, cross-country, and track, as well as team national championships in baseball, basketball, and skiing. C of I is among national leaders in Academic All-Americans and NAIA Scholar-Athletes every year. For those who enjoy the game but might not make the team, there is an active intramurals program and the large Albertson Activities Center. "Intramurals are huge at our school," says a sophomore.

C of I has much to offer its Yotes. They enjoy a well-designed liberal arts education and personal academic attention on a campus striving to keep its offerings on the cutting edge. What's more, students here are encouraged to take an active role in the school's future. "The C of I community is absolutely incredible," cheers one happy junior.

Over four years, students earn a major and three minors spread across four knowledge "peaks."

The student-run Outdoor Program offers trips, classes, and equipment rentals for skiing, camping, and white-water rafting.

Overlaps

Boise State, University of Idaho, Idaho State, College of Western Idaho, Westminster, Earlham, Northwest Nazarene

University of Illinois at Urbana–Champaign

901 West Illinois Street, Urbana, IL 61801

Half a step behind Michigan and neck and neck with Wisconsin among top Midwestern public universities. U of I's strengths include business, communication, engineering, architecture, and the natural sciences. Three-quarters of the undergraduates hail from in state.

Like many of its Midwestern neighbors, the University of Illinois has its roots in agriculture. The Morrow Plots, the oldest experimental fields in the nation, still rest in the middle of campus—and when the wind blows the wrong way, students are not-so-subtly reminded of their heritage as a farm school. Like most big, public universities, U of I has a barn full of choices, and with a strong Greek system and 1,000 clubs, social activities are more than plentiful. Homecoming weekend was invented at the University of Illinois, and whether cheering for the Illini, pledging one of nearly 100 Greek houses, or celebrating Moms', Dads', or Siblings' Weekends, students here stir up a vibrant mix of school spirit and good times. This may look and feel like a laid-back Midwestern campus, but make no mistake: Illinois's stellar academics and learning communities are among the best of any of the country's public flagships.

Befitting the oldest land grant institution, the Illinois campus was built in farm country between the twin cities of Champaign and Urbana. The parklike campus was designed along a mile-long axis where trees and walkways separate stately white-columned Georgian structures made of brick. Physically challenged students tend to appreciate the campus because it is flat and well equipped with ramps and widened doorways. The impressive Illinois library system, the largest public university collection of its kind worldwide, makes it easier to keep up with classwork. A 250,000-square-foot computer science center and the physical education center are notable, as is the Technology Commercialization Laboratory, which provides faculty and students the opportunity to benefit from the commercialization of their research.

> **"[Professors] are truly invested in our success."**

Illinois has eight undergraduate colleges and more than 150 undergraduate programs; if nothing strikes your fancy, you may design your own. Requirements include composition, quantitative reasoning, cultural studies, natural sciences and technology, humanities and arts, social and behavioral sciences, and proficiency in a foreign language. Students may fulfill some of their gen-ed requirements by taking newly launched Grand Challenge Learning courses, interdisciplinary courses that explore three main "pathways," or real-world challenges facing today's society: Inequality and Cultural Understanding; Health and Wellness; and Sustainability, Energy, and the Environment. Partially because of its size, Illinois can afford to support excellent programs across the university, including the expansion of undergraduate minors campuswide. Engineering, business, communication, education, and the sciences—especially agriculture and veterinary medicine—get high marks

Website: www.illinois.edu
Location: Small City
Public
Total Enrollment: 41,279
Undergraduates: 31,552
Male/Female: 56/44
SAT Ranges: CR 570–680, M 700–790
ACT Ranges: 26–31
Financial Aid: 44%
Pell Grant: N/A
Expense: Pub $ $ $ $
Student Loans: 50%
Average Debt: $ $
Phi Beta Kappa: Yes
Applicants: 34,271
Accepted: 66%
Enrolled: 34%
Grad in 6 Years: 85%
Returning Freshmen: 93%
Academics: ✍ ✍ ✍ ✍ ✍
Social: ☎ ☎ ☎
Q of L: ★ ★ ★
Admissions: (217) 333-0302
Email Address: admissions@illinois.edu

Strong Programs:
Engineering
Business
Communication
Architecture
Natural Sciences
Social Sciences
Education

from students and lots of resources from administrators. Another notable program is the Beckman Institute for Advanced Science and Technology, an interdisciplinary center designed to bring biological and physical sciences together to pursue new insights in human and artificial intelligence.

Students may fulfill some of their gen-ed requirements by taking newly launched, interdisciplinary Grand Challenge Learning courses.

"Overall, classes are demanding," says a senior. A junior describes the academic climate as "engaging." Freshmen and sophomores, who register last, may have trouble getting into certain general education classes, such as foreign languages. Professors and academic advisors can usually help if classes you need are full, and students appreciate their dedication. Illinois has its share of stellar faculty, including Nobel laureates, National Medal of Science winners, and dozens of members of the National Academy of Sciences. "The quality of teaching is high with few exceptions," says a psychology major. "They are truly invested in our success," adds one senior. Even freshmen stuck in large lectures (750 seats) will find some personal attention in the associated discussion sections, led by graduate teaching assistants. (Although many students note that due to budget cutbacks, even these classes are getting larger.)

Freshman Discovery Courses, seminars limited to 19 students, enable first-year students to interact closely with full professors. The undergraduate honors program includes faculty mentoring, intensive seminars, advanced sections of regular courses, and access to special resources. About 6 percent of undergraduates travel and study abroad each year, roaming 60 countries around the globe, while the Ronald E. McNair Scholars Program helps fund independent, original research by minority, low-income, and first-generation college students who are completing bachelor's degrees.

"It is a big campus that likes to have a lot of fun."

Seventy-three percent of Illinois undergrads are homegrown and "the school is continuously getting more diverse," a sophomore says. Since Illinois stretches from the wealthy north suburbs of sophisticated Chicago to the unspoiled rural hills bordering Kentucky and encompasses classic farm towns as well as factory towns, students do come from multiple backgrounds and fit less into the stereotypical "Midwest" mold than one might think. African Americans make up 6 percent of the student body, Hispanics 10 percent, and Asian Americans 17 percent, while international students account for another 17 percent. Merit scholarships averaging $4,983 and 217 athletic awards are doled out annually. The Illinois Promise program provides financial aid for qualified in-state freshmen whose family income is at or below the federal poverty level.

U of I claims to have the largest Greek system anywhere.

Fifty percent of students live in U of I's co-ed and single-sex residence halls, which range in size from 51 to 660 beds and are arranged in quadrangle-like groups. Some dorms are quite a hike from classrooms, veterans warn. The university offers 10 themed living/learning communities, such as WIMSE (Women in Math, Science, and Engineering) and Innovation LLC (entrepreneurship and creativity), that combine in-hall courses with specialized cocurricular activities. Each residence hall is a mini-neighborhood, with dining halls, darkrooms, libraries, music practice rooms, computers, and lounges creating a sense of community. Chefs keep the food interesting, and campus security maintains a visible presence.

Illinois claims to have the largest Greek system anywhere, with nearly 100 chapters drawing 21 percent of the men and 27 percent of the women. Illinois attracts many socially oriented students who love parties and intramural sports, which may be why the Greek influence is particularly strong.

"The school is continuously getting more diverse."

Independents don't have to suffer boredom, though, as there are also more than 1,000 registered student clubs and organizations, ranging from the rugby team to ethnic advocacy groups. "It is a big campus that likes to have a lot of fun," a student says. Though drinking is prohibited in the dorms, the campus policies regarding alcohol are a "token gesture," a business major says. On most weekends, the Illini Union showcases bands, comedians, and hypnotists in its central café. The impressive Krannert Center for the Performing Arts, with four theaters and more than 350 annual performances, serves as the area's cultural center, while Assembly Hall hosts national touring acts, including popular musicians and musicals. Students get a discount at both facilities. For those who itch for the stimulation of a big city, the campus is just about equidistant from Chicago, Indianapolis, and St. Louis, and Mardi Gras makes for a good road trip in the dead of winter.

The Division I Illini compete in the Big Ten, and men's basketball and baseball have winning traditions. Other solid programs include women's soccer, softball, and tennis and men's wrestling and gymnastics. The intramural program is extensive, with available facilities that include 16 full-length basketball courts, five pools, 19 handball/racquetball courts, a skating rink, a baseball stadium, and the $5.1 million Atkins Tennis Center, with six indoor and eight outdoor courts. Eighty-five percent of the student body participates in recreational sports. Illinois has a strong athletic program for students with disabilities, including wheelchair basketball, which Illinois invented.

While the University of Illinois may seem mammoth to some students, don't be scared off by this giant institution. Academic and social opportunities are incredibly diverse, and classroom sizes, while growing, are supplemented by smaller group discussions. The breadth of the programs offered combined with an active campus life makes for a well-rounded college experience, students say. "We have a great reputation and it only grows stronger and stronger."

Illinois invented wheelchair basketball.

Overlaps

University of Iowa, University of Michigan, Northwestern, Purdue, University of Wisconsin–Madison, Washington University in St. Louis

If You Apply To > **Illinois:** Early action: Nov. 1. Regular decision: Dec. 1. Financial aid: Mar. 15. (Priority financial aid: Nov. 30.) Housing: May 15. Application fee: $50. Campus interviews: recommended, informational. No alumni interviews. SATs or ACTs: required. No Subject Tests. No letters of recommendation. Essay: required. Apply to particular schools or programs. Music, dance, and theater applicants must audition.

Illinois Institute of Technology

10 West 33rd Street, Chicago, IL 60616

Forget about cheerleaders, homecoming games, and other traditional trappings of college life. IIT is about learning about technology, getting a degree, and landing a job. IIT is all engineering with a little bit of architecture thrown in for good measure. If your goal is a technical job in the Chicago area, this is your place. Though private, IIT is relatively inexpensive.

Engineers unite at the Illinois Institute of Technology, where classwork and real-world experience promise to propel students to the top of their fields. After all, when you're engaged in comprehensive undergraduate research and able to take advantage of state-of-the-art labs, you're nearly guaranteed a high-paying job after graduation. IIT programs may be hard, says a junior, but the work "will pay off in the end" as students enter the workforce. Indeed, kids here tend to burn the midnight oil, but frequently escape to downtown Chicago for culture and much-deserved fun.

IIT's home is an urban, 120-acre campus designed by Ludwig Mies van der Rohe, the influential 20th-century architect who directed the architecture school for 20

Website: www.iit.edu
Location: City Center
Private
Total Enrollment: 6,575
Undergraduates: 2,789
Male/Female: 70/30
SAT Ranges: CR 520–650, M 630–730
ACT Ranges: 25–30

Incoming first-years receive Apple iPads; students work with professors to create new applications.

years. Founded in 1890, the school is just three miles south of Chicago's Loop, and one mile west of Lake Michigan. U.S. Cellular Field, home of the White Sox, is located directly across from the campus. Miesian-style buildings are adorned by trees and grassy open parks. The S.R. Crown Hall, home of IIT's College of Architecture, is considered a landmark.

Along with humanities and social science courses, students must fulfill general education requirements that include mathematics, computer science, natural science, and engineering; writing is emphasized across the curriculum. Computer literacy is demanded of all students. All freshmen take an introduction to the professions seminar, which includes discussion of innovation, ethics, teamwork, communication, and leadership. Incoming first-years also receive Apple iPads; students work with professors to create new applications in order to "enhance their educational experience." Multidisciplinary, group-based learning is big at IIT. Every student must complete two semester-long interprofession projects that sharpen real-world skills. The architecture curriculum emphasizes a team approach that mixes third- through fifth-year students under the supervision of a master professor.

Engineering is the most popular major, and it sets the tone at IIT. Every engineering department is outstanding. Architecture is also popular and highly regarded.

"Professors take an active role in their students' education."

"Architecture has a strong faculty," says one student, "and biomedical engineering is very new and well funded." Computer science and business round out the most popular majors, and the sciences, physics in particular, are first-rate. Guided by an academic reorganization, the physical sciences have been bolstered, grouped together with career-oriented fields such as psychology, political science, and computer information systems. Other academic options include majors in consumer research analytics, applied science, and dual admissions programs in pharmacy, optometry, and osteopathic medicine.

IIT's academic climate is pretty unforgiving, students say. Both the workload and the competition are fierce. "The courses are very difficult," says a junior. Fifty-four percent of the classes have fewer than 20 students, and professors always teach their own classes, while TAs are available for labs and extra help. "Professors take an active role in their students' education," states a biochemistry major.

In addition to meeting outside of class to go over problem sets or for career direction, IIT students and professors often work side by side on research projects. The College of Science awards several $5,000 scholarships to undergrads to perform research work under the supervision of faculty during the summer. Engineering students make use of sophisticated labs and have access to independent research labs in Chicago. Two dozen on-campus research centers, such as the Pritzker Institute of Biomedical Science and Engineering and the Wanger Institute for Sustainable Energy Research, provide additional opportunities. The five-year co-op program—another possibility for hands-on experience—helps lead IIT students into high-paying jobs after graduation. Study abroad programs send students to more than 50 nations around the globe, including France, Greece, Chile, and Singapore; 10 percent of IIT students—mostly architecture majors—participate.

"Students at IIT are nerds," reports a communication major, but "in a good way." In-state students account for 57 percent of the undergraduate population, and

"Students at IIT are nerds, in a good way."

27 percent hail from foreign countries, one of the highest rates of any U.S. college or university. African Americans constitute 6 percent of the student body, Hispanics 15 percent, and Asian Americans 13 percent. Students say International Fest is one of the year's most popular events, and IIT offers a multitude of cultural awareness workshops and sponsors "awareness" weeks and months on different

diversity-related topics. Merit scholarships averaging $22,595 are available, and 29 percent of incoming students are Pell-eligible.

As befits the school's urban location, a large chunk of students commute. The 64 percent of students who live in residence halls report that rooms are nice but can be difficult to get. The McCormick Student Village is popular, and students note that Fowler has the biggest rooms, but no air-conditioning; the rest of the dorms have AC. The newly implemented Women in Social Engagement learning community attracts female students who are interested in leadership, civic engagement, and social change. Some students live in apartments in the area or on Chicago's North Side; others inhabit one of the eight fraternity houses. The dining hall has several meal plans and a special vegetarian menu. Breakfast and lunch can also be eaten in the student union's cafeteria. Engineers and architects—notorious late-night studiers—have to hit the library early, since it closes at 10 p.m.

Twenty-seven percent of undergrads hail from foreign countries, one of the highest rates of any U.S. college or university.

IIT's six-block campus is contiguous to Chicago's "Gap" community, where historic but rundown homes are being rehabilitated to form one of the city's hottest new urban residential areas. Most students love exploring Chicago; the city skyline is beautiful and a veritable museum, with buildings designed by the likes of Frank Lloyd Wright, Louis Sullivan, and, of course, Mies van der Rohe. "Chicago provides educational opportunities, internship opportunities, and countless things to do," says one biomedical engineering major. Lake Michigan is within jogging distance, Chinatown is a walk away for lunch or dinner, and the school provides free shuttle bus service to downtown on weekends.

"This school is for people who want to make a lot of money after college."

Although students who stick around campus on weekends must work hard to find social events, "The social life at IIT has improved over my four years," says a senior. Fraternities claim 11 percent of the men and sororities attract 15 percent of the women, and many students say the social aspect of Greek life is a welcome addition to campus. The Union Board offers movies, concerts, and comedians, and the Bog brings in bands on Thursdays and Saturdays. Students can also plan events like a formal on the *Odyssey*, a sightseeing boat, or an outing to the Chicago Symphony.

In sports-crazy Chicago, IIT's Division III athletic teams (the Scarlet Hawks) are not much of a draw. Still, students praise the men's baseball, cross-country, and basketball teams, along with women's volleyball. Men's and women's soccer are competitive, as is men's swimming and diving, which has produced more than 20 All-Americans. Twelve recreational sports, ranging from water polo to Quidditch, are available, but students lament the fact that the facilities close at 5 p.m. on weekends.

Shipping off to Chi-town to take on the mammoth workload at IIT means hitting the books for hours upon hours and a fair share of all-nighters. But the payoff is undeniable. One student says bluntly, "This school is for people who want to make a lot of money after college." Indeed, students who take advantage of this small school's ever-improving engineering departments are likely to have their pick of careers after graduation. And with the innumerable diversions offered in the Windy City, students at IIT revel in the best of two worlds: a challenging academic climate and a great city in which to let off all that steam.

Overlaps

Carnegie Mellon, Loyola University Chicago, Marquette, Rensselaer Polytechnic, University of Illinois at Urbana–Champaign

If You Apply To > **IIT:** Rolling admissions: Aug. 1. (Priority deadline: Dec. 1.) Financial aid: Feb. 7. No application fee. Campus and alumni interviews: optional, informational. SATs or ACTs: required. Subject Tests: optional. Letters of recommendation: required. Essay: required. Accepts the Common Application. Applicants to architecture program may submit optional portfolio.

Illinois Wesleyan University

Bloomington, IL 61702

IWU is a small Midwestern college with an emphasis on creativity and the spirit of inquiry. The curriculum is basic liberal arts with additional divisions devoted to fine arts and nursing. An optional three-week term in May allows students to travel or explore an interest. IWU's reputation is limited outside Illinois and surrounding states.

Website: www.iwu.edu
Location: Small City
Private
Total Enrollment: 1,821
Undergraduates: 1,821
Male/Female: 44/56
SAT Ranges: CR 490–620, M 660–760
ACT Ranges: 25–30
Financial Aid: 99%
Pell Grant: 20%
Expense: Pr $ $
Student Loans: 69%
Average Debt: $ $ $ $
Phi Beta Kappa: Yes
Applicants: 3,744
Accepted: 62%
Enrolled: 19%
Grad in 6 Years: 81%
Returning Freshmen: 93%
Academics: ✐ ✐ ✐ ½
Social: ☎ ☎ ☎
Q of L: ★ ★ ★ ★
Admissions: (309) 556-3031
Email Address: iwuadmit@iwu.edu

Strong Programs:
Business Administration
Psychology
Biology
Accounting
English
Chemistry
Mathematics
Nursing

Illinois Wesleyan University has its sights set on a special breed of student—the kind who isn't afraid to be many things at once. Students here are very much encouraged to pursue multiple passions, and IWU is a mecca for students who have preprofessional interests, especially those with unusual pairings like management and music. "What makes Wesleyan really stand out is its care and attention for each student as an individual," says a junior. "You will feel at home here."

Founded in 1850, IWU occupies an 80-acre campus site in a north-side residential district of Bloomington. The heart of campus is the central quadrangle, and tree-lined walkways connect buildings that range in style from gray stone Gothic to ultramodern steel and glass. The College of Fine Arts houses the three separate schools of music, art, and drama; music is the standout, having turned out such talents as opera star Dawn Upshaw. Illinois Wesleyan's new main classroom building, State Farm Hall, includes state-of-the-art classrooms and research spaces.

Illinois Wesleyan's general education requirements emphasize critical thinking, imagination, intellectual independence, social awareness, and sensitivity to others. All first-year students must take a Gateway Colloquium, a topic-based, seminar-style class of 15 that stresses critical reading, writing, discussion, and analytical skills, and introduces students to the intellectual life

> **"Students can easily find themselves a mentor who is passionate about…the personal success of their students."**

of the university. Recent topics include Jesus at the Movies, American Inequality, Writing New Russia: From Gorbachev to Putin, and Did You Freely Choose This Class?. Among the top-notch programs in the College of Liberal Arts are biology, English, chemistry, and math, and some of the most popular majors include business administration, psychology, and accounting. The business administration department offers a Portfolio Management course, in which students buy and sell orders overseen by a client board composed of university trustees. A new design, technology, and entrepreneurship major allows students to flex their creative, technical, and management muscles as they practice all phases of successfully conceiving, developing, and bringing a product to market; administrators say the program aims to turn out "creative people who can actually implement their ideas."

"The classes inside of one's major are typically rigorous," says one student. Professors are lauded for their knowledge and accessibility. "Students can easily find themselves a mentor who is passionate about their teaching as well as about the personal success of their students," a senior says. In addition to the usual fall and spring semesters, IWU has an optional three-week May term. The courses during this term must have one of five features: curricular experimentation, nontraditional approaches to traditional subject matter, student/faculty collaboration, crossing of disciplinary boundaries, or experiential learning through travel, service, or internships. The majority of students take a May term class, and about half take off-campus travel courses. The university's study abroad program sends students packing to more than 70 countries, including England, Denmark, and Japan.

Research opportunities are also plentiful, and IWU hosts an annual student research conference that attracts people from all disciplines.

Undergraduates at IWU are mostly the homegrown variety, with 78 percent hailing from Illinois and 9 percent from outside the country. "Students at Illinois Wesleyan have a passion for what they do academically and professionally, and overall they are just good people," a senior says. Although IWU began admitting African American students in 1867, the campus is still overwhelmingly white. African Americans account for 4 percent of the student body, Hispanics 7 percent, and Asian Americans 4 percent. A multicultural task force has been working to address the issue of diversity. Students here are socially conscious and active in groups like Circle K, the Alpha Phi Omega service fraternity, and Habitat for Humanity. Merit scholarships averaging $16,936 are available to qualified students; there are no athletic scholarships.

A new design, technology, and entrepreneurship major allows students to flex their creative, technical, and management muscles.

Housing is guaranteed for four years, and 70 percent of the students live in the dorms, which receive high marks from residents. "There are almost no maintenance issues, but when there are, the Physical Plant department is quick to respond," according to one theater design and technology major. Students must be 21 to live off campus. "The food is considerably diverse," says a philosophy major. Most students say campus security is good, though common sense must be exercised. The university has placed great emphasis on educating students about sexual harassment and violence through a variety of programs.

"IWU allows you to become who you want to be, but only if you let it."

Twenty-eight percent of the men and 32 percent of the women go Greek, and fraternities and sororities are the focus of IWU's social life. Non-Greeks also use the system for social life, but if partying isn't your thing, there are plenty of other options. "There are opportunities to socialize in the residence halls," says a senior, "and many other organizations provide a social outlet for students. The majority of social activity takes place either on campus or directly off campus in a house or apartment." The alcohol policy allows drinking on campus for those of legal age, and students admit that the policies don't always stop underage drinkers. "Lots of students drink," one junior says. Each fall during homecoming, Greeks and dorm dwellers compete in the Titan Games to get appropriately psyched. Other annual festivities include the Far Left Carnival, the Gospel Festival, and Earthapalooza (on Earth Day). The Student Senate also sponsors guest speakers; Spike Lee, Bonnie Blair, and the late Maya Angelou have addressed audiences in recent years.

Each fall during homecoming, Greeks and dorm dwellers compete in the Titan Games to get appropriately psyched.

Thanks to the proximity of Illinois State University in nearby Normal, IWU offers more than the typical small college town atmosphere. The total area's student population of about 25,000 helps to offer students at tiny IWU "the best of both worlds," says a senior. An accounting major says, "Bloomington has the highest restaurant-per-capita ratio of any community. The students love this." The best road trips are to Peoria or Urbana–Champaign (home of the University of Illinois) or to Chicago or St. Louis, each two and a half hours away.

The IWU Titans compete in the Division III College Conference of Illinois and Wisconsin. Baseball and football are well and good, but Titans basketball really gets students going. In 2016 the women's track and field team claimed the national championship title, and the softball team brought home its third straight regular season conference championship. The Fort Natatorium houses a whopping 14-lane swimming pool, and the swim team has had its share of stars. Forty percent of IWU men and 10 percent of women participate in intramural sports.

One of the Midwest's better-kept secrets, Illinois Wesleyan is at once cozy and diverse, loaded with opportunities for ambitious students with traditional or offbeat interests. As one junior advises, "The school provides a multitude of paths down which one can travel, and it is up to the student to decide which path to take. IWU allows you to become who you want to be, but only if you let it."

Overlaps

University of Illinois at Urbana–Champaign, Washington University in St. Louis, Northwestern, Notre Dame, Augustana, University of Illinois at Chicago, University of Chicago, DePaul

Indiana University

300 North Jordan Avenue, Bloomington, IN 47405

Though men's basketball has traditionally been IU's most famous program, it may not be its best. That distinction could easily go to the world-renowned music school or to the distinguished foreign language program. IU enrolls three times as many out-of-staters as the University of Illinois. Bloomington is a great college town, and most students live off campus after freshman year.

Website: www.iub.edu
Location: Small City
Public
Total Enrollment: 37,750
Undergraduates: 31,559
Male/Female: 50/50
SAT Ranges: CR 520–630, M 540–660
ACT Ranges: 24–30
Financial Aid: 78%
Pell Grant: N/A
Expense: Pub $ $
Student Loans: 48%
Average Debt: $ $ $
Phi Beta Kappa: Yes
Applicants: 34,483
Accepted: 78%
Enrolled: 23%
Grad in 6 Years: 77%
Returning Freshmen: 89%
Academics: ✍ ✍ ✍ ✍
Social: ☎ ☎ ☎ ☎
Q of L: ★ ★ ★ ★
Admissions: (812) 855-0661
Email Address: iuadmit@ indiana.edu

Strong Programs:
Finance
Management
Accounting
Economics
Music
Foreign Languages

With more than 31,000 undergraduates on its enormous campus, Indiana University is the prototype of the large Midwestern school. With strong academics, a thriving social scene, and some of the best sports teams around, this top-notch public institution is a testament to Hoosier determination.

Located in southern Indiana's gently rolling hills, the 1,900-acre campus boasts architecture from Italianate brick to collegiate Gothic limestone to the distinctive style of world-famous architect I. M. Pei. Other unique campus features include fountains, gargoyles, an arboretum of more than 450 trees and shrubs surrounding two reflecting pools, a limestone gazebo, and the Jordan River, a pretty creek that runs alongside a shaded path. A new Student Activities and Events Center recently opened, and construction is under way on a new Arts and Sciences Building.

Indiana prides itself on its liberal arts education—freshmen are admitted not to preprofessional schools but to the "university division." Majors are declared after one or two years, and the university discourages premature specialization. General education requirements vary from school to school but usually include math, science, arts and humanities, social and behavioral sciences, English and writing, culture, and a foreign language.

IU's schools and colleges offer many majors and minors, cross-disciplinary study, an individually designed curriculum, and intense honors and research programs. The highly touted business school, with its respected global studies component, is among the most popular on campus. Overall, the finance, management, accounting, and economics majors enroll the most students. The internationally known Kinsey Institute for the Study of Human Sexual Behavior is housed on IU's campus, and the music school is tops in its field, setting the, ahem, tone for much of the campus. The Media School gives students the language, communication, research, and technological skills they need to excel in media-related careers, while the Environmental Science Joint Program is an undergraduate degree program that specifically considers the environment as a scientific entity. The new School of Global and International Studies brings together language, area studies, and international studies programs to prepare students in the global competencies of the 21st century. For those seeking study abroad opportunities, the university offers more than 300 programs in 52 countries and 18 languages, for students in nearly every field of study. A major in

"With 4,000 different courses per semester, a variety of intensity levels exist."

intelligent systems engineering, with concentrations in computer engineering and cyberphysical systems, is the newest academic offering.

Students describe the academic climate as rigorous but not cutthroat. "With 4,000 different courses per semester, a variety of intensity levels exist," says a marketing major. "There is a balance with room for both competitive overachievers and laid-back, carefree individuals." Students say they regularly share ideas with each other, and group projects are commonplace. Faculty members bring their research results directly to students, and some profs bring undergrads into their labs to assist with ongoing projects. "The professors here are remarkable," says an art history/telecommunications major. As for advising, many students seem surprised by the personal attention they receive at such a large university, and they soon learn that many available resources are helpful to those students who seek them out.

Sixty percent of IU undergraduates are from in state, and 11 percent are international, coming from more than 100 countries. Out-of-staters face much more rigorous minimum admissions standards, including rank in the top quarter of their high school class and SAT scores in the 1050 to 1100 range. African Americans comprise 4 percent of the student body, Hispanics 5 percent, and Asian Americans 4 percent. By and large, students do not seem to dwell on political or social issues. And while IU does not guarantee to meet the full demonstrated need of every student, it does admit on a need-blind basis. Merit scholarships are awarded to qualified students and average $5,548 annually; applicants must be in the top 10 percent of their graduating class and have a combined SAT score of 1200. More than 300 athletic scholarships are available for qualified jocks. The Finish in Four program waives any increases in tuition and fees for juniors and seniors who are on track to complete their degrees in four years.

"There is no trouble getting a room, but preference of dorm may be harder."

Housing is guaranteed to all incoming freshmen and ranges from Gothic quads (co-ed by building) to 13-floor high-rises (co-ed by floor or unit, except for one all-women's dorm). Halls are considered "clean and comfortable." One student explains the housing situation this way: "All dorms have laundry facilities, cafeterias, computer clusters, and undergraduate advisors, and some even have special amenities like language-speaking floors." A junior adds, "There is no trouble getting a room, but preference of dorm may be harder." Academic floors are popular with more serious students who are not interested in intense nightlife. Some dining halls have been modernized to resemble mall food courts with outlets offering international and healthful menus sprinkled among the fast-food options. Alcohol is prohibited in the dorms, which may help explain why 65 percent of the student body lives off campus. Most off-campus residents choose apartments or small houses with big front porches within walking distance of the campus or the IU bus system. A number of student-driven initiatives, including Culture of Care, MARS (Men Against Rape and Sexual Assault), and Safe Sisters, are working to promote student wellness and safety on campus.

Although campus organizations host numerous events, the most active on-campus groups, in terms of social life, seem to be the Greeks, which attract 21 percent of the men and 19 percent of the women. Some complain of a polarized atmosphere. "There is a large separation between the Greek community and the rest of the student body," says a senior. With concerts, ballets, recitals, and festivals right on campus, students are not lacking for things to keep them busy. The IU student union is the largest in the nation, and the range of extracurricular organizations is also impressive. The Little 500 bike race, which was modeled after the Indianapolis 500, is one of the most highly attended events of the year. Every fall there is a

"There is a large separation between the Greek community and the rest of the student body."

(continued)

Education
Environmental Science

The university offers more than 300 study abroad programs in 52 countries and 18 languages.

The Finish in Four program waives increases in tuition and fees for juniors and seniors who are on track to complete their degrees in four years.

36-hour Dance Marathon to raise money for Riley's Children's Hospital in Indianapolis. The Office of Diversity Programs, Committee on Multicultural Understanding, and Students Organized Against Racism are a few more ways students can make a difference on campus.

Students say Bloomington is a great college town. There are many excellent bars, shops, and restaurants, including one of the few Tibetan restaurants in the country. Locally, the area offers some impressive rock quarries (often used as illegal but refreshing swimming pools), miles of public forests, and three nearby lakes. Spelunkers will find heaven down below in the many nearby caves. Chicago, Cincinnati, Indianapolis, St. Louis, and even New Orleans are popular road trips.

Although dozens of intramural and club sports are available, recreational sports pale in comparison with Division I varsity athletics here; basketball is an established religion in the state of Indiana. Students and faculty are all eligible for tickets, but they've got to get requests in early—and even those lucky enough to get tickets don't count on going to more than a quarter of home games. In recent years, the Hoosiers men's basketball, baseball, and cross-country and women's swimming and diving teams have claimed Big Ten championships, and even the football team draws red-and-white crowds. Purdue is IU's traditional athletic rival, and teams play for the Old Oaken Bucket, found on a farm in southern Indiana in 1925 and alleged to have been used during the Civil War.

Along with IU's reputation as a basketball powerhouse, it also provides committed students with stellar programs ranging from foreign languages to music, and a social scene that's hard to beat. For those not frightened away by throngs of classmates, Indiana University may be a great fit.

If You Apply To ➢ **Indiana:** Early action: Nov. 1. Regular decision: Feb. 1. Financial aid: Mar. 10. Housing: May 1. Application fee: $60. Campus and alumni interviews: optional, evaluative. SATs or ACTs: required. Subject Tests: recommended. Letters of recommendation: optional. Essay: required. Accepts the Common Application.

International Universities

Do you thrive on new experiences? Like to meet new people? Want to learn about different cultures? You can do all that at a college or university in the United States, but if you really want to jump in with both feet, think about attending a school in a foreign country. This section highlights the opportunities available in Canada, Great Britain, and Ireland, by far the most common destinations outside the United States for degree-seeking undergraduates.

The absence of a language barrier is the most obvious reason why these three countries are the preferred destinations for study abroad. Plenty of students do a junior year abroad where the language is Spanish or Swahili, but only a handful can realistically expect to earn an entire degree in a foreign tongue. A growing number of European universities are offering instruction in English, not only to Americans but to students from throughout the world. A smattering of American universities do exist in places ranging from Paris to Cairo, but most are small and the majority of their enrollment is students from other countries seeking an American-style education. If you're willing to venture halfway around the world, Australia is an English-speaking destination that might be worth a look for its combination of beautiful scenery, quality universities, and, at least by American standards, reasonable tuition.

Look for coverage of Australian institutions in a future edition of the *Fiske Guide*. The following sections examine Canada, Britain, and Ireland in more detail, followed by full-length articles on selected institutions.

Canadian Universities

Horace Greeley told ambitious young men of his generation to "go West." Today his admonition to young men and women seeking a quality college education at a relatively modest cost would probably be to "go North"—to Canada. A growing number of American students are discovering the educational riches that lie just above their northern border in this huge land of 35 million people that is known for its rugged mountains, bicultural politics, spirited ice hockey, and cold ale. What's drawing them is easy to discern.

The top Canadian universities are the academic equals of most flagship public universities and many leading privates in the United States. Canadian campuses and the cities in which they are located are safe places and, unless one opts for a French course of study, there are no language and few cultural barriers. Canadian schools are strong on international exchange programs, and their degrees carry weight with U.S. graduate schools.

Canada has 90 institutions of higher learning, ranging from internationally recognized research universities to the small undergraduate teaching institutions in the country's more rural areas. Most of the larger universities are located in highly urban centers, but some are situated in smaller towns where they dominate the life of the community. Most are almost literally next door to the United States, within 100 miles of the Canada–U.S. border. In this guide, we feature four of Canada's strongest universities: the University of British Columbia, McGill University, Queen's University, and the University of Toronto.

Institutions of higher learning in Canada were established from the earliest days of French settlement in the mid-17th century, making them some of the oldest in North America. The precursors to the public universities in Canada were the small, elite, denominational colleges that sprang up in Quebec, in the Maritimes, and later in Ontario. A few private denominational colleges and universities still exist in Canada, but most have been subsumed into affiliations or associations with the larger universities. Education in Canada, including university education, became the exclusive jurisdiction of provincial governments.

One of the key differences between Canadian and U.S. universities is that Canadian universities (and this is what they are, not "colleges") are primarily funded from public monies. Calculating the cost for an American to attend a Canadian university can be tricky. For one thing, the exchange rate between the U.S. and Canadian dollar fluctuates (at this writing, it favors the U.S. dollar). Moreover, tuition and fee rates vary by field of study. The cost of pricey majors such as medicine and other hard sciences can easily be double or triple that of less expensive ones such as social work or theology. Canadian citizens, of course, pay far less than visitors from south of the border. Depending on the factors just described, tuition and fees at the four universities included in the *Fiske Guide* range from less than US $15,000 to more than US $70,000. For many U.S. students, education at one of the top Canadian universities is comparable to out-of-state rates at a flagship public university in the States.

Federal and provincial loans and grants that are readily available to Canadian students are generally not available to students from the United States and other countries. However, the majority of universities with competitive admissions, particularly those featured in the *Fiske Guide*, offer merit-based awards and scholarships to students of all nationalities. American students who attend leading Canadian schools can apply their U.S. student assistance funds, including federal Direct Loans and Pell Grants.

The requirements for obtaining a degree are set by each institution, as are the admissions requirements and prerequisites. Unlike the United States, Canada does not offer nor require its own students to take a Canadian college entrance test. Some Canadian universities admitting students from the United States will require SAT or ACT scores along with high school marks from academic subjects in the last two or three years of high school. In general, top universities are about as selective as their American counterparts.

Application fees vary by institution, as do deadlines. Canadian universities are aware of the May 1 deadline operative in the United States, and they try to accommodate. Applications to the University of Toronto and Queen's University in Ontario are handled centrally through the Ontario Universities' Application Service. McGill handles applications directly and accepts both Web-based and paper applications. British Columbia has its own application; it can be mailed, but students are encouraged to apply online. Canadian universities differ widely in the amount of credit and/or advanced standing they offer for Advanced Placement examinations or International Baccalaureate Higher Level examinations.

The following admissions requirements apply to applicants from an American school system. The University of British Columbia bases admissions decisions on the average of eight full-year academic courses over the last two years of high school, and there are also specific program requirements for students entering the science-based faculties. SAT test results are not required, but if students submit them, the results can be helpful in the evaluation process. McGill bases its assessment of American high school graduates on the overall record of marks in academic subjects during the final three years of high school, class standing, and results obtained in SAT I and SAT II and/or ACT tests. Queen's wants applicants with a minimum score of 1200 on SAT I (with at least 580 in Critical Reading and 520 in Mathematics) and looks at class rank. There are also program-specific requirements for programs where mathematics and/or biology, chemistry, and physics are a requirement. Toronto's Arts and Science faculties want a high grade point average and good scores on the SAT I and on three SAT II subject tests. ACT and CEEB Advanced Placement Examination scores are also considered.

It is hard to beat Canadian universities for the quality of student life. Although many students commute, most of the universities in Canada offer on-campus housing; some even guarantee campus housing for first-year students. Universities offer active intramural and intercollegiate sports programs for both men and women, and the usual student clubs, newspapers, and radio stations provide students with opportunities to get involved and develop friendships. As in the United States, student-run organizations are active participants in university life, with leaders serving on university committees and lobbying on issues ranging from creating more bicycle paths to keeping tuition low. Few Canadian campuses are troubled by issues of student safety or rowdiness. In the larger urban centers, Canadian campuses reflect the rich diversity of Canada's cultural mosaic, and most encourage their students to gain international experience by spending a term or a full year abroad.

Americans wondering about the currency of a Canadian degree in the United States should be reassured that top American and multinational companies—the likes of Chase, IBM, Microsoft, and Nortel—actively recruit on Canadian campuses, as do American graduate schools. According to the Institute of International Education in New York, more than 10,000 Canadians are currently enrolled in graduate schools in the United States.

The one thing that is different for U.S. and other international students intending to study in Canada is that they will have to obtain a Student Authorization, equivalent to a visa, from Canadian immigration authorities, as well as a passport. Getting a Student Authorization is fairly straightforward for American citizens, but this slight bureaucratic hurdle is a reminder that Canada, for all of its similarities in language and culture with the United States, is still another country.

The Association of Universities and Colleges of Canada has a website at www.aucc.ca. Another source of information is the website of the Canadian Embassy in Washington, D.C., at http://www.can-am.gc.ca/washington/index.aspx?/ang=eng&lang=eng.

Canadian universities are currently playing host to about 1,600 American students on their campuses and, as a result of funding cutbacks and internationalization policies in the early 1990s, they have become increasingly active in recruiting students from south of the border. This is but one more reason why it makes sense for more young Americans to check out the "Canadian option." Canada, eh?

University of British Columbia

Vancouver, British Columbia V6T IZI CAN

Natural beauty is the first thing that draws Americans to Vancouver—and Canada's premier western university. A similar scale to places like University of Washington but with two major differences—no big-time sports to unite the campus and limited dorm life. The university is active in recruiting overseas, which creates an international ambience.

Website: www.ubc.ca
Location: City Outskirts
Public
Total Enrollment: 43,755
Undergraduates: 34,075

What do three prime ministers of Canada, three provincial premiers, an astronaut, a world-renowned opera singer, and two Nobel Prize winners have in common? They are all graduates of the University of British Columbia. Founded in 1908, UBC offers students hundreds of solid programs, such as business, science, engineering, the social sciences, and fine arts, as well as ready access to beaches and mountains and a diploma with instant name recognition. Though the massive campus can sometimes feel isolating, students are nevertheless happy to be here in such illustrious company.

Located just 25 minutes from downtown Vancouver, UBC's striking Point Grey campus covers a peninsula that borders the Pacific Ocean and is bounded by an old-growth forest. Mountains—perfect for skiing—loom in the distance. Architectural styles are a mix of Gothic and modern, and students can enjoy a leisurely stroll through the university's botanical gardens. Other notable campus facilities include the Kaiser Building (the central hub of engineering), the Barber Learning Centre, and the Mitchell Thunderbird Sports Arena. The university also has a smaller campus—UBC Okanagan—located in Kelowna, in the Okanagan Valley. Newer facilities include the student union, alumni center, and student life center.

Strong programs include psychology, biology, English, computer science, and political science. Asian studies is highly regarded, and music majors benefit from the Chan Centre for the Performing Arts. Microbiology, international relations, economics, and business administration are popular too. The administration concedes

> **"The professors are extremely intelligent people who are truly dedicated to their discipline."**

that some home economics and agricultural science courses could be strengthened, and one student grumbles about his 8 a.m. philosophy lecture: "Who can focus on the big questions at that time of the morning?" Additional programs include majors in applied animal biology, applied plant and soil sciences, geographical biogeosciences, and zoology.

Freshmen benefit from a wide array of first-year programs, including Imagine UBC and Create UBC Okanagan, a first-day orientation. Arts One and the Coordinated Arts programs offer enriched, integrated approaches to broad interdisciplinary themes in arts and humanities. Qualified students can take advantage of Science One, featuring team-taught courses in biology, chemistry, math, and physics. The UBC study abroad program has 176 institutional partners in 38 countries, and co-op programs in engineering, science, arts, commerce, and forestry give students an opportunity to earn while they learn. In addition, honors and double-honors programs are available to superbrains and budding geniuses. Students in the School of Human Kinetics choose from one of three majors at the end of their second year; choices include kinesiology and health science, physical and health education, and interdisciplinary studies in human kinetics. Additionally, applicants to undergrad programs following the U.S. curriculum are required to submit test scores for the SAT or ACT with writing.

The academic climate is exactly what you would expect from a university of UBC's international stature. "Courses can be hard," says one student, "but success is based on your interest and willingness to learn." Most classes have fewer than 50 students, while larger lectures are supplemented with smaller labs and discussion groups. Overall, the faculty receives good marks. "The professors are extremely intelligent people who are truly dedicated to their discipline," says a junior. Academic advising is a mixed bag, with some students complaining that finding a knowledgeable advisor can be time-consuming.

With 34,000 undergraduates attending the Vancouver campus, it's no surprise that UBC's student population is a melting pot—22 percent come from outside Canada. "There is a huge diversity here that many smaller schools may lack," says a sophomore. The typical UBC student is bright, hardworking, and gregarious. A history major divides his classmates into two categories: commuters and "those who live on campus and enjoy the community spirit." Minorities are well represented (Asians make up the largest contingency), and the university encourages diversity through a series of special programs and active recruiting. Hot political issues

(continued)

Male/Female: 45/55
SAT Ranges: 1700 or above (combined)
ACT Ranges: 26 or above
Financial Aid: N/A
Pell Grant: N/A
Expense: Pub $
Student Loans: N/A
Average Debt: N/A
Phi Beta Kappa: No
Applicants: 30,939
Accepted: 68%
Enrolled: 51%
Grad in 6 Years: 76%
Returning Freshmen: 93%
Academics: ✍ ✍ ✍ ✍ ½
Social: ☎ ☎
Q of L: ★ ★ ★ ★
Admissions: (604) 822-8999
Email Address: N/A

Strong Programs:
Psychology
Biology
English
Computer Science
Political Science
Asian Studies
International Relations
Business Administration

Arts One and the Coordinated Arts programs offer enriched, integrated approaches to broad interdisciplinary themes in arts and humanities.

include LGBTQ rights, abortion, and global genocide. UBC offers merit scholarships to qualified students and athletic scholarships in many varsity sports.

Theme houses, which offer like-minded students the opportunity to mingle, include three international houses.

Nearly one-third of students currently live on campus. A major expansion of on-campus housing is under way, and UBC now guarantees a spot to all incoming first-time, first-year students. On-campus options include co-ed complexes (primarily for freshmen), university apartments, and family units for upperclassmen. Theme houses, which offer like-minded students the opportunity to mingle, include three international houses—Korea University/UBC House, Tec de Monterrey/UBC House, and Ritsumeiken House. "Housing is awesome," chirps one senior. Those seeking off-campus accommodations must contend with Vancouver's pricey rental market. Hungry students will find a wide variety of meal options, including "Japanese, Lebanese, Italian, and vegetarian" plates, according to one student.

On such a large campus, isolation is a real threat. "You need to get in touch with other students quickly when you get here or you could feel lost on such a big campus," says a freshman. A history major offers another point of view, "One of the biggest complaints is that UBC is too big. I totally disagree with this. I think that the school's biggest strength is its size; there are so many opportunities here." Social life happens mostly on campus but largely "depends on the crowd you hang with," according to one student.

"There is a huge diversity here that many smaller schools may lack."

For partying types, there are the requisite bashes, courtesy of UBC's small but active Greek scene—one of the few places where underage drinkers may sneak a sip of booze. Alternatives include university-sponsored events, such as movies and guest speakers. Popular campus events include Storm the Wall, long-boat racing, and the Arts County Fair.

Vancouver offers students countless opportunities, though one health science major says, "It isn't a college town. It is a well-developed semicosmopolitan city." Another adds, "Vancouver is one of the most livable cities in the world and UBC is located in the nicest, most beautiful part—it's not too hard to imagine what a pleasure it is to go to school with that surrounding you." Beautiful weather draws students outdoors and to nearby beaches and mountains for in-line skating, snowboarding, and swimming. Fifteen recreational sports leagues and 23 intramural events are a huge draw for students; popular sports include soccer, basketball, hockey, volleyball, and skiing. UBC has 37 varsity teams in 14 sports and those teams have brought home more than 120 championships—the most of any institution in Canada.

"If you don't get involved in the nonacademics, you'll graduate with only half an education. Academics aren't everything," counsels a junior. Indeed, spending four years at this mammoth university can be isolating for the shy student. But for those willing to take control of their social lives, UBC offers an impressive academic milieu.

Overlaps

University of Toronto, McGill, University of Washington, University of Victoria, Simon Fraser, UC–Berkeley, University of Alberta

If You Apply To ➤ **British Columbia:** Regular decision: Jan. 15. Housing: May 1. Application fee: $112. No campus or alumni interviews. SATs or ACTs (with writing): required for those following the U.S. curriculum. Subject Tests: optional. Letters of recommendation: optional. Essay: required. Apply to specific program. Requirements vary by program.

McGill University

Montreal, Quebec H3A 0C8 CAN

The Canadian university best known south of the border. Though instruction is in English, McGill is located in French-speaking Montreal, a world-class city that has it all. Individualism is encouraged, and there's a strong international flavor. Just over 10 percent of students live in university housing, and anyone coming here will be on their own for housing after freshman year.

With such strong preprofessional programs and a diverse student body, it's easy to see why enterprising men and women from around the world flock to McGill University. But beware: this is not a cookie-cutter school, and fitting in actually seems to be discouraged. "McGill is a university where people are allowed to become individuals," a senior says. "Difference and creativity are celebrated here."

Montreal's climate alternates between hot summers and freezing winters. A junior describes McGill's 88-acre main campus as "an oasis in the heart of the city." Located in downtown Montreal amidst the hustle and bustle, the campus provides students with ample green space and a welcome respite from the decidedly urban atmosphere of the city. Campus buildings range from "Gothic-like" structures with vines growing up the sides to more modern structures. Trees and greenery dot the campus landscape, and the sprawling recreation trails of Mount Royal rise to its immediate north. Newer construction includes a $71 million life sciences complex that serves as the centerpiece of the largest research complex of its

> **"Difference and creativity are celebrated here."**

kind in Eastern Canada and the Montreal Neurological Institute. The Schulich School of Music offers an ultra-modern symphony and multimedia hall that functions as a recording studio, performance venue, and research studio. A short drive west of downtown, the Macdonald Campus occupies 1,600 acres of woods and fields on the shores of Lac St-Louis, providing unique opportunities for fieldwork and research.

Though the most popular majors are psychology, political science, commerce, and education, there is no denying that the university's strengths lie in preprofessional programs such as medicine, law, and engineering. The sciences receive uniform praise, as does the School of Environment. For those who want to escape Montreal's brutal winters, there are internships; field studies in Barbados, Africa, and the Smithsonian Tropical Research Institute in Panama; exchange programs with more than 500 partner universities around the world; and study abroad options via the Canadian University Study Abroad Program.

To fulfill the university's general education requirements, students must first choose which discipline (or faculty) to enter. A senior says, "It is important to consider the university on the basis of which faculty you would be interested in, because they vary greatly and operate almost as independent units." On average, students must earn 120 credits to graduate with a four-year degree. Freshmen must accumulate six to 12 credits in three of four disciplines, including languages, math and science, social sciences, and humanities, and declare a major before their sophomore year. Upon entering their major, students have a menu of course options that includes honors programs and double majors. A double-degree interdisciplinary program allows students to combine a bachelor of arts program with one in the sciences. Several programs help freshmen with the transition to college, and some are tailored to international students, which includes those from the United States.

Regardless of the major, students can expect classes to be demanding. "McGill has a very stressful and competitive atmosphere," a finance major says. Classes tend

Website: www.mcgill.ca
Location: City Center
Public
Total Enrollment: 30,163
Undergraduates: 22,311
Male/Female: 43/57
SAT Ranges: 1180 or above (combined)
ACT Ranges: 26 or above
Financial Aid: 18%
Pell Grant: N/A
Expense: Pub $
Student Loans: N/A
Average Debt: N/A
Phi Beta Kappa: No
Applicants: 41,970
Accepted: 46%
Enrolled: 46%
Grad in 6 Years: 86%
Returning Freshmen: 93%
Academics: ✐ ✐ ✐ ✐ ½
Social: ☎ ☎ ☎ ☎
Q of L: ★ ★ ★ ★
Admissions: (514) 398-7878
Email Address:

Strong Programs:
Psychology
Political Science
Commerce
Education
Medicine
Law
Engineering

to be large—especially for freshmen, who have more than 100 students in two-thirds of their classes—and students must be willing to seek out professors and advisors. "The quality of teaching is generally above average," a student says. "Many of the professors are kind, intelligent, and devoted to their students." Students grumble that academic advising is a bureaucratic tangle. "There is way too much red tape and dealing with the administration can be horrible," says one senior.

Forty-six percent of undergraduates are Quebecers (or Québécois, as Francophones would say), and 29 percent are international, representing more than 140 countries. Indeed, McGill students are a diverse lot, and the only common thread among them seems to be their fierce independence. A geography major says McGill students are "hardworking, driven, very intellectual, and research-oriented." Environmental issues are a big concern, and students report that political and social concerns receive ample attention on campus. Qualified students are eligible for merit scholarships, but there are no awards for athletes. There is also a work-study program for those in need of financial assistance.

The university's traditional and alternative residence halls house 13 percent of undergrads in dorms, apartments, and shared facilities houses. Dorms run the gamut, but one recent acquisition is, according to a senior, a "four-star hotel, turned into a six-star dorm." Party animals will feel free to crank up the stereo in Molson or McConnell, while bookworms might be better suited for Gardener. Douglas denizens enjoy their hall's quaint charm, and women who want to skip the co-ed scene can find a room in Royal Victoria College, an all-female dorm. Off-campus apartments are a popular alternative for upperclassmen, who take advantage of Montreal's clean, affordable housing. "The dining facilities are good," says a sophomore. Despite its urban location, the McGill campus is safe and security is considered more than adequate. "There are student organizations like 'Walksafe' and 'Drivesafe' that will walk or drive students to their residences at night regardless of where they are or where they are going," reports one student.

"McGill students are very sociable and love to party!" says one student. Though there are "considerable on-campus social activities, with many clubs and associations," many students venture off campus into Montreal for fun and adventure. "A cultural epicenter, Montreal is home to some of the world's best museums, galleries, restaurants, shops, and music," a senior says. "There are always free concerts and festivals all over the city throughout the year." Drinking is a popular pastime, but underage drinkers are few and far between since the legal age in Quebec is 18. "McGill treats its students as mature, educated adults and offers them the decision to choose whether or not to drink. Their decision is respected," reports a senior English major. Greek organizations sign up about 3 percent of the men and 2 percent of the women, and McGill boasts Canada's first social fraternity for gay, bisexual, transgender, and progressive men. Well-attended campus events include homecoming, Winter Carnival, and Frosh Week activities. Popular road trips include New York City, Ottawa, and Toronto. Ski slopes are less than an hour away.

"McGill students are very sociable and love to party!"

Men's and women's basketball and ice hockey, men's rugby, and women's soccer are among the most popular varsity sports; men's baseball and lacrosse and women's synchronized swimming have captured recent national championships. According to one student, "The McGill–Harvard rugby match is a must-watch." Intramurals offer would-be jocks an opportunity to blow off steam after classes and on weekends, with soccer and ice hockey attracting the most interest.

In recent years the government of Quebec has been less than enthusiastic about funding its English-speaking academic gem, and large classes and mountains of red tape are undeniably part of the McGill experience. Nevertheless, most denizens seem happy. "The students who go to McGill are very invested in their academic life and are proud of their school," a student says.

Queen's University

Kingston, Ontario K7L 3N6 CAN

With about 18,000 undergraduates, Queen's is the smallest of the major Canadian universities. It is also the only one set in a metropolitan area of modest size. Engineering and business are the strongest areas of study, followed by nursing. Toronto and Montreal are both about three hours away. With 90 percent of its first-year students in the dorms, Queen's has a more active residential life than other Canadian universities.

Students at Queen's University approach work and play with equal zeal and enjoy a potent mix of school spirit and intellectual drive. Success requires energy and a willingness to get into the thick of things. "People who aren't interested in being a part of the school community are better off at a school that isn't such a big family," warns a sophomore. Solid academics, a pervasive school spirit, and long-standing traditions make life at this storied university unique—and demanding. "Getting into Queen's is just the first challenge," says a senior. "Succeeding at Queen's is another battle."

The 161-acre Queen's campus is located on the north shore of Lake Ontario, just minutes from the heart of Kingston, Ontario ("the limestone city"), and directly between Montreal and Toronto. "Almost all buildings are constructed using limestone," explains a senior. Historically significant buildings have been maintained, and "there are

"Courses are often theory-driven and require a substantial amount of work."

some modern buildings with a lot of glass to provide a bright and welcoming atmosphere." Ample greenery and open spaces provide students a place to stretch out under the sky and hit the books. Queen's recently opened the 80,000-square-foot Isabel Bader Centre for the Performing Arts, featuring common teaching rooms and shared public spaces designed to encourage interactivity.

Established in 1841 by Royal Charter of Queen Victoria, Queen's University offers undergraduate degrees in a variety of faculties, including science, engineering, commerce, education, music, nursing, and creative arts. Academics are unilaterally solid, but the most demanding are engineering and commerce, and nursing is popular. The bachelor of commerce program was the first of its kind in Canada and provides students with an internationally focused liberal business education, enhanced by leadership modules and the integration of technology. The School of Computing offers bachelor of computer degrees in biomedical computing, cognitive science, and software design, as well as B.A. and B.S. degrees. Computing and the Creative Arts is a multidisciplinary program that allows students to use cutting-edge software programs for music, drama, art, and film production. General education requirements vary by program, but all students can expect to complete a rigorous series of core and elective courses. Students participating in programs at the Queen's Bader International Study Centre are whisked away to the university's campus in East Sussex, England, where they enjoy small classes and integrated field studies

Website: www.queensu.ca
Location: Small City
Public
Total Enrollment: 22,630
Undergraduates: 18,013
Male/Female: 40/60
SAT Ranges: 1200 or above (combined)
ACT Ranges: 26 or above
Financial Aid: 58%
Pell Grant: N/A
Expense: Pub $ $
Student Loans: 34%
Average Debt: N/A
Phi Beta Kappa: No
Applicants: 30,999
Accepted: 49%
Enrolled: 28%
Grad in 6 Years: 85%
Returning Freshmen: 94%
Academics: ✏ ✏ ✏ ✏ ½
Social: ☎ ☎ ☎ ☎
Q of L: ★ ★ ★
Admissions: (613) 533-2218
Email Address: admission@queensu.ca

Strong Programs:
Commerce
Engineering
Nursing
Computing
Arts
Sciences

while residing in a 15th-century castle. In addition, there are exchange programs with 180 universities in 45 countries around the world. Queen's is considered a leader in study abroad; 20 percent of students participate. Opportunities for undergraduate research are abundant as well.

"The academic climate is quite competitive, and the courses are often theory-driven and require a substantial amount of work to prepare for class and complete assignments," says one senior. The general consensus among struggling students is that As are hard to come by. "After working your butt off and reading stacks of textbooks, your grades pale in comparison to the marks of students at other universities," gripes a biology major. The QSuccess program helps orient first-year students academically and socially, and Bounce Back is an opt-in academic support program for first-year students who earn low GPAs in their first term. Participating students are paired with Bounce Back Facilitators, peer mentors who help them set goals and identify strategies for academic success.

Classes tend to be large for freshmen and sophomores, but dwindle in size as one approaches graduation. The majority of classes are taught by full professors, who receive praise for their accessibility and intelligence. "The teachers I have had have been thorough, challenging, and concerned about my success," says a junior. Office hours and special "wine and cheese" functions give students ample opportunity to mingle with faculty. Students report that there is little trouble getting into desired classes, and "there is lots of counseling available for students who need it."

> "The teachers I have had have been thorough, challenging, and concerned about my success."

Queen's students are an industrious, intelligent group, and most are used to academic success. "Students take pride and honor in their work and are deeply involved in the Queen's community," asserts one student. School spirit runs high and campus issues include rising tuition fees—and determining just who is responsible for the cost. Students come from every Canadian province and 80 countries; 78 percent are from Ontario and 7 percent are international. A sociology major says that "Queen's is very PC and inclusive, regardless of gender, race, religion, or sexual orientation." Though there are no athletic scholarships, hundreds of merit awards averaging $2,000 are handed out annually. "I have had great help through scholarships and financial aid," relates a senior. "There is quite a lot of money for you. You just have to go after it." International students are automatically considered for available merit awards.

Ninety percent of undergraduates live in 17 residence halls, and all freshmen are guaranteed a place to hang their hats. The residence halls are "comfortable, extremely well maintained, and offer a number of services for students," says a senior. Co-ed and single-sex dorms are available. A mandatory meal plan gives freshmen a wide variety of foods to choose from, including pasta, salad, pizza, and a soup-and-salad bar. The surrounding city also offers a plethora of dining options. After freshman year, most students pack their bags and head off campus to the "student village," where comfortable apartments are available. Most Queen's students live within a reasonable walk of campus. Though always a concern, safety is practically a nonissue on campus. Students report that they feel quite safe and that security is more than adequate.

> "Campus pubs and city pubs have both found their niche."

Make no mistake about it, Queen's students know how to have a good time. "Social life is huge at Queen's," says a student. Adds another, "Campus pubs and city pubs have both found their niche." On Thursday nights, students flock to the campus pub, The Underground, for a drink or two, while Saturday nights are reserved for city bars and nightclubs. The legal drinking age is 19, and kiddies will have a tough time skirting the law. "The bouncers in Kingston actually have a couple of brain cells and can spot a fake ID from 90 kilometers away," says a senior. Nonalcoholic alternatives include school-sponsored movies and extracurricular clubs (there are more than 220). "Extracurricular activities are a must, not an option!" says one student. Frosh Week is a favorite event, with "cheers that even the most blasé of students will be shouting out with pride by the end of the week." The school is steeped in Scottish tradition, and it's normal to see kilt-wearing bandsmen at important campus events.

Once the capital of Canada, Kingston is described as "very much a university town." There are several universities in the area (including the Royal Military College), and downtown provides students with places to shop. "Kingston itself has several clubs, three malls, a number of museums, numerous gyms, and three or four movie theaters," says a student. The city's relative isolation makes it the favored stomping ground for students without wheels. Town/gown relations are good, and students are very active in the community. Toronto and Montreal (less than three hours away) are popular road trips.

With 13 varsity teams, 35 varsity clubs, and 30 recreational clubs, Queen's athletic program is not only the largest in Canada, but also ranks with Harvard University and MIT for the largest programs in North America. Competitive Gaels teams include men's and women's rugby, ice hockey, soccer, and volleyball. Men's rugby won the regional title in 2015. The annual "kill McGill" football game against rival McGill University draws pigskin-crazed students from every corner of campus; homecoming is reputed to be a lively affair. Intramural competition is fierce too, and nearly half of the students are involved on some level. A student says, "There is so much school spirit, sometimes it makes you sick."

Life at Queen's University is one of extremes. "Our spirit is second to none," says a senior. Though the academic climate can be tough and the winters long, students here find much to praise. "One of the great things about Queen's is that it's constantly growing and expanding to meet the needs of its students," says one senior, "but at the same time, it never loses sight of where it came from or what it stands for."

The school is steeped in Scottish tradition, and it's normal to see kilt-wearing bandsmen at important campus events.

Overlaps

Western University of Ontario, University of Toronto, McMaster, McGill, University of Alberta, University of British Columbia, Dalhousie

If You Apply To ➢

Queen's: Rolling admissions: Feb. 1. Application fee: $150 CAD. No campus or alumni interviews. SATs or ACTs: required for U.S. applicants. Subject Tests: optional (required for engineering candidates only). No letters of recommendation. Essay: recommended (personal statement of experience and supplemental essay).

University of Toronto

Toronto, Ontario M5S 1A1 CAN

U of T is one of the largest institutions in the *Fiske Guide* and one of the biggest in the world. If ever there were a place where go-getterism is a necessity, this is it. In the absence of American-style school spirit, U of T students cut loose to find their fun in the city. Toronto is one of the most diverse and cosmopolitan cities in the world, with nearly half of its citizens born outside of Canada.

Students at the University of Toronto avoid getting lost in the shuffle by taking part in a unique residential college system that allows them to model their educational experience after their own personalities. Each college has a distinct character and appeal, yet blends seamlessly into the university's overall academic milieu. And when it comes to academics, the U of T delivers, says a senior: "The students were

Website: www.utoronto.ca
Location: City Center
Public
Total Enrollment: 76,537

As befitting such a gargantuan institution, the university's endowment is the largest of any Canadian college or university.

likely at the top of their class in high school and are very competitive—more so than at Queen's or York universities."

The University of Toronto is so large that it spans three campuses. The St. George campus in downtown Toronto features Gothic architecture and historic buildings. The suburban campuses in Mississauga and Scarborough feature more modern structures. Other facilities include the Centre for Biological Timing and Cognition, where researchers study how sleep cycles affect learning and physical and mental health, and the Goldring Centre for High Performance Sport.

Students apply directly to one of Toronto's nine colleges, seven of which are on the St. George campus. U.S. citizens who are admitted typically have a high school diploma, SAT or ACT (including the essay or writing test) results, plus two SAT II or AP/IB scores in appropriate subjects. Students are expected to present composite scores of at least 1700 for the SAT or 26 for the ACT; most programs require higher scores. Scores below 500 on any component of the SAT or SAT II are not acceptable. Prerequisite courses should be taken at a twelfth-grade level. The most popular majors include arts, sciences, commerce, engineering, and physical health and education. The concurrent education program allows undergraduates to complete the requirements for a bachelor of education, professional teacher certification, and a second undergraduate degree simultaneously.

> "Professors have been consistently engaging and well-versed."

In the Faculty of Arts & Science, students can pursue academic interests from a selection of more than 300 programs and more than 4,000 courses in a wide array of disciplines that span the arts, science, and business. Distinctive learning options include First-Year Learning Communities, Summer Abroad, and a wide range of research opportunities. First-Year Seminars, capped at 24 students each, are "a good transition from high school to university," says a senior, and give incoming freshmen the chance to learn from leading faculty members in a less intimidating environment. In addition, the Trinity One and Vic One programs each offer 25 to 50 highly capable students the opportunity to develop their critical-thinking, speaking, and writing skills, while fostering close relationships with fellow students, instructors, guest lecturers, and visiting scholars. The U of T Music Faculty is the oldest in Canada and offers bachelor's, master's, and doctoral degrees in all of their programs. As befitting such a gargantuan institution, the university's endowment is the largest of any Canadian college or university.

Courses require a great deal of reading outside the classroom and are typically demanding. "During exam periods and the final weeks of each semester, the academic climate can understandably become quite intense," says one senior. Large lecture classes are accompanied by smaller tutorials, facilitating personal attention, and professors get high marks for their teaching skills and their smarts. "Even in classes of 1,500 students, professors have been consistently engaging and well-versed," says a student.

"Students are from all over the world and represent the full spectrum of values and backgrounds," says an anthropology major. "U of T is very diverse and the student body is generally intelligent, progressive, and open-minded." Twenty-one percent of those enrolled are "foreign"—from outside Canada, that is—and the most significant issues on campus include "tuition fees, unequal pay, the environment, and critical social justice," according to one student. The Ontario Public Interest Research Group and Amnesty International attract sizable followings. There are no athletic scholarships.

> "Students are from all over the world and represent the full spectrum of values and backgrounds."

Roughly 15 percent of students live in campus housing, and first-years are guaranteed rooms. "There are new buildings and historic old buildings that are beautiful," says an anthropology major. "They are cozy and comfortable and pretty well maintained." All of the dorms are affiliated with one of the nine undergraduate colleges, which act as "local neighborhoods" and center on specialties, including Buddhism, Celtic studies, and criminology. "Every cafeteria always has a vegetarian, vegan, halal, kosher, gluten-free, or dairy-free option," a junior reports. "Security is pretty good on campus, and our campus is in a good part of Toronto," a bioethics major says.

All of the dorms are affiliated with one of the nine undergraduate colleges, which act as "local neighborhoods."

"Social life here revolves around the very energetic city in which the school is located," says a sociology and English major. Another student adds, "Social events are balanced between off-campus pubs, clubs, skating rinks, banquet halls, and stadiums to on-campus pubs, event spaces in Hart House, and student lounges." Toronto boasts great culture, super shopping, a clean and safe nightlife district—and the picturesque shores of Lake Ontario, lovely in warmer weather. "Toronto has a huge club scene, and U of T pub nights happen in the city," a student explains. The legal drinking age here is 19; students who are of age may have alcohol in their rooms but not in common spaces, and anyone caught violating local laws or the open-container policy is reported to the dean of the residence. Those wishing to party alcohol-free will find plenty of school-sponsored events, such as movies, guest

"Social life here revolves around the very energetic city in which the school is located."

speakers, and countless clubs. There are no fraternities or sororities, but there is a club for nearly every interest. "There isn't much of a party culture at U of T, because we are much more focused on studying," one student says. Students turn out in droves to celebrate PRIDE, the largest gay pride event in North America, along with Frosh Week, which includes wacky fun such as bed races between the colleges, and the annual Fireball formal dance.

Sports are not a focus of campus life at Toronto, though hockey, volleyball, and basketball are among the varsity teams that draw something of a following, especially when the opponent is Queen's University or the University of Western Ontario. The intramural program, however, is another story. It's the largest in Canada, involving more than 10,000 students in 26 sports and 57 leagues each year. Residence halls and groups of friends compete in everything from badminton to indoor cricket, inner-tube water polo, squash, triathlon, and ultimate Frisbee. Students can also be found cheering the city's many professional teams, including the Blue Jays (baseball), the Raptors (basketball), and the Maple Leafs (hockey).

Toronto's biggest liability, its sheer and sometimes overwhelming size, may also be its biggest asset, students say—as long as they learn to speak up and proactively take advantage of all of the school's resources. "A prospective student should choose the University of Toronto due to its outstanding academic reputation and convenient location in the social hub of Toronto's downtown core," says a senior.

Overlaps

McGill, Queen's, Western University, York, Ryerson, University of Guelph, Waterloo, University of British Columbia

If You Apply To ➤

University of Toronto: Regular decision: Jan. 13 (varies by program). Application fee: $150 (CAD). No campus or alumni interviews. SATs (with essay) or ACTs (with writing): required. Subject Tests or AP or IB exams: required (any two). No letters of recommendation. No essay question. Apply to specific program.

British and Irish Universities

If going to college in Canada sounds adventuresome, you'll need even more moxie to venture overseas. But give it some thought. As the most popular overseas destination, Great Britain currently has about 2,300 Americans enrolled in undergraduate degree programs, and another 30,000 per year are pursuing shorter study abroad stints. Hundreds more have found their way to the Republic of Ireland. Depending on your course of study, studying in Britain or Ireland may or may not turn out to be less expensive than a flagship public university in the U.S., but the top British and Irish universities offer a richer international experience, infused with historical and cultural perspectives, than you will find on this side of the Atlantic.

Before we go further, here's a word to moms and dads: you may get queasy at the thought of sending your little cherub across a 3,000-mile ocean, but a flight to Dublin or London is quicker than driving 10 hours to get to First Choice U. Once you're there, the cities are at least as safe as those in the U.S., and the small towns have a crime rate roughly equivalent to that of the town of Mayberry on *The Andy Griffith Show*. The best part for parents: you'll need to visit at least once—and preferably more.

For those who are hazy on their geography, England, Scotland, and Wales make up Great Britain; throw in Northern Ireland and the moniker changes to the United Kingdom. The Republic of Ireland, occupying the southern part of the Emerald Isle across the Irish Sea, used to be part of Great Britain, but won its independence in 1921. Ireland is the closest European nation to the East Coast of the U.S., and the only English-speaking country in the eurozone. Britain and Ireland make the most sense for American students interested in studying English literature, history, foreign languages, and anything related to international studies. If medieval history is your passion, why not go to school where the remains of that long-ago world still dot the landscape? If you're looking for a career in international business, perhaps consider a country where the global village has been a way of life, and you will be making lifelong friends from around the world. Though Britain is an English-speaking country, it offers far better instruction in European and other languages than you can get in the U.S., and Ireland's favorable corporate tax rates have led U.S. companies such as Google, Microsoft, and GlaxoSmithKline to make it their European headquarters (think internships). No matter what your academic interests, your classmates will include a cross section of nationalities that would be the envy of any North American institution. Most importantly, study in Britain and Ireland has the potential to be a life-changing experience that will broaden your horizons and deepen your understanding of our increasingly globalized world. With cheap flights and trains readily available, travel to Continental Europe and beyond becomes a way of life.

With all of these benefits come some challenges. American students in Britain need to adjust to a different tenor of academic life than is found at U.S. colleges and universities. There are no campus "bubbles" to protect you from the real world. Students are treated as adults and expected to behave accordingly. The legal drinking age is 18, which obviates the need for fake IDs but puts the onus on students to behave responsibly. Dorms are generally the domain of first-year students; expect to find a "flat" (apartment) for subsequent years. "Sport" means playing, not watching. The student body will not come out on a Saturday afternoon for the big game for a simple reason: there are no big games. Most faculty members (a.k.a. tutors) are ready to help you if you are struggling with your studies, but only if you take the initiative. There is no Dean of Student Hand-Holding in British universities (nor do they offer landing pads for helicopter parents).

Americans thinking about studying in Britain and Ireland should also be aware of differences in the academic system "across the Pond." Most important: whereas American universities generally require students to sample a variety of fields for two years before choosing a major, British and Irish institutions expect students to identify their field of concentration before they set foot on campus. That's because students take their general education courses in high school. Thus students in Britain and Ireland take only two or three courses at a time, mostly related to their major. American-style distribution requirements are all but unheard of—good news for students who want to get out of those nasty math or foreign language requirements. But keep in mind that since British and Irish students tend to take courses only in subjects that seriously interest them, all classes are taught at a high level, even introductory ones. Moreover, although students get fewer hours in class, they are expected to put in more hours of study per course outside of class. Anyone who wants to change majors after a year or two may encounter difficulty.

Another important academic difference is that British and Irish universities evaluate applicants almost entirely on the basis of academic credentials, with emphasis on demonstrated ability in their field of study. No essays about page 236 of your autobiography or need to present yourself as a well-rounded overachiever who will enrich the campus environment. As one administrator put it, "We don't do social engineering." Along with Trinity College Dublin, the top British universities, especially the four "ancient" Scottish universities, are thus a good bet for U.S. students who may have the smarts to do Ivy League work, but whose résumés do not include an Olympic medal or building a school in Belize during spring vacation. Standards are high; St Andrews, for example, looks for a minimum score of 1950 on the SAT I, and 28 on the ACT. Institutions tend to prefer the SAT over the ACT, though many will accept either. Scores from SAT II or AP tests may also be required. For the application essay, the British usually ask about commitment to your intended major and why you want to study it. They view American-style personal essays as fluff.

As with Canadian universities, the cost for an American studying at one of the leading Scottish and Irish universities will vary with fluctuating exchange rates. To complicate matters, tuition and fee levels vary not only across universities but also according to the course of study and academic level within each institution. Total tuition and fees among the five universities described in the *Fiske Guide* range from US $17,000 to more than US $50,000—roughly equivalent to the costs for out-of-state students at flagship public universities in the U.S. but less than the sticker price of selective privates. The downside is that the sticker price is also the final price; academic scholarships are scarce and institutional financial aid all but nonexistent. British and Irish students, along with those from the European Union, generally receive government funding. Federal aid such as federal Direct loans and Pell Grants can be transported, but many, if not most, families will find themselves paying the full freight. For a searchable database of the few scholarships available for study in Great Britain, visit the British Council at www.britishcouncil.org/usa. One reason that financially strapped British universities have recently begun showing a greater interest in recruiting U.S. students is that they are a source of much-needed revenue. By and large, the academic bars for U.S. students are slightly lower than for native Brits.

If you are considering a British university, you may be picturing yourself in England, the most populous region of Great Britain that includes London as well as fabled universities Oxford and Cambridge. But here's the rub: the English have a system of higher education that makes degree study impractical in many cases. In England, undergraduate degrees are completed in three years, not four, and students are generally assumed to have completed 13 years of schooling rather than 12. As a result, the most selective English universities are reluctant to admit American high school graduates—some refuse to admit any—and the students who do get in will find themselves navigating a world more appropriate for juniors and seniors in college. One note on terminology: in Britain and Ireland, a program of study is called a "course." The British word for what we call a course is "module."

The University of Cambridge (www.cam.ac.uk) is particularly blunt about "the possible mismatch between the broad liberal arts curriculum of the North American high school and the specialist emphasis of British degree courses." The University of Oxford (www.ox.ac.uk) does offer a glimmer of hope for a select few superachievers; Oxford will consider American students who graduate in the top 2 percent of their class, and it has recently stepped up its recruiting efforts in U.S. high schools. In a recent year it enrolled about 30 U.S. students. Even so, the odds of admission to Oxford are lower than at any college in the U.S., including Harvard. The vast majority of American undergraduates at both Oxford and Cambridge are there for a second bachelor's degree after earning one from an American institution. Students with their hearts set on the Oxbridge institutions should consider them for graduate school, where both welcome Americans (and their dollars) in significant amounts.

Students will hear a similar story at the third-most recognized name in English higher education, the London School of Economics (www.lse.ac.uk), which enrolls about 5,000 undergraduates. The LSE says it will not normally consider U.S. students until they have a year of higher education under their belts. Less selective English institutions are more receptive to Americans, but, once again, only those who feel certain of what they would like to study should apply. If you are in this category, there is one potential benefit to an English degree: the three-year degree program will save you a year of tuition bills.

So what to do? One answer is to cast your gaze on Scotland, England's less populous neighbor, where universities offer four-year degrees that are much better suited to the needs of American high school graduates. Scotland, which lies north of England, was an independent nation until 1706 and has its own parliament that exercises considerable power when it comes to domestic policy. It has an illustrious intellectual history and has produced the likes of David Hume, Adam Smith, Rudyard Kipling, Robert Louis Stevenson, J. K. Rowling, and the world's most famous ogre, Shrek. Scotland is more egalitarian in feel than England—less hung up on social class.

The Scots take great pride in their universities, which are central to their national identity and have deep historical ties with American higher education. The American-style liberal arts institution was imported directly from Scotland in the person of John Witherspoon, a graduate of the University of Edinburgh who was lured to the U.S. in 1768 to head Princeton University. With the model of his alma mater in mind, Witherspoon transformed Princeton from a small-time school for ministers into a broad-based institution that taught philosophy, history, geography, science, mathematics, and theology. Like their U.S. counterparts, Scottish universities offer four-year programs; thus, they represent something of a middle ground between the American system and that of Oxford and Cambridge with their three-year, entirely specialized programs. Scottish universities expect early specialization, but there is some room to explore fields outside your major during the first two years. One downside of studying in Scotland is its northern location, which makes for long winter nights. Scotland has also been historically regarded as a "dreich" corner of Britain—a Highland term referring to weather variously described as dull, overcast, drizzly, cold, misty, and miserable, or a combination thereof. Scottish higher education is noted for its four "ancient" universities—Aberdeen, Edinburgh, Glasgow, and St Andrews—each of which is profiled in the pages that follow.

There are seven universities in Ireland, but Trinity College Dublin is by far the most distinguished, and it is the only one that operates on a four-year system for undergraduates. TCD was founded in 1592 by Queen Elizabeth as an Irish counterpart to Oxford and Cambridge to train Anglican clergymen. While TCD follows the Scottish system, its cultural ties remain distinctly English, and graduates who subsequently enroll in Oxford or Cambridge are automatically entitled to an "ad eundem" courtesy degree from the English university. TCD was founded as the University of Dublin with the expectation that it would serve as "the mother of a university" and other colleges would grow up around it à la Oxbridge. This never happened, though, so for all practical purposes Trinity College Dublin is the University of Dublin. Roman Catholics make up the overwhelming majority of students despite the fact that until as late as 1972 they needed special permission from church authorities to attend this bastion of Anglican scholarship.

Students applying to UK institutions should generally use the Universities and Colleges Admissions Service (UCAS, www.ucas.com), which functions like the Common Application group in the U.S. The UCAS form asks you to list all your courses and the grades you received in them, as well as your SAT and/or ACT scores. It also requires an essay and a letter of recommendation. Most institutions will accept applications through the spring, though we recommend that you apply by the deadline for British students, January 15. The deadline for applying to Oxford and Cambridge, or to apply to any program in medicine, is October 15 for entrance the following fall. Many institutions have rolling admissions, another reason to apply early. Applicants to Trinity College Dublin apply directly to the university, which has rolling admissions.

A high proportion of U.S. students currently enrolled in British universities come from families with international connections, such as close relatives living in other countries or diplomat parents, but prior international experience is by no means required. College in Britain is not for the faint of heart, but it can be richly rewarding for those with the initiative to take the plunge. After college in Britain, students will have the skills and savvy to succeed almost anywhere in the world.

University of Aberdeen

Aberdeen, Scotland AB24 3FX GB

Located in Scotland's third largest city, Aberdeen is the most accessible of the four "ancient" universities. Notable for the flexibility of its curriculum and emphasis on independent learning. Major attractions include engineering, life sciences, and anything related to Europe. City of Aberdeen combines charm with the bustle of a small city. Outdoor enthusiasts will love the Scottish Highlands at arm's length.

Website: www.abdn.ac.uk
Location: Small City
Public
Total Enrollment: 14,500
Undergraduates: 11,000

The University of Aberdeen was founded in 1495, three years after a certain well-known explorer sailed from Spain to the New World. Students seeking the flavor of old Europe will not be disappointed. With plenty of cobblestone streets and buildings made of ancient stone (it's the Granite City), the university has a distinctly medieval aura. It offers top-notch academics, a curriculum that is unusually flexible by UK standards, and a slice of life far richer than any U.S. institution can muster. "It's great fun and has a lot of opportunities," says a senior, "both academically and socially."

With a population of 240,000, the port city of Aberdeen is Scotland's third largest city. Once a center for fishing, shipbuilding, and textiles, it is now a center for the thriving oil extraction business in the North Sea. With two universities—the other is Robert Gordon—it is the educational capital of Northeastern Scotland. Aberdeen is perched at a latitude roughly the same as Juneau, Alaska, but because of the Gulf Stream, winter temperatures are generally milder than those on the East Coast of the United States. December days are short in winter, but sky-gazers are often treated to glimpses of the fabled Northern Lights.

Most university buildings are concentrated in a quiet enclave known as "Old Aberdeen." The campus is crowned, literally, by a 16th-century tower in the shape of an imperial crown. Lightly traveled streets pass through the campus, and the multitude of green lawns and picturesque courtyards are ideal for lounging on sunny days. As part of its Sixth Century Campaign, the university began investing $450 million in infrastructure and facilities, starting with the Sir Duncan Rice Library, which officially opened in 2011, and the Sports Village. The Aquatics Centre, which includes an Olympic standard swimming pool and diving boom, opened in 2014.

Aberdeen is divided into three colleges: the College of Arts and Social Sciences, the College of Life Sciences and Medicine, and the College of Physical Sciences. In 2010, the university decided to broaden its curriculum and add more flexibility, bringing it in line with the academic systems of Harvard, Melbourne, Hong Kong, and top universities around the world.

"We do a lot of group work, and student interaction is really key."

Thus it has introduced a series of interdisciplinary Sixth Century Courses, such as Science and the Media or Oceans and Society, that students are expected to sample during their first two years. Other curriculum innovations are designed to encourage students to pursue interests outside their core disciplines—what might be called "electives" in an American context. Popular majors include English literature, biology, religious studies, environmental science, and a joint international relations/politics concentration. Engineering is also strong, especially for programs related to the oil industry. The Centre for Learning and Teaching helps faculty members find ways to enhance the learning experience, while the Student Learning Service helps students develop their academic skills.

With approximately 14,500 undergraduate and graduate students, Aberdeen is a medium-sized university by U.S. standards. The academic climate is described as relaxed. "The academic climate at Aberdeen is largely collaborative. We do a lot of group work, and student interaction is really key," says a business major. Courses in the first two years generally consist of lectures supplemented by smaller weekly discussion sections. "In my first year I was taught by a mixture of Ph.D. students and lecturers (professors). In my honours years, my lecturers were leading experts in their fields and widely published," says a student. Professors typically team-teach introductory "modules," with each covering the topics that are his or her specialty. As in other Scottish universities, students generally take only three subjects at a time in the first two years, with extensive reading and research outside of class generally taken for granted. "Often we are expected to come to class prepared to discuss certain topics, but given no minimum reading assignment. The professor gives out a list of selected readings from which we can choose," says a history major. Grades are typically determined by end-of-the-term evaluations with few intermediate assignments. At the end of their second year, students must typically pass exams in order to advance to "honors level," the equivalent of the junior and senior years of college in the States. Upper-level

(continued)

Male/Female: 49/51
SAT Ranges: 1750
  (combined)
ACT Ranges: 26 or above
Financial Aid: N/A
Pell Grant: N/A
Expense: Pub $
Student Loans: N/A
Average Debt: N/A
Phi Beta Kappa: No
Applicants: 13,000
Accepted: 27%
Enrolled: N/A
Grad in 6 Years: N/A
Returning Freshmen: N/A
Academics: ✑ ✑ ✑ ✑ ½
Social: 🍷 🍷 🍷 🍷
Q of L: ★ ★ ★ ★
Admissions: (+44) 1224 272090
Email Address: sras@
  abdn.ac.uk

Strong Programs:
English Literature
Biology
Religious Studies
Environmental Science
International Relations
Politics
Engineering

Professors typically team-teach introductory "modules," with each covering the topics that are his or her specialty.

science students typically spend long hours in the lab. One nice feature: there is generally no limit to the number of students who can enroll in a particular course, thereby giving students the freedom to sign up for anything that strikes their fancy.

Overall, 56 percent of undergraduates hail from Scotland, 13 percent from the rest of the UK, and 30 percent arrive from 120 different countries. "We have a very international student body," says one senior. The political climate on campus is described as conservative and relatively subdued. Upon their arrival at the university, students partake of Freshers Week, when student organizations sponsor informational meetings. Aberdeen is a selective institution for U.S. students, though less so than the other three "ancient" universities.

On-campus housing at Aberdeen is varied and guaranteed to all first-year students who apply before the deadline. "Accommodations themselves are basic," notes one student, "but you get what you pay for." A majority of the international students live in Hillhead Halls of Residence, a complex of houses and flats that is about a 15-minute walk from the campus. Students may elect catered rooms (two meals per day) or self-catering, wherein they cook their own food with kitchen facilities generally located down the hall from the rooms.

"We have a very international student body."

Many students choose to move off campus after their first year, and a variety of housing options are available near the campus. Only a few students own cars, as the university is within easy walking distance of the city center and the North Sea and is on a regular bus route. Parking permits are made available to those students who require them.

"Social life is great," raves one student. "There's always something going on." Another adds, "We have around 200 societies and sports clubs, and most students are involved in at least one." Since the drinking age in Britain is 18, social life at Aberdeen revolves around legal consumption rather than drinking on the sly. "There is not pressure to drink, and we do not have Greek organizations," reports a student. Aberdeen offers a varied nightlife with clubs and bars to suit all tastes. You may find yourself doing what Britons call "the pub crawl," which means sampling the refreshment of several pubs before heading home in the wee hours. For those who overdo it, the university has a standing deal with a local cab company to take home any student who needs a ride, with the fare put on the student's university bill. Popular campus social events include periodic formal balls, to which the men wear kilts and the women wear evening gowns. Perhaps the biggest event of the year is the Torcher's Parade, which is held every spring and features floats made by various student organizations. Sports are mainly for playing, rather than watching, with 50 sports clubs at students' disposal. Individual sports rather than team intramurals are the staple of weekend warriors, and students can purchase passes for various athletic facilities, depending on their interests.

Aberdeen is described by one student as "a fantastic college town!" The city center offers a variety of pubs and clubs as well as inexpensive cinemas, music, and theater. The city has plenty of old-world charm, and outdoorsy types will love the dramatic scenery that is everywhere in northeast Scotland. Picturesque cliffs overlooking the North Sea are within an easy bus or train ride. Fifteen miles south of Aberdeen is breathtaking Dunnottar Castle, a 14th-century ruin set high on a rocky outcrop that was the set for Mel Gibson's film rendition of *Hamlet*. Within a half-hour ride inland is the edge of the legendary Scottish Highlands. Famous castles are in all directions, including the royal family's summer hideaway, Balmoral. For the Scottish version of

"It is such a carefree atmosphere with that special touch of Scottish tradition."

the big city, Glasgow and Edinburgh are close by and two hours on a plane will get you to most places in Western Europe.

Though Aberdeen may lack some of the conveniences of home, most Americans are happy they came. "Between classes on a sunny day, students will buy something from the bakery and sit on the grass in the midst of 500-year-old buildings and cobblestone streets. It is such a carefree atmosphere with that special touch of Scottish tradition," says a satisfied history major. If you're the kind of person who likes to meet new people and learn about different cultures, you might thrive on the Aberdeen air.

If You Apply To > **Aberdeen:** Rolling admissions: Jun. 30. (Priority deadline: Jan. 15.) Application fee: $29. Campus Interviews: informational, optional. No alumni interviews. SATs or ACTs: required. Subject Tests: required (varies by program). Letters of recommendation: required. Essay: required.

University of Edinburgh

Old College, South Bridge, Edinburgh, Scotland EH8 9JS UK

With close ties to the city that founded it in the 16th century, Edinburgh is the most prestigious of Scotland's major research universities. Combines deep roots in Scottish culture and history with the cosmopolitan flavor and cultural riches of a sophisticated capital city. Competitive admissions for top British students, but better odds for Americans with Ivy-level academic credentials. More diverse student body than St Andrews.

The largest and best-known of the ancient Scottish universities, the University of Edinburgh is part and parcel of Scotland's most vibrant urban center. The city of Edinburgh is home to the Scottish Parliament, reconstituted in 1999 after nearly three centuries under the political thumb of London, as well as to the national museum, abundant historical sites, winding streets, and countless restaurants and pubs. The university, like the city, has an unmistakable international feel, including long-standing connections across the pond. In addition to the likes of Charles Darwin and J. K. Rowling, eminent graduates include two signatories of the U.S. Declaration of Independence, Benjamin Rush and John Witherspoon. "Students know that by coming to Edinburgh they are attending not only a prestigious university but the city that goes along with it," says a modern language student.

Edinburgh is unique among the major Scottish universities in that it was founded (in 1583) by a municipality rather than under religious auspices. There is no central campus per se. Its buildings are spread throughout the city, which, with 483,000 residents, is really an overgrown town. Public transport is good, but just about everything is within walking distance. The older university buildings are Georgian and tend to bear names from the Scottish Enlightenment (David Hume and Dugald Stewart), while more modern ones date to the '60s and '70s. The George Square complex is home to the School of Business. A spate of new construction and renovation is under way.

The university is organized around three colleges: Arts, Humanities, and Social Sciences; Science and Engineering; and Medicine and Veterinary. Edinburgh has traditionally been strong in the sciences, and historical ties to economists like Adam Smith and philosophers like John Locke have contributed to strong programs in

Website: www.ed.ac.uk
Location: City Center
Public
Total Enrollment: 27,971
Undergraduates: 20,823
Male/Female: 40/60
SAT Ranges: CR 600–700, M 600–700
ACT Ranges: 28–31
Financial Aid: N/A
Pell Grant: N/A
Expense: Pub $ $
Student Loans: N/A
Average Debt: N/A
Phi Beta Kappa: No
Applicants: 57,019
Accepted: 39%
Enrolled: 26%
Grad in 6 Years: 94%
Returning Freshmen: 95%
Academics: ✍ ✍ ✍
Social: ☎ ☎ ☎
Q of L: ★ ★ ★

(continued)

Admissions: (+44) 1316 514296

Email Address: usa.enquiries@
ed.ac.uk

Strong Programs:

English Literature

International Relations

Art and Design

Law

Linguistics

Sociology

History

Economics

those fields. English literature, international relations, art and design, and law attract a lot of U.S. students, and linguistics, sociology, and history are strong, Scottish and otherwise. Unlike in the U.S., the programs in medicine and veterinary science are five-year programs for undergraduates. Veterinary graduates can go on to practice immediately in the U.S. A new program in sustainable development is attracting a diverse group of students, as is an interdisciplinary major in government, policy, and society. A merger with the Edinburgh College of Art has made possible a concentration in studio-based art. Some 200 study abroad programs are offered at leading universities around the world.

Applicants apply to study a particular subject, such as physics or English literature, but, unlike the situation in the leading English universities, it is possible to make changes once enrolled. There is no core curriculum, and no one has to endure a science or any other subject in which they have little interest. Students normally take three courses for each of their first two years in a variety of fields and then concentrate on one or two subjects the last two years. Each course involves a combination of lectures, which are taught by full professors, and weekly tutorials, or groups of 10 to 20 students led by tutors. "Although not full professors, my tutors have been fantastic," reports an international relations student. Another student adds, "The faculty is very international, so you don't have to worry about having a professor with too thick of a Scottish accent."

> "By coming to Edinburgh [students] are attending not only a prestigious university but the city that goes along with it."

Coursework throughout the year mostly involves essays, with final exams in late April or May accounting for most of the final grade. The academic system is built around self-study. "Students are expected to find their own way," reports an American student. "We are not hand-held or told what to do—which breeds a very different kind of learner and academic." The academic pressure at Edinburgh is said to be intense, with little grade inflation. "As befits one of the elite universities in the UK, the students are highly intelligent, and this intelligence is reflected inside the classroom," reports a sophomore. "Students know how to study and get their work in on time, but they also know how to go out and have fun." Faculty members do not see their role as seeking out students who may need help. "That being said, professors and tutors are more than happy to help out when you ask," says one American denizen.

Veterinary science is a five-year program for undergraduates, who can go on to practice immediately in the U.S.

Edinburgh is the leading destination for top-performing Scottish students, who face tighter admissions standards than North Americans. Thirty-seven percent of undergraduates hail from Scotland, with 20 percent from the United Kingdom and Europe, and 33 percent international. There are more than 650 regular American undergrads and 600 postgrads, as well as more than 800 study abroad students. Edinburgh students tend to be more middle class than their counterparts at St Andrews, which is more upper class. With total costs of about U.S. $36,000,

> "We are not hand-held or told what to do—which breeds a very different kind of learner and academic."

Edinburgh is slightly more expensive than the other ancient Scottish universities but a bargain compared to the Ivies in the U.S. The university makes scholarships available to international students, and American students can use their U.S. student loans to attend. Like all the prestigious Scottish universities, admissions and financial aid decisions are based entirely on academic grounds, with test scores playing a big role. The fact that you spent a spring vacation helping build housing in the slums of Honduras won't bolster your chances of admission. Given the nature of the student body, there is plenty of discussion of global issues. "Scotland is inherently left-leaning as a country," reports a language student, "but the international students want to share their views while also listening to the opinions of others." Not surprisingly, the most pressing issue is possible increases in tuition fees for British and Scottish students.

Edinburgh guarantees housing to all international first-year students. Catered accommodations are available in the Pollock Halls and come with 14 meals per week in the university dining hall—breakfast and dinner during the week and brunch on the weekends. Pollock accommodates 2,000 students with various styles of rooms (and prices), including some with private bathrooms. Nine out of 10 are singles. "There are common rooms and communal pantries with basic amenities such as a refrigerator and a microwave," explains one resident. Students can also choose self-catered options in which they make their own cooking arrangements. Self-catered flats (apartments) generally consist of three to five students, each with an individual room, sharing a large common living and kitchen area. All accommodations are described as clean and well maintained. Most students move off campus after their first year. "Edinburgh is a student-oriented city with many cheap flats which are directed especially at students," says a third-year student. The Student Union Advice Place will help you find a flat. Cafeteria food is described as "fine but not that diverse," and one student adds that "there are many cheap cafés near the university to grab sandwiches or baked potatoes."

> **"First-years tend to explore club life in the city center."**

Since the university is so closely tied to the city, it's no surprise that social life takes place both on and off campus. "First-years tend to explore club life in the city center," explains an American student, "and as they get into their second and third years, the partying transfers homeward into flat parties." But the two student unions offer their own entertainment options. "Teviot has several bars inside, most notably the Library Bar, which is a popular student hangout for a pint as well as for lunch or dinner during the week," explains a language student. "Potterow during the day has a café for coffee but on weekend nights becomes a nightclub that plays cheesy '90s music." All in all, he adds, the social options include "pub crawls, comedy nights, amazing music, top-notch student theater, cinema, dance, and book fairs." Since the drinking age is 18, the university has no school policy on the serving of alcohol. The city of Edinburgh offers its own menu of ancient and contemporary traditions. The Beltane Fire Festival, with roots in pagan times, celebrates the arrival of spring, and every August the city is host to the huge Fringe Festival, which draws artists and spectators from all over the world. Thanks to affordable trains and low-cost airlines like Ryanair and easyJet, trips throughout Britain and all over Europe are easy to arrange. "You get good at traveling," says one American undergrad.

The Edinburgh University Student Association and the Edinburgh University Sports Union combine to offer what one American describes as "just about every sport, charity, or special interest society/club conceivable." A fair is held during Freshers' Week to give first-year students a sense of the options. Does the Chocolate Lovers Society sound tasty? Edinburgh's varsity athletic teams, which compete against other Scottish and European universities in sports like rugby, soccer, and field hockey, do well, "but the competition is laid-back." Most attention goes to the "very strong and popular intramural sports program, which, depending on the sport, has quite a high caliber of play." Many of the teams are co-ed, and there are eight levels of rugby. One student adds that "ancient Scottish sports like shinty that aren't well known globally make us unique." The Centre for Sport and Exercise has "top-notch, newly renovated sports equipment, studios, weight rooms, archery ranges, and stretching stations," adds a third-year student. In all, Edinburgh hosts more than 260 societies and 64 sports clubs.

> **"[Edinburgh is] incredibly international but still Scottish."**

Much of the fun of going to college in Scotland comes from taking part in centuries-old traditions, of which Edinburgh has an abundance. Various societies and degree programs sponsor weekly or monthly ceilidhs, or traditional Scottish Dance Nights. Robert Burns Night is a big deal, as is Guy Fawkes Night on November 5, when students set off fireworks throughout the city. Whereas American commencements feature students moving the tassel of their mortarboards from one side to the other, Edinburgh places a common cap on the head of each student in turn that contains a piece of the trousers of John Knox and a NASA emblem that accompanied an Edinburgh graduate on a space mission.

American students tend to do well at Edinburgh. "They are smart and well traveled and tend to be independent thinkers," observes a faculty member. "This university has allowed me to become an adult and challenge myself because of the independent style of the education," reports an international studies major. Another American transplant hails the fact that Edinburgh is "incredibly international but still Scottish," adding that "the bagpipes playing in the city streets, the ethereal castle, and the wee pubs constantly remind me where I am."

If You Apply To ➤

Edinburgh: Rolling admissions: Jun. 30. (Priority deadline: Jan. 15.) Financial aid: Apr. 1. Housing: Jul. 31. Application fee: $34. No campus or alumni interviews. SATs or ACTs: required for some. Subject Tests: required for some. Letters of recommendation: required. Essay: required. Apply to particular program.

University of Glasgow

University Gardens, Glasgow, Lanarkshire, Scotland G12 8QQ UK

A major urban research university located in the bohemian section of a working-class city. U of Glasgow is slightly smaller than U of Edinburgh and the atmosphere somewhat more laid-back. The West End is student-friendly, with lots of cafés and shops. Glasgow is a financial and shopping center also known for its nightlife. Locals claim "you can have more fun at a Glasgow funeral than at an Edinburgh wedding." Glasgow students get the point.

Website: www.gla.ac.uk
Location: City Center
Public
Total Enrollment: 23,082
Undergraduates: 16,669
Male/Female: 41/59
SAT Ranges: 1200 or above (combined)
ACT Ranges: 27 or above
Financial Aid: N/A
Pell Grant: N/A
Expense: Pub $
Student Loans: N/A
Average Debt: N/A
Phi Beta Kappa: No
Applicants: 5,779
Accepted: N/A
Enrolled: N/A

The second oldest of Scotland's major universities, the University of Glasgow shares the history and culture of Scotland's largest city. Glasgow (population 599,000) was a major center of the 18th-century Scottish Enlightenment and the 19th-century Industrial Revolution, and it now ranks as Britain's largest financial center after London. The University of Glasgow was founded in 1451 with quarters in Glasgow Cathedral before moving to its own main campus in Gilmorehill in the city's West End in 1870. In contrast to the elitist traditions of other ancient British universities, Glasgow pioneered in serving the educational needs of the growing urban and commercial classes and in 1894 became the first Scottish university to grant degrees to women. Along with Edinburgh, it belongs to the two major groups of research universities: the Russell Group (British) and Universitas 21 (global).

Not surprisingly for a place with more than five centuries of history, the dominant architectural style on campus is neo-Gothic, with a healthy mix of Victorian thrown in. While other sections of Glasgow retain the hardscrabble feel of a depressed industrial area, the West End is a bohemian residential area with an abundance of restaurants, cafés, and shops catering to the college crowd. "The area is very student-oriented, with plenty of venues offering student discounts," reports one student. A literature major describes the university as "a huge school with a small-town feel." The city center, a 15-minute walk from the university, offers an abundance of historical sites and museums, as well as the best shopping in Britain outside London. Kelvingrove Park and the Botanical Gardens are down the street from the main gate of the university. The university has embarked on a $1.2 billion development plan that will expand the campus footprint by more than 25 percent by 2026. Construction on the first stage of the plan, a new Learning and Teaching Hub, is set to commence in 2017.

Students describe the academic climate as pressured but balanced. "Professors know their field and are excellent at providing students with an enormous amount of insight into the courses and subjects," says a European politics major. But another warns, "Specific assignments aren't given. You're told which books go with the course, and you'd better read them on your own!" The workload is said to increase noticeably in later years, but because students apply to study in a particular field, they "rarely find themselves in courses they would prefer to avoid because of distribution requirements." All undergraduates complete a dissertation or research project based on independent research, supervised by a faculty member in their major. First-year students go through a Fresher's Week, with tours of the university, concerts, and other events, and special orientation is also provided for international students.

> "[The West End] is very student-oriented, with plenty of venues offering student discounts."

Slightly smaller than Edinburgh, Glasgow is the only Scottish university with the full range of both professional and academic offerings. The university is divided into four colleges: Arts; Social Sciences; Science and Engineering; and Medical, Veterinary, & Life Sciences. Befitting the alma mater of physicist Lord Kelvin, the sciences are strong, notably veterinary medicine and geography. The economics department is proud that it turned out Adam Smith, and history is well regarded. English language and literature is a traditional strength, and Glasgow maintains the only department of Scottish literature anywhere. Eastern European languages like Czech and Polish are specialties. One student suggests that "visiting students would do well to take a literature course in this department to gain an understanding of the country which they are visiting." For U.S. students, the most popular majors by enrollment are politics, history, business and management, and English literature. The university has faculty of education and offers a five-year joint studies program in product design engineering with the Glasgow School of Art.

Students describe faculty members as respected and well published in their fields. Lectures are offered by full professors, and tutorials of about 15 students are occasionally handled by graduate students, whose teaching is described as "hit-or-miss." Semester-long or yearlong study abroad programs are popular, especially through the Erasmus program, which allows students to take courses at European universities, and a year of foreign study is mandatory for foreign language students during their third year. "The university seems to believe that a world culture is very important and values it," says a Scottish literature major.

> "Professors know their field and are excellent at providing students with an enormous amount of insight."

Consistent with the university's cosmopolitan setting and traditions, the student body is a diverse lot with regard to nationality, race, religion, and socioeconomic backgrounds. Nearly one-third of students are international, hailing from 120 countries; roughly 40 percent are native to Scotland and the balance come from elsewhere in the UK. Expats include more than 800 Americans. "You don't have an exclusive student body," reports a sophomore. "Dealing and working with people from different backgrounds is the norm." The university offers a fourth-year tuition

(continued)

Grad in 6 Years: N/A
Returning Freshmen: N/A
Academics: ✐ ✐ ✐
Social: ☎ ☎ ☎
Q of L: ★ ★ ★
Admissions: (+44) 141 3302000
Email Address: student .recruitment@glasgow.ac.uk

Strong Programs:
Politics
History
Business and Management
English Literature
Veterinary Medicine
Geography
Economics
Scottish Literature

All undergraduates complete a dissertation or research project based on independent research, supervised by a faculty member in their major.

waiver as a merit scholarship for qualified international students, including those from the U.S., and it also accepts U.S. federal loans, as determined by the FAFSA.

Freshmen usually live in university housing, which is not on campus but spread throughout the northwest sections of the city, and then move into readily available independent housing in later years. The dorms are generally comfortable, and international students are guaranteed housing. One student recalls, "My first year I was in a student apartment in an old Victorian tenement flat. It was very beautiful. I had friends who stayed in the more modern student flats, and those were nice as well." Students describe campus security as good. "I always feel safe on campus," says an archaeology major. The university is launching a new campaign, Let's Talk, aimed at building a system for reporting sexual assault, providing resources to survivors, and educating the community on bystander intervention. As for dining, only one of the seven residence halls offers catered food, and it is located away from the main campus. The others are self-catered, which means that students cook for themselves or savor the offerings of dining facilities sprinkled throughout the campus. "The on-campus dining is very good, and they have a range of foods from Indian to Scottish on various days," reports one denizen. "There is also typically a vegan dish available upon request." A psych major reports living in a noncatered hall with an ample and well-equipped kitchen. "I enjoyed the independence of making all my own meals and found that I was able to save a lot of money by doing so," she says.

> **"The university seems to believe that a world culture is very important and values it."**

Glasgow offers a fourth-year tuition waiver as a merit scholarship for qualified international students, including those from the U.S.

Social life is equally divided between on- and off-campus activities. Glasgow offers an abundance of quality restaurants, clubs, and pubs. There are plenty of ceilidhs, or Gaelic social gatherings, and the city sponsors an International Comedy Festival each March. Glasgow has a vigorous music scene, hosting an average of 130 music events every week. Much of the on-campus social life revolves around the two student-run university unions, the Glasgow University Union (GUU) and the Queen Margaret Union (QMU), which host student organizations, provide dining and social activities and, of course, have their own bars. Since most students are above the drinking age of 18, underage imbibing is a nonissue. GUU favors sports and debates, while QMU is big on music. One popular event is GUU's Daft Friday, a black-tie affair at the end of the first term where the entire building is elaborately decorated around a secret theme. The Student Representative Council sponsors an annual Raising and Giving week to aid volunteer organizations and raise awareness of volunteer opportunities. Social activism tends to be most vigorous when the issue involves cuts to the university budget and increases in tuition levels, but there are plenty of student groups organized around issues such as the environment, gender equality, and LGBTQ rights. Road trips are a major attraction of studying in Scotland, both to in-country destinations like Edinburgh and beyond. "It's easy to get to visit Europe while studying in Glasgow with cheap flights and accommodations," reports one student. "I recently visited Paris with an 18-pound return flight!"

> **"It's easy to get to visit Europe while studying in Glasgow with cheap flights and accommodations."**

Intercollegiate debating is taken seriously, and the university has won the national championship several times. More than 60 percent of students belong to the Glasgow University Sports Union and more than 3,000 students take part in 49 sports teams. Competitive team sports include rugby, soccer, hockey, basketball, volleyball, American football, rowing, cricket, golf, and many others, and recreational clubs are available for everything from cycling to skydiving to surfing. The only athletic rivalry of any consequence in town is the off-campus competition between the two Glasgow soccer clubs, Celtic (Roman Catholic) and the Rangers (Protestant). A

More than 60 percent of students belong to the Glasgow University Sports Union.

student warns, "It's better not to get involved, as the games are just staging grounds for sectarian hatred. Much of the city's police funding goes to monitoring these violent affairs."

The city of Glasgow is shedding its rough reputation, and undergrads describe their experience living and studying in the West End as rewarding. One American sums up her experience as follows: "Glasgow offers a good mix of academics and fun. It's a highly rated school with many good departments, not too competitive, and has all types of students. And other than the weather, Glasgow is a great city to live in."

If You Apply To ➤ **Glasgow:** Rolling admissions: Jun. 30. No application fee. No campus or alumni interviews. SATs or ACTs: required. Subject Tests: required (at least two; AP exams also accepted. Subjects relevant to degree program). Letters of recommendation: required. Essay: required. Accepts the Common Application with supplement.

University of St Andrews

St Andrews, Scotland KY16 9AJ GB

The most international of Scotland's four "ancient" universities and the most popular destination for Americans studying in the UK. Small by British standards and comparable in feel and stature to Brown. Major drawing cards range across English literature, international relations, medieval history, the sciences, and modern languages. St Andrews is inseparable from the town, which boasts the famed "Old Course" where the British Open is played every five years. With 600 years to gestate, traditions reign supreme.

Harvard likes to brag about the fact that it was founded back in 1636. Think that's old? Try 1413, the date Pope Benedict XIII issued a Papal Bull recognizing the University of St Andrews as Scotland's first university and the third in the English-speaking world. Set in an ancient town on the North Sea opposite Norway, St Andrews is an ideal spot for adventuresome Americans who want a world-class education and an introduction to life outside North America. It now numbers more than 900 Yankees among its 6,700 undergrads, with the number on the rise. Success here requires a go-getter mentality. Support services are available, but students on this side of the Atlantic are accustomed to being treated like adults. "They don't hold your hand," says one U.S. student.

St Andrews is the only institution in the *Fiske Guide* whose most prominent landmark is the spot where a student was burned at the stake. In 1528, a Protestant reformer named Patrick Hamilton fell victim to a prolonged burning imposed by the local archbishop. Tradition deems that if you step on the stones that mark the spot where he was martyred, you will fail your final exams, unless you submerge yourself in the North Sea just before dawn the first day of May as part of a tradition called the May Dip. Academic buildings are interspersed through the town's narrow medieval streets, and for all practical purposes, says one student, "The university *is* the town." Buildings are constructed of ancient stone and include the ruins of a 13th-century castle and a cathedral. Narrow alleys, called "wynds" by the Scots, lead to secluded gardens and courtyards that add to the old-world charm. A number of academic buildings are perched on cliffs overlooking the North Sea, and white beaches are a

"The university *is* the town."

Social: ☎ ☎ ☎

Q of L: ★ ★ ★

Admissions: (+44) (0) 1334462194

Email Address: international@ st-andrews.ac.uk

Strong Programs:

International Relations

Psychology

Physics

Marine Biology

Modern Languages

English Literature

Medicine

Management

A number of academic buildings are perched on cliffs overlooking the North Sea.

two-minute walk from some of the dorms. The library, known as the Palace of Mustard because of unfortunate color choices by an apparently color-blind interior decorator, has been completely refurbished.

Though more flexible than most British universities, St Andrews offers less latitude to explore a variety of subjects than U.S. institutions, and so is best suited to those who arrive with clear academic goals in mind. "It's the best of both worlds—an academic focus, but you can still take some courses outside your major," says a junior. Students typically take three yearlong courses, or "modules," in each of their first two years, continue with two of them in the second year, and then opt for a single or double honors program the final two years. "Pick your courses carefully," counsels one U.S. student. "You can't major in something you haven't taken the first year." Modules generally consist of three lectures per week with 100 or more students and a tutorial with 10 to 20, while honors-level courses are generally taught in seminar format. Fewer courses means less time in class and more emphasis on outside reading—"much more than in the States," says a UCLA study abroad student. Modules typically end with papers or exams that account for most of the grade, and there is a full week without classes prior to exams. More so than in the United States, the onus is on the students to keep current with their work and seek help from faculty when necessary. "St Andrews is a very rigorous environment, where you are encouraged to take on independent research," says a junior. "If you make it through, you'll be strong." Nevertheless, the faculty gets high marks, and students like having professors who are internationally known in their fields. "Our lecturers are very good," comments a junior. And when students do reach out for help, they find ample academic and personal support from Student Services and wardens (RAs) in the residence halls; indeed, nearly all freshmen return for their sophomore year.

> "Pick your courses carefully. You can't major in something you haven't taken the first year."

Signature offerings at St Andrews include international relations (IR), psychology (especially neuroscience), physics, marine biology, and modern languages, and the university is a world leader in the study of international terrorism. The most popular majors include medicine, IR, management, and English. Americans at St Andrews tend to cluster in a few departments, notably psychology and international relations. "I thought doing international relations in the U.S. would be a bit silly," says one American. Standards in foreign language are higher than in the United States, an opportunity but also a challenge. "I got close to 700 on my SAT IIs in French and I was completely lost," says a second-year student. As at many U.S. universities, natural science students tend to work the hardest.

St Andrews is one of the world's most international universities, with one-third of its students from Scotland and the European Union, another third from elsewhere in the UK, and another third from the rest of the world, including sizable contingents from Scandinavia, Eastern Europe, Asia, the Middle East, and, of course, the U.S. In fact, Americans represent the largest international group. Having friends from around the world is both enriching and convenient because, as one American student explains, "you have lots of choices of places to go on vacation." The international melting pot seems to work, although the upper-middle-class background of some English students lends a more conservative tenor to the campus than some Americans might expect—as is generally true of top universities in the UK.

St Andrews is inviting enough to have attracted the likes of Prince William and Kate Middleton, who met there. While it is competitive for European students, who must be in the top 10th academically, it is more accessible for U.S. students who have the brains to make it into the Ivies but can't throw a football or play a Liszt concerto. Many of the Americans at St Andrews arrive with an international orientation, including "diplobrats" whose parents have worked in international organizations such as the World Bank or the State Department. The British and internationals typically give Americans a warm welcome. Tuition varies depending on the course, but the total bill for a year at St Andrews is likely to be roughly $25,000, depending on the exchange rate. Students in the International Honours joint-degree program spend two years at the College of William and Mary and two years at St Andrews and earn degrees in classical studies, economics, English, film studies, history, or international relations from both institutions.

Housing is guaranteed for first-year students only, and students can request a single or shared room; 42 percent of students reside in university housing. They also have the option of the university meal plan or "self-catering," in which they use kitchens in the dorms to prepare their food. Catered dorms are the most central and ancient, although students tend to give the food less-than-enthusiastic reviews. Meals are served at specified times with standard portions, so don't expect the glitzy food courts or all-you-can-eat service typical in the States. On the plus side, dorm life includes once-a-week maid service. After their first year, students generally move to one

> "I thought doing international relations in the U.S. would be a bit silly."

of the many apartments (flats) in town. "There is a bit of a scramble for flats in February, but most students are able to find good accommodations," reports an IR and French major.

Given the symbiosis of town and gown, social life "takes place in the town's pubs, the student union, the dorms, and apartments," says an English major. A peek inside the student union reveals something never seen on a U.S. campus: a fully equipped bar with, of course, an ample array of scotch. The drinking age is 18 in Britain, and St Andrews boasts 18 pubs. Though there may not be more alcohol than at an American institution, it is certainly more out in the open and thus less of an issue. Black-tie balls are also a staple, as are ceilidhs (pronounced "kaylees"), which feature traditional Scottish dancing akin to square dancing. Like other Scottish universities, St Andrews offers "a society for everything you can think of," says a senior. Interested in whiskey tasting? Philosophical debate? Belly dancing? Harry Potter? Tunnocks Caramel Wafers? Then there's a society just waiting for you, probably with meetings at a pub. The St Andrews debating society was founded in 1793 and continues to do well in international competitions. Political activism is muted—"It's not the place to start protesting," reports a junior—but the annual Charities Campaign is well supported by students.

As befitting a 600-year-old institution, St Andrews is rife with traditions. Red gowns, once the student uniform, are only worn on special occasions, but pubs are still forbidden to serve anyone wearing one. The aforementioned May Dip, aimed at purging oneself of academic bad luck, has roots in pagan times. One student explains that during Raisin Weekend in November, first-year students "equipped with multiple cans of shaving foam and dressed up in costume are taken by their adopted academic

> "[Social life] takes place in the town's pubs, the student union, the dorms, and apartments."

parents (older students who will take the first-years under their wing) to a huge shaving foam fight in one of the school squares." Students emerging from their last exam are greeted by their friends and doused with buckets of cold water.

The nearest road-trip destination is the medium-sized city of Dundee, about 20 minutes away, which offers nightclubs, a mall, movie theaters, and a McDonald's. (Subway is the only American fast-food joint to crack the St Andrews market thus far.) Scotland's two largest cities, Edinburgh and Glasgow, are about an hour away, and for outdoorsy types, the legendary Scottish Highlands are within easy reach. The Student Association helps with overseas travel.

Though more flexible than most British universities, St Andrews offers less latitude to explore a variety of subjects than U.S. institutions.

St Andrews is a world leader in the study of international terrorism.

Soccer, a.k.a. football, is the national sport, and students congregate to watch pro teams in the pubs or on the big-screen TV at the union. Rugby, tennis, golf, soccer, rowing, and water polo are among the school's most competitive sports teams, although these draw fewer spectators than do varsity sports in the U.S.— "you don't have 40,000 screaming fans," notes one student. Students tend to be much more enthusiastic about their "hall sport" competitions (the equivalent of intramurals in the U.S.), in sports ranging from rugby and ultimate Frisbee to shinty, a violent Scottish mix of field hockey and lacrosse. Students can also join the sports center, which has recently been renovated and upgraded with top-of-the-line facilities and equipment. The fabled Old Course, where golf was invented in the 1500s, offers student discounts, but the sport is not as popular among students here as one might assume.

Although St Andrews comes the closest of any of the Scottish universities to having the feel of a liberal arts college, this is not the United States. Those who come here must be ready to adjust to a different way of life, and the tight identification of the university and the town can eventually make for a bit of claustrophobia. But these are small prices to pay for Scotland in all its ancient glory. U.S. institutions may trumpet their diversity, but nothing stateside compares to the richness of living abroad among the best and brightest from all corners of the globe. St Andrews delivers it all against a hauntingly beautiful backdrop that will remain forever etched in the minds of all who come here. And there's always the chance that you will hit it off with a future king or queen of England.

Overlaps

Georgetown, Brown, NYU, Columbia, Tufts, Harvard, McGill, Yale

If You Apply To ➤

St Andrews: Rolling admissions: May 1 (if applying via the Common Application) or Jun. 30 (if applying via UCAS). Housing: Jun. 30. Application fee: $75. No campus or alumni interviews. SATs (with essay) or ACTs (with writing): recommended. Subject Tests: optional. Letters of recommendation: required. Essay: required. Accepts the Common Application with supplement.

Trinity College Dublin

College Green, Dublin 2, Ireland

The youngest four-year university in Ireland, Trinity College Dublin belongs to a peer group consisting of Oxbridge and the four ancient Scottish universities—albeit with a more European feel. Trinity combines rich academic offerings across the curriculum with life in one of the world's youngest and most vibrant capital cities. Traditions abound, academic and otherwise. Where else do honors students get the right to graze their sheep on the college green?

Website: www.tcd.ie
Location: City Center
Public
Total Enrollment: 17,511
Undergraduates: 11,457
Male/Female: 43/57
SAT Ranges: CR 600–700, M 600–700
ACT Ranges: N/A
Financial Aid: N/A

Founded in 1592 by Queen Elizabeth as an Irish counterpart to Oxford and Cambridge, Trinity College Dublin is the largest and most distinguished of the seven universities in Ireland and one of the strongest anywhere. Although best known for its offerings in the humanities and social sciences, Trinity is strong across the curriculum, including in new specialties such as nanoscience. The university has produced enough distinguished alumni to fill an encyclopedia (Jonathan Swift, Oscar Wilde, Edmund Burke, and Ernest Walton for starters), and its students bathe in centuries-old academic traditions while enjoying life in one of Europe's most vibrant capital cities. "Dublin is an incredibly student-friendly city," says a junior. "It offers students whatever the university doesn't."

Trinity College Dublin occupies a 47-acre oasis in the heart of Dublin, within easy walking distance of the national museums, government buildings, and other major cultural attractions. "When you pass under the archway you move from the bustle of the city to a traditional liberal arts setting, complete with rugby and cricket pitches," explains a sophomore. Most of the central buildings are built of light gray Georgian stone, including its iconic Campanile, whose bells ring on the hour and 10 minutes before exams. The Trinity College Library is Ireland's deposit library and home to the Book of Kells, an illuminated Latin manuscript of the Gospels that draws a steady stream of tourists onto the campus. Another library bears the name of James Ussher, the university's first student, who went on to make a name for himself by calculating that the world started at 6:00 p.m. on October 22, 4004 BC. Trinity College Dublin essentially coexists with a city that, with four large universities in its midst, has the youngest population in Europe and boasts a vibrant music and cultural scene. Where else can you go pub crawling in the footsteps of James Joyce and Bram Stoker? "Everything Dublin has to offer is within walking distance of the Front Gate," says one student. A freshman describes Dublin as "a fantastic city in all regards," but cautions, "Let's not go overboard. There is also a lot of rain."

> "Dublin is an incredibly student-friendly city."

Trinity is organized around three schools in each of the traditional areas: arts, humanities, and social sciences; engineering, math, and science; and health sciences. Unlike other universities in Ireland, Trinity offers a four-year undergraduate program parallel to the four "ancient" universities in Scotland. There are no "core" courses that everyone is required to take. The college has traditionally been best known for its English and literature courses along with history, geography, political science, and international studies. Mathematics and the sciences are also strong, especially molecular biology and genetics, immunology, and chemistry. The Trinity Biomedical Sciences Institute is a new state-of-the-art research facility, while the Trinity Long Room Hub opened in 2010 for research in the arts and humanities. In fact, all students are required to complete an undergraduate research project. Nanoscience, Physics, and Chemistry of Advanced Materials (N-PCAM) is a four-year honors degree dealing with the physics and chemistry of small-scale matter. The BESS program (Business, Economics, and Social Studies) is particularly popular among American students, who are also beginning to pursue the sciences in greater numbers. The college has also recently introduced a specialized business studies degree. Trinity has a strong interdisciplinary culture, and the Broad Curriculum option encourages students to exercise their curiosity in a module (course) outside their specialty, such as film studies or globalization.

Trinity's academic climate offers "a healthy balance between prescribed work and suggested, voluntary endeavors that students can undertake if they so wish," explains a history and economics double major. "The vast majority of students are open to collaborative learning and prove helpful to each other outside of the lectures and seminars." The academic year runs for 12 weeks each in the fall and spring, followed by three weeks of exams. Students accumulate 60 credits per year through modules offering various numbers of credits, with strong weight given to final exams, although the balance of continuous and final assessment varies by module. "The major difference between Trinity and American universities is that the onus falls much more on the students," says a junior. Lectures coupled with weekly tutorials are common the first two years but then give way to small seminars the last two years. A junior observes that Trinity "invests some of its best faculty toward teaching undergraduate freshmen." Each entering student is assigned a faculty tutor, not one of his or her professors, who will be available for personal, academic, and professional advice over four years and, if necessary, become

> "The vast majority of students are open to collaborative learning."

(continued)

Pell Grant: N/A
Expense: Pub $
Student Loans: N/A
Average Debt: N/A
Phi Beta Kappa: No
Applicants: 21,590
Accepted: 18%
Enrolled: 74%
Grad in 6 Years: 90%
Returning Freshmen: 95%
Academics: ✍ ✍ ✍ ✍ ✍
Social: ☎ ☎ ☎ ☎
Q of L: ★ ★ ★
Admissions: (+353) 1 896 4500
Email Address:
  academic.registry@tcd.ie

Strong Programs:
Business, Economics, and
   Social Studies
English Literature
History
Geography
Political Science
International Studies
Nanoscience
Molecular Biology

an advocate. American students can also sign up for the weeklong Trinity Smart-Start Program to help them get the hang of the university and its setting.

As the top university in Ireland, Trinity is highly competitive academically. There are about 200 Americans pursuing four-year degrees, most of whom would probably qualify on strict academic grounds for admission to Ivy League schools. Since Trinity is the closest European university to the East Coast of the U.S., it draws heavily from New York and New England, but it is attracting an increasing number of Texans and Californians who find access to the University of California frustrating. "I feel that students here are exceedingly hardworking," says a freshman. Ten percent of undergraduates are international students from 122 nations, with the U.S. and Canada making up the largest group. Most U.S. students have no Irish family connections, hail from elite public high schools and prep schools, and have traveled abroad. "I've never had a student who had to apply for a passport," says an administrator. Admission is based entirely on test scores and a 300-word academic statement, which makes Trinity an option for top students who are strong on academics but who neglected to edit their high school newspaper, star on the soccer team, or do community service in Bujumbura.

> **"Students here are exceedingly hardworking."**

Trinity has a strong interdisciplinary culture, and the Broad Curriculum option encourages students to exercise their curiosity.

Trinity students are encouraged to take advantage of the nearly 300 foreign study options, including those with leading institutions in Australia, Canada, India, China, and Singapore; 23 percent take part. Trinity participates in the Erasmus Program with other European universities and has special relationships in the U.S. with such prestigious institutions as Brown, Chicago, and Columbia. A political science major warns that some of the non-European universities "have still not worked out the kinks in transferring grades." Dublin serves as the European headquarters for several major companies, such as Google, Airbnb, Microsoft, and Facebook, which frequently recruit students for internships, summer jobs, and post-graduation careers.

While Trinity is less expensive than the four historic Scottish universities, it offers no institutional financial aid to U.S. students, although it does accept U.S. federal student loans. Nevertheless, all students can try their luck in a series of competitive tests that sophomores can take just after Christmas known as the Foundation Scholarship Exams. More than 400 students typically sit for the exams, with about 90 becoming either "scholars" or "foundation scholars." Scholars become members of the university's governing board. Other benefits include five years of free or heavily discounted tuition, free accommodations and evening meals, and, best of all, the privileges of carrying a sword into an exam and grazing their sheep on the campus green.

> **"Trinity students are spoiled for choice in terms of eating establishments extremely close to the university."**

Dublin serves as the European headquarters for companies such as Google and Airbnb, which frequently recruit students for internships.

One drawback of Trinity's self-contained campus is that it can accommodate only 11 percent of undergrads. Most first-year students live in Trinity Hall, a modern residence about 20 minutes by bus that offers comfortable six-person apartments with kitchens and living areas. "It is pretty much where all freshmen live, all together, so it is lots of fun," says a political science major. "It should be noted that after first year, students are generally expected to find their own housing within Dublin unless they are deeply involved in a club," says a freshman. Students say it's becoming more difficult to find affordable housing near campus. Preference for on-campus rooms goes to seniors, students with the highest grades, campus leaders, and international students. Trinity offers no university-wide meal plan, so students learn to cook for themselves or head to the two main restaurants or smaller cafés on campus, which provide simple meals. And as a senior points out, given the school's prime location, "Trinity students are spoiled for choice in terms of eating establishments extremely close to the university." Despite its urban setting, the campus is said to be safe, and a freshman comments, "My personal advice? Be street smart and savvy as you would in any large city and you'll be—as the Irish would say—*grand*."

Extracurricular activities may not help you to get into Trinity, but they play an important role in campus culture once you get there. There are more than 200 sports clubs and student societies devoted to activities from yoga to traditional Irish music to entrepreneurialism. "Most students sign up for a bunch of them when they first arrive and then gradually concentrate on just a few," reports an economics major. The most famous are the Philosophical Society ("the Phil"), which is the oldest debating club in the English-speaking world (1684), and its rival, the Historical Society ("the Hist"). The two groups share a building, sponsor weekly public debates, and award medals to notable visiting speakers. The Metaphysical Society ("the Metafizz") also gives students a chance to show off how much they know about Plato or Bertrand Russell. As far as the political climate on campus is concerned, protests against rising student fees are commonplace, and students cite a growing interest in advocating for women's and LGBTQ rights.

Social life takes place both on and off campus. "The social scene is fantastic," exudes an English major. "There is a big pub scene—it is Ireland, after all—and we are in the city center." Student clubs are mandated to throw events once a month, so there is plenty to choose from every day of the week. The drinking age is 18, and most students attend "Pav Fridays," where the lively on-campus Pavilion Bar offers cheap beer and cider. "As the student bar is the designated drinking spot, there are very few people who choose to drink elsewhere on campus, so that works well," says a theoretical physics major. St. Patrick's Day is always a time to celebrate, but unquestionably the biggest event is the weeklong Trinity Week. It starts on Monday, when the new Scholars are announced, given black robes, and invited to take on current Scholars in a game of marbles on the steps of the chapel. Festivities culminate on Friday with the Trinity Ball, frequently described as "the largest private party in Europe." "It's a massive music festival where many popular Irish and European bands perform," says a recent graduate. "It draws 8,000 students, staff, and alumni in formal dress and takes over the city." Recent headliners have included Bastille and Ellie Goulding. Trinity is ideally located for travel to European and other destinations. "There are cheap buses from Dublin to any corner of Ireland," reports a senior. "It is also possible to fly to continental Europe or the UK for well under 50 euros."

Sports are for playing, not watching. Says a history major, "There is no school mascot or particular set of colors that students wear. People tend to do sport mainly as an extracurricular activity. It's not really a status symbol." Nevertheless, there are at least 60 club and intramural sports, with Gaelic football, rugby, and rowing among the most popular. The annual dodgeball tournament is also a highlight. Although the English invented rugby, students at Trinity started the first club, and the boat (rowing) club is also one of the oldest. The university does hire coaches for some intercollegiate sports, such as rugby and soccer, and team leaders are eligible for scholarships.

Trinity College Dublin combines strong academics with the benefits of a beautiful campus in the midst of a thriving capital city that is also a gateway to the rest of Europe. "You get a top-tier degree that costs less than most private colleges in the U.S. and gives you the international experience of a lifetime," comments one American denizen. "And I met the nicest, most interesting, and hilarious people— the Irish."

There are more than 200 sports clubs and student societies devoted to activities from yoga to traditional Irish music to entrepreneurialism.

"As the student bar is the designated drinking spot, there are very few people who choose to drink elsewhere on campus."

Overlaps

University of St Andrews, University of Edinburgh, King's College London, University College Dublin, Brown, NYU, University of California

University of Iowa

107 Calvin Hall, Iowa City, IA 52242

A bargain compared with other Big Ten schools such as Michigan and Illinois. Iowa is world-famous for its creative writing program and Writers' Workshop. Other areas of strength include health sciences, social and behavioral sciences, and space physics. Future scientists should check out the Research Fellows Program. The university is a regional draw, with 34 percent of the students from out of state.

Website: www.uiowa.edu
Location: Small City
Public
Total Enrollment: 24,398
Undergraduates: 19,712
Male/Female: 48/52
SAT Ranges: CR 460–630,
   M 540–690
ACT Ranges: 23–28
Financial Aid: 58%
Pell Grant: 21%
Expense: Pub $
Student Loans: 51%
Average Debt: $ $ $
Phi Beta Kappa: Yes
Applicants: 26,222
Accepted: 81%
Enrolled: 23%
Grad in 6 Years: 70%
Returning Freshmen: 85%
Academics: ✍ ✍ ✍ ✍
Social: ☎ ☎ ☎
Q of L: ★ ★ ★
Admissions: (319) 335-3847
Email Address: admissions@
   uiowa.edu

Strong Programs:
Creative Writing
Finance
Psychology
Communication Studies
Health and Human Physiology
Nursing

At first glance, one might dismiss Iowa as a standard-issue Midwestern State U. But look beyond the endless miles of fields and corn and you'll find one of the most dynamic schools in the country—and one of the best values to boot. Iowa is known for breeding stellar nurses, future doctors, and of course, wrestlers. "I feel like I'm at home when I'm here," says a sophomore. "Iowa has a great vibe." Iowa was the first public university in the 19th century to admit men and women on an equal basis and the first to accept theater, music, and the other arts as equal to more traditional areas of academic research. The university has long been a major player in the creative worlds, particularly writing, and its small-town atmosphere is just one of many reasons students nationwide flock to this "budget Ivy."

The 1,770-acre campus is located in the rolling hills of the Iowa River valley. Among the 298 major buildings is Old Capitol, the first capitol of Iowa, a national historic landmark and the symbol of the university. The primary architectural styles of the campus buildings are Greek Revival and modern. Notable facilities include a 216,000-square-foot, state-of-the-art recreation and wellness center and the College of Public Health Building. The new Visual Arts Building serves students from across the curriculum, including about 400 design-oriented engineering students per year.

Each of the three undergraduate colleges has its own general education requirements. Liberal arts students must take courses in rhetoric, natural science, social sciences, foreign language, historical perspectives, humanities, and quantitative or formal reasoning. Also required are general education courses in the areas of cultural diversity, foreign civilization and culture, and physical education. On Iowa! immerses incoming freshmen in the campus culture and introduces them to traditions that will define their Iowa experience.

> **"The English department is stellar."**

Iowa has a long tradition in creative arts. It was one of the first universities to award graduate degrees for creative work and is also the home of the famed Writers' Workshop, a two-year graduate program for emerging authors whose graduates have included Jane Smiley and John Irving. The school also prides itself on its International Writing Program. "The English department is stellar," raves one English major. "It's possibly the best in the country—at least for creative writing." Iowa's on-campus hospital is one of the largest teaching hospitals in the United States. Undergraduates benefit from the strong programs in health professions such as physician's assistant and medical technician. The most popular majors are finance, psychology, communication studies, and health and human physiology. Iowa is also strong in the social and behavioral sciences, space physics, and paleontology. Combined degree programs permit students to earn degrees in liberal arts and their choice of business, engineering, nursing, or medicine. Agriculture, veterinary medicine, forestry, architecture, and animal science are not offered at Iowa but are taught at its sister institution, Iowa State.

(continued)

Social and Behavioral Sciences
Space Physics

"The academic climate is extremely competitive," says one sophomore, although most agree the intensity can vary by program. Just over half of the classes have fewer than 20 students, and "freshmen do tend to spend a majority of their time in large lectures," says a senior. Professors are a mixed bag, students report. "I have had a few really amazing teachers become mentors and I've had more than a few terrible teachers who don't care," a journalism major says. The University of Iowa's Four-Year Graduation Plan guarantees that students who fulfill certain requirements will not have their graduation delayed by unavailability of a needed course. The University Honors Program provides special academic, cultural, and social opportunities to undergraduates who maintain a cumulative grade point average of 3.3 or higher. About 150 students, across all disciplines, are chosen each year to be ICRU Research Fellows, earning scholarships of up to $2,500 to engage in faculty-mentored research. Roughly 800 undergraduates study abroad, mostly in UI-sponsored programs; in all, programs are available in 75 countries worldwide.

"Freshmen do tend to spend a majority of their time in large lectures."

Iowa's on-campus hospital is one of the largest teaching hospitals in the United States.

"I think that the students here are more open-minded than at our closest rival," says a premed student. "I think this is because of the strong artistic and performing culture present here." Fifty-five percent of the undergraduates hail from Iowa, with most of the rest coming from contiguous states, especially Illinois; 11 percent are international. African Americans account for 3 percent, Hispanics 7 percent, and Asian Americans 4 percent. Students say the campus is extremely tolerant and a community atmosphere is fostered in and out of the classroom. As part of its efforts to welcome diversity on campus, the university's application now includes an optional question regarding sexual identity. Twenty-one percent of freshmen qualify for Pell Grants. In addition to the 585 athletic scholarships, there are academic scholarships averaging $4,776 for eligible students. Twenty Roy J. Carver Scholarships are awarded each year to juniors who have "overcome unusual or debilitating circumstances in life."

Students say that campus residence halls are very sociable and therefore not very quiet. "The dorms have a very comfortable atmosphere and are cleaned daily," says a sophomore. All are co-ed by floor or wing. Twenty-six percent of undergrads live in university housing, and one student warns, "For the past several years, a few hundred students get put in temporary housing until rooms open up." Students can choose to live in one of more than 30 living/learning communities, such as Craftastic, Green Adventures, and Justice for All. Most students move off campus after their first year, often to apartments or houses adjacent to the campus. The "very nice" dining halls are "set up like food courts, with numerous options for varying ethnic and special taste backgrounds," says a senior. The student union includes a pastry and coffee shop, two cafeterias, and the State Room Restaurant.

"The dorms have a very comfortable atmosphere."

About 150 students, across all disciplines, are chosen each year to be ICRU Research Fellows, earning scholarships of up to $2,500.

"The weekends are a major part of college life," a student says. Thirteen percent of the men and 18 percent of the women belong to fraternities and sororities, respectively, and these groups tend to play less of a role in the social life than they do elsewhere. Football, basketball, and wrestling events are especially popular on campus. On weekends, students often venture to the downtown area, across the street from campus, which "is built with the college student in mind," a student says. "There are two university theaters right on campus and many affordable cultural events take place at Hancher Auditorium. The Union Bar and Grill, Mickey's, Sports Column, and George's are all popular hangouts with students." The school officially follows the state policy regarding alcohol. "Students disobey the policy," says a student, "but there are fines and academic ramifications." Riverfest, held at the Iowa Memorial Union and on the banks of the Iowa River, is a weeklong, all-campus event celebrating the long-awaited spring. "It is a unique tradition that brings the campus and the community together," says a sophomore. Students also look forward to the annual Iowa City Jazz Festival, homecoming, Dance Marathon, and Big Ten football, especially the game against Iowa State. For a change of scene, Chicago, Kansas City, or St. Louis are all within four to six hours by car, a short road trip by Midwestern standards.

Iowa's Hawkeyes compete in the Division I Big Ten Conference. The football team is a national powerhouse and regularly appears in New Year's Day bowl games. Hawkeye fans are serious about their team: "The whole town is basked in black and gold," a freshman says. Men's and women's basketball are especially competitive, as are wrestling, football, field hockey, and softball. Sixteen percent of undergrads participate in the extensive intramural program, which offers more than 40 individual, dual, or team sports with a variety of leagues. Among the most popular are flag football, indoor soccer, basketball, volleyball, and spikeball.

Much more than a campus among the cornfields, Iowa boasts a beautiful university that is ever evolving. "The University of Iowa is continually renovating and improving its facilities to stay modern and keep up with technology," says a sophomore. The scope of its academic programs is broad and social activities abound—especially when it comes to rooting for their Hawkeyes.

Overlaps

University of Illinois at Urbana–Champaign, Iowa State, University of Missouri, Indiana University, Illinois State, University of Minnesota, University of Wisconsin–Madison, University of Illinois at Chicago

If You Apply To ➤ **Iowa:** Rolling admissions: May 1. Priority financial aid: Dec. 1. Housing: Jun. 15. Application fee: $40. No campus or alumni interviews. SATs or ACTs: required. No Subject Tests. Letters of recommendation: optional. Essay: optional. Applicants have option of selecting gender pronouns of reference, preferred name, and sexual orientation.

Iowa State University

100 Alumni Hall, Ames, IA 50011

Agriculture and engineering are the twin pillars of the curriculum, and the university is a magnet for prevets. Ames is a small city and ISU must still endure barbs from certain snobby people in Iowa City. In truth, ISU is relatively cosmopolitan, with students hailing from more than 100 foreign countries. While others retrench, ISU continues to expand.

Website: www.iastate.edu
Location: Small City
Public
Total Enrollment: 31,572
Undergraduates: 28,073
Male/Female: 57/43

Love for Iowa State University runs as deep as its Midwestern roots. Strong programs in engineering, business, and agriculture attract students from around the globe. The close-knit, small-town atmosphere fostered at this school of more than 28,000 undergraduates keeps them here. At a time when many state universities are tightening the purse strings and retrenching, Iowa State has its eyes set on future growth. The university is planning to add more than 200 faculty members, mostly in research-oriented fields such as agricultural biotechnology and biorenewable energy.

The university has lavished attention on its parklike setting, located on a 1,984-acre tract in the middle of Ames, population 60,000. The campus, which boasts a combination of dignified old buildings and award-winning new ones, is a model of landscape design with numerous shady quadrangles with floral plantings and artwork that create a garden-like quality. History and tradition prevail, from the campanile, which serenades the campus with its carillon bells, to the huge public art collection including sculptures by Danish artist Christian Petersen. Howe Hall, home to aerospace engineering, boasts a virtual reality application center and a six-sided virtual reality cave. Along with Hoover Hall, the complex provides the teaching and research home for the College of Engineering. Much of the campus is closed to cars, largely for the benefit of walking, bicycling, and in-line skating students, as well as the swans (named Sir Lancelot and Lady Elaine) and ducks that reside on Lake LaVerne. The CyRide fare-free bus system delivers students around campus and the city. Recent construction includes a state-of-the-art biorenewables research lab.

> "We have some world-class profs here who are doing important research."

All undergraduates must take two semesters of ISUComm, foundational courses covering written, oral, visual, and electronic communication, and demonstrate proficiency in English prior to graduation. Other general education requirements, which vary by college, focus on gaining breadth in the natural and social sciences, but everyone takes a half-credit course on the use of the library and must satisfy a three-credit requirement in diversity. When Iowa State opened in 1869 as a land grant university, agriculture and engineering ruled the academic roost. These days, though, the liberal arts are nearly as popular, and the College of Liberal Arts and Sciences is the largest of ISU's seven undergraduate colleges. Other colleges include business, design, veterinary medicine, and human sciences. Among the university's 100-plus majors, the College of Agriculture still fields outstanding programs in animal science, turf grass management, agribusiness, and agronomy. Mechanical, electrical, and computer engineering are the most popular majors, followed by kinesiology and animal science. Programs in biosystems engineering, chemistry, and civil engineering are also strong.

Students find the academic climate competitive, but report that it varies by program. Twenty-four percent of classes have more than 50 students. Despite the university's size, professors teach most classes, with the exception of some freshman English options. "We have some world-class profs here who are doing important research," one senior says. Academic and career counseling draw praise too, and advisors are "always readily available" to help students.

> "We have a lot of farmers and small-town Iowans."

Students can also use the AccessPlus system of electronic kiosks sprinkled around campus to check the status of their university bill or financial aid package, print an unofficial transcript, or get their current schedule. Seventy percent of freshmen join ISU's 80 highly touted learning communities, which offer the opportunity to join a group of other newcomers who share similar academic interests in taking a common set of classes together or living together on the same residence hall floor. An honors program enrolls 400 outstanding freshmen each year, many of whom live in honors housing. Roughly 5 to 10 percent of undergrads study overseas; popular destinations include Italy, the United Kingdom, China, Australia, and Costa Rica. Participation in undergraduate research and capstone programs is on the rise.

Sixty-four percent of ISU's undergraduates are Iowans, though all 50 states and more than 100 countries are represented here. Foreign students comprise 7 percent of the student body. Iowa State was the first co-ed land grant institution, but attracting minorities has proven more difficult: Hispanics comprise 5 percent, Asian Americans 3 percent, and African Americans 3 percent. "We have a lot of farmers

(continued)

SAT Ranges: CR 460–620, M 500–640
ACT Ranges: 22–28
Financial Aid: 51%
Pell Grant: N/A
Expense: Pub $
Student Loans: 64%
Average Debt: $ $ $
Phi Beta Kappa: No
Applicants: 19,164
Accepted: 87%
Enrolled: 37%
Grad in 6 Years: 69%
Returning Freshmen: 87%
Academics: ✍ ✍ ✍
Social: ☎ ☎ ☎ ☎
Q of L: ★ ★ ★
Admissions: (515) 294-5836
Email Address: admissions@iastate.edu

Strong Programs:
Engineering
Agriculture
Agronomy
Agribusiness
Animal Science
Kinesiology
Chemistry
Business

Seventy percent of freshmen join ISU's 80 highly touted learning communities.

and small-town Iowans," says a senior. "This is a pretty white campus." To help remedy this situation, ISU launched a $25 million campaign aimed at increasing the number of scholarships available for minority students, athletes, and student leaders. In addition to need-based financial aid and 400 athletic scholarships, thousands of merit awards, which average $2,979 annually, are available.

Forty-one percent of students live in on-campus residence halls and apartments, including about 2,000 students who live in college-affiliated Greek housing. Eaton Residence Hall offers suite-style rooms. Single-sex and co-ed dorms are available, and rooms are said to be comfortable and well maintained. "The dorms are sterile to begin with but the traditions are very strong here and students transform them into home with their own personal touch," explains a junior. Special floors are available for international students, teetotalers, and particularly studious undergraduates. Students dine at 21 campus locations, including four main dining centers.

Iowa State is not simply located in Ames—in many respects it *is* Ames, but whether or not it qualifies as a college town depends on whom you ask. Des Moines, the state capital, is about 30 minutes away, and Iowa City, Minneapolis, and Chicago are other easy and enjoyable road trips. Socializing tends to stay on campus, with big-name bands playing at Hilton Coliseum and parties always rocking. There are also 500 student organizations that cater to just about any interest. Twelve percent of the men and 20 percent of the women go Greek. The campus is officially dry but, according to one sophomore, many older students will buy alcohol for minors. Across the street from campus, Campustown offers several bars for those of age, as well as a variety of cafés and ethnic restaurants. One long-held tradition is campaniling, where students must kiss under the campanile at the stroke of midnight to be considered "true" co-eds. And students have learned not to walk over the zodiac sign in the Memorial Union—it brings bad luck. The traditional weeklong campus festival called VEISHEA, a longtime favorite, has been canceled by the administration because students were getting too rowdy.

> "Students transform [the dorms] into home with their own personal touch."

In sports, Cyclones basketball is king; the men's and women's teams are usual invitees to the NCAA Division I tournament, and the men's team brought home the Big 12 title in 2013 and 2015. The university boasts college wrestling's only four-time undefeated champion and an Olympic gold medalist as the head coach. Football, track and field, and women's volleyball are also competitive. The Hawkeye rivalry is one of the strongest in the nation. A majority of students participate in the intramural program, which is one of the largest in the country, offering more than 40 sports—and if that's not enough, students have their pick of 52 club sports too.

From its first class of 28 men and two women in 1869, Iowa State has taken to heart Abraham Lincoln's land grant ideal: to open higher education to all, to teach practical courses, and to share that knowledge beyond the borders of the school. According to one junior, it's this dynamic combination that draws "hardworking, kind students" from near and far.

Overlaps

University of Iowa, University of Minnesota, Purdue, University of Wisconsin–Madison, University of Illinois at Urbana–Champaign, University of Nebraska–Lincoln, Michigan State

If You Apply To ➤

Iowa State: Rolling admissions. Priority financial aid: Dec. 1. Housing: Sept. 1. Application fee: $40. No campus or alumni interviews. SATs or ACTs: required. No Subject Tests. Letters of recommendation: optional. Essay: optional.

100 Job Hall, Ithaca, NY 14850

Ithaca offers an unusually wide array of programs for a smallish university. Students looking at Ithaca College also apply to Boston University, NYU, and Syracuse. The common thread? Outstanding programs in the arts and media. Students also clamor to get into physical therapy. Crosstown neighbor Cornell adds curricular and social opportunities.

Over South Hill, at the center of the upstate New York Finger Lakes region, sits Ithaca College. The school has a close-knit community, along with strong programs in music, theater, communications, and health sciences, such as physical and occupational therapy. With a "gorges" campus and a size that allows for easy friendships with peers and professors alike, Ithaca draws students from all over the U.S.—and dozens of other countries. Ithaca's special focus on undergraduate education and hands-on learning helps prepare students for the rigors of life outside institutional walls. "Ithaca is a diverse college," says one freshman, "with so much to offer in creating the well-rounded, successful person you will become."

Ithaca's campus, midway between Syracuse and Binghamton, in the beautiful Finger Lakes region, lies on the city's southern hill overlooking Cayuga Lake. None of the streamlined, modern campus buildings on the 757-acre plot are more than a few decades old, since the college did not move to its present location until the 1960s. The surrounding area is dotted with forests, waterfalls, rolling hills, and, of course, those ever-present gorges. Author Tom Wolfe dubbed the college "the emerald eminence at the fingertip of Lake Cayuga." Recent construction includes a new human anatomy lab and the refurbished Ford Hall, which features a new projection screen and improved sound system.

Ithaca has five schools—music, communications, business, health sciences and human performance, and humanities and sciences. Together, they offer nearly 100 undergraduate majors and 70 minors. All students complete the Integrative Core Curriculum (ICC), the centerpiece of which is a Themes and Perspectives sequence that includes courses from the natural sciences, creative arts, humanities, and social sciences, all focusing on one of six themes, such as Power and Justice or The Quest for a Sustainable Future. All first-year students enroll in an Ithaca Seminar during the first semester that emphasizes the transition to college life. These classes are limited to about 15 students each, and professors and students decide together how to use the fourth hour of instruction each week, covering themes such as personal, social, and academic responsibility. Recent examples of the more than 100 offerings include Creativity and Mindfulness, Exile and Immigration, and The Right-Brain Revolution. Additional ICC elements include coursework in writing, diversity, and quantitative literacy; a senior capstone experience; and a learning portfolio.

> **"The academic climate at Ithaca is very positive and hands-on."**

Ithaca is best known for its preprofessional programs—and for its school of music, which dates to 1892, when the college was founded as a music conservatory. "The music school has always been lauded and maintained an excellent academic program," a freshman says. The school requires an in-person audition, making it a destination for already-accomplished musicians, composers, and sound-recording technologists. Professional programs in the School of Health Sciences and Human Performance range from athletic training and speech-language pathology to health education and the highly regarded physical therapy program. The Roy H. Park

Website: www.ithaca.edu
Location: Small City
Private
Total Enrollment: 6,567
Undergraduates: 6,197
Male/Female: 42/58
SAT Ranges: CR 550–640, M 550–630
ACT Ranges: 24–29
Financial Aid: 93%
Pell Grant: 21%
Expense: Pr $ $
Student Loans: 72%
Average Debt: $ $ $ $
Phi Beta Kappa: No
Applicants: 16,519
Accepted: 67%
Enrolled: 16%
Grad in 6 Years: 76%
Returning Freshmen: 86%
Academics: ✍ ✍ ✍
Social: 🐧 🐧 🐧 🐧 🐧
Q of L: ★ ★ ★
Admissions: (800) 429-4274
Email Address: admission@ithaca.edu

Strong Programs:
Business Administration
Television and Radio
Physical Therapy
Integrated Marketing
  Communications
Music
Theater Arts
Occupational Therapy
Speech-Language Pathology

School of Communications houses programs in TV and radio, integrated marketing communications, photography, sport media, and others. The business school offers programs in accounting and business administration (the college's most popular major), as well as an M.B.A. Cross-registration is available at Cornell University and Wells College, and Ithaca also offers a 3–2 physics and engineering program.

"The academic climate at Ithaca is very positive and hands-on," says a senior, and students are often encouraged to work together. A sophomore adds, "If you do struggle, as I have, there are lifelines in the form of TAs, free tutoring (in most cases), and persistent professor interaction." Sixty percent of classes have fewer than 20 students, and professors are praised for their knowledge and enthusiasm. "The teaching approach here is discussion-based and hands-on. Students don't learn from simply reading and listening, we learn from applying course material," says a junior. The Honors Program offers special, intensive seminars and an array of out-of-class activities to qualified students. Those seeking real-world experience may apply for semester-long programs in New York City or Los Angeles that combine an internship with industry-related courses. Ithaca offers study abroad programs at the Ithaca College London Center and in more than 50 countries; 28 percent of students study off campus.

"Students don't learn from simply reading and listening, we learn from applying course material."

What are the characteristics of a typical Ithaca student? "Imagine band geeks, jocks, preppy kids, hippies, and every other group you can see sitting at the same table, talking and laughing," says one sophomore. "That—multiplied by about 6,000—is what it feels like to be a student at Ithaca." Forty-four percent of Ithaca students hail from New York State; many of the rest come from elsewhere in New England, and 2 percent come from other nations. African Americans represent 6 percent of undergraduates, Asian Americans 4 percent, and Hispanics 8 percent. The campus leans liberal, and according to a biochemistry major, "Some of the very hot topics at the moment are racism and ensuring that all students are treated fairly and equally, as well as advocating for women's rights." Twenty-one percent of incoming freshmen are eligible for the Pell Grant, and merit scholarships averaging $14,088 are available to top-performing applicants; there are no athletic awards.

Sixty-nine percent of Ithaca's students live on campus, thanks in part to the college's Circle and Garden Apartments, which have full kitchens and space for 630 upperclassmen in units that house two to six students each. "Housing is pretty easy at Ithaca College," a senior reports. First-year students participate in the First-Year Residential Experience, living in communities focusing on themes like diversity and inclusion and sustainability. Campus residents can eat in any of three dining halls, each with a different daily menu. "There's a big emphasis on local foods and vendors," says one student, adding, "They make it really easy for you to eat healthy, but there's still unlimited ice cream in every dining hall too." Public safety officers and a blue-light system help keep the campus safe, and a sophomore says, "As a woman, I have never felt threatened or uneasy about being around at night or by myself."

"There's a big emphasis on local foods and vendors."

Ithaca recognizes only academic fraternities and sororities, not social ones, but that doesn't slow down the campus social scene. "Between music school concerts, theater performances, Student Activities Board movies, club events, open-mic nights, comedy shows, or athletic events, it is impossible to be bored on campus," one sociology major says. More than 200 student organizations also keep students busy. Bars and clubs in Ithaca are 18 to enter, 21 to drink, and there are a mall, bowling alley, movie theaters, and go-karting in town. Students agree that the party scene is laid-back and they don't feel pressured to drink. Each fall brings Applefest, a local

Ithaca's school of music dates to 1892, when the college was founded as a music conservatory.

Semester-long programs in New York City and Los Angeles combine an internship with industry-related courses.

The First-Year Residential Experience houses students in communities focusing on themes like diversity and inclusion and sustainability.

downtown festival that celebrates the harvest, and in the winter, Chilifest helps students warm up. The area's hilly terrain provides abundant opportunities for hiking, biking, sledding, and skiing. Popular road trips include Syracuse and Binghamton (each an hour away), and New York City, Philadelphia, Boston, Washington, D.C., and Toronto, each between a four and six hours' drive.

Ithaca fields 27 competitive Division III varsity athletics programs. The Bombers won 12 Empire 8 conference titles during the 2015–16 season, and the women's outdoor track and field team produced two individual national champions. The biggest annual athletic tradition is the "Cortaca Jug" football game that pits the Ithaca Bombers against rival SUNY–Cortland. (The winner gets the jug-shaped "firkin" as a trophy, and the game is "the only Division III football game you can bet on in Vegas," boasts a sophomore.) There are two levels of intramural competition at Ithaca, depending on just how competitive you want to be, and popular options include soccer, flag football, basketball, and volleyball.

> "It is impossible to be bored on campus."

If you can endure the harsh winters ("Come mid-February or so, we hate the snow!" gripes one senior), you'll appreciate the small size and personal attention characteristic of Ithaca College. "Everybody who is part of the Ithaca College community knows that they are part of something special," observes one student. "At other schools, you're a number. At Ithaca, we know your name."

If You Apply To ➤ **Ithaca:** Early decision: Nov. 1. Early action: Dec. 1. Regular decision and financial aid: Feb. 1. Application fee: $60. Campus and alumni interviews: optional, informational. SATs or ACTs: optional. Subject Tests: optional. Letters of recommendation: required. Essay: required. Accepts the Common Application with supplement.

James Madison University

Harrisonburg, VA 22807

JMU has carved out a comfortable niche among Virginia's superb public universities. More undergrads than UVA and nearly three times as many as William and Mary, though the city of Harrisonburg gives JMU a more down-home feel. Strong in preprofessional fields such as business, health professions, and education. Undergraduates rule the roost.

No doubt about it: students at James Madison University get down to business. In fact, the school's business programs continue to garner national attention and attract top-notch students from coast to coast. The university has been growing at a phenomenal rate, causing some to feel growth pains. But an emphasis on undergraduate teaching, close student/faculty interaction, and a warm and welcoming climate are business as usual at JMU, so students have plenty of things to cheer about. "Every student 'bleeds purple,'" says a junior.

JMU is in the heart of the Shenandoah Valley, two hours from Washington, D.C., and Richmond, Virginia. Three types of architecture make up the campus. The buildings on Front campus have red-tile roofs and are constructed of a distinctive limestone block known as bluestone. Back campus has more modern, redbrick structures. The College of Integrated Science and Technology campus features modern beige buildings. The university straddles Interstate 81, an outlet to several major East Coast cities.

(continued)

Average Debt: $ $
Phi Beta Kappa: Yes
Applicants: 21,439
Accepted: 73%
Enrolled: 28%
Grad in 6 Years: 82%
Returning Freshmen: 91%
Academics: ✍ ✍ ✍
Social: ☎ ☎ ☎ ☎
Q of L: ★ ★ ★ ★
Admissions: (540) 568-5681
Email Address: admissions@
jmu.edu

Strong Programs:
Business
Education
Social Sciences
Communication Sciences and
Disorders
Community Health
Psychology
Biology
Geology

*Outdoor Adventures
gives first-year
students an
opportunity to meet
while hiking and
mountain climbing
in the Shenandoah
Mountains.*

The General Education Program requires each student to take courses in several clusters, including Skills for the 21st Century, Arts and Humanities, the Natural World, Social and Cultural Processes, and Individuals in the Human Community. The idea is to offer students a basis for lifelong learning by challenging them to become active in their own education and to explore the foundations of knowledge. Freshmen are offered a variety of programs to help smooth their transition into the university. Outdoor Adventures, held before classes begin, gives first-year students an opportunity to meet while hiking and mountain climbing in the Shenandoah Mountains.

James Madison University is recognized nationally for its programs within the business major, while social sciences and education are also strong. Some of the

"Every student 'bleeds purple.'"

most popular majors include communication sciences and disorders, community health, psychology, and biology. Undergraduates in the biology department have even employed recombinant DNA technology to help develop organisms that produce biodegradable plastics. Also worth noting is the geology and geography departments' summer geology field camp for undergraduates. A mathematical modeling laboratory is used by select undergrads to solve real-world applied math problems.

"For the most part, classes are challenging and competitive," says a sophomore. A junior adds, "JMU definitely has its difficult courses. There were some that I really struggled with and others that I was able to breeze through without a problem." Thirty-four percent of classes have fewer than 20 students. With undergraduates far outnumbering grad students, JMU's main mission is undergraduate teaching. "All of the teachers are professors with degrees in their field and no classes are taught by grad students or TAs," says one psychology major. Those looking for a more intense intellectual experience can check out the honors program, which offers small classes and opportunities for independent study. Many upper-level programs encourage undergraduate participation with faculty research. JMU offers semester abroad programs in England, Spain, China, Belgium, Italy, and Scotland. In addition, there are summer programs in Argentina, Kenya, the Philippines, and several other countries.

You won't find a lot of ethnic diversity among fellow students at JMU, but "anyone can find their niche here," assures one student. "We've got athletes, punk rockers, preps, nerds, tree huggers, and politicians!" Most undergrads attended public high school, and 74 percent are from Virginia. In fact, there's a general effort to keep out-of-state enrollment below 30 percent; international students represent 2 percent. African Americans account for 4 percent of JMU's student body, Hispanics 6 percent, and Asian Americans 4 percent. As for political involvement, students are "very justice-oriented and politically active," according to one sociology major. A group calling itself Orange Band tries to get people talking about current issues, and students say all views on the political spectrum are represented on campus. JMU offers merit scholarships averaging $3,628 and hundreds of athletic scholarships.

Just 13 percent of the students live in the dorms, which run the gamut from the old high-ceiling variety to newer, air-conditioned rooms that come complete with carpet and a fitness center in the building. "The dorms are well maintained and a close walk to everything," says a junior. Freshmen are guaranteed a room, but the

"Social life is really fun for a rural area."

school's enrollment growth means some students wind up in triples, and most move off campus after their first year. Students rave about the meal plan, which has a growing number of options to choose from, including a salad bar and low-calorie meals. "There are 14 dining halls on campus, so you can get literally anything that you could ever want. They have vegetarian, vegan, and gluten-free options all over the place," cheers an international affairs major.

"Social life is really fun for a rural area," reports one student. "The students mostly gather at off-campus apartments via a bus that runs into the late hours. Bars and clubs are not particularly popular because there aren't that many." The Greek system attracts 1 percent of the men and 5 percent of the women. Greeks and independents alike participate in JMU's many annual rites, including homecoming and Christmas on the Quad. The school cracks down on underage drinking on campus and after three strikes "students are asked to leave," says a student. Most students find Harrisonburg a friendly Southern town, though it doesn't necessarily embrace the college. As for road trips, the favorite destination seems to be the University of Virginia, almost an hour's drive to the south. Equally enticing, however, are the many natural delights of the Shenandoah Valley, including hiking, camping, and even skiing, all nearby.

With undergraduates far outnumbering grad students, JMU's main mission is undergraduate teaching.

Sports fans here are known as the Electric Zoo and are enthusiastic about their Dukes teams, which are all Division I. Among the most competitive sports are football, women's basketball, baseball, and men's and women's soccer. The field hockey team has brought home conference titles, as have the softball team and the lacrosse team. More than two-thirds of students participate in the intramural program's many offerings. JMU's debate team was named the top public debate program in the nation by the Cross Examination Debate Association.

Though JMU still has a ways to go before establishing itself as a front-rank national university, it is making progress. The school is growing, but not outgrowing its Southern charm. "The school spirit is really what sets us apart," says an elementary education major. "No matter where you go on campus, you are always going to find someone wearing purple and gold."

Overlaps

George Mason, Penn State, University of Delaware, University of Virginia, Virginia Commonwealth, Virginia Tech

If You Apply To >	**James Madison:** Early action: Nov. 1. Regular decision: Jan. 15. Financial aid: Mar. 1. Housing: May 1. Application fee: $70. No campus or alumni interviews. SATs or ACTs: required. No Subject Tests. Letters of recommendation: optional. Essay: optional.

The Johns Hopkins University

3400 North Charles Street, Baltimore, MD 21218

The Hop's reputation as a premed factory can be misleading. It's true, but Hopkins also has fine programs in international studies (with D.C. close at hand) as well as in the humanities and social sciences. With total enrollment just over 7,200—5,300 of them undergraduates—Hopkins is smaller than most people think.

One of the few U.S. universities initially founded as a graduate school, The Johns Hopkins University has garnered widespread acclaim for its exceptional professors, incredible resources, and unparalleled research opportunities. Though the university has a reputation as a top-notch premed factory, the administration has been working for a number of years to make it clear that this mid-sized Baltimore university has plenty to offer those undergrads whose interests are decidedly nonmedical or nonscience based. Students who attend this elite university know they are at the top of the game, and they burn the midnight oil to stay there.

The arts and sciences and engineering schools are on the picturesque 140-acre Homewood campus, just three miles north of Baltimore's revitalized Inner Harbor. Tree-lined quadrangles, open lawns, and playing fields make for an idyllic setting

Website: www.jhu.edu
Location: City Outskirts
Private
Total Enrollment: 7,224
Undergraduates: 5,326
Male/Female: 51/49
SAT Ranges: CR 690–760, M 710–790
ACT Ranges: 32–34
Financial Aid: 51%

(continued)

Pell Grant: 13%
Expense: Pr $ $ $ $
Student Loans: 42%
Average Debt: $ $
Phi Beta Kappa: Yes
Applicants: 24,716
Accepted: 13%
Enrolled: 40%
Grad in 6 Years: 94%
Returning Freshmen: 97%
Academics: ✍ ✍ ✍ ✍ ✍
Social: ☎ ☎ ☎
Q of L: ★ ★ ★
Admissions: (410) 516-8171
Email Address: gotojhu@
    jhu.edu

Strong Programs:
Premed
Public Health Studies
Biomedical Engineering
Neuroscience
Molecular and Cellular Biology
International Studies
Engineering
Creative Writing

As much as some try to deny it, students bound for medical school dominate the campus.

on the edge of a major urban center. The architecture on this woody urban campus is mainly Georgian redbrick, with several recently built, more modern structures scattered throughout. Decker Quadrangle includes Mason Hall, a 28,000-square-foot visitor center, an interdisciplinary computational sciences building, and a 604-space underground parking garage. Malone Hall is a new, state-of-the-art building that houses several collaborative research institutions. Hopkins's medical campus is easily accessible via a crosstown shuttle. Hopkins opened a new building in 2016 that combines 157 student apartments with 31,000 square feet of commercial space, to encourage new business development in the Charles Village neighborhood that surrounds the Homewood campus.

Although Johns Hopkins is a firm supporter of traditional scholarship, there are no university-wide requirements, other than a four-course writing component. Each major has its own distribution requirements, and there are several creative seminar offerings for freshmen. Freshmen are assigned a premajor advisor, and arts and sciences students are encouraged to wait until at least their sophomore year to declare a major. For freshmen who enter Hopkins in the fall 2017 semester or later, the university will no longer "cover" first-semester freshman grades by recording them as satisfactory or unsatisfactory—ending a policy that had been in place since 1971. Freshmen must now buckle down to a Herculean workload right from the get-go. Even so, the university has developed and strengthened several student support resources over the last few years to help ease the transition to college. Students may also get some relief from the optional January intersession, during which they can take courses or pursue independent study for one or two credits.

> **"I feel like I'm part of a conversation, engaged, and enjoying my time in class."**

As much as some try to deny it, students bound for medical school dominate the campus. Public health studies is among the most popular majors, along with biomedical engineering, neuroscience, molecular and cellular biology, and international studies. The Johns Hopkins Hospital and Medical School play such a major role in the identity of Hopkins that students sometimes fear it "overshadows the vibrant undergrad life that exists at Homewood." But administrators say the school is paying more attention to the undergraduate programs and emphasizing interdisciplinary, collaborative approaches to the coursework. Engineering majors enjoy strong departments, such as mechanical engineering, chemical and biomedical engineering, electrical and computer engineering, and computer science. Many say the engineering programs are the hardest, thanks to the intense workload. But that doesn't deter a Hopkins student. "Hopkins is a rigorous institution, but with its collaborative academic culture, learning is very manageable and enjoyable," says a behavioral biology major.

Students can receive a B.A. in creative writing through the Writing Seminars program, where they study with authors and poets such as Alice McDermott and Andrew Motion. The Humanities Center espouses a casual, interdisciplinary approach, and with the maximum curriculum flexibility allowed them, undergraduates are free to range as broadly or focus as specifically as they want. Students can get a dual degree in music performance with the university's Peabody Conservatory. There also are broad "area majors," such as humanistic studies, behavioral biology, or natural sciences, and students can choose from a cluster of related disciplines to design their own program. New minors are available in computational medicine; medicine, science, and the humanities; and visual arts. Students are generally happy with the quality of teaching at Hopkins, which is enhanced by small class sizes—73 percent of classes enroll fewer than 20 students. "The professors here are *awesome*," enthuses a neuroscience and music double major. "I feel like I'm part of a conversation, engaged, and enjoying my time in class."

The well-developed graduate side of Johns Hopkins proves to be a boon to undergraduates as well. The international studies program, for example, is enriched by its offerings at the university's Bologna Center in Italy, its Nanjing Center in China, and its Nitze School of Advanced International Studies in nearby Washington, D.C. Thirty-four percent of all undergraduates study abroad in these and other locations across the globe. Undergraduate research is a hallmark of the Johns Hopkins experience, with 75 percent of students having at least one research experience. "The opportunities here are unparalleled," affirms a civil engineering major. "Students can become involved in groundbreaking research as early as freshman year." Programs such as the Woodrow Wilson Undergraduate Research Fellowship Program and the Provost's Undergraduate Research Awards offer funding and faculty support for research projects. Those interested in service can apply for one of 50 paid summer internships with Baltimore area nonprofits and government agencies through the Community Impact Internships program.

The Community Impact Internships program offers 50 paid summer internships with Baltimore area nonprofits.

The image Johns Hopkins students once had as antisocial bookworms is giving way to a more balanced social life. "Students at Hopkins are competitive, motivated, and innovative," says one chemical engineering major. Geographically, most students come from the mid-Atlantic states and New England; only 11 percent are Maryland natives, and another 11 percent are international. Ninety-two percent

"Students can become involved in groundbreaking research as early as freshman year."

graduated in the top 10th of their high school class. Twenty-three percent of students are Asian American, 6 percent African American, and 13 percent Hispanic. The campus is fairly liberal and according to a freshman, "Students here are unafraid to bring attention to important and undiscussed issues." At $2.9 billion, Hopkins's endowment is among the top 25 in the country, and the school strives to meet the full demonstrated financial need of every admit. Hopkins rewards the extraordinarily talented with hefty Hodson Trust scholarships worth $30,500 annually, regardless of need, and renewable annually for those who keep a 3.0 GPA. The need-based Hodson Success Scholarship replaces the loans in the aid packages of selected students from underrepresented minority groups. Fifty athletic scholarships are also awarded in women's and men's lacrosse, where Hopkins is a perennial national powerhouse.

The nationally acclaimed Division I men's lacrosse team is a recent Big 10 conference champion.

Fifty-two percent of Hopkins students live in student housing; freshmen and sophomores are required to do so. "The freshman-year dorms are classic and encourage social interactions," explains a writing major. "The sophomore-year dorms are spacious, new, and have excellent amenities." Upperclassmen often choose to scope out the row houses and apartment buildings that surround Hopkins, but 25 percent are now guaranteed housing in the Charles Commons or one of six other residence halls or university-owned "luxury" apartments. Campus dining gets positive reviews, as does security, which includes call boxes, security patrols, and a consistent presence;

"Students here are unafraid to bring attention to important and undiscussed issues."

an English major says, "I've never once felt like I was in any danger." The Sexual Assault Resource Unit student organization is active in raising awareness about sexual violence.

Rowdy dorm parties and all-campus events are few and far between, but fraternity parties can be found on the weekends; 17 percent of the men and 26 percent of the women belong to Greek life. There are also more than 350 clubs and student organizations, and according to a junior, "The party culture isn't defined by Greek life—it's defined by all student organizations." The biggest and most popular undergraduate social event of the year is the annual student-organized Spring Fair, which draws crowds from the surrounding communities as well.

"What is nice about Hopkins is that if none of the multitude of things going on on campus entice you, you have the whole city of Baltimore and its social scene to explore," says a senior. Downtown and the famed Inner Harbor are not too distant, and some of the city's best attractions, such as the Baltimore Museum of Art, Wyman Park, and the funky Hampden neighborhood, are right near campus. Trendy Baltimore hot spots—like Canton, Fells Point, and Little Italy—are favorites. Students

"The party culture isn't defined by Greek life—it's defined by all student organizations."

also head downtown for plays, the symphony, films, clubs, restaurants, the zoo, and major league sports; Camden Yards, home of baseball's Orioles, is the most commodious park in the country. Students with wheels can take off for Annapolis, less than an hour away. Washington, D.C., only an hour's train ride, beckons with tourist activities and ample nightlife. In the warmer months, a trek out to the Delaware and Maryland beaches takes the mind off the books.

When the nationally acclaimed Division I men's lacrosse team—Big 10 conference champion in 2015—takes to the road to meet opponents, students often take advantage of the opportunity to road-trip with them and cheer them on. Women's lacrosse is Division I as well, but the rest of the Blue Jays athletic program competes in Division III. Recent Centennial Conference champions include men's basketball, baseball, and football; women's cross-country and soccer; and men's and women's tennis and indoor and outdoor track. The Woodrow Wilson Debate Council is ranked fourth in the nation in the American Parliamentary Debate Association. Twenty percent of undergraduates compete in intramurals.

With one of the world's premier medical schools, top science programs, and first-rate programs in areas as diverse as writing, international studies, environmental engineering, and philosophy, The Johns Hopkins University is clearly among the best schools in the country. Students here take pride in the fact that they belong to the cream of the academic crop. "Hopkins students are incredibly passionate about their unique interests," says a senior. "It is a really contagious culture to be a part of, because it inspires you to pursue your passions as well."

Overlaps

Cornell University, University of Pennsylvania, Harvard, Columbia, Stanford, Duke, Brown, Princeton

If You Apply To >

Johns Hopkins: Early decision: Nov. 1. Regular decision: Jan. 2. Financial aid: Feb. 1. Housing: May 29. Application fee: $70. Campus and alumni interviews: optional, informational. SATs or ACTs: required. Subject Tests: recommended. Letters of recommendation: required. Essay: required. Biomedical engineering students must apply to that program. Accepts the Common Application with supplement.

Juniata College

1700 Moore Street, Huntingdon, PA 16652

Located in the middle of rural Pennsylvania, Juniata boasts one of the best undergraduate science programs among liberal arts colleges. Students are encouraged to design their own majors and to think globally. Peace and conflict studies are a specialty. Lots of merit scholarships, but not much diversity among students.

Website: www.juniata.edu
Location: Small Town
Private
Total Enrollment: 1,583

Set amid the ridges and valleys of central Pennsylvania, Juniata College offers students a tantalizing mix of academic flexibility, small classes, and surprisingly solid programs in the natural sciences. Students here create their own majors, conduct research alongside faculty, and pack their bags for study abroad opportunities around the world. What's more, Juniata students share a desire to change themselves and the world.

Juniata's 110-acre campus features a central stand of structures reflecting three architectural styles. The college's landmark building, Founders Hall, is a colonial Revival structure, built of brick atop a stone foundation. Halbritter Center for the Performing Arts, Ellis Hall, and the von Liebig Center for Science are all Classical Revival buildings, the prominent pillars on each visible all over campus. The college also boasts a Beaux-Arts building, Carnegie Hall, originally built as a Carnegie library in 1907 and redesigned on the interior to house the college's art museum. Juniata recently dedicated its first single-room residence hall, offering informal gathering spaces and lounges for a sense of community, as well as features to improve environmental sustainability, including geothermal heating and a bike shelter to encourage less driving.

In order to graduate, all Juniata students must complete six credit hours of coursework in five specific liberal arts-related areas: fine arts, international studies, social sciences, humanities, and natural sciences. Students also are expected to complete at least four communications courses—two of which must be writing-based—and must demonstrate that they

> **"We work hard, there is no doubt about that, but we are not overworked."**

have a basic competency in statistics and an understanding of basic mathematical skills. All freshmen take the College Writing Seminar, an interdisciplinary course that covers reading and writing skills, as well as topics like research skills, study habits, and career planning. After attaining sophomore standing, students complete an Interdisciplinary Colloquia course and a Cultural Analysis course.

In lieu of preset majors, Juniata students may develop their own Programs of Emphasis (POEs) and approximately one-third do so. Each student works with two advisors to combine two existing POEs into a third course of study or create an entirely new program. Students may also choose a course of study from more than 50 existing POEs, and some of the most popular are biology, physical sciences, environmental science, wildlife conservation, business, and marketing. "Juniata has long been known as a school for the natural sciences," confirms a senior. Peace and conflict studies is one of the oldest and most comprehensive programs of its kind in the United States, and includes study abroad opportunities and internships. Museum studies teaches students how to curate art (and provides internships at prestigious galleries around the nation) while the Center for Entrepreneurial Leadership provides $15,000 in seed capital for budding business leaders. New POEs have recently been added in business analytics and fisheries and aquatic sciences.

"Juniata College challenges its students to think critically about what they are learning and why it is important," says a secondary education math major. "We work hard, there is no doubt about that, but we are not overworked." "Juniata is very community-centered," adds another student, making for a supportive atmosphere in the classroom. Seventy-two percent of classes have fewer than 20 students, which allows for plenty of interaction between professors and students. "The professors have a strong relationship with each student that allows their teaching to be more personalized and therefore more

> **"[Students] are not interested in learning in the conventional way."**

efficient," asserts one communication and conflict studies major. The Inbound program allows new students to spend a week on campus as part of a particular club or activity in order to "make their first few days of immersion into college life easier," according to one student. Juniata has international exchange/study abroad agreements with colleges and universities in 21 countries, and 42 percent of all Juniata students participate in study abroad. About 47 percent of students participate in faculty-guided undergraduate research projects.

"The types of students who are attracted to Juniata are those who have a motivation to learn, but are not interested in learning in the conventional way," says a

(continued)

Undergraduates: 1,512
Male/Female: 44/56
SAT Ranges: CR 510–630, M 510–620
ACT Ranges: N/A
Financial Aid: 100%
Pell Grant: 22%
Expense: Pr $ $
Student Loans: 71%
Average Debt: $ $ $
Phi Beta Kappa: No
Applicants: 2,604
Accepted: 77%
Enrolled: 18%
Grad in 6 Years: 73%
Returning Freshmen: 86%
Academics: ✍ ✍ ✍
Social: ☎ ☎ ☎
Q of L: ★ ★ ★
Admissions: (814) 641-3420
Email Address: admissions@ juniata.edu

Strong Programs:
Biology
Physical Sciences
Environmental Science
Wildlife Conservation
Business
Marketing
Peace and Conflict Studies
Museum Studies

psychology major. Fifty-six percent of Juniata students hail from Pennsylvania, and 8 percent come from foreign nations. African Americans comprise 3 percent of the student body, Asian Americans 4 percent, and Hispanics 4 percent. Although the campus tends to lean left, students report that all viewpoints are represented and respected. "We're big on sustainability," says a student. "Students will literally pick plastic bottles out of the trash to recycle them." Another adds, "Compared to schools in New England, we're Bible-thumpers, whereas compared to schools in the South, we're socialists." Hundreds of merit scholarships are available, averaging $19,051, but there are no athletic scholarships. Twenty-two percent of freshmen are eligible for the Pell Grant.

Eighty-two percent of the students live on campus in traditional residence halls, and upperclassmen must apply to move off campus to apartments. "Some dorms are newer, some are bigger, but they're all good dorms," says a sophomore. For grub, "Juniata provides two main dining facilities as well as several coffee and a la carte stops throughout campus," a student reports. "The one main cafeteria is a buffet-style that provides several sections such as stone-oven pizza and a gluten-free, organic area for those with potential allergies." Students report feeling safe on campus thanks to an active security program that includes patrolling officers, locked dorms, and initiatives to prevent sexual assault.

> "Compared to schools in New England, we're Bible-thumpers, whereas compared to schools in the South, we're socialists."

"Without barriers such as Greek life, the students at Juniata are able to cross different boundaries and interact with those who may be completely different than themselves," says a senior. Social life is mostly on campus, and activities include live bands, trivia shows, poker tournaments, dinners, and dances. Students of legal age may drink on campus, and students say that while the enforcement of alcohol policies is fairly lenient, the drinking and party culture is low-key. Students enjoy a number of traditions, including Madrigal Dinner and Mountain Day, on which classes are canceled for the day and students attend outdoor activities at nearby Raystown Lake ("Food, carnival games, kayaking, Slip'N Slides, and the president's dog with a GoPro on—it is a great time," says a junior). Students also take part in the "storming of the arch," in which "freshmen attempt to run into an arch defended by the rugby team," according to one student. Huntingdon (population 7,000) is "a relatively small place for a college," says one student, but does provide the basic necessities for college students, including several restaurants and a movie theater. Community service is popular, as are road trips to Penn State (40 minutes away), Baltimore, Philadelphia, and Pittsburgh.

The Juniata Eagles compete in Division III, and Juniata teams have earned 54 conference championships. The most successful sports include women's volleyball, field hockey, and, of late, women's basketball, men's tennis, and men's volleyball. The athletics program is expanding, adding new varsity teams in men's and women's golf and women's lacrosse in 2017. Juniata students also have the chance to participate in a variety of club, intramural, and individual activities; women's rugby, Quidditch, and mixed martial arts are among the most popular.

Although students sometimes complain about the limitations of attending a small college in a small town, most seem excited to be part of such an inviting academic institution. Those seeking "big football games, raging frat parties, and a vibrant urban setting" should look elsewhere, a senior adds. However, "if you are more interested in an intensive and personal academic environment with an extremely tight-knit and supportive community, then Juniata is the place for you."

Overlaps

Penn State, Allegheny, Susquehanna, University of Pittsburgh, Ursinus, Gettysburg, McDaniel, Goucher

Kalamazoo College

1200 Academy Street, Kalamazoo, MI 49006

Kalamazoo is a small liberal arts school that opens up the world to its students—literally. An impressive 75 percent of Kalamazoo Hornets study abroad thanks to the ingenious K-Plan, a quarter system that allows students to study abroad one, two, or three academic terms. And if you need an extra boost to round out that résumé, there is an extensive internship program.

Kalamazoo College is a small school in America's heartland. But college subsidies enable the majority of students to go abroad during their years here, making the school a launching pad to the world. In addition to international education, the school's K-Plan emphasizes teaching, internships (80 percent of students have at least one), and independent research (as seniors, all students complete a senior individualized project, with one-on-one faculty supervision). Students are exposed to a demanding academic schedule and high expectations from faculty. "K is a very rigorous place," warns one student, "characterized by people who want to do well and are passionate about their work."

Life on Kalamazoo's wooded, 60-acre campus centers on the Quad, a green lawn where students ponder their destinies and play ultimate Frisbee with equal ease. With its rolling hills, Georgian architecture, and brick-laid streets, the campus has the quaint look more typical of historic New England than of nearby Kalamazoo, which, with surrounding communities, has 225,000 residents. A new 30,000-square-foot fitness and wellness center opened in 2016.

Founded in 1833 and formerly associated with the American Baptist Churches, Kalamazoo is the oldest college in Michigan. The college operates on the quarter system, and students must spend their entire first year on campus. But many first-years begin the year with a LandSea trip, three weeks of climbing, rappelling, canoeing, and backpacking in the mountains of the Adirondacks. By the end, they're convinced they can survive anything, including the rigors of a Kalamazoo education and the long Michigan winters. Once back on campus, they take a liberal arts curriculum that includes language proficiency, a first-year writing seminar, sophomore and senior seminars, as well as a senior individualized project—an internship, directed research, or a traditional thesis—basically anything that caps off each student's education in some meaningful way.

> **"[Study abroad] was a huge learning and growing experience."**

After their sophomore year, most of Kalamazoo's undergrads meet life's challenges with suitcase in hand, studying wherever their heart takes them, for the regular tuition price. The college offers three-, six-, and nine-month immersive study abroad programs that are available to all students, regardless of major; all credit earned during study abroad transfers back to Kalamazoo College. "I studied abroad in Clermont-Ferrand, France, for nine months. I went to a French university, lived with a French family, and was completely immersed in French culture. It was a huge learning and growing experience, and I am very thankful to have been

Website: www.kzoo.edu
Location: Small City
Private
Total Enrollment: 1,406
Undergraduates: 1,406
Male/Female: 44/56
SAT Ranges: CR 530–660, M 540–690
ACT Ranges: 26–30
Financial Aid: 97%
Pell Grant: 37%
Expense: Pr $ $
Student Loans: 61%
Average Debt: $ $ $
Phi Beta Kappa: Yes
Applicants: 2,455
Accepted: 72%
Enrolled: 21%
Grad in 6 Years: 82%
Returning Freshmen: 92%
Academics: ✑ ✑ ✑
Social: ☎ ☎ ☎
Q of L: ★ ★ ★
Admissions: (800) 253-3602
Email Address: admission@kzoo.edu

Strong Programs:
Biology
Psychology
Business and Economics
English
International and Area Studies
Foreign Languages

(continued)

Community and Global Health
Critical Ethnic Studies

able to do it," says one student. Seventy-five percent of students take part in study-abroad programs, including those offered by the Great Lakes College Association*. In fact, Kalamazoo offers students the opportunity to study via dozens of programs in 26 countries. Kalamazoo's Center for Experiential Education is another resource for information on careers, internships, and study abroad.

Kalamazoo aims to prepare students for real life by helping them synthesize the liberal arts education they receive on campus with their experiences abroad. "The rigor of classes makes the academic climate seem competitive at times but it is pretty collaborative," says a sophomore. The natural sciences are exceptionally good, and interdisciplinary programs in international and area studies and community and global health are also strengths. Students heap praise on the psychology, business and economics, English, and language departments. "People are doing very cool and exciting things in all of the departments," one student says. Professors give students lots of individual attention and are rewarded with some of Michigan's highest faculty salaries. "Every professor I've had has been passionate about what they teach and accessible outside of class," says a senior. A junior adds, "Professors here are also doing research or work in their fields, so you may be able to work in a professor's lab during the school year or summer, or hear about their clinical practice in psychology, or learn about the process of writing a book." New minors in economics, business, and international economics and business are available, as is a new critical ethnic studies major.

"People are doing very cool and exciting things in all of the departments."

"K students are very passionate and determined to make a difference not just in their lives but in the lives of others," says a computer science major. "Everybody here has a certain amount of weirdness to them, and we love each other for it," another student adds. Fifty-nine percent of students come from Michigan and 7 percent from foreign nations. The student body is 6 percent African American, 10 percent Hispanic, and 7 percent Asian American. Many Kalamazoo students crave more diversity on campus. The administration says it is continuing efforts to educate students on intercultural understanding, and the campus has a decidedly progressive tone. "Students here are not afraid to state their opinions and push for what they want and believe the school needs," offers one biology major. Thirty-seven percent of incoming students receive Pell Grants, and merit scholarships averaging $18,317 are available to qualified students. Athletic scholarships are not available.

The senior individualized project can be basically anything that caps off each student's education in some meaningful way.

Sixty-six percent of students live on campus. "The dorms are older and they don't look new on the inside, but they are ridiculously spacious," a student explains. With 200 to 300 students away each term thanks to the study abroad program, a certain instability pervades all activities, from athletics to student government to living groups in the co-ed residence halls, where suites hold one to six students. Dorms are divided by class standing, and three dorms are available for first-year students. For those who tire of campus life, "Off-campus housing is both cheap and located close to campus, so it is a popular option," says a sophomore. While there are no Greek organizations at Kalamazoo, nine living/learning houses offer a more community-oriented atmosphere, including family-style dinners. "The food is great and the cooks are very friendly," says a student. Another describes Kalamazoo as "a very safe environment."

"Students here are not afraid to state their opinions."

The Day of Gracious Living is a spring day where students relax by taking day trips or helping beautify the campus.

"There are always tons of things to do on campus, like movies, concerts, speakers, and events," an economics major reports. A senior adds that although "drinking and partying does happen at Kalamazoo, I have never felt pressure to do so." Students look forward to a casino night called Monte Carlo, homecoming, Spring Fling, and the Day of Gracious Living, a spring day where, without prior warning, classes are canceled and students relax by taking day trips or helping beautify the campus. (One popular T-shirt: "The end of learning is gracious living.") About three-fourths of students participate in volunteer programs with the Center for Civic Engagement, working with community partners to address issues such as neighborhood development, sustainability, prison reform, and migrant rights. The city of Kalamazoo is a "fun city with lots going on," according to one political science major. In addition to the typical collection of restaurants, theaters, and bars, Kalamazoo students benefit from the physical proximity of colleges such as Western Michigan University, where they may use the library or attend cultural events. Lake Michigan's beaches and Chicago's urban playground are easy road trips for students with cars.

For those who equate college with athletics, Kalamazoo has something to offer—even if it's not nationally televised games or tens of thousands of screaming fans. The Kalamazoo Hornets have a long-standing rivalry with Hope College, culminating in the football teams' annual competition for the "infamous wooden shoes," where the Hornets are cheered on by fans known as "the stingers." Kalamazoo also has an outstanding men's tennis team, which has won conference titles for 78 (!) consecutive years, as well as seven national championships. Baseball claimed the conference title in 2016, and the women's tennis and men's and women's swimming and soccer squads are also highly competitive. Fifty percent of students participate in intramural sports.

Kalamazoo is best suited for those "looking for a place where everyone is really enthusiastic about learning and thrives in that kind of environment," says one student. A classmate adds that it can be tough for students to "find a balance between the academic life and recreation." Despite the somewhat disruptive nature of the study abroad program, Kalamazoo offers students a truly global education.

> *The men's tennis team has won conference titles for 78 consecutive years.*

Overlaps

University of Michigan, Michigan State, Hope, Grand Valley State, College of Wooster, Albion, Macalester, Beloit

If You Apply To ➤ **Kalamazoo:** Early decision I and early action: Nov. 1. Regular decision: Jan. 15. Early decision II: Feb. 15. Financial aid: Feb. 1. Housing: May 30. No application fee. Campus interviews: recommended, informational. Alumni interviews: optional, informational. SATs or ACTs: optional. Subject Tests: optional. Letters of recommendation: required. Essay: required. Accepts the Common Application with optional supplement.

University of Kansas

1502 Iowa Street, Lawrence, KS 66045

Often overlooked because of its heartland location, KU has the sophistication of the leading Big Ten universities but is much easier to get into. Stereotypes of Kansas to the contrary, Lawrence is not flat as a pancake. Offers a solid slate of professional schools and an honors program that is among the nation's best.

Despite its conservative Midwest location, the University of Kansas is a welcoming oasis of progressive activism and tolerance. Those students who are extremely dedicated can plunge into a great honors program that the school provides to court them in its efforts to raise its academic profile. With sound academics and extracurriculars, winning athletics, and a stellar social life, the University of Kansas has a bounty of opportunities for motivated Jayhawks. "You name it, we have it," cheers one satisfied junior.

The 1,000-acre campus is set atop Mount Oread ridge—once a lookout point for pioneer wagon trains—and spread out on rolling green hills overlooking valleys.

Website: www.ku.edu
Location: Small City
Public
Total Enrollment: 22,801
Undergraduates: 16,946
Male/Female: 50/50
SAT Ranges: N/A
ACT Ranges: 22–28

(continued)

Financial Aid: 66%

Pell Grant: 24%

Expense: Pub $ $ $

Student Loans: 52%

Average Debt: $ $ $

Phi Beta Kappa: Yes

Applicants: 15,155

Accepted: 93%

Enrolled: 30%

Grad in 6 Years: 61%

Returning Freshmen: 80%

Academics: ✍ ✍ ✍ ✍

Social: 🐓 🐓 🐓 🐓

Q of L: ★ ★ ★ ★

Admissions: (785) 864-3911

Email Address: adm@ku.edu

Strong Programs:

Journalism

Psychology

Accounting

Biology

Architecture

Health Professions

Music

Engineering

The School of Journalism & Mass Communications perpetuates the legacy of famed journalist William Allen White.

Many of the buildings are made of indigenous Kansas limestone and are famed for their red roofs. But the real beauty of the campus lies in its landscape, particularly the breathtaking foliage that appears each autumn. The Dole Institute of Politics is home to one of the world's largest congressional archives and a World Trade Center memorial. A new residence hall and dining center is slated to open in 2017, and a new 708-bed, on-campus apartment complex in 2018.

KU applicants apply to the individual school of their choice. Freshmen may apply to the schools of Architecture, Business, Engineering, Journalism & Mass Communications, Music, and the College of Liberal Arts & Sciences. Those not admitted to one of the professional schools will automatically be considered for admission to the College of Liberal Arts & Sciences, where nearly 60 percent of the undergraduate population is enrolled. Students wishing to enter the schools of Health Professions, Nursing, Pharmacy, and Social Welfare must complete prerequisite courses and meet the schools' entry requirements. All KU undergraduates must complete a university-wide curriculum as part of their degrees; this curriculum, the KU Core, spans the entire undergraduate experience. The majority of degrees at KU require 120 hours for graduation.

> "There isn't a time at KU where your academics and instruction are not made a top priority."

Of KU's 13 schools, those most noted for their undergraduate programs are journalism, architecture, business, engineering, health professions, music, and social welfare. The School of Journalism & Mass Communications perpetuates the legacy of famed journalist William Allen White, and the School of Engineering has been significantly expanding its resources and facilities, recently adding a Structural Testing and Student Projects Center. Journalism, psychology, accounting, and biology are the most popular majors. A new major in Jewish studies has recently been added, as has a minor in visual art.

"Students are encouraged to collaborate with others while also being challenged to achieve their individual best," says a senior. Fifty-two percent of all undergraduate classes have fewer than 20 students. "The quality of teaching is certainly very good, but not perfect," a student reports. While TAs do teach some classes, students often have access to leading professors early on. "My calculus course freshman year was taught by the head of the math department—showing that there isn't a time at KU where your academics and instruction are not made a top priority," says an architecture major. The Office of Student Affairs, run by its own vice provost, wins praise for its academic advising and for its help with internships, disability services, and extracurriculars. It also publishes a monthly newsletter to parents.

Incoming freshmen can apply for the highly selective University Honors Program, which provides academically motivated students with honors courses, special advising, tutorials, and opportunities for scholarships and research grants. Other options for undergraduates include independent study, completion of one of KU's undergraduate certificate programs, and participation in study abroad programs in more than 70 countries, including Costa Rica, Germany, Ireland, Singapore, and Spain. KU provides several area study programs supported by language instruction in more than 40 languages.

"Proud and passionate. These two words invoke to me what it means to be a Jayhawk," says one student. Sixty-seven percent of undergrads are from Kansas, and

> "The social climate of KU offers something for everyone."

most of the rest are fellow Midwesterners (many from Chicago), although 6 percent are international. African Americans account for 4 percent, Hispanics 7 percent, and Asian Americans 4 percent. According to a communications and sociology double major, "The political climate is unique in that the state of Kansas is more conservative and the town of Lawrence is more liberal—therefore we get individuals with a wide variety of opinions, beliefs, and values." KU grants four-year renewable merit scholarships to eligible freshmen, and student-athletes vie for 308 scholarships in 18 sports. Twenty-four percent of students are Pell-eligible, and for those who also meet certain academic criteria, the KU Pell Advantage program provides a combination of scholarships and grants to fund students' tuition and fees.

One-quarter of Kansas students live in KU housing, either in residence halls, scholarship halls, or on-campus apartments. "Most freshmen live in very comfortable, spacious dorms," says one junior. Groups of 20 students can live in thematic learning communities on their residence hall floors—past themes include aerospace engineering and the meaning of film. A vast majority of KU students live off campus in Lawrence apartments, which are considered expensive only by Kansas standards. Three dining complexes provide extended-hour access to food-court-style dining, and the campus also offers 17 retail cafés and snack shops, along with a full-service restaurant. "You can get anything from a simple sandwich to sushi," says a student. Security is said to be good, and one student explains, "KU Saferide and Safebus provide transportation for late at night, while Lawrence police and university police constantly patrol the streets."

> **"Lawrence is *the* American college town. Period."**

"The social climate of KU offers something for everyone," says a senior. The Greek system, which attracts 18 percent of men and 25 percent of women, tends to be a major force in the social scene. Hard liquor is not allowed in fraternity houses, and no alcohol of any kind is allowed in sorority houses. All students are required to complete a sexual harassment training each year they're enrolled, and incoming students receive alcohol education training. On campus, more than 600 organized groups keep things lively; other activities include movies, poetry readings, and concerts. Scholarship halls, residence halls, and other student groups also sponsor large campus parties and events. The university's bus system is much appreciated by tenderfeet, especially because that great big hill seems to double in size during the cold, windy winters. With its myriad boutiques, restaurants, and bars, Lawrence is a favored destination for off-campus fun, and students also enjoy getting involved in the community through KU's Center for Community Outreach. "Lawrence is *the* American college town," says one enthusiastic Jayhawk. "Period." City slickers can trek off to Topeka, the state capital, or to Kansas City, each less than an hour's drive. The KC airport makes for easy long-distance transportation, and the area is also served by Amtrak.

KU varsity teams—the only ones in the nation that carry the name Jayhawks—compete in the rough-and-tumble Big 12 Conference. Twenty-nine teams represented KU in NCAA postseason competition during the 2013–16 seasons, including women's basketball, volleyball, and track and field. After winning its 12th straight conference title in 2016, the men's basketball team made its 27th consecutive appearance in the national tournament (an NCAA record), advancing to the Elite Eight. James Naismith, who invented basketball, was KU's first coach—and the only one with a losing record. Twelve percent

> **"The Rock Chalk chant… creat[es] a sort of bond between all Jayhawks, past and present."**

of students take part in more than 30 intramural sports, the most popular of which is—you guessed it—basketball, which signs up more than 140 teams.

Jayhawk traditions certainly run deep. The school year kicks off with Hawk Week, the official welcome for new students. To demonstrate their loyalty to the Jayhawks, thousands of students show up for the first basketball practice of the season. This nocturnal tradition is lovingly labeled "Late Night in the

The KU Pell Advantage program provides a combination of scholarships and grants.

In 2016, the men's basketball team made its 27th consecutive appearance in the national tournament (an NCAA record).

Overlaps

Kansas State, University of Texas at Austin, Texas A&M, University of Arizona, University of Oklahoma, University of Colorado–Boulder

Phog"—an allusion to the late, great coach Phog Allen. The traditional "Rock Chalk Jayhawk" KU cheer and steam whistle denoting class change is enough to bring a pang of nostalgia to the heart of even the most grizzled Kansas alum. "The Rock Chalk chant is widely recognizable, creating a sort of bond between all Jayhawks, past and present," says one student.

KU's academic value is hard to beat. With nearly 50 nationally ranked academic programs, Kansas's reputation (the nonbasketball one) continues to grow. Comprehensive study abroad programs, a distinctive honors program, and a robust sense of school spirit are just some of the reasons students choose to be a Jayhawk. "To put it simply," says one proud student, "greatness is our greatest tradition."

If You Apply To ➤ **Kansas:** Rolling admissions. (Priority deadline: Nov. 1.) Financial aid: Mar. 1. Application fee: $30. No campus or alumni interviews. SATs or ACTs: required. No Subject Tests. No letters of recommendation. No essay. Apply to particular school or program.

University of Kentucky

100 Funkhouser Building, Lexington, KY 40506

The state of Kentucky is better known for horses and hoops than higher education, but the University of Kentucky is working to change that. The basketball team, with it's one-and-done approach to recruiting, is always a championship contender, but so too are programs in business, engineering, and health fields. About one in three students comes from out of state, mostly from Tennessee and Ohio.

Website: www.uky.edu
Location: City Center
Public
Total Enrollment: 26,753
Undergraduates: 21,058
Male/Female: 46/54
SAT Ranges: CR 500–620, M 510–630
ACT Ranges: 22–28
Financial Aid: 40%
Pell Grant: N/A
Expense: Pub $ $ $
Student Loans: 54%
Average Debt: $ $ $
Phi Beta Kappa: Yes
Applicants: 18,432
Accepted: 91%
Enrolled: 31%
Grad in 6 Years: 61%
Returning Freshmen: 83%
Academics: ✍ ✍ ✍
Social: ☎ ☎ ☎ ☎

You probably recognize the University of Kentucky Wildcats as a perennial force in the NCAA postseason basketball tournament. But the University of Kentucky's claim to excellence stretches beyond its winning athletic teams—into outstanding medical and premedical programs, scientific research involving both professors and students, and a social calendar packed so full of Southern tradition that it would make even the most composed debutante's head spin. UK is a national leader in efforts to support first-generation college students and has established a living/learning community for such students. Nothing if not ambitious, the college has initiated a strategy that seeks to make UK a top-20 public research university by 2020, but budget cuts have stymied the effort for the time being. Stay tuned and cross your fingers.

The University of Kentucky campus contains a mixture of old and new, modern and traditional buildings that date back to the late 1890s. The campus buildings indicate a transition beginning with the original redbrick structures to designs using contemporary glass and concrete as one moves south following the path of development. Most visitors would agree that the grounds are well maintained, organized around the comfortable parklike spaces influenced by Frederick Law Olmsted's design. The campus contains a vast amount of mature trees and lawns set in a natural arrangement of open spaces, typical of the great land grant universities. Of course, UK's location in the heart of one of the finest horse-breeding areas in the world makes it a natural place for the Gluck Equine Research Center, a headquarters for research into horse diseases.

"I do wish I had more assistance from my advisors on which classes to take."

To graduate, all students must take mathematics and a foreign language, as well as written and oral communication classes and a statistics, calculus, or logic course. The core program, called University Studies, also requires exposure to natural and social sciences, humanities, an introduction to cross-disciplinary education, and experience with non-Western ways of thinking. Additionally, all freshmen are encouraged to take an academic orientation class called UK101, designed to help them adjust to college life.

Students sing the praises of many departments at UK, but several unique programs stand out. The Lexington campus is home to the Gaines Center of the Humanities, which is unusual in its study of public higher education. Lexington also hosts the Patterson School of International Diplomacy, one of the smallest yet most respected schools of its type in the country. The chemistry department has turned out three National Science Foundation fellowship winners. For upperclassmen, UK offers a number of joint programs with other colleges and universities, including Transylvania, Centre, and Georgetown (in Kentucky). There's also a cooperative program with the Army and Air Force ROTC. Students studying prevet at UK will find coveted slots reserved for them at Auburn and Tuskegee in the advanced veterinary medicine program, at in-state tuition rates. UK is a member of the Academic Common Market, which provides students in 15 states the opportunity to pay in-state tuition at any of these states' schools if they want to enroll in a program not offered in their home state. UK received a national award for its efforts to improve the international experience of students.

The academic climate is laid-back, but students shouldn't expect easy As. "When it comes to study time and classwork, the students are always competing with themselves to earn the best grades they can," explains a junior. About a third of classes have fewer than 20 students, but lower-level "monster" science classes are common, and one student describes them as "extremely large and not at all personalized." Undergrads complain about trouble getting into courses they need; according to a marketing major, students "have difficulty if they are freshmen, because most of them have to take the same classes, and sometimes they don't get the right times—or the classes at all." It's hard to complete the engineering, health, business, and architecture programs in four years, students say. Term-time internships, known as co-ops, also complicate—but enliven—the picture. The Central Advising Service, or CAS, is helping to

"UK students are typically self-assured, slightly competitive, and outgoing."

improve the quality of academic guidance, though one student notes, "I do wish I had more assistance from my advisors on which classes to take." TAs and full professors teach about the same number of freshman classes, and students praise UK's professors. "My professors have always shown a genuine concern for my grades," says a sophomore.

"UK students are typically self-assured, slightly competitive, and outgoing," says a psychology major (perhaps practicing analysis for her future career). UK undergraduates hail from all 50 counties in Kentucky, while 30 percent are from out of state and 3 percent are international. The student body is predominantly white; African Americans account for 8 percent of students, Hispanics 4 percent, and Asian Americans 2 percent. Despite these small numbers, students say diversity is valued. "Respectfulness is an issue," says one student, "but Southern hospitality abounds." Merit scholarships averaging $8,446 are offered to qualified students, as are more than 500 athletic scholarships.

Kentucky's dorms are clean and convenient, as well as a great way to meet people, students say, though there's quite a range of what amenities you may get. Dorms are located on three parts of the campus—north, central, and south. North campus housing is old, but the halls are small, so they afford a chance

(continued)

Q of L: ★ ★ ★
Admissions: (866) 900-4685
Email Address: admissions@ uky.edu

Strong Programs:
Business
Engineering
Premed
Prevet
Nursing
Education
International Diplomacy
Chemistry

Prevet students will find coveted slots reserved for them at Auburn and Tuskegee in the advanced veterinary medicine program.

The Green Dot Bystander Intervention program, designed to prevent sexual assault and domestic violence on college campuses, originated at UK.

to form close relationships. They're also within a short walking distance of classrooms, the student center, and the bookstore. South campus offers newer dorms with small rooms and air-conditioning, while central campus offers the biggest rooms. Recommended for freshmen: Kirwan-Blanding Complex, because "everything seems to happen there." Since students are not required to live on campus, only 15 percent do so. The Green Dot Bystander Intervention program, designed to prevent sexual assault and domestic violence on college campuses, originated at the University of Kentucky and has been adopted by hundreds of colleges and universities across the country.

Students say that while Lexington is a great place to go to school, it's not a typical college town. "Lexington is over 300,000 people strong," an upperclassman explains. "It's small enough to drive across town easily, but large enough not to see everyone you know when you go to Walmart." Despite the lack of diversity on campus, Lexington abounds with a multitude of ethnic eateries, as well as theaters, shopping malls, and nightspots. On campus, students enjoy movies, presentations, seminars, and athletic events, the most popular being basketball games at the legendary Rupp Arena. Other campus activities include the Little Kentucky Derby, a weeklong student-run festival that features a balloon race and concerts. Among the highlights of any student's career at UK are two one-month periods—one in the fall, one in the spring—when students spend afternoons at Keeneland Race Track enjoying the tradition of Kentucky horse racing.

> **"In Kentucky, basketball is like a second religion."**

Twenty percent of Kentucky men and 34 percent of the women go Greek, and fraternities and sororities offer the great majority of on-campus activities, as well as opportunities for volunteer work in the community. The university has a strict no-alcohol-on-campus policy, but it doesn't tend to affect students with fake IDs. When it's time for a road trip, UK students head to Cincinnati or Louisville (one hour away), or to Atlanta or Chicago (six hours)—that is, if they're not taking leisurely Sunday drives through nearby Bluegrass country.

The best road-trip destinations are anywhere there's a steamy, noisy gym and a basketball team ready to do battle with UK's always-solid Wildcats. Home games at Lexington's Rupp Arena—what one student calls "a magical experience"—are consistently packed. "In Kentucky, basketball is like a second religion," agrees another true-blue Wildcat fan. Although screaming yourself hoarse for five guys hitting the hardwood may not be as genteel as cheering while sipping a mint julep at the track, for many students, the mix of collegiate craziness and old-world Southern hospitality found at the University of Kentucky is just what they want.

Overlaps

Indiana University, University of Louisville, Miami University (OH), Ohio State, University of Tennessee

If You Apply To ➤

Kentucky: Early action: Dec. 1. Regular decision and financial aid: Feb. 15. Housing: May 1. Application fee: $50. Campus and alumni interviews: optional, informational. SATs or ACTs: required. No Subject Tests. Letters of recommendation: required. Essay: required. Accepts the Common Application.

Kenyon College

Ransom Hall, Gambier, OH 43022

Kenyon is a vintage liberal arts college plunked down in the middle of the Ohio countryside. More mainstream than Oberlin, more serious than Denison, and more selective than Wooster, Kenyon is best known for English and a small but distinguished drama program. Located in a tiny village where faculty and staff are the main residents. Swimming and diving teams make a huge splash.

Kenyon College provides students with an accessible and pure liberal arts experience that rivals those of leading East Coast institutions. Students here are proud of what they see as setting Kenyon apart from other liberal arts colleges. "The one thing that unites us all is that we are passionate about something," explains one student. "Whether it be drama, physics, writing, activism—Kenyon students care!" The college continues to increase its selectivity and build on its reputation as a supportive academic environment.

The oldest private college in Ohio, Kenyon's 1,200-acre campus sits on a hillside overlooking a scenic view of river, woods, and fields in a secluded village of roughly 600 residents. The college's oldest building, Old Kenyon, dating from 1826, is said to be the first collegiate Gothic building in America, and the campus is on the National Register of Historic Places. The campus also includes a butterfly garden and extensive perennial gardens planted with community donations. New facilities include the Hillel House and a health and counseling center.

The hallmark of Kenyon's academic philosophy is an almost fanatical devotion to the liberal arts and sciences. While there is no core curriculum at Kenyon, all students must have proficiency in a second language and complete requirements in quantitative reasoning. A bevy of academic counselors, including upperclassmen and professors, help ensure that freshmen stay on the right track. The culmination of each student's course-work at Kenyon is the senior exercise, which may take the form of a comprehensive examination, an integrative paper, a research project, a performance, or some combination of these. Approximately 11 percent of students graduate with departmental honors.

> **"Whether it be drama, physics, writing, activism— Kenyon students care!"**

English, a nationally renowned subject at Kenyon since the 1930s, is the most popular major, and it, along with the drama department (which turned out Paul Newman), sets the tone of campus life. Kenyon is the home of the *Kenyon Review*, a prestigious literary quarterly, and a school about which alum E. L. Doctorow has said, "Poetry is what we did at Kenyon, the way at Ohio State they played football." Economics, international studies, and biology round out the list of popular majors, and the modern languages and literatures department is also strong. Political science draws undecided majors with its introductory class, Quest for Justice. The Integrated Program in Humane Studies concentration, which incorporates English, history, political science, and art history, is also popular. Opportunities for independent study abound, such as a unique farming program that places students on nearby farms for fieldwork each week. Preprofessional opportunities include 3–2 engineering programs with several universities and high access to graduate programs in law, business, and medicine.

Kenyon's focus on liberal arts makes for a challenging, but largely collaborative, learning environment. "Despite the academic rigor of many classes and departments at Kenyon, I have never felt competitive with my fellow students," says a psychology

Website: www.kenyon.edu
Location: Rural
Private
Total Enrollment: 1,698
Undergraduates: 1,698
Male/Female: 45/55
SAT Ranges: CR 630–730, M 610–690
ACT Ranges: 28–32
Financial Aid: 35%
Pell Grant: 10%
Expense: Pr $ $ $ $
Student Loans: 36%
Average Debt: $ $
Phi Beta Kappa: Yes
Applicants: 7,076
Accepted: 24%
Enrolled: 29%
Grad in 6 Years: 89%
Returning Freshmen: 93%
Academics: ✍ ✍ ✍ ✍
Social: ☎ ☎ ☎
Q of L: ★ ★ ★
Admissions: (800) 848-2468
Email Address: admissions@ kenyon.edu

Strong Programs:
English
Drama
Film
Economics
International Studies
Biology
Modern Languages and Literatures
Political Science

major. Classes are small and even the larger introductory courses use a two-part format in which students meet for lectures one week and split up for discussion sections with the professor the next. "Kenyon's professors are active researchers and exemplary teachers," says a math major. "They are passionate about their fields, and they love getting their students excited about the material as well." Many profs live close to campus, which enhances the close-knit environment. On-campus Summer Science research scholarships provide opportunities for collaborative research for aspiring scientists and doctors. Half of the student body takes part in study abroad, choosing from more than 150 programs in more than 50 countries, including Kenyon-sponsored programs in England and Italy.

"Kenyon students are very friendly and intelligent and easy to talk to," says a student. Twelve percent of Kenyon students are Ohioans, one-third hail from New England and Mid-Atlantic states, and 5 percent come from abroad. African Americans account for 4 percent of the student body, Hispanics 7 percent, and Asian Americans

> **"Kenyon's professors are active researchers and exemplary teachers."**

4 percent, and the college is actively working to increase diversity. The liberal student body is politically engaged, especially when it comes to social justice issues, but a sophomore says, "Students at Kenyon thrive on open conversation and do not silence opinions that contradict theirs." Kenyon meets the full demonstrated financial need of admitted students and awards merit scholarships averaging $15,204. Thanks in part to a $10 million gift from the late Paul Newman, the college also guarantees a loan-free education for 25 selected students with the greatest need who bring the qualities of creativity, community service, and leadership to Kenyon.

All students live on campus, with housing guaranteed for four years. Freshmen start in five dorms at the north end of campus, and most move to the south end the next year. Renovations and expansions are always in the works, with more than a dozen north campus townhouses recently opened, but students say some accommodations still need improving. Rooms are selected via a sometimes harrowing housing lottery, and upperclassmen typically try to get into one of the historic dorms. Everyone, including those in the apartments with kitchens, must buy the unlimited meal plan. "Kenyon is in an isolated area of Ohio, and is generally very safe," a senior says. The college has recently adopted a new Title IX policy and hired a civil rights coordinator to enforce it.

The school's Greek system draws 18 percent of the men and 20 percent of the women, and the frats throw lively parties that are open to all. "Social life takes place on campus mostly because Kenyon is in a very rural area," says one student, and there are more than 100 student clubs. A senior adds, "Every student performance—sports games, public presentations, music recitals, art shows—is incredibly well attended." With its deli, market, coffeehouse, inn, restaurant, couple of bars, bank, and post office, Gambier is at least quaint, even if it is a bit of a culture shock for urbanites. Students enjoy buying real maple syrup, fresh bread, and cheese from

> **"Students at Kenyon thrive on open conversation and do not silence opinions that contradict theirs."**

Amish farmers with stands on the main street on Saturdays. There are a few more options 10 minutes away in Mount Vernon, to which the college runs a daytime shuttle bus, and two small ski areas lie near campus. For those seeking adventure farther from home, Columbus and Ohio State University are a 45-minute drive south. The adventurous sometimes take road trips to Cleveland (home of the Rock and Roll Hall of Fame), Cincinnati, Chicago, or even Canada.

Kenyon remains defined by its traditions, the most hallowed of which is renewed each year as incoming freshmen sing college songs to the rest of the community from the steps of Rosse Hall. Departing seniors sing the same songs at graduation. On Matriculation Day each October, after a formal ceremony, freshmen sign a book that contains the signatures of virtually every Kenyon student since the early 1800s. To break February's icy cold, the school holds a formal ball called Philander's Phling, remembering founder Philander Chase; an alum donates money for the dance. Summer Sendoff is an outdoor concert celebrating the end of spring semester classes.

Kenyon's varsity teams are known as the Lords and the Ladies. Women's and men's tennis and soccer are competitive, but the flagship sport is definitely swimming. Kenyon's swimming and diving teams dominate Division III competition, with the men's team having won 34 titles. "Kenyon's rivalry with Denison is huge," says one student, "especially between the swim teams." Kenyon was instrumental in establishing the North Coast Athletic Conference, which includes a number of academically strong Midwestern schools. The annual hockey game against Denison and soccer games against Ohio Wesleyan draw large crowds. Club and intramural sports attract about half of the students and sponsor everything from ultimate Frisbee to ballroom dance.

Kenyon students are liberal, global thinkers who are as devoted to one another as they are to their studies and their traditions. The *Kenyon Review*, the legend of alumnus Paul Newman, and national-championship swimming give the college an identity that's hard to match. As one sociology major advises, "It can be tough at times dealing with the location or the intense academics, but if students embrace Kenyon, it is a quirky school that can be extremely rewarding to attend."

> *Kenyon is the home of the Kenyon Review, a prestigious literary quarterly.*

> **"Social life takes place on campus mostly because Kenyon is in a very rural area."**

Overlaps

Oberlin, Brown, Middlebury, Wesleyan, Grinnell, Bowdoin, Carleton, Vassar

If You Apply To > **Kenyon:** Early decision I: Nov. 15. Early decision II, regular decision, and financial aid: Jan. 15. Housing: May 1. No application fee. Campus and alumni interviews: recommended, evaluative. SATs or ACTs: required. Subject Tests: optional. Letters of recommendation: required. Essay: required. Accepts the Common Application.

Knox College

2 East South Street, Galesburg, IL 61401

This friendly and progressive Illinois college was among the first in the nation to admit African Americans and women. Offers a strong writing program and exceptional sciences. More mainstream than Beloit and Grinnell and smaller than Illinois Wesleyan. With a hugely diverse student body of about 1,400, Knox offers an unusual degree of personal attention, even by the standards of small colleges.

With the unconventional Prairie Fire as its mascot, Knox College has long made a name for itself by breaking away from the conventions of the day. Founded by abolitionists in 1837 as the Knox Manual Labor College, this liberal arts college has a tradition of debate that extends beyond the Lincoln-Douglas event that occurred here in 1858. And through a warm, supportive academic community and emphasis on experiential learning, the college continues to foster a strong sense of individualism.

Located in the heart of the Midwest—almost midway between Chicago and St. Louis—the 82-acre campus has spacious, tree-lined lawns and a dynamic mixture of architecture that reflects the 160-year span of construction dates of existing buildings. Old Main, constructed in 1857, is a National Historic Landmark and the only building remaining from the 1858 Lincoln-Douglas debates. Alumni Hall recently

Website: www.knox.edu
Location: Small Town
Private
Total Enrollment: 1,365
Undergraduates: 1,365
Male/Female: 41/59
SAT Ranges: CR 580–630, M 590–660
ACT Ranges: 23–29
Financial Aid: 98%

re-opened after a yearlong, $12.5 million renovation that earned it LEED Gold certi-fication. Construction on a new $8 million center for art and art history is scheduled for completion in 2017.

Students say the academic relationships at Knox are infused with a spirit of cooperation and equality. Beyond the classroom, students, faculty, and administra-tors make decisions on boards together, each with identical voting power. First-year students confront the core issues of liberal education in Preceptorial, a one-term seminar examining questions of ethics and truth through multidisciplinary reading and critical writing.

The general education curriculum requires students to take one course each in the arts, the natural and social sciences, and the humanities, as well as courses in writing, speaking, mathematics, information technology, foreign language, and human diversity. All students participate in an experiential learning activity of their choice, such as research or an internship, that serves as a capstone experience. Popular majors include economics, education, cre-ative writing, computer science, and psychology, and the theater and biology depart-ments are also strong, with biology attracting lots of research grant money. Knox offers 3–2 or 3–4 programs in engineering, nursing, medical technology, law, and architecture, as well as a cooperative program with The George Washington University School of Medicine and Health Sciences. The college is also a member of the Associated Colleges of the Midwest* consortium.

> **"Students who attend Knox are involved in their community (campus and otherwise) and are independent thinkers."**

Knox operates on an honor system that allows students to take tests unproctored in any public area. "Knox is challenging but not overwhelming," says a senior. Where faculty is concerned, students offer uniformly glowing reviews for their performance in the classroom and availability outside of it. "The quality of teaching is very high," a student says. Seventy-one percent of classes have fewer than 20 students. Knox's tri-mester system packs a great deal of studying into a short period, but students are only required to take three courses per term. They may also opt to participate in immersive terms that allow them to engage in a hands-on exploration of a single field of study for an entire term; the six available subjects include clinical psychology, Japanese language and culture, studio art, repertory theater, start-ups, and fieldwork and community living at the off-campus Green Oaks prairie restoration site. Students praise Knox's student advising system for helping them navigate the multitude of options avail-able. "Academic advising has been excellent for me, and advisors are always available to discuss anything ranging from future plans to personal problems," says a junior.

As part of the Artists, Scholars, Scientists, and Entrepreneurs of Tomorrow pro-gram, students complete intensive individual projects and work together to identify and discuss connections across disciplinary boundaries. Knox also awards $350,000 annually for independent student research and creative work, and more than 85 percent of students do some type of independent study. Knox's COAST (Creating Opportunities and Access in Science and Technology) Program offers qualified first-year students planning to major in biology, biochemistry, and chemistry a package of personalized attention that includes tutoring, seminars with visiting scientists, career exploration activities, and scholarships for select students. First priority goes to students who are the first in their families to attend college and those who are from groups underrepresented in STEM-related fields. For those interested in ser-vice, Knox was the first college in the country to establish an official Peace Corps Preparatory Program. Knox also offers more than 30 study abroad and off-campus programs in 18 countries, and 37 percent of students participate.

"Students who attend Knox are involved in their community (campus and other-wise) and are independent thinkers," says a senior. Forty-five percent of students are

Knox was the first college in the country to establish an official Peace Corps Preparatory Program.

from Illinois, and 14 percent hail from foreign countries. While Knox is not a terribly politically active school—one senior reports the biggest issue to be student governance—there appears to be a commitment to diversity across campus. Students of color make up a third of the student body (8 percent African American, 7 percent Asian American, and 18 percent Hispanic) and maintain an active profile on campus. Socioeconomically, 39 percent of freshmen qualify for Pell Grants. Merit scholarships averaging $18,304 are available, but athletic scholarships are not.

"Galesburg is a small town with a lot of hidden treasures."

Eighty-seven percent of students reside in campus digs, and renovations have improved housing for most students, though some complain that most rooms are not air-conditioned. Still, "The dorms are comfortable and have adequate space," one senior reasons. Co-ed living arrangements are available, although most freshmen live in single-sex suites. Students suggest freshman women would be happiest in Post Hall, while men should try to live anywhere in Old Quad. It takes a minor miracle for students to obtain permission to move off campus, which has become a common complaint among juniors and seniors. Students say campus dining options are edible if not overly diverse. Knox Guardian is a new mobile safety app, and the college recently revamped its policies and resources aimed at preventing and responding to campus sexual assault.

Thirty-two percent of men and 18 percent of women go Greek, and weekends are filled with dances, campus activities, and fraternity parties. "Most of the social life happens on campus," a creative writing major says. The alcohol policy is strict, students say, and the administration is quick to deal with underage drinkers. Galesburg is a small Midwestern railroad town, and the Amtrak station makes travel easy and relatively cheap. At one time this city of about 32,000 was a center of abolitionism, and the honorary degree that the college bestowed on then-presidential candidate Abraham Lincoln was his first formal title. A senior says, "Galesburg is a small town with a lot of hidden treasures." Nearby Lake Storey offers boating, water slides, and nature trails, and students looking for more excitement can travel to Peoria, about 40 miles away. Slightly farther away, Chicago is about 140 miles to the northeast. One of the best all-time campus traditions is Flunk Day. At 5:30 on a spring morning, Old Main's bell rings, whistles blow, and classes are canceled to make way for dunk tanks and Jell-O pits.

"There is a 'freedom to flourish' at Knox. My opportunities are limitless."

Prairie Fire athletics' 20 Division III teams also generate a reasonable degree of enthusiasm. Both the men's and women's soccer teams are strong; the men's team is a recent Midwest Conference regular season champ. Every fall, the football team endures lots of hard "Knox" against archrival Monmouth to bring home the highly prized Bronze Turkey Award, a throwback to the time when the game was played on Thanksgiving Day. About 25 percent of students participate in intramurals; basketball and indoor futsal are the most popular. The college's biannual literary magazine, *Catch*, has won several national and international awards.

Knox may not be a well-known school, but students here have little else to complain about. Academics and hands-on experiences are the priority, and students are encouraged to be individuals, but the close-knit atmosphere helps them form strong connections with different types of students and down-to-earth professors. Says a student, "There is a 'freedom to flourish' at Knox. My opportunities are limitless."

The college's biannual literary magazine, Catch, has won several national and international awards.

Overlaps

University of Illinois at Chicago, University of Illinois at Urbana–Champaign, DePaul, Beloit, Loyola University Chicago, Marquette, Augustana, Illinois Wesleyan

If You Apply To ➤ **Knox:** Early decision and early action I: Nov. 1. Early action II: Dec. 1. Regular decision and financial aid: Jan. 15. Housing: May 1. Application fee: $50. Campus interviews: recommended, evaluative. No alumni interviews. SATs or ACTs: optional. Subject Tests: optional. Letters of recommendation: required. Essay: required. Accepts the Common Application with supplement.

Geographically close to Lehigh, but closer kin to Colgate and Hamilton and boasting a strong global orientation. Does offer engineering, as do Bucknell, Swarthmore, Trinity (CT), and Union. Attracts relatively conservative, athletic students who work hard and play hard. A recent spate of building shows Lafayette's financial health. One of the smallest institutions to play Division I sports.

Lafayette College has become one of the small elite liberal arts colleges with a huge presence abroad. Lafayette is a national leader in undergraduate faculty-mentored research and is ranked among the top colleges in study abroad participation. The liberal arts curriculum mixes nicely with engineering in a small college atmosphere. The number of applications has increased, signaling that the world beyond the Lafayette campus has taken notice.

Lafayette is situated on a stately hill in Easton, Pennsylvania, just an hour and a half west of New York City and even closer to Philadelphia. The campus has an eclectic blend of architectural styles and more than 125 species of trees. A $22 million expansion of the Skillman Library has added 30,000 square feet of open learning space—a common theme in many Lafayette buildings. The 90,000-square-foot Acopian Engineering Center stays open all night and weekends and features lots of open workspaces and glass walls to build a sense of shared purpose—and allow for extra mingling. The newest campus addition is the environmentally friendly Oechsle Center for Global Education, which houses programs in international affairs, Africana studies, anthropology, and sociology.

A Common Course of Study (CCS) includes a first-year seminar and courses in lab science, social sciences, mathematics, humanities, writing, global and multicultural proficiency, and a foreign language. "It is a tough workload, but there is not cutthroat competitiveness," says a biology major. Lafayette's economics, government and law, psychology, mechanical engineering, and biology programs are among the most popular majors. The Economic Empowerment and Global Learning Project allows students from all disciplines to relate classroom lessons to real-world problems in the U.S. and abroad. The Center for Innovation, Design, Entrepreneurship, and Leadership provides hands-on, multidisciplinary opportunities for collaboration in the liberal arts and engineering. The EXCEL program pays students who take research positions with faculty. One student states, "The quality of teaching in the classroom ranges, but all professors are accessible and seek to help students one-on-one." Newly added minors include aging studies, health and life sciences, and literature in translation. Students also benefit from cross-registration opportunities with other schools in the Lehigh Valley Association of Independent Colleges*.

> "All professors are accessible and seek to help students one-on-one."

Lafayette has one of the highest study abroad participation rates among liberal arts colleges and offers programs in 50 countries. Options include several semester-long, faculty-led programs as well as short-term, faculty-led programs for credit during the January and May interim terms. "Study abroad is life-changing," marvels one student. Even engineering students are encouraged to explore foreign cultures; programs led by Lafayette faculty at Jacobs University in Germany and Saint Louis University in Spain allow them to study abroad for a semester while maintaining normal progress toward their degrees.

Lafayette students are by and large "compassionate, hardworking, and extremely talented," says one senior. Seventy-two percent of Lafayette students are from out

---

Website: www.lafayette.edu
Location: Small City
Private
Total Enrollment: 2,491
Undergraduates: 2,491
Male/Female: 51/49
SAT Ranges: CR 580–670, M 620–710
ACT Ranges: 27–31
Financial Aid: 58%
Pell Grant: 11%
Expense: Pr $ $ $
Student Loans: 55%
Average Debt: $ $ $
Phi Beta Kappa: Yes
Applicants: 7,465
Accepted: 30%
Enrolled: 30%
Grad in 6 Years: 90%
Returning Freshmen: 95%
Academics: ✏ ✏ ✏ ✏
Social: 🍷 🍷 🍷 🍷 🍷
Q of L: ★ ★ ★
Admissions: (610) 330-5100
Email Address: admissions@lafayette.edu

Strong Programs:
Economics
Government and Law
Psychology
Mechanical Engineering
Biology
Social Sciences

of state, and another 9 percent are drawn from abroad. African Americans account for 5 percent of the student body, Hispanics 6 percent, and Asian Americans 4 percent. "Students are less political than one might imagine," a student explains, "even though the College Democrats, Republicans, and Libertarians all have a pretty loud voice on campus." Roughly 10 percent of incoming freshmen receive merit-based Marquis Scholarships worth $25,000 per year, while 30 top achievers are awarded Marquis Fellowships worth $40,000 per year. Student-athletes vie for athletic scholarships in 11 sports. Additionally, Lafayette guarantees to meet the full demonstrated need of admitted students, and it reduces or eliminates loans from financial aid packages for students from families with annual incomes less than $100,000.

Lafayette has one of the highest study abroad participation rates among liberal arts colleges and offers programs in 50 countries.

Ninety-four percent of students live on campus, and housing is guaranteed for all four years. Possibilities include Greek houses as well as independent dormitories and college-owned apartments with a variety of living and eating arrangements. "I have had friends visit who are shocked by how roomy my double is. Upperclassmen may live off campus, but many do choose to stay because the housing options are excellent," a freshman says. There's a lottery system that determines which dorm a student will live in, but most get into the dorm of their choice. Ruef and South College are more social, while Watson Hall and Kirby House are quieter, students say. Campus dining gets good reviews: "There are definitely a lot of choices and they cater to all of those with special needs," says one student. Another reports, "The campus is very well lit at night, and feels very safe. The blue light system is in place, but I've never heard of anybody using it (which is a good thing!)."

"Students are less political than one might imagine."

"The social scene takes place primarily on College Hill. Students pregame in dorm rooms or off-campus apartments and parties take place at off-campus apartments," says one senior. Greek life attracts 17 percent of the men and 34 percent of the women. "I think there is some pressure to drink, with the tone being set by Greeks and athletes," observes one senior, although all sororities and some fraternities are dry, at least on campus. The arts program brings a range of performers to campus, and the most important nonathletic event of the year is Spring Concert, an outdoor event to celebrate the season. For students with cars, or those willing to hop a bus or train, the bright lights of Philadelphia, New York, and Atlantic City beckon on weekends; for a change of pace, there is also hiking the Appalachian Trail. Another popular excursion is touring the nearby Binney & Smith factory where Crayola crayons are made. Blue-collar Easton "gets a bad rap, but is really nice," says a senior. "A lot of restaurants on the hill, lots of nice shops, great health and beauty salons. I really like Easton." From College Hill and Downtown to the South Side, the city offers plenty of opportunities for volunteer work in schools, prisons, rehabilitation centers, hospitals, and environmental sites, under the auspices of Lafayette's Community Outreach Center.

The annual football game against nearby Lehigh is intense—it's the most-played rivalry in college football.

"I have had friends visit who are shocked by how roomy my double is."

Division I sports add much flavor to the Lafayette experience. Recent Patriot League champions include men's basketball, football, and women's field hockey. Other competitive Leopard teams include men's soccer, baseball, and lacrosse and women's basketball. The annual football game against nearby Lehigh is intense—it's the most-played rivalry in college football. For those not up to varsity level, there is an extensive intramural program, buoyed by the state-of-the-art, $35 million Kirby Sports Center.

Students seeking close contact with professors, research opportunities, and a global outlook—and who aren't afraid of some serious study—should take a close look at Lafayette College. "If you want to make lifelong friends, have professors and alumni who mentor you, and get involved on campus and in the local community," says a senior, "Lafayette is for you."

Overlaps

Lehigh, Bucknell, Villanova, University of Richmond, Northeastern, Boston College, Cornell University, Franklin & Marshall

If You Apply To ➤

Lafayette: Early decision I: Nov. 15. Early decision II, regular decision, and financial aid: Jan. 15. Application fee: $65. Campus interviews: recommended, evaluative. Alumni interviews: optional, evaluative. SATs or ACTs: required. Subject Tests: recommended. Letters of recommendation: required. Essay: required. Accepts the Common Application with supplement.

Lake Forest College

555 Sheridan Road, Lake Forest, IL 60045

The only small, selective, private college in the Chicago area, Lake Forest generally attracts middle-of-the-road students. In the exclusive town from which the school takes its name, students can babysit for corporate CEOs at night and get internships at their corporations during the day. Large numbers of Foresters also study abroad.

Website: www.lakeforest.edu
Location: Suburban
Private
Total Enrollment: 1,557
Undergraduates: 1,546
Male/Female: 44/56
SAT Ranges: N/A
ACT Ranges: 23–28
Financial Aid: 96%
Pell Grant: 41%
Expense: Pr $ $
Student Loans: 68%
Average Debt: $ $ $ $
Phi Beta Kappa: Yes
Applicants: 3,373
Accepted: 55%
Enrolled: 19%
Grad in 6 Years: 73%
Returning Freshmen: 85%
Academics: ✐ ✐ ✐
Social: ☎ ☎ ☎ ☎
Q of L: ★ ★ ★
Admissions: (847) 735-5000
Email Address: admissions@lakeforest.edu

Strong Programs:
Biology
Finance
Communication
Psychology
Business
English
Entrepreneurship and Innovation

Located just 30 miles north of the downtown Loop, Lake Forest College offers excellent programs in business, communication, and psychology, along with abundant opportunities for study abroad and professional internships at Chicagoland companies such as *Rolling Stone*, the Chicago Blackhawks, and the Chicago Board of Trade. Academic improvements at Lake Forest are drawing attention; applications are up significantly and the school is attracting high-caliber students from around the nation. Indeed, the school is shedding its image as a haven for spoiled rich kids, says a senior, in favor of "increasingly challenging academics, more student engagement, and more responsible students."

With its mixture of century-old Gothic and modern glass structures, Lake Forest's 107-acre campus is storybook beautiful. Located on Chicago's North Shore in a wealthy, quiet city of 20,000, the campus has three contiguous parts divided by natural wooded ravines: North, Middle, and South. Each has a mix of residence halls and academic buildings. The state-of-the-art Donnelley and Lee Library offers a 24-hour computer lab, wireless access to the campus network, and "smart classrooms," along with space where students can work collaboratively on projects. The Johnson Science Center, a $43 million project, is slated for completion in 2018.

> **"It's not uncommon to find an entire class sitting in a study room going over material for an upcoming exam."**

General education requirements include the First-Year Studies Program, featuring "very small classes designed to help freshmen integrate into the college," says an English major. "These courses are writing intensive and offer a variety of opportunities, including trips to Chicago for plays and museum visits." Students also complete two credits in each of three liberal arts areas (humanities, social sciences and natural sciences, and math), two cultural diversity courses, and a senior studies capstone course. Students may pursue up to two majors and one minor or one major and two minors.

Students say Lake Forest's best and most popular departments include biology, finance, communication, psychology, business, and English. An entrepreneurship and innovation minor has also proven popular. Accelerated and dual-degree programs—including three-year degree programs in philosophy and communication and dual-degree programs in law, engineering, pharmacy, accounting, and international studies—are available. A major in African American studies and a minor in journalism have recently been added. Academic self-starters benefit from the self-designed major program, which allows undergrads to create their own majors outside the boundaries of traditional disciplines.

The academic climate at Lake Forest is described as intense but collaborative. "The small class sizes allow for a lot of group discussion, group projects, and peer mentoring," says a biology major. "It's not uncommon to find an entire class sitting in a study room going over material for an upcoming exam." Foresters especially enjoy the large doses of individual attention that they receive from the faculty. "Overall, the teaching is outstanding," says one student. "The professors go above and beyond, and they are all at Lake Forest College because they want to teach." The Career Advancement Center is run by the same person who oversees admissions, meaning that the person who brings you to Lake Forest is also looking out for you as you graduate and move into the workforce. The center offers symposia, workshops, and résumé clinics, and students benefit from the college's proximity to downtown Chicago, just an hour away by train. Many pursue term-time internships in the city's business district, known as the Loop, or at nonprofits and other organizations in surrounding communities.

Study abroad is also integral to the Lake Forest experience, and 40 percent of students travel abroad via more than 200 programs in approximately 70 nations, including programs offered through the Associated Colleges of the Midwest* consortium. Lake Forest's program in Greece uses archaeological sites and museums to study the ancient Aegean world, while the international program in Paris allows aspiring international executives to hone their language and financial skills. Students in the Honors Fellows program are expected to conduct independent research and present their findings at the annual Student Symposium. Each year, about 35 students become Richter Apprentice Scholars. They participate in an interdisciplinary seminar and a 10-week paid research assistantship during the summer before their sophomore year. As upperclassmen, Richter scholars live and work together and take part in a weekly student/faculty colloquium designed to help them learn about—and pursue—careers in academics and primary research.

> **"Our dining hall is multicultural, so you can have Mexican food one day and Indian the next."**

Sixty-four percent of Lake Forest students hail from the Land of Lincoln, and most are serious about their studies and having fun. "There are a lot of intelligent, bright students who attend, and many of them put their knowledge to good use in extracurriculars as well," says one student. African Americans make up 7 percent of the student body, Hispanics 17 percent, and Asian Americans 5 percent; 13 percent are international. The campus is generally liberal, and a senior notes, "When big topics come up like the election or Black Lives Matter, the school puts together meetings and activities for students to engage in politics and social problems." Competitive financial aid packages are helping to bring more students of color and those from less-advantaged backgrounds to LFC. Forty-one percent of freshmen are eligible for Pell Grants. LFC awards numerous merit scholarships averaging $17,885 but does not offer athletic scholarships.

Seventy-four percent of students live in the dorms, and they are required to do so through their junior year. An English major says, "Different halls attract different people. I preferred living in the older buildings because they felt homier than the new buildings, which felt more like a hotel." Freshmen are assigned rooms by the dean of students, while housing selection for upperclassmen is prioritized by seniority and GPA, "so there's a definite incentive to do well in your classes," says a senior. Everybody eats in the central dining hall, where food is prepared to order at pizza, pasta, stir-fry, and other stations, and helpings are unlimited. "Our dining hall is multicultural, so you can have Mexican food one day and Indian the next," explains a sophomore. "Public Safety does an excellent job at making us feel safe and actually keeping us safe," says one student. Adds a senior, "We have regular programming events and student panels dedicated to educating the campus on sexual assault."

The admissions officer who brings you to Lake Forest is also looking out for you at the Career Advancement Center.

The Richter Apprentice Scholars program is designed to help students learn about—and pursue— careers in academics and primary research.

Forty-one percent of freshmen are eligible for Pell Grants.

"The social life on campus is always active because a majority of students live on campus and are involved in multiple organizations," says a biology major. The Campus Entertainment Committee books movies, comedians, and big-name bands, while the Garrick Players also put on several productions per year. The school's three fraternities and five sororities attract 19 percent of the men and 21 percent of the women, respectively, and though they don't have houses, their parties are open to all. Students say the party culture is relatively low-key, and underage students caught drinking on campus are strictly penalized. Everyone enjoys the tradition of homecoming, as well as the semiformal Winter Ball, the annual Day of Service, the Spring Concert, and the Drag Show lip-synch contest planned by PRIDE.

The town of Lake Forest is mostly residential, and one student says, "The town is actually in a forest, so the whole place is beautiful, and it feels like you live tucked away in a safe haven." There's a commuter train station five minutes away and the Lake Michigan beach is just as close. LFC also offers a weekend shuttle service to local malls and movie theaters, though a car is helpful. Several student organizations are devoted to community service, and Greek organizations sponsor blood drives, bake sales, and car washes. One program sends students to the Appalachian Mountains in Virginia and Tennessee every spring break to help local townspeople repair substandard housing.

> "The town is actually in a forest... and it feels like you live tucked away in a safe haven."

Division III varsity athletics have begun to draw more attention from Foresters. In recent years more than a dozen varsity sports teams have qualified for their respective conference or national postseason championships. Recent conference champions include women's soccer, tennis, and softball, as well as men's swimming and diving. Club and intramural sports programs attract more than half of the student body; lacrosse and indoor soccer are especially popular.

Although Lake Forest still has its fair share of "preppy" types, students are quick to emphasize that the college is taking steps to increase diversity, foster a collaborative atmosphere, and encourage school pride. "Lake Forest takes very good care of its students by providing challenging academics, comfortable living, lots of entertainment, and a small-town feel with access to a big city," concludes a senior. "What more could anyone want?"

Overlaps

University of Illinois at Urbana–Champaign, DePaul, Loyola University Chicago, Augustana, Denison, Knox, Illinois Wesleyan

If You Apply To ➤

Lake Forest: Early decision and early action I: Oct. 15. Early action II: Jan. 1. Regular decision and financial aid: Feb. 15. Housing: May 1. No application fee. Campus interviews: recommended, evaluative. No alumni interviews. SATs or ACTs: optional (ACTs preferred). Subject Tests: optional. Letters of recommendation: required. Essay: required. Accepts the Common Application.

Lawrence University

711 East Boldt Way, Appleton, WI 54911

One of three small colleges in the nation that combines the liberal arts with a first-rate music conservatory (Bard and Oberlin are the others). Lawrence is half the size of Oberlin and comparable to Beloit and Grinnell, though Lawrence's personality is more mainstream than any of the three. Occupies a scenic bluff in northeastern Wisconsin.

Lawrence University is an unpretentious school that can appeal to both the left and right side of students' brains. For those with an analytical bent, there is Lawrence's uncommon physics program. More creative types can take advantage of the school's renowned Conservatory of Music. "I came to Lawrence because I found no other school where I could seriously study music and academics," says a senior. "At all the other schools, you had to pick one or the other." It's this eclectic, individualized approach to learning that attracts interested and interesting students from around the world. "Lawrence allows students to explore individual and intellectual interests in greater depth than most institutions," confirms a neuroscience major.

Lawrence's campus is on a wooded bluff above the Fox River, perfect for long walks, jogging, or simply meditating underneath the trees. It was chosen in 1847 by one of Appleton's earliest settlers. The pristine 84-acre campus reflects several architectural styles of the past 150 years, including classical revival, 1920s Georgian-inspired, and 1950s and 1960s institutional, unified by their limestone color. The award-winning Wriston Art Center and the Conservatory's Shattuck Hall of Music (both designed by Lawrence graduates) bring contemporary architectural touches to the campus. The university's stadium has been revamped and now includes new seating, synthetic turf, and an LED scoreboard.

One of the first coeducational colleges established in the nation, Lawrence was founded to educate German immigrants and Native Americans. While coeducation was shocking, innovators at Lawrence didn't stop there. More than 50 years ago, administrators introduced the Freshman Studies program, a required two-term course that focuses primarily on the great works of art, music, and literature of both Western and non-Western origin and gives all incoming students a shared intellectual experience. General education requirements at Lawrence include Freshman Studies; distribution requirements; and diversity, foreign language, and writing-intensive courses. All seniors—in all degree programs—are required to produce a final project demonstrating proficiency in their major field of study.

"Lawrence allows students to explore individual and intellectual interests in greater depth than most institutions."

At the school's Conservatory of Music, the instrument collection includes an 1815 Broadwood piano identical to Beethoven's Broadwood, and a Guarneri violin. There are first-rate jazz ensembles along with classical and world music programs. The college offers a bachelor of music degree within its liberal arts environment, and students may opt to complete a five-year, double-degree program to earn both a bachelor of music and a bachelor of arts in another field. "Music is the unifying theme at Lawrence," says one student. "Almost everybody plays it or studies it or likes to listen to it and talk about it." Music is also the most popular major, followed by biology, psychology, government, and English. Languages offered include Chinese, Japanese, and Arabic. New interdisciplinary areas include museum studies and innovation and entrepreneurship, and a new major in global studies has also been added.

Lawrentians appreciate their professors' expertise and experience. Despite the "occasional dud professor who hides behind tenure, the teaching quality is phenomenal," says a student. Small class sizes—80 percent of classes have fewer than 20 students—enable professors to take a personal approach to their teaching. Because of the three-term calendar, the academic climate is intense but "extremely collaborative," a sophomore says. "As long as you stay on top of reading and notes, it is not overwhelming."

Students are encouraged to spend at least one term of their college career off campus, and 38 percent of undergrads do so. The university is known for its London Centre, which allows students to take classes "across the pond" while taking

Website: www.lawrence.edu
Location: Small City
Private
Total Enrollment: 1,494
Undergraduates: 1,494
Male/Female: 45/55
SAT Ranges: CR 560–690, M 610–730
ACT Ranges: 26–32
Financial Aid: 98%
Pell Grant: 16%
Expense: Pr $ $
Student Loans: 62%
Average Debt: $ $ $ $
Phi Beta Kappa: Yes
Applicants: 3,014
Accepted: 68%
Enrolled: 19%
Grad in 6 Years: 76%
Returning Freshmen: 89%
Academics: ✑ ✑ ✑ ✑
Social: ☎ ☎ ☎
Q of L: ★ ★ ★
Admissions: (800) 227-0982
Email Address: admissions@lawrence.edu

Strong Programs:
Music
Biology
Psychology
Government
English
Physics
Innovation and Entrepreneurship

A five-year, double-degree program allows students to earn both a bachelor of music and a bachelor of arts in another field.

advantage of the city's many cultural activities. Other off-campus programs include a Francophone seminar in Dakar, Senegal, and a marine biology term in the Cayman Islands. In all, 45 international programs are available in more than two dozen countries. About 65 percent of students participate in research opportunities, especially those in the sciences. The LU-R1 program pairs qualified students with Lawrence alumni who are conducting research at tier-one universities across the country for 10-week research assistantships during the summer.

"Lawrence University has passionate, supportive, and thoughtful undergraduates," observes one student. Twenty-six percent of Lawrentians hail from Wisconsin, and another quarter come from elsewhere in the Midwest. At 11 percent, the international population is sizable and represents more than 40 countries. African Americans make up 3 percent of the student body, Asian Americans 5 percent, and Hispanics 7 percent. The political climate on campus is generally liberal—there's a leftist newspaper—and a junior says, "Students here are very quick to speak their mind and express their opinions, regardless of what they are." There are no athletic scholarships, but top achievers vie for merit scholarships averaging $19,988 each.

The dorms at Lawrence are well populated; all but 4 percent of students live on campus. "Because we have to live on campus for our first four traditional years of college, there are tons of options for housing: dorms, theme houses, group houses, lofts, etc.," explains a junior. All halls are co-ed, by room or by floor, and all have laundry facilities, kitchens, televisions, and lounges. On-campus students have a choice of meal plans and report that the food is diverse and friendly to those with dietary restrictions. "The food is all made from scratch from organic and locally sourced food. Some of our produce comes from a student-run garden right across the street from the dining hall," reports one student. The administration is in the process of overhauling its sexual misconduct policies, with input from students and faculty, and a junior notes, "We are working together to make campus safer than it already is."

"Students here are very quick to speak their mind and express their opinions."

Social life at Lawrence is as varied and eclectic as the students. "Most of social life takes place on campus because the surrounding city of Appleton is rather small," a psychology major says. Greek life attracts 20 percent of the men and 14 percent of the women; students say Greek organizations do not set the tone for social life and the party culture tends to be laid-back. The President's Ball in the winter and LU-aroo, a music festival in the spring, are favorite annual traditions. The Great Midwest Trivia Contest takes place during January each year; held since 1965, it's the longest running trivia contest in the nation. Octoberfest is also a big weekend event, held in conjunction with the city of Appleton, which draws people in from nearby cities.

Relations between Lawrence and Appleton are good. "The town is safe and has lots to do," says a student, including "cafés, restaurants, shops, nightlife, performing arts, and farmers markets." The nearest grocery store is a five-minute drive away, as is the nearest theater, and many students see a car as a necessity. Volunteerism is popular, and students regularly take part in activities such as tutoring at local schools. The best road trips are to Milwaukee (two hours), Green Bay (half an hour), and Chicago (four hours). There are also weekend seminars at Björklunden, the college's 425-acre estate on the shores of Lake Michigan.

"I've always felt that this school is a hidden gem."

And what would a Midwest fall Saturday be without football? The Division III Lawrence Vikings draw good crowds almost every weekend. Men's hockey, cross-country, and tennis, women's swimming, and softball are among the most competitive teams. The sparkling recreation center helps students fend off midwinter blues.

Participating in a rousing game of intramural broomball, which is ice hockey played on shoes with brooms as sticks and kickballs as pucks, is a must for students, even if all you do is watch. Ultimate Frisbee is a popular club sport.

With its outstanding liberal arts curriculum, knowledgeable and caring faculty, an administration that treats students like adults, and a charming country setting, Lawrence University is easily one of the best little-known schools in the country. "Lawrence really does provide the tools and opportunities necessary to become an effective leader. I've always felt that this school is a hidden gem," raves a film studies major. And for students with a musical ear, Lawrence's symphony of offerings strikes just the right chord.

If You Apply To ➢

Lawrence: Early action I: Nov. 1. Early action II: Dec. 1. Regular decision: Jan. 15. Financial aid: Jan. 22. Housing: May 1. No application fee. Campus interviews: recommended, evaluative. Alumni interviews: optional, evaluative. SATs or ACTs: optional. Subject Tests: optional. Letters of recommendation: required. Essay: required. Accepts the Common Application with supplement. Music applicants must audition.

Lehigh University

27 Memorial Drive West, Bethlehem, PA 18015

Built on the powerful combination of business and engineering, Lehigh occupies a middle ground between techie havens such as Drexel and Rensselaer and the liberal arts/engineering institutions such as Bucknell and Union. By graduation, students are primed for the global job market. Hillside campus means that students get plenty of exercise. A wrestling powerhouse.

From the College of Arts and Sciences to the College of Business and Economics, Lehigh University combines the academic resources of a large research university with the collegial atmosphere of a much smaller institution. Because much of Lehigh's reputation rests on its consistently strong engineering program, the school has invested millions of dollars to enhance critical academic programs such as nanotechnology, biotechnology, bioscience, and optoelectronics. And with its robust approach to experiential learning, students are well prepared for life after college. Says one engineering major, "Lehigh students have the know-how to jump right into the workforce and tackle any challenges that they may face."

Grand old oaks shade the buildings on Lehigh's 2,358-acre campus, which is tucked into the side of an eastern Pennsylvania mountain. Architectural styles range from ivy-covered collegiate Gothic to modern glass and steel. In an apt symbol of Lehigh's efforts to link tradition with what it takes to be part of a global workforce, the 1878 collegiate Gothic Linderman Library in the center of campus has been completely gutted and rebuilt with attention to computer access, group study areas, and a café. The Goodman Campus provides first-class practice and playing facilities for Lehigh's Division I and intramural sports teams alike.

> "I love the flexibility that I have had with my major."

Distribution requirements are divided into four domains—the mathematical sciences, the natural sciences, the social sciences, and the arts and humanities. Additionally, some degrees include a mandatory internship. Finance, mechanical engineering, accounting, and chemical engineering are the most popular majors. Lehigh is big on connecting traditionally separate disciplines, so students interested in interdisciplinary study will find a wealth of options, including integrated business

Website: www.lehigh.edu
Location: Small City
Private
Total Enrollment: 6,195
Undergraduates: 4,986
Male/Female: 55/45
SAT Ranges: CR 590–680, M 640–740
ACT Ranges: 29–32
Financial Aid: 46%
Pell Grant: 16%
Expense: Pr $ $ $
Student Loans: 54%
Average Debt: $ $ $ $
Phi Beta Kappa: Yes
Applicants: 12,843
Accepted: 30%
Enrolled: 32%
Grad in 6 Years: 88%
Returning Freshmen: 95%
Academics: ✑ ✑ ✑ ✑
Social: ☎ ☎ ☎
Q of L: ★ ★ ★ ★

(continued)

Admissions: (610) 758-3100
Email Address: admissions@
lehigh.edu

Strong Programs:
Finance
Mechanical Engineering
Accounting
Chemical Engineering
Marketing
Industrial Engineering

and engineering, computer science and business, environmental engineering, design arts, and minors in business, ethics, engineering leadership, and engineering. "I love the flexibility that I have had with my major, and it is really cool that I have been able to study both engineering and psychology," says a senior. Several dual-degree options are available, such as a medical program with Drexel University, a dental program with the University of Pennsylvania, and a five-year arts and engineering program. Expanded offerings in health studies are on the drawing board.

Lehigh prides itself on offering innovative special programs. Integrated Product Development brings engineering, business, and arts students together to design and make products for sponsoring companies. The IDEAS (Integrated Degree in Engineering, Arts, and Sciences) program is a four-year honors curriculum that allows students to blend two focus areas—engineering and the arts, humanities, or natural sciences—into a single course of study. The innovative Mountaintop program gives nearly 175 students a chance to work with faculty mentors on cutting-edge projects during the summer. Recent projects include Smart Schools, Transitions for Refugees, Low-Energy Sustainable Farming, and 3D Printed Exoskeletons. Co-ops allow students to spend eight months working for a major-related company—and getting paid to do so—while still graduating in four years.

More than 250 study abroad options in 80 countries are also offered, with exchange programs in nine countries and winter and summer faculty-led programs in 13 countries; twenty-two percent of students participate. In recent years, Lehigh summer programs have been conducted in England, China, and the Czech Republic, while winter-term programs have been offered in Costa Rica, Ghana, and Spain. Through the President's Scholars program, top Lehigh students who meet certain requirements and maintain a 3.75 GPA or better are eligible for a fifth year of study tuition-free.

Lehigh is big on connecting traditionally separate disciplines.

Lehigh students are ambitious, and many pursue double majors. "Lehigh's academic climate is one that sets students up for success," says a biopharmaceutical engineering major. "The workload does get heavy at times, and that's why collaboration between students is essential and easy to find." The burden is lightened somewhat by exceptional teachers, who one senior describes as "the most intellectual but approachable people I have ever met." Adds another, "Every Lehigh professor really wants to see their students succeed, and they will all dedicate the time needed to see that happen." Forty-seven percent of courses contain fewer than 20 students, and courses aren't hard to get into. Students praise the wide range of services made available to them, including career counseling. "Career services is especially good at bringing large numbers of employers at a time to campus," says one junior, "and I think that sort of behind-the-scenes activity is more vital than students realize. Our placement numbers speak for themselves."

"The students at Lehigh are all very bright, talented students who also know how to relax and enjoy themselves," says one civil engineering major. Twenty-four percent of Lehigh's students come from Pennsylvania,

"Lehigh's academic climate is one that sets students up for success."

and many others hail from other Northeastern states; 8 percent are international, coming from 50 countries. African Americans account for 4 percent of the population, Hispanics 9 percent, and Asian Americans 9 percent. One student notes that although the campus could be more ethnically diverse, "You can always find someone with a different perspective, as well as background." Special-interest housing, including the UMOJA House (the Swahili word for "unity") and the new PRIDE Community, exists to promote positive cultural exchanges between students. Merit scholarships averaging $13,602 are awarded annually, and student-athletes vie for more than 200 athletic scholarships in 25 sports. Lehigh now guarantees to meet 100 percent of every student's demonstrated financial need. Additionally,

Lehigh caps loans in its financial aid packages at $5,000 per year for students with demonstrated need, and has eliminated loans entirely for students with need whose total annual family income is less than $75,000.

Sixty-seven percent of Lehigh students live on campus; first- and second-year students are required to do so. Accommodations are described as "decent." Many upperclassmen choose to live in apartment-style dorms, Greek houses, and off-campus apartments. Other options include Campus Square, a residential and commercial complex that houses 250 upper-class students. Lehigh's dining service has been honored with the Ivy Award, given by the restaurant industry to first-class restaurants as well as to educational institutions. "The dining on campus is great! I am an extremely picky eater and can always find something delicious to eat," cheers one student. Campus security draws cheers, too, and students note that the new Office of Gender Violence Education and Support has done much to educate the campus community, including rallies and prevention-awareness training.

An active Greek scene (40 percent of the men join fraternities and 45 percent of the women belong to sororities) fuels the campus social life. "Students who live off campus often host parties, and it creates a really great social scene," says one student. Lehigh takes underage drinking very seriously, according to a junior, although underage students still find ways to skirt the rules. And although students agree that a drinking and party culture does exist, according to a finance major, "There isn't pressure from anyone to become involved in those activities." Plenty of other social options are available too, says a cognitive psychology major: "The proliferation of campus clubs

> "You can always find someone with a different perspective, as well as background."

and organizations makes for a very vibrant evening and nightlife, and a plethora of daytime activities all week long." Favorite traditions include the Founder's Day celebration as well as bed races and other spirit activities during the week leading up to the big football game against Lafayette. Students volunteered more than 75,000 hours last year both locally and nationally with a variety of charities, including the Boys and Girls Club of America and America Reads.

The bustling campus has helped revive Bethlehem, a once-great steel town in the heart of the Lehigh Valley. Just five minutes from campus, "Bethlehem is an up-and-coming community," a senior explains; town-gown relations are described as "strained at best." Still, students look forward to some events the city has to offer, including Musikfest in early August, a 10-day music festival that attracts more than one million people and showcases nearly every musical style. For those with wheels, Philadelphia is 50 miles to the south and New York City is 75 miles to the east. Skiers will appreciate the close proximity of the Poconos in the winter, while sun worshippers can enjoy the nearby Jersey shore in the early fall and late spring.

The Lehigh Mountain Hawks field a number of competitive teams. Lehigh's wrestling program is a powerhouse, having brought home numerous EIWA championships, and women's softball won the Patriot League championship in 2015. Other solid programs include men's and women's basketball, men's cross-country, men's lacrosse, and men's and women's golf. Fans flock to the annual Lehigh versus Lafayette football game, said to be the most played rivalry in college football. In addition, about 85 percent of students participate in intramural sports and club programs, and weekend warriors make ample use of the expansive facilities in Taylor Gymnasium.

Lehigh students proudly juggle rigorous classes and a packed extracurricular calendar. "The type of student who will do best at Lehigh is the one who prefers to be too involved rather than sit back and observe," advises one senior. They give college life more than the old college try—and expect to succeed (with a little help from others along the way). Says one student, "We are developing the world-changers of tomorrow."

The innovative Mountaintop program gives nearly 175 students a chance to work on cutting-edge research projects during the summer.

Lehigh now guarantees to meet 100 percent of every student's demonstrated financial need.

Overlaps

Cornell University, Villanova, Bucknell, University of Pennsylvania, Northeastern, Penn State, Drexel, Lafayette

Lewis & Clark College

Portland, OR 97219

The West Coast's leader in international and study abroad programs. Politically liberal, but not as far out as crosstown neighbor Reed. Portfolio Path to admission allows students to finesse standardized tests. With Mount Hood visible in the distance (sometimes), there is a wealth of outdoor possibilities. Located in suburban Portland, at arm's length from the bustle of downtown.

Website: www.lclark.edu
Location: City Outskirts
Private
Total Enrollment: 3,062
Undergraduates: 2,078
Male/Female: 38/62
SAT Ranges: CR 600–720, M 590–670
ACT Ranges: 27–31
Financial Aid: 91%
Pell Grant: 16%
Expense: Pr $ $ $
Student Loans: 56%
Average Debt: $ $
Phi Beta Kappa: Yes
Applicants: 7,368
Accepted: 63%
Enrolled: 14%
Grad in 6 Years: 79%
Returning Freshmen: 83%
Academics: ✐ ✐ ✐
Social: ☎ ☎ ☎
Q of L: ★ ★ ★
Admissions: (503) 768-7040
Email Address: admissions@lclark.edu

Strong Programs:
International Affairs
Psychology
Sociology and Anthropology
Biology
English
Entrepreneurship

The 19th-century explorers Lewis and Clark struck out from Middle America to find where the trail ended, and their travels took them to Portland, a lush, green paradise by the Willamette River. The college that bears the explorers' names encourages students to explore too. Since 1962, almost 12,000 students and 300 faculty members have participated in programs in 68 countries. Each year, Lewis & Clark offers more than 30 programs in different parts of the world. Without a doubt, Lewis & Clark students receive, as one junior puts it, "an excellent, hands-on education."

Lest students become too enchanted overseas, Lewis & Clark lures them back with a gorgeous campus perched atop fir-covered bluffs overlooking the river. The campus is an old estate, complete with elaborate gardens, fountains, and pools, where cement is almost nonexistent and the roads are paved with cobblestones. Lewis & Clark demonstrated its commitment to the environment by signing the Talloires Declaration, an agreement with other colleges to promote sustainable development. With that in mind, it built the 50,000-square-foot Howard Hall, which earned a gold certification from the U.S. Green Building Council. Howard Hall is one of five energy-saving, environmentally friendly buildings that also include three residence halls and Wood Hall. A new career center opened in 2015.

Lewis & Clark requires that all students achieve competency in a foreign language and international studies; 60 percent of students fulfill these requirements by studying overseas for a semester or more. Students may travel to such locales as Australia, China, Ecuador, and Morocco—some even study in two or three countries—and may also study in a number of American cities. In addition to the international studies requirement, students must complete courses in scientific and quantitative reasoning, creative arts, and physical education. Not surprisingly, one of the most popular majors at Lewis & Clark is international affairs; others include psychology, sociology and anthropology, biology, and English. Minors in dance, ethnic studies, and political economy are offered, as are 3–2 programs in engineering. Honors programs are available in all majors. The Rogers Science Research Program teams students and faculty on research projects ranging from the adhesive power of geckos to molecular science. The Center for Entrepreneurship allows students to collaborate with faculty, mentors, and outside professionals to reframe problems using entrepreneurial thinking.

> **"Most of the classes are small and discussion-based, so there is a lot of time for personal questions."**

Lewis & Clark offers a Portfolio Path to admission, where students present a package representing their talents and interests. PP students supply two teacher recommendations and two graded samples of high school work: one quantitative sample and one analytical writing sample. The key to a good portfolio is a "well-rounded approach," administrators say. "The more creative, the better, but be sure it's not solely artwork or writing samples."

Despite this open attitude, L&C students, once enrolled, are expected to follow through with a challenging workload. The required six-week Pioneer Success Institute at the beginning of the year helps ease new students into the college transition, and the yearlong Exploration and Discovery course introduces them to college-level academic work. "Classes are hard but not impossible," says a freshman. Freshmen and graduating seniors get priority in the registration process, helping ensure graduation in four years for those who plan a way to fit in all of the requirements and declare majors early. Professors get high marks for being knowledgeable and passionate. "The quality of teaching is excellent," says a sophomore. "Most of the classes are small and discussion-based, so there is a lot of time for personal questions."

"Students here are socially conscious, motivated, and involved," says an international affairs major. Lewis & Clark tends to attract West Coasters (almost half of the student body) who are seeking an emphasis on the liberal arts; it is also a haven for well-off Easterners who see L&C as an escape from the social claustrophobia of the typical prep school scene. Five percent of students are drawn from foreign countries.

"There is a big divide between athletes and nonathletes."

"There is a big divide between athletes and nonathletes," says one student. "This doesn't exactly mean that the two groups don't associate with each other, but the two groups do sit on different sides of the cafeteria. It just feels awkward." The campus is politically active and predominantly left-leaning. The student body is 6 percent Asian American, 2 percent African American, and 10 percent Hispanic. The college appointed its first dean of diversity and inclusion in 2016, to promote and expand campus diversity. Merit scholarships averaging $14,571 are available for qualified students, but there are no athletic awards.

Lewis & Clark's residency requirement keeps students on campus their first two years; 70 percent of all undergraduates stay in campus housing, which is described as convenient. "The most common room is a double, but there are also quads and singles, all of which have sufficient room for their respective residents," reports a student. Owing to the college's hilltop location, lucky dorm residents have views of Mount St. Helens, Mount Hood, or the Portland skyline—at least when they are not fogged in. Students involved in performing arts, multicultural engagement, outdoor pursuits, and other programs can join living/learning communities. Dining halls cater to different diets and "the food is honestly really good," says a student. Despite L&C's location in a residential section of Portland, safety is a priority—residence halls have card-swipe entry systems and door alarms, and campus security has officers on duty 24 hours a day.

Fun seekers at Lewis & Clark rely primarily on the Campus Activities Board for on-campus movies, contests, dances, and talent shows; there is no Greek life. Yearly events include the Fall Ball and Spring Fling dances and the Watzek Rocks Concert, which takes place in the library. Students 21 and older are permitted to consume alcohol on campus, and alcohol policies for underage drinkers are enforced. "You can get in trouble if you get caught," says a sophomore, "but the repercussions aren't that severe." The neighborhood immediately surrounding the college is pleasant, affluent suburbia, which means a few stores, restaurants, and bars. Students get involved in the local community through Saturdays in Service days and a variety of

Sixty percent of students fulfill foreign language and international studies requirements by studying overseas.

The college appointed its first dean of diversity and inclusion in 2016, to promote and expand campus diversity.

campus organizations. The activity of downtown Portland—mostly on Hawthorne Boulevard in the southeast section, and in the Pearl District or on 23rd Street in the northwest quadrant—is 15 minutes away on the city's public transit system or the free campus shuttle service, the Pioneer Express. On the weekends, College Outdoors sponsors trips to Mount Hood (great skiing, about an hour distant) or the coastal beaches (an hour and a half). Seattle and Vancouver, BC, three- and six-hour drives, are favorite road trips, as are San Francisco and Las Vegas when there's more time.

> **"Students here look outside their lives and experiences in order to find something greater."**

Pioneer teams compete in the Division III Northwest Conference, and the most successful teams include women's tennis (conference champs in 2016), men's tennis and basketball, and men's and women's rowing. As might be expected at a school in the outdoorsy Pacific Northwest, Lewis & Clark has a well-organized intramural program and plenty of outdoor activities. Ultimate Frisbee, basketball, and volleyball are student favorites. The L&C debate team brought home back-to-back national titles in 2014 and 2015.

Lewis & Clark's many outdoor enthusiasts and champions of social causes thrive in the college's rather laid-back atmosphere. Students are knowledge-seeking pioneers—ones who would have made the school's namesakes proud. "Students here look outside their lives and experiences in order to find something greater," says a senior. "We constantly question and search for the answers."

If You Apply To ➤ **Lewis & Clark:** Early decision and early action: Nov. 1. Regular decision: Jan. 15. Financial aid: Feb. 15. Housing: May 1. No application fee. Campus interviews: optional, evaluative. Alumni interviews: optional, informational. SATs or ACTs: required (except for Portfolio Path applicants). No Subject Tests. Letters of recommendation: required. Essay: required. Accepts the Common Application.

Louisiana State University

1146 Pleasant Hall, Baton Rouge, LA 70803

In the state that invented Mardi Gras, students come to LSU for a great time as well as a good education. Finding the former is a no-brainer. The latter can be had in business, engineering, and life sciences fields. Administrators are trying to make LSU a more serious place with higher admissions standards and less underage drinking, but they face draconian budget cuts. A quarter of students live in the upgraded dorms.

Website: www.lsu.edu
Location: City Center
Public
Total Enrollment: 27,595
Undergraduates: 23,450
Male/Female: 48/52
SAT Ranges: CR 510–620, M 510–640
ACT Ranges: 23–28
Financial Aid: 79%
Pell Grant: 7%
Expense: Pub $ $

From abundant azaleas and Japanese magnolias and the smell of Cajun cuisine, to the sororities' antebellum mansions and the "huge and legendary" rivalries with Alabama and Florida, few schools evoke the spirit of the South like Louisiana State University in Baton Rouge. The university continues to offer solid programs in business, engineering, and the life sciences, and admissions standards continue to rise. "I feel that LSU's academic achievements have been underrated," says one senior. "There are so many ways to learn and grow, both in and out of the classroom."

LSU sits on 2,000 acres along the banks of the Mississippi River on the grounds of a former plantation. Most of the 250 buildings are Italian Renaissance in style, with tan stucco walls and red tile roofs. Lakes and huge oak trees dot the landscape, helping to diffuse the strong sun and temper Louisiana's legendary humidity. Recent campus projects include a digital media center, a parking garage, and an expansion to Tiger Stadium that increased its capacity to more than 102,000.

LSU was once an open-admissions university for state residents, but standards have gone up in recent years, and with them, the caliber of students. Students must complete a broad core curriculum, with six hours of coursework in each of three disciplines (English composition, analytical reasoning, and social sciences), nine hours in the humanities, nine hours in the natural sciences, and three hours in the arts. Classes can be large, with 22 percent enrolling upward of 50 students, to the chagrin of many. "Some classes can have hundreds of students in an auditorium," says one student. "That changes the dynamic of the classroom experience." Especially motivated students may opt to join the honors college, to enjoy smaller class sizes and produce a senior thesis.

> **"I feel that LSU's academic achievements have been underrated. There are so many ways to learn and grow."**

LSU students choose from 70 undergraduate degrees and tend to focus on practical courses of study, which will help them get into graduate school or find jobs after graduation. To that end, popular majors include biological sciences and psychology—both typical for premeds—as well as mechanical engineering, petroleum engineering, and kinesiology. LSU's programs in business and landscape architecture are highly regarded. Given its location and history as a sea grant college, LSU's offerings in coastal studies and coastal ecology are notable as well. The multidisciplinary LSU Center for Internal Auditing was the first university-based internal auditing training program to be established. Professors are lauded for their enthusiasm and skill behind the lectern. "Overall the professors here at LSU love their material and are dedicated to teaching," one student says. Students interested in working on projects at the interface between the biological and computational sciences are encouraged to apply to the Louisiana Biomedical Research Network Undergraduate Research Program, which hosts nine-week research opportunities. The President's Future Leaders in Research Program provides undergraduates the chance to work side by side with professors in a research setting, such as a laboratory or in the field, to learn what a career in that area might be like. Three percent of the student body study abroad and may choose from programs in 60 countries.

Eighty-two percent of LSU Tigers are Louisiana natives, and 2 percent come from abroad. "Many of the students here are partiers and social butterflies," says one sophomore. "They tend to hang out, go to clubs, bars, and restaurants on a regular basis." African Americans make up 12 percent of the student body, Asian Americans 4 percent, and Hispanics 6 percent. "The big-

> **"Many of the students here are partiers and social butterflies."**

gest political issue is concerning budget cuts in the state and how they affect higher education," says a student. Thousands of merit scholarships are available, averaging $4,096, but the state merit scholarship has been suspended. LSU also hands out 500 athletic scholarships each year in 21 sports. The Pelican Promise Scholarship provides additional financial aid to low-income students; to qualify, students must be Pell Grant eligible (a mere 7 percent of a recent freshman class qualified) and come from a family whose income is no more than 150 percent of the federal poverty level.

Twenty-four percent of the students live on campus. Over the past decade, the university has invested more than $150 million in housing facilities and new programs, with more than 50 percent of undergraduate housing either newly constructed or renovated. A junior calls the dorms that have not been upgraded "small and dated." A quarter of first-year students choose to live in 10 residential colleges organized by academic interest. Campus dining halls offer a variety of dishes, and students say most are tasty. There are also a variety of eateries near campus that are "delicious and inexpensive," according to one student. Despite Baton Rouge's high crime rate, students report feeling safe on campus. LSU has nearly 100 full-time officers and a transit system so that students don't have to walk alone after dark.

(continued)

Student Loans: 40%
Average Debt: $ $
Phi Beta Kappa: Yes
Applicants: 17,429
Accepted: 77%
Enrolled: 42%
Grad in 6 Years: 67%
Returning Freshmen: 85%
Academics: ✍ ✍
Social: ☎ ☎ ☎ ☎ ☎
Q of L: ★ ★ ★
Admissions: (225) 578-1175
Email Address: admissions@lsu.edu

Strong Programs:
Biological Sciences
Psychology
Mechanical Engineering
Petroleum Engineering
Kinesiology
Business
Landscape Architecture
Coastal Environmental Science

The LSU Center for Internal Auditing was the first university-based internal auditing training program to be established.

Social life at LSU "is never-ending," cheers a student. "Plenty of students enjoy off-campus fun with house parties and plenty of bars nearby in Tigerland," adds another. Seventeen percent of the men and 28 percent of the women go Greek, and while doing so "is always a good way to meet people, it can be expensive," says a finance major. When it comes to drinking, you must be 21, though all bets are off on game days. "Tailgating on game day is a big party for everyone," says a senior, and the rowdy LSU contingent at away games has earned a reputation comparable to that of English soccer fans. Everyone looks forward to homecoming and to annual festivals such as Groovin', "where big-name bands come play for the students, with lots of food and games—all free!" says a junior. Road trips to the Florida beaches are common during spring break.

Tiger football is king in Baton Rouge, having won national championships in 2003 and 2007 and a conference title in 2011. The men's golf team earned a national championship in 2015, and women's gymnastics was the national runner-up that same year. The Tiger baseball team is a dynasty, having brought home its most recent Southeastern Conference title in 2015. When the Tigers are on the road, many students follow the team (and the fun) to Oxford, Mississippi (home of Ole Miss), or Auburn, Alabama (home of the Auburn Tigers). Intramural soccer, flag football, and softball are popular, and even those who don't play may work out at the well-equipped recreation center.

"There is never a boring day at LSU," gushes one psychology major. The trees and traditions date back more than 100 years, but change is the new norm here. "Just a few years ago, LSU was named the number-one party school," notes one student. "Today, it's not even listed in the top 10." Flagship 2020 focuses on the goals of learning, discovery, diversity, and engagement, and though it may be a while before the school's academic profile matches its athletic prowess, that's what administrators are aiming for. In the meantime, students are happy to *laissez les bons temps roulez*!

Overlaps

Louisiana Tech, Tulane, University of Alabama, University of Georgia, University of Louisiana, Texas A&M, Mississippi State, University of Mississippi

If You Apply To ➤

LSU: Rolling admissions: Apr. 15. Priority financial aid: Nov. 15. Application fee: $40. No campus or alumni interviews. SATs or ACTs: required. No Subject Tests. No letters of recommendation. No essay (only required for Honors College and scholarship candidates).

Loyola University Maryland

Baltimore, MD 21210

Vintage Jesuit school with a rigorous liberal arts curriculum, caring faculty, and a strong sense of community. Baltimore location a plus for those with "I don't want to miss anything" attitude. Same size as Providence, smaller than BC, Fordham, and other Roman Catholic schools in urban settings. No varsity football, but top-ranked men's lacrosse team evokes plenty of school spirit.

Website: www.loyola.edu
Location: City Outskirts
Private
Total Enrollment: 4,583
Undergraduates: 4,002

Four U.S. universities bear the name of St. Francis Loyola, founder of the Jesuit order, but this one is the granddaddy of them all. Founded in 1851 (and the one that laid claim to www.loyola.edu), Loyola University Maryland combines the virtues of a residential campus with ready access to a major city on the Amtrak corridor. Loyola jumped up from "college" to "university" status in 2009, and, with a "big enough but not too big" feel, manages to strike a balance between real-world experience and the traditional Jesuit ideals of academic excellence, a liberal arts curriculum, and *cura personalis* (a.k.a. education of the whole person).

Loyola's Evergreen campus, the home to undergraduates, sits on 80 green and wooded acres in a mixed residential area in northern Baltimore, about 15 minutes from the heart of the city. (Graduate students are shunted off to their own campuses in Columbia and Timonium, Maryland.) The academic Quad features the largest collection of Collegiate Gothic buildings in Baltimore, including the Alumni Memorial Chapel with its lovely stained-glass windows. Architectural variety is provided by the Tudor-style Humanities Center, built in 1895, and the Sellinger School of Business and Management, a contemporary 50,000-square-foot facility notable for its atrium and five-story glass façade.

Undergraduate academics at Loyola are organized around the School of Education, the Sellinger School of Business and Management, and Loyola College, the arts and sciences college. Consistent with Jesuit academic tradition, Loyola students pursue a core curriculum that covers "basic knowledge and concepts in the humanities, math, science, and the social sciences" and "encourages students to think and to solve problems in a variety of ways and to critically examine a cross-section of ideas." Among the requirements are two theology courses, an ethics course, and the choice of a course designated "diversity"—with a focus on global or domestic diversity or justice awareness. First-year students jump-start their college careers with various pre-orientation programs in which they meet a small group of fellow students and focus on some special interest. Loyola 101 is a one-credit course in the fall semester that brings in guest speakers and introduces students to the resources available throughout Baltimore. Messina is a first-year living/learning program in which students enroll in two small seminar classes guided by a professor and an older student who also lives with the same students. "It makes new students feel like they are a part of the Loyola community and realize how many people care about them here," says a biology major.

> **"I cannot imagine what it would be like not to have a professor know my name."**

The business program is said to be strong, as are most of the humanities, where "professors find ways to make the humanities relevant to real life," says a psych major. Business, communication, social sciences, and psychology are the most popular majors. Other strong areas, students say, include education, speech pathology, biology, and engineering. Fine arts "does not attract very many people," reports a global studies major. Students describe the academic program at Loyola as challenging but supportive. "Students are generally not competing against each other for the best grades, but rather tend to work together on projects or while studying," says a senior. Teaching assistants are an unknown species, and an English major reports, "Classes are rarely bigger than 30. Most of mine have ranged from 15 to 30 students." Students praise their professors' emphasis on teaching and getting to know students. "I cannot imagine what it would be like not to have a professor know my name," says a senior. A political science major reports that "professors tend to shy away from boring lectures in favor of engaging discussions."

Each summer, 10 to 12 undergraduates are selected to work side by side with faculty from the six natural science departments to conduct research in the students' area of interest and participate in seminars, journal clubs, and social activities. For top students, the Honors Program provides an interdisciplinary route through a more ambitious core curriculum. Sixty-four percent of students study abroad for a semester or more. Venues for business students range from Bangkok and Singapore to Melbourne and Accra, while language students set out for Spain, France, China, and elsewhere in search of native speakers. Loyola students are encouraged to do community service while abroad and to submit an Immersion Research Project

(continued)

Male/Female: 42/58
SAT Ranges: CR 550–650, M 560–640
ACT Ranges: 25–29
Financial Aid: 73%
Pell Grant: 17%
Expense: Pr $ $ $
Student Loans: 58%
Average Debt: $
Phi Beta Kappa: Yes
Applicants: 13,867
Accepted: 61%
Enrolled: 13%
Grad in 6 Years: 83%
Returning Freshmen: 87%
Academics: ✍ ✍ ✍
Social: ☎ ☎ ☎
Q of L: ★ ★ ★
Admissions: (800) 221-9107
Email Address: admissions@ loyola.edu

Strong Programs:
Business
Communication
Social Sciences
Psychology
Education
Speech Pathology
Biology
Engineering

Messina is a first-year program in which students enroll in two small seminar classes guided by a professor and an older student.

upon return. "I studied in Cork, Ireland, and it was one of the highlights of my college experience!" cheers a senior.

Students at Loyola tend to be, in the words of one senior, "fairly preppy." Eighteen percent of undergraduates hail from Maryland, and 1 percent come from other countries. African Americans represent 6 percent, Hispanics 10 percent, and Asian Americans 4 percent. At least 75 percent of undergrads describe themselves as Catholics, and there are seven Jesuits on the faculty. "Religion has a huge impact on campus," says one non-Catholic, who adds, "As a Christian, I love the fact that I can openly talk about my religion and that others accept my beliefs." A political science major says that "social justice is a huge initiative at Loyola, with abortion, immigration reform, gay marriage, homelessness, hunger, and gender equality just some of the issues that students at Loyola are fighting for/against." Merit awards average $14,960, and Loyola offers 114 athletic scholarships in 17 men's and women's sports.

At least 75 percent of undergrads describe themselves as Catholics.

Loyola students cheer about the residence halls, which are located west of the main campus and connected by a pedestrian bridge spanning Charles Street. Facilities are spacious and modern, with air-conditioning, laundry facilities, vending machines, and recreation areas. "We have some of the best dorms in the country," says a senior. A senior English major's experience is typical: "My first year included dorm-style living, sophomore and junior years [were] apartment living with six people, and my senior year included an on-campus townhouse." Not surprisingly, 81 percent of students live on campus, at least until their senior year. The main dining facility is Boulder Garden Café, but other options range from the Reading Room to Starbucks. Loyola offers a "meal swipe" or "declining balance" dining plan. Campus security is not an issue. "We are in a relatively dangerous part of the city," says an accounting major, "but the Loyola police do a good job to make us all feel safe on campus."

"The passion for service runs very strong through the veins of Loyola."

Loyola has no fraternities or sororities, but given the proximity to Baltimore, this arrangement is just fine with students. "Most of Loyola's social life takes place off campus," says a student. "Bars and clubs are very close to campus, and the penalties for throwing a party in your room are pretty steep." That's not to say that on-campus life is monastic. "The campus is always buzzing with things like concerts and festivals," says an English major. The undisputed high point of the social calendar is Loyolapalooza, the spring festival held on the last weekend before final exams to celebrate the academic year. Students gather on the Quad for a concert, games, and food. A close second is Luck O'Loyola, the annual St. Patrick's Day celebration that features traditional Irish bagpipes, dancing, and music. "It's a fun time for everyone, whether Irish for a day or Irish for the year," says a communication major. Students raise funds for charity at the 12-hour Relay for Life, a series of running events that "transforms our gym into a track for hope."

Luck O'Loyola is the annual St. Patrick's Day celebration that features traditional Irish bagpipes, dancing, and music.

Community service also plays a prominent role in campus life. "The passion for service runs very strong through the veins of Loyola," reports a senior. The Center for Community Service and Justice helps students find opportunities ranging from one-time volunteer activities to service-oriented international trips and service-learning courses. The city of Baltimore offers an abundance of sights, including the famed Inner Harbor, with its many restaurants and museums, as well as major league sports. A senior calls it "a city with a hometown feel." Loyola's neighbors include numerous other colleges and universities, including Johns Hopkins and Towson University. "Loyola students do not regard this as a 'college town' per se, but it has plenty of young-adult neighborhoods and pockets of entertainment," reports an accounting major.

"We care for each other, and our Jesuit mission rings true in our day-to-day lives."

Public transportation is poor in Baltimore, but a "college town" shuttle takes students between the various schools, the mall, and downtown attractions. Popular road-trip destinations are the nearby Towson Mall as well as the Inner Harbor and Washington, D.C.

Loyola eschews varsity football, but the Greyhounds compete in the Division I Patriot League in eight men's and nine women's sports. Consistent with its Maryland location, both men's and women's lacrosse are strong, with both taking home national championships in 2014. For those with more modest athletic ambitions, Loyola sponsors 26 co-ed and single-sex club sports teams and 30 intramural events that draw about 40 percent of students. Flag football, lacrosse, volleyball, and soccer are popular. "The teams are great outlets to make friends and form connections with peers in a healthy way," says an English major. The state-of-the-art Fitness and Aquatic Center boasts a well-equipped 6,000-square-foot fitness center, while the Mangione Aquatic Center features an eight-lane pool as well as a sauna and hot tubs.

Some Loyola denizens lament the absence of football and the dearth of parties on campus, but such complaints seem a small price to pay for four years as part of a close-knit community that takes its humanistic, academic, and social values seriously. "We care for each other, and our Jesuit mission rings true in our day-to-day lives," says a senior. A classmate adds, "You will always have someone who cares about you here. The good food, residence halls, and location don't hurt either."

If You Apply To ➢ **Loyola:** Early decision: Nov. 1. Early action: Nov. 15. Regular decision and financial aid: Jan. 15. Housing: May 1. Application fee: $60. No campus or alumni interviews. SATs or ACTs: optional (test-optional applicants must submit additional essay or additional teacher recommendation). No Subject Tests. Letters of recommendation: required. Essay: required. Accepts the Common Application.

Loyola Marymount University

I LMU Drive, Suite 100, Los Angeles, CA 90045

LMU is a Roman Catholic university known for its strategic L.A. location and strong programs in film and television, business, and communication. Compare to Chapman, Santa Clara, and University of San Diego. Strong international emphasis in film and theatre arts. To take full advantage of L.A., access to a car is highly beneficial.

At Loyola Marymount University, students are treated to ideal weather year-round, a vast array of internship opportunities, and a stellar academic lineup that includes solid programs in television and film, liberal arts and sciences, and business. What's more, LMU has the distinction of being the only Roman Catholic university in Los Angeles. "LMU is more than an academic institution," says a junior. "It is a community dedicated to helping students grow and thrive."

Established in 1911, LMU occupies a 142-acre Westchester campus perched on a bluff overlooking the Pacific Ocean and Marina del Rey in a peaceful residential neighborhood of Los Angeles. As part of an ambitious 10-year construction program, the university opened two new apartment buildings and a traditional residence hall. The William H. Hannon Library is located on the bluff, between the Leavey Residence Halls and the Jesuit Community, and provides a variety of seating and work space, including 33 small-group study rooms that may be reserved in advance online. A $110 million, LEED Gold–certified life sciences building opened

Website: www.lmu.edu
Location: Suburban
Private
Total Enrollment: 8,219
Undergraduates: 6,018
Male/Female: 43/57
SAT Ranges: CR 550–640, M 560–660
ACT Ranges: 25–30
Financial Aid: 87%
Pell Grant: 19%
Expense: Pr $ $
Student Loans: 56%

(continued)

Average Debt: $ $ $
Phi Beta Kappa: No
Applicants: 13,288
Accepted: 51%
Enrolled: 20%
Grad in 6 Years: 79%
Returning Freshmen: 91%
Academics: ✍ ✍ ✍
Social: ☎ ☎ ☎
Q of L: ★ ★ ★
Admissions: (310) 338-2750
Email Address: admissions@
  lmu.edu

Strong Programs:
Marketing
Communication Studies
Psychology
English
Film and Television Production
Theatre Arts
Engineering
Business

Students in the School of Film and Television have the chance to study in Bonn, Germany, and produce their own documentaries.

in 2015 and features 35 research and teaching labs, an auditorium, courtyards, and a green roof.

LMU offers 57 baccalaureate majors and 51 minors in six colleges and schools. The general education requirements (known as the Core Curriculum) are designed to encourage intellectual breadth, tackling themes such as faith and reason; virtue and justice; culture; art and society; and science, nature, and society. "The nice thing about LMU's academics is that the core requirements encourage students to be open to various studies," says a freshman, "from science to theology to philosophy." Freshmen may take part in a number of programs designed to support first-year students, including an honors program and a first-year seminar. "The first-year program begins helping freshmen before they even arrive on campus," says one student. "The program seeks to integrate the freshmen so their first year will be successful."

The most popular programs include marketing, communication studies, psychology, English, film and television production, and theatre arts; these are also among the university's strongest. Other solid programs include engineering and business. Students in the School of Film and Television have access to a number of resources, including a student-run production office, a television stage, and a film

> **"The [first-year] program seeks to integrate the freshmen so their first year will be successful."**

soundstage with a professional "green screen" (for those cool CGI effects!). They also benefit from the program's strong international emphasis, including the chance to study in Bonn, Germany, and produce their own documentaries that are exhibited at festivals in Germany and the U.S. Those in the College of Science and Engineering take part in national competitions to design steel bridges and race eco-friendly cars. Thanks to its hip Los Angeles locale, LMU offers a plethora of internships to experience-hungry students, including stints at Disney, MTV, and Warner Bros. LMU offers 64 study abroad options on six continents, including 30 faculty-led programs. Exchange, semester, and summer study abroad programs are available in a wide range of disciplines; about 16 percent of students participate each year.

Like nearby Tinseltown, LMU manages to be both competitive and relaxed. "Depending on the course, a lot of work might be required or barely any homework could be given," says a freshman. A theology major adds, "Most of the intro classes seem more laid-back and the upper division classes are more rigorous." Fifty-one percent of classes have fewer than 20 students and students say teacher-student interaction is a given. "Professors truly know their students and take a personal interest in their learning," says a junior. Another student adds, "All of them encourage students to interact and to get to know them better."

LMU undergraduates hail from 49 states and 94 foreign countries; 70 percent come from California and 9 percent from abroad. "LMU is known for its sense of community and its friendliness," says a student. Another adds, "There is an optimistic atmosphere on this campus because students want to be here." African Americans comprise 6 percent of the student body, Hispanics 21 percent, and Asian Americans 11 percent. Student activism is alive and well on campus and

> **"There is an optimistic atmosphere on this campus because students want to be here."**

diversity is a perpetually hot issue. Merit scholarships averaging $10,293 are available for qualified students, and the athletically inclined vie for 231 athletic scholarships in 16 sports.

Fifty-one percent of LMU students live on campus, where a student says, "Housing is pretty nice." A number of themed living communities are available, including those dedicated to social action, substance-free living, and multicultural living; roughly 22 percent of first-year students participate. The university offers a variety of meal plan options and dining facilities and "all types of food are available," according to a political science major. Students describe campus security as good too; "I have never felt unsafe," a junior says.

The social life at LMU takes place "both on and off campus," says one student. "There is always something to do on campus," a senior explains, "whether it is a party or events hosted by different clubs." Student service organizations and clubs frequently host activities, and Greek life influences the scene too, attracting 22 percent of the men and 37 percent of the women. Students say there is little pressure to drink. "If students want to drink, they can find alcohol," says a freshman. "Those that don't want to, don't have to." The university's Jesuit heritage promotes a social atmosphere that "motivates students to improve themselves by helping others," a student says. "Whether it's Greek life, service organizations, or intramurals, students have a number of possibilities." Students volunteer nearly 200,000 hours of service every year in hospitals, legal-aid clinics, after-school programs, and other settings. The area of Westchester is "definitely not a college town," groans a sophomore. Fortunately, Marina del Rey and Santa Monica are a short car or bus ride away, and it's only a mile to the beach. "Since L.A. is a big city, there are plenty of places for a college student to eat, shop, and find entertainment." Popular road trips include San Diego, Santa Barbara, Las Vegas, and Mexico.

Back on campus, LMU's varsity teams compete in the Division I West Coast Conference. Women's water polo and men's soccer each won their respective conference titles within the last few years; women's soccer and volleyball are also competitive. The Lions' rivalry with nearby Pepperdine always draws a huge crowd and the basketball team's annual pep rally—Madness at Midnight—"is a pretty big event," says a student. Intramurals are popular and include softball, basketball, soccer, volleyball, and ultimate Frisbee. LMU's debate team is a standout too, having placed first in more than 250 national and international tournaments over the past 40 years.

With its dynamic mix of solid academics, Jesuit tradition, and thriving social life, LMU offers students substance and style. "We're very friendly with a gorgeous campus," says a student. Whether you're a budding scientist or a future filmmaker, Loyola Marymount University may be worth a look.

Students volunteer nearly 200,000 hours of service every year.

Overlaps

University of Southern California, UCLA, Santa Clara, University of San Diego, Chapman, Cal Poly–San Luis Obispo, UC–Berkeley, UC–Santa Barbara

If You Apply To >

LMU: Early decision and early action: Nov. 1. Regular decision: Jan. 15. Financial aid: Feb. 1. Application fee: $60. No campus or alumni interviews. SATs or ACTs: required. Subject Tests: optional. Letters of recommendation: required. Essay: required. Accepts the Common Application with supplement. Applicants to animation, dance, music, and theatre arts are required to submit a portfolio or audition.

Loyola University New Orleans

6363 St. Charles Ave., Box 89, New Orleans, LA 70118

Of the four Loyolas in the nation, this is the only one where you can go to Mardi Gras and still get up in time for class. New Orleans is an ideal setting for this Roman Catholic university with strengths in business, communication, and the arts. New Orleans is the most free-wheeling Deep South city, and Loyola's politics are mainly liberal.

Website: www.loyno.edu
Location: Suburban
Private
Total Enrollment: 3,019
Undergraduates: 2,432
Male/Female: 40/60
SAT Ranges: CR 520–620,
   M 480–610
ACT Ranges: 22–28
Financial Aid: 89%
Pell Grant: 22%
Expense: Pr $
Student Loans: 66%
Average Debt: $ $ $
Phi Beta Kappa: No
Applicants: 3,591
Accepted: 90%
Enrolled: 21%
Grad in 6 Years: 66%
Returning Freshmen: 77%
Academics: ✍ ✍ ✍
Social: ☎ ☎ ☎
Q of L: ★ ★ ★
Admissions: (504) 865-3240
Email Address:
   admit@loyno.edu

Strong Programs:
Mass Communication
Music Industry Studies
Psychology
Criminal Justice
International Business
Digital Filmmaking
Popular and Commercial
   Music
Creative Writing

Minors in jazz studies and New Orleans studies are available.

Loyola University New Orleans is a Jesuit liberal arts school that continues to enhance its rich tradition through extensive service-learning programs, increasing admissions standards, and a renewed commitment to diversifying the student body. As a Loyola student, "you will be challenged, motivated, and inspired to do more," says one happy senior.

The school's attractive and well-kept 20-acre main campus, in the University section of Uptown New Orleans, mixes Tudor, Gothic, and modern structures. It overlooks acres of Audubon Park and, beyond, the mighty Mississippi River. Two blocks up St. Charles Avenue, Loyola's Broadway campus has an additional four acres. The Monroe Library houses approximately 500,000 volumes, the Lindy Boggs National Center for Community Literacy, and an art gallery. More recent additions include state-of-the-art science labs, new high-tech design studios, and a seventh-floor greenhouse, all located in newly renovated Monroe Hall, which houses 40 percent of all Loyola classes.

The Loyola Core requires all students to take courses in critical reading and writing, mathematics, natural sciences, social sciences, history, writing about literature, philosophy, religious studies, and creative arts and cultures. They must also complete a First-Year Seminar designed to introduce students to college-level work and the Jesuit tradition of "thinking critically, acting justly." First-years also participate in a three-day orientation followed by a comprehensive first-year experience that includes a common reading program, a series of lectures and panel discussions, educational excursions, exhibits, and service-learning projects coordinated around a common academic theme. An Executive Mentoring program lets freshman business students meet regularly with local business leaders to discuss their career and personal development, while a peer mentoring program helps new students adjust to college life during their initial semester.

> "Classmates study together, seek each other out for help, and wish one another good luck."

Loyola offers dozens of comprehensive undergraduate degree programs. The School of Mass Communication, whose students do well in national competitions, wins praise, as do the international business program in the College of Business and virtually any major in the College of Music and Fine Art, which allows students to take advantage of creative professions such as digital filmmaking and commercial music in a city where these are specialties. Indeed, mass communication and music industry studies are two of the most popular majors, along with psychology and criminal justice. Creative writing is another strength, and minors in jazz studies and New Orleans studies are available. Loyolans also benefit from the New Orleans Consortium, with cross-registration and library access at other schools in the area.

Fifty-four percent of classes have fewer than 20 students, and the academic climate is challenging but collaborative. "Classmates study together, seek each other out for help, and wish one another good luck," one freshman says. Undergraduate science courses offer the chance to participate in research projects, and many programs require a senior capstone experience. Honors options are available in all majors. "Faculty are extremely accessible to students and are always open to discussion," says one international business major. Every year, 30 percent of undergraduates exercise their wings in study abroad programs available in more than 50 countries, from Mexico and Brazil to the Netherlands, Japan, and Korea.

"The students here are very laid-back and kind," a junior says. Forty percent of Loyola undergraduates are Louisiana natives and many of the remaining students are from the Southeast; 3 percent are international. Undergraduates at Loyola are a diverse lot: 16 percent are Hispanic, 17 percent are African American, and 4 percent are Asian American. Religion—specifically Roman Catholicism—has a significant influence on campus. Daily mass is voluntary, but many students attend. Students are generally well-informed and passionate about political and social issues, and many volunteer their sweat equity with the Loyola University Community Action Program, a student-led coalition of 11 organizations that provides community service opportunities that take on issues such as hunger and homelessness. With the help of the service-learning office, about 500 students make service learning part of their studies. Loyola awards merit scholarships averaging $16,148 each year and 127 athletic scholarships in 10 sports. Twenty-two percent of freshmen are Pell-eligible.

Many Loyola students commute from home or off-campus apartments; 59 percent of all undergraduates reside on campus. "The residences are spacious and comfortable," a freshman says. The transition to college is eased by Themed Living Communities, which house classmates together in a common living space within one of the residence halls. Campus dining is good and students may choose from an array of culinary delights, including "sushi, salads, and sandwiches," says a sophomore. Students feel safe on campus, according to one junior. "We have a police force specifically for our campus."

Major events include the annual "Sneaux Day" that blankets Loyola's front lawn with "snow," and the senior crawfish boil.

"Loyola gives us lots of cool things to do on campus," a philosophy major says, including musical performances and sporting events. Fraternities and sororities are rarities at Jesuit schools, but make themselves felt at Loyola, with 9 percent of the men and 21 percent of the women choosing to belong.

"We have a police force specifically for our campus."

Major campuswide social events include the annual "Sneaux Day" that blankets Loyola's front lawn with "snow," the senior crawfish boil, family weekend featuring a New Orleans-style jazz brunch, and the musical event "Christmas at Loyola," held on the first Sunday in December. Loyola even allows students to register overnight visitors for the Mardi Gras holidays. As for underage drinking, Louisiana law requires that you be at least 21 to buy alcohol, but only 18 to consume it in a private residence. New Orleans is always bustling and offers "tons of live music, bars, clubs, and restaurants all easily accessible to students," according to one senior.

Wolf Pack teams compete in the NAIA Division I as a member of the Southern States Athletic Conference. The most competitive teams are women's golf and women's basketball. Other successful teams include baseball, women's soccer, and volleyball. About 60 percent of undergraduates participate in intramural and club sports, and Loyola's wellness program offers a range of fitness classes, club sports, and recreational activities for jocks and non-jocks alike. Basketball, flag football (no real pigskins at Loyola), and volleyball are popular pastimes.

Students at Loyola know how to pull together and draw strength from their faith. Whether they're working closely with caring professors or relaxing with friends amid the Big Easy's boundless energy, students are satisfied with their choice. A sophomore says, "Overall, Loyola is an awesome small Jesuit college with a lot to offer as a community and academic institution."

Overlaps

Tulane, Louisiana State, Fordham, University of Miami (FL), Loyola University Chicago

If You Apply To ➤

Loyola: Rolling admissions. Early action: Nov. 15. Regular decision: Apr. 15. (Priority deadline: Feb. 15.) Financial aid: Mar. 1. No application fee. Campus interviews: optional, evaluative. No alumni interviews. SATs or ACTs: required. Subject Tests: optional. Letters of recommendation: required. Essay: required. Accepts the Common Application with supplement. Audition or portfolio required for admission to the College of Music and Fine Arts.

1600 Grand Avenue, St. Paul, MN 55105

A small school that pulls above its weight, Macalester offers an internationalist and multiculturalist view of the world with a pronounced Scottish flavor. One of a handful of leading liberal arts colleges in a metropolitan setting. Carleton has a slightly bigger national reputation, but Mac has St. Paul, a progressive capital city. Eighty-five percent of the student body hails from outside Minnesota.

Website: www.macalester.edu
Location: City Center
Private
Total Enrollment: 2,138
Undergraduates: 2,138
Male/Female: 40/60
SAT Ranges: CR 620–730,
  M 620–740
ACT Ranges: 29–32
Financial Aid: 78%
Pell Grant: 15%
Expense: Pr $ $ $ $
Student Loans: 69%
Average Debt: $
Phi Beta Kappa: Yes
Applicants: 6,030
Accepted: 39%
Enrolled: 25%
Grad in 6 Years: 90%
Returning Freshmen: 95%
Academics: ✑ ✑ ✑ ✑ ½
Social: ☎ ☎ ☎
Q of L: ★ ★ ★ ★
Admissions: (800) 231-7974
Email Address: admissions@
  macalester.edu

Strong Programs:
International Studies
Geography
Community and Global Health
Chemistry
Biology
Economics
Political Science
Mathematics

Macalester College is an international island in the heart of the Great Plains. Liberal describes not only its curriculum, but also its politics. Students here get riled up over all sorts of issues with local, national, or international import—from sweatshops and fair trade to gay rights. Mac students come to the school "deeply caring about a social justice issue," says one student, "and throughout their years at Mac, their passions expand and deepen." Bagpipes lead all major processions and are heard frequently on campus as a stirring reminder of the college's historic Scottish roots. Says one senior, "Bagpipes are like the Macalester anthem. They begin all official events, bringing happy tears to my eyes every time."

Macalester takes its name from a Scotsman named Charles Macalester, an adviser to Abraham Lincoln and other U.S. presidents. The college is located in a friendly, family-oriented neighborhood in St. Paul, Minnesota, one mile from the Mississippi River, which divides St. Paul from Minneapolis. Summit Avenue, a tree-lined street with the longest, best-preserved stretch of Victorian homes in the nation, forms the campus's northern boundary. The self-contained, 53-acre campus is arranged around 115-year-old Old Main, a splendid Victorian structure listed on the National Register of Historic Places. The unifying theme is redbrick, the better to set off the octagonal Weyerhauser Chapel, constructed of black glass. A comprehensive renovation of the Mondale Hall of Studio Art was recently completed.

Mac's general education requirements include two courses in social sciences, a course in quantitative reasoning, three courses in writing, and two in natural sciences and math, plus one to two courses in fine arts and in humanities. Two courses must address cultural diversity, in the United States and internationally. Every student also completes a capstone experience during his or her senior year, such as an independent research project, performance, artistic work, or other original work. In addition to international studies, Mac's academic strengths include geography, community and global health, and chemistry. The most popular majors are biology, economics, political science, and mathematics. The school's impressive science facilities include an observatory, an animal operant chamber, and labs for electronic instrumentation and laser spectroscopy. Students may also take advantage of a critical theory concentration.

> **"Professors cater to students' passion for learning by making classrooms safe spaces for discussion and community."**

The academic environment is "very rigorous," says one economics major. A sophomore adds, "At Macalester, students, staff, and professors want you to excel, but it is understood that this means something different to every student, so the climate is very collaborative." Mac emphasizes small class sizes and working together to handle the challenging workload, and students say most pressure to do well comes from within. Teaching is paramount, with professors often having students over for dinner or taking their students for drinks at a local watering hole. "Professors cater to students' passion for learning by making classrooms safe spaces for discussion and community," says an international studies major.

Former UN secretary general Kofi Annan, class of '61, typifies one of Macalester's hallmarks: internationalism, not just in its curriculum and its student body, but also in its emphasis on international, off-campus experiences. Sixty percent of students go abroad to complete traditional coursework, independent research, and internships, choosing from more than 90 faculty-led, exchange, and partner programs on six continents. More than 100 students do stipend-supported research with Mac professors each summer, and since a number of faculty members play intramurals, students may find professors dishing off passes on the basketball court. Before graduation, 54 percent of students complete an internship at a Twin Cities business, law firm, hospital, financial institution, government agency, or nonprofit organization, and almost all students get involved in volunteer work.

Bagpipes lead all major processions and are heard frequently on campus as a reminder of the college's historic Scottish roots.

"Mac students are smart, and they know it," boasts one geography major. "They care about a lot of things; social and political activism is huge here." Fifteen percent of Macalester students hail from Minnesota, and the rest come from every state, the District of Columbia, and dozens of other countries—the proportion of international students is substantial, at 14 percent. Two percent of students are African American, 6 percent are Hispanic, and 7 percent are Asian American. Merit scholarships averaging $12,957 are available to eligible students; there are no athletic scholarships. Macalester guarantees to meet 100 percent of admitted students' demonstrated financial need.

"[Students] care about a lot of things; social and political activism is huge here."

All freshmen and sophomores are required to live in college housing; 61 percent of students remain in college-owned digs, and more say they'd stay, if only they could get rooms. They live in traditional residences, with double rooms for the first two years and suites for upperclassmen. Single-sex floors are guaranteed to those who want them, and many students have single rooms. "Housing is really good, overall," a student says. "The residence halls are high quality and rooms are fairly clean and spacious." Residents of the Hebrew House and the Veggie Co-op prepare their own meals, while others enjoy vittles in the campus center. "It's really easy to hate on Café Mac, the one dining hall here," says a junior, "but honestly the food here is much better than people give it credit for." Students praise campus security and the college's proactive approach to sexual assault awareness. "We are constantly holding dialogues, having discussions, bringing in outside speakers, and addressing policy about this growing issue," reports a junior.

Sixty percent of students go abroad to complete traditional coursework, independent research, and internships.

Given the proximity of a major metropolitan area, much of Mac's social life takes place off campus, although there are plenty of events in the "Macalester bubble" for those loath to leave. "There is no Greek life on campus, which I think is really positive. No one is dictating the party culture on campus and there is no pressure to drink," says one student. Popular events include Spring Fest and the annual Brain Bowl football game against in-state rival Carleton. Minneapolis and St. Paul offer bookstores, coffee shops, restaurants, bars, and movie theaters, plus dance and jazz clubs and professional sports teams. The Mall of America

"Whenever the weather's nice, students dot the lawns playing Frisbee, soccer, or cricket—yes, cricket!"

is also nearby, though Mac students tend to tire of it quickly, and the Twin Cities' public transportation isn't the greatest. Still, with about a dozen colleges and universities in town, there's plenty to do and the Twin Cities are an excellent place to live. For those with wheels, the best road trips include Chicago, Madison, and Duluth—and Bemidji, Minnesota, "to see Babe the Blue Ox," according to a senior.

Competitive Division III Scots teams include men's soccer and football (both recent conference champions), along with women's soccer, men's tennis, and men's and women's cross-country and track and field. Macalester has one of the oldest competitive debate programs in the nation, and the mock trial program is ranked in the top 10 nationally. Nearly half of the students compete in intramurals, and the Club Sports Program offers a variety of sports, including crew, rugby, and hockey. "Although the student body seems to take pride in being much more focused on academia, whenever the weather's nice, students dot the lawns playing Frisbee, soccer, or cricket—yes, cricket!" says one student.

Macalester provides high-powered scholarship and Scottish heritage, pairing academic rigor with global perspective. As the school's story travels, the skill and diversity of the student body are rising. Students here appreciate their freedom to grow within a supportive community. "We are all encouraged to explore ourselves, and we are all encouraged to find our passions and commit to them," says one student. "It is what binds us all."

If You Apply To ➤

Macalester: Early decision I: Nov. 15. Early decision II: Jan. 1. Regular decision: Jan. 15. Financial aid: Feb. 1. Housing: May 1. Application fee: $40. Campus interviews: recommended, evaluative. Alumni interviews: optional, evaluative. SATs or ACTs: required. Subject Tests: optional. Letters of recommendation: required. Essay: required. Accepts the Common Application.

University of Maine–Orono

Orono, ME 04469

A sleeper choice for out-of-staters amid better-known public universities such as UMass, UNH, and UVM. Not coincidentally, Maine is the least expensive—and easiest in admission—of the four. A popular marine sciences program flourishes here, as does engineering. Offers a solid honors program and one of the top varsity hockey programs in the nation. Aggressively recruiting out-of-state students.

At the University of Maine–Orono, roughly 8,000 undergraduates help themselves to a range of strong academic programs at a reasonable cost. UMaine is not only the state's only land grant university, but also the only sea grant, and attracts top students to its marine sciences program. "Here at UMaine there seems to be a widely accepted and shared value of the opportunity to further one's education," says a junior.

Situated on an island between the Stillwater and Penobscot rivers, UMaine's campus is 660 acres, centered on a large, tree-shaded grass mall. Architectural themes at this flagship of the state university system range from English academic to contemporary. Many of UMaine's facilities have recently been renovated or newly built, such as the Innovative Media Research and Commercialization Center, which contains a computer-driven 3-D router, a video production lab, and rich-media classrooms; the Wyeth Family Studio Art Center, which houses studios for printmaking, painting, and drawing; and the $5.2 million Emera Astronomy Center, home to the state's largest planetarium and telescope.

> "The atmosphere is very relaxed and allows for a more comfortable exploration of your education."

As Maine's flagship public university, UMaine offers more than 90 undergraduate majors and academic programs. The university's colleges are the College of Education and Human Development; the College of Engineering; the College of Liberal Arts and Sciences; the College of Natural Sciences, Forestry, and Agriculture; and the Honors College (which now enrolls approximately 850 students)—as well as the Maine Business School. Specific general education requirements vary from college to college, though all students must demonstrate writing proficiency and take two physical or biological science courses, 18 credits in human value and social context, six credits in math (including statistics and computer science), and at least one ethics course. A capstone experience is also mandatory.

"Unless you're in a very competitive major, the atmosphere is very relaxed and allows for a more comfortable exploration of your education," says a junior. The engineering programs are widely viewed as the most demanding on campus. Other best bets include business, forestry, and the health professions. UMaine's Climate Change Institute is renowned. The most popular majors include psychology, business man-

> **"Most of my professors have been very thorough, passionate, and enthusiastic."**

agement, nursing, and elementary education. Marine sciences undergrads can spend a semester by the sea at UMaine's renowned Darling Marine Center. Forty-one percent of all classes have fewer than 20 students, which means a fair amount of personal attention from professors. "Most of my professors have been very thorough, passionate, and enthusiastic about the subject," says a communication major.

Research is a key part of an undergraduate education at UMaine and is woven into many areas of the curriculum, as is real-world experience. UMaine's Explorations program lets first-year students work with professionals in different areas before declaring their degree choices. SPIFFY, the student investment club, manages a $2.3 million, real-money portfolio. Ocean Classroom Foundation (OCF) and the University of Maine offer a semester at sea experience for students aboard a 19th-century-style schooner. In all, UMaine students may choose from more than 700 study abroad programs in more than 40 countries.

"Students at UMaine are laid-back but also exhibit a love for learning," states one student. Most are immune to the frigid New England temperatures, since 71 percent are from Maine and many of the rest hail from other parts of New England. Faced with a declining youth population in Maine, the university is seeking to lure out-of-state students from nearby states with several new programs, including the new Flagship Match program, which allows them to pay the same in-state tuition they would pay at their home flagship university. African Americans account for 2 percent of the student body, Asian Americans 2 percent, and Hispanics 3 percent; international students comprise 2 percent. "UMaine is pretty homogeneous," admits one journalism major. Socioeconomic diversity is better represented on campus than ethnic diversity, with 36 percent of students qualifying for Pell Grants. Merit scholarships offer an average of $5,218 a year for qualified students, and 221 athletic scholarships are available in 16 sports.

Thirty-nine percent of UMaine students live on campus; the remainder seek shelter in Orono, nearby Bangor, or the sparsely populated area in between. "After sophomore year, unless someone is in the Honors College, getting housing on campus is a serious challenge," complains a senior, adding that while off-campus housing is generally more affordable and more comfortable, commuting to campus can be a pain, especially given limited parking and long, snowy winters. Dorms are co-ed; some have gyms, computer labs, or apartment-style suites. First-years may opt to

> **"The party scene is pretty lively at UMaine."**

join one of seven living/learning communities organized around themes like wellness, green living, and first-generation college students. Dining options have been overhauled, but students agree that the food could still be improved, especially for the health-conscious. "Campus feels incredibly safe to me," says one student. "The dorms are very well-secured and can only be accessed with our student ID cards."

Despite—or possibly because of—UMaine's relatively isolated location, the campus pulses with social life; 200 student groups and organizations plan plays,

(continued)

Social: ☎ ☎ ☎ ☎
Q of L: ★ ★ ★
Admissions: (207) 581-1561
Email Address: umaine admissions@maine.edu

Strong Programs:
Psychology
Business Management
Nursing
Elementary Education
Marine Sciences
Engineering
Forestry
Health Professions

The new Flagship Match program allows some out-of-staters to pay the same in-state tuition they would pay at their home flagship university.

carnival nights, concerts, and comedy hours, with a different activity offered each night. "Whatever your lifestyle, you can find something to do," one student says. Partiers find their niche off campus at bars, clubs, Greek parties, and house parties. According to a junior, "The party scene is pretty lively at UMaine, with many different parties happening every weekend and sometimes on several weeknights," and underage drinking on campus, though prohibited, is common. The annual Maine Day features a parade, cookout, and campuswide cleanup.

The midsized town of Orono—described by one sophomore as a "great college town"—offers a few bars, a theater, and some other hangouts. Buses to Bangor, a fair-sized city 10 minutes away, run every 15 to 20 minutes. UMaine students tend to be outdoor enthusiasts, and popular road trips include Acadia National Park, skiing at Sugarloaf USA, L.L. Bean's 24-hour store in Freeport, and the real-life Mount Katahdin, which appears on Bean's logo. More urban types enjoy Bar Harbor and Boston, or Montreal, just four hours away (and with a lower drinking age).

UMaine is the state's only Division I school, and athletic events are a big part of student life. Hockey reigns supreme, especially when played against Boston College, Boston University, or New Hampshire, and the Black Bears are perennial champions. Women's softball claimed the America East conference title in 2016, and women's basketball, field hockey, men's and women's track and field, and football are also competitive. The popular intramural program covers more than 30 sports, from swimming and wrestling to hoopball (golf with a basketball) and broomball (ice hockey with a dodgeball and a broom, played with shoes instead of skates).

"People here are relaxed and generally very friendly," says an accounting and finance major, "and the school does a good job of making anyone feel welcome and at home." Indeed, UMaine is a medium-sized school with a small-school atmosphere. Combine the state's natural beauty with an increased emphasis on top-quality facilities and more intimate student/faculty interaction, and it's no surprise that this campus draws more die-hard "Maine-iaks" each year.

If You Apply To ➢ **Maine:** Rolling admissions. (Priority deadline: Feb. 1.) Early action: Dec. 1. Priority financial aid: Mar. 1. Application fee: $40. Campus interviews: optional, evaluative. No alumni interviews. SATs or ACTs: required. No Subject Tests. Letters of recommendation: required. Essay: required. Accepts the Common Application with supplement.

Manhattanville College

2900 Purchase Street, Purchase, NY 10577

Though co-ed for more than 40 years, Manhattanville is still two-thirds female. Strong programs include art, education, and psychology. Among the few small colleges in the NYC area, Manhattanville is a quick train ride from the city. Despite its roots as a commuter school, two-thirds of Manhattanville's students live on campus.

Founded in 1841 by the Sisters of the Sacred Heart as an all-women's boarding school, Manhattanville College today is a private, nondenominational, coeducational, liberal arts college with a mission to "educate students to become ethical and socially responsible leaders in the global community." The Portfolio System, Manhattanville's distinct approach to undergraduate education, has been placed on hiatus while administrators move from a paper format to a modernized e-portfolio. In the meantime, Manhattanville continues to encourage individuality and personal growth.

Manhattanville College pulled up stakes from its original location on Houston Street in New York City in the 1950s for a 125-acre estate in Purchase, New York. The estate is located in wealthy Westchester County, near the town of White Plains—home to several major corporations, and just 28 miles from the excitement of the Big Apple. The focal point of the campus, which was designed by Central Park architect Frederick Law Olmsted, is Reid Hall, a 19th-century replica of a Norman castle.

Manhattanville recently introduced a new general education program, called Inquiry, in which students must fulfill coursework in four pillars: Investigator (scientific, mathematical, humanistic, and social scientific reasoning), Inventor (creativity and aesthetics), International Citizen (global systems and civilizations, foreign language, and applied liberal learning), and Interpreter (written and oral communication and digital literacy). Freshmen take a First-Year Seminar and two semesters of First-Year Writing. Seminar professors serve as faculty mentors, and all incoming students are also assigned academic advisors and peer mentors to help ease the transition to college life.

"Students often engage with peers and professors."

The college's strongest offerings include art and design (enhanced by the proximity of New York City's many museums and galleries), music, and education, while psychology, communication and media, business management, and finance are also popular. Manhattanville's School of Education, which offers two five-year master's programs, boasts a near-perfect passage rate for the New York State Teaching Exam. A major in sport studies prepares students for a wide range of careers, such as sports business management, sport psychology, physical education, and sports journalism. Students may choose from a bevy of new programs, including degrees in music technology, music business, musical theater, and digital media production, or opt to design their own major.

"The academic climate is collaborative, as students often engage with peers and professors," explains an English major. "It can be relaxed or intense depending on the professor and the expectations the students set for themselves." The quality of teaching, and the low student/faculty ratio, get high marks. Sixty-three percent of classes have fewer than 20 students. "The faculty members are extremely accessible and freshmen are often taught by full professors," a junior says. Students studying psychology, biology, or chemistry can conduct research with faculty. Qualified freshmen may apply for the Castle Scholars Honors Program, for

"[The housing lottery is] a little *Hunger Games*-ish."

a more intensive curriculum. The college has exchange programs with Mills College and with American University's World Capitals Program, plus more than 100 study abroad options in 30 countries, in which 11 percent of students participate. The Center for Career Development is "phenomenal," securing internship placements at more than 350 locations in and beyond the New York Metro area, such as MTV, the Metropolitan Museum of Art, Fox News, U.S. Senate offices, MasterCard, PepsiCo, and the Westchester County Board of Legislators.

Females outnumber males 2 to 1, and students describe themselves as friendly and accepting of diverse backgrounds and viewpoints. Nine percent of undergraduates come from overseas, while 65 percent are in-staters. Hispanics comprise the largest minority group at 17 percent, followed by African Americans at 8 percent, and Asian Americans at 1 percent. Thirty-nine percent of freshmen are eligible for Pell Grants. While there are no athletic scholarships, hundreds of merit scholarships averaging $17,762 are awarded to qualified students.

Sixty-six percent of Manhattanville's students live on campus in one of four dorms, which have lounges, communal kitchens, and laundry rooms. Freshmen are assigned rooms that are "spacious and very comfortable" according to a student,

(continued)

SAT Ranges: CR 480–580, M 480–570

ACT Ranges: 21–26

Financial Aid: 96%

Pell Grant: 39%

Expense: Pr $

Student Loans: 84%

Average Debt: $ $ $

Phi Beta Kappa: No

Applicants: 4,033

Accepted: 74%

Enrolled: 15%

Grad in 6 Years: 57%

Returning Freshmen: 82%

Academics: ✍ ✍ ✍

Social: ☎ ☎ ☎

Q of L: ★ ★ ★

Admissions: (800) 328-4553

Email Address: admissions@mville.edu

Strong Programs:
Art and Design
Music
Education
Psychology
Communication and Media
Business Management
Finance
Sport Studies

A new gen ed program, called Inquiry, requires coursework in four pillars: Investigator, Inventor, International Citizen, and Interpreter.

while upperclassmen hoping to score coveted singles or suites enter a lottery that a senior describes as "a little *Hunger Games*-ish." Campus dwellers can choose 15- or 19-meal-a-week plans, and can also use their meal cards at The Pub (a deli-type eatery) and vending machines. The dining hall has been renovated and offers fresh-baked goods and a well-stocked salad bar. "The meals are pretty consistent, but it isn't mom or dad's homemade cooking," a junior says. Security is perceived as hit or miss: "I think that campus safety could do a little better to patrol and monitor the front gate," says one senior. Campus sexual assault is said not to be a problem, but an English major adds, "The school as a whole has been promoting more awareness on the topic."

With increasing numbers of male students enrolling, the social scene seems to be picking up, and with no fraternities or sororities, off-campus parties are usually open to all. Students say Manhattanville is no party school, though, and "there is no pressure to drink." Still, for those of age, one student says, "the social life often takes place at local bars." The student programming board is working to improve the

"The social life often takes place at local bars."

campus social life with weekend events such as dinners, formals in the castle, comedy and talent shows, movies, plays, and concerts. Every spring, students look forward to Quad Jam, an all-day concert and carnival. There's also a Fall Fest'ville and an International Bazaar, in which students give cultural performances and share ethnic foods.

Manhattanville students contribute nearly 30,000 hours of community service each year through more than 50 local and global programs. The college's hometown, Purchase, "is not a college town. It is an affluent area with mansions all over," a junior says. Students frequently take the school's free bus to White Plains to enjoy a variety of restaurants, bars, and shops, and as one student points out, "Manhattanville is only 30 miles from New York City, so students can also go to the city for fun." Road trips include Rye Beach in the warmer months and upstate New York or Vermont for skiing in the winter.

Manhattanville has invested heavily in athletics as a way of making the school better known and attracting more males. Valiant teams have earned more than 40 regular-season conference championships and dozens of conference tournament titles in program history, and as a result, the school has made more than two dozen NCAA Tournament appearances. Men's and women's basketball and ice hockey, baseball, softball, and men's golf are particularly strong. Intramural and club sports draw 20 percent of students, and weekend warriors and letter-winners alike applaud the college's gym, fitness center, swimming pool, tennis courts, and athletic fields.

"Manhattanville really feels like a close-knit community," a junior says. The familial atmosphere can get claustrophobic at times, but for those wishing to be part of a close but growing community where values matter, Manhattanville may be worth a look.

If You Apply To ➤

Manhattanville: Rolling admissions. (Priority deadline: Mar. 1.) Early action: Dec. 1. Financial aid: Mar. 1. Application fee: $50. Campus and alumni interviews: recommended, evaluative. SATs or ACTs: recommended. No Subject Tests. Letters of recommendation: required. Essay: required. Accepts the Common Application with supplement.

Marlboro College

Marlboro, VT 05344

Marlboro is a hilltop home to a couple hundred nonconformist souls. Each develops a Plan of Concentration that culminates in a senior project. One of the few colleges in the country that is governed in town-meeting style, where student votes carry the same weight as those of faculty members. About 60 percent of the students graduate in six years. Where else can you cheer for the Fighting Dead Trees?

Founded in 1946, Marlboro College is known far and wide as an innovator in liberal arts education. It was founded on the principles of independent and in-depth study just after World War II, when returning GIs renovated an old barn as the college's first building while living in Quonset huts. And today's Marlboro students are just as trailblazing; they prepare for the future by digging into self-developed Plans of Concentration. With fewer than 200 undergrads and fewer than 50 faculty members, Marlboro is its own little world, which students enter as novices and leave as pros.

Positioned atop a small mountain, surrounded by maples and pines and with a gorgeous view of southern Vermont, Marlboro's physical beauty is striking. Buildings are adapted from barns, sheds, and houses that stood on three old farms that today make up the more than 450-acre campus. Among the renovated structures, many with passive solar heating, are nine dormitories, a science building, a 350-seat theater, and a campus center. The new Snyder Center for the Visual Arts opened in 2016. In the old independent Yankee spirit, Marlboro's library operates on the honor system, where students sign out their own books 24 hours a day. Furthermore, the college employs a New England town-meeting style of government involving students, faculty, and the staff and their spouses in every aspect of policymaking. Students can veto Faculty Meeting decisions on academic policy, and it takes a two-thirds vote of the faculty to override such a veto.

The cornerstone of a Marlboro education is the Plan of Concentration, which each undergraduate student develops independently. Juniors and seniors "on plan" take most coursework in one-on-one tutorials with their faculty sponsors. Seniors present their thesis or project to their sponsors, who are backed up by outside examiners, experts in the student's field unaffiliated with the college. The administration boasts that by bringing in these outsiders for two- to three-hour oral examinations of its seniors, Marlboro has created its own accountability system, ensuring that neither students nor faculty at this isolated institution are cut off from the most current academic thinking. Faculty members often find the exams as stressful as the students, as it means outsiders are judging their teaching. The only other requirement is the Clear Writing Program, usually completed by the end of the third semester, with a 21-page portfolio reviewed by faculty. Marlboro offers solid instruction in literature, writing, social sciences, and fine arts, with the physical and natural sciences also well integrated into the curriculum. The world studies program requires students to complete a six- to eight-month internship in a foreign country, as well as a graduate-level course at the nearby School for International Training. Marlboro has direct exchange programs with Heilongjiang University in China, Bratislava International School of Liberal Arts in Slovakia, and Charles University in Prague, and 24 percent of students do some type of study abroad.

While some schools see growth as a sign of success, Marlboro intends to remain one of the nation's smallest liberal arts institutions. Academics are modeled after the

> "I consistently find myself saying, 'This is the best class I've ever taken,' every semester."

Website: www.marlboro.edu
Location: Rural
Private
Total Enrollment: 189
Undergraduates: 189
Male/Female: 51/49
SAT Ranges: CR 580–760, M 510–600
ACT Ranges: 24–29
Financial Aid: 96%
Pell Grant: 40%
Expense: Pr $
Student Loans: 83%
Average Debt: $ $ $ $
Phi Beta Kappa: No
Applicants: 144
Accepted: 94%
Enrolled: 26%
Grad in 6 Years: 59%
Returning Freshmen: 74%
Academics: ✐ ✐ ✐
Social: ☎ ☎ ☎
Q of L: ★ ★ ★ ★
Admissions: (800) 343-0049
Email Address: admissions@marlboro.edu

Strong Programs:
Literature
Writing
History
Visual Arts
Film Studies
Political Science
World Studies

Oxford system of tutorials and seminars, and administrators believe the college's small size stimulates dynamic relationships between students and faculty, making learning happen both inside and outside the classroom. This isn't a place where students can fade into the background: none of the classes exceed 20 students, and the institution relies on everyone to share their talents and skills. Marlboro's flexibility should not be confused with academic flabbiness. Grades are an integral part of the evaluation process, professors are stingy with As, and most students work hard. Students agree that the school has an "intellectually intense" but "collaborative academic climate that is centered on the individual." One student says, "Teachers are very knowledgeable, quick to answer questions, spark discussion, and explore new territory." Another adds, "I consistently find myself saying, 'This is the best class I've ever taken,' every semester."

"Marlboro students are passionate learners with insurmountable curiosity, always excited to see how deep the academic rabbit hole can go," says one religion and dance major. Marlboro remains a liberal-leaning campus, and students are politically active. Eighty-eight percent of students hail from outside Vermont, and minority enrollment continues to be low: Asian Americans, African Americans, and Hispanics each make up less than 1 percent. Socioeconomic diversity is far more present on campus, with 40 percent of students qualifying for Pell Grants. Marlboro aims to increase campus diversity through its new Renaissance Scholars program, which offers free tuition to one student from each U.S. state; recipients must demonstrate a strong commitment to community engagement and leadership. The college offers merit awards but no athletic scholarships.

> **"Most rooms are large and include wood paneling and views straight into the forest."**

The dorms house 78 percent of Marlboro students and are mostly co-ed; students say they have a "rustic" appeal. "Most rooms are large and include wood paneling and views straight into the forest," says one dorm dweller. Generally, first-years live in doubles or triples, sophomores live in singles or doubles, and upperclassmen have access to cabins in the woods nearby. Students with the highest number of credits get housing priority. A small percentage of students live off campus in Brattleboro, 20 minutes away, and shuttle to and from campus in a school van. As part of the Real Food Campus Commitment, Marlboro has increasingly been sourcing campus food from local or community-based, fair, ecologically sound, and humane food sources. "The meals are generally very healthy, with many vegetarian/vegan options available," reports a physics major. "On the other hand, if you like Indian food, or really any spices at all, prepare for disappointment." "I feel really safe here," says one freshman. "Everyone is out at night and nobody's worried about assault—except maybe by bears."

"For miles in every direction there is nothing but mountains, forests, and small farms," says a junior. "The view is incredible, but it's hard to deny that it can feel cramped and isolated." The college's location means that social life takes place almost exclusively on campus. "The social scene gets strange in the best way," says an economics major. "Students may throw a large punk show on Saturday night and attend a classical pianist performance the next morn-

> **"It's hard to deny that it can feel cramped and isolated."**

ing." As might be expected, Marlboro has no Greek organizations. The school sponsors activities like poetry readings, trips to Boston and New York City, vans to local movie theaters, and pumpkin-carving contests. On Work Day, students and faculty skip class and work together to improve the campus through various manual labor projects. The annual President's Fall Ball, Goth Prom, and Hogwarts Dinner are popular social events, and regular open-mic nights are always well attended. Students agree that the town of Marlboro, recognizable by a post office and general store, has little to write home about. "Marlboro isn't a town so much as a few buildings with a college a mile or so down the road," observes one literature major. Many students head to Brattleboro for its restaurants, bookstores, and coffee shops.

The school mascot, the Fighting Dead Trees, is emblazoned on the shirts of the ever-popular co-ed soccer team. The annual broomball tournament, offering a variation of ice hockey played using shoes instead of ice skates, brooms instead of sticks, and a kickball instead of a puck, is always popular for athletes and spectators. The rather informal intramural program also offers dodgeball, ultimate Frisbee, and volleyball, among other sports. The "incredibly dynamic" Outdoor Program ensures plenty of opportunities to enjoy the local wilderness, including hiking and cross-country skiing on runs that radiate from the center of campus. Excellent downhill skiing is only a few minutes' drive away.

> "I feel very empowered here to express and explore different aspects of myself and our community."

"Marlboro College is a place for students with a passion for academia, a desire to join and maintain a small democratic community, and an interest in designing their own course of intellectual study," muses one student. This iconoclastic school continues to push the academic envelope and remains proud of doing—and being—the unexpected. And that suits its students just fine. Says a freshman, "I feel very empowered here to express and explore different aspects of myself and our community."

The annual President's Fall Ball, Goth Prom, and Hogwarts Dinner are popular social events.

Overlaps

Bennington, Hampshire, Bard, Warren Wilson, St. John's College, Beloit, Reed, Sarah Lawrence

If You Apply To ➤

Marlboro: Early decision: Nov. 15. Early action: Jan. 15. Regular decision: Mar. 15. Financial aid: Mar. 1. Application fee: $50. Campus interviews: required, evaluative. Alumni interviews: optional, informational. SATs or ACTs: optional. No Subject Tests. Letters of recommendation: required. Essay: required. Accepts the Common Application with supplement. Submission of an academic expository writing sample required in addition to essay. Encourages "nontraditional" students.

Marquette University

Milwaukee, WI 53201

Marquette is an old-line Roman Catholic university that is actively engaged in strengthening its Jesuit character. Milwaukee is not a selling point, and the university's student body is mainly from the southern Wisconsin/northern Illinois corridor. Two-thirds of students are Catholic. Relatively inexpensive, in keeping with its middle- and working-class roots. Compare to Saint Louis University and Loyola of Chicago.

At Marquette University, students practice what they preach. The college experience at this Roman Catholic institution includes an emphasis on personal growth, civic responsibility, and community service. The university may have hired its first lay president in 2014, but it has also worked in recent years to strengthen its Jesuit traditions and character, while at the same time connecting students with more practical, real-world experiences. Service learning, which helps students put classroom theories to the test through volunteer work in the local community and across the globe, is a cornerstone of campus life, helping to shape well-rounded students who graduate ready, as the school puts it, to "be the difference" in the world.

Marquette occupies more than 80 acres of "concrete with interludes of grass and trees" just a few blocks from the heart of downtown Milwaukee. While offering the advantages of an urban setting, its campus does have plenty of open spaces suitable for everything from throwing a Frisbee to throwing a barbecue. Although most of

Website: www.marquette.edu
Location: City Center
Private
Total Enrollment: 10,043
Undergraduates: 7,952
Male/Female: 47/53
SAT Ranges: CR 530–640, M 540–660
ACT Ranges: 24–30
Financial Aid: 99%
Pell Grant: 17%
Expense: Pr $

(continued)

Student Loans: 62%
Average Debt: $ $ $ $
Phi Beta Kappa: Yes
Applicants: 20,486
Accepted: 74%
Enrolled: 12%
Grad in 6 Years: 79%
Returning Freshmen: 90%
Academics: ✍ ✍ ✍
Social: ☎ ☎ ☎
Q of L: ★ ★ ★
Admissions: (414) 288-7302
Email Address: admissions@
  marquette.edu

Strong Programs:
Biomedical Sciences
Accounting
Psychology
Nursing
Social Welfare and Justice
Operations and Supply Chain
  Management
Bioinformatics
Theatre Arts

Each semester, more than 1,000 students enroll in service-learning courses that connect them with service opportunities in more than 130 community agencies.

the buildings are relatively modern, the campus is the site of the St. Joan of Arc Chapel, which was built in France more than 500 years ago and later transported to Wisconsin. It is said to be the only medieval structure in the Western Hemisphere dedicated to its original purpose. Construction is under way on the university's first new residence hall in 50 years, a $96 million facility that will house 750 freshman and sophomore students.

The 36-hour general education core curriculum is composed of nine "knowledge areas": diverse cultures, human nature and ethics, histories of cultures and societies, individual and social behavior, theology, literature/performing arts, mathematical reasoning, rhetoric, and science and nature. All freshmen take a mandatory rhetoric course after reading the same book over the summer, and those who want to get a head start on the Marquette experience in a close-knit group can opt to participate in the five-week Freshman Frontier program, which offers credit and noncredit courses, along with intensive assistance from academic advisors.

> "The professors I've had have really instilled the idea of teamwork."

The most popular majors at Marquette include biomedical sciences, accounting, psychology, and nursing. The social welfare and justice major is well regarded, as are more specialized majors in operations and supply chain management and bioinformatics. Through an affiliation with the Milwaukee Institute of Art and Design, four art minors (studio art, photography, graphic design, and motion narrative) are available. Marquette has its own art museum and an active theatre program. Newly added programs include majors in data science, environmental studies, and innovation and entrepreneurship. Perhaps the most popular academic offerings are Marquette's service-learning courses. Each semester, more than 1,000 students enroll in service-learning courses that connect them with service opportunities in more than 130 community agencies. Roughly 83 percent of students overall take part in some type of community service experience prior to graduation.

Forty percent of classes have fewer than 20 students, and students report little difficulty getting into the ones they want. The academic climate is described as challenging and competitive, although this varies by program. A student says, "Marquette is pretty collaborative. The professors I've had have really instilled the idea of teamwork." The school's Jesuit influence is felt in the classroom, and the Manresa project, named for the Spanish town where St. Ignatius spent a year praying about his vocation, helps professors incorporate Ignatian teaching into their classes—focusing particularly on community-based learning and service, social justice, and personal reflection on faith and vocation.

> "We are the type of students who love debate, and love the free-flowing exchange of ideas."

Twenty-four percent of Marquette students travel to more than 30 countries each year for study abroad programs. The flagship South Africa Service-Learning Program in Cape Town, South Africa, is particularly popular; participants combine their studies at the University of Western Cape with two full days of volunteer work per week in areas like education, literacy, public health, and economic development. The university is also home to the Les Aspin Center for Government in Washington, D.C., which allows students to take courses while participating in an internship with a federal government agency. Closer to home, students intern with local and state government agencies. Twenty percent of students assist faculty members with their research, and about 100 top freshmen per year join the University Honors Program, which offers small seminars and an optional living/learning community.

Although Marquette actively recruits in 35 or so states and several U.S. territories, most of the undergraduate student body is from the Midwest, 30 percent from

Wisconsin itself. Four percent come from foreign countries. In general, Marquette boasts a friendly collection of traditional, middle-class students. Student religious organizations are active, and students, faculty, and staff can attend mass every day of the week. Catholics are understandably predominant in the student body, but religious practice is left to the individual. According to one sophomore, "We are the type of students who love debate, and love the free flowing exchange of ideas." African Americans make up 4 percent of the student body, Hispanics 10 percent, and Asian Americans 6 percent. Marquette's successful Educational Opportunity Program enables low-income, disadvantaged students to have the benefit of a college education. Merit scholarships averaging $10,772 are available, as are 231 athletic scholarships in 16 sports.

Fifty-two percent of Marquette students make their home on campus; all but two residence halls are co-ed, and there are more than 400 apartments (which come with a separate electric bill). Residency is required for freshmen and sophomores, but by junior year an overwhelming majority of students choose to move off campus, though housing is guaranteed for all undergraduate students through a lottery. "Dorms are decent," says one digital media major. Within the residence halls are four different living/learning communities, including the honors, social justice, inclusive leadership, and Spanish language and culture communities. Dining hall fare has plenty of choices on the menu. Regarding campus security, a senior says, "Although Marquette is located in an urban environment, public safety does an absolutely outstanding job ensuring that students are safe and know how to remain safe in the area." The Gender and Sexuality Resource Center supports students with an interest in LGBTQ, gender identity, and sexual violence and prevention issues.

Four living/learning communities include the honors, social justice, inclusive leadership, and Spanish language and culture communities.

Social life is mainly on campus, and "there are always things to do," says a senior. Students don't characterize Milwaukee as a college town, but still say there are many good things about being there, including plenty of opportunities for community service. An old advertising slogan once claimed that "Milwaukee Means Beer," and few Marquette students would disagree. Students report that Marquette is stricter than most universities in enforcing the drinking age, but getting served off campus is not as difficult. Fraternities and sororities attract 4 percent of the men and 9 percent of the women, respectively. A well-loved tradition is the Miracle on Westowne Square, the annual lighting of the campus Christmas tree and accompanying mass.

"Marquette students really are a community."

The Golden Eagles Division I men's basketball, golf, lacrosse, tennis, and track and field teams are highly competitive, as are women's basketball, volleyball, and soccer. Women's track and field is a recent Big East conference champion. Seventy percent of students participate in at least one of roughly two dozen intramural sports, and 36 club teams are another option. Sports fans will be impressed with Milwaukee's BMO Bradley Center, close to campus and home to Marquette basketball and the NBA's Milwaukee Bucks. Nature lovers can head to Lake Michigan, a 40-minute walk from campus, or to Kettle Moraine, a glaciated region ideal for hiking and cross-country skiing. Chicago is only 95 miles away.

Students at Marquette University are engaged not only in their own personal growth but also in the betterment of their local and global communities through service. Students say it's the supportive, familial atmosphere that makes them excited about those goals, and that makes Marquette what it is. Confirms a senior, "Marquette students really are a community. Everyone supports everyone else."

Overlaps

University of Wisconsin–Madison, University of Illinois at Urbana–Champaign, Loyola University Chicago, University of Minnesota, Saint Louis University, University of Iowa, DePaul, Indiana University

If You Apply To ➤

Marquette: Regular decision: Dec. 1. Financial aid: Feb. 1. Housing: May 1. No application fee. No campus or alumni interviews. SATs or ACTs: required. Subject Tests: optional. No letters of recommendation. Essay: required. Accepts the Common Application.

University of Mary Washington

1301 College Avenue, Fredericksburg, VA 22401

Situated in historic Fredericksburg, Mary Washington could easily be mistaken for one of Virginia's elite private colleges. A public liberal arts college, it offers just as much history and tradition albeit for a much lower price. Once a women's college, it is still about two-thirds female, and administrators failed in an effort to drop "Mary" from the name to attract more men.

Website: www.umw.edu
Location: Small City
Public
Total Enrollment: 3,917
Undergraduates: 3,789
Male/Female: 36/64
SAT Ranges: CR 510–620,
M 490–590
ACT Ranges: 22–27
Financial Aid: 39%
Pell Grant: 13%
Expense: Pub $ $ $
Student Loans: 50%
Average Debt: $
Phi Beta Kappa: Yes
Applicants: 5,549
Accepted: 83%
Enrolled: 21%
Grad in 6 Years: 70%
Returning Freshmen: 82%
Academics: ✍ ✍ ✍ ½
Social: ☎ ☎ ☎
Q of L: ★ ★ ★
Admissions: (540) 654-2000
Email Address:
admit@umw.edu

Strong Programs:
Biology
Business Administration
English
Psychology
Historic Preservation
Political Science
International Affairs
Communication and Digital
Studies

Strolling among the university's elegant buildings of redbrick with white columns has led more than one pleased parent to declare, "Now this is what a college should look like." Indeed, for an aura of history and tradition, few schools stack up to this small college in Fredericksburg, a site of Civil War action and the boyhood town of George Washington. Mary Washington is a good place to spend four years "because it is a strong community of socially conscious and academically focused students," says one senior.

The University of Mary Washington campus features classical Jeffersonian buildings, sweeping lawns, brick walkways, and breathtaking foliage. If the campus architecture puts some people in mind of the University of Virginia, it's no accident: UMW (formerly Mary Washington College) was the all-female branch of that august institution before going co-ed in 1970 and cutting its ties in 1972. The new University Center opened in 2015 and provides much-improved dining facilities, student lounge areas, a retail store, student club and organization offices, and a ballroom.

Mary Washington has gained a reputation as one of the premium public liberal arts colleges in the country. The core curriculum emphasizes a strong liberal arts focus. The general education requirements include a first-year seminar (which involves a living/learning cluster, dedicated advising, and a common book reading) and courses in quantitative reasoning; natural science; human experience and society; global inquiry; language, arts, literature, and performance; experiential learning; a writing intensive course; and two speaking intensive courses. Nearly every major requires students to complete a capstone project or experience or to take a senior-level initiative seminar. The program in historic preservation is solid: "It's pretty unique and has great local partners for internships," says a senior. Among the sciences, biology is the clear favorite, and other popular majors include business administration, English, and psychology. New programs have been added in communication and digital studies and international business.

> **"I never imagined that I would find such a highly engaged and compassionate set of professors my first year of college."**

"The academic climate has the ability to squeeze as much potential out of you so you can graduate knowing you have nothing more to learn at UMW," says a journalism major, "but it is up to you to challenge yourself to make the commitment." The close ties between students and faculty are a great source of pride at Mary Washington. Classes rarely have more than 25 students, and instructors are described as intelligent and accessible. "I never imagined that I would find such a highly engaged and compassionate set of professors my first year of college," says one student. Students are encouraged to take on research projects of their own design, and science students are eligible for a 10-week summer research program. Several departments offer grants for work abroad or in the United States, and 29 percent of students study abroad each year. The college's location, roughly an hour from both

Washington, D.C., and the state capital, Richmond, is a handy asset for the approximately 350 budding politicos who seek internships every year. A large majority of students continue on to jobs after graduation, rather than graduate school.

"UMW's community is a little quirky, and it definitely embraces that," says a senior. "A lot of students…aren't afraid to mix ideas that most people wouldn't connect together or to try new things." Eighty-seven percent of the student body is from Virginia and just 1 percent arrive from foreign countries. African Americans make up 6 percent of the student population, Hispanics 8 percent, and Asian Americans 4 percent. "We have an amazing Multicultural Center that puts a lot of effort into bringing together diverse cultures and backgrounds and blending our community," says a sophomore. Students cite feminism and divestment from fossil fuels as hot topics on campus. Eligible undergraduates receive merit awards averaging $2,768, but there are no athletic scholarships.

A first-year seminar involves a living/learning cluster, dedicated advising, and a common book reading.

All told, 57 percent of students live in university housing, and an unusually strong sense of community characterizes everything from academics to dorm life. The residence halls offer a variety of living arrangements, including suites, singles, doubles, quads, and the aforementioned living/learning clusters. "All of the residence halls have a different feel to them and have unique qualities,"

"Students…aren't afraid to mix ideas that most people wouldn't connect together or to try new things."

says a senior, and that includes how well maintained and up-to-date they are. Students say the recent opening of a new main dining hall has been a "rough" transition but are optimistic that the quality and variety of food will improve with the help of student feedback. Security is described as good and students report feeling safe on campus. In response to recent incidents, the university has increased its efforts to deal with sexual assault on campus, hiring new staff and implementing a range of new prevention and support programs.

Although there are parties both on and off campus, alcohol does not dominate the social scene, and a good number of students go home on the weekends. Still, "Students are incredibly involved outside of the classroom," says an English major. "There are over 120 active clubs on campus." There are no fraternities or sororities, but other student organizations offer special events each Friday, such as a student film festival or a Mardi Gras celebration, and volunteering is a big part of campus life. Mary Washington students take an uncommon interest in traditions. Several annual outdoor parties, including the Homecoming Bonfire and Rocktoberfest, never fail to attract a large crowd. All third-year students brace themselves for Junior Ring Week, during which they are the victims of practical jokes prior to receiving their rings from the school's president. The favorite tradition is Devil-Goat Day, an all-day competition pitting odd- and even-year classes against each other in events such as sumo wrestling, jousting, and the Velcro wall. The annual Multicultural Fair draws many residents and vendors from the local community to campus.

Devil-Goat Day is an all-day competition pitting odd- and even-year classes against each other.

Small and friendly, nearby Fredericksburg is an "interesting mix of Civil War relics, antique shops, museums, and Mary Washington," according to a history major. While it lacks some of the nightlife of a larger community, there are historic homes to visit, museums with Civil War exhibits, a mall, and restaurants that offer discounts to students. For dance

"Students are incredibly involved outside of the classroom."

clubs and bars, students drive to Richmond or D.C. Also an hour's drive away is the scenery of the Chesapeake Bay, due east, and the Blue Ridge Mountains, due west.

Mary Washington doesn't have a football team, but its 21 Division III Eagles sports teams are alive and well. Since the inception of the Capital Athletic Conference, UMW has won more conference championships than all other conference members

Overlaps

James Madison, George Mason, Christopher Newport, Virginia Commonwealth, University of Virginia, Virginia Tech, College of William and Mary

combined. The men's swim team has won four national championships, and the men's basketball team recently advanced to the NCAA quarterfinal competition. Men's and women's tennis and women's swimming and lacrosse are also top performers. Nonvarsity types also use the 76-acre sports and field complex, complete with an Olympic-size pool, for 29 club sports, including men's and women's rugby and crew, and a variety of intramurals, ranging from flag football and soccer to indoor Wiffle ball. "'Intramural Champions' is the most coveted T-shirt on campus," says a senior.

"Students looking for an easy pass and wild parties should look elsewhere," advises one English major. Instead, the University of Mary Washington offers a first-rate liberal arts education, the feel of a private school, and a public school price tag. "What's more," says one senior, is that "students are connected and feel like a family."

If You Apply To >

Mary Washington: Early decision: Nov. 1. Early action: Nov. 15. Regular decision and financial aid: Feb. 1. Housing: May 1. Application fee: $50. Campus interviews: optional, evaluative. No alumni interviews. SATs or ACTs: required for some (optional for applicants with minimum 3.5 GPA). Subject Tests: optional. Letters of recommendation: required. Essay: required. Accepts the Common Application with supplement.

University of Maryland

College Park, MD 20742

The name says Maryland, but the location says Washington, D.C. Students in College Park can jump on the Metro just as they do at American or Georgetown. Maryland is nothing if not big, and savvy students will look to programs such as the honors program and living/learning communities for some personal attention.

Website: www.umd.edu
Location: Suburban
Public
Total Enrollment: 33,327
Undergraduates: 25,272
Male/Female: 53/47
SAT Ranges: CR 590–690, M 620–730
ACT Ranges: N/A
Financial Aid: 55%
Pell Grant: 14%
Expense: Pub $ $
Student Loans: 43%
Average Debt: $ $
Phi Beta Kappa: Yes
Applicants: 28,301
Accepted: 45%
Enrolled: 31%
Grad in 6 Years: 86%
Returning Freshmen: 95%
Academics: ✐ ✐ ✐

For good luck on exams, University of Maryland students rub the nose of Testudo, the school's terrapin mascot. But even without touching the storied statue, most students here feel lucky to be at a diverse school that offers a multitude of programs, from living/learning communities to special opportunities for freshmen, that make it feel smaller and more personal, despite its daunting size. "With hundreds of different student organizations," says a senior, "students will always be able to find their niche."

Maryland's 1,200-acre campus embraces an array of architectural styles, including the Georgian brick buildings ringing the oak-lined mall at the heart of the campus. Students now have a new athletic arena—the Comcast Center. Clark Hall, which houses the bioengineering department and state-of-the-art labs and project spaces, and the St. John Teaching and Learning Center are the newest additions to campus.

Maryland has earned a strong reputation for its engineering and computer science departments, as well as the Smith School of Business and Merrill College of Journalism. The most popular majors are biological sciences, criminology and criminal justice, economics, and psychology. General education requirements entail 40 to 46 credits in a number of areas, including writing, oral communication, mathematics, analytic reasoning, history and social sciences, humanities, natural sciences, and diversity. Students must also take an "I-Series" course that emphasizes "broad, analytical thinking about significant issues." Curricular innovations include an institute that supports technology start-ups and an entrepreneurship center in the business school. For students at the extremes of the academic spectrum, there are several honors programs and an intensive educational development and tutoring program. Students participating in individual studies can combine established majors and create their own programs.

Maryland's coursework is "intense" but "more collaborative than competitive," according to one student. Lower-level courses tend to be large and impersonal ("easy to hide in, even easier to skip"), but the corresponding weekly discussion sections led by teaching assistants offer personal attention. The situation improves by junior year, when classes of 20 to 40 students become the norm. "The quality of teaching here has been pretty good. Faculty members are accessible," a senior says. The university is putting more emphasis on helping students make timely progress toward their degrees. A two-day orientation, seminars, and course clusters are offered for freshmen, while more than 20 living/learning programs offer students experiential learning opportunities in more intimate settings. The FIRE (First-Year Innovation and Research Experience) program allows qualified freshmen to join faculty-led research groups for research and mentorship experiences. Students also benefit from internships in nearby Washington, D.C., and Baltimore, and study abroad options in locations such as Costa Rica, Israel, and Sweden.

> "With hundreds of different student organizations, students will always be able to find their niche."

Seventy-six percent of undergraduates are Maryland natives, while New York and New Jersey are also well represented; 4 percent hail from foreign nations. Diversity is more than just a buzzword: 13 percent of students are African American, 9 percent are Hispanic, and another 18 percent are Asian American. Major social and political issues on campus revolve around greater awareness of racial and LGBTQ+ issues. The Maryland Pathways program provides three avenues to help students from low-income families attend the university without assuming excessive amounts of debt. In addition, qualified undergrads receive merit awards averaging $6,682, and athletes vie for 418 scholarships in 19 sports.

Forty-two percent of students live on campus in single-sex or co-ed dorms; freshmen are guaranteed housing. While many juniors and seniors seek off-campus accommodations, those who stay on campus all four years will find that their digs improve as they gain seniority—upperclassmen have the option of on-campus apartments and suites. Freshmen generally live in high-rises or low-rises; South Campus (more relaxing than the louder North Campus) features air-conditioning, carpeting, and new furniture. "Dorms are great and an essential part of the freshman experience," one senior says. Campus safety features include triple locks on dorm-room doors, blue-light emergency phones, and walking and riding escort services to transport students after dark. "The area has its rough spots but it is constantly becoming safer," a sophomore says, noting that the campus itself tends to be "extremely safe."

> "Terrapin pride runs rampant around here."

The university's reputation as a haven for those who prefer partying to studying is changing as students with better credentials apply, but there is still always something happening in the dorms, at local pubs, and in nearby Baltimore and Washington, D.C. Students enjoy frequent school-sponsored concerts, movies, and speakers, as well as the traditional fraternity parties and football and basketball games. "Social life is epic here," raves one history and education double major. Fifteen percent of men and 19 percent of the women go Greek, but they don't dominate the tone of campus life. As for drinking, "They say no tolerance and in recent years, there have been crackdowns. As a result, policies have increased in effectiveness," says one student. Art Attack is a favorite annual event in which local artists share their crafts and national touring artists perform an evening concert. Other popular events include Maryland Day and homecoming. When Maryland's suburban

(continued)

Social: ☎ ☎ ☎
Q of L: ★ ★ ★
Admissions: (800) 422-5867
Email Address:
applymaryland@umd.edu

Strong Programs:
Biological Sciences
Criminology and Criminal Justice
Economics
Psychology
Engineering
Computer Science
Business
Journalism

The FIRE program allows qualified freshmen to join faculty-led research groups for research and mentorship experiences.

The Terrapins now compete in the Big Ten Conference, and five teams won conference championships in the 2015–16 season.

campus feels too small, a few bucks and a few minutes on the Metro (Washington's subway system) brings Terrapins into downtown D.C. at a hare's pace.

Division I sports are a big deal here, and the Terrapins now compete in the Big Ten Conference, and five teams won conference championships in 2015–16. Women's field hockey, basketball, and lacrosse, along with men's soccer and lacrosse, were all conference champions in the 2015–16 season. Women's lacrosse brought home the national championship in 2015. Basketball fans are intrepid and not always civilized, turning out en masse to cheer against opponents. "Students here have a lot of school spirit," a junior says. "Terrapin pride runs rampant around here." A handful of intramural sports draw strong participation, and 45 club-level sports are available as well.

The University of Maryland's overwhelming size is both a blessing and a curse for the increasingly capable undergraduates here. On one hand, "the diversity of the student body and the opportunities afforded are infinite," a sophomore says. On the other, largeness can translate into crowded dorms, big classes, parking problems, and other hassles. Still, most students agree that the threat of anonymity is overshadowed by the countless opportunities for success. "Our campus is gorgeous, academics are competitive, and we have school spirit," says one student. "Why wouldn't you want to be a Terp?"

If You Apply To ➤

Maryland: Regular decision: Jan. 20. (Priority deadline: Nov. 1.) Financial aid: Jan. 1. Application fee: $75. No campus or alumni interviews. SATs or ACTs: required. No Subject Tests. Letters of recommendation: required. Essay: required. Students who do not meet academic standards may submit additional information for consideration.

University of Maryland Baltimore County

Baltimore, MD 21250

A midsize public university with the feel of a private one. Strategically located in a suburban setting between Washington, D.C., and Baltimore, UMBC invests heavily in learning communities and other efforts to ensure that its undergraduates thrive. Nationally known for its selective Meyerhoff Scholars Program and a chess team that routinely bests its Ivy League competition. Working on its commuter reputation.

Website: www.umbc.edu
Location: Suburban
Public
Total Enrollment: 10,737
Undergraduates: 9,577
Male/Female: 57/43
SAT Ranges: CR 540–640, M 570–670
ACT Ranges: 24–29
Financial Aid: 84%
Pell Grant: N/A
Expense: Pub $ $ $
Student Loans: 50%
Average Debt: $ $

At the University of Maryland Baltimore County, you can be king or queen of your academic world. Students here are given access to academic and social resources usually reserved for those attending mammoth public institutions or pricey private colleges. In addition to solid programs in the sciences and humanities, UMBC offers students a seemingly endless menu of social options. "There are so many ways to get involved academically and socially," says a student, "whether it's through clubs, research, internships, or service learning." What's more, the school fields a killer chess team that regularly keeps competitors in check. UMBC encourages exploration and expects students to support one another and the community at large. It's your move.

UMBC's 500-acre suburban campus is located between D.C. and Baltimore, offering students access to an array of cultural attractions including restaurants, art galleries, specialty shops, and museums. In the past decade, the university has invested more than $300 million in new facilities and landscaping, including a new LEED Gold–rated performing arts and humanities building, a redesigned and pedestrian-friendly entrance plaza, and more than 3,000 trees.

All students must complete general foundation requirements, which include three courses in the arts and humanities, three social science courses, one math course, and two biological/physical science courses. In addition, students must complete a foreign language requirement. The university offers a number of programs designed to help freshmen ease into college life. First-Year Academic Seminars allow students to partner with faculty members to explore course material in an intimate, active learning environment. Students focus on creative and critical-thinking skills and written and oral communication, and take part in faculty and peer critiques. The Small Study Groups program encourages freshmen and sophomores to form study groups, and Campus Connect provides additional mentoring to undecided freshmen who appear at risk for not completing their degrees.

"The academic climate is more collaborative than competitive, but intense," says one English major. UMBC's most popular programs are also its strongest, including biological sciences, computer science and information systems, psychology, financial economics, and engineering. Programs in bioinformatics and theatre are also well regarded. The interdisciplinary studies major gives students a chance to create individualized majors drawing on a wide range of disciplines; past majors include biomechanics, criminal justice, medical illustration, and intercultural conflict resolution. Students also take advantage of new programs in Asian studies, Africana studies, and global studies. Thirty-nine percent of classes have fewer than 20 students, and the quality of teaching is hit or miss, students say. "Some of my professors are very engaged and focused on student success," says a junior, while "others seem to be disinterested. Most are in the middle."

> **"The academic climate is more collaborative than competitive, but intense."**

The Brown Center for Entrepreneurship sponsors programs and courses to inspire entrepreneurial thinking among students and faculty, while budding researchers may compete for undergraduate research awards through the Provost's Office and via Undergraduate Research and Creative Achievement Day. The highly selective Meyerhoff Scholars Program addresses the shortage of African Americans in the sciences and engineering; today, it is one of the nation's top producers of African American science, engineering, and math undergrads who matriculate into Ph.D. programs. Each year, the Shriver Center places more than 1,200 UMBC students in internship and co-op experiences, and several hundred students participate in study abroad programs.

Eighty-six percent of students hail from Maryland, while 6 percent come from abroad. "Students here tend to be on the nerdy end of the spectrum," says one senior, "but we embrace it." African Americans account for 12 percent of the student body, Hispanics 6 percent, and Asian Americans 24 percent. "The biggest social and political issues on campus would be the Black Lives Matter march and a growing awareness of LGBTQIA issues," a senior says. UMBC awards merit scholarships worth an average of $8,815 and more than 160 athletic scholarships.

Thirty-five percent of students live on campus. "Dorms are small, and first priority goes to new students. Housing is also expensive," laments one student. Students say off-campus housing is plentiful and cheap, although parking on campus can be a chore. Living/learning communities connect students with similar interests and house them together in themed residence halls, which include the Center for Women and Information Technology, Emergency Health Services, Honors College, and Exploratory Learners. Campus dining options include a dining hall and the Commons, which offers a variety of fare, including Italian, Chinese, and Mexican cuisines. Campus security is described as "decent" and "UMBC actually has its own police force

> **"UMBC is not a place where alcohol and partying dictates who is cool or not."**

(continued)

Phi Beta Kappa: Yes
Applicants: 10,629
Accepted: 59%
Enrolled: 26%
Grad in 6 Years: 63%
Returning Freshmen: 87%
Academics: ✎ ✎ ✎
Social: ☎ ☎ ☎
Q of L: ★ ★ ★
Admissions: (410) 455-2292
Email Address: admissions@ umbc.edu

Strong Programs:
Biological Sciences
Computer Science and
    Information Systems
Psychology
Financial Economics
Engineering
Bioinformatics
Theatre

Campus Connect provides additional mentoring to undecided freshmen who appear at risk for not completing their degrees.

located on campus," says a junior. In addition, students must swipe their student ID to get into residence halls, and emergency call boxes are stationed throughout the campus.

Students complain that social life can be slow on campus. "Most of the social life at school takes place off campus. The surrounding area offers a better social scene," one senior reports. On campus, a student says,

"We're focused on doing big things and being influential people."

"Most social groups are formed through the organizations on campus—volunteer, cultural, religious, academic, and others." Only 4 percent of the men and 6 percent of the women go Greek, and you're unlikely to find any alcohol-fueled toga parties here. "UMBC is not a place where alcohol and partying dictates who is cool or not," says a junior. "For this reason, alcohol abuse is not prevalent among the students." National acts—including comedians and rock stars—have been known to make an appearance at Quadmania, much to the students' delight. Block Party is "another carnival where all the residential students can win prizes and play games," enthuses a student. "Last year I got to hit my community director in the face with a pie at one of the booths!" Homecoming always draws big crowds and popular road trips include treks into Baltimore (10 minutes away) and Washington, D.C. (40 minutes away).

The UMBC Retrievers compete in Division I and field a number of competitive teams, including men's soccer and lacrosse, volleyball, and men's and women's swimming and diving, track and field, and tennis. The men's soccer team made it to the Final Four in 2016, and swimming and diving have captured multiple America East conference titles in recent years. UMBC is a perennial collegiate chess powerhouse (and regularly makes the Final Four of College Chess), and the university lures talented players with a bevy of scholarships. Intramurals are strong too, and offer more than 15 sports and activities each semester. The Retriever Activities Center offers students 18,000 square feet of fitness and recreation space, including a gymnasium, weight room, fitness studio, indoor pool, and tennis courts.

"I would say that UMBC is a school just coming into its own," says a student. Unlike the gargantuan University of Maryland at College Park, UMBC capitalizes on its small size by providing students with intimate learning communities, solid academics, and ample resources on a manageable scale. It's a combination that appeals to a certain kind of student, according to one junior: "We're focused on doing big things and being influential people."

The highly selective Meyerhoff Scholars Program addresses the shortage of African Americans in the sciences and engineering.

Overlaps

Towson, University of Maryland, University of Delaware, Johns Hopkins, Virginia Tech

If You Apply To ➤ **UMBC:** Early action: Nov. 1. Regular decision: Feb. 1. Financial aid: Dec. 14. Housing: May 1. Application fee: $50. No campus or alumni interviews. SATs or ACTs: required. No Subject Tests. Letters of recommendation: required. Essay: required. Accepts the Common Application.

University of Massachusetts Amherst

Amherst, MA 01003

A liberal mecca in cosmopolitan and scenic western Massachusetts. UMass boasts strong study abroad programs and an international flavor. Business and engineering are also strong. Ready access to privates Amherst, Hampshire, Mount Holyoke, and Smith via the Five College Consortium*. Lack of big-time sports makes for a lower national profile than the likes of Michigan or UNC.

A leading flagship and land grant university with more than 150 years of tradition, the University of Massachusetts Amherst offers students a dizzying array of majors and extracurricular options and the chance to take courses at nearby private colleges that are among the best anywhere. Students can live in one of the nation's top college towns, take advantage of an extensive research program and strong honors program, and enjoy an endless supply of social opportunities—without emptying their wallets.

UMass's sprawling 1,463-acre campus is centered on a pond full of ducks and swans, while architectural styles range from colonial to modern. The school is located on the outskirts of Amherst, a city that combines the energy of a bustling cosmopolitan center with the quaintness of an old New England town. Students agree that Amherst caters to college life. UMass's library system is the largest of any public institution in the Northeast. The campus is undergoing a spate of new construction, including the recently opened Integrative Learning Center, which offers 2,000 seats of new classroom space as well as space for several academic departments.

> "We have nerds, jocks, theater buffs, hippies, and future CEOs."

UMass offers more than 100 undergraduate degree programs, and among them management and engineering are top-ranked. Psychology, biology, kinesiology, and communication are the most popular majors. The English department is notable, and computer science, food science, and linguistics also draw praise. Students report little difficulty getting into courses they want or are required to take, but some regard math, computer science, and the natural sciences as especially tough, and some engineering programs are subject to more than the standard 120 credit hours required by most programs. Students seeking to stand out from the "masses" might consider the interdisciplinary major in social thought and political economy, or the bachelor's degree in individual concentration, a design-it-yourself major. The new Exploratory Track Program places undeclared first-years into one of eight academic advising tracks, based on the interests and academic strengths demonstrated in their admissions applications.

All undergraduates must complete two courses in writing, two courses in basic mathematics and analytic reasoning, two courses in the biological and physical world, four courses in the social world, two courses in social and cultural diversity, and an integrative experience. The writing requirement includes a freshman course taught in sections of 24 or fewer. Commonwealth Honors College offers

> "[Amherst] is a lively— if small—college town."

qualified students special courses and sponsors interdisciplinary seminars, student gatherings, service projects, and a state-of-the-art, $192 million residential complex that includes 1,500 beds, nine classrooms, faculty residences, and space for gathering, advising, and program administration. UMass offers more than 500 study abroad programs in more than 70 countries to about 1,000 students each year. Programs are available in Africa, Asia, Australia, Latin America, South America, and Europe. The Center for Student Business offers one of the most imaginative programs at UMass, allowing students to staff and manage nine campus businesses and learn how to work with others and resolve conflicts professionally.

UMass's intellectual and political climate is extraordinarily fertile for a state university, perhaps in part because of its membership in the Five College Consortium*. This special alliance allows students to attend UMass and take courses (for no extra charge) at the other four consortium schools: Amherst College, Hampshire, Mount Holyoke, and Smith. The university is "definitely competitive," says a student. "The faculty have responded to the demands of serious students by challenging us to learn how to succeed." Full professors teach most courses, and some of the larger courses are broken down into smaller sections with graduate-level teaching

---

Website: www.umass.edu
Location: Small Town
Public
Total Enrollment: 23,133
Undergraduates: 20,962
Male/Female: 52/48
SAT Ranges: CR 550–640, M 580–670
ACT Ranges: 25–30
Financial Aid: 50%
Pell Grant: 21%
Expense: Pub $ $ $ $
Student Loans: 70%
Average Debt: $ $ $
Phi Beta Kappa: Yes
Applicants: 40,010
Accepted: 58%
Enrolled: 20%
Grad in 6 Years: 78%
Returning Freshmen: 91%
Academics: ✐ ✐ ✐ ½
Social: 🕿 🕿 🕿 🕿
Q of L: ★ ★ ★
Admissions: (413) 545-0222
Email Address: mail@admissions.umass.edu

Strong Programs:
Management
Engineering
Psychology
Biology
Kinesiology
Communication
English
Computer Science

The new Exploratory Track Program places undeclared first-years into one of eight academic advising tracks.

assistants; overall, half of all undergraduate classes have fewer than 20 students. "I have had some amazing, out-of-this-world professors," says a junior, "and some abysmal ones." Academic and career counseling receive mixed reviews, and it is usually up to students to pursue career help.

The majority of students are white public school graduates from Massachusetts; 76 percent are in-staters, while 4 percent hail from more than 60 foreign countries. "We have nerds, jocks, theater buffs, hippies, and future CEOs," says a senior. Four percent of UMass students are African American, while 9 percent are Asian American, and another 5 percent are Hispanic. The university has established cultural centers on campus, providing activities and support for students from different backgrounds, but affirmative action is still an issue, students report. "There are always rallies about better programs and aid for minorities," says a senior. Merit scholarships averaging $4,825 are handed out each year, and athletes vie for 260 athletic scholarships in 21 sports. Twenty-one percent of incoming students are eligible for the Pell Grant.

UMass has the third-largest residence-hall system in the country. Fifty-eight percent of students are housed among seven residential areas. The Residential First-Year Experience assigns first-years to living/learning communities with peers who share common interests and experiences. About half of the freshmen end up in the Southwest Area, a "huge, city-like complex" with five high-rise towers and 11 low-rise residence halls. "It is not a problem for students to get housing on campus, the only trouble is getting the housing that they want," says a student. Dining services get good reviews. A senior comments, "The campus is very self-contained, and so I have felt safe on campus even late at night." The UMatter at UMass program works to address issues of bias, sexual assault, hazing, high-risk drinking, and other community challenges.

"If we don't have what you want, we'll give you the opportunity to create it!"

UMass offers "a vast social life," says a student, with noisy dorms, overflowing frat houses, frequent off-campus parties, and more than 300 student organizations of all types. "Most of my social interactions occur on campus during my extracurriculars. On the weekends, we frequent the restaurants and bars in Amherst center, which is a lively—if small—college town," a chemical engineering major says. Both on campus and off, alcohol policies are strict and well enforced; underage drinking is many times confined to students' rooms, if they can get away with it. First-time underage offenders are sent to alcohol-education programs. Eight percent of the men and 6 percent of the women belong to one of the nearly two dozen fraternities and sororities, but they are somewhat out of the mainstream. The Fine Arts Center brings nationally known theater, music, and dance performances to campus year-round. A free public transportation system allows maximum mobility—not only among the Five Colleges, but also to nearby towns, which are graced with a number of exceptional bookshops.

Settled in the Pioneer Valley and surrounded by the Berkshire foothills, Amherst is close to good skiing, hiking, and canoeing areas. It's also 90 miles west of Boston, 150 miles north of New York City, and 25 miles south of Vermont and New Hampshire, making a car very useful (and very expensive if you get too many tickets from overzealous campus cops, students say).

Division I varsity sports are popular, and UMass Minutemen have been a model for achieving gender equity in athletics. Teams compete in the Atlantic 10 Conference; women's field hockey and men's swimming and lacrosse are recent conference champs. Rowing and men's basketball are also solid. Intramural offerings are extensive, and two on-campus gyms offer facilities for the recreational athlete, while two Olympic-size skating rinks mark the recent reintroduction of intercollegiate hockey to the university.

UMass is big enough to offer a vast number of academic and extracurricular opportunities, though at times it can feel impersonal and overwhelming. But with special residential programs that group students with similar languages, cultures, and lifestyles, many students will easily find a home in Amherst. And as one junior cheers, "We have so many resources. If we don't have what you want, we'll give you the opportunity to create it!"

<table>
<tr><td>If You Apply To ➤</td><td>UMass: Early action: Nov. 1. Regular decision: Jan. 15. Financial aid: Mar. 1. Application fee: $75. No campus or alumni interviews. SATs or ACTs: required (SAT essay or ACT writing recommended). No Subject Tests. Letters of recommendation: required. Essay: required. Accepts the Common Application.</td></tr>
</table>

Massachusetts Institute of Technology

Room 3-108, 77 Massachusetts Avenue, Cambridge, MA 02139

If you're a science genius, come to MIT to find out how little you really know. No other school makes such a massive assault on the ego. Technology is a given, but MIT also prides itself on leading programs in economics, political science, and architecture, with unmatched undergraduate research opportunities. Those who don't study 24/7 can let off steam via the surprisingly extensive athletics offerings or enjoy MIT's prime location near downtown Boston.

Founded in 1861, the Massachusetts Institute of Technology continues to attract the brightest minds from near and far. MIT teachers and students have discovered many of the technological innovations that we take for granted, from electromagnets and radar to the decoding of the human genome. The school is a magnet for minds like Tim Berners-Lee, the Brit who invented the World Wide Web, to Noam Chomsky, the linguist and antiwar activist. Graduates have formed more than 25,000 companies that, among other things, employ a quarter of the workforce of Silicon Valley. While Harvard stuck to the English model of Oxbridge classical education, with its emphasis on Latin and Greek, MIT looked to the German system of learning based on research and hands-on experimentation. This emphasis is enshrined in the school motto—*Mens et Manus*, or Mind and Hand—as well as its muscular logo, showing a gowned scholar standing beside an ironmonger bearing a hammer and anvil. Intellect and craftsmanship pervade the classrooms, and students here are not so much taught as engaged and inspired.

MIT is located on 168 acres that extend more than a mile along the Cambridge side of the Charles River basin facing historic Beacon Hill and the central sections of Boston. The main campus of neoclassical architecture carved from limestone was designed by Welles Bosworth and constructed between 1913 and 1920. Since then, more modern designs in brick and glass have been added. The buildings have a utilitarian aura; most are even known by number instead of by name. Athletic playing fields, recreational buildings, dorms, and dining halls are closely arranged on the campus and provide a sense of unity. Sculptures and murals, including the works of Alexander Calder, Henry Moore, and Louise Nevelson, are found throughout the campus. The university's Brain and Cognitive Sciences Complex is the world's largest neuroscience center.

> "Some professors really know how to engage the interest of the student."

Website: web.mit.edu
Location: City Center
Private
Total Enrollment: 11,049
Undergraduates: 4,440
Male/Female: 54/46
SAT Ranges: CR 680–780, M 750–800
ACT Ranges: 33–35
Financial Aid: 91%
Pell Grant: 18%
Expense: Pr $ $ $
Student Loans: 32%
Average Debt: $ $
Phi Beta Kappa: Yes
Applicants: 18,306
Accepted: 8%
Enrolled: 73%
Grad in 6 Years: 92%
Returning Freshmen: 98%
Academics: ✑ ✑ ✑ ✑ ✑
Social: ☎ ☎ ☎
Q of L: ★ ★ ★
Admissions: (617) 253-3400
Email Address: admissions@mit.edu

Whatever their major, all students must fulfill a set of General Institute Requirements consisting of a six-course "science core" that includes calculus and a lab and eight courses in the humanities, arts, and social sciences; there's also an eight-credit physical education requirement. Some of these requirements, most notably calculus, can be fulfilled by AP or International Baccalaureate exams, and students have a choice of focus in the basic science offerings. A basic biology course, for example, might emphasize either genetics or the environment. To fill much of their science core, many students will join one of four Freshman Learning Communities that offer a coherent freshman curriculum, small classes, and common meeting spaces. In addition to the four learning communities, flexible, small-group alternatives for freshmen include the Experimental Study Group, which allows a self-paced course of study based on tutorials instead of a traditional lecture format. Not only can these offer support, but they can also engage geniuses who excel on exams without attending the lectures.

Originally called Boston Tech and now frequently referred to as "the 'Tute," MIT stresses science and engineering studies with a "concern for human values and social goals." Every science and engineering department is superb. The biology department is a leader in medical technology and the search for designer genes. Nevertheless, pure sciences tend to play second fiddle to the engineering fields that, along with computer science, draw the bulk of the majors. Electrical engineering and computer science are almost universally credited as tops in the nation. Students in these two areas may pursue a five-year-degree option, where they can obtain a professional master's degree upon completion of their studies. Biological engineering, chemical engineering, and mechanical engineering; physics; and the aeronautics and astronautics department are also highly praised programs. The most popular majors include computer science and engineering, electrical engineering, mechanical engineering, and biology.

> "MIT is intense and will take you for quite a ride."

For all of its emphasis on science and technology, MIT takes the arts and humanities as well as the social sciences—especially economics—seriously. Technology is, after all, the point where science and the humanities intersect over matters of values. Beyond that, the administration worries that engineers of the future will need first-rate technical skills coupled with a good understanding of technology's social context and marketplace. As one dean puts it, "Too many MIT graduates end up working for too many Princeton and Harvard graduates." Hence, new majors in management, business analytics, and finance are now offered "in response to employers seeking graduates who are better prepared for today's increasingly complex responsibilities." Perhaps to help ensure that they will be able to make their future discoveries known, students must take four communication-intensive subjects. Architecture, political science, urban studies, linguistics, graphics for modern art, and holography—and just about anything else that can be linked to a computer—are strong, and the minority who major in these subjects receive enough personal attention to make any college student envious. "Some professors really know how to engage the interest of the student," says a senior.

New majors in management, business analytics, and finance are now offered.

A pass/no record grading system helps freshmen adjust to "MIT brainstretching": in the first semester, freshmen receive grades of P, D, or F in all subjects they take. P means a C-or-better performance; Ds or Fs do not receive credit or appear on the permanent record. In the second semester, the Ps are replaced by A, B, or C; Ds and Fs do not receive credit and are only noted internally. Grades or not, most MIT students set themselves a breathtaking pace. "MIT is intense and will take you for quite a ride," a biology/premed student says. "The courses demand your full attention and a lot of extra work," another adds. The traditionally humongous introductory physics lectures have been replaced with smaller, hands-on classes that emphasize collaboration. In fact, 64 percent of all undergraduate classes have fewer than 20 students. Along with Harvard, the university has founded an online learning consortium called edX that allows students around the world access to many courses. On campus, students have access to world-renowned professors and the Nobel Prize winners who carry lighter teaching loads to allow them time for research and interaction with students. Faculty advising is "pretty good for freshmen," one student says, but after that, "it's as good as you make it." The vast library system includes some one-of-a-kind manuscripts on the history of science and technology. One library is even open 24 hours a day, and "some students spend the majority of their time (awake or asleep) there," one student reports.

One of MIT's most successful innovations is the Undergraduate Research Opportunities Program, a year-round program that facilitates student/faculty research projects. Considered one of the best programs of its kind in the nation, it allows students to earn course credit or stipends for doing research. Ninety percent of students get involved with collaborative or independent research during their time at MIT. Relief from "tooling" (that is, studying) is found through the optional January Independent Activities Period, which offers noncredit seminars, workshops, and activities in fields outside the regular curriculum, as well as for-credit subjects. Participation in the engineering co-op program, junior year abroad (including a major program at Cambridge University in England), or cross-registration at all-female Wellesley College are other helpful ways to get young noses away from the grindstone.

A pass/no record grading system helps freshmen adjust to "MIT brainstretching."

While MIT somewhat justly earned an image as a "conservative, rich, white boys' school" in the past, there is certainly enough racial and ethnic variety to beat that rap today. African Americans account for 6 percent of the undergraduate student body, Hispanics 15 percent, and Asian Americans a hefty 25 percent. To further welcome diversity, MIT's application now includes an optional question regarding gender identity and sexual orientation, including a "straight" option. Ninety-eight percent of incoming freshmen come from the top 10th of their high school class, and average SAT and ACT scores are simply mind-boggling. In a concession to growing demand, MIT has increased undergraduate enrollment to just over 4,400. Just 8 percent of students are residents of Massachusetts, and 10 percent are international. "The average MIT student can be characterized as having a passion and singular drive for what they really want in life," offers a chemical engineering major. Although there are no merit or athletic scholarships, MIT meets undergraduates' full demonstrated financial need. For students with family incomes less than $75,000 a year, the Institute ensures that scholarship funding from all sources will allow them to attend MIT tuition-free.

"Some students spend the majority of their time (awake or asleep) [at the library]."

Ninety-five percent of undergraduates live on campus, and all freshmen are required to live in the dorms. Guaranteed housing is either single-sex or co-ed; the dorms are in the middle of campus, and most of the fraternities and living groups are a mile or less away across the Charles. Meal plans can be mandatory for dorms that don't have kitchens, or optional for equipped quarters. Frat types feast on spreads prepared by their full-time cooks, and the Kosher Kitchen provides some refuge for others. MIT has recently increased its Title IX staffing, training programs, and educational outreach in an effort to combat campus sexual assault.

Ninety percent of students get involved with collaborative or independent research during their time at MIT.

MIT's social scene is varied. There are campus movies and lectures if one can escape the ubiquitous workload worming its way into the uneasy consciousness of a techie's every waking hour. On-campus dances, parties, and dorm activities also keep students busy. Supposedly, there are more clubs and organizations at MIT than at any other school in the country, and a sampling of the offerings explains why. The Rocket Society, the Guild of Bell Ringers, and a singing group called the Chorallaries are only a few of the diverse interests on this campus. Most on-campus drinking for 21-and-over students is relaxed and accepted, "as long as the alcohol does not result in unlawful behavior or cause any problems," a student explains. MIT's alcohol-prevention program is considered a national model, and drug-prevention initiatives are also comprehensive. The Greek scene attracts 48 percent of the men and 36 percent of the women. For those with the urge to roam, the multifaceted greater Boston metropolis sits only a few subway stops away. The student-friendly city boasts many restaurants, clubs, parks, shopping opportunities, and more than 50 other colleges.

When the MIT megabrains take a break, practical jokes, or "hacks" (described by one student as "practical jokes with technical merit") are sure to follow. In past years, popular hacks have included disguising the dome of the main academic building as a giant breast, dismantling a campus police car and reassembling its body at the top of the tower, unscrewing and reversing all the chairs in a 500-seat lecture hall, and, of course, welding shut Harvard's gates. Hacking can also involve Harry Potter-style late-night explorations by students in the tunnels and shafts that run through restricted parts of the campus, a practice that's definitely frowned upon by the school.

When not studying or hacking, these engineering jocks often turn into real jocks. MIT has 33 varsity sports, the most of any Division III school. Known as the Engineers

with a beaver named Tim (if you can't figure it out, don't bother to apply) as their mascot, teams have earned 17 New England Men's and Women's Athletic Conference titles in the past two years. Men's and women's tennis, cross-country, track and field, and swimming and diving are among the most competitive teams; MIT is also nationally ranked in crew, sailing, and water polo. Hockey is popular, and even more popular is the extensive, well-organized intramural program (roughly 30 percent participate), with sports ranging from Ping-Pong, billiards, and bowling to the more traditional basketball and volleyball. More than 30 instructional and competitive club sports are also available, and everyone has access to MIT's extensive athletic facilities.

Though students often wonder what life at a so-called typical college would have been like, chances of survival and even satisfaction at MIT are excellent. Students are able to comprehend the incredible experience of attending one of the nation's leading academic powerhouses. A biology major puts it bluntly: "It will take you right up to what you think your limits are, and then MIT will shatter them and make you realize how great your potential is."

If You Apply To ➢

MIT: Early action: Nov. 1. Regular decision: Jan. 1. Financial aid: Feb. 15. Application fee: $75. No campus interviews. Alumni interviews: recommended, evaluative. SATs or ACTs: required. Subject Tests: required (one math and one science). Letters of recommendation: required. Essay: required. Application includes optional question regarding gender identity and sexual orientation.

McGill University: See page 369.

University of Miami (FL)

P.O. Box 248025, Coral Gables, FL 33124

Football is a major reason UM is on the map, but it's hardly the only one. Renowned programs in marine science and music are big draws; business is also strong. Housing takes the form of a distinctive residential college system that offers living/learning opportunities. Attracts more Northerners than other leading Florida universities, with geographic reach continuing to expand.

Year-round sunshine and the colorful Miami culture could make even the most dedicated students forget why they are at college. But at the University of Miami, students can have their fun and get a solid education at the same time. The university boasts a boatload of strong programs, including red-hot preprofessional offerings. Sound academics, a diverse and energetic student population, sandy beaches, and a subtropical climate create a perfect storm that attracts talented Hurricanes from far and wide. "At UM you will find diversity, tradition, unity, and rivalry," says one senior, "while getting an exceptional education."

Twenty minutes from Key Biscayne and Miami's beaches, and 10 minutes from downtown Miami, the university's 239-acre campus is located in tranquil suburbia and features tall palms, wide lawns, flowering vines, outdoor sculptures, and even a butterfly garden. The campus, with its own lake right in the middle, is architecturally varied, from postwar, international-style structures to modern buildings, most with open-air breezeways to let in the warm winds. Recent Coral Gables campus additions include a new Enrollment Center to house the undergraduate admissions office and the Center for Experiential Music.

UM's Cognates Program of General Education requires students to take at least three courses in each of three areas of knowledge: arts and humanities, people and society, and STEM (science, technology, engineering, and math). With nine undergraduate schools and colleges and more than 180 majors and programs, UM offers a broad range of preprofessional options as well as those across the liberal arts. The university has one of the nation's top programs in marine biology, and its architecture program is well regarded. UM was the first American university to offer a four-year undergraduate degree in music engineering. It has also developed a unique program in jazz. The university's dual-degree programs in medicine, marine geology, Latin American studies, exercise physiology, law, biology, biochemistry and molecular biology, and computer science receive high marks. The Foote Fellows Honors Program provides high-achieving students more academic flexibility, opportunities for faculty-mentored research, and additional resources. Popular degree programs include business/marketing, biological/life sciences, social sciences, communication/journalism, and engineering.

> "At UM you will find diversity, tradition, unity, and rivalry, while getting an exceptional education."

UM's academic environment manages to be "both competitive and collaborative," says one junior. "Everyone wants to get into the best graduate programs, but they want their peers to do so as well. It can be intense, as students here are some of the best and brightest." Nearly two-thirds of the students graduated in the top 10th of their high school class. Full professors teach most courses, including those with freshmen. Professors "are extremely accessible through office hours, and teaching assistants often reach out to students to help with workshops and extra study sessions," says a business management major. Students looking for a change of pace can take advantage more than 85 study abroad options in dozens of countries,

Website: www.miami.edu
Location: Suburban
Private
Total Enrollment: 15,198
Undergraduates: 10,291
Male/Female: 49/51
SAT Ranges: CR 590–690, M 610–700
ACT Ranges: 28–32
Financial Aid: 74%
Pell Grant: 15%
Expense: Pr $ $ $
Student Loans: 40%
Average Debt: $
Phi Beta Kappa: Yes
Applicants: 33,415
Accepted: 38%
Enrolled: 16%
Grad in 6 Years: 81%
Returning Freshmen: 92%
Academics: ✍ ✍ ✍
Social: ☎ ☎ ☎ ☎
Q of L: ★ ★ ★
Admissions: (305) 284-4323
Email Address: admission@miami.edu

Strong Programs:
Marine Science
Architecture
Music
Business
Biology
Social Sciences
Communication
Engineering

including seven UM semester-on-location programs in Italy, the Czech Republic, Ecuador, South Africa, Argentina, India, and China.

"The students at UM are culturally and academically diverse, with so many interests and passions," says one student. Fifty-seven percent of UM's full-time degree-seeking undergraduate students come from out of state, including quite a few from the Northeast and upper Midwest, seeking respite from harsh weather. UM's student body is impressively diverse; Hispanics account for a substantial 22 percent of the total, African Americans 8 percent, and Asian Americans 6 percent. International students, who represent 14 percent of undergraduates and more than 120 countries, play an integral role in the life of the university. Numerous merit scholarships, averaging $19,071, are available, as are athletic scholarships.

UM offers a distinctive system of five co-ed residential colleges, modeled after those at Oxford and Cambridge. Each residential college is directed by a master—a senior faculty member who organizes seminars, concerts, dinners, social events, and lectures, including guest speakers from all walks of life to discuss current issues.

"Everyone wants to get into the best graduate programs, but they want their peers to do so as well."

Generally, students give the dorms average marks; 37 percent of undergrads live on campus, and others bunk in off-campus apartments or commute. "Housing is slightly dismal in the beginning, but you soon become so engulfed in campus life that you don't mind the dorms at all," says a senior. Scrounging up food on campus is easy. "Our food court is very diverse with just about every food option you can think of," says a senior. Students also report feeling safe on campus, thanks to a robust security program that includes safety escorts and campus shuttles.

UM offers a plethora of social opportunities. "Miami is an incredible city, so there is always something fun to do with friends. The university is also constantly hosting activities on campus in order for students to have the opportunity to enjoy themselves without having to leave campus," says one student. On the weekends, UM students frequent nearby bars or Rathskeller, a popular student meeting place on campus that offers food, entertainment, a venue for postgame parties, and alcohol to students at least 21 years old. Campus alcohol policies are strict for underage students. Fraternities still manage to thrive, accounting for 16 percent of the men. The sororities, with no housing of their own, attract 19 percent of the women. "The drinking and party culture on campus is not something that proves to be a massive issue," says an art history major, and "Greek organizations don't typically set the tone for social life." Students anticipate annual events such as International Week and Sportsfest, which pits dorms against each other in sports ranging from flag football to obstacle courses. The biggest non-sports-related event each year is Gandhi Day, which students spend doing community service.

Coral Gables is not a college town. "We are a college in a big city," says a junior, which means access to events such as Art Basel, Ultra Music Festival, and professional sports teams (Dolphins, Heat, Marlins). Those who shun sand between their toes head to the boutiques in Coconut Grove, Bayside, or South Beach. Public transportation and the Hurry 'Cane Shuttle service run in front of the residential colleges, but most students recommend a car in order to get "the full Florida effect." Parking can be a problem, though, says a senior: "If you want a parking space, you need to get to school by 8:00 a.m." The best road trips are Key West, Key Largo, the Everglades, and, of course, UM football games against the University of Florida and Florida State.

The Hurricanes compete in the Atlantic Coast Conference. The most competitive intercollegiate teams for men are football, baseball, basketball, and diving. Women's tennis, basketball, track, and diving are solid too. Men's diving brought home a recent individual national championship title, while women's tennis is

UM was the first American university to offer a four-year undergraduate degree in music engineering.

International students represent 14 percent of undergraduates and more than 120 countries.

Each residential colleges is directed by a master—a senior faculty member who organizes social events.

a recent conference champ. In a bow to Harry Potter fans, the extensive club sports program includes Quidditch. The university also has a state-of-the-art fitness, recreation, and wellness facility that includes an 18,000-square-foot fitness room and basketball, racquetball, squash, and tennis courts, plus an indoor pool and a juice bar.

It's hard to imagine a school in the Sunshine State without a generous allotment of fun, and UM is no exception. "Though we're not the number one party school in the nation anymore, we still really love to have a great time," observes a junior. That said, UM students these days are just as likely to search long and hard for the perfect instrumental phrase or mathematical proof as they are to scope out the perfect wave. Says one happy Hurricane, "The biggest complaint is that students don't have enough time in four years to access all the amazing things available."

> "You soon become so engulfed in campus life that you don't mind the dorms at all."

If You Apply To ➤ **Miami:** Early decision I and early action: Nov. 1. Early decision II, regular decision, and financial aid: Jan. 1. Housing: May 1. Application fee: $70. Campus interviews: optional, informational. No alumni interviews. SATs (with essay) or ACTs (with writing): required. Subject Tests: required for some (math and one science required for dual-degree program in medicine and biochemistry/molecular biology). Letters of recommendation: required. Essay: required. Apply to particular schools or programs. Accepts the Common Application with supplement.

Miami University (OH)

301 S. Campus Avenue, Oxford, OH 45056

Rather than disappear into the black hole of Ohio State, top students in the Buckeye state come here to feel as if they are going to an elite private university. MU is the honors public university in one of the nation's largest states. Twice the size of William and Mary, Miami has the same classic look but is much less selective. Miami's top draw is business, and its tenor is preppy/conservative. Bring your best clothes.

This Miami is about 1,000 miles from South Beach, but that doesn't mean it's without sizzle. The academic kind, that is. Miami University is actually tucked into a corner of Ohio and is gaining national recognition as an excellent state university that has the true look and feel of a private, with a picture-perfect campus and high-caliber student body.

The university is staked out on 2,100 wooded acres in the center of an urban triangle of approximately three million people, encompassing Cincinnati and Dayton, Ohio, and Richmond, Indiana. The campus is dressed in the modified Georgian style of the colonial American period, and it remains as impeccably groomed as its sharply attired students. Recent campus additions

> "[Professors] are dedicated to assisting students both in their educational and personal development."

include residence halls on Miami's scenic Western Campus and a dining hall featuring special selections, including vegan options. Renovations to Shideler Hall, home to the geology and geography departments and the Institute for the Environment and Sustainability, were completed in 2016.

Miami University was founded in 1809 to provide a classical liberal education and has never strayed from its central commitment to the liberal arts. All undergraduates must complete the Global Miami Plan for Liberal Education, which provides them with a background in fine arts, humanities, social sciences, natural sciences,

Website: www.miamioh.edu
Location: Small City
Public
Total Enrollment: 16,650
Undergraduates: 15,667
Male/Female: 49/51
SAT Ranges: CR 550–650, M 590–690
ACT Ranges: 26–30
Financial Aid: 72%
Pell Grant: 10%
Expense: Pub $ $ $ $
Student Loans: 53%
Average Debt: $ $ $
Phi Beta Kappa: Yes
Applicants: 27,454
Accepted: 66%
Enrolled: 21%
Grad in 6 Years: 79%

(continued)

Returning Freshmen: 90%
Academics: ✏ ✏ ✏ ✏ ½
Social: ☎ ☎ ☎
Q of L: ★ ★ ★
Admissions: (513) 529-2531
Email Address: admission@
  miamioh.edu

Strong Programs:
Finance
Marketing
Accountancy
Psychology
Architecture and Interior
  Design
Biology
International Studies
Interactive Media Studies

The Scripps
Gerontology Center,
which offers a major
and a minor in
gerontology, is one
of the oldest of its
kind in the country.

mathematics, formal reasoning, technology, and globally oriented courses/study abroad. Additional components include an experiential learning opportunity and an advanced writing requirement; all Miami Plan courses promote competency in written communication as well as critical-thinking skills. Students must also fulfill a thematic sequence requirement by taking three related courses outside their major, and they must complete a capstone experience their senior year.

Popular majors include finance, marketing, accountancy, and psychology. Programs in architecture and interior design, biology, and international studies have also been traditional strengths. Students majoring in interactive media studies investigate the impact of a wide range of digital technologies, such as ecommerce, game design, social media marketing, and virtual and augmented reality,

"The majority of students at my school are the typical rich white American who is Republican."

and take a consulting course in which they work with a real corporate client. The Scripps Gerontology Center, which offers a major and a minor in gerontology, is one of the oldest of its kind in the country.

"The academic climate at Miami is both competitive and collaborative," says a biology major. "Students are encouraged to work together, but each student is also individually motivated to succeed." Professors are lauded for their knowledge and willingness to help. "The professors are extremely knowledgeable and accomplished within their fields of study and are dedicated to assisting students both in their educational and personal development," one student says. Thirty-two percent of classes have fewer than 20 students, and most are taught by full professors, though graduate students do appear behind the lectern from time to time.

The three-week Winter Term allows students to take a class, study abroad, conduct research, or participate in an internship. A hefty forty-two percent of students head for foreign climes each year. Miami's Dolibois European Center in Luxembourg offers summer, semester, or year-long study and an opportunity to live with a foreign family. Other opportunities spanning more than 90 countries include exchanges with foreign universities, as well as summer and winter programs. Undergraduate research gets a lot of attention at Miami too. The Office of Research for Undergraduates sponsors several competitive programs, including the Undergraduate Summer Scholars Program, which gives 100 students a stipend, free tuition, and a project allowance to complete a nine-week faculty-mentored project. Each year, more than 2,000 Miami undergraduates work with professors on funded research, many starting in their freshman year.

"The majority of students at my school are the typical rich white American who is Republican," says a sophomore. Racial and socioeconomic diversity are lacking, although the university is working to boost both; 3 percent of undergraduates are African American, 4 percent are Hispanic, and 2 percent are Asian American, while just 10 percent qualify for Pell Grants. Another 10 percent come from foreign countries. Fifty-eight percent of students are from Ohio, and the campus has a reputation

"Every time I step foot on campus, I just want to be a better version of me."

for conservatism. Paul Ryan, the Republican Speaker of the House of Representatives, learned his trickle-down economics here. The *New York Times* suggested that Miami appeals to Republican families as "a place unlikely to turn their children against them." The Office of Diversity Affairs, the Center for American and World Cultures, and various student groups regularly hold events designed to encourage awareness of diversity, difference, and privilege. Thousands of merit scholarships, averaging about $8,000 each, and 270 athletic scholarships in 19 sports are awarded annually.

Forty-six percent of the student body call the campus home. "Students tend to live off campus after their second year, but the dorms are comfortable and typically well maintained," says one junior. Miami offers 29 theme-based living/learning communities (LLCs); 24 are for first-year students. The LLCs center on interests such as the arts, leadership, premedicine, entrepreneurship, and cultural perspectives, among others. Students report that campus dining options are diverse and tasty, and campus security is good, "mostly due to the fact that we are in a sleepy little town in Ohio." Students say sexual assault is not a big problem on campus, and according to administrators, the university is working to "create a culture where sexual and interpersonal violence is unacceptable and survivors are supported."

"Social life is a vital part of college at Miami, as students enjoy going out at night and on the weekends. Most of the social events take place off campus," says one student. Drinking is a popular pastime, but the school is "very strict about alcohol violations," explains one student. "There is no tolerance for minors drinking on campus." A lot of socializing takes place in the restaurants, bars, and clubs of Oxford, although students say on-campus activities organized by Late Night Miami, such as movie screenings, musical performances, craft nights, and casino nights, are a fun alternative. Miami also offers more than 400 student organizations. Annual events include homecoming and continued rivalries with Ohio University. Twenty-three percent of the men and 31 percent of the women belong to fraternities or sororities, respectively. In fact, Miami is known as the "Mother of Fraternities" because several national ones began here. Despite the hard-partying reputation of the Greeks, Miami boasts one of the best graduation rates in the nation among public institutions. "Oxford may be a small town, but there is plenty to do," says a strategic communications major. For students who crave brighter lights and a bigger city, Cincinnati is about 35 miles away.

In the past two years, a number of Miami's Division I RedHawks teams have won championships, including women's tennis (eighth straight MAC championship and NCAA appearance), men's golf, men's ice hockey, field hockey, softball, and synchronized skating (12th consecutive Division I national title and finished ninth at the world championships). The mock trial team has placed in the top five at the American Mock Trial Association national championships for three consecutive years. Intramurals and club sports attract more than 12,000 participants annually, and popular sports include women's ice hockey, broomball, soccer, and ultimate Frisbee.

Miami University, with its strong emphasis on liberal arts and its opportunities for research, travel abroad, and leadership, is looked upon as one of the rising stars among state universities. The school effectively combines a wide range of academic programs with the personal attention ordinarily found only at much smaller, upscale institutions. Says one premed major, "Every time I step foot on campus, I just want to be a better version of me, and it is amazing that I am able to do that through the resources of the institution."

Each year, more than 2,000 Miami undergraduates work with professors on funded research.

Miami is known as the "Mother of Fraternities" because several national ones began here.

Overlaps

Ohio State, Indiana University, University of Michigan, University of Illinois at Urbana–Champaign, University of Dayton, Purdue, Penn State, Michigan State

If You Apply To >

Miami (OH): Early decision: Nov. 15. Early action: Dec. 1. Regular decision: Feb. 1. Priority financial aid: Dec. 1. Housing: May 1. Application fee: $50. No campus or alumni interviews. SATs or ACTs: required. No Subject Tests. Letters of recommendation: required. Essay: required. Accepts the Common Application.

1220 Student Activities Building, 515 East Jefferson Street, Ann Arbor, MI 48109

The most interesting mass of humanity east of UC–Berkeley. UM is among the nation's best in most subjects, but undergraduates must elbow their way to the front to get the full benefit. Superb honors and living/learning programs are the best bet for highly motivated students. Out-of-state families may need a second mortgage to cover pricey tuition.

Website: www.umich.edu
Location: Small City
Public
Total Enrollment: 40,758
Undergraduates: 27,161
Male/Female: 50/50
SAT Ranges: CR 630–730, M 660–770
ACT Ranges: 29–33
Financial Aid: 53%
Pell Grant: 15%
Expense: Pub $ $ $ $
Student Loans: 44%
Average Debt: $ $
Phi Beta Kappa: Yes
Applicants: 51,761
Accepted: 26%
Enrolled: 45%
Grad in 6 Years: 90%
Returning Freshmen: 97%
Academics: ✍ ✍ ✍ ✍ ✍
Social: ☎ ☎ ☎
Q of L: ★ ★ ★
Admissions: (734) 764-7433
Email Address: N/A

Strong Programs:
Business Administration
Psychology
Economics
Political Science
Engineering
Foreign Languages
Pharmaceutical Sciences
Public Health Sciences

One of the nation's elite public universities, Michigan offers an excellent faculty, dynamite athletics, an endless number of special programs, and the most interesting collection of students east of Berkeley. It also produces more Fulbright scholars than any other U.S. university. "Michigan is a special place because it has a deep history and reputation," says a senior. "It is an excellent school and no matter what degree you have, it is respected."

Situated on 3,211 acres, Michigan's campus is so extensive that newcomers may want to come equipped with maps and a GPS system to find their way to class. The university is divided into two main campuses. Central Campus, the heart of the university, houses most of Michigan's 19 schools and colleges. North Campus, which is two miles northeast of Central, is home to the College of Engineering; the School of Music, Theatre, and Dance; the Stamps School of Art and Design; and the Taubman College of Architecture and Urban Planning. Other campus areas include the Medical Center Complex, containing seven hospitals and 15 outpatient facilities, and South Campus, featuring state-of-the-art athletic facilities. Architecturally, the main drag of campus

> **"Michigan is a special place because it has a deep history and reputation."**

features a wide range of styles, from the classical Angell Hall to the ultracontemporary Museum of Art addition. Recent construction includes the 78,000-square-foot School of Nursing Building, which features a high-tech clinical learning center.

Michigan offers more than 600 active degree programs, including more than 250 undergraduate majors, as well as individualized concentrations. No courses are required of all freshmen at Michigan, but all students must complete some coursework in English (including composition), foreign languages, natural sciences, social sciences, and humanities. Students in the College of Literature, Science, and the Arts must also take courses in quantitative reasoning and race or ethnicity.

The university ranks among the best in the nation in many fields of study, mainly because it attracts some of the biggest names in academia to teach and research in Ann Arbor. The College of Literature, Science, and the Arts is the largest school at Michigan, offering the most undergraduate majors, including a number of foreign language majors not found at many other places, such as Arabic, Armenian, Persian, Russian, and Turkish. The screen arts and cultures major balances studies and production with studies occupying approximately two-thirds of a student's coursework and the remaining one-third devoted to creative, hands-on projects. The College of Engineering and Ross School of Business are well respected, and the university's programs in health-related fields are also top-notch. A preferred admissions program guarantees 150 top high school students admission to Michigan's programs in architecture, business, education, information, pharmaceutical sciences, or social work, provided they make satisfactory progress during their first years. The most popular majors are business administration, psychology, economics, and political science. New offerings include a B.S.E. degree in climate and meteorology and a B.S. or B.A. degree in gender and health.

Academically, students describe the courses as challenging and rigorous but not cutthroat competitive. "People always want to do their best, and they work very hard to do so," says a senior. Fifty-seven percent of classes have fewer than 20 students, and one student says, "The professors here are intelligent and seem to enjoy teaching." Students claim there is excellent academic and career advising available, but only for those who seek it. The administration, however, notes that the advising offices on campus, which serve more than 30,000 clients each year, offer individually tailored services and workshops. The campus Career Center processes about 120,000 transactions each year, provides individual and group career counseling/planning and individual job placement, and works with 950 companies annually in recruiting UM graduating students.

Michigan's special academic programs seek to offer the best of both worlds—personalized attention and a large university setting. The First Year Experience is a themed living community, paired with an introductory course taught in the residence halls, designed to support students through the transition to college; past programming has included movie nights, ice cream socials, a trip to Michigan's Upper Peninsula to learn dog sledding, and discussions about how to promote environmental sustainability. The university's long-established honors program, considered to be one of the best in the nation, offers qualified students special honors courses and seminars, opportunities to participate in individual or collaborative research, and access to special academic advisors. The Comprehensive Studies Program offers specialized academic support designed to help first-generation and underrepresented students best realize their potential. About 1,300 students each year work outside the classroom with a small group of students and a faculty member of their choice through the Undergraduate Research Opportunities Program. Off-campus opportunities abound at UM too. Students have the chance to visit and study abroad in more than 60 countries. Specific programs include a year abroad in a French or German university, a business program in Paris, summer internships in selected majors, and special trips organized by individual departments.

Fifty-eight percent of undergraduates hail from Michigan, and 7 percent come from abroad. The student body is notably diverse for a midwestern state university. African Americans make up 4 percent of the student body, Hispanics 5 percent, and Asian Americans 13 percent. Michigan's Program on Intergroup Relations has served as a national model for supporting diversity on college campuses, offering a variety of intergroup dialogues, courses and workshops on social justice, and community outreach programs. There are large and well-organized Jewish and LGBTQ communities here too. While the student body is more conservative today than it was a decade ago, it is still "most noticeably liberal," says a history major, and political issues flare up from time to time on campus. Students can vie for thousands of merit scholarships averaging $7,813, as well as 638 athletic scholarships for men and women in 27 sports. Michigan is the only public university in the state that meets the full demonstrated financial need of all in-state students. And although the university really socks it to out-of-staters with a hefty surcharge roughly triple the in-state tuition rate, the Provost's Award meets the full demonstrated need of the neediest out-of-state admits.

Dormitories at UM traditionally have well-defined personalities. East Quad, as the home to the Residential College, the Michigan Community Scholars Program, and the Gender-Inclusive Learning Experience, is perhaps the most "open-minded" dorm on campus. North Quad is the newest dorm and the focal point for international

First Year Experience programming has included a trip to Michigan's Upper Peninsula to learn dog sledding.

"People always want to do their best, and they work very hard to do so."

Michigan's Program on Intergroup Relations has served as a national model for supporting diversity on college campuses.

"Ann Arbor is a quintessential college town, with a wide range of cultural opportunities."

and intercultural programming. On-campus housing is comfortable and well maintained, and 34 percent of students reside there. Lodgings are guaranteed for all incoming freshmen, leaving many upperclassmen to play the lottery. "Many of the juniors and seniors live off campus. The housing is nothing to write home about," says a senior. Other alternatives include fraternity and sorority houses, and a large number of college- and privately owned co-ops. As for concerns about safety on campus, a student says, "Campus security is pretty good and most people I know feel safe." The university recently expanded its mandatory sexual assault prevention education programming beyond incoming freshmen to also include new staff, faculty, and graduate students.

Detroit is a little less than an hour away, but most students become quite fond of the picturesque town of Ann Arbor. "Ann Arbor is a quintessential college town, with a wide range of cultural opportunities and ways for students to get involved," a sophomore says. A surprising variety of visual and performing arts are offered in town and on campus. A senior has a stern warning for any potential underage drinkers: "Your fake ID will be taken. Plan on it. Do not be surprised, no matter how good it is." An art fair held each summer in Ann Arbor draws craftspeople from throughout the nation and Canada. Many lakes and swimming holes lay only a short drive away and seem to keep the large summer-term population happy. Michigan winters, though, are known for being cold and brutal. Seventeen percent of the men and 24 percent of the women go Greek. As one junior says, "We are ranked high enough to be known for our academic success, but we still have a reputation for having a good time."

Division I football overshadows nearly everything each fall as students gather to cheer, "Go Blue." Despite a few shaky seasons on the gridiron, the Wolverines are rebounding under new leadership. Attending football games is an integral part of the UM experience, students say, although one sophomore quips, "You shouldn't be allowed to graduate if you haven't gone to a hockey game." The Little Brown Jug football competition with Minnesota is popular.

"We still have a reputation for having a good time."

Men's cross-country, men's and women's swimming and diving, and women's gymnastics, water polo, and softball each brought home Big Ten championships in the past year. Intramurals, which were invented at the University of Michigan, provide students with a more casual form of athletics. The university's Solar Car Team has won numerous American Solar Challenge competitions in recent years.

The University of Michigan strives to offer its students a delicate balance between academics, athletics, and social activities. On one hand, this is an American college with the usual interest in football and fraternities. But it's also a world-class university with a fine faculty and top-rated programs, intent on making America competitive in the 21st century. For assertive students who crave spirit and action as well as outstanding academics, Michigan is an excellent choice.

Overlaps

Michigan State, Northwestern, Cornell University, University of Illinois at Urbana–Champaign, Washington University in St. Louis, University of Wisconsin–Madison, UC–Berkeley, UCLA

If You Apply To >

Michigan: Rolling admissions: Feb. 1. Early action: Nov. 1. Financial aid: Apr. 30. Application fee: $75. Campus and alumni interviews: optional, informational. SATs (with essay) or ACTs (with writing): required. Subject Tests: required for homeschooled students (English, math, science, foreign language, and social studies). Letters of recommendation: required. Essay: required. Accepts the Common Application with supplement. Apply to particular school or program. Policies and deadlines vary by school.

Michigan State University

250 Administration Building, East Lansing, MI 48824

Most people don't realize that Michigan State is significantly bigger than the University of Michigan. Students can find a niche in strong preprofessional programs such as hospitality business management, prevet, business, and engineering. MSU's self-contained campus is like a town unto itself, with shuttle buses available to get from one side to the other.

Michigan State's roots are agricultural—the school became the state's land grant institution in 1862—and future farmers and veterinarians still flourish here. So do those with wanderlust, thanks to study abroad programs on each of the world's seven continents. MSU's programs in natural sciences and multidisciplinary social sciences offer students the feel of a small, liberal arts college and the resources of a large research university. "Resources here abound," says a senior.

The heart of the MSU campus, north of the Red Cedar River, boasts ivy-covered brick buildings, some of which predate the Civil War and are listed on the National Register of Historic Places. This area houses five colleges plus the MSU Union and 10 residence halls. Across the river are the medical complex, newer dorms, and two 18-hole golf courses. Most notably, MSU is home to the National Superconducting Cyclotron Laboratory. Current construction includes the $730 million Facility for Rare Isotope Beams, which is operated in partnership with the U.S. Department of Energy and expected to be completed in 2022. On the southernmost part of campus are farms and animal research and teaching facilities.

Michigan State students tend to be preprofessional and clear about their interests; the premed and prevet programs are strong, and the most popular majors include business, communications and journalism, education, various fields in the social sciences, and engineering. More unusual options include museum studies, supply-chain management, and hospitality business management; students in the latter program

"Resources here abound."

get real-world experience by staffing the university hotel. To graduate, all students must satisfy university requirements in math and writing, complete a major, and take a minimum of 26 credits in the integrative studies program, which includes arts and humanities; social, behavioral, and economic sciences; and biological and physical sciences.

The climate at MSU gets tougher as students advance through their majors, according to a junior. "Many of our courses are very competitive because they play a part in determining whether or not you are accepted into a specific program," adds a classmate. Courses are large, with 23 percent enrolling more than 50 students. Students say that, for the most part, professors are accessible and dedicated. "I've learned so much from my professors," says one senior. Freshmen may participate in special study-away programs or take part in residential programs that focus on international themes, political science, and the environment, among others. The Honors College emphasizes individualized academic program planning, rather than a tightly prescribed set of courses, and offers the intimacy of a small-college atmosphere. MSU has a strong international component as well, with more than 275 study abroad programs in 60 countries.

"Students here are friendly and diverse," says an elementary education major. "We also have a large international population, which is really cool because it gives you the opportunity to get to know people and cultures from all over the world." Seventy-five percent of undergraduates are Michigan residents, and 13 percent are

Website: www.msu.edu
Location: Suburban
Public
Total Enrollment: 43,248
Undergraduates: 35,425
Male/Female: 49/51
SAT Ranges: CR 450–580, M 530–680
ACT Ranges: 23–28
Financial Aid: 53%
Pell Grant: N/A
Expense: Pub $ $ $ $
Student Loans: 43%
Average Debt: $ $
Phi Beta Kappa: Yes
Applicants: 35,300
Accepted: 66%
Enrolled: 34%
Grad in 6 Years: 79%
Returning Freshmen: 93%
Academics: ✍ ✍ ✍
Social: ☎ ☎ ☎ ☎
Q of L: ★ ★ ★
Admissions: (517) 355-8332
Email Address:
admis@msu.edu

Strong Programs:
Business
Communications and Journalism
Education
Social Sciences
Engineering
Premed
Prevet
Hospitality Business Management

international. Whether they come from gritty Motor City or pretty Traverse City, or from somewhere outside the Midwest, Michigan State students care about the world around them. Indeed, more than 2,300 alumni have served in the Peace Corps since the school first partnered with the agency in 1961, a milestone reached by only four other universities. There's a balance between conservative and liberal factions on campus, says a premed student. African Americans make up 7 percent of the student body, Asian Americans add 5 percent, and Hispanics constitute 4 percent. Scholarships are offered in 25 Division I sports, and thousands of students also receive grants and awards based on academic merit, which average $9,055 annually.

Thirty-nine percent of MSU students—but nearly all freshmen—live in Michigan State's dorms, which one sophomore describes as "very convenient and well maintained." Those seeking the "traditional" college experience can bunk in one of three huge living/learning complexes, each with about four residence halls plus libraries, faculty offices, classrooms, cafeterias, and recreation areas. There are also residential colleges housing fewer than 1,000 students each. Other living/learning programs,

"Many of our courses are very competitive."

known by their catchy acronyms, include RISE (focus on the environment), ROIAL (arts and letters), ROSES (science and engineering), and STAR (Support Teamwork Achievement Resources). All 27 of the school's residence halls are to be updated by 2020. MSU's dining services dish out 32,000 meals a day at 11 cafeterias, where salad, soup, and dessert bars help satisfy those who crave variety. "All the food is edible," says a senior.

Safety is not a huge issue here; green-light emergency telephones are sprinkled throughout the campus, walking escorts are available for those who stay late at the library, and Lansing's bus system offers cheaper night-owl rates for those living farther away. Still, parking places are in chronically short supply, and students complain about the tickets they receive as a result. Once they've earned 28 credits, which can be as soon as the spring of the first year, students may move off campus. Many do so because the city of East Lansing, just outside Michigan's capital, offers all the positive aspects of a large urban area (the population more than doubles when school is in session), along with the safety and community feel of a much smaller town. According to one student, "The social life at MSU is very lively on the weekends." Eight percent of MSU men and 7 percent of the women go Greek. Other weekend alternatives include bands, dances, and comedians brought in by the Student Activities Board. Second-run movies are also shown in Wells Hall—free for campus dwellers, and a couple of bucks for those who live off campus.

Weekends are dominated by Division I Big Ten athletic competitions, with the Michigan–MSU rivalry especially fierce. "Our large campus is filled from end to end with individuals sporting green and white; alcohol-free tailgating is also available,"

"The social life at MSU is very lively on the weekends."

says a junior. "Seeing 150,000 people in a space that usually has about 60,000 is quite an experience." The football team brought home the 2015 Cotton Bowl championship, while men's basketball reached the Final Four. After more than six decades of standing guard at Kalamazoo Street and Red Cedar Road, the school's mascot, affectionately known as "Sparty," has moved indoors to protect him from the elements (and predatory Wolverines). However, a replica stands outside and is guarded by students when the University of Michigan comes to town. Students are still able to paint "the Rock," a large boulder donated in the 1960s, to advertise campus events, birthdays, anniversaries, and the like.

Although the majority of MSU students are from the state of Michigan, they're a cosmopolitan lot. Future leaders, physicians, and financiers happily coexist here, in a "diverse, friendly, and expressive" bunch. And despite the university's size, a food science major says, "The majority of people are incredibly nice, outgoing, and laid-back."

Middlebury College

Middlebury, VT 05753

Set in the picturesque and ski-friendly Green Mountains of Vermont, Middlebury is a magnet for students with serious interests in environmental sciences and international studies. Known worldwide for its summer foreign language programs. Varsity and intramural sports play big role in campus culture, which may help explain why Middlebury was the first college to play Quidditch.

For some, Middlebury College's campus, with its picturesque sunsets, excellent skiing, and rural Vermont charm, may bring to mind a resort, but this school's rigorous workload means four years here is far from a vacation. Middlebury is a paradise for those interested in environmental studies, second and third languages, and a tight-knit community where highly motivated and intelligent students and faculty truly care about each other.

The college's 350-acre main campus overlooks the village of Middlebury, Vermont, which a junior describes as a "small, quaint Vermont town of 8,500 people and five stoplights." The 1,800-acre mountain campus, site of the Bread Loaf School of English, the Bread Loaf Writers' Conference, and the college's Snow Bowl, is nearby. Old Stone Row cuts across the campus, where buildings with simple lines and rectangular shapes evoke the mills of early New England. (Middlebury was founded in 1800.) Academic halls and dormitories of marble and limestone sit in quadrangles and feature views of the Adirondack and Green mountains. The new, 110,000-square-foot Virtue Field House provides a bevy of athletic facilities and exercise equipment.

"Midd kids" must take a discussion-based, writing-intensive First-Year Seminar with only 15 students; the instructor serves as advisor to those enrolled until they declare a major. By the end of sophomore year, students must complete a second writing-intensive course. In addition to a 10- to 16-credit major, students must also satisfy distribution requirements in seven of eight academic areas: literature, the arts,

> **"The small class sizes make it so that students form deep connections with their professors."**

philosophical and religious studies, history, physical and life sciences, deductive reasoning and analytical processes, social analysis, and foreign language. Students also take four cultures and civilizations classes and two noncredit courses in physical education. With all of these requirements, it's no wonder students and faculty become close. Students agree that the academic atmosphere is very collaborative, and the quality of teaching is "extremely high," according to one political science major. An economics major adds, "The work is rigorous, but the small class sizes make it so that students form deep connections with their professors and hence receive more personalized help with assignments." About 20 percent of students per semester collaborate with faculty on research projects.

Between June and August, Middlebury banishes English from its campus and hundreds of students live, learn, and, hopefully, think only in their chosen language.

Website: www.middlebury.edu
Location: Small Town
Private
Total Enrollment: 2,502
Undergraduates: 2,502
Male/Female: 48/52
SAT Ranges: CR 630–750, M 640–750
ACT Ranges: 29–33
Financial Aid: 45%
Pell Grant: 16%
Expense: Pr $ $ $ $
Student Loans: 41%
Average Debt: $
Phi Beta Kappa: Yes
Applicants: 8,891
Accepted: 17%
Enrolled: 38%
Grad in 6 Years: 94%
Returning Freshmen: 97%
Academics: 🖎 🖎 🖎 🖎 ½
Social: ☎ ☎ ☎
Q of L: ★ ★ ★
Admissions: (802) 443-3000
Email Address: admissions@middlebury.edu

Strong Programs:
Foreign Languages
English
Geography
Psychology
Economics
Political Science

The language departments continue their excellent instruction during the school year; especially notable are German, Chinese, Japanese, and Hebrew. Although there is no foreign language requirement, just about everyone studies another tongue, if only to take advantage of Middlebury's campuses at 37 universities in 17 countries around the world, from Italy and India to China and Cameroon. The school is also a member of the Maritime Studies Program* and there are 90 college-approved study abroad programs in total; about 60 percent of juniors take advantage of them. "Middlebury is renowned for its language departments, but the departments across the board are strong. The sciences are phenomenal, with one of the most beautiful science buildings I've ever seen," says a student. Other highly touted Middlebury departments include English (one of the school's most popular majors, bolstered by its connections to the famed Bread Loaf Writers' Conference), geography, and psychology. Economics, political science, neuroscience, and environmental studies are also popular.

"Middlebury students are driven, passionate, humble, and have a multitude of interests," says one sophomore. "Although all students are incredibly intelligent, they are also compassionate and generally easy-going." Seventy-four percent of Middlebury's students graduated in the top tenth of their high school class, and just 7 percent come from within the state; 11 percent come from abroad. Six percent of students are Asian American, 9 percent are Hispanic, and 3 percent are African American. All first-year students participate in a one-day, student-run program called JusTalks, which facilitates discussions on race and other topics. The campus leans left politically, and hot-button issues include human rights and environmental causes. In fact, the Sierra Club rates Middlebury top in the nation for its environmental efforts, which include reliance on a wind turbine and systematic efforts to help students recycle. There are no merit or athletic scholarships, but the college is committed to a need-blind admissions policy and to meeting 100 percent of admitted students' demonstrated financial need.

> "The dining facilities require no swipes or meal plans."

> Middlebury has campuses at 37 universities in 17 countries around the world.

Few Middlebury students live off campus (5 percent), since housing is guaranteed for four years. For the first two years, students live in traditional residence halls grouped into living/learning communities called Commons. Upperclassmen can choose from a range of options, such as suites, college-owned townhouses, the Environmental House (where residents cook all of their own food), and academic interest houses, while still remaining members of their original Commons. A student says, "Housing is quite nice in my opinion. There isn't any air-conditioning though, so bring a fan for the first few weeks of school!" The school's five dining halls get high marks for their tasty victuals, friendly staff, and accommodations for students with dietary restrictions. "The dining facilities require no swipes or meal plans: you simply walk in, grab food, and leave (and maybe come back for more)," says a junior. Students say they feel safe on campus—"It's hard to feel *unsafe* in rural Vermont," reasons one sophomore—and appreciate the school's responsiveness to sexual assault prevention. "The college provides a ton of resources for students and survivors, and it fosters a strong social community in which students work together to prevent cases of sexual violence," reports a junior.

> "[Middlebury is] the quintessential New England town, straight out of Norman Rockwell."

> The Sierra Club rates Middlebury top in the nation for its environmental efforts.

Students at Middlebury play as hard on the weekends as they work during the week. "Most social scenes or parties are what you make of them and almost any kind of Saturday night (from staying in, to watching a movie with friends, to going to a party) can be found and is acceptable," says a sophomore. Those who stay on campus are treated to school-sponsored dances, plays, dance performances, or parties at the Greek-like co-ed social houses, which draw 9 percent of students. (Middlebury has banned fraternities and sororities.) There are more than 170 student organizations, and Middlebury was the first college to play Quidditch. Kegs are prohibited in the dorms but permitted at parties, which must be registered and also offer nonalcoholic drinks and snacks. Despite the policies, alcohol consumption is common among underage students and "the college is pretty lenient about alcohol," a Spanish and geography double major reports. The three-day Winter Carnival is a major annual extravaganza including parties, cultural events, an all-school formal, sporting competitions, snow sculpture, and ice-skating at an outdoor rink.

Off campus, Middlebury is "the quintessential New England town, straight out of Norman Rockwell" that is "intrinsically linked to the school." It has necessities such as fast food, grocery stores, drug stores, hardware stores, and clothing shops, and students are actively involved in the community. "Community service is a big part of who we are here at Midd," says a sophomore. February can be grim because the snow here comes early and stays late, so road trips are popular. The progressive city of Burlington is 45 minutes away, while Montreal is a three-hour drive, Boston four, and New York City five. Middlebury's own Snow Bowl and proximity to most Vermont ski slopes make this a paradise for ski fanatics, a breed Middlebury attracts in predictably large numbers.

> *For the first two years, students live in traditional residence halls grouped into living/learning communities called Commons.*

"We're a small liberal arts college [that is] big on individuality and character."

Middlebury athletics draw rabid fans, especially when cheering on the powerful Panthers ice hockey teams—men's and women's—that compete in Division III against archrival Norwich; townspeople support the hockey games and the teams' members give back by tutoring in local schools. The college offers 31 varsity sports and has won more than 30 national titles since 1995, most recently in women's lacrosse in 2016 and field hockey in 2015. Recent conference champs include men's tennis and golf. About half of the student body is active in the large intramural and club sports program, with soccer, basketball, softball, and, of course, Quidditch drawing the most interest.

Students have noticed physical changes at Middlebury over the past few years, with more in the works, and have seen the school grow more rigorous and competitive. But some things have remained the same—namely, the combination of "excellent academics with endless extracurricular opportunities," says a student. "We're a small liberal arts college [that is] big on individuality and character," a sophomore says. "Whatever your character, you'll find your niche."

Overlaps

Dartmouth, Yale, Brown, Williams, Princeton, Harvard, Amherst, Bowdoin

If You Apply To > **Middlebury:** Early decision I: Nov. 1. Early decision II and regular decision: Jan. 1. Financial aid: Feb. 1. Housing: May 1. Application fee: $65. No campus interviews. Alumni interviews: optional, evaluative. SATs or ACTs or three Subject Tests: required. Letters of recommendation: required. Essay: required. Accepts the Common Application.

Mills College

5000 MacArthur Boulevard, Oakland, CA 94613

One of two major women's colleges on the West Coast. Mills has the San Francisco Bay area to fall back on, including UC–Berkeley, where students can take classes. Mills is strong in the arts and math, though it does offer smaller programs in preprofessional areas such as business economics. Still the only women's college to turn back coeducation with a massive protest, which it did in 1990.

Mills was the first single-sex college to implement an admissions policy for transgender applicants.

At Mills College, students receive more than just a liberal arts education. They are expected to graduate with a deeper understanding of social issues and a broad knowledge base to help ensure they will be technologically savvy and artistically aware of the world around them. The school's dedication to equality is obvious: Mills was the first women's college in the West to award bachelor's degrees, the first to offer a computer science major, the only women's college to reverse a decision to go co-ed, and the first single-sex college to implement an admissions policy for transgender applicants. "Mills is a magnet for students passionate about social justice and the world around them," says a music major, and "an environment where differences are celebrated."

The school's fascinating history started in 1852, when it began as a young ladies' seminary serving the children of California Gold Rush adventurers who were determined to see their daughters raised in an atmosphere of gentility. Now, the combination of student diversity and educational opportunity helps guarantee that no one will graduate without having her horizons well expanded. The enclosed, park-like 135-acre campus boasts both historic and modern architecture set among rolling meadows, woods, and a meandering creek.

Requirements of Mills's new Core Curriculum fall into three main categories: Foundational Skills (critical analysis, information literacy, written and oral communication, and quantitative literacy), Modes of Inquiry (race, gender, and power; scientific inquiry; foreign language; and international perspectives), and Contributions to Knowledge and Society (community engagement and creativity, innovation, and experimentation).

> **"Mills is a magnet for students passionate about social justice and the world around them."**

A required first-year seminar allows students to work in small classes, participate in living/learning communities, and share a weekly lunch with their professor (who also serves as their academic advisor). Nearly all majors involve a senior thesis or capstone project.

"We are a very collaborative school, always thinking in interdisciplinary terms, and even when the work gets hard, we enjoy working with each other," observes a biology major. The professors are highly regarded, friendly, and accessible, and since 70 percent are women, there's no shortage of strong female role models. "My professors are some of the most intelligent and caring people that I have ever met, whom I have shared meals and laughs and philosophical chats with," one sophomore says. English, psychology, and biology are some of the most popular majors, and computer science and public policy are also strong. Popular among prelaw students is the interdisciplinary program in politics, economics, law, and policy. The fine arts department is Mills's traditional stronghold, and electronic and computer music specializations within the music program are worthy of note. Mills has concurrent cross-registration agreements with UC–Berkeley and many other Bay Area colleges, a five-year engineering program in conjunction with USC, and exchanges with several East Coast colleges. Mills students are encouraged to explore beyond the Oakland campus, and 15 percent take advantage of programs abroad.

"Our students are radical and hoping to change the world," says one senior. Eighty percent of Mills undergraduates are from California, and 1 percent are international. African Americans constitute 7 percent of the student body, Hispanics make up 24 percent, and another 9 percent are Asian Americans. An influential subgroup of students consists of "resumers"—women who are returning to college after a break of several years. The LGBTQ community is also strong here; approximately half of the student body identifies as heterosexual and half as other sexual orientations. Forty-one percent of freshmen are Pell-eligible, and 30 percent are the first in their families to attend college. A junior cites "gender equality, racial equality, locally sustained foods, water conservation, land conservation, [and] hedging against gentrification," as issues in which students are most engaged—along with "too many others to name." Merit scholarships averaging $21,342 are doled out annually to qualified students, but Mills does not award athletic scholarships.

Fifty-seven percent of students live on campus. "Overall, I have been very happy with my experience. It has been clean, safe, convenient, and a lot of fun to live in close proximity with my friends," explains a student. Most students, even freshmen, are housed in single rooms. Campus dining receives cheers from students for its "endless" variety of tasty options and accommodations for students with all manner of needs or tastes. Mills is a gated campus with one entrance, and students say they feel safe on campus. "We are a small school, but we are not immune to issues of sexual assault," comments a senior. "Our revised policies for dealing with these situations are very strong and have done wonders to make our school safe and responsive."

Since 70 percent of the professors are women, there's no shortage of strong female role models.

"Party culture is nonexistent on campus. People go off campus to party, stay on campus to study and relax," explains a business economics major. Popular annual events include the Black and White Ball, Midnight Breakfast, and Spring Fling, as well as Latina Heritage Month and a spring powwow sponsored by the ethnic studies department. Most of the time, though, the campus is quiet, and students head to UC–Berkeley for parties and to San Francisco for culture and urban adventures. Both are accessible via public transportation, beginning with a bus stop outside the front gate. Those with the means can take ski trips to Lake Tahoe or go to the sunny Santa Cruz beaches. Most students also stay busy volunteering in the local community.

"We are a very collaborative school, always thinking in interdisciplinary terms."

The Cyclones compete in the Association of Division III Independents in six sports: cross-country, rowing, soccer, swimming, tennis, and volleyball; swimming is the most competitive. About 15 percent of students play recreational and intramural sports, with volleyball being the most popular, and students also enjoy college-organized hiking, kayaking, and camping trips.

Despite some complaints about campus life, Mills students enjoy small classes with excellent teaching in one of the country's most desirable locations close to San Francisco. With an educational program that emphasizes skills critical for understanding today's society and succeeding in the real world, Mills students are sure to graduate as independent thinkers capable of making it on their own. "Mills does not create a cookie-cutter student," says one senior. "Everyone has a voice, everyone has opportunity, and everyone is challenged to reach their own potential."

Overlaps

UC–Berkeley, UCLA, Smith, Saint Mary's College of California, University of San Francisco, UC–Santa Cruz, Mount Holyoke, UC–Irvine

If You Apply To ➤

Mills: Early action: Nov. 15. Regular decision: Jan. 15. Financial aid: Feb. 15. Housing: Jun. 1. Application fee: $50. Campus interviews: recommended, evaluative. Alumnae interviews: optional, evaluative. SATs or ACTs: optional. Subject Tests: optional. Letters of recommendation: required. Essay: required. Accepts the Common Application with supplement. Accepts applications from students who are self-identified women or who were assigned female sex at birth but do not identify with the gender binary.

1701 North State Street, Jackson, MS 39210

Millsaps is the strongest liberal arts college in the deep, Deep South and by far the most progressive. Its largely preprofessional student body typically has sights set on business, law, or medicine. Usually compared to Hendrix, Rhodes, and Sewanee. More than half the students come from out of state, generally from other Deep South states.

Website: www.millsaps.edu
Location: City Center
Private
Total Enrollment: 810
Undergraduates: 749
Male/Female: 50/50
SAT Ranges: CR 520–630,
  M 525–630
ACT Ranges: 23–28
Financial Aid: 98%
Pell Grant: 23%
Expense: Pr $
Student Loans: 65%
Average Debt: $ $ $
Phi Beta Kappa: Yes
Applicants: 3,657
Accepted: 53%
Enrolled: 12%
Grad in 6 Years: 66%
Returning Freshmen: 79%
Academics: ✑ ✑ ✑
Social: ☎ ☎ ☎
Q of L: ★ ★ ★
Admissions: (601) 974-1050
Email Address: admissions@
  millsaps.edu

Strong Programs:
English
Education
Business Administration
Biology
Accounting
Psychology
Prehealth
Religious Studies

Millsaps College has long been thought of as a finishing school for well-bred Southern belles and gentlemen. Less well-known outside the Deep South is that this is also one of the region's top liberal arts institutions. Millsaps's motto, *ad excellentiam*, means "promoting excellence"—which is what the college still does. What characterizes the school is its focus on scholarly inquiry, spiritual growth, and community service. "Millsaps is the perfect package," says a freshman, "strongly academic, small enough to build relationships, yet big-thinking enough to build the mind."

Millsaps's 100-acre campus sits in the center of Jackson, on the highest point in the city. A mix of modern and traditional buildings is arranged around the Bowl, a sequestered glen surrounded by old-growth trees and shrubs that serves as a main student gathering place.

Millsaps requires students to complete 128 semester hours to earn a degree, all but eight of which must be taken for a letter grade. The newly implemented Compass Curriculum is built on four learning outcomes: Foundations (covering thinking and reasoning), Communication in Humanities, Integrative and Collaborative Learning, and Problem Solving and Creative Practice. A Writing Across the Curriculum initiative ensures that every student develops writing skills, and all students must complete the Major Experience, a capstone learning experience that may involve research, a field- or community-based course, study abroad, an internship, or an honors project.

"The campus is very activist and very political—well split between conservatives and liberals."

Millsaps offers more than 30 majors and 40 minors, including the option of a self-designed major. Among the best programs at Millsaps are English and education, where students get involved with the Jackson Public Schools from introductory-level classes. Each year, a few select upperclassmen join the Ford Teaching Fellows Program, letting them work closely with a faculty member to learn about teaching—and paying them for their time in the classroom. The Millsaps College Writing Program is top-notch, and the religious studies program is well regarded. The most popular majors are business administration, biology, accounting, and psychology. Premed courses, including those in biology and chemistry, are strong, and the college's prehealth mentoring program pairs students with practitioners in their chosen field, allowing them to earn credit for real medical experience. The Wiener Premedical Summer Research Fellowships are available to students seeking careers in medicine, while cooperative agreements allow students to opt for nursing degrees in partnership with the University of Mississippi Medical Center and Vanderbilt University. Millsaps also offers engineering opportunities in cooperation with Auburn, Columbia, Vanderbilt, and Washington universities. Millsaps is a founding member of the Associated Colleges of the South* consortium, and students eager to see how government works may participate in the Washington Semester*.

"The courses are rigorous as the professors continue to push the students' academic boundaries," says a sophomore. Eighty-three percent of courses at Millsaps have fewer than 20 students, and none exceed 50. "The quality of the teaching surpasses all of my expectations," says a student. Students may do research for credit at the Blue Ridge Center for Environmental Stewardship in Virginia and at Yellowstone National Park, or they may intern for credit with local businesses or in state government offices in Jackson. The college also maintains a 4,000-acre biological reserve in the rainforest of the Yucatán Peninsula, which hosts courses exploring Mayan culture and the Mayan coral reef, with course topics ranging from the literature of the Spanish conquest to Mayan mathematics and astronomy. Approximately 40 percent of Millsaps students study abroad, and courses are offered in nearly 20 nations, including Albania, Israel, Tanzania, China, Greece, and Costa Rica.

The Ford Teaching Fellows Program lets students work closely with a faculty member to learn about teaching.

"The students at Millsaps are very diverse," says a sophomore. "They range from athletes to scholars, from the outspoken to the quiet, from liberal to conservative, and from religious to atheist." Millsaps has broadened its recruiting efforts, and 57 percent of students now come from out of state, in addition to 4 percent who come from foreign countries. Millsaps was the first college in Mississippi to voluntarily open its doors to minority students, and African Americans now make up 13 percent of the student body, Asian Americans 3 percent, and Hispanics 4 percent. "The campus is very activist and very political—well split between conservatives and liberals," says a political science major. "All views are respected; poverty and human rights are hot topics." Twenty-three percent of freshmen are Pell-eligible. Qualified students are awarded academic merit scholarships averaging $22,048 each year, but there are no athletic awards.

"Greek life is the center of Millsaps's social life."

Many Mississippians view Millsaps as a hotbed of liberalism, and the school's co-ed dorms confirm their worst fears, though freshmen must still live in single-sex halls. Ninety percent of students stay in campus housing—mostly, grouses a sophomore, because those who move off campus lose 30 percent of their financial aid. "Housing is average," a psychology major says. The robust Greek system claims 62 percent of men and 58 percent of women; sophomore, junior, and senior men may live in one of four fraternity houses, but there is no sorority housing. Students say campus food is decent and "there is something for everyone," according to a senior.

Millsaps maintains a 4,000-acre biological reserve in the rainforest of the Yucatán Peninsula.

"Greek life is the center of Millsaps's social life," a student explains, and the fraternity houses are usually open and rocking from Wednesday through Saturday nights. Greek rush is now held after fall midterms instead of during the first hectic week of school, but that hasn't dampened the party spirit. Underage students caught drinking are fined, but students say enforcement of the policy is lax. Major Madness is a favorite annual event, offering a week of open-mic nights, hypnotists, and comedians and culminating in a weekend-long festival in the Bowl, with a crawfish boil, carnival games, and live music. The city of Jackson also offers a wealth of options, including professional symphony, opera, and ballet, and the city is a nexus for Mississippi's legendary blues and "roots rock" musical traditions. The "1 Campus 1 Community" program connects students with local volunteer opportunities. Easy road trips include New Orleans, Memphis, and the riverfront casinos in Vicksburg, Mississippi; closer to campus, 10 miles to the north, is a huge reservoir that is popular for weekend water sports. For students who enjoy the great outdoors, the Natchez Trace offers easy access to wooded trails and bicycling paths.

"We offer the sort of prestigious education generally only available in New England."

The Millsaps Majors compete in Division III as a member of the Southern Athletic Association, so it isn't nearly as sports crazy as most Southern campuses. Men's soccer, baseball, and football and women's basketball and softball have brought home conference championships in recent years. There are more than

Overlaps

Tulane, Loyola
University New
Orleans, University
of Mississippi,
University
of Alabama,
Mississippi State

25 intramural sports, plus group exercise classes and sports clubs, so even students with recreational interests and abilities can find a game to play. Everyone benefits from the 65,000-square-foot Hall Activities Center, which has facilities for weight training, aerobics, basketball, racquetball, squash, and volleyball, along with an outdoor pool.

In a state renowned for blues, booze, barbecue, and the tradition of old magnolia trees and grand plantations, progressive Millsaps College is an anomaly. "We offer the sort of prestigious education generally only available in New England," states a junior. "Millsaps is a magnet for accomplished students from strong backgrounds and the kind of college not usually found in the South." Small classes ensure plenty of time to get to know fellow students and faculty members. And that's one tradition that never gets old.

If You Apply To ➤

Millsaps: Early action: Nov. 15. Regular decision: Feb. 1. Financial aid: Mar. 1. Housing: May 1. No application fee. No campus or alumni interviews. SATs or ACTs: required. No Subject Tests. Letters of recommendation: required. Essay: required. Accepts the Common Application.

University of Minnesota

240 Williamson, 231 Pillsbury Drive SE, Minneapolis, MN 55455

Not quite as highly rated as the University of Michigan or the University of Wisconsin, but not nearly as expensive for nonresidents either. In a university the size of Minnesota, the best bet is to find a niche, such as the honors program. Strong programs include engineering, management, and health fields.

Website: www.umn.edu
Location: City Center
Public
Total Enrollment: 37,879
Undergraduates: 28,206
Male/Female: 49/51
SAT Ranges: CR 560–700, M 620–740
ACT Ranges: 26–31
Financial Aid: 48%
Pell Grant: 19%
Expense: Pub $ $ $ $
Student Loans: 59%
Average Debt: $ $
Phi Beta Kappa: Yes
Applicants: 46,165
Accepted: 45%
Enrolled: 28%
Grad in 6 Years: 77%
Returning Freshmen: 93%
Academics: ✍ ✍ ✍ ✍
Social: ☎ ☎ ☎

The University of Minnesota, like the nearby Mall of America, can be overwhelming, given its seemingly limitless variety of offerings and gargantuan size. With nearly 150 majors and the largest study abroad program in the nation, the U of M offers an abundance of academic choices. Be warned, though—winters can be frigid and it can take a cool customer to navigate the endless choices here.

The vast Twin Cities campus actually consists of two campuses with three main sections, and within each the architecture is highly diverse. The St. Paul campus encompasses the College of Food, Agricultural, and Natural Resource Sciences; the College of Biological Sciences; the College of Veterinary Medicine; and the College of Continuing Studies. The Minneapolis campus is divided by the Mississippi River into an East Bank and a West Bank that are home to the other colleges and most of the dormitories, as well as most of the fraternities and sororities. Both campuses offer a blend of traditional and modern architecture, with columned buildings seated next to sleek geometric structures.

> "We have a dedicated police force as well as a free escort program."

The two campuses are five miles apart and linked by a free bus service. Academic facilities are excellent, beginning with the five-million-volume library system, which is the 14th largest in North America. Every one of the colleges has its own library, many of which are good places to study. A 695-acre arboretum is used for research and teaching. The West Bank Arts Quarter makes the U of M the only public university in the nation with all of its art disciplines in the same district.

Minnesota offers nearly 150 undergraduate majors among seven separate schools. The College of Science and Engineering is notable for its tutorial and internship options; the electrical and mechanical engineering programs are particularly strong and well subscribed. The Carlson School of Management is well regarded and offers majors in entrepreneurial management, international business, and other areas. Psychology, communication studies, journalism, and mechanical engineering are the most popular majors. Undergraduates also have access to more esoteric fields such as mortuary science, and newer majors include special education, environmental engineering, and Biblical studies.

"The classes are relatively difficult," a junior says, but "it really depends on the subject." The university is on a semester system, and almost all classes have a pass/fail option (limited to no more than a quarter of a student's courses). Efforts to limit class size have been stepped up—38 percent of classes have fewer than 20 students—and the university is focusing more on undergraduates. While undergraduates have had a difficult time enrolling in courses, one junior reveals, "If a class is closed and somebody really needs it, they can usually get a magic number from the department to be able to register for it." The administration attributes the school's low six-year graduation rate to the fact that students are likely to center their lives in spheres outside the university—in work and off-campus homes. However, the four-year plan guarantees graduation in four years provided students follow program requirements, including frequent academic counseling and specific coursework. Helpful teaching assistants are abundant. Professors receive high marks from most students as being approachable and knowledgeable. "The instructors have been exemplary due to their passion for the subject matter and commitment to their students," an archaeology major says.

The excellent honors program in the liberal arts college allows close contact with faculty members as well as leeway to enroll in certain graduate courses and seminars. The Undergraduate Research Opportunities Program provides scholarships of up to $1,500 for students to conduct research with faculty. Students find plenty of internship opportunities at the many corporations and government agencies in the Twin Cities area, and the university pushes its more than 300 study, work, and volunteer programs in more than 60 nations. These draw 30 percent of undergrads, including engineering students.

Most U of M students are "motivated and hardworking," says a junior. Seventy-two percent of undergraduates are from Minnesota, and 10 percent hail from outside the U.S. Four percent are African American, 4 percent are Hispanic, and 9 percent are Asian American. Need-based financial aid is available, as are merit scholarships averaging $5,088 and athletic awards in all major sports.

Dorm life at Minnesota follows the big school, wait-in-line mantra. Twenty-three percent of undergraduates live in residence halls; there are eight traditional halls and three university-run apartment facilities. Students can also choose to join one of three dozen living/learning communities, such as Design House, STEM Diversity House, and Lavender House. "Dorms are adequate," says one student, although "some can be a bit cramped." Dorm rooms are hard to obtain, and parking spaces for all those commuters are almost as scarce. Students who have rooms get the chance to keep them for the next year, and they're also required to purchase a meal plan. Meals are said to be hit or miss, but, "Fresh fruit and veggies are always available," notes a junior, who also adds (lest anyone fear the campus dietitians are excessively health-obsessed), "they have the best chocolate-chip cookies." Campus security is adequate. "We have a dedicated police force as well as a free escort program," notes a junior.

Many U of M students live in apartments and have a thriving social life away from campus. "Most social life takes place right off campus," says one student, "but there are loads of activities available on campus, such as bowling, theater, late-night activities, and movies." About 11 percent of students go Greek. Underage drinking is

(continued)

Q of L: ★ ★ ★
Admissions: (800) 752-1000
Email Address: admissions@umn.edu

Strong Programs:
Psychology
Communication Studies
Journalism
Mechanical Engineering
Electrical Engineering
Entrepreneurial Management
International Business

U of M boasts nearly 150 majors and the largest study abroad program in the nation.

"Most social life takes place right off campus."

Students can choose to join one of three dozen living/learning communities, such as STEM Diversity House and Lavender House.

banned, and students say the policy usually works. The union's bowling alley, pool tables, movie theater, and live music dance club are good places to meet people. And there are more than 500 student groups on campus. The Carnival Weekend put on by the Greeks each April to raise funds for charity is a huge event. Spring Jam is described by one student as "homecoming in spring—but better," and Campus Kickoff Days in the beginning of the fall quarter is much anticipated.

Here, being "under the weather" can be a good thing, as campus designers found a way to get around—or under—wet or wintry conditions by linking many of the

"[U of M] offers unparalleled opportunities for students to grow academically, socially, and personally."

campus buildings with tunnels. For those who love winter, there is Snow Week, and happy skiers and skaters become colorful spots all over the state's white backdrop. In the spring and summer, Minnesota's famed 10,000 lakes offer swimming, boating, and fishing. The downtown areas of the Twin Cities are easy to get to by bus, and there are scores of good bars, restaurants, nightspots, and movie theaters.

This is an athletically inclined bunch of students, as both intramural and Division I varsity sports are popular. Students always hope the current season will be one in which the gridiron Gophers take home the roses in a bowl victory, but short of that, a win over Michigan for custody of the Little Brown Jug is cause for celebration. Women's ice hockey scored its sixth national championship in 2016. Men's ice hockey, tennis, and baseball and women's soccer, softball, swimming, and volleyball have all won Big Ten conference championships in the last two years. Intramural competition can go on well past midnight.

Anonymity is almost a given at a university of this size, but then size does have its virtues in the countless array of campus resources. A senior says, "It offers unparalleled opportunities for students to grow academically, socially, and personally." The University of Minnesota is ideal for those who appreciate an urban setting and a good, old-fashioned, button-up-your-overcoat winter.

If You Apply To ➤

U of M: Rolling admissions: Dec. 15. (Priority deadline: Nov. 1.) Financial aid: Mar. 1. Housing: May 1. Application fee: $55. No campus or alumni interviews. SATs or ACTs: required (SAT essay or ACT writing recommended). No Subject Tests. No letters of recommendation. No essay. Accepts the Common Application with supplement.

University of Minnesota, Morris

600 East 4th Street, Morris, MN 56267-2199

The plains of western Minnesota may seem an unlikely place to find a liberal arts college—and a public one at that. Morris is cut from the same cloth as Mary Washington, UNC Asheville, and St. Mary's of Maryland. The draw: private college education at a public university price. Remote location pulls students to Minneapolis–St. Paul for city life.

The University of Minnesota, Morris is far more comprehensive than the small size of its student body might suggest. The first buildings on its 130-year-old campus were originally home to an American Indian boarding school, which was succeeded in 1910 by an agricultural school. Morris opened its doors in 1960, and since then it has grown into a solid public liberal arts college. Morris "strives to encourage students to push their limits and go out on limbs," says an English and history double major, and a junior adds, "There is a place for everyone here."

The 130-acre Morris campus includes 26 traditional brick-and-mortar buildings, loosely arranged around a central mall. Two high-powered wind turbines generate 60 percent of the power Morris requires each day. The renovated Welcome Center is LEED Gold–certified and is the first building in Minnesota (and the first on the National Register of Historic Places) to use energy-efficient chilled-beam technology.

General education requirements at Morris span 60 credits. Everyone starts with the Intellectual Community seminar, which introduces students to college-level work and active interaction with faculty. Students then move on to as many as five courses under the umbrella of Skills for the Liberal Arts, along with eight courses in Expanding Perspectives. Seniors must participate in a senior seminar or capstone project, and some do both. The most popular majors are psychology, biology, management, and English. Other well-regarded programs include environmental science and environmental studies, as the Morris campus itself serves as a study in renewable energy, and American Indian studies, which benefits from the campus's unique history. A creative writing minor for non-English majors was recently added.

> **"[Morris] strives to encourage students to push their limits and go out on limbs."**

Students describe the academic climate as challenging yet "informally comfortable." "Almost everything at UMM is a collaborative effort," says a biology major, and students are encouraged to reach out to professors for individual help. Sixty-six percent of classes have fewer than 20 students, and professors are respected for their knowledge and real-world experience. "Every professor I've had seems focused on their teaching skills," reports a sophomore.

Morris offers service-learning projects as part of the classroom experience, and more than half of the student body conducts research projects. Morris's Center for Small Towns, which works with small towns, local schools, and nonprofits to address challenges specific to rural communities, offers opportunities for service projects, internships, and research. The Morris Honors Program allows high achievers to enjoy various honors courses, an honors capstone project, and a core course titled Traditions in Human Thought. Morris continues to integrate study abroad opportunities into the curriculum, offering more than 300 options for students wishing to study overseas; half of undergraduates participate by the time they graduate.

"Students at UMM are characteristically intelligent, well-rounded individuals," says a psychology major. Seventy-eight percent of Morris students are Minnesota natives, and 10 percent are international. American Indians comprise 6 percent, Asian Americans add 4 percent, and African American and Hispanic students combine for 5 percent. Political issues don't dominate campus conversation, but students tend to be engaged in issues of local and national concern. "Particularly, the rights and treatment of women, ethnic and racial minorities, and the LGBTQ community are of high consideration," notes one student. Merit scholarships averaging $4,206 are available, but there are no athletic awards. Financial incentives for low-income students include the University of Minnesota Promise Scholarship, awarded to Minnesota residents with a family income up to $100,000. Thirty percent of current freshmen qualify for Pell Grants. Honoring a policy that dates back to the campus's late-19th-century origins, a tuition waiver is available for American Indian students.

Fifty-six percent of Morris students live on campus in one of the six residence halls, which offer several living/learning communities, or in an apartment complex reserved for upperclassmen. It's easy to get a room, though many opt for

(continued)

Undergraduates: 1,674
Male/Female: 46/54
SAT Ranges: CR 500–660, M 510–640
ACT Ranges: 22–28
Financial Aid: 93%
Pell Grant: 30%
Expense: Pub $ $ $
Student Loans: 65%
Average Debt: $ $
Phi Beta Kappa: No
Applicants: 3,619
Accepted: 60%
Enrolled: 19%
Grad in 6 Years: 65%
Returning Freshmen: 77%
Academics: ✐ ✐ ✐ ½
Social: ☎ ☎
Q of L: ★ ★ ★
Admissions: (888) 866-3382
Email Address: admissions@ morris.umn.edu

Strong Programs:
Psychology
Biology
Management
English
Environmental Science
American Indian Studies
Elementary Education

Well-regarded programs include environmental science, as the Morris campus itself serves as a study in renewable energy.

less expensive housing off campus. "The rooms themselves are not cramped, and each comes already equipped with a desk, a dresser, a nightstand, an adjustable loft/bed, a closet, and a fan," a student says. Campus dining is tasty and diverse, students say, and most report feeling safe on campus. "I have never felt unsafe on this campus as there is virtually no crime. It is really nice to be able to relax," says a student.

There is no Greek system, but students say there's always something to do. "Lots of events such as concerts, movies, presentations, and shows occur on campus, incentivizing on-campus socialization and making the campus a fun hub for hanging out," explains an English major. "On campus is where all the action is," another student agrees. The drinking age is 21, and it's strictly enforced on campus and in local bars. "There is a small party culture on campus. There is zero pressure to drink or do any drugs," says a computer science major.

"Almost everything at UMM is a collaborative effort."

Campus traditions include the annual tug-of-war competition between two dorms, Clayton A. Gay Hall and David C. Johnson Independence (Indy) Hall. "Hundreds of students show up!" says one. Students also look forward to the Zombie Prom in the fall and the Yule Ball, a holiday dance inspired by the Yule Ball from *Harry Potter and the Goblet of Fire*. Morris itself is described as "small but very friendly," and for those pining to get away, "Road trips are usually taken by small groups of friends, who get together on the weekends to go to Perkins in Alexandria, or to the mall in St. Cloud," says a sophomore. Minneapolis-St. Paul, about three hours away, is also a popular destination.

The Cougars compete in the Division III Upper Midwest Athletic Conference. Women's basketball is particularly successful and has won six conference championships in the last seven years. Women's volleyball and men's and women's soccer are also strong. In addition, students enjoy access to more than 90 student-led clubs and associations. Co-ed flag football, basketball, volleyball, and badminton are among the most popular intramurals, and students also use the Regional Fitness Center or hiking and biking trails to stay fit.

One of the smaller campuses in the University of Minnesota system, Morris may just epitomize the idea of "Minnesota nice." Tucked away from the state's big cities, some students might find the campus isolated. But the school's location means fewer distractions—and more time for its happy students to focus on independent reading and research, or just getting to know their peers. "We are the University of Minnesota's gem on the prairie," says a senior. "We have the intimacy of a private school, and the academic excellence of the state's largest educational institution, all for an affordable price."

Overlaps

University of Minnesota, University of Minnesota Duluth, Gustavus Adolphus, St. Cloud State, Minnesota State, Hamline, University of St. Thomas, St. Olaf

If You Apply To ➤

Morris: Rolling admissions. Priority deadline: Dec. 15. Regular decision: Mar. 15. Financial aid: Mar. 1. Housing: May 1. Application fee: $35 (paper), $25 (online). Campus interviews: optional, evaluative. No alumni interviews. SATs (with essay) or ACTs (with writing): required. No Subject Tests. Letters of recommendation: optional. Essay: recommended.

University of Mississippi

University, MS 38677

Located in the progressive town of Oxford, Ole Miss is doing its best to put the state's redneck past in the rearview mirror. Strong on public policy and international studies, and the honors college is one of the best anywhere. Location near Faulkner's old hangouts is ideal for soaking up Southern literary traditions, and Rebel Black Bear continues to stoke school spirit, especially against LSU and Mississippi State. Tailgating remains world class.

The University of Mississippi (more commonly known as "Ole Miss" after the nickname of the yearbook) offers students an educational experience steeped in tradition and thick with school spirit. Students have access to a host of academic offerings, including a top-notch honors college and an innovative public policy leadership major, and to a vibrant community of like-minded Rebels always ready to have a good time. Whether they're hitting the books, cheering on their teams, or simply hanging out, Ole Miss students display a love for their school that is hard to miss.

Founded in 1844, the University of Mississippi's central campus occupies 640 acres of rolling land in the center of Oxford. The main campus consists of 199 buildings and a mix of architectural styles, including Greek Revival, Beaux-Arts Classicism, Georgian Revival, and modern. The white-columned Lyceum, which served as a hospital during the Civil War, is the campus's oldest building and now houses administrative offices. Construction on a 200,000-square-foot, $138 million STEM education building is underway, slated for completion in 2018.

All students at Ole Miss must complete six hours of English composition, three hours of mathematics, six hours of laboratory science, nine hours of humanities and fine arts, and six hours of social and behavioral sciences. Approximately 80 percent of first-year students sign up for the Freshman Year Experience, a seminar-style course that helps new students transition from high school into a successful college career. The newly established Center for Writing and Rhetoric administers two mandatory composition courses for freshmen.

Students say coursework is what you make of it and varies by program, but the atmosphere is collaborative rather than competitive. "The classes are definitely challenging at times," says one freshman, "but doable with the right amount of work." The most popular majors include general studies, elementary education, marketing, and accountancy; programs in pharmaceutical sciences and Chinese language are also strengths. The Lott Leadership Institute is a standout that offers a public policy leadership major and an innovative curriculum that combines the systematic study of public policy with the development of leadership qualities. "The atmosphere of the Lott Institute is conducive to learning and team building," says one broadcast journalism major. "Conversational and debate classes are a change from the regular classroom, and Lott offers both." New majors have been added in applied gerontology and recreation administration. Professors are highly rated across the university. "The quality of teaching is superior," boasts one senior. "It is not at all uncommon for full professors to teach freshmen and even offer tutoring to freshmen during their office hours."

> **"It is not at all uncommon for full professors to teach freshmen and even offer tutoring."**

Website: www.olemiss.edu
Location: Small Town
Public
Total Enrollment: 18,657
Undergraduates: 17,120
Male/Female: 44/56
SAT Ranges: CR 490–600, M 500–600
ACT Ranges: 21–28
Financial Aid: 49%
Pell Grant: 23%
Expense: Pub $
Student Loans: 50%
Average Debt: $ $ $
Phi Beta Kappa: Yes
Applicants: 18,059
Accepted: 79%
Enrolled: 28%
Grad in 6 Years: 61%
Returning Freshmen: 87%
Academics: ✍ ✍ ✍
Social: ☎ ☎ ☎
Q of L: ★ ★ ★
Admissions: (662) 915-7211
Email Address: admissions@olemiss.edu

Strong Programs:
General Studies
Elementary Education
Marketing
Accountancy
Pharmaceutical Sciences
Chinese
Public Policy Leadership
International Studies

For students itching to have their passports stamped, Ole Miss offers numerous study abroad options in diverse locations around the world, including Botswana, China, Greece, Peru, and Thailand. "Our study abroad program is exceptional," gushes one senior. "Not only do they offer you the opportunity to travel basically anywhere that you want, they offer many different scholarships to make study abroad less costly." Another option is the Croft Institute for International Studies, which accepts 55 students each fall into the international studies program. Participating students study international politics, economics, and culture both in the classroom and via study abroad. Gifted students may apply for the highly competitive Sally McDonnell Barksdale Honors College, where they take part in small, discussion-based honors courses offered in a number of disciplines and engage in community service; roughly 1,400 students from 70 majors currently participate. Honors students complete research and a senior thesis to graduate as an SMBHC Scholar and have access to foreign study fellowships.

"Ole Miss students are ambitious, hospitable, and well rounded," says one public policy leadership major. The student body is largely home grown: 58 percent of undergraduates are Mississippi natives and 3 percent hail from abroad. African Americans make up 15 percent, Hispanics 3 percent, and Asian Americans

"[Ole Miss] offer[s] many different scholarships to make study abroad less costly."

2 percent. "The outside view of UM is that everyone is a sorority girl or a frat guy," a mathematics major complains. "We have people of all categories and cultures." Twenty-three percent of incoming freshmen are eligible for Pell Grants. Merit scholarships averaging $7,827 are awarded annually, as are 523 athletic scholarships in 16 sports.

Twenty-seven percent of students live in the dorms, which are a hit-or-miss affair. "Some of the older dorms have seen better days, but there is a new focus on campus to renovate and rebuild housing," a student reports. Options include apartments, traditional residence halls, and residential colleges. According to one student, the residence halls "provide a sense of community and family that makes Ole Miss unique." Campus dining options are reported to be plentiful and tasty. "We offer several different dining halls," says a student, "some of which are all you can eat and some of which are cafeteria style." Campus security gets a thumbs-up too. "Ole Miss is the kind of place where people look out for each other," comments a student. "We have a campus police department that works diligently to make sure the campus is safe."

The Ole Miss social scene is dominated by Greek life, which attracts 35 percent of the men and 48 percent of the women, although non-Greeks find plenty to enjoy as well. "Ole Miss social life is one of a kind," says a senior. The Student Activities Association hosts a variety of on-campus activities each week, including movies, pageants, concerts, and multicultural events. Alcohol is forbidden on campus and students say the "two strikes and you're out" policy is effective at curbing consumption. Campus worship organizations have a strong presence, and students also get involved in 250 student groups, as well as volunteer opportunities in Oxford. One enthusiastic junior describes the city as "the best college town in the nation." A senior adds, "There are lots of locally owned businesses and restaurants that are unique to the area and very charming."

Famed author William Faulkner grew up here and attended Ole Miss for three semesters before dropping out, and the slew of local cultural events includes the annual Faulkner and Yoknapatawpha Conference, featuring lectures and discussions by literary scholars and critics. Although it lost out to the University of Virginia as repository of Faulkner's sessions, Ole Miss operates Rowan Oak,

Faulkner's home, and has a sizable collection of Faulkner materials. Blues legend B.B. King gave Ole Miss his personal record collection to help establish its Blues Archive. Colonel Reb, the longtime school mascot now deemed politically problematical, is long gone—replaced by Rebel Black Bear.

The Ole Miss Rebels compete in the gauntlet known as the Southeastern Conference, where they face the likes of Alabama's Crimson Tide, the Florida Gators, and the LSU Tigers. Solid teams include football, baseball, and men's and women's tennis, golf, basketball, and track and field. The baseball team made its first College World Series appearance in 42 years in 2014, while the football team has played in a bowl game for four consecutive seasons. School spirit is on full display, especially when LSU is in town. On game days, frenzied fans gather on the Grove—10 acres of oak and maple trees in the center of campus—for tailgating, which draws more than 100,000 loyal supporters who pitch 2,500 tents and must drink from red and blue cups (no beer cans allowed). Jackets, ties, and cowboy boots are common, and food is sometimes served on silver trays. Says one happy Rebel, "The Grove is a place where people come together regardless of their differences to support our Ole Miss Rebs and share in a community that we all love." Dozens of intramural and club sports also prove to be popular diversions.

Overall, students at Ole Miss seem to be a contented lot, especially those in the honors college. Despite the lack of diversity and standard complaints about parking, it's clear that these Rebels have much to cheer about, including solid academics, game days in the Grove, and a healthy dose of school spirit.

> **"Ole Miss is the kind of place where people look out for each other."**

Overlaps

Mississippi State, University of Southern Mississippi, University of Alabama, Auburn, University of Memphis, University of Tennessee Knoxville

If You Apply To ➤

Ole Miss: Rolling admissions. Priority financial aid: Mar. 1. Application fee: $40 (residents), $60 (nonresidents). No campus or alumni interviews. SATs or ACTs: required. Subject Tests: required for some. No letters of recommendation. Essay: required.

University of Missouri

230 Jesse Hall, Columbia, MO 65211

Renowned for having one of the top journalism schools in the nation, Mizzou boasts the country's only commercial university-owned TV station, as well as a National Public Radio outlet. Also strong in agriculture and the health sciences, as well as business and music. Comparable in size to Iowa and Iowa State, smaller than Illinois and Indiana.

In 1839, the residents of Boone County, Missouri, raised enough money to create the state university in Columbia. Today, Missouri's flagship university has evolved into a top research institution, yet continues to uphold the belief of its founders in the great value of higher education that is accessible to all. Currently in the thick of its second $1 billion development campaign, the university continues to expand programs and facilities in ways that benefit students, including 11 new residential halls and renovations to 19 others.

The oldest public university west of the Mississippi, Mizzou's 1,262-acre campus is flanked by mansionlike fraternity and sorority houses and features 42,000 plants and trees and numerous thematic gardens. The Francis Quadrangle Historical

Website: www.missouri.edu
Location: Small City
Public
Total Enrollment: 30,838
Undergraduates: 25,909
Male/Female: 48/52
SAT Ranges: CR 530–650, M 530–650
ACT Ranges: 24–29

(continued)

Financial Aid: 59%
Pell Grant: N/A
Expense: Pub $ $
Student Loans: 51%
Average Debt: $ $
Phi Beta Kappa: Yes
Applicants: 21,988
Accepted: 78%
Enrolled: 36%
Grad in 6 Years: 69%
Returning Freshmen: 87%
Academics: ✎ ✎ ✎
Social: ☎ ☎ ☎ ☎
Q of L: ★ ★ ★
Admissions: (573) 882-7786
Email Address:
  mu4u@missouri.edu

Strong Programs:
Journalism
Agriculture
Health Sciences
Business
Music
Engineering

Mizzou boasts the country's largest alternative breaks program, which sends students on 130 trips each year to work on service projects.

District, with 18 National Historic Landmark buildings, is the core of the Red Campus (so named for the predominant color of brick). Central to this area are the 60-foot granite columns of the original Academic Hall that was destroyed by fire in 1892. To the east of the columns is the original tombstone of Thomas Jefferson, which the Jefferson family gave to Mizzou (not UVA!) in the 19th century as a symbol of his championing of state-supported education. The White Campus consists of vine-covered limestone buildings by the Memorial Union Tower.

An array of general education requirements includes courses in exposition and argumentation, algebra, math reasoning proficiency, and American history

"There is a nice mix of classes in regards to difficulty."

or government. Students also must complete 27 hours in three content areas: social and behavioral sciences, physical and biological

sciences and mathematics, and humanities and fine arts. All students must take a course in computer literacy, although the content of those courses varies by degree program. Two writing-intensive courses are also required, and all undergrads complete a senior-year capstone course. Full professors teach the lecture courses at Mizzou, supplemented by a weekly discussion session led by a teaching assistant to go over material presented in class. Professors "make a conscious effort to convey their knowledge in a way that allows [students] to discover new facts and evidence on their own," a senior explains. Owing to MU's size, classes can fill up quickly, but professors do give overrides for students who must take certain credits at specific times. Missouri guarantees the availability of coursework to complete a degree in four years.

With more than 270 degree programs and 18 schools and colleges, Mizzou offers a comprehensive set of choices for basic and advanced study. Aspiring journalists can get hands-on experience working on the *Columbia Missourian*, the 7,000-circulation local daily paper edited by J-school faculty members and students, or at KOMU-TV, the nation's only university-owned commercial television station. KBIA, MU's National Public Radio station, is popular among journalism students and listeners alike. The J-school has created a convergence sequence to introduce students to new digital technologies and recently began offering a documentary journalism program. Agriculture is also nationally ranked, especially in the areas of agricultural economics and applied research for farm communities, and the music program is noteworthy. The College of Engineering maintains several strong undergraduate segments, including biological and civil engineering. The College of Business is competitive and features a five-year bachelor's/master's accounting program.

"The academic climate is relatively competitive, depending on the major," says one senior. "In my experience, there is a nice mix of classes in regards to difficulty." Committed preprofessionals will be glad to know that MU offers ambitious freshmen guaranteed admission to its graduate-level programs in medicine, law, veterinary medicine, nursing, and health professions. Mizzou is also one of the leading public research institutions in the country for the number and range of lab and scholarly opportunities it offers undergraduates, a task made easier through the undergraduate research office. Five percent of students study abroad each year, choosing from programs in more than 50 countries. In addition, a cooperative agree-

"I loved my residence hall experience."

ment allows Southeastern Conference university students access to education abroad programs offered at other SEC universities. The university also boasts the

country's largest alternative breaks program, which sends students packing on roughly 130 trips each year to contribute 40,000 hours of work on service projects in the U.S. and abroad during spring, winter, and weekend breaks.

Seventy-two percent of Mizzou students hail from the Show-Me State, though every state in the union is represented; the 3 percent of international students come from more than 100 countries. One biological sciences major says, "The typical Mizzou student is a well-rounded individual who values academics, involvement, and social opportunities." African Americans account for 8 percent of the undergraduate student body, Asian Americans 2 percent, and Hispanics 4 percent. To boost its minority population, Mizzou has established several scholarship and support programs designed especially for minorities. It's also opened a Black Culture Center and an Asian Affairs Center and offers extensive programming, such as Diversity Week, which features workshops, speakers, and other events. Nevertheless, protests in 2015 over chronically poor race relations on campus attracted national attention and led to the resignation of the UM System president. They also motivated the UM System to appoint its first ever chief diversity, inclusion, and equity officer, and to develop a new orientation training program on diversity for all incoming students. Merit scholarships are available averaging $5,531, and student-athletes may compete for 303 awards in 20 Division I sports.

More than 100 Freshman Interest Groups allow students with shared academic interests to live in the same residence hall.

Twenty-five percent of MU students live on campus, and freshmen under age 20 are required to do so. "I loved my residence hall experience," says one sophomore. "I had a lot of space in my room and the closets were huge!" Residence halls have double rooms and are often crowded and noisy—and thus are fun places to be, though single-sex halls, a few single rooms, and round-the-clock quiet floors are also available. About 30 percent of new students choose a Freshman Interest Group—there are more than 100 to choose from—where 15 to 20 students with shared academic interests live in the same residence hall and enroll in three core classes together. All other undergrads living in the dorms participate in 31 general and thematic living/learning communities. Dorm dwellers are also required to purchase meal plans, and credits can be used at all-you-can-eat dining halls, coffee bars, and take-out stands. "If you are vegetarian, vegan, or have any special dietary needs, our dining halls do a great job with providing a range of food and drink," says a hospitality management major. The fraternity and sorority houses are livable (the frat houses less so); 23 percent of Mizzou men and 32 percent of women go Greek.

> **"Columbia is a bustling college town that is high-energy most weekends."**

Mizzou's Greek system is one of the largest in the nation to go dry.

Students say MU's social life is packed with options, including movies, shopping, eating out, the usual Greek parties, and great parks and hiking areas on the outskirts of town. Says a senior, "There is always something going on at Mizzou, whether it be a free event being put on by campus or a social event happening in Greek Town." Mizzou is a champion of tough alcohol policies, and students have adopted the school's stance and agreed to ban alcohol from all fraternities and sororities, making it one of the largest Greek systems in the nation to go dry. The rule is lifted when alumni come home to visit. "Columbia is a bustling college town that is high-energy most weekends," says one student. Students support the town by engaging in community service, and the community caters to them in return. Road trips to St. Louis, Kansas City, and Lake of the Ozarks offer a change of scenery.

> **"[Mizzou] will shape your life and help guide you into the future."**

Mizzou's Tigers compete in the rough-and-tumble Southeastern Conference, and basketball and football games draw big crowds. In fact, the entire town turns out in black and gold for any football game. The women's softball team recently won its 11th regional championship, and the wrestling team took home its second consecutive Mid-American Conference regular season championship in 2016. MU's popular intramural program has nearly two dozen sports and two skill divisions, attracting more than a quarter of the student body.

Overlaps

University of Illinois at Urbana–Champaign, Indiana University, University of Iowa, Iowa State, University of Kansas, Kansas State

Mizzou is a school on the rise. "It is a college that will shape your life and help guide you into the future," says a student. It continues to grow academically and physically, as evidenced by the ambitious capital campaign, while sticking with its longtime traditions.

If You Apply To ➢

Mizzou: Rolling admissions. (Priority deadline: Dec. 1.) Priority financial aid: Mar. 1. Housing: May 15. Application fee: $55. Campus interviews: optional, informational. No alumni interviews. SATs or ACTs: required. No Subject Tests. No letters of recommendation. No essay.

Morehouse College: See page 35.

Mount Holyoke College

50 College Street, South Hadley, MA 01075

One of two women's colleges, along with Smith, that are members of the Five College Consortium* in the scenic Pioneer Valley of western Massachusetts. Less nonconformist than Bryn Mawr and Smith. MHC is strongest in the natural and social sciences, and one of few colleges to have a program devoted to leadership.

Website: www.mtholyoke.edu
Location: Small Town
Private
Total Enrollment: 2,107
Undergraduates: 2,081
Male/Female: 0/100
SAT Ranges: CR 620–730, M 610–735
ACT Ranges: 29–32
Financial Aid: 78%
Pell Grant: 16%
Expense: Pr $ $
Student Loans: 69%
Average Debt: $ $
Phi Beta Kappa: Yes
Applicants: 3,858
Accepted: 50%
Enrolled: 27%
Grad in 6 Years: 85%
Returning Freshmen: 90%
Academics: ✍ ✍ ✍ ✍
Social: ☎ ☎ ☎
Q of L: ★ ★ ★ ★
Admissions: (413) 538-2023
Email Address: admission@ mtholyoke.edu

The women who choose Mount Holyoke College value achievement, leadership, inclusivity, and tradition. Mount Holyoke pioneered women's higher education in 1837 and continues to pave the way as a diverse research liberal arts institution. While students sometimes complain about the heavy workload, most bring that challenge upon themselves as they seek intellectual fulfillment within the supportive, caring environment that MHC fosters. "Mount Holyoke is a campus of empowered and passionate changemakers. We strive to seek the best in ourselves and others," says one confident senior.

Mount Holyoke is located in the heart of New England on 800 acres of rolling hills dotted with two lakes, miles of hiking trails, and waterfalls. Modern glass-and-stone buildings stand alongside more traditional ivy-covered brick and sandstone structures. Campus highlights include the Japanese Meditation Garden and Teahouse, the Talcott Greenhouse, an art building with studios and a bronze-casting foundry, an 18-hole championship golf course, and an equestrian center. The $33 million science center continues to advance the college's reputation as a leader in science education and houses classrooms, labs, and offices for eight departments. A new community center that will serve as the main campus destination for student life and dining is in the works, to be completed by spring 2018.

"We strive to seek the best in ourselves and others."

Despite changes to the campus, curriculum at this 180-year-old institution remains rooted in the traditional liberal arts and sciences. Students are required to complete 128 total credits to graduate—with at least 32 credits completed in their major field. All students must take a first-year seminar, and the college offers roughly 36 seminars each fall and 5 in the spring, covering a wide variety of topics and disciplines. The focus of these courses is developing skills in analysis and critical inquiry. Some also include field trips to museums or events in Boston, New York, and Washington, D.C.

Chemistry is a traditional strength at Mount Holyoke, bolstered by top-of-the-line labs, a scanning electron microscope, several nuclear magnetic resonance spectrometers, and a linear accelerator. The most popular majors are psychology, economics, English, and international relations. The dance program is also strong. Five-year dual-degree programs enable students to combine degrees from MHC with B.S. degrees in engineering from the University of Massachusetts, California Institute of Technology, or Dartmouth. A new minor in organizations, entrepreneurship, and society has recently been added. As an alternative to pursuing a minor or second major, the college also offers the Nexus program, which builds in opportunities for internships, off-campus research, and public presentations, along with traditional coursework. Participating students select from one of nine preprofessional tracks, such as global business, nonprofit organizations, and a new track in data science.

"Students have high expectations for themselves and push themselves to excel, but are extremely supportive of each other's endeavors," says a sophomore. Students rave about the quality of teaching and the small classes. "Faculty are warm, sensitive, incredibly intelligent, and highly invested in their students," says a psychology and education double major. "They are very accessible and interested in the lives of their students." Although some of Mount Holyoke's intro courses have 50 or more students, 70 percent of classes have fewer than 20. Since the required curriculum is so diverse, there is little trouble getting into the smaller classes and finishing in four years. The school's honor code makes possible self-scheduled, self-proctored final exams. Students say the Career Development Center's assistance with résumés, cover letters, and interview preparation is particularly effective. "They even have 40 full suits for students to rent for free!" adds a senior.

> **"Faculty are warm, sensitive, incredibly intelligent, and highly invested in their students."**

Many students choose to take advantage of an optional January winter term to take a noncredit, nontraditional course, or do an internship in major cities or points abroad. The Lynk curriculum-to-career experience guarantees all students funding for an internship or research opportunity and offers students access to special resources, workshops, and networking opportunities with alumnae. "Every student is guaranteed between \$3,000 and \$3,600 in funding for a summer internship or research project following their sophomore or junior years!" cheers one psychology major. Forty-four percent of MHC students seeking a complete change of scenery spend all or part of junior year in another country. The Twelve College Exchange Program offers opportunities in more than two dozen locales, while Mount Holyoke also sponsors its own study abroad programs, including stints in France, China, Japan, and Costa Rica.

> *The Nexus program offers nine preprofessional tracks, such as global business, nonprofit organizations, and a new track in data science.*

"Mount Holyoke students are all different, and we pride ourselves on our diversity," asserts a senior. Indeed, the college attracts students from 45 states and 74 countries; 18 percent are Massachusetts natives and 26 percent are international. African Americans make up 6 percent of the student body, Asian Americans 10 percent, and Hispanics 8 percent. "Social justice and human rights are big issues on campus," says one student, and others add that transgender rights have been a particular focus recently. CAUSE (Creating Awareness and Unity for Social Equality) is a large and popular campus group dedicated to community-building and student leadership. While only 16 percent of freshmen are eligible for the Pell Grant, Mount Holyoke's financial aid packages do meet 100 percent of applicants' demonstrated financial need. Merit scholarships are available, averaging \$16,888, but there are no athletic scholarships.

> **"We pride ourselves on our diversity."**

Ninety-five percent of Mount Holyoke students live in the residence halls. "All the residence halls at Mount Holyoke are great. They all have their own personality, which makes it very difficult to choose sometimes," says a student. Most dorms are also very homey, with living rooms, TV lounges, and baby grand pianos; all serve milk and cookies (as well as healthier fare like hummus and vegetables) most nights at 9:30 p.m. Students from all four classes live together and housing is guaranteed for all four years. Some residence halls also offer apartment-style living. Campus dining gets good reviews, as does security. "We're a really well-lit campus, and we're on the blue-light system."

Students find the Five College Consortium* one of Mount Holyoke's greatest assets. A free bus service runs every 20 minutes between MHC and Amherst, Hampshire, UMass, and Smith, multiplying a Mount Holyoke student's access to academic, social, and cultural opportunities. Social life on campus is described as "mellow." "Many students stay on campus and party or hang out with friends or watch a movie," one student explains, "but a bunch of students also socialize off campus." On-campus options include parties, plays, concerts, speakers, and cultural events. "There really isn't pressure to drink at Mount Holyoke," says one student. If on-campus activities aren't appealing, road trips to Boston, Vermont, and New York City are also popular. Closer to campus, the South Hadley Center has eateries, a pub, shops, a movie theater, and apartments, though students say that Amherst and Northampton provide more shopping options.

"There is a unique bond and desire for empowerment on campus."

Mount Holyoke students take pride in tradition. Each class has a color and a mascot, and class spirit is huge, especially for the annual Junior Show and Convocation. Every fall on Mountain Day, students wake up to ringing bells, classes are canceled (even the library is closed), and everyone treks up Mount Holyoke to picnic and see the foliage. The *Mount Holyoke News* is the oldest continuously running college newspaper in the country, and the campus is also home to the Mount Holyoke College V8s (Victory Eights), the oldest continuing female collegiate a cappella group in the United States. Community service is an important emphasis, and 52 percent of students regularly volunteer.

In addition to academic pursuits, Division III athletics at Mount Holyoke, such as crew, riding, field hockey, and lacrosse, are popular. The Lyons field hockey team capped its 2015 season by winning a third NEWMAC tournament title, and the riding team won the regional championship and placed second at the 2016 IHSA national championships. Swimming and diving and track and field are also competitive. The college encourages athletic participation at all levels with a state-of-the-art fitness center. Mount Holyoke's Model United Nations team brought home top honors in the 2015 national competition, ranking among the top 25 schools overall.

Mount Holyoke's diverse student body makes for a globally aware community, and its identity as a women's college promotes a culture where deep, personal relationships are the norm. As one senior explains, "There is a unique bond and desire for empowerment on campus." Academic excellence and easy access to New York and Boston provide a small college atmosphere that's infused with art and culture. A history major says, "Students who are interested in a welcoming student body, challenging classes, an active schedule, and wonderful memories should really consider Mount Holyoke."

Overlaps

Smith, Wellesley, Bryn Mawr, Brown, Barnard, Vassar, Tufts, University of Massachusetts Amherst

If You Apply To ➤ **MHC:** Early decision I: Nov. 15. Early decision II: Jan. 1. Regular decision: Jan. 15. Priority financial aid: Feb. 15. Financial aid: Mar. 1. Application fee: $60 (paper), free (online). Campus and alumnae interviews: recommended, evaluative. SATs or ACTs: optional. Subject Tests: optional (required for homeschooled students). Letters of recommendation: required. Essay: required. Accepts applications from students who are female or who identify as women. Accepts the Common Application with supplement.

2400 Chew Street, Allentown, PA 18104

There is a definite Muhlenberg type: ambitious, studious, and preprofessional. Takes its Lutheran affiliation and values seriously, but one-third of students are Jewish and another third are Roman Catholic. Strong in premed, prelaw, pre-anything. Has a more humble, middle-class persona than more upscale Dickinson and Lafayette and boasts a nurturing atmosphere.

When a popular school pseudonym is "The Caring College" rather than some line referring to sun or booze, you know you're in for a different experience. That's the case with Muhlenberg College, a small liberal arts school that nurtures its students. School administrators characterize the students as having "Muhlenberg goodness"—meaning that they share a strong sense of community and mutual support. Founded on solid Lutheran roots, the school continues to encourage religious diversity among students and to attract the best and brightest to its top premed school.

Set on 91 parklike acres, the 'Berg campus is a combination of older Gothic stone structures and newer buildings in a variety of architectural styles. Prominent facilities include a lovely chapel, the high-tech Trexler Library, a 40-acre biological field station and wildlife sanctuary, and a 48-acre arboretum with more than 300 species of wildflowers, broadleaf evergreens, and conifer trees. The campus also boasts a football stadium and all-weather track, and the 50,000-square-foot Trexler Pavilion for the Performing Arts that has a dramatic 45-foot glass outer shell and houses a variety of performance spaces.

Muhlenberg's popular First-Year Seminars are small, writing-intensive, discussion-intensive courses capped at 15 students. Other general education requirements include two additional writing-intensive courses, a two-course cluster in the sophomore or junior year aimed at helping students connect different disciplines, a two-course diversity and global engagement requirement, and a capstone experience in the major. The fun-filled, three-day freshman orientation program carries just one requirement: learning the alma mater and then hightailing it to the president's house to serenade him.

Muhlenberg's regional reputation rests on its premedical program, which continues to attract large numbers of students. An agreement with Philadelphia's Drexel University College of Medicine guarantees seats for up to six Muhlenberg students each year. A new major in public health was recently added, the neuroscience major has been gaining prominence, and there are joint programs in physical

> **"[Muhlenberg] urges you to compete with yourself, to question your thinking, and to reach your full potential."**

therapy and occupational therapy available with Thomas Jefferson University. The college's theater arts program is also a national draw, and a few alumni have even gone on to star on Broadway. Science lab equipment at Muhlenberg is cutting-edge, and a comprehensive natural science major allows for a sampling of it all. The Living Writers course is offered every other year and has brought a number of noted authors to campus, including Robert Pinsky, Jay Wright, and Alice Fulton. Business administration is Muhlenberg's most popular major, followed by psychology, theater, media and communication, and biology.

Students agree that the academic climate at Muhlenberg is collaborative, and a mathematics major adds, "I feel that Muhlenberg is competitive in the sense that it urges you to compete with yourself, to question your thinking, and to reach your full potential." Seventy-seven percent of courses have fewer than 20 students, and

Website: www.muhlenberg.edu
Location: City Outskirts
Private
Total Enrollment: 2,278
Undergraduates: 2,278
Male/Female: 41/59
SAT Ranges: CR 550–660, M 560–660
ACT Ranges: 25–31
Financial Aid: 89%
Pell Grant: 13%
Expense: Pr $ $ $
Student Loans: 57%
Average Debt: $ $ $
Phi Beta Kappa: Yes
Applicants: 5,015
Accepted: 49%
Enrolled: 24%
Grad in 6 Years: 85%
Returning Freshmen: 93%
Academics: ✑ ✑ ✑
Social: ☎ ☎ ☎
Q of L: ★ ★ ★ ★
Admissions: (484) 664-3200
Email Address: admissions@ muhlenberg.edu

Strong Programs:
Business Administration
Psychology
Theater
Media and Communication
Biology
Premed
Public Health
Neuroscience

since there are no graduate students, there are no teaching assistants. "Professors go out of their way to make students feel comfortable and valued both within the classroom and out," says a senior. "It is easy for students to find faculty mentors and establish relationships that will last post-graduation." Advising is strong here too, and seniors may take advantage of the Senior Year Experience program that helps them make the transition from college to "whatever comes next." The program is organized around the concepts of transition, integration, and reflection and includes workshops and seminars.

An agreement with Philadelphia's Drexel University College of Medicine guarantees seats for up to six Muhlenberg students each year.

The college offers three honors programs: the Muhlenberg Scholars Program, the Dana Scholars Program, and the RJ Fellows Program, which focuses on the ramifications of change. They carry an annual $4,000 stipend and culminate in an in-depth mentored senior research project; about 20 percent of students participate. Students speak highly of the college's array of service-learning course offerings. Muhlenberg sends study groups to Washington, D.C., and there is a semester-long program at the Jewish Theological Seminary in New York City. Those seeking international experiences may study abroad via 150 programs in countries around the globe, and about a third do so. Muhlenberg is also a member of the Lehigh Valley Association of Independent Colleges*.

"It is easy for students to find faculty mentors and establish relationships that will last post-graduation."

"There is a niche for everyone at the 'Berg," says a senior, "whether your interests are in knitting or theater, comedy or football, politics or hip-hop dancing." Muhlenberg draws 27 percent of its students from Pennsylvania, and many from adjacent New Jersey, as well as 3 percent from foreign nations. African Americans account for 3 percent of the student body, Hispanics 7 percent, and Asian Americans 3 percent. Cultural appreciation is emphasized as Muhlenberg continues to foster a religiously varied campus and works to increase ethnic diversity. "Many student organizations are making efforts to make progress toward social justice, such as the Muhlenberg Trans* Advocacy Coalition," says a psychology major. Merit scholarships averaging $12,057 are available, but there are no athletic scholarships.

The college offers three honors programs that carry an annual $4,000 stipend.

Muhlenberg encourages students to live on campus and guarantees housing to all undergraduates except transfers, so 91 percent of students live in campus residences. "Freshmen are required to live in one of three dorms, which is actually nice because it brings them all together in one area of campus," explains a senior. All dorms have computer labs, study lounges, and vending machines. Upperclassmen praise the Muhlenberg Independent Living Experience townhouses and other suite-style options. Two dorms, Robertson and South, house 140 students in single, air-conditioned rooms overlooking Lake Muhlenberg. Freshmen choose from a seven- or five-day meal plan, and students rate dining options highly. "The food is fresh and locally sourced as often as possible," reports a student. "There is specific labeling for foods that are vegan, vegetarian, gluten-free, and kosher." A senior says, "With a Title IX coordinator and judicial panel, the college puts a great deal of effort into making sure that students and members of the Muhlenberg community feel safe."

"There is a niche for everyone at the 'Berg."

Most social life at Muhlenberg takes place on campus. "The most fun I've had at school has been in my dorm hallway," says a student. "Just hanging out with people I meet is fun." The Muhlenberg Activities Council provides comedians every Thursday evening, current movies in the Red Door Café, live band concerts, and new movies on the lawn. "For those who enjoy different entertainment, it is easy to get together a group of friends, go somewhere, or make your own fun," says one student. Hillel is among the largest of the more than 100 student organizations, as are the theater and dance associations. Students stay involved in the community by volunteering as tutors and with groups such as Habitat for Humanity and America Reads. City buses stop five minutes from campus for trips to Allentown proper and area malls. There also are daily bus runs to New York City (for clubbing and theater), Philadelphia (for nightlife and cheesesteaks), and Baltimore and Washington, D.C. Outdoorsy students can pick up the Appalachian Trail for a little hiking.

Nineteen percent of Muhlenberg men and 27 percent of the women pledge their undergraduate years to fraternities and sororities, respectively, but Greek life does not dominate the social scene. Alcohol is forbidden if you're underage, per Pennsylvania law, and the school takes its policies seriously. Big social events include homecoming, West Fest in the fall, East Fest in the spring, the Scotty Wood basketball tournament, the Mr. Muhlenberg awards—which parody the Miss America pageant—and the Henry Awards, the college's version of the Oscars. There's also a candlelight ceremony where freshmen write down their college goals, to be reexamined the day before graduation.

For the athletically inclined, the Muhlenberg Mules compete in the Division III Centennial Conference. Women's basketball, men's soccer, and men's football have won conference championships recently. Women's soccer and softball are also competitive and popular spectator sports on campus. Students say any contest against Johns Hopkins draws crowds. Muhlenberg's Life Sports Center offers a pool, a basketball court, other all-purpose courts, and a jogging track. Also popular is Frisbee golf; there's an 18-hole course on campus, where play goes on during all seasons and all hours of the day and night.

Muhlenberg earns its moniker as "The Caring College" by offering students a warm, intimate academic milieu and plenty of support. It's a winning formula that draws students from far and wide. Put simply, says one senior, "Muhlenberg believes in students and their ability to learn."

The theater and dance associations are among the largest of the more than 100 student organizations.

Overlaps

Lafayette, Dickinson, NYU, Skidmore, Ithaca, Gettysburg, Franklin & Marshall, College of New Jersey

If You Apply To > **Muhlenberg:** Early decision, regular decision, and financial aid: Feb. 15. Application fee: $50. Campus interviews: recommended, evaluative (required, along with a graded paper, if students choose not to submit SAT scores). Alumni interviews: optional, evaluative. SATs or ACTs (with writing): optional. No Subject Tests. Letters of recommendation: required. Essay: required. Accepts the Common Application with supplement.

University of Nebraska–Lincoln

12 Administration Building, Lincoln, NE 68588

Everybody knows Nebraska football, but in other areas UNL, the smallest public university in the Big Ten, flies under the radar. With relatively few out-of-staters, has a corner on the market for Nebraskans without a major competitor like Iowa State. Psychology, business administration, and advertising and public relations top the list of majors. Because of the state's demographic makeup, diversity is a challenge.

On crisp fall weekends, when spirits are high and the Big Red football arcs through the air, Huskers cheer and paint the town of Lincoln red and white in a show of appreciation for their alma mater. In fact, on home-game Saturdays, the stadium is the third largest "city" in the state, holding 5 percent of the population. Away from the stadium, students at the University of Nebraska–Lincoln have more reasons to cheer, with notable programs ranging from biological systems engineering to digital humanities to professional golf management.

Website: www.unl.edu
Location: Small City
Public
Total Enrollment: 21,407
Undergraduates: 18,817
Male/Female: 53/47

(continued)

SAT Ranges: CR 500–630,
  M 500–660
ACT Ranges: 22–28
Financial Aid: 60%
Pell Grant: 26%
Expense: Pub $
Student Loans: 57%
Average Debt: $ $
Phi Beta Kappa: Yes
Applicants: 9,724
Accepted: 76%
Enrolled: 62%
Grad in 6 Years: 67%
Returning Freshmen: 83%
Academics: ✍ ✍ ✍
Social: ☎ ☎ ☎ ☎
Q of L: ★ ★ ★
Admissions: (800) 742-8800
Email Address: admissions@
  unl.edu

Strong Programs:
Psychology
Business Administration
Advertising and Public
  Relations
Accounting
Agricultural Sciences
Animal Science
Biochemistry
Early Childhood Education

*The UCARE program
provides a stipend
for students to
participate in one-
on-one research
with a professor.*

UNL spreads across two campuses. The East Campus, referred to by many as the "Ag Campus," is home to the College of Agricultural Sciences and Natural Resources, law, and dentistry. Most entering students end up on the larger City Campus, home of seven undergraduate colleges: architecture, arts and sciences, journalism and mass communications, business administration, fine and performing arts, engineering, and education and human sciences. On City Campus, the architectural style ranges from the modern Sheldon Art Gallery designed by Philip Johnson to the architecture building, which is on the National Register of Historic Places. There are also several malls, an arboretum, and a sculpture garden. New campus additions include a soccer and tennis complex and the Outdoor Adventures Center.

> **"The professors do a good job of making students feel valued."**

Nebraska's Achievement-Centered Education Program provides students with a common set of educational experiences across the majors and colleges, and all UNL students must take a capstone course their senior year. To help freshmen get oriented, Big Red Welcome combines entertainment, information booths, and food in a carnival setting. Nebraska's College of Agricultural Sciences and Natural Resources is known for its outstanding programs in food science and technology, agribusiness, and animal science. Biochemistry and early childhood development are also traditional strengths. The school of music's opera program has received national attention, and the performing arts programs benefit from the Lied Center for the Performing Arts, which seats 2,300. The most popular majors are psychology, business administration, advertising and public relations, and accounting. Newly added programs include B.S. degrees in software engineering, agricultural and environmental sciences communication, and integrated science.

"Students help each other become better by challenging each other," says an accounting major. "The workload is fairly intensive, if you want to get good grades."

> **"[My learning community] helped make the campus seem smaller and less intimidating."**

Getting into courses in the most popular areas, especially education, business, and engineering, can be a problem, students say; preregistration is a must. Although many classes are large, 37 percent have fewer than 20 students. Graduate students teach some freshman courses, but top professors can be found inside the classroom too. "For a university this big, I think that the professors do a good job of making students feel valued," says a prenursing student. "It is hard to be recognized in classes with 100 students, but I don't think that the quality of teaching is any less. And there are always office hours for students."

The UNL Honors Program gives qualified students research opportunities to complement their coursework. Also, the UCARE (Undergraduate Creative Activity and Research Experience) program provides a stipend for students to participate in one-on-one research with a professor after freshman year. The Jeffrey S. Raikes School of Computer Science and Management is a highly selective program that focuses on a curriculum in technology, business, and real-world projects, and that awards scholarships to participants. Study abroad opportunities are offered in 45 countries and include 40 faculty-led programs; 21 percent of students take part. Career Services shows students how to make a professional résumé, holds mock interviews, and hosts potential employers, among other activities.

A junior says UNL students' "social etiquette and values are high, embodying 'Nebraska Nice,'" adding, "The political climate is more liberal than the state as a whole." Seventy-two percent of undergraduates hail from in state, and 9 percent come from abroad. Asian Americans make up 2 percent of the student body, African Americans 3 percent, and Hispanics 5 percent. Many students say diversity—or the lack thereof—is an issue, but one notes, "I feel like my institution has really made an effort to expand diversity." Twenty-six percent of incoming freshmen are eligible for Pell Grants. Merit scholarships are available, with an average award of $6,486, in addition to 267 athletic scholarships in 19 sports.

Forty-one percent of students live in the university's single-sex or co-ed dorms, and there's usually no trouble getting a room. "Most of the dorms are up-to-date and are pretty sizable, but there are a few that are smaller," explains a science education major. "There are options, however, for suite-style dorms that are available to everyone, including freshmen." Apartment-style housing is fairly competitive for underclassmen, and dorm lotteries favor those wanting to stay in the same room or on the same floor. Freshmen must live on campus, but many students move off campus after their sophomore year. Students praise the 25 living/learning communities offered for first-years with common majors. "I was a member of a learning community my freshman year and it helped make the campus seem smaller and less intimidating," recalls a nutrition and dietetics major. Dining facilities are "new and wonderful," says one student, "and always have a wide variety of food selections." Campus security is said to be strong. "'Dial 2 for Blue' is a slogan everyone on campus knows," reports a chemistry major. A sophomore adds that sexual assault "has been a minor issue on campus. The response has been one of zero tolerance, though, and various organizations are working to raise awareness about sexual assault."

"A lot of the social life starts on campus but then moves off," says a communication studies major. "You meet people on your floor or in a club, and then you hang out and go out off campus." Fraternity and house parties, concerts and theater performances, the movies, eating out, visiting coffee

> **"UNL is rooted in tradition, kindness, and Husker pride!"**

shops and bars (for those of age), and road trips to Omaha or Kansas City are just some of the activities that keep students busy. For many, the fall semester revolves around football weekends and postseason bowl games. Fraternities draw 19 percent of UNL men and sororities attract 22 percent of the women. They offer both social events and a chance to get involved in the Lincoln community. Homecoming, Greek Week, the spring concert, and The Big Event (a major community service occasion) are among the most anticipated campus events.

"Lincoln is a great college town, especially during football season!" exclaims one business administration major. Another student points out that the "thirty bars within a two-minute walk of campus" are appreciated by those of age, given UNL's dry campus. Town/gown relations are good and "the community is always eager for students to return in the fall," according to one premed student. Pachyderm enthusiasts will be delighted by the Nebraska Museum of Natural History's outstanding collection of prehistoric elephant skeletons. Beyond the town's sidewalks are miles of flat roads and plains, ideal for biking, cross-country skiing, and snowmobiling, and Omaha is only 45 minutes away by car.

The Cornhuskers have a reputation as a powerhouse in a number of sports and hold consecutive NCAA sell-out attendance records in volleyball (2015 national champions) and, of course, football. Women's bowling also claimed the national title in 2015, and women's basketball, soccer, softball, and gymnastics, along with men's track and field, have all brought home recent conference titles. Men's and women's hoopsters frolic in the new 16,000-seat Haymarket Arena, which also serves as a venue for concerts and other events. And who hasn't heard of the classy Nebraska football? Having only recently joined the Big Ten, Nebraska has not yet developed long-term rivalries to replace the likes of Oklahoma, though the annual Black Friday bowl game against the University of Iowa may be a likely candidate. Nevertheless, home football games are not to be missed. "There is nothing like Game Days in Nebraska," says a senior. "The entire city of Lincoln is full of Husker fans." Recreational and intramural sports are popular, with flag football and basketball drawing the most participants.

The Cornhuskers hold consecutive NCAA sell-out attendance records in volleyball (2015 national champions) and football.

Apartment-style housing is available, but fairly competitive, for underclassmen.

Overlaps

University of Nebraska Omaha, University of Nebraska at Kearney, Iowa State, Nebraska Wesleyan, Creighton, University of Missouri, University of Kansas, University of Iowa

At Nebraska, future agricultural experts mingle with techno-whizzes, while teachers-in-training brush elbows with architecture mavens. Whether studying overseas, immersing themselves in internships, or going wild on Saturday afternoon, students here know how to make the most of their time as Cornhuskers. Cheers one happy Husker, "UNL is rooted in tradition, kindness, and Husker pride!"

If You Apply To ➤

Nebraska: Rolling admissions: May 1. Financial aid: Apr. 1. Application fee: $45. No campus or alumni interviews. SATs or ACTs: required. No Subject Tests. No letters of recommendation. No essay (personal statement required for scholarship consideration).

New College of Florida

5800 Bay Shore Road, Sarasota, FL 34243

New College is the South's most liberal institution of higher learning—apologies to Guilford. With an enrollment of just over 850, New College is about one-third the size of a typical liberal arts college. The kicker: it's a public institution and a great bargain. Don't expect to hear many Southern accents; most students are transplants even if they went to high school in Florida.

Website: www.ncf.edu

Location: Suburban

Public

Total Enrollment: 852

Undergraduates: 852

Male/Female: 39/61

SAT Ranges: CR 610–720, M 560–660

ACT Ranges: 27–31

Financial Aid: 97%

Pell Grant: 27%

Expense: Pub $

Student Loans: 48%

Average Debt: $

Phi Beta Kappa: No

Applicants: 1,655

Accepted: 61%

Enrolled: 26%

Grad in 6 Years: 71%

Returning Freshmen: 81%

Academics: ✍ ✍ ✍ ✍

Social: ☎ ☎ ☎

Q of L: ★ ★ ★

Admissions: (941) 487-5000

Email Address: admissions@ncf.edu

Strong Programs:
Psychology

The mere existence of New College of Florida is proof that it's possible to find success through individualism. This school has done away with grades and GPAs, and the laid-back student body and rigorous academic program "proves to students that learning can be a self-directed, fun, and productive experience," a sophomore says. Indeed, college alumni include winners of various prestigious national scholarships, among them 64 Fulbright scholars since 2005. Strong programs in psychology, biology, and anthropology complement the liberal arts offerings and boost the reputation of this fast-rising star. "New College does not produce cookie-cutter graduates," asserts a senior. "We are intellects, activists, and sometimes a little self-righteous."

New College began in 1960 as an alternative private college for academically talented students, but when inflation threatened its existence in the mid-1970s, it offered its campus to the University of South Florida. Today, NCF serves as Florida's honors college but is an academically independent entity. New College's campus is adjacent to Sarasota Bay and consists of historic mansions from the former estate of circus magnate Charles Ringling, abutting modern dorms designed by I. M. Pei. The central quad is filled with palm trees, and sunsets over the bay are spectacular.

> **"We are intellects, activists, and sometimes a little self-righteous."**

The administration once had no required core curriculum, but has added requirements to provide "each student with the depth and breadth of knowledge characteristic of a good liberal arts education." All undergraduates must complete at least eight courses in the liberal arts curriculum, including courses in humanities, social sciences, and natural sciences, and show literacy in math and computers. The school calendar, however, is still unusual: the two 14-week semesters are separated by a month-long January Interterm, during which students devise and carry out their own research, conduct group projects, or pursue short-term internships. Students work out a "contract" with their advisor each semester and receive written evaluations instead of grades. The seven semester-long contracts and three independent study projects lead to an area of concentration, capped by a senior thesis project and an oral baccalaureate examination.

New College doesn't offer the specialized courses of a large university, but there's still plenty to choose from across the academic spectrum. Anthropology wins raves, and many students also gravitate to biology, psychology, international and area studies, political science, and sociology. Academic programs are constantly changing to best suit students' needs; an example is the beefing up of offerings in STEM fields, environmental studies, and economics. A 1,100-gallon seawater system is available for lab experiments in animal behavior and physiology. The Jane Bancroft Cook Library makes up for its small size—fewer than 300,000 volumes—with a language lab, an interlibrary loan program with the entire state university system of Florida, and a classroom equipped for teleconferences. "For a small college with limited resources, we have an incredibly thought-provoking and challenging curriculum," says one student.

Due to the highly individualized nature of the curriculum, getting into some classes can be a challenge. Courses are rigorous, but students say the lack of grades negates any competitive airs. "I would describe the academic climate of our school as collaborative," reflects an applied mathematics major. "Students who attend our institution are here to learn and progress in a way that promotes individuality rather than competition." Students praise the personalized attention they receive from professors; graduate students and teaching assistants don't lead classes here, and 73 percent of classes have fewer than 20 students. "The classroom environment is personalized and intimate," says one student. Another describes profs as "tremendously helpful and willing to listen or give advice when needed." The shape of any student's program depends heavily on the outlook of his or her faculty sponsor, and students say advising—both academic and career—is readily available. All disciplines provide the opportunity for original research, and students also may conduct field research around the globe. Seventeen percent of students study abroad in roughly 25 countries.

In keeping with the revolution theme, students on this relatively cosmopolitan campus tend to be creative liberal types with '60s nuances and social habits. "New College is full of hippies with a strong social justice agenda," says a biology major. "We are very, very, very liberal, though inclusive." Students rally around issues that run the gamut from women's rights to poverty and commercialism. Hispanics account for 16 percent of the student body, 3 percent are Asian Americans, and African Americans make up 3 percent; 4 percent come from foreign countries. Socioeconomic diversity is strong, with 27 percent of freshmen qualifying for Pell Grants. Seventy-eight percent of undergrads hail from Florida, perhaps because New College has yet to make a national name for itself, although the college is attempting to change that by offering all admitted out-of-state students automatic Presidential Scholarships worth $60,000 over four years. All admitted Florida residents are guaranteed automatic scholarships too, in amounts that vary based on academic standing. There are no athletic awards.

Seventy-six percent of students live in campus housing. "We just built five new dorms," says one student, "which some people like but others think are too stiff." The Dort dorms, two apartment-style halls, accommodate 140 students in two-bedroom, two-bath suites with a kitchen, living area, and—of course—air-conditioning. Rooms are chosen by lottery and there has been a room shortage as of late, forcing some to find off-campus alternatives. Campus dining has long been a student grievance, especially among the school's sizable vegan population, but meals are showing signs of improvement following a recent change in food providers. A literature major says,

(continued)

Anthropology
Biology
International and Area Studies
Political Science
Sociology

Students work out a "contract" with their advisor each semester and receive written evaluations instead of grades.

"For a small college with limited resources, we have an incredibly thought-provoking and challenging curriculum."

All admitted out-of-state students are offered automatic Presidential Scholarships worth $60,000 over four years.

"Our campus is very secure, with emergency blue phones placed every few yards and police available 24/7."

The abundance of students sporting T-shirts and shorts on Friday night reflects the laid-back campus social scene. A senior says, "We do not have a Greek system, so the drinking and party culture stems more from blowing off steam from a challenging week of classes rather than peer pressure." Resident advisors organize substance-free events, and a multitude of student organizations also keep students busy, from the New College Student Alliance (the student government) to "Cloud Watching Club (it is what it sounds like)," says a sophomore, adding, "It's a small campus, so it's easy to become involved in new activities." The COUPs (Center of the Universe Parties) are "blow-out-of-proportion" social gatherings that occur during Halloween, Valentine's Day, and graduation. Students also flock to the annual Cardboard Regatta, in which they build and race cardboard boats; Midnight Breakfast, where faculty and staff serve students free breakfast foods at night during exam weeks; Chocolate Fest, where students bring chocolate-containing dishes to a large potluck; and Queer Pride Week, in which students host events centered on LGBTQ history, awareness, and pride.

> **"The beaches are gorgeous—white sand and blue water."**

> *COUPs (Center of the Universe Parties) occur during Halloween, Valentine's Day, and graduation.*

Sarasota offers little more than "beaches and old people," according to one sophomore, although 57 percent of students get involved in volunteer work through more than 30 local community organizations. The Ringling Museum of Art and the Asolo State Theater adjoin the campus, and many New College instrumentalists perform with the Sarasota Orchestra, the city's professionally led symphony orchestra. The open road to Tampa, Gainesville, Key West, Orlando, New Orleans, Atlanta, and even Washington, D.C. ("to protest stuff"), beckons when Sarasota becomes too quiet.

New College is definitely no haven for jocks; it fields no varsity teams, although its Intercollegiate Sailing Association sailing team is nationally competitive. The fledgling quiz bowl team, founded in 2015, has already made a name for itself by qualifying for the Academic Competition Federation's national tournament in 2016. Nineteen percent of students take advantage of club and intramural sports, which range from flag football and fencing to soccer and scuba diving. The annual Ringling College of Art and Design/New College flag football game draws crowds, as does the nearby ocean. "The beaches are gorgeous—white sand and blue water," says a student.

Without a Greek scene, grades, or crazy football games, New College of Florida is definitely not your typical Southern institution. But the eccentricity doesn't impede students' academic motivation; in fact, it encourages an atmosphere that celebrates learning for the sake of curiosity, persistence, and thoughtfulness—whether the subject at hand is biology, belly dancing, psychology, or origami. "If you want to get hands-on experience, work side by side with published professors, and leave with knowledge greater than what can get you a good score on a standardized test, then go to New College," says one proud senior.

Overlaps

University of Florida, Florida State, University of South Florida, University of Central Florida, Eckerd, University of Miami (FL), NYU, Vassar

If You Apply To ➤

New College: Regular decision: Apr. 15. (Priority deadline: Nov. 1.) Priority financial aid: Nov. 1. Application fee: $30. No campus or alumni interviews. SATs or ACTs: required. Subject Tests: optional. Letters of recommendation: required. Essay: required. Accepts the Common Application.

University of New Hampshire

Grant House, 3 Garrison Avenue, Durham, NH 03824

UNH is a public university that looks and feels like a private college, and its tuition hits the pocketbook with similar force. Expensive though it may be, UNH draws half of its students from out of state. Well known for engineering, space science, and life science programs—especially marine biology—and its business school is nationally ranked. With graduate students accounting for less than one-tenth of total enrollment, UNH's focus is squarely on undergrads.

Students at the University of New Hampshire know how to get their hands dirty, and this solid public institution provides them with countless opportunities to do so. UNH is one of just 17 universities in the nation to receive land grant, sea grant, and space grant designations. Its research mission has grown dramatically in the last decade, yet the university remains a moderate-sized institution that emphasizes undergraduate instruction. Unlike many large research universities, the UNH faculty teach all students, including freshmen, and value teaching as much as they do their research. A love of the outdoors is a must, as well as the ability to withstand long, cold winters. "Every day is a great day to be a Wildcat!" cheers one student.

The university's wide-open, grassy Durham campus hosts a mix of modern facilities and ivy-covered brick buildings. The sprawling lawns are surrounded by nearly 3,000 acres of farms, fields, and woods. During the past few years, UNH has invested in large-scale construction and renovation projects, including new residence halls, a new physics building, a new veterinary diagnostic lab, and an addition to one of its coastal marine labs. A major expansion of the student health and fitness center was completed in 2016, as was construction on a brand-new stadium for the football team.

The university's core curriculum, the Discovery Program, includes general education requirements that apply across the board and mandate completion of one course from each of eight categories: biological science; physical science; historical perspectives; world cultures; social science; fine and performing arts; humanities; and environment, technology, and society.

> **"A lot of weight is placed on grades and academic standing."**

Freshman composition is also mandatory as part of a four-course writing intensive requirement, as is a course in quantitative reasoning. All first-years must complete an Inquiry course involving an experiential learning component, and all seniors must complete a capstone experience.

Interdisciplinary programs enhance UNH's emphasis on traditional academic programs and the many research opportunities offered by its seven schools and colleges. Engineering and business are among the most respected programs. The Peter T. Paul College of Business and Economics is nationally ranked, offering a spate of majors and the opportunity for students to design their own tracks; the college also boasts one of the first student-run angel investment funds. Marine biology is considered stellar, enhanced by UNH's proximity to the ocean and a brackish bay, and nursing and creative writing are also strengths. The most popular majors are business administration, psychology, biomedical science, and communication. New offerings include ocean engineering, biotechnology, and analytics, as well as a new dual major that allows students to pair a degree in sustainability with any other major.

The academic climate at UNH can be fairly competitive, and a junior says, "A lot of weight is placed on grades and academic standing," but students agree that

Website: www.unh.edu
Location: Small Town
Public
Total Enrollment: 13,823
Undergraduates: 12,585
Male/Female: 46/54
SAT Ranges: CR 500–600, M 510–610
ACT Ranges: 22–27
Financial Aid: 80%
Pell Grant: 24%
Expense: Pub $ $ $ $
Student Loans: 77%
Average Debt: $ $ $ $
Phi Beta Kappa: Yes
Applicants: 19,255
Accepted: 79%
Enrolled: 21%
Grad in 6 Years: 79%
Returning Freshmen: 85%
Academics: ✑ ✑ ✑
Social: 🐗 🐗 🐗 🐗
Q of L: ★ ★ ★ ★ ★
Admissions: (603) 862-1360
Email Address: admissions@unh.edu

Strong Programs:
Business Administration
Psychology
Biomedical Science
Communication
Engineering
Marine Biology
Nursing
Creative Writing

the level of intensity varies by school and college. Classes are relatively small, with 83 percent enrolling fewer than 50 students, and TAs only facilitate discussion sections or labs. "We have world-class professors, many of whom participate in research and include students as research assistants," says a senior, and a junior notes that professors are accessible and "easy to speak to."

UNH prides itself on producing undergraduates with research experience. The Hamel Center for Undergraduate Research provides about 100 research awards each year for undergraduates to work closely with faculty on original projects. Budding scientists and sociologists have opportunities to work at research centers for space science and family violence; other students can take advantage of opportunities to conduct research on NASA partner projects or within the Institute for Policy and Social Science Research; the Institute for the Study of Earth, Oceans, and Space; and the Center for Humanities. The UNH InterOperability Lab lets students work with professors and businesses on cutting-edge compatibility testing, and the Isle of Shoals Marine Laboratory, six miles off the coast, provides an offshore research setting. UNH's Center for International Education and Global Engagement offers more than 500 study abroad programs and other opportunities; 22 percent of students study abroad. And for the especially motivated, the University Honors Program, featuring small classes, is available for qualifying students in any major to begin during freshman year.

"Meals are amazing, and the school…[caters] to gluten-free students and students with allergies."

While UNH is New Hampshire's major public institution, it has long been popular with out-of-staters, who make up 51 percent of its students; international students add another 2 percent. African Americans account for 1 percent of the student population, Asian Americans 2 percent, and Hispanics 3 percent. A special task force at the university is working on keeping minority students in school until graduation and helping them network. Social issues at UNH include alcohol awareness and—as might be expected in a place with such lush natural beauty—the environment. The school offers hundreds of merit scholarships, averaging $6,834, and 350 awards are available for gifted athletes. Twenty-four percent of incoming students qualify for Pell Grants.

Fifty-six percent of UNHers live in the school's co-ed dorms. "Some of the freshman dorms are too far away from the main area of campus (Williamson and Christenson)," complains one senior, but accommodations are said to be generally nice. Freshmen and sophomores are guaranteed dorm rooms; most upperclassmen live off campus or in two on-campus apartment complexes. More than a dozen themed residence halls are available and are an increasingly popular option. Campus dining receives rave reviews: "Meals are amazing, and the school is nationally ranked when it comes to catering (no pun intended) to gluten-free students and students with allergies," says a political science major. A mathematics major says, "I feel safe on campus. Nearly every path is well lit at night." UNH is a national leader in efforts to prevent sexual assaults on campus. In addition to its student-praised training programs and support services, UNH established the Prevention Innovations Research Center to develop evidence-based prevention strategies and policies.

"Get involved early on, as that will help you become acclimated to the campus."

UNH offers more than 200 student organizations covering just about any interest. "Get involved early on, as that will help you become acclimated to the campus," advises a social work and women's studies major. "U Day is a great way to do that." Service organizations are popular, and half of the student body gets involved with community service activities. The Campus Activities Board organizes weekend social events including concerts, dances, movies, and gatherings at local coffeehouses.

Greek groups claim 11 percent of the men and 12 percent of the women. The party culture at UNH is lively, but Greek parties are subject to the university's no-tolerance alcohol policy, which evicts underage students caught with alcohol more than once from on-campus housing. Homecoming, Winter Carnival, Casino Night, and Spring Fling are favorite annual events.

Less than a five-minute walk from campus is the beautiful little town of Durham, which caters to the student clientele. Durham is UNH, students say, and its Main Street is lined with restaurants and coffeehouses, a grocery store, an ice-cream parlor, and a few bars, which have been divided into separate sections (for legal consumers of alcohol and everyone else). The on-campus Amtrak station makes weekend escapes to Boston and Portland, Maine, easy—if students can find time off. (The school's nickname is the University of No Holidays, since an exceptionally generous winter break limits the number of days off during other seasons.) The White Mountains are popular with outdoor enthusiasts, and late nights at L.L. Bean have also become commonplace. Every four years, New Hampshire takes the spotlight when the state holds the nation's earliest presidential primary.

UNH has 20 Division I athletics teams, of which ice hockey is a fan favorite. Students celebrate the first Wildcats goal of each game by inexplicably throwing a large fish onto the ice, and during games against its rival, the University of Maine–Orono, students wear white to "white out" the stadium. The women's volleyball team won the America East conference championship in 2016, and other solid teams include football, women's field hockey, and men's and women's skiing. Club and intramural sports enlist thousands of students. Broomball—played with brooms, balls, and sneakers on the ice—is very popular, as are activities organized by the Outing Club, including skiing, surfing, camping, fishing, and hiking.

New Hampshire's only major public university offers a huge variety of programs. That's one reason it attracts so many students from out of state. The laid-back atmosphere and multitude of both academic and social opportunities in a beautiful natural setting make the UNH experience worth every dime.

UNH is a national leader in efforts to prevent sexual assaults on campus.

Overlaps

University of Massachusetts Amherst, University of Vermont, University of Rhode Island, University of Connecticut, University of Maine–Orono, University of Massachusetts Lowell, University of Delaware, Quinnipiac

If You Apply To ➤

New Hampshire: Early action: Nov. 15. Regular decision: Feb. 1. Financial aid: Mar. 1. Housing: May 1. Application fee: $50 (residents), $65 (nonresidents). No campus or alumni interviews. SATs or ACTs (with writing): required. No Subject Tests. Letters of recommendation: required. Essay: required. Accepts the Common Application with supplement. Additional materials required for applicants to music, theatre, and studio art programs.

The College of New Jersey

P.O. Box 7718, Ewing, NJ 08628

A public liberal arts institution in the mold of UNC Asheville or William and Mary. Also offers business and education. With more than nine-tenths of the students homegrown Garden Staters, TCNJ has little appeal beyond Jersey. On the other hand, it is now the state's second most selective institution, after a certain school up the road in Princeton. A smaller, more personal alternative to Rutgers.

The College of New Jersey is an up-and-coming public institution with special focus on undergraduates, an emphasis more commonly found at a private school. TCNJ offers professors focused on teaching and a campus physically similar to one found up the road at Princeton University—without the Ivy League price tag. Formerly a teachers' college, TCNJ strives to provide students opportunities in a host of other

Website: www.tcnj.edu
Location: Suburban
Public
Total Enrollment: 6,711

(continued)

Undergraduates: 6,486
Male/Female: 41/59
SAT Ranges: CR 550–640,
   M 570–670

ACT Ranges: 26–30
Financial Aid: 49%
Pell Grant: N/A
Expense: Pub $ $ $ $
Student Loans: 64%
Average Debt: $ $ $ $
Phi Beta Kappa: Yes
Applicants: 11,290
Accepted: 49%
Enrolled: 26%
Grad in 6 Years: 87%
Returning Freshmen: 95%
Academics: ✎ ✎ ✎ ✎
Social: ☎ ☎ ☎
Q of L: ★ ★ ★
Admissions: (609) 771-2131
Email Address: tcnjinfo@
   tcnj.edu

Strong Programs:
Elementary Education
Business Administration
Psychology
Biology
Communication Studies
Nursing

Campus Town, a $120 million complex adjacent to the campus, features 612 apartments for upperclassmen, retail shops, and restaurants.

fields. The small size makes for closeness among students and faculty. Says one student, "TCNJ is really big on the 'community' feel."

TCNJ is set on 289 wooded and landscaped acres in suburban Ewing Township, six miles from Trenton. The picturesque Georgian colonial architecture centers on Quimby's Prairie, surrounded by the original academic buildings of the 1930s. A flock of Canada geese makes its home in one of the two campus lakes. In partnership with a private developer, the college has recently opened Campus Town, a 12-acre, $120 million complex adjacent to the campus that features 612 apartments for upperclassmen, a new campus gym, and retail shops and restaurants open to both the campus community and the public.

Liberal Learning, TCNJ's general education program, requires coursework centered on three fundamental areas: intellectual and scholarly growth, broad areas of human inquiry, and civic responsibilities. Freshmen participate in several programs to prepare them for college life and academics, including a summer reading program; welcome week; an online, noncredit course on information literacy; a writing seminar; and a First Seminar course, in which they take a small seminar on a topic outside of their intended major and live with their classmates in the same residence hall. Freshmen must also complete at least eight hours of community service.

Consistent with the school's origins as a teachers' college, elementary education is popular. The business school is strong, as are the natural sciences. The most popular majors include psychology, biology, communication studies, and nursing. The college offers a combined four-and-a-half-year B.S./M.A. in law and justice, taught jointly by TCNJ and Rutgers; a seven-year B.S./M.D. degree program with the University of Medicine and Dentistry of New Jersey; and a seven-year B.S./O.D. degree with SUNY College of Optometry.

"TCNJ is really big on the 'community' feel."

Academically, TCNJ is competitive and getting more so. "The academic climate is somewhat intense," confides a sophomore. "Some students and professors try to downplay the competitive nature, but overall it's pretty driven." An honors program is available for those who wish to challenge themselves with an even more rigorous curriculum. Forty-three percent of undergraduate classes have fewer than 20 students. The college has no teaching assistants, and faculty members get high marks, though quality can vary by department. "My professors are very passionate about their work and field of study," says a psychology major. Another student adds, "Some have had a great influence on my life, and some would be better off choosing another profession." TCNJ runs foreign study and exchange programs in 13 countries, including South Africa, the Czech Republic, and Thailand, and preapproved partner programs give students access to dozens of other countries around the globe. Roughly a quarter of students get their passports stamped to study, intern, or volunteer overseas.

The typical TCNJ student is "overly book smart" with "low social skills," according to one junior. The school has no cap on out-of-state admissions, but only 6 percent of TCNJ's students are non-Jerseyans, including less than 1 percent who are foreign nationals. The college has aggressively pursued minority students, and today, African Americans account for 6 percent of the student body, Hispanics 12 percent, and Asian Americans 10 percent. "If you don't leave this school very well educated in political correctness, then you were obviously unconscious," says a marketing major, who praises the school for its diversity. Merit scholarships averaging $5,156 are available to qualified students. The Educational Opportunity Fund Promise Award covers full tuition, room and board, and other expenses, and provides specialized academic support services, for qualifying New Jersey residents from disadvantaged backgrounds.

Dorm housing is only guaranteed for freshmen and sophomores, though 60 percent of students live on campus. "Most of the dorms are really nice," says a student, "but a few are older and outdated." Freshmen hang their hats in one of four residence halls, two of which, Centennial and Norsworthy, have recently been renovated. After that, students can enter the lottery to secure spots in traditional residence halls, townhouses, or the new Campus Town apartments. Many upperclassmen opt for nearby off-campus apartment complexes, which are plentiful.

Although suburban Ewing doesn't really cater to students, funky New Hope, Pennsylvania, and preppy Princeton, New Jersey, are nearby; restaurants, bars, movie theaters—and, this being New Jersey, many malls—are within a short drive. Road trips to Philadelphia and New York, each about an hour away and accessible by train, are also highly recommended. State alcohol policies are strictly enforced; students 21 and over can enjoy adult beverages at the campus restaurant, Traditions, which also features a bar and a stage area for performances. Fourteen percent of the men and 11 percent of the women belong to fraternities and sororities, respectively, which provide many of the off-campus parties. Campus programming includes dances, concerts, and movies. TCNJers look forward to several annual events, including homecoming, a Family Fest Day, and—the springtime favorite—Senior Week.

Freshmen must complete at least eight hours of community service.

"If you don't leave this school very well educated in political correctness, then you were obviously unconscious."

The College of New Jersey's 21 varsity teams (the Lions) are the pride of the New Jersey Athletic Conference and make frequent appearances in national Division III tournaments. Women's lacrosse, tennis, and field hockey, and men's and women's cross-country and swimming and diving have claimed recent conference titles. Students rally around the football and basketball squads, especially when archrival Rowan comes to town. The college also offers 14 intramural and 21 club sport programs.

The College of New Jersey is one of the few public liberal arts colleges with reasonable tuition and a location that offers media types, artists, and budding scientists a relaxed suburban haven within shouting distance of the editors, producers, directors, curators, and pharmaceutical companies of New Jersey, Pennsylvania, and New York.

Overlaps
University of Delaware, Drexel, Lehigh, University of Maryland, NYU, Penn State, Rutgers, Villanova

If You Apply To > **TCNJ:** Early decision I: Nov. 1. Early decision II: Jan. 1. Regular decision: Feb. 1. Financial aid: Feb. 15. Housing: May 1. Application fee: $75. No campus or alumni interviews. SATs or ACTs: required. No Subject Tests. Letters of recommendation: required. Essay: required. Accepts the Common Application. Art applicants must submit portfolio. Music applicants must audition.

New Jersey Institute of Technology

University Heights, Newark, NJ 07102

NJIT is one of the few public technical institutes in the Northeast. It occupies a middle ground between the behemoth Rutgers and smallish Stevens Institute. Primarily offers engineering, computing, architecture, and management. At four to one, NJIT's gender ratio is particularly skewed. Then again, no one comes to NJIT for the social life.

The Murray Center for Women in Technology offers scholarships and resources to help female students and faculty advance in their chosen fields.

The New Jersey Institute of Technology provides a no-frills technological education that prepares students for a future in an ever-changing global workplace. NJIT's challenging programs emphasize education, research, service, and (not surprisingly) economic development. The combination is enticing—as is the price tag, relative to some of NJIT's closest competitors.

NJIT's urban 48-acre campus is dotted with 27 buildings of diverse architectural styles, ranging from Elizabethan Gothic to contemporary design. Some of New Jersey's greatest cultural institutions are just blocks away, including the Newark Museum, Symphony Hall, and the New Jersey Center for the Performing Arts.

To graduate, students must fulfill general education requirements in areas ranging from English to management. All freshmen take Calculus I and II, English composition, computer science, physical education, and Freshman Seminar, a course that introduces students to university life. NJIT is composed of the Newark College of Engineering, the College of Computing Sciences, the College of Architecture and Design (which includes the New Jersey School of Architecture and the School of Art and Design), the School of Management, the College of Science and Liberal Arts, and the Albert Dorman Honors College.

"I love housing. We get free cable, fast Internet connections. We have very big rooms."

Information technology, civil engineering, mechanical engineering, and architecture are the most popular majors, and computer science is also a strength. Mechanical and electrical engineering are said to be especially challenging. The administration acknowledges that interdisciplinary studies is among the weaker programs. NJIT has worked with Rutgers to create a number of joint-degree programs from biology to history. The university has also launched a prelaw program with an emphasis on technology.

While some say the atmosphere can be low-pressure in certain fields, most agree that the workload across the board is demanding. According to a history major, "Students do not come in prepared for the arduous courseload." The administration assists students if they are having a difficult time, arranging for leaves of absence or extra semesters with a lighter load. Most NJIT courses have fewer than 50 students. Some have problems getting into enrollment-capped classes that are offered only once a year. But one student calculates that if a freshman has all of the prerequisite courses, he or she has a good chance of graduating on time. Academic advising isn't as helpful as it could be, say some students, but professors are given average to high marks. Since most have worked in their industry, they can offer job information along with academic assistance. And students say career counseling services are helpful in preparing them for the job hunt.

NJIT's most-favored academic option is the co-op program, which enables juniors to get paid for two six-month periods of work at technical companies. Top freshman applicants are offered a spot in the Honors College, and they can stay as long as they keep their grades up; more than 700 undergraduates in all majors are enrolled in the Honors College. Perks include guaranteed dorm rooms, research opportunities, and acceptance into the B.S./M.S. program after completion of five courses for the undergraduate major. NJIT also has a chapter of Tau Beta Pi, the national engineering honor society. Learning communities in selected majors are available for incoming freshmen. In the midst of this heavily male-dominated campus, the Murray Center for Women in Technology offers scholarships, networking opportunities, and resources to help female students and faculty alike advance in their chosen fields.

As New Jersey's comprehensive technological public university, NJIT attracts a wide range of students with different interests. "There are students who are very driven and want to achieve their absolute best," observes a sophomore. "However, there are a large number of students who are coasting." In-state residents represent 94 percent of the undergraduate student body, and international students add 2 percent.

Eight percent are African American, 22 percent are Hispanic, and 23 percent are Asian American. Tolerance is not a problem here as it is on some other campuses. One student praises the Educational Opportunity Program, saying, "If it weren't for them, I would not be here. They make it easy to be a minority." Forty percent of students qualify for Pell Grants. The university awards merit scholarships averaging $12,643 to qualified students, and athletic scholarships are also available.

NJIT's four residence halls can accommodate one-third of the students, and 23 percent live on campus. "I love housing," says a junior. "We get free cable, fast Internet connections. We have very big rooms." Students are advised, however, to get their applications in on time in order to get one of those roomy rooms. Freshmen get first crack at lodgings, and those who get in are guaranteed space the next year. Consensus has it that the best freshman dorms are Redwood Hall and Cypress. Upperclassmen move into fraternity or sorority houses or nearby off-campus apartments. The dorms and Greek houses both have kitchen facilities, which many students welcome, as the dining service fare sometimes draws complaints from students left with grumbling stomachs after dinner. Because of its urban location, safety is always a consideration at NJIT, and students praise the security efforts. "Public safety officers are always around," says an electrical engineering major.

Diwali, the Indian festival of lights, and Chinese New Year give undergrads pause to party.

Newark is hardly a college town, students report. "I think the school would attract more students by transforming the surrounding areas into a more 'college town' atmosphere," offers one sophomore. The 4 to 1 male/female student ratio definitely puts a crimp in the social life. There are some outlets, though. Five percent of the men and 3 percent of the women join the Greek system. One of the

"Students here are certainly intelligent and come off as nerds, but everyone has their own niche."

best annual campus events is Spring Week, which includes bands, novelties, and a semiformal. Diwali, the Indian festival of lights, and Chinese New Year also give undergrads pause to party. "We have a lot of barbecues that bring people together," says an architecture major. Another option is the beach, an hour away. Most students agree that the administration's strict alcohol policies are effective.

NJIT students do take pride in their athletic prowess, though their 19 varsity teams operate at the bottom of the Division I food chain. Unable to join a regional conference, the Highlanders belong to the Great West Conference that pits them against unlikely and distant rivals, such as Texas-Pan American and North Dakota, as far as 1,950 miles from Newark. Swimming, tennis, and men's basketball are the most competitive teams. The outstanding athletic facilities are open to all and feature an indoor running track, a fitness center, a six-lane pool, a multiuse soccer stadium, and numerous courts for squash, sand volleyball, and other pursuits. A proud (and sweaty) tradition is the Hi-Tech Soccer Classic, which pits NJIT athletes against rivals from MIT, RPI, and Stevens Institute.

"Students here are certainly intelligent and come off as nerds, but everyone has their own niche," says a biomedical engineering student. NJIT students choose their school because they want a top-notch technical education without the topflight price tag. Academics are the priority here, and if the social life is less than electrifying, students deal with it. After all, they know highly skilled jobs will beckon after graduation. Getting through is a challenge, but there's ample compensation available for NJIT alums in the technologically dependent workplaces of today—and tomorrow.

Overlaps

Rutgers, Stevens Institute of Technology, Rowan University, Drexel, The College of New Jersey, Penn State, Montclair State, Seton Hall

If You Apply To ➤ **NJIT:** Rolling admissions: Mar. 1. Early action I: Nov. 15. Early action II: Dec. 15. Priority financial aid: Mar. 15. Housing: Jun. 2. Application fee: $75. Campus and alumni interviews: optional, informational. SATs or ACTs: required. No Subject Tests. Letters of recommendation: required. Essay: required. College of Architecture and Design applicants must submit portfolio of work. Accepts the Common Application with supplement.

P.O. Box 4895, Albuquerque, NM 87131

UNM gives new meaning to cultural diversity. Studies related to Hispanic and Native cultures are strong, and in a land of picture-perfect sunsets, photography is a major deal. Technical programs are fueled by government labs in Albuquerque and Los Alamos, while the business school produces an outsized percentage of New Mexico's commercial elite.

Website: www.unm.edu
Location: City Center
Public
Total Enrollment: 19,368
Undergraduates: 15,851
Male/Female: 45/55
SAT Ranges: CR 480–610, M 470–600
ACT Ranges: 19–25
Financial Aid: 85%
Pell Grant: N/A
Expense: Pub $
Student Loans: N/A
Average Debt: N/A
Phi Beta Kappa: Yes
Applicants: 13,517
Accepted: 50%
Enrolled: 49%
Grad in 6 Years: 48%
Returning Freshmen: 80%
Academics: ✍ ✍ ✍
Social: ☎ ☎ ☎
Q of L: ★ ★ ★
Admissions: (505) 277-8900
Email Address: apply@unm.edu

Strong Programs:
Latin American Studies
Native American Studies
Photography
Business
Anthropology
Education
Social Sciences
Health Professions

The University of New Mexico's heritage stretches back to 1889 when New Mexico wasn't even a state, and the university's strengths are still rooted in the rich history of the American Southwest. New Mexico excels in areas such as Latin American affairs and Southwest Hispanic studies. Lest you think it is a typical state school, consider that many students are commuters or of nontraditional age. UNM also boasts New Mexico's only law, medical, and architecture and urban planning schools.

Seated at the foot of the gorgeous Sandia Mountains in the lap of Albuquerque, the beautifully landscaped campus sports both Spanish and Pueblo Indian architectural influences, with lots of patios and balconies. The duck pond is a favorite spot for sunbathing, and the mountains, which rise majestically to the east, are visible from virtually any point on campus. Newer facilities include a technology and education center and a science and math learning center.

UNM offers more than 4,000 courses in 13 colleges, running the gamut from arts and sciences, education, and engineering to management, fine arts, and the allied health fields. Academic and general education requirements vary, but the core curriculum mandates three English courses focused on writing and speaking; two courses each in the humanities, social, and behavioral sciences, and physical and natural sciences; and one course each of fine arts, a second language, and math. Those reluctant to specialize can spend a few semesters in the broad University College, which offers a bachelor of liberal arts and a bachelor of integrative studies degree. The Honors College offers a bachelor of arts in interdisciplinary liberal arts. The Tamarind Institute, a nationally recognized center housed at UNM's School of Fine Arts, offers training, study, and research in fine-art lithography. Anthropologists may root around one of New Mexico's many archaeological sites, and engineers may join in major solar-energy projects. Other solid programs include Native American studies, Chicano-Mexicano-Hispano studies, and Latin American studies. Students may also enroll in a Navajo language program.

"Social life takes place both on and off campus."

The academic climate is "very laid-back and depends on what field of study you are going into," according to a senior. Students are quick to help one another study, and competition for grades is the exception rather than the rule. Fifty-five percent of classes have fewer than 20 students. As for professors, "I would have to give them a B," says a student. "There have been some very good ones and some that were very knowledgeable but didn't know how to teach." Freshman Learning Communities and academic coaching help ease the transition from high school to the college environment. Many classes, and several complete degree programs, are offered in late afternoon and evening sessions, and about half of the student body takes advantage of these after-hours options. And for those who yearn for more exotic locales, study abroad programs beckon from Mexico, Brazil, Venezuela, Costa Rica, and Scotland.

By virtue of its location, UNM enjoys a diverse mix of cultures, even though the vast majority of students are state residents. A large minority student enrollment—

47 percent Hispanic, 6 percent Native American, 3 percent Asian American, and 2 percent African American—reflects this cultural diversity. Two percent of undergraduates are from overseas. UNM hosts a number of programs that encourage diversity and healthy race relations, including the Arts of the Americas, a broad cross-cultural program that involves U.S. and Latin American artists in festivals, classes, and exhibits. "Students here are pretty chill," says a journalism major. "We hang out and stuff, but for the most part we are focused on school." The average merit award is more than $2,000. More than 250 athletic scholarships are available as well.

Many UNM students commute, and they complain that finding parking spots continues to be difficult. Even with new residence halls, a scant 8 percent of students live on campus. Students are happy with the variety of food available to them, and note that the remodeled student union building includes chain restaurants and one that serves food from different cultures every week. An escort service, emergency phones, good lighting, and police who patrol around the clock help students feel safe.

Many students are commuters or of nontraditional age.

> **"People here are serious and accepting, which makes UNM a comfortable environment."**

Alcohol, though banned on the UNM campus, is readily available, according to most students, especially at Greek parties. Five percent of the men and 6 percent of the women join the Greek system. Other students find their fun off campus in Albuquerque's clubs and restaurants. "Social life takes place both on and off campus," a junior says. For the more socially conscious, the college sponsors Spring Storm, an outing of roughly 1,000 students who volunteer around the city on a Saturday. Annual social events include Welcome Back Days in the fall and Nizhoni Days, a celebration of Native American culture. Each spring, the whole campus turns out for a four-day fiesta with food and live music.

Solid programs include Native American studies, and students may also enroll in a Navajo language program.

Albuquerque—sometimes referred to as ABQ—is New Mexico's largest city, and it offers a variety of cultural attractions, including the nation's largest hot air balloon fiesta, a growing artists' colony, and concert tours to charm the ears. Santa Fe is an hour away. Those with cars take advantage of the state's natural attractions: superb skiing in Taos, the Carlsbad Caverns, the Sandias, as well as excellent hiking and camping opportunities. For the historically inclined, numerous Spanish and Indian ruins are within an easy drive.

The UNM Lobos (Spanish for "wolves") compete in the Division I Mountain West Conference and the men's basketball and football squads and the women's softball, soccer, and volleyball teams usually draw crowds. Recreational and intramural sports are popular; students flock to flag football, volleyball, soccer, and basketball.

UNM offers a sun-drenched location that satisfies—precisely because its academic climate is as relaxed as the rolling desert dunes. "People here are serious and accepting," says a senior, "which makes UNM a comfortable environment."

Overlaps

Arizona State, University of Colorado, Eastern New Mexico, Highlands, New Mexico State, University of Texas at El Paso

If You Apply To ➢ | **UNM:** Rolling admissions. (Priority deadline: May 1.) Financial aid: Jan. 6. Housing: Jul. 12. Application fee: $20. No campus or alumni interviews. SATs or ACTs: required. No Subject Tests. No letters of recommendation. No essay.

Eugene Lang College–The New School for Liberal Arts: See page 252.

New York University

22 Washington Square, New York, NY 10012

Don't count on getting into NYU just because Big Sis did. From safety school to global brand, NYU's rise has been breathtaking. The siren song of Greenwich Village now includes the School of Engineering in Brooklyn, degree-granting campuses in Abu Dhabi and Shanghai, and a dozen global academic centers around the world. Major draws include the renowned Tisch School of the Arts and the best undergraduate business school this side of Penn.

Website: www.nyu.edu
Location: City Center
Private
Total Enrollment: 40,275
Undergraduates: 24,252
Male/Female: 43/57
SAT Ranges: CR 620–720, M 630–750
ACT Ranges: 29–32
Financial Aid: 51%
Pell Grant: 21%
Expense: Pr $ $ $
Student Loans: 49%
Average Debt: $ $ $
Phi Beta Kappa: Yes
Applicants: 56,092
Accepted: 33%
Enrolled: 31%
Grad in 6 Years: 84%
Returning Freshmen: 93%
Academics: ✍ ✍ ✍ ✍ ½
Social: ☎ ☎ ☎
Q of L: ★ ★ ★
Admissions: (212) 998-4500
Email Address: admissions@nyu.edu

Strong Programs:
Business
Economics
Drama
Film and Television
Dance
Accounting
English
Journalism

With the world at its doorstep, New York University invites its student body to jump right in. Firmly planted in the heart of Greenwich Village, arguably one of the most eclectic and energizing neighborhoods in New York City, NYU has set its sights on becoming the world's first truly global university. Its growing student body, burgeoning new facilities, and multiple opportunities for high-level internships and research projects have made it a top option for a rising number of students. One senior observes, "The prestige of the university has certainly increased." What's more, "NYU is a place to gain street smarts in addition to book smarts," says a senior. "The combination of strong academics and an amazing location give NYU a big advantage."

It doesn't get more real world than the venue that NYU calls home. NYU has campuses and centers throughout the city but is centered on Washington Square. Trendy shops, galleries, clubs, bars, and eateries crowd neighboring blocks; SoHo, Little Italy, and Chinatown are just blocks away. Academic NYU buildings—both modern and historic—blend with 19th-century brick townhouses surrounding Washington Square Park (the closest thing NYU has to a quad). Kimmel Center for University Life houses meeting space for NYU's nearly 400 student clubs, plus areas for the frequent recruitment fairs and lectures featuring national and international leaders. It also holds the Skirball Center for the Performing Arts' 860-seat theater, which is the largest performing arts facility south of 42nd Street.

The city scene is a core element of the NYU experience. So, too, is the wide range of academic programs. Under the Morse Academic Plan, freshmen and sophomores take courses including foreign language, expository writing, foundations of contemporary culture, and foundations of scientific inquiry. The language offerings, though, go beyond the typical Spanish-French-German—among the choices are Arabic, Cantonese, Hindi, Modern Irish, Swahili, and Tagalog—and NYU operates a language exchange program with Columbia University as well. The Tisch School of the Arts trained such famed actors and directors as Marcia Gay Harden, Alec Baldwin, Martin Scorcese, and Spike Lee, and current undergrads continue to win many national student filmmaker awards. Tisch also boasts excellent drama, dance, photography, and television departments, and it's not uncommon to see students who haven't yet finished B.F.A. degrees performing in Broadway shows.

> **"The prestige of the university has certainly increased."**

Wall Street's future bulls and bears make their home at the Stern School of Business, where they benefit from a business and political economy program. The new Leslie eLab provides space for aspiring entrepreneurs. Another favorite department among students (and the New York corporations who recruit them after graduation) is accounting, known for its high job-placement rate. The arts and sciences are strong, with economics, English, journalism, history, political science, and applied math winning highest marks. The Gallatin School of Individualized Study provides flexible schedules and freedom from requirements for those wishing to engage in independent study or develop their own programs. The Polytechnic School of Engineering, the Steinhardt School, the Silver School of Social Work, the College of Nursing, and the School of Professional Studies offer a bevy of career-based programs, including art, education, engineering, media, music, nutrition, hotel and sports management, and real estate. In fact, the variety of degree options here may tempt students to hang around the Village for more than four years. There's a seven-year dental program and a five-year joint bachelor's/master's program in engineering with New Jersey's Stevens Institute of Technology.

It's not uncommon to see students who haven't yet finished B.F.A. degrees performing in Broadway shows.

Finding a cheap New York apartment may be easier than sailing through NYU's academics. "The classes can be very challenging," says a senior, "but students have a plethora of resources to help them succeed." Premed, prelaw, and prebusiness students may encounter packed schedules and competitive classes, while Gallatin and Tisch students may have lots of spare time, students say. Regardless of major, everyone is very focused on career preparation—it's never enough to just concentrate on your classes. "It's hard to avoid the pressure," says a student majoring in drama and politics, with nine hours of acting class a day and writing-intensive academic courses too. At least the NYU library is accommodating—it's one of the largest open-stack facilities in the country, with millions of volumes. And despite the university's mammoth size, 60 percent of classes taken by undergraduates have fewer than 20 students. Graduate students might lead foreign language sections, writing workshops, and the recitations that accompany lectures, but students still say teaching is top-notch. "Surprisingly, most of our introductory courses are taught by really great and well-known professors," says one student. "I have found professors to be accessible and willing to help their students succeed," a history major adds.

Point to a spot on a world map and you'll likely hit a country hosting undergraduates from NYU, which sends more of them abroad than any other school. In addition to its campuses in Abu Dhabi, Shanghai, and Singapore, NYU has 11 academic sites in cities ranging from Buenos Aires and Prague to Sydney and Tel Aviv, as well as exchange agreements with universities in other locations throughout the world. Students may study abroad as early as their freshman year through the University's Core Program in Liberal Studies. Locally, internships range from jobs on Wall Street to assignments with film industry giants. The career center is "amazingly personal and well run," says an econ major, and has thousands of listings for on-campus jobs, full-time jobs, and internships. Students qualifying for freshmen honors seminars study in small classes under top faculty and eminent visiting professors. An annual undergraduate research conference at the College of Arts and Science gives students the chance to present findings from their research. Many students graduate in less than four years.

"Students have a plethora of resources to help them succeed."

An international politics major says NYU students are "high achieving individuals, cosmopolitan, independent, self-driven, confident, and able to manage academics, part-time jobs, and internships while having active social lives." Thanks in part to the university's investment in new housing, 47 percent of undergraduates now come from outside New York State and another 17 percent from outside the United States. In-staters come primarily from the city and nearby suburbs. African Americans make up 5 percent of the student body, Asian Americans 20 percent, and Hispanics 12 percent. Twenty-one percent are Pell-eligible. On this generally liberal campus, gender issues, social justice, the Israeli-Palestinian conflict, and rights of all kinds—gay, lesbian, transgender, animal, human, and workers'—are important now, students say. "NYU is primarily a pretty liberal university," says a sophomore, "but conservative folks are welcome here too!" Although most financial aid is need based, merit awards averaging $12,688 are available; athletic scholarships are not.

NYU sends more undergraduates abroad than any other school.

While NYU students once had to fend for themselves in New York's outrageous housing market, the university guarantees four years of housing to all freshmen (and most transfers) who seek it. Twenty-one residence halls, ranging from old hotels to a converted monastery, provide a wide range of accommodations. Most rooms have private baths and are larger, cleaner, newer, and better equipped than many city apartments, enticing 44 percent of students to stay on campus. Freshmen are housed largely in freshman residence halls, many of which have theme floors, and rooms are assigned by lottery each spring. Amenities include central air-conditioning, computer centers, musical practice rooms, kitchens, and even, in some buildings, small theaters. The university provides free shuttle buses to dorms that are farther uptown or downtown. The dining halls offer extensive choices—from wraps to sushi to Burger King. "The dining halls really try to accommodate everyone," says one student. Of course, downtown's array of ethnic restaurants also offers a variety of food at cheap prices.

> "[The career center is] amazingly personal and well run."

> *Most residence hall rooms have private baths and are larger, cleaner, newer, and better equipped than many city apartments.*

Because NYU is large and fairly decentralized, the Student Resource Center helps students navigate university resources and services. The university's Wellness Exchange provides students with a hotline that connects them with professionals who can help them address daily challenges or crises they may encounter. Students also meet with academic advisors—usually professors in their major department—at least once a semester. For concerned parents and students, NYU hosts a series of workshops on keeping safe, and programs like the NYU Trolley and Escort Van Service provide door-to-door service for students until 3:00 a.m. "I always feel safe," says a linguistics major. "I can't walk more than one block without seeing an NYU security officer or an NYPD car just patrolling the area."

As for NYU's social life, "You're in New York City," says a student. "Why would you bother staying in your dorm at night when you're within minutes of internationally renowned art, world-class theater on Broadway, shopping in SoHo, and dining in Little Italy?" Another adds, "Greenwich Village is full of students, professors, artists, families; it's the most exciting, alive, cultural part of New York City."

> "To be an NYU student is to be part college student, part New Yorker."

On campus, there are concerts, movies, fraternity and sorority events (only 7 percent of the men and 6 percent of the women go Greek), and more than 600 clubs and organizations. The springtime Strawberry Festival includes free berries, cotton candy, outdoor concerts, and carnival amusements. Many students march in the city's Halloween Parade, which takes over Greenwich Village, while most spring and fall weekends find a city-sponsored street fair somewhere nearby. The Violet Ball, a dinner/dance held each fall in the atrium of Bobst Library, is an excuse to get dressed up. Underage students caught with alcohol in public areas of dorms may lose their housing. The rest take their chances with the notoriously strict bouncers at bars and clubs around Manhattan. "They card like crazy," says one junior.

While sports have not traditionally been NYU's strength, successful Violets programs include men's and women's swimming and diving, men's wrestling, and women's golf, softball, and soccer, all of which compete in Division III. Roughly half of undergrads participate in intramural sports, which include flag football, bowling, and indoor cricket. The Palladium Athletic Facility boasts a big swimming pool and a 30-foot-high indoor climbing wall.

The heartbeat of New York City thumps day and night; NYU students thrive on all that energy and know how to capture it in their studies and social lives. "To be an NYU student is to be part college student, part New Yorker," a senior says. "Don't come here if you're not up to working hard and moving fast."

Overlaps

UC–Berkeley, Columbia, Cornell University, Harvard, Northwestern, University of Southern California

<table>
<tr><td>**If You Apply To** ▷</td><td>**NYU:** Early decision I: Nov. 1. Early decision II and regular decision: Jan. 1. Financial aid: Feb. 15. Housing: May 1. Application fee: $70. Campus interviews: optional, evaluative. No alumni interviews. SATs or ACTs or three Subject Tests or three AP exams: required. Letters of recommendation: required. Essay: required. Accepts the Common Application with supplement. Portfolio or audition required for some programs.</td></tr>
</table>

University of North Carolina Asheville

I University Heights, Asheville, NC 28804

The "other" UNC happens to be one of the best educational bargains in the country. With 3,200 full-time, degree-seeking students, UNC Asheville is about half the size of fellow public liberal arts college William and Mary and somewhat smaller than Mary Washington. Picturesque mountain location in one of the most livable small cities anywhere. By Southern standards, a progressive university in a progressive city.

Whether it's the lush environment or the money you're saving, the University of North Carolina Asheville will have you seeing green. This public liberal arts university offers all of the perks that are generally associated with pricier private institutions: rigorous academics, small classes, and a beautiful setting. And it does it for a fraction of the cost. The university continues to integrate experiential learning into its traditional curriculum, emphasizing undergraduate research, internships, and service-learning experiences. Any way you look at it, UNC Asheville is a bargain that may have your friends turning green with envy.

Located in the heart of North Carolina's gorgeous Blue Ridge Mountains, the 360-acre campus lies in the middle of one million acres of federal and state forest near the tallest mountain in the East and the most heavily visited national park in the country. The campus was built in the 1960s, and much of the brick architecture reflects the style of that decade, although half of the buildings were added within the past few years, including a high-tech science and multimedia building, a health and wellness center, and a campus observatory. The Botanical Gardens at Asheville, adjacent to the main campus, features thousands of labeled plants and trees, and serves as a wildlife refuge and study center for biology students. Highsmith University Union features modern space for gatherings and student organizations, as well as an Intercultural Center, bookstore, game room, gallery space, and food court.

> **"Our faculty's mentorship and close relationships are especially evident in undergraduate research."**

Asheville's general education curriculum, the Liberal Arts Core, is required of all undergraduates. In addition to first-year and senior-capstone liberal arts colloquia, students must take courses in eight areas spanning the humanities, sciences, and mathematics, as well as a Diversity Intensive, and must demonstrate competency in information literacy and writing. The most popular majors at Asheville are psychology, environmental studies, biology, and management. Students can take advantage of Asheville's strengths as a global source of information for weather forecasting and as a center of digital imaging, computer science, and, of course, fine arts and studio crafts. A joint B.S. degree in engineering (with a concentration in mechatronics) with North Carolina State University is the only such program in the state and is one of the fastest-growing majors. The university introduced a new Creative Fabrication course in 2016, in which sculpture and engineering students team up in the state-of-the-art River Arts Makers Place to develop assistive technologies.

Website: www.unca.edu
Location: Small City
Public
Total Enrollment: 3,194
Undergraduates: 3,191
Male/Female: 45/55
SAT Ranges: CR 530–640, M 520–610
ACT Ranges: 23–28
Financial Aid: 48%
Pell Grant: 32%
Expense: Pub $
Student Loans: 57%
Average Debt: $ $
Phi Beta Kappa: No
Applicants: 3,324
Accepted: 79%
Enrolled: 28%
Grad in 6 Years: 64%
Returning Freshmen: 79%
Academics: ✍ ✍ ✍ ✍
Social: ☎ ☎ ☎
Q of L: ★ ★ ★ ★
Admissions: (828) 251-6481
Email Address: admissions@unca.edu

Strong Programs:
Psychology
Environmental Studies
Biology
Management
Atmospheric Sciences

"I find UNC Asheville to be a very collaborative and easy-going school," says one sophomore. Half of all classes have fewer than 20 students, and a number of them have service-learning components. "All of my professors have been incredibly helpful and understanding whenever I have approached them with a problem," cheers one psychology major. As a French and political science double major points out, "Our faculty's mentorship and close relationships are especially evident in undergraduate research." Research is indeed a key emphasis here: Asheville founded the National Conference on Undergraduate Research and has hosted the conference five times, most recently bringing 4,000 scholars to campus in 2016. Sixty-three percent of Asheville students will have an undergraduate research experience by graduation. The UNC Asheville honors program offers special courses—as well as cultural and social opportunities—to motivated students who can make the grade. Study abroad is an option too, and 17 percent of students participate in programs in more than 50 countries.

"[Students] like to be green in a number of ways."

The head count at Asheville has risen steadily over the past decade, but only 11 percent of the student body come from out of state and another 1 percent from abroad. (The state limits its out-of-state admits to 18 percent.) Asheville is moving away from its early reputation as a hippie haven, but students still value this individualism—with more "geeks than beer-swillers." Students "like to be green in a number of ways," one student reports, "from recycling to being vegan to conserving water." Currently, the student body is 4 percent African American, 5 percent Hispanic, and 2 percent Asian American, but Asheville is making special efforts to bring more students who are underrepresented to the campus. A substantial number of transfer students add their own brand of diversity. Thirty-two percent of current freshmen are Pell-eligible. Asheville offers 164 athletic scholarships, as well as merit scholarships averaging $2,702.

Asheville is a global source of information for weather forecasting.

Asheville is working hard to build up its on-campus housing; 39 percent of the students live in six residence halls that offer a variety of accommodations. "I would be comfortable living in any of our residence halls on campus and was very glad that none of them have hall-style bathrooms and all of them have nice kitchens, lounges, and study spaces," says a senior. There is no lottery, and freshmen are mixed in with upperclassmen. "The residence halls are not dorms where students are stuffed in and hope to survive," says one student. "They are communities." Living/learning communities offer special residential and academic options for students with similar interests, such as LEAD (for leadership and social justice), Go Local, and The Cloud (for computer science and atmospheric sciences majors). For meals, students may eat dining-hall fare or grab something quick at retail outlets around campus, including local cuisine and nationally known Argo Tea. "Our dining service does a great job of serving a variety of food to meet students' needs," cheers a senior. A sophomore says, "Our campus security is excellent. We have an on-campus police force that patrols regularly around campus."

"The residence halls are not dorms where students are stuffed in and hope to survive. They are communities."

In the new Creative Fabrication course, sculpture and engineering students team up to develop assistive technologies.

After class, there are plenty of opportunities for fun, especially for the many Asheville students with a hankering for the great outdoors. The university is surrounded by the Blue Ridge Mountains and the Smokies, where students can hike and rock climb; water buffs can go rafting and kayaking on the nearby rivers. Preorientation wilderness trips help build friendships among freshmen.

"The social life could be improved, but overall everyone is really fun to hang out with," says one student. Most parties take place off campus, especially since RAs stalk underage drinkers in the dorms. "There is no tolerance for unsafe, underage, or unwise drinking," says a student. Greek life is not an influential presence, with only 3 percent of the men and 3 percent of the women joining up. There are more than

60 student organizations, including a student newspaper, the *Blue Banner*. Several campuswide events bring the school together each year, including the Turning of the Maples in October, homecoming, a spring lawn party, and a mock casino night with an auction. "There are lots of annual events, but the one I feel makes our campus unique is the annual Greenfest," says a student. "All groups on campus—faculty, staff, and students—come together for two or three days to help make a designated section of campus more beautiful."

The city of Asheville, an increasingly popular retirement destination, offers a tame but inviting nightlife, with popular hangouts like Mellow Mushroom, Urban Burrito, Tupelo Honey, and Rosetta's Kitchen, and the city has been named Beer City USA several times. Asheville is also home to a bevy of street performers, outdoor music festivals, and live entertainment events. For students with cars, the Blue Ridge Parkway is a short drive away, while Spartanburg and Charlotte are one and two hours away, respectively. Real big-city action takes extra effort, though, since Atlanta is a four-hour trek.

The Division I Bulldogs boast Big South Conference teams in 14 sports. Men's and women's basketball are the most successful, with each team taking home conference championship titles in 2016. Men's and women's soccer, men's tennis, and women's volleyball are also competitive. "We have a great rivalry with Western Carolina," says a health and wellness major. Intramurals and club sports are at least as popular as the varsity sports, as are outdoor adventure trips and the on-campus challenge course and bike shop.

"Everyone who works here is dedicated to the student experience in some way," says a senior. "That means you won't be a number." Indeed, all the ingredients for a superior college experience lie in wait at Asheville: strong academics, dedicated professors, and an administration that continues to push for excellence. It's a place to get the kind of liberal arts education usually associated with private colleges—but for a lot fewer greenbacks.

> *The university is surrounded by the Blue Ridge Mountains and the Smokies.*

Overlaps
Appalachian State, North Carolina State, UNC at Chapel Hill, UNC Greensboro, Western Carolina, UNC Wilmington, UNC Charlotte, Elon

If You Apply To ➤ **UNC Asheville:** Early action: Nov. 15. Regular decision: Feb. 15. Financial aid: Mar. 1. Housing: May 1. Application fee: $75. Campus interviews: optional, informational. No alumni interviews. SATs or ACTs (with writing): required. Subject Tests: optional. Letters of recommendation: optional. Essay: required. Accepts the Common Application with supplement.

University of North Carolina at Chapel Hill

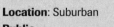

CB 2200, Jackson Hall, Chapel Hill, NC 27599

Close on the heels of UVA as the South's most prestigious public university. With nearly 80 percent of the spots in each class reserved for in-staters, admission is selective but not impossible for out-of-staters who aren't 6'9" with a 43-inch vertical jump. But they keep trying by the thousands. Chapel Hill is a quintessential college town that is morphing into a medium-sized city.

Welcome to "the Southern part of heaven," a place where the sky is Carolina Blue and the academics are red-hot. As the flagship campus of the state university system, UNC at Chapel Hill has earned its place among the South's most prestigious universities. The atmosphere here is a unique brand of Southern, a rowdy mixture of hard work, sports fanaticism, progressive social values, and traditions that seems to attract bright, fun-loving students from everywhere.

Website: www.unc.edu
Location: Suburban
Public
Total Enrollment: 24,022
Undergraduates: 17,606

The nearby Research Triangle Park employs many students as research assistants.

Chartered in 1789, UNC was the first public university in the United States to open its doors, and North Carolinians still take pride in Carolina's identity as "the University of the people." UNC's gorgeous and comfortable campus occupies 730 acres lush with trees and lawns and brick-paved walkways. The architecture ranges from Palladian, Federal, and Georgian to postmodern, with redbrick the prevailing motif. The Old Well, the university's symbol, stands at the center of the campus. Newer additions include the nine-story Marsico Hall, dedicated in 2014 as a center for medical research.

The general education curriculum requires all students to complete 38 to 44 credit hours of coursework in three broad themes: Foundations, Approaches, and Connections. Coursework includes physical and life sciences, social and behavioral sciences, humanities and fine arts, composition and rhetoric, foreign language, quantitative reasoning, and lifetime fitness. About two-thirds of first-years participate in the First-Year Seminar program, which allows them to work closely with professors in small classes of 20 students each, as an introduction to the university's research-oriented environment. The "Maymester" provides undergraduates with additional opportunities for work and study off campus.

> **"Although it is a prestigious university, I don't feel a sense of competition at all."**

Chapel Hill offers more than 75 undergraduate degree programs. Some of the strongest are communication and media studies, computer science, English, and philosophy. The chemistry and sociology programs are highly regarded, and other popular majors include biology, psychology, and economics. UNC's honors program is nationally recognized as among the best in the country. With original funding from the Ewing Marion Kauffman Foundation, the university has developed a broad range of opportunities to help students in business, liberal arts, and sciences become entrepreneurial, including an entrepreneurship minor and the Carolina Challenge, a student-run competition that awards up to $50,000 in prizes each year for the best business plan. Global studies is one of the fastest-growing majors, and a new joint-degree program in biomedical and health sciences engineering has been developed in partnership with North Carolina State University.

The academic climate is challenging but not overwhelming. "Although it is a prestigious university, I don't feel a sense of competition at all," says one sophomore. Academic and social life are governed by a student-run honor system. Forty-two percent of classes enroll fewer than 20 students, and access to registration is based on seniority. If you get closed out of a class, "be persistent," advises a freshman. The Carolina faculty is, for the most part, top-notch. Professors keep regular office hours, and a history major says, "The majority of professors go out of their way to help students and make sure that they are learning everything they possibly can." Regarding career preparation, a senior cheers, "Our career services department on campus puts effort into each and every student."

Undergraduate research opportunities are available to students in all disciplines, and students may be eligible to present their findings at professional conferences, publish results in academic journals, and win fellowships to support summer research in the United States and abroad. For those tired of the classroom rush, Research Triangle Park, a nearby research and corporate community and home of the National Humanities Center, employs many students as research assistants. UNC offers more than 325 study abroad programs in 70 countries, in which 30 percent of students participate.

> **"Our career services department on campus puts effort into each and every student."**

"Carolina students are unlike any others. They are proud to attend this school and they bleed Carolina blue," says one Tar Heel. Out-of-state admission is extremely tough; 78 percent of students hail from North Carolina, and another 5 percent from foreign countries. Big social and political issues on campus include multiculturalism, gender roles, and religious issues. African Americans account for 8 percent of the student body, Asian Americans 10 percent, and Hispanics 8 percent. UNC awards a limited number of highly competitive merit scholarships, along with more than 600 athletic scholarships in 28 sports. What's more, the university is need-blind in admissions and commits to meeting the full demonstrated financial need of all admitted students—one of only two public universities in the U.S. to do so (see also University of Virginia). Twenty percent of incoming students are eligible for Pell Grants, and the Carolina Covenant program, which has served as a national model to universities seeking to increase socioeconomic diversity, offers grants and work-study to dependent students below 200 percent of the poverty level, giving eligible low-income students the chance to graduate debt-free. The program offers extensive mentoring and other support to Covenant Scholars, many of whom are the first in their families to attend college.

The Carolina Covenant program gives eligible low-income students the chance to graduate debt-free.

Fifty-two percent of undergraduates live in university housing, which "is an invaluable part of the experience because you are connected to campus resources and also have the ability to make friends and connections easily," according to one student. Housing on the north side of campus offers old and newly renovated dorms; the south side offers several new housing options, which are a good hike from academic buildings (not to worry—there's a free campus shuttle). "The pickiest of the picky could be happy with Carolina dining services," says a freshman. UNC has a fully accredited campus police department, which is praised for its constant presence, and the university has implemented a number of new training and support programs to address the issue of sexual assault.

"[Students] bleed Carolina blue."

"'College town' in the dictionary should show a picture of Chapel Hill," boasts one senior. Franklin Street, the main drag in town that runs across the northern boundary of campus, offers Mexican and Chinese restaurants, ice-cream parlors, coffeehouses, vegetarian eateries, bakeries, a dance club, and a generous supply of bars. Fraternities and sororities may account for only 18 percent of the men and 18 percent of the women, but they exert an influence far beyond their numbers. "Fraternities are a social hub, and many students flock to their off-campus parties," confirms one student. Between Greek life and other campus-sponsored activities, "There are always five or six things happening on any given day," says a political science major. FallFest kicks off the school year with an emphasis on the idea that you don't have to drink to have fun. Students look forward to several annual festivals: the Carolina Jazz Festival and Halloween Celebration on Franklin Street are always, shall we say, raucous. The North Carolina Literary Festival is held biannually. Students are involved in the community, many through a service-learning program for which they receive academic credit.

Men's basketball were national runners-up in 2016, and men's and women's lacrosse were both national champions.

UNC's reputation for balancing high-level athletics and academics took a major hit following embarrassing reports of longstanding special academic treatment of athletes that has spurred a continuing series of well-publicized academic and athletic reforms over the past several years. Student and alumni loyalty remains high, and the word "popular" doesn't do justice to the basketball games. A contest between Tar Heel hoopsters and NC State makes any Carolina fan's heart beat faster, but Duke takes the prize as the most reviled of all devils. The Tar Heels play in the 21,750-seat Smith Center, named for the late coach Dean Smith, one of the winningest college basketball coaches of all time. Men's basketball were national champions in 2017, as were men's and women's lacrosse in 2016. Men's field hockey, men's soccer, and

"'College town' in the dictionary should show a picture of Chapel Hill."

women's tennis are also highly competitive, but the team with one of the best records in college sports history is women's soccer, which has won nearly two dozen national championships since 1981. Carolina has also finished in the top 10 nationally for the Directors' Cup for across-the-board athletic excellence a dozen times in as many years. Extensive intramural and club sports programs draw heavy participation; intramural basketball and soccer alone each boast rosters of more than 200 teams. Those who crave fresh air can take advantage of the Outdoor Education Center's mountain bike trails, rope courses, and one of the longest double zip lines on the East Coast.

As a popular saying goes, "If God is not a Tar Heel, why is the sky Carolina Blue?" It's a cute turn of phrase, but also points to something that is well-known in these parts: as one of the best college buys in the country, the University of North Carolina at Chapel Hill gives students everything they want, both academically and socially. Despite recent budget cuts enacted by Philistine forces in the state legislature and governor's mansion, the 200-year history of this school creates an atmosphere of extreme pride, a love of tradition, and monumental school spirit. One freshman, full of that school spirit, says, "Southern hospitality blended with a high level of thinking, an overwhelming dose of friendliness and pep, and a spectacularly gorgeous campus make Chapel Hill my favorite place in the world."

Overlaps

North Carolina State, Duke, University of Virginia, Vanderbilt, Wake Forest, Harvard, University of Pennsylvania, Yale

If You Apply To ➤

UNC at Chapel Hill: Early action: Oct. 15. Regular decision: Jan. 15. Financial aid: Mar. 1. Housing: May 1. Application fee: $80. No campus or alumni interviews. SATs or ACTs: required. Subject Tests: optional. Letters of recommendation: required. Essay: required. Accepts the Common Application with supplement.

University of North Carolina Wilmington

Wilmington, NC 28403

Still overshadowed by Chapel Hill and the other biggies in the strong UNC system, but making a name for itself. Strong in marine biology and other sciences. You won't see the Seahawks in the NCAA Final Four anytime soon, but you will be able to get to know your professors. About 13 percent of incoming students come from out of state, most of those hailing from Mid-Atlantic, Northeast, and New England states.

Website: www.uncw.edu
Location: Small City
Public
Total Enrollment: 12,295
Undergraduates: 11,635
Male/Female: 39/61
SAT Ranges: CR 560–630, M 560–630
ACT Ranges: 23–27
Financial Aid: 60%
Pell Grant: 29%
Expense: Pub $
Student Loans: 39%
Average Debt: $ $

At the University of North Carolina Wilmington, students enjoy extensive undergraduate research opportunities, a slate of solid sciences, and a close-knit community of like-minded individuals who like their modern academics mixed with a bit of old-fashioned Southern charm. The university's close proximity to the ocean provides motivated students with ample opportunities for fun in the sun and a natural lab for the school's stellar marine biology program. Whether diving into the sea or their studies, UNCW students are filled with school spirit.

Founded as Wilmington College in 1947, UNCW moved to its present location in the heart of New Hanover County in 1961. The 650-acre campus is only minutes from Wrightsville Beach and historic downtown Wilmington and features Georgian architecture and designated conservation areas. These conservation areas are significant zones of natural beauty with their longleaf pines, oaks, dogwoods, and native magnolias. Notable campus landmarks include the clock tower, the Leutze Hall portico, Chancellor's Walk, and the Teaching Laboratory. The Campus Life complex serves as the hub of the university community and includes the Fisher Student

Center, which houses a bookstore, game room, 360-seat movie theater, and student meeting space.

UNCW's University Studies curriculum requires students to complete coursework in three main categories—Foundations, Competencies, and Approaches and Perspectives—and to complete one approved Explorations Beyond the Classroom experience, such as an internship or a study abroad program. Freshmen benefit from a slate of special programs designed to ease the transition into college life, including a required two-day orientation, a common reading, and a first-year seminar. Each seminar is limited to 25 students and has a Seahawk "link": students who help with the transition into UNCW life. The Cornerstone Learning Communities are home to approximately 225 freshmen, who complete coursework together. "Learning communities are a game changer," says a communication studies major. "They allow freshmen to get used to a college workload, but in a familiar environment where they feel comfortable."

Some of the most popular majors offered are business administration, psychology, biology, communication studies, and nursing. The university's strengths lie in the natural sciences, especially marine biology, biology, chemistry, and other disciplines that form the core of the marine sciences. "Our university places a large emphasis on lab and field work," says one geography major. Outside of the

"Though academics can be challenging, the university provides many tools for academic success."

sciences, UNCW offers solid programs in film studies and creative writing. Students say the academic climate is collaborative, and according to a biology major, "Though academics can be challenging, the university provides many tools for academic success." Freshmen are taught by full professors, and a sophomore says, "The teaching is superb!" A junior adds, "Professors at UNCW want to help their students." Enrollments in introductory courses sometimes swell to more than 100, but 30 percent of all classes have fewer than 20 students.

A hallmark of the UNCW student experience is known as eTEAL: experiencing Transformative Education through Applied Learning. Applied learning places students in hands-on experiences, such as directed independent study, undergraduate research, internships, and service-learning projects, requiring them to integrate the theories, ideas, and skills they have learned in new contexts. Research opportunities include the Hosier Undergraduate Research and Creativity Fellowship, which awards $1,000 for innovative research. For those yearning to experience new vistas, the university offers more than 800 approved study abroad programs in 50 countries; 8 percent of students participate. The UNCW Honors College accepts approximately 125 students each year to participate in living/learning communities, advanced coursework, and experiential seminars; honors students must also complete a senior honors capstone research project.

According to a marketing major, UNCW students are "hardworking beachgoers. Every student here is hardworking and motivated but enjoys a little time off as well." Eighty-seven percent of undergrads are native to North Carolina, and 1 percent are international. African Americans represent 5 percent of the student body, Hispanics 7 percent, and Asian Americans 2 percent. Students say there is a balance of liberal and conservative political views on campus. Outstanding students can vie for merit scholarships averaging $3,182, as well as 164 athletic

"[Students are] hardworking beachgoers."

scholarships in 18 sports. Twenty-nine percent of students qualify for Pell Grants, and under UNCW's Support Opportunity Access Responsibility (SOAR) program, high-achieving students from low-income families may receive grants and scholarships equaling the cost of in-state tuition and fees, in addition to federal loans or work-study funding if needed.

(continued)

Phi Beta Kappa: Yes
Applicants: 12,505
Accepted: 55%
Enrolled: 31%
Grad in 6 Years: 72%
Returning Freshmen: 85%
Academics: ✐ ✐
Social: ☎ ☎
Q of L: ★ ★ ★
Admissions: (910) 962-3243
Email Address: admissions@ uncw.edu

Strong Programs:
Marine Biology
Biology
Chemistry
Film Studies
Business Administration
Psychology
Communication Studies
Nursing

Students complete one Explorations Beyond the Classroom experience, such as an internship or a study abroad program.

Thirty-one percent of all undergraduates live on campus, and a variety of options are available. "We have the traditional, hallway-style housing; upperclassmen apartments; sophomore suites; and specialty housing for fraternities, sororities, athletes, honors, international, and Cornerstone students," says one student. "The dorms are very nice and have a current, fresh vibe to them," adds a sophomore. All students living on campus purchase a meal plan; campus eateries include Wagoner Hall, the Hawks Nest food court, Dubs Café, and Einstein Bros. Bagels. "For students with allergies, when they swipe their UNCW One Card at a dining location, the employees will be notified of the allergy and a separate meal will be prepared," explains a student. Another student says security is solid thanks to an ever-present security staff. "They patrol on foot, in cars, and on bikes. We also have emergency call boxes." Students praise the CARE office for helping to combat sexual assault on campus.

"There are so many organizations on our campus that it is hard not to get involved," says one senior. Fraternities and sororities attract approximately 4 percent of the men and 9 percent of the women, respectively. The party scene is far from raucous, students say, and underage drinkers face stiff penalties if caught. "There will be serious consequences to deal with," warns a business major. Popular events include homecoming, the Dub Idol and Hawk It Out singing and dance competitions, and the annual

> **"Maybe it's the Southern charm in us, but whatever it is, it sure helps make this laid-back college an awesome place to attend."**

Oozeball Tournament, "where teams of six compete in games of volleyball that take place on a court filled a foot deep with mud," according to a film studies major. Downtown Wilmington offers its share of restaurants, shops, and bars, and is "a very scenic and beautiful city," says a marine biology major. "Wilmington is one of the best locations in North Carolina. From the many bars to the many beaches, we have hundreds of social spots to hang out," says a senior. Road trips include jaunts to Myrtle Beach, the Outer Banks, Washington, D.C., and the Appalachian Mountains.

UNCW fields varsity teams that compete in Division I, and recent Colonial Athletic Association conference champions include volleyball, men's basketball, and baseball. The women's basketball and softball teams are also competitive, as are men's and women's golf, tennis, and soccer. "Seahawk basketball is huge!" raves one freshman. Club and intramural sports are also popular, especially flag football, basketball, and outdoor and indoor soccer, and the sea kayaking and paddleboarding trips organized by Seahawk Adventures are other favorite diversions.

Despite complaints of limited parking, expensive food, and the lack of football, students at the University of North Carolina Wilmington seem to be a happy lot. "Everyone here always seems to be in a good mood and goes out of their way to speak to and help others," says a senior. "Maybe it's the Southern charm in us, but whatever it is, it sure helps make this laid-back college an awesome place to attend."

Overlaps

East Carolina, North Carolina State, UNC Charlotte, Appalachian State, UNC at Chapel Hill, UNC Greensboro, Western Carolina, University of South Carolina

If You Apply To ➤

UNC Wilmington: Early action: Nov. 1. Regular decision: Feb. 1. Financial aid: Mar. 1. Housing: May 1. Application fee: $75. No campus or alumni interviews. SATs or ACTs: required. No Subject Tests. Letters of recommendation: required. Essay: required. Accepts the Common Application with supplement.

North Carolina State University

Box 7103, Raleigh, NC 27695

NC State lacks the high national profile of neighbors Duke and UNC at Chapel Hill, but it's an equally important player in North Carolina's Research Triangle—just ask the thousands of graduates who have moved into jobs in the area. Engineering, business administration, and biology are the most popular programs. Location in the state capital a big plus. Compare to Clemson and Virginia Tech.

Whether you're looking for a stellar education or a top-rated basketball program, North Carolina State University offers students the benefits of a large school—highly regarded professors, a diverse student body, and plenty to do on weekends—while making sure that no one feels left out. Says a communication major, "At NCSU, you will be welcomed and able to find your niche easily."

The 128-year-old, 2,100-acre campus consists of redbrick buildings, brick-lined walks, and cozy courtyards dotted with pine trees. There is no dominant style, but more of an architectural stream of consciousness that reveals a campus that grew and changed with time. Holladay Hall has been designated as a historic site by the Raleigh City Council, while the ultramodern James B. Hunt Jr. Library features a game lab, visualization studio, digital production suites, and more than 100 collaborative spaces. For amusement you can always stroll over and watch the robotic book retrieval system in action. The $115 million facility received the Stanford Prize for Innovation in Research Libraries. A major renovation to the Talley Student Union was recently completed. NCSU's Centennial Campus is a 1,227-acre, public-private research campus for university, government, and industrial partners.

General education requirements cover a broad range of liberal arts courses and include 13 hours of math and natural sciences; 12 hours of humanities and social sciences; four hours of writing; three hours of additional breadth in an area clearly distinct from the major; five hours of interdisciplinary perspectives; and two hours of physical education. Students also must demonstrate proficiency in a foreign language. An Exploratory Studies program provides guidance and counseling for incoming students to introduce them to possible majors.

> "At NCSU, you will be welcomed and able to find your niche easily."

NC State excels in the professional areas of engineering, statistics, mathematics, agriculture, and forestry, which are the largest and the most demanding divisions. Not surprisingly, given its location in the heart of textile country, the school also boasts a first-rate textile school, the largest and one of the best programs in the country. It also has one of the nation's top veterinary schools. Engineering tops the list of most popular majors, followed by business, biological sciences, and agriculture. The College of Humanities and Social Sciences is the second largest school in the university, and strong nontechnical areas include communication, English, international studies, and social work. Notable programs are also available in genetics, soil and land development, mechatronics engineering (with UNC Asheville), sport management, and turfgrass science. "The academic climate is very competitive at my college and the courses are very difficult," says a psychology major. "They push you to not only use the material in the class, but also apply it outside the classroom." Many classes at NC State are large, but the faculty gets high grades for being accessible, interested in teaching, and friendly. "Teachers take time out of their schedule to make the most of students' education by offering office hours,

Website: www.ncsu.edu
Location: City Center
Public
Total Enrollment: 26,532
Undergraduates: 20,894
Male/Female: 54/46
SAT Ranges: CR 570–650, M 590–680
ACT Ranges: 27–31
Financial Aid: 47%
Pell Grant: 18%
Expense: Pub $
Student Loans: 55%
Average Debt: $
Phi Beta Kappa: Yes
Applicants: 21,099
Accepted: 50%
Enrolled: 40%
Grad in 6 Years: 76%
Returning Freshmen: 94%
Academics: ✍ ✍ ✍ ½
Social: ☎ ☎ ☎
Q of L: ★ ★ ★
Admissions: (919) 515-2434
Email Address: undergrad-admissions@ncsu.edu

Strong Programs:
Engineering
Business
Biological Sciences
Agriculture
Textiles
Statistics
Communication
Genetics

going above and beyond with interesting lectures, and maintaining a healthy student/teacher relationship," says one senior.

An important feature of NC State's approach to education is the cooperative education program, through which students in all schools can alternate semesters of on-site work with traditional classroom time. The university benefits greatly from its relationships with Duke, UNC at Chapel Hill, and private industry through the state's high-tech Research Triangle Park, located nearby. NC State offers approximately 400 study abroad programs in more than 60 countries, and 16 percent of students participate. In the University Scholars program, academic standouts live together and participate in weekly activities such as cultural events, honors classes, and outdoor recreation trips. Students in the University Honors Program take small seminars and complete a capstone project, and they can join a dedicated living/learning community.

In the University Scholars program, students live together and participate in cultural events, honors classes, and outdoor recreation trips.

NC State's star continues to rise as it becomes more selective. The students here are largely hardworking, bright North Carolinians; 86 percent are in-state students, and 3 percent are international. "Our students are committed to their studies but know how to enjoy themselves," says a communication major. Six percent of undergraduates are African American, 5 percent are Hispanic, and 5 percent are Asian American. Conservatism abounds, and the largest political organization is the College Republicans. Jocks and sports fans are visible, and the university offers 404 athletic scholarships in 24 sports. Those with outstanding academic qualifications can compete for one of thousands of merit scholarships, which average $6,251. The Pack Promise guarantees that every North Carolina resident admitted to NC State with a family income at or below 150 percent of the federal poverty level will receive an aid package that meets 100 percent of their demonstrated financial need.

"[Courses] push you to not only use the material in the class, but also apply it outside the classroom."

Thirty-two percent of students choose to live on campus, and as of fall 2017, all freshmen are required to do so. "Dorms are like home away from home," says a student, "and if anything is wrong, maintenance can fix it in a flash." Rooms range in size from spacious to cramped, and students report that dorm dwelling is actually more expensive than some off-campus units, which are plentiful. A small percentage of students are housed in fraternities and sororities, and the international house is also an option. The university manages a number of Living and Learning Villages where students can live and socialize with others who share their interests. The dining halls feed all freshmen and anyone else who cares to join the meal plan. "The food really is good," says a student. "There is such a variety that things don't get boring." The university has recently expanded its Title IX education programs to reach all incoming students and new employees.

The never-ending fight to "Beat Carolina!" permeates the campus year-round.

The 28 fraternities and 21 sororities attract 11 percent of the men and 17 percent of the women. The Greek scene provides much of the entertainment, but dorm and suite parties are also popular. With home close by for so many students, the campus does tend to thin out on weekends. Still, one student says, "There are endless possibilities and never a dull moment on NC State's campus." Alcohol policies are enforced, and if you're thinking about grabbing a brew, "don't try unless you're 21," warns a senior. Public transportation affords easy access to downtown, with its shops, restaurants, theaters, and night spots. Many students also like to head to the beach, which is about two hours away, or to the mountains for skiing, which is about a three-and-a-half-hour trip. Volunteering is popular too.

"Dorms are like home away from home."

Students love to cheer on their Division I teams, which do well in baseball, wrestling, softball, gymnastics, women's cross-country and golf, and men's and women's swimming and diving. But needless to say, basketball reigns supreme—the Wolfpack plays in the high-powered Atlantic Coast Conference. Some crazy NC State fans have stormed nearby Hillsborough Street following game-day victories, especially those over archrival UNC at Chapel Hill. Indeed, the annual State versus Carolina football game always packs the stadium, and the never-ending fight to "Beat Carolina!" permeates the campus year-round. Intramurals also thrive.

North Carolina State seems to have overcome many of the obstacles associated with large land grant universities. It has attracted a dedicated and friendly student body independent enough to deal with the potential anonymity of a state school, but spirited enough to cheer the Wolfpack to victory. NC State works well for both those who can shoot hoops and those who can calculate the trajectory of the same three-point shot.

If You Apply To >

NC State: Early action: Oct. 15. Regular decision: Jan. 15. Financial aid: Mar. 1. Application fee: $85. No campus or alumni interviews. SATs or ACTs: required. Subject Tests: optional. Letters of recommendation: optional. Essay: recommended. Accepts the Common Application with supplement.

Northeastern University

360 Huntington Avenue, Boston, MA 02115

Northeastern is synonymous with preprofessional education and hands-on experience. By interspersing co-op jobs with academic study, students can help finance their education while getting a leg up on the job market—domestic and global. Aided by a huge spike in applications and an ambitious building program, NU has transformed itself from blue-collar urban into Boston chic. With the city and the rest of the world beckoning and students always coming and going, campus life is minimal.

Long known for its co-op program and hands-on learning experiences, Northeastern University has set its sights on becoming one of the region's top-tier institutions. More selective than ever, NU has added lavish new facilities and recruited big-name professors while continuing to combine liberal arts requirements with up to 18 months of challenging work placements. "The school has encouraged and empowered me to explore the world through research and study abroad," cheers one mechanical engineering major, "experiences that will stay with me forever."

Northeastern's 73-acre campus is an unlikely oasis located in the heart of Boston, just minutes away from Fenway Park, shopping centers, nightclubs, cafés, Symphony Hall, and the Museum of Fine Arts. The campus's green spaces are interspersed with brick walkways, sculptures, and outdoor art. Older buildings are utilitarian gray-brick, while newer structures are modern glass and brick. During inclement weather, students

> **"Professors want to make sure that you are as attractive as possible to potential employers."**

can be found navigating the underground tunnel system that connects many campus buildings. No longer a commuter college, NU has the rare luxury for an urban institution of having erstwhile parking lots available for new construction. The newest additions to campus include the Interdisciplinary Sciences and Engineering Complex, a state-of-the-art facility that furthers NU's emphasis on applied—or, to use the local jargon, "use-inspired"—research, and the East Village residence hall.

Website: www.northeastern.edu
Location: City Center
Private
Total Enrollment: 23,962
Undergraduates: 17,913
Male/Female: 50/50
SAT Ranges: CR 660–740, M 680–770
ACT Ranges: 31–34
Financial Aid: 70%
Pell Grant: 13%
Expense: Pr $ $ $
Student Loans: N/A
Average Debt: N/A
Phi Beta Kappa: No
Applicants: 50,523
Accepted: 28%
Enrolled: 19%

(continued)

Grad in 6 Years: 84%
Returning Freshmen: 97%
Academics: ✎ ✎ ✎
Social: ☎ ☎
Q of L: ★ ★
Admissions: (617) 373-2200
Email Address: admissions@
neu.edu

Strong Programs:
Business and Marketing
Social Sciences
Health Professions
Engineering
Biological and Life Sciences

*Students may select
from a slew of
combined majors
that cross disciplines,
such as information
science and cognitive
psychology.*

Northeastern's core curriculum (known as NUpath) embraces writing-intensive instruction, mathematical/analytical thinking, comparative understanding of religions and cultures, and knowledge domains. Students must also take part in a first-year learning community, integrated experiential learning, and a capstone experience. Woven into the Northeastern experience is its signature co-op education program, which places students in full-time positions related to their major and personal interest. Students complete at least two co-ops, four to six months in length, if they seek to graduate in four years and head on to graduate school, or three co-ops if they enroll in the university's traditional five-year bachelor's degree programs. Consistent with the global nature of today's economy, internship destinations range from nonprofits in Boston to a soft-drink maker in Nigeria, an electronics firm in China, or even an Antarctic research station. Faculty members prepare students for their co-ops with a special course beforehand, check in with them while they are out in the field, and organize academic reflection on the experience afterwards. "Professors want to make sure that you are as attractive as possible to potential employers," says a political science major.

"I feel extremely safe on campus even though it is in the middle of the city."

NU's undergraduate programs are divided among seven colleges and schools: the College of Arts, Media, and Design; the D'Amore-McKim School of Business; the College of Computer and Information Science; the College of Engineering; the Bouvé College of Health Sciences; the College of Science; and the College of Social Sciences and Humanities. The Program for Undeclared Students offers experiential learning opportunities to help students explore potential majors and careers. Students with diverse interests may select from a slew of combined majors that cross disciplines, such as computer science and interactive media, information science and cognitive psychology, political science and communication studies, and international affairs and cultural anthropology. The most popular majors fall under the categories of business and marketing, social sciences, health professions, and engineering. The international business program features an "expat year," in which students spend one semester studying at an overseas university and six months pursuing an international co-op. Health sciences students may pursue six-year doctor of pharmacy or doctor of physical therapy degrees.

"The climate on campus can be both competitive and collaborative at the same time," says one student. "Students strive to work hard and achieve academically, but also never fail to help a friend out in their time of need." Sixty-five percent of Northeastern's classes have fewer than 20 students. Scheduling can be difficult, as students sometimes find that courses they want are offered only when they're scheduled to be away on a job. "The quality of teaching is unparalleled," according to one senior. "Faculty members make themselves totally accessible via email, face to face for meetings, and phone conferences." Under the Dialogue of Civilizations program, faculty members take about 1,000 students abroad each summer. The Northeastern University Scholars Program, limited to 50 students, offers customized global experiences, personalized advising and mentoring, access to university resources, and financial support. An honors program is also available for the highly motivated.

"You are pushed to meet new people and develop networking skills."

"Northeastern students are driven," says one senior. The university, which was founded as a YMCA educational program, has traditionally served local students from diverse socioeconomic backgrounds. These days, only 30 percent of undergraduates are from Massachusetts, and just 13 percent qualify for Pell Grants. Consistent with Northeastern's efforts to promote a global culture, 19 percent come from overseas—more than at any other New England school. Asian Americans comprise 12 percent of the student body, Hispanics 7 percent, and African Americans 4 percent. Outstanding students can compete for merit scholarships as part of a program that evaluates students' potential through a combination of traditional and nontraditional assessments, including interviews and personality tests. There are more than 250 athletic scholarships—including at least one for each sport.

Forty-eight percent of undergraduates live on campus. All freshmen reside in living/learning communities organized around particular interests, and freshmen honors students live together in their own housing. On-campus housing is now guaranteed for all four years, though many students find it less expensive to live off campus, where options include privately owned apartments or suites located adjacent to the residence halls. The dining halls offer "a lot of options and good food," according to students, who also speak highly of NU Public Safety: "I feel extremely safe on campus even though it is in the middle of the city," says one senior. The university hired a Title IX coordinator in 2016 to oversee its new Office for Gender Equity and Compliance.

The international business program features an "expat year," involving one semester of overseas study and a six-month international co-op.

When it comes to Northeastern's social scene, "Most of the social life happens off campus," one student says. Clubs and activities abound, but the continuous flow of students on and off the campus for co-ops tends to be disruptive. "I may see a friend one quarter in class and then not again for six months. It's hard to stay connected," a student explains. The upside of this, says an engineering student, is that "you are pushed to meet new people and develop networking skills." Fraternities and sororities attract 8 percent of NU men and 12 percent of women, respectively.

"Hockey is king here at Northeastern."

Regular traditions include Springfest, an annual concert that draws the likes of Snoop Dogg and Kid Cudi, and the annual Underwear Run during Parent Weekend in the fall, when students run through the city at night in their underwear or crazy costumes. Boston is, of course, the "ultimate college town" and offers a seemingly endless array of concerts, museums, clubs, and eateries. In the winter, students head to the ski slopes of Vermont, and in balmier weather, they're off to the beaches of Cape Cod and the North Shore.

Outstanding students can compete for merit scholarships through assessments that include interviews and personality tests.

Northeastern fields 18 Division I varsity teams (the Huskies) as part of the Colonial Athletic Association and the Hockey East Association. The biggest sports series of the year is the Beanpot Hockey Tournament ("Hockey is king here at Northeastern"), which pits Northeastern against rival teams from Boston College, Boston University, and Harvard. "It is all about bragging rights and pride, and the fans from the schools make it fun," reports a student. One T-shirt reads, "No—we don't want to B.U.," epitomizing the competitive nature of the sports teams in the Boston area. The fleet-footed men's and women's track and cross-country teams, who work out in the Bernard Solomon Indoor Track Facility, regularly leave their opponents blinking in the dust. The recreation program offers 30 options, from intramural flag football and sand volleyball to group fitness classes led by a trained instructor, and Northeastern is well represented in nonvarsity competition with other schools.

Students gripe about the so-called NU Shuffle, which a junior explains as, "Want to take more than 19 credits in a semester or start a new club? Please track down 14 administrators from your department and get their signatures." Bureaucracy aside, Northeastern is a school on the rise. It has moved well beyond its origins as an open admissions commuter school and—through aggressive fund-raising, an ambitious building program, and unabashed marketing—adapted its decades of experience with co-op education to the emerging global economy. Northeastern students tend to be serious about their studies but learn to wear many hats. "We are employees at co-op, students in class, friends and roommates in our free time," explains one denizen. "We balance work and play while still meeting deadlines." Northeastern

Overlaps

Boston University, NYU, Boston College, Cornell University, University of Pennsylvania, Tufts, Columbia, UC–Berkeley

students graduate with a broad reservoir of experiences that they know will serve them well once they start scouring those job listings—both in the U.S. and around the world.

If You Apply To ➤ **Northeastern:** Early decision and early action: Nov. 1. Regular decision: Jan. 1. Financial aid: Feb. 15. Application fee: $75. Campus and alumni interviews: optional, evaluative. SATs or ACTs: required. Subject Tests: optional. Letters of recommendation: required. Essay: required. Accepts the Common Application. Music technology and studio art applicants must submit portfolio.

Northwestern University

1801 Hinman Avenue, P.O. Box 3060, Evanston, IL 60208

The Big Ten is not the Ivy League, and NU has more school spirit than its Eastern counterparts. Much more preprofessional than its nearby rival University of Chicago or any of the Ivies except Penn, and students identify strongly with their school. More similar to Duke and Stanford. World-renowned in journalism. Suburban setting on the shore of Lake Michigan, with quick access to Chicago.

Website: www.northwestern .edu

Location: Suburban

Private

Total Enrollment: 17,006

Undergraduates: 8,134

Male/Female: 50/50

SAT Ranges: CR 690–760, M 710–800

ACT Ranges: 31–34

Financial Aid: 44%

Pell Grant: 15%

Expense: Pr $ $ $ $

Student Loans: 45%

Average Debt: $ $

Phi Beta Kappa: Yes

Applicants: 32,122

Accepted: 13%

Enrolled: 48%

Grad in 6 Years: 93%

Returning Freshmen: 97%

Academics: ✎ ✎ ✎ ✎ ✎

Social: ☎ ☎ ☎

Q of L: ★ ★ ★

Admissions: (847) 491-7271

Email Address: ug-admission@ northwestern.edu

Strong Programs:
Economics

On Sunday nights before finals begin at Northwestern University, students are encouraged to let off steam with a campuswide "primal scream." The ear-shattering event illustrates two big themes at NU: students work really hard, but they also know how to have some fun. Regarded as the most elite school in the Midwest, this top-tier university, the only private school in the Big Ten, boasts some of the most well-respected preprofessional programs in the country. Plus, Northwestern is ideally located just outside of Chicago. "I love being at a place where I can learn and have a great social life," says one student.

Northwestern is situated on 231 acres about a dozen miles north of the Chicago Loop. An eclectic mix of stone buildings with abundant ivy, the leafy campus is set off from the town of Evanston and runs for a mile along the shore of Lake Michigan. Students migrate between the North Campus (techy) and the South Campus (artsy). The newer buildings are located adjacent to a 14-acre lagoon, part of an 85-acre lakefill addition built in the '60s. This area provides students with a prime location for picnicking, fishing, running, cycling, rollerblading, or just daydreaming. The new, state-of-the-art Visitors Center for prospective students and their families includes an auditorium with approximately 160 seats, meeting rooms, offices for admissions staff, and a two-story reception area. The Garage, located in a repurposed facility whose origins you can guess, offers meeting and workshop spaces, classrooms, and a café on a 24/7 basis for entrepreneurs from across the university. Amenities include design software and 3-D printers.

Half of Northwestern's undergraduates are enrolled in arts and sciences, while the other half are spread out among five professional schools, all with national reputations. Indeed, students tend to identify more strongly with their school than with Northwestern as a whole. The Medill School of Journalism, the only such program at a top private university, sends student reporters out with iPads and video cameras as well as spiral notebooks. The curriculum integrates multimedia techniques with the study of "audience understanding" and features internships at dozens of top newspapers, magazines, and television stations across the nation. There's also a four-year accelerated B.S.J./M.S.J. program. A dazzling electronic

> "I love being at a place where I can learn and have a great social life."

studio centralizes Medill's state-of-the-art broadcast newsroom and the communication school's radio/TV/film department. The McCormick School of Engineering and Applied Science is strong in all aspects of engineering and pairs students with clients with practical problems. Five-year co-op options are available. The School of Music wants students who can combine conservatory-level musicianship with high-level academics. It requires auditions and offers a five-year program from which students emerge with two B.A. degrees. The School of Education and Social Policy is the only school of its kind in the country and competes with Vanderbilt for education majors. Students and faculty members alike are encouraged to range across traditional disciplinary barriers—a policy that has led to the creation of some entirely new fields such as materials science—and students are free to switch schools once they are enrolled.

(continued)

Journalism
Psychology
Political Science
Engineering
Education
Communication Studies
Premed

Consistent with this approach, students say the university's best programs include the Integrated Science Program, the Honors Program in Medical Education, and Mathematical Methods in Social Sciences, a selective program that gives students the technical skills to move into various areas of the social sciences. Strong arts and sciences departments include chemistry and history, although the humanities as a group are less strong. Economics, journalism, psychology, and political science enroll the most majors. Each of the undergraduate schools determines its own general education requirements, but broad outlines are similar. Each school requires a graduate to have coursework in "the major domains of knowledge"—science, mathematics and technology, individual and social behavior, historical studies, values, the humanities, and the fine arts. Incoming students take part in Wildcat Welcome, a weeklong orientation designed to ease the transition into college life.

Students migrate between the North Campus (techy) and the South Campus (artsy).

Unlike most schools on a 10-week quarter system, Northwesterners take four (not three) courses each quarter, except in engineering, where five are permitted. "Students tend to be supportive and collaborative," says a senior, but "the academics are rigorous and will take some adjustment from high school." Virtually all undergraduate courses, including required freshman seminars in arts and sciences, are taught by regular faculty members. Introductory courses are larger than most, but the average 100-level class has about 30 students.

"The academics are rigorous and will take some adjustment."

"The quality of teaching at Northwestern depends on the department and the professor," confides a senior, "but overall I would say is a very high quality." The Office of Undergraduate Research helps students apply for research assistantships and faculty-mentored independent projects, often with the support of grants. Students can take a break from the campus through any of the numerous field-study programs and programs abroad.

Upon graduating, NU students tend to pursue business fields like consulting and finance, with technology, education, and communication distant followers. "Students at Northwestern are always passionate about something," says a social policy major. "That could be theories of relativity like my roommate, wildlife conservation like myself, or film criticism like one of my good friends. So it's really easy to have interesting conversations and learn from each other." Twenty-eight percent of undergraduates hail from Illinois, and 9 percent come from overseas. Minorities represent a sizable contingent of the student body, with Asian Americans accounting for 18 percent, African Americans 6 percent, and Hispanics 11 percent. There are no academic merit scholarships, but NU does guarantee to meet the full demonstrated need of every admit, and offers hundreds of scholarships for its athletes. In addition, the university has eliminated loans for families with incomes below $55,000 a year and capped loans at $5,000 for others.

The Medill School of Journalism's curriculum integrates multimedia techniques with internships at dozens of top media companies.

Fifty percent of undergraduates reside in university housing, mostly in double rooms, although there are also singles, triples, and quadruple rooms, as well as suites.

"Dorms range from 50 students to 600 students, and some are general dorms while others have themes that the communities are based around," one student reports. Several residential colleges bring students and faculty members together during faculty "firesides" or simply over meals. The newer Slivka Hall houses the engineering residential colleges; there are also special dorms for students in communication, international studies, humanities, commerce and industry, performing arts, and public affairs. Fraternities and sororities also have their own houses. Students can choose to eat at the coffeehouse or at any one of six dining halls on campus. A variety of meal plans are available, including one that provides Sunday brunch and one offering kosher food, and the university staff includes a dietitian who consults with and designs nutrition programs for students who have food allergies or other special dietary needs. Those who head off campus to apartments are mostly juniors and seniors. Students generally feel safe on campus, but crime has been a concern in Evanston, especially after dark.

Much of the social life on NU's campus is centered on the Greek system, with 29 percent of the men and 32 percent of the women going Greek. Some students say finding a social niche can be tough, especially for those who aren't involved in Greek life, athletics, journalism, or theater. The school's alcohol policy is tough, but not always effective, "like the

"Students at Northwestern are always passionate about something."

vast majority of campuses nationwide," says a student. The student government and Activities and Organizations Board sponsor an array of campuswide events, including theater productions, concerts, and movies. The 30-hour Dance Marathon and Dillo (Armadillo) Day, an end-of-the-year "festival of music, debauchery, and Greek life," in the words of a journalism major, are popular annual events. Another tradition is upheld when representatives of student organizations slip out in the dead of night to paint their colors and slogans on a centrally located rock. In all, there are more than 350 student organizations, ranging from an African drum and dance ensemble to Adshop, an advertising agency that lets students hone their marketing skills by promoting local businesses. Upscale Evanston is "the restaurant haven of Chicago's North Shore," says a junior, and "very quaint with tons of flowers that bloom every spring." A short stroll off campus brings you to the town's myriad restaurant options, trendy bars, and coffee shops with space to plug in a laptop and study. For a night out, of course, Chicago is right across the border.

Football and tailgate parties are a traditional way of bringing alumni back and rousing the students to support the smallest and only private school in the Division I Big Ten. Although the football team's trip to the

"[Evanston is] the restaurant haven of Chicago's North Shore."

1996 Rose Bowl remains the stuff of legend, the Wildcats tend to be strongest in country club sports. In the last two years, wrestling, women's golf, women's soccer, men's swimming, and fencing have brought home team and individual championship titles. As far as facilities, NU is on par with many schools its size and larger, with the beautiful Norris Aquatics Center/Henry Crown Sports Pavilion and the Nicolet Football and Conference Center used for conditioning of varsity athletes. The student-sponsored intramural program provides vigorous competition among teams from dorms and rival fraternities. Northwestern also boasts the winningest debate team in the country.

Northwestern occupies a unique niche in U.S. higher education. It has the academics of the Ivies, the spirited atmosphere of the Big Ten publics, and, along with Duke, Stanford, and perhaps Vanderbilt, combines success in Division I sports with quality instruction. With a strong work ethic and an equally strong desire for play, Northwestern students bask in their school's balance of challenging academics, preprofessional bent, and myriad opportunities to get off campus to learn and let loose.

University of Notre Dame

220 Main Building, Notre Dame, IN 46556

The Holy Grail of higher education for many Roman Catholics. ND's heartland location and 80-percent-Catholic enrollment make it a bastion of solid education and equally solid values. Offers business, science, architecture, and engineering in addition to the liberal arts. ND's personality is much closer to Boston College or Holy Cross than Georgetown. Only school ever ranked #1 in both football and graduation rates.

Founded in 1842 by the French priest Edward Sorin from the Congregation of the Holy Cross, the University of Notre Dame has come a long way from its fledgling days in a rustic log cabin. While described as "a Catholic academic community of higher learning," its students need not be affiliated with the Roman Catholic Church. Notre Dame takes pride in fostering a culture that values open discussion of religious, spiritual, and social issues—witness the willingness of its president to stick by a controversial decision in 2009 to award former president Obama an honorary doctorate even though Obama does not share Catholic views on abortion. The school appeals to non-Catholics who are committed to social justice or seek a broadly spiritual dimension to their education. A soft spot for football doesn't hurt either.

With 1,250 acres of manicured quads, twin lakes, and woods, the university offers a peaceful setting for studying. The lofty Golden Dome that rises above the ivy-covered Gothic and modern buildings and the old brick stadium, where Knute Rockne made the Fighting Irish almost synonymous with college football, are national symbols. Newer campus additions include the Jordan Hall of Science, the Stinson-Remick Hall of Engineering, and the Keough School for Global Affairs. The university's $10 billion endowment is the largest of any of the country's Roman Catholic colleges and universities.

> "[The workload] requires the student to have very good time-management skills."

Liberal education is more than just a catchphrase at Notre Dame. No matter what their major, students must take the First Year of Studies, one of the most extensive academic and counseling programs of any university in the nation. The core of the program is a one-semester writing-intensive university seminar limited to 20 students per section. The remainder of each freshman's schedule is reserved for the first of a comprehensive list of general education requirements: one semester each in writing and mathematics and two semesters in natural science, as well as one semester chosen from theology, philosophy, history, social science, and fine arts. It also includes a strong counseling component in which peer advisors are assigned to each student, as are academic advisors and tutors if necessary. Administrators are quick to point out that, due in part to the success of the first-year support program, a whopping 98 percent of freshmen make it through the year and return for sophomore year. (It also doesn't hurt that 91 percent of freshmen are high achievers who graduated in the top 10th of their high school class.)

Website: www.nd.edu
Location: Small Town
Private
Total Enrollment: 12,018
Undergraduates: 8,413
Male/Female: 52/48
SAT Ranges: CR 670–760, M 680–770
ACT Ranges: 32–34
Financial Aid: 81%
Pell Grant: 11%
Expense: Pr $ $ $
Student Loans: 50%
Average Debt: $ $ $
Phi Beta Kappa: Yes
Applicants: 18,157
Accepted: 20%
Enrolled: 56%
Grad in 6 Years: 97%
Returning Freshmen: 98%
Academics: ✑ ✑ ✑ ✑
Social: ☎ ☎ ☎
Q of L: ★ ★ ★
Admissions: (574) 631-7505
Email Address: admissions@nd.edu

Strong Programs:
Finance
Economics
Accountancy
Psychology
English
Theology

(continued)

Physics
Chemical Engineering

The First Year of Studies is one of the most extensive academic and counseling programs of any university in the nation.

In the College of Arts and Letters, highly regarded departments include English, theology, and philosophy, while physics and chemistry are tops in the College of Science. Within the engineering school, chemical engineering rules. The Mendoza College of Business's accountancy program is ranked among the nation's best, and the chemistry labs in the Nieuwland and Jordan Science Halls have first-rate equipment. The most popular majors overall are finance, economics, accountancy, and psychology. Students describe the academic climate as fairly rigorous. "The workload is very demanding," says a senior. "It requires the student to have very good time-management skills." And while the atmosphere is competitive, students agree that it is not cutthroat by any measure. Faculty members are praised for being dynamic, personable, knowledgeable, and accessible. "The professors here care a great deal about their students, and it shows," says a biology major. Sixty percent of classes enroll fewer than 20 students, and students report it can be hard to get all the classes they want during a particular semester, but say it's not difficult to graduate in four years.

Notre Dame offers a variety of special academic programs and options. One of the most popular is the Program of Liberal Studies (PLS), in which students study art, philosophy, literature, and the history of Western thought within their Great Books seminars. The Kaneb Center for Teaching and Learning, the university's most recent commitment to teaching, is based in DeBartolo Hall, an 84-classroom complex with state-of-the-art computer and audiovisual equipment. Roughly half of the students take part in Notre Dame's extensive international study program, which includes opportunities at the university's Global Gateways in London, Dublin, Rome, Beijing, and Jerusalem.

"The professors here care a great deal about their students, and it shows."

The president is a priest of the Congregation of the Holy Cross, and each dorm has its own chapel with daily Masses.

With a predominantly lay board of trustees and faculty, Notre Dame remains committed to "the preservation of a distinctly Catholic community," and it has a more self-consciously Catholic identity than any other major research university, including Boston College and Georgetown. The president and several other top administrators are priests of the Congregation of the Holy Cross, and each dorm has its own chapel with daily Masses, though attendance is not required. Eighty percent of the students are Catholic, and students are required to take two theology courses. The main social issues discussed on campus include abortion, gender and racial issues, homosexuality, and faith. African Americans make up 4 percent of the undergraduate student body, Hispanics 11 percent, and Asian Americans 6 percent. Despite its relative cultural homogeneity, Notre Dame recruits from all over the country; 93 percent of the students are from states outside of Indiana, and 1 percent hail from other countries. Competitive merit awards, averaging $15,230, are offered to students with outstanding high school records, and the university meets 100 percent of accepted students' demonstrated financial need. The Division I powerhouse deals out hundreds of athletic scholarships as well.

Seventy-nine percent of ND students choose to live on campus. "Notre Dame dorm life is extraordinary," says a junior. "The dorm rooms are all very well kept and very comfortable." For their freshman year, students are assigned to a dorm, mixed among the other classes, and they are encouraged to stay in the same one until graduation. Since Greek organizations are banned, the single-sex dorms really become surrogate fraternities and sororities that breed a similar spirit of community and family. Parietal rules (midnight on weekdays, 2 a.m. on weekends) are strictly enforced. Boarders eat in either the North Quad or South Quad cafeterias and must buy a 19-meal plan. For those who tire of institutional cuisine, the Huddle offers plenty of fast-food options, as well as a pay-as-you-go snack bar. Students can also reserve their residence hall kitchen to cook their own meals.

"Notre Dame dorm life is extraordinary."

Notre Dame has been open to women since 1972, and the gender split in the undergraduate student body is now comparable to many other formerly all-male schools. ND's social life isn't as rambunctious as it once was, thanks to the policy that forbids alcohol at campus social events. The rules relating to alcohol in the dorms are a bit more relaxed. For those who choose not to indulge, there are several groups dedicated to good times without alcohol. Most activities take place on campus and include parties, concerts, and movies. A popular event is the An Tóstal (Gaelic for "the pageant") festival, which comes the week before spring finals and guarantees to temporarily relieve academic anxiety with its "childish" games, such as pie-eating contests and Jell-O wrestling. The annual Notre Dame Literary Festival is entirely student-run and draws prominent writers and poets from across the country. Students are involved in the community through volunteer work—more than 10 percent of grads enter public service positions. The best outlet for culture is nearby Chicago, about 90 minutes away. South Bend, with a metro area population of 300,000, offers plenty of opportunities for entertainment as well.

In 2013, ND moved to the Division I Atlantic Coast Conference for all sports except football and ice hockey. With its proud gridiron heritage, there's nothing like Notre Dame football. From Knute Rockne and the Gipper right on down to modern-day greats such as Joe Montana, the spirit of the Fighting Irish reigns supreme and has regained its former glory under head coach Brian Kelly. It wasn't intentional—at least that's what they say—but the giant mosaic of Jesus Christ on the library lifts his hands toward the heavens as if to signal yet another Irish touchdown. Tailgate parties are celebrated events, occurring before and after the game. Notre Dame offers one of the strongest all-around athletic programs in the country, with several teams—both men's and women's—bringing home conference and national titles in recent years. Die-hard jocks who can't make the varsity teams will find plenty of company in ND's very competitive club and intramural sports, which attract more than three-quarters of students. The Bookstore Basketball Tournament, the largest 5-on-5, outdoor hoops tournament in the world with more than 700 teams competing, lasts for a month.

Although temperatures here can drop below freezing, few dispute that Notre Dame is red-hot. Everyone at the university, from administrators to students, is considered part of the "Notre Dame family." Traditions are held in high esteem. For those looking for high-quality academics; a friendly, caring environment with a Catholic bent; and an excellent athletic scene, ND could be an answer to their prayers.

From Knute Rockne right on down to modern-day greats such as Joe Montana, the spirit of the Fighting Irish reigns supreme.

Overlaps

Duke, Northwestern, Vanderbilt, Boston College, Harvard

If You Apply To >

ND: Early action: Nov. 1. Regular decision: Jan. 1. Financial aid: Feb. 15. Housing: May 1. Application fee: $75. No campus or alumni interviews. SATs or ACTs: required. Subject Tests: optional. Letters of recommendation: required. Essay: required. Accepts the Common Application with supplement.

Oberlin College

101 North Professor Street, Carnegie Building, Oberlin, OH 44074

The college that invented nonconformity. From the Underground Railroad and coeducation to the modern peace movement, Obies have long been in the forefront. As at Grinnell and Reed, Oberlin's curriculum is less radical than its students. Oberlin is especially strong in the sciences, and its music conservatory is among the nation's best. The annual Drag Ball is quintessential Oberlin.

Website: www.oberlin.edu
Location: Rural
Private
Total Enrollment: 2,914
Undergraduates: 2,897
Male/Female: 45/55
SAT Ranges: CR 640–740, M 620–710
ACT Ranges: 29–32
Financial Aid: 85%
Pell Grant: 7%
Expense: Pr $ $ $ $
Student Loans: 46%
Average Debt: $ $
Phi Beta Kappa: Yes
Applicants: 7,815
Accepted: 29%
Enrolled: 35%
Grad in 6 Years: 88%
Returning Freshmen: 92%
Academics: ✏️ ✏️ ✏️ ✏️ ½
Social: 🍷 🍷 🍷 🍷
Q of L: ★ ★ ★ ★
Admissions: (440) 775-8411
Email Address: college
.admissions@oberlin.edu

Strong Programs:
Music
Biology
Chemistry
Politics
Economics
English
Creative Writing
Environmental Studies

New and contrasting ideas are a way of life at Oberlin College, a liberal arts school where nonconformity is a long tradition. Tucked away in a small Ohio town, Oberlin was the first American college to accept women and minorities, and it was a stop on the Underground Railroad. That pioneering spirit has not faded. With diverse academic challenges ranging from cinema studies to neuroscience, Obies thrive on higher thinking and exploring their myriad talents. A junior says Oberlin appeals to those students "who love to be active, help their communities, challenge themselves, and want to learn."

Oberlin's attractive campus features a mix of Italian Renaissance buildings (four designed by Cass Gilbert), late 19th- and early 20th-century organic stone structures, and some less interesting 1950s barracks-type dorms. The buildings rise over flatlands typical of the Midwest, which do little to stop brutal winter winds. The Allen Memorial Art Museum, sometimes mentioned in the same breath as Harvard's and Yale's, is one of the loveliest buildings on campus, with a brick-paved, flower-laden courtyard and a fountain. The Oberlin College Science Center offers state-of-the-art classrooms, wireless Internet areas, a science library, and laboratory space. In a nod to environmental concerns, the college produces half of its energy from renewable resources, and the new Hotel at Oberlin is designed to meet LEED Platinum criteria.

There are no requirements for freshmen at Oberlin, but general education requirements include proficiency in writing and math and nine credit hours in each of the three divisions—arts and humanities, natural sciences and math, and social and behavioral sciences—plus another nine credit hours in cultural diversity courses, including a foreign language. Students must also participate in three January terms during which they pursue month-long projects, traditional or unique, on or off campus. About 40 different First-Year Seminar classes are available every semester, with enrollment limited to 14 students each, and although optional, "it's a great way to make friends," says a student. "It also introduces you to the Oberlin academic experience."

> **"I've never felt like I was competing with people for grades."**

Oberlin's Conservatory of Music holds a well-deserved spot among the nation's most prominent performance schools; the voice, violin, and technology in music and related arts programs are especially praised. It is the oldest continuously operating music conservatory in the country, and Oberlin is one of only three liberal arts colleges with a conservatory (see also Bard and Lawrence). The conservatory also boasts 150 practice rooms, a substantial music library, and Steinway pianos—one of the world's largest collections. It enrolls about a fifth of Oberlin undergrads, who must audition to gain acceptance. Each year, 25 to 35 students enter the dual-degree program, which allows them to earn both a B.M. and a B.A. in as little as five years; these students must be admitted to both the college and the music conservatory.

Oberlin has been a leader among liberal arts colleges seeking to promote their science offerings; biology and chemistry are two of the college's strongest departments, and undergraduates may major in interdisciplinary programs like neuroscience and biopsychology. Students also flock to the politics, economics, and English departments. Oberlin is one of the few liberal arts colleges to offer a major in creative writing. Other notable majors include environmental studies and East Asian studies. Interdisciplinary and self-created majors, such as African American, Latin American, Russian, Third World, and women's studies, are popular—not surprisingly at such a liberal school. One of Oberlin's more unusual offerings is EXCO, an experimental college that offers students and interested townsfolk the chance to learn together. Most classes are taught by students, and topics can range from fairy tales to knitting to salsa dancing, and much more.

"There are more protests, awareness and advocacy groups, and campaigns here than I can keep track of."

Oberlin's students are as serious about their schoolwork as they are about politics, justice, and other social causes. Courses are rigorous; heavy workloads and the occasional Saturday morning class are the norm. "Oberlin can be very intense, especially in certain majors. That being said, I've never felt like I was competing with people for grades," says one student. Seventy-seven percent of classes have fewer than 20 students, and an English major says, "I've been able to form close relationships with many of my professors—both in my major as well as in other departments—which is extremely valuable." A credit/no-entry policy allows students to take an unlimited number of grade-free courses. Recognizing that students at Oberlin are gifted and want to challenge themselves, most departments offer group and individual independent study opportunities and invite selected students to pursue demanding honors programs, especially during their senior year. Two-thirds of students conduct undergraduate research, and a whopping 75 percent of students study abroad in Oberlin-directed programs in Italy, Spain, and the UK, or more than 85 other affiliated programs.

Oberlin's Conservatory of Music boasts one of the world's largest collections of Steinway pianos.

Oberlin students are—in a word—*passionate*. "Talk to a dozen different students and you'll probably have in-depth conversations about things like swing dancing, the co-op system, technical stage lighting for theater, Russian cinema, minerals and geology, and Japanese woodblock prints," says one political science major. Eighty-six

"There are students on every green area between the dorms, playing ultimate Frisbee."

percent of undergraduates are from states outside of Ohio, primarily from the Mid-Atlantic states, and 8 percent come from abroad. But achieving diversity in rural Ohio has been a challenge: African Americans account for 5 percent of the student body, Asian Americans 4 percent, and Hispanics 8 percent. And although Oberlin promises to meet students' full demonstrated financial need, a mere 7 percent of incoming freshmen are eligible to receive Pell Grants. Merit scholarships averaging $13,671 are available to qualified students. "Though the student body is homogeneously liberal," says a junior, "there are more protests, awareness and advocacy groups, and campaigns here than I can keep track of." A popular annual event is the Drag Ball, in which half the student body comes in full drag. "It's very Oberlin, because it's all about challenging social norms," says a student. For all its talk of nonconformity, Oberlin is also a model of political correctness. The director of dining services recently issued an apology of sorts for offering "culturally insensitive" items such as inauthentic sushi, and 1,300 students recently signed a petition calling for students who skimp on their studies to engage in social activism to be protected from receiving low grades.

A mere 7 percent of incoming freshmen are eligible to receive Pell Grants.

Ninety percent of Oberlin students live on campus in the dorms, including several program houses focusing on various foreign languages and cultural backgrounds. Students are required to live on campus for their first three years. "Some of the dorms are beautiful (Talcott, Asia House) and some are large concrete blocks

(Dascomb)," says one East Asian studies major. For five dollars, students can rent up to two original works of art to decorate their rooms. Students may eat in any of seven dining rooms. Appetizing alternatives to institutional fare can be found at the eight co-ops that comprise the Oberlin Student Cooperative Association, a nearly $3-million-a-year corporation run entirely by students. Students say they feel safe on campus, and the college has recently implemented a new sexual misconduct policy and added staff and other resources aimed at preventing campus sexual assault.

Social life, like so much of the Oberlin experience, is what you make of it, students say. "Everything takes place on campus, and there is a *ton* going on," raves one senior. Even in the middle of the day, "it's hard to walk across campus without becoming distracted by a pick-up game of Frisbee, the construction of a snow fort, or some students dancing contact improvisation on the lawn," says another. The monthly midnight Organ Pump concerts in Finney Chapel combine serious classical music with musical oddities, such as the school police blotter performed as Anglican chant. House parties, plays, movies, and conservatory performances are planned every other night. And since there's no Greek system, nothing is exclusive. As for drinking, underage students can finagle booze, and of-age students are allowed to imbibe in their rooms. "I think the rules work well," a chemistry major says. "Not too many students get into trouble."

When the need to wander strikes, Cleveland is only 30 miles away, but students enjoy their small town. "There's only really two square blocks of downtown," says one student, "but within it is basically everything that you need." Another student adds, "Pretty much all of the restaurants downtown are used to working until at least 2 a.m., delivering pizza to hungry late-nighters or having special offers for college students." And Obies are very enthusiastic about giving back to the community through volunteer activities at local schools, hospitals, and nursing homes. "Our motto is 'Think one person can make a difference? So do we!'" says a student.

> **"Oberlin is a place where you can be yourself, but also learn and grow as a person."**

The Yeomen and Yeowomen, terms that originated with British warriors of old, appear to be building a loyal fan base: the women's cross-country team won six consecutive Division III North Coast Athletic Conference championships (2009–14); baseball and women's lacrosse are competitive as well. As for intramural sports, "as soon as the rain stops in the spring, there are students on every green area between the dorms, playing ultimate Frisbee," says a sophomore. Fencing and Quidditch are other student favorites.

Oberlin may be small, but its emphasis on global learning, undergraduate research, and a vibrant liberal arts education helps it burst those statistical seams. Students are more likely to discuss local poverty than the quality of cereal choices in the dining halls, and can be found playing a Steinway or plugging away at astronomy. One Obie sums it up this way: "Oberlin is a place where you can be yourself, but also learn and grow as a person in a diverse environment enhanced by people equally interested in personal growth."

Eight co-ops comprise the Oberlin Student Cooperative Association, a nearly $3-million-a-year corporation run entirely by students.

Overlaps

Brown, Vassar, Wesleyan, Yale, University of Chicago, Kenyon, Northwestern, Macalester

If You Apply To ➤

Oberlin: Early decision I: Nov. 15. Early decision II: Jan. 2. Regular decision: Jan. 15. Financial aid: Mar. 1. No application fee. Campus and alumni interviews: recommended, evaluative. SATs or ACTs: required. Subject Tests: optional. Letters of recommendation: required. Essay: required. Accepts the Common Application with supplement. Applicants to Conservatory of Music must audition.

Occidental College

1600 Campus Road, Los Angeles, CA 90041

Oxy is a streetwise cousin to the more upscale and suburban Claremont Colleges. Plentiful internships and study abroad give Oxy students real-world perspectives. Oxy's innovative diplomacy and world affairs program features an internship at the UN. One of the most socially and economically diverse liberal arts colleges in the nation.

Occidental College is one of a handful of small colleges located in a big city, in this case La La Land. But unlike the sprawling and impersonal City of Angels, Oxy emphasizes a strong sense of community and a decidedly diverse student population. Notable alums include former president Barack Obama. "Students dream big at Oxy," says a senior. "Whether a student wants a career in Hollywood or on Wall Street, everyone knows that it starts in the classroom."

Set against the backdrop of the San Gabriel Mountains, Oxy's self-contained Mediterranean-style campus is a secluded enclave of flowers and trees between Pasadena and Glendale, minutes from downtown Los Angeles. A renovated and expanded career center opened in late 2015, while the McKinnon Center for Global Affairs features a two-story, LED-lit wall of sculpted glass with embedded interactive screens that display a shifting array of student and faculty research and coursework.

Inside this urban oasis resides a thriving community of high achievers who don't for a moment believe that the liberal arts are dead, or even wounded. Required first-year cultural studies seminars include topics in human history and culture, with an emphasis on writing skills. Each seminar has 16 students, some of whom also share the same residence hall; it's called the Learning Communities Program. In addition, all Oxy students must show proficiency in a foreign language and complete 12 units of world cultures courses, a fine arts course, preindustrial-era coursework, and 12 units of science and math. In their final year, all students complete a senior comprehensive, or "com," such as a project, paper, or exam that shows mastery in their field. Many of Occidental's academic departments are excellent; economics, politics, diplomacy and world affairs, biology, urban and environmental policy, and art and art history among the strongest and most popular majors. There are also 3–2 engineering programs with Caltech and Columbia University, an exchange program with Spelman College in Atlanta, and cross-registration privileges with Caltech and Pasadena's Art Center College of Design. Students may also take advantage of a 4–2 biotechnology program with Keck Graduate Institute (of the Claremont Colleges).

"Occidental provides an academically challenging environment," says a junior. "I was pleasantly surprised at how much my professors challenged me, pushing me to grow intellectually." Faculty members are readily available in and out of the classroom, and students say the teaching, in general, is excellent. "Every student is instructed by qualified and worldly professors who really go that extra mile to help students," one sophomore says. Nearly two-thirds of classes have fewer than 20 students, and as academic advisors are responsible for about four students per class (16 total), personal relationships develop quickly. "I have had in-home lunch, dinner, museum outings, and hour-long office discussions with my professors," explains one senior.

Oxy encourages diverse learning experiences through independent study, internships, and study abroad—including one of only a few undergraduate programs to

> **"I was pleasantly surprised at how much my professors challenged me, pushing me to grow intellectually."**

Website: www.oxy.edu
Location: City Center
Private
Total Enrollment: 2,112
Undergraduates: 2,112
Male/Female: 43/57
SAT Ranges: CR 600–690, M 600–690
ACT Ranges: 28–31
Financial Aid: 69%
Pell Grant: 20%
Expense: Pr $ $ $ $
Student Loans: 55%
Average Debt: $ $ $
Phi Beta Kappa: Yes
Applicants: 5,911
Accepted: 45%
Enrolled: 22%
Grad in 6 Years: 87%
Returning Freshmen: 93%
Academics: ✍ ✍ ✍ ✍
Social: ☎ ☎ ☎
Q of L: ★ ★ ★ ★
Admissions: (800) 825-5262
Email Address: admission@oxy.edu

Strong Programs:
Economics
Politics
Diplomacy and World Affairs
Biology
Urban and Environmental Policy
Art and Art History

offer internships with UN-related organizations in New York City, as well as the opportunity to work full time on political campaigns and then return to campus for a seminar where students reflect on their experiences. The California Environment Semester is a team-taught, interdisciplinary course for freshmen that involves extended field trips throughout the state. Fifty-five percent of students broaden their horizons in study abroad programs in more than 50 countries on six continents. On average, Oxy supports more than 300 student research projects in the sciences, social sciences, and humanities every year, and many students publish and present their work.

"Students are very socially conscious and have a deep passion for diversity," says an economics major. Forty-eight percent of the students are from California, and 6 percent hail from foreign nations. African Americans make up 5 percent of the student population, Hispanics 15 percent, and Asian Americans 13 percent. Perhaps not surprisingly, students tend to be liberal, and the raging social concerns are "racial and social inequalities, environmentalism, and gender issues," according to

"Students are very socially conscious and have a deep passion for diversity."

one student. In response to student protests over racial justice, the administration has hired a new chief diversity officer, increased funding for diversity programs, and is working to establish a minor in Black studies. Merit scholarships are doled out to qualified students each year—averaging $11,638—but there are no athletic scholarships. Occidental typically meets the full demonstrated need of admitted students, and special financial packages are available to low-income students; the college administers Pell Grants to 20 percent of its incoming freshmen. The college's financial aid staff visits local high schools to help families fill out applications, offering sessions in English, Spanish, and Vietnamese.

The residence halls are small—almost all house fewer than 150 students—and co-ed by floor or room. Eighty-two percent of students live on campus, but what you get depends on your luck in the housing lottery. Students from all four classes live together, many in special-interest houses like the Multicultural Hall, the Food Justice House, or the Substance-Free Quad. Freshmen, sophomores, and juniors are required to live on campus and eat in the dining hall (tip from a junior: don't try anything that has an unusual name, like "Mayan tofu"). In an effort to combat the national issue of campus sexual assault, Occidental has expanded its mandatory preventative education programs to reach the entire student body.

While the bustle of L.A. often beckons on weekends, the Oxy campus provides its share of fun too, whether it be a "basketball game, concert, dance, or party," says one student. Fraternities and sororities, though declining on the Oxy social ladder, attract 13 percent of the men and 19 percent of the women, but they are neither selective nor exclusive; students choose which to join, rather than being chosen,

"Students have a voice at Oxy and can easily relay their views to people at the top."

and the frats must invite everyone to their functions. As for alcohol, "like most other colleges, there is underage drinking even though this is illegal," says a junior. Dance Production—a decades-old tradition in which student dancers perform works by student choreographers—sells out both performances each year. Other big events include Apollo Night (a talent contest), Winter Formal, and A Taste of Oxy, a student potluck that showcases the diversity of the Oxy community through food and performance. You may want to keep your birthday a secret, or on that unhappy day a roaring pack of your more sadistic classmates will carry you out to the middle of campus and mercilessly toss you in the Gilman Fountain. It's a tradition, after all.

A student characterizes the surrounding neighborhood of Eagle Rock as "a quaint little community with an eclectic combination of 'ma and pa' restaurants and plenty of hole-in-the-wall stores." Community outreach is important at Occidental and dates back to the mid-1960s, when the college opened its Community Literacy Center and one of the country's first Upward Bound programs for under-served students. Today, Oxy's Upward Bound is one of the largest in the country, and half of Oxy students participate in some kind of community project, most through the Center for Community Based Learning. When students become weary of the social life in the "Oxy fishbowl," they head for the bars, restaurants, muse-ums, and theaters of downtown Los Angeles and Old Pasadena, where, one student notes, "You can find almost anything except snow." But the ski slopes of the San Gabriel Mountains are not far away, and neither is Hollywood nor the beautiful beaches of Southern California. When they tire of California, students try their luck in Las Vegas—or trek south of the border, into Tijuana. A car (your own or someone else's) is practically a necessity, though the college runs a weekend shuttle service to Old Town Pasadena. The weather is warm and sunny, but the air is often thick with that infamous L.A. smog.

The college opened one of the country's first Upward Bound programs for underserved students.

Oxy's sports teams (the Tigers) compete in Division III and draw a modest fol-lowing. Football is the most popular, while baseball and men's track and field have won recent conference championships. Women's basketball and cross-country are solid too. And don't forget that L.A. is home to the NBA's Lakers, the NHL's Kings, and the MLB's Dodgers. Oxy has a small intramural program, in which 20 percent of students take part; popular club sports include rugby and ultimate Frisbee.

"Students have a voice at Oxy," says a sophomore, "and can easily relay their views to people at the top." Occidental's creative, motivated, and diverse students are not here for the bright lights and beautiful people of Los Angeles; those are just fringe benefits. Instead, students are drawn to this intimate oasis of learning by professors who hate to see anyone waste one whit of intellectual potential. And stu-dents here are only too happy to live up to these lofty expectations.

Overlaps

UCLA, University of Southern California, UC–Berkeley, Pomona, Scripps, Claremont McKenna, Pitzer, Macalester

If You Apply To ➤ **Oxy:** Early decision I: Nov. 15. Early decision II: Jan. 1. Regular decision and financial aid: Jan. 15. Housing: May 1. Application fee: $65. Campus and alumni interviews: optional, evaluative. SATs or ACTs: required (SAT essay or ACT writing recommended). Subject Tests: optional. Letters of recommendation: required. Essay: required. Accepts the Common Application with supplement.

Oglethorpe University

4484 Peachtree Road NE, Atlanta, GA 30319

Small wonder that brochures for Oglethorpe trumpet Atlanta as the college's biggest drawing card. In a region where most liberal arts colleges are in sleepy towns, Oglethorpe has the South's most exciting city at its fingertips. Highly diverse student body. Oglethorpe Idea stresses broad academic values, while interdisciplinary Core Program gives shape to the curriculum. Strong Greek system provides the main social life.

Founded in 1835, Oglethorpe University is named for the idealistic founder of the state of Georgia, James Edward Oglethorpe. His idealism is well captured in the school's motto, *Nescit cedere* (He does not know how to give up), and in its ambition to become the first-choice university for high-achieving students in a region where it faces tough competition from much bigger names. Even as it seeks to boost enroll-ment, the university remains committed to the Oglethorpe Idea and to connecting

Website: www.oglethorpe.edu
Location: City Outskirts
Private
Total Enrollment: 1,055
Undergraduates: 1,055

(continued)

Male/Female: 41/59
SAT Ranges: CR 530–630,
    M 510–610
ACT Ranges: 22–28
Financial Aid: 90%
Pell Grant: 40%
Expense: Pr $
Student Loans: 68%
Average Debt: $ $
Phi Beta Kappa: No
Applicants: 2,768
Accepted: 78%
Enrolled: 20%
Grad in 6 Years: 51%
Returning Freshmen: 73%
Academics: ✍ ✍ ✍
Social: ☎ ☎ ☎
Q of L: ★ ★ ★ ★
Admissions: (404) 364-8307
Email Address: admission@
    oglethorpe.edu

Strong Programs:
Business Administration
English
Biology
Accounting
Psychology
Communication and Rhetoric
    Studies

*The Oglethorpe
Idea is based on
the conviction that
education should help
students make both
a life and a living.*

students with real-world experiences. Says a junior, "Although few outside of the Southeast have heard of it, this school provides a top-notch education."

Its 118-acre campus is strategically located in Brookhaven, one of Atlanta's most popular inner suburbs, with a picturesque Gothic campus that gives a traditional college feel. The heavily wooded, slightly rolling terrain is perfect territory for walks or long runs, and the beautiful campus has served as the backdrop for several movies and TV shows. Oglethorpe's academic buildings and some residence halls are in the English Gothic style. A recently opened campus center features a dining hall, coffee shop, bookstore, and outdoor patios. The building is also home to campus life offices and serves as the hub of the experiential learning program.

The university's guiding principle is the Oglethorpe Idea, which says students should develop academically and as citizens. This philosophy is based on the conviction that education should help students make both a life and a living. All students take the sequenced, interdisciplinary Core Curriculum program at the same point in their college careers, providing them with a model for integrating information and gaining knowledge. In addition to the ability to reason, read, and speak effectively, the core asks students to reflect on and discuss matters fundamental to understanding who they are and what they ought to be. The core requires Narratives of the Self (freshmen), Human Nature and the Social Order (sophomores), Historical Perspectives on the Social Order (juniors), and Science and Human Nature (seniors), plus a fine arts core course in music and culture or art and culture, and coursework in modern mathematics or advanced foreign language.

> **"Although few outside of the Southeast have heard of it, [Oglethorpe] provides a top-notch education."**

Oglethorpe's strengths are business administration, English, biology, accounting, psychology, and communication and rhetoric studies. Weaker bets are the fine arts and foreign language departments, though the latter does offer courses in Japanese, German, French, and Spanish. One student offers this assessment: "Many self-proclaimed premed majors change programs within their first semester because of its difficulty. The science departments are particularly demanding." Aspiring engineers may take advantage of 3–2 dual-degree programs with Auburn, Georgia Tech, the University of Florida, and the University of Southern California. The school also offers cross-registration with other schools in the Atlanta area and additional resources as a member of the Atlanta Regional Council for Higher Education*.

"I have never breezed through a class," says an art history major. "The academics are so rigorous." Oglethorpe's faculty may be demanding, but they're also friendly and helpful. "They really do care for you intellectually and personally," says one junior. Classes are generally small—70 percent of courses have fewer than 20 students—and most students notice few problems at registration. Advising services are said to be helpful. Oglethorpe offers a wide variety of study abroad programs, including a semester at Seigakuin University in Japan and sister-school exchanges in Argentina, the Netherlands, Germany, France, Russia, and Monaco. The Global Oglethorpe program sends students to Rome and Barcelona.

What's an Oglethorpian like? "We tend to be open-minded, thoughtful, and intellectual," explains one student. Most come from public schools and 70 percent are Georgians; 7 percent hail from abroad. "Our campus is pretty small—however, cliques do form." Oglethorpe prides itself on being one of the first Georgia colleges to admit African American students, and today 18 percent of students are African American, 3 percent are Asian American, and 10 percent are Hispanic. There's a level of comfort with racial differences, students report. Socioeconomic diversity is also strong, with 40 percent of students receiving Pell Grants. Merit scholarships are also available, worth an average of $17,571.

Fifty-seven percent of Oglethorpe's students choose to live on campus—and most love it. "The dorms are big and have nice furniture," says an accounting major. Most rooms are suites with private bathrooms, and some singles are available. Some students commute to campus; a quarter live in Atlanta—not a college town, but where the wild life is. "Some weekends, everyone stays around and life is great, and then there are others when campus is deserted," one student explains. Fraternities and sororities, which claim 20 percent of the men and 12 percent of the women, respectively, throw parties that draw big numbers. Officially, the campus is dry, but underage students can find alcohol if they try, students agree. The campus celebrates its origins once a year during Oglethorpe Day. Each Christmas brings a particularly unique tradition: the Boar's Head Ceremony celebrates a medieval scholar who halted a stampeding wild boar by ramming his copy of Aristotle down the animal's throat.

It's rumored that Oglethorpe barflies do more hopping than Georgia bullfrogs, and bars, clubs, and cafés abound within 10 minutes of campus. Students can also find excitement on the campuses of the dozen or so other colleges in the area or in downtown Atlanta, which one student describes as "the heart of Atlanta and a few minutes from Buckhead, a party district, and two great malls." Atlanta proper offers everything you can imagine—arts, professional

Oglethorpe's mascot, the Stormy Petrel, is a sea bird that flies in the face of storms. James Oglethorpe was inspired by them in 1733.

"We tend to be open-minded, thoughtful, and intellectual."

sports (including basketball's Hawks, football's Falcons, and baseball's Braves), and entertainment (ride the Great American Scream Machine at Six Flags). Oglethorpe always has a big contingent going to Savannah for St. Patrick's Day and to New Orleans for Mardi Gras, and sunny Florida beckons too.

Oglethorpe's mascot, the Stormy Petrel, is a sea bird that flies in the face of storms. James Oglethorpe was inspired by them on his first visit to Georgia in 1733. Intramurals are important at Oglethorpe, sometimes more so than varsity sports. Perhaps Atlanta's diversions or the relatively small number of students on campus cause varsity sports to be a weak draw. Still, the men's golf team is a Division III powerhouse, making regular NCAA Tournament appearances and winning two national titles. Basketball games against cross-city rival Emory are popular. The Georgia landscape makes possible a plethora of outdoor activities, including hiking at nearby Stone Mountain and boating or swimming in Lake Lanier (named for Georgia poet Sidney Lanier—Oglethorpe Class of 1860).

Though Oglethorpe may lack widespread name recognition, its diverse group of students get all the attention they need from a caring faculty on a close-knit campus. And being in a large city like Atlanta provides anything else that might be lacking, ranging from great nightlife to internships and postgraduate employment with big-name corporations. In a sea of large Southern state schools, Oglethorpe stands out as a place where students come first.

Overlaps

University of Georgia, Georgia State, Emory, Mercer, Kennesaw State, Georgia Southern, Berry, Georgia Tech

If You Apply To >

Oglethorpe: Rolling admissions. Early action and financial aid: Nov. 15. Housing: May 1. Application fee: $50. Campus and alumni interviews: optional, evaluative. SATs or ACTs: required. No Subject Tests. Letters of recommendation: required. Essay: required. Accepts the Common Application.

Ohio State University

Student Academic Services Building, 381 West Lane, Columbus, OH 43210

The biggest school in the Big Ten, Ohio State lacks the prestige of a Michigan or a Wisconsin, in part because it competes with two other Ohio publics, Miami and Ohio U, for top students. Operates the mother of all college sports programs that claims multiple national titles. Check out the top-notch honors program. Columbus is a major city and the capital of Ohio.

Website: www.osu.edu
Location: City Center
Public
Total Enrollment: 50,720
Undergraduates: 40,898
Male/Female: 52/48
SAT Ranges: CR 560–670, M 610–720
ACT Ranges: 27–31
Financial Aid: 69%
Pell Grant: 17%
Expense: Pub $ $
Student Loans: 55%
Average Debt: $ $ $
Phi Beta Kappa: Yes
Applicants: 40,240
Accepted: 49%
Enrolled: 35%
Grad in 6 Years: 83%
Returning Freshmen: 94%
Academics: ✐ ✐ ✐ ½
Social: ☎ ☎ ☎ ☎
Q of L: ★ ★ ★
Admissions: (614) 292-3980
Email Address:
  askabuckeye@osu.edu

Strong Programs:
Psychology
Finance
Communication
Biology
Business
Engineering
Data Analytics
African American and African Studies

Envision a campus with 50,000 students and too many opportunities to count. What might come to mind is Ohio State University, located in the heart of the state's capital, offering 15 colleges and 12,000 courses in more than 200 undergraduate majors. If those numbers aren't staggering enough, consider the fact that OSU has 36 varsity sports, nearly 30 intramural sports, 60 sports clubs, and the third largest campus in the nation. It also has an operating budget larger than that of the state of Delaware. While students cite the school's size as both a blessing and a curse, all seem to agree that at OSU, the sky is the limit for those with a desire to sample its academic and other resources. "Knowing what you want is great, but to get it, you'll need to work hard," warns one student. "Because if you want it, there are likely hundreds of other people who want it too."

This megauniversity stands on 1,777 acres in the middle of the city, rubbing the edge of downtown Columbus on one side. Across the Olentangy River from campus is a teaching and research farm associated with the College of Food, Agricultural, and Environmental Sciences. "One part of the campus maintains a nostalgic air while another is relatively modern," observes a student. The grounds are nicely landscaped, and a centrally located lake provides a peaceful setting for contemplation.

> **"I do not know a single student who wouldn't help another out if they were struggling academically."**

OSU's rich array of academic resources includes 15 libraries, all linked electronically, with 7 million volumes. Other facilities include the Recreation and Physical Activity Center (RPAC)—the nation's largest facility dedicated to student fitness, wellness, and recreation—and the Chemical and Biomolecular Engineering and Chemistry Building, the university's first LEED-certified lab building, which opened in 2015.

The university's fundamental commitment to liberal arts learning means all undergrads must satisfy rigorous general education requirements that include courses in math, writing, foreign language, social science, natural science, and arts and humanities. Business, engineering, education, geography, and industrial design are among the school's most celebrated departments; political science and dance are also strong. OSU bills itself as the place to go for computer graphics and has a supercomputer center to back up its claim. The strong African American and African studies program, which grew out of the civil rights movement of the 1960s, offers the most extensive offering of African languages of any U.S. university. Furthermore, the university has the nation's only programs in welding engineering and geodetic science, the state's only program in medical communications, and the nation's first undergraduate program in data analytics. The College of Arts and Sciences, in collaboration with Ohio State's Center for Aviation Studies, has launched the Social Sciences Air Transportation major, which combines study of the science of aircraft and flight with the social, economic, and political considerations of the air transportation industry. The majors that enroll the most students include psychology, finance, communication, and biology. A personalized study program enables students to create their own majors.

"Although everyone strives to do well, I do not know a single student who wouldn't help another out if they were struggling academically," says a sophomore. Freshmen may take advantage of numerous first-year programs, including the First Year Success Series, and pre-enrollment programs like Camp Buckeye and the Leadership Collaborative. Once the academic year is underway, they experience a variety of class formats and sizes, ranging from intimate Freshman Seminars to large lectures; 23 percent of all undergraduate classes have more than 50 students. Teaching assistants, not professors, hold smaller recitation sections and deal on a personal level with students. Students find that class sizes are whittled down as they continue in their fields of study. At such a large institution, the quality of instruction can vary greatly and students report this to be the case.

The university's RPAC is the nation's largest facility dedicated to student fitness, wellness, and recreation.

OSU's honors program allows selected students to take classes that are taught by top professors and limited to 25 students each. "The whole system of honors classes, priority scheduling, honors housing, and cocurricular activities really adds to the overall experience at OSU," a biology major says. Twenty percent of undergraduates participate in research opportunities coordinated by the Undergraduate Research Office. Internships are required in some programs and optional in others, and Columbus affords students access to the state government, Fortune 500 companies, and major tech and research organizations, including the IBM Analytics Solutions Lab and Battelle. Roughly 3,000 students study abroad each year through more than 100 programs in 40 countries.

"The dorms are very good, though they tend to have an industrial feel."

"Most students are extremely well-mannered, ambitious, open-minded, and obsessed with the Buckeyes," says a sophomore. Seventy-seven percent of Ohio State's students come from Ohio, and the remainder come largely from Illinois, Pennsylvania, California, New York, and Michigan—many of them lured by one of the most generous merit aid programs of any public university in the country. Eight percent come from foreign countries. The student body is 6 percent African American, 4 percent Hispanic, and 6 percent Asian American. "The diversity on campus is striking," says a senior. Several programs are aimed specifically at "enhancing" efforts to attract and retain minority students, including a statewide Young Scholars Program that begins working with students when they start the seventh grade. Sixty-two percent of incoming freshmen graduated in the top 10th of their high school class. Qualified students compete for merit scholarships averaging $6,943, and hundreds of athletic scholarships go to talented athletes each year.

OSU has the most extensive offering of African languages of any U.S. university.

The residence halls, which house 26 percent of the Ohio State masses, are located in three areas: North, South, and Olentangy (that is, those closest to the Olentangy River). Freshmen and sophomores are required to live in residence halls unless they are commuting from home, and freshmen are scattered among each of OSU's 42 residence halls. "The dorms are very good, though they tend to have an industrial feel," says a student. "Most upperclassmen live off campus." Those who stay on campus find the South campus section among the most desirable (it's more sociable, louder, and full of single rooms). The Towers in the Olentangy section have

"As hard as students may work during the school week, everything stops on game day."

gained more popularity since their conversion to eight-person suites. A system of variable room rates based on frills (air-conditioning, private bath, number of roommates), as well as a choice of four meal-plan options, give students flexibility in determining their housing costs. "The food at OSU is fantastic," chirps one student. BuckeyesACT is a comprehensive program to combat sexual misconduct and relationship violence on campus.

OSU is a bustling place on weekends. "Social life is never-ending," cheers one student. Various social events are planned by on-campus housing groups—floors, dorms, or sections of the campus. The student union runs eateries as well as movies and other activities. Campus policies prohibit underage drinking in dorms, but one partier discloses, "I can get served in almost any bar on campus." Still, another reports, "It's a laid-back party atmosphere with not much pressure." Nine percent of OSU men and 10 percent of the women go Greek. By one account, these students make the Greek system "a way of life and isolate themselves from the rest of the student population."

Such a large student market has, of course, produced a strip of bars, fast-food joints, convenience stores, bookstores, vegetarian restaurants, and you-name-its along the edge of the campus on High Street, and downtown Columbus is just a few minutes away. "Columbus is a vibrant town," says a junior. The fine public transportation system carries students not only throughout this capital city but also around the sprawling campus. In addition to the usual shopping centers, restaurants, golf courses, and movie theaters, Columbus boasts a symphony orchestra, a ballet, and professional hockey and soccer teams; OSU's D-Tix program offers students discounted or free tickets to cultural and sporting events. The city's central location in the state makes it easily accessible to Cleveland and Cincinnati. Outdoor enthusiasts can ski in nearby Mansfield, canoe and sail on the Olentangy and Scioto rivers, hike around adjacent quarries, or camp in the nearby woods.

Ohio State operates perhaps the most lavish—and successful—college sports program in the nation. The Buckeyes field 16 men's, 17 women's, and three co-ed varsity teams, from golf to gymnastics to riflery. The football team won both the Big Ten and national Division I championships in 2014; other recent national champions include wrestling, synchronized swimming, women's rowing, men's volleyball, and pistol. Recent conference winners include baseball and men's and women's tennis. "Football is somewhat like religion," says one student. "As hard as students may work during the school week, everything stops on game day." Rivalries abound, and nonrecruited students should not expect to make any varsity team as walk-ons. Many take advantage of an ambitious intramural program that boasts a dozen basketball courts and 26 courts for handball, squash, and racquetball.

OSU's sheer size is sometimes overwhelming to be sure, but students here seem to thrive on the challenge and excitement of a big university. For those who really want to be Buckeyes, be prepared to jump in with both feet and get involved in plenty of activities.

If You Apply To ➤ **OSU:** Rolling admissions: Feb. 1. Early action: Nov. 1. Financial aid: Feb. 1. Housing: Jun. 16. Application fee: $60. No campus or alumni interviews. SATs or ACTs: required. Subject Tests: optional. Letters of recommendation: optional. Essay: required. Accepts the Common Application with supplement.

Ohio University

Chubb Hall 120, Athens, OH 45701

OHIO is one-third the size of Ohio State and plays up its homey feel compared to the cast of tens of thousands in Columbus. The Honors Tutorial College is a draw for top students who want close contact with faculty. Communication and journalism top the list of prominent programs. OHIO is not in the Big Ten, but the Mid-American Conference has begun to generate more excitement.

With top-notch programs in journalism and business, Ohio University has become a competitive public research institution without shedding its small-town roots. Faculty interests range from dinosaur anatomy to rural diabetes rates. Students here love to hit the town for fun but are quick to hit the books too. Those who choose to attend OHIO receive ample returns, says a senior, including "a quality education, lifelong friends, supportive faculty, and a beautiful campus."

Established in 1804 as the first institution of higher learning in the old Northwest Territory, Ohio University is located in Athens, which lies about 75 miles southeast of Columbus, the state capital, and was named after a certain ancient center of learning in Greece. Encircled by winding hills, the campus features neo-Georgian architecture, tree-lined redbrick walkways, and white-columned buildings all clustered on "greens," which are like small neighborhoods. Long walks are especially nice during the fall foliage season. The Living Learning Center, a multipurpose building with classrooms, meeting rooms, and offices for residential housing staff, is among the newest additions to campus.

General education requirements at OHIO involve a minimum of one course in math or quantitative skills, two courses in English composition, one senior-level interdisciplinary capstone course, plus additional coursework in applied sciences and technology, social sciences, natural sciences, humanities, and cross-cultural perspectives. Students enroll in nine undergraduate colleges, and the College of Communication now contains five distinct schools: the schools of journalism, information and telecommunication systems, communication studies, media arts and studies, and visual communication. The most popular majors are nursing, health services administration, business, and communication studies. The journalism program is highly regarded and offers tracks in news and information and strategic communication, in addition to an emphasis on learning to use current and emerging technology. Engineering and education are also strengths. New majors include geological sciences, dance studies, and physical activity and sport coaching.

> "All of us have a very deep interest in our chosen subject matter."

The academic environment is far from cutthroat, but courses can be demanding. "The climate is laid-back," says one student, "but people do work hard." Freshmen are often taught by full professors with TAs handling study sessions. Classes of 100-plus students do exist, but 31 percent of undergraduate classes have fewer than 20 students. Budget cutbacks have limited access to some classes, and "we need more professors to cut down the class sizes," says a finance major. Even so, students praise professors for making themselves as available as possible. "My professors have always been willing to work with me and offer out-of-class time to make sure that me and my peers could excel in the courses," a senior says.

One of the best advantages of an Ohio University education, and something that sets the school apart from run-of-the-mill state institutions, is the Honors Tutorial College. Founded in 1972, it's the nation's first multidisciplinary,

Website: www.ohio.edu
Location: Small Town
Public
Total Enrollment: 20,167
Undergraduates: 17,355
Male/Female: 48/52
SAT Ranges: CR 490–600, M 500–610
ACT Ranges: 22–26
Financial Aid: 79%
Pell Grant: 33%
Expense: Pub $ $ $
Student Loans: 66%
Average Debt: $ $ $
Phi Beta Kappa: Yes
Applicants: 21,000
Accepted: 74%
Enrolled: 28%
Grad in 6 Years: 67%
Returning Freshmen: 79%
Academics: ✍ ✍ ✍
Social: ☎ ☎ ☎ ☎
Q of L: ★ ★ ★
Admissions: (740) 593-4100
Email Address: admissions@ohio.edu

Strong Programs:
Nursing
Health Services Administration
Business
Communication Studies
Journalism
Engineering
Education
Visual Communication

degree-granting honors program modeled on the tutorial method used in British universities, notably Oxford and Cambridge. It is ranked as one of the best programs on campus, and the most selective: only about 70 freshmen get in every year. Students take an individualized curriculum in a major field and spend most of their time in one-on-one weekly tutorials with profs. Special opportunities abound for those not in the honors program too. Co-op programs are available for engineering students, and nearly anyone can earn credit for an internship. The Provost's Undergraduate Research Fund provides financial support for undergraduate research, and students showcase more than 500 research and creative projects at the university's annual Student Research Expo. The Global Leadership Center (GLC) offers an innovative certificate program that prepares students for leadership opportunities in a rapidly changing world. First-year GLC students work in binational teams with students from universities in Hungary, Ecuador, Thailand, and elsewhere. Study abroad offers worldwide destinations for anywhere from one week to one year; 10 percent of students take part.

The Honors Tutorial College is modeled on the tutorial method used in British universities.

OHIO students are easygoing, yet driven in the classroom. "All of us have a very deep interest in our chosen subject matter," says one student. "I see so much passion among my peers for their work." Eighty-three percent of undergraduates are Ohioans, and 4 percent are international. The student body is overwhelmingly white, although administrators are trying to attract more minority students and have established an Office of Multicultural Programs. Five percent of undergraduates are African American, 3 percent are Hispanic, and 1 percent are Asian American. Thirty-three percent are Pell-eligible. The OHIO Signature Awards program provides merit scholarships and need-based grants for outstanding students who show academic excellence, financial need, or a combination of both. The athletically gifted can vie for 233 scholarships in 16 sports. The new OHIO Guarantee initiative sets fixed rates for each incoming class for tuition, housing, dining, and other fees that are guaranteed not to increase for six years.

"Most freshmen drink in their dorm rooms, and the bars are almost always crowded."

The new OHIO Guarantee sets fixed rates for tuition, housing, dining, and other fees that are guaranteed not to increase for six years.

Forty-six percent of students live in campus housing. The university supports more than 200 residential learning communities, in which approximately 80 percent of first-year students participate. At the "mods," six men and six women occupy separate wings but share a living room and study room. Upperclassmen usually move to fraternity or sorority houses, nearby apartments, or rental houses. The university recently launched an extensive renovation effort that includes updates to existing housing and construction of four new residence halls. All three campus dining halls have also been renovated recently, and students can choose from five different meal plans.

Eighty percent of first-year students participate in more than 200 residential learning communities.

According to a sophomore, "OHIO offers a very cohesive and communal social life" that includes guest speakers and performers, plays, and other events. Approximately 8 percent of the men and 11 percent of the women choose to participate in Greek life. Freshmen are required to pass an online alcohol education course in order to register for OHIO classes, and the administration and some students have tried to downplay OHIO's party-school image by strictly enforcing the alcohol policy. But despite these efforts, students say that drinking continues. "Most freshmen drink in their dorm rooms, and the bars are almost always crowded," a student explains. Students look forward to university events such as homecoming and International Festival. Uptown Athens is dotted with bars and clubs, and the city's fabled Halloween celebration is a huge street party that draws people from all over the Midwest. "Athens is its own place," says a senior. "You feel at home. It's beautiful and friendly and like no other." Volunteer opportunities, such as Habitat for Humanity and a local homeless shelter, are available through the Center for

Campus Involvement. Students also love to hike and camp at the nearby state parks or trek to Columbus for shopping.

Division I sports are a big draw at OHIO. The Bobcats field 16 varsity teams, and baseball, women's basketball, and volleyball are recent conference champions. The Bobcat football team has made multiple bowl game appearances, and men's basketball garnered national attention by reaching the Sweet 16 round of the 2012 NCAA Tournament. The university also has a nationally ranked forensics program. Twenty intramural and 35 club sports draw 60 percent of students; popular choices include teams for broomball and wallyball (think volleyball using walls).

> "Athens is its own place. You feel at home. It's beautiful and friendly and like no other."

Students say Ohio University has a lot to offer, from a vibrant social life to quality professors and challenging academics. "I love this school and the city's community," says one student. "I think most students would not regret their decision to come here."

If You Apply To ➤

OHIO: Rolling admissions. (Priority deadline: Feb. 1.) Early action: Dec. 1. Financial aid: Jan. 15. Housing: May 1. Application fee: $50. No campus or alumni interviews. SATs or ACTs: required (SAT essay or ACT writing recommended). No Subject Tests. Letters of recommendation: optional. Essay: optional. Accepts the Common Application. Honors Tutorial College applicants must interview.

Ohio Wesleyan University

South Sandusky Street, Delaware, OH 43015

OWU serves up the liberal arts with a popular side dish of business-related programs. In a region of beautiful campuses, Ohio Wesleyan's is nondescript. Like Denison, OWU is working hard to make its fraternities behave. Attracts middle-of-the-road to conservative students with preprofessional aspirations. Offers a variety of programs to raise social awareness, notably Wesleyan in Washington.

Ohio Wesleyan University is a small school with a big commitment to providing its students with a well-rounded education. Affiliated with the Methodist Episcopal Church, OWU hallmarks include strong preparation for graduate and professional school, a solid grounding in the liberal arts, and an emphasis on having fun outside the classroom. Once known for its raucous students, this small university has overcome its hard-partying past and now offers students a rewarding academic experience.

Situated in the center of the state and on the outskirts of Columbus, OWU's spacious 200-acre campus is peaceful and quaint. Several buildings are on the National Register of Historic Places. The architecture ranges from Greek Revival to colonial to modern, with ivy-covered brick academic buildings on one side of a busy thoroughfare and dormitories and fraternities on the other side of the highway. Stately University Hall, with its majestic spire and bell tower, is the main campus landmark and houses the president's office and the 1,100-seat Gray Chapel, home to the largest Klais organ in the United States. The new Simpson Querrey Fitness Center houses a workout area, fully equipped dance studio, classroom space, and other areas.

To graduate, OWU students must take a year of foreign language; three courses each in the social sciences, natural sciences, and humanities; one course in the arts; and one course in cultural diversity. Students must also pass three mandatory writing classes to sharpen their written communication skills, but these aren't burdensome.

Website: www.owu.edu
Location: Small City
Private
Total Enrollment: 1,658
Undergraduates: 1,658
Male/Female: 48/52
SAT Ranges: CR 510–630, M 510–620
ACT Ranges: 22–28
Financial Aid: 98%
Pell Grant: 31%
Expense: Pr $ $
Student Loans: 67%
Average Debt: $ $ $ $
Phi Beta Kappa: Yes
Applicants: 3,949
Accepted: 75%
Enrolled: 15%

Students interested in public policy may choose to pursue a semester-long internship through the Wesleyan in Washington program.

Preprofessional education has always been Ohio Wesleyan's forte. More than 80 percent of students applying to medical school are accepted. "The academics here are intense and challenging," says one sophomore. The curriculum includes majors in neuroscience and health and human kinetics, and the highly popular zoology, psychology, and botany and microbiology departments are interesting alternatives to the traditional premed route. Dentistry, optometry, veterinary medicine, law, public administration, and theology round out the list of preprofessional offerings. The Woltemade Center for Economics, Business, and Entrepreneurship caters to budding entrepreneurs, and the music and fine arts programs offer both professional and liberal arts degrees. Classes are small, with 72 percent enrolling fewer than 20 students, and a sophomore says, "The professors are very accessible and are willing to help students however they can."

A member of the Great Lakes Colleges Association* consortium, OWU offers numerous curricular and cocurricular programs. The most prominent is the Sagan National Colloquium, a series of lectures, classes, events, and projects around a theme that unites the liberal and civic arts. OWU Connection allows students to study a particular topic (such as water or poverty) in-depth over a long period of time, selecting courses from disciplines and departments throughout the university. It also includes a component of real-world experience, such as international travel opportunities to study or conduct original research, as well as internships and culminating senior projects. The honors program offers qualified students one-on-one tutorials and a chance to conduct research with faculty members in areas of mutual interest. The Special Languages program offers the opportunity for self-directed study and tutoring by native speakers in languages such as Arabic, Chinese, Japanese, and Modern Greek. Students interested in public policy and service may choose to pursue a semester-long internship through the Wesleyan in Washington program, while others may spend a semester in New York City in apprenticeships with working professionals. The school's study abroad offerings are enhanced by Theory-to-Practice Grants that support students in projects ranging from a field dig on the Aegean coast to the study of HIV/AIDS in South Africa and Tanzania.

> **"The academics here are intense and challenging."**

OWU students are "the opposite of ordinary," according to one senior. Forty-one percent of students come from Ohio and 6 percent are international. Students agree that diversity, although lacking, is valued on campus; African Americans make up 8 percent of the student body, Hispanics 5 percent, and Asian Americans 3 percent. Liberals and conservatives are well represented on campus and hot topics include racial, gender, and sexual equality. Merit scholarships averaging $22,311 are available for qualified students, and 31 percent of freshmen qualify for Pell Grants.

Ninety-one percent of OWU students live in university-sponsored housing. All but one of the dorms are co-ed, and rooms are mostly apartment-style, four-person suites or doubles. Fraternities, unlike sororities, offer a residential option. "We have small-living units or SLUs, which are essentially themed houses," says a senior. "The members of these houses do house projects every semester for the campus and are an extremely important part of the OWU community." Each meal eaten on the college plan subtracts a certain number of points (far too many in the opinion of most students) from students' accounts, but there are numerous culinary choices, from all-you-can-eat in the three dining halls to pizza and snacks from the college grocery store. A sophomore reports, "We have a Safewalk program at night, so students do not have to walk alone. Also, Public Safety is very active in engaging with the students."

> **"The members of [themed] houses do house projects every semester for the campus."**

"There are many social events on campus to keep students busy and entertained. The school hosts many functions, like laser tag or roller-skating or different events with free food," says a sophomore. Does the buttoned-down seriousness of recent years mean that OWU has forsaken its heritage of raucous partying? Administrators certainly hope so. Part of OWU's commitment to mend its partying ways includes dry rush for all fraternities and an armband policy at parties—and two fraternities have been shut down since 2015 for various violations. Still, Greek membership attracts 46 percent of men and 34 percent of women. "There is definitely pressure to drink, because so many people do it every weekend," says one student. Among OWU's best-loved traditions are homecoming in the fall and Alumni Weekend in the spring, as well as the President's Ball in December.

Delaware is "adorable," says one junior. "There are several small shops and restaurants that are also relatively diverse from Greek to Cajun to just regular pizza and burger joints." The Little Brown Jug, one of harness racing's Triple Crown events, takes place each autumn, bringing thousands of people to the city of Delaware. Most students are involved in service, either through mission trips or community service learning in such projects as Habitat for Humanity, Delaware Reads, and the Delaware County Humane Society. "Because of the high amount of volunteering that OWU students do in Delaware, we have a fairly good relationship with the town," one student says. Ohio's capital and largest city, Columbus, is only 30 minutes away by car and offers many internship and job opportunities. Lakes, farms, and even ski slopes are within a few hours' drive.

OWU's Battling Bishops are a North Coast Athletic Conference powerhouse. Men's soccer consistently dominates and advanced to the 2014–15 Final Four. Women's track and field, men's lacrosse, and men's basketball are solid too. Sports fever carries over into single-sex and co-ed intramurals (nearly 80 percent of students take part), and a massive annual game of Capture the Flag begins at 11:00 at night and lasts until the wee hours.

Ohio Wesleyan University offers a solid liberal arts education devoid of bells and whistles. "Ohio Wesleyan is a place where the education goes well beyond the classroom," explains one student. "The family atmosphere and the opportunities that the college provides you...enrich the entire college experience."

> *OWU mandates dry rush for all fraternities—and two fraternities have been shut down since 2015 for various violations.*

> **"The family atmosphere and the opportunities that the college provides you...enrich the entire college experience."**

Overlaps

Ohio State, Wittenberg, Miami University (OH), Ohio University, Otterbein, College of Wooster, Denison, Capital University

If You Apply To >

OWU: Early decision: Nov. 15. Early action I: Dec. 1. Early action II: Jan. 15. Regular decision: Mar. 1. Priority financial aid: Dec. 1. Application fee: $35 (paper), free (online). Campus and alumni interviews: optional, evaluative. SATs or ACTs: required (optional for students with minimum qualifying GPA). No Subject Tests. Letters of recommendation: required. Essay: required. Accepts the Common Application.

University of Oklahoma

1000 Asp Avenue, Room 127, Norman, OK 73019

Tops among public universities in attracting National Merit Scholars, OU is strong in engineering and geology-related fields. Check out the nationally recognized Honors College, which features living/learning options. Football aside, OU has traditionally lacked the visibility of rival UT Austin. Putting a recent scandal involving a racist chant by fraternity members in the rearview mirror.

Website: www.ou.edu
Location: Small City
Public
Total Enrollment: 23,945
Undergraduates: 18,670
Male/Female: 49/51
SAT Ranges: CR 520–670,
   M 540–670
ACT Ranges: 24–29
Financial Aid: 74%
Pell Grant: 20%
Expense: Pub $ $
Student Loans: 44%
Average Debt: $ $ $
Phi Beta Kappa: Yes
Applicants: 12,002
Accepted: 78%
Enrolled: 35%
Grad in 6 Years: 66%
Returning Freshmen: 86%
Academics: ✐ ✐ ✐
Social: ☎ ☎ ☎
Q of L: ★ ★ ★
Admissions: (405) 325-2252
Email Address: admrec@
   ou.edu

Strong Programs:
Nursing
Accounting
Psychology
Administrative Leadership
Petroleum Engineering
Meteorology
Entrepreneurship
Western American History

The University of Oklahoma has more to boast about than its powerhouse football program. The university is also producing a population of high-achieving students. In fact, OU is the only university in the country where students have won Rhodes, Marshall, Mitchell, Truman, Goldwater, and Fulbright scholarships in the same year. Couple that with a rigorous honors program and a genuine friendliness among the student body, and it's easy to understand this favorite saying: "Sooner born and Sooner bred, when I die, I'll be Sooner dead!"

Located about 20 miles south of Oklahoma City, OU's 3,500-acre Norman campus features tree-lined streets and predominantly redbrick buildings. Many are historic in nature and built in the Cherokee Gothic or Prairie Gothic style. The Norman campus houses 16 colleges; six medical and health-related colleges are located on the OU Health Sciences Center campus in Oklahoma City, and programs from colleges on both campuses are also offered at OU's Schusterman Center in Tulsa. OU is also home to the Sam Noble Oklahoma Museum of Natural History, which has more than 7 million artifacts, including the largest Apatosaurus on display in the world and the oldest work of art ever found in North America—a lightning bolt painted on an extinct bison skull. Over the last two decades, more than $2 billion in construction projects have been completed or are under way on OU's three campuses.

> **"Eating at the Caf is like eating dinner with the whole freshman class every night."**

OU's general education requirements consist of three to five courses in symbolic and oral communication, including English composition; two courses in natural science; two courses in social science; four humanities courses; an upper-division general education course outside the major; a Diversity and Inclusion Experience; and a Senior Capstone Experience. All OU freshmen start out in University College before choosing among OU's degree-granting colleges.

The most popular majors include nursing, accounting, psychology, and administrative leadership. The Gallogly College of Engineering offers aerospace, civil, mechanical, and environmental engineering, among others. The Mewbourne College of Earth and Energy provides resources related to petroleum and geological engineering, geology, and geophysics. In fact, OU's petroleum engineering program ranks among the best in the nation. OU is home to the largest meteorology department in the country and the National Weather Center. In the College of Arts and Sciences, the natural sciences, notably chemistry, are strong. The Michael F. Price College of Business, named for the superstar investment manager, class of '73, offers a major in entrepreneurship and venture management. Other well-recognized programs at OU include majors in Western American history, Native American studies, and energy management. The Jeannine Rainbolt College of Education's rigorous five-year teacher-certification program, Teacher Education Plus, incorporates field experience, mentoring, and instruction from 30 full-time professors. A B.S. in biomedical engineering is the newest academic offering.

"While most students are very personally driven to succeed academically, the atmosphere among students is far from competitive," says a psychology major. "If anything, you'll find that students help each other do well by forming study groups, tutoring each other, and sharing their resources." OU has made efforts to address large classes and is now one of the nation's few public universities to cap the class size of first-year English comp courses at no more than 19; overall, 43 percent of undergraduate classes have fewer than 20 students. In the past decade, increased private support has helped OU nearly quadruple its endowed faculty positions, helping the school attract and retain talented professors. "Professors do a great job of engaging students and making the material easy to understand and fun to learn," says one sophomore.

OU is the only university where students have won Rhodes, Marshall, Mitchell, Truman, Goldwater, and Fulbright scholarships in the same year.

The Honors College offers small classes with outstanding faculty members and independent study, along with its own dorm. Top students may also apply for the Scholar-Leadership Enrichment Program, under which well-known lecturers give seminars at the university for academic credit. Students across the university compete for Undergraduate Research Opportunities Program grants of up to $1,000 to support faculty-mentored research and creative work. Study abroad opportunities are available in more than 80 countries, including programs at OU's study centers in Italy, Brazil, and Mexico. Students are often able to apply their financial aid to study abroad, and special scholarships, including Presidential International Travel Fellowships, are available for qualified students as well.

OU is home to the largest meteorology department in the country and the National Weather Center.

"Sooners are down-to-earth, passionate, and focused not only on goals for their college careers, but on big dreams for changing the world outside of this campus," says a senior. The student body is primarily homegrown; 64 percent of undergraduates hail from the Sooner state, and 4 percent come from abroad. African Americans account for 5 percent, Asian Americans 6 percent, Hispanics 9 percent, and American Indians 4 percent. "Students are very informed here," one junior says, citing environmental issues as a hot topic. Qualified students receive scholarships based on academic merit, with awards averaging $2,554, and there are also 257 athletic scholarships in 12 sports. OU also offers a variety of special aid programs aimed at making the university more affordable for low-income students; 20 percent of incoming students are eligible for the Pell Grant.

"I consider game days an all-day festival."

Thirty percent of students live on campus, and the university is making living/learning communities a major focus. Renovations to existing residence halls, which are mostly occupied by freshmen, have recently been completed. Freshmen can choose to live on specific academic floors or at the Honors College, and a faculty-in-residence program has been established to support a cohesive academic and social transition to college. Construction is under way on new residential colleges for upperclassmen; modeled after those at Yale and Oxford, the residential colleges will also serve as living/learning communities. Upperclassmen may also choose the OU Traditions Square apartment community, featuring fully furnished units, fitness areas, and other amenities. And how about the food? According to one student, "Eating at the Caf is like eating dinner with the whole freshman class every night, and the community feeling is tangible. Out of the hundreds of times I have eaten here, there have been only a couple of incidents of gross food." Students say they feel safe on campus. "Campus security is excellent. We have our own police department at OU and we are also covered by Norman PD. So we are kind of double covered," reasons one premed student.

Construction is under way on new residential colleges for upperclassmen, modeled after those at Yale and Oxford.

The OU social scene is vibrant. "Most things happen on campus so they are easy to go to," says one student. Greek life at OU sparked a scandal in 2015 when two members of Sigma Alpha Epsilon were videotaped saying a racist chant, and university officials have been taking steps to improve race relations, including a required five-hour course on diversity. Twenty-two percent of men and 29 percent of women go Greek. Although the dorms and Greek houses are dry, fraternity parties are the highlight of weekends at OU. "Campus Corner provides a lot of the nightlife with

"A student can come from anywhere and find that they are part of something special."

great restaurants and bars located directly across the street from campus," a junior says. The "three-strikes" alcohol policy "has greatly cut down on alcohol incidents" on campus, says one student. The town of Norman, population 120,000, is Oklahoma's third-largest city, and Oklahoma City is just 20 minutes away. Popular diversions include the annual road trip to Dallas for the OU–Texas football game, the Medieval Festival, and the University Sing talent show. The Big Event sends thousands of students into the community for a day of service each year.

OU has a reputation for powerhouse Division I athletic teams. Sooner football remains strong under coach Bob Stoops and has brought home the Big 12 Conference title multiple times in recent years. "Every football game day, the town swells to over 500,000 people, and I consider game days an all-day festival," says a letters major. Women's and men's gymnastics each won national titles in 2016. Men's and women's basketball make regular NCAA Tournament appearances, and softball and men's tennis are recent conference champs. Recreational and intramural programs attract a quarter of the undergraduate population, and flag football and basketball are especially popular.

"OU offers the classic college experience," says a senior. Indeed, students at Oklahoma have a lot to brag about. "The educational opportunities are top-notch," says one junior, and "a student can come from anywhere and find that they are part of something special." If you're searching for a school with plenty of spirit and a feeling of family, OU may be worth a look—sooner, rather than later.

Overlaps

Oklahoma State, University of Texas at Austin, Texas A&M, Texas Tech, Baylor, University of Arkansas, Texas Christian, Southern Methodist

If You Apply To ➤

OU: Rolling admissions: Feb. 1. Financial aid: Mar. 1. Application fee: $40. No campus or alumni interviews. SATs or ACTs: required. No Subject Tests. Letters of recommendation: required. Essay: required. Accepts the Common Application.

Olin College of Engineering

Olin Way, Needham, MA 02492

Olin opened its doors in 2002 with an innovative project-based curriculum and a commitment to turning out "technologists with soul." Already an elite institution that competes with Caltech and MIT. Every enrolled student gets a hefty merit scholarship. Located in Needham, near Wellesley, on the outskirts of Boston.

Website: www.olin.edu
Location: Suburban
Private
Total Enrollment: 332
Undergraduates: 332
Male/Female: 52/48
SAT Ranges: CR 710–800, M 730–800
ACT Ranges: 32–35
Financial Aid: 100%
Pell Grant: 12%
Expense: Pr $ $ $
Student Loans: 43%
Average Debt: $
Phi Beta Kappa: No
Applicants: 1,075
Accepted: 11%
Enrolled: 64%
Grad in 6 Years: 93%
Returning Freshmen: 91%

In the mid-1990s, leaders of the F. W. Olin Foundation began daydreaming about what "state-of-the-art" engineering education for the 21st century would look like. Two decades and $470 million later they have their answer: the Franklin W. Olin College of Engineering. This elite engineering school aims to turn out Steve Jobs-style graduates who are not only technically competent but who can "come up with innovative ideas and products." The curriculum is project-based, and students become as comfortable in the machine shop as in labs and classrooms. The foundation fathers also decided that, rather than gradually building up the quality and reputation of their new school, they would invest in excellence from the get-go. By offering every admitted student a half-tuition scholarship worth more than $93,000 over four years, Olin has succeeded in luring super-bright students away from Caltech, MIT, and other engineering highfliers. Sure, the college lacks the rich tradition and reputation for research of more established institutions. But that doesn't seem to bother the more than 300 students who have latched onto perhaps the best deal in U.S. higher education.

> **"The professors value feedback from the students very highly."**

Olin's 70-acre campus is located adjacent to Babson College in a pleasant suburb less than 20 miles west of Boston. The campus design is an innovative blend of the traditional and futuristic. Five buildings curve around a central green space, creating a sense of community and echoing the design of the traditional New England college. The entire campus is wired for high-tech communications and designed for easy updating to stay on the cutting edge. The classrooms make use of state-of-the-art instructional media, and there are plenty of meeting and public spaces to encourage the kind of collaboration called for in modern-day engineering.

Olin's innovative curriculum emphasizes science and engineering, business and entrepreneurship, and the liberal arts. Students choose from three majors—electrical and computer engineering, mechanical engineering, or a self-designed major in engineering with a concentration, such as bioengineering, computing, design, or robotics. In addition, students must complete 30 credits of math and science (10 of which must be in math) and 28 credits of arts, humanities, social sciences (AHS), and entrepreneurship, 12 of which must be in AHS. The course catalog is thin, especially in liberal arts subjects, but students can and do take courses at nearby Babson, Wellesley, and even Brandeis. The hands-on nature of Olin's curriculum means that students start out with relatively simple projects, such as designing water rockets, and progress to more sophisticated challenges like building a wall-climbing gecko—a project that involves analyzing the physics of the natural world and then figuring out how to replicate it mechanically. Concern for "engineering design" is built into every subject. Each student also completes one of two options—SCOPE (Senior Capstone Program in Engineering) or ADE (Affordable Design and Entrepreneurship)—for a yearlong, team-based senior capstone project, in which they apply their knowledge to solving real-world problems, in partnership with outside organizations or communities.

"We're all engineers, but we have social skills!"

Courses are rigorous, but working in teams and across disciplines is the norm for faculty as well as students. "We work very hard, and we work a lot," says one senior, "but there's no real feeling of anything but the friendliest competition. Students are encouraged to work together on homework and help others, and we generally enjoy doing so." Grading starts after the first semester. Fifty-six percent of classes have fewer than 20 students, and all are led by professors, with whom students are on a first-name basis. Faculty members do not have tenure. Like their students, many of them have been lured from the likes of MIT because they like the challenge of helping to create what one of them termed "the model of engineering for the future." A sophomore explains, "The professors value feedback from the students very highly—courses are often altered halfway through the semester with suggestions from the students."

First-year students have an opportunity to participate in an interactive week-long orientation program that includes team-building exercises, meetings, and meals with faculty and advisors, as well as a trip into Boston. The college also encourages students to engage in "Passionate Pursuits" by enabling them to pursue personal interests via faculty-guided projects, for which they receive nondegree academic credit and, often, funding. A sampling of student projects includes rock climbing, guitar making, marathon training, gelato making, and Bhangra (Indian folk dancing). Although students can find it a challenge to fit study abroad into their demanding schedules, Olin does offer several direct-exchange options, as well as pre-approved programs at more than 30 institutions around the world.

"We're all engineers, but we have social skills!" asserts a senior. Only 14 percent hail from Massachusetts, and 8 percent come from abroad. African Americans comprise 1 percent of the student body, Asian Americans 16 percent, and Hispanics 5 percent. "Students are generally liberal, but not particularly active in promoting political issues," according to a sophomore, and while students appreciate the balanced male/female ratio as "very uncommon" for an engineering school, many express a desire to see their campus become more racially diverse. To make sure that it selects students who are a good fit for Olin's

"You can leave your laptop in the lounge, and it won't walk off."

(continued)

Academics: ✏️ ✏️ ✏️ ✏️ ✏️
Social: ☎ ☎ ☎
Q of L: ★ ★ ★ ★ ★
Admissions: (781) 292-2222
Email Address: info@olin.edu

Strong Programs:
Engineering
Electrical and Computer
 Engineering
Mechanical Engineering

Every admitted student is offered a half-tuition scholarship worth more than $93,000 over four years.

unique approach to engineering, the admissions office invites 220 applicants to attend one of three "candidates' weekends" in the spring, where they learn about the school, take part in team projects such as building a weight-bearing bridge out of Styrofoam, and go through a 25-minute interview with faculty, staff, students, and an alumnus. About 130 of these students are accepted, and about 30 are placed on a waiting list. In addition to awarding half-tuition scholarships, Olin guarantees to meet 100 percent of any remaining demonstrated financial need for all enrolled domestic students.

All students live on campus in Olin's two residence halls, freshmen and sophomores in doubles in West Hall and upperclassmen in either doubles or suites in East Hall. "The dorms are wonderful," reports one student. Meal options in Olin's sole dining hall have been described as "mediocre," but students are optimistic that the newly hired dining-service provider will turn things around. Olin operates with a student-designed honor system that makes for unlocked rooms and take-home exams. "You can leave your laptop in the lounge, and it won't walk off," said a senior. Campus security is good and "students do feel physically safe," says one student, but others note that there have been incidents of campus sexual assault recently. "The administration has handled it bureaucratically," says a senior. "The college continues to refine its policies at the behest of vocal students and the student government."

> "I think our healthy disregard for tradition makes life a little more interesting."

When students aren't laboring over the latest Structural Biomaterials assignment, they tend to congregate on campus for fun. "There are parties in the residence halls, and the Student Activities Committee hosts some sort of schoolwide event every weekend," says a junior. There are no Greek organizations, and students say the social scene does not revolve around alcohol. "The campus alcohol policies are quite reasonable," says a student, "relying largely on student responsibility." The student orchestra has no conductor—or, as the joke goes, "not even a semiconductor." When the campus scene grows tiresome, students often travel to nearby Babson (on foot) or Wellesley (by shuttle bus) to mingle. There are also frequent road trips to Boston, Vermont, or the beaches of Maine.

The surrounding town of Needham "isn't a great college town, but does have some good restaurants," says a sophomore. Still, students take advantage of volunteer opportunities, and the college organizes community-oriented events, such as a Halloween labyrinth for local school children and a charity auction where students offer up everything from original artwork to haircutting services. Campus traditions, however, are few and far between. "I think our healthy disregard for tradition makes life a little more interesting," says a senior, adding, "We do have a traditional spring formal and an academic exposition at the end of each semester."

Although Olin does not offer varsity sports, "a number of pick-up leagues have evolved for soccer, Frisbee, football, and basketball," says a junior, and students are allowed to participate in intramural sports at Babson and Wellesley. Many students join extracurricular project teams that participate in competitions like Formula SAE, SAE Baja, the ASME Human-Powered Vehicle competition, and robotic sailing.

For those who have what it takes, Olin College offers a top-notch engineering degree at a bargain price. Olin students have watched their school grow up and blossom before their eyes, frequently taking part in shaping its innovative approach to engineering education. It's not at all clear that future employers are ready for the freethinking graduates that Olin is producing, but students here value interdisciplinary, project-based instruction and the importance of "learning to learn." As one junior comments, "Olin is pretty quirky, and we like to think we're different—passionate, weird, and doing fun things."

Overlaps

MIT, Stanford, Caltech, Yale, Carnegie Mellon, Harvey Mudd, Rose–Hulman, Worcester Polytechnic

University of Oregon

1585 E 13th Ave, Eugene, OR 97403-1226

A flagship university of manageable size in a great location, UO is notable for its emphasis on the undergraduate educational experience. The liberal arts are more than just a slogan, and programs in the sciences, business, and communication are strong. Splashy sports program plays a big—faculty members say too big—role in shaping the vibrant campus life and culture. Lagging state funding assures that it lacks the academic range of larger flagship universities. Less selective than the University of Washington.

Blend two vegetarians, one track star, one fraternity brother, two tree huggers, three hikers, and one conservative. What have you got? Ten UO students. Sure, the joke's hokey, but its offbeat humor is typical of the laid-back, slightly eccentric attitude that prevails here in Eugene, where bicycling is the main form of transportation, recycling is a requirement, and littering is déclassé. As the most accessible of the West Coast flagship universities, the University of Oregon attracts brainy students who are proud of their quirky ways.

UO's buildings date from as early as 1876 and are surrounded by the university's lush 295-acre arboretum-like campus, which boasts more than 4,000 trees representing nearly 500 species. Most academic buildings were built before World War II and represent a blend of classical styles, including Georgian, Second Empire, Jacobin, and Lombardic. Residential facilities range from 19th-century colonials to modern high-rises. In a move to make undergraduate life more pleasant, the Student Recreation Center, complete with a 16-seat hot tub and a climbing wall, recently underwent a $50 million renovation. A $95 million facelift to Erb Memorial Union, the campus social hub, was completed in 2016.

While a liberal arts emphasis underlies Oregon's entire curriculum, general education requirements are not highly structured. The calendar is composed of quarters, and students must take two terms of English composition, two years of foreign language (for a B.A.), one year of math (for a B.S.), and two courses

> **"[Students] find what they love and work hard for it."**

exploring American or international culture, identity, pluralism, and tolerance, plus four courses in each of three areas: arts and letters, social sciences, and natural sciences. Each July, the university offers IntroDUCKtion to new students, featuring opportunities for orientation, registration, and advisement. First-Year Seminars introduce students to top professors in small-group settings, and professors have to apply to teach them, a process students applaud. First-Year Interest Groups help new students develop close working and advising relationships with faculty members and other students.

Due to steadily declining state funding, UO has a relatively modest array of academic offerings for a major research university and a higher ratio of tenured faculty members to students than many of its peer institutions. UO's professional schools—journalism, architecture and allied arts, education, law, business, and music

Website: www.uoregon.edu
Location: Small City
Public
Total Enrollment: 21,606
Undergraduates: 18,604
Male/Female: 47/53
SAT Ranges: CR 500–620, M 500–610
ACT Ranges: 22–27
Financial Aid: 76%
Pell Grant: 25%
Expense: Pub $ $
Student Loans: 51%
Average Debt: $ $
Phi Beta Kappa: Yes
Applicants: 22,000
Accepted: 74%
Enrolled: 25%
Grad in 6 Years: 72%
Returning Freshmen: 88%
Academics: ✍ ✍ ✍ ½
Social: ☎ ☎ ☎
Q of L: ★ ★ ★ ★
Admissions: (800) 232-3825
Email Address: uoadmit@uoregon.edu

Strong Programs:
Business Administration
Psychology
General Social Science
Economics

and dance—are highly regarded, and considered to be more accessible to entry-level students than similar programs elsewhere. The most popular majors include business administration, psychology, general social science, economics, and human physiology. The School of Architecture and Allied Arts is the home of Oregon's only accredited degrees in architecture, landscape architecture, and interior architecture. In the College of Arts and Sciences, the science departments enjoy advanced resources and offer many opportunities for research in fields like nanotechnology, optogenetics, and neuropsychology. In keeping with Oregon's eco-friendly reputation, the Green Chemistry Laboratory and Instrumentation Center was the first in the nation to use nontoxic materials in experiments. Pine Mountain Observatory, a field-study resource for astronomy and physics students located high in the Cascade Mountains, and the Oregon Institute of Marine Biology give students a chance for intimate studies in their major.

"I would say that the academic climate at the University of Oregon is collaborative yet challenging," says an accounting major. "Above all else, it is what you make of it." Forty-four percent of classes have fewer than 20 students. Professors are lauded for their knowledge, although it's not uncommon to find TAs handling some of the teaching duties. "The quality of teaching varies," says one educational foundations major. "It is painfully obvious when a professor does not care or they simply allow a graduate student to teach the class."

Highly motivated undergraduates may apply to the Clark Honors College, a small liberal arts college with its own four-year curriculum, including a senior thesis, or to the College Scholars program, which offers enrichment opportunities like freshman colloquia and research assistantships. The student-run community internship programs provide credit for community volunteer work. About a quarter of undergrads study or complete internships abroad during their time at UO, and more than 200 programs are offered in more than 90 countries.

"The university is working hard to create a safer campus community."

UO students "find what they love and work hard for it," says a journalism major. Only 53 percent of undergraduates are native Oregonians, largely because the university has increasingly relied on revenue from full-paying outsiders to balance the budget. "There are a lot of people from California," says a freshman, and "a lot of artsy hipsters." There is a noticeable contingent of international students, who account for 15 percent of the student body. Asian Americans account for another 6 percent, African Americans 2 percent, and Hispanics 10 percent. Numerous merit scholarships worth an average of $5,139 are awarded to qualified students, as are 361 athletic scholarships in 18 sports. Twenty-five percent of students are eligible for the Pell Grant.

Twenty percent of UO students choose to live in the university's nine residence halls, and construction on a 10th is scheduled for completion by fall of 2017. A student says of the rooms, "They are pretty small, but I love the cozy feeling." There are a number of thematic living arrangements, including the new Global Scholars Hall, which provides a living/learning environment for students enrolled in language immersion programs in Chinese, Japanese, French, German, and Spanish, as well as the Clark Honors College and the College Scholars program. Any student can sign up for the meal plan in the 13 dining halls; restaurants in the student union and off-campus fast food round out the menu. "The dining halls are so good," says one student, and another adds, "The food in the dining halls is designed with dietary restrictions in mind." Regarding sexual violence on campus, a junior comments, "I think that the university is working hard to create a safer campus community," citing several administrative initiatives and student groups dedicated to educating students about "remaining aware and watching out for your fellow Ducks," as well as providing resources to survivors.

UO's professional schools are highly regarded, and considered to be more accessible to entry-level students.

Fifteen percent of UO men and 20 percent of the women join Greek organizations, which provide living space, interesting social diversions, and a wealth of leadership and community service opportunities. "The university plays host to a variety of concerts, culture nights, film viewings, guest lecturers, sporting events, and dances," one journalism and history double major says. Regarding alcohol, one student explains, "The only students who are allowed to drink must be of age and do so with their doors closed." A junior adds, "There are large parties happening around campus most nights of the week for people who would like to spend their time on such activities," but there is no pressure to do so. Major events include the Whiteaker Block Party, the Oregon Country Fair, and semiannual street fairs attended by local vendors. University Day, which happens each spring, offers students, faculty, and staff an opportunity to clean up their campus.

Eugene is "the best college town ever! Everything about Eugene is based around the Ducks!" one student raves. Popular hangouts include Taylor's and Rennie's Landing, and community and public service projects also draw crowds. The one drawback to all this fun is Oregon's weather: it rains and

"Everything about Eugene is based around the Ducks!"

rains. "Eugene gets some sunny days in early fall, late spring, and summer," reports a veteran. Still, the moist climate rarely dampens enthusiasm for the many expeditions available through the university's well-coordinated outdoor program, from rock climbing to skiing. An hour to the west, the rain turns to mist on the Pacific Coast; an hour to the east, it turns to snow in the Cascade Mountains.

UO's official mascot is a whimsical yellow-and-green likeness of Donald Duck. The athletic program is financially independent of the university, and the Ducks continue to dominate their Division I athletic rivals. In recent years, seven programs have finished their respective seasons with a top-five national ranking, including multiple national championships in men's and women's track and field and one in men's golf. Football, men's basketball, women's acrobatics and tumbling, and softball have had impressive successes as well. UO's "quacker backers" love cheering on their teams, especially during the Civil War football game against Oregon State, a rivalry that has been playing out since 1894. Intramurals are another time-honored pastime here, and roughly 46 percent of students take part.

UO has embarked on a $2 billion capital campaign that will be used in part to hire more tenured faculty and shore up its status among major research universities. A recent University of Oregon Orientation Week T-shirt sported a picture of a duck and a simple exhortation: "Let your future take flight." UO offers ample opportunities for those with lofty ambitions to succeed. Indeed, UO's accessible academics, expert faculty, and abundance of social activities reveal that UO is all it's quacked up to be.

Overlaps

University of Washington, University of Colorado, Oregon State, Caltech, University of Arizona, UC–Santa Barbara, UC–Santa Cruz, San Diego State

If You Apply To ➤ **UO:** Early action: Nov. 1. Regular decision: Jan. 15. Financial aid: Mar. 1. Application fee: $65. No campus or alumni interviews. SATs or ACTs: required. Subject Tests: optional (required for homeschooled students). Letters of recommendation: optional. Essay: required.

Oregon State University

Corvallis, OR 97331

The biggest dilemma facing the typical 18-year-old Oregonian is whether to be a Beaver or a Duck. Choose Duck and hang with the ex-hippies in cosmopolitan Eugene. Choose Beaver and get small-town life with professional programs in business, engineering, and life sciences in Corvallis. OSU offers a less-selective option for frustrated UO hopefuls. Strong global emphasis.

Website: www.oregonstate.edu
Location: Small City
Public
Total Enrollment: 21,472
Undergraduates: 18,080
Male/Female: 54/46
SAT Ranges: CR 480–610,
    M 490–630
ACT Ranges: 21–28
Financial Aid: 70%
Pell Grant: 30%
Expense: Pub $ $
Student Loans: 61%
Average Debt: $ $
Phi Beta Kappa: No
Applicants: 14,058
Accepted: 78%
Enrolled: 33%
Grad in 6 Years: 63%
Returning Freshmen: 85%
Academics: ✍ ✍ ✍
Social: ☎ ☎ ☎
Q of L: ★ ★ ★
Admissions: (541) 737-4411
Email Address: osuadmit@
    oregonstate.edu

Strong Programs:
Computer Science
Human Development and
    Family Sciences
Kinesiology
Public Health
Business
Engineering
Forestry
Agricultural Sciences

With a wide range of academic programs, Oregon State University could very well be the setting of its own movie, titled *Planes, Trains, and Submarines*. You see, Oregon State is one of just two universities in the country with land, sea, space, and sun grant designations. Though the school might be happy to forget its many years of being called Moo U, that doesn't mean its agriculture department should go unnoticed. In fact, many of the contributions made by Oregon State researchers center on the field of agriculture. Still, there's more to OSU than fruits and vegetables. The most accessible West Coast public university, OSU is strong in many departments, including biotechnology, forestry, and engineering. Says one satisfied student, "Anyone would be lucky to be at Oregon State."

Located in the pristine but rainy Willamette Valley, OSU's campus is a mix of older, ivy-covered buildings and more modern structures. In addition to the 500-acre main campus, OSU owns 13,000 acres of forestland near campus and numerous agricultural tracts throughout Oregon. Thousands of azalea and rhododendron bushes welcome springtime on campus with their colorful blooms, and summers are unfailingly sunny. A bevy of newly renovated, LEED-certified facilities have been added over the past few years, and the new, $65 million Oregon Forest Science Complex is slated to open in spring 2018.

OSU's extensive Baccalaureate Core requires courses in a variety of areas, including skills; perspectives; and difference, power, and discrimination. One writing-intensive course is required as well. Perhaps the core's most innovative facet is its "synthesis" requirement, in which upperclassmen take two interdisciplinary courses on global issues in the modern world. The campus's global awareness is also evident in the international degree, which can be coupled with any other course of study. Thus, students can earn a B.S. in forestry and a B.A. in international studies in forestry simultaneously. The level of academic

> **"Classes are highly challenging and collaborative."**

pressure varies by major, but even those in the various honors programs say they don't feel overworked. "Classes are highly challenging and collaborative," says a senior. Most professors are "so captivated by their area of study that they are eager to enlighten others with their knowledge and interests," says a sophomore. Freshmen have full professors for most courses, excluding recitation.

OSU's College of Liberal Arts ranks with business and engineering as the largest on campus, but there are many more preprofessionals than poets. With the exceptions of history and English, the liberal arts—including such standard fare as sociology, psychology, economics, and philosophy—play second fiddle to more practical, technical fields. The business school offers some of the finest business-related programs in the state, and the departments of forestry and engineering (with its up-to-date electrical and computer engineering building) are major drawing cards. Even though agriculture doesn't lure as many students as it used to, those who do come find excellent programs, including agricultural sciences, animal sciences, and fisheries and wildlife science. Computer science, human development and family sciences, kinesiology, and public health are among the most popular majors.

Of particular note is OSU's Experimental College, where undergraduates spice up their semesters with noncredit courses in a range of imaginative subjects—everything from wine tasting to the art of bashing (a medieval war technique). Students in the Honors College participate in small seminars with top professors and hands-on research, culminating in a senior thesis. The university's small-town location makes it difficult to find much career-oriented part-time employment, and internships are hard to come by. (OSU operates on a quarter system.) Students in almost all majors, however, can participate in the cooperative education program, which allows them to alternate terms of study with several months of work in a relevant job. Those who choose a semester abroad may select from 200 study abroad programs or research and internship opportunities on all seven continents.

> "[Students are] very all-American—not cowboys and not city slickers, but very middle-of-the-road in all respects."

Says an engineering major, "The college has its intelligentsia, its social butterflies, its determined athletes, and any combination of those." Seventy-one percent of undergraduates are from Oregon, and 6 percent hail from foreign countries. One percent are African American, 9 percent are Hispanic, and 7 percent are Asian American. The Office of Diversity and Cultural Engagement sponsors several cultural resource centers, conferences, social justice retreats, an internship program, and other diversity initiatives to support students from underrepresented backgrounds. Most Oregon Staters are conservative and "very all-American—not cowboys and not city slickers, but very middle-of-the-road in all respects," a business major observes. Merit scholarships averaging $4,106 are awarded annually, as are 291 athletic awards in 17 sports. Thirty percent of students qualify for Pell Grants, and the Bridge to Success program allows roughly 3,000 in-state students per year to attend the university tuition-free.

Oregon State is one of just two universities in the country with land, sea, space, and sun grant designations.

Freshmen are expected to live in college housing, though fraternity pledges have the option of living in their houses. Co-ed and single-sex options are available in the dorms, which house 17 percent of the students. "I loved living in my hall because it is where I made many friends, however, I much prefer living off campus because it is not as expensive," a student says. In addition to standard rooming situations, a new "wellness" hall offers an exercise room and low-calorie meals; several other living/learning communities are options too. Students can also choose life in one of eight cooperatives or the plentiful off-campus apartments. "Our campus security is top-notch. I have never felt unsafe," says a junior.

> "Civil War games between OSU and U of Oregon are a big part of every season."

Six percent of the men and 13 percent of the women go Greek. Alcohol still flows freely at Greek affairs, but crackdowns by the administration and local police have begun to curb the most wanton debauchery. "Most social events happen on campus or close to campus," says a student. Favorite campus traditions include the Greeklife Sing (featuring musical numbers staged by fraternity and sorority members) and the annual Fall Festival. A popular student activity is complaining about the Willamette Valley weather: "People in the valley don't tan, they rust," warns one native. One reward for this sogginess, however, is the abundance of flowers that bloom in every color and shape each May. Many students consider Corvallis a good-size town; a number of bars and cheap theaters cater to their entertainment needs. Beautifully rugged beaches are less than an hour away, and some of the best skiing in the country can be found in the Cascade Mountains, two hours east. Hiking and rafting are nearby too, and trips to powwows in the area and camping on the coast provide other good times.

The Bridge to Success program allows roughly 3,000 in-state students per year to attend the university tuition-free.

Overlaps

University of Oregon, University of Washington, Washington State, Portland State, University of Portland, Arizona State, Western Oregon, Cal Poly–San Luis Obispo

Cheering for the Beavers' nationally ranked wrestling team, which has had several top-10 national finishes in the past few years, demands a lot of students' time and energy here, as does participation in the well-rounded intramural and club sports programs. Benny Beaver, the school's former (and somewhat benign) mascot, has been replaced by a more aggressive beaver that students have dubbed the "angry beaver." Recent Pac-12 conference champs include baseball, wrestling, and women's basketball and gymnastics. The football team won the 2014 Hawaii Bowl, and the men's basketball team has one of the top-10 winningest programs of all time among Division I schools. As for rivalries, one student says, "Civil War games between OSU and U of Oregon are a big part of every season."

OSU continues to build on its solid reputation as an agricultural institution, marching forward as a faithful part of the state's university system. OSU doesn't scream for attention. Instead, it's content to be a "nice" college, in "a safe and pleasant little town," where professors are "helpful" and, even if everyone doesn't know your name, they'll let you stand under their umbrella whenever the skies open up.

If You Apply To ➤

Oregon State: Early action: Nov. 1. Regular decision and financial aid: Feb. 1. Application fee: $60. No campus or alumni interviews. SATs or ACTs: required (SAT essay or ACT writing recommended). Subject Tests: required for some. No letters of recommendation. Essay: required. Application includes optional questions regarding gender and sexual identity.

University of the Pacific

3601 Pacific Avenue, Stockton, CA 95211

The university's name dates from a time when there were no other universities near the Pacific. Still the only small, independent university in California north of L.A., it offers an eye-popping array of programs for an institution its size, including business, engineering, pharmacy, and education. The student body is just as diverse.

Website: www.pacific.edu
Location: Suburban
Private
Total Enrollment: 5,531
Undergraduates: 3,630
Male/Female: 48/52
SAT Ranges: CR 490–620, M 520–660
ACT Ranges: 22–29
Financial Aid: 73%
Pell Grant: N/A
Expense: Pr $ $
Student Loans: 69%
Average Debt: $ $ $ $
Phi Beta Kappa: Yes
Applicants: 14,449
Accepted: 65%
Enrolled: 10%

University of the Pacific looks like more than 100 acres of New England plunked down in California wine country. With its stately combination of redbrick and ivy, it could be mistaken for an East Coast liberal arts college. But instead of a blanket of snow, Pacific is surrounded by the lush greenery of the San Joaquin Valley. On campus, this increasingly competitive bastion of learning offers its 3,600 undergrads a solid and diverse academic program and scores of things to do when not hitting the books.

With majestic evergreens and flowering trees, Pacific is home to six undergraduate schools and the College of the Pacific, the university's liberal arts and sciences division. There is also a school of law in Sacramento and a superlative school of dentistry in San Francisco. A biological sciences building provides 54,000 square feet of space for the biological sciences program.

The university-wide general education program has three components: the Pacific seminars, the breadth program, and fundamental skills. All entering students must complete Pacific Seminar I (What Is a Good Society?) and Pacific Seminar II (Topical Seminars on a Good Society) in sequence during their first year, and Pacific Seminar III (The Ethics of Family, Work, and Citizenship) in their senior year. In addition to the seminars, students must complete six or nine courses

"Our academic climate is collaborative and relaxed."

in the breadth program and must demonstrate competence in writing, math, and reading. Strong departments abound in the schools of engineering, pharmacy, education, and business (with special programs in the arts/entertainment management and entrepreneurship). The sciences, English, communication, and international studies are also strong. A freshman says, "The best academic departments tend to be prepharmacy, predentistry, and the health, exercise, and sports sciences programs, because they do an astounding job of preparing students for their future professions." Students may also design their own majors with faculty approval.

Students report that studying accounts for anywhere from 10 to 40 hours a week. "Our academic climate is collaborative and relaxed. Instead of students who do whatever it takes to be at the head of the class, everyone works together," says an international relations major. Fifty-six percent of classes taken by freshmen have fewer than 20 students, and TAs teach labs only. "The faculty members are very accessible and always willing to help," says one sophomore. The university guarantees graduation in four years (assuming the student follows all university guidelines), or it will pay for the extra schooling. Students are also guaranteed to have the opportunity for some type of experiential learning, and a number of internship and co-op programs are available. An extensive study abroad program offers 200 choices in dozens of countries, and international studies majors are required to participate.

> **"You instantly feel like you are surrounded by very friendly and loving people."**

Pacific students are "genuinely nice and friendly," says one freshman. Eighty-six percent of undergraduates are California residents, and 7 percent hail from foreign countries. As for ethnic diversity, Asian Americans account for 35 percent, African Americans 3 percent, and Hispanics 18 percent. The school is middle-of-the-road to conservative, though politics in general play a small role on campus. "We're very open to all political, religious, sexual orientations, etc.," says a senior. "We have a little bit of everything." Though not unusually expensive by national standards, the university price tag can seem steep when compared to the University of California system. So Pacific has stepped up efforts to compete, using merit scholarships, which average $11,480 annually, as well as athletic scholarships in several sports.

Freshmen and sophomores are required to live on campus, and 46 percent of all undergrads make their home on campus. "Housing is generally pretty clean and the sense of community is felt all across the halls," says one student. With three meal plans, two dining halls, and one fast-food-type facility, residents are well fed. A senior reports, "Campus security is pretty effective," and includes a blue-light system.

"The social life happens on campus, whether it is at sporting events, going to events for different fraternities, sororities, or clubs, or simply playing games out on the UC Lawn," says a student. Six percent of men and 6 percent of women go Greek. Other social opportunities are offered by the Residence Hall Association, intramural and club sports, conservatory and drama/dance programs, campus movies, and more than 100 student clubs. Students caught violating the alcohol policy must take an online course in alcohol education. The majority of Greek houses are designated substance-free, following a trend enforced by their national organizations. "I only recently attended my first party where there was alcohol," one student says. "There was no pressure for me to drink." Annual campus festivities include Diversity Week, International Spring Festival, the popular Fall Festival, and Greek Week. For weekend excitement, Pacific students love to hit the road: within about two hours, they can be skiing, shopping in San Francisco, or surfing in Monterey. Stockton itself (population

(continued)
Grad in 6 Years: 70%
Returning Freshmen: 85%
Academics: ✍ ✍ ✍
Social: ☎ ☎ ☎
Q of L: ★ ★ ★ ★
Admissions: (209) 946-2211
Email Address: admission@ pacific.edu

Strong Programs:
Engineering
Pharmacy
Education
Business
English
Communication
International Studies

All entering students must complete Pacific Seminar I (What Is a Good Society?) and Pacific Seminar II (Topical Seminars on a Good Society).

Students are guaranteed to have the opportunity for some type of experiential learning.

300,000) offers shopping and plenty of fast-food joints, as well as numerous volunteer opportunities.

Pacific dropped its football program in 1995, but the Tigers field a number of competitive Division I teams. The women's volleyball team makes regular NCAA Tournament appearances, and men's and women's basketball, water polo, and golf are also strong. The university also sponsors a solid speech and debate team.

Pitted against the state's immense public university system, Pacific stands out for offering major university opportunities in a small-college setting. The administration is striving to place more focus on its student body, which is becoming more top-notch and diverse. A political science major says, "When you come here, you instantly feel like you are surrounded by very friendly and loving people."

If You Apply To ➤

Pacific: Early action: Nov. 15. Regular decision and financial aid: Jan. 15. Application fee: $35. Campus interviews: optional, informational. No alumni interviews. SATs or ACTs: required. Subject Tests: recommended. Letters of recommendation: required. Essay: required. Accepts the Common Application.

University of Pennsylvania

1 College Hall, Philadelphia, PA 19104

An Ivy League institution in name, Penn has more in common with places like Georgetown and Northwestern—where the liberal arts share center stage with preprofessional programs. At Penn, that means business, engineering, and nursing. Penn has something else other Ivies don't: school spirit. It's a good idea to apply early decision if Penn is your first choice.

Website: www.upenn.edu
Location: City Center
Private
Total Enrollment: 19,967
Undergraduates: 9,444
Male/Female: 50/50
SAT Ranges: CR 680–760, M 700–790
ACT Ranges: 31–34
Financial Aid: 43%
Pell Grant: 16%
Expense: Pr $ $ $ $
Student Loans: 28%
Average Debt: $ $
Phi Beta Kappa: Yes
Applicants: 37,268
Accepted: 10%
Enrolled: 64%
Grad in 6 Years: 95%
Returning Freshmen: 98%
Academics: ✐ ✐ ✐ ✐ ✐
Social: ☎ ☎ ☎

Benjamin Franklin would be proud of the way his university has surged in recent years. Once relegated to the bottom of the Ivy League (and confused with Penn State), the University of Pennsylvania is now the first choice for top students who see no conflict between high-level academics and having a life. The undergraduate School of Arts and Sciences—once on the university's back burner—is now central not only to its undergraduates, but also to the remaining three undergraduate schools that tap into its programs and course offerings. Penn established the nation's first medical school, the first business school, the first journalism curriculum, and the first psychology clinic, and is a pioneer in service learning and service research. In her inaugural address, a former president paid tribute to Franklin as "the ultimate visionary and pragmatist. Franklin thought education should be for the body as well as for the soul—that it should enable a graduate to be a breadwinner as well as a thinker, that it should produce socially conscious citizens as well as conscientious bankers and traders."

Penn is situated in a tree-shaded, self-contained, 278-acre nest called University City, which is adjacent to downtown Philadelphia. Its 155 buildings range from Victorian Gothic to postmodern. There are very old structures, such as College Hall, and newer ones, such as Wharton's Huntsman Hall

"Teachers are always willing to meet with students."

and Skirkanich Hall, home to Penn's bioengineering programs. While many students thrive on Philadelphia's cultural abundance, the school is located in the western part of town, once considered to be dangerous. Even so, a senior explains, "there are a wealth of cultural resources at the tip of your fingers, and more and more students are able to find jobs in the Philadelphia area after graduation."

Penn's reputation is primarily wrapped up with its 12 graduate schools, especially the prestigious Wharton School of Business; the Annenberg School of Communication; and the well-known law, medical, and veterinary schools. Three of four undergraduate schools—engineering, nursing, and the undergraduate division of Wharton—are also professionally oriented and offer an education that's hard to beat anywhere. The undergraduate College of Arts and Sciences (a.k.a. "The College") has come into its own in recent years and provides students with high-quality instruction as well as the chance to run into a Nobel laureate here and there.

Finance is among the most popular undergrad majors, followed by economics and nursing. Penn's anthropology department ranks with Chicago's as perhaps the best in the country, while the management and technology program is also outstanding. Penn has earned applause in the field of cognitive and computer sciences because of its special program linking psychology, linguistics, and computers with philosophy. Another popular crème-de-la-crème interdisciplinary major, biological basis of behavior, combines psychology, biology, and anthropology. Students are allowed to design their own individualized majors, and they can hop from school to school—undergraduate or graduate—in doing so. Students in the Vagelos Program in Life Science and Management pursue studies in both the College of Arts and Sciences and the Wharton School, exposing them to research and development, biotech start-ups, managed care, and other related issues.

At the Wharton School, officials have introduced the Joseph Wharton Scholars program, which emphasizes breadth in the arts and sciences. All undergraduates must attain proficiency in one of the 45 foreign languages taught at Penn. Another added plus that comes with a Penn undergraduate education is the opportunity for early entry (submatriculation) into the university's graduate programs. Juniors may apply to any master's program (continuing into the Wharton M.B.A. program is especially popular) and begin completing graduate requirements during their senior year. Penn offers no co-op programs and discourages full-time internships for credit, remaining true to the Ivy League belief that learning should be based in academic settings. Those who want to explore more exotic classrooms may study abroad at Penn's programs in Italy, Scotland, Japan, China, Nigeria, and Russia, among others. Freshmen are encouraged (but not required) to participate in a seminar program that explores various areas of academic interest, and also in the Penn Reading Project, which involves student and faculty discussion of a common text.

> "Penn students have historically been extremely involved with the local community."

Sixty-eight percent of undergraduate classes have fewer than 20 students, and while professors at Penn take their research responsibilities seriously, they are surprisingly accessible to freshmen. "Most departments have fantastic professors who are top in their field," says one student, "and have developed a great teaching style." Another student adds, "Teachers are always willing to meet with students." The academic program at Penn is well supplemented by its huge and busy library, which houses more than six million volumes.

Despite all the preprofessional programs, Penn never lets its undergraduates stray too far from the liberal arts. The general education requirements mandate that students take at least one course in each of seven "sectors": society; history and tradition; arts and letters; living world; physical world; humanities and social sciences; and natural sciences and mathematics. Students must also complete one course in each of five "skills and methods" areas, including the study of a foreign culture as well as a mandatory writing requirement. Strict academic policies and demanding professors exacerbate the academic pressure. "Penn is a competitive university," says one nursing major, "but is also intellectually stimulating." Each year students evaluate every class themselves and publish their findings in a guide.

(continued)

Q of L: ★ ★ ★
Admissions: (215) 898-7507
Email Address: info@
  admissions.upenn.edu

Strong Programs:
Business
Engineering
Nursing
Finance
Economics
Anthropology
Management and Technology
Cognitive Science

Penn established the nation's first medical school, the first business school, the first journalism curriculum, and the first psychology clinic.

Thousands of faculty and students give expression to Benjamin Franklin's adage that service to humanity is "the great aim and end of all learning." To wit, Penn is a national leader in service learning and service research. Students work with local public school students as part of academic coursework in disciplines as diverse as history, anthropology, and mathematics. There are tons of opportunities to volunteer—from tutoring to Big Brothers Big Sisters to the Ronald McDonald House. "Penn students have historically been extremely involved with the local community and have taken the experiences they've had in the neighborhood with them to the real world," an economics and history double major says.

Students in the Vagelos Program in Life Science and Management are exposed to research and development, biotech start-ups, and managed care.

Ninety-five percent of Penn freshmen ranked in the top 10th of their high school class and more than half come from public high schools. Nineteen percent are Pennsylvania natives, and 12 percent are international. "There are all kinds of people with all kinds of personalities, interests, and backgrounds," says a student, "all of which makes Penn a vibrant place to live and study." Seven percent of undergrads are African American, 10 percent are Hispanic, and 20 percent are Asian American. Penn admits students regardless of need—and meets full demonstrated need—but does not offer any merit, athletic, or academic scholarships. The No-Loan initiative expands Penn's commitment to need-blind admissions and is highlighted by an outreach program targeting hundreds of schools and thousands of students from low- and middle-income families.

"The best kept secret on campus is the kosher cafeteria."

Fifty-four percent of all undergraduates live on campus and enjoy a wide range of living options in Penn's 11 co-ed "College Houses." The Quad, home to three of the 11 houses, seems to be the hot spot, described as "well maintained and incredibly comfortable." There are living/learning programs in most College Houses for those who are interested in the arts, Asian studies, etc., and want to be surrounded by others with the same interests. Upperclassmen reluctantly move to the high-rises across campus that look like "prefabricated, 24-story monsters" but do offer more space, as well as kitchens. Rather than compete in the lottery for rooms, many juniors and seniors simply head off campus—"for the freedom, plus it's a lot cheaper," a junior says. Some end up in nearby renovated three-story houses in the neighborhood. "Off-campus living is just an extension of student neighborhoods, as we tend to stay in large groups," explains a senior. Like housing, the meal plans are optional (though strongly recommended freshman year as an important source of social life), and the food isn't all that bad for institutional fare. "The best kept secret on campus is the kosher cafeteria," a finance and management major says.

Penn is a national leader in service learning and service research.

Undergraduates may work hard during the week, but in contrast to most Ivy League achievers, they leave it behind them on weekends. "Social life at Penn centers around frats," a junior explains. The university prohibits underage drinking, but "parties freely serve alcohol to underage drinkers," says another student. More than two dozen fraternities attract 30 percent of the men and provide "your basic meat-market scene"; sororities claim 27 percent of the women. The frats' exclusive claim to the houses along Locust Walk, the main artery on campus, has been undone: after some controversy, it was determined that non-Greeks, too, must be able to live at the social nexus of the campus.

"There is a great balance between academics and social activities."

Two big annual events at Penn are Spring Fling, a weekend "nothing short of absolutely incredible fun," and Hey Day, when juniors, donning Styrofoam hats, march down Locust Walk to officially become seniors, taking chomps out of each other's hats as they go. Downtown Philadelphia, only a few minutes away by foot, cab, or public transportation, offers enough social and cultural activities to make up for the less-attractive aspects of city living. "Philly is large and very developed," a sophomore says. Students frequent sporting events, malls, South Street ("a miniature

Greenwich Village"), and, of course, myriad bars and dancing joints. "There is a lot of social intermingling among the schools, and university students dominate the nightlife," a student explains. Road trips include New York City, Washington, D.C., Atlantic City, and even Maine and Florida.

Penn is more sports-minded than most Ivy schools, and Division I football is the biggie. The team has grown accustomed to sitting on the top of the Ivy League and has sparked a widespread revival of school spirit. Tickets are free for those with a student ID. The Penn–Princeton rivalry is always a crowd pleaser. At the end of the third quarter of each home game, everyone in the stands begins belting out the lyrics of the Penn fight song, and when they get to "Here's a toast to dear old Penn," the students shower the field with burnt toast, "a moment that makes all Penn students proud," according to a senior. Aside from football, solid Quakers teams include men's and women's basketball, men's lacrosse, and women's field hockey and fencing. A bevy of intramural sports bring thousands of less-seasoned athletes out to play each year, and all types of athletes benefit from the swanky track and weight-lifting facilities. Each spring, Penn hosts the prestigious Penn Relays, a track-and-field extravaganza that attracts the nation's best track athletes.

While its students work hard, Penn lacks the intellectual intensity of some of the other top Ivies, and you can detect preprofessional undercurrents. But most accept it for what it is: a first-rate university where you can live a relatively normal life. Penn is one Ivy League university where no one apologizes for having fun. Says one sophomore, "There is a great balance between academics and social activities, which is rare in such highly competitive institutions."

> *Penn is more sports-minded than most Ivy schools.*

Overlaps
Brown, Columbia, Cornell University, Harvard, Stanford, Yale

If You Apply To ➤ **Penn:** Early decision: Nov. 1. Regular decision: Jan. 5. Financial aid: Feb. 2. Housing: May 1. Application fee: $75. No campus interviews. Alumni interviews: optional, evaluative. SATs or ACTs: required. Subject Tests: optional. Letters of recommendation: required. Essay: required. Accepts the Common Application with supplement.

Pennsylvania State University

201 Old Main, University Park, PA 16802

Although its athletic programs have tended to grab most of the headlines, Penn State remains one of the premier public universities academically. With a student body the size of a small city, the university is strong in fields from meteorology to film and television. The 2,000-student Schreyer Honors College is one of the nation's elite programs.

Once viewed as the model of how the values of big-time football and academic excellence could coexist, Penn State's image took a major hit five years ago with the conviction of a former assistant football coach as a sexual predator that made front-page news around the world. Since then a new administration has enacted governance and other changes aimed at shoring up institutional values. Fortunately, the legendary school spirit of the 39,000 undergraduate denizens of what sportswriters have long called Happy Valley is still alive, as are Penn State's stellar choices in engineering, the sciences, and other fields appropriate to a land grant university.

With an eclectic architectural mix, including white-columned brick, stone, and some modern apartments, Penn State continues to experience growth as major renovation and expansion projects proceed. New facilities are added every year, and

Website: www.psu.edu
Location: Small City
Public
Total Enrollment: 45,179
Undergraduates: 39,294
Male/Female: 53/47
SAT Ranges: CR 530–630, M 560–670
ACT Ranges: 25–29
Financial Aid: 58%

(continued)

Pell Grant: N/A
Expense: Pub $ $ $ $
Student Loans: 56%
Average Debt: $ $ $ $
Phi Beta Kappa: Yes
Applicants: 53,472
Accepted: 51%
Enrolled: 28%
Grad in 6 Years: 86%
Returning Freshmen: 93%
Academics: ✍ ✍ ✍ ✍ ½
Social: 🖵 🖵 🖵 🖵 🖵
Q of L: ★ ★ ★
Admissions: (814) 865-5471
Email Address: admissions@
psu.edu

Strong Programs:
Business
Engineering
Communications
Social Sciences
Meteorology
Food Sciences
Agricultural Sciences
Information Science and
Technology

Penn State's food sciences program is one of the best in the nation, and dairy products from the school's cows are sold at an on-campus store.

renovations and other improvements are constantly under way. "Penn State just keeps growing and improving itself," says one student.

Penn State's general education requirements consist of 45 credits that include several communications and quantification courses as well as humanities, arts, natural sciences, social and behavioral sciences, and health and physical education courses. The incorporation of critical-thinking skills has been a priority in redesigning the general curriculum. In addition, undergrads must enroll in "diversity-focused" courses that encourage awareness of minority concerns. One helpful program offered to freshmen is LEAP (Learning Edge Academic Program), which gives new students the benefit of a big university while making it seem small. Students in LEAP take a team approach by taking classes together and living together. About 2,000 of the university's best and brightest are invited to participate in the Schreyer Honors College, which offers opportunities for research and an honors thesis, as well as honors options in regular courses.

"Your academic experience is completely what you make it."

The most popular majors at Penn State fall under the categories of business, engineering, communications, and social sciences. The university maintains strong programs in the scientific and technical fields such as earth sciences, engineering, agricultural sciences, and life sciences, as well as nutrition and family studies. The meteorology program boasts alumni worldwide, including the founder of AccuWeather, an internationally renowned private forecasting firm. The College of Information Sciences and Technology is designed to prepare students for the digital age. The College of Agricultural Sciences has extensive facilities that include huge livestock barns. Its food sciences program is one of the best in the nation. Dairy products from the school's cows are sold at an on-campus store, and courses are offered in the production of its famous ice cream. Students can choose from more than 260 baccalaureate programs and more than 160 graduate fields spread over 24 locations statewide, including the College of Medicine and the Dickinson School of Law, both located near Harrisburg, and Penn State Law on the University Park campus. At a school of Penn State's size, there are bound to be some weaknesses, but the curriculum is in a seemingly constant state of change, with programs added and dropped on a regular basis. Combined undergraduate/graduate degree options are available, as are co-op programs in engineering, distance learning, and student-designed majors.

According to one student, "The one thing about Penn State is that your academic experience is completely what you make it." Some of the intro-level lecture courses draw up to 400 students at University Park, yet most of the students seem to agree—classes are excellent and require your full attention. Students report that professors are accessible and engaging—when they are teaching. "I must say I was surprised that I was taught by grad students," says one senior. "For the amount of money I am paying to go here, I would have thought all my classes would be taught by professors." For cramming outside of class, the Penn State library system contains 7 million volumes. A large number of students study abroad through more than 300 summer, semester, and full-year programs in roughly 50 countries.

"Penn State students are active, fun, and open-minded," says one student. Sixty-one percent of undergraduates are residents of Pennsylvania, with 11 percent hailing from foreign nations. More than half of Penn State's undergraduates who finish at University Park began their education at one of the university's 19 campuses across the state. Many students note that race and diversity issues can be pronounced on a campus that is still pretty homogeneous for a public university: Asian Americans make up 6 percent of the undergrad population, African Americans 4 percent, and Hispanics 6 percent. A whopping 633 athletic

"Penn State students are active, fun, and open-minded."

scholarships are available, covering all of the university's NCAA-approved varsity sports, as are thousands of merit awards, averaging $4,020.

Freshmen must live in the dorms, which students say are comfortable and located near classroom buildings and dining facilities. Overall, thirty-four percent of students live on campus; the balance find a home off campus, often in downtown apartments. "I loved living in the dorms," reports one public relations major. "I think it's part of the whole college experience and I made some great friends along the way." The meal plan operates on a point system where you pay for what you eat. Stand for State, launched in 2016, is a comprehensive bystander intervention program covering sexual assault, drug and alcohol use, acts of bias, and mental health concerns.

Partying at Penn State is almost as legendary as the football team. "Social life at Penn State is huge," says a freshman. "Most of the parties happen at fraternities, which are both on and off campus." Students also hit the bars in State College, where "it's very difficult for underage students to be served at the bars," according to a student. While the administration strives to keep booze out of underage hands on campus, "there are places students can get alcohol, mostly at other people's apartments," says a junior. The HUB (the campus union building) offers nonalcoholic entertainment. Eighteen percent of Penn State men and 19 percent of the women go Greek. Favorite annual events include the mid-July arts festival, the Dance Marathon, and, of course, homecoming.

> **"A majority of the students get involved in community service to maintain and constantly improve town relations."**

University Park students take advantage of the picturesque and peaceful locale by engaging in outdoorsy activities, including skiing and snowboarding at a nearby slope, and sailing, canoeing, hiking, and renting cabins in Stone Valley. State College offers cultural events such as symphonies, theatrical shows, and ballets, while the Bryce Jordan Center hosts top-notch performers. The town may be small, but according to a biochem major, "a majority of the students get involved in community service to maintain and constantly improve town relations."

When thousands of alumni converge to cheer on their Nittany Lions in blue and white, the festivities include tailgate parties replete with marshmallow throwing, pregame parties, and postgame revelry. As a member of the Big Ten, Penn State's foes include Michigan and Ohio State, both of which make great road trips. Nittany Lions teams have won more than 75 national titles in a wide variety of sports, including men's and women's volleyball, women's soccer and field hockey, and fencing. The men's wrestling team was the national champ in 2016. There are three large gyms, a competitive-size pool, an indoor ice rink, and an extensive program of intramural and club sports for the recreational athlete, including a large angler's club.

For better or worse, Penn State's reputation for academic excellence had been closely linked in the public mind with the success of its Division I football team and the personal image of its famous coach, the late Joe Paterno. After a period of soul-searching about what went wrong, Penn State's sense of pride and community spirit are reasserting themselves. As one proud Lion explains, "Imagine a family of 40,000—the excitement, compassion, and sense of belonging, which is unparalleled at any institution."

A whopping 633 athletic scholarships are available, covering all of the university's NCAA-approved varsity sports.

Stand for State, launched in 2016, is a comprehensive bystander intervention program.

Overlaps

University of Pittsburgh, Temple, University of Maryland, Indiana University (PA), University of Delaware, Rutgers

If You Apply To ➤ | **PSU:** Rolling admissions. (Priority deadline: Nov. 30.) Priority financial aid: Feb. 15. Application fee: $65. No campus or alumni interviews. SATs or ACTs: required. No Subject Tests. No letters of recommendation. Essay: optional. Apply to particular school or program.

Pepperdine University

24255 Pacific Coast Highway, Malibu, CA 90263

Pepperdine has arguably the most beautiful campus setting in America. The buildings are nothing special, but the views of the Pacific Ocean are incomparable. With L.A. nearby, small wonder its popularity is soaring. Students should come to Pepperdine ready to embrace an evangelical Christian emphasis. Pepperdine is not the Stanford of SoCal.

Website: www.pepperdine.edu
Location: Suburban
Private
Total Enrollment: 5,529
Undergraduates: 3,219
Male/Female: 40/60
SAT Ranges: CR 550–650,
   M 550–670
ACT Ranges: 25–30
Financial Aid: 54%
Pell Grant: 16%
Expense: Pr $ $ $ $
Student Loans: 57%
Average Debt: $ $ $ $
Phi Beta Kappa: No
Applicants: 9,923
Accepted: 38%
Enrolled: 20%
Grad in 6 Years: 84%
Returning Freshmen: 94%
Academics: ✏ ✏ ✏
Social: ☎ ☎
Q of L: ★ ★ ★ ★
Admissions: (310) 506-4392
Email Address: admission
   -seaver@pepperdine.edu

Strong Programs:
Business Administration
Communication
Psychology
Economics
Biology
Computer Science
Sports Medicine

With picturesque surroundings, it's easy to confuse Pepperdine University with its nicknames—Pepperdine Resort and Club Med. Surrounded by the beautiful Southern California seashore, Pepperdine University might seem paradise found for students seeking sunshine rather than studies at this conservative, Christian-affiliated university, though students take their work and their worship seriously. "The philosophy of the school is that God and the academic experience must be married," says a senior communication major. "This creates an intimate learning environment that prides itself on moral integrity and a high academic standard." Business and communication are the blessed programs, though other departments deserve recognition too. Undergrads praise their educational opportunities, the strength of their school's spiritual community, and the vast sandy beaches beckoning below their hilltop campus.

There's no denying that Pepperdine's location—high in the Santa Monica Mountains, about 25 miles northwest of Los Angeles—is a strong selling point. The 830-acre Malibu campus, to which the school moved in 1972, overlooks the Pacific Ocean and features fountains, hillside gardens, mountain trails, and a 20-minute walk to the beach. Cream-colored, Mediterranean-style buildings topped with red terra-cotta roofs dot the landscape. A 125-foot-tall white stucco cross stands near the center of campus, reminding students and faculty of the school's affiliation with the Churches of Christ. Pepp's 10-facility library system boast nearly 500,000 volumes.

> **"The philosophy of the school is that God and the academic experience must be married."**

Pepperdine was founded in 1937 by George Pepperdine, a lifelong member of the Churches of Christ who had amassed a fortune through his mail-order auto parts supply company. The church's continued influence on the school pervades many aspects of campus life, from the prohibition of overnight dorm room visits by members of the opposite sex to the requirement that students attend convocation—similar to chapel—14 times each semester. Students at Seaver College, Pepp's undergraduate school, must also take three religion courses. While drinking is officially prohibited on campus, the administration has lifted the ban on dancing and now allows students to choose their own seats at convocation. Though restrictions like this would drive the average kid up a wall, most at Pepperdine like the "highly moral" atmosphere. Says one student: "In comparison to other schools, Pepperdine students generally have a more religious foundation and thus have high standards of moral integrity."

Seaver's academic programs aim to provide students "with a liberal arts education in a Christian environment and relate it to the dynamic qualities of life in the 21st century." Individual classes are demanding, as is the required General Studies program, which includes a freshman seminar, a physical education course, three courses in Western heritage, two courses each in American heritage and English composition, and one class each in a foreign language and a non-Western culture. However, faculty members are said to be accessible and responsive—not surprising when 69 percent of classes have fewer than 20 students. "The quality of teaching is very personal and exceptional," says an art major. Another student adds, "Because it is a small school, professors don't accept excuses or laziness. They demand a lot from their students and expect a high standard and quality of work."

The business administration department is unequivocally the strongest and most popular department at Pepperdine, and it tends to set the tone on campus. Those seeking to pursue advanced business education can enroll in a B.S./M.B.A. program that allows them to earn a bachelor's degree in business administration, international business, or accounting from Seaver College and an M.B.A. from the university's graduate business school in five years. The communication department, with majors including advertising, public relations, and journalism, is also highly touted, and boasts radio and television broadcasting studios. Psychology, economics, biology, and computer science are said to be strong, and sports medicine, rare at the undergraduate level, is both popular and well respected. Music studios and a $10 million humanities and visual arts center have been built to enhance the fine arts division. The well-organized Career Center allows students to sign up for job fairs, interviews, and individual and group career-counseling sessions. Juniors interested in European culture may spend a year at Pepperdine's own facilities in Heidelberg, London, Florence, or Lausanne. Locations for summer study include East Africa, the Galapagos Islands, Honduras, Madrid, Oxford, and Pepperdine-owned properties. Eighty-seven percent of students participate in short- and long-term study abroad programs.

> **"The quality of teaching is very personal and exceptional."**

Students are required to attend convocation—similar to chapel—14 times each semester.

One might expect students at this religiously oriented school to be politically conservative, and they most definitely are. Many come from well-to-do California Republican families; there are also quite a few wealthy international students. Students joke that there's never a shortage of Porsches and BMWs on campus, but there is a shortage of places to park them. Overall, 49 percent of undergraduates are California natives, and 10 percent come from abroad. Hispanics account for 16 percent of the students, Asian Americans 12 percent, and African Americans 6 percent. The Republican influence is felt far and wide. Pepperdine has received millions of dollars from conservative donors, including the late Pittsburgh financier Richard Mellon Scaife. One student sums up the political climate gently: "Pepperdine tends to shy away from political activism." The university awards merit scholarships averaging $17,979 to top achievers, in addition to 105 athletic scholarships in 15 sports.

> **"Parties on weekends are well attended, and probably draw a larger portion of students than church on Sunday."**

Fifty-seven percent of undergraduates live on campus; students who are married, over 21, or commuters are permitted to live off campus. A senior declares that Pepperdine's single-sex dorms are "comfortable, convenient, and really quite nice." Rooms are assigned on a first-come, first-served basis, and the housing stock consists of 22 dorms, a 135-room tower, and a 75-unit apartment complex for juniors and seniors. Freshmen are typically assigned to suites with bathrooms, living rooms, and four double bedrooms. Some consider these arrangements crowded, but a junior says they "connect freshmen instantly to seven suitemates and friends." Despite the above-average cost of living in the Malibu area, many upperclassmen choose to live off campus.

Eighty-seven percent of students participate in short- and long-term study abroad programs.

Some say flashy student vehicles fit into the small, very wealthy community of Malibu better than the students themselves; the city sees the university as a catalyst for development, and that hurts town/school relations. Because the social scene in Malibu is pretty slack, with a 10 p.m. noise curfew and high price tags for everything, students typically head to L.A., Hollywood, Westwood, and Santa Monica for fun. "For a large proportion of students, academics and their social lives take priority over religious matters," says a public relations major. "Parties on weekends are well attended, and probably draw a larger portion of students than church on Sunday." Six percent of the men and nine percent of the women join one of five national fraternities or eight national sororities, which are playing a larger role in social life. Along with student government, they sponsor dances, movies, and other typical college activities, including the occasional illicit drink. "Pepperdine enforces a 'dry' campus, but 'damp' would be a better way of describing the residential community," says one student. The student union serves as the main campus social center, and annual events including Songfest, Family Weekend, and Midnight Madness draw crowds.

Sports receive a lot of attention at Pepperdine. The Waves compete in the West Coast Conference. Recent conference champions include baseball, men's and women's golf, and women's tennis and beach volleyball. Eleven club and intramural sports, including lacrosse, rugby, cycling, surfing, and soccer, keep students busy, as does the physical education department, with classes in everything from surfing to horseback riding. A tennis pavilion and recreation center serves varsity jocks and weekend warriors alike.

Pepperdine has taken up the challenge of trying to marry the Christian focus of a Bible college with the academic rigor of a secular university—all in a location not known for the strength of its moral fiber. Students love to tease their well-manicured university with T-shirts proclaiming, "Pepperdine. 8-month party. 45K cover charge." But most seem to think the solid, values-oriented education they receive is worth the stiff price tag.

Overlaps

Loyola Marymount, UCLA, UC–San Diego, UC–Santa Barbara, University of Southern California

If You Apply To ➢

Pepperdine: Regular decision: Jan. 5. Financial aid: Feb. 15. Application fee: $65. No campus or alumni interviews. SATs or ACTs: required. No Subject Tests. Letters of recommendation: required. Essay: required. Accepts the Common Application with supplement.

University of Pittsburgh

Alumni Hall, 4227 Fifth Avenue, Pittsburgh, PA 15260

As its home city has risen in stature, Pitt has become a hot commodity along with next-door neighbor Carnegie Mellon. A state-related university in the mold of the University of Cincinnati—not the state flagship, but strong in a host of preprofessional programs, especially in health fields. Curiously, Pitt is among the nation's best in philosophy. Admissions is rolling, so apply early.

Website: www.pitt.edu
Location: City Outskirts
Public
Total Enrollment: 25,368
Undergraduates: 17,815
Male/Female: 49/51
SAT Ranges: CR 580–660, M 600–690
ACT Ranges: 26–31

Pittsburgh has joined the ranks of the most livable cities in the United States. The University of Pittsburgh has matured too, becoming a formidable public research institution that is moving toward national stature. The school offers numerous opportunities for students pursuing business, medical, and engineering careers, but leaves a great deal of room for exploration in the liberal arts. Students are encouraged to be individuals and carve out their own academic niche, either with multiple majors or with certificate programs. "The great thing about Pitt is they are always adding and adapting programs to fit the students' needs and interests," says a junior.

Pitt began as a tiny, private educational academy in the Allegheny Mountains in 1787. Oh, how times have changed. The university, which became state-related in 1966, is adjacent to Carnegie Mellon and is now part of the landscape of shops, museums, and galleries that make up Oakland, the heart of Pittsburgh's cultural center. Spacious, light-filled, contemporary buildings and generic modern office buildings make up the Pitt campus, but the architectural delight is a 42-story, neo-Gothic academic building, appropriately called the Cathedral of Learning, a national historic landmark. The stately and towering cathedral, with its unique Nationality Rooms, attracts 30,000 visitors annually. And contrary to images you may hold of inner-city Pittsburgh, the campus borders a 456-acre city park.

The Dietrich School of Arts and Sciences has academic requirements that include skill requirements in writing, quantitative and formal reasoning, foreign languages, and distribution requirements in the humanities, social and natural sciences, and foreign cultures. First-year students undergo an extensive orientation that includes three days in the summer focused on academics, another five days before the term starts, and a one-credit freshman studies seminar. Pitt offers guaranteed admission into a wide variety of graduate programs for outstanding freshman applicants.

With 16 undergraduate, graduate, and professional schools and more than 450 degree programs across its five-campus system, Pitt rightfully claims to accommodate students with diverse needs. The schools of engineering and nursing are excellent and attract high-caliber students. Premed students can watch transplants at the famed University of Pittsburgh Medical Center, one of the world's leading organ transplant centers. Pitt's highly competitive physical therapy program is the top one in the country. The most popular majors include psychology, biological sciences, nursing, and finance. The interdisciplinary politics and philosophy major is a unique offering, and a new undergraduate degree in gender, sexuality, and women's studies was recently added.

> **"Pitt is…always adding and adapting programs to fit the students' needs and interests."**

"It is an intense and collaborative learning environment," says one sophomore. "Generally, people aren't in competition with one another." Forty percent of classes have fewer than 20 students. Pitt faculty members are often at the top of their fields, leading the way in areas like astronomical discoveries and medical advances. Its physicians were the first to utilize gene therapy on a person with rheumatoid arthritis. Still, students report that the quality of teaching is hit or miss. "In some classes, professors were only teaching because it is a requirement to do research at Pitt. However, these professors weren't common, and the overall experience was positive."

The academically motivated can take advantage of the excellent University Honors College, and those who do graduate with a distinctive bachelor of philosophy degree. Pitt is one of the top 10 institutions in the nation in terms of annual research support awarded by the National Institutes of Health. Seventy percent of undergrads pursue research projects, facilitated by the university's 300 centers, institutes, laboratories, and clinics. For those who want to travel, the university offers hundreds of study abroad options in 65 countries. Closer to home, Pitt is a partner with Carnegie Mellon University and Westinghouse Electric Company in the Pittsburgh Supercomputing Center. Students praise the career center's internship guarantee program, which places students in local internships after they've completed a set of workshops and other requirements. The Outside the Classroom Curriculum is an optional cocurricular program in which students participate in activities in 10 goal areas, such as leadership development, sense of self, wellness, and appreciation of the arts, in order to round out their college experience.

"There isn't really one type of Pitt student, and I think that's what makes us so unique," says an applied developmental psychology major. Seventy-one percent of all undergraduates are from Pennsylvania, including a substantial number from the Pittsburgh area, and 4 percent are international, coming from 104 countries. African

(continued)

Financial Aid: 54%
Pell Grant: 16%
Expense: Pub $ $ $ $
Student Loans: 63%
Average Debt: $ $ $ $
Phi Beta Kappa: Yes
Applicants: 30,626
Accepted: 54%
Enrolled: 24%
Grad in 6 Years: 82%
Returning Freshmen: 92%
Academics: ✐ ✐ ✐ ½
Social: ☎ ☎
Q of L: ★ ★
Admissions: (412) 624-7488
Email Address: oafa@pitt.edu

Strong Programs:
Psychology
Biological Sciences
Nursing
Finance
Engineering
Premed
Rehabilitation Science
Philosophy

Pitt's highly competitive physical therapy program is the top one in the country.

American students account for 5 percent of the student body, Asian Americans 9 percent, and Hispanics 3 percent. The university created a new Office of Diversity and Inclusion in 2015 to support diversity, and every student must pledge to promote civility on campus. When it comes to political and social issues, "our campus is very vocal," says a senior. Pitt offers merit awards averaging $10,680, and 248 athletic scholarships are available in 19 varsity sports.

While student housing may have been scarce in the past, Pitt continues to increase the amount of on-campus living space and guarantees housing for three years. Forty-four percent of students live on campus in 20 co-ed and single-sex dorms with all kinds of rooming situations, from singles to seven-person suites. Students say the quality varies, but "for the most part, students tend to be really happy with wherever they end up," says a junior. Living/learning communities are popular, and the university offers 17 options for first-years and eight for upperclassmen. Hungry students may choose from more than 20 dining spots, and the food is "significantly better than the average college," cheers a senior. Campus safety is bolstered by a consistent police presence. Additionally, "The It's On Us campaign has been very prevalent on campus," according to a history major. "Our campus has done such a good job with sexual assault prevention that Vice President Joe Biden came and visited."

> **"Bars tend to be big here, as Pittsburgh has the most bars per capita in the entire United States."**

As for social activities, "The city is our campus," says a nursing major. Within minutes are shops, parks, museums, professional sporting events, and performing arts venues, and Pitt Arts provides students with low-cost tickets to attend cultural events in the city. For students of age, a senior says, "Bars tend to be big here, as Pittsburgh has the most bars per capita in the entire United States." On campus, students have more than 350 clubs and organizations to choose from, and 10 percent of the men and 10 percent of the women belong to the Greek system. "Greek life is small on campus, so they don't take over the scene like at other schools," says one senior. Fall Fest and Bigelow Bash are favorite annual concerts that bring recognizable performers like OneRepublic, Kesha, and X Ambassadors to campus. Adjacent Schenley Park offers jogging trails and facilities for outdoor recreation. Ski slopes and mountain trails are not far away, and road trips to Penn State and Philadelphia, Boston, and New York City are popular.

> **"Students and faculty want the best for each other."**

The Pitt Panthers compete in the Division I Atlantic Coast Conference, and solid teams include baseball, volleyball, softball, men's and women's swimming and diving, and men's and women's track and field. Women's gymnastics won the 2016 Eastern Gymnastics League team title. Approximately 70 percent of undergrads take part in intramurals and club sports; basketball, football, soccer, and volleyball are the most popular.

"The best word to describe the University of Pittsburgh is 'family,'" says a junior. "The atmosphere is incredibly welcoming, and students and faculty want the best for each other." Indeed, Pitt is a large university made to feel small. Its flexibility in adapting to students' needs and its commitment to community breed a kind of loyalty and pride that students say can't be found elsewhere. Case in point, one senior declares, "I have two separate friends who have our unofficial slogan, 'Hail to Pitt,' tattooed on them." Now *that's* commitment.

Overlaps

Penn State, Ohio State, University of Maryland, Boston University, Carnegie Mellon, Case Western Reserve, NYU, Temple

If You Apply To ➤

Pitt: Rolling admissions. Financial aid: Mar. 1. Application fee: $45. No campus or alumni interviews. SATs or ACTs: required. Subject Tests: optional. Letters of recommendation: optional. Essay: recommended.

Pitzer College: See page 155.

Pomona College: See page 157.

Presbyterian College

503 Broad Street, Clinton, SC 29325

A South Carolina liberal arts college that competes head-to-head with Wofford for students who want their education served up with plenty of personal attention. Programs in business and engineering complement those in the liberal arts. Lacks the urban allure of Furman or Oglethorpe. Nearly two-thirds of PC students are from South Carolina.

Presbyterian College students live up to the motto *Dum Vivimus Servimus* ("While we live, we serve."). Approximately 75 percent of students participate in some kind of community service while at PC. Current PC students seem a far cry from the orphans for whom William Plumer Jacobs founded the school way back in 1880. And although today's Presbyterians largely come from stable, economically secure families, they continue to pursue personal, spiritual, and academic growth. "Our students are top-notch in academics and athletics, and practice servitude and Christian love in their daily lives," a senior says. "Only great things are in PC's future!"

The Presbyterian campus sits on 240 acres in the South Carolina piedmont. The redbrick buildings are largely Georgian in style, with tall, white columns and lots of shade trees; many structures are listed on the National Register of Historic Places. The campus resembles Thomas Jefferson's University of Virginia, with buildings grouped around three plazas just perfect for reading, studying, or throwing a Frisbee. A major renovation and expansion to the campus's most recognizable building, Neville Hall, is to be completed in fall 2017.

Presbyterian's curriculum emphasizes the traditional liberal arts and requires an electronic portfolio, cross-cultural education, and experiential learning for all students. All incoming freshmen are introduced to the college's mission and resources through a First-Year Experience course that focuses on critical thinking, academic skills,

> "This is obviously not a school for apathetic college students. PC students are hard workers."

and personal exploration of vocation and calling. Additional course requirements include English composition and literature, fine arts, history, math, science, physical education, religion, foreign language, and a social science. Students must also participate in a senior capstone course.

Academically, PC is challenging, and students strive to do well, says an education major. "Our college has a very competitive academic atmosphere," offers one junior. "Our courses are extremely rigorous." Classes are small, with two-thirds enrolling fewer than 20 students. Presbyterian doesn't use teaching assistants, and students praise their teachers. "Our professors are outstanding in the classroom," says a senior. The most popular majors are business administration, biology, psychology, and political science. English and music are strong, and biochemistry is one of the fastest-growing majors. Those desiring a degree in pharmacy can take advantage of the Early Entry Pre-Pharmacy Program that allows select students to

Website: www.presby.edu
Location: Small Town
Private
Total Enrollment: 1,379
Undergraduates: 1,064
Male/Female: 46/54
SAT Ranges: CR 480–590, M 490–600
ACT Ranges: 20–27
Financial Aid: 99%
Pell Grant: N/A
Expense: Pr $
Student Loans: 59%
Average Debt: $ $ $
Phi Beta Kappa: No
Applicants: 2,078
Accepted: 62%
Enrolled: 20%
Grad in 6 Years: 70%
Returning Freshmen: 81%
Academics: ✍ ✍ ✍
Social: ☎ ☎ ☎
Q of L: ★ ★ ★ ★
Admissions: (800) 960-7583
Email Address: admissions@ presby.edu

Strong Programs:
Business Administration
Biology
Psychology
Political Science
English

(continued)

Ten to 25 Summer Fellows receive stipends to live on campus and undertake independent research guided by faculty.

Student Volunteer Service is the largest organization on campus, sending students to local orphanages, nursing homes, schools, and other facilities.

earn a Doctor of Pharmacy degree in six years. Accepted students who complete all requirements of the two-year program, including coursework and community service opportunities, will have a seat reserved for them in the PC School of Pharmacy.

Options for off-campus study include semester-long exchange programs as well as highly popular, short-term Maymester trips, led by faculty, to destinations such as Australia, Greece, South Africa, India, and Scotland. Faculty-led trips during spring break are also available in Cuba, Guatemala, and Turkey. For eight weeks each summer, 10 to 25 Summer Fellows receive stipends to live on campus, undertake independent research guided by faculty, and present the findings of their work. The president and provost also work with 10 to 12 Presidential Fellows in an academic seminar; Fellows receive full scholarships and work in various campus offices to gain leadership experience. A biology major praises honors programs, which "are valuable because they allow the top students to share ideas, participate in debates, and learn from other scholars."

PC students are "passionate," observes one student. "This is obviously not a school for apathetic college students. PC students are hard workers." Thirty percent of undergraduates hail from states outside South Carolina, and 5 percent come from nations abroad. Minorities are a small but increasing presence on campus: African Americans make up 14 percent of the population, Hispanics 3 percent, and Asian Americans less than 1 percent. And while you don't have to be Presbyterian to attend PC, it does help, as roughly one-third of the students define themselves as such. "Most students have high Christian morals," a student says. Campus politics tend to be conservative, and some debate centers around religious affiliation, one student says. Merit scholarships worth an average of $17,000 are handed out to eligible students, as are 225 athletic awards in 15 sports.

Ninety-eight percent of Presbyterian students live on campus, where all dorms are air-conditioned, and accommodations range from traditional rooms with hall baths to suites and apartments. Where you live is determined by a random lottery, though everyone is guaranteed a bed. "Housing is not too bad," a student says. Another adds, "I really enjoy the dorm life. I believe it allows everyone to stay close and connected." There are two dining halls on campus, both overseen by Aramark. "Around Thanksgiving and Easter, they serve wonderful meals," says an English major. "The Sunday buffet is awesome—after church, people from the community pay to eat in our cafeteria."

"I really enjoy the dorm life. I believe it allows everyone to stay close and connected."

Thirty-eight percent of PC's men and 47 percent of the women join Greek groups, and "social life is very active," says one student. "Fraternity Court is the popular spot on weekend nights." The school has taken a firm stand against underage drinking, and three violations lead to a two-semester suspension. Many students join campus clubs, which typically have at least one off-campus retreat each semester. Owing to PC's aforementioned motto, Student Volunteer Service is the largest organization on campus. The group routinely sends students to local orphanages, nursing homes, schools, and other facilities where their time and talents can be helpful. Favorite annual traditions include Spring Fling, a weekend carnival featuring four or five bands, and the Student Government Association's midnight breakfast, served during exam weeks. Students also look forward to the candlelight Christmas service and to the outdoor graduation ceremony under the oaks, with bagpipes heralding students and faculty in full academic regalia. Students with cars enjoy heading to Greenville, Columbia, or Spartanburg for a bite to eat or some shopping—or, if there's more time, to Charleston or Atlanta. PC is equidistant from South Carolina's mountains and beaches, providing many opportunities to enjoy the outdoors. "Any road trip is a good road trip," says a junior.

PC's 15 varsity sports teams compete in Division I. The college's mascot is the Blue Hose, a reference to the stockings of their Scottish ancestors. (While some students wear kilts during athletic events, most are more restrained, says a junior.) Men's tennis is a recent Big South Conference winner, and other strong programs include women's basketball and softball. Recreational sports are divided into three divisions, depending on how competitive you are. All students may take advantage of PC's 31-acre recreational facility, with lighted softball, football, and soccer fields, volleyball courts, a basketball court, a track, and an amphitheater.

Presbyterian College students take pride in the school's history and traditions, including its very own tartan. PC's church affiliation keeps them focused on service, and on bettering the broader world, giving their classroom experiences added dimension. Says one student, "Students at PC have class. They genuinely care about one another and develop a close sense of family."

If You Apply To ➤

Presbyterian: Early decision: Nov. 1. Early action: Nov. 15. Regular decision: Feb. 1. Priority financial aid: Mar. 15. Housing: May 1. No application fee. Campus and alumni interviews: optional, evaluative. SATs or ACTs: optional (required for applicants with GPA below 3.25). Subject Tests: optional. Letters of recommendation: optional. Essay: recommended (required for test-optional applicants). Accepts the Common Application with supplement.

Prescott College

220 Grove Avenue, Prescott, AZ 86301

Not a place where students fresh out of high school typically go. Those who succeed here love the outdoors and are looking for an alternative college experience. Has ready access to northern Arizona and southern Utah, the nation's most exotic outdoor playground. College of the Atlantic is the only remotely comparable college in the *Fiske Guide*. If you loved Outward Bound, consider Prescott.

Future *Hunger Games* contestants take note: this tiny outpost in the wilderness of central Arizona is a perfect spot for the nature lover who seeks adventure, wants to learn survival skills, and likes studying outdoors. Where else but Prescott College could you major in adventure education or take courses like Mountain Search and Rescue, Ecopsychology, and Wilderness Rites of Passage? Before any Prescott student sets foot in a classroom, the college sends him or her to the outback for three weeks of hiking and camping. Wilderness Orientation is an introduction to everything Prescott stands for: hands-on experience, personal responsibility, cooperative living, and stewardship of the environment. "We attract a fairly liberal student body that is passionate about the environment and social justice," says one junior.

Founded in 1966 and still the only private liberal arts college in Arizona, Prescott retains the air of a 1960s commune. Surrounded by national forest, the college's "campus" consists of a two-block-long handful of buildings in the small town of Prescott. The architectural style of the campus ranges from the historic to the modern. The largest of the college's buildings is the Crossroads Center, an all-green building, which houses the library, computer labs, classrooms, conference centers, and the Crossroads Café. The administrative building was once a convent; its chapel is now used for meetings, art shows, and performances.

> **"[Students are] passionate about the environment and social justice."**

Website: www.prescott.edu
Location: Small City
Private
Total Enrollment: 431
Undergraduates: 304
Male/Female: 38/62
SAT Ranges: CR 440–580, M 460–570
ACT Ranges: 19–27
Financial Aid: 100%
Pell Grant: N/A
Expense: Pr $
Student Loans: 67%
Average Debt: $ $ $
Phi Beta Kappa: No
Applicants: 328
Accepted: 70%
Enrolled: 15%
Grad in 6 Years: 37%
Returning Freshmen: 70%

(continued)

Academics: ✍ ✍ ✍
Social: ☎ ☎
Q of L: ★ ★ ★ ★
Admissions: (877) 350-2100
Email Address: admissions@
    prescott.edu

Strong Programs:
Adventure Education
Psychology
Education
Environmental Studies
Global Studies
Marine Biology
Natural History and Ecology
Ecopsychology

Wilderness Orientation is an introduction to everything Prescott stands for: hands-on experience, personal responsibility, cooperative living, and stewardship of the environment.

Prescott bills itself as a college "for the liberal arts and the environment," and most students envision themselves becoming teachers, researchers, park rangers, or wilderness guides. Adventure education, a major including everything from alpine mountaineering to sea kayaking, is a specialty. Also popular are psychology, education, and global studies; the environmental studies major provides offerings of impressive breadth and depth for such a small school. The major in social and human development—a hodgepodge of sociology, psychology, and New Age mysticism—includes such unorthodox courses as Dreamwork Intensive. Integrative studies has been separated into cultural and regional studies and human development, and is home for core humanities and liberal arts areas such as religion, philosophy, and social sciences, as well as an "incubator" for programs such as peace studies. Among the college's few concessions to practicality is the teacher preparation program, which offers students teaching credentials in elementary, secondary, special, and bilingual education, and English as a second language. Prescott does not offer a comprehensive program in advanced math, chemistry, physics, or foreign languages other than Spanish. Students may take advantage of majors in creative writing, visual arts, interdisciplinary arts and letters, and sustainability management.

Prescott's requirements for graduation are characteristically unorthodox. Instead of grades, faculty members give narrative evaluations, although students may elect to receive grades. And rather than accruing credits, students design individualized "degree plans" that outline the competence (major) and breadth (minor) areas they will pursue, and the Senior Project (thesis) they will complete to demonstrate competence (graduate). Students must obtain two levels of writing certification (college level and thesis level) and math certification, showing knowledge of college-level algebra. Students also take a set of required interdisciplinary Core Curriculum courses, which are cotaught by faculty from multiple fields.

"You can interact with your coursework in a way that's more meaningful to you."

"People are inspired to work hard because their projects reflect their passions, not because they're worried about getting an A," observes one senior. "The courses are as rigorous as you want to make them." A human consciousness major adds, "Because you're not cramming for the next test (I never took one here), you can interact with your coursework in a way that's more meaningful to you." There's no tenure track at Prescott, so publishing and research take a backseat to teaching, and with 99 percent of classes having fewer than 20 students, the academic atmosphere is intimate, to say the least. "Teachers encourage you to follow your passions in your presentations, and it's really inspiring to be in an environment where your fellow students are excited to learn," says a student.

Prescott's calendar is divided into three periods, each with one 10-week quarter and one four-week block. During the quarters, students follow a traditional schedule, studying liberal arts and spending time doing fieldwork and student teaching. During the blocks, students pursue intense immersion in one course, most likely in the field, perhaps the backcountry of Baja California, the alpine meadows of Wyoming, or even a local service clinic. Students can even take a one-month rafting trip down the Colorado River for credit. Summers may be spent studying field methods in agroecology at Prescott's 30-acre Wolfberry Farm. Though Prescott does not offer a traditional study abroad program, students are encouraged to take courses in marine biology and cultural studies at the Kino Bay Center for Cultural and Ecological Studies in Mexico, as well as a social justice course in Kenya and a biodiversity course in Costa Rica.

Environmental issues predominate and one student declares, "Students here are liberal, enthusiastic, and outgoing. They will be the world's future mountaineering guides, peacemakers, and environmentalists." Despite gradually declining enrollment, Prescott's unconventional approach entices many well beyond Arizona. Sixty-eight percent of undergraduates are out-of-staters, although there are no international students. The minority population is small, with African Americans making up 2 percent of the total, Hispanics 9 percent, and Asian Americans 2 percent. Prescott offers merit awards averaging $6,126, and administrators note that tuition decreased by 12 percent recently.

During four-week blocks, students pursue intense immersion in one course, most likely in the field.

Sixteen percent of students call the housing units home. "Our dorms are so amazing we don't even call them dorms," cheers one senior. "The Village is a series of eight-person townhouses. Each townhouse has two single rooms and three double rooms." The vast majority of students fend for themselves in the town of Prescott, a rapidly growing community of approximately 40,000 where almost everything is accessible by bicycle. The college assists with the apartment hunt by providing lists of available properties and by cosigning leases when necessary. The Prescott meal plan draws praise for being tasty and fresh. "Omnivores, vegetarians, vegans, and gluten-free folk all love the food in the café," cheers one student. "We don't have a formal dining hall, but the freshman dorms do have full kitchens and the café staff offer cooking lessons throughout the semester. There's also free community lunch every Wednesday."

Social life at Prescott is informal and spontaneous. "There are plenty of social events on campus and the main part of town with bars and restaurants is only a short walk from the school," says an education major. As for the townsfolk, students describe them as "a mix of artists, activists, students, locals, retirees, and ranchers." Aside from environmental activities, Prescott offers a nationally

"We don't have a formal dining hall, but...the café staff offer cooking lessons throughout the semester."

recognized literary magazine, *Alligator Juniper*, and a chapter of Amnesty International. Those looking for nightlife can hit Whiskey Row, the town bar scene, or drive to Flagstaff (90 minutes) or Phoenix (two hours).

Though the college offers no athletics, students often participate in city sports leagues. "Our school has bike jousting, juggling, barefoot soccer, ultimate Frisbee, and capoeira—none of which involve competing against other schools," says one student. Cycling is also a popular sport among students. Prescott's personal touch extends to graduation, a unique experience where a faculty member speaks about each student personally and then the student speaks on his or her own behalf.

Prescott may not have the huge campus or financial resources that are typically associated with larger schools; however, the small classes and specialized programs appeal to a student who would not be interested in your "typical" college. A human development senior explains, "PC students are a unique and self-motivated group of individuals. Our passion and dedication to education springs from a deep and inner desire to effect positive change in the world."

Overlaps

Warren Wilson, Evergreen State, Green Mountain, Northland, College of the Atlantic, University of Redlands, Northern Arizona

If You Apply To ➤

Prescott: Rolling admissions. (Priority deadline: Mar. 1.) Early decision: Dec. 1. Financial aid: Mar. 1. Housing: May 1. No application fee. Campus interviews: optional, informational. No alumni interviews. SATs or ACTs: required. No Subject Tests. Letters of recommendation: required. Essay: required. Accepts the Common Application with supplement. Apply to particular school or program.

110 West College, Princeton, NJ 08544

More conservative than Yale and a third the size of Harvard, Princeton is the smallest of the Ivy League's Big Three. That means more attention from faculty and plenty of opportunity for rigorous independent work. Offers engineering but no business major. The affluent small-town location contrasts with urban New Haven and Cambridge. Princeton continues to develop residential colleges modeled on Yale's.

Website: www.princeton.edu
Location: Suburban
Private
Total Enrollment: 7,964
Undergraduates: 5,260
Male/Female: 52/48
SAT Ranges: CR 690–790,
   M 700–800
ACT Ranges: 32–35
Financial Aid: 60%
Pell Grant: 21%
Expense: Pr $ $
Student Loans: 16%
Average Debt: $
Phi Beta Kappa: Yes
Applicants: 27,290
Accepted: 7%
Enrolled: 68%
Grad in 6 Years: 97%
Returning Freshmen: 97%
Academics: ✍ ✍ ✍ ✍ ✍
Social: ☎ ☎ ☎
Q of L: ★ ★ ★
Admissions: (609) 258-3060
Email Address: uaoffice@
   princeton.edu

Strong Programs:
Public and International Affairs
Economics
Computer Science
History
Mathematics
Philosophy
Operations Research and
   Financial Engineering
Molecular Biology

Princeton occupies a distinctive niche among America's super-elite universities. It is a major research university with a world-class corps of professors who, in the absence of lots of graduate and professional students, lavish their attention on a relatively modest number of undergraduates. Princeton has an engineering school as well as programs in applied science, architecture and public planning, public policy, and a new Entrepreneurial Hub near campus, but it is basically an "arts and sciences university." The academic atmosphere across campus is dominated by commitment to the liberal arts—with a carefully structured set of core requirements and a heavy emphasis on independent study, including a mandatory senior thesis. "Many schools brag about great buildings and great professors, but it's really your fellow students that end up making or breaking your college experience," says one sophomore. "What sets Princeton students apart is that they come here not just for an excellent education, but they come to share knowledge with others." Princeton has strong historic links to the South, which helps explain its conservative and stratified social climate. For better or worse, Princeton has been known as a bastion of exclusivity, although its undergraduates are just as racially and ethnically diverse as any other Ivy League school.

But Princeton is changing. University leaders are looking to make Princeton's particular brand of high-powered undergraduate liberal arts education available to an increasingly diverse group of students. New four-year residential colleges are being established, aimed at broadening the range of social options available to students, and the administration is making major investments in the creative and performing arts and the biological sciences. The university has backed off from a decade-long effort to curb grade inflation, but, sensitive to faculty complaints that

> **"[Students] come here not just for an excellent education, but they come to share knowledge with others."**

Princeton draws too many bright students whose main claim to fame is that they have learned to work the system, the admissions office is on the lookout for more students with demonstrated intellectual curiosity—including more high-ability/low-income students and creative types. Princeton has replaced all loans in its financial packages with grants, so just about any qualified student should be able to afford the place (about 84 percent of students graduate debt-free, and those who do borrow graduate with debt well below the national average). Support for first-generation and low-income students is offered through the Freshman Scholars Institute, which offers an academic and social introduction to Princeton over the summer before classes start, and the Scholars Institute Fellows Program that covers all four years.

Cloistered in a secluded but upscale New Jersey town, Princeton's architectural trademark is Gothic, from the cavernous and ornate university chapel to the four-pronged Cleveland Tower rising majestically above the treetops. Interspersed among the Gothic are examples of colonial architecture, most notably historic Nassau Hall, which served as the temporary home of the Continental Congress in 1783 and has defined elegance in academic architecture ever since. A host of modern structures, some by leading American architects Robert Venturi, Frank Gehry, and I. M. Pei, add variety and distinction to the campus, but the ambiance is still quintessential Ivy League at its best. The outstanding library facilities embrace five million volumes and provide 500 private study carrels for seniors working on their theses; there are another 700 enclosed carrels in other parts of the campus. Princeton's campus is self-contained, but those who venture outside its walls will find the surroundings quite pleasing. One side of the campus abuts quaint Nassau Street, which is dominated by chic (and pricey) boutiques and restaurants, most out of the range of student budgets, although coffee shops and affordable restaurants are becoming more prevalent. The other side of campus ends with a huge man-made lake that was financed by Andrew Carnegie so that Princetonians would not have to forgo crew. Recent campus projects include the new Andlinger Center for Energy and the Environment.

Princeton became the model for American-style liberal arts colleges after John Witherspoon was lured from the University of Edinburgh to become president in 1768. Today, Princeton is distinctive in its scale (among the Ivies, only Dartmouth has a lower total enrollment) and its emphasis on undergraduates. Each student's Princeton experience begins with a week of orientation; 800 each year participate in Outdoor Action, a few days of wilderness activities immediately preceding orientation. For a major research institution, the university offers its students unparalleled faculty contact. "We have some of the most brilliant professors in the world here," says a junior. An economics major adds, "I can open the newspaper and read my professor's article or turn on the TV and see him giving a speech, then go to a lecture to hear him speak, then go to his office to speak with him one-on-one." Seventy percent of undergraduate classes have fewer than 20 students. With fewer graduate students to siphon off resources or consume faculty time than at large research universities, undergraduates get the lion's share of both; at last count, 70 percent of Princeton's department heads taught introductory undergraduate courses. Special opportunities to work closely with senior faculty members come with the freshman seminar program, taken by two-thirds of new students, which offers the opportunity to go deep into dozens of topics ranging from the Physics of Music to the Search for Life in the Universe. Lovers of literature can study with Tracy K. Smith, Paul Muldoon, Chang-rae Lee, or Toni Morrison, and nearly every other department has a few stars of its own. Senior professors lead at least one or two of the small discussion groups that accompany each lecture course.

Every liberal arts student must fulfill distribution requirements in epistemology and cognition, ethical thought and moral values, historical analysis, literature and the arts, quantitative reasoning, social analysis, and science and technology. Students must also take a writing seminar. During their junior year, liberal arts students work closely with a faculty member of their choice in completing two junior papers—about 30 pages of independent work each semester in addition to the normal courseload. Princeton also requires every graduate to complete a senior thesis—an enterprise that serves as a culmination of their work in their field of concentration. As a result, "seniors develop close personal relationships with their thesis advisors," says one student. Alumni often note the thesis as one of their best experiences at Princeton.

As one might expect, Princeton's small size means the number of courses offered is smaller than at other Ivies. But lack of quantity does not beget lack of quality. Princeton's math and philosophy departments are among the best in the nation, and economics, history, public policy, English, physics, molecular biology, and romance languages are right on their heels. As part of a major effort to become a national center in the field of molecular biology, the university supports a

Eighty-four percent of students graduate debt-free, and those who do borrow graduate with debt well below the national average.

"We have some of the most brilliant professors in the world here."

laboratory for teaching and research staffed by 28 faculty members. Princeton is one of the few top liberal arts universities with equally strong computer science and engineering programs, most notably chemical, mechanical, electrical, and aerospace engineering. In fact, the department of civil engineering and operations research is split into two departments: civil and environmental engineering, and operations research and financial engineering, with the latter becoming one of the most popular majors. There is also a five-year program that leads to a B.S.E. and M.E. in mechanical and aerospace engineering. One of Princeton's best-known programs is the prestigious Woodrow Wilson School of Public and International Affairs ("Woody Woo" to the students). The school's name recently survived a well-publicized campaign to change it, in protest of former president Wilson's strong advocacy of racial segregation. Fifty-five percent of students study abroad in one of 100 programs in 44 nations. For those wishing to postpone their entry into the university in favor of an international experience, Princeton's Bridge Year program covers the full cost of one-year service abroad programs in Bolivia, Brazil, China, India, and Senegal.

"Seniors develop close personal relationships with their thesis advisors."

Princeton's Bridge Year program covers the full cost of one-year service abroad programs in Bolivia, Brazil, China, India, and Senegal.

"The courses are very challenging and rigorous," a junior reports, "but perhaps because of that, people are very cooperative. They realize that no one can really succeed alone." Princeton's semester system gives students a two-week reading period before exams in which to catch up, with first-term exams postponed until after New Year's, much to the dismay of many ski buffs and tropical sun worshipers. The university honor code, unique among the Ivies, allows for unproctored exams. A limited number of courses can be taken on the pass/fail option, and the University Scholars program provides especially qualified students with what the administration calls "maximum freedom in planning programs of study to fulfill individual needs and interests." Although the faculty gets high ratings for its academic advising, students are rather cool on the university's nonacademic counseling programs.

"Our students are tight-knit, extremely hardworking, highly cooperative, and supportive of one another's activities," says an economics major. Just 6 percent of undergraduates are New Jersey natives, and 12 percent are international. African Americans account for 8 percent of the student body, Hispanics 9 percent, and Asians 22 percent. While diversity is present, mixing sometimes isn't. "As an African American, I can say that even the African Americans are subdivided based on economics, place of origin, and whether you went to public or private school," explains one senior. And the campus remains socially conservative, with tweed and penny loafers adorning many students. Although students report that there can be a general air of apathy around campus, administrators are quick to point to the numerous political organizations on campus as evidence of students' interest in political and social issues. Princeton undergraduates are admitted to the university without regard to their financial need, and those who qualify for aid receive generous support that covers their full demonstrated need. In fact, Princeton was the first university in the U.S. to replace loans with grants for all aid recipients. Twenty-one percent of the most recent freshman class qualified for Pell Grants.

"[The residential colleges system] creates a gulf between underclassmen and upperclassmen."

In an attempt to improve the quality of life for freshmen and sophomores, Princeton has grouped many of its dorms into residential colleges, each with its own dining hall, faculty residents, and an active social calendar. Under this system, nearly all the freshmen and sophomores live and dine with their residential college unit, alleviating the formerly fragmented social situation. However, by providing a separate social sphere for these students, the system also "creates a gulf between underclassmen and upperclassmen." All upperclassmen maintain an affiliation to the residential colleges, taking many meals there and even continuing residence there if they prefer. Just 4 percent of undergraduates live off campus. The university's turn-of-the-century Gothic dorms may look like crosses between cathedrals and castles, and some halls have amenities like living rooms and bay windows. But conditions on the inside are sometimes less glamorous. All dorms are renovated on a rotation schedule, and new dorms have helped ease the housing crunch. The modern and roomy Spelman dorms, which come complete with kitchens, are the best on campus and fill up quickly every year with seniors who do not belong to eating clubs.

The university honor code, unique among the Ivies, allows for unproctored exams.

Princeton's eating clubs are its most firmly entrenched bastions of tradition. Run by students and unaffiliated with the school, they line Prospect Avenue, and have, for more than a century, assumed the dual role of weekend fraternity and weekday dining hall. Of the 11, five admit members through an open lottery, but the others still use a controversial selective admissions process called bicker (because of the wrangling over whom to admit), to the chagrin of the administration and most of the students. While many of the clubs opened their doors to women back when Princeton went co-ed, two of the oldest and most exclusive—the Ivy Club and the Tiger Inn—remained all-male until 1991, when a court decision compelled them to admit women. Now, all the clubs are co-ed.

Catering exclusively to upperclassmen, the eating clubs provide a secure sense of community for their members. More than half of all sophomores join one of the clubs at the end of the year, becoming full-fledged members by the fall of their junior year. Annual dues vary; the most expensive is the Ivy Club, which charges its members almost $10,000 a year. Financial aid covers eating costs for those who qualify and

"Virtually all social life takes place on campus, both at the eating clubs and at dorm parties."

want to join. Unfortunately, the social options for those who choose not to join may feel limited. All too often the upper-level eating clubs steal the thunder from college-sponsored social events. As a result, "the underclassmen spend too much time pining for the day when they, too, can join the closest thing Princeton has to cliques," says one student. Some opt for life in independent dormitories or join the handful of Greek fraternities and sororities (not sanctioned by the administration) that have sprung up on campus over the past few years and have become feeders to particular eating clubs.

"Virtually all social life takes place on campus, both at the eating clubs and at dorm parties," says a sophomore. Princeton has the oldest licensed college radio station in the nation, plenty of journalistic opportunities, a prestigious debating and politics society (Whig-Clio) whose ranks included James Madison and Aaron Burr, and a plethora of arts offerings. McCarter Theatre, adjacent to campus, is the nation's seventh-busiest performing arts center and houses Princeton's Triangle Club, which counted Jimmy Stewart and Brooke Shields as members. The roundup of annual campus events includes Communiversity Day, an international festival, and the P Party in the spring, which features a big-name band. Each year about 3,000 students engage in volunteer activities such as tutoring, working in soup kitchens, or helping the elderly. Few students complain about boredom, and many praise the affluent town of Princeton for the parks, woods, bike trails, and, most important, the quiet and safety it offers students. Students rarely venture much farther than New York or Philadelphia, each one hour away (in opposite directions) on the train.

Princeton's eating clubs have, for more than a century, assumed the dual role of weekend fraternity and weekday dining hall.

Athletics are a big deal at Princeton, both varsity and intramural. Fourteen Tigers teams took home Ivy League conference titles in 2015–16, among them men's indoor track, women's ice hockey, and men's and women's fencing. Men's squash and women's field hockey are recent Division I national champions. Dozens of club and intramural sports are available, ranging from rugby to ballroom dancing to wallyball, and the eating clubs and residential colleges offer recreational athletic programs too. Every fall the freshman and sophomore classes square off in Cane Spree, an intramural Olympics that has been a tradition since 1869.

Princeton's unofficial motto is "Princeton in the nation's service and the service of all nations," and the oft-repeated notion that with privilege comes responsibility lives on as part of its culture. It's easy to be humbled at Princeton. Even the most jaded students must be awed and inspired when they think of those who've traversed the campus paths before them, including former U.S. presidents James Madison and Woodrow Wilson. While some may find the ambiance too insular, not many turn down membership in this very rewarding club.

If You Apply To ➤ **Princeton:** Single choice early action: Nov. 1. Regular decision: Jan. 1. Financial aid: Feb. 1. Application fee: $65. No campus interviews. Alumni interviews: optional, evaluative. SATs (with essay) or ACTs (with writing): required. Subject Tests: recommended (any two; engineering applicants required to take either physics or chemistry and math I or II). Letters of recommendation: required. Essay: required. Accepts the Common Application with supplement. Applicants with a special talent may submit an optional arts form.

Principia College

Elsah, IL 62028

Prin is a tiny college in a tiny town about an hour from St. Louis. All students have ties to Christian Science. Prin is mainly liberal arts, though its most popular program is business administration. Nearly two-thirds of the students study abroad. Campus tenor is similar to places like Pepperdine and Wheaton (IL).

Website: www.principiacollege .edu
Location: Rural
Private
Total Enrollment: 450
Undergraduates: 450
Male/Female: 49/51
SAT Ranges: CR 460–590, M 470–608
ACT Ranges: 21–27
Financial Aid: 96%
Pell Grant: N/A
Expense: Pr $
Student Loans: 81%
Average Debt: $
Phi Beta Kappa: No
Applicants: 159
Accepted: 75%
Enrolled: 66%
Grad in 6 Years: 80%
Returning Freshmen: 88%
Academics: ✍ ✍ ✍
Social: ☎ ☎ ☎
Q of L: ★ ★ ★ ★

Students come to Principia College with a common bond—ties to Christian Science. They shun smoking, drinking, drugs, and sex in favor of God and learning. Prin graduates are culturally, spiritually, and intellectually well rounded, the product of a liberal arts education that promotes critical thinking and a broad worldview. As the only college anywhere for Christian Scientists, Prin attracts a lot of international students. The historic campus is reminiscent of Harry Potter's Hogwarts. But the fictional school of wizardry never had a woolly mammoth to unearth between the dormitories as Prin did. Says one senior, Prin "has a warm, calm, and cozy atmosphere that reminds me of a second home."

Principia's 2,600-acre campus, on limestone bluffs above the mighty Mississippi River, was designated a National Historic Landmark in 1993. The dominant architectural influences are colonial American, Tudor, and medieval, and many buildings—including most dormitories—were designed by California architect Bernard Maybeck. A contemporary of Frank Lloyd Wright, Maybeck urged Principia trustees to bring the college to its current spot when they relocated from St. Louis in 1935. The College Chapel, whose bells ring out hymns every Sunday evening, is the symbolic center of campus.

> **"[Prin] has a warm, calm, and cozy atmosphere that reminds me of a second home."**

In addition to 10 to 12 courses in their major, students must complete a broad range of distribution requirements in the arts, humanities, social sciences, and natural sciences, as well as two physical education courses. All freshmen participate in a first-year experience program their first semester, and all seniors must complete a capstone course or project. Of the 25 majors offered, the most popular are business administration, educational studies, mass communication, and biology. Students say that the music, political science, and religion programs are also strong. The sociology and anthropology major was recently dropped, but a new dual-degree program was added in engineering science, in conjunction with the University of North Dakota.

Academics are challenging, but students can count on each other and their professors for help. "The atmosphere in the classroom is very friendly," says a senior. "Most classes take advantage of group work in small teams, and this helps you develop teamwork, leadership, and collaborative skills." Most of the faculty members receive high marks. "Professors at Principia take a personal interest in your learning and challenge you to not only be better students, but better people as well," says an educational studies major. Fifty-nine percent of Principia students participate in the five or six study abroad programs the school organizes each year. Each program enrolls 18 to 22 students and sites are determined by academic subject and focus. Recent locations have included Greece, Turkey, the Czech Republic, Slovenia, and Ireland. Others participate in a prairie restoration program, gather data for the study of the Mississippi River's aquatic life, or build solar cars to be entered in races around the world.

"We are all Christian Scientists who strive to be the most moral people we can be," says one junior. The minority population is minuscule—2 percent are African American, 4 percent are Hispanic, and 1 percent are Asian American. Still, 16 percent of students arrive from abroad, one of the largest percentages of international students on a college campus in the country, and only 4 percent of students are from Illinois. One international student says of the student population, "I've found that diversity positively impacts me. I've learned that there are more good things that bind us than negative things that divide us as human beings." Principia does not accept any governmental financial aid, so Pell Grants and the typical federal loans are not available to students, but the school does offer merit scholarships averaging $21,792, grants, and private, institutionally funded loans. No athletic scholarships are available.

All students live in Prin's dorms, except for the few who are married or live locally with their parents. "The housing at Principia is superb, in the form of large, historical houses rather than the typical dormitory," says a senior. The rooms are large and comfortable, and those that aren't air-conditioned have ceiling fans. Students are expected not to be in the wings of dorms where the opposite sex lives during "house hours" every night. Freshmen live in two modernized dorms with upper-class resident advisors trained to help new students adjust to college life. "Each house has its own sense of house culture and traditions, and houses have brother-sister relationships as well as rivalries," explains a business administration and mass communication major. A sit-down pub and restaurant on campus provides a nice alternative to traditional dining-hall fare. "Dining facilities are improving, but vegetarians and vegans are still struggling," says a junior. Students agree that they feel safe on campus, citing the rural location and a strong security presence.

"We are all Christian Scientists who strive to be the most moral people we can be."

In addition to eschewing alcohol, tobacco, and drugs, students are also asked to sign a pledge of abstention from premarital and extramarital sexual relationships. "Those who sign the contract are committed to those morals for religious reasons," a political science major says. "It's a wonderful thing not to have to deal with alcohol on campus," says a senior. It goes without saying that Greek organizations are nonexistent; instead of partying, students keep busy at school-sponsored concerts, movies, dances, or intramural sporting events that pit one dorm against another. "Prin is remote enough where people stay on campus during the weekends to attend

(continued)

Admissions: (618) 374-5181
Email Address: college admissions@principia.edu

Strong Programs:
Business Administration
Educational Studies
Mass Communication
Biology
Music
Political Science
Religion

A new dual-degree program was added in engineering science, in conjunction with the University of North Dakota.

The Public Affairs Conference is the oldest student-run event of its type, bringing in big-name speakers.

our awesome social events," says one student. Each dorm organizes its own annual celebration, and international students show off their native cuisines at the Whole World Festival. The Public Affairs Conference is the oldest student-run event of its type, bringing in big-name speakers to give talks, lead workshops, and provide networking opportunities to students; recent themes have included innovation, sustainability, and youth empowerment. "Elsah is not a college town. I think it was established in the 1800s and not much has changed," a junior says. Stores, restaurants, and movie theaters are about 30 minutes away, and St. Louis is about an hour's drive.

Principia's Panthers compete in Division III, and rugby, women's soccer, and men's and women's tennis and cross-country are especially competitive. Intramural sports including lacrosse, soccer, basketball, and softball are popular. On sunny afternoons, students can be found playing ultimate Frisbee. Campus athletic facilities include a four-court indoor tennis center, a field house with gym and pool, and outdoor courts and running trails.

Prin students embrace the conservative environment at their Christian Scientist school. Gone are the pressures that take hold of most college students. Prin graduates leave their collegiate bubble ready to take on the world. "The school promotes character development and personal growth," says a political science major, "[it] doesn't just crank out diplomas."

> **"Houses have brother-sister relationships as well as rivalries."**

If You Apply To ➤

Principia: Rolling admissions. Priority financial aid: Mar. 1. No application fee. Campus interviews: recommended, evaluative. No alumni interviews. SATs (with essay) or ACTs (with writing): required. No Subject Tests. Letters of recommendation: required. Essay: required. Only college in the world that admits only Christian Scientists. Accepts the Common Application with supplement.

Providence College

Providence, RI 02918

Strong Roman Catholic atmosphere makes Providence more comparable to Notre Dame than to Boston College or Holy Cross. Liberal arts emphasis rooted in required two-year interdisciplinary Western Civilization sequence, though 35 percent of students opt for business disciplines. Friars athletic teams do well in small but high-profile Big East Conference. No fraternities or sororities, but Providence is a vibrant college town.

Website: www.providence.edu
Location: Small City
Private
Total Enrollment: 4,123
Undergraduates: 3,906
Male/Female: 43/57
SAT Ranges: CR 520–620, M 530–630
ACT Ranges: 23–28
Financial Aid: 77%
Pell Grant: 15%

As the nation's only college or university operated by the Dominican Friars, Providence College wears its Roman Catholic and Dominican identities on its sleeve. Three-quarters of students are Catholic, friars in habits walk the campus grounds, crucifixes adorn the walls of classrooms and offices, and St. Dominic's Chapel stands tall in the heart of the campus. The school's mission is grounded in these identities too, as it aims to "provide an education for the whole person—body, mind, and soul—that bridges the common divides between matter and spirit, God and creation, faith and reason." Students here enjoy solid offerings in the sciences and liberal arts—including a unique and rigorous two-year Western Civ course—and a tight-knit community of like-minded men and women.

Located only an hour's drive from Boston and just a few hours' drive from New York City, Providence College's 105-acre campus is situated in Rhode Island's capital city. The campus boasts open spaces, beautiful lawns, and student-centered facilities. The traditional brick and stone academic buildings, residence halls, and campus chapel coexist with several contemporary structures. The Canavan Sports Medicine Center is a 4,000-square-foot facility featuring a 920-square-foot hydrotherapy room and other amenities. Now in the midst of a massive, five-phase campus transformation plan, the campus currently resembles a construction site.

A recently revised core curriculum brought "comprehensive revisions designed to provide students with a liberal arts education responsive to today's complex and rapidly changing global environment," according to administrators. The heart of the curriculum is a sequence of seminar-based classes that comprise the Development of Western Civilization (DWC). This 20-credit course spans students' freshman and sophomore years and introduces them to the seminal ideas and primary texts in history, literature, theology, and philosophy, as well as the music and visual arts that shaped the Western world and other civilizations. Students also take coursework in theology, philosophy, natural science, social science, quantitative reasoning, and fine arts, and they must demonstrate proficiency in intensive writing, oral communication, diversity, and civic engagement.

Providence comprises four schools: arts and sciences, business, professional studies, and continuing education. Popular majors include marketing, finance, biology, and psychology, and the chemistry and education programs are strong. The School of Business, which draws 35 percent of the students, offers a number of solid programs, including majors in accountancy and management. All School of Business majors share a common set of core courses to ensure that business graduates have a broad understanding of all essential business disciplines. A student says, "Although biology is a very popular major here, many seem to complain about the workload." The biology department offers a combined degree program with the New England College of Optometry, which allows for the completion of the B.A. and doctorate in seven years. The premedical/dental option is designed to prepare students intending to pursue careers in medicine and dentistry.

> "[Professors] are enthusiastic, willing, and available to us."

"The academic climate at Providence College is rigorous but supportive," says a junior. Fifty-two percent of classes have fewer than 20 students and are taught by tenured or junior faculty. "Freshmen are always taught by full professors," says one student. "We do not have TAs here." A Spanish and global studies double major adds, "Professors here go the extra mile for their students. They are enthusiastic, willing, and available to us. They never treat us like we are a number." The Liberal Arts Honors Program offers students of high academic ability and initiative a more in-depth and rigorous version of PC's core curriculum, and honors courses are offered in virtually all areas. Small, seminar-style classes of 12 to 15 students allow for extensive one-on-one contact among students and professors. Students have ample opportunity for experiential learning through internships and faculty-directed laboratory or field research. PC's Center for International Studies sends 30 percent of students to more than 40 countries, including Argentina, Italy, New Zealand, and South Africa.

Fifteen percent of PC's students come from Rhode Island, and the remainder "tend to be mostly from the Northeast," according to one junior. In addition, most students are "preppy, white, Catholic, and generally upper middle class," according to a sophomore. Two percent are foreign nationals. African Americans account for 4 percent of the student body, Hispanics 9 percent, and Asian Americans 1 percent. Many students are vocal when it comes to social and political issues. "The most heated debates are generally about religion and race as they are

> "The most heated debates are generally about religion and race as they are key issues on our campus."

(continued)

Expense: Pr $ $ $
Student Loans: 64%
Average Debt: $ $ $ $
Phi Beta Kappa: No
Applicants: 10,215
Accepted: 57%
Enrolled: 18%
Grad in 6 Years: 86%
Returning Freshmen: 90%
Academics: ✍ ✍ ✍
Social: ☎ ☎ ☎
Q of L: ★ ★ ★
Admissions: (401) 865-2535
Email Address: pcadmiss@ providence.edu

Strong Programs:
Marketing
Finance
Biology
Psychology
Chemistry
Education
Accountancy
Management

All School of Business majors share a common set of core courses to ensure a broad understanding of essential business disciplines.

key issues on our campus," a marketing major says. The lack of diversity draws near-universal concern: "I think it is felt very strongly among the minority students that we need more diversity on campus, even with all of our cultural clubs," says a junior. Merit scholarships averaging $19,280 are available to qualified students, and gifted athletes may vie for 176 awards in 19 sports.

Owing to the college's strong Catholic identity, community service and volunteer work are popular pastimes.

Seventy-six percent of students live in the dorms, where conditions are said to be adequate if not spacious. "Dorms vary from very comfortable to a tight squeeze," reports one finance major. "They are usually well maintained, and I have never experienced or heard of anyone having trouble getting a room." Options include nine traditional halls, five apartment buildings, and a suite-style residence. Many juniors and seniors move off campus into the surrounding neighborhoods. Campus dining is "good and constantly getting better," says a global studies major. "With the blue-light system, Intelliguard system, escort service, and good line of communication between administration and students, I feel as if PC has implemented all that they can to keep students safe," says an English major.

A junior says the social life is varied and, "There are free events for students to attend almost every day of the week, including weekends." Absent a Greek presence, students find other ways to let off steam. Owing to the college's strong Catholic identity, community service and volunteer work are popular pastimes. Annual traditions include a spring concert featuring top national acts and Civ Scream, held at midnight on the eve of Western Civ finals: "The entire sophomore class circles around the quad and screams to let out their frustration over Civ.

"Basketball and hockey games are very important to PC students because we can show our school spirit."

People do crazy things and it is always something to remember," says a student. And although the college is located in "kind of a rundown area," students say the city of Providence has much to offer. "Providence is full of opportunities," reports an English major, including a mall, a movie theater, and a cultural district with all sorts of shops and eateries. The city is also home to six other colleges, which enhances the social scene. Popular road trips include treks into Boston and New York City.

The Providence Friars compete at the Division I level, and most varsity teams play in the competitive Big East Conference (men's and women's hockey are part of the Hockey East Association). The most competitive teams include men's ice hockey (2015 national champs) and soccer, women's ice hockey, and men's and women's basketball and cross-country. "Basketball and hockey games are very important to PC students because we can show our school spirit," says a sophomore. Students get especially rowdy when rivals UConn, URI, or Syracuse are in town. Intramurals and recreational programs are popular too, and attract 75 percent of the student body.

Providence College appeals primarily to those students who want to challenge themselves academically without compromising their faith. Despite frequent complaints about the length and rigor of the Western Civ requirement, students here seem content with what the college has to offer and are proud to be part of the PC community. "We are all very similar, which some people might consider a weakness," says one elementary and special education major, "but in the end I feel that everyone here is my friend and that I can relate to them."

Overlaps

Boston College, College of the Holy Cross, Villanova, Loyola University Maryland, Fordham, Fairfield, Stonehill, University of Massachusetts Amherst

If You Apply To ➤ **Providence:** Early action: Nov. 1. Early decision I: Nov. 15. Early decision II and regular decision: Jan. 15. Financial aid: Feb. 1. Application fee: $65. Campus interviews: recommended, informational. No alumni interviews. SATs or ACTs: optional. Subject Tests: optional. Letters of recommendation: required. Essay: required. Accepts the Common Application.

University of Puget Sound

1500 North Warner, Tacoma, WA 98416

Ask anyone in Tacoma about Puget Sound and they'll tell you that UPS (the college, not the package service) delivers solid liberal arts programs with a touch of business. Within easy reach of the Sound and Mount Rainier, the university specializes in all things Asia, including a nine-month university-sponsored trip. Compare to Whitman and Willamette.

An ambitious building program and revised core curriculum have raised the profile of the University of Puget Sound, transforming it from a regional liberal arts college in Tacoma to an undergraduate institution with growing national reach. What hasn't changed is the school's close-knit community and its emphasis on Asia. "People don't come here because they have heard of us before," says one contented senior. "They come here because they visit and they don't want to leave."

Founded in 1888, Puget Sound is cradled by the Cascade Range and the rugged Olympics, with easy access to the urban energy of Seattle and the natural beauty of Mount Rainier. The 97-acre campus boasts carefully maintained lawns, native fir trees, and plenty of other greenery, thanks to the moist climate. Most buildings, with distinctive arches and porticos, were built in the 1950s and '60s. Additional facilities include an all-weather track and a 3,850-square-foot Sculpture House, with facilities for welding, woodwork, and painting. A new athletics and aquatics center opened in 2016.

Puget Sound students must complete an eight-course core curriculum, which includes a freshman seminar in writing and rhetoric, and another in scholarly and creative inquiry; they must also demonstrate foreign language proficiency. In their first three years at Puget Sound, students also study five Approaches to Knowing—fine arts, humanities, math, natural sciences, and social sciences. An upper-level capstone course, Connections, challenges traditional disciplinary boundaries and examines the benefits and limits of an interdisciplinary approach to learning.

After navigating UPS's requirements, students may pursue a B.A., B.S., or B.M. (bachelor of music) degree. Some of the most popular majors are psychology, business, politics and government, economics, and international political economy. Newer programs include a major in environmental policy and decision making and a minor in education. The university has developed a reputation as a jumping-off point to Asia—both literally and figuratively. Its curriculum stresses two of the fastest-growing fields in the region: Asian studies and Pacific Rim economics. Nearly one-third of Puget Sounders take at least one Asian studies course, and once every three years, there's a nine-month, school-sponsored trip through Japan, Thailand, Korea, India, China, and Nepal, where participants study native art, architecture, politics, population, and philosophy. In all, more than 100 study abroad programs are available in more than 40 nations; 34 percent of students participate. Other special offerings include a classics-based honors program, the Business Leadership Program, residence-based humanities programs, and the Social Justice Residence Program.

> "Students at Puget Sound are definitely outdoorsy. Lots of Birkenstocks and plaid."

Students say the atmosphere at Puget Sound is relatively relaxed. "Academics are definitely a focus here, but most students recognize that their Puget Sound experience is more than just inside the classroom," explains a studio art major. Sixty-one percent of classes have fewer than 20 students, and you won't find grad students

Website: www.pugetsound.edu
Location: Small City
Private
Total Enrollment: 2,687
Undergraduates: 2,459
Male/Female: 41/59
SAT Ranges: CR 560–680, M 540–660
ACT Ranges: 25–30
Financial Aid: 100%
Pell Grant: 17%
Expense: Pr $ $ $
Student Loans: 58%
Average Debt: $ $ $ $
Phi Beta Kappa: Yes
Applicants: 5,827
Accepted: 79%
Enrolled: 14%
Grad in 6 Years: 76%
Returning Freshmen: 86%
Academics: ✍ ✍ ✍ ½
Social: ☎ ☎ ☎
Q of L: ★ ★ ★ ★
Admissions: (253) 879-3211
Email Address: admission@pugetsound.edu

Strong Programs:
Psychology
Business
Politics and Government
Economics
International Political Economy
Asian Studies
Music

leading classes here. "I have been struck by the number of faculty that remember details about me, or will still stop me around campus to say hello three years after I took an introductory class with them," comments a sociology and anthropology major. Students also praise the plentiful opportunities for undergraduate research, which recently have ranged from studying bacteria on lizard eggs to summer field-work in Europe researching "graffiti that has emerged from the Syrian refugee crisis," according to one student.

"Students at Puget Sound are definitely outdoorsy," says a Hispanic studies junior. "Lots of Birkenstocks and plaid. Politically liberal, for the most part." Most UPS students come from western states, with 20 percent hailing from Washington; 1 percent come from abroad. African Americans make up 1 percent of the student body, Hispanics 7 percent, and Asian Americans 6 percent. A junior acknowledges that the campus community is working to address "issues of microagression, racial bias, and diversity and inclusion." An active Hawaiian student organization sponsors a number of events, including a luau each spring, with "great food and lots of traditional dances." There are no athletic scholarships, but merit awards averaging $15,389 are doled out annually.

Sixty-six percent of Puget Sound students live on campus, and freshmen and sophomores are required to do so. "First-year students all live in first-year residence halls that have plenty of space and are routinely renovated," says a sophomore. After the first year, students may go Greek and live in chapter housing, pursue a single room in the dorms, or apply for one of 60 university-owned theme houses, which focus on interests like substance-free lifestyles, social justice, or outdoor adventures. Other options include four foreign language houses. Aside from the main campus dining area, students can chow down at two campus cafés and the Cellar. "They do a good job of buying local and having fresh options," says one student. "Students here understand the risks and the signs of sexual assault and have risen up to speak out against it," says a biology major.

"The vibe is laid-back, but purposeful at the same time."

Twenty-seven percent of Puget Sound men and 31 percent of the women go Greek, though fraternities and sororities don't dominate the social scene. "Social life at UPS is fairly intimate. In my experience, people tend to hang out more off campus on the weekends, at people's houses and such. Parties aren't large," a philosophy major says. A senior adds, "There is no pressure to drink and it's not hard to have fun without alcohol." Popular school-sponsored activities include the Log Jam BBQ, which kicks off the school year, Midnight Breakfasts, and Foolish Pleasures, a festival of short student-produced films. The Repertory Dance Group and Puget Sound Outdoors are among the most popular campus organizations. A few Tacoma bars and restaurants are within walking distance, and a junior says the university is working "to give students pipelines to the local community through volunteering and social justice programs, free and discounted museum passes, and more." With the mountains and beaches so close—Seattle is 30 minutes away by car, Portland is two hours south, and Vancouver, British Columbia, is three hours north—road trips are *de rigueur*. That's especially true during ski season, and the school rents out all the necessary equipment.

Students are fond of saying that Puget Sound's Division III varsity teams, the Loggers, "Kick Axe." Solid teams include men's baseball, basketball, crew, and cross-country, and women's lacrosse, softball, tennis, and volleyball. The women's soccer team won its 13th consecutive conference title in 2014–15. The school's archrival is Pacific Lutheran University; "football and basketball games against PLU are a big deal and always packed," says a fan.

Don't let UPS students' slacker-chic clothes and casual demeanor fool you. Puget Sound means business and serious study for students seeking immersion in the liberal arts and the natural beauty of the outdoors. As a molecular and cellular biology major explains, "The vibe is laid-back, but purposeful at the same time. People who come to this school are passionate and love to share those passions with others."

If You Apply To ➤

Puget Sound: Early decision I: Nov. 15. Early action: Dec. 1. Early decision II: Jan. 1. Regular decision and financial aid: Jan. 15. Housing: May 1. Application fee: $50. Campus and alumni interviews: optional, evaluative. SATs or ACTs: optional (test-optional applicants must submit two short essay questions). Subject Tests: optional. Letters of recommendation: required. Essay: required. Accepts the Common Application with supplement.

Purdue University

1080 Schleman Hall, West Lafayette, IN 47907

Purdue is Indiana's STEM university—with side helpings of business, health professions, and liberal arts. Compare to Kansas State and Big Ten rival Michigan State. Does better than most large universities in giving students hands-on opportunities such as internships and co-ops. Flight technology and aerospace—and turning out future astronauts—are long-time specialties.

Successful Indiana colleges typically have three things in common: a solid agricultural program, a powerhouse basketball team, and a conservative student body. Purdue University has all of these—plus one of the nation's strongest engineering programs, and the distinction of having awarded more bachelor's degrees in the field than any other institution. Purdue is also home to the nation's first computer science department, and its programs in pharmacy, nursing, and management are top-notch. Budding classicists, dramatists, and literary critics probably should look elsewhere, as liberal arts are not Purdue's forte. But those seeking small-school friendliness with big-school spirit may be very happy here. "Purdue has great academic programs, incredible organizational and social opportunities, and an awesome sense of community," says one sophomore. "Boiler Up!"

Purdue is the main attraction in the small industrial town of West Lafayette, where the population triples when students return each fall. The campus features redbrick and limestone buildings arranged around lush shaded courtyards. Recent construction includes the Third Street Suites, a new residential facility. Purdue is also home to Amazon.com's first ever brick-and-mortar locations, where students are able to have textbooks shipped overnight to campus for no cost.

Students apply to and enroll in one of Purdue's 10 colleges, and academic requirements vary by school and major. Typically, they include English, math, a lab science, and foreign language proficiency. Management is the most popular major, followed by mechanical engineering, health and kinesiology, and biology. Students flock to the five-year engineering co-op program, one of the most competitive on campus, because it marries classroom study with real-world work. Purdue also offers three-year degree programs for five majors within the Brian Lamb School of Communication; the goal is to make college more affordable in fields where three-year degrees are feasible. Additionally, Purdue offers a strong undergraduate program in professional flight technology, which includes hands-on training at the university's own airport. Purdue has produced more than 20 astronauts, including Neil Armstrong and Gus Grissom. Students

> "[Purdue has] an awesome sense of community. Boiler Up!"

Website: www.purdue.edu
Location: Small City
Public
Total Enrollment: 35,849
Undergraduates: 28,108
Male/Female: 57/43
SAT Ranges: CR 520–630, M 560–700
ACT Ranges: 25–31
Financial Aid: 63%
Pell Grant: 15%
Expense: Pub $ $
Student Loans: 48%
Average Debt: $ $ $
Phi Beta Kappa: Yes
Applicants: 45,023
Accepted: 59%
Enrolled: 26%
Grad in 6 Years: 76%
Returning Freshmen: 92%
Academics: ✏ ✏ ✏ ½
Social: ☎ ☎ ☎
Q of L: ★ ★ ★
Admissions: (765) 494-1776
Email Address: admissions@purdue.edu

Strong Programs:
Management

Purdue is home to the nation's first computer science department.

in the retail management program may spend their junior year at the Fashion Institute of Technology (FIT) in New York and return to Purdue for their senior year. Upon completion of the four-year program, they receive both a Purdue bachelor's and FIT associates' degree. Twenty percent of students study abroad, and options are available for students in all majors in more than 60 countries. Undergraduates also participate in more than 2,000 research projects each year.

"The academic climate is fairly competitive and intense," says a sophomore. Despite the university's size, many freshman classes are seminar-style, taught by graduate students and academic advisors who help answer students' questions and provide career advice. "I've had some teachers who were phenomenal at connecting with the students and having them understand the concepts," one student confides, "and other teachers act like they are presenting to an empty room."

"The students here are very academically focused and driven," says a junior. "They have fun and relax on weekends but everyone knows the reason we are here is to get a degree to be successful in the future." Purdue's undergraduate student body is fairly homogeneous, with 54 percent from Indiana, although there is a healthy proportion of international students, at 18 percent. Three percent are African American, 6 percent are Asian American, and 4 percent are Hispanic. Boilermaker pride does stretch across boundaries of race, gender, and socioeconomic background. Thousands of merit scholarships averaging $6,592 are awarded annually to qualified students; athletes vie for 240 scholarships in 16 sports. The Purdue Promise program grants financial assistance and specialized academic and leadership coaching to eligible Indiana residents from lower-income backgrounds.

Thirty-eight percent of students live in Purdue's residence halls; the numbers may be so low because of rules governing male and female visitation hours. (The

"The students here are very academically focused and driven."

notion of a "co-ed dorm" here means that both sexes share a lobby.) Almost all freshmen live on campus, though they aren't required to, and Harrison Hall is said to be a good pick for newbies. "Some are definitely nicer than others," a sophomore admits. "Many of them still do not have air-conditioning." Most upperclassmen find inexpensive housing just off campus. Those with a grumbling stomach are treated to tasty options on campus. "Our food is fantastic," cheers one junior. "It's all-you-can-eat." Walking and riding escorts, blue-light phones, and more than 40 campus police officers help students feel safe.

"The social life typically takes place on campus," reports one philosophy major. Alcohol is prohibited in dorms, and "people have been kicked out of the residence halls for being caught with alcohol," says a sophomore. Still, underage students get served at the frats, or—as at most schools—when friends over 21 are buying. Those of age may also frequent Harry's Chocolate Shop—a longtime bar, not a candy store. Greek life draws 18 percent of Purdue men and 20 percent of the women and offers many social opportunities. But there are other options too, including football, basketball, soccer, and baseball games. "Outside of class, you can do anything from skydiving, paintball, choir, rock climbing, salsa dancing—anything. It's up to you," encourages a senior mechanical engineering major. Purdue's more than 1,000 student organizations range from the BBQ society to professional development clubs.

Undergraduates participate in more than 2,000 research projects each year.

As far as college towns go, West Lafayette "would not exist if it weren't for Purdue," one student says. Another adds, "The surrounding area has a good social scene for those 21 [and over], with excellent bars and nightlife. There are also many great nearby restaurants within walking distance for all students." Chicago and Indianapolis are favored weekend destinations for students with cars, and each spring, a week of fun and parties leads up to the Grand Prix go-kart races. Students also look forward to the Bug Bowl, an annual event sponsored by Purdue's entomology department, including cricket-spitting and cockroach races.

Purdue's athletic facilities offer opportunities for weekend warriors and varsity athletes alike. Boilermaker pride manifests itself at Division I games of all types, especially when the opposing team is Indiana University, known derisively as "that school down south," in the annual struggle for the Old Oaken Bucket. Every year, the winner adds a link to a chain on the bucket in the shape of either an "I" or "P." Women's volleyball, men's basketball, and men's and women's golf and track and field are among the most competitive sports on campus. Thirty-three club sports and more than 40 intramurals are a big draw for those looking for friendly competition. Solar car racing and Rube Goldberg machine contests are some of the more popular activities among STEM students.

Happy students here have discovered that learning is fun when academics are mixed with a healthy dose of school spirit and general carousing. "Students obtain incredible jobs, make lifelong friendships, meet their future spouses, and have the best balance between academics and social life that you could find at a university," cheers one enthusiastic junior.

If You Apply To ➤

Purdue: Rolling admissions: Jan. 1. Financial aid: Mar. 1. (Priority financial aid: Jan. 1.) Housing: May 5. Application fee: $60. No campus or alumni interviews. SATs or ACTs: required. No Subject Tests. Letters of recommendation: recommended. Essay: required. Accepts the Common Application. Apply to particular schools or programs.

Queen's University: See page 371.

Quinnipiac University

275 Mount Carmel Avenue, Hamden, CT 06518

For those who can't get into Conn College or Trinity (CT), here comes Quinnipiac University to the rescue. Aggressive expansion of programs and facilities has put it on the map of New England liberal arts colleges with a preprofessional bent. Business and health sciences are big attractions, though Quinnipiac is best known to the public for its political polling. Midway between NYC and Boston.

Under the leadership of entrepreneurial president John L. Lahey, Quinnipiac University has experienced a massive growth spurt, including mushrooming enrollment, more than a dozen new graduate programs, a slate of new facilities, and two new campuses. While the expansion has helped to increase the school's national prominence, it hasn't come without some growing pains. Quinnipiac's debt load has quadrupled, elbow room is at a premium, and some complain that class sizes are too large. Still, administrators show no signs of slowing the school's rapid growth. Talented students from around the nation are attracted to the university's solid programs in health, communications, and business, and most seem to take Quinnipiac's explosive expansion in stride. Says a senior, "The campus is constantly evolving for the betterment of student life."

Quinnipiac's 250-acre Mount Carmel campus sits adjacent to Sleeping Giant Mountain State Park, with its 1,700 acres of hiking and walking trails, 90 minutes from New York City and two hours from Boston. The academic, student life, and residence hall buildings are built of traditional New England redbrick, and a large

Website: www.quinnipiac.edu
Location: Suburban
Private
Total Enrollment: 8,062
Undergraduates: 6,703
Male/Female: 39/61
SAT Ranges: CR 490–590, M 500–620
ACT Ranges: 22–27
Financial Aid: 84%
Pell Grant: 15%
Expense: Pr $ $
Student Loans: 67%
Average Debt: $ $ $ $

The newest majors include four flavors of engineering, and 17 new engineering labs have recently been completed.

center quad is surrounded by the library, the law school, the student center, the Lender School of Business Center, and the Echlin Center for Health Sciences. The landscape is enhanced by convenient walkways and broad lawns. The three-building College of Arts and Sciences Center features a spacious quad that overlooks Clark's pond and its family of swans. The Bernhard Library is home to one of the world's largest collections of art commemorating the Great Irish Famine. The 250-acre York Hill campus is just across Whitney Avenue. The North Haven campus (expansively updated from its origin as the headquarters of Anthem/Blue Cross), located four miles from the Mount Carmel Campus, serves as home to the Center for Medicine, Nursing, and Health Sciences, as well as the School of Education and the School of Law.

"The campus is constantly evolving for the betterment of student life."

Quinnipiac's liberal arts philosophy is evident in its general education curriculum, which includes three interdisciplinary freshman seminars, freshman composition, and quantitative literacy requirements. There is also a breadth requirement that includes 28 hours of foundational courses in the sciences, social sciences, humanities, and fine arts. All freshmen take part in QU 101, a common reading assignment that explores the role of the individual in the local community. "It gives the student an idea of how he or she fits into the community," a math major says.

Quinnipiac offers more than 50 undergraduate majors; the newest include four flavors of engineering (civil, industrial, software, and mechanical), and 17 new engineering labs have recently been completed to accommodate them. The most popular majors include health science studies, nursing, psychology, and communications. Physical therapy students enroll in a six-year, combined B.S./D.P.T. program, aspiring physician assistants may choose a six-year B.S./M.H.S., and there is also a combined B.S./M.O.T. in occupational therapy. The Lender School of Business offers strong programs in entrepreneurship and finance, while students in the School of Communications may enroll in the media production program, which emphasizes the technical aspects of digital media preproduction, production, and postproduction. The communications and journalism programs

"Just about every club or organization has some kind of volunteer program happening every semester."

also benefit from several university-owned media outlets, including two radio stations and a television station. The university is home to the renowned Quinnipiac Polling Institute, which regularly surveys residents of nine key swing states about political races, state and national elections, and issues of public concern.

"Students will find courses challenging, but reasonable," says a junior. Thirty-eight percent of all classes have fewer than 20 students, and "there are no massive lecture halls," says one journalism major. There are no TAs or graduate assistants, either; all classes are taught by professors. "The quality of teaching is stellar. Professors care about their students on a very personal level, and will always know your name," says a physical therapy major. Gifted students may enroll in the University Honors Program, which features special seminars, close relationships with professors, and a slew of enrichment and leadership opportunities. Internships and clinical experiences abound: communications students may elect to spend their summer on production sets or on-air, while political science majors have the opportunity to assist elected officials at the state capital or in Washington, D.C. Study abroad options include jaunts in France, England, Spain, Italy, and Australia; 12 percent of students take part. The semester program in Ireland, at University College Cork, is very popular in both the fall and the spring semesters.

Twenty-two percent of Quinnipiac's undergraduates come from Connecticut, and 3 percent come from foreign countries. "Each student at Quinnipiac is unique, but on the whole they are kind, respectful of one another, and enthusiastic," says a broadcast journalism major. The student body is 5 percent African American, 9 percent Hispanic, and 3 percent Asian American. Political and social issues aren't a huge concern on campus, students say. Qualified undergraduates receive merit awards averaging $15,389, and gifted athletes vie for 320 athletic scholarships in 21 sports.

Housing is guaranteed for four years to incoming freshmen, and 77 percent of students reside in school-owned housing. Freshmen and sophomores live on the Mount Carmel campus; freshmen can expect to live in triples and quads, while sophomores get suite-style housing. Juniors and seniors live on the York Hill campus and in nearby university-owned apartment complexes and residences. Students are required to purchase a meal plan, and food options at the main dining hall (Café Q) and the Bobcat Den get positive reviews. "I love that I can pay per item, so I can grab a snack without wasting an entire meal swipe like at other colleges," says a senior. As for campus security, one student says, "Officers are available 24/7 by phone, [and] are often seen walking or biking around campus." Another adds, "Quinnipiac is tackling sexual assault head-on, raising awareness during Sexual Assault Awareness Month (April) and creating a conversation about it on campus."

The Quinnipiac social scene is bustling. The campus hosts a variety of events, including guest speakers, concerts, comedians, and film screenings; there are also more than 150 student clubs to whet the appetite of those seeking a good time. "Getting involved made Quinnipiac home

The renowned Quinnipiac Polling Institute regularly surveys people about political races and issues of public concern.

"The Yale rivalry is fierce, and student pride comes alive."

to me and really enhanced my collegiate experience," says a senior. The university sponsors two fraternities and three sororities; 24 percent of the men and 25 percent of the women go Greek. Quinnipiac is a "wet" campus—students 21 or older are allowed to possess alcohol in the dorms—but underage drinkers face stiff penalties. "The alcohol policy certainly stops things from getting out of hand," says one student.

When students tire of the campus scene, they trek into surrounding towns in search of fun. Hamden offers the usual mix of chain restaurants, movie theaters, and bowling alleys, although "many students like to take the free shuttle into New Haven to enjoy food, shopping, and the nightlife," says a junior. Eighty-six percent of students choose to get involved in the local community through volunteer work, including the Quinnipiac Future Teachers Organization and Habitat for Humanity. A student says, "Just about every club or organization has some kind of volunteer program happening every semester."

The Quinnipiac Bobcats field 21 Division I teams—7 for men and 14 for women—and all compete in the Metro Atlantic Athletic Conference, except for men's and women's ice hockey, which compete in the powerful Eastern College Athletic Conference. The university recently agreed to expand athletic opportunities for women (and keep women's volleyball) to settle a legal battle. Women's rugby brought home a national championship in 2016, and recent conference champs include men's and women's ice hockey; women's tennis, golf, and cross-country; and men's lacrosse. Nothing brings out the Bobcat faithful like the annual hockey match versus rival Yale. "The Yale rivalry is fierce, and student pride comes alive," says a student. Eighty percent of students join Quinnipiac's "large and very popular intramural sports program," which includes competition in more than a dozen sports.

The Quinnipiac Bobcats field 21 Division I teams—7 for men and 14 for women.

"The feeling of community is why I chose Quinnipiac University, and why I would recommend it to prospective students," says one junior. New campuses, expanding academics, and increased selectivity are all part of the university's continuing mission to attract bright students. It's an expensive gamble that administrators and students feel will pay off. "There are more resources here than I can think of," says one satisfied student. "Any student who wants to succeed will succeed."

Overlaps

University of Connecticut, University of Massachusetts Amherst, Sacred Heart, University of New Hampshire, Penn State, Fairfield, Ithaca, Syracuse

Randolph College

2500 Rivermont Avenue, Lynchburg, VA 24503

Co-ed since 2007, Randolph College continues to pursue its traditional mission of strong liberal arts programs in the spirit of its motto *Vita abundantior* (the life more abundant). Males now make up more than a third of undergrads. Its suburban location on the James River is rich in history, though of limited appeal to those of college age.

Website: www.randolphcollege.edu

Location: Suburban

Private

Total Enrollment: 673

Undergraduates: 661

Male/Female: 34/66

SAT Ranges: CR 460–570, M 450–550

ACT Ranges: 19–24

Financial Aid: 99%

Pell Grant: 34%

Expense: Pr $

Student Loans: 80%

Average Debt: $ $ $ $

Phi Beta Kappa: Yes

Applicants: 1,207

Accepted: 81%

Enrolled: 19%

Grad in 6 Years: 69%

Returning Freshmen: 78%

Academics: ✍ ✍ ✍

Social: ☎ ☎

Q of L: ★ ★ ★ ★

Admissions: 434-947-8100

Email Address: admissions@randolphcollege.edu

Strong Programs:
Biology
English
Art
Psychology
History

With rich traditions, cozy dorms, and challenging, seminar-based classes, Randolph College has preserved the best elements of its past while evolving into an institution that remains relevant today. The college, formerly known as Randolph–Macon Women's College, offers men and women a place to be themselves. "Fitting in isn't what Randolph is about," says a sophomore. "One of our mottoes is 'Be an Original,' and you can see that throughout the school."

The college's 100-acre campus sits in the historic neighborhood of Lynchburg, on the banks of the James River. Graceful old buildings are covered with purple wisteria and linked by glass corridors called trolleys; the surrounding trees burst into riotous bloom each spring. Main Hall, dating from 1893, houses dorm rooms, classrooms, and faculty and administrative offices. The Maier Museum of Art has one of the best college collections of American art in the country. The school's Riding Center offers indoor and outdoor arenas in the nearby Blue Ridge foothills.

Randolph's general education requirements are reflected in a matrix of study areas, with artistic expression, cultural inquiry, global issues, gender issues, and quantitative literacy and analysis on one axis, and arts and literature, humanities, natural sciences and math, wellness, and interdisciplinary courses on the other. "It forces you to explore different areas and take classes in almost every department," explains a sophomore. "I never thought I would major in psychology, but I took a psych class my spring semester and loved it!" All freshmen take the First-Year Seminar, which examines how to maximize academic success, and participate in the Passport Program, which orients them to campus resources and events. Every major culminates in a senior-year capstone experience.

> "Fitting in isn't what Randolph is about. One of our mottoes is 'Be an Original.'"

Biology, English, art, psychology, and history are some of the most popular majors at Randolph—and among the school's best departments. Programs in global studies, sport and exercise studies, and dance are also well regarded. A program in American culture combines classroom study with guest speakers and visits to historic sites; in past years, topics have focused on the Deep South, American capitalism, and the Lewis and Clark expedition. SUPER (Step Up to Physical Science and Engineering at Randolph) is an immersive scholarship program for first-year students emphasizing science, math, and engineering. In addition to a two-week residential academic program in the summer, students receive specialized academic services and mentoring.

"The academic climate of the school is collaborative without losing its competitive edge," says a sophomore, and a senior adds that the workload is "just heavy enough to promote academic growth, but still reasonable enough to keep you sane." The student-run Honor System has been in effect for more than a hundred years. Since 85 percent of classes enroll fewer than 20 students, and there are no TAs, it's easy for students to form friendships with their professors. "The professors genuinely care that the students learn the material and even have fun doing it," one student says.

Randolph makes cocurricular opportunities a priority, and all students are eligible to apply for a $2,000 RISE grant, which they can use to fund research, international travel, and other academic pursuits. Those interested in research may compete to assist professors with ongoing projects during an eight-week summer session, and many present their findings at the National Conference on Undergraduate Research. Twenty-two percent of students study abroad, many in the school's flagship program at the University of Reading in England, and others in programs that are thematic in nature, such as examining peace studies in Nagasaki and Hiroshima. The college also participates in the Seven-College Exchange*, the Tri-College Exchange, and in American University's Washington Semester program*. Two-thirds of Randolph students secure off-campus internships, with organizations from the Chicago Lyric Opera and London's Imperial College to businesses such as clothing maker Tommy Hilfiger.

"Students are very charged and passionate about equal rights," says one student. "Sometimes I feel like I'm in the midst of a socialist movement." Sixty percent of Randolph students hail from Virginia, and 82 percent graduated from public schools; 8 percent are international. Minorities have a notable presence, with African Americans comprising 12 percent of the student body, Hispanics 5 percent, and Asian Americans 2 percent. Socioeconomic diversity is present on campus as well, with 34 percent of students qualifying for Pell Grants. Randolph awards merit scholarships averaging $20,886 each year, but there are no athletic awards.

"The academic climate of the school is collaborative without losing its competitive edge."

Eighty-four percent of Randolph students live in the dorms, many of which have "high ceilings, carpet or hardwood floors, and large windows with crown molding," according to one history major. Everyone gets a room, eventually, though one student cautions that room draw in the spring can take a long time to sort out. Main Hall, a.k.a. "the Hilton," is the largest dorm, and its central location makes it the most convenient. As for campus dining, a biology major says, "The actual dining hall is very nice; the food is mediocre at best." Security officers patrol continuously and take pride in knowing students by name, and a sophomore says, "The college is very intent on making sexual assault as nonexistent as possible on the campus."

"The surrounding area does offer a good social scene, but the real scene is inside the Red Brick Wall. We have a number of secret societies, clubs, and other social organizations," says a sophomore. The Macon Activities Council makes sure no one is bored by hosting comedians, bands, and other entertainers, as well as talent shows and outdoor parties. Randolph's close-knit community can get too close at times (a junior warns, "You may learn things about your personal life from other people before you knew them yourself"), so students occasionally escape to other nearby colleges like Hampden–Sydney, Washington and Lee, and the University of Virginia, for those seeking frat parties and football. Underage drinking is prohibited at Randolph, in accordance with both law and the honor code, and there is no Greek life, but sports teams and other organizations offer a moderate party scene.

(continued)
Global Studies
Sport and Exercise Studies
Dance

The Maier Museum of Art has one of the best college collections of American art in the country.

All students are eligible to apply for a $2,000 RISE grant, which they can use to fund research, international travel, and other academic pursuits.

Randolph traditions include the Even/ Odd class rivalry, Ring Week, and the Pumpkin Parade.

The town of Lynchburg (population 80,000) hosts two other colleges and has a shopping mall and some retail chains like Target and Barnes & Noble, but

"The real [social] scene is inside the Red Brick Wall." is otherwise "less than exhilarating," says a biology major. Most clubs in the area are 21 and over, and the restaurants, stores, and movie theaters are closed by 10 p.m. Thankfully, the college's coffee bar satisfies students' caffeine cravings. Students often get involved in the local community via volunteering.

Randolph's WildCats compete in Division III, and the school's top rival is Lynchburg College. The softball team is the most competitive of the women's sports; men's soccer is solid too. But more than athletic contests, students look forward to Randolph traditions, such as the Even/Odd class rivalry, Ring Week (in which a freshman anonymously decorates the door of a junior and leaves small gifts all week, culminating with a scavenger hunt for their class ring), and the Pumpkin Parade (during which sophomores present lit jack-o'-lanterns to seniors, who show them off in an evening parade). The Never-Ending Weekend each fall includes both a formal and the annual Tacky Party, for which tasteless attire is *de rigueur*.

The students of Randolph aren't shy about their academic goals, career drive, or sense of campus unity. "The college went co-ed years ago and so the population changed," says one student. "But the core dynamic and value system did not. Students still value respect and responsibility."

Overlaps

Virginia Commonwealth, Lynchburg, Randolph–Macon, Roanoke, James Madison

If You Apply To ➤

Randolph: Early action: Nov. 15. Regular decision: Mar. 1. Financial aid: Apr. 1. (Priority deadline: Feb. 1.) Housing: May 1. No application fee. Campus interviews: recommended, informational. Alumni interviews: optional, informational. SATs or ACTs: required. Subject Tests: optional. Letters of recommendation: optional. Essay: optional. Accepts the Common Application with supplement.

University of Redlands

1200 East Colton, P.O. Box 3080, Redlands, CA 92373

If you like the thought of palm trees against a backdrop of snow-covered peaks, Redlands may be your place. As a "university," Redlands is double the size of Occidental and Whittier. The alternative Johnston Center for Integrative Studies makes an odd contrast to the buttoned-down conservatism of the rest of Redlands.

Website: www.redlands.edu
Location: Small City
Private
Total Enrollment: 4,168
Undergraduates: 2,698
Male/Female: 42/58
SAT Ranges: CR 510–610, M 510–610
ACT Ranges: 22–28
Financial Aid: 91%
Pell Grant: 24%
Expense: Pr $ $ $

Amid the dozens of gigantic and well-known universities in the state of California stands the University of Redlands. With its innovative living/learning college and strong preprofessional emphasis, this versatile school is one of higher education's better-kept secrets, and a place where students receive all the personal attention and intellectual stimulation they could want. One student describes it as a "small liberal arts college in sunny Southern California with great financial aid packages."

The University of Redlands's 160-acre campus, covered in majestic oak trees, is designed around "The Quad," a group of dorms that face one another. The two main landmarks are the Memorial Chapel and the administration building. Redlands's facilities are a mixture of older, more historical columned buildings and more modern, renovated ones. The view from the college can only be described as breathtaking. Mountain ranges form the backdrop, and neighboring Big Bear Lake and

Arrowhead ski resorts give endless getaway opportunities. Also nearby are the San Gorgonio Wilderness and Joshua Tree National Park.

Redlands's most distinctive attribute is the experimental living/learning college, where students create their own course of study and are judged by professor and self-evaluations rather than grades. The Johnston Center for Integrative Studies was established in 1969 to function as an "alternative" college within a traditional setting; now that it is a program rather than a separate college, about 10 percent of the students take advantage of this opportunity. The program offers unusual academic freedom; there are no departments, majors, or distribution requirements. Instead, students "contract" with professors for their entire plan of study. At the beginning of each course, students make up the syllabus by consensus and then set their own research and writing goals. Each student develops four-year goals—which are reviewed by a student/faculty board for direction and breadth—within one or more broad areas: the social sciences, behavioral sciences, humanities, and fine and performing arts.

> "Education becomes a conversation, and students' original ideas are not only allowed but encouraged."

Compared with other Redlands students, Johnston undergrads have higher test scores, with average SATs that are 50 to 75 points above the Redlands median. One student explains, "Johnston Center students tend to be independent thinkers, self-motivated, and [don't] take classes just because they have to." Recent participants have designed degrees such as urban agriculture, social behavior across cultures, and neuroscience of oneirology.

Aside from Johnston, Redlands is unusual among liberal arts institutions mainly in that it also offers preprofessional programs. The schools of education and music provide strong career training, as does the excellent program in communicative disorders. The environmental studies program consists of courses in natural science, humanities, and social science, focusing on values-based environmental problem solving. Premed/prehealth and prelaw students receive advising on requirements for graduate school. Redlands has also emerged as a national leader in science curriculum reform. Business is the most popular major, followed by environmental studies, biology, and communicative disorders. Regardless of major, all students must take a freshman seminar and complete a capstone requirement in order to graduate.

> "The breadth of student involvement and diversity of activities at Redlands is almost overwhelming."

"I love Redlands's small, discussion-based classes," says a Johnston Center student. "Education becomes a conversation, and students' original ideas are not only allowed but encouraged." Sixty-three percent of classes have fewer than 20 students, meaning "interaction with professors is common and camaraderie is abundant," says a psychology and Spanish double major. Professors are said to be very accessible outside of class too, even occasionally coming by the dorms for "fireside chats." With its 4–4–1 calendar, Redlands affords students the option to take one intensive course each May, and some use this time to study abroad. Students may embark on Redlands's signature programs in Salzburg, Austria, or Oaxaca, Mexico, or choose from among 100 other options worldwide; 58 percent study abroad. The highly acclaimed freshman seminar program places small groups of first-year students with some of the school's best professors, while the selective honors program enables outstanding students to work individually with professors.

"Redlands students are bright, friendly, and involved," says one senior. Sixty-nine percent of the student body come from within the state, creating a mellow, Southern California atmosphere on campus. The climate is a definite plus, with temperatures rarely below 50 degrees. The typical Redlands student tends to be fairly

(continued)

Student Loans: 74%
Average Debt: $ $ $
Phi Beta Kappa: Yes
Applicants: 4,790
Accepted: 68%
Enrolled: 16%
Grad in 6 Years: 72%
Returning Freshmen: 85%
Academics: ✍ ✍ ✍
Social: ☎ ☎ ☎
Q of L: ★ ★ ★
Admissions: (909) 748-8074
Email Address: admissions@ redlands.edu

Strong Programs:
Business
Environmental Studies
Biology
Communicative Disorders
Education
Music
Integrative Studies

Recent Johnston Center participants have designed degrees such as urban agriculture and neuroscience of oneirology.

conservative, although the student body as a whole "is not the most politically engaged," according to one senior. Three percent of students are international, and the racial makeup of the school is diverse, with Hispanics representing 27 percent, Asian Americans 6 percent, and African Americans 5 percent. Redlands annually awards a variety of merit scholarships averaging $12,360. There are talent awards in art, writing, music, and theater, but there are no athletic scholarships. Twenty-four percent of incoming students are Pell eligible.

Sixty-five percent of the students live in the residence halls, and a senior raves, "The quality of our residence halls is spectacular even without AC. The university does an amazing job at creating a community." Most of the residence halls are co-ed, and other housing options include on-campus apartments and student-run co-ops. Students enjoy their food at the Irvine Commons or Plaza Café, part of the Hunsaker University Center, which has a "town square" atmosphere. Students praise Redlands's safety and its approach to sexual assault prevention; says one, "My school has taken measures to protect students by being very transparent with them."

Social life mostly takes place on campus, and a senior says, "The breadth of student involvement and diversity of activities at Redlands is almost overwhelming."

"Students are given such access to opportunity that it should be celebrated."

Local fraternities and sororities claim 13 percent of the men and 20 percent of the women, respectively, and their generally well-controlled parties are open to all. Alcohol is accessible but "there is no pressure to drink or party," according to one senior. The nearby city of Redlands offers a variety of coffee shops and restaurants, and students are highly involved in the local community, contributing more than 120,000 hours of service each year. As the Southern California heat and smog can become unpleasant, road trips to Los Angeles, Palm Springs, San Francisco, and even Mexico are common.

The University of Redlands sponsors 21 intercollegiate teams, all of which consistently vie for spots among the top of the Division III Southern California Intercollegiate Athletic Conference (SCIAC). Men's and women's soccer and women's golf are recent conference champs; men's and women's tennis and track and field, women's cross-country, and women's swimming and diving are also competitive. Games against rival Occidental always draw crowds, and the "Och Tamale" school chant—a string of "complete gibberish" invented in 1921 in mockery of Oxy's Latin chant—is a beloved school tradition ("Och tamale gazolly gazump!"). Half of students participate in at least one intramural sport, and weekend adventurers strike out on regular excursions organized by Outdoor Programs.

The University of Redlands is a lot of different things to a lot of different people. With 170 faculty members, it manages to be a preprofessional institute, a liberal arts college, and an alternative school all in one. The Johnston Center is clearly a path to travel for the innovative individualist, but even those who don't join Johnston can find what they want and need at Redlands. As one senior enthuses, "Students are given such access to opportunity that it should be celebrated."

Reed College

3203 S.E. Woodstock Boulevard, Portland, OR 97202

Reed is a West Coast version of Grinnell or Oberlin, mixing nonconformist students with a traditional and rigorous curriculum. Sends huge numbers of grads on to Ph.D.s. Students who were square pegs in high school often find Reed a square hole.

Reed College is one of the most intellectual colleges in the country. It's the place where the late Steve Jobs—cofounder of Apple—attended for a semester before dropping out to rule the world and where students complain that the library, which closes its doors at midnight on Fridays and Saturdays, shuts down too early. Letter grades are de-emphasized as a form of evaluation. Instead, students receive lengthy and detailed commentaries from professors, which fosters continued dialogue and eliminates grade inflation. "Reed is the absolute best place for someone who likes to think, to read, to question, and to work," says a student. "It's a community of scholars."

Located in Southeast Portland, Reed's 116-acre campus boasts rolling lawns, winding lanes, a canyon creek, and protected wetlands. A fish ladder was installed to help salmon reach their spawning grounds, and nonnative plants are being removed from the area to protect the natural habitat. In addition to the canyon, the campus hosts 125 different species of trees. Two thousand majestic arbors shade a mix of original campus buildings, constructed of brick, slate, and limestone in the Tudor Gothic style, as well as lodges in the homey Northwest Timber style and some more modern facilities, such as the Performing Arts Building. Major renovations are underway to Reed's older residence halls and its sports center.

Although Reed emphasizes personal freedom and responsibility, especially through its Honor Principle, the curriculum and academic requirements are remarkably traditional. Freshmen must complete Humanities 110, a yearlong interdisciplinary course focused on society and culture in classical Greece, imperial Rome, and the ancient Mediterranean. The course, which has been taught for more than 50 years and creates a shared intellectual experience for new students, draws on the expertise of 25 professors, including some of Reed's most senior and distinguished faculty.

> "Reed is the absolute best place for someone who likes to think, to read, to question, and to work."

Students must also take courses in four "breadth" areas: literature, philosophy, religion, and the arts; history, social sciences, and psychology; the natural sciences; and mathematics, logic, linguistics, or foreign languages. Seniors must submit a research-based thesis to graduate. On the due date, just after spring classes have ended, seniors march from the library steps to the registrar's office in the Thesis Parade. This marks the beginning of Renn Fayre (originally "Renaissance Fayre"), a weekend-long celebration that involves a bug-eating contest, Glow Opera, and live human chess.

"The academics here are very rigorous, but not highly competitive," says an economics major. Reed's most popular majors include biology, English, psychology, and art. Dual-degree (3–2) programs are offered in engineering, computer science, and forestry/environmental science. Students take full advantage of the range of academic options, which often keep them tethered to their computers and study carrels. You'll never find a TA at the lectern here or leading a group discussion, so students rarely attend class unprepared for the lively intellectual banter that typically ensues between inquiring and active minds. Reed has "the best profs from anywhere around," says a psychology major. "They want to be at Reed, meaning that their top priority is teaching." Reed has improved its retention and graduation rates considerably in the last decade or two by becoming more selective in admissions,

Website: www.reed.edu
Location: Small City
Private
Total Enrollment: 1,388
Undergraduates: 1,388
Male/Female: 46/54
SAT Ranges: CR 670–760, M 620–720
ACT Ranges: 29–33
Financial Aid: 53%
Pell Grant: 17%
Expense: Pr $ $ $ $
Student Loans: 53%
Average Debt: $
Phi Beta Kappa: Yes
Applicants: 5,396
Accepted: 35%
Enrolled: 22%
Grad in 6 Years: 79%
Returning Freshmen: 88%
Academics: ✑ ✑ ✑ ✑ ½
Social: ☎ ☎ ☎
Q of L: ★ ★ ★ ½
Admissions: (503) 777-7511
Email Address: admission@reed.edu

Strong Programs:
Biology
English
Psychology
Art
Environmental Science
Physics
Mathematics

increasing on-campus housing for a stronger residential community, and bolstering student support services, including a popular peer tutoring program.

Despite Reed's small size—80 percent of the courses taken by undergraduates have fewer than 20 students—the school offers unsurpassed research opportunities in the liberal arts and sciences. Budding physicists and environmental scientists can work with college staff at the 250-kilowatt Triga nuclear reactor after passing an Atomic Energy Commission examination. "Reed has a fantastic science program for a liberal arts school," says one physics major. "The sciences are an active and thriving branch of inquiry." Reed also has a tradition of respect for calligraphy that, among other things, inspired Steve Jobs to build traditional graphics into Apple computers. Fifty-two exchange programs attract 23 percent of each graduating class, taking students to 22 countries, from Germany and China to Ecuador and Russia. Reed also offers domestic exchange programs with Howard, Sarah Lawrence, and the Woods Hole Oceanographic Institute. Over the years, a quarter of Reed's grads have gone on for Ph.D.s—the highest percentage of any liberal arts college in the country.

On the senior thesis due date, seniors march from the library steps to the registrar's office in the Thesis Parade.

"Students who attend Reed are ridiculous, silly, cerebral, passionate, critical, and questioning," says one observant Reedie. "If we have one thing in common, we are people whose lives center on learning." While Reed is located in Oregon, its quirky brand of intellectualism means only 9 percent of the students are in-staters. Ten percent hail from other nations. Five percent are Asian American, 12 percent are Hispanic, and 2 percent are African American. "The Multicultural Resource Center provides resources—guest speakers, lecturers, Tuesday Talks, and more—to keep diversity an ongoing discussion on campus," says an English major. When it comes to political and social issues, "Students are very, very, very liberal," according to one sophomore, and another student cites "racial, gender, low socioeconomic status, and LGBTQ+ issues on and off campus" as particularly important. All financial aid at Reed is need-based, and the school covers 100 percent of admitted students' demonstrated need.

"Reed has a fantastic science program for a liberal arts school."

Sixty-seven percent of Reed students live on campus. "The dorms are comfortable and the staff keeps them clean and in shape," reports one senior. Some rooms feature such homey touches as fireplaces or balconies. Freshmen are guaranteed housing, and usually get divided doubles; upperclassmen get singles. There are six language houses (French, German, Russian, Spanish, Chinese, and Arabic) and each is staffed with a native speaker. For those who lose out in the housing lottery, or upperclassmen seeking a taste of post-college independence, off-campus houses are cheap and plentiful. On-campus students must buy the meal plan, and students say outside caterer Bon Appétit does a good job. "The food is surprisingly good and diverse," one student says, "and the kitchen is happy to help with any particular dietary needs." As for campus security, "I know the community safety officers on campus," says one student. "They aren't uniformed nameless entities patrolling dorms." Another adds, "Our student body really promotes a strong culture of [sexual] consent."

Students look forward to Paideia, a weeklong program of wacky, noncredit alternative classes before spring semester begins.

"There's always a ton going on, both on campus and off. On campus, there are always small parties, or plays, or giant Student Union dances, or fire-dancing shows, or bands playing," says one student. Something of a drug culture persists on campus, although the administration—led by the current president, a former Oregon attorney general who presumably knows something about drug enforcement—is making vigorous efforts to uphold the drug and alcohol policies governed by the college's Honor Principle. Students look forward to Paideia (which means "education" in Ancient Greek), a weeklong program of wacky, noncredit alternative classes before spring semester begins. Past Paideia workshops have

"Portland is a college student's dream come true."

ranged from Bollywood dance and the history of Batman to how to speak with a French accent. Each April, students celebrate Nitrogen Day, honoring our atmosphere's most plentiful—and underappreciated—element.

Reed owns a ski cabin on Mount Hood that sleeps 15.

"Portland is a college student's dream come true," raves one student. "There is live music every night, a steady stream of literary events, and constant film screenings." Many students get involved in community service projects organized by SEEDS (Students for Education, Empowerment, and Direct Service). Reed students love to road-trip—whether to the mammoth Powell's bookstore downtown (about a 15-minute drive) or to Oregon's coastal beaches, mountains, or high desert, all about two hours away. The school also owns a ski cabin on Mount Hood that sleeps 15.

The closest thing Reed has to a school mascot is the Doyle Owl, a 300-pound concrete sculpture that dorms regularly plot to steal from one another. While Reed doesn't have varsity athletics, club teams in basketball, rugby, soccer, and ultimate Frisbee do compete with other clubs in the area. A variety of intramural and recreational sports are available for the less competitive, such as mountaineering, rowing, and curling. Reedies must also fulfill a three-semester-long physical education requirement.

Reed attracts seriously intellectual, unconventional students, but it is not without a sense of humor—the school's unofficial, tongue-in-cheek slogan is "Atheism, Communism, Free Love." If you're a lover of learning who prefers to spend Saturday nights with your nose in a book, this Portland school is definitely worth a look. "Reed is a really special place," says one sociology major. "Being able to go through college with the brilliant and interesting people I get to call my friends has been a privilege in and of itself."

Overlaps

Brown, University of Chicago, Lewis & Clark, UC–Berkeley, Stanford, Columbia, Yale, Oberlin

If You Apply To ➤

Reed: Early decision I: Nov. 15. Early decision II: Dec. 20. Regular decision and financial aid: Jan. 1. Housing: Jun. 15. No application fee. Campus and alumni interviews: recommended, evaluative. SATs or ACTs: required. Subject Tests: optional. Letters of recommendation: required. Essay: required. Accepts the Common Application with supplement.

Rensselaer Polytechnic Institute

110 Eighth Street, Troy, NY 12180

If you can spell Rensselaer, you've already got a leg up on many applicants. RPI is one of the nation's great technical universities—along with Caltech, Harvey Mudd, MIT, and Worcester Polytech—and one of the most innovative. The beauty of RPI is the chance for hands-on learning and synergy between technology and management. Building boom and faculty hiring spree have raised its profile, and now much more selective in admission than a few years ago.

It would be an exaggeration to say that technology is god at RPI, though the school's conversion of a Gothic chapel into a computer lab does hint in that direction. Even if it's not deified, technology remains omnipresent at this school, which pioneered the teaching of calculus via computer in the early '90s. Students attend class in fully wired studio classrooms where they work on team projects and collaborate to solve real-world problems. Since 1998, the institute has more than doubled its research funding, and it's one of six original National Science Foundation Nanotechnology Centers in the country. For students who may have been known as geeks in high school, coming to Rensselaer is like coming home.

Website: www.rpi.edu
Location: Suburban
Private
Total Enrollment: 6,798
Undergraduates: 5,778
Male/Female: 69/31
SAT Ranges: CR 610–720, M 670–770

(continued)

ACT Ranges: 28–32
Financial Aid: 89%
Pell Grant: 17%
Expense: Pr $ $ $ $
Student Loans: 68%
Average Debt: $ $ $
Phi Beta Kappa: Yes
Applicants: 17,752
Accepted: 42%
Enrolled: 19%
Grad in 6 Years: 81%
Returning Freshmen: 94%
Academics: ✍ ✍ ✍ ✍
Social: ☎ ☎ ☎
Q of L: ★ ★ ★
Admissions: (518) 276-6216
Email Address: admissions@ rpi.edu

Strong Programs:
Engineering
Computer and Information Sciences
Business/Marketing
Biological Sciences
Mechanical Engineering
Aeronautical Engineering
Architecture

The Computational Center for Nanotechnology Innovations is among the world's most powerful university-based supercomputers.

Set high on a bluff overlooking Troy, New York, Rensselaer's 260-acre campus mixes modern research facilities and classical, ivy-covered brick buildings dating to the turn of the century. Almost the entire campus is wireless, allowing students to study and collaborate with each other from anywhere on campus. The cutting-edge Center for Biotechnology and Interdisciplinary Studies houses more than 400 researchers in biotechnology and related disciplines who work in such areas as regenerative medicine, bioinformatics, biocatalysis, metabolic engineering, and others.

In order to graduate, all students must complete at least 24 credits in humanities and social sciences, as well as at least 24 credits in physical, life, and engineering sciences; a minimum of 30 credits in their majors; and two communication-intensive courses, including one writing-intensive course. RPI made its reputation as one of the

"[Professors] bring a personal, applicable perspective to the material they teach."

nation's premier engineering schools and continues to excel in traditional favorites such as mechanical and aeronautical engineering, as well as newer specialties like environmental and computer systems engineering. Engineering majors tend to be the most popular, followed by computer and information sciences, business/marketing, and biological sciences. Architecture is also a strength. The nuclear engineering department has its own linear accelerator, while graduate and undergraduate students participate in research at the Center for Industrial Innovation. The Computational Center for Nanotechnology Innovations is among the world's most powerful university-based supercomputers and is designed to advance semiconductor technology to the nanoscale.

RPI's Lally School of Management and Technology combines elements of a business school with the latest technical applications. Entrepreneurship is one of its specialties; budding entrepreneurs from all majors may participate in a business incubator program, a support system for start-up companies run by Rensselaer students and alumni. RPI is a national leader in the study and application of electronic media and offers a B.S. program in electronic arts. The B.S. program in information technology attracts top students who often combine it with coursework in e-commerce or the arts. Majors in the humanities and social sciences are limited, and their quality is directly related to their applicability to technical fields. Students with long-term professional goals may enter a seven-year dual-degree program in medicine; a six-year program in law; or four- and five-year master's programs in biology, geology, or mathematical science.

"The courses are challenging, but not completely overwhelming," says one junior. About three-quarters of Rensselaer students are undergraduates, a high percentage for a top engineering school; because of this, RPI has worked hard to ensure that classes are smaller and more attention is paid to individual needs. Fifty-four percent of classes enroll fewer than 20 students. "The professors are all involved in research and so they bring a personal, applicable perspective to the material they teach," a student says. Students say career counseling and academic advising are also helpful.

Juniors and seniors enjoy self-paced courses and occasionally paid positions helping with faculty research. For students who can't wait to start working, popular co-op programs in more than a dozen fields help them earn both money and credit.

"Politics? Not so much on this campus."

Although most engineering schools discourage studying abroad, Rensselaer expects and encourages undergrads to participate in some sort of international study, internship, or service-learning experience, offering study and exchange programs in more than 15 countries on four continents.

Thirty-three percent of RPI students are New Yorkers, and 11 percent are international. Seventy-two percent ranked in the top 10th of their high school class.

RPI is fairly diverse, with Asian Americans comprising 10 percent of the student body, African Americans 3 percent, and Hispanics 8 percent. "The students at RPI are driven and motivated. They want to get ahead and change the world," says one student. Despite that ambition, RPI is far from a center of political activism; students say they're just too busy. "Politics? Not so much on this campus," says a student. The biggest campus issue may be choosing the Grand Marshal, who oversees a boisterous weeklong carnival celebrating campus elections, during which professors are barred from giving tests. Merit scholarships averaging $17,156 are available, as are 41 athletic scholarships.

Fifty-seven percent of students live in university residence halls; freshmen and sophomores are required to live on campus as part of the student life model known as Clustered Learning, Advocacy, and Support for Students. The program features common living arrangements and a team of faculty and peer advisors with the aim of creating smaller, more tightly knit student communities. "The freshman dorms are pretty typical but the upper-class residence halls are great," one senior reports. Upperclassmen may keep their current room, enter the lottery to get something better, or live in college-owned apartments off campus, widely considered the nicest option. A business management major says, "Public safety does a great job and they are very underappreciated."

Rensselaer encourages undergrads to have some sort of international study, internship, or service-learning experience.

"Hockey at RPI equals insanity."

A senior says, "There are things to do on campus, but a majority of the social students go to celebrations in the Greek houses and off-campus apartments." Thirty percent of men and 16 percent of women go Greek and, other than Greek parties, weekend options at RPI include sporting events, live entertainment, concerts, movies, and a half-dozen local pubs—some of which students find easily accept fake IDs. Those under 21 can't have alcohol in the dorms, and fraternities aren't allowed to have "containers of mass distribution" (i.e., kegs) at parties; students say alcohol isn't an issue on campus. Extracurricular clubs, organized around such interests as chess, dance, judo, and skiing, are chartered and funded by a student-managed body that doles out more than $8 million annually.

Freshmen and sophomores are required to live on campus in common living arrangements with a team of faculty and peer advisors.

Free shuttle buses run regularly from campus to downtown Troy, a former industrial revolution town, but there aren't many good reasons to make the trip. "Troy is not a college town," says a senior, "but it does have good places to eat and some beautiful parks." Students and Greek groups get involved with community service projects, and the town offers opportunities for internships. Rensselaer has helped generate economic growth in Troy by investing in the downtown area and providing grants to homebuyers. A six-screen movie theater is within easy reach, and for a taste of bigger-city nightlife, Albany is a half-hour drive. For scenic excursions, the Berkshires, Catskills, Adirondacks, Lake George, Lake Placid, the Saranac Lakes, Montreal, and Boston are popular destinations.

The athletic scene at Rensselaer revolves around hockey, hockey, hockey—the school's only team playing in Division I. One of the biggest weekends of the year is Big Red Freakout, when all festivities center around cheering on the beloved Big Red. "Hockey at RPI equals insanity," one student

"Students at RPI are all a little bit nerdy, and proud of it."

says. "If you go to one hockey game all season, go to the men's hockey season opener. The place is packed with rowdy RPI students who scream and chant in unison." Other varsity teams play in Division III, and the football, baseball, men's and women's basketball, and women's field hockey teams are most successful. There are many intramural sports to choose from, but the most popular may be the D-level hockey team (meaning "I really don't know how to play this," says a junior).

Rensselaer provides cutting-edge technology to students constantly wondering how things work. Computer geeks and video game junkies aren't the only ones who will find a home at RPI—students who thrive on teamwork and collaboration will also find it to their liking. RPI students work hard, sometimes to the detriment of a social life, but they don't seem to mind. Says a computer engineering major, "Students at RPI are all a little bit nerdy, and proud of it."

<table>
<tr><td>If You Apply To ➤</td><td>RPI: Early decision I: Nov. 1. Early decision II: Dec. 15. Regular decision: Jan. 15. Financial aid: Feb. 1. Application fee: $70. No campus or alumni interviews. SATs or ACTs: required. Subject Tests: optional (required for all accelerated program applicants). Letters of recommendation: required. Essay: required. Apply to particular program. Accepts the Common Application with supplement.</td></tr>
</table>

University of Rhode Island

Kingston, RI 02881

URI is a smallish alternative to UConn and UMass. With Boston, Providence, and vacation hot spot Newport within easy reach, there is plenty to do. Strong programs include engineering, marine sciences, nursing, and pharmacy. Nearly half of URI's students are out-of-staters.

Website: www.uri.edu
Location: Small Town
Public
Total Enrollment: 14,035
Undergraduates: 12,213
Male/Female: 46/54
SAT Ranges: CR 500–590, M 510–600
ACT Ranges: 22–26
Financial Aid: 59%
Pell Grant: N/A
Expense: Pub $ $ $
Student Loans: 71%
Average Debt: $ $ $ $
Phi Beta Kappa: Yes
Applicants: 21,261
Accepted: 71%
Enrolled: 21%
Grad in 6 Years: 63%
Returning Freshmen: 84%
Academics: ✍ ✍
Social: 🐦 🐦 🐦 🐦
Q of L: ★ ★ ★
Admissions: (401) 874-7100
Email Address: admission@ uri.edu

Strong Programs:
Nursing
Communication Studies

No longer an unabashed party school, the University of Rhode Island has earned a reputation for challenging academics with an emphasis on innovation and inter-disciplinary learning. URI offers an environment in which students engage in service learning, do research with top faculty, and find a much heavier emphasis on alternative styles of learning. "Our college is an amazing place to learn, prosper, and have fun," boasts one sophomore.

URI's 1,200-acre campus is located in the small town of Kingston. Surrounded by farmland and only six miles from the coast, it is also within easy driving distance of cities such as Providence—the Renaissance City and home to Brown, the Rhode Island School of Design, and several other colleges and universities—Boston, and New York. The main academic buildings at URI, a mixture of modern and "old New England granite," surround a central quad on Kingston Hill. At the foot of Kingston Hill lie the athletic buildings and agricultural fields. Dozens of construction projects have been completed since 2014, and plans are in the works for a major upgrade to the College of Engineering facilities and a 500-bed residence hall.

New students initially enroll in the University College, which offers academic and career guidance, as well as advice on selecting from among required general education courses. All new students take URI 101, a one-credit course intended to acquaint them with support services, cocurricular activities, and academic majors and career options. After a year or two in University College, students choose more specialized colleges, such as the well-regarded College of Pharmacy. Programs in engineering, business, and marine sciences are also strong, and the most popular majors include nursing, communication studies, kinesiology, and psychology. Some programs—such as the international engineering dual-degree program, which combines degrees in engineering and a foreign language with a year abroad—require students to stay for five or six years, but many students graduate in four years. There is also a new Winter J Term session in January (students may earn up to 4 academic credits) as well as new undergraduate degrees in sustainable agriculture and Chinese.

> "Our college is an amazing place to learn, prosper, and have fun."

(continued)

Kinesiology
Psychology
Pharmacy
Engineering
Business
Marine Sciences

"The academic climate of URI is mostly collaborative, but there are definitely some competitive programs on campus," one senior says. Professors receive generally good marks for their teaching, but their accessibility can be hit or miss. "At times, it can be difficult to work with faculty, but overall there is always someone available to speak with you, as long as you have found a professor or faculty member who is invested in you and your studies," advises a marine affairs major. The Academic Enhancement Center, along with its Writing Center, provides active learning enhancement for all students through peer tutorials, course-specific collaborative learning projects, supplemental instructional sessions, and special programs for high-risk students.

URI offers nationally recognized international exchange programs with universities in such diverse locales as Australia, France, Korea, and Venezuela, as well as domestic exchange programs with state colleges and universities. Twenty percent of undergraduates participate in the more than 200 available programs each year. Students interested in research can collaborate on projects with multidisciplinary teams of faculty through established research partnerships, such as the Partnership for the Coastal Environment. The Center for Student Leadership Development offers for-credit leadership development classes, as well as conferences, retreats, and workshops.

The international engineering dual-degree program combines degrees in engineering and a foreign language with a year abroad.

Although URI gives preference to in-state students who meet certain requirements, 45 percent of the entering freshmen are from outside Rhode Island, including 2 percent from foreign countries. "Students here are involved and outgoing," one junior says. Minority enrollment stands at 5 percent African American, 9 percent Hispanic, and 3 percent Asian American. "There is no doubt about it that URI is a predominantly white institution," says one student of color, "but diversity comes in many shapes and forms. We are diverse when it comes to socioeconomic status, nationality, sexual orientation, political affiliation, gender, and many other ways." The university has been investing in resources to support diversity in recent years, and a senior says, "URI has great women's services as well as LGBTQ services," including a brand-new facility for the Gender and Sexuality Center. The academic profiles of the incoming class have risen steadily over the past 10 years, in large measure due to the Centennial and Merit Scholarship Programs for outstanding freshmen. Merit awards average $6,261, and athletes vie for 194 athletic scholarships in 22 sports.

Though most freshmen live on campus, 56 percent of all undergraduates choose to find off-campus digs. The majority of residence halls have recently been renovated, and hundreds of new bed spaces have been added. "Housing isn't the best aspect of URI," one student reports, but adds, "Some of the freshman dorms are gorgeous." About half of freshmen participate in living/learning communities in a variety of disciplines. Dining options include two new dining halls, and a junior says, "They are very accommodating for dietary restrictions." Another student adds, "Campus security does rounds around campus throughout the night."

"URI is mostly collaborative, but there are definitely some competitive programs on campus."

"Most of the social life takes place off campus," a senior says. "There is not much for underage students to do at night on campus." The campus coffeehouse hosts open-mic nights, and movie theaters, clubs, and malls beckon just off campus. Greek life attracts 17 percent of the men and 22 percent of the women. The student newspaper that covers it all has one of the most original names anywhere: *The Good 5¢ Cigar* (as in, "what this country needs is"). As for Kingston, it's a sleepy New England college town. "There is nothing in Kingston," complains one student, "but we are ten minutes from the beach and thirty minutes from Providence." Students get involved in the town through clubs or URI 101, which requires volunteer work. Newport, with its thriving social scene, is just 20 minutes away, and those feeling

About half of freshmen participate in living/learning communities in a variety of disciplines.

lucky can get to the Foxwoods Resort and Casino in 45 minutes. Other fun road trips include Boston (90 minutes) and New York City (four hours). Travel is facilitated by the fact that there is an Amtrak stop on campus.

Division I sports are big at Rhode Island, and basketball games are especially exciting. Midnight Madness (the team's first sanctioned practice of the year) is always well attended, and URI fans love it when the Rams defeat archrival Providence College. Recent Atlantic 10 conference champs include men's indoor and outdoor track and field, and men's soccer and baseball teams each reached the conference finals. Other solid teams include men's golf and women's rowing. A favorite student tradition is oozeball, an April volleyball tournament played in about two feet of mud. As befits the school's locale, sailing draws much interest, and the team regularly produces All-Americans.

URI offers students a large-school feel in a small state. Consistent efforts by the administration to invest in campus upgrades and new educational opportunities have paid off, evidenced by the changing face of the student body and their achievements. Once ground zero for wild drinking and carousing, students here now work hard to achieve good grades and lay the foundation of lifelong learning.

Overlaps

Boston University, University of Connecticut, University of Delaware, University of Massachusetts Amherst, Northeastern

If You Apply To >

URI: Early action: Dec. 1. Regular decision: Feb. 1. Financial aid: Mar. 1. Housing: May 1. Application fee: $65. No campus or alumni interviews. SATs or ACTs: required. No Subject Tests. Letters of recommendation: required. Essay: required. Accepts the Common Application with supplement.

Rhode Island School of Design

2 College Street, Providence, RI 02903

The nation's best-known art and design school, RISD sits on a hillside adjacent to Brown. The campus offers easy access to downtown Providence, but it can't match the location of rival Parsons in New York's Greenwich Village. Offers 16 undergraduate majors in architecture, fine arts, and design. Industrial design is also a specialty.

Website: www.risd.edu
Location: City Center
Private
Total Enrollment: 2,481
Undergraduates: 2,014
Male/Female: 32/68
SAT Ranges: CR 560–680, M 580–720
ACT Ranges: 25–32
Financial Aid: 39%
Pell Grant: N/A
Expense: Pr $ $ $
Student Loans: 48%
Average Debt: $ $ $
Phi Beta Kappa: No
Applicants: 2,516
Accepted: 36%

Founded in the late 19th century to address the country's need for more artisans and craftsmen, Rhode Island School of Design has grown into a premier arts incubator. It's a place where today's artists and designers gather to share ideas and create tomorrow's masterpieces and architectural icons. In fact, the cofounders of Airbnb, Brian Chesky and Joe Gebbia, met and developed their creative instincts here. RISD (pronounced "Rizdee") grants degrees in virtually every design-related topic, and like the varied curriculum, the students and their creations are as diverse as the colors on an artist's palette. The one thing everyone shares here is an intense workload and a highly competitive spirit. "RISD students are masochists," says one freshman.

Though you might expect an art school like RISD to occupy funky, futuristic buildings, the predominant look here is colonial New England. Set on the upgrade of College Hill, RISD sits at the edge of Providence's beautifully preserved historic district, adjacent to Brown University. Many campus buildings date from the 1700s and early 1800s; the mostly redbrick-and-white-trim group includes converted homes, a bank, and even an old church. Recent renovations have been made to the Illustration Studies Building as well as the building that houses the Apparel Design department.

While RISD looks traditionally New England on the outside, behind its historic walls lies something else entirely. Perhaps RISD's most prized facility is the RISD museum, a superlative collection of more than 91,000 works that includes everything from Roman and Egyptian art to works by Monet, Matisse, and Picasso. In addition, the Edna Lawrence Nature Lab allows for examining, exploring, and understanding patterns, structures, and interactions of design in nature. To graduate, students must be in residence for at least two years and must complete a final-year project. They must also finish 126 credit hours—54 in their major, 18 in the Experimental and Foundation Studies program (an integrated year of "functional and conceptual experiences" that leads to "an understanding of visual language"), 42 in the liberal arts (art and architecture history; English; history, philosophy, social sciences; some electives), and 12 in nonmajor electives.

(continued)

Enrolled: 51%

Grad in 6 Years: 89%

Returning Freshmen: 95%

Academics: ✍ ✍ ✍ ✍

Social: ☎ ☎

Q of L: ★ ★ ★

Admissions: (401) 454-6300

Email Address: admissions@ risd.edu

Strong Programs:

Illustration

Industrial Design

Architecture

Graphic Design

Film/Animation/Video

Painting

Photography

The most popular majors include illustration, industrial design, architecture, and graphic design. Students may choose to supplement their degrees with one of four concentrations in history of art and visual culture; history, philosophy, and the social sciences; literary arts and studies; and nature-culture-sustainability studies. RISD also offers cross-registration at adjacent

"I have had positive and supportive professors, but I have also had professors who lacked a sense of criticality."

Brown University for students seeking more diverse courses. Hands-on studio courses abound at RISD, and 76 percent of classes have fewer than 20 students. Still, a sophomore says, "Sometimes classes fill very quickly because they are really interesting, but there are always ample alternatives to choose from." While students at RISD don't "hit the books" in the traditional sense, the in-studio workload is considerable. "RISD is very intense with a huge workload. Students need to be willing to sacrifice some daily leisure to make sure work gets done," says a sophomore. Students say teaching here is generally good, although it can be a mixed bag. "The quality of teaching at RISD seems to be inconsistent," says a senior. "For the most part, I have had positive and supportive professors, but I have also had professors who lacked a sense of criticality." Career and academic counseling both get high marks.

During RISD's Wintersession, five weeks between the first and second semesters, students are encouraged to take courses outside their major. And each year, about 60 juniors and seniors venture to Rome for one of two six-month experiences offered through the European Honors Program, which provides independent study, projects with critics, and immersion in Italian culture. There is also an international exchange program where students study abroad at approved art institutions.

The Edna Lawrence Nature Lab allows for exploring patterns, structures, and interactions of design in nature.

RISD students (referred to as "RISDoids") come to Providence to form a distinctly urban mix of styles and personalities. "RISD students are amazing, talented, unique, diverse, and inclusive," says a painting major. A mere 5 percent of students are native Rhode Islanders, not surprising given the state's small size, while an impressive 26 percent hail from foreign countries. Though highly selective, RISD will sometimes take a chance on students who did not perform well in high school by the usual academic criteria but who make up for that with special artistic talent. The racial makeup of the campus is fairly mixed, with Asian Americans making up 19 percent of the student body, African Americans 2 percent, and Hispanics 8 percent. Overall, students say the campus is not politically charged. "There are students who

"On-campus housing is…grossly overpriced."

pay attention to world issues and incorporate them into their work, but we also exist in a bit of a bubble," says one student. Tuition and fees here are steep; though RISD offers a limited number of merit scholarships, athletic scholarships are nonexistent, and the school does not guarantee to meet financial need.

Sixty percent of undergraduates reside on campus; all noncommuting freshmen must live in co-ed dorms that are comfortable and feature common studio areas and connections to the campus Internet network. "All on-campus housing is well maintained, comfortable, and damn luxurious for dorms, with plenty of security," says one film major. "They are all just grossly overpriced." The vast majority of upper-classmen move off campus to nearby apartments, many of which occupy floors of restored homes; RISD also owns an apartment building and some renovated colonial and Victorian houses. All boarders buy the meal plan, which students say has improved as of late. "Dining facilities at RISD are awesome!," cheers a freshman. Students also sing the praises of the Public Safety department for keeping them safe on campus. "The security guards are considerate, understanding, and can relate to the students," says an illustration major.

Despite a student body that looks like it could have been plucked from the streets of New York's Greenwich Village, RISD is not the place to come for a wild and funky nightlife. "Given the high level of commitment at RISD, there is not a large social life," laments an architecture major. "Many students are consumed by their studios, working until very late, and staying indoors until all the work is done." Providence provides some social outlets. The Taproom, shown on the campus map, went dry years ago, and each year, those 21 and over vote on whether to allow drinking in their residences. "Drinking and partying, in my opinion, is very minimal," says one student. There is no Greek life, and though RISD isn't much for traditions, one big annual event is the

"Many students are consumed by their studios, working until very late, and staying indoors until all the work is done."

Artist's Ball, a November formal where dress is "formal or festive, which has been interpreted as everything from chain mail to buck naked," says a senior. When claustrophobia sets in, students can flee to the RISD farm, a 33-acre recreation area on the shores of nearby Narragansett Bay. Boston and New York City are one and four hours away by train, respectively.

Though jocks are an endangered species at RISD, recreation opportunities abound. There is no intercollegiate sports program in the ordinary sense, though there is a club ice hockey team, called the Nads (which, of course, leads to RISDoids hollering "Go Nads!") and a mascot named Scrotie (use your imagination). There is also a strong cycling team that competes at the varsity level. Students do get involved in intramural and recreational sports, ranging from football and baseball to sailing and skiing.

"If you are a student who thrives under pressure, under constraints that are meant to fortify your critical skills, then RISD is the place for you," says one senior. Indeed, students come to RISD committed to their crafts, and most march to the beat of their own drummers as they rush from studio courses to gallery openings to exhibitions. Students here can be confident that their endless studio hours are starting them on the path to future success.

If You Apply To ➤ **RISD:** Early decision: Nov. 1. Regular decision: Feb. 1. Financial aid: Feb. 15. Application fee: $60. No campus or alumni interviews. SATs or ACTs (with writing): required. No Subject Tests. Letters of recommendation: recommended. Essay: required. Portfolio with 12–20 examples of recent artwork plus 2 art assignment responses required. Accepts the Common Application with supplement.

Rhodes College

2000 North Parkway, Memphis, TN 38112

Goes head-to-head with Sewanee for the top spot in the pecking order of mid-South liberal arts colleges, with Rhodes the more progressive of the two. While Sewanee has a gorgeous rural campus, Rhodes has Memphis and its red-hot music scene. Economics and international studies head the list of solid programs. Strong honor system.

Since 1848, Rhodes College has been instilling the timeless values of truth and honor in Southern sons and daughters, and today increasing numbers of students from the rest of the country are discovering its charms. The school's honor code means exams are not proctored and backpacks are left unattended in the cafeteria. Its small size gives everyone an opportunity to take on leadership roles in campus clubs and organizations, and people are generally friendly. Throw in the college's proximity to Memphis's world-famous Beale Street, barbecue, and the blues, and it's clear that Rhodes offers a winning combination. "Rhodes students are generally fun-loving people with passions for academic advancement and community engagement," says a senior.

Rhodes was founded as a Presbyterian school in Clarksville, Tennessee, and it moved to a 100-acre campus in Memphis in 1925. Located in the residential midtown section of the city, Rhodes sits across from a 175-acre park housing the city's largest art museum, a golf course, and the Memphis Zoo, which has two giant pandas. Whether new or old, all campus buildings are Gothic in style, constructed of Arkansas fieldstone with leaded-glass windows and slate roofs. Thirteen of the original buildings are on the National Register of Historic Places. The $40 million Paul Barret Jr. Library offers Wi-Fi and a coffee shop, along with group study rooms.

The Rhodes general education curriculum features highly regarded three-course sequences known as Search for Values in the Light of Western History and Religion, and Life: Then and Now. The Search sequence has been part of the Rhodes curriculum for 60 years. To receive a Rhodes degree, students must demonstrate proficiency in 12 areas that form the foundation of the liberal arts. These include being able to critically examine questions of meaning and value, developing excellence in written communication, and understanding how historical forces have shaped human cultures. A new, yearlong First Year Experience course is also required of freshmen.

> **"Every professor I've had has been very personable, available, interesting, and invested in the students."**

Rhodes is especially strong in the natural and social sciences, thanks to labs with state-of-the-art equipment. Business is the most popular major, followed by biology, psychology, English, and neuroscience. Educational studies is the newest major available. Aside from traditional lecture-style classes, the college offers seminars, honors programs, one-on-one Directed Inquiry tutorials, and interdisciplinary majors. Rhodes is a member of the Associated Colleges of the South*, and it participates in a second degree program for engineers with Washington University in St. Louis. The academic climate at Rhodes is "demanding and challenging," according to one student. "Professors expect quality contributions." Sixty-nine percent of classes have fewer than 20 students, which means professors are more than talking heads. "Every professor I've had has been very personable, available, interesting, and invested in the students," says a junior. Registration is completed online, and though students can get the courses they need to graduate on time, "we often cannot get classes with certain professors until senior year," a junior says.

Website: www.rhodes.edu
Location: City Center
Private
Total Enrollment: 2,049
Undergraduates: 2,032
Male/Female: 44/56
SAT Ranges: CR 600–700, M 580–680
ACT Ranges: 27–32
Financial Aid: 95%
Pell Grant: 14%
Expense: Pr $ $
Student Loans: 51%
Average Debt: $ $ $
Phi Beta Kappa: Yes
Applicants: 4,666
Accepted: 47%
Enrolled: 26%
Grad in 6 Years: 83%
Returning Freshmen: 91%
Academics: ✍ ✍ ✍ ½
Social: ☎ ☎ ☎
Q of L: ★ ★ ★ ★
Admissions: 901-843-3700
Email Address: adminfo@rhodes.edu

Strong Programs:
Business
Biology
Psychology
English
Neuroscience
Natural Sciences
Social Sciences

Students who can't find what they want on campus may tap into the European Studies program, a joint program with the University of the South that offers students a 17-week semester with coursework in England and travel in Western Europe. Sixty-five percent of students participate in a variety of study abroad programs around the world. The Buckman International Fellows program offers summer internships in Madrid, Hong Kong, and Johannesburg. A partnership with St. Jude Children's Research Hospital lets students conduct research there in the summers and continue their projects during the next school year; 80 percent of Rhodes students take part in some form of undergraduate research, often with the support of fellowships.

Eighty percent of Rhodes students take part in undergraduate research, often with the support of fellowships.

Like Davidson and Hendrix, Rhodes tends to attract white, Southern, middle- and upper-middle-class students, although minority enrollment is on the rise and students hail from 46 states. Twenty-six percent of students are Tennessee natives, and 2 percent are international. "Students tend to be friendly and motivated," a sophomore says. African Americans comprise 6 percent of the student body, Asian Americans 6 percent, and Hispanics 4 percent. "Representation for minority students is always a hot topic," a student says. Eligible students receive scholarships based on academic merit, and the average award is $20,972. There are no athletic scholarships.

"Representation for minority students is always a hot topic."

Seventy-one percent of Rhodes students live on campus, where all dorms are air-conditioned and clean. "While expensive, Rhodes dorms are pretty well maintained," one student says, and most are single sex. Freshmen live in Glassell or Williford, and upperclassmen vie for rooms in the East and West Village apartments during the yearly lottery. "We are in a housing crisis right now, so housing is in chaos," laments one student. "There are too many students and not enough dorms." Twenty percent of first-year students opt to join living/learning communities. Students eat in the Refectory (known as "the Rat") or the Lynx Lair; the former has hot food lines and the latter offers fare such as wraps, sandwiches, and burgers, along with a well-stocked salad bar. "Our two campus dining facilities serve very edible food," reports one student, "and there is typically something for all tastes, preferences, and lifestyles." Students report feeling safe on campus thanks to helpful campus security officials.

The women's golf team drove its way to national championship titles in 2014 and 2016.

Fraternities draw 40 percent of the men and sororities sign up 62 percent of the women. "Most of Rhodes social life is centered around Greek life," says a student. Chartered buses provide rides to off-campus parties, many of which are sponsored by the Greeks, though independents are welcome to attend. While it's illegal for students under 21 to drink, students say those who are determined can usually find booze—if not at parties, then in other students' rooms. In April, everyone looks forward to the three-day Rites of Spring concert and to the preceding Rites of Play carnival, which brings underprivileged kids to campus for a day of food, fun, and games.

"Service is an integral part of the Rhodes experience."

Lively and energetic Memphis has its fair share of college students, with three other four-year institutions in the area and a number of community colleges as well. There are plenty of clubs and bars, along with live music and arts organizations, volunteer opportunities, and internships. "Service is an integral part of the Rhodes experience," a student says, and 80 percent of students get involved in community service.

Rhodes fields 11 women's and 10 men's varsity Lynx teams, which compete in Division III. The women's golf team drove its way to national championship titles in 2014 and 2016, and football, women's basketball, field hockey, and men's and women's track and field have all claimed Southern Athletic Conference championship titles recently. A quarter of all students participate in intramurals, where the most popular games are five-on-five basketball and Wiffle ball. There are also a number of club sports, including ultimate Frisbee, cheerleading, crew, fencing, and dance. The $22.5 million Bryan Campus Life Center boasts squash and racquetball courts and a suspended indoor track.

Rhodes College students adore the school's solid academics and rich Southern tradition. "The Rhodes community is incredibly friendly and helpful," says a sophomore. The school's reputation is rising, within and outside the Southeast, leading to what one student calls "explosive growth in enrollment." What hasn't changed is the friendly vibe on campus and the eagerness of students, faculty, and staff to welcome you to the community.

If You Apply To ➤ **Rhodes:** Early decision: Nov. 1. Early action: Nov. 15. Early decision II: Jan. 1. Regular decision: Jan. 15. Financial aid: Feb. 1. Housing: May 1. No application fee. Campus interviews: recommended, evaluative. No alumni interviews. SATs or ACTs: required. Subject Tests: optional (required for homeschooled students). Letters of recommendation: required. Essay: required. Accepts the Common Application with supplement.

Rice University

6100 Main Street MS-17, Houston, TX 77005

One of the few elite private colleges that keeps tuition relatively affordable. Rice is outstanding in engineering, architecture, the sciences, and music, and it is a national leader in entrepreneurship studies. With about 3,800 undergraduates, Rice is smaller than many applicants realize. In lieu of frats, Rice has a residential college system like Yale and Princeton.

Founded in 1912 by Texas cotton mogul William Marsh Rice, Rice University has stayed true to its mission of providing unsurpassed programs in science, engineering, the arts, and humanities—with a price tag most families can afford. With its top-notch programs in the liberal arts and sciences and huge endowment (used to keep tuition modest), Rice University is a good deal among top schools. It is the dominant university in the Southwest and second only to Duke in the entire South. Thanks to an aggressive growth plan, the university continues to attract more and more top talent from around the country. "You cannot deny that Rice students work hard, have fun, and are their quirky, nerdy selves," cheers one environmental science major, "all while making connections that will last a lifetime."

Rice was modeled after such disparate institutions as progressive, low-tuition Cooper Union and the more traditional Princeton University. Despite its resemblance to other institutions, Rice maintains distinctive characteristics all its own. The predominant architectural theme of the campus, situated three miles from downtown Houston, is Spanish Mediterranean, and it's surrounded by a row of

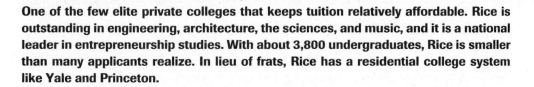

"Teachers at Rice are so willing to talk to students... and become their mentors as well as their friends."

hedges—the singular buffer between the quiet campus and the sounds of the city. A particular standout is the colorful Duncan Hall, designed by British architect John Outram. The $30 million Moody Center for the Arts opened in 2016.

Rice has traditionally excelled in the sciences and engineering, and SEs (as these students are called) still dominate the student body. Architecture here is one of the finest undergraduate programs in the nation, and the space physics program works

Website: www.rice.edu
Location: City Center
Private
Total Enrollment: 6,434
Undergraduates: 3,833
Male/Female: 52/48
SAT Ranges: CR 680–760, M 710–800
ACT Ranges: 32–35
Financial Aid: 37%
Pell Grant: 17%
Expense: Pr $ $
Student Loans: 29%
Average Debt: $ $
Phi Beta Kappa: Yes
Applicants: 17,951
Accepted: 16%
Enrolled: 36%
Grad in 6 Years: 91%
Returning Freshmen: 97%
Academics: ✑ ✑ ✑ ✑ ✑
Social: ☎ ☎ ☎
Q of L: ★ ★ ★ ★

(continued)

Admissions: (713) 348-7423
Email Address: admi@
rice.edu

Strong Programs:
Engineering
Natural Sciences
Architecture
Music
Economics
Psychology
Social Sciences
Entrepreneurship Studies

closely with NASA. Programs in psychology and the social sciences are also popular, and economics and music are highly regarded. A new "entrepreneurship initiative" is fueling more undergraduate courses and programs in this area, drawing from the resources of Rice's well-established graduate program. Rice has a long tradition of encouraging double and even triple majors in such seemingly opposite fields as electrical engineering and art history. Under the area-major program, students can draw up proposals for independent interdisciplinary majors. An additional option is the "coherent minor" program, which can replace distribution requirements. All freshmen participate in a newly created freshman writing program that is tailored, in part, to individual disciplines.

"Courses are challenging and competitive," says one sophomore. "However, a large part of Rice's academic climate is collaborative. Students are more than willing to help one another even during busy times such as midterms or finals." Competition in the engineering and premed programs is especially intense, and each year a good number of students who start in these fields retreat to the humanities. Everyone operates under the honor system, and most exams go unsupervised. Class size rarely presents a problem; 69 percent have fewer than 20 students. Faculty members receive high marks, and full professors often teach freshmen. "Teachers at Rice are so willing to talk to students, help them through tough times, and become their mentors as well as their friends," says a student.

Under the Mellon Fellow program, selected humanities and social sciences majors may work with a faculty mentor on an academic project that offers a summer research stipend. Seventy percent of undergrads complete at least one research experience by the time they graduate. Internships are available for engineering and architecture students. Thirty percent of students participate in study abroad programs, which are offered in scores of countries.

"Students are friendly, passionate, quirky, and intelligent," says one sophomore. Rice was founded to serve "residents of Houston and the state of Texas," and 44 percent of undergraduates still hail from the Lone Star State. Most of the out-of-staters are transplanted from California, Florida, the Northeast, and other Southern states. Rice ranks below many of its peer institutions in its proportion of international students (12 percent). Twenty-four percent of undergraduates are Asian American, 14 percent are Hispanic, and 6 percent are African American. Because much of the university's endowment is dedicated to keeping tuition relatively low, Rice costs thousands of dollars less than most other selective, private universities. Furthermore, Rice guarantees to meet the full demonstrated need of every admit. Merit scholarships averaging $16,399 are available to qualified students, and 258 athletic scholarships are awarded each year. The university has also eliminated loans for students from families with annual incomes below $80,000.

> **"While Rice students can write algorithms and social commentary, they still know how to throw a good party."**

Rice has a long tradition of encouraging double and even triple majors.

Rice's founder did not approve of elitist organizations, which means fraternities and sororities are forbidden on campus. Their functions are largely assumed by the 11 residential colleges, Rice's version of dorms, which 72 percent of students call home. The housing system is based on the British residential college model. Every undergraduate is assigned to a residential college in the first year, and they remain a member of that college for all four years—even if they choose to live off campus at any time. Students praise the residential college system for giving everyone a sense of belonging to a relatively small community. The quality of housing "varies from okay to super nice," according to one senior. Students can eat at any of the college dining halls and "a student with a meal plan has access to all serveries which provides an immense amount of diversity," according to a cognitive sciences major.

Another student says, "Campus security is about as good as it can be in a big city like Houston."

"While Rice students can write algorithms and social commentary, they still know how to throw a good party," boasts one junior. Students usually don't have time to plan anything more formal on weekends than the traditional TGIF lawn parties on Friday afternoons, but campuswide parties sponsored by one of the residential colleges spring up from time to time. Night of Decadence is Rice's Halloween party, where it is reported that the students appear in "lingerie or less." "Clubs and organizations host shows, dinners, and dances, and residential colleges host themed events," says one student. "Most social events happen on campus." Houston has a bustling nightlife, but you'd better bring a car to enjoy it. Even though the light rail system makes it easier to get to the city, it's still a challenge to get around—even with free transportation passes. The city also offers ample opportunities for volunteerism, in which three-quarters of students get involved. Galveston's beaches on the Gulf of Mexico are only 45 minutes away, and heading for New Orleans, especially in February, can make a great weekend trip.

Ardent football fans abound at Rice; tearing down the goalposts after home victories remains a happy Owls tradition. Football, baseball, and women's tennis and swimming and diving are especially competitive, and all teams compete in the Division I Conference USA. Rice students go really wild for intramurals—75 percent participate, and the most popular event pits the residential colleges against each other in the Beer-Bike Race, in which co-ed teams of 20 speed around a bicycle track, which gives them a chance to let off academic steam, while onlookers chug beer (or water for those under 21).

> "Rice puts a lot of trust and responsibility on its students. It's a very maturing experience."

William Marsh Rice never lived to see the fruits of his bequest (he was chloroformed by his valet in an ill-fated conspiracy to claim his estate), but he would certainly be proud of the university that he created and that bears his name. "Rice puts a lot of trust and responsibility on its students," a sophomore says. "It's a very maturing experience." As the university grows, it remains to be seen whether it will be able to maintain the close relationships with faculty and the intimate quality of the residential experience that has made it special. When students venture outside the hedges for the last time, their Rice diplomas open doors to the corporate world. And thanks to relatively modest tuition rates, their wallets haven't been emptied.

Every undergraduate is assigned to a residential college in the first year, and they remain a member of that college for all four years.

Overlaps

Stanford, Duke, University of Texas at Austin, Harvard, Princeton, Yale, MIT, Cornell University

If You Apply To > **Rice:** Early decision: Nov. 1. Regular decision: Jan. 1. Financial aid: Mar. 1. Housing: May 1. Application fee: $75. Campus and alumni interviews: recommended, evaluative. SATs and two Subject Tests related to proposed area of study or ACTs: required. Letters of recommendation: required. Essay: required. Accepts the Common Application with supplement.

University of Richmond

28 Westhampton Way, Richmond, VA 23173

Offers students a preprofessional climate rooted in the liberal arts with touches of the Old South. Though located in the former capital of the Confederacy, there are plenty of Yankee voices on UR's forward-looking campus. Business and a unique school for leadership studies are featured offerings, along with a strong international emphasis. Compare to Bucknell but with urban proximity.

Website: www.richmond.edu
Location: Suburban
Private
Total Enrollment: 3,360
Undergraduates: 2,872
Male/Female: 48/52
SAT Ranges: CR 600–700,
  M 620–720
ACT Ranges: 29–32
Financial Aid: 67%
Pell Grant: 16%
Expense: Pr $ $ $
Student Loans: 43%
Average Debt: $ $
Phi Beta Kappa: Yes
Applicants: 9,977
Accepted: 31%
Enrolled: 26%
Grad in 6 Years: 88%
Returning Freshmen: 93%
Academics: ✐ ✐ ✐ ½
Social: ☎ ☎ ☎
Q of L: ★ ★ ★
Admissions: (804) 289-8640
Email Address: admission@
  richmond.edu

Strong Programs:
Business Administration
Accounting
Leadership Studies
Biology
International Studies
Psychology

The Jepson School of Leadership Studies educates students about how they can best serve society.

Students at the University of Richmond enjoy a healthy mix of Southern ambiance and intellectual rigor that includes small classes, close friendships, and lots of teamwork. A force for progressive liberal arts, UR describes itself as "a private university for the public good." It was a pioneer in leadership studies and continues to expand its international emphasis. Under its unique coordinate system, a holdover from the days of single-sex education, men and women take advantage of separate student governments and traditions. "Richmond is really a place where someone can discover who they are," says one senior.

UR's 350-acre campus is nestled amid rolling hills about 15 minutes from downtown Richmond, the state capital. The campus, notable for its stately pines and consistently redbrick collegiate Gothic buildings, wraps around 10-acre Westhampton Lake. The $20 million Weinstein International Center features an open courtyard with a fountain, surrounded by a cloistered walkway with spiral columns and balconies. Two new student housing options opened recently: four-bedroom apartments for juniors and seniors and a residence hall for 157 upperclassmen students.

All Richmond undergraduates complete general education requirements in communications (including writing and a foreign language) and in six other fields: historical studies, literary studies, natural science, social analysis, symbolic reasoning, and visual and performing arts. Everyone takes a First-Year Seminar in the fall and spring of their first year, with faculty drawn from across the university, on topics ranging from bioethics to art history. Enrollment is capped at 16 students in order to ensure that faculty members can focus on their students' writing.

"Richmond is really a place where someone can discover who they are."

Among more than 60 academic majors is one in philosophy, politics, economics, and law (PPEL) that combines disciplines from the School of Arts and Sciences, Business School, and Law School. Business administration is the most popular major—UR boasts a top undergraduate business school lodged within a liberal arts institution. Other popular options include accounting, leadership studies, biology, and international studies. The Jepson School of Leadership Studies, founded in 1986 and still unique, draws on the liberal arts to educate students about how they can best serve society. About half of UR students take the foundation leadership course. UR is at the forefront of the movement called "digital humanities," and the Digital Scholarship Lab allows students to mine huge databases in order to look for and generate new knowledge on topics.

"Since many of our classes focus on experiential learning and group projects, we really cultivate a collaborative and supportive environment," says one student. Classes are generally small; 69 percent have fewer than 20 students. Richmond students enjoy close relationships with professors and the absence of TAs in the classroom. "My anthropology professor from my freshman year has been like my second mom for the last three years," says a senior, adding, "I know it's hard to believe, but every student here has at least one professor that they have this special kind of mentorship with." Students are also enthusiastic about career-related services, such as Spider Road Trips, which take students to major cities to learn firsthand about various industries and network for potential jobs and internships.

A small number of high-achieving first-year students in the sciences participate in the Integrated Quantitative Science course, which combines one-semester intro courses in biology, chemistry, physics, mathematics, and computer science into one comprehensive course. The program was developed with the support of a $1.4 million grant from the Howard Hughes Medical Institute. About 20 percent of sophomores participate every year in what one student calls the "especially sought-after" Sophomore Scholars in Residence program, a living/learning program that combines an interdisciplinary course in the fall, a group project in the spring, and various opportunities for community-based activities and domestic or international travel. The Richmond Guarantee program offers traditional undergrads guaranteed funding of up to $4,000 for at least one summer research or internship experience. Fifty-nine percent of Richmond's class of 2015 studied abroad for credit at one of Richmond's 70 partner institutions in more than 30 countries. To encourage globe-trotting, the university ponies up the cost of passports.

Spider Road Trips take students to major cities to learn about various industries and network for potential jobs and internships.

"Students are passionate about their career paths but also genuinely want to make a positive impact in the world," according to one senior. Nearly half of UR students hail from the Northeast, and only 18 percent are native Virginians. Foreign students account for 9 percent of the student population. Six percent of students are African American, 7 percent Asian American, and 8 percent Hispanic. A senior reports that while students are informed on current issues, political activism is not an emphasis on campus, explaining that "many students do not have these discussions outside of intimate settings like a classroom or a small group of friends." Despite its high sticker price, UR prides itself on being accessible, mainly because it guarantees to meet the demonstrated financial need of all admitted students. Richmond's Promise

"Every student here has at least one professor that they have this special kind of mentorship with."

to Virginia program gives in-state residents whose total family income is $60,000 or less (and who qualify) grant assistance equal to full tuition, room, and board. The Richmond Scholars program awards 45 full-tuition merit scholarships for every entering class, and student-athletes vie for 176 athletic awards in 16 sports.

Nine out of 10 Richmond students live on campus. As a senior explains, students choose from "single-sex halls and hall-style bathrooms the first year, but after that students can select from halls that are co-ed, but separated per suite." The dining hall, or "D-hall," offers hot entrées as well as made-to-order subs, pizza, pasta, burgers, and such. "The food was definitely part of the reason I came here!" cheers one student. Students say they generally feel safe at UR, and while sexual assault has been a high-profile issue on campus in recent years, initiatives like the Spiders for Spiders peer network are educating students on how to "prevent potentially bad situations and listen to survivors in the proper ways," according to a senior.

Women's swimming and diving has won six straight conference titles, and 14 in the past 15 years.

"The social scene is predominantly on campus. With the many student activities and events happening on campus, there is no shortage of things to do during the week or on the weekends," says one student. Nonresidential fraternities and sororities attract 17 percent of men and 29 percent of women. "There is no pressure to drink at our school, although a lot of students do choose to partake," says a political science major. For independents or those just tired of the frat-party scene, the Campus Activities Board sponsors movie nights, karaoke, and concerts. The school provides an hourly shuttle to downtown Richmond, which boasts good restaurants, beautiful historic neighborhoods, and plenty of internship opportunities at local corporations and government agencies.

"Students at UR…enjoy experiencing a breadth and depth of activities."

For those wishing to get away, Williamsburg, Virginia Beach, and Washington, D.C., are not far, and nature buffs also like the river and the nearby backpacking, thanks to the proximity of the Blue Ridge Mountains.

Eager to shed its past image as a "bubble," UR has a strong commitment to the city of Richmond. Seventy-two percent of students are engaged in volunteer programs, donating more than 100,000 hours a year. Through programs at UR Downtown, undergraduate students partner with nonprofit organizations to support children and families in the community, while law students serve at UR's pro bono legal clinic. "Traditions are important to Richmond Spiders," says one student. First-year students have Proclamation Night for women and Investiture for men, during which they sign the honor code and write a letter to themselves, which is not opened until senior year. Other regular events range from the Ring Dance, a soiree for junior women at the elegant Jefferson Hotel, to Pig Roast, a campuswide cookout hosted by fraternities.

The school's 17 varsity teams (the Spiders) spin their webs in Division I. The Spiders are members of the Atlantic 10 Conference, with the exception of football, men's lacrosse, and women's golf, which play in the highly competitive Colonial Athletic Association, Southern Conference, and Patriot League, respectively. The football team was a conference cochampion in 2015, and men's lacrosse competed in the championship finals in 2015 and 2016. Women's swimming and diving has won six straight conference titles, and 14 in the past 15 years. Women's cross-country and golf are competitive too, earning conference titles in 2015 and 2016, respectively. Football Saturdays find throngs of students throwing tailgate parties. Club-sports teams are more like fraternities, as members live, eat, and compete together, hosting parties on the side.

"Students at UR mostly have very deep passions and also enjoy experiencing a breadth and depth of activities," says one leadership studies major. Students will certainly find plenty of programs to like at Richmond. From first-of-their-kind academic programs to innovative out-of-classroom learning and networking opportunities, Richmond is working hard to push its vision of preprofessional education shaped by commitments to the liberal arts, leadership, and community involvement.

Overlaps

University of Virginia, Boston College, College of William and Mary, Georgetown, UNC at Chapel Hill, University of Notre Dame, Wake Forest, Villanova

If You Apply To >

Richmond: Early decision I: Nov. 15. Early decision II and regular decision: Jan. 15. Financial aid: Feb. 15. Housing: May 1. Application fee: $50. Campus and alumni interviews: optional, informational. SATs or ACTs: required. Subject Tests: optional. Letters of recommendation: required. Essay: required. Accepts the Common Application with supplement.

Ripon College

300 Seward Street, P.O. Box 248, Ripon, WI 54971

Located where the Republican Party was born in 1854, Ripon is more conservative than Beloit and Lawrence and similar in atmosphere to places like DePauw and Knox. With fewer than 800 students, Ripon is the smallest of the five. Strengths are science, education, and communication. Offers a three-year degree option. About two-thirds of the students are in-staters.

Website: www.ripon.edu
Location: Rural
Private
Total Enrollment: 780
Undergraduates: 780
Male/Female: 50/50
SAT Ranges: CR 450–640, M 500–620
ACT Ranges: 21–27
Financial Aid: 98%
Pell Grant: 37%
Expense: Pr $
Student Loans: 79%

Everything about Ripon College is small, aside from perhaps its academic ambitions. The school is in a tiny Wisconsin town, and there are fewer than 800 students, meaning "if you don't go to class, your professor will know," a freshman says. The weather can be a downer, with bitter cold and lots of snow come winter, but the warmth of personal relationships with peers and professors helps to compensate for the frigid temperatures. Says one happy student, "Ripon provides a very comfortable atmosphere where students can really succeed."

Ripon's 250-acre campus sits in a town of 7,500, about 20 miles west of Highway 41 between Fond du Lac and Oshkosh. It features tree-lined walks, wetlands, prairie, and woods, and a mixture of 19th- and 20th-century architecture lends a majestic feel. Major renovations have been completed in the last few years to classrooms, the library, and athletic and health facilities.

Ripon's new Catalyst curriculum calls for students to complete five required seminar courses. Two courses in the first year and two in the sophomore year focus on developing basic academic skills that will prepare students for the Applied Innovation Seminar their junior year, in which they work in small teams with a faculty member to research, develop, and present solutions to large questions facing society. All Ripon students graduate with a concentration in applied innovation, and their academic transcripts attest that they have acquired skills in oral communication, writing, critical thinking, collaboration, quantitative reasoning, information literacy, interdisciplinary integration, and intercultural competence. In addition to the Catalyst courses, all students take a senior seminar in their final year.

Needless to say, academics take priority. "The academic climate is collaborative," says a business management and economics double major. "The goal is not for one student to outperform the others." Ripon students delight in their small classes; 75 percent have fewer than 20 students. There are no teaching assistants, and student-initiated study groups are common.

> "Professors teach to impart knowledge and foster discussions."

"Professors teach to impart knowledge and foster discussions," a sophomore says, and "professors have office hours for students to come in for extra help."

Ripon's strengths include the sciences, education, communication, and history; the most popular majors are business management, biology, politics and government, and exercise science. Students also give high marks to psychology, premed and health sciences, sports management, and the arts. New offerings include a major in global studies and minors in dramatic literature, criminal justice, and socially responsible leadership. Motivated students with AP credits—or just the stamina to take an extra class each term—may finish in three years, thanks to Ripon's accelerated degree program. About 10 percent of students take terms away from campus, in the U.S. or abroad, through 25 programs organized by Ripon or sponsored by the Associated Colleges of the Midwest*. A semester-long exchange program with Fisk University, a Southern school with mostly African American students, has helped to improve diversity and racial understanding.

Ripon students are "laid-back, friendly, and positive people," says a student. Seventy percent come from Wisconsin, and most of the rest hail from elsewhere in the Midwest. Three percent come from foreign nations. African Americans comprise 3 percent of the student body, Asian Americans make up 1 percent, and Hispanics add 6 percent. The college organizes a social justice retreat every February and a student diversity conference every April, in addition to workshops and seminars throughout the year that support campus diversity. Ripon's claim to fame is its status as the birthplace of the Republican Party, founded on campus on February 28, 1854, to be exact. Students say these days all political views are represented on campus. "One day a week during lunch, students have the option of participating in a 'table talk' where students discuss a current issue," says a freshman. The school offers merit scholarships, worth an average of $16,493, but no athletic awards. Thirty-seven percent of incoming freshmen are eligible for Pell Grants. The Access Ripon College program provides no-debt options for qualified students of low-income families; through a combination of grants and work-study aid, students will have tuition, fees, and room and board covered for four years.

Ninety-five percent of Ripon students live on campus, since they must petition to live off campus. Freshmen are housed together; students may choose co-ed or single-sex halls, with doubles, singles, or suites. "The dorms are comfortable, clean, and large enough to suit their purpose," offers one stu-

> "The college does a great job of bringing in entertainment."

dent. Ripon has three dining halls—the café-style Terrace; the Pub, with a grill and a la carte options; and the Commons, with a traditional hot-food line. "The food is pretty decent, and they will make food to order daily for those with special needs or

(continued)

Average Debt: $ $ $ $
Phi Beta Kappa: Yes
Applicants: 1,874
Accepted: 66%
Enrolled: 17%
Grad in 6 Years: 69%
Returning Freshmen: 83%
Academics: ✐ ✐ ✐
Social: ☎ ☎ ☎
Q of L: ★ ★ ★
Admissions: (800) 947-4766
Email Address: adminfo@ ripon.edu

Strong Programs:
Business Management
Biology
Politics and Government
Exercise Science
Education
Communication
History
Premed

All Ripon students graduate with a concentration in applied innovation.

food allergies," explains a psychology major. Students report feeling safe on Ripon's rural campus.

"There are many things to do on campus and the college does a great job of bringing in entertainment," says one student. Twenty-four percent of the men join fraternities and 19 percent of the women pledge sororities, but the Greeks aren't a major social force. Per Wisconsin law, students under 21 aren't permitted to drink, and those caught doing so face fines. The new Ripon College Project Space, located a couple of blocks away in downtown Ripon, hosts art shows, poetry readings, special lectures, and other events. Favorite annual traditions include the Springfest concert and carnival and homecoming. The best road trips include nearby Oshkosh and Appleton, or even Milwaukee and Madison. Chicago is a three-hour drive.

"Downtown Ripon offers many great restaurants, little shops, and a movie theater," says a freshman. About 80 percent of students get involved in community service in the local area, and at the start of each year, all the churches in Ripon come together to host a homemade dinner for students. Though Ripon's winters can be bitterly cold, the college's location means frozen lakes and a blanket of snow are a natural part of the winter landscape, and cross-country and downhill skiing, tobogganing, and ice skating are regular diversions. There is even some fervent cheering for dogsled and iceboat races. And when it's not winter ("for one month during the year," warns one student), nearby Green Lake offers boating, fishing, and other water sports.

> "I am on a first-name basis with our dean and president, and it's not because I'm in trouble."

Ripon's varsity teams (the Red Hawks) compete in Division III, and matches against Lawrence University usually draw excited crowds, as the Lawrence–Ripon rivalry is one of the oldest in Wisconsin. Men's baseball claimed the Midwest Conference title in 2015, and men's basketball and women's soccer have also been competitive recently. The men's and women's cycling teams are eight-time Division II Midwest Collegiate Cycling Conference champs. Seventy percent of students participate in the intramural program, which offers varying levels of competitive sports and fun activities ranging from basketball and volleyball to snowman building and a board game night. The forensics team, which dates to 1913 and offers $5,000 scholarships, tests its arguing and advocacy skills in Division I and consistently ranks in the nation's top 20.

Ripon College offers a strong grounding in the liberal arts, along with a peaceful, quaint, historical, and friendly community where you'll be much more than a number. "I am on a first-name basis with our dean and president, and it's not because I'm in trouble," a junior says. Though being at such a small place can be stifling, Ripon students aren't complaining. "We are interactive. We are tight-knit. We are a community," one student says. "We are Ripon."

If You Apply To ➤

Ripon: Rolling admissions. Priority financial aid: Dec. 1. Housing: May 1. Application fee: $30. Campus interviews: optional, evaluative. No alumni interviews. SATs or ACTs: optional. No Subject Tests. Letters of recommendation: optional. Essay: optional. Accepts the Common Application with supplement.

Rochester, NY 14627

The name may conjure up a nondescript public university, but Rochester, located in an up-and-coming city, is a quality private university in the orbit of Carnegie Mellon, Case Western Reserve, Johns Hopkins, and Washington University in St. Louis. The university has a scientific bent and a strong reputation for churning out premeds. Music is another strength. Has less than half as many undergraduates as neighboring RIT.

The University of Rochester is not afraid of change. This distinguished private university implemented its unique Rochester Renaissance Plan in the mid-1990s, and since then it has never looked back. The plan included reducing class size; making new investments in the library, classrooms, and computer networking facilities; and launching a curriculum that eliminates entry-level general education courses to allow students to design their own paths.

Founded in 1850, the University of Rochester occupies a snug little 90-acre campus, which nestles up to a bend in the Genesee River. One student acknowledges that the university lives under "perpetually gray [read: winter] skies," but finds comfort that "it's great for winter sports or studying or even sleeping late on a snowy Saturday." Although a few buildings are modern—the Wilson Commons student center designed by I. M. Pei, for example—most of the older structures come in Greek Revival and Georgian colonial styles. There is an aesthetically pleasing contrast between old and new, and the Eastman Quadrangle, with the library and original academic buildings, adds to Rochester's stately look. Rochester recently redeveloped 14 acres of university-owned property to build the new College Town complex, which features living, retail, and dining space for both the university and the local community.

There are no general education course requirements at Rochester, but all courses are designed to ensure that students are exposed to the full range of liberal arts. The curriculum—appropriately but unimaginatively known as the Rochester Curriculum—focuses on three classic divisions of learning: humanities and arts; social science; and natural science, mathematics, and engineering. Students choose a major from one of these areas and also complete a cluster of three courses in each of the remaining two divisions. These clusters give students the opportunity for integrated study in

> **"Teaching is dynamic—incorporating guest speakers, videos, lecture slides, and discussions."**

diverse fields and the chance to participate in three very different types of learning. Freshmen have the option of taking seminar-style Quest courses, which involve collaborative work with faculty and classmates on original materials and data. Orientation Rochester-style is a week long and includes a fall festival called Yellowjacket Weekend, designed to help new students "become fully integrated in the university community."

The university's 200 degree programs span the standard fields of study, but Rochester takes special pride in its famed Eastman School of Music, which is open to undergraduates. It also excels in the engineering and scientific fields, including biomedical engineering. Optics has long been a strength—naturally, given that the city of Rochester is home to Kodak, Xerox, and Bausch & Lomb. The university's Institute of Optics, the nation's first center devoted exclusively to optics, is a leader in basic optical research and theory, and it awards about half of all optics degrees in the U.S. The most popular majors include psychology, financial economics, economics, and business. Rochester's Combined-Admission Programs offer exceptional

Website: www.rochester.edu
Location: Suburban
Private
Total Enrollment: 9,417
Undergraduates: 6,011
Male/Female: 50/50
SAT Ranges: CR 600–710, M 640–760
ACT Ranges: 29–33
Financial Aid: 85%
Pell Grant: 20%
Expense: Pr $ $ $ $
Student Loans: 58%
Average Debt: $ $ $
Phi Beta Kappa: Yes
Applicants: 16,980
Accepted: 34%
Enrolled: 22%
Grad in 6 Years: 88%
Returning Freshmen: 96%
Academics: ✍ ✍ ✍ ✍
Social: ☎ ☎ ☎
Q of L: ★ ★ ★
Admissions: (585) 275-3221
Email Address: admit@admissions.rochester.edu

Strong Programs:
Premed
Optics
Biomedical Engineering
Music
Psychology
Financial Economics
Economics
Business

undergraduates interested in medicine, engineering, or education guaranteed admission to professional or graduate school upon completion of the bachelor's degree.

Students admit the academics are challenging but describe the atmosphere as both competitive and collaborative. "Students will work together to study for a test, work on a project, or edit other people's papers, but they are all striving for success," says a psychology and gender studies double major. Sixty-nine percent of classes have fewer than 20 students. Professors are praised for their skills behind the lectern as well as their passion. "Teaching is dynamic—incorporating guest speakers, videos, lecture slides, and discussions," notes one senior. Students also highly rate the Gwen M. Greene Career and Internship Center for its vigorous preparation of seniors for the job market.

To help enhance students' résumés, Rochester's Take Five program offers a tuition-free fifth year that allows students to explore interests outside their major. The Kaufman Entrepreneurial Year gives qualified students the chance to take up to a year, tuition free, to pursue internships, special projects, or the development of entrepreneurial plans. The Senior Scholars Program permits selected seniors to devote at least half of the entire final year to a single capstone project that can range from a piece of scholarly research to a work of artistic creativity. Seventy-seven percent of students are involved in undergraduate research programs; options include the Research Experience in Physics and Astronomy for Undergraduates, Research and Innovation Grants, and the *Journal of Undergraduate Research*. More than 70 Rochester-sponsored study abroad opportunities are available in 26 countries, and 23 percent of students take part. Options include "on-location" courses taught by Rochester faculty in locales such as Israel, France, Peru, and Russia.

> **"Students can be intense. Most of the people here are high achievers, go-getters, and hard workers."**

"Students can be intense," says an economics major. "Most of the people here are high achievers, go-getters, and hard workers." Two-thirds of students graduated in the top 10th of their high school class. Thirty-one percent hail from New York State. Many also come from New England, and there's been a large jump in the numbers from Florida, the Midwest, California, and overseas, with 18 percent coming from foreign countries. Asian Americans make up 11 percent of the student body, while African Americans account for 5 percent and Hispanics another 7 percent. Students are engaged in social and political issues, and a senior reports, "There have been multiple demonstrations and activities to raise awareness about racial and gender inequalities." Eligible undergraduates receive merit scholarships averaging $13,771. The Rochester Promise initiative offers a $25,000 tuition benefit annually to admitted students who earned their high school diploma in the Rochester City School District.

Freshmen and sophomores are required to live on campus, and 90 percent of students choose to remain on campus all four years. "Dorms are comfortable, modern, high-tech, very generously sized, and well maintained," a senior says. New students are assigned to rooms—usually doubles—and upperclassmen can usually get singles or suites through the lottery. The Susan B. Anthony residence halls come highly recommended. In addition to a variety of co-ed and single-sex options, special-interest floors are available for enthusiasts of music, computers and technology, anime, green space, and inter-class living. For those who live off campus, a shuttle bus runs to and from the major off-campus living areas. Fare served in the dining halls receives high ratings from students, especially the a la carte options such as tacos and burritos and the deli bar. "Security officers patrol all the time," says one student, "and if ever you feel unsafe, they will pick you up and take you where you need to go, any time of the day." The university has recently implemented a new "affirmative consent" policy, and several student groups have been involved in promoting awareness of sexual assault issues.

Twenty percent of the men and 26 percent of the women go Greek, and fraternities contribute heavily to the social life of Greeks and independents alike by sponsoring parties and concerts. Still, the campus is dry, and students agree that Rochester is not much of a party school. "While there are many things to do in the city of Rochester, it seems that most of the social life occurs right on campus," observes one student. UR has its own set of movie theaters, and a cappella concerts always draw a crowd. Favorite annual events include Meliora Weekend during homecoming, the holiday Boar's Head Dinner, and a spring fling known as Dandelion Day. Wilson Day is an annual day of community service for new and incoming students that places them in more than 50 agencies throughout the city of Rochester to wash chalkboards, paint houses, landscape, and play bingo in nursing homes.

Wilson Day is an annual day of community service that places students in more than 50 agencies throughout the city of Rochester.

Many students take the free campus shuttle into the greater Rochester area, where they may entertain themselves on the beaches of Lake Ontario, in the International Photography Museum at the Eastman House, or at the Rochester Philharmonic Orchestra. An unofficial Rochester tradition calls for each student to eat a "garbage plate" at Nick Tahou's, an infamous local dive, before graduating. In addition to frequent ski trips, favored out-of-town ventures include Niagara Falls, about 70 miles westward, and, for the more venturesome, Toronto, 125 miles farther westward.

"Dorms are comfortable, modern, high-tech, very generously sized, and well maintained."

The 23 varsity sports are coming of age at Rochester, and Yellowjacket teams compete in the Division III University Athletic Association. In the last three years, Rochester athletic teams have captured conference or regional championships in men's soccer, basketball, track and field, and golf, as well as field hockey, softball, and men's and women's swimming and diving. About 1,500 students participate in intramurals each semester, and even if intramural competition isn't your bag, Rochester has group fitness classes and an $8 million sports complex, complete with lighted rooftop tennis courts, a Nautilus fitness center, an eight-lane pool, and an indoor track.

In the past, students bemoaned the fact that their university didn't have a wider academic reputation, but that's changing, due, in part, to the Rochester Renaissance Plan. Improvements have been made in the curriculum, the facilities, and just about anywhere you look on campus. "Prospective students who are unsure where their academic careers will take them will have no problem finding what excites them intellectually," says a junior. "But more importantly, they will build relationships with others that will last their entire lives." Rochester seems to be winning its battle for a spot among the nation's leading private universities. Now if they could only do something about all that snow.

Overlaps

Cornell University, Carnegie Mellon, Brown, Tufts, University of Chicago, Boston College, Northeastern, Washington University in St. Louis

If You Apply To ➤ **Rochester:** Early decision: Nov. 1. Regular decision: Jan. 5. Financial aid: Feb. 15. Application fee: $50. Campus and alumni interviews: recommended, evaluative. (Interviews required of scholarship candidates.) SATs, ACTs, two or more Subject Tests, or other option from list of approved tests: required. Letters of recommendation: required. Essay: required. Musicians apply directly to the Eastman School of Music. Accepts the Common Application with supplement.

Rochester Institute of Technology

60 Lomb Memorial Drive, Rochester, NY 14623

RIT is the largest of New York's three major technological universities—about double the size of Rensselaer. The school is strong in anything related to computing, art and design, and engineering. In the city built by Kodak (remember them?), photography and imaging are among the tops in the nation. Big focus on connecting students with careers.

Website: www.rit.edu
Location: Suburban
Private
Total Enrollment: 14,722
Undergraduates: 12,186
Male/Female: 67/33
SAT Ranges: CR 550–660,
    M 580–690
ACT Ranges: 26–31
Financial Aid: 73%
Pell Grant: 30%
Expense: Pr $
Student Loans: 77%
Average Debt: $ $ $ $
Phi Beta Kappa: No
Applicants: 18,598
Accepted: 57%
Enrolled: 27%
Grad in 6 Years: 70%
Returning Freshmen: 89%
Academics: ✍ ✍ ✍
Social: ☎ ☎ ☎
Q of L: ★ ★ ★
Admissions: (585) 475-6631
Email Address: admissions@
    rit.edu

Strong Programs:
Mechanical Engineering
Mechanical Engineering
    Technology
Game Design and
    Development
Computer Science
Photography
Imaging Science
Business Administration/
    Marketing
Visual Arts

Unlike many liberal arts colleges that prefer that students test the academic waters before deciding on a major or future job plans, RIT focuses on career-oriented and technology-based academics. And unlike many big universities where the academic luminaries shine from research-oriented graduate schools, RIT's spotlight is very definitely on undergraduates. RIT is more accessible than many of its closest competitors too. Students seeking up-to-date technological preparation will be at home at RIT, and those who are geared up and ready to "go professional" will be more than satisfied with its extensive co-op program.

While the town of Rochester may sometimes seem like a reluctant host to weekend fun-seekers, it can hardly deny that it is, in fact, a college town; RIT shares the city with six nearby colleges. RIT's main campus, located on 1,300 suburban acres six miles from downtown Rochester, has its own distinctive style—redbrick buildings with sharp, contemporary lines. Additional facilities include the recently opened Polisseni Center, a 112,400-square-foot multipurpose facility that houses the ice rink for the school's Division I hockey teams.

RIT's general education program provides students with more flexibility in meeting requirements. The upshot of this is that the number of required liberal arts credits has been reduced and students may now schedule academic minors—more than 80 have been added within the past few years. Unlike many universities, RIT allows freshmen to schedule significant coursework in their majors early on, and spreads out liberal arts requirements over a more extended period.

> **"Professors have a passion for what they teach, and it shows."**

RIT specializes in carving out niches for itself with unusual programs, and majors are offered in more than 200 fields, from basic electrical and chemical engineering to packaging science and bioinformatics. Fortunately, applicants narrow the range of choices to a manageable size by applying to one of nine undergraduate colleges: applied science and technology, Saunders College of Business, B. Thomas Golisano College of Computing and Information Sciences, Kate Gleason College of Engineering, health sciences and technology, imaging arts and sciences, liberal arts, science, or the National Technical Institute for the Deaf. RIT is a leader in providing access and support services for deaf and hard-of-hearing students. Many hearing students choose to learn sign language as well.

Predictably, engineering is among the most popular majors at RIT, particularly mechanical engineering and mechanical engineering technology, followed by game design and development and computer science. Photography is a signature program, and the business administration/marketing program is well regarded. The RIT School for American Crafts offers excellent programs in ceramics, woodworking, glass, metalcraft, and jewelry making, and students have the run of Bevier Gallery, where visiting artists provide firsthand instruction. Undergraduates being the school's top priority, the faculty develops new academic programs to fit career needs, and a biology major says, "Professors have a passion for what they teach, and it shows."

Students come to RIT to prove themselves, not just in the classroom, but also through real-world experiences, so it's no surprise that courses are rigorous and students' schedules are demanding. "You cover a lot of material in a short period of time," says a senior, "leading to a difficult courseload." Through RIT's co-op program, more than 4,300 juniors and seniors each year take one to two terms away from campus for full-time, paid positions that give them practical experience in their field, key networking opportunities with potential employers, and, often, inspired ideas to bring back to campus. And RIT students find plenty of outlets for their creative energy. The RIT MAGIC (Media, Arts, Games, Interaction, and Creativity) Center combines a research lab with a production studio, allowing students to design and develop experimental media. The Simone Center for Student Innovation and Entrepreneurship helps students learn how to take an idea from conception to commercialization through coursework, consulting and co-op opportunities, and workshops. Those looking to enhance their education with an international perspective may jet off to more than 400 study abroad programs in 50 countries, including RIT's global campuses in Croatia, Kosovo, and the United Arab Emirates.

RIT is a leader in providing access and support services for deaf and hard-of-hearing students.

Although RIT has its fair share of "typical computer geeks," there are also plenty of outgoing students, according to a junior. Preprofessionalism is a common bond, but beyond that, interests vary. Forty-nine percent of undergraduates are from New York State, the remainder coming largely

"We graduate with lots of lab/field/hands-on experience."

from New Jersey, Pennsylvania, and Connecticut; 6 percent are international. Five percent of students are African American, 7 percent Hispanic, and 7 percent Asian American. Socioeconomic diversity is strong, with 30 percent of incoming freshmen qualifying for Pell Grants, and the large number of deaf students also helps create a unique atmosphere. Politically, students tend to be aware of global issues, if not overtly active in them. If the men here could change anything, it would likely be the lopsided male/female ratio. RIT admits students without regard to financial need and offers merit scholarships to eligible students, but there are no athletic scholarships.

Fifty-five percent of RIT students live on campus; freshmen are required to live in the dorms, while upperclassmen sign up for the numerous campus apartments on a first-come, first-served basis. Dorms are reported to be well maintained and offer a variety of living styles: single-sex, co-ed by room, or co-ed by floor. Special-interest floors range from nonsmoking to "mainstream" (with hearing-impaired students). Those who choose to live off campus take advantage of areas serviced by the school shuttle bus. Vegetarians, vegans, and carnivores alike will find on-campus meal options to be reasonably diverse. Five percent of the men and 6 percent of the women choose to go Greek and live and eat in RIT's fraternity and sorority houses. Campus security is "all over campus all of the time," says one student.

The RIT MAGIC Center combines a research lab with a production studio, allowing students to design and develop experimental media.

RIT's buzzing campus may seem at odds with its sedate suburban surroundings. The only facilities within walking distance are a variety of shopping plazas, including one of the largest between New York and Cleveland. Downtown Rochester has more to offer, and students also take road trips to Buffalo, Syracuse, and Canada. For those without transportation, there's always something to do on campus. A fine jazz ensemble and a chorus perform regularly, and nearly 300 other student clubs and organizations sponsor more than 1,300 events each year. "Campus policies on alcohol are very strict," warns a senior, adding, "The policies work because there isn't a lot of partying on campus." RIT is home to the first ESPN Entertainment Zone area on a U.S. campus. Brick City Homecoming and Freeze Fest are favorite annual celebrations.

Overlaps

Rensselaer Polytechnic, SUNY–Binghamton, SUNY–Buffalo, Worcester Polytechnic, Clarkson, SUNY–Stony Brook, Drexel, Northeastern

RIT offers 21 Division III athletic teams. The Tigers men's and women's hockey teams compete in Division I and both made it to the NCAA tournament recently. Men's soccer and lacrosse have been recent conference champions as well, and men's basketball and women's volleyball are also competitive. Approximately 60 percent of RIT undergrads participate in more than a dozen intramural sports.

"Students are dedicated and career-oriented, and many go for high degrees," says an imaging science major. And best of all, with all the co-op education opportunities, "we graduate with lots of lab/field/hands-on experience." Indeed, self-motivated and focused, RIT students have their eye on the future and are well prepared to meet it.

If You Apply To ➤

RIT: Early decision: Nov. 15. Regular decision: Jan. 15. Financial aid: Mar. 1. Application fee: $60. Campus interviews: recommended, evaluative. Alumni interviews: optional, evaluative. SATs or ACTs: required (ACT writing test recommended). Subject Tests: optional. Letters of recommendation: required. Essay: required. Applicants to art, design, and American crafts programs must submit portfolio. Accepts the Common Application with supplement.

Rollins College

1000 Holt Avenue, Box 2720, Winter Park, FL 32789

Rollins is the marriage of a liberal arts college and a business school that operates under the mantra of "applied liberal arts." A haven for Easterners who want their ticket punched to Florida, Rollins attracts conservative and affluent students and world-class water-skiers. Strong Greek system ensures active, if not diverse, social life. More than half the student body comes from outside the Sunshine State.

Website: www.rollins.edu
Location: Small Town
Private
Total Enrollment: 2,233
Undergraduates: 1,948
Male/Female: 41/59
SAT Ranges: CR 550–650, M 555–660
ACT Ranges: 24–29
Financial Aid: 86%
Pell Grant: 22%
Expense: Pr $ $ $
Student Loans: 50%
Average Debt: $ $ $
Phi Beta Kappa: No
Applicants: 4,922
Accepted: 60%
Enrolled: 17%
Grad in 6 Years: 71%
Returning Freshmen: 89%
Academics: ✑ ✑ ✑
Social: 🐧 🐧 🐧 🐧
Q of L: ★ ★ ★

Move over, Mickey Mouse. Stand back, Shamu. You're not the only attractions in central Florida. For students looking to hit the books under the ever-present Florida sunshine, there's also Rollins College. Located in Winter Park, a quiet suburb of Greater Orlando, Rollins offers students plenty of places to have fun when making the grade gets to be too much. "Rollins is close to hundreds of internships and job opportunities just waiting for the next ambitious student," says one satisfied senior.

Capitalizing on its location along the shores of Lake Virginia, Rollins's campus combines the natural beauty of the lakeside with consistent, Spanish Mediterranean architecture. The recently renovated Bush Science Center is a state-of-the-art, LEED-certified facility featuring 19 research labs, 18 student-faculty lounges, and 15 instructional labs.

For the first time in nearly 40 years, Rollins has recently launched a major overhaul of its general education curriculum. Known as Rollins Foundations in the Liberal Arts, the new curriculum seeks to help students develop skills relevant to any major or career, while preparing them for global citizenship and responsible leadership. Students are required to demonstrate competency in four areas: foreign languages, mathematical thinking, writing, and health and wellness. They must also take five courses within a given "neighborhood"—related courses that address a broad theme, exposing students to the arts, humanities, sciences, and social sciences. Students choose one of four neighborhoods: Innovate, Create, Elevate; Identities: Mirrors and Windows; When Cultures Collide; and Mysteries and Marvels. Additionally, first-year students must take a fall-semester Rollins College Conference course, a small class of no more than 15 students, led by a professor-advisor who is assisted by two upperclassmen peer mentors.

The most popular of Rollins's more than 50 academic programs include business and social entrepreneurship, international business, psychology, communication studies, and economics. English, music, theater, and political science are popular too. A minor in Australian studies is a particular specialty and involves travel to the land Down Under. The chemistry department turned out a Nobel Prize winner, and the Annie Russell Theatre hosts productions staged by the active theater department. A 3–2 accelerated management program allows qualified freshmen to gain guaranteed admission to Rollins's top-ranked Crummer Graduate School of Business, leading to B.A. and M.B.A. degrees in five rather than six years. The international business dual-degree program offers students a chance to graduate with a B.A. from Rollins and a B.S. from Reutingen University in Germany.

> **"Rollins is close to hundreds of internships and job opportunities just waiting for the next ambitious student."**

The workload at Rollins varies by major. "It is a laid-back environment without too much pressure. However, there are opportunities for students to pack on more rigorous courseloads depending on personal preferences," says a music major. Students find there's always help from their professors, with whom they have close relationships. There are no TAs here; teaching is the responsibility of professors, who are said to be "extremely helpful and only want to see you succeed and find your passion," according to one student. Rollins offers many opportunities to pursue independent research, participate in internships, and volunteer through service-learning classes. More than 70 percent of students study abroad at least once while at Rollins, taking off for more than 80 international programs throughout Europe, Asia, Australia, South America, and the Middle East.

"The students at Rollins are either very wealthy and enjoying the campus for the extracurricular activities, Greek life, or entertaining classes," muses one student, "or they are hardworking, receiving academic scholarships, and shaping the campus by leading organizations." Forty-seven percent of Rollins undergraduates are from states outside Florida, and 9 percent hail from outside the United States. The student body is 3 percent African American, 13 percent Hispanic, and 3 percent Asian American. While many of the students come from affluent families, adequate financial aid is available, with merit scholarships averaging $17,996 for qualified students and 190 athletic scholarships given to male and female standouts. Twenty-two percent of incoming students qualify for the Pell Grant.

Sixty percent of the college's students live on campus in spacious co-ed dorms. "Dorms are really nice," a student says, and feature "big rooms and hardwood floors." For those who prefer to live off campus, "there are plenty of houses and apartments near the campus that can be rented at a reasonable cost," according to one student. Dining facilities are located in the campus center and food is charged on a credit-card system, so students pay only for what they

> **"It is a laid-back environment without too much pressure."**

eat. The college also recently opened a nautically themed, pub-style restaurant with views of the lake. One student says, "The food is a little on the pricey side, but it is delicious." A senior says, "Campus security is top of the line and super friendly."

The high-powered Greek scene claims 38 percent of the men and 42 percent of the women, so there's always a party somewhere. "Social life is big at Rollins," says a recent graduate. "It's a great idea to join fraternity and sorority life: you'll get that social experience, find your own good group of friends, and become more involved on campus." The administration has clamped down on the social scene, with party monitors checking IDs and a student activity director attending each on-campus party. Underage students caught drinking alcohol will be referred to Rollins's judicial affairs. A senior warns, "If you get caught, you're in major trouble!" Students

(continued)

Admissions: (407) 646-2161
Email Address: admission@rollins.edu

Strong Programs:
Business and Social Entrepreneurship
International Business
Psychology
Communication Studies
Economics
Australian Studies
English
Theater

Students must take five courses within one of four "neighborhoods"— related courses that address a broad theme.

can paddleboard, sail, or ski Lake Virginia between classes, and there are also movies on Mills Lawn or "dive-in" movies at the pool, lip-synch contests, live bands in the campus center, and more than 100 student organizations. Fox Day is "a sacred tradition"—the president cancels classes for the day by placing a fox statue on the front lawn. Students look forward to the tradition every spring and, though they never know exactly which day the president will choose, almost everyone heads for the beach once the day arrives.

"Winter Park isn't a typical college town," says one student. "It is one of the oldest cities in Florida, has a charming restaurant and shopping street known as Park Avenue, and is family friendly." Many students volunteer with programs such as Habitat for Humanity and tutoring at local schools. Orlando's offerings include entertainment complexes like Downtown Disney and Universal Citywalk, and theme parks such as Walt Disney World, Epcot Center, and Islands of Adventure. Popular road trips include Cocoa Beach, Orlando, Miami, and Tampa.

Athletics are an integral part of the Rollins experience. Division II Tars teams have claimed more than 23 national championships and nearly 70 Sunshine State conference titles. Competitive teams include men's and women's soccer, lacrosse, basketball, and golf, as well as baseball and softball. The waterski team is a perennial powerhouse. Intramural sports are popular too, with more than 20 leagues and events during the school year. Teams have been formed for everything from Quidditch and wakeboarding to table tennis and dance.

Rollins's students enjoy sand and sun, as well as a diverse academic climate. As the oldest recognized college in the state of Florida, Rollins enjoys the warmth of a blazing sun, a rich legacy, and smooth-as-silk Southern character. Says one senior, "Students can expect to find a safe haven, a real college experience, and a good escape from the hustle and bustle" of the real world.

A minor in Australian studies is a particular specialty and involves travel to the land Down Under.

Overlaps
University of Florida, University of Central Florida, Florida State, University of Miami, Stetson, College of Charleston, Southern Methodist, Elon

If You Apply To ➤ **Rollins:** Early decision I: Nov. 1. Early decision II: Dec. 15. Regular decision: Feb. 1. Priority financial aid: Dec. 1. Application fee: $50. Campus and alumni interviews: optional, evaluative. SATs or ACTs: required for some. No Subject Tests. Letters of recommendation: required. Essay: required. Accepts the Common Application.

Rose–Hulman Institute of Technology

5500 Wabash Avenue, Terre Haute, IN 47803

Co-ed since 1995, Rose–Hulman offers the rare combination of technical education and personal attention. Only Caltech, Clarkson, and Harvey Mudd offer comparable intimacy and a technical academic environment. Nearby Indiana State and St. Mary's of the Woods help mitigate the skewed gender ratio. RHIT is among the few engineering schools with significant study abroad offerings.

Website: www.rose-hulman.edu
Location: Suburban
Private
Total Enrollment: 2,270
Undergraduates: 2,219
Male/Female: 78/22

The Rose–Hulman Institute of Technology may not be as well known as Caltech, MIT, or even Carnegie Mellon, but it was the first private college to offer an undergraduate degree in chemical engineering, and it continues to innovate today. If you can handle the lopsided male/female ratio and the limited list of majors (all in engineering and the sciences), Rose offers an outstanding technical background and bright prospects for future employment. Students are smart, motivated, and highly competitive, and love using their computers for work and play. "We are all dorks," says a senior. "Some of us just hide it better than others."

Established in 1874, Rose–Hulman is the oldest private engineering school west of the Alleghenies. Its benefactors were Chauncey Rose, an entrepreneur who brought the railroad to Indiana, and the Hulman family, owners of the Indianapolis Motor Speedway, who gave their fortune to the institution in 1970. (A member of the Hulman family starts the Indianapolis 500 race every year with the famous words, "Ladies and gentlemen, start your engines.") The 200-acre campus includes numerous trees, two small lakes, and a student apartment complex.

General education requirements at Rose include math, physics, chemistry, and humanities and social sciences. Humanities professors "are very eager to educate and expose science- and engineering-oriented people to a different way of thinking," an applied biology major says. In the first quarter, freshmen must take a College and Life Skills course that covers such topics as time management and study skills.

"The courses at Rose are very challenging and demanding," says one sophomore, "and most people who come here want to do very well academically." Thirty-eight percent of classes have fewer than 20 students. Mechanical engineering, chemical engineering, computer science, and electrical engineering are the most popular majors, but regardless of which discipline you choose, odds are you'll

"Our professors love to teach. Research and side projects come in as a distant second to teaching."

find faculty members eager to help. "Our professors love to teach," one student explains. "Research and side projects come in as a distant second to teaching." A software engineering major adds, "There is no such thing as a teaching assistant at Rose."

Students in every program except math must work in a team and complete a project for an outside company. The Interdisciplinary Research Collaborative affords selected students the opportunity to work on ongoing research projects for 10 weeks during the summer. The HERE (Home for Environmentally Responsible Engineering) program for freshmen integrates residential learning with a curriculum that incorporates sustainability topics and design projects into special sections of required courses. ESCALATE is an entrepreneurially focused living/learning community, and Rose–Hulman Ventures is a business incubator program that allows students to gain experience in product development. For those in need of new vistas, there are opportunities to study abroad in a bevy of international locales, including Spain, Sweden, South Korea, New Zealand, and Egypt; 4 percent of students participate. In addition to semester- and yearlong programs, students may enroll in study abroad courses that combine traditional on-campus coursework with a two- to three-week trip at the end of the quarter.

The typical Rose–Hulman student is "very motivated and curious," says a senior. "We have everything from multisport athletes to introverted gamers," adds a junior, "but since we're all engineers it kind of keeps everyone together." Thirty-two percent of students are Indiana natives, and 12 percent come from abroad. African Americans comprise 2 percent of the student body, Asian Americans 4 percent, and Hispanics 3 percent. Hot issues tend to center on campus issues rather than those of global concern. "Students are conservative but don't really get involved politically," one senior explains. Merit scholarships are available, averaging $11,557, but there are no athletic awards.

Fifty-seven percent of students live on campus. Freshmen are guaranteed rooms in the dorms, as are any sophomores who want them. The residence halls boast weekly maid service, and "we're allowed to do almost anything to the rooms, like add lofts or decks to gain space," says a civil engineering major. (At an engineering school, would you expect anything less?) All but two dorms have air-conditioning. Most upperclassmen move into Greek houses or find other off-campus digs, students say. There's a traditional cafeteria, as well as a restaurant-style dining facility,

(continued)

SAT Ranges: CR 550–670, M 630–750

ACT Ranges: 28–32

Financial Aid: 95%

Pell Grant: 14%

Expense: Pr $ $ $

Student Loans: 64%

Average Debt: $ $ $ $

Phi Beta Kappa: No

Applicants: 4,331

Accepted: 58%

Enrolled: 22%

Grad in 6 Years: 77%

Returning Freshmen: 93%

Academics: ✐ ✐ ✐

Social: ☎

Q of L: ★ ★

Admissions: (800) 248-7448

Email Address: admissions@rose-hulman.edu

Strong Programs:
Mechanical Engineering
Chemical Engineering
Computer Science
Electrical Engineering
Biomedical Engineering
Mathematics
Physics

Students in every program except math must work in a team and complete a project for an outside company.

and students report there are typically at least five entrée choices at each meal plus fresh fruit, and steak and seafood on Friday nights. "They certainly make provisions for vegans, vegetarians, and students who are allergic to certain types of food, and will even make sack lunches if you are unable to attend lunch during the day," a senior says. As for safety, "there is essentially zero crime on campus," according to one student, and the school is introducing new training programs to prevent sexual assault.

The town of Terre Haute has some restaurants, a mall, a Starbucks, and two movie theaters, but generally, it's "sleepy and lacking in nightlife, so we create our own," says a physics major. Various groups, including the Greek organizations and Habitat for Humanity, help the town out with service projects. There are eight fraternities and three sororities, which draw 35 percent of the men and 36 percent of the women, respectively. "The girl/guy ratio here definitely hurts social life," confides a student, "but overall it's not bad." When it comes to alcohol, Rose–Hulman allows students 21 and over to imbibe, provided it's behind closed doors. Students say the best weekend activities are usually road trips to Chicago, Cincinnati, Indianapolis, or St. Louis, all within a few hours' drive. Everyone looks forward to the homecoming bonfire, and to basketball games against DePauw. "Homecoming is very big," says a sophomore. "Freshmen build up and guard the bonfire the week preceding homecoming while upperclassmen try to sabotage it," explains a junior.

> **"We have everything from multisport athletes to introverted gamers, but since we're all engineers it kind of keeps everyone together."**

Varsity teams (the Engineers) play in Division III, and men's cross-country, soccer, track and field, swimming, and tennis, along with women's basketball, all earned conference championships recently. Competitive tech teams like the Human Powered Vehicle Team, Team Rose Motorsports, and Cyber Defense Team are strong, but if you're envisioning Rose–Hulman students as pasty-faced lab dwellers, you're sorely misinformed. Approximately half of the student body participate in 22 intramural sports, with flag football, basketball, and ultimate Frisbee the most popular.

Students committed to careers in engineering or the sciences will find a top-flight education at this Midwestern technical school. While Rose "doesn't have that big-school pride" so common in this part of the country, students appreciate the feel created by the small classes and the school's small size. "Our community atmosphere makes us different from anywhere else," a junior says. "Where else do you know the dean of students by his first name? Or talk to your professors while you are working out?"

If You Apply To ➢   **Rose–Hulman:** Early action: Nov. 1. Regular decision: Feb. 1. Financial aid: Mar. 1. Application fee: $40 (paper), free (online). Campus interviews: optional, evaluative. No alumni interviews. SATs or ACTs: required. No Subject Tests. Letters of recommendation: required. Essay: optional.

Rutgers–The State University of New Jersey

65 Davidson Road, Piscataway, NJ 08854

Rutgers is a huge institution spread over three regional campuses and 29 colleges and schools. Rutgers College on the New Brunswick campus is the most prominent. Everything is available: engineering, business, pharmacy, the arts, and the nation's largest women's college (Douglass College in New Brunswick). Recent plunge into big-time sports has been a financial and academic disaster.

Life at Rutgers University is all about choice. Choices between the more than 100 undergraduate majors and 4,000 courses offered among its campuses in New Brunswick, Newark, and Camden. Choices about which of the more than 450 student organizations to join. Even choices about which library to visit, as there are 18 branches with holdings of more than three million volumes university-wide. "Rutgers's best quality is its wide variety of majors, classes, and social activities," confirms one junior.

Rutgers University has three regional campuses (Camden, Newark, and New Brunswick/Piscataway). Rutgers–New Brunswick/Piscataway, which has the largest concentration of students, is composed of five smaller campuses located along the Raritan River. The campuses are connected by a free university bus system, and students travel among campuses to take classes. Rutgers–Newark is in a downtown section of Newark, giving the campus neighborhood a collegiate feel. The smallest campus in the Rutgers system is in Camden, located one stop away from the shopping and cultural offerings of downtown Philadelphia. For those seeking a broad-based education, the university has eight liberal arts schools spread out among its campuses. Seven colleges cater to the needs of students wanting a preprofessional school (business, nursing, life and environmental studies, fine and performing arts, engineering, and pharmacy).

Among the more than 100 majors, the most popular include psychology, biology, criminal justice, and nursing. Especially strong academic programs include history, political science, and chemistry. The workload is steady for most students; science majors and pharmacy students can expect the heaviest load. "The courses here require a great deal of thought and outside preparation if you want to be successful," says a political science major. Other majors include cell biology and neuroscience, genetics and microbiology, biomedical engineering, evolutionary anthropology, and allied health technology. As at any big state university, classes can be large and registration can sometimes be a headache. Professors generally get high marks. "I completely revere most of my professors," says a junior. "They are intelligent, well respected in their fields, and present dynamic lectures."

> **"Rutgers's best quality is its wide variety of majors, classes, and social activities."**

In an effort to reverse the traditional exodus of New Jersey high school superstars from the state, Rutgers offers a variety of honors programs, including special seminars, internships, independent projects, and research opportunities with faculty. Biology students have the run of the 370-acre Rutgers Ecological Preserve and Natural Teaching Area. In addition, Rutgers is home to more than 100 specialized research centers and institutes dedicated to the study of topics ranging from ancient Roman art to mountain gorillas. Rutgers also provides its undergraduates with a chance to study abroad in more than 55 countries, including Cuba, Romania, South Africa, and Thailand.

Although the administration has been attempting to increase the number of out-of-staters, 88 percent of Rutgers students hail from New Jersey. Nevertheless, the

Website: www.rutgers.edu
Location: Small City
Public
Total Enrollment: 54,661
Undergraduates: 43,425
Male/Female: 49/51
SAT Ranges: CR 510–630, M 550–690
ACT Ranges: N/A
Financial Aid: 53%
Pell Grant: N/A
Expense: Pub $ $ $ $
Student Loans: 58%
Average Debt: $ $
Phi Beta Kappa: Yes
Applicants: 37,641
Accepted: 67%
Enrolled: 33%
Grad in 6 Years: 77%
Returning Freshmen: 91%
Academics: ✍ ✍ ✍ ✍
Social: 🕿 🕿 🕿
Q of L: ★ ★ ★
Admissions: (732) 932-4636
Email Address: admissions@ugadm.rutgers.edu

Strong Programs:
Psychology
Biology
Criminal Justice
Nursing
History
Political Science
Chemistry
Business Administration

Rutgers is home
to more than 100
specialized research
centers and institutes.

student population is as diverse as that of the state, with a good proportion of students from cities, suburbs, farms, and seaside communities; 6 percent come from abroad. Minorities account for roughly half the students: 10 percent are African American, 15 percent are Hispanic, and 23 percent are Asian American. "I feel I've grown so much here and learned so much about being a member of a rich and diverse community," explains one senior. The school's administration takes pride in its Committee to Advance Our Common Purposes, which works to reduce prejudice and promote diversity on campus. About 400 students receive athletic scholarships in a wide range of sports, and qualified students receive merit scholarships averaging $8,332.

On-campus housing in New Brunswick accommodates approximately 48 percent of full-time students. "There has been a big push recently to renovate the dorms, so most of them are really nice," says a history major. Another student says, "With the exception of a few mediocre dorms for freshmen, most are extremely large and have air-conditioning; some have free cable TV; and a good number are hardwired for Internet access." Other on-campus housing options include special-interest areas and apartment complexes with kitchens and living rooms. The university also offers a special dormitory for students who are trying to overcome addictions to drugs and alcohol. Rutgers has its own police department that possesses the same training and powers as the New Jersey State Police.

"I completely revere most of my professors."

"The variety of activities at Rutgers provides you with the opportunity to have fun any way you desire," says one student. "There are lots of on-campus social activities," a senior explains, including "movies, coffeehouses, local and bigger bands, lectures, and parties. Off-campus activities include frat parties and bars." Each college has its own student center with pinball machines, pool tables, bowling alleys, and a snack bar. Major social events include Reggae Day at Livingston, Agricultural Field Day at Cook, and Oktoberfest for the campus as a whole. Pioneer Pride Night is Camden's big party. During homecoming, tailgate parties are held in the stadium parking lot, featuring tons of food (including roast pigs and whole sides of beef), continuous music, and thousands of revelers. Reportedly, it is "difficult to drink in dorms," but underage students drink if they really want to. The Greek system, which attracts only a small percentage of men and women, is entirely off campus. While the school neither owns nor administers any of the Greek organizations, it does have a university office for Greek affairs, which oversees the welfare of those belonging to fraternities and sororities. Students say a lot of the nightlife for the New Brunswick campus takes place at the Greek houses.

The Committee to
Advance Our Common
Purposes works to
reduce prejudice and
promote diversity
on campus.

The city of New Brunswick is an attractive place to go for a drink or dinner on the town. Just don't stray too far from campus. "I personally don't feel safe in New Brunswick, so I restrict my outings to on-campus locations," one student admits. A senior says, "Students definitely get involved in the surrounding community and do a lot of volunteer work." Over a recent five-year period, students enrolled in the Citizenship and Service Education Program at Rutgers contributed more than 90,000 hours of service to communities across New Jersey. For those who want to hit the road for fun, New York City and Philadelphia are each only about an hour's drive or train ride, and students flood the Jersey Shore in springtime. The Rutgers College Program Council offers trips ranging from white-water rafting to mountain climbing to skiing.

"[I've] learned so much about being a member of a rich and diverse community."

Varsity, intramural, and club sports fill whatever gap is left by the social scene. The university fields more than 1,000 Division I athletes, among the most of any university in the nation, and successful Scarlet Knights teams include baseball, men's track and field, and women's basketball and soccer. The school's 2012 decision to embrace big-time sports and join the Big Ten, however, has produced more scandals and red ink than athletic glory. The athletic program regularly runs deficits in excess of $20 million annually, much of it to cover severance pay for disgraced coaches and administrators. The average undergraduate pays more than $300 in activities fees to support varsity teams.

Rutgers has a plethora of people and programs characteristic of a large state university. It also offers a lot more, including loyal support from the state's legislature and private sector and tuition that is relatively affordable. Says one satisfied student: "From the diversity of its majors and courses to the hundreds of student organizations on campus, Rutgers gives me a chance to explore a world of options."

> **Overlaps**
>
> **Montclair, College of New Jersey, NYU, Penn State, Rowan University**

> **If You Apply To >**
>
> **Rutgers:** Early action: Nov. 1. Regular decision: Dec. 1. Financial aid: Mar. 15. Application fee: $70. No campus or alumni interviews. SATs or ACTs: required (SAT essay and ACT writing recommended). No Subject Tests. No letters of recommendation. Essay: required. Apply to particular school.

University of St Andrews: See page 387.

University of St Andrews: See page 387.

College of St. Benedict and St. John's University

37 South College Avenue, St. Joseph, MN 56374

The College of St. Benedict (CSB) and St. John's University (SJU) are throwbacks to the way colleges were 50 years ago: women and men on separate campuses and copious amounts of school spirit. Roman Catholics comprise about 54 percent of the students, and monastic communities are very active on both campuses. Nearly 80 percent of the students are from Minnesota.

Remember when women's colleges had nearby brother schools, when dorms were single-sex, and when visitors of the opposite gender were only welcome at certain times? Doesn't ring a bell? Well, you might ask your grandparents. Or you could visit the College of St. Benedict and St. John's University. These two single-sex campuses—all-female CSB and all-male SJU—are five miles apart and have their own presidents, but they share a common heritage and mission: students and faculty join together in a shared liberal arts education, guided by principles of their Benedictine founders. The schools' small sizes and respect for tradition give rise to a tight-knit community. "We have a strong sense of school pride and alumni connection," says one happy student. "Once a Bennie or a Johnnie, always a Bennie or a Johnnie."

Owned and operated by the largest men's Benedictine monastery in the world, St. John's occupies 2,500 pristine acres in rural Minnesota, an area filled with forests, lakes, and the wide-open spaces perfect for outdoorsy types. The two colleges are connected by a free and frequent shuttle bus. Alongside a 130-year-old quadrangle erected by monks is a strikingly modern church designed by Marcel Breuer. St. Benedict is a cohesive 800-acre campus comprised of redbrick buildings and cobblestone walks. Together, the colleges have invested millions in facilities in recent years. A major renovation of the SJU Learning Commons, including its existing library space, is scheduled for completion in 2017.

> **Website:** www.csbsju.edu
> **Location:** City Outskirts
> **Private**
> **Total Enrollment:** 3,692
> **Undergraduates:** 3,639
> **Male/Female:** 47/53
> **SAT Ranges:** CR 480–570, M 450–580
> **ACT Ranges:** 22–28
> **Financial Aid:** 93%
> **Pell Grant:** 26%
> **Expense:** Pr $ $
> **Student Loans:** 71%
> **Average Debt:** $ $ $ $
> **Phi Beta Kappa:** No
> **Applicants:** 3,465
> **Accepted:** 74%
> **Enrolled:** 36%

(continued)

Grad in 6 Years: 81%
Returning Freshmen: 88%
Academics: ✎ ✎ ✎
Social: ☎ ☎ ☎
Q of L: ★ ★ ★
Admissions: (800) 544-1489
Email Address: admissions@
   csbsju.edu

Strong Programs:
Global Business Leadership
Accounting
Psychology
Biology
Communication
Music
Nursing
Environmental Studies

Entrepreneurial Scholars travel to Silicon Valley and China/Hong Kong and start their own entrepreneurial ventures.

Seventy-one percent of students engage in community service, often through Campus Ministry programs.

St. Benedict and St. John's share a joint academic program through which students take classes together on both campuses. The core curriculum requires a first-year seminar, Ethics Common Seminar, and a capstone project. Students must also fulfill requirements in a number of areas, including the humanities, natural sciences, social sciences, fine arts, theology, and foreign language. The Global Business Leadership program prepares students to be leaders in a global economy and is the most popular major, followed by accounting, psychology, and biology. Programs in communication, music, and nursing are also well regarded. The interdisciplinary environmental studies program is enhanced by access to the area's natural resources and the largest solar farm in the upper Midwest. The theology program benefits from abundant resources, including the Hill Museum & Manuscript Library, one of the foremost microfilm collections of centuries-old handwritten manuscripts. New programs include majors in integrated science and European studies and minors in book arts and teaching English as a second language.

"There is a lot of emphasis on sharing of ideas, discussions, and collaborative work," says one sociology major. Very few classes have more than 30 students, and some fill up fast. The small classes encourage a community atmosphere and strong student/faculty ties. "The quality of instruction that I have received at CSB/SJU has been extraordinary," says a nursing major. "Faculty members encourage students to ask them questions and will go out of their way for the success of their students." Members of the monastic communities make up under 5 percent of the CSB/SJU faculty.

For those who tire of the Minnesota winters, which can start in October and run until April, faculty-led international study programs are offered in 20 countries on six continents. Each program is limited to about 30 students, and 57 percent of students take part. Numerous shorter trips are also offered during semester break and summer break. The Donald McNeely Center for Entrepreneurship is an educational resource that provides classes, coaching, and assistance to budding entrepreneurs from a range of disciplines. The program's Entrepreneurial Scholars travel to Silicon Valley and China/Hong Kong, and all of them start their own entrepreneurial ventures. Undergraduate research is becoming more prevalent at CSB/SJU (41 percent of students participate), and there is an endowed summer research program in the health and medical areas. An honors program serves exceptional freshmen, and upper-class students may also apply.

Known as "Bennies" or "Johnnies," CSB/SJU students "tend to be honest, fun, hardworking, and—most importantly—loyal and respectful," according to a junior.

"Once a Bennie or a Johnnie, always a Bennie or a Johnnie." Fifty-four percent of students are Roman Catholic, 78 percent are from Minnesota, and most are white. African Americans constitute 3 percent of the student body, Hispanics 6 percent, and Asian Americans 5 percent. International students account for 5 percent of the student population. A senior notes that despite the lack of diversity on campus, the schools offer "a lot of programming events encouraging students to learn about diversity," and a junior adds that, politically, "We encompass all viewpoints, from ultraconservative to ultraliberal." Merit scholarships averaging $16,165 are available, and 26 percent of first-year students qualify for the Pell Grant, but there are no athletic scholarships.

Through a four-year residential program, 90 percent of students live on campus. The residence halls are staffed partly by members of the monastic communities, but students aren't made to feel like a nun is watching their every move. "First-year residence halls are your typical dorm, and then each year the housing gets better," reports an elementary education major. Other options include on-campus apartments, such as Flynntown, an independent living area for juniors and seniors that has a central student center. Students can choose from four dining halls on either campus and most report the fare to be tasty and diverse. "Campus security is excellent," says one student. "They are not only there to enforce the laws and punish rule breakers, they are also a great resource and compassionate people."

Since there are no fraternities or sororities here, students have learned to make their own fun. The Joint Events Council organizes regular weekday and weekend events, including "campus bands performing, poetry readings, comedians, magicians, and big concerts every semester," says a student. Students 21 and older are allowed to consume alcohol in their rooms, but underage drinkers face stiff penalties if caught. Each year, students look forward to the Festival of Cultures, the Fruit at the Finish Triathlon, the Senior Farewell, and spring break trips involving community service. Also popular is the annual Pines music festival, which welcomes the spring with a day of concerts featuring popular national acts. Says a sophomore, "Off campus, there are many things to do in St. Cloud and also in St. Joseph, such as parties, coffee shops, restaurants, shopping, and movies." Seventy-one percent of students engage in community service, often through Campus Ministry programs. St. Cloud (metro population 195,000) is less than 10 minutes away by car, and the Twin Cities are about an hour away.

> "There is a lot of emphasis on sharing of ideas, discussions, and collaborative work."

The CSB Blazers field 10 Division III teams, and the SJU Johnnies boast 11. The football team is a perennial powerhouse (and the winningest Division III team in history), and its rivalry with St. Thomas is as strong as ever. Curiously enough, a team of guys known as the Rat Pack gets students psyched up for games. Men's golf has participated in the Division III national tournament 14 of the last 17 years, and the Johnnie baseball team was the 2015 conference champ. The Blazers volleyball team advanced to the national tournament for the fifth straight year in 2015; women's soccer and track and field are also competitive. Nonvarsity students can participate in a variety of club and intramural sports, and activities like kayaking and indoor rock climbing, offered through the Outdoor Leadership Center, are popular year-round.

Students who attend CSB/SJU revel in the schools' small-town setting, their traditions, and the grounding that comes from their shared Benedictine values. Perhaps more than anything, they treasure the community spirit that allows them to grow both individually and together. Says a senior, "Students challenge and push one another to be the best version of themselves that they can be: academically, athletically, socially, spiritually, and as informed citizens."

Overlaps

University of Minnesota, University of St. Thomas, University of Minnesota Duluth, St. Cloud State, Winona State, Gustavus Adolphus, Minnesota State University Mankato, College of Saint Scholastica

If You Apply To ➤ **St. Benedict and St. John's:** Early action I: Nov. 15. Early action II: Dec. 15. Regular decision: Jan. 15. Financial aid: Mar. 15. Housing: Jun. 1. No application fee. Campus and alumni interviews: optional, evaluative. SATs or ACTs: required. No Subject Tests. Letters of recommendation: optional. Essay: optional. Accepts the Common Application.

St. John's College

Annapolis Campus: P.O. Box 2800, Annapolis, MD 21404-2800
Santa Fe Campus: 1160 Camino Cruz Blanca, Santa Fe, NM 87505-4599

Books, books, and more books is what you'll get at St. John's—from Thucydides to Tolstoy, Euclid to Einstein. St. John's attracts smart, intellectual, and nonconformist students who like to talk (and argue) about books. Easy to get in, not so easy to graduate. One of the few institutions with two coequal campuses. Students admitted to one can spend time at the other. St. John's is a croquet powerhouse.

Annapolis
Website: www.sjc.edu
Location: Suburban
Private
Total Enrollment: 451
Undergraduates: 406
Male/Female: 55/45
SAT Ranges: CR 620–750,
   M 590–700
ACT Ranges: 23–30
Financial Aid: 90%
Pell Grant: 19%
Expense: Pr $ $ $ $
Student Loans: 55%
Average Debt: $ $
Phi Beta Kappa: No
Applicants: 332
Accepted: 78%
Enrolled: 40%
Grad in 6 Years: 71%
Returning Freshmen: 79%
Academics: ✍ ✍ ✍ ✍ ½
Social: ☎ ☎ ☎
Q of L: ★ ★ ★ ★
Admissions: (800) 727-9238
Email Address: annapolis
   .admissions@sjc.edu

Strong Programs:
The Great Books Program
Liberal Arts

Santa Fe
Website: www.sjc.edu
Location: Small City
Private
Total Enrollment: 373
Undergraduates: 318
Male/Female: 58/42

With no traditional professors, departments, or majors, and a combined total of fewer than 1,000 students on its two campuses, St. John's College is about as far from the typical postsecondary experience as you can get. Or maybe it's much closer to what college used to be—after all, the Annapolis campus traces its roots to King William's School—the Maryland colony's "free" school—founded in 1696. More than two centuries later, in 1964, St. John's opened a second campus in Santa Fe, New Mexico, to facilitate a doubling of enrollment and offer its super-serious students a change of scenery. While the campuses may be a thousand miles apart, the Johnnies who populate them share an all-consuming quest for knowledge in the classical tradition. Their true teachers are the Great Books, about 150 of the most influential works of Western civilization. "One of the beautiful things about the St. John's program and its focus on the unchanging questions of mankind is that it changes very little," says a student. "I appreciate the sense that I am studying something permanent and real."

Physically, the two St. John's campuses are more than just two time zones from one another. The colonial brick structures of the small urban campus in Annapolis, where the central classroom building dates from 1742, are squeezed into the city's historic district. With the Maryland state capitol and the U.S. Naval Academy in the neighborhood, this campus exudes old-world charm, and its location at the confluence of the Severn River and the Chesapeake Bay allows students to participate in sailing, crew, and individual sculling. The Santa Fe campus sits on 250 acres in the sun-drenched capital of New Mexico, just two and a half miles from downtown. The adobe-style buildings reflect Spanish and Native American traditions, and their perch in the Sangre de Cristo Mountains offers beautiful views of the city below. Students at St. John's in Santa Fe can get back to nature in several nearby national parks, which offer hiking, mountain biking, snowboarding, and skiing. Students may attend both campuses during their academic careers, and many do so.

> **"I appreciate the sense that I am studying something permanent and real."**

The St. John's curriculum, known as "the program," has every student read the Great Books in roughly chronological order. All students major in liberal arts, discussing the books in seminars, writing papers about them, and debating the riddles of human existence they raise. Classes are led by tutors, who would be tenured professors anywhere else, but here are just the most advanced students. Each tutor is required to teach any subject within the curriculum (resisting the general trend in American academia toward more and more specialization). As a group, the tutors help students divine wisdom from each other and from great philosophers and thinkers, from Thucydides and Tolstoy to Euclid and Einstein. "Because St. John's is not a research institution, the tutor's only job is teaching and engaging with students," says one junior. Both campuses follow a curriculum that would have delighted poet and educator Matthew Arnold, who argued that the goal of education is "to know the best which has been thought and said in the world."

There are no registration or scheduling hassles at St. John's; the daily course of study is mapped out before students set foot on campus. The curriculum includes four years of mathematics, two years of ancient Greek and French, three years of laboratory science, two years of music, and, of course, four years of Great Books seminars. Freshmen study the Greeks, sophomores advance through the Romans and the Renaissance, juniors cover the 17th and 18th centuries, and seniors do the 19th and 20th centuries. Readings are from primary sources only: math from Euclid and Ptolemy, physics from Maxwell, psychology from Freud, and so on. For about seven weeks in the junior and senior years, seminars are suspended and students study a book or topic one-on-one with a tutor. The assumption is that the Great Books can stand on their own, representing the highest achievements of human intellect. "There is a real sense of community and a collaborative feel to all of the academic work we do," says one sophomore. "Our class conversations carry over into the dining hall, the quad, the common rooms, and coffee shop."

> "Because St. John's is not a research institution, the tutor's only job is teaching and engaging with students."

Students say the junior year, with its advanced curriculum in math and the natural sciences, is the most challenging. Still, the climate is anything but cutthroat. "Preparing for a class is not for the sake of competing with classmates rather for the sake of being able to bring something to the table," says a first-year student. While there are no multiple-choice tests and no formal exams, since everyone's doing the same thing, there's a lot of peer pressure not to slack off. Many St. John's students find they need a year off between the sophomore and junior years to decompress; some switch from Annapolis to Santa Fe or vice versa, and a relatively high percentage of students take more than six years to graduate. St. John's prefers that all eight semesters be completed in residence. Twenty students per year (10 from each campus) receive academic credit for study abroad, via a semester-long program in Aix-en-Provence, France, that teaches the established junior curriculum in a living European context.

A fifth of St. John's students are transfers from more conventional colleges—a true act of devotion, since St. John's requires everyone to begin as freshmen. Though the reasons students choose St. John's are never simple, the common thread is a fierce love of learning. "There is a universal desire for knowledge here and a spirit of inquiry that I would say is unparalleled. A heated discussion about Plato on the grassy knoll is the type of sight that reminds me why I love this place," one student reflects. The vast majority of students at both campuses are out-of-staters; international students represent 9 percent of the student body in Annapolis and 20 percent in Santa Fe. In Annapolis, 6 percent are Hispanic, 4 percent are Asian American, and 2 percent are African American, while in Santa Fe those groups account for 12 percent, 3 percent, and less than 1 percent, respectively. One student reports that students are "more interested in political philosophy and theory" than in actually engaging in political or social activism. Admissions are need-blind, and limited merit awards are available, but no athletic ones. Nineteen percent of incoming Annapolis freshmen are eligible for the Pell Grant, compared to 33 percent in Santa Fe. Qualified international students may take advantage of special financial aid packages.

> "Our class conversations carry over into the dining hall, the quad, the common rooms, and coffee shop."

Roughly two-thirds of students in Annapolis and 85 percent of those in Santa Fe live on campus in the co-ed dorms; freshmen are guaranteed a room. In Annapolis, the six "historic" residence halls are arranged around a central quad, while the two modern halls face College Creek. (Students warn that "historic" is code for "old,"

(continued)

SAT Ranges: CR 600–730, M 560–690
ACT Ranges: 26–31
Financial Aid: 87%
Pell Grant: 33%
Expense: Pr $ $ $ $
Student Loans: 76%
Average Debt: $ $
Phi Beta Kappa: No
Applicants: 177
Accepted: 81%
Enrolled: 53%
Grad in 6 Years: 47%
Returning Freshmen: 82%
Academics: ✐ ✐ ✐ ✐ ½
Social: ☎ ☎ ☎
Q of L: ★ ★ ★ ★
Admissions: (800) 331-5232
Email Address: santafe.admissions@sjc.edu

Strong Programs:
The Great Books Program
Liberal Arts

The St. John's curriculum, known as "the program," has every student read the Great Books in roughly chronological order.

and complain about "schizophrenic heating and cooling" and a lack of hot water for morning showers.) In Santa Fe, the dorms are small, modern units clustered around courtyards. Most students get singles or divided double rooms. Upperclassmen typically live off campus in apartments and group houses; those who stay in the dorms usually get single rooms. "I think the food is consistently good and underrated," says one Santa Fe campus resident. There are no fraternities or sororities.

"With the amount of reading and thinking done here, students most definitely need to find ways to have well-rounded lives. There are pick-up sports, dance groups, musical ensembles, and many other interest-based clubs to participate in," says one student. Drinking is a favored release for Johnnies, who have, of course, read Plato's Symposium and are familiar with the likes of François Rabelais ("Drink constantly. You will never die."). Still, hard liquor is not allowed on campus, and parties and kegs must be registered. And although no one under 21 may be legally served at college-sponsored events, which are patrolled to prevent underage drinking, young-

"Students most definitely need to find ways to have well-rounded lives."

sters tip their share of brew at smaller gatherings and in their rooms. Only students who are extremely rowdy or disruptive are reported to the dean's office to face penalties. "Campus security really only makes it an issue if you do first," one student explains. Road trips to Washington, D.C., Baltimore, New York, and Assateague State Park are options for Annapolis students with cars. In Santa Fe, nearby blues and jazz clubs are popular, though one student cautions that the town shuts down around 9 p.m.

Popular annual events on both campuses include Lola's, a casino night sponsored by the senior class, and Reality, a three-day festival of food, games, and general debauchery thrown for the seniors the weekend before commencement. There's Melee, the club where "combatants" fight epic battles with foam weapons of their own creation, and Tuesday Nite Fites, where students vote for line-ups like Funk versus Dinosaurs and then debate the winner. There's also the Arc party, held to celebrate the sophomores' completion of the Old Testament, and Oktoberfest. Intercollegiate club teams in crew, fencing, croquet, and women's soccer are available. In fact, the Johnnies hold more national croquet titles than any other college, and the match against The Naval Academy each spring is the occasion for a genteel lawn party. Annapolis students relish their intramural teams, with names like the Druids and the Furies. In Santa Fe, the nearby Rio Grande and Chama rivers offer excellent white-water canoeing, kayaking, and rafting, while the Hueco Tanks area offers rock climbing and bouldering; the Taos Ski Valley and Ski Santa Fe are excellent in the winter months. The Outdoor Programs Office organizes trips and makes athletic equipment available for use.

Students at St. John's are as passionate about learning as their peers at other schools are about basketball rivalries or blowout parties. And while those larger colleges and universities try desperately to grow and change, St. John's cherishes its tradition—including the mandate that seniors wear formal academic dress to their oral examinations, which are open to the public. As one happy Johnnie simply sums up, "Everyone is passionate and engaged. The program wouldn't work if students and tutors were not engaged."

Overlaps

University of New Mexico, Reed, Kenyon, Bard, Occidental, Colorado College, Smith, Mills

If You Apply To ➤ **St. John's:** Early action I: Nov. 15. Early action II: Jan. 15. Regular decision: Feb. 15. Financial aid: Feb. 1. Housing: May 1. No application fee. Campus interviews: recommended, evaluative. Alumni interviews: optional, informational. SATs or ACTs: optional. Subject Tests: optional. Letters of recommendation: required. Essay: required. Accepts the Common Application with supplement. Apply to one campus only.

College of St. Benedict and St. John's University: See page 635.

St. Lawrence University

Canton, NY 13617

St. Lawrence is perched far back in the north country, closer to Ottawa and Montreal than to Syracuse. Isolation breeds camaraderie, and SLU students have a special bond similar to that at places like Dartmouth and Whitman. Compare to Allegheny and Hobart and William Smith. Environmental studies is the crown jewel: where else can you live and work in a Mongolian-style yurt?

St. Lawrence University seeks snow lovers who place equal value on their experiences inside and outside the classroom. Its upstate New York location offers quick access to both pristine ski slopes and rugged hiking trails—and to the bright lights of Ottawa and Montreal. Classes are small and there are no TAs, meaning it's as easy to form friendships with faculty members as it is with fellow students. A flood of new facilities has helped to make the campus almost as breathtaking as the natural beauty that surrounds it. "The students at SLU are here to learn," says one sophomore. "They come for a liberal arts education that will teach them to be a well-rounded individual who can speak about everything from great American literature to microbiology or the Ottoman Empire."

Hiking trails, a river, and a golf course surround SLU's 30 buildings, which sit on a 1,000-acre tract; facilities are clustered, so even the most distant buildings are only 10 minutes from one another. Many buildings date from the late 19th century, and though their exteriors have been preserved, their interiors are fully modernized. In all, the school has invested $200 million to beautify and better its campus over the past decade. The LEED Gold–certified Johnson Hall of Science supports the biology, chemistry, biochemistry, neuroscience, and psychology programs. A 155-bed residence hall opened recently and is powered by geothermal energy.

St. Lawrence offers a classical liberal arts education, placing a premium on small classes and team teaching. General education requirements include courses in the following areas: The Human Experience and the Natural World; Human Diversity: Culture and Communication; Quantitative/Logical Reasoning; Environmental Literacy; and Integrated Learning. Everyone also participates in the two-semester First-Year Program (FYP), which emphasizes critical thinking, communication, and interdisciplinary content. "Students are separated into first-year 'colleges' for housing, and each college is enrolled together in a unique course," an economics major explains. There are more than a dozen "residential colleges," each with 30 to 45 students, and FYP professors also serve as academic advisors. "This program creates an instant living and learning community the moment you step on campus, and students within FYPs become like family," says one student.

> **"The First-Year Program creates an instant living and learning community the moment you step on campus."**

Economics is the most popular major, followed by psychology, business in the liberal arts, performance and communication arts, and biology. Programs in conservation biology, government, and neuroscience are notable, and a new major in statistics was recently introduced. Students in the signature environmental studies program are encouraged to pursue combined majors that integrate the study of

Website: www.stlawu.edu
Location: Small Town
Private
Total Enrollment: 2,444
Undergraduates: 2,402
Male/Female: 45/55
SAT Ranges: CR 550–650, M 550–660
ACT Ranges: 26–30
Financial Aid: 96%
Pell Grant: 23%
Expense: Pr $ $ $ $
Student Loans: 60%
Average Debt: $ $
Phi Beta Kappa: Yes
Applicants: 5,876
Accepted: 46%
Enrolled: 25%
Grad in 6 Years: 87%
Returning Freshmen: 89%
Academics: ✍ ✍ ✍
Social: ☎ ☎ ☎
Q of L: ★ ★ ★
Admissions: (315) 229-5261
Email Address: admissions@stlawu.edu

Strong Programs:
Environmental Studies
Economics
Psychology
Business in the Liberal Arts
Performance and
    Communication Arts
Biology
Conservation Biology
Government

environmental issues with substantial study in one of 10 other fields, such as geology, psychology, English, or sociology. The academic climate demands that students pay attention and keep up with coursework, but competition is hardly a concern. "The academic climate is focused and intense. Sunday through Friday, students are working diligently to finish work and study for tests," observes a business major. Since there are no teaching assistants, full professors teach even the introductory courses; 62 percent of all classes have fewer than 20 students. "Teachers value the input of each student, and oftentimes a significant part of the overall class grade is based on participation," says a junior.

In an effort "to make the world our classroom," St. Lawrence encourages students to spend time away from campus. Sixty-three percent do so, and while some participate in one of the school's 25 international programs, others choose the nearby Adirondack Semester at Saranac Lake, about an hour from campus. Under this program, offered each fall, a small group of students live and study in a yurt village in a park, where they learn wilderness survival skills and take courses on topics such as environmental philosophy and nature writing. The St. Lawrence University Fellows Program offers 25 to 30 students housing and $3,500 stipends for summer research.

"Everyone at St. Lawrence smiles. This is easy, as everyone's so good-looking," quips a senior. Thirty-seven percent of the students are New Yorkers, and 9 percent are international. Three percent are African American, 5 percent Hispanic, and 2 percent Asian American. "Politics can be important" on campus, says one student, "although peripherally for most students." Twenty-three percent of incoming freshmen are Pell-eligible. The university awards merit scholarships averaging $20,151 to top students and also hands out 41 athletic scholarships for Division I men's and women's ice hockey.

> **"Sunday through Friday, students are working diligently to finish work and study for tests."**

Virtually all SLU students live in the dorms, and seniors definitely have it best, with access to "new and spacious townhouses that sit along the golf course," says a sophomore. Everyone else makes do in the "adequate" residence halls, which have mostly double rooms featuring Wi-Fi access, cable TV, computer and study lounges, laundry rooms, and kitchens. The dining halls serve up themed dinners once a month, as well as ethnic foods, vegetarian options, and organic items. Other options include the pub and convenience store, both in the student center, and a café in the physical education building. In addition, 10 percent of the men and 15 percent of the women go Greek; fraternity and sorority members may live and eat in their chapter houses.

"Students will sometimes go to Ottawa and Montreal if they crave a city scene, but there are always fun, social activities on campus," says one student. University-sponsored activities include a campus nightclub, four different first-run movies each week, and the campus coffeehouse—a great place to hear a live band, acoustic guitarist, or comedian. On campus, students under 21 aren't permitted to drink. One sophomore says, "There is a social drinking culture on campus, where students are not raging and binge drinking, but rather having a few beers and hanging out with friends. There is no pressure to drink."

The "charming" town of Canton is "a speck on the state map," says one student. "We do not live in a college town at all." Still, Canton does have everything from bagels to handmade jewelry to bars and restaurants, and Potsdam, 10 minutes away, offers more. But students say the most popular pastimes include skiing, hiking, rock climbing, and canoeing down the Grasse River (when it's not frozen over), as well as road trips to Ottawa and Montreal, where there's better shopping and dining, and the drinking age is lower too. "Being in the Adirondacks means you can escape to

Environmental studies students are encouraged to pursue combined majors that integrate substantial study in one of 10 other fields.

Favorite annual traditions include Peak Weekend, when students, faculty, and staff summit all 46 of the Adirondack High Peaks.

the mountains, or the river, when you need a break or want to hang out with your friends," says a freshman. Favorite annual traditions include Winter Weekend, a two-day celebration of the season, and Peak Weekend, when students, faculty, and staff summit all 46 of the Adirondack High Peaks.

In varsity sports, the Division I Skating Saints hockey teams are the top draw, especially when the opponent is archrival Clarkson. Solid Division III teams include men's lacrosse and men's and women's soccer and track and field. The school's fine athletic facilities include two field houses, one with more than a dozen courts, a pool, a three-story climbing wall, and a ropes course. The school's golf course doubles as a running route in warmer weather and a cross-country ski trail during the winter. Seventy percent of all students participate in intramural and club sports; available sports range from club hockey to broomball, co-ed soccer, and an annual fall quadathlon.

"Teachers value the input of each student."

St. Lawrence makes up for frigid winters with the warmth of a close-knit, caring community. As the frenzied pace of construction winds down and academic standards are ratcheted up, SLU is a school on the rise, especially for those wanting to get back to nature.

Overlaps

Colby, Hamilton, Hobart and William Smith, Union, University of Vermont

If You Apply To ➢ **St. Lawrence:** Early decision, regular decision, and financial aid: Feb. 1. Housing: May 1. Application fee: $60. Campus interviews: recommended, evaluative. Alumni interviews: optional, evaluative. SATs or ACTs: optional. Subject Tests: optional. Letters of recommendation: required. Essay: optional. Accepts the Common Application.

Saint Louis University

221 North Grand Boulevard, St. Louis, MO 63103

This is not your father's SLU. The campus and surrounding neighborhood have been spiffed up in the past three decades, and SLU's campus is a pleasant oasis in the bustle of midtown St. Louis. In addition to strengths in premed and theology, SLU has an unusual specialty in aviation science. Competes with Loyola Chicago and Marquette for bragging rights among Midwestern Jesuit institutions.

Within sight of St. Louis's famed Gateway Arch, the historical gateway to the American West, sits Saint Louis University, the first university established west of the Mississippi River. The school's academic atmosphere is shaped by its Jesuit tradition; administrators ensure that each student receives personal care and attention and expect graduates to contribute to society and lead efforts for social change. In return, students find an atmosphere where their faith is encouraged. SLU offers students many nationally recognized programs, from premed to aviation and, of course, theology. "SLU is the type of university that prepares the whole person to go out into the world," says a freshman.

Since 1987, the SLU campus has undergone an $840 million renovation and features pedestrian walkways, lush greenery, fountains, and sculptures, as well as the signature Saint Louis University gates at all entrances. Cupples House, a beautiful old mansion in the middle of campus, houses 19th-century furniture and an art gallery—and is just a short walk from a new, modern focal point on campus, the Busch Student Center. The center is home to a bookstore, copy center, eateries, lounges, and conference facilities. Numerous renovations and additions have been

Website: www.slu.edu
Location: City Outskirts
Private
Total Enrollment: 11,539
Undergraduates: 7,488
Male/Female: 41/59
SAT Ranges: CR 540–660, M 550–670
ACT Ranges: 25–30
Financial Aid: 89%
Pell Grant: 21%
Expense: Pr $
Student Loans: 61%
Average Debt: $ $ $ $
Phi Beta Kappa: Yes

(continued)

Applicants: 13,236
Accepted: 63%
Enrolled: 20%
Grad in 6 Years: 74%
Returning Freshmen: 90%
Academics: ✍ ✍ ✍
Social: ☎ ☎
Q of L: ★ ★ ★
Admissions: (314) 977-2500
Email Address: admission@
   slu.edu

Strong Programs:
Premed
Aviation Science
Theology
Nursing
Biology
Accounting
Exercise Science
Psychology

The Manresa Program offers interdisciplinary and integrated study in the intellectual and social traditions of the Church.

Greek life at SLU— unusual for a Jesuit institution—claims 18 percent of the men and 26 percent of the women.

completed over the last few years, including Cook Hall, which doubled the size of the business school facilities; the Saint Louis University Museum of Art; and the Salus Center, which houses the School of Public Health.

In keeping with its strong Jesuit commitment to education in the broadest sense, all SLU undergrads must complete distribution requirements in cultural diversity, world history, fine arts, literature, science, social science, mathematics, languages, and foundations of discourse. Additionally, students must take philosophy and theology courses, such as SLUVision, which integrates community service with the philosophy and theology component. The most popular majors are nursing, biology, accounting, exercise science, and psychology. Premed, philosophy, and theology are also outstanding programs. SLU attracts scholars from around the globe with one of the world's most complete microfilm collections of Vatican documents. Parks College, America's first certified college of aviation, offers degree programs in aviation science and is a legacy of the days when St. Louis was a flying hub. (Remember Charles Lindbergh's "Spirit of St. Louis"?) The meteorology program in the College of Arts and Sciences provides students with an opportunity to study with specialists in satellite, radar, and mesoscale meteorology.

> **"SLU is the type of university that prepares the whole person to go out into the world."**

The academic climate at SLU is "very competitive," according to one junior. "This school sets high standards for its students," adds a classmate, "thereby creating opportunities for a good learning environment." Fifty-four percent of classes have fewer than 20 students, but the quality of teaching varies greatly by professor, students say. "I have had horrible professors and wonderful professors," a sophomore says. More than 300 SLU students study outside of the United States each year. In Madrid, Spain, SLU has one of the largest and most charming American campuses in Europe. The Micah House Program is a living/learning program integrated around themes of peace and justice—it takes its name from the biblical prophet Micah, who spoke out against social injustice in ancient Israel. The Manresa Program offers interdisciplinary and integrated study in the intellectual and social traditions of the Church from the New Testament period to the present.

SLU students tend to be "friendly and pretty laid-back," says a senior, but "most take school seriously." Many undergraduates come from private, religiously affiliated high schools; 28 percent are Roman Catholic. Twenty-eight percent hail from the Show-Me State, while 6 percent are international, coming from more than 70 countries. African Americans comprise 6 percent of the student body, Asian Americans 9 percent, and Hispanics 6 percent. Because SLU is a Jesuit institution, human rights and abortion are prominent issues of debate. The residential life department trains diversity advocates who serve as programmers and facilitators for the dorms; they get in-depth training about diversity, racism, and oppression. Billiken World Festival is a weeklong celebration of diversity that includes a citywide festival of African and Caribbean culture and music. The school offers 118 athletic scholarships, along with merit scholarships worth an average of $15,025.

Fifty-two percent of the student body lives on campus and 49 percent take part in residential learning communities, which are centered on a specific theme or interest. Upperclassmen can move into spacious courtyard-style apartments, but many opt for less expensive apartments off campus. "The dorms are sufficient," one student says. "They're nothing to brag about." The dining options are tasty, but students complain about the lack of healthy options. "The campus isn't really vegetarian/vegan friendly," laments one sophomore. Students say they feel safe on campus thanks to an active public safety department and the continuing improvement of surrounding neighborhoods.

Social life at SLU includes campus events, such as movies in the Quad, dances, and Greek parties, and the plethora of restaurants and coffee shops in St. Louis, as well as movie theaters, museums, bars, sporting events, and nightlife. A student says, "The social life is very active. Students know how to juggle personal with academic lives." Greek life at SLU—unusual for a Jesuit institution—claims 18 percent of the men and 26 percent of the women. Students say most parties take place in off-campus apartments or at an off-campus fraternity house, and despite the rules limiting alcohol on campus, it's common in the apartments. Spring Fever and Fall Homecoming, both annual events, feature bands, club-sponsored booths, and vendors. True to tradition, Sunday evening mass is usually packed with students of all beliefs, and "practically everyone" participates in community service and outreach projects. Road trips to Kansas City, Chicago, and nearby schools like the University of Illinois and Indiana University are also popular.

> **"This school sets high standards for its students."**

SLU has no varsity football team, but Billiken squads more than compensate for this deficit. (A billiken was a common good-luck charm in the early 1900s. A popular sportswriter of the time said the charm resembled the then-football coach, and the name stuck.) Teams compete in Division I, and the Billiken's men's basketball and baseball teams are recent Atlantic 10 Conference champions. Women's tennis and softball are also competitive. For weekend warriors, the Simon Recreation Center boasts a 40-meter pool, six racquetball courts, and loads of equipment.

Saint Louis University is winning students' devotion and increasing its national visibility by offering a slew of strong programs. The Jesuit education prepares students to work for a more just and humane world. "SLU is a good choice for its relatively moderate-sized classrooms, its dedication toward a Jesuit mission, and its enjoyable learning environment," says a senior. "I am very happy that I chose SLU."

Overlaps

University of Missouri, Marquette, University of Illinois at Urbana–Champaign, Washington University in St. Louis, Loyola University Chicago, Creighton, University of Dayton, Xavier

If You Apply To ➤

SLU: Rolling admissions. (Priority deadline: Dec. 1.) Priority financial aid: Feb. 1. Housing: May 1. No application fee. Campus and alumni interviews: recommended, evaluative. SATs or ACTs: required. No Subject Tests. Letters of recommendation: recommended. Essay: required. Accepts the Common Application. Apply to particular programs. Music applicants must audition. Studio art applicants must submit portfolio.

St. Mary's College of Maryland

St. Mary's City, MD 20686

A public liberal arts institution of the same breed as Mary Washington, UNC Asheville, and much larger William and Mary. St. Mary's historic but sleepy environs are 90 minutes from D.C. and Baltimore on Maryland's western shore. With the Chesapeake Bay close at hand, St. Mary's is a haven for sailors. Maryland's public "honors college" is a well-kept secret beyond Maryland's borders; less than 10 percent of students come from out of state.

Twenty-five years ago, St. Mary's College of Maryland was just another public college, albeit one with a gorgeous waterfront campus in the oldest continuously inhabited English settlement in the New World. In 1992, the state of Maryland decided to make St. Mary's its public "honors college"—and the rest, as they say around there, is history. Students can easily design their own majors, undertake independent research projects, or work closely with professors to investigate whatever interests them. "This is truly a home away from home," says a biology major.

Website: www.smcm.edu
Location: Rural
Public
Total Enrollment: 1,706
Undergraduates: 1,679
Male/Female: 43/57

(continued)

SAT Ranges: CR 530–640,
   M 500–620
ACT Ranges: 22–28
Financial Aid: 72%
Pell Grant: 25%
Expense: Pub $ $ $ $
Student Loans: 51%
Average Debt: $
Phi Beta Kappa: Yes
Applicants: 1,675
Accepted: 79%
Enrolled: 30%
Grad in 6 Years: 78%
Returning Freshmen: 86%
Academics: ✍ ✍ ✍ ✍
Social: ☎ ☎ ☎
Q of L: ★ ★ ★ ★
Admissions: (800) 492-7181
Email Address: admissions@
   smcm.edu

Strong Programs:
Biology
Psychology
Economics
English
Anthropology
Music
Chemistry
Environmental Studies

*The school has its own
marina right on the
St. Mary's River, with
a shoreline that gets
beautiful sunset views.*

"This place will allow you to try new things, understand yourself better, and open your eyes to the world."

St. Mary's has never been owned by any religious denomination and takes its name from its founding in 1840 in St. Mary's City, the original capital of Maryland. The campus sits on a peninsula in southern Maryland where the Potomac River meets the Chesapeake Bay. Not surprisingly, it has an excellent center for estuary research, as well as a strong working relationship with the Chesapeake Biological Laboratory; the school even has its own marina right on the St. Mary's River, with a shoreline that gets beautiful sunset views. Architectural styles range from colonial to modern buildings, though the land on which the campus is built belongs to a 1,100-acre national historic landmark, commemorating Maryland's first colonial settlement. For that reason, students may step over archaeological digs as they stroll to class. The 33,000-square-foot Anne Arundel Hall opened in 2016, housing classrooms, labs, and research spaces for anthropology, archaeology, and international languages and cultures.

The cornerstone of a St. Mary's education is the small, discussion-focused First Year Seminar. Students may choose from dozens of topics—ranging from The Many Lives of Abraham Lincoln to The Future of Nature—taught by professors from every discipline at the college, in order to cultivate an area of particular interest while building critical-thinking, researching, writing, and speaking skills. St. Mary's core curriculum also mandates that students complete coursework in arts, cultural perspectives, humanistic foundations, mathematics, natural sciences, and social sciences. They must also demonstrate foreign language proficiency and fulfill a minimum of four credits to complete the Experiencing the Liberal Arts in the World requirement, which may involve an internship, community service, study abroad, or off-campus research. All seniors complete a capstone requirement.

"Because of the nature of an honors college, all students who attend St. Mary's are academically focused."

Biology is among the most popular majors, and also one of the more difficult programs; students can spend time on the college's research boat when they tire of the lab. Students also sign up in droves for psychology, economics, and English. Anthropology and chemistry are traditional strengths, and the standout music department includes prize-winning pianist Brian Ganz. Environmental studies, added in 2015, is the school's fastest-growing major. Aside from the 23 established majors and seven cross-disciplinary study areas, more freethinking types may design their own majors.

"Because of the nature of an honors college, all students who attend St. Mary's are academically focused, and there is a common goal to succeed," explains a senior. Another adds that, although rigorous, "Classes are only competitive in the sense that we push each other to try harder and learn more. But it's in a positive, supportive way." Seventy-two percent of classes have fewer than 20 students, and graduate students do not teach courses. Professors are said to be accessible and well respected. "Professors at St. Mary's are always engaged in research and like to involve students in the process," says a psychology major.

Students with exceptional academic potential may participate in the Global Scholars Program, which offers a special first-year seminar on global citizenship, followed by a college-funded international study tour at the end of the semester. For all students, St. Mary's offers study programs at the University of Heidelberg in Germany, Fudan University in China, University College Dublin, and James Cook University in Australia, as well as short-term study tours in several other countries. The Washington Program places students in top summer internships with the

"Our closeness to D.C. means that trips to protest a law or Supreme Court case are regular."

government, nonprofits, and think tanks in Washington, D.C., and also offers mentoring from alumni.

"Students at St. Mary's are not afraid to be themselves and to try new things," says a psychology major. Ninety-two percent of St. Mary's students come from Maryland, which helps give the campus a homegrown feel. More minority students are finding their way to the peninsula: African Americans account for 8 percent of the student body, Hispanics 8 percent, and Asian Americans 3 percent. Twenty-five percent are Pell-eligible. Students are said to be left-leaning and very engaged in social and political issues. According to an economics major, "Our closeness to D.C. means that trips to protest a law or Supreme Court case are regular." St. Mary's is more expensive than other publics in Maryland but less expensive than the private liberal arts colleges with which it also competes. Qualified students receive merit scholarships, worth an average of $4,826. There are no athletic awards.

Campus housing is "comfortable and popular among students," according to a student. Eighty-three percent of full-time students live on campus, and most residence halls are co-ed. Apartments and townhouses—arguably among the most attractive student digs anywhere—are reserved for upperclassmen, and students select rooms based on the number of credits they have. Open (gender-neutral) housing is available, as are living/learning centers for women in science, African studies, environmental sustainability, and substance-free living. There are some choices off campus too, including old farmhouses and riverside cottages for rent. "The food at St. Mary's is not only consistently delicious, but it is healthy, diverse, and made with local ingredients," cheers a biology major. Those who tire of the food line may join the vegetarian co-op.

> **"It's virtually impossible to graduate without knowing how to sail."**

St. Mary's doesn't have fraternities or sororities, and its secluded location means there's little nightlife off campus, but one senior confirms, "The fun that happens on campus is more than enough to make up for that!" The student-run Programs Board organizes events like concerts, comedians, and festivals, and for the culture-hungry, there are also theaters, an art gallery, lectures, and films on campus. The St. Mary's River offers a wealth of outdoor activities too. "Most days if we aren't in class, you'll find us paddleboarding, sailing, kayaking, swimming, or just studying on the docks. On nice days, there's a summer-camp atmosphere to it all," says one student. Another adds, "It's virtually impossible to graduate without knowing how to sail." The waterfront also becomes the focus of campuswide activities, including the bamboo boat race held each fall, Earth Day in April, and the end-of-year World Carnival.

St. Mary's fields 19 varsity Seahawks teams; men's basketball, women's lacrosse, and the sailing program are among the most successful. Men's and women's rowing were newly added in 2016. Overall, nearly half of the students at St. Mary's take part in intramurals; floor hockey, badminton, and basketball are the most popular.

"Students work hard and have opportunities to find their academic niche," says a psychology major. St. Mary's has worked hard too, to establish itself as one of the nation's premier public liberal arts colleges. Though its small size and remote location can feel confining to some, students leave with a solid grounding in the liberal arts—and the close bonds that they forge with friends during peaceful days on the St. Mary's River. For those looking to be part of an intellectual community in a small-town setting, St. Mary's just might be a place to set sail.

> *St. Mary's is more expensive than other publics in Maryland but less expensive than the private liberal arts colleges with which it also competes.*

Overlaps

University of Maryland, Salisbury, Towson, University of Maryland Baltimore County, Washington College, McDaniel, Frostburg State, Mary Washington

---

If You Apply To ➤ **St. Mary's:** Early action: Nov. 15. Regular decision: Feb. 15. Priority financial aid: Feb. 28. Housing: May 1. Application fee: $50. Campus interviews: optional, evaluative. Alumni interviews: optional, informational. SATs or ACTs: required. Subject Tests: optional. Letters of recommendation: required. Essay: required. Accepts the Common Application with supplement.

Saint Michael's College

One Winooski Park, Colchester, VT 05439

Roman Catholic liberal arts college located in a top college town with breathtaking views of the Adirondack and Green mountains. Cheerful academic community with most students being New Englanders. Proximity to Burlington helps make for vibrant social scene. Easy access to Montreal and to some of the best skiing and snowboarding in the East.

Saint Michael's College carries the distinction of being the only Edmundite institution of higher learning in the world. The college was established by the Society of Saint Edmund, a group of Catholic country priests who took Saint Edmund, Archbishop of Canterbury, as their patron and spiritual inspiration. The Society maintains an on-campus presence to this day, and the influence of the patron saint can be found in the college's dedication to meaningful residential experiences, comprehensive liberal arts, and social justice. A junior says, "Saint Michael's teaches students to go out into the world and work to make it a better place."

Founded in 1904, Saint Michael's sits on 440 acres overlooking Vermont's Green Mountains and the Winooski River. Just five minutes from Burlington, the campus features redbrick architecture, themed gardens, and a central quad. To the east, Mount Mansfield—Vermont's tallest peak—provides a spectacular backdrop. The Dion Family Student Center and Quad Commons residence hall overlook the mountains and use geothermal heating and cooling, among other green technologies. Another energy-efficient residence hall opened in 2016, featuring apartments that house 188 students.

The general education curriculum includes a writing- and research-intensive First-Year Seminar, and other requirements that fall into the categories of Foundations in Faith, Values, and Thought (courses in philosophy, religious studies, and ethical decision-making); Pathways to Understanding the World (including courses in literary and historical studies, scientific and quantitative reasoning, human behavior, global issues, and second-language acquisition); and Participatory Learning and Competencies, which includes an experiential learning requirement for all students. Many majors also include a capstone course.

> **"Students are encouraged to succeed not only by their professors, but by their peers as well."**

Saint Michael's offers a plethora of solid programs, including business, psychology, biology, English, education, religious studies, and media studies. The newly added neuroscience major is a top draw too. A popular 3–2 engineering program with nearby University of Vermont enrolls about 30 students, and there are hybrid summer courses, including an art history course based partly at the Metropolitan Museum in New York City. Students may also take advantage of cross-registration options with Champlain College and apply to take part in a semester exchange with any other private college in Vermont.

Regardless of major, students agree that courses are demanding, but many are taught in a discussion-based format that "allows for a more relaxed environment and the opportunity to work with other students," says a sophomore. Adds another, "Students are encouraged to succeed not only by their professors, but by their peers as well." Students praise professors for their knowledge and willingness to make themselves available. "The professors, though some are highly kooky, are all very well educated, invested, and caring when it comes to their students," says a junior. Fifty-nine percent of classes taken by freshmen have

---

Website: www.smcvt.edu
Location: Small City
Private
Total Enrollment: 1,968
Undergraduates: 1,931
Male/Female: 45/55
SAT Ranges: CR 540–630,
   M 530–630
ACT Ranges: 24–28
Financial Aid: 96%
Pell Grant: 14%
Expense: Pr $ $
Student Loans: 73%
Average Debt: $ $ $ $
Phi Beta Kappa: Yes
Applicants: 4,767
Accepted: 76%
Enrolled: 13%
Grad in 6 Years: 79%
Returning Freshmen: 87%
Academics: ✍ ✍ ✍
Social: ☎ ☎ ☎ ☎
Q of L: ★ ★ ★
Admissions: (800) 762-8000
Email Address: admission@smcvt.edu

Strong Programs:
Business
Psychology
Biology
English
Education
Religious Studies
Media Studies
Neuroscience

fewer than 20 students and "freshmen are taught by full professors," according to a sophomore.

The Honors Program offers 20 percent of undergraduates the opportunity to take specialized honors core courses and a colloquium, live-in honors housing, and complete a senior honors project. Approximately 33 percent of Saint Michael's students take part in undergraduate research, and many receive stipends for full-time work as research partners with faculty during the summer. Study abroad options include international study trips to such far-flung locales as Cuba, Ghana, India, Tanzania, and Costa Rica; 34 percent of undergraduates participate.

> **Many students receive stipends for full-time work as research partners with faculty during the summer.**

"Students at Saint Michael's are extremely well-rounded," says an American studies major. "Everyone has found their niche on campus, creating a community that is open and accepting." African Americans account for only 3 percent of the student body, Hispanics 4 percent, and Asian Americans 2 percent. Eighteen percent come from Vermont and 3 percent from foreign countries. Campus politics lean left, students say, although conservatives are well represented too. A media studies, journalism, and digital arts student reports that student organizations like the Diversity Coalition and Martin Luther King Jr. Society "work together to put on events throughout the year to encourage discussion around the topic of diversity. It is definitely a hot-button topic here." The college offers merit awards averaging $16,295 to qualified students, and a limited number of athletic scholarships are available for basketball players.

> **"Students stick around on weekends because there is so much going on."**

Students are required to spend all four years on campus in the residence halls, which a sophomore says "creates a sense of community among the different classes, and people really get to know their peers well." All first-year students are housed in living/learning communities organized around four main themes: leadership, service, wellness, and approaches to transition. Residence halls include traditional dorms with double and single rooms, suites with shared living spaces, townhouses, and apartment-style accommodations. Campus dining options include an unlimited meal plan at the Green Mountain Dining Room. A freshman says, "There is always a variety of options to eat at the dining hall, and the meals are decently good." Students report feeling safe on campus, and while there have been instances of sexual assault, they say the school has taken a proactive approach and always informs them of "what steps they are taking to protect the community and hold those who were responsible accountable," says a student.

> **All first-year students live in living/learning communities with four main themes: leadership, service, wellness, and approaches to transition.**

Despite the lack of a Greek scene, "the social life is outstanding," raves one student. "St. Mike's is not a suitcase school. Students stick around on weekends because there is so much going on," adds a sophomore. While there is a party scene, students agree that parties are "pretty well controlled," and the Residential Initiative Program delivers a slew of alternative weekend programs. Campuswide activities include comedians, coffeehouse music and poetry performances, and talent shows. Every Friday and Saturday night, the college hosts the Weekend Grilling Program, which provides free food (hamburgers, hot dogs, or chicken patties) between 11 p.m. and 1 a.m. Spring and Fall concerts are popular campus events, and students appreciate the annual P-Day (or Preparation Day) tradition, which is "a time for students to relax before finals" with free food, bouncy houses, tricycle races, a movie screening, and other activities, according to an English major. Apart from senior housing, the campus is dry, and students report that underage drinking is dealt with swiftly; those who want to imbibe travel off campus to take part in Burlington's bar scene. Popular road trips "are to downtown Burlington

> **"Volunteering is a huge aspect of life at Saint Michael's."**

or to the mountains and great outdoors like Mount Mansfield or Camel's Hump," says one student. Montreal is a popular weekend trip.

Burlington (population 43,000) is "a great college town, as it contains [two] other colleges: UVM and Champlain," a sophomore says. "The area consists of young people and entrepreneurs, offering a fun atmosphere to eat, shop, and go out in." Saint Michael's students receive a free bus pass that will take them downtown, and the Saint Michael's Cultural Pass gives students unlimited access to performances at Burlington's Flynn Theater for little or no cost. An unrestricted (and deeply discounted) season pass to Smuggler's Notch is available as well. Students can often be found volunteering in the surrounding community. "Volunteering is a huge aspect of life at Saint Michael's," confirms one student. Seventy percent of students get involved in at least one service program over the course of their college careers.

Saint Michael's fields a number of Division II sports, the majority of which compete in the Northeast-10 Conference. Competitive Purple Knights teams include men's and women's lacrosse, women's cross-country, field hockey, men's and women's basketball, and men's ice hockey. Recreational and intramural programs are popular too, and include the Wilderness Program, which organizes about 75 outings per semester, including sea kayaking, rock and ice climbing, white-water rafting, and other outdoor activities.

"St. Mike's is a school that cares not only about the academic growth of students, but their personal growth as well," reflects a political science major. The college attracts students who appreciate the unique vision inspired by Saint Edmund so many years ago and who want to use their education for the betterment of the world. And that all starts, says a sophomore, with being a part of the intimate community that is Saint Michael's: "I feel connected with my peers, and with my professors, and I think we really do a good job of making this place feel like home."

Overlaps

University of Vermont, University of Massachusetts Amherst, University of New Hampshire, Quinnipiac, Saint Anselm, Providence, University of Maine–Orono, University of Rhode Island

If You Apply To ➤ **St. Michael's:** Early action I: Nov. 1. Early action II: Dec. 1. Regular decision and financial aid: Feb. 1. Housing: May 5. Application fee: $50. Campus and alumni interviews: optional, evaluative. SATs (with essay) or ACTs (with writing): optional. Subject Tests: optional. Letters of recommendation: required. Essay: required. Accepts the Common Application with supplement.

St. Olaf College

1520 St. Olaf Avenue, Northfield, MN 55057

Notable for its deep Lutheran roots and strong international orientation, St. Olaf has more of a Midwestern feel than crosstown rival Carleton. The music program—especially its choir—is world famous, and more than two-thirds of students study abroad. Daily chapel is not mandatory, but many students go. With nearly 3,000 students, St. Olaf is on the big side of small.

Website: www.stolaf.edu
Location: Small Town
Private
Total Enrollment: 2,997
Undergraduates: 2,997

St. Olaf College's home is Northfield, Minnesota, which bills itself as the city of "Cows, Colleges, and Contentment." Founded by Norwegian Lutheran immigrants and affiliated with the Evangelical Lutheran Church in America, St. Olaf provides a solid liberal arts education and plenty of opportunities to study abroad. One Ole describes her peers at St. Olaf as "Minnesota nice." Students differ in this respect from the school's namesake, St. Olaf, an 11th-century Norwegian king prone to violence and brutality. The student also adds, "I feel personally valued and supported by the faculty and administrators. I felt at home here from day one."

St. Olaf's meticulously landscaped 350-acre campus, featured in several architectural journals, is located on Manitou Heights, overlooking the Cannon River valley and Northfield. More than 10,000 trees, native prairie, and a wetlands wildlife area surround the 34 native limestone buildings that form the campus. Regents Hall of Natural and Mathematical Sciences, a 200,000-square-foot science center, is one of the largest and most complex academic facilities in the nation to earn the prestigious LEED Platinum rating. The recently opened Digital Scholarship Center features media production workstations, 3-D printers, and other equipment designed to encourage students and faculty to apply technology to their work.

All students at St. Olaf complete a general education requirement that covers three areas: foundation studies, core studies, and integrative study. Typically, 14 to 16 courses satisfy the general education requirements; some courses may fulfill requirements in more than one area. All first-year students also complete a writing course and an introductory course in Biblical and Theological Studies.

Biology, mathematics, economics, chemistry, and psychology are the most popular majors and some of the school's best. The music department draws high praise; it offers many performance opportunities with eight school choirs and seven instrumental ensembles. The choirs perform in major venues around the nation and can be heard singing

> **"I feel personally valued and supported by the faculty and administrators."**

with the Minnesota Orchestra. The Center for Integrative Studies allows students to form their own majors. The Conversation Programs are interdisciplinary, team-taught programs that bring together students and faculty with a broad range of academic interests for a critical exploration of specific topics within their historical, cultural, and social contexts. Programs include the Great Conversation, American Conversations, Asian Conversations, Environmental Conversations, the Science Conversation, and the Public Affairs Conversation. These programs, which can be one to two years in length, "take care of a ton of general requirements, but they are extremely rigorous," warns one freshman.

Faculty members are highly praised by students. "There are some fantastic professors at St. Olaf, and almost all of them are accessible," says an English major. Fifty-four percent of classes have fewer than 20 students, and instructors reportedly have as many as 10 hours of open-office time a week. Academically, students have their work cut out for them. "I consider it very rigorous," admits one junior. Students look forward to the annual, stress-relieving study break where professors serve them ice cream.

In the last quarter-century, the college has cultivated an international agenda for its students and faculty and has created one of the largest international studies programs in the country among liberal arts colleges, in which 71 percent of students participate. More than 110 programs are available in 46 countries, including St. Olaf's faculty-led Global Semester, Mediterranean Semester, and Environmental Science in Australia programs. Additional programs are offered through membership in the Associated Colleges of the Midwest* consortium and other partnerships. There are also several opportunities to spend a semester studying elsewhere in the U.S. Research opportunities are available in all disciplines, and are especially robust in the sciences; about half of the students take advantage of them.

"The typical St. Olaf student is fairly outgoing, extremely involved, and interested in trying new things," says a freshman. "Everyone loves meeting new people and supporting one another." Forty-two percent of students hail from Minnesota, and 8 percent come from overseas. Asian Americans make up 6 percent, Hispanics 5 percent, and African Americans 2 percent, and the college is actively recruiting

(continued)

Male/Female: 43/57
SAT Ranges: CR 560–710, M 580–700
ACT Ranges: 26–31
Financial Aid: 90%
Pell Grant: 17%
Expense: Pr $ $
Student Loans: 57%
Average Debt: $ $ $
Phi Beta Kappa: Yes
Applicants: 7,571
Accepted: 36%
Enrolled: 28%
Grad in 6 Years: 87%
Returning Freshmen: 93%
Academics: ✎ ✎ ✎ ✎
Social: ☎ ☎ ☎
Q of L: ★ ★ ★ ★
Admissions: (800) 800-3025
Email Address: admissions@stolaf.edu

Strong Programs:
Biology
Mathematics
Economics
Chemistry
Psychology
Music
Religion

The Conversation Programs are interdisciplinary, team-taught programs that explore topics within their historical, cultural, and social contexts.

more students from diverse backgrounds. Most students are high achievers from Midwestern public schools, drawn in part by hundreds of merit scholarships, which average $14,291 each year. St. Olaf has a tradition of meeting the full demonstrated need of all admitted students.

Ninety-three percent of undergrads live in on-campus housing or in college-owned houses available off campus. "Dorms are comfortable and usually well maintained, but outdated," comments a student. Dorms are co-ed by floor, and each has its own personality. Rooms are selected by lottery, and it can be difficult to get a room at times. Students eat in a large modern cafeteria, where they say the food is generally quite good. "While there are those days when the options seem slim, I never feel like I'm eating cafeteria food," reasons a student. Another adds, "Campus security is wonderful!"

St. Olaf's social life takes place mostly on campus, and weekend spots include a nightclub called Lion's Pause and a coffeehouse, the Cage. "The Pause, an entirely student-run organization complete with TVs, hangout areas, food, and a main stage,

"[Conversation Programs] take care of a ton of general requirements, but they are extremely rigorous."

is the place to go for entertainment," says a junior. The fine arts department provides many music, theater, and dance performances. "Most social life is defined by small dorm parties," adds a sophomore. The campus is officially dry,

and there are no fraternities or sororities at St. Olaf, but alcohol is available to those determined enough to seek it out, students say, and can also be found at local bars, for those of age. The Student Activities Committee sponsors frequent dances, speakers, and cultural events, covered by student fees and at-the-door ticket sales. Daily chapel services, though not mandatory, are well attended.

Northfield is "friendly and intimate," but there is little of social interest for St. Olaf students aside from neighboring Carleton. Each September, the locals reenact the failed 1876 attempt by Jesse James to rob the town bank. The most talked-about annual event, which has been running for more than 100 years, is the four-day Christmas Festival, during which five choirs and the St. Olaf Orchestra combine in televised concerts celebrating Christmas. Many students volunteer in Northfield and report a friendly rapport with the community. "Students are actively involved in community mentor, volunteer, and outreach programs," one student says. For those with wanderlust, buses leave regularly for the twin cities of Minneapolis and St. Paul, less than an hour's drive, where one can experience a shopper's paradise at the huge Mall of America.

St. Olaf has outstanding Division III athletic programs. The Oles men's basketball team reached the Sweet Sixteen for the first time in 2015. Recent Minnesota Intercollegiate Athletics Conference champions include men's cross-country and

"Students are actively involved in community mentor, volunteer, and outreach programs."

soccer; men's track and field and cross-country have produced individual national champions. Women's skiing and swimming and diving are also competitive. The St. Olaf football team competes against rival Carleton for the honor of having the statue in the town's square face the winning campus. The chorus of St. Olaf's fight song is "Um! Yah! Yah!" which has become a popular chant on campus. There is also an extensive intramural program, in which 70 percent of students compete, and broomball—ice hockey played with brooms instead of sticks and shoes rather than skates—is the sport of choice in the winter.

For those yearning for a school where spirituality and scholarship exist on the same exalted plane, St. Olaf could be the right place to spend four years. It's a school where students work hard, are encouraged by good teachers, toughened by Minnesota winters, and nourished by strong moral values—in addition to hearty

Scandinavian food. Says one satisfied senior, "It is an experience that will change your life and challenge you in ways you never thought possible."

If You Apply To ➤

St. Olaf: Early decision I: Nov. 15. Early decision II: Jan. 8. Regular decision and financial aid: Jan. 15. Housing: May 1. No application fee. Campus and alumni interviews: recommended, evaluative. SATs or ACTs: required. Subject Tests: optional. Letters of recommendation: required. Essay: required. Accepts the Common Application with supplement. Music applicants must submit additional application.

University of San Diego

5998 Alcala Park, San Diego, CA 92110

With a panoramic view of the Pacific Ocean, USD is riding a wave of popularity due to its sun-drenched location. Not to be confused with its UC counterpart across town, USD is now often preferred to Roman Catholic peers the University of San Francisco and Santa Clara. Strong in business and engineering.

Students at the University of San Diego have many reasons to cheer: a beatific ocean-side campus, a rich Roman Catholic heritage centered around ethical conduct and compassionate service, and an array of superb academics. "USD is becoming more and more competitive, and the academic programs continue to get better," says one freshman. "There has never been a better time to come to USD than right now."

Founded in 1949, the USD campus occupies 180 acres on a mesa overlooking San Diego's Mission Bay and is only two miles north of downtown San Diego. The buildings are designed in 16th-century Spanish Renaissance architectural style in a nod to San Diego's Catholic heritage and the Universidad de Alcalá in Spain. In a fitting architectural juxtaposition, at one end of campus is the Joan B. Kroc (of McDonald's fame) Center for Peace and Justice; at the other end is the Jenny Craig Athletic Center, where you can work off your Big Macs. The university recently opened the Cymer Ideation Space and Donald's Garage to provide space for inventing and designing new innovations in engineering.

Core curriculum requirements are grouped into three clusters: indispensable competencies (written literacy, mathematical competency, logic, second language); traditions (theology and religious studies, philosophy); and horizons (humanities and fine arts, natural sciences, social sciences, diversity of human experience). Freshmen take part in USD's First Year Experience, which features small preceptorial classes taught by faculty advisors.

"There has never been a better time to come to USD than right now."

Students are assigned a preceptorial assistant, a current student who serves as a mentor and organizes out-of-class activities. They also choose from one of nine living/learning communities, such as Change, Natural World, and Faith and Reason, which students describe as integral to their transition to college life. "Four years ago I was nervous about starting college, but being a part of programs such as these really enabled me to find out more about myself and what I am passionate about," says a communication studies major.

USD offers more than 60 degree programs—an impressive number given its relatively small student body—across seven schools: the School of Business, the School of Leadership and Education Sciences, the School of Law, the Hahn School of Nursing and Health Science, the College of Arts and Sciences, the Shiley-Marcos School of Engineering, and the Joan B. Kroc School of Peace Studies. The most

Website: www.sandiego.edu
Location: City Center
Private
Total Enrollment: 6,909
Undergraduates: 5,390
Male/Female: 46/54
SAT Ranges: CR 550–640, M 560–670
ACT Ranges: 26–30
Financial Aid: 72%
Pell Grant: 13%
Expense: Pr $ $ $
Student Loans: 51%
Average Debt: $ $ $
Phi Beta Kappa: Yes
Applicants: 13,675
Accepted: 52%
Enrolled: 16%
Grad in 6 Years: 79%
Returning Freshmen: 87%
Academics: ✍ ✍ ✍
Social: 🍸 🍸 🍸 🍸
Q of L: ★ ★ ★ ★
Admissions: (800) 248-4873
Email Address: admissions@sandiego.edu

Strong Programs:
Finance
Business Administration
Communication Studies
Accounting

(continued)

Psychology
Engineering

popular undergraduate majors include finance, business administration, communication studies, accountancy, and psychology. Engineering is a traditional strength.

Forty percent of classes have fewer than 20 students, but none exceed 50, which allows for classroom discussions and collaborative projects. "The workload is substantial, but it is also feasible," says a political science major. Professors are said to be knowledgeable and accessible. "All of my professors know me by name and are always available when I need them," says a business administration major. When it comes to finding employment after college, one senior comments, "I wish that the individual departments on campus were a little more focused on helping you in the job search, but career services has done a wonderful job."

The Honors Program offers small classes and a core curriculum of innovative courses to qualified students. Those who overdose on Southern California's ubiquitous blue skies and sunshine may take part in USD's robust study abroad program, which sends students to live and study in more than 30 countries and more than 80 programs, including a newly established permanent program at the University of San Diego Madrid Center in Spain. Seventy-eight percent of students participate in year, semester, summer, or intersession programs.

USD offers more than 60 degree programs— an impressive number given its relatively small student body— across seven schools.

A junior says that USD students are "driven and strive to be successful in all aspects of life, but at the end of the day they know how to enjoy themselves." Fifty-six percent hail from the Golden State and 8 percent are international. USD has a considerable minority population: African Americans account for 3 percent of the student body, Hispanics 19 percent, and Asian Americans 7 percent. There is a healthy conservative presence on campus, but one freshman notes, "The university is making a big push toward acceptance and understanding of all people and beliefs." The school offers merit awards averaging $14,656 to qualified students, and there are 196 athletic awards in 15 sports.

Forty-five percent of undergraduates live on campus, and they are required to do so for both their first and second year. Residence halls are a mix of singles, doubles, triples, and limited quads, with singles and doubles representing the majority of the units. Apartments range from one room to four bedrooms. When the dinner bell rings, students have plenty to cheer about. "Meals are delicious," says one junior. "Dining facilities are nice, clean, and a hot place to be at all hours of the day." Campus security is excellent, students say, with officers on duty around the clock. "A huge sexual assault awareness task force has...done a lot of good things after a few accusations in the past few years," according to a senior.

"Mission Beach, where most upperclassmen live, has a vibrant social scene."

And how about the campus social scene? "Mission Beach, where most upperclassmen live, has a vibrant social scene. Many USD students congregate in the area on weekends," a finance major explains. For those who choose to eschew the sand and waves, USD offers a slate of on-campus activities, including movies, concerts, and mass (lest you forget, USD is a Catholic university). The Greek scene attracts 24 percent of the men and 40 percent of the women. Alcohol is allowed only in designated areas for those students of legal age, and "this policy is heavily enforced by the RAs," says a marketing major. Downtown San Diego has plenty to offer, including a bevy of bars, eateries, and shopping centers. The USD community is big on giving back too, via more than 300,000 hours of service. Popular road trips include Las Vegas and Big Bear. Back on campus, students enjoy annual festivals such as International Week and Greek Week, the Alcalá Bazaar, and homecoming.

The University of San Diego Madrid Center in Spain is a newly established permanent study abroad program.

USD sponsors nearly 20 Division I intercollegiate teams and is a member of the West Coast Conference for all sports except football, which competes in the Pioneer League. Between 2008 and 2012, the Toreros earned a record-setting five consecutive WCC Commissioner's Cups, an all-sports award presented at the end of each academic year to the league's top-performing school in conference play. Students are especially rowdy when the USD basketball team takes on rival Gonzaga. Twenty-two sports and recreational clubs are available to students, and nearly a quarter participate; among the most popular are basketball, lacrosse, inner-tube polo, and kickball.

Don't underestimate USD—this small, first-year friendly institution offers a rich variety of academic programs, and its students seem to understand that they are living out their college careers in one of the most beautiful spots in the country. As a sophomore reflects, "The great thing about USD is you can get a great education in a challenging academic environment and in one of the most beautiful cities in the nation."

If You Apply To ➤

USD: Regular decision: Dec. 15. Financial aid: Mar. 2. Housing: May 1. Application fee: $55. Campus interview: recommended, informational. Alumni interviews: optional, informational. SATs (with essay) or ACTs (with writing): required. Subject Tests: optional. Letters of recommendation: required. Essay: required. Accepts the Common Application.

University of San Francisco

2130 Fulton Street, San Francisco, CA 94117

Talk about prime real estate: USF is next door to the legendary Haight–Ashbury district, down the street from Golden Gate Park, and within five miles of the Pacific Ocean. Though USF is a Jesuit institution, only about a third of its students are Roman Catholic. Asia Pacific studies is a standout. Nearly 40 percent of the students are from outside California.

In the heart of one of the nation's most liberal cities is a thriving Jesuit university that has become an integral part of its community. Instead of shunning the city's reputation, the University of San Francisco embraces it with a strong social conscience. With an incredibly diverse student body and an emphasis on programs such as nursing and business, students encounter a broad set of cultures, academic challenges in a liberal arts setting, and the chance to put all that experience to good use.

USF's 55 well-kept acres, spotted with beautiful basilica-type buildings and modern facilities, are, as one student puts it, "wedged into the heart of San Francisco." The campus stands atop one of San Francisco's seven hills, adjacent to Golden Gate Park, overlooking San Francisco Bay and the city skyline. The One Stop Services Office combines registrar, financial aid, and payment services in one convenient location. The newest campus addition is the LoSchiavo Center for Science and Innovation, which features cutting-edge classrooms, laboratories, and community gathering places.

The 44-unit core curriculum requires students to take courses in six major categories: foundation of communication; math and sciences; humanities; philosophy, theology, and ethics; social sciences; and visual and performing arts. A three-part series of success courses emphasizes study skills, critical thinking, and career and major exploration. First-year seminars give students insights into unique topics and a taste of the city through excursions and other enrichment activities; recent topics include Independent Film, Speaking of Bicycles, and The Right to the City: Community Movements in San Francisco.

"USF is extremely quirky, and it really is a reflection of the city."

Website: www.usfca.edu
Location: City Center
Private
Total Enrollment: 9,696
Undergraduates: 6,398
Male/Female: 38/62
SAT Ranges: CR 530–620, M 540–640
ACT Ranges: 24–28
Financial Aid: 69%
Pell Grant: 24%
Expense: Pr $ $
Student Loans: 58%
Average Debt: $ $ $ $
Phi Beta Kappa: No
Applicants: 15,462
Accepted: 64%
Enrolled: 13%
Grad in 6 Years: 71%
Returning Freshmen: 83%
Academics: ✍ ✍ ✍
Social: ☎ ☎ ☎

(continued)

Q of L: ★ ★ ★ ★
Admissions: (415) 422-6563
Email Address: admission@
usfca.edu

Strong Programs:
Nursing
Finance
Psychology
Biology
Data Science
Business Administration
Asian Studies
Visual Arts

Nursing students interact with state-of-the-art mannequins that simulate symptoms and conditions of real-life patients.

USF places a strong emphasis on its preprofessional programs, especially nursing, health studies, communications, and business, and these tend to draw the most students. Nursing, finance, psychology, and biology are the most popular majors, and data science is also a strength. In the School of Nursing's Simulation Lab, nursing students interact with state-of-the-art mannequins, including adult, pediatrics, and obstetrics, that simulate symptoms and conditions specific to real-life patients and scenarios. The Center for Asia Pacific Studies enhances interdisciplinary majors with an Asian focus, as does the Asian studies program. The visual arts program provides courses in art education, graphic and fine art, drawing, painting, art history, and museum studies. There's also a joint B.A./B.S.-J.D. program.

Some of the preprofessional majors are demanding, but students say the climate is generally relaxed and collaborative. "All professors and students encourage others to succeed," says a business administration major. Extensive and mandatory academic advising ensures that students' courseloads are manageable. Forty-eight percent of classes taken by freshmen have fewer than 20 students, and nearly all faculty hold terminal degrees in their academic discipline. According to a senior, "Professors do not just care about the bottom line or the letter grade, but really make sure their students understand the material."

"Internships and service learning are definitely big parts of the education here at USF," says one senior. Community-minded students take advantage of volunteer programs, often through University Ministries, and the student body as a whole contributes more than 600,000 hours of community service each year. USF is also the official host of the Human Rights Watch Festival, which is integrated into the curriculum. USF offers more than 120 study abroad programs in 50 countries, and 44 percent of the student body choose to participate. The St. Ignatius Institute offers an integrated four-year, honors-based

> "I haven't met a student who doesn't want to change the world."

curriculum centered on the great books of Western civilization presented in an unusual seminar/lecture combination. The program is not restricted to top students, and participants can spend their junior year studying in Oxford, Rome, or Budapest. "USF also has a partnership with UC–San Francisco, so a lot of people are able to do research at the various UCSF campuses," notes a junior.

"USF is extremely quirky, and it really is a reflection of the city," says a comparative literature and culture major. Sixty-three percent of undergraduates are from California, and 20 percent hail from abroad. Asian Americans account for 21 percent of the population, African Americans 3 percent, and Hispanics 20 percent. Student groups advocating for LGBTQ rights and racial justice are said to be particularly active on campus. Twenty-four percent of freshmen qualify for Pell Grants. Admission is need-blind, and USF offers merit scholarships averaging $11,874, as well as 136 athletic scholarships in 15 sports.

Thirty-two percent of undergrads choose to live in on-campus housing, which is guaranteed for the first year. After that, most students brave San Francisco's budget-busting rental market. "The dorms are comfortable, well-maintained, and updated," says a communication studies major. On-campus students say the dining facilities offer a range of vegan, vegetarian, and other choices. "Campus safety officers are constantly roaming the campus making sure that the students are safe," reports a student. And while students say sexual assault has not been a problem on campus, "USF encourages a lot of dialogue" on the issue.

"Freshman year, most social life happens on campus," says a senior, "with events and activities being offered almost every day." Notable campus activities include the Hawaiian Club's annual luau, the Barrio Festival held by the Filipino American Club, and the springtime Donaroo music festival. The College Players is the oldest continuously performing college theater group in the West. Fraternities attract 3 percent of the men and sororities draw 4 percent of the women, although they don't have houses. Underage drinking is officially prohibited, and the school's zero-tolerance policy is strictly enforced. USF's greatest social asset is undoubtedly its location. "Many students take advantage of going into the city rather than sticking around campus for fun," says a junior. San Francisco is a cosmopolitan city where students can take advantage of reliable public transportation, including the famous cable cars, to get to a variety of cultural attractions, ranging from Chinatown to the symphony. Nightlife is great for those who want to dance at the clubs or meet in the bars.

Varsity athletics provide a popular diversion as well, and the Division I USF Dons women's basketball team claimed the West Coast Conference title in 2016, advancing to the national tournament for the first time in 19 years. Men's soccer and women's cross-country are perennial powerhouses, and the boxing club has won multiple U.S. Intercollegiate Boxing Association national championships. The university sponsors two dozen club and intramural sports, and students make ample use of the Koret Health and Recreation Center, which touts an Olympic-size swimming pool, exercise and weight rooms, and a variety of playing courts.

The core mission of USF is to use the Jesuit tradition, which views "faith and reason as complementary resources in the search for truth and authentic human development," as the backdrop for a solid liberal arts and preprofessional education. Students take advantage of the cosmopolitan setting to get involved and make the most of their time here. "Students at USF truly care about learning and we desire to achieve great things in life," says a kinesiology major. "I haven't met a student who doesn't want to change the world."

USF is the official host of the Human Rights Watch Festival, which is integrated into the curriculum.

Overlaps

Loyola Marymount, UC–Santa Barbara, Cal Poly–San Luis Obispo, UC–Davis, Santa Clara, UC–Berkeley, UC–Santa Cruz, San Diego State

---

If You Apply To >

USF: Early decision and early action: Nov. 15. Regular decision: Jan. 15. Financial aid: Feb. 1. Housing: May 1. Application fee: $65. No campus or alumni interviews. SATs (with essay) or ACTs (with writing): required. (Writing scores required for placement purposes only.) No Subject Tests. Letters of recommendation: required. Essay: required. Accepts the Common Application with supplement.

Santa Clara University

500 El Camino Real, Santa Clara, CA 95053

Santa Clara is a selective midsized California university now drawing increased national attention. Gorgeous Silicon Valley campus is within easy reach of San Francisco, and the large endowment also contributes to an air of prosperity. A well-developed core curriculum keeps students focused on basic academic and other values. Offers engineering and business in addition to the liberal arts.

Steeped in history and tradition, Santa Clara University was founded by Jesuits with a mission that emphasizes a commitment to academics and the community. The class schedule is based on quarters (10 weeks), classes stay small and intimate, and the revised curriculum focuses on an expanding global society. "The students here genuinely care for one another and create a real community and culture of support," cheers one junior.

SCU's old-world charm includes 106 acres complete with lush green lawns, palm trees, and luscious rose gardens, accented by authentic Spanish architecture. The Mission Gardens, replete with olive trees, are a beautiful escape from the pressures of school. The famous classic mission church was rebuilt in 1926 in the design

Website: www.scu.edu
Location: Small City
Private
Total Enrollment: 7,254
Undergraduates: 5,268
Male/Female: 51/49
SAT Ranges: CR 590–690, M 620–710
ACT Ranges: 27–32

The Core Pathways program offers 24 sets of courses with innovative common themes across disciplines.

of the six previous churches that were destroyed by seemingly biblical disasters ranging from fires to floods. The new Dowd Art and Art History Building was completed in 2016.

The Core Curriculum is designed to express the school's "most basic values." It prescribes courses in three broad categories—Knowledge, Habits of Mind and Heart (skills), and Engagement with the World—as well as in 16 subcategories, including global cultures, science and technology, religious reflection, and civic engagement. The Core Pathways program supplements the major and core curriculum by offering 24 sets of courses with innovative common themes across disciplines, such as design, hunger and poverty, justice and the arts, and values in science and technology; students choose one Pathway and complete three or four courses. It culminates in an integrative Pathway Reflection Essay. All first-year students are members of a Residential Learning Community (RLC) and take a two-quarter sequence of Critical Thinking & Writing or Cultures & Ideas linked to their RLC. All students must complete a requirement that involves community service, and most majors require a capstone experience or senior project.

In addition to liberal arts, Santa Clara offers preprofessional programs in engineering and business. Students can opt for the 3–2 engineering program, which allows them to get a bachelor's and master's degree in five years, while the Leavey School of Business is renowned along the West Coast, with finance, marketing, and accounting all strong. In the College of Arts and Sciences, psychology and communication remain popular. Other notable majors include environmental studies, public health, bioengineering, and computer science and engineering. The Silicon Valley location means that internship opportunities abound.

> "Every 10 weeks you can change your workload to something that fits best for you."

While courses are challenging, students say the quarter system gives them more control over the intensity of their workload. "Every 10 weeks you can change your workload to something that fits best for you," explains a public health major. "SCU has a generally collaborative environment that encourages students to work with one another and (especially) the professors," says a junior. Small classes taught by full professors mean "the quality of teaching is good and professors are really there to help the students rather than do research," says a senior.

For students looking for more of a challenge, the honors program places 45 to 50 selected freshmen in seminar-style classes, and an endowed scholarship sponsors one student's junior year at Mansfield College, Oxford University. The LEAD (Leadership, Excellence, and Academic Development) Scholars Program invites students whose parents did not attend college to join a small community of 60 to 75 peers who work closely with faculty and staff to cultivate leadership skills. Multiple opportunities are available to all students to engage in research supervised by a faculty member, much of it subsidized by grants. About one-third of students participate in the extensive study abroad program that allows travel and study in more than 50 countries on every continent except Antarctica.

Santa Clara students are "driven and smart but know how to have fun and let go," according to one senior. About half are Roman Catholic, and religion, while not intrusive, is a force in many aspects of campus life. The campus ministry provides counseling and opportunities for spiritual development, and many students are active in local volunteer organizations. Seventy-three percent of undergraduates hail from California, 4 percent come from foreign countries, and the rest are from nearly 40 states. The student body is almost evenly split between public school graduates and alumni of religiously affiliated or other private schools. The racial diversity on campus is impressive; 17 percent of the students are Asian American, 3 percent are African American, and 18 percent are Hispanic. Socioeconomically, the school is less diverse, with just 9 percent of incoming freshmen qualifying for the Pell Grant. A variety of academic and athletic scholarships are available to those who qualify; the Johnson Scholars Program rewards up to 10 outstanding incoming students with four-year, full-tuition scholarships and special opportunities to develop leadership skills.

Almost all freshmen and sophomores live on campus before packing up and heading for apartments for the last two years. Most residence halls are co-ed by floor. "The housing options are very nice. Every building has been updated," says one senior. All first-year students, including commuters and those living off campus, participate in one of the eight Residential Learning Communities, living in themed dorms and taking courses with students who share similar academic or social interests. The campus offers one central dining hall. "Everything is made to order, so it is very customizable and easy to accommodate any dietary needs," says an economics major. "Food on campus is organic and locally grown and always tastes fresh." A marketing major reports, "Campus always feels safe and is patrolled by a 24/7 campus safety team." On the topic of campus sexual assault, a senior comments, "Our school has recently reworked our reporting system, and there are multiple clubs on campus working to raise awareness."

Santa Clara ended its support of fraternities and sororities, but Greek organizations persist, albeit independently. "There's a great social life both on and off campus and over a hundred clubs and programs to get involved in," says one student. Those who choose to party on or near campus can take advantage of the school's attempt at enforcing "no drinking and driving" by providing the students with transportation called the Bronco Bus. "There is no pressure to drink at all, though many of the students do," says a bioengineering major. The Bronco is a sports and recreation area where students can hang out, play billiards, and enjoy a late-night meal. The town of Santa Clara is mostly residential, and getting away requires a car. But for those who want to bask in the sun, Santa Cruz is only 20 miles away. San Francisco lies within 45 minutes, and other short road trips include Napa Valley, Monterey, and Palo Alto.

The Santa Clara Broncos compete in Division I, and competitive programs include men's and women's soccer and tennis, women's volleyball, and men's basketball, baseball, and water polo. The 13 intramural sports draw roughly half of undergraduates, and students may also choose from 17 club sports teams. "Every patch of grass usually has someone either chucking a Frisbee or kicking a ball around," says a political science major.

Santa Clara University is a warm place in every sense of the word. The physical setting is comfortable and scenic. More important, it gives meaning to the traditional Jesuit ideals of infusing morality and ethics into strong and coherent academics. Says a sophomore, "Because our school is Jesuit, we have an incredible sense of community, helping others, and drive for the best and most well-rounded education you can get."

All first-year students, including commuters, participate in one of the eight Residential Learning Communities.

"Every patch of grass usually has someone either chucking a Frisbee or kicking a ball around."

Overlaps

Cal Poly–San Luis Obispo, Loyola Marymount, UC–Berkeley, UC–Davis, University of Southern California

If You Apply To ➢ | **SCU:** Early decision and early action: Nov. 1. Regular decision: Jan. 7. Financial aid: Feb. 1. Housing: May 1. Application fee: $60. No campus or alumni interviews. SATs or ACTs: required. Subject Tests: optional. Letters of recommendation: required. Essay: required. Accepts the Common Application.

Sarah Lawrence College

1 Mead Way, Bronxville, NY 10708

A pricey and free-spirited sister of East Coast alternative institutions like Bard and Bennington where individualism reigns supreme. Though co-ed, women significantly outnumber men. Strong in the humanities and fine arts with a specialty in creative writing. Full of quirky, headstrong intellectuals who hop the train to New York City every chance they get.

Sarah Lawrence College attracts creative, highly motivated individuals who are both critical thinkers and devotees of independent learning. They love literature and the fine arts and take pride in their academic prowess. Indeed, freedom and exploration are valued more highly than any tradition here. And although some students lament Sarah Lawrence's move toward the mainstream (including more sports teams than ever), they also appreciate the things that haven't changed on campus, such as the emphasis on small classes and one-on-one conferences with professors. "If you are an independent, academically curious student who passionately cares about what you want to learn, Sarah Lawrence might be the place for you," says one happy student.

Founded in 1926, Sarah Lawrence sits on a quaint, 44-acre tract in the city of Yonkers called Lawrence Park West, a wealthy Westchester County community close to the village of Bronxville, where even the public library boasts Oriental rugs and fireplaces. On campus, the prevailing architectural theme is English Tudor, including the mansion from the founder's converted estate, but more modern structures are present as well. The landscape is hilly and green, with more than a hundred types of trees and abundant rock outcroppings. Because the school's founders believed that there should be as little physical separation as possible between life and work, many classrooms, dormitory suites, and faculty offices are all housed in the same ivy-covered buildings. A science center furnishes students with 22,500 square feet of classrooms, lab benches, and computer technology. Though its holdings are small—fewer than 350,000 volumes—the charming library takes the sting out of studying with a café for those wanting a snack or cup of tea.

Regardless of what they choose to focus on, all students at Sarah Lawrence become intimately acquainted with the written word; writing begins in the first year and continues relentlessly "across the curriculum" for the next three. General education requirements include credits in at least three of four academic areas, leaving lots of room for students to dabble in whatever strikes their fancy. Though there are formal grades, more important is the student's portfolio of work, accompanied by in-depth, written evaluations from professors, filed twice a year. To ease the transition to college, all first-years take a First-Year Studies seminar. Students choose from more than 30 subjects, and the professor of their chosen course becomes their "don," the person who guides their academic development throughout their four years.

> **"Sarah Lawrence students are intellectually free-thinking, independent people."**

The academic climate is "neither particularly competitive, nor is it incredibly collaborative," according to one student. "Our academics are so independently driven that it's rare for any two students to be working on the same topic." Indeed, every student designs his or her own program of study, and almost no subject is out of bounds. Writing, literature, and visual arts are among the college's traditional strengths, and the most popular concentrations include chemistry, biology, inter-active media, and computer science. Aspiring psychologists—also a significant group on campus—may participate in fieldwork at the college's Early Childhood Center. The premed program, more structured than other offerings, places nearly all eligible graduates into medical school.

Courses "are generally demanding," says a student studying computer science. That's because everyone takes only three courses per semester. Still, professors meet one-on-one with their students weekly or biweekly, in a system modeled after Oxford University's tutorials, so there's no time to slack off—or fall behind. "While I have had professors who I don't quite jive with, this group of faculty is absolutely stunning," says a senior, calling out the "love and hard work they put into teaching the next generation." Perhaps because of the college's emphasis on personal rela-tionships with professors, even the registration process requires deep thought: stu-dents interview teachers to ensure that courses fit into their academic plans, and that the professor is someone they respect and want to study with. Classes are inti-mate, with 93 percent of them enrolling fewer than 20 students, but students warn that getting into popular classes can sometimes be a problem.

All students at Sarah Lawrence conduct research as part of their one-on-one work with professors. Ninety percent of all courses include this research, known as "conference work." The Sarah Lawrence Center for the Urban River is a new facility on the banks of the Hudson River that affords research opportunities for students pursuing environmental and social sciences. The college runs its own semester, yearlong, and summer study abroad programs in such locales as Cuba, England, Japan, Turkey, and Zimbabwe. Students are encouraged to study abroad for their entire junior year, and 48 percent of students undertake some sort of international experience. Those interested in service learning may participate in the Intensive Semester in Yonkers, in which they take three classes in Yonkers centered on the history of the city and community empowerment, while also work-ing with local nonprofit organizations.

"Sarah Lawrence students are intellectually free-thinking, independent people on the whole," says one sophomore. Twenty-one percent are natives of New York State—the bulk from nearby New York City—and 16 percent come from abroad. Four percent of students are African American, 4 percent Asian American, and 10 per-cent Hispanic. Students report that political and social issues attract much attention. "Students are very active in fighting against racism, inequality, and sexism, and are more than happy to start a protest," says an economics and public policy-focused student. Thirty-three percent of freshmen are eligible for the Pell Grant, and merit scholarships averaging $15,793 are available.

Nearly all first-year students live on campus, and housing is guaranteed for all four years. "The college is great at accommodating any living preferences students may have," says a sophomore. Campus food receives fair reviews, and there are plenty of options for students with special needs. A sociology student says, "Campus secu-rity is very attentive and works around the clock" to keep students safe. A senior reports that students and administrators have worked closely together to adjust sexual assault policies, create education around consent and respect, and "fix the reporting process to make it more accessible and simple."

With a plethora of student organizations hosting on-campus activities, and the school's proximity to New York City, social life is varied and active. "Anything you do here will be new, interesting, and fun," cheers one student. Theater fans and aspiring actors flock to discounted Broadway shows, and clubs, bars,

The professor of students' chosen First-Year Studies seminar course becomes their "don."

"Anything you do here will be new, interesting, and fun."

Every student designs his or her own program of study, and almost no subject is out of bounds.

"We have very unofficial rivalries with Vassar and Bard—more ironic than not."

museums, and concert halls also beckon. Campus policies require party hosts who serve alcohol to register. Although alcohol policies are "rigorous," students report that they are not effective at curbing underage drinking. Favorite traditions include May Fair, the "actually interesting" sex education program called Sleaze Week, fall and spring formals, and midnight breakfast, served during the last week of each semester.

The Sarah Lawrence Gryphons, a mythical figure that was part lion, part eagle, compete in the Division III Skyline Conference. Women's cross-country and swimming were both conference runners-up in 2015; women's tennis and men's swimming are also competitive. The men's basketball and co-ed equestrian teams attract the most fans. "We have very unofficial rivalries with Vassar and Bard—more ironic than not," claims a senior. The intramural program revolves around monthly invitational events—squash matches, dodgeball tournaments, fitness challenges—rather than league play.

Sarah Lawrence offers a close-knit community for writers and artists in a lush setting just outside the hustle and bustle of Manhattan. "The education students get at Sarah Lawrence is unlike any other. You can truly have it all here," says a writing student. "You can play sports and perform in the theater. You can study botany and poetry at the same time. I think everyone could benefit from the Sarah Lawrence education."

Overlaps

Bard, Barnard, Boston University, Brown, Emerson, Fordham, NYU, Oberlin

If You Apply To ➤   **Sarah Lawrence:** Early decision I: Nov. 1. Early decision II: Jan. 2. Regular decision: Jan. 15. Financial aid: Feb. 1. Housing: Jun. 15. Application fee: $60. Campus and alumni interviews: recommended, informational. SATs or ACTs: optional. Subject Tests: optional. Letters of recommendation: required. Essay: required. Accepts the Common Application.

Scripps College: See page 159.

Seattle University

Seattle, WA 98122

Unlike the University of Washington, Seattle U is a stone's throw from downtown and within walking distance of the waterfront. Jesuit tradition guarantees a nurturing environment and student growth both academically and in community service. Transitioning to a national institution but remains true to its humble roots. Out-of-staters are drawn as much by the city of Seattle as by the university itself.

Website: www.seattleu.edu
Location: City Center
Private
Total Enrollment: 5,791
Undergraduates: 4,455
Male/Female: 40/60
SAT Ranges: CR 530–650, M 530–630
ACT Ranges: 24–32

Although Seattle has cultivated a reputation based largely on software, Starbucks lattes, and perpetually gray skies, the city is also home to Seattle University, a vibrant Jesuit institution that attracts nearly 4,500 undergraduates to its urban campus. With strong preprofessional programs and a commitment to social and spiritual engagement, SU continues to express its mission to empower leaders for a just and humane world. A marketing major says, "Students at Seattle University are interested in self-reflection and creating a better world once they leave the university."

SU's campus is a 45-acre urban sanctuary in the heart of Seattle. Bordered by busy city streets, the diverse campus buildings are united by a recurring theme of redbrick and light-filled atriums. The Chapel of St. Ignatius is a prize-winning building designed by Steven Holl around the concept of a "gathering of different lights." New buildings are designed to meet environmentally friendly standards, and energy efficiency and sustainability are top priorities for renovations. Campus grounds have long been pesticide-free, and special areas like the Ethnobotanical Garden and Japanese American Remembrance Garden highlight native plants and local history. The James Tower Clinical Nursing Lab is a state-of-the-art training facility for nursing students.

The 60-credit University Core Curriculum introduces all students to the "unique tradition of Jesuit liberal education" and aims to develop the whole person for a life of service, provide a foundation for questioning and learning in any major or profession, and provide a common intellectual experience to all SU students. The core features seminars in writing, quantitative reasoning and creative expression, humanities, social sciences, and natural sciences, as well as coursework in philosophy and theology. Freshmen complete a first-year seminar built around a central theme or problem (enrollment is limited to 19 students), and seniors must complete a capstone course. In addition, the writing-across-the-curriculum initiative requires all sophomores to submit a writing sample for assessment.

> "Students at Seattle University are interested in self-reflection and creating a better world."

SU students choose from more than 60 undergraduate degree programs, and popular majors include nursing, finance, marketing, accounting, and management. The B.S. in diagnostic ultrasound degree is a particular specialty, and criminal justice, computer science, and biology are also strengths. The university has recently added a six-year, dual-degree program in business and law. "The courses are definitely demanding. When the professors include the Jesuit value in their lectures and exams it really proves how dedicated Seattle University is to fulfilling their mission," says a sophomore. Another adds, "Being on the quarter system is conducive to fostering academic growth as a community because students are aware that there is no time to slack off." Fifty-six percent of classes have fewer than 20 students, and professors are accessible.

Motivated students may enroll in the University Honors program, which offers three concurrent classes in every term. The program focuses on the history of ideas, offering tracks in Intellectual Traditions and Innovations, and makes extensive use of the seminar format. According to a strategic communications major, "Many of our majors require some sort of internship, and professors are more than willing to get students connected with opportunities in the area." When students want to escape Seattle's dreary skies and near-constant drizzle, they can take part in the university's study abroad program. Twelve percent of students pack their bags each year for 45 nations around the world, including China, France, Ghana, Japan, and Sweden. SU also sends approximately 20 students to the National Conference for Undergraduate Research each year as part of a robust undergraduate research program.

> "As a queer student, I feel more than safe—I feel embraced."

Forty-three percent of SU undergraduates hail from Washington, and 11 percent are from other nations. African Americans comprise 3 percent of the student body, Asian Americans 16 percent, and Hispanics 9 percent. Despite its Jesuit ties, "Seattle University is a very liberal and progressive institution," states one junior. "We're all feminists, agents against racism, and allies," says a sophomore, adding, "As a queer student, I feel more than safe—I feel embraced." Merit scholarships worth an average of $13,502 are awarded annually, and athletes vie for 217 scholarships in 18 sports.

Forty-six percent of SU students live in university housing. "The residence halls are comfortable and definitely well maintained," a student says. All first-year

(continued)

Financial Aid: 88%
Pell Grant: 18%
Expense: Pr $ $
Student Loans: 68%
Average Debt: $ $ $
Phi Beta Kappa: No
Applicants: 7,806
Accepted: 73%
Enrolled: 18%
Grad in 6 Years: 78%
Returning Freshmen: 85%
Academics: ✍ ✍ ✍
Social: ☎ ☎ ☎
Q of L: ★ ★ ★ ★
Admissions: (206) 220-8040
Email Address: admissions@ seattleu.edu

Strong Programs:
Nursing
Finance
Marketing
Accounting
Management
Diagnostic Ultrasound
Criminal Justice
Computer Science

The University Honors program focuses on the history of ideas, offering tracks in Intellectual Traditions and Innovations.

students participate in one of 14 learning communities, including options for those interested in eco-awareness, global affairs, wellness, outdoor adventure and leadership, and the arts. First-years and sophomores are required to live on campus; after that, housing is not guaranteed, and students complain that growing enrollment has made getting a room "very competitive." "The surrounding area is very expensive, so most students who move off campus share bedrooms in apartments or townhouses," explains a biology major. Dining, on the other hand, gets rave reviews for being local, seasonal, organic, sustainable, and made to order; one sophomore describes it as "delicious, Instagram-ready food." Vegan, vegetarian, and other diets are well accommodated for. Students report feeling safe on campus, day and night.

"There are events to attend on campus every day, and it often seems like there is too much going on at once," says a senior, including more than 100 student clubs and organizations. Consistent with Jesuit traditions, there are no fraternities or sororities, and "not a whole lot of drinking occurs on campus," according to one student. Instead, students head off campus to enjoy Seattle's vibrant nightlife. "The campus overlooks the urban center of Seattle," explains a student, "and it's a 10-minute walk to the heart of downtown." Once there, students can take advantage of the city's ubiquitous coffeehouses, eateries, and shops, or engage in volunteer work and service-learning opportunities. Everyone anticipates the annual Quadstock festival. "For one Saturday during spring quarter, the campus turns into a huge block party, with live music, games, and food," says a senior; Talib Kweli, OK Go, and Saint Motel have been recent headliners.

SU's Redhawks compete in the Western Athletic Conference (and Division I). Men's and women's soccer, baseball, and women's cross-country are all recent conference champs. "There has always been a rivalry between Seattle University and Seattle Pacific University," a political science major says. Intramural and club sports draw active participation; popular options include baseball, flag football, softball, crew, and cycling.

With its emphasis on the liberal arts, civic engagement, and Jesuit principles, SU affords students an experience "which focuses on educating the entire person," according to one junior. For those students who are not averse to hard work and overcast skies, Seattle University might be an inspired choice—just be sure to pack a parka.

Overlaps

University of Washington, University of Portland, Gonzaga, Western Washington, Seattle Pacific, Washington State, University of San Francisco, University of Oregon

If You Apply To ➤ **Seattle:** Early action: Nov. 15. Regular decision: Jan. 15. Financial aid: Feb. 1. Application fee: $55. Campus interviews: optional, informational. No alumni interviews. SATs or ACTs: required. No Subject Tests. Letters of recommendation: required. Essay: required. Accepts the Common Application with supplement.

Skidmore College

815 North Broadway, Saratoga Springs, NY 12866

Founded in 1903 as the Young Women's Industrial Club of Saratoga, co-ed Skidmore College still excels in the fine and performing arts that were then deemed proper for young ladies. Little else remains the same. Compare to Connecticut College, Vassar, and Wheaton (MA), all institutions that made the successful transition to coeducation. Unique wooded campus gives the feel of living in a forest.

Skidmore College serves up solid academics with a decidedly nontraditional flair. These politically liberal and free-spirited students seem a happy lot, thanks to small classes and accessible faculty members. "The college has a charm, sort of like a summer camp," says a junior. Thanks to an emphasis on interdisciplinary learning, students can "have diverse interests and be able to dabble in anything," a senior says.

In 1961, as enrollment surged and Skidmore's turn-of-the-century Victorian buildings grew obsolete, Skidmore traded its campus in the heart of Saratoga Springs for 750 acres on the northwest edge of town. Since then, the campus has grown to more than 50 buildings on 1,200 acres, and the student body has doubled in size (men were welcomed in 1971). While contemporary in style, the new buildings on Skidmore's Jonsson campus reflect the Victorian heritage of the school's original Scribner campus. Covered walkways connect the residential, academic, and social centers, and the prevailing views are of surrounding mountains, woods, and fields. The Zankel Music Center features a 600-seat performance hall. A bevy of apartment-style student residences have added 350 beds in recent years.

Skidmore's First-Year Experience includes a classwide summer reading project and a choice from among 45 Scribner seminars. Each seminar is capped at 16 students and taught by a professor who also becomes the mentor and advisor for that group. Seminar topics are broad and varied, in keeping with Skidmore's nearly 50 majors. They range from Voting and Game Theory to Disney's America to Stress and the Human Brain. Students in each seminar receive guidance and support from an upper-class peer mentor, and themes raised in the summer reading crop up again during the year in campuswide programming.

The most popular majors at Skidmore are psychology, art, business, environmental studies, and political and social sciences. Not coincidentally, students say these are some of the college's best programs as well. Biology, environmental studies, and geoscience majors, in addition to students in certain first-year seminars and interdisciplinary classes, may conduct fieldwork in

"The college has a charm, sort of like a summer camp."

the college's 300-acre North Woods, a natural laboratory. Skidmore augments liberal arts and sciences offerings with preprofessional majors in business, education, exercise science, and social work. There are also cooperative programs in engineering with Clarkson, Dartmouth, and Rensselaer Polytechnic Institute; the Washington Semester with American University*; a semester at the Marine Biological Laboratory in Woods Hole, Massachusetts; M.B.A. programs with Clarkson, Rochester Institute of Technology, and Syracuse; 4+1 accountancy programs with Wake Forest and Syracuse; a 4+1 finance program with Syracuse; cooperative nursing and physical/occupational therapy programs with New York University and Sage Graduate School, respectively; and an early assurance program with Albany Medical College. Through the Hudson-Mohawk Association of Colleges and Universities, students may take courses at most other colleges nearby.

Most students agree that coursework is challenging but not competitive. "Skidmore is a very collaborative working environment. Professors challenge students to constantly improve communication skills by working with other students and submitting work in both written and oral forms," says a sophomore. A senior adds, "The professors have a huge passion for whatever they're studying, which makes for a great academic climate. They are always accessible." Seventy-two percent of classes have fewer than 20 students, enhancing that accessibility. Students speak highly of off-campus study options, especially Skidmore-run programs in France, England, and Spain, in addition to 120 other approved programs in 45 countries. Some 60 percent of students spend at least one semester off campus. Skidmore's Summer Research Program provides roughly 80 students an opportunity to work

Website: www.skidmore.edu
Location: Small City
Private
Total Enrollment: 2,600
Undergraduates: 2,600
Male/Female: 39/61
SAT Ranges: CR 550–670, M 560–673
ACT Ranges: 26–30
Financial Aid: 45%
Pell Grant: 11%
Expense: Pr $ $ $ $
Student Loans: 42%
Average Debt: $ $
Phi Beta Kappa: Yes
Applicants: 8,508
Accepted: 37%
Enrolled: 22%
Grad in 6 Years: 86%
Returning Freshmen: 94%
Academics: ✍ ✍ ✍ ✍
Social: ☎ ☎ ☎
Q of L: ★ ★ ★
Admissions: (800) 867-6007
Email Address: admissions@skidmore.edu

Strong Programs:
Psychology
Visual and Performing Arts
Business
Environmental Studies
Political Science
Social Sciences

Students in first-year seminars receive guidance and support from an upper-class peer mentor.

individually with faculty mentors for five to 10 weeks on original research in disciplines ranging from biology to business. Internships are popular too.

"Skidmore has a very diverse student body in terms of sexual, religious, geographic, and gender identities. There is also a diverse field of interests," says a student. Many students are well-off. They hail primarily from New York (22 percent are in-staters), New Jersey, and New England; 10 percent come from foreign countries. Asian Americans constitute 6 percent of the student body, Hispanics 8 percent, and African Americans 4 percent. Awards for academic merit—five annually in music ($48,000 over four years) and five annually in math and science ($60,000 over four years)—are avail-

The riding program has won seven Intercollegiate Horse Show Association national championships.

> **"Professors challenge students to constantly improve communication skills."**

able, although there are no athletic scholarships. Grant-funded science scholarships for economically disadvantaged students have recently been instituted. Additionally, the college meets the full demonstrated financial need of all enrolled students.

Ninety-two percent of Skidmore students live in the dorms, and most students get singles after freshman year. Dorms are integrated by class and co-ed by floor or suite, with kitchenettes and lounges on every floor. "Housing is great. It's guaranteed all four years, and the on-campus apartments are unbelievably nice," says a student. Most buildings have carpeting, air-conditioning, and cozy window seats. Some upperclassmen move to apartments—whether on campus in the Northwoods Village Apartments or the new Sussman Village Apartments, or off campus in Saratoga Springs. The Murray-Aikins Dining Center provides students with fresh food choices in a state-of-the-art facility. "I have friends come and visit me from other schools and demand to be sneaked into our dining hall," says a freshman.

"Most of the social life revolves around campus clubs and organizations," says one chemistry major. "Since we don't have Greek Life, we don't have the stereotypical party scene on campus." Skidmore's more traditional activities, which have continued even after nearly a half century of coeducation, include Junior Ring Weekend, when juniors receive their class rings and a dance is held in honor of their initiation. Other annual events include Club Fair, Oktoberfest, Winter Carnival, Spring Fling, and Fun Day in the spring, with games and an inflatable obstacle course on the college green.

The nearby Adirondacks and Green Mountains make Skidmore a haven for backpackers, skiers, and members of the popular Outdoors Club, while the old

> **"I have friends come and visit me from other schools and demand to be sneaked into our dining hall."**

resort town of Saratoga Springs, with its healing waters and antique shops, offers plenty of culture, including the Saratoga Performing Arts Center and the country's oldest thoroughbred racetrack. Saratoga is also the summer home of the New York City Ballet, the Lake George Opera, and the Philadelphia Orchestra. Students reach out to the community through BenefAction, a volunteer group connected to several local agencies and schools. The best road trips include Albany, New York City, Boston—and especially Montreal, where you don't need a fake ID to drink at 18.

Skidmore's men's and women's varsity teams (the Thoroughbreds) compete in Division III; the men's baseball, basketball, tennis, and golf teams have claimed league championships in recent years, as have the field hockey, volleyball, and women's tennis teams. The riding program has won seven Intercollegiate Horse Show Association national championships. Varsity athletes and weekend warriors alike enjoy the 400-meter, all-weather track and the athletic center, which includes a fitness center, a six-lane pool, and an intramural gym.

Skidmore continues to win the hearts of motivated students with gorgeous scenery; caring faculty; and its flexibility, openness, and receptivity to change and

Overlaps

Vassar, Wesleyan, Brown, Tufts, Middlebury, NYU, University of Vermont, Bates growth. Students here are also a bit quirky, says a sophomore, "wearing shorts in the winter, for example." They're more likely to cheer on the fall of a foreign dictator than a goal by the lacrosse team. The point is, there's room for—and encouragement of—all types of students.

If You Apply To ➤

Skidmore: Early decision I: Nov. 15. Early decision II and regular decision: Jan. 15. Financial aid: Feb. 1. Housing: May 1. Application fee: $65. Campus and alumni interviews: recommended, evaluative. SATs or ACTs: optional. Subject Tests: optional. Letters of recommendation: required. Essay: required. Accepts the Common Application.

Smith College

College Lane, Northampton, MA 01063

The furthest left-leaning of the nation's leading women's colleges. Liberal Northampton provides sophisticated social life, and the Five College Consortium* adds depth and breadth all around. With a total enrollment of about 2,800, Smith is the biggest of the top women's colleges, strong in the sciences, and the first women's college to offer engineering. Compare to Bryn Mawr.

Heaven only knows what Sophia Smith would think of the women's college she founded in 1871 with the hope it would be "pervaded by the Spirit of Evangelical Christian Religion." There are still Evangelicals at Smith, but today they join the rest of their schoolmates in crusading against racism, classism, sexism, and homophobia. Though the all-female school remains strongly committed to its liberal arts mission, it is also focused on placing women at the forefront of science and technology. Students here have the opportunity to become leaders in the male-dominated field of engineering, or pursue interdisciplinary fields such as landscape studies. "Smith has an open curriculum, a great college town, and a very strong science program," says one sophomore.

Smith is in the small city of Northampton, an artsy oasis within an hour's drive of the Berkshire Mountains. The 147-acre campus resembles a medieval fortress from the front gate, but inside it sparkles with many gardens, Paradise Pond, and a plant house. Buildings cover a range of styles from late 18th century to modern, and the college has successfully retained its historic atmosphere while keeping facilities up-to-date. The college's science and engineering building, Ford Hall, has earned LEED Gold certification and boasts a myriad of high-tech equipment, including two electron microscopes. Smith's four libraries have almost two million holdings among them, making it one of the largest collections of any liberal arts college in the country. Work is underway on a new, state-of-the art main library, designed by famed architect Maya Lin, to replace the historic Nielson Library.

> "[Smith is] not too competitive because we all want to grow together."

With the exception of at least one writing course, Smith women have unusual freedom to plan a course of study. They must take half of their credits outside of their major, and first-year students can take small seminars on topics such as Biography in African History. Students can expand their options by registering for courses at Five College Consortium* member schools, studying for a semester or two at one of 12 well-known New England colleges through the Twelve College Exchange Program*, or taking advantage of the innovative Maritime Studies Program*.

Website: www.smith.edu
Location: Small City
Private
Total Enrollment: 2,764
Undergraduates: 2,455
Male/Female: 0/100
SAT Ranges: CR 620–740, M 620–720
ACT Ranges: 28–32
Financial Aid: 71%
Pell Grant: 23%
Expense: Pr $ $ $
Student Loans: 63%
Average Debt: $
Phi Beta Kappa: Yes
Applicants: 5,006
Accepted: 38%
Enrolled: 32%
Grad in 6 Years: 87%
Returning Freshmen: 90%
Academics: ✍ ✍ ✍ ✍ ½
Social: ☎ ☎ ☎
Q of L: ★ ★ ★ ★
Admissions: (413) 585-2500
Email Address: admission@smith.edu

Strong Programs:
Government

Government is among the most popular majors on campus, followed by psychology, art, economics, English, and biological sciences. Four in 10 Smith women major in science and thereby enjoy numerous opportunities to assist professors with their research. The Picker Engineering Program is the first of its kind at a women's college and offers students the opportunity to pursue an ambitious engineering program taught within the full depth and breadth of the liberal arts. Those who complete it are among the most sought-after graduates of any U.S. college, and administrators hope the curriculum will lead to greater gender parity in engineering. Members of the first graduating class headed to prestigious graduate programs at Cornell, Harvard, MIT, Princeton, and other colleges, and two received highly competitive National Science Foundation fellowships; others were quickly snatched up by employers. Smith's art history department is among the best in the nation and enjoys access to the college's superb museum. Newer offerings include landscape studies, which focuses on the relationship between humans and natural and built environments; it's the only such program in the country.

Be ready to hit the books with your newfound sisters at Smith. Coursework is described as "very intense and very difficult," although the atmosphere is "not too competitive because we all want to grow together," according to one student. Smith's student-run honor system, which covers everything from exams to library checkout, is widely praised and enforced. Students generally refrain from discussing grades, choosing instead to focus on helping each other. All courses are taught by professors, and 68 percent of them have fewer than 20 students. Students seem to be pleased with the quality of teaching and their access to the professors. "My professors have all been accessible and supportive as well as open-minded and articulate," says a sophomore.

> **"[Smithies are] women who know what they want and know how to get things done."**

With the exception of at least one writing course, Smith women have unusual freedom to plan a course of study.

Qualified students may enter the Smith Scholars program and embark on one or two years of independent study or extra college research for full credit. The STRIDE program allows freshmen and sophomores to become paid research assistants to professors. Students are also enthusiastic about the opportunity to take part in Smith's well-known study abroad program, which usually sends about half of the junior class to a number of countries for at least a semester. The Praxis program allows each student to participate in at least one summer internship funded by the college. About 100 older students are enrolled in the Ada Comstock Scholars program for women going back to college.

Smithies are "women who know what they want and know how to get things done," says a government major. Sixty-five percent of Smith first-years ranked in the top 10th of their high school class. Less than 20 percent of undergraduates hail from Massachusetts, and 14 percent come from abroad. African Americans account for 5 percent of the student body, Asian Americans 12 percent, and Hispanics 10 percent. Nobody disputes that Smith is a liberal place, with social issues of the day dominating conversations, though some students are surprised to find themselves in such a freewheeling atmosphere. With an endowment of more than a billion dollars, Smith has deeper pockets than many of its competitors. And though it's got a hefty price tag, 23 percent of the most recent freshman class qualified for Pell Grants, and the school meets the full demonstrated financial need of admitted students. It also offers a limited number of merit-based awards that average $14,178 annually.

> **"The house system builds strong community."**

Housing at Smith, which consists of houses, not dorms, is unabashedly adored, and is home to 95 percent of students. "The house system builds strong community, and each house has its own traditions," a student explains. Each of the 37 houses, accommodating from 10 to 100 students, is a self-governing unit, responsible for everything from visiting hours to weekend parties and concerts. The atmosphere is less that of a sorority than of an extended family. Except for one senior house, classes are mixed in each house, and first-year students easily mingle with seniors. Incoming students can indicate a preference for size and location of their first house, and changes are possible by entering a lottery. Two alternatives offered are a vegetarian cooperative and an apartment complex. A house system is also used for the dining halls, and the food is highly praised. There are 15 dining halls on campus open at specific times for breakfast, lunch, and dinner on the weekdays and brunch and dinner on the weekends. Some houses even have family-style Thursday dinners to which students invite faculty members.

You will not be greeted with a rocking social scene at Smith, but there are plenty of parties to be had and great places to visit. "The student organizations on campus are pretty good at organizing events like movie nights and sundae parties," says a senior. Meeting men (or non-Smith women) is made easier by the five-college system; a free bus service runs to the other four campuses of the consortium, which offer a broad range of social and cultural opportunities. In addition, each house throws an average of two parties a semester. For special weekends, a whole fraternity may be invited from Dartmouth or another nearby college, an arrangement that is only slightly more civilized than the typical college bar scene. Students say the alcohol policies are getting stricter, and IDs are checked and hands are stamped at campus parties. Smith also offers time-honored traditions like Mountain Day, when the president cancels class for a day of hiking and female bonding, complete with brown-bag lunches.

> "Northampton is one of my favorite places. It's small and artsy."

Northampton, known as NoHo after New York City's SoHo neighborhood, is a college town of about 30,000 that is known for its freewheeling culture and funky bohemianism. The town is home to multiple subcultures, and is generally tolerant of everyone. "Northampton is one of my favorite places," says a senior. "It's small and artsy, has multiple venues for music and dance, a dance club, bowling alley, and a lot of great restaurants. There is never a lack of nightlife." The Community Service Office arranges for students to volunteer in about 600 placements in Northampton, the surrounding communities, and on campus. The New England countryside has numerous special charms, including ski slopes only an hour away. The best road trips are to Boston (two hours) or New York City (three hours).

Smith has a long tradition of success in Division III athletics; the college was the first women's college to join the NCAA and still places a premium on recruiting scholar-athletes. Top Pioneer teams include crew, basketball, soccer, and equestrian. The crew and volleyball teams have brought home recent championships. Smith's multimillion-dollar sports complex includes indoor tennis and track facilities, a six-lane swimming pool, and a riding ring. Inter-house competitions include everything from kickball to inner-tube water polo to rugby.

"It can be hard to adapt to the environment of a women's college," acknowledges one senior. "But it's been the most valuable thing I've ever done." The strict evangelism is gone, and today's Smith women are far from Sophia Smith wannabes. But her namesake and spirit live on at this eclectic, open-minded institution where women don lab coats, power suits, combat boots, and even white dresses at graduation. This "community of close, intelligent, interesting, and compassionate women" readies them to be and do just about anything.

Administrators hope the first-of-its-kind Picker Engineering Program will lead to greater gender parity in engineering.

The Praxis program allows each student to participate in at least one summer internship funded by the college.

Overlaps

Barnard, Brown, Bryn Mawr, Mount Holyoke, Oberlin, Scripps, Wellesley

If You Apply To ➤

Smith: Early decision I: Nov. 15. Early decision II: Jan. 1. Regular decision: Jan. 15. Financial aid: Jan. 25. No application fee. Campus and alumnae interviews: recommended, evaluative. SATs or ACTs: optional (required for international applicants). Subject Tests: optional. Letters of recommendation: required. Essay: required. Accepts the Common Application with supplement. Accepts applications from students whose birth certificates reflect their gender as female or who identify as female.

735 University Avenue, Sewanee, TN 37383

Easily mistaken for an Oxford or a Cambridge plunked down in the highlands of Tennessee. Traditions loom large at Sewanee, including its honor code and the wearing of "class dress" and academic gowns. Affiliated with the Episcopal Church, it is more conservative than Davidson and Rhodes and continues to have old-line Southern feel. Burgeoning environmental studies, prebusiness, and study abroad programs. If you have a horse, bring it along.

Website: www.sewanee.edu
Location: Small Town
Private
Total Enrollment: 1,755
Undergraduates: 1,681
Male/Female: 48/52
SAT Ranges: CR 580–670,
 M 560–650
ACT Ranges: 26–30
Financial Aid: 79%
Pell Grant: 15%
Expense: Pr $ $
Student Loans: 42%
Average Debt: $
Phi Beta Kappa: Yes
Applicants: 4,509
Accepted: 41%
Enrolled: 26%
Grad in 6 Years: 78%
Returning Freshmen: 89%
Academics: ✍ ✍ ✍ ✍
Social: ☎ ☎ ☎
Q of L: ★ ★ ★ ★
Admissions: (800) 522-2234
Email Address: admiss@
 sewanee.edu

Strong Programs:
Economics
English
History
Psychology
Environmental Studies
Natural Resources and the
 Environment
Premed
International and Global
 Studies

Tradition is respected at University of the South, known simply as Sewanee. Leonidas Polk, an Episcopal bishop and later a Confederate general, founded the school in 1857, envisioning it as a distinguished center of learning in the region. When Sewanee's campus was destroyed during the Civil War, Anglican parishes in England gave money to restart the school, and Oxford and Cambridge donated the library's first volumes. Sewanee opened again in 1868, with nine students and four professors. Though many traditions remain alive and well—including calling academic semesters Advent and Easter—students say some traditions are disappearing as the school modernizes and emphasizes a broader national appeal. Still, one junior says, "This is a great academic college that will provide you with fun and unique experiences that will be burned into your mind for the rest of time."

Sewanee is located atop Tennessee's Cumberland Plateau, between Chattanooga and Nashville. The atmosphere is like "attending Oxford in England," a freshman says, "only with mountains!" Stately English Gothic buildings are carved from beige-and-pink sandstone native to the region, and each has plenty of space, as the school spreads out over a 13,000-acre forested plot fondly known as "the Domain." Particularly noteworthy structures are St. Luke's and All Saints' Chapel, and Convocation Hall, built in 1886. Gailor Hall, once a dorm and dining facility, is now a center for languages and literature, with offices for the *Sewanee Review*—the oldest continuously published literary quarterly in the United States—and the Sewanee Writers' Conference. A new residence accommodating 110 students opened in 2016.

> **"The professors are brilliant and, on top of that, they care deeply about their students."**

To graduate, all Sewanee students must take at least 32 courses, achieve a GPA of at least 2.0, and spend at least four semesters in residence. Students pursue six learning objectives in their first two years: Reading Closely, Understanding the Arts, Seeking Meaning, Exploring Past and Present, Observing and Experimenting, and Cross-Cultural Comprehension. In addition to preorientation, a new Finding Your Place program enhances the first-year experience with academic, social, and geographical exploration, including outdoor and community-based studies. In keeping with European tradition, Sewanee seniors must also pass comprehensive exams in their majors to earn their diplomas. While students are tested, friends decorate their cars to celebrate.

Economics, English, history, and psychology are the most popular majors. Sewanee's English department is nationally recognized, thanks in part to a bequest from playwright Tennessee Williams. The sciences are also strong, especially variations on environmental studies, given the campus's rich natural setting. The school's unique natural resources and the environment major focuses on geology and forestry, and offers cooperative master's programs with Duke and Yale. Premed and preprofessional programs are also highly regarded; about nine of every 10 students applying to medical, dental, and veterinary schools in the last decade have been admitted. Although Sewanee does not offer a business major, its prebusiness program, consisting of special experiential learning opportunities and a business minor with managerial, international, and finance tracks, is gaining popularity. The international and global studies major is another fast-growing program, and 43 percent of all students study abroad in nearly 400 approved programs.

Most professors wear black academic gowns when they teach, as do members of Sewanee's signature honor society, the Order of Gownsmen. Administrators say students and professors voluntarily observe these traditions to demonstrate their commitment to teaching and learning. "The professors are brilliant and, on top of that, they care deeply about their students," says a cultural anthropology major. Women often wear dresses or skirts to class, and many men wear jackets and ties. Sewanee also takes its honor code very seriously. Violations—such as lying, cheating, or stealing—usually result in expulsion. Sewanee is "steeped in tradition that almost all students abide by, no matter how archaic," a sophomore says. Sixty-three percent of courses enroll fewer than 20 students, and classwork is taken seriously too. "The courses can be quite challenging," says a junior. "They are the perfect fit for the hardworking, motivated, intelligent, and articulate students that Sewanee tends to attract."

The school spreads out over a 13,000-acre forested plot fondly known as "the Domain."

"[Sewanee is] steeped in tradition that almost all students abide by, no matter how archaic."

Sewanee students are not simply a "large group of privileged preps," argues one senior. Rather, they are "personable, intelligent, motivated, honest, and friendly," says an art major. Twenty-four percent of Sewanee's students are Tennessee natives, though many of the rest come from the Southeast; 3 percent are international. Southern culture is strong here and the atmosphere can be quite familial—almost a quarter of entering freshmen are legacies. The student body is overwhelmingly Christian. Minorities have a small but growing presence on campus, with African Americans making up 4 percent of the student body, Asian Americans 2 percent, and Hispanics 5 percent. Each year, the school hands out academic scholarships averaging $10,939, but no athletic awards. Sewanee also guarantees the tuition rate for four years for each incoming class. Students who maintain a 3.0 cumulative GPA may have the loan portion of their financial aid award replaced with grant money.

Almost a quarter of entering freshmen are legacies.

Ninety-nine percent of Sewanee students live in the dorms, and the most sought-after bunk is Humphreys Hall, which houses 119 students from all classes in singles, doubles, and suites—and is air-conditioned. "Most of the dorms are really wonderful," says a student. Language and theme houses are also available. McClurg Dining Hall serves a wide variety of food and accommodates students' requests, students say. Life on the mountain is peaceful and "students most always feel safe and secure," according to one junior. The FOG program sends students who are trained in alcohol and sexual misconduct intervention strategies to parties to mingle with (and monitor) their classmates and step in to offer help when necessary.

Greek life is a huge deal here, with approximately 60 percent of the men and 60 percent of the women signing up. "Social life takes place mainly on campus," a student reports. "Greek life rules the social scene, but university-funded programs help keep life from becoming one long frat-a-thon." Still, drinking is a fact of life, even though it's against the law for anyone under 21. "Alcohol policies are enforced in the dorms and glass bottles are a huge no-no," says a senior. Annual Fall and Spring Party Weekends draw alumni and friends back to campus, and students also enjoy the Perpetual Motion dance performances and Sewaneroo music festival. Popular road trips include Atlanta, Nashville, and Chattanooga, so it helps to have a car. Nearby lakes, waterfalls, and caverns also offer rafting, hiking, camping, and other active day trips.

The FOG program sends students trained in intervention strategies to parties to mingle with (and monitor) their classmates.

Sports are popular at Sewanee, where virtually no one gets cut from varsity squads because they compete in Division III. The most popular Tigers sport on campus is probably football—not so much because the team is any good, but because games are important social events, where everyone shows up in coats, ties, and dresses (presumably, not all at once). And then there's the cheer: "Sewanee, Sewanee, leave 'em in the lurch. Down with the heathens and up with the Church. Yea, Sewanee's right." The men's and women's lacrosse, swimming and diving, and tennis teams, along with the women's golf team, are competitive, with teams and/or individuals regularly competing in the NCAA championships. The equestrian team competes in International Horse Show Association events and regularly ranks among the top teams in the country. About two-thirds of students participate in intramural sports and the Outing Program, which sponsors outdoor adventures.

> **"University-funded programs help keep life from becoming one long frat-a-thon."**

Sewanee's small size means it offers students plenty of opportunity to really make a difference. The rich traditions tap into the university's long history and give the campus a life and personality all its own. "The [Sewanee] community ebbs and flows like all communities tend to do," says a student, "but its sentiment remains the same: it is and will always be home."

<table>
<tr><td>

Overlaps

Rhodes, University of Tennessee Knoxville, Furman, Washington and Lee, University of Georgia, University of Virginia, UNC at Chapel Hill, Wake Forest

</td></tr>
</table>

If You Apply To ➤ **Sewanee:** Early decision I: Nov. 15. Early action: Dec. 1. Early decision II: Jan. 15. Regular decision: Feb. 1. Financial aid: Dec. 1. Housing: May 1. No application fee. Campus interviews: recommended, evaluative. Alumni interviews: optional, informational. SATs or ACTs: optional. Subject Tests: optional. Letters of recommendation: required. Essay: required. Accepts the Common Application.

University of South Carolina

Columbia, SC 29208

Among public flagship universities in the South, USC struggles against the image of being one giant step behind UNC at Chapel Hill. The university has paid big money to attract star professors and boasts one of the top international business programs in the nation. Criminal justice is also a specialty. In contrast to Clemson, USC is in a major city. Check out the Honors College, which is one of the best anywhere.

<table>
<tr><td>

Website: www.sc.edu
Location: City Center
Public
Total Enrollment: 28,987
Undergraduates: 23,501
Male/Female: 46/54
SAT Ranges: CR 550–640, M 560–650
ACT Ranges: 25–30
Financial Aid: 75%
Pell Grant: N/A
Expense: Pub $ $ $
Student Loans: 55%
Average Debt: $ $ $

</td></tr>
</table>

Whether it's football or international business, students at the University of South Carolina are game—after all, they're the Gamecocks and, like their mascot, they've got plenty of fighting spirit. Students love to cheer on the school's football and basketball teams, especially if the opponent is longtime rival Clemson. South Carolina is working hard to give its campus a more global feel through programs such as SEED, which stands for Students Educating and Empowering for Diversity. "Diversity and loyalty are two words to describe Gamecock students," says a chemical engineering major.

South Carolina's mostly modern campus is located in the heart of Columbia (population 133,000), which also happens to be the state capital. Government buildings and downtown businesses are within an easy walk, allowing students to secure internships or even part-time jobs during the school year. The old section of the campus, which dates to the school's 1801 founding, includes the glorious oak-lined Horseshoe; 10 of its 19th-century buildings are now listed in the National Register of Historic Places. The $250 million Innovista complex integrates public and private sector research in high-tech facilities. The new Darla Moore School of Business opened recently. This "green" building houses more than 2,000 classroom seats in 35 classrooms, more than 40 meeting rooms/project spaces, and 136 faculty offices.

Regardless of the program in which they enroll, students must complete the Carolina Core, a series of distribution requirements that includes courses in problem solving, writing, global citizenship and multicultural understanding, and scientific literacy (among others). Foreign language proficiency is required for graduation, as is the three-hour University 101 seminar, designed to help freshmen adjust to college. University 101 is "an incredible class," according to one student. "You learn about student skills, time management, all the resources at USC, and have a ton of fun." To build community, there's the Freshman Reading Experience, in which entering students read the same book before coming to campus then discuss it in small groups upon arrival.

South Carolina offers a slew of undergraduate degree programs; business administration is popular, as is psychology, nursing, exercise science, and biological sciences. Students in the journalism and mass communications program benefit from an excellent film library right on campus, while budding marine scientists may study and do research at a 17,000-acre facility about three hours away. With South Carolina's coastal economy

"Diversity and loyalty are two words to describe Gamecock students."

depending on foreign trade, the university has also developed a top-notch international business program. Art students, neglected at many universities, here have access to the latest cameras, editing stations, and computers, as well as pottery kilns and other necessary equipment. Musicians enjoy a four-level building with classrooms, a music and performance library, rehearsal rooms, recording studios, and a 250-seat lecture hall. The English program benefits from sizable collections of research material on F. Scott Fitzgerald and Ernest Hemingway. An unusual minor in medical humanities gives doctors-to-be an introduction to the ethical, cultural, legal, economic, and political factors that affect medical practice today.

"For the most part, the courses are challenging and the environment is laid-back," says one senior. A classmate adds, "Students share notes, study together, and help out others." Thirty-four percent of undergraduate classes have fewer than 20 students, and the quality of teaching is generally high: "All my professors are passionate about what they teach and do a great job of sharing their passion with us," one student says. Unlike many honors programs that focus on lower-division education, the University of South Carolina's Honors College provides curricular and research opportunities across all four years. More than 300 courses are available through the Honors College annually. Nineteen percent of undergraduates study, intern, volunteer, or conduct independent research abroad in 52 different countries.

USC draws students from all 50 states and from more than 100 countries; 59 percent of undergrads are in-staters and 2 percent are international. The university also has the highest number of minority students of any public university in the state; 9 percent are African American, 3 percent are Asian American, and 4 percent are Hispanic. "It is the norm to be

"The courses are challenging and the environment is laid-back."

involved with at least two or three student organizations and to be very active on campus," says one student. Another says hot-button issues include education funding, gay rights, and marijuana laws, but since there are about 300 religious, social, athletic, and professional clubs on campus, you'll probably be able to find a niche, no matter where you fall on the political spectrum. The university awards merit scholarships averaging $5,057, as well as 513 athletic scholarships. The Gamecock

---

(continued)

Phi Beta Kappa: Yes
Applicants: 25,736
Accepted: 65%
Enrolled: 31%
Grad in 6 Years: 73%
Returning Freshmen: 88%
Academics: ✍ ✍ ✍
Social: ☎ ☎ ☎
Q of L: ★ ★ ★
Admissions: (803) 777-7700
Email Address: admissions-ugrad@sc.edu

Strong Programs:
Business Administration
Psychology
Nursing
Exercise Science
Biological Sciences
Journalism
Marine Science
International Business

Entering students read the same book before coming to campus then discuss it in small groups upon arrival.

Guarantee promises that each eligible student's undergraduate tuition and technology fee will be covered for up to four years, if the student meets the program's academic, financial, and participation criteria.

Only 29 percent of USC students live on campus because housing can be expensive and difficult to get, students say. The nicest rooms in the stately old Horseshoe section of campus, for example, cost considerably more than traditional double rooms with hall baths located elsewhere. The best advice? Apply early, since the system is first come, first served, and freshmen compete with upperclassmen for space. The surest way to beat the housing system? Get into the Honors College, which entitles you to some of the best rooms. "I loved living on campus," says one junior. "It was so easy to walk to class from my residence hall. I never had to worry about parking or being late to class, as long as my alarm went off in time!" Dining options range from fast-food stands to all-you-can-eat lines, with plenty of vegetarian and healthy choices—and of course, some junk food too. "You will never go hungry," promises one student. Students report feeling safe while roaming campus. "There are over 160 emergency call boxes located throughout campus," notes one junior.

> *More than 300 courses are available through the Honors College annually.*

"Most social life takes place off campus," says a psychology major. "We have cool bars and restaurants close to campus that are geared toward younger people." Seventeen percent of South Carolina's men and 35 percent of the women go Greek,

"We have cool bars and restaurants close to campus that are geared toward younger people."

and their chapters provide much of the weekend social life on campus. While students under 21 may not legally drink, some "sneak it in, and are not bothered if they behave themselves," says a speech/language pathology major. Still, administrators have become more concerned about binge and underage drinking, and funding for alternative activities during high-risk times for alcohol has recently tripled. Those activities include films, dance performances, theatrical productions, concerts, and comedy shows. Downtown Columbia offers more theaters, a comedy club, a performing arts center, and Five Points, a strip boasting six different bars. Outdoorsy types will appreciate Myrtle Beach, just three hours away, and the mountain ranges four hours north for hiking, skiing, and camping.

Fall football weekends are always a big deal at South Carolina, which competes in the Division I Southeastern Conference. The enduring USC–Clemson rivalry is one of the oldest and most colorful in college sports, with festivities beginning weeks in advance; their annual game (the Palmetto Bowl) has been played for more than a century. "We do an annual Tiger Burn, where the engineering students build a 30-foot-tall tiger and burn it to the ground before the big game," says one Gamecock. "That's really fun!" Winter weekends welcome another of USC's strong sports, basketball, played in the 342,000-square-foot Colonial Center. The women's basketball team won its second consecutive conference championship in 2016, while the equestrian team brought home the 2015 National Collegiate Equestrian Association national championship. USC's baseball, soccer, and women's golf teams are also competitive. Students can also choose from dozens of club and intramural sports, or dip into the indoor and outdoor pools at the Strom Thurmond Fitness and Wellness Center, which also features an indoor track, volleyball and basketball courts, a climbing wall, and racquetball courts.

> *The enduring USC–Clemson rivalry is one of the oldest and most colorful in college sports.*

"Carolina is amazing and Clemson is stuck up and snobby," sniffs one diehard Gamecock. The pace of change is picking up at South Carolina's flagship university. With a campus beautification initiative underway, along with scholarships and small, seminar-style courses working to draw more capable students, it seems that no place could be finer.

Overlaps

Clemson, College of Charleston, Furman, University of Georgia, UNC at Chapel Hill

University of Southern California

University Park, Los Angeles, CA 90089

USC's old handle: "The University of Spoiled Children." USC's new handle: highly selective West Coast university with preeminent programs in cinematic arts and business. The difference: a deluge in applications of historic proportions as students flock to the region's only major private university that just happens to have a top football team. L.A.'s answer to SMU on the one hand and NYU on the other.

Once dismissed as little more than an academic bastion of privilege, the University of Southern California has come into its own as a West Coast destination for students seeking the advantages of study in a center for the arts, technology, communication, and international trade. The school's lush campus and prime Los Angeles location has led to a flood of applicants, making it continually tougher to win admission. Students cheer on national championship teams and solid engineering, cinematic arts, business, and communication programs, and give high marks to the Trojan alumni network as well. Often accused of being elitist, USC is nevertheless turning out the next generation of Los Angeles business leaders.

USC's University Park campus has an unmistakably upscale vibe and offers a mix of traditional ivy-covered and modern structures, arranged around fountains and reflecting pools, well shaded from the Southern California sun. Sitting on 226 parklike acres, just minutes from downtown Los Angeles, USC is a veritable urban oasis. Some nearby areas are pretty rough, but thanks to USC's police department, most students say they've never felt unsafe. The new, $700 million USC Village complex includes apartment-style housing for 2,700 undergraduates, a dining hall modeled after Harry Potter's Hogwarts, a fitness center, landscaped courtyards, and retail stores that include Target and Trader Joe's.

> "I have come across professors who seemed to care more about research than the students."

USC's Core Curriculum requires nine courses: six general education, two intensive writing, and one diversity. Together, administrators say, they "provide a coherent approach to fundamental areas of learning, and give students the tools to think critically, communicate clearly, and locate themselves in history." Students with high GPAs and test scores may choose the Thematic Option—a.k.a. the "Traumatic Option"—in place of regular general education courses. The 200 or so who do get smaller classes with some of the university's best teachers and a handpicked group of writing instructors. Freshmen may also join one of the school's Learning Communities, groups of 20 students with common academic interests, such as business, medicine, technology, or languages. Each community takes four common courses during the first year and meets with a dedicated faculty mentor and staff advisor three to six times a semester.

Aside from a strong alumni network, USC offers undergraduates the chance to pursue degrees not only in the College of Letters, Arts, and Sciences, but also at any of its 17 professional schools and schools of the arts. In fact, USC strongly

Website: www.usc.edu
Location: City Center
Private
Total Enrollment: 33,447
Undergraduates: 18,014
Male/Female: 49/51
SAT Ranges: CR 620–730, M 650–770
ACT Ranges: 30–33
Financial Aid: 63%
Pell Grant: 17%
Expense: Pr $ $ $ $
Student Loans: 44%
Average Debt: $ $ $
Phi Beta Kappa: Yes
Applicants: 51,924
Accepted: 18%
Enrolled: 32%
Grad in 6 Years: 91%
Returning Freshmen: 96%
Academics: ✐ ✐ ✐ ½
Social: ☎ ☎ ☎
Q of L: ★ ★ ★
Admissions: (213) 740-1111
Email Address: admitusc@usc.edu

Strong Programs:
Cinema Arts
Business
Engineering
Communication
Journalism
Visual and Performing Arts
Social Sciences

encourages students to pursue double majors or a combination of majors and minors in unrelated academic fields. This means business majors may minor in bioethics or Russian, that international relations majors may double major in urban planning or international urban development, and art history majors may study cinema and television, the music industry, or business too. The Renaissance Scholars program recognizes those who excel in two or more disparate areas of study by finishing their majors and minors in no more than five years and achieving a GPA of 3.5 or higher in those disciplines. The progressive degree program allows students to apply to a master's-level program during their junior year; depending on the field, one can earn a bachelor's and master's degree in as little as 10 semesters.

The academic climate is challenging and new students "often have to adjust because either they are not the best in their class anymore or they have to work harder to be the best," says a senior. Sixty-one percent of undergraduate classes enroll fewer than 20 students, but the quality of teaching varies, especially in some introductory courses for freshmen, which can be huge. "I have come across professors who seemed to care more about research than the students," says an accounting major, but, overall, "the professors are truly amazing." The Discovery Scholars program honors original research and creativity among undergraduates, and the Global Scholars program singles out students who excel both at home and abroad. USC offers 52 semester- and year-long study abroad programs in 30 countries, in addition to several short-term options offered during summer and winter breaks and the May term.

USC students are a healthy mix of "artistic brilliance and ambitious drive," says one senior. Forty-three percent of USC undergrads come from within the state, and the university consistently boasts one of the highest proportions of foreign students in the country, at 15 percent. Even aside from the international presence, this campus is one of the most diverse in the U.S., with African Americans making up 4 percent of the student body, Hispanics 14 percent, and Asian Americans 22 percent. Most students here are "outgoing and friendly," says a music industry major—and most pride themselves on their ability to multitask, maintaining decent grades along with an active social life. Hundreds of merit scholarships, averaging $19,351, are awarded each year, as are more than 340 athletic awards. USC also meets 100 percent of accepted students' demonstrated financial need, and is need-blind in its admissions.

Thirty percent of USC undergrads live on campus. Freshmen are guaranteed university housing, and students say dorm rooms, which come with microwaves and refrigerators, are comfortable. Halls are co-ed, and, "New 1 North is definitely the social dorm that everyone in surrounding residence halls wishes they lived in," says a sophomore. Since swimming pools, tennis courts, carpeting, and air-conditioning are just some of the luxuries to be found in USC dorms, it's no wonder more upperclassmen would like to stay on campus. But because there isn't enough space for everyone, sophomores, juniors, and seniors typically move to fraternity and sorority houses or apartments, which are just a short walk away. (Twenty-six percent of the men and 27 percent of the women go Greek.) Dining halls offer plenty of options, including an international buffet in the Parkside complex. Blue-light phones, tram and taxi services, and escorts from the campus police mean most students don't worry too much about crime.

Though Los Angeles is hardly a "college town" in the traditional sense, "it does allow you to experience a wide variety of cultures," says an accounting major. Whether you're looking for an internship at a law firm or a movie studio, you want to learn to

The new, $700 million USC Village complex includes apartment-style housing and a dining hall modeled after Harry Potter's Hogwarts.

The Renaissance Scholars program recognizes those who excel in two or more disparate areas of study.

"[L.A.] allow[s] you to experience a wide variety of cultures."

"We are drawing an academically competitive and involved student body."

surf, or you're eager to check out a new band before they get signed to a major label, L.A. delivers. Famous Venice Beach is just a few miles from USC's campus, and in the winter months, students can reach the San Gabriel Mountains (and its ski resorts) in less than an hour (by car, not by skis). USC students are also active in the community, tutoring in 10 local schools through the Joint Educational Project.

On campus, Division I sports are pretty much the biggest thing going. Trojan athletics, which compete in the Pac-12 Conference, have won more than 115 team national championships in a dozen men's and women's sports—from baseball to water polo. Women's beach volleyball claimed the national title in 2016. USC has won more national championships than all but two NCAA member institutions and is one of only three universities in intercollegiate athletics history to win five national championships in one year (1962–63 and 1976–77). Two of USC's biggest schoolwide traditions revolve around the ol' pigskin. The first is Troy Week—the week leading up to the UCLA game—which culminates with a pep rally and concert in the middle of campus. Then there's the Weekender, when USC students take off en masse for northern California to see their beloved Trojans face off against Stanford or Berkeley. Throngs of USC undergrads, alumni, and fans gather in San Francisco's Union Square for a huge pep rally, featuring the band, cheerleaders, and university personalities.

USC is a university on the move. Students here enjoy solid academics, a thriving social scene, and enough sunshine to craft the perfect tan. "We are drawing an academically competitive and involved student body," says a geography and communication major. "We have received major donations. And USC athletics are back on par." Pack your sunscreen, flip-flops, and some assertiveness, and you'll fit right in. Shrinking violets, on the other hand, should probably look elsewhere.

Trojan athletics have won more than 115 team national championships in a dozen men's and women's sports.

Overlaps

UCLA, UC–Berkeley, Stanford, NYU, Boston University, University of Michigan, Northwestern, Cornell University

If You Apply To ➤ | **USC:** Regular decision: Jan. 15. Financial aid: Feb. 14. Application fee: $80. Campus interviews: optional, evaluative. No alumni interviews. SATs or ACTs: required. Subject Tests: optional (required for some programs). Letters of recommendation: required. Essay: required. Accepts the Common Application with supplement.

Southern Methodist University

P.O. Box 750181, Dallas, TX 75275

With a reputation as the official alma mater of the Dallas corporate and professional elite, SMU is best known for business, performing arts, and upscale conservatism. Go-getter mentality is pervasive, and students benefit from internships and other opportunities in nearby Dallas. Opulent suburban campus adds to its appeal. Methodist, but mainly in name.

Southern Methodist University is on a mission to shed its long-standing image as a party school for the business elite of Dallas. Admissions standards are on the rise, and recent years have brought an updated curriculum, a new residential model, and, in the words of one senior, "tons of new campus buildings." The highly regarded Cox School of Business sets the no-nonsense tone for SMU's success-driven academic climate. Although founded by what is now the United Methodist Church, SMU is nondenominational and welcomes students of all faiths.

SMU's lush, well-landscaped campus is located in the toney suburb of University Park, located "five minutes from downtown Dallas and within 30 minutes of

Website: www.smu.edu
Location: City Center
Private
Total Enrollment: 8,836
Undergraduates: 6,156
Male/Female: 50/50
SAT Ranges: CR 600–690, M 620–720

(continued)

ACT Ranges: 28–32
Financial Aid: 69%
Pell Grant: 9%
Expense: Pr $ $ $ $
Student Loans: 38%
Average Debt: $ $ $
Phi Beta Kappa: Yes
Applicants: 12,992
Accepted: 49%
Enrolled: 22%
Grad in 6 Years: 77%
Returning Freshmen: 90%
Academics: ✍ ✍ ✍
Social: ☎ ☎ ☎ ☎
Q of L: ★ ★ ★ ★
Admissions: (800) 323-0672
Email Address:
 ugadmission@smu.edu

Strong Programs:
Economics
Finance
Accounting
Psychology
Advertising
Performing Arts
English
History

SMU is nondenominational and welcomes students of all faiths.

everything else," according to one student. Flower beds, fountains, and neatly trimmed lawns surround stately brick buildings, most of them collegiate Georgian. Dallas Hall, with its four-story rotunda, is the centerpiece. The Embrey Engineering Building is one of the first academic buildings in the nation to be designed and constructed to LEED Gold Standards of environmental design. SMU is the only private college in the country to host a presidential library on its main campus, the George W. Bush Presidential Center.

Students describe the academic climate as serious but supportive. "While the classes are extremely challenging and push your intellectual limits, the professors want students to excel," explains an electrical engineering major. General education requirements are laid out in the new three-pronged University Curriculum. Foundations courses emphasize reading and writing, quantitative reasoning, applied critical thinking, and wellness, while Pillars embrace the natural sciences, the arts and humanities, and the social and behavioral sciences. Students also complete a capstone course, project, or experience in which they must reflect on what they have learned. Additionally, students fulfill requirements in eight proficiencies and experiences through coursework or out-of-class activities.

Students hail the Cox School of Business and the Meadows School of the Arts, which turns out professional artists, actors, and singers and has one of the finest collections of Spanish art outside Spain, as SMU's strongest suits. The most popular field of study is economics, followed by finance, accounting, psychology, and adver-

"Some of my professors have practically been my life coaches."

tising. Engineers have access to an extensive co-op program, thanks to the proximity of more than 800 high-tech companies, including Nokia and Texas Instruments, which have facilities in the Dallas suburbs. The John Goodwin Tower Center for Political Studies, named for the former senator, focuses on international relations and comparative politics, while the on-campus Tate Forums give students a chance to interact with national and international figures. The applied physiology and health management program teaches the biological basis of health while offering the business skills needed in the health and fitness industries. Creative computing, a new interdisciplinary major, combines theory and methodology from computer science, engineering, and the arts. As for the humanities, English and history are particularly strong, and SMU publishes *Southwest Review*, one of the four oldest continuously published literary quarterlies in the nation. SMU is the first university in the South and one of the few anywhere to offer a major in human rights. The Simmons School of Education and Human Development offers undergraduate and graduate teaching certifications.

Students praise professors for their accessibility. "Some of my professors have practically been my life coaches," says an advertising major. "They've helped me excel in classes and prepare for interviews. They've provided recommendation letters and answered my emails at two in the morning. They never stop caring for their students." SMU prides itself on small classes; 58 percent of undergraduate courses have fewer than 20 students. Teaching assistants are available for extra help, students say, but they never teach classes.

Freshmen have a variety of special programs available to them that "help students to gain experience and knowledge about the university and its programs," including "Mustang Corral, which is an off-campus retreat," explains one student. The Honors Program enables about 850 students to take seminars on topics not offered broadly, with enrollment in each course capped at 15 to 20 students. Study abroad programs take participants to 50 nations. Each year, about 25 exceptional students are named President's Scholars and awarded full-tuition scholarships as well as opportunities to study abroad and to rub elbows with world leaders at a retreat in Taos. The Academic Learning Enhancement Center, staffed by students, offers tutoring. A management major points out that since SMU is "the only game in town when it comes to colleges in Dallas, there are many companies based just a few miles away looking to hire SMU graduates."

A marketing major describes SMU students as passionate and driven to succeed, adding, "There's a big go-getter mentality all throughout campus." Forty-six percent of undergraduates are from the Lone Star State, and 8 percent come from outside of the U.S. The student body is fairly evenly divided between graduates of public and private or parochial schools. Hispanics account for 11 percent of the student body, Asian Americans 7 percent, and African Americans 5 percent. SMU offers merit scholarships averaging $21,757, as well as 250 athletic scholarships, but socioeconomic diversity is lacking—just 9 percent of incoming freshmen qualify for Pell Grants.

> "There are many companies based just a few miles away looking to hire SMU graduates."

Fifty-seven percent of undergrads live on campus; all first- and second-year students are required to live on campus in one of 11 Residential Commons living/learning communities, each with a resident faculty member, intended to integrate academic, residential, and social experiences. Students are assigned to them randomly. The Academic-Community Engagement house, known as Service House, gives students the opportunity to engage in community service in struggling East Dallas. All residence halls are co-ed by floor, and options include single and double rooms, some with their own bathrooms. The traditional, all-you-can-eat meal plans include dining dollars that can be used at the two main dining halls and at on-campus Subway and Chick-fil-A outposts. "The dining facilities are unbelievable," a senior says. Campus security, which falls under the jurisdiction of four police departments, is strong, students say. "We have many resources such as the blue-light system, sexual assault hotline, and more," reports a Spanish major. Students praise the Not On My Campus campaign aimed at raising awareness of the issue of sexual assault.

Service House gives students the opportunity to engage in community service in struggling East Dallas.

When the weekend comes, the nearly 200 student groups sponsor speakers and other diversions. "Social life at SMU is vibrant both on and off campus," says a sophomore. With Dallas so close and the campus officially dry, much social life takes place in the city. Those under 21 and caught drinking are referred to the Judicial Council, but "if you act like a responsible adult you will be treated like one," reports a senior. Thirty-seven percent of the women join sororities and 28 percent of the men pledge fraternities. SMU students are active in community service projects, including one that promotes micro loans to budding entrepreneurs in low-income areas. According to a management major, "There is a large amount of competition between students outside of the classroom to lead and start different organizations on campus." Highlights of the campus calendar include Peruna Palooza, a birthday carnival in honor of the Mustang mascot (a pony). Students mark the end of the winter semester with the Celebration of Lights featuring holiday lights and carols at Dallas Hall. Favorite road trips are to Austin, with its abundance of restaurants, bars, and live music, and South Padre, Texas, a popular spring break spot with a great beach.

> "There's a big go-getter mentality all throughout campus."

Football games are a big deal here—after all, this is Texas—and SMU students get riled up for the annual battle against Texas Christian University for possession of the Iron Skillet. For home games, there is SMU's answer to tailgating known as Boulevarding, with lavish tents, family activities, music, and food on the main quad. When basketball season arrives, students camp out with their friends to get tickets and pack into the student section known as the "Mob." SMU Mustangs compete in the Division I American Athletic Conference with considerable success. Recent conference champs include men's basketball and golf, and women's cross-country,

Boulevarding is SMU's answer to tailgating, with lavish tents, family activities, music, and food on the main quad.

Overlaps

University of Southern California, Texas Christian, University of Texas at Austin, Vanderbilt, NYU, Texas A&M, Baylor, Duke

swimming and diving, and track and field. Slightly more than a quarter of students participate each year in the intramural program, which offers more than 30 different individual and team sporting activities. Flag football draws more than 1,000 participants to its 81 teams.

Although known for its beautiful people and striking campus, SMU offers solid preprofessional training along with an active social life and ample opportunities to give back to the city of Dallas through community service. The administration is struggling to increase diversity but may actually be making progress. "I never wanted to attend because I didn't feel like I fit the 'SMU mold,'" confesses a senior psychology major. "It wasn't until I visited campus and met students and professors that I began to question what the 'SMU mold' really is."

If You Apply To ➤   **Southern Methodist:** Early decision I and early action: Nov. 1. Early decision II, regular decision, and financial aid: Jan. 15. Housing: May 1. Application fee: $60. No campus or alumni interviews. SATs or ACTs: required. No Subject Tests. Letters of recommendation: required. Essay: required. Accepts the Common Application with supplement.

Southwestern University

1001 E. University Avenue, Georgetown, TX 78627

The oldest institution of higher education in Texas, Southwestern is one of its top liberal arts colleges. Compare to more conservative Austin and much larger Trinity. Southwestern prides itself on individual attention and down-to-earth friendliness. Academic strengths include psychology, fine arts, and the natural sciences, including premed, with big emphasis on interdisciplinary and inquiry-based learning. Recently went native and revived football after 30 years in the Texas athletic wilderness.

Website: www.southwestern.edu

Location: Small City

Private

Total Enrollment: 1,499

Undergraduates: 1,499

Male/Female: 43/57

SAT Ranges: CR 520–640, M 520–630

ACT Ranges: 23–29

Financial Aid: 98%

Pell Grant: 29%

Expense: Pr $

Student Loans: 58%

Average Debt: $ $ $ $

Phi Beta Kappa: Yes

Applicants: 3,736

Accepted: 44%

Enrolled: 22%

Grad in 6 Years: 73%

In a state known for political conservatism and an assumption that bigger is better, Southwestern University stands out like a monadnock. Small and agile, it pursues a flexible and innovative brand of teaching and learning in a culture where the liberal arts are not always appreciated. "You learn to express and defend your opinions," says one student. "I learned how to think."

Founded in 1840 when Texas was still part of Mexico, Southwestern sits on 700 acres at the edge of the rolling Texas Hill Country, although the city of Austin has expanded to meet Georgetown. The Texas limestone buildings, built in the Romanesque style, date from the early 20th century, and there are plenty of open spaces and new athletic facilities. Southwestern's commitment to sustainability includes two LEED-certified buildings and an agreement with the city of Georgetown that allows it to use wind power for the campus's electrical needs. The Fondren-Jones Science Hall is undergoing a major, two-phase renovation.

To graduate, Southwestern students must complete a First-Year Seminar; one math or computer science course; one natural science course with a lab; and two each in humanities, social sciences, fine arts, and fitness and recreational activities. Students must also demonstrate proficiency in a foreign language and satisfy requirements around intercultural perspectives, social justice, and a capstone experience. All students participate in the Paideia program, whereby they pursue a particular theme, such as global health or gender identity, in multiple courses and thus come to see how the various disciplines are interconnected. A sociology and English double major explains, "It's nice to be able to get a taste of how others may see and understand the world in various other disciplines."

The most popular majors include biology, psychology, English, communication studies, and business, which is taught as one of the liberal arts. Student work in the fine arts, where pottery is a specialty, approaches graduate-level quality, and environmental studies, sociology, and anthropology are also strengths. Political science majors benefit from proximity to Austin, the state capital. Southwestern is affiliated with the United Methodist Church and is also a member of the Associated Colleges of the South*.

"The academic climate of Southwestern is rigorous but not competitive," reports a junior. "Students go out of their way to help each other succeed." Seventy-six percent of classes have fewer than 20 students, and professors are appreciated for their hard work and willingness to help students with course concepts and research opportunities. Academic support and career services are highly praised as well, from departmental student mentors, such as the SCI Guides in the natural sciences, to the comprehensive resources offered by the Office of Career Services, including one-on-one counseling, alumni panels, and campuswide internship and job fairs. "I definitely feel prepared for life after college because everything is a process that has been put in motion since I arrived my first semester," says a junior.

SU encourages undergraduate research (75 percent of students participate), and each year holds a symposium to showcase students' scholarly endeavors. The King Creativity Fund provides grants to support up to 20 "innovative and visionary projects" each academic year. Thirty-five percent of Southwestern's students choose to study abroad, and SU hosts faculty-led programs in England, Spain, Peru, and Argentina, plus a service-learning program in Jamaica. The university also sponsors an internship program in Washington, D.C., and an arts apprenticeship program in New York City.

Nearly nine out of 10 Southwestern students come from Texas, and many are the first in their families to go to college. Two percent of students come from foreign countries. Hispanics are the largest minority group at SU, comprising 22 percent of the student body; African Americans add 5 percent and Asian Americans 4 percent. Students describe a fairly even mix of conservative and liberal political views, and campus diversity has drawn attention recently. "The CDSJ (Coalition for Diversity and Social Justice) is a fantastic umbrella organization that has a place for everyone to get involved and be an activist on and off campus," says a computer science major. SU's tuition is markedly less than at institutions of similar quality elsewhere, and 29 percent of incoming freshmen qualify for the Pell Grant. In addition, eligible students receive scholarships based on academic performance; talent awards are also available for fine arts majors, though there are no athletic scholarships.

Seventy-seven percent of SU students live in the residence halls, where the number of stars definitely improves as you get older—juniors and seniors usually get apartment-style facilities with their own bedrooms, bathrooms, and kitchens. "First-year dorms weren't glamorous," says one student, "but I loved everyone in my hall, including the RAs. We were a little family!" Most rooms are suite-style, with house-keepers cleaning up several times a week. All freshmen participate in living/learning communities tied in with their First-Year Seminar. The a la carte fare at the Cove receives good reviews, but the all-you-can-eat Commons dining hall is said to need improvement. Students can also swipe their "Pirate cards" at pizzerias and other local merchants. Students generally feel safe on campus, although a junior reports that after several protests related to alleged incidents of campus sexual assault, the university "has responded by creating student forums to promote discussion,

> **"You learn to express and defend your opinions. I learned how to think."**

The university sponsors an internship program in Washington, D.C., and an arts apprenticeship program in New York City.

(continued)

Returning Freshmen: 86%
Academics: ✎ ✎ ✎ ½
Social: ☎ ☎ ☎
Q of L: ★ ★ ★
Admissions: (512) 863-1200
Email Address: admissions@ southwestern.edu

Strong Programs:
Business
Biology
Psychology
English
Communication Studies
Fine Arts
Environmental Studies
Sociology

mandating that all Greek organizations go through an educational course on how to respond to and support victims of sexual assault, and creating a Title IX student group who works with the university."

Almost all the social life at Southwestern takes place on campus. "Wednesday, Friday, and Saturday nights are the main party nights, but there is always something going on," says one political science major. Southwestern has a strong Greek system, drawing 22 percent of the men and 21 percent of the women, "but you do not have to be Greek to have a fabulous social life," says a sociology major. Students 21 and older are permitted to consume alcohol in designated areas on campus. Annual traditions include the Soundwave concert and Late Night Breakfast, in which "faculty and staff serve students breakfast during finals week while karaoke and other fun stuff happens!"

Georgetown, the county seat, caters mainly to families and retirees, but things are getting more exciting thanks to the mall, two movie theaters, several restaurants, and live music on Friday evenings. Two-thirds of students get involved in the community through service-learning and volunteer work. The Blue Hole, popular for swimming, is within walking distance of campus. The bars and clubs of Austin's Sixth Street are just a half hour away, and San Antonio, College Station, and Houston aren't that much farther.

"It's nice to be able to get a taste of how others may see and understand the world in various other disciplines."

The Southwestern Pirates field 20 Division III varsity sports. The school belongs to the Southern Collegiate Athletic Conference; men's golf won the 2016 conference championship, while women's basketball and volleyball took home conference titles in 2015. Men's basketball and soccer draw the biggest crowds, especially during games against archrival Trinity in San Antonio. Sixty percent of students compete in 18 intramural and club sports, with basketball, flag football, and volleyball being the most popular.

With its emphasis on in-depth and student-centered learning, Southwestern is doing its best to push the frontiers of liberal arts instruction in the 21st century. "SU allows you to continue to grow and challenge yourself in a safe and accepting atmosphere," says a freshman. Couple that sense of growth with caring professors and a campus full of natural beauty, and the attraction of this Hill Country college becomes clear. In a state where things tend to be huge and overwhelming, Southwestern University is out to show that good things can come in small packages.

If You Apply To ➤ **Southwestern:** Early action: Dec. 1. Regular decision: Feb. 1. Financial aid: Mar. 1. Housing: May 1. No application fee. Campus interviews: optional, evaluative. No alumni interviews. SATs or ACTs: required. No Subject Tests. Letters of recommendation: required. Essay: required. Accepts the Common Application with supplement.

Spelman College: See page 36.

Stanford University

Stanford, CA 94305-3005

If you're looking for an Eastern counterpart to Stanford, think Duke with a touch of MIT mixed in. Stanford's big-time athletics, preprofessional feel, and laid-back atmosphere set it apart from Ivy League competitors. In contrast to the hurly-burly of Bay Area rival Berkeley, Stanford's aura is upscale, spacious, and green. Bring your bike and a pair of sunglasses.

You might think the only difference between Stanford and the Ivy League is a couple hundred extra sunny days each year. You'd be wrong. From the red-tiled roofs to the lush greenery and California vibe, Stanford is a world away from the Gothic intellectual culture of the Ivies. Virtually all the great Eastern universities began as places to ponder human existence and the meaning of life, with European institutions as their models. Stanford, by contrast, built its academic reputation around science and engineering, fields characterized by American ingenuity, and only later cultivated excellence in the humanities and social sciences. Stanford is, without a doubt, the nation's first great "American" university. Now the most selective university in the country—turning down 19 of every 20 applicants—Stanford hopes to expand the size of its entering classes until it reaches a new comfort level. Starting with an increase of about 100 students in the fall of 2016 (making for a class of about 1,800 freshmen), the university also intends to expand its dormitories and number of faculty proportionately.

The differences between Stanford and other institutions it competes against for the country's top high school seniors are evident everywhere, from the architecture to the curriculum. The school's mission-style buildings look outward to the world at large, rather than inward to ivy-covered courtyards. And unlike its Colonial-era predecessors, Stanford—founded in 1885 by Leland and Jane Stanford in memory of their son Leland Jr.—has been co-ed from the beginning. During its centennial, the school became the first U.S. university to successfully launch a billion-dollar capital campaign; today Stanford's endowment is $22.2 billion. Some architectural critics say the campus looks like the world's biggest Mexican restaurant, even though Frederick Law Olmsted, designer of New York City's Central Park, planned many of the buildings. The campus stretches from the foothills of the Santa Cruz Mountains to the edge of Palo Alto in the heart of Silicon Valley, smack in the middle of earthquake country. The campus is nationally recognized as "bicycle friendly" and the university operates free bike repair stations. Recent construction includes the McMurtry Building, which houses the department of art and art history, and three new undergraduate residences.

> "People are always working together on projects and assignments."

Stanford requires students to complete one course in Thinking Matters and 11 in a series called Ways of Thinking/Ways of Doing. The series includes two courses in aesthetic and interpretive inquiry, two courses in social inquiry, two courses in scientific analysis, one course in formal reasoning, one course in quantitative reasoning, one course in engaging diversity, one course in moral and ethical reasoning, and one course in creative expression. Stanford also requires writing and rhetoric courses and one year of a foreign language. More than 200 optional, small-group Introductory Seminars are available to freshmen and sophomores, covering topics like What is Nanotechnology? and Mark Twain and American Culture, in which about half of students enroll; one student credits these courses with helping freshmen "develop relationships with really engaging professors."

Website: www.stanford.edu
Location: City Outskirts
Private
Total Enrollment: 15,778
Undergraduates: 6,999
Male/Female: 52/48
SAT Ranges: CR 690–780, M 700–800
ACT Ranges: 31–35
Financial Aid: 85%
Pell Grant: 16%
Expense: Pr $ $ $
Student Loans: 22%
Average Debt: $
Phi Beta Kappa: Yes
Applicants: 42,497
Accepted: 5%
Enrolled: 80%
Grad in 6 Years: 95%
Returning Freshmen: 98%
Academics: ✑ ✑ ✑ ✑ ✑
Social: 🕿 🕿 🕿 🕿
Q of L: ★ ★ ★ ★ ★
Admissions: (650) 723-2091
Email Address: admission@stanford.edu

Strong Programs:
Computer Science
Human Biology
Engineering
Science, Technology, and Society
International Relations
Political Science
Economics

Computer science is the most popular major on campus, followed by human biology; engineering; and science, technology, and society. The newly created CS+X program allows students to complete one of 14 joint degrees that combine computer science with disciplines in the humanities, such as foreign languages, history, linguistics, and philosophy. Stanford has also developed a particularly interesting set of interdisciplinary programs. The Haas Center for Public Service offers more than 100 service-learning courses in a wide range of disciplines, while the communications department offers paid positions at various California media outlets. The Stanford Hopkins Marine Station is located on a mile of coastland in Pacific Grove, next to the Monterey Bay Aquarium, and offers courses in marine and biological sciences.

"People are a bit quirky, but everyone is generally happy and easy to get along with."

Don't let Stanford's California location fool you into thinking studying is optional—it's more like a full-time job. "I think Stanford is a very collaborative school. People are always working together on projects and assignments. That said, this might be because it is intense, and many students do take on a heavy workload," one student says. Students sometimes compare themselves to ducks: they look peaceful on the surface, but they're paddling like mad underneath. Stanford's faculty ranks among the best in the nation, with impeccable credentials, and most departments boast a nationally known name or two. Class sizes are generally small, with 71 percent enrolling fewer than 20 students, and 93 percent are taught by faculty, as opposed to graduate students. "Overall, professors do seem to care about the students. They are definitely accessible, almost all having open office hours," says one computer science major. Befitting its location in Silicon Valley, Stanford is pioneering the use of mobile technologies, including replacing paper textbooks with tablet-based digital ones.

Stanford is the most selective university in the country, turning down 19 of every 20 applicants.

For students who are inclined to study abroad, programs are offered at Stanford's campus in Cape Town, South Africa, as well as several other locations around the globe, including Australia, Chile, Japan, Germany, and Turkey. Fifty-three percent of each graduating class takes advantage of these programs. Closer to home, the Stanford-in-Washington program allows 60 students to live, study, and intern in the nation's capital each quarter, and a similar program is offered in New York City. The Summer Research College is designed to create community among undergraduates engaged in full-time summer research on campus, and there are three honors programs. Three-quarters of students undertake independent study projects with faculty. For those seeking additional academic support, the Schwab Learning Center—named after alum Charles Schwab—offers services for students with learning disabilities and ADHD.

Stanford students may be Olympic champions and future Rhodes scholars, but students say there isn't a sense of elitism on campus. One notes, "People are a bit quirky, but everyone is generally happy and easy to get along with." Fifty-eight percent of undergraduates attended public high school. Thirty-six percent are from California, while international students represent 9 percent of the student population. Minority enrollment is well above average, with Asian Americans accounting for 20 percent of the student body, Hispanics 15 percent, and African Americans 6 percent.

"Party culture is not exclusively Greek, and social life is not exclusively partying."

Students on this liberal campus are keen to be heard, and recent hot topics include "divestment from Israel, divestment from fossil fuels, and race relations," according to one senior. Admissions are need-blind, and the university guarantees to meet the full demonstrated financial need of every domestic admit. Academic scholarships are based on need (meaning no merit awards), and Stanford has eliminated parent contributions for families with annual incomes below $65,000. The university also awards more than 300 athletic scholarships annually in 34 sports.

Freshmen must live on campus, and Stanford guarantees housing for four years; 93 percent of students stay on campus, in part because of the lack of affordable off-campus options in the extraordinarily expensive Silicon Valley. As students gain seniority, a lottery system decides where they'll live. "Junior year I lived in an old faculty mansion for 30 students that had a Thai chef," one student says. The multimillion-dollar Governor's Corner complex includes all-oak fixtures, homey rooms with views of the foothills, microwave ovens in the kitchenettes, and Italian leather sofas in the lounges. Dorm dwellers must sign up for a meal plan. "Campus security is quite good. We have an AlertSU program that texts emergency messages to the school whenever there is any sort of security violation, and Stanford is extremely well-lit at night," says a freshman.

Like most things at Stanford, social life and activities vary a great deal, although most take place on campus, with a constant lineup of events and performances. Greek organizations claim 20 percent of the men and 20 percent of the women, and provide their share of happy hours and weekend bashes, which are open to all. Underage drinking happens, but is kept under control. As one freshman puts it, "Party culture is not exclusively Greek, and social life is not exclusively partying." As tradition goes, freshmen aren't "true Stanford students" until they've been kissed at midnight in the quad by a senior. Full Moon on the Quad occurs at the first full moon and features a bevy of first-year students eager to receive their initiation (courtesy of a well-timed entrance by upperclassmen). The Viennese Ball is a February event that may make you wish you'd taken ballroom dancing lessons, and Halloween finds students partying at the Mausoleum, the Stanfords' final resting place.

Palo Alto "has a few fun hangouts and is slightly overpriced," a political science major says, and students love to seek refuge in the outdoors—nearby hills are perfect for jogging and biking. Trips to the Sierra Nevada mountains (four hours away) or to the Pacific coast (45 minutes) are popular, as are jaunts to San Francisco, Los Angeles, or the Napa Valley.

Stanford has a proud athletic tradition. In 2016, Stanford took home its 21st consecutive Directors' Cup, which recognizes the best overall collegiate athletic program in the country. Men's soccer, women's tennis, and women's synchronized swimming all won their respective national championships in the 2015–16 season. Men's and women's basketball consistently make it to at least the Sweet 16. The baseball team has been to the College World Series, and the football team has become a powerhouse, claiming victory in the 2016 Rose Bowl and finishing third in the nation. The annual contest against archrival Cal (Berkeley) is dubbed the "Big Game." The marching band proudly revels in its raucous irreverence, to the delight of students and the dismay of conservative types. For those not inclined to varsity play, Stanford offers 24 club sports and 27 intramural activities, and its vast sports complex includes 26 tennis courts, two gymnasiums, a stadium, an 18-hole golf course, and four swimming pools.

Stanford University's sunny demeanor and infectious West Coast optimism offer an appealing alternative to the gloom and gray weather that seem to hang over some of its East Coast counterparts, with the same high-caliber academics and deep athletic traditions that have made them great. Stanford is hard to fit into a box," muses one student, "but there is a very innovative and individualistic personality that is also a collective culture on campus."

The newly created CS+X program offers 14 joint degrees that combine computer science with disciplines in the humanities.

"There is a very innovative and individualistic personality that is also a collective culture on campus."

Halloween finds students partying at the Mausoleum, the Stanfords' final resting place.

Overlaps

Harvard, Yale, MIT, Princeton, Columbia, Brown, Duke, UCLA

If You Apply To ➤ **Stanford:** Single choice early action: Nov. 1. Regular decision: Jan. 3. Financial aid: Feb. 15. Application fee: $90. Campus and alumni interviews: optional, evaluative. SATs (with essay) or ACTs (with writing): required. Subject Tests: strongly recommended (Math II and one other). Letters of recommendation: required. Essay: required. Accepts the Common Application with supplement.

State University of New York

As the largest university system in the world, the State University of New York provides more than 440,000 students with a vast landscape of educational opportunities—both figuratively and literally. Encompassing 64 widely dispersed campuses and 21,000 acres of property, SUNY's staggering physical presence is exceeded only by the scope of its academic offerings. Under the brand new New York State Excelsior Scholarship program, the first of its kind in the U.S., in-state students from households earning up to $100,000 qualify for free tuition at the state's two- and four-year colleges and universities.

The statistics of SUNY (pronounced "SOOney") are awesome. The university has an annual operating budget of billions, greater than the gross national product of many countries and larger than the budget of more than a dozen American states. It has more than 440,000 students, about 4,400 undergraduate academic programs, and 34,000 faculty members, and it maintains more than 2,200 buildings. Every year it awards approximately 95,000 degrees (80,000 of which are undergraduate degrees), from associate to Ph.D., in thousands of different academic fields. And—you're not going to believe this one—it has nearly three million living graduates.

Such figures are all the more remarkable considering that until 1948, New York had no state university at all. That year, the legislature created the State University around a cluster of 29 institutions, the best of which focused on the training of teachers, to handle the flow of returning World War II veterans. But a "gentleman's agreement" not to compete with the state's private colleges (which for generations had enjoyed a monopoly on higher education in New York) hindered SUNY's movement into the liberal arts. Not until Nelson A. Rockefeller became governor in 1960 and made the expansion of the university his major priority did SUNY begin its dramatic growth. SUNY has now ripened into a network of four "university centers," 13 arts and sciences colleges, seven technological colleges, 11 statutory and specialized institutions, and 29 locally sponsored community colleges.

Despite this seeming diversity, leaders of the SUNY system are making concerted efforts to improve diversity among the students and to make students of all backgrounds feel welcome. The establishment in 2007 of the Office of Diversity, Equity, and Inclusion has helped to increase minority enrollment, but the student body is still nearly 60 percent white. SUNY's definition of diversity is sweeping and covers not only race and ethnicity but also religion, sexual orientation, gender, gender identity and expression, age, and socioeconomic status. The system has enacted numerous programs aimed at increasing the retention and graduation rates of underrepresented students.

Prospective students apply directly to the SUNY unit they seek to attend. Fifty-one of the colleges use a "common form" application that enables a prospective student to apply to as many as four SUNY campuses at the same time. The central administration runs a SUNY Admissions Assistance Service that helps rejected students find places at other campuses. Students who earn associate degrees at community or other two-year colleges are guaranteed the chance to continue their education at a four-year institution, though not necessarily at their first choice. The level of selectivity varies widely. Most community colleges guarantee admission to any local high school student, but the university centers, as well as some specialized colleges, are among the most competitive public institutions in the nation. As part of a recent "standards revolution," SUNY trustees voted to adopt a new budgeting model designed to financially reward campuses that increase enrollment. Undergraduates at all liberal arts colleges and university centers pay the same tuition, but the rates at community colleges vary (and are lower). Out-of-state students, who make up only 6 percent of SUNY students, pay about double the amount of in-state tuition. Annual costs at institutions like SUNY–University at Albany have traditionally been well below those at such hoary and prestigious publicly supported flagship campuses as UC–Berkeley and the University of Michigan, but they are now slightly above the national average.

Mainly for political reasons, the State University of New York chose not to follow the model of other states and build a single flagship campus the likes of an Ann Arbor, Madison, or Chapel Hill. Instead, it created the four university centers with undergraduate, graduate, and professional schools and research facilities in each corner of the state. When they were created in the 1960s, each one hoped to become fully comprehensive, but there has been a certain degree of specialization from the beginning. Albany is strongest in education and public policy, Binghamton is best known for undergraduate arts and sciences, and Stony Brook is noted for its hard sciences. Buffalo, formerly a private university, maintains a strong reputation in the life sciences and geography and comes the closest of any of the four to being a fully comprehensive university.

Critics say that the decision to forgo a flagship campus guarantees that the system won't achieve national prominence, and the lack of big-time Division I football and prestigious Ph.D. programs has affected SUNY's reputation as well. Still, many insist that somewhere in the labs and libraries of these four university centers are lurking the Nobel Prize winners of this century. To these supporters, it's only a matter of time before SUNY achieves excellence in depth as well as breadth.

The 13 colleges of arts and sciences likewise vary widely in size and character. They range from the 25,000-student University at Buffalo, whose 1,346-acre campus reflects the urban flavor of the state's second-largest city, to the small, rural College at Geneseo. Still others are suburban campuses, such as Purchase, which specializes in the performing arts, and Old Westbury, which began as an experimental institution to serve minority students, older women, and others who have been "bypassed" by more traditional institutions.

With the exception of Purchase and Old Westbury, which were started from scratch, the four-year colleges are all former teachers' colleges that have, for the most part, successfully made the transition into liberal arts colleges on the small, private New England model. Now they face a new problem: the growing desire of students to study business, computer science, and other more technically oriented subjects. Some have adjusted to these demands well; others are trying to resist the trend.

SUNY's technical and specialized colleges, while not enjoying the prominence of the colleges of arts and sciences, serve the demand for vocational training in a variety of two- and four-year programs. Five of the seven agricultural and technical colleges—Alfred State, Canton, Cobleskill, Delhi, and Morrisville—are concerned primarily with agriculture, but also have programs in engineering, nursing, medical technology, data processing, and business administration. Farmingdale offers the widest range of programs, from ornamental horticulture to aerospace technology. The SUNY Polytechnic Institute, created in 2014 through a merger of two technical schools, offers degrees in nanoscience and nanoengineering at its campuses in Albany and Utica–Rome.

Four of the five statutory schools are at Cornell University—agriculture and life sciences, human ecology, industrial and labor relations, and veterinary medicine—while the internationally known College of Ceramics is housed at Alfred University, another private university. The six specialized colleges consist of the College of Environmental Science and Forestry at Syracuse, the Maritime College at Fort Schuyler in the Bronx, the College of Optometry in New York City, the Upstate Medical University, the Downstate Medical Center, and the Fashion Institute of Technology, whose graduates are gobbled up as fast as they emerge by employers in the Manhattan Garment District.

The 29 community colleges have traditionally been the stepchildren of the system, but the combination of rampant vocationalism and the rising cost of education elsewhere is rapidly turning them into the most robust members of the family. Students once looked to the community colleges for terminal degrees that could be readily applied in the marketplace. Now, with the cost of college soaring, a growing number of students who otherwise would have been packed off to a four-year college are saving money by staying home for the first two years and then transferring to a four-year college—or even a university center—to get their bachelor's degrees.

Following are full-length descriptions of SUNY–Purchase, which is the liberal arts institution best known beyond New York's borders, SUNY–Geneseo, and the four university centers (the University at Albany, Binghamton University, the University at Buffalo, and Stony Brook University).

SUNY–University at Albany

1400 Washington Avenue, Albany, NY 12222

Like the rest of the SUNY system, University at Albany is much better than its relative anonymity would suggest. Strong in anything related to public policy, including criminal justice and social welfare. Study abroad programs in Europe and Asia are also strengths. Only 11 percent of undergrads are from outside New York. Campus is a living testament to just how bad 1960s architecture could be.

Founded in 1844 to train teachers, UAlbany offers a bevy of outstanding programs in arts and sciences, business administration, and preprofessional programs. Study abroad is solid too, but it's the university's public policy programs that truly shine.

Designed by Edward Durrell Stone, who also designed the Kennedy Center and Lincoln Center, UAlbany's main uptown campus is stark, modern, and suburban. Almost all the original academic buildings are clustered in the center of the campus,

Website: www.albany.edu
Location: Suburban
Public
Total Enrollment: 14,350
Undergraduates: 12,151

(continued)

Male/Female: 51/49

SAT Ranges: CR 490–580,
  M 510–590

ACT Ranges: 22–26

Financial Aid: 61%

Pell Grant: 29%

Expense: Pub $

Student Loans: 69%

Average Debt: $ $

Phi Beta Kappa: Yes

Applicants: 22,337

Accepted: 56%

Enrolled: 21%

Grad in 6 Years: 66%

Returning Freshmen: 82%

Academics: ✐ ✐ ✐ ✐

Social: ☎ ☎ ☎

Q of L: ★ ★ ★

Admissions: (518) 442-5435

Email Address:
  ugadmissions@albany.edu

Strong Programs:

Public Policy and Management

Social Welfare

Criminal Justice

Biology

Psychology

Business Administration

Communication

Education

The New York State Writers Institute, headed by William Kennedy, is the least traditional of Albany's offerings.

while students are housed in symmetrically situated quads so similar in appearance that it usually takes a semester to figure out which one is yours. (Hint: the quads are named for periods in New York history—Indian, Dutch, Colonial, State, and Freedom—and progress clockwise around the campus.) A spate of new construction has changed the face of the uptown campus over the past decade. The latest, an expansion of the Campus Center, was completed in 2015.

UAlbany's general education requirements consist of 30 credits, including one course in each of 10 areas: math and statistics, writing and critical inquiry, arts,

> **"There are some superstar professors and a bad apple here and there."**

humanities, natural sciences, social sciences, U.S. history, international perspectives, foreign languages, and challenges for the 21st century. All freshmen take a required introductory seminar. In addition, all students complete academic competencies in the areas of advanced writing, oral discourse, information literacy, and critical thinking.

For the career-minded, most of the preprofessional programs are among the best of any SUNY branch. Students in the public policy and management, social welfare, and criminal justice programs may take advantage of their proximity to the state government to participate in internships. Biology, psychology, communication, education, and anthropology are other notable majors, and undergrads are clamoring for admittance to the university's business administration program, which is especially strong in accounting. Students can sign up for one of 30 B.A./M.A. programs or opt for a law degree with the bachelor's in only six years in conjunction with UAlbany Law School. The New York State Writers Institute is the least traditional of UAlbany's offerings, and with William Kennedy as head of the institute, the university's dream of becoming distinguished for its creative writing is well on its way. The university has recently established two new colleges from expanding programs: the College of Emergency Preparedness, Homeland Security, and Cybersecurity and the College of Engineering and Applied Sciences.

The academic climate is challenging and courses tend to be demanding. "There's a lot of importance placed on academic achievement," says one junior. "In certain classes—especially the honors classes—there is a competitive climate." Classes can be

> **"The cost of apartments is as cheap (or cheaper) than living on campus."**

large, but 30 percent enroll fewer than 20 students. Students form study groups to help one another through the coursework, and professors are always available to offer support. "The quality of teaching is excellent overall," a physics major says. "There are some superstar professors and a bad apple here and there, but usually very good instructors." Qualified students can take part in the Honors College, which allows freshmen and sophomores to enroll in up to six introductory courses that have been designed by distinguished faculty. The courses emphasize research, service learning, and a creative component. Senior honors students design and complete a yearlong research or creative project. About 5 percent of students take advantage of UAlbany's superior offerings in foreign study. The Office of Study Abroad and Exchanges offers more than 130 programs in 40 countries where students can earn credits in their major or minor, or even general education credits.

The student body comprises "bits and pieces of every Long Island high school and a dash of upstate, topped off with a Big Apple or two," according to one student. Another adds, "There are a handful that I think made it into UAlbany by some kind of miracle. Most of the students I interact with, though, are the opposite." Just 5 percent of undergraduates come from states outside New York, and another 6 percent come from foreign countries. African Americans comprise 16 percent of the student body, Hispanics 15 percent, and Asian Americans 8 percent. UAlbany makes available merit scholarships, averaging $3,326, and 210 athletic scholarships in 17 sports. Low-income students may qualify for the Equal Opportunity Program, which offers additional academic and financial support. Twenty-nine percent of first-year students are Pell-eligible.

Fifty-nine percent of students live in university housing; freshmen and sophomores are required to live in dorms. Living/learning communities allow incoming freshmen who share similar interests or majors to live together in the same residence hall and take some courses together. "Dorms are sometimes small," says one student, "but you get used to it." Others report that the co-ed quads are exceptionally friendly, surprisingly quiet, and comfortable. Each floor is divided into four- to six-person suites. Many students move off campus because "the transportation system to and from campus is convenient and the cost of apartments is as cheap or cheaper than living on campus," says a junior. Students on the main campus take their meals at any of the four dorms or at the campus center that includes a food court and bookstore, while downtowners haunt the cheap local eateries as well as their own cafeterias.

The Student Association owns and operates Dippikill, a wilderness retreat described as UAlbany's "own little Walden" in the Adirondacks.

"You can spend months without leaving campus," says one student. "It's relatively large and there's always something going on." Students have more than 200 clubs and organizations to choose from, many of which are involved in community service. While most people are serious about their work, a UAlbany weekend starts on Thursday night for many, with parties or barhopping about town. Students warn that alcohol policies forbidding underage drinking are strict and well enforced. "You can get into a lot of trouble if you're caught on campus with alcohol," says a student. Fraternities and sororities attract 1 percent of the men and 2 percent of the women and have become the main party-throwers on campus. Rites-of-spring festivals, mandatory after enduring the

"This is not a school that will educate you when you're not looking."

miserable upstate winters, have produced Guinness records for the largest games of Simon Says, Twister, and Musical Chairs, as well as the all-school pillow fight. Parkfest is a huge all-school concert that brings in well-known as well as up-and-coming bands. The natural resources of the upstate region keep students busy skiing and hiking, and the Student Association owns and operates Dippikill, a wilderness retreat described as UAlbany's "own little Walden" in the Adirondacks. Treks to Montreal and Saratoga are also popular.

Men's and women's varsity basketball and lacrosse, and women's tennis, soccer, and field hockey are highly competitive, and the Great Danes are members of the Division I America East Conference. The men's and women's indoor and outdoor track and field teams have dominated the conference; each of the four teams have claimed the last dozen or so of their respective championships. Intramurals and club sports engender a great deal of student enthusiasm, and participation numbers in the thousands.

The University at Albany is not the concrete, sterile diploma mill it may appear to be. It's a place of opportunity for those willing to put in the hours and hard work. As one veteran warns, "You can find an outlet here for even the most obscure interest, but this is not a school that will educate you when you're not looking."

Overlaps
SUNY–Binghamton,
SUNY–Stony Brook,
SUNY–Buffalo

If You Apply To ➤

SUNY–Albany: Early action: Nov. 15. Regular decision and financial aid: Mar. 1. Application fee: $50. No campus or alumni interviews. SATs or ACTs: required. No Subject Tests. Letters of recommendation: required. Essay: required. Accepts the Common Application with supplement.

SUNY–Binghamton University

P.O. Box 6001, Binghamton, NY 13902-6000

If 100,000 screaming fans on a Saturday afternoon tickles your fancy, head 200 miles southwest to Penn State. Binghamton has become one of the premier public universities in the Northeast because of its outstanding academics and commitment to undergraduates. It is writing the rules on how to integrate global awareness and international experiences into undergraduate study.

Website: www.binghamton.edu
Location: Suburban
Public
Total Enrollment: 15,093
Undergraduates: 13,045
Male/Female: 52/48
SAT Ranges: CR 600–680, M 630–703
ACT Ranges: 27–31
Financial Aid: 70%
Pell Grant: 28%
Expense: Pub $
Student Loans: 53%
Average Debt: $ $
Phi Beta Kappa: Yes
Applicants: 30,616
Accepted: 42%
Enrolled: 85%
Grad in 6 Years: 81%
Returning Freshmen: 91%
Academics: ✎ ✎ ✎ ✎ ½
Social: ☎ ☎ ☎
Q of L: ★ ★ ★ ★
Admissions: (607) 777-2171
Email Address: admit@ binghamton.edu

Strong Programs:
Psychology
Accounting
Biological Sciences
Economics
Business Administration
Global Studies
Foreign Languages

Binghamton University offers a private-school experience at a public-school price, even for out-of-staters. With more than 280 clubs and an emphasis on small classes—86 percent of those taken by undergraduates have fewer than 50 students—it's no wonder that students who apply here are also considering schools such as Cornell and NYU. Binghamton offers an intellectually challenging environment with an emphasis on global experiences, including more than 600 study abroad opportunities in more than 100 countries, area studies programs that focus on specific regions of the world, and the unique Languages Across the Curriculum program. "The biggest complaint," muses one student, "is the one thing that no one can change: the weather."

Binghamton's campus sits on 930 acres of open grassy space and includes a nature preserve, trails, fountains, and a pond. The oldest buildings date from 1958, so the prevailing architectural style is modern and "functional." Some students say that, from the air, the circular campus bears a striking resemblance to the human brain, but administrators say that's merely a coincidence. A slew of renovations and construction has taken place recently, including the new Center of Excellence and the Smart Energy Research and Design Facility, slated for completion in 2017.

Students apply to one of the university's six schools with undergraduate programs: the Decker School of Nursing, the Harpur College of Arts and Sciences, the College of Community and Public Affairs, the School of Management, the Thomas J. Watson School of Engineering and Applied Science (named for the founder of IBM), and a new School of Pharmacy and Pharmaceutical Sciences. A seventh unit, the Graduate School of

> **"Beating the test is usually more important than beating other students."**

Education, offers only graduate-level degrees. Regardless of the school they choose, students face the same general education requirements, which span five thematic areas: language and communication, creating a global vision, sciences and mathematics, aesthetics and humanities, and physical activity and wellness. All undergraduates must complete one of the global interdependence (or "G") courses offered in all departments as part of the effort to equip students with "a basic understanding of the complex dimensions of contemporary global issues." The Discovery program provides freshmen with peer mentors and assistance in exploring experiential learning opportunities and career paths.

Popular majors include psychology, accounting, biological sciences, economics, and business administration. Students also have the option to design their own majors via the Individualized Major Program in Harpur College. New programs include combined B.A./M.A. programs in sociology and history and minors in computational biosystems and biomedical devices and instrumentations. Binghamton's academic reputation is enhanced by a tough grading policy, which includes pluses and minuses as well as straight letter grades, and Fs on the transcripts of failing students rather than no credit. "Students are usually self-motivated and cooperative," says a sophomore. "Beating the test is usually more important than beating other students." According to a biology major, "There are some great teachers here and some not so great. All faculty members, however, have made themselves very accessible."

Binghamton operates student exchanges with universities around the world and directly sponsors more than 40 study abroad programs in locations as diverse as the United Kingdom, Costa Rica, India, Morocco, Korea, and Australia. "Study abroad at Binghamton is huge!" says an English major. Nineteen percent of students study abroad at some point in their undergraduate careers. Programs in global and international affairs, information systems, and management bring more than 300 students a year to Binghamton from four of Turkey's most prestigious universities. Binghamton administrators hope the programs will also encourage more of their students to travel to Turkey and the Middle East. Undergraduate research is also emphasized here, and the new, invitation-only Freshman Research Immersion program involves enriched courses, taught by teams of faculty from multiple STEM disciplines, that incorporate authentic research experiences for outstanding freshmen. Faculty-supervised independent research, often culminating in a senior honors thesis, is common in Harpur College. The Binghamton University Scholars Program is a four-year honors program offering special seminars and leadership training to exceptional students, along with opportunities for experiential learning and junior- and senior-year capstone projects.

All undergraduates must complete one of the global interdependence (or "G") courses offered in all departments.

"Study abroad at Binghamton is huge!"

Although Binghamton offers a top-notch liberal arts and sciences education, word of its excellence has been slow to cross state lines: only 8 percent of domestic students come from outside of the Empire State, and another 8 percent of undergraduates hail from foreign nations. By other measures, though, Binghamton's student body is rather diverse: African Americans make up 5 percent of the total, while Hispanics add 10 percent and Asian Americans 14 percent, and 28 percent are Pell-eligible. "The biggest social and political issues on campus relate to social equality," a student reports. "Students at Binghamton are very proactive and we hold meetings that raise questions and provoke ideas." The university is taking several steps to create a more inclusive campus environment, including the establishment of a new LGBTQ center. Binghamton offers merit scholarships worth an average of $7,114, as well as 334 full or partial athletic scholarships in 21 sports.

The Freshman Research Immersion program involves enriched STEM courses that incorporate authentic research experiences.

Fifty-two percent of Binghamton's students live in the dorms, where options range from traditional double rooms with bathrooms down the hall to suites and apartments. As one student explains, "Binghamton models the housing system after Oxford. We have five different residential communities, comprised of four to five buildings each. This makes a rather large university seem smaller and more comfortable." Each community is led by a collegiate professor who helps link students' residential and academic experiences. Dining halls have plenty of options, including sushi. Students report feeling safe while trekking around the university grounds. "The university works hard to make our campus feel like a home; students have enough to worry about and safety does not need to be one of those things," a senior says.

"The housing system…makes a rather large university seem smaller and more comfortable."

When the weekend comes, Binghamton students know how to let off steam. "On campus there are activities going on every single day and night. The options are endless: bowling, concerts, performances, Late Nite Binghamton, sports, and much more," notes a senior. Late Nite Binghamton brings free movies, games, a coffee bar, and other nonalcoholic fun to campus, from 8 p.m. until 1 a.m. every Friday and Saturday. Frat parties occur off campus; 12 percent of the men and 10 percent of the women go Greek. "I have friends who are in Greek Life and friends who aren't, and we all get along fine," says one student. "It's not something that defines you at this school." While some underage students manage to find alcohol, any caught violating the school's policy "will be taken care of accordingly," says a senior. Annual campus traditions include Stepping on the Coat during the Spring Fling carnival (to celebrate the arrival of warm weather) and Picnic in the Park, the annual senior barbecue.

Binghamton itself is "far from the most exciting place on earth, but the community is still alive and has its own distinct pulse," according to a biomedical engineering major. "The nearest Walmart is infested with students no matter what time of day," adds a senior. The downtown area offers restaurants and bars, and "many students volunteer with local groups, such as food drives and mentoring children," says a nursing major. Students also get involved in Special Olympics and various fund-raising walks, and "there is even a co-ed service fraternity." Popular road trips include Ithaca, for parties at Ithaca College and Cornell, and Syracuse, for Destiny USA, as well as Cortland and Oneonta, about an hour away by car. The toughest part about going away may be finding a parking space when you return, as permits currently outnumber spaces by about three to one.

> **"The nearest Walmart is infested with students no matter what time of day."**

Binghamton teams compete in Division I, but the school doesn't field a football squad. As a result, some of the most significant rivalries are with Cornell in men's lacrosse and co-rec football, where teams have three men and three women and always a female quarterback. In recent years, women's volleyball and softball, along with men's cross-country, tennis, and baseball, have brought home America East Conference championships. Binghamton's debate team is among the best in the nation, and computer science students placed first or second for seven consecutive years in the FAA National Design Competition. Intramurals, club sports, and fitness programs attract about 80 percent of the student body.

With a four-year graduation rate that is among the highest of any public university, Binghamton has a reputation for an excellent education at a reasonable price that continues to draw smart New Yorkers to its vibrant and growing campus. "When you walk on the campus, you instantly feel at home and a huge sense of camaraderie," says a senior. Despite the hubbub of city life, the university maintains a cozy feel. Says a biology major, "It really only takes one campus visit to fall in love."

If You Apply To ➤ **SUNY–Binghamton:** Early action: Nov. 1. Regular decision: Jan. 15. Priority financial aid: Jan. 1. Housing: May 1. Application fee: $50. No campus or alumni interviews. SATs or ACTs: required (SAT essay or ACT writing strongly recommended). No Subject Tests. Letters of recommendation: required. Essay: required. Accepts the Common Application with supplement.

SUNY–University at Buffalo

15 Capen Hall, Buffalo, NY 14214

Glamorous it may not be, but the University at Buffalo offers solid programs in everything from business and engineering to geography and English. The majority of students come from Western New York and New York City, and a high percentage commute from home. The largest of the SUNY campuses, it is slowly building visibility with bigtime sports.

Although part of the mammoth State University of New York system, the University at Buffalo takes steps to ensure it gets noticed. Very few universities share its strength in medicine, engineering, and computer science, and UB is one of the world's leading supercomputer sites. Its resources are large enough to warrant three campuses: North, South, and Downtown. In addition to the sciences, the former private university offers strong professional schools. Students interested in pharmacy find Buffalo has the only accredited school in the SUNY system. "As large as we are, we have a very diverse and welcoming atmosphere," says a senior.

The North Campus of the University at Buffalo, home to most undergraduate programs, stretches across 1,100 acres in the suburbs just outside the city line and boasts buildings designed by world-renowned architects such as I. M. Pei. Meanwhile, the South Campus, along Main Street, favors collegiate ivy-covered buildings and is the home of the schools of architecture, pharmacy, and health sciences, including UB's highly rated programs in medicine and dentistry. The university provides connecting bus service—known as the UB Stampede—between the North and South campuses. The academically oriented student body spends plenty of time in UB's six main libraries, which are, for the most part, comfortable and well stocked at more than three million volumes. The university continues building and renovating at a steady pace. The medical school is constructing an extensive new campus in Downtown Buffalo in the heart of Buffalo's expanding medical corridor.

> **"Success through hard work and innovative thinking is really stressed."**

UB has a new general education program aimed at providing more cohesion to the undergraduate experience. Components include small-group seminars for all new students; required coursework in diversity, writing, math, and natural sciences; pathways that allow students to explore interests thematically; and a capstone e-portfolio aimed at integrating their learning. "First-year seminars and classes help make the college transition a successful and enjoyable one," says a sociology major. The engineering and business management schools are nationally prominent, and architecture is solid. Occupational and physical therapy programs are also quite good, while the English department is notable for its emphasis on poetry. Well-known poets visit the campus frequently, and students not only compose and read poetry, but study the art of performing it as well. French, physiology, geography, and music are well regarded, but other humanities vary in quality. The most popular majors are psychology, engineering, business administration/marketing, and social sciences. The university has a multitude of special programs, combined degrees (such as a five-year business administration B.S./M.B.A.), and interdisciplinary majors, as well as opportunities for self-designed majors and study abroad.

Students agree that the academic atmosphere in most disciplines at UB is competitive. "Success through hard work and innovative thinking is really stressed," says an occupational therapy major. "You are measured against your peers in many classes and labs." Twenty-one percent of classes have more than 50 students, and class size has been a challenge, especially for first-years, but the Finish in 4 program helps students graduate in four years in part by providing special advising and expanding class availability. Students seem to accept that some degree of faculty unavailability is the necessary trade-off for having professors who are experts in their fields at a school where graduate education and research get lots of the attention. "The quality of teaching depends on the subject as well as the professor," says one junior. An international business major adds, "Students oftentimes do not build relationships with professors." But where personal attention from faculty may be lacking, students say the career services office steps in to provide helpful guidance. "I feel very prepared for post-UB since I have

Website: www.buffalo.edu
Location: Suburban
Public
Total Enrollment: 24,647
Undergraduates: 18,336
Male/Female: 57/43
SAT Ranges: CR 510–610, M 550–650
ACT Ranges: 24–29
Financial Aid: 68%
Pell Grant: 31%
Expense: Pub $ $
Student Loans: 45%
Average Debt: N/A
Phi Beta Kappa: Yes
Applicants: 23,629
Accepted: 60%
Enrolled: 26%
Grad in 6 Years: 74%
Returning Freshmen: 88%
Academics: ✍ ✍ ✍ ✍
Social: ☎ ☎
Q of L: ★ ★
Admissions: (716) 645-6900
Email Address: ub-admissions@buffalo.edu

Strong Programs:
Psychology
Engineering
Business and Marketing
Social Sciences
Medicine
Computer Science
Occupational and Physical Therapy
English

UB has a new general education program that includes a capstone e-portfolio aimed at integrating students' learning.

taken advantage of our wonderful career office," says a senior. Students accepted into the UB Honors College enjoy smaller classes, priority class registration, and faculty mentors.

"Students like to be involved but at the same time are very studious," says one senior. "They also like to party." Eighty-three percent hail from New York State, and 14 percent come from nations outside the U.S. African Americans account for 7 percent of the student body, Hispanics 6 percent, and Asian Americans 14 percent. The campus is socioeconomically diverse as well, with 31 percent of entering first-years qualifying for Pell Grants. UB's considerable efforts in increasing awareness of diversity include the Intercultural and Diversity Center and the Office of Equity, Diversity, and Inclusion. Students report that campus politics tend to lean left and current issues include environmental sustainability, the economy, and LGBTQ concerns. Scholarships are offered to the top incoming students, regardless of financial need, and student-athletes compete for 435 athletic scholarships in 12 sports.

Efforts to increase awareness of diversity include the Intercultural and Diversity Center and the Office of Equity, Diversity, and Inclusion.

Thirty-five percent of students live on campus in traditional dorms or apartments for upper-class students; the rest commute from home or find apartments near Main Street. "The dorms are a lot better than some schools I have seen," says an electrical engineering major. "The on-campus apartments are excellent but are quickly becoming pricier than more elegant and affordable off-campus housing." Most of the on-campus dwellers reside on the North campus. Governors is known as the smallest and quietest dorm, while social butterflies prefer Ellicott. Greiner Hall is a sustainably designed addition for sophomores only. Gender-inclusive housing is also available for first-year and returning students who wish to live in a mixed-gender housing environment. With the recent addition of the marché-style dining in the Crossroads Culinary Center dining hall, students have a smorgasbord of choices, including options for those with special dietary concerns. "I am super impressed with the dining facilities at UB," reports a junior. "Everything is clean, well organized, with great service, and fantastic food." Along with three dining halls, two full-service restaurants, pizza grills, and food courts, there are popular snack stops all around campus, including local favorite Tim Hortons. Security on campus is adequate, with a full-time police station and emergency call lights all around.

One senior says, "There are so many sports teams, club teams, frats, sororities, and student life activity clubs; there's something for everyone." The Greek scene is small; 1 percent of UB men and 2 percent of women participate. UB supports more than 150 other student organizations ranging from break-dancers to math enthusiasts. Drinking is banned in the "dry" dorms, but students 21 and over are allowed to drink in the "wet" dorms. Underage drinkers face "severe punishments" if caught, a junior reports. Students tend to gravitate to downtown Buffalo on the weekends; Friday night happy hour centers on beer and the chicken wings that spread the fame of Buffalo cuisine. Also popular are the Albright-Knox Art Gallery, with its world-renowned collection of modern art, and the Triple-A baseball Bisons, who play downtown. The two major pro teams, the Buffalo Bills in football and the Sabres in hockey, are both top draws.

"Students oftentimes do not build relationships with professors."

UB is the only major SUNY unit to field a Division I football team.

The winters are cold in Buffalo, but students can take refuge inside a series of enclosed elevated walkways that connect most of the North Campus academic buildings. The flip side is that the outlying areas of the city offer great skiing, skating, and snowmobiling—and the ski club even offers free rides to the slopes. Having a car might be a good idea, but students warn that parking can be a problem on campus. Although most students are content to stay in Buffalo, those who want a change of scene can drive to Niagara Falls, just a few minutes away, or to Rochester, Cleveland, or Toronto, where the drinking age is lower. "The best road trip is 10 minutes to Canada," says an anthropology and geology double major.

UB has been trying to enhance its visibility by getting its name on the sports pages. It is the only major SUNY unit to field a Division I football team, and the Bulls have played in a couple of bowl games in recent years. The men's basketball team went to its second NCAA tournament in a row in 2016, while its female counterparts went to their first NCAA tournament. Women's soccer and men's tennis were

"Students like to be involved but at the same time are very studious. They also like to party."

also Mid-American Conference champs, and men's outdoor track and field celebrated an individual national champion. School spirit is sometimes generated at the student union and UB's impressive sports complex, which boasts a 10,000-seat arena, squash and racquetball courts, and other amenities. Intramural sports are popular, especially soccer, and earthy types revel in the annual Oozefest—a mud-volleyball tournament.

UB students love the size of their school, with its huge range of academic programs, social events, and people to meet. Yes, students are exposed to the long Buffalo winter, but they also get exposed to some top-notch professors. And they get to meet a diverse mix of native New Yorkers, other East Coast residents, and international students drawn to the university's outstanding programs and extensive resources.

Overlaps

SUNY–Albany, SUNY–Binghamton, SUNY–Stony Brook, Cornell University, NYU, Syracuse

If You Apply To ➤   **University at Buffalo:** Rolling admissions. Early action: Nov. 15. Priority financial aid: Mar. 1. Housing: May 1. Application fee: $50. No campus or alumni interviews. SATs (with essay) or ACTs (with writing): required. No Subject Tests. Letter of recommendation: required. Essay: required. Accepts the Common Application with supplement.

SUNY–College at Geneseo

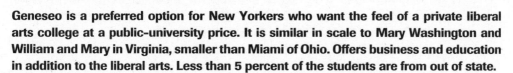

1 College Circle, Geneseo, NY 14454

Geneseo is a preferred option for New Yorkers who want the feel of a private liberal arts college at a public-university price. It is similar in scale to Mary Washington and William and Mary in Virginia, smaller than Miami of Ohio. Offers business and education in addition to the liberal arts. Less than 5 percent of the students are from out of state.

The SUNY–College at Geneseo offers a seriously academic environment at an affordable price. This public institution attracts high achievers from around the nation. Students here "tend to be friendly, liberal, and hardworking, and most like to have fun on the weekends," says a junior. Responsive, attentive professors help compensate for the long winters and somewhat isolated location. And excellent preprofessional programs have been making it harder to win admission to this most bucolic campus of the New York State university system.

Geneseo sits in the scenic Genesee Valley of western New York. Campus architecture ranges from Gothic to modern, and the surrounding community has been designated a National Historic Landmark Community by the U.S. Department of the Interior. An elementary education major calls the town "small and inviting" and says the historic buildings and nearby forests and mountains make for "lots of beautiful scenery." Recent campus projects include a new college sports stadium and a renovated social sciences building.

Regardless of their course of study, all students must demonstrate foreign language proficiency. General education requirements also include two courses

Website: www.geneseo.edu
Location: Small Town
Public
Total Enrollment: 5,491
Undergraduates: 5,441
Male/Female: 40/60
SAT Ranges: CR 550–640, M 550–650
ACT Ranges: 25–29
Financial Aid: 39%
Pell Grant: 21%
Expense: Pub $
Student Loans: 49%
Average Debt: $
Phi Beta Kappa: Yes

(continued)

Applicants: 9,118
Accepted: 73%
Enrolled: 20%
Grad in 6 Years: 78%
Returning Freshmen: 89%
Academics: ✍ ✍ ✍ ½
Social: ☎ ☎ ☎
Q of L: ★ ★ ★ ★
Admissions: (585) 245-5571
Email Address: admissions@
geneseo.edu

Strong Programs:
Psychology
Biology
Business Administration
English
Communication
Accounting
Education

Students are active in the community, volunteering 200,000 hours of service each year.

Outdoorsy types will appreciate the nearby Letchworth State Park, often referred to as the "Grand Canyon of the East."

each in the natural sciences, social sciences, and fine arts; a two-semester sequence in Western humanities; and one course each in non-Western traditions, U.S. history, and numeric and symbolic reasoning. All first-year students take a seminar in persuasive writing and critical reading in a small class, focusing on a unique topic related to the instructor's discipline. Psychology is the most popular major, followed by biology, business administration, English, and communication. Accounting and education are also strengths, and new majors in neuroscience and applied mathematics are now available. Cooperative programs with other SUNY campuses in dentistry, optometry, business, physical therapy, and other disciplines allow students to finish their graduate degrees a year ahead of schedule.

"The workload depends on the professor," says a sophomore. "Geneseo is challenging but never unreasonable." Twenty-nine percent of classes have fewer than 20 students, and the quality of teaching is high, according to a political science major. "Most professors are accessible, friendly, and intelligent." Thirty students from each class are invited to join the prestigious Edgar Fellows scholarship program;

"We do not have a huge nightlife…but there is a very charming Geneseo social scene."

membership includes a $2,000 annual scholarship, five honors courses designed specifically for the program, and an opportunity to complete a senior thesis. The acclaimed Geneseo Opportunities for Leadership Development program, which is open to all students, seeks to prepare students for college and community leadership roles via workshops and symposia. Thirty-six percent of students study abroad, and the college offers more than 50 programs in 43 nations; through other SUNY campuses, students have access to more than 600 programs in 50 nations.

Ninety-six percent of Geneseo students are from New York State, and 2 percent come from abroad. "The students here are friendly, intelligent, and driven," says a history major. Asian Americans make up 7 percent of the student body, Hispanics 7 percent, and African Americans 3 percent. Twenty-one percent of freshmen qualify for Pell Grants. Geneseo offers merit scholarships averaging $1,494 each, but no athletic awards.

Fifty-six percent of Geneseo students live in the residence halls and townhouses, where rooms are guaranteed for four years. "There is no trouble getting a room, though we did have to triple this year for the first time in over five years," notes one student. Several residence halls have been newly renovated, and five academic living/learning communities are available. Students say they feel safe at Geneseo, and while campus food doesn't get enthusiastic reviews, "it has improved over the years," says a senior. A classmate adds, "There are gluten-free options, but not as many diet-friendly options, other than boring salads."

"We do not have a huge nightlife like you would have on a larger campus, but there is a very charming Geneseo social scene. There are a lot of activities on campus as well as great festivals and events in the town itself," says one psychology major. Fraternities and sororities, which draw 22 percent of the men and 26 percent of the women, set the tone on campus. "Greek life is a loud, influential minority," says one student. Thanks to strict alcohol policies, "Most drinking and partying takes place off campus," according to a senior. If Greek parties don't appeal, students can get involved in any of the more than 200 student organizations or partake in college-sponsored late-night activities at the College Union. Students are active in the community, volunteering 200,000 hours of service each year through annual days of service, events like Relay for Life, and numerous student groups, including Alpha Phi Omega, the co-ed service fraternity. Students also look forward to monthly multicultural club dinners and shows and the annual Spring Fest.

The "gorgeous small town" of Geneseo "really caters to college students," says an education major. There's a Wegman's supermarket and a Walmart, and restaurants and shops on Main Street. Outdoorsy types will appreciate the nearby Letchworth State Park, often referred to as the "Grand Canyon of the East"; rowers will enjoy beautiful Conesus Lake, only a 10-minute drive from campus. Popular road trips include Rochester, 30 miles north, and Buffalo, 60 miles west; don't forget your hat, mittens, and parka!

> "[Students] tend to be friendly, liberal, and hardworking."

Half of Geneseo students participate in intramural sports, and "broomball is the most popular," says a sophomore. Basketball and volleyball are also favorites. Geneseo's varsity teams, the Knights, compete in Division III, and the men's ice hockey, women's basketball, and men's and women's cross-country, track, and swimming teams are competitive on the national level. Ice hockey stirs up the most school spirit: "Hockey is huge here," says a senior.

The SUNY–College at Geneseo gives students the best of two worlds. Given its size, professors can provide the kind of personal attention normally seen only at private liberal arts colleges; because of its public status, that attention comes at bargain-basement cost. Those factors have made it more and more difficult to get in—and, it turns out, getting in is only half the battle. "Students are very serious about their education," says a sophomore. "Once you are here, you must work hard."

Overlaps

Colgate, Hamilton, NYU, SUNY–Binghamton, University of Rochester, Cornell University, Boston College, Skidmore

If You Apply To ➤ | **SUNY–Geneseo:** Early decision: Nov. 15. Regular decision: Jan. 1. Financial aid: Feb. 1. Housing: May 1. Application fee: $50. Campus interviews: optional, evaluative. No alumni interviews. SATs or ACTs: required. Subject Tests: optional. Letters of recommendation: required. Essay: required. Accepts the Common Application.

SUNY–Purchase College

735 Anderson Hill Road, Purchase, NY 10577

One of the few public institutions that is also an arts specialty school. The visual and performing arts are signature programs, though Purchase has developed some liberal arts specialties in areas like environmental studies. Percentage-wise, tied with Stony Brook as the most selective institution in the SUNY system. Limited campus life because students head for the city.

SUNY–Purchase College is a dream come true for aspiring artists of all kinds—an academic environment that provides a strong sense of community and support, yet celebrates individuals for their unique talents and contributions. A literature major says, "There's a raw energy that exists on campus—in the students and professors—that I don't think many other colleges have."

Set on a 500-acre wooded estate in an area of upscale Westchester County's most scenic suburbia, Purchase has a campus described by one student as "sleek, modern, ominous, and brick." The college has earned a national reputation for its instruction in music, dance, visual arts, theater, and film. Almost all the faculty members in the School of the Arts are professionals who perform or exhibit regularly in the New York metropolitan area, and the spacious, dazzling facilities here rank among the best in the world. The college also boasts the Neuberger Museum, the sixth-largest public college museum. The four-theater Performing Arts Center is huge, and dance students, whose building contains a dozen studios, whirlpool rooms,

Website: www.purchase.edu
Location: Suburban
Public
Total Enrollment: 3,772
Undergraduates: 3,686
Male/Female: 43/57
SAT Ranges: CR 490–610, M 470–570
ACT Ranges: 22–27
Financial Aid: 74%
Pell Grant: N/A
Expense: Pub $
Student Loans: 67%

(continued)

Average Debt: $ $ $
Phi Beta Kappa: No
Applicants: 7,928
Accepted: 41%
Enrolled: 24%
Grad in 6 Years: 59%
Returning Freshmen: 81%
Academics: ✐ ✐ ✐ ½
Social: ☎ ☎ ☎
Q of L: ★ ★ ★
Admissions: (914) 251-6300
Email Address: admissions@
  purchase.edu

Strong Programs:
Music
Dance
Visual Arts
Theater
Film
Environmental Studies
Literature
Psychology

Almost all the faculty members in the School of the Arts are professionals who perform or exhibit regularly in the New York metropolitan area.

and a "body-correction" facility, may never again work in such splendid and well-equipped surroundings.

Purchase has two separate sets of degree requirements, one for the liberal arts and sciences and one for the performing and visual arts, although students in each category must sample coursework from the other. Students in the liberal arts and sciences spend one-third of their time fulfilling the general education requirements, which include 10 knowledge areas. Students take mathematics, natural sciences, social science, American history, Western civilization, other world civilizations, the arts, humanities, foreign language, and basic communications. In addition to these core requirements, they also must take critical thinking and information management as skill areas, and everyone must complete a senior project. Students in the arts divisions usually have many more required courses, culminating in a senior recital or show.

Mingling with highly motivated and talented performers and artists can make some students in the liberal arts and sciences feel a little drab and out of place. "Dancers, actors, visual artists, and music students pull the most weight as far as campus life is concerned," says a student. The academic atmosphere at Purchase reportedly varies between programs too. "The courses are very generic in the liberal arts and quite heavy and rigorous in the conservatories," reports a music major. Still, Purchase is a fine place to study humanities and the natural sciences, particularly environmental studies, literature, psychology, art history, and biology. Most of the shaky liberal arts and sciences programs are confined to some majors in the social sciences and language and culture, where "there are not a lot of class options," according to one junior. Students tend to be serious about their own personal achievements, and with 62 percent of classes enrolling fewer than 20 students, professors are said to be accessible and friendly. "The professors are engaged, extremely qualified, and very interested in our education," says a student. Faculty members lead short-term study abroad programs during the summer on such topics as Tibetan Buddhist philosophy and art in India, art history and language in Italy, and political theater in Prague; affiliated programs in the SUNY system provide access to hundreds of other options.

> **"There's a raw energy that exists on campus—in the students and professors."**

Purchase attracts "all the students from high school who weren't the cheerleaders and football players," says one student, describing classmates as "artsy, creative, hippies, gay, vegans, and open-minded, liberal activists." A senior adds, "We believe strongly in animal rights, civil rights, women's rights, etc." Indeed, the largest student organization on this politically active campus is the gay and lesbian union. Roughly three-quarters of the student body are from New York State, most from New York City and Westchester County. Others are from Long Island, New Jersey, and Connecticut; 2 percent are international. African Americans account for 10 percent of the student body, Hispanics 18 percent, and Asian Americans 4 percent. In addition to need-based aid, hundreds of merit scholarships averaging $2,440 are awarded each year on the basis of academic achievements, auditions, and portfolios.

Approximately one-third of the student body commutes from nearby communities, though housing in the surrounding suburbs is expensive and hard to find. On campus, "Housing is very limited," confides one student. "There are older and newer dorms and their condition definitely reflects their age." The two eating facilities offer decent fare, and for those who tire of institutional cuisine, there is a student-run co-op that specializes in health food.

> **"Our 'teams' are our dancers, our vocalists, our musicians, and our theater companies."**

The campus is a neighbor to the world headquarters of IBM, Texaco, AMF, General Foods, and PepsiCo, and the town of Purchase is not student-oriented.

The Big Apple provides a regular weekend distraction, to the extent that it inhibits the formation of a tight campus community. "Because so many students are from New York, the weekends are pretty dead," complains one student. Since the campus shuttle bus runs only once on the weekend, students started their own van service, which goes into Manhattan three times a day. Still, "a car is a definite must at Purchase," counsels one student. The Performing Arts Center is host to at least two student or faculty performances every weekend, and there is a constant flow of New York artists and celebrities. Notes a music major, "Campus is very quiet, but the student center always has something going on," and the over-21 crowd often frequents the Pub. Fraternities and sororities are definitely out. "The closest we come to Greek are the two guys from Athens [New York] who go here," quips a staunch independent. Besides, as one artist explains, "individuality is far more important to the artist than being part of a group." Despite the unconventional aura of the place, Purchase is not without its traditions, including Fall Ball ("a big dance where everyone dresses in drag"), Fall Fest, Zombie Prom, Culture Shock, and Purchase Prom.

Purchase athletes compete in Division III, and the few competitive Panthers teams include men's basketball, women's volleyball, and women's soccer. Men's basketball and the women's swim team have won the Skyline Conference championship in recent years. Intramural programs draw 30 percent of students, but informal Frisbee-tossing remains more popular than organized sports. Says a student: "Our 'teams' are our dancers, our vocalists, our musicians, and our theater companies."

Despite a conspicuous lack of a college-town atmosphere, Purchase is a perfect place to study the arts and still be able to indulge in academics of all kinds, or vice versa. "It's a great place to come and devote yourself to your craft," says a senior. Those willing to put up with what a student calls "an isolated campus full of ugly architecture" may find that Purchase offers the opportunity for a personalized, diverse education unique within the SUNY system.

> *The largest student organization on this politically active campus is the gay and lesbian union.*

Overlaps

Ithaca, NYU, SUNY–Albany, SUNY–Binghamton, SUNY–New Paltz, SUNY–Stony Brook

If You Apply To ➤	**SUNY–Purchase College:** Rolling admissions. (Priority deadline: Mar. 1.) Early action: Nov. 15. Financial aid: Feb. 1. Application fee: $50. Campus interviews: recommended, evaluative (required of theater design/technology and film program applicants). No alumni interviews. SATs or ACTs: required. No Subject Tests. Letters of recommendation: required. Essay: required. Accepts the Common Application. Apply to particular school or program. Auditions held for acting, dance, and music.

SUNY–Stony Brook University

118 Administration Building, Stony Brook, NY 11794

Strategically located 60 miles east of New York City, Stony Brook has risen a few notches in the SUNY pecking order. The natural sciences, engineering, and health fields are the major drawing cards. Situated in the lap of Long Island luxury, Stony Brook offers easy access to beachfront playlands. Still caters mainly to students from the New York tristate area.

Stony Brook, one of the academic leaders in the SUNY system, aims to be the model of a student-centered research university. The six Undergraduate Colleges provide a small college community experience with all the assets of a leading research university. The public university has made a name for itself with its top-notch programs in the hard sciences. It has also become known for its highly competitive learning

Website: www.stonybrook.edu
Location: Suburban
Public
Total Enrollment: 20,792

(continued)

Undergraduates: 15,532

Male/Female: 55/45

SAT Ranges: CR 550–660,
   M 600–720

ACT Ranges: 26–31

Financial Aid: 65%

Pell Grant: 32%

Expense: Pub $

Student Loans: 58%

Average Debt: $ $

Phi Beta Kappa: Yes

Applicants: 34,146

Accepted: 41%

Enrolled: 20%

Grad in 6 Years: 68%

Returning Freshmen: 90%

Academics: ✑ ✑ ✑ ✑

Social: ☎ ☎ ☎

Q of L: ★ ★

Admissions: (631) 632-6868

Email Address: enroll@
   stonybrook.edu

Strong Programs:
Health Science
Nursing
Premed
Psychology
Biology
Business Management
Engineering
Physics

*The comprehensive
university hospital and
research center make
health sciences strong.*

environment and the high quality of its professors. In short, "Stony Brook is the complete package," boasts one senior.

The school's location on Long Island's plush North Shore (Gatsby's stomping grounds) is a wonderful drawing point. Sitting on 1,040 wooded acres just outside of the small, picturesque village of Stony Brook, and only 90 minutes from New York City and half an hour from the beaches of the South Shore, the campus is a conglomeration of redbrick buildings interspersed with several modern brick and concrete designs. Campus beautification and sustainability are priorities, and grass and trees have replaced much of the uninspiring campus concrete. Recently completed construction includes a 70,000-square-foot computer science building.

The new Stony Brook Curriculum is based on a series of learning outcomes and is organized into four categories: Demonstrate Versatility, Explore Interconnectedness, Pursue Deeper Understanding, and Prepare for Life-Long Learning. All freshmen—residents and commuters alike—enter the university as members of one of six Undergraduate Colleges. Each college has its own faculty director, as well as both academic and residential advisors. Freshmen participate in theme-based academic and cocurricular programs, which include two small seminar courses.

Coming of age in the high-tech era, Stony Brook quickly became known and respected for its science departments. Facilities are extensive, and the science faculty includes a number of internationally known researchers. The comprehensive university hospital and research center make health sciences strong, especially nursing and physical therapy. The hospital, which has been ranked among the nation's best for teaching, attracts grants and offers many opportunities for research programs for undergrads as well as graduate students.

> "The Residential Safety Program is made up of students who…will walk with you anywhere you need to go after dusk."

Health science is the most popular major, followed by psychology, biology, and business management. Engineering and physics are also strong. The school's arts program benefits from a fine arts building, complete with studios and a reference library. The building complements Stony Brook's beautiful five-theater Staller Center for the Arts. The Grammy-winning Emerson String Quartet is in residence in the music department. A new major in polysomnographic technology has been introduced, as have minors in energy science and entrepreneurship.

Students spend a lot of time studying. "Stony Brook is a fairly competitive place. The larger classes, like general chemistry and biology, are difficult but not impossible. A solid work ethic is vital for success," a senior advises. Twenty-one percent of classes enroll more than 50 students, and freshmen are the last to register, so they sometimes have to wait a semester or two to get into the most popular electives. A recent graduate says, "On the whole, the quality of teaching was excellent. The professors were talented lecturers, passionate about the material, and involved in cutting-edge research."

An Undergraduate Research and Creative Activities program offers undergraduates the opportunity to work on research projects with faculty members from the time they are freshmen until they graduate. Unique to Stony Brook, the WISE (Women in Science and Engineering) program encourages women entering the university as freshmen to pursue study in the sciences, engineering, and mathematics. The program provides mentoring from women professors in these fields, as well as research experiences during the freshman year. About 500 students per year take advantage of one of Stony Brook's wonderful study abroad programs (France, England, Italy, Japan, and Tanzania are just some of the possibilities), while others choose established internships in the fields of policy analysis, political science, psychology, foreign language, or social welfare. University Scholars is a by-invitation program for students who rank in the top 7 percent of the incoming freshman class that offers specialized support, programming, and events during the first year.

Eighty percent of Stony Brook undergraduates hail from New York, and about half commute from Long Island homes; 12 percent arrive from foreign countries. "In addition to being extremely bright and high-achieving, Stony Brook's students are by far one of the most diverse of all student bodies on Long Island," a senior says. The student body is 7 percent African American, 11 percent Hispanic, and 24 percent Asian American, and to promote multicultural understanding, students are required to take classes focusing on different cultures. Merit scholarships averaging $4,357 are given out each year, in addition to several hundred athletic scholarships. Thirty-two percent of freshmen receive Pell Grants.

Stony Brook, which has one of the largest residential programs in the SUNY system, has a slew of robust facilities that provide students access to state-of-the-art fitness centers, computing facilities, Internet, and widescreen TVs. Fifty-one percent of undergrads live in university housing. "The dorms are nice," says one student. While residential freshmen must take a meal plan, upperclassmen who live in suites on campus either opt for a flexible food-service plan or pay a nominal fee to cook for themselves. Kosher and vegetarian food co-ops keep

The WISE (Women in Science and Engineering) program provides women with mentoring and research experiences during the freshman year.

"Though we are a rather new university, Stony Brook is like its students: we grow and learn quickly."

interested students well supplied with cheap eats. The university has a Campus Relations Team, composed of university police officers who educate the community on topics ranging from personal safety to rape prevention to drug and alcohol awareness, and it has recently hired several new Title IX staff members and implemented new mandatory training programs. Students report feeling safe on campus. "The Residential Safety Program is made up of students who check to make sure the buildings are secure and will walk with you anywhere you need to go after dusk so that you don't have to walk alone," explains a senior.

"There is a big social life on campus and a smaller one off campus," notes one senior. Because many students go home on the weekends, Thursday is the big party night. The university has fairly strict policies on alcohol consumption, and "the policies are as effective as possible with young students in college," a student reports. The fledgling Greek system draws 3 percent of the men and 3 percent of the women. Current and classic movies are screened during the week, and student organizations coordinate other entertainment in the form of frequent concerts, plays, and other performances. Annual festivals in the fall and spring, as well as the Roth Pond Regatta and the homecoming football game are among the biggest social events of the year.

Because many students go home on the weekends, Thursday is the big party night.

"Stony Brook is a wealthy residential town that cannot be categorized as a 'college town,'" one student says. "It doesn't appreciate the large campus located within its limits." Nearby Port Jefferson offers small shops and interesting restaurants. Beachcombing on the nearby North Shore, or on the Atlantic Ocean shore of Long Island, and heading into New York City are popular ways to pass the weekends. "You absolutely need a car if you want to get around the town at all," says a junior. Still, many students make do with trains, and a station is conveniently located at the edge of campus.

Stony Brook's 20 Division I teams compete in the America East Conference, except for football (Colonial Athletic Association) and men's tennis (Missouri Valley Conference). The Seawolves achieved their first NCAA Tournament berth in men's basketball in 2016. Intramurals, ranging from soccer and flag football to handball and table tennis, provide one of the school's greatest rallying points, and the university also offers more than 30 club sports.

Overlaps
SUNY–Binghamton, Cornell University, NYU, SUNY–Albany, SUNY–Buffalo, Boston University, Columbia, Northeastern

Though Stony Brook is not old enough to have ivy-covered walls, it does offer some of the best academic opportunities in the SUNY system. Students have to maneuver around lots of rough spots, including increasing class sizes. Yet despite

"A solid work ethic is vital for success."

these budget-crisis-induced problems, students share in the promise of Stony Brook's future. In the meantime, they tout their school's diversity and creativity, as well as the feeling of hospitality that pervades campus life. "Though we are a rather new university," says a senior, "Stony Brook is like its students: we grow and learn quickly."

Stetson University

421 N. Woodland Boulevard, DeLand, FL 32723

The oldest private university in Florida, Stetson keeps company with the likes of Baylor and Furman among prominent Deep South institutions with historic ties to the Baptist Church. The common thread is conservatism, and business is traditionally the strongest program. Stetson also excels in music and has a specialty in integrative health science. More like a small college than a university.

Website: www.stetson.edu
Location: Small City
Private
Total Enrollment: 4,027
Undergraduates: 2,995
Male/Female: 43/57
SAT Ranges: CR 530–640, M 520–620
ACT Ranges: 24–28
Financial Aid: 100%
Pell Grant: 36%
Expense: Pr $ $
Student Loans: 69%
Average Debt: $ $ $
Phi Beta Kappa: Yes
Applicants: 11,216
Accepted: 63%
Enrolled: 14%
Grad in 6 Years: 64%
Returning Freshmen: 77%
Academics: ✐ ✐ ✐
Social: ☎ ☎ ☎
Q of L: ★ ★ ★
Admissions: (386) 822-7100

Stetson University, named for the maker of the famed 10-gallon hat, draws students from around the Southeast with its small size and emphasis on the liberal arts. Long a bastion of conservatism, students say the school has become more liberal since cutting ties with the Southern Baptists. With top-notch business courses and surprising strengths in music and Russian, East European, and Eurasian studies, this Florida university continues to attract students who aren't afraid to wear a variety of hats during their stay.

Located halfway between Orlando and Daytona Beach, Stetson's 170-acre campus features mainly brick structures in styles from Gothic to Moorish to Southern colonial. While some modern wood buildings are scattered about, the theme is decidedly Southern, complete with royal palms and oak trees. An $8 million Welcome Center recently opened, and a major renovation and expansion of the Carlton Union Building is underway, slated for completion in 2018.

Stetson has three undergraduate colleges—music, business administration, and arts and sciences—and its general education requirements apply to all of them. Requirements are divided into three categories: Foundations, Knowledge of Human Cultures and the Natural World,

"The academic climate at Stetson is challenge by choice."

and Personal and Social Responsibility. All entering students take a First Year Seminar, which allows them to work closely with Stetson faculty to ease the transition to college. All freshmen who are undecided on a major participate in the Discovery program, and all students take a Junior Seminar that focuses on personal and social responsibility. Students in the college of arts and sciences must complete a capstone research project, while music students perform a senior recital and business students take a senior capstone course on strategy and in-depth case studies. Additionally, all students must pass four writing-enhanced courses in order to graduate.

Stetson is known for its business program, particularly majors in accounting, business systems and analytics, and finance. Would-be money managers benefit from the award-winning Roland George Investments program, where they oversee a cash portfolio worth more than $3 million. Students who hope to work for themselves can tap into the Prince Entrepreneurial Program, which connects them with successful business owners, while the Family Enterprise Center was one of the first in the nation in educating students for work in family businesses. The most popular majors are psychology, finance, integrative health science, and biology. The education department has received national acclaim for its research on single-gender classrooms and their impact on performance in public schools. Stetson's music school is notable (ahem) for its programs in brass instruments, organ, and voice. Aspiring lawyers may take advantage of 3+3 or 4+3 B.A./J.D. programs with Stetson's College of Law. A new major in public health has recently been introduced, as has a minor in public management.

"The academic climate at Stetson is challenge by choice," says a junior. "There are students who choose to work very hard and challenge themselves academically, then there are students who choose to take the easy way out and cruise." Fifty-four percent of classes have fewer than 20 students. Professors are always willing to help; a management major says many have worked in the field they are teaching before stepping in front of the lectern. "The teaching at Stetson is top-notch. From my experience, every professor is fully engaged in and supportive of each student in their course and department," says a social science major.

Students with wanderlust can choose from more than 100 faculty-led, exchange, or affiliate programs, and international internships are an option too; 28 percent of undergrads study abroad. Stetson's honors program incorporates international study, community service, and a senior colloquium, and also allows students to create their own majors. The Summer Undergraduate Research Experience program awards funding to students for summer research or creative projects with faculty members.

"The university has faced an issue of overcrowding, making housing a difficult situation."

Sixty-three percent of Stetson Hatters are native Floridians; they tend to be white, wealthy, and friendly, a sociology major says. A political science major describes Hatters as "very driven and personable." African Americans constitute 8 percent of the student body, Hispanics make up 15 percent, and Asian Americans add 2 percent; 5 percent hail from foreign countries. Thirty-six percent of current freshmen are Pell-eligible. Students describe a mix of political views on campus and say that concerns about the transparency of the university's administration tend to spark student activism. Merit scholarships and non-need-based grants averaging $21,025 are awarded each year, and Stetson also hands out athletic scholarships in 17 sports.

First-year students are required to live on campus, and sixty-five percent of all undergrads live in the residence halls. Although students say that accommodations in the residence halls, all of which have been upgraded in recent years, have significantly improved, a junior warns, "Because of the rising enrollment, the university has faced an issue of overcrowding, making housing a difficult situation." Others add that more upperclassmen would probably move off campus if the school didn't cut financial aid awards for doing so. Stetson's traditional cafeteria is known as the Commons, and although the food tends to get poor reviews, renovations are underway to expand dining offerings. As for campus safety, one student says, "I always feel safe on the central part of campus, but avoid the outer parts of campus at night because there seems to be less patrolling there." Students

(continued)

Email Address: admissions@ stetson.edu

Strong Programs:
Psychology
Finance
Integrative Health Science
Biology
Accounting
Business Systems and
    Analytics
Music
Russian, East European, and
    Eurasian Studies

In the award-winning Roland George Investments program, students oversee a cash portfolio worth more than $3 million.

report that administrative handling of campus sexual assault cases has been a topic of some debate.

"Greek organizations are usually the place to find parties or connections to party life," says a junior, adding that "music organizations also offer a type of subculture partying." Fraternities attract 31 percent of the men and sororities draw 32 percent of the women, but students say that tightened alcohol policies have pushed most partying off campus to nearby apartments or bars. The Council for Student Activities offers plenty of on-campus alternatives, bringing in big-name acts, and students also get involved in the more than 140 student organizations. Students look forward to annual events such as Greek Week, when sorority and fraternity chapters compete in a lip-synch contest and other events to raise money for charity, and Greenfeather, aimed at promoting community service. Three-quarters of students participate in community service activities, often through service-learning courses. When your birthday rolls around, don't forget to wear your bathing suit—it's a tradition for fellow students to toss you into the midcampus Holler Fountain.

As for the "adorable, small Southern town" of DeLand, it boasts "shops, galleries, and cafés," but only a handful of bars, so students often head to Orlando (40 minutes from campus) or Daytona Beach (20 minutes) to eat out, shop, or dance the night away. In addition to the omnipresent beaches, Blue Spring and DeLeon Springs offer canoeing and nature watching. Popular road trips include Miami for clubbing and the Keys for camping.

Stetson's teams compete in Division I, and a football team took the field in 2013 for the first time in 58 years, competing against the likes of Butler, Dayton, and Drake. The women's basketball program has been the standard-bearer for Hatters Athletics, qualifying for NCAA postseason play multiple times in the past several seasons. Other solid teams include softball, beach volleyball, baseball, and women's golf. The Hollis Wellness Center offers a variety of fitness facilities, and about a third of students participate in club and intramural sports, ranging from ultimate Frisbee and bass fishing to flag football and pool battleship.

Stetson students savor the one-on-one attention freely given at this small Sunshine State university with a strong sense of what it is. After four years spent enjoying great weather and forming close friendships with peers and professors, they emerge with solid academic foundations for future work or study. Says one happy student, "Stetson may not be perfect or have the shiniest bells and whistles, but I can promise that if you put the work in, this institution will reward you tenfold."

Aspiring lawyers may take advantage of 3+3 or 4+3 B.A./J.D. programs with Stetson's College of Law.

Overlaps

University of Central Florida, University of Florida, Florida State, University of South Florida, Florida Gulf Coast, Florida Atlantic, Florida International, University of North Florida

If You Apply To ➤ **Stetson:** Rolling admissions. Priority deadline: Mar. 1. Financial aid: Feb. 15. Housing: May 1. Application fee: $50. Campus interviews: recommended, evaluative. No alumni interviews. SATs or ACTs: optional. No Subject Tests. Letters of recommendation: required. Essay: required. Accepts the Common Application with supplement.

Stevens Institute of Technology

1 Castle Point Terrace, Hoboken, NJ 07030

Stevens ranks with Clarkson and Worcester Polytechnic among East Coast technical institutes that offer intimacy and personalized education. Youth–oriented Hoboken is a major plus and a quicker commute to Manhattan than most places in Brooklyn. Plan to work hard.

At Stevens Institute of Technology, students accept intense classwork, all-nighters, and trips to the Big Apple as givens. The school is located just across the Hudson River from Manhattan, which means that students have the cultural, athletic, and gastronomic resources of New York City at their fingertips. Engineering and the sciences dominate campus life, but students seem prepared to take on the challenge of balancing work and play. "Stevens is a great place to embrace one's inner nerd and party too," says one satisfied student.

An eclectic mix of architectural styles compose Stevens's 55-acre campus. Many of the residence halls and administrative buildings are redbrick; classroom and lab facilities range from traditional, ivy-covered brownstones to modern glass-and-steel structures. The Altorfer Academic Complex offers 13,500 square feet of modern spaces dedicated to classrooms and a graduate student research center.

Stevens is organized into four schools—the Schaefer School of Engineering and Science, the Howe School of Technology Management, the College of Arts and Letters, and the School of Systems and Enterprises—and offers 35 majors. Each major has its own requirements, but most programs require calculus, chemistry, physics, humanities courses, and physical education. In the engineering school, the core curriculum is followed by technical electives that culminate in a senior design project. All entering students are required to participate in the Freshman Experience, which is a sequence of two common courses: Writing and Communications Seminar and Humanities Colloquium.

> "Students are challenged to push themselves, but never at the expense of their peers."

Engineering has long been king of the hill at Stevens; programs in biomedical, chemical, civil, electrical, environmental, naval, and computer engineering are all highly regarded, as is the major in mechanical engineering, not surprising since Stevens was the first school to award a degree in the field. Business programs are popular, and the university offers the only undergraduate quantitative finance degree in the nation. Graduates of the program are prepared for such roles as trading assistants, risk managers, or analysts. Other notable programs include cybersecurity, music and technology, information systems, and science communications. Two five-year programs are available; one allows students to incorporate co-op internships into their studies, and the other enables students to take fewer courses per term, without extra tuition charges, to make the workload a little more manageable. "Classes are competitive, but collaboration is essential when performing experiments, preparing reports, or studying for exams," observes a mechanical engineering major. "Students are challenged to push themselves, but never at the expense of their peers." Thirty-eight percent of classes have fewer than 20 students, and students agree that, despite a few professors more interested in their research than their teaching, the quality of instruction is high. "Professors have office hours every week and administrators keep their doors open," says a junior.

Professional practice is an important part of the Stevens environment, with nearly all students participating in cooperative education, internships, or mature research projects. Stevens also has an active on-campus recruiting program with major corporations, start-up firms, and the government. Women on this heavily male-dominated campus are supported through the Women's Programs initiative, which offers events ranging from health and wellness activities to leadership conferences and professional dinners with successful women in industry. Study abroad opportunities include exchange programs with universities in Australia, Scotland, and Turkey; a chemical ecology program in the Dominican Republic; and programs run by the International Student Exchange.

"Stevens students are generally really hardworking and have a full schedule," says one chemical biology major. "They somehow balance schoolwork with

---

Website: www.stevens.edu
Location: Small City
Private
Total Enrollment: 5,084
Undergraduates: 2,955
Male/Female: 71/29
SAT Ranges: CR 590–680, M 650–745
ACT Ranges: 29–32
Financial Aid: 93%
Pell Grant: 17%
Expense: Pr $ $ $
Student Loans: 75%
Average Debt: $ $ $ $
Phi Beta Kappa: No
Applicants: 6,540
Accepted: 44%
Enrolled: 24%
Grad in 6 Years: 82%
Returning Freshmen: 94%
Academics: ✍ ✍ ✍
Social: ☎ ☎
Q of L: ★ ★ ★
Admissions: (201) 216-5194
Email Address: admissions@stevens.edu

Strong Programs:
Mechanical Engineering
Civil Engineering
Chemical Engineering
Business
Quantitative Finance
Cybersecurity
Music and Technology
Information Systems

Stevens was the first school to award a degree in the field of mechanical engineering.

involvement in school organizations, including professional societies, media outlets, ethnic organizations, and many other activities." Fifty-nine percent of the students at Stevens are from New Jersey; another third come from the greater New York City portion of New York State, and 4 percent hail from foreign nations. Eleven percent of undergraduates are Asian American, 9 percent are Hispanic, and 2 percent are African American. Politics doesn't receive a lot of attention on campus, although the Stevens Political Awareness Committee can be quite active. Unlike some of Stevens's peer institutions, admissions officers here look more closely at high school grades, especially in math and science, than at test scores. In addition to need-based financial aid, qualified students receive merit-based scholarships that average $17,751.

Stevens guarantees housing for a student's entire four- or five-year stay, but students warn that housing is increasingly becoming a headache as the university continues to grow. After living in the "pretty standard" dorms freshman year, most students are housed in university-leased, off-campus apartments, which a computer science major says are "very nice" but "are a significant distance from campus, cost a lot more, and do not come with included meal plans." Seventy-one percent of undergraduates live in housing provided by Stevens, while others find their own, often less expensive, off-campus apartments. Students say the dining hall has improved greatly, thanks to a recent renovation and a new service provider. One student reports, "Campus security is great. The open campus is patrolled by Stevens police, who couldn't be more friendly." Regarding campus sexual assault, a junior says, "While I have heard of a few, extremely rare, alleged cases on campus, I put the utmost trust in the school officials to be doing right by all parties."

Twenty-five percent of Stevens men join fraternities, and 25 percent of the women pledge sororities. "People like to party here, but they keep it in check," says a quantitative finance major. "Greek houses follow campus policies regarding alcohol and usually hold registered parties where bouncers check IDs." An Entertainment Committee plans weekly events, from comedy nights to hypnotists and musical guests. The student-run TechFest and Boken festivals are favorite annual events, and a senior notes that festivals are organized "by proposal only, which makes each year different and unique." Greenwich Village, Times Square, and the bright lights of Broadway are just 15 minutes away on the PATH train. There is also Hoboken, which offers popular pubs and clubs right next to campus. Road trips, often taken by train, include Yankee Stadium in the Bronx and Six Flags Great Adventure, a New Jersey amusement park. Beaches and ski slopes are both within a 90-minute drive.

> **"Stevens has taught me the importance of entrepreneurial thinking and efficiency in everything that I do."**

Students cheer enthusiastically when the Division III Stevens Ducks are competing. Men's volleyball won the national championship in 2015, earning the school its first ever team national title. Men's soccer brought home its ninth consecutive conference championship in 2015, and women's soccer, field hockey, track and field, men's and women's swimming, and men's tennis have also claimed titles recently. For those without the time or talent to play at the varsity level, there are intramurals in everything from basketball, soccer, and football to dodgeball and even bowling.

Stevens's urban location and relatively small size can make for fun times, but the emphasis here is on hard work and innovation. Stevens graduates go on to make a dent in the world; notable alums include Nobel Laureate Frederick Reines, who detected the subatomic world of the neutrino; Frederick Winslow Taylor, father of scientific management; and Alfred W. Fielding, inventor of bubble wrap. Says a civil engineering major, "Stevens has taught me the importance of entrepreneurial thinking and efficiency in everything that I do."

Overlaps

Rensselaer Polytechnic, Rutgers, Northeastern, Worcester Polytechnic, College of New Jersey, New Jersey Institute of Technology, Columbia University, Lehigh

<table>
<tr><td>**If You Apply To** ➢</td><td>**Stevens:** Early decision I: Nov. 15. Early decision II: Jan. 15. Regular decision: Feb. 1. Financial aid: Feb. 15. Housing: Jun. 1. Application fee: $65. Campus and alumni interviews: recommended, evaluative (required for students applying to accelerated programs and international students). SATs or ACTs: required (applicants to music or visual arts and technology programs may choose to submit portfolio in lieu of test scores). Subject Tests: required for some. Letters of recommendation: required. Essay: required. Accepts the Common Application with supplement.</td></tr>
</table>

Susquehanna University

Selinsgrove, PA 17870

Susquehanna offers welcome relief from the plodding, unimaginative education at many small-scale universities. Its innovative core curriculum includes personal development and transition skills (e.g., computer proficiency) in addition to more conventional topics. Best known for its business program. With a more down-to-earth atmosphere than at upscale competitors like Bucknell and Dickinson, it is a national leader in promoting socioeconomic diversity.

"Susquewho?" That's the question many students ask when they're first introduced to this undergraduate institution. While it may not be a household name, Susquehanna University is earning a reputation as an innovator. Friendly faculty, personal attention, and an increasing emphasis on community make SU a good place to expand your mind. "The institution cares about the students, and the campus is well maintained and has a lot to offer," says a senior. "SU truly feels like home."

Susquehanna's campus is beautiful, set on 325 lush acres in the small town of Selinsgrove on the Susquehanna River. Most of the 60 buildings on campus are brick, with Georgian the predominant architectural style. Selinsgrove Hall, built in 1858, and Seibert Hall, built in 1901, are on the National Register of Historic Places. The campus is compact and serene. The 18th Street Commons provides townhouse living for upper-class students on the edge of campus. The Blough-Weis Library was recently renovated and now includes a new café, new teaching lab, and spaces for study and collaboration.

Susquehanna's Central Curriculum emphasizes coursework in five areas: Richness of Thought (fine arts and math); Natural World; Human Interactions (history, sociology, ethics, and language); Intellectual Skills (writing, oral presentation, and teamwork); and Connections (an off-campus, cross-cultural experience matched

> **"The honors program significantly widens the range of classes open to students."**

with diversity classes). All freshmen must complete a summer Common Reading assignment based on a specific theme, participate in an orientation program, take a Writing and Thinking course, and take a Perspectives seminar that helps them make the transition to college-level work. Freshmen also have access to Leadership Passport, a series of workshops and mentoring to help them develop their leadership potential. Finally, all students must take a capstone course in their major.

The Weis School of Business is not only one of the most striking buildings on campus, but also a prestigious business program that attracts the most Susquehanna students. Weis also sponsors a semester in London exclusively for its junior business majors. Communications, psychology, and creative writing are also popular majors. Susquehanna is increasingly recognized for its science programs, especially biology, biochemistry, and environmental science. New majors include physical chemistry, global management, public policy, and luxury brand marketing and management. SU students may also take classes at nearby Bucknell University.

Website: www.susqu.edu
Location: Small Town
Private
Total Enrollment: 2,104
Undergraduates: 2,104
Male/Female: 45/55
SAT Ranges: CR 500–610, M 510–610
ACT Ranges: 23–27
Financial Aid: 97%
Pell Grant: 26%
Expense: Pr $ $
Student Loans: 83%
Average Debt: $ $ $ $
Phi Beta Kappa: No
Applicants: 5,304
Accepted: 76%
Enrolled: 17%
Grad in 6 Years: 71%
Returning Freshmen: 86%
Academics: ✎ ✎ ✎
Social: ☎ ☎ ☎
Q of L: ★ ★ ★ ★
Admissions: (570) 372-4260
Email Address: suadmiss@susqu.edu

Strong Programs:
Business Administration
Communications
Psychology
Creative Writing
Biology

"The academic climate is challenging, yet it is common to have multiple group projects," says one psychology major. Fifty-seven percent of classes have fewer than 20 students, and student/faculty interaction is one of Susquehanna's strong points. "All Susquehanna students are taught by full professors and most of these professors hold a doctorate or the highest degree possible in their field," says one student. An assistantship program for outstanding first-year students combines a $16,000 scholarship with hands-on work with a professor or staff member for 10 hours per week. Past recipients have worked on academic research, university publications, the Writers' Institute, and marketing research. Students enjoy a bevy of support services too. "We have a great counseling center, health center, financial aid office, and gym," a senior says.

For 10 percent of each class, the academic experience is defined by the Susquehanna Honors Program. Unlike other programs in schools of similar size, SU's program does not separate its students from the rest of the campus. Instead, it allows students to take most of their classes with the general student body, thus creating a balance between freedom of choice and a challenging education. "The honors program significantly widens the range of classes open to students and allows them to fulfill their core requirements in creative ways," says a participant. Through the Global Opportunities Program, all students are guaranteed an opportunity to study away from campus for as little as two weeks or as long as a semester, to fulfill their curricular Connections requirement. Students may choose from 100 options on six continents, and about 90 percent of students study abroad, while the remaining 10 percent head to locations across the U.S. Most students also do summer internships as a crucial part of their education and future job searches.

Through the Global Opportunities Program, all students study away from campus for as little as two weeks or as long as a semester.

"SU students are genuine and truly care about making a difference in the community and the world," says one student. Forty-nine percent of SU students are from Pennsylvania, and the majority attended public high school; 2 percent of students are international. Six percent are African American, 6 percent are Hispanic, and 2 percent are Asian American. A communications major explains, "Diversity and multiculturalism are big issues. The university wants the student body to be more diverse." To wit, faculty and staff focus on educating students on issues of diversity, including "invisible differences" such as socioeconomic status, religion, and sexual orientation. Twenty-six percent of freshmen receive Pell Grants. Susquehanna guarantees to meet the full demonstrated financial need of students who are accepted under their early decision plan, but not necessarily that of other students. Merit scholarships averaging $17,885 are available for resident Einsteins, but there are no athletic scholarships.

"SU students are genuine and truly care about making a difference in the community and the world."

All Susquehanna students are required to live on campus, except for the 8 percent who are commuters. There is no problem getting a room, says one student, "but there isn't any off-campus housing, which seems to be an issue for a lot of the students." Freshmen are assigned to four dorms, and after the first year, students choose from a variety of options, including suites, townhouses, and on-campus apartments. Campus vittles are described as "not bad" to "very good." A senior says students feel safe on campus. "Public Safety is constantly patrolling and there are blue emergency lights in various places around campus." The SAFER program offers monthly educational events covering issues of sexual violence, bystander behavior, and how to build a safe community.

Favorite campus traditions include a candlelight Christmas service and a Thanksgiving dinner at which faculty members serve students.

"Social life at Susquehanna is very active and gatherings occur throughout the week," explains a student, "typically on campus." Eighteen percent of the men and 14 percent of the women belong to fraternities or sororities, respectively, but Greeks do not set the tone for the social scene. Fall Weekend, homecoming, and Spring

Weekend are the big annual events. Favorite campus traditions include a candlelight Christmas service and a Thanksgiving dinner at which faculty members serve students "the best meal of the year." Outside the university, Selinsgrove is "small and quaint" with several restaurants and stores. SU was originally founded to prepare students for the ministry, and the university's commitment to the community has remained strong. Each year, half of the student population volunteers on significant community service projects. In the surrounding countryside, "it's not uncommon to see an Amish family go by in their horse and buggy," says a student. For those with cars, it's a short drive to additional shopping and entertainment options. Penn State is an hour away.

Division III sports are popular among Susquehanna students, and the River Hawks (formerly known as the Crusaders) field a number of competitive teams. Baseball, women's swimming and diving, men's track and field, and men's and women's lacrosse are recent conference champs. Students also enjoy the recreational sports program, with 45 percent participating in 9 club and 8 intramural sports; crew, rugby, and ice hockey sign up the most students.

At Susquehanna, "the professors care about their students," a biochemistry major says. A classmate adds that the "personal atmosphere, great faculty/student relationships, and beautiful campus" make Susquehanna worthwhile—and a name worth learning.

If You Apply To ➤ **Susquehanna:** Early action I: Nov. 1. Early decision: Nov. 15. Early action II: Dec. 1. Regular decision: Feb. 1. Priority financial aid: Dec. 1. Housing: May 1. No application fee. Campus interviews: recommended, evaluative. No alumni interviews. SATs or ACTs: optional. No Subject Tests. Letters of recommendation: required. Essay: required. Accepts the Common Application with supplement.

Swarthmore College

500 College Avenue, Swarthmore, PA 19081

Don't mistake Swarthmore for a miniature version of an Ivy League school. Swat is more intellectual (and liberal) than its counterparts in New Haven and Cambridge. The college's honors program gives hardy souls a taste of graduate school, which is where many Swatties invariably end up. Geekier than Wesleyan, more grounded than Reed, more collaborative than just about anywhere.

Swarthmore College's leafy green campus may be just 11 miles from Philadelphia, but students often don't have the time or the inclination to make the jaunt. That's because they have opted for one of the country's most self-consciously intellectual undergraduate environments. Swatties are bright, hardworking, and eclectic in their interests, and campus life is fabled for its intensity. But the intensity doesn't come from huge amounts of coursework (à la Yale) as much as the self-imposed drive of talented students who want to do lots of things simultaneously—from academics to social protests to rugby—and do them well. "Swat is a truly intellectual place where people love ideas with all of their hearts," a senior philosophy major says. "But that doesn't prevent them from having an eye for activism and a knack for partying hard."

Swarthmore's 425-acre campus is a nationally registered arboretum, distinguished by rolling wooded hills. Multistory buildings with natural stone exteriors from local quarries, shaped roofs, and cornices are the norm, fostering a quiet,

Website: www.swarthmore.edu
Location: Small Town
Private
Total Enrollment: 1,566
Undergraduates: 1,566
Male/Female: 50/50
SAT Ranges: CR 670–760, M 670–770
ACT Ranges: 30–34
Financial Aid: 51%
Pell Grant: 20%
Expense: Pr $ $ $
Student Loans: 33%

(continued)

Average Debt: $

Phi Beta Kappa: Yes

Applicants: 7,818

Accepted: 12%

Enrolled: 42%

Grad in 6 Years: 94%

Returning Freshmen: 98%

Academics: ✍ ✍ ✍ ✍ ✍

Social: ☎ ☎ ☎

Q of L: ★ ★ ★ ★

Admissions: (610) 328-8300

Email Address: admissions@
swarthmore.edu

Strong Programs:
Economics
Biology
Computer Science
Political Science
Psychology
Visual and Performing Arts

Swarthmore is among the top five in the nation for the number of graduates who go on to earn Ph.D.s, at 27 percent.

collegiate atmosphere. Newer residence halls feature loft-style rooms and environmentally friendly "green" roofs, while the Wister Education Center and Greenhouse is LEED Gold–certified and includes classrooms, exhibit areas, and greenhouse space. The Matchbox, a 21,000-square-foot facility for fitness and theater, is the newest addition to campus.

Students are required to take three courses in each of the college's three divisions—humanities, natural sciences and engineering (unusual for a liberal arts college), and social sciences—and at least two of the three must be in different departments. Students must also complete 20 courses outside their majors, demonstrate foreign language competency, and fulfill a physical education requirement, which includes a swimming test. Students fulfill the writing requirement by taking three writing courses from at least two divisions. Freshman seminars emphasize close interaction with faculty members in a seminar format; about 86 percent of students participate. The most popular majors are economics, biology, computer science, political science, and psychology, and students also give high marks to majors in visual and performing arts. Cross-registration is offered with nearby Bryn Mawr, Haverford, and Penn, and a semester exchange program includes Harvey Mudd, Middlebury, Mills, Pomona, and Tufts.

> "While the courses are generally very challenging, the environment of Swat is not competitive at all."

Freshmen at Swarthmore are graded on a pass-fail system for their first semester, there is no class rank or dean's list, and there is a big emphasis on group projects. A freshman explains, "While the courses are generally very challenging, the environment of Swat is not competitive at all. You will often see students reminding each other of assignments, giving each other tips on how to succeed, and studying in the library together." Indeed, the administration has encouraged a spirit of collegiality by sprinkling small lounges and cappuccino bars around the dorms and academic spaces. Class sizes are intimate as well, with 76 percent enrolling fewer than 20 students. "All the classes are taught by professors, many of them world-class, and they are always accessible and very, very friendly," says a classics and fine arts double major. Aside from teaching, Swarthmore professors also serve as advisors, and students are likewise assigned to Student Academic Mentors, who shepherd them through the first year on campus.

Undertaken by about a third of Swat's juniors and seniors, the acclaimed honors program features small seminars or independent study and collegial relationships between students and professors. Setting it apart from any other program in the United States are the written and oral examinations, which are reviewed by external faculty at the end of the senior year and gauge the students' ability to hold their own with experts in the field. One student describes honors as "like a pre-Ph.D. program"; indeed, Swarthmore is among the top five institutions in the nation for the number of graduates who go on to earn Ph.D.s, at 27 percent. The college has boosted the number of programs in which students may pursue honors to include studio and performing arts, as well as study abroad. Forty percent of Swarthmore students study abroad in countries such as France, Japan, Poland, and Spain. Roughly two-thirds of students get involved with research or independent creative projects. A sophomore adds, "We have a great group of networked alumni who are always willing to help students, especially with externships, in which students stay with their Swat alum host family one week before winter break and shadow them."

> "We have a great group of networked alumni who are always willing to help students."

"Ultimately, we are all nerds here," a history major says. "Each of us in our own way has found a place where our passionate, geekiest interests are validated, appreciated, and celebrated by our fellow Swatties." Swarthmore is home to a diverse student body; 13 percent are native Pennsylvanians and 11 percent are international. Six percent of students are African American, 17 percent Asian American, and 13 percent Hispanic. Consistent with its Quaker roots, Swarthmore encourages students to be as educated as possible on issues of cultural, racial, and socio-economic pluralism, and the entire community is brought into decisions on issues such as socially responsible investments and pay scale of campus workers. Liberals far outnumber conservatives, students say, but students on both sides are keen to stand up for issues they are passionate about. The Eugene Lang Center for Civic and Social Responsibility has made Swarthmore a national force in the area of service learning. "Swarthmore is characterized by a genuine will to do good in the world," a senior engineering major says. Swarthmore is need-blind in its admissions and meets 100 percent of admitted students' demonstrated financial need. In an effort to reduce the burden of loans, the college has replaced loans with grants in its financial aid packages.

Ninety-five percent of undergraduates live on campus, and housing is guaranteed for all four years. "The dorms each have their own personality," says a senior, "and for the most part they are quite comfortable and well maintained." Dining options are said to be diverse and plentiful, if not always outstanding, and a handful of local eateries are also covered by the meal plan. Campus safety personnel are "quick to respond in any circumstance," and a sophomore says, "We have a *very* active Title IX office that works on prevention and resolution equally."

Most social life at Swarthmore takes place on campus, and it often begins late, since students hit the books until 10 or 11 p.m. and then head out for fun. "In order to receive funding from the Social Affairs Committee, an event has to be open to all members of campus," explains an economics major. "Because of this regulation, you don't have to worry about getting in to a party or having to pay for most events." When it comes to alcohol, Swarthmore follows Pennsylvania law, which states that you must be 21 to drink. "Campus police are not disciplinarians," a student says. "They want students to be safe." Swarthmore's two fraternities attract 11 percent of the men; a newly formed sorority draws 6 percent of the women. Annual activities include Primal Scream, the tradition where everyone screams at midnight the night before exams, and the McCabe Mile, where everyone decorates the McCabe Library with toilet paper around shelves (the founder of Scott Tissue is an alumnus and contributor).

Students' biggest complaints include lack of sleep and too much work, self-imposed or otherwise. If they're not studying, Swatties are volunteering, often in Philadelphia or the nearby smaller city of Chester, or out pursuing a personal whim. The village of Swarthmore, known as the "'Ville," has some stores, a pizza parlor, and a Chinese restaurant. Students say there's not much in the way of off-campus social activity. For that, they hop from the on-campus train station into city-center Philadelphia, where many temptations await, including concerts, dance clubs, museums, and four professional sports teams. The King of Prussia mall, with a movie theater and department stores, isn't far either.

With Swarthmore's focus on academics, athletics aren't a high priority. The school scrapped its football program because the need to recruit enough males to remain competitive in the increasingly intense Division III environment was undermining efforts to recruit students with other interests and talents. Swarthmore is a founding member of the Centennial Conference, and women's soccer and volleyball, along with men's lacrosse, have won conference championships in recent years. Other competitive Garnet teams include women's track and field and men's soccer,

Consistent with its Quaker roots, Swarthmore encourages students to be as educated as possible on issues of pluralism.

"We have a *very* active Title IX office that works on prevention and resolution equally."

Social life often begins late, since students hit the books until 10 or 11 p.m. and then head out for fun.

"We really are dedicated to learning just because we like to learn, not because we want the A."

basketball, and tennis. Any victory over archrival Haverford will have Swatties swelling with pride. Intramurals are also popular, and Prom Dress Rugby is a beloved annual event. In the Crum Regatta, student-made boats float in nearby Crum Creek—Swarthmore's answer to the America's Cup.

Swarthmore is a place where the administration supports the student body completely, and students are given a voice in a variety of issues ranging from faculty hiring decisions to making campuswide policies. Students who want to take an active role in their education beyond the classroom door may find the right fit here. "Swarthmore will show you just how much you can take on and accomplish," says a student. Adds another, "We really are dedicated to learning just because we like to learn, not because we want the A."

If You Apply To ➤ **Swarthmore:** Early decision I: Nov. 15. Early decision II and regular decision: Jan. 1. Financial aid: Feb. 15. Housing: May 1. Application fee: $60. Campus and alumni interviews: optional, evaluative. SATs or ACTs: required. Subject Tests: optional. Letters of recommendation: required. Essay: required. Accepts the Common Application with supplement.

Syracuse University

900 South Crouse Avenue, Syracuse, NY 13244

Syracuse has defined itself as a research university that takes undergraduates seriously. World famous in its signature field of communications, SU is also strong in information studies, architecture, and public affairs. The university has been a national leader in promoting socioeconomic diversity. Basketball provides solace during frigid winter nights.

Website: www.syr.edu
Location: City Center
Private
Total Enrollment: 18,879
Undergraduates: 14,127
Male/Female: 45/55
SAT Ranges: CR 530–630, M 560–660
ACT Ranges: 24–29
Financial Aid: 73%
Pell Grant: 20%
Expense: Pr $ $
Student Loans: 64%
Average Debt: $ $ $ $
Phi Beta Kappa: Yes
Applicants: 33,254
Accepted: 48%
Enrolled: 22%
Grad in 6 Years: 80%
Returning Freshmen: 91%
Academics: ✍ ✍ ✍
Social: ☎ ☎ ☎

Anyone who has watched college sports on TV is familiar with the bright orange color associated with Syracuse University. They've seen the screaming fans and the stadiums overflowing with cheering hordes. But beyond all the athletic fanfare is passion of another sort: Syracuse has set out to become a student-centered research university. In recent years, the university has launched academic programs in emerging areas such as global enterprise technology and sport management and created integrated learning majors in fields such as forensic science and neuroscience. By fostering close working relationships between students and faculty, expanding course offerings, and pouring loads of money into facility upgrades, Syracuse has made its former reputation as an academic assembly line with killer sports teams a thing of the past.

The Syracuse campus is located on a hill overlooking the city of Syracuse in central New York State. The character and mixture of architectural styles depict a continuously changing campus, which is grassy, full of trees, and bordered by residential neighborhoods. Fifteen of SU's 140 buildings are listed in the National Register of Historic Places. Many schools and colleges have restructured facilities to accommodate more faculty/student research, as well as social interaction between the two groups. Ensley Athletic Center opened in 2015 and features 87,000 square feet of space for fitness and athletic pursuits.

> **"Students on campus are very vocal and advocate greatly for what they believe in."**

General education requirements vary by school, but all Syracuse students are expected to take writing courses. Several schools and colleges subscribe to the Arts and Sciences core requirements, which include coursework in the sciences, math, social sciences, humanities, and contemporary issues. Entering freshmen must complete a writing seminar, and each school and college offers a small-group experience course, known as the Freshman Forum, to share common first-year academic and personal experiences.

The Newhouse School of Public Communications is undoubtedly Syracuse's most prestigious academic offering and affords students the opportunity to choose any one of the eight Newhouse majors and have a dual major in information management and technology. Also well known is the Maxwell School of Citizenship and Public Affairs, whose faculty members teach sought-after undergraduate courses in economics, history, geography, political science, and social sciences. The College of Arts and Sciences is the largest college at Syracuse and offers recognized programs in creative writing, philosophy, geography, and chemistry. Majors in marketing, psychology, architecture, entrepreneurship and emerging enterprises, and visual and performing arts are also popular and well regarded.

> "I was in the engineering learning community, and it was where I met my closest friends."

A civil engineering major says that "each school at Syracuse has its own academic climate, and some are more competitive or collaborative than others," but students can expect challenging coursework across the board. Classes are usually small; 59 percent have fewer than 20 students. "Faculty members do care, and are very accessible," says a sophomore. Their approaches to teaching, however, can vary considerably, according to a senior: "Some professors go above and beyond to teach material, while others stick to the old PowerPoint presentations."

Teaming with NASA, the university has a $3 million virtual aerospace engineering facility—one of three in the nation—where students have helped design a reusable space launch vehicle. SU students have also participated in NASA's reduced-gravity student flight programs. The university offers an honors program for a small number of the most motivated students, and a large portion of students participate in undergraduate research. Thirty-seven percent study abroad via centers in eight countries, as well as more than 65 World Partner programs. SU centers in Los Angeles and New York City offer semester-long programs for those pursuing careers in the entertainment industry.

"Students on campus are very vocal and advocate greatly for what they believe in," says a sophomore. Thirty-seven percent of the students are from New York State, and most of those hail from New York City and Long Island, and 12 percent are international. The number of students of color has been steadily increasing, with African Americans now comprising 8 percent of the student body, Asian Americans 8 percent, and Hispanics 11 percent. Despite pushback from faculty members concerned about the university's academic image, the administration insists that Syracuse remains committed to admissions policies that made Syracuse a national leader in promoting socioeconomic diversity. Twenty percent of first-year students—and 24 percent of all graduates—qualify for Pell Grants. "Two of the current biggest issues on campus are diversity/self-segregation and sexual safety," reports a political science major. "These two issues have resulted in multiple events organized by the university and students to discuss problems, solutions, and more." Student-athletes are well supported with 351 athletic scholarships in 16 sports. Merit scholarships are also available.

Seventy-five percent of undergraduates live in university housing, which is described as comfortable and well maintained. "Freshmen are only allowed to live in dorms, but after that year you have the option to reside in on-campus apartments," a student explains. One-third of students, mostly first-years, participate in roughly two dozen living/learning communities. "I was in the engineering learning

(continued)

Q of L: ★ ★ ★
Admissions: (315) 443-3611
Email Address: orange@ syr.edu

Strong Programs:
Communications
Information Management and Technology
Marketing
Psychology
Architecture
Entrepreneurship and Emerging Enterprises
Visual and Performing Arts

The Newhouse School of Public Communications is undoubtedly Syracuse's most prestigious academic offering.

Teaming with NASA, the university has a $3 million virtual aerospace engineering facility.

community, and it was where I met my closest friends," says a senior. "These people were my ultimate support system." The campus offers 18 eateries, including five residential dining centers. As for campus safety, SU has emergency alarms throughout the campus, a key-card access system in all dorms, and bus service for students studying late on campus.

Twenty-eight percent of men belong to fraternities, and 32 percent of women join sororities. "Greek Life definitely plays a huge role on this campus. I have never felt pressured to drink, however," a student says. Students over 21 spend many an evening barhopping on Marshall Street, a lively strip near campus. Orange After Dark puts on activities like movie nights, bowling, and dancing. Students also enjoy the annual Juice Jam, Mayfest, and Martin Luther King Jr. celebrations.

Students generally enjoy the city of Syracuse, which offers a variety of off-campus retreats, including an excellent art museum, a resident opera company, a symphony, and a string of movie theaters and restaurants. The city's Armory Square is flanked with coffee shops, upscale boutiques, clubs, and eateries. Many students are involved in the community through internships and volunteer work, and SU education majors give more than 40,000 hours in community service. If students tire of the life in Syracuse, several quaint country towns, complete with orchards, lakes, and waterfalls, are nearby, as are several ski resorts. Destiny USA, about 10 minutes away, is the country's sixth-largest shopping center and has an 18-theater cinema and indoor go-kart track. Popular road trips include Ithaca, Niagara Falls, Montreal, and Rochester.

"On game days we're all bleeding orange."

"Whether you are a socialite who loves Greek life or a nerd who loves science, on game days we're all bleeding orange," says one senior. Now belonging to the Atlantic Coast Conference, the Syracuse Orange continue to rock the spacious Carrier Dome. Football games make for great fun and much enthusiasm during the year, and a new Duke–Syracuse basketball rivalry has been established. Five programs reached their respective NCAA Final Fours in recent years: women's field hockey, men's and women's lacrosse, and men's and women's basketball. The women's basketball team also competed in the 2016 championship game. The "painters" are famous at SU—they are groups of students who each paint a letter of the school's name on their bare chests and run through rain, sleet, or snow to each home game in the Carrier Dome. Syracuse extends its enthusiasm for sports to 62 club and intramural programs as well.

From special partnerships with NASA to opportunities to study abroad or help out right at home, students at Syracuse know they've got something special. The wintry climate can be problematic, but the ubiquitous bright orange paraphernalia all over campus is enough to warm anyone. For many, one senior's words prove to be true: "You'll never find a school that has more school spirit than we do."

University of Tennessee Knoxville

Knoxville, TN 37996

UT is in the middle of the pack among its Southeastern rivals—behind Florida, U of Georgia, and UNC; ahead of Alabama, Arkansas, and Ole Miss. As the only major public university in Tennessee, UT comes close to being all things to all students. Strong in business, engineering, and communication. One of the few Southern flagship universities located in a major city.

Students at the University of Tennessee put a premium on school spirit, athletics, and academics—usually in that order. In the fall, boisterous fans pack into one of the nation's largest on-campus football stadiums to watch the Volunteers play against national powerhouses like Alabama, Arkansas, and Florida. Also competitive are the SEC-dominating women's basketball and soccer teams and the men's baseball team. Amid this excitement, it's easy to forget that UT also prides itself on some strong academic programs. "Bleeding orange is the only way to go!" cheers one happy Volunteer.

Set in the foothills of the Great Smoky Mountains, UT is in the heart of east Tennessee's urban hub and only a few miles away from Oak Ridge, Tennessee, home to the prominent Oak Ridge National Laboratory. The 560-acre campus has an array of architectural styles ranging from Gothic to Georgian to modern. Particularly noteworthy is the Hodges Library—the largest one in the state—built in the shape of a ziggurat. The university has spent $1.4 billion in the last three years on new construction, renovations, and landscaping improvements. Streets that once ran through the center of campus have been transformed into landscaped pathways, and several parking lots have been replaced by grassy lawns. A new student union is slated for completion in 2018 and will double the size of the current center by adding a new book and technology store, auditorium, and upgraded event spaces.

UT's general education requirements are fairly extensive and include courses in written and oral communications, quantitative reasoning, arts and humanities, culture and civilizations, social sciences, and natural sciences, plus intermediate proficiency in a foreign language or multicultural studies. Business majors are immersed in a broad liberal arts program, including a foreign language requirement, during their first

> **"Some classes are harder than anything I could imagine and some require little effort."**

two years of study. Many strong academic programs are in preprofessional fields, most notably business (particularly supply chain management), architecture, engineering, and nursing. On the liberal arts side, psychology, social work, and communication are popular majors. The modern foreign languages and literatures major allows students to combine a concentration in a language, such as German, Spanish, or Japanese, with one in international business. The sustainability major is well regarded, and a new minor has been added in leadership studies.

Academic competition varies, as does course difficulty. "Some classes are harder than anything I could imagine and some require little effort," says one junior. Twenty-eight percent of classes have fewer than 20 students. Students report occasional problems with registration because preference is given to seniors. Students are expected to meet with their advisors each semester before registering, although advising also gets mixed reviews, depending on the field of study. UT faculty get a generally positive rating. "I have had some really good professors and some mediocre ones as well," a logistics major says.

UT is the managing partner of Oak Ridge National Laboratory—the federal government's largest nonweapons lab—which bolsters science and technology offerings,

Website: www.utk.edu
Location: City Center
Public
Total Enrollment: 22,808
Undergraduates: 20,467
Male/Female: 50/50
SAT Ranges: CR 520–630, M 530–630
ACT Ranges: 24–30
Financial Aid: 93%
Pell Grant: 30%
Expense: Pub $ $ $
Student Loans: 52%
Average Debt: $ $
Phi Beta Kappa: Yes
Applicants: 17,081
Accepted: 76%
Enrolled: 36%
Grad in 6 Years: 70%
Returning Freshmen: 85%
Academics: ✐ ✐ ✐
Social: 🏮 🏮 🏮 🏮
Q of L: ★ ★ ★
Admissions: (865) 974-2184
Email Address: admissions@utk.edu

Strong Programs:
Business
Supply Chain Management
Architecture
Engineering
Nursing
Psychology
Social Work
Communication

and involves more than 400 students and faculty in majors as diverse as English and physics. Up to 10 percent of undergraduates are members of the university-wide Chancellor's Honors program, and most of UT's colleges also offer honors tracks. UT established the Haslam Scholars program for 15 of the nation's top students; selection criteria include scholastic achievement, leadership potential, and special talents. Haslam scholars enjoy such benefits as study groups mentored by top UT faculty, a study abroad experience, and research support. Each year about 1,000 students study abroad, selecting from programs in more than 60 countries on six continents. The most popular options are short-term, faculty-led programs that provide students the opportunity to study under the guidance of a faculty member during the summer terms.

UT students are "levelheaded but tend to get a little crazy on the weekends," says a student. Eighty-seven percent of the student body are homegrown Tennesseans, and 2 percent are international. Minority enrollment remains low—African Americans account for 7 percent of the students, while Asian Americans and Hispanics each account for 3 percent—but the university has hired a vice chancellor for diversity and inclusion to promote and support campus diversity. Financial aid opportunities have been generous, with thousands of merit scholarships available (averaging $2,016) and 260 athletic scholarships in 20 sports. Thirty percent of freshmen qualify for the Pell Grant.

> **"[UT students are] levelheaded but tend to get a little crazy on the weekends."**

Thirty-three percent of UT students live on campus. Although a few older buildings remain, the university has undertaken a multiphase housing development plan that will produce seven new residence halls by 2019. Each of the dorms has a residence hall association, which for a token fee provides checkout of sports equipment, games, cooking utensils, and other useful items. Freshmen may choose from 21 living/learning communities, where they collaborate with peers on shared academic interests. The university goes out of its way to ensure the security of the campus and the students. To this end, UT has installed remote alarm units that allow students to report a crime from anywhere on campus and has developed comprehensive sexual assault prevention programs.

Students say that the social life is "very important" and active both on and off campus. Greek life is growing more popular—16 percent of the men and 24 percent of the women go Greek. The social calendar is dotted with numerous major events, including River Fest on the nearby Tennessee River, Saturday Night on the Town, and the Dogwood Arts Festival. Cumberland Avenue (a.k.a. The Strip), a few blocks away, offers a lively variety of bars and eateries.

But nothing compares to the sea of orange that engulfs the campus on Saturday afternoons in the fall. More than 100,000 people jam the football stadium to see the Volunteers (a term dating to the Mexican War) take on their Southeast Conference rivals. Denizens liken football in Knoxville to religion, and according to one, "'Alabama' is a four-letter word" in these parts. UT has claimed 189 team and 987 individual SEC regular-season and tournament titles, along with 23 team and 247 individual national championships, and UT has finished in the Top 20 of the National Association of Collegiate Directors of Athletics (NACDA) Directors' Cup seven times in the last 10 years. Recent conference champs include women's basketball, rowing, volleyball, and softball and men's tennis. The intramural program attracts 23 percent of undergraduates, and the most popular sports are flag football, indoor and outdoor soccer, basketball, and softball.

The University of Tennessee is well known for its athletics, and administrators and students are hoping that it can develop the same reputation for its academics. Though the oft-sluggish bureaucracy may turn some off, many will find the myriad opportunities here at the "Big Orange" to be well worth the squeezing.

UT: Regular decision: Dec. 15. (Priority deadline: Nov. 1.) Financial aid: Feb. 15. Application fee: $50. No campus or alumni interviews. SATs or ACTs: required. No Subject Tests. Letters of recommendation: optional. Essay: required. Accepts the Common Application with supplement. Additional essay required for nursing program applicants.

University of Texas at Austin

John Hargis Hall, Austin, Texas 78712

UT is on anybody's list of the top 10 public universities in the nation. The Plan II liberal arts honors program is one of the country's most renowned. Though it is also the capital of Texas, Austin ranks among the nation's best college towns—a progressive enclave in a conservative state. Boot camp for aspiring political types in the Lone Star State and beyond.

The University of Texas at Austin has come a long way from where it began in 1883 as a small school with only one building, eight teachers, two departments, and 221 students. Today, the UT campus is Texas-sized home to more than 45,000 students. From its extensive academic programs to its powerful athletic teams to its location in one of the nation's ultimate college towns, the University of Texas has everything a Longhorn could ask for. "Our university is a diverse community with amazing opportunities for success," says a junior.

A 400-acre oasis near downtown Austin, replete with rolling hills, trees, creeks, and fountains, the campus features buildings ranging from "old, distinguished" limestone structures to contemporary Southwest architecture. The fabled UT Tower is adorned with a large clock and chimes (a lifesaver for the disorganized) and is illuminated in Longhorn orange after big athletic wins. From the steps of the Tower, one can see the verdant Austin hills and the state capitol. The outstanding library system at the University of Texas has more than seven million volumes located in 19 different libraries across campus, and is the sixth-largest academic library system in the United States. Construction on three new buildings to house the recently established Dell Medical School was completed in 2016.

Each college within the university has established basic requirements for all majors: four English courses, with two writing intensives; five courses in social sciences; five courses in natural sciences and math; and one course in the fine arts or humanities. Entering freshmen are expected

> **"My professors are above and beyond my expectations."**

to complete a "Signature Course" within their first year of attendance. Signature Courses, which are usually small and taught by senior professors, introduce undergraduates to academic discussion and analysis of issues from an interdisciplinary perspective. Freshmen can also take University 101, which covers everything from major requirements to healthy lifestyle choices and cultural diversity.

The list of academic strengths at the University of Texas is impressive for such a large school. Undergraduate offerings in accounting, architecture, botany, biology, business, foreign languages, and history are first-rate. The engineering and computer science departments are excellent and continue to expand, and engineering, communication, social sciences, and business represent the most popular majors. The English department is huge (nearly 100 tenure-track professors) and students give it high marks, but the art/photography department is said to need improvement. UT's McDonald Observatory, based in West Texas, boasts one of the world's largest telescopes.

Website: www.utexas.edu
Location: City Center
Public
Total Enrollment: 46,799
Undergraduates: 36,357
Male/Female: 47/53
SAT Ranges: CR 570–680, M 600–710
ACT Ranges: 26–31
Financial Aid: 42%
Pell Grant: 23%
Expense: Pub $ $
Student Loans: 46%
Average Debt: $ $
Phi Beta Kappa: Yes
Applicants: 43,592
Accepted: 39%
Enrolled: 46%
Grad in 6 Years: 81%
Returning Freshmen: 96%
Academics: ✍ ✍ ✍ ✍ ½
Social: ☎ ☎ ☎ ☎
Q of L: ★ ★ ★ ★
Admissions: (512) 475-7399
Email Address: bealonghorn@utexas.edu

Strong Programs:
Engineering
Communication
Social Sciences
Business
Accounting
Architecture

(continued)

Botany
History

Students say the academic climate is competitive and demanding. "There are many rigorous majors that have accelerated courses or competitive programs," says a student. Many UT classes are quite large—26 percent enroll more than 50 students—and smaller sections fill up quickly. UT is a research university, so the professors are often busy in the laboratories or the library. They do, however, have office hours. "My professors are above and beyond my expectations," says a psychology major. "Their own interest in their topics is obvious, and the determination to aid the students is admirable."

The Plan II liberal arts honors program, a national model, is one of the oldest honors programs in the country and one of the best academic deals anywhere. It offers qualified students a flexible curriculum, top-notch professors, small seminar courses, and individualized counseling, and provides them with all of the advantages of a large university in a small-college atmosphere. Business, engineering, liberal arts, and natural sciences honors programs are also available. Engineering majors can alternate work and study in the co-op program, while education and health majors hold term-time internships. Being in the capital city should have its advantages, and it does. Almost 200 UT undergrads work for lawmakers in the Texas Legislature, only a 10-minute walk from campus. A strong Reading and Study Skills Lab services students in need of remedial help. Study abroad options are available in more than 70 countries, and UT sends roughly 3,000 students to foreign locales annually.

> **"[Students are] intelligent, involved, and proactive in their education."**

> *The fabled UT Tower is illuminated in Longhorn orange after big athletic wins.*

UT students are "intelligent, involved, and proactive in their education," says a senior. Ninety percent of UT undergraduates are Texans, and 5 percent hail from outside the U.S. Students say there is no dominant political pattern on campus—despite the fact that historically UT has been integral in the careers of big-time (conservative) Texas politicians. The liberals are not exactly hiding out on this huge campus. Political issues, such as human rights, gun control, and abortion, can get students on both sides pretty riled up here. Hispanics account for 22 percent of undergrads, Asian Americans 20 percent, and African Americans 4 percent. The university offers special "welcome programs" for African American and Hispanic students, with social and educational events and peer mentoring. The university also awards merit scholarships averaging $5,938, as well as hundreds of athletic scholarships in 20 sports. Twenty-three percent of incoming freshmen receive Pell Grants.

University housing accommodates only 19 percent of students, and it ranges from functional to plush. "Most of the dorms are old," says a student, "but they have nice facilities." Dorms offer a variety of living options based on common social and educational interests. Apartments and condos close to campus are lovely—and very expensive. More reasonably priced digs can be found in other parts of town, a free shuttle ride away. But be forewarned: with more than 110 buildings, UT life requires lots of walking, especially for commuters, though bus stops and parking lots are scattered about. As for food, there is a wide variety of options, including healthy, vegetarian, kosher, and vegan fare. What's more, "other cafés and convenience stores on campus offer even more selection," says one student. Security can be a concern (Austin is an urban area, after all), but students report feeling safe on campus, thanks to an active and highly visible campus police. Texas law permits people to carry firearms on campus.

> **"I love [Austin]… It has a great live music scene and is beautiful."**

> *Almost 200 UT undergrads work for lawmakers in the Texas Legislature, only a 10-minute walk from campus.*

The Texas Union sponsors movies and social events, and its Cactus Café is a popular venue for musical acts. It also boasts the world's only collection of orange-topped pool tables in its arcade and bowling alley. For those more interested in octaves than eight balls, the Performing Arts Center has two concert halls that attract nationally known performers. There are also more than 1,100 student organizations from which to choose. Fifteen percent of the men and 18 percent of the women go Greek. Annual festivals include 40 Acres Fest, a sprawling carnival of the campus organizations. A pep rally gets students psyched before the Longhorns play rival Oklahoma. And Texas Independence Day provides an occasion for celebration in March.

As the state capital, Austin is hardly a typical college town, but it is one of the best ones. "I love it," exclaims a junior. "It was really the deciding factor on going to UT. It has a great live music scene and is beautiful." Nightlife centers on nearby Sixth Street, full of pubs and restaurants of all types, and the well-known music scene that features everything from jazz to rock to blues to folk, as well as the Austin City Limits and South by Southwest festivals. Along with live music, bat-watching is one of Austin's most popular activities—the city is known as "Bat City" after the colony of Mexican free-tailed bats that lives under the Congress Avenue Bridge in the spring and summer. It's the largest urban bat colony in North America. Halloween draws an estimated 80,000 costumed revelers to Sixth Street (and sometimes up its lampposts). When the weather gets too muggy (quite often in spring and summer), students head for off-campus campgrounds, lakes, and parks. The most popular road trips are to San Antonio or Dallas. For spring break, students travel to Padre Island, if not New Orleans.

Athletics are as vital as oxygen to most Texans, and the Longhorns compete in the Division I Big 12 Conference. The athletic department has a budget in excess of $160 million, and students look forward to the annual Texas–Oklahoma football game played in the Cotton Bowl in Dallas. "Football games pull the student body together and give us a chance to show our school spirit," says one student. Bevo XV, the

"Football games pull the student body together and give us a chance to show our school spirit."

famed UT mascot, is the latest in a long line of live longhorn steer mascots who have at various times been known to bolt loose from their handlers, rip their shirts, and, on one occasion, lie down in the end zone during a football game. Basketball is also popular, and the men's and women's teams regularly reach their respective NCAA tournaments. The baseball program has many alumni in the major leagues, and the annual spring game between UT's baseball alumni and the current college squad is quite a contest. The men's swimming and diving team claimed the national championship in 2016, and women's swimming and diving, volleyball, men's and women's track and field, and men's golf are recent conference champs. The chess team is a perennial powerhouse too, and the Quidditch team has won multiple national championships. UT's extensive intramural program is also very popular and offers weekend athletes access to the same great facilities that the big-time jocks use.

The University of Texas may seem overwhelming because of its imposing size, but students say the school spirit and sense of community found here make it feel smaller. UT prides itself on having one of the most reasonably priced tuitions in the country for a flagship public research university. It also offers one of the best all-around educational experiences a student could ask for, especially if you make it into Plan II.

Overlaps

Baylor, Duke, University of Houston, MIT, NYU, Rice, Texas A&M, Vanderbilt

If You Apply To > **UT Austin:** Rolling admissions: Dec. 1. Financial aid: Mar. 15. Application fee: $75. No campus or alumni interviews. SATs (with essay) or ACTs (with writing): required. Subject Tests: not used for admissions decisions (may be used for placement purposes). Letters of recommendation: optional. Essay: required. Apply either to institution as a whole or particular program. Certain departments have additional requirements.

Richardson, TX 75080

A rising star in the Lone Star State, UTD is now the most selective of the regional campuses of the UT system. Has put on a full-court press to attract top students in science and technology. Good living conditions and a serious honors program. Football here is of the flag variety. Has a lower acceptance rate than both Texas A&M and Texas Tech.

Website: www.utdallas.edu
Location: Suburban
Public
Total Enrollment: 18,674
Undergraduates: 12,585
Male/Female: 56/44
SAT Ranges: CR 560–670,
M 600–700
ACT Ranges: 25–31
Financial Aid: 75%
Pell Grant: 28%
Expense: Pub $ $ $
Student Loans: 36%
Average Debt: $
Phi Beta Kappa: Yes
Applicants: 11,237
Accepted: 61%
Enrolled: 40%
Grad in 6 Years: 67%
Returning Freshmen: 84%
Academics: ✍ ✍ ✍
Social: ☎ ☎ ☎
Q of L: ★ ★ ★
Admissions: (972) 883-2270
Email Address: interest@
utdallas.edu

Strong Programs:
Biology
Accounting
Business Administration
Psychology
Speech-Language Pathology
and Audiology
Neurology
Nanotechnology
Engineering

Founded in 1961 as a graduate research center, the University of Texas at Dallas did not begin awarding undergraduate degrees until 1975. It wasn't until 1990 that UT Dallas admitted its first freshman class. Since that time, the university has continued to grow and hone its chops as a four-year university with an emphasis on engineering, mathematics, the sciences, and the management of new technologies. "UTD is a young, vibrant, and promising institution," raves one senior. "Even freshmen have the chance to create new organizations and traditions, work in real labs with full professors, and be in contact with top administrators." Although the university may not fit the typical Texas "frats and football" mold, students here still find plenty of reasons to cheer.

Situated on 700 rolling acres in the Dallas suburb of Richardson, UT Dallas has the feel of a large corporate campus. Most buildings are positioned around an interior mall that features a variety of blooming trees, low flower beds, and fountains. The predominant architectural style is 1970s tilt wall concrete, and many buildings are interconnected by a series of glass sky bridges. The Natural Science and Engineering Research Laboratory provides 192,000 square feet of state-of-the-art labs, including "class 1000" clean rooms that have highly controlled environments to prevent contamination. The building is playfully referred to as the "mermaid building" for its iridescent blue, green, and magenta shingles, which resemble fish scales. A new, $110 million bioengineering and sciences building opened in 2015.

> **"UTD is a young, vibrant, and promising institution."**

To graduate, UT Dallas students must complete a general education curriculum consisting of 42 credit hours across eight disciplines: communication, mathematics, natural science, humanities, fine arts, American history, government, and social and behavioral sciences. Freshmen are expected to take a first-year rhetoric class, which is a small group seminar designed to teach college survival skills and to ensure that students receive appropriate advising.

UTD offers budding scientists an especially solid choice of majors, including highly respected programs in speech-language pathology and audiology, neurology, and nanotechnology. In fact, all of the hard sciences draw praise from students, especially the engineering and computer science programs. Those seeking to add a pinch of the humanities to their science may opt for the innovative arts and technology program, which unites art and engineering. The most popular majors are biology, accounting, business administration, and psychology. Students say the academic climate is collaborative, but courses can be grueling. "The workload can be intense, depending on the amount of hours per semester that you take, but it is doable," says one sophomore. Seventy-eight percent of classes have fewer than 50 students. "Professors do their best to be accessible to students with office hours and review sessions," says one student. "Many of them are particularly involved in the community and clubs on campus, so it is easy to get to know them."

Qualified first-year students may take part in the Honors College, which houses eight programs that grant students access to personal mentoring and special social and academic opportunities. The program is valuable because it "gets smaller groups together to form real communities and resource networks," according to one junior. The Undergraduate Research Program offers students stipends specifically to pursue short-term research proposals, and the university has opened the state's first Confucius Institute, which promotes a better understanding of Chinese language and business through classes and travel. Study abroad options are available in more than 15 countries. The McDermott Scholars program offers a full ride plus stipends for international travel, field trips, and other benefits; approximately 25 freshmen are selected every year.

UTD opened the state's first Confucius Institute, which promotes a better understanding of Chinese language and business.

"Students here are weird, in the best way possible," says a marketing major. "Being called weird is like being called limited edition, meaning you won't see it often." Ninety-four percent of undergraduates hail from the Lone Star State and 3 percent from abroad. African Americans account for 6 percent of the student body, Asian Americans add 29 percent, and Hispanics comprise 18 percent. When it comes to political and social issues, students don't show much concern. "Ha!" scoffs one computer science major. Adds another student, "Whenever an event is put on with candidates in upcoming elections, or information about current political topics, attendance tends to be pretty low." The university hands out merit scholarships averaging $11,891 each year, but no athletic scholarships. Twenty-eight percent of incoming freshmen qualify for the Pell Grant, and students whose annual family income is less than $25,000 are eligible for the Tuition Promise program, which covers full tuition and fees. Academic Bridge takes 160 local students whose academic credentials are not quite high enough to meet UTD standards and pays them to attend an intensive summer prep experience, including classes and off-campus trips. Those who perform well are admitted to the university.

"Dorms are some of the best dorms I've seen at any university."

Twenty-seven percent of undergrads live on campus in apartment-style residence villages. "Dorms are some of the best dorms I've seen at any university," says one student. Freshmen participate in a living/learning community (LLC); options include arts and technology, computer science, engineering, prehealth, social sciences, management, and exploration. LLC students live in the same apartment building, attend classes together, and participate in various group activities. A bevy of new dining options are available, including choices for the health-conscious. A junior says, "Campus security is solid." Under Texas law, people are permitted to carry firearms on campus.

Freshmen reside in living/learning communities, living in the same apartment building and attending classes together.

Students say the social scene is slowly heating up. "There is a decent Greek presence, intramural games are fun to go to, and student government helps create fun student events," according to one senior. There are frequent concerts, dinners, movies, and dances, and the aforementioned Greek scene attracts 2 percent of the men and 3 percent of the women. Alcohol policies prohibit underage drinking, and the university is "fairly strict" when it comes to enforcing the rules. Popular traditions include homecoming, the Cometville Carnival, and the oozeball tournament (that's mud volleyball, for the uninitiated). "We're still young and traditions are still forming," says a sophomore.

"We're still young and traditions are still forming."

Richardson is "definitely not a college town, but the surrounding community is pleasant and relaxed," says a senior. Students frequent the neighborhood grocery stores and restaurants and get involved with the locals through volunteering and community service projects. When it's time for off-campus fun, many head into downtown Dallas, which is "lively, artsy, and sophisticated," according to a molecular biology major.

UTD may be one of the few places in Texas where football isn't considered a way of life. In fact, you won't find football listed among the university's 13 varsity teams. Nevertheless, with 15 conference titles since 2002, the UT Dallas Comets are powerhouse contenders in the Division III American Southwest Conference. The chess team is a juggernaut as well, having made more than a dozen appearances in the Final Four of College Chess. Roughly one third of the student body takes part in recreational or club sports, and the most popular activities include flag football, basketball, and soccer. Students also enjoy a wide array of individual and group fitness programs.

UTD appeals to those students seeking a science- or business-centric curriculum, access to undergraduate research and top-notch facilities, and administrators who value their input. "Students actually matter here," says a junior. Thanks to UTD's relative youth, "undergraduates see a lot more lab time. Students can get involved across programs. Non-theater majors can participate in university productions, non-prelaw students are on the mock trial team, science majors participate in model UN, and the list goes on," says a freshman. Indeed, students here aren't bound by tradition—they're creating it.

Overlaps

University of Texas at Austin, Texas A&M, University of North Texas, University of Texas at Arlington, Texas Woman's, University of Houston, Southern Methodist, Texas Tech

If You Apply To ➢

UT Dallas: Rolling admissions: May 1. (Priority deadline: Jan. 15.) Financial aid: Mar. 15. Housing: May 22. Application fee: $50. No campus or alumni interviews. SATs (with essay) or ACTs (with writing): required. Subject Tests: required for some. Letters of recommendation: optional. Essay: optional.

Texas A&M University

College Station, TX 77843

Coming to A&M is like joining an elite club with 55,000 members. In addition to fanatical school spirit, Texas A&M offers leading programs in the natural sciences, business, and engineering. To succeed in this mass of humanity, students must find their academic niche. The student body is 95 percent Texan, and out-of-staters should be prepared for major culture shock.

Website: www.tamu.edu
Location: Small City
Public
Total Enrollment: 55,224
Undergraduates: 43,411
Male/Female: 51/49
SAT Ranges: CR 520–640, M 550–670
ACT Ranges: 25–30
Financial Aid: 68%
Pell Grant: 24%
Expense: Pub $ $
Student Loans: 43%
Average Debt: $ $
Phi Beta Kappa: Yes
Applicants: 33,970
Accepted: 66%
Enrolled: 46%

Known for its top-notch engineering program and its unsurpassed school spirit, Texas A&M opened in 1876 as a land-grant college and military academy. Today, as one of only 17 universities in the nation to hold federal land, sea, and space grant designations, A&M would seem to have the whole universe covered. This school of more than 43,000 undergrads boasts a massive endowment and more traditions than Vatican City. When they're not studying for rigorous classes, Aggies are likely to be found at Midnight Yell before each home and away football game or yelling— "Aggies don't cheer, they yell!," as the saying around campus goes—for their teams at other high-energy athletic events.

Texas A&M is now the largest university campus in the country, in terms of acreage (5,200)—something made obvious to students every time they walk to class. The A&M campus combines historic brick buildings from the turn of the century with newer structures in more modern styles, and is pulled together by a heavy cover of live oak trees. The campus is in a constant state of flux, as renovations and new construction take place on a regular basis, the most recent being a $480 million renovation of Kyle Field.

Incoming Aggies can expect some heavy coursework in general education requirements, which consist of communications, math, natural sciences, humanities, social/behavioral sciences, kinesiology, visual/performing arts, and U.S. history/

political science. They are also expected to have at least two years of a foreign language, complete a cultural diversity requirement, and demonstrate computer literacy. Texas A&M is best known for its agriculture and engineering colleges, and for veterinary medicine, although the university is cultivating a strong liberal arts program and an even stronger business school. Business, agriculture, and engineering-related majors are the most popular, although two interdisciplinary studies majors in education also garner high enrollment. Aggies also stand by science programs, especially chemistry and physics, and have done outstanding research in oceanography. Technical programs of virtually all kinds are heartily supported at A&M, especially nuclear, space, and biotechnical research.

Students generally agree that academics are taken seriously at A&M, but the climate is "definitely collaborative," says a junior. Professors receive rave reviews, although TAs and grad students are often behind the lectern, and 27 percent of classes have more than 50 students. "The faculty at Texas A&M is phenomenal, drawing from the most esteemed professionals and researchers in their respective fields to teach you from day one," enthuses an electrical engineering major, although a biology major warns that some professors are, "so focused on their own work that they forget sometimes how to teach."

> **"No matter who you are, you'll be greeted with a smile and a 'Howdy!' and all of the courtesy the South is known for."**

Coursework sometimes takes students far from Aggieland. Fourteen percent of students study abroad in more than 90 faculty-led programs and hundreds of additional options available through partnerships and exchange programs worldwide. Undergraduate research is, unsurprisingly, important here, and many professors "open positions for current students to help and participate," explains a junior. Highly motivated students also recommend the University Honors Program as a good way to make friends and enjoy perks like "priority registration, access to smaller classes with better professors, and networking with the brightest minds here at Texas A&M," according to a biomedical sciences major.

Ninety-five percent of students are from Texas, and the political climate is decidedly conservative. Students are known for their characteristic friendliness. Says one, "From your first tour on campus to the day you graduate, no matter who you are, you'll be greeted with a smile and a 'Howdy!' and all of the courtesy the South is known for." Just 1 percent of students come from abroad, and 24 percent qualify for the Pell Grant. The school's departments of Multicultural Services and Student Life offer numerous programs to enhance minority student recruitment and retention. African Americans comprise 3 percent of the student body, Asian Americans 6 percent, and Hispanics 22 percent. Athletes compete for the hundreds of scholarships parceled out among 11 sports each year, while scholars vie for thousands of merit awards averaging $3,580.

A&M's single-sex and co-ed dorms range from cheap and not-so-comfortable to expensive and cushy (with private bathrooms and in-unit laundry machines), but only 23 percent of undergrads reside in them. "Apply for housing as quickly as you can to ensure you get a residence hall, because not many students have the opportunity to live on campus," a sophomore says. Most upperclassmen live in the numerous apartments and houses in College Station or its twin city, Bryan, and the university offers an extensive bus system throughout the community. Several meal plans are offered in the dining halls, and fast-food chains and snack shops are all over campus. Campus security is lauded, but the school is not incident-free. Texas law permits people to carry firearms on campus. Students report that the Step In, Stand Up campaign has done much to raise awareness about sexual assault.

When it comes to social life, a junior advises, "It is imperative that you join a student organization in order to make A&M feel a little smaller and to really find your niche and purpose." With more than 1,000 student-led clubs and organizations to

(continued)

Grad in 6 Years: 79%
Returning Freshmen: 90%
Academics: ✎ ✎ ✎ ✎
Social: ☎ ☎ ☎
Q of L: ★ ★ ★
Admissions: (979) 845-3211
Email Address: admissions@ tamu.edu

Strong Programs:
Business
Agriculture
Engineering
Interdisciplinary Studies
Veterinary Sciences
Biological and Biomedical Sciences
Chemistry
Physics

A&M is one of only 17 universities in the nation to hold federal land, sea, and space grant designations.

New construction takes place regularly, the most recent being a $480 million renovation of Kyle Field.

choose from, students should have little trouble doing so. Greeks attract 3 percent of the men and 6 percent of the women, and students say that neither Greek life nor partying define the social scene. Still, despite the Texas Alcoholic Beverage Commission being stationed in town, "those who choose to drink have no problem getting alcohol." Students appreciate the amenities of the surrounding area, especially in the Northgate district, which offers ample restaurants and bars. "College Station is a model college town," asserts a senior. When the school empties out for a holiday, the town does too. Students are actively involved in the community, including the Big Event, which draws 22,000 Aggies each year. Those seeking a getaway can drive an hour and a half to either Houston or Austin, and the beaches of the Gulf Coast beckon.

> **"It is imperative that you join a student organization in order to make A&M feel a little smaller."**

The treasured Corps of Cadets is the single most important conservator of the spirit and tradition in Aggieland.

Texas A&M is practically synonymous with tradition. Boasts one senior, "We have the same traditions as were created years ago and, young or old, Aggies know them all." Favorites include "Twelfth Man," in which all students stand for the entirety of every football game as a symbol of their loyalty and readiness to take part, and the Aggie Muster, a memorial service for A&M alumni around the world who died within the year. There's also the 400-plus member Fightin' Texas Aggie Band and the senior "boot line" at the end of the halftime show. The treasured Corps of Cadets is one of the largest military training programs in the country. While less than 10 percent of the school belong to the Corps, it remains the single most important conservator of the spirit and tradition in Aggieland. Yet another ritual: thousands of seniors join hands and meander through the campus visiting favorite spots for the last time during the Elephant Walk, which takes its name from elephants, who wander away from their herds before they die.

Athletics, whether on the varsity level or for recreation, are tops on anyone's list here. The school competes in the ultra-competitive Division I Southeastern Conference, where they line up against powerhouses such as Alabama and LSU. Football fans rock Kyle Field with cries of "Gig 'em, Aggies," or "Hump it, Ags," and after touchdowns are scored, Aggie fans kiss their dates. Men's baseball routinely fields outstanding teams, and women's swimming and diving brought home the conference championship in 2016. Women's golf and volleyball and men's tennis are also recent conference champs. Basketball, flag football, racquetball, and soccer are among the most popular sports in the well-organized and extensive intramural program. Aggie jokes abound, much to the chagrin of A&M students, who don't take too kindly to being the object of ridicule. Example: "How do you get a one-armed Aggie out of a tree?" "Wave."

> **"We have the same traditions as were created years ago and, young or old, Aggies know them all."**

"A great school will challenge and nurture you to become an individual who is ready to conquer any problem in the world—and that right there is Texas A&M," says one satisfied biology major. While extremely large, Texas A&M is uniquely familial. Being a student here is being a part of something seemingly so much bigger, which is what the Aggie spirit embodies. With varied educational opportunities and memorable traditions worth cheering (that is to say, "yelling") about, it's no wonder students here are so devoted to their "Aggie Family." As one English major avouches, "You always have a home and a friend with fellow Aggies."

Overlaps

University of Texas at Austin, Baylor, Texas Tech, Texas Christian, University of North Texas, University of Houston, Rice

If You Apply To ➤

Texas A&M: Regular decision: Dec. 1. Priority financial aid: Mar. 15. Application fee: $75. No campus or alumni interviews. SATs (with essay) or ACTs (with writing): required. Subject Tests: optional. Letters of recommendation: optional. Essay: recommended. Apply to particular schools or programs. Primarily committed to state residents.

Texas Christian University

TCU Box 297013, Fort Worth, TX 76129

The personalized private alternative to Texas-sized state universities. Tuition is less, and the student body less affluent, than that at archrival SMU. Though affiliated with the Disciples of Christ, TCU goes lighter on religion than, say, Baylor. Strengths include business, communication, and the fine arts. Strong sense of community and school spirit.

You know a school has spirit when its students paint themselves purple to cheer raucously for a horny toad. Although outsiders might be baffled by such a display, Texans know these folks are TCU fans cheering for the home team (known officially as the Texas Christian University Horned Frogs) at a Saturday afternoon football game. There's a true sense of school spirit and solidarity here. And while TCU is more selective than rivals Southern Methodist and Baylor, it also has a reputation for being more accessible. "Your TCU visit experience is very personal, from the folder to your name tag, the staff want to know you for you, and not you as a number, from the very beginning," says a senior, adding, "TCU is a community, a real family."

The spacious 277-acre campus is kept in almost perfect condition and features tree-lined walkways and grassy areas. Nearby is a lovely residential neighborhood not too far from the shops and restaurants of downtown Fort Worth. The campus features an eclectic mix of architecture, ranging from neo-Georgian to contemporary. Facilities also include the Walsh Center for Performing Arts, a 56,000-square-foot performance hall and theater complex. New construction includes a two-story multipurpose building that provides multiple dining venues and common areas, as well as a residence hall that houses 160 students.

Students choose their majors from 117 disciplines, with the core curriculum embodying the base of the liberal arts education. The core emphasizes critical thinking and is divided into three areas: essential competencies; human experience and endeavors; and heritage, mission, vision, and values. There are freshman seminar courses, along with a student orientation and Frog Camp (an optional summer

> **"TCU is a community, a real family."**

camp that emphasizes team building and school spirit). TCU's standout programs are business, nursing, communication, education, and fine arts. The most popular majors are nursing, finance, communication studies, and strategic communication. In the Neeley School of Business, some students manage a $1.5 million investment portfolio that is one of the largest student-run investment funds in the nation. The university also offers an innovative dance program with a ballet major, a strong theatre internship program, and a major in ranch management. A new major in interdisciplinary inquiry was recently added.

The academic climate at TCU is challenging, but not overwhelming. "TCU students are definitely concerned about academics and grades, but there is also a feeling of support and open cooperation between students," says an English major. Classes are small, with 42 percent enrolling fewer than 20 students, which a senior says makes for "an inclusive and comfortable classroom setting." Professors often take on the role of mentors, and one student adds, "The quality of teaching is unbeatable." Academic advising receives high marks too. "My advisor is so eager to help," says a student. "I think he really enjoys giving me advice."

Top achievers may be invited to join the Roach Honors College. Participants live together in the honors dorm their first year and pursue individual research opportunities as part of their honors thesis senior year. Globally minded students travel to

Website: www.tcu.edu
Location: City Outskirts
Private
Total Enrollment: 9,831
Undergraduates: 8,574
Male/Female: 40/60
SAT Ranges: CR 530–630, M 550–650
ACT Ranges: 25–30
Financial Aid: 74%
Pell Grant: 11%
Expense: Pr $ $
Student Loans: 39%
Average Debt: $ $ $ $
Phi Beta Kappa: Yes
Applicants: 18,423
Accepted: 43%
Enrolled: 26%
Grad in 6 Years: 76%
Returning Freshmen: 90%
Academics: ✍ ✍ ✍
Social: ☎ ☎ ☎
Q of L: ★ ★ ★
Admissions: (800) TCU-FROG
Email Address: frogmail@tcu.edu

Strong Programs:
Nursing
Finance
Communication Studies
Strategic Communication
Education
Dance
Theatre
Business

45 countries to study abroad in more than 200 programs. "I would highly encourage students to get involved with Student Development Services and the Leadership Center," says a psychology and religion double major. "They offer...leadership programs that students can participate in as a first-year student and then lead as they grow older."

TCU's student body is fairly homogeneous; 52 percent are from Texas, many from affluent, conservative families. Only 11 percent of students qualify for Pell Grants, a number notably lower than the population of Pell-eligible students at upscale rival Southern Methodist. African Americans account for 5 percent of the student body, Hispanics 11 percent, and Asian Americans 3 percent; 4 percent of students are international. This is hardly an activist campus, and although TCU is affiliated with the Christian Church (Disciples of Christ), the atmosphere is not overtly religious. TCU offers merit awards averaging $15,405 and 344 athletic scholarships in 17 sports.

"My advisor is so eager to help. I think he really enjoys giving me advice."

Forty-nine percent of the student body lives on campus. Dorm life is a good experience, with up-to-date facilities and helpful staff. Many juniors and seniors move off campus, and fraternity and sorority members may live in their Greek houses after freshman year. Campus meals receives average reviews, but a variety of other options are available, and school spirit is evident even in the dining facilities. "Chick-fil-A offers Go Purple Fridays where we get free meals if we wear purple!" cheers a student. An evening transportation service, Froggy Five-O, takes you wherever you want to go on campus, and students say they feel safe. The annual, weeklong Not On My Campus campaign works to raise awareness of sexual assault, and a senior says, "I am proud of TCU for addressing it head on."

Greek life is important at TCU; 41 percent of the men and 55 percent of the women join Greek organizations. They party in the esprit de corps tradition, but there's plenty of fun left on campus and in Fort Worth to keep the non-Greek Frogs hopping. The alcohol rules on campus are fairly strict for minors and involve a three-strike system. "Alcohol violations are a big deal," one student says. Homecoming and the traditional lighting of the Christmas tree are special events, and students look forward to annual fall and spring festivals that bring big-name acts like Macklemore & Ryan Lewis and Fred Armisen to campus. "Fort Worth is cultured and has plenty of things to do," says a senior. "The stockyards let you get in touch with the inner country in you, and no one should miss a visit to Billy Bob's, the world's largest honky-tonk." Dallas is only 45 minutes to the east, and other road trips include Austin, San Antonio, the Gulf Coast, and Shreveport, Louisiana.

TCU fields 21 athletic programs, which compete in the tough Big 12 Conference. In the 2014–15 and 2015–16 seasons, the Horned Frog football, baseball, and men's tennis programs all won conference championships. Ten TCU teams were nationally ranked in the 2015–16 season, with the women's rifle and equestrian teams each finishing second nationally. Intramurals are a popular choice with students as well.

Overlaps

Baylor, Southern Methodist, University of Texas at Austin, Texas A&M, University of Alabama, University of North Texas, University of Southern California, University of Oklahoma

From its student-friendly admissions process to its dedication to supporting and developing students once they arrive on campus, TCU is an accessible university offering a personalized educational experience. Its warm, spirited student body completes the feeling of community. "TCU is welcoming," confirms a senior. "That's why I came as a freshman and stayed until graduation."

If You Apply To ➤ **TCU:** Early decision and early action I: Nov. 1. Early action II: Jan. 1. Regular decision: Feb. 15. Financial aid: Feb. 15. Housing: May 1. Application fee: $40. Campus interviews: optional, evaluative. No alumni interviews. SATs or ACTs: required. No Subject Tests. Letters of recommendation: required. Essay: required. Accepts the Common Application. Optional Freedom of Expression question allows space for any information not included elsewhere in application.

Texas Tech University

Lubbock, TX 79409

A child of the remote West Texas plains, Texas Tech is emerging from the large shadow of Texas A&M as one of the state's top research universities. It takes big-time sports to be on the map in Texas, and the Red Raiders have taken up the challenge. Bills itself as smaller and more personal than UT or A&M.

Texas Tech University has come a long way from its humble beginnings. It opened its doors in 1925 in the West Texas city of Lubbock with fewer than 1,000 students, and courses in the liberal arts, agriculture, engineering, and home economics. Today, Tech hosts more than 25,000 undergraduates, more than 500 student organizations, hundreds of academic programs, and schools of medicine and law, and it aspires to become a leading research university on the national level. "We are enjoying increasing emphasis on undergraduate research, service learning and community engagement, personal and professional ethics, and internationalization," administrators say.

Tech's 1,839-acre campus features expansive lawns, impressive landscaping, and Spanish Renaissance-style red-tile-roofed buildings. The school has completed more than $1 billion in construction projects in recent years, including the West Village Residential Complex and the Bayer Plant Science Building. Tech also has a slew of other facilities around Texas, such as a 16,000-acre agricultural facility and research farm.

The university's 10 undergraduate colleges and schools boast more than 150 degree programs. Tech's general education requirements span all of the colleges and schools, and include courses in written and oral communication, math, natural science, humanities, visual and performing arts, social and behavioral sciences, and multiculturalism. Most degree programs include a capstone course as well. The College of Agricultural Sciences and Natural Resources "has the strongest financial foothold on campus, with the largest endowment," says an economics major. "Within the College of Human Sciences lies the department of personal and family financial planning, the best of its type in the country." Mechanical engineering, kinesiology, sport management, and accounting are among the most popular majors, and the business and music programs are also well regarded.

> **"Each year that I have been here, the classes have gotten harder and the professors more experienced."**

Despite Tech's massive size, 79 percent of classes have fewer than 50 students. "The academic climate is very strong," says one senior. "Each year that I have been here, the classes have gotten harder and the professors more experienced." Those professors "have changed my life and made me think for myself," explains a communication studies major. Graduate assistants may lead discussion sections or labs, but they aren't the main force at the lectern. A one-credit freshman seminar helps with the transition from high school to college, and learning communities provide students with ample service-learning opportunities.

Outstanding students may enroll in Tech's Honors College, where they sit on committees, help with recruiting, make decisions about course content, and evaluate faculty. They can also work on research projects, either independently (with a professor's guidance) or as part of a student/faculty team. Tech invested $2 million in undergraduate research in one recent year, and about 2,500 students participated, investigating topics such as pain management, wind engineering, and sick-building syndrome. Those yearning to leave the hardscrabble plains of Texas may study abroad in more than 70 countries; Tech also has its own campus in Seville, Spain,

---

Website: www.ttu.edu
Location: City Center
Public
Total Enrollment: 30,257
Undergraduates: 26,055
Male/Female: 55/45
SAT Ranges: CR 510–600, M 520–620
ACT Ranges: 23–27
Financial Aid: 52%
Pell Grant: 23%
Expense: Pub $ $
Student Loans: 55%
Average Debt: $ $ $
Phi Beta Kappa: Yes
Applicants: 23,010
Accepted: 63%
Enrolled: 36%
Grad in 6 Years: 60%
Returning Freshmen: 84%
Academics: ✍ ✍ ✍
Social: ☎ ☎ ☎
Q of L: ★ ★ ★
Admissions: (806) 742-1480
Email Address: admissions@ttu.edu

Strong Programs:
Mechanical Engineering
Kinesiology
Sport Management
Accounting
Agriculture
Personal Financial Planning
Business
Music

where courses are taught by Tech professors (in English and Spanish) and students live with local families.

The Tech student body is largely homegrown; 92 percent hail from the Lone Star State and 2 percent come from foreign nations. "'Techsans' are truly down-to-earth and friendly," says one student. "We come from small, West Texas towns and some of the largest cities in the United States." African Americans account for 6 percent of the undergraduate population, Hispanics 23 percent, and Asian Americans 3 percent. Diversity and the role of Greek life on campus are among the hottest political and social issues. Tech offers merit scholarships worth an average of $3,516, as well as 333 athletic awards in 17 varsity sports. Elite chess players can vie for a handful of scholarships as well. Twenty-three percent of freshmen are Pell-eligible. The Red Raider Guarantee offers free tuition and fees to qualified freshmen who are Texas residents and whose families earn less than $40,000 per year.

Only 25 percent of the students at Tech live in the dorms, mainly freshmen who are required to do so. "The dorms are the ultimate college experience," says one senior. Co-ed, single-sex, and quiet study dorms are available, as are 19 living/learning communities. Dining options are plentiful, and a junior says, "Whether you're a vegetarian or on a protein diet, you'll eat well here." About 50 restaurants in the area also take the university's Tech Express debit card, and many have student specials one night a week. Under Texas law, people are permitted to carry firearms on campus. Blue-light emergency phones and a safe-ride shuttle service help students feel safe, and the newly created Risk Intervention and Safety Education office is working to prevent sexual violence and support personal wellness on campus.

> **"Whether you're a vegetarian or on a protein diet, you'll eat well here."**

Tech is officially dry and "punishments are quite harsh" for those who attempt to skirt the university's alcohol policies, a senior warns. Since so many students live off campus, that's where most of the weekend action is. Still, the more than 500 student organizations offer plenty of activities to keep students busy on campus. Four percent of the men pledge fraternities and 8 percent of the women join sororities, so a sizable contingent heads to the parties at Greek Circle. The Depot District is also a popular destination, as most bars and clubs admit anyone 18 and over.

The city of Lubbock (population 240,000) offers many opportunities to get involved with the community through work with the Boys & Girls Clubs of America, Habitat for Humanity, animal shelters, or Bible study at local churches. Annual traditions include homecoming, complete with a chili cook-off; the Carol of Lights during the first weekend in December; and Arbor Day, when hundreds of students fan out across campus to plant flowers and trees for the spring. Popular road trips include any of the four nearby lakes (for picnicking, boating, or camping), skiing in New Mexico (four hours away), and anywhere the Red Raiders are playing, especially if it's against the University of Texas Longhorns.

The Division I Red Raiders compete in the Big 12 Conference, and the football, baseball, and men's track and field teams are among the school's best. When the football team takes the field, the Masked Rider, replete with red and black cape and cowboy hat, motivates the crowd by galloping up and down the sidelines. Women's soccer claimed the conference championship in 2015; softball and men's and women's tennis and cross-country are strong too. The university's livestock and meat judging teams have also won several national championships in recent years. Intramural sports, which attract more than 50 percent of undergraduates, include everything from the typical soccer and flag football to mud volleyball, dodgeball, and table tennis.

Texas Tech has come a long way in a short time and over the past 90 years has done much to carve out its own niche. "We have a good mix of 'small-town' students and 'big-town' students," says a communications major. If you can stand the heat and relative isolation of the West Texas Plains, and the effort it takes to be more than a number at a school of this size, Texas Tech may be worth a look.

<table>
<tr><td>If You Apply To ➤</td><td>Texas Tech: Rolling admissions. (Priority deadline: Feb. 1.) Financial aid: Mar. 1. Application fee: $75. No campus or alumni interviews. SATs or ACTs: required. Subject Tests: optional. Letters of recommendation: recommended. Essay: recommended.</td></tr>
</table>

University of Toronto: See page 373.

Trinity College

300 Summit Street, Hartford, CT 06106

Long known both for its quality academics and its well-to-do students, Trinity is shaking up its admissions practices and diversifying its student body. Abundant community-based learning and service opportunities take imaginative advantage of the school's troubled urban setting. Trinity joins Lafayette, Smith, Swarthmore, and Union as a small liberal arts college that offers engineering.

For students at Trinity College, the learning experience doesn't stop at the campus borders. At first glance, the small liberal arts college and the large, gritty city of Hartford, Connecticut, seem like an uneasy match. But instead of insulating itself from outside problems, Trinity takes advantage of its surroundings by using Hartford as its classroom. In addition to the Learning Corridor, a $175 million community revitalization effort led by Trinity in the late 1990s and composed of an eclectic mix of schools, Trinity partnered with Hartford Public Schools to create in 2011 the Hartford Magnet Trinity College Academy, a public middle/high school designed to prepare students for college-level work. On campus, academic standards continue to rise, and students graduate with a strong liberal arts background. "Students are the priority here," says one senior. "The personal attention I found at Trinity is unrivaled."

Splendid Gothic-style stone buildings behind wrought-iron fences decorate Trinity's 100-acre campus. The large, grassy quadrangle is home to pickup games of hackeysack and lazy relaxation on warm spring and fall afternoons. Along with revitalizing the neighborhood that surrounds it, Trinity's campus is undergoing its own revitalization, including the creation of the Gates Quadrangle. Recent renovations include the restoration and modernization of the "Long Walk" dormitory and classroom facilities in some of the college's original buildings. The college also recently completed construction of the Crescent Street Townhouses, which provide accommodations for 340 upperclassmen.

> **"The personal attention I found at Trinity is unrivaled."**

Trinity's general education requirements include one course each in the arts, humanities, natural sciences, numerical and symbolic reasoning, and social sciences. Students must also demonstrate proficiency in writing and mathematics and fulfill a foreign language requirement. The First-Year Seminar emphasizes writing, speaking, and critical thinking; the seminar instructor serves as students' academic advisor. Freshmen may also choose one of four "gateway" programs in the arts; natural

Website: www.trincoll.edu
Location: City Center
Private
Total Enrollment: 2,138
Undergraduates: 2,137
Male/Female: 53/47
SAT Ranges: CR 570–670, M 580–670
ACT Ranges: 27–30
Financial Aid: 43%
Pell Grant: 10%
Expense: Pr $ $ $ $
Student Loans: 43%
Average Debt: $ $ $
Phi Beta Kappa: Yes
Applicants: 7,570
Accepted: 33%
Enrolled: 22%
Grad in 6 Years: 86%
Returning Freshmen: 88%
Academics: ✍ ✍ ✍ ✍
Social: ☎ ☎ ☎ ☎
Q of L: ★ ★ ★
Admissions: (860) 297-2180
Email Address: admissions.office@trincoll.edu

(continued)

Strong Programs:
English
Economics
Computer Science
Engineering

sciences; European cultures; or the history, culture, and future of cities, which one student calls "phenomenal—very challenging and rewarding." A global engagement requirement can be completed by coursework or study abroad.

Students give rave reviews to Trinity's English, economics, and computer science departments, and say the school's small but accredited engineering program is likewise strong. That department sponsors the Fire-Fighting Home Robot Contest, the largest public robotics competition in the U.S., open to entrants of any age, ability, and experience. Through the BEACON program, biomedical engineering students can take courses at UConn, the UConn Health Center, and the University of Hartford while conducting research at three area health centers. Trinity's close ties to the community also are apparent in the curriculum; students can take courses on urban development and the history of the city of Hartford, or choose from service-learning courses that incorporate opportunities to work with more than 80 local community service organizations.

Faculty/student collaboration is a tradition at Trinity. Two-thirds of students work with professors on research and scholarly papers, and many students join their mentors to present findings at symposia. "The academic climate is rigorous but not overly competitive," says a senior. Seventy-three percent of classes have fewer than 20 students. Students say that professors have high expectations of students, and most go the extra mile to provide support. "The quality of teaching is truly outstanding," says a student. "Most professors are distinguished as authorities in their fields."

Through the BEACON program, biomedical engineering students can conduct research at three area health centers.

More than half of the students seek internships in businesses, government (including the Legislative Internship Program at the state capital), and nonprofit organizations in Hartford (the insurance capital of the world), and some also take terms at other schools through the Twelve College Exchange*. Trinity's study-away program includes Trinity's own international program sites in Cape Town, Rome, Barcelona, Vienna, Buenos Aires, Port of Spain, Shanghai, and Paris, as well as more than 90 approved and affiliated programs. Other enticing choices include the Trinity/La MaMa Urban Arts program in New York City; the Washington Semester* in D.C.; the Associated Colleges of the Midwest* program in Chicago; and the SEA Semester* at Woods Hole.

Under a new president, Trinity has retreated from its recent policy of consistently increasing freshman enrollment, a practice that undermined the academic quality of entering students and strained faculty resources. It has also become test-optional in its admissions and has reintroduced optional essays that encourage students to write about their interest in Trinity and its Hartford home. Although the school has had a reputation for enrolling, in the words of a sophomore, "prep school students from privileged families," it is moving away from its traditionally heavy

"[Hartford offers] unique opportunities for internships, mentoring, and community service."

recruitment of New England boarding school grads, seeking to diversify the student body. Sixteen percent of Trinity students are Connecticut natives; an increasing number come from California, and 11 percent are international. Asian Americans account for 4 percent of the student body, Hispanics 7 percent, and African Americans 6 percent. Although no one would mistake the campus for a political hot zone, students remain aware of global issues and local concerns. The college offers no athletic scholarships, but does provide special financial packages to replace student loans for students with the most need. In addition, the majority of admissions decisions are made without regard to financial considerations, and the college guarantees to meet the full demonstrated need for four years.

Ninety-one percent of Trinity's students live in the co-ed dorms. Each incoming class is assigned to one of five Houses in residential clusters. Freshmen must eat in

Trinity's dining hall. The Bistro, an upscale but reasonable café, is another choice for students on the meal plan, and others hibernate in the Cave, which offers sandwiches and grilled fare. Overall, students report the campus dining options to be edible and adequate.

"The social life revolves around on-campus activity," a sophomore says. Students praise the Trinity College Activities Council, which brings in comedians and musical performers and organizes parties, study breaks, and community service days. "The campus dances are very popular with the entire student body," says a senior. The Underground Coffeehouse and the Bistro's weekly comedy nights are also student favorites. But the action on Thursday, Friday, and Saturday nights is mostly at the Greek houses (20 percent of the men and 16 percent of the women join up). An effort by the administration to force the single-gender organizations to go co-ed was abandoned after houses failed to attract members of the opposite sex and alumni donors with Greek ties pulled back. Students say alcohol is not hard to come by, but "the campus policies on alcohol are fairly severe on underage drinkers and abusers," says a student. Spring Weekend brings bands to campus for a three-day party outdoors. Popular road trips include Montreal, Boston, New York City, and the beaches and mountains of Maine.

Trinity's location in Hartford has been problematic; some students describe the surrounding area as "scary" and "a terrible college town." In part because Connecticut has not done a good job of investing in its cities, downtown Hartford does not attract visitors from outside the city, and the administration worries about urban problems, such as drugs thrown through dorm windows. Even so, one philosophy major says things are improving: "Hartford has a terrific assortment of restaurants, ranging from cheap but delicious ethnic fare to upscale, parent-friendly places." A college-sponsored "culture van" takes students downtown to catch a show at the Bushnell or visit the Wadsworth Atheneum, the nation's oldest public art museum. Many see the city's troubles as offering "unique opportunities for internships, mentoring, and community service," according to a sophomore. The Office of Community Service and Civic Engagement coordinates opportunities for students to work and learn in the city. Students have created and run organizations that provide housing, tutoring, meals, and other services to youth, families, and senior citizens.

Trinity's Bantams compete in Division III, and thanks to its international recruits, both men's and women's squash are powerhouses (the men's team has won 15 national titles in the last 18 years). Other solid programs include men's and women's rowing, baseball, and women's lacrosse. Homecoming typically brings Wesleyan or Amherst to campus for a football game, which gets under way after Trinity students burn the opposing school's letter on the quad. Fifty percent of students take part in the intramural and club sports programs.

Trinity is ahead of the curve in liberal arts education, and, a sophomore says, "you can appreciate it much better if you are interested in more than one subject." Even more importantly, Trinity students have taken their civic responsibility to heart. "Our average student is self-motivated and active, whether it be in sports or in clubs or community service," a senior says. "It's a place where everyone can have their voice heard."

Service-learning courses incorporate opportunities to work with more than 80 local community service organizations.

"You can appreciate [Trinity] much better if you are interested in more than one subject."

The men's squash team has won 15 national titles in the last 18 years.

Overlaps
Boston College, Boston University, Brown, Colby, Tufts

If You Apply To ➤ **Trinity College:** Early decision I: Nov. 15. Early decision II and regular decision: Jan. 1. Financial aid: Feb. 1. Application fee: $65. Campus interviews: recommended, evaluative. Alumni interviews: optional, evaluative. SATs or ACTs: optional. Subject Tests: optional. Letters of recommendation: required. Essay: required. Accepts the Common Application.

Trinity College Dublin: See page 390.

Trinity University

One Trinity Place, San Antonio, TX 78212-7200

One of the few quality Southwestern liberal arts colleges in a major city. Trinity is twice as big as nearby rivals Austin College and Southwestern University and offers a diverse curriculum that includes business, education, and engineering in addition to the liberal arts. Upscale and conservative. San Antonio runs neck and neck with Austin as the most desirable city in Texas.

Website: www.trinity.edu
Location: City Center
Private
Total Enrollment: 2,381
Undergraduates: 2,223
Male/Female: 47/53
SAT Ranges: CR 580–690,
   M 580–680
ACT Ranges: 27–32
Financial Aid: 90%
Pell Grant: 15%
Expense: Pr $
Student Loans: 51%
Average Debt: $ $ $ $
Phi Beta Kappa: Yes
Applicants: 5,563
Accepted: 48%
Enrolled: 23%
Grad in 6 Years: 81%
Returning Freshmen: 90%
Academics: ✑ ✑ ✑
Social: ☎ ☎ ☎
Q of L: ★ ★ ★
Admissions: (800) 874-6489
Email Address: admissions@
   trinity.edu

Strong Programs:
Business Administration
Biology
Communication
Economics
Education
Engineering
Accounting
Chinese

Trinity University is a small school with big bucks. Thanks to that liquid that gushes out of the Texas soil, Trinity has one of the nation's largest educational endowments at a school its size. The wealth is used unashamedly to lure capable students with bargain tuition rates and to entice talented professors from around the nation. The result? A student body composed of smart, ambitious men and women, and a stellar faculty. Students here enjoy challenges but still manage a laid-back Texas attitude. "It's friendly, warm, personal, engaged, and academically stimulating," a senior says.

Trinity was founded in a small central Texas town just after the end of the Civil War. In 1952, the school moved to its current location, a residential area about three miles from downtown San Antonio, one of the most beautiful cities in the Southwest. The 117-acre campus, filled with the Southern architecture of O'Neil Ford, is located on what was once a rock quarry. Everything fits the school's aesthetically pleasing and somewhat well-to-do image, from the uniform redbrick buildings to the stately pathways that wind along gorgeous green lawns and through immaculate gardens spotted with Henry Moore sculptures. Trinity's most dominant landmark is Murchison Tower, which rises in the center of campus and is visible from numerous vantage points throughout San Antonio. The university recently completed the Center for the Sciences and Innovation, a 280,000-square-foot, state-of-the-art, LEED-certified integrated science and engineering center.

> **"People are smart and competitive, but they are also willing to help one another."**

Trinity has implemented a new general education curriculum, called Pathways, which contains five new signature curricular elements: the Enhanced First-Year Experience; Core Capacities (Written, Oral, and Visual Communication; Digital Literacy; and Engaged Citizenship); Approaches to Creation and Analysis (the humanities, the arts and creative disciplines, the social and behavioral sciences, the natural sciences, and quantitative disciplines); Interdisciplinary Clusters; and Experiential Learning. Trinity has a highly praised education department, with a five-year Master of Arts in Teaching program and a good health professionals advising program. Other strong departments include economics, business, engineering, and chemistry. The communication department offers students hands-on training with television equipment or the chance to produce a newscast. The five-year accounting program allows students to serve an internship with the big four accounting firms in offices around the nation while earning a salary and receiving college credit. Trinity has one of the fastest-growing Chinese language programs in the country, and the Languages Across the Curriculum program features classes such as business, religion, and anthropology taught in languages including German, Spanish, and Russian.

Students report that the academics are demanding, but the climate is not competitive. "The courses can be rigorous and thought-provoking, challenging and inspiring," says a junior. Another student adds, "The people are smart and competitive, but they are also willing to help one another and are generally modest about their level of intelligence." The classes at Trinity are small; 63 percent have fewer than 20 students, and freshmen are assigned to a faculty advisor and to mentor groups of 10 to 15 students for academic and guidance counseling, as well as peer tutoring from upperclassmen. The professors at Trinity are "available, brilliant, and helpful," according to a junior. "They always hold office hours for students to come in and talk or ask questions." Forty-five percent of students participate in research projects with faculty mentors, while 38 percent study abroad in locations as varied as Madrid, Shanghai, and Cuba.

> "[Residence halls are] fantastic, with walk-in closets, private balconies, suite-style rooms, and a cleaning service."

The school makes a concerted effort to maintain its admissions standards, keeping enrollment low and recruiting high achievers with greater energy than is possible from larger universities. Seventy percent of Trinity students are Texans, and 7 percent are international. The school is fairly diverse; Hispanics alone account for 20 percent, Asian Americans another 6 percent, and African Americans 4 percent. Politically, the campus leans conservative, and activism isn't a main focus for most students. Merit scholarships averaging $17,955 are available to academically gifted students; there are no athletic scholarships.

Trinity requires students to live on campus through their junior year. In fact, 77 percent of the students live in the residence halls, which one student describes as "fantastic, with walk-in closets, private balconies, suite-style rooms, and a cleaning service." Residence halls are co-ed by suite, with one single-sex residence hall that is off-limits to freshmen; all rooms are wired for cable and the Internet. "We are spoiled!" boasts one junior. Most seniors move off campus so they can have single rooms. Campus dining is "delicious," according to a student. "I've been eating on campus for four years and I'm still not sick of the food."

"Most of the social life occurs on campus," says a philosophy major. "There are over 100 student organizations that put events on every weekend. You more often than not have to choose which event you are going to attend as opposed to whether or not to attend an event." Seventeen percent of the men and 29 percent of the women join the local fraternity and sorority organizations. Most of the parties are within walking distance of the school and are primarily hosted by Greek groups—but open to all students. Country line dancing is also a popular activity, and the university sponsors an excellent lecture series that brings notable politicians and public figures to campus. Beer and wine may be consumed on Trinity's campus by those of legal age in any of the upper-class residence halls, except for designated substance-free floors. The school year kicks off with a party at the school's bell tower, which students can climb to get a knockout view of San Antonio. Students look forward to the Tigerfest dance and parade on homecoming weekend and the Chili Cook-Off that pits Greek and other clubs against one another. They also anticipate Fiesta, a weeklong, annual celebration of San Antonio's mixed culture that features bands, dancing, food, and drink.

> "There are no rivalries in sports since we win at everything."

San Antonio, with its famed River Walk, receives a well-deserved "thumbs-up" from students. "San Antonio is a great place to be, because there are so many things to do. That being said, you need a car to get almost anywhere," says one student. And it doesn't hurt that the city is home to several colleges. Students frequent the many outdoor shops and cafés in the historic Pearl district, as well as touristy hangouts such as Six Flags and SeaWorld. There are also many cultural and musical attractions

The five-year accounting program allows students to serve an internship while earning a salary and receiving college credit.

The school year kicks off with a party at the school's bell tower, which students can climb to get a knockout view of San Antonio.

and students get involved in city life by contributing more than 60,000 hours of community service every year. The city's beautiful, warm weather provides plenty of activities for the students year-round, but there are also many fun road trips. The funky state capital of Austin is 90 miles north, and students can also road-trip to the Texas Gulf Coast and the Hill Country.

Trinity's varsity sports teams compete in the Division III Southern Collegiate Athletic Conference. One student brags, "there are no rivalries in sports since we win at everything." The baseball team won the national championship in 2016, the first Division III Texas team to do so. Other successful Tiger teams include volleyball and men's and women's soccer and tennis, all of which make regular NCAA Tournament appearances. Football and basketball are strong too. About two-thirds of students take advantage of intramural, club, and recreational sports; flag football is the most popular.

A big state and big money give students at this small university many of the advantages of a larger school. If you are looking for a small community feel with quality professors, look no further than Trinity. "It is a very nice campus, students hold a lot of school pride, and the teachers are very welcoming," one satisfied student says.

If You Apply To ➤ | **Trinity University:** Early decision I and early action I: Nov. 1. Early decision II and early action II: Jan. 1. Regular decision: Feb. 1. Financial aid: Feb. 15. Housing: May 1. No application fee. Campus and alumni interviews: optional, evaluative. SATs or ACTs: required. Subject Tests: optional. Letters of recommendation: required. Essay: required. Accepts the Common Application.

Truman State University

100 East Normal, Kirksville, MO 63501

Truman has more in common with private institutions than with nondescript regional publics. Looking for a public ivy niche like Miami of Ohio and William and Mary. Rural setting encourages strong focus on academics. Nearly a quarter of the students are from out of state, mainly from Illinois.

Truman State University, Missouri's only public liberal arts college, attracts overachievers from across the Show-Me State. Founded in 1867 as a regional teacher training institution, the school became a statewide university in 1985 and 11 years later took the name of the only Missourian to serve as a president of the United States. Indeed, since shifting to a liberal arts and sciences mission, Truman has worked to become a "public ivy" on the order of Miami University (OH) or the College of William and Mary. True, the small town of Kirksville, Missouri, is no Williamsburg, Virginia—or even Oxford, Ohio. But the school's relative isolation makes it easier to concentrate on academics. "I would call Truman a nerd school," says one focused physics and mathematics double major. "Nearly everyone at Truman is there to learn first, so education and work take priority over almost everything else."

"Education and work take priority over almost everything else."

Truman is located in the northeastern corner of Missouri, about 200 miles from both Kansas City and St. Louis. The flower-laden campus includes approximately 40 buildings on 210 acres, many of which are Georgian in style—in fact, the oldest portion of the campus, dating to 1873, is modeled on Thomas Jefferson's University of

Virginia. The Robison Planetarium and Multimedia Theater is the campus's newest facility, and renovations to all seven residence halls were recently completed.

Truman's general education requirements revolve around the liberal arts and sciences. The Liberal Studies Program forms the core of all academic majors; students must complete six "Modes of Inquiry," which include courses in fine arts, math, science, philosophy/religion, humanities, foreign language, and social science. Students take an interdisciplinary, writing-enhanced seminar in their junior year, and all students complete a capstone course. All first-year students are required to participate in a one-day orientation session during the summer as well as the weeklong Truman Transformation, which is designed to help freshmen adjust to college life.

The most popular major is exercise science; business administration, psychology, and biology round out the list of programs with the highest enrollment. An interdisciplinary studies major allows students to combine coursework from two or more disciplines to create a specialized major. Nursing is a traditional strength, and there are also five-year programs for students interested in education or accounting, which culminate in the awarding of bachelor's and master's degrees.

"Truman's academic climate is very competitive. Each student wants to do the best, and it is a consistent challenge to try to do better than a classmate," says one junior. "Academics are taken seriously at Truman," agrees another student, "and professors work hard to create a valuable and intellectually engaging learning experience." Ninety-eight percent of classes have fewer than 50 students, which makes access to professors the norm, but some students warn that it can be difficult to get a seat in essential required courses, especially in the sciences. A health science major says, "Most professors are warm and helpful. They love teaching and have a real passion for the material." Students praise the career center as well, and a freshman notes, "There are tons of seminars to talk about practical ways to improve your hirability."

The Honors Scholar program offers a challenging curriculum to motivated students; since Truman State is considered Missouri's "honors college," all students are welcome to participate. Study abroad opportunities are available in roughly 500 programs in more than 65 countries around the world; 20 percent of students participate. About 40 percent of students conduct independent research or collaborate with faculty members on research projects, and Truman typically sends one of the largest delegations of undergraduates to the National Conference on Undergraduate Research every year.

"Students at Truman are academically minded and super involved in extracurricular activities," offers one junior. Seventy-six percent of Truman students are native to Missouri, and 7 percent hail from abroad. Hispanics comprise 3 percent and Asian Americans 2 percent of the student body; African Americans add 4 percent. Social and political issues are met with much discussion and debate. "The biggest social issues tend to be LGBT rights and empowerment. The attitude toward this is supportive and accepting," says one student. Merit scholarships are available to qualified students; the average award is $5,489. The school also hands out 335 athletic scholarships in 16 sports. Twenty-four percent of students are eligible for the Pell Grant. Additionally, the Truman Access Grant provides funding to a limited number of students who have unmet need after their federal financial aid and Truman scholarship award have been packaged.

> **"There are tons of seminars to talk about practical ways to improve your hirability."**

Forty-eight percent of Truman students live on campus in the residence halls, and "each hallway is decorated so they have more of a warm feeling—not like the feel of a prison," a junior says. Students say it's easy to get a room, but most students seek less expensive options off campus after their sophomore year. Campus

(continued)

Accepted: 79%
Enrolled: 41%
Grad in 6 Years: 73%
Returning Freshmen: 89%
Academics: ✍ ✍ ✍
Social: ☎ ☎ ☎
Q of L: ★ ★ ★
Admissions: (660) 785-4114
Email Address: admissions@ truman.edu

Strong Programs:
Exercise Science
Business Administration
Psychology
Biology
Nursing
Education
Accounting

Since Truman State is considered Missouri's "honors college," all students are welcome to participate in the Honors Scholar program.

dining is described as "average" and "tolerable" and campus safety as adequate. "There is a full-time staff of police officers who operate only on Truman's campus," says a junior.

Social life at Truman is robust, according to students. "Because of Truman's semi-isolated location, the Student Activities Board brings in various musicians, comedians, YouTube stars, speakers, and performers to campus for free," explains a freshman. The Greek system plays an integral part in Truman's social life; 27 percent of men and 24 percent of women sign up. Since the campus is dry, according to an exercise science major, "Most parties take place off campus, where they're hosted by Greek organizations, athletic teams, or one of the five bars in town." Students also venture out on road trips to St. Louis, Kansas City, various destinations in Iowa, and Quincy, Illinois. Everyone looks forward to homecoming in the fall and the Final Blowout carnival in the spring, with wacky games, inflatables, free food, and prizes.

The town of Kirksville (population 17,500) grows on you, say students. "All of the essentials of a college town are present, including a Walmart, a bowling alley, a good movie theater, and a beautiful state park," a business administration major says. Two-thirds of students take advantage of various opportunities to get involved in volunteer work and service learning. The Big Event is a popular one-day service event that brings more than 1,500 campus volunteers to Kirksville. Truman hosts 12 service organizations, which provide thousands of hours of service every year.

When not competing academically, Truman's Bulldogs, members of the Great Lakes Valley Conference, are succeeding in the pool and on the playing field. The men's and women's swim teams have won multiple Division II titles, the women's team most recently in 2016. The baseball and softball teams each reached their respective national tournaments in 2015, and the women's volleyball team is also competitive. Truman's Forensics Team, the school's longest-running cocurricular activity, has brought home several state titles. About one-third of students participate in more than 30 intramurals, which include everything from basketball and soccer to pickleball and baggo.

"With the highest admissions standards of any public university in the state, Truman has a distinct culture of academic excellence," says a student. Indeed, Truman State offers challenging academics, pursued within a close-knit community. Though its rural Missouri location can feel isolating, its bargain-basement price is certainly worth considering. "Truman offers an incredibly well-rounded college experience," says one history major. "Not only do we have challenging and rewarding academics, but we also have more than 200 organizations to get involved with that can change your college experience."

Overlaps

University of Missouri, Missouri State, Saint Louis University, University of Missouri–Kansas City, Missouri S&T, Rockhurst, Washington University in St. Louis, Maryville

If You Apply To ➤

Truman State: Rolling admissions. Priority deadline: Dec. 1. Priority financial aid: Feb. 1. Housing: May 1. No application fee. Campus interviews: optional, informational. No alumni interviews. SATs or ACTs: required. No Subject Tests. Letters of recommendation: optional. Essay: required. Accepts the Common Application with supplement.

Tufts University

Bendetson Hall, Medford, MA 02155

One of the smallest and most undergraduate-focused of the major research universities, Tufts is known for its global focus. Strengths run the gamut from classics and philosophy to engineering and international relations, and opportunities for undergraduate research abound. Located just outside student-friendly Boston, it has more in common with Brown than any other Ivy. Compare to other top urban schools such as Georgetown, Northwestern, and Wash U. The Experimental College lets student take nontraditional courses for credit.

Once considered a safety school for those who couldn't get into an Ivy, Tufts isn't so safe anymore. Applications are up dramatically, propelling Tufts into the ranks of the more selective schools in the country. With its strong academics, high-achieving student body, and attractive setting, some might say that not all that much more separates Tufts University from its illustrious neighbors, Harvard and MIT, than a few stops on the T. Says one senior, "Tufts is a school for people who aren't afraid to speak their mind but are also open to having someone change their mind."

Tufts's 150-acre, tree-lined campus on Walnut Hill overlooks the heart of nearby Boston and is a striking scene. The main campus, with its brick and stone buildings, sits on the Medford/Somerville boundary. Medford, the fifth-oldest city in the country, was a powerful shipbuilding center during the 19th century. Somerville lies adjacent to the Tufts campus, and in 1776, the first American flag was raised on its Prospect Hill. For years, Tufts, founded in 1852 by Universalist businessman Charles Tufts, has devoted resources to traditional areas of graduate strength—medicine, dentistry, veterinary, and diplomacy—as well as new ventures, such as a Nutrition Research Center. In 2016, Tufts acquired the School of the Museum of Fine Arts in Boston, expanding opportunities for study in fine arts and design.

Undergraduate teaching is what attracts students to Tufts. They get highly personalized attention from faculty, and they enjoy wide freedom to pursue independent study and to complete research and internships for credit. Tufts students also get a healthy diet of traditional academic fare. For liberal arts students, distribution requirements include a World Civilization course in addition to art, English and foreign languages, social sciences, humanities, natural sciences, and math. Engineers must take six courses in the arts, humanities, and social sciences, with one of those fulfilling a writing requirement. The most popular majors include international relations, economics, biology, and engineering. Tufts also boasts strong classics and philosophy departments, and there is an excellent child study and human development program. Interdisciplinary programs such as human factors engineering (or, engineering psychology) are growing in popularity as well, and a new science, technology, and society program has recently been added.

> "Professors are willing to sit with you and explain topics you don't understand…or give you general advice on life."

Tufts has two popular programs in which students who need a break from being students can develop and teach courses: the Experimental College, which annually offers more than 100 nontraditional, full-credit courses taught by students, faculty, and outside lecturers; and the Freshman Explorations seminars, taught by two upperclassmen and a faculty member. Explorations courses are a way for freshmen to get to know each other and ease into the college experience, since the teachers double as advisors. Recent Experimental College offerings include Race in Human Development, American Witches, and Pharmacology and Therapeutics.

Website: www.tufts.edu
Location: Suburban
Private
Total Enrollment: 10,143
Undergraduates: 5,196
Male/Female: 50/50
SAT Ranges: CR 680–750, M 690–770
ACT Ranges: 30–33
Financial Aid: 51%
Pell Grant: 11%
Expense: Pr $ $ $ $
Student Loans: 38%
Average Debt: $ $
Phi Beta Kappa: Yes
Applicants: 19,063
Accepted: 16%
Enrolled: 44%
Grad in 6 Years: 92%
Returning Freshmen: 97%
Academics: ✍ ✍ ✍ ✍ ½
Social: 🏮 🏮 🏮
Q of L: ★ ★ ★ ★
Admissions: (617) 627-3170
Email Address: undergraduate.admissions@tufts.edu

Strong Programs:
International Relations
Economics
Biology
Engineering
Classics
Philosophy
Child Study and Human Development
Human Factors Engineering

"The academics are tough but rewarding," says one junior, and students agree that the atmosphere is supportive and collaborative, rather than competitive. Sixty-seven percent of classes have fewer than 20 students, and most courses are taught by full professors, who are praised for being "knowledgeable, engaging, and caring." "Professors are willing to sit with you and explain topics you don't understand, give recommendations on research opportunities, or give you general advice on life," says an economics and international relations double major.

For those looking to get off campus, Tufts offers the Washington Semester*, exchanges with Swarthmore and Spelman, and cross-registration at a number of Boston schools. Tufts is among the top 10 research universities for the percentage of undergrads who study abroad—at 42 percent—and frequently ranks as one of the top Peace Corps suppliers. Students may choose to spend their summer at Tufts's overseas campus in Talloires, France, embark on a semester or year abroad at one of more than 170 preapproved programs, or select one of Tufts's own full-immersion programs in nine countries around the globe. The Institute for Global Leadership includes the popular, interdisciplinary Education for Public Inquiry and International Citizenship (EPIIC) program. The yearlong intensive experience revolves around a theme and includes a weekly colloquium, international symposium, and a research project or internship. Recent EPIIC themes have been The Future of Europe and Global Health and Security.

"We're proud of our different interests and quirks."

"We're proud of our different interests and quirks, and that's what makes the student body so vibrant," says a senior. Twenty-four percent of students hail from Massachusetts; New Jersey, New York, and California are also well represented. The university's reputation in international relations attracts a substantial number of international students (12 percent) and Americans living abroad. Asian Americans make up 11 percent of the population, Hispanics 6 percent, and African Americans 4 percent. The campus is largely liberal, and many students are enthusiastically engaged in social and political issues, to the point that student activism itself has become a hot-button topic. "The level of social activism has caused a fissure in the student body between those who are fighting for a cause and those who channel their energies elsewhere," remarks a senior. No merit or athletic scholarships are available, but several prepayment and loan options are, and in the past the school has met the full demonstrated need of all admits. There are additional financial incentives for students from low-income families.

Sixty-five percent of students live on campus. Accommodations in the Uphill and Downhill (the two quads joined by a great expanse of grass and trees) campus dorms vary from long hallways of double rooms to apartment-like suites, old houses, and co-ops—and a good-natured rivalry exists between the two areas. Freshmen and sophomores must live on campus in the dorms, while upperclassmen compete in a lottery or move to affordable apartments just a short walk from campus. "When you're a freshman, go all-freshman housing. Nothing is more special than a community of all freshmen where everyone's looking for a niche to fit in," a student advises. All first-years are required to have the unlimited meal plan, and one freshman cheers, "The food at Tufts is probably my favorite thing. We are incredibly lucky to have diverse options and a dining staff that is committed to the happiness of students." The campus police department is said to be effective, and a chemical engineering major says that an ongoing dialogue is "pushing the administration in the right direction for handling sexual assault on campus, and positive changes have been made."

"The level of social activism has caused a fissure in the student body."

While suburban Medford is not very exciting for those of the college class, the T metro system extends to the Tufts campus, so it's easy to make a quick jaunt to "student city" (a.k.a. Boston) for work or play. Davis Square in Somerville is even closer and provides plenty of restaurants, nightlife, and music stores. Tufts has earned a national reputation for its programs to promote the "responsible" use of alcohol. "Drinking is a significant part of life at Tufts, but it's not overwhelming," says a sophomore.

A small band of fraternities and sororities provides many of the on-campus weekend parties; 18 percent of the men and 18 percent of the women join the Greek system. According to a senior, "Partying at a frat is just as acceptable as staying in with your roommate and watching Netflix." University-sponsored activities include concerts, plays (Aidekman Arts Center stages 15 to 20 productions each year), and parties, and there are free movies on weekend nights. Several a cappella groups thrive at Tufts, and a favorite student group is the Tufts Dance Collective, where "groups of students practice goofy dances all semester" and put on two shows per year that draw big crowds. Other major campus events include homecoming and Halloween on the Hill, the latter of which is a carnival for children in the community, as well as Spring Fling, an outdoor concert that helps students relax before final exams. Of all student activities, the largest by far, with more than 1,000 students, is the Leonard Carmichael Society, the umbrella group for volunteer activities ranging from adult literacy and blood drives, to work with battered women and the homeless.

Tufts fields 29 teams in the New England Small College Athletic Conference (NESCAC) and finished fourth in the Directors' Cup standings for the 2015–16 season, its eighth top-10 finish. Tufts Jumbos have captured 15 national titles, most recently in softball, men's lacrosse, and men's soccer. Nearly one-third of the student body plays in more than 20 intramural and club sports. The Tufts Sabermetrics team, which grew out of the Experimental College, is a national powerhouse in competitions to apply sophisticated statistical techniques to the sport of baseball.

Tufts is in the midst of a modern-day renaissance. This, along with a swelling applicant pool, makes Tufts a much hotter school than it was just a few years ago. And its proximity to Boston, an intellectual and educational mecca, makes it even more attractive. "If you have something that you uncontrollably geek about and love to be able to share that passion," says a senior, "then Tufts is the place for you." Tufts gives every indication that it's going to keep scaling the university ranks until it reaches the summit—and that's not too far from Walnut Hill.

Tufts is among the top 10 research universities for undergrads who study abroad—at 42 percent.

Overlaps

Brown, University of Pennsylvania, Cornell University, Washington University in St. Louis, Northwestern, Georgetown, NYU, Boston University

If You Apply To > | **Tufts:** Early decision I: Nov. 1. Early decision II and regular decision: Jan. 1. Financial aid: Feb. 15. Application fee: $70. No campus interviews. Alumni interviews: optional, evaluative. SATs and two Subject Tests or ACTs: required. Letters of recommendation: required. Essay: required. Portfolio optional for applicants to arts programs. Application includes optional gender identity field. Accepts the Common Application with supplement.

Tulane University

6823 St. Charles Avenue, New Orleans, LA 70118

The map may say that Tulane is in the South, but Tulane has the temperament of an East Coast institution. The university is trying to shoehorn its way into the front rank of Southeastern universities, though it still trails Emory and Vanderbilt. Tulane has developed a strong emphasis on community service. High achievers should shoot for the Tulane Scholars program.

Website: www.tulane.edu

Location: City Center

Private

Total Enrollment: 11,009

Undergraduates: 6,624

Male/Female: 41/59

SAT Ranges: CR 620–710, M 620–700

ACT Ranges: 29–32

Financial Aid: 37%

Pell Grant: N/A

Expense: Pr $ $ $ $

Student Loans: 42%

Average Debt: $ $ $

Phi Beta Kappa: Yes

Applicants: 26,257

Accepted: 30%

Enrolled: 21%

Grad in 6 Years: 83%

Returning Freshmen: 92%

Academics: ✐ ✐ ✐ ½

Social: 🐿 🐿 🐿 🐿

Q of L: ★ ★ ★

Admissions: (800) 873-9283

Email Address: undergrad.admission@tulane.edu

Strong Programs:
Business
Marketing
Social Sciences
Biological Sciences
Health Professions
Environmental Studies
International Studies
Latin American Studies

All Tulane students must complete a service-learning course as well as a service-learning project.

Once a staid, genteel choice for students seeking a traditional education, Tulane University has rebranded itself with an emphasis on community service. It now attracts service-minded students from all 50 states who choose from more than 130 service-learning opportunities, many of them existing courses that were revamped to include a service-learning component after Hurricane Katrina. Indeed, Tulane promises a solid education to those who are ready to take up residence in the Big Easy.

The school's 110-acre campus is located in an attractive residential area of uptown New Orleans, about 15 minutes from the French Quarter and the business district. Tulane's administration building, Gibson Hall, faces St. Charles Avenue, where one of the nation's last streetcar lines still clatters past mansions. Across the street is Audubon Park, a 385-acre spread where students jog, walk, study, or feed the ducks in the lagoon. The buildings of gray limestone and pillared brick, separated by live southern oak trees, are modeled after the neocollegiate/Creole mixture indigenous to Louisiana institutional-type structures. One particular point of pride is the university's 13 Tiffany windows, one of the largest collections in existence.

All Tulane students must complete a rigorous set of general education and distribution requirements that include a service-learning course as well as a service-learning project, such as doing urban archaeology or teaching in a local school. In the process of satisfying the requirements, students must take at least one course in Western and non-Western civilization and complete a public service component, as well as a writing-intensive class, although freshmen with Advanced Placement or International Baccalaureate credit can place out of some classes. Several programs help freshmen make the transition from high school to college. One is TIDES, where students can join groups on such topics as Understanding Your Classmates, World Religions, and Cultures. Another offering for freshmen is the First-Year Experience, one-credit courses on such subjects as Metacognition (Thinking about Thinking), Campus Life, and Women and Leadership.

"It's impossible to escape the Southern influence of the city."

Tulane remains committed to its mission as a major research university that emphasizes undergraduate opportunities. The most popular majors include business, marketing, social sciences, biological sciences, and health-related programs. Tulane's strength lies in the natural sciences, environmental sciences, and the humanities; international studies in general and Latin American studies in particular are especially strong. The Stone Center for Latin American studies includes the 200,000-volume Latin American Library and offers more than 150 courses taught by 80 faculty members. An interdisciplinary program in political economy (economics, political science, and philosophy) stands out among the social sciences and is very popular with prelaw students. The School of Science and Engineering is composed of five distinct divisions: biological sciences and engineering; chemical sciences and engineering; physical and material sciences; earth and environmental sciences; and mathematics and computational science. Environmental studies majors benefit from the Tulane/Xavier Center for Bioenvironmental Research, where faculty members and students work together on research projects that include hazardous-waste remediation and the ecological effects of environmental contaminants.

Sixty-four percent of classes have fewer than 20 students, and although the majority of those classes are taught by full professors, graduate instructors are most likely to teach the beginning-level classes in English, foreign languages, and math. Overall, students praise Tulane's faculty, and the academic atmosphere can be very intense, depending on the class. Each year the university's highly acclaimed honors program invites about 700 outstanding students to partake in accelerated courses taught by top professors. Students may also apply for the Tulane Scholars Program.

Tulane offers more than 80 study abroad programs in 30 nations, including one-semester programs to locations such as Japan to study sociology and culture, Mexico City to delve into the language, and London to study liberal arts. In addition, the Tulane/Newcomb Junior Year Abroad program is one of the country's oldest and most prestigious programs, in which the student is fully immersed in the language and culture of the particular country.

Tulane has a somewhat Southern feel and is a sophisticated and cosmopolitan institution. Says one student, "If you're a Northerner, it's impossible to escape the Southern influence of the city, and if you're a Southerner, it's impossible to escape the Northern influence that exists on campus." Twenty-four percent of undergraduates are Louisiana natives, and 3 percent come from outside the U.S. The student body is 4 percent African American, 6 percent Hispanic, and 4 percent Asian American. Tulane awards hundreds of merit scholarships, averaging $23,847, and 151 athletic scholarships in 15 sports.

> *The Tulane/Newcomb Junior Year Abroad program is one of the country's oldest and most prestigious study abroad programs.*

Forty-five percent of students live on campus; nonlocal freshmen and sophomores must do so. Many upper-class students opt to move off campus, claiming that it's much cheaper than university housing, but others are concerned about the safety factor of living in New Orleans. Some Greek students live in their chapter houses. Freshmen have to stomach the cost of Tulane's meal plan, but alternatives exist at the University Center food court.

Social life at Tulane goes almost without saying. "New Orleans itself never stops partying!" boasts a junior. Fraternities and sororities are a presence—31 percent of the men and 41 percent of the women join—but do not dominate the social life. Though you're supposed to be 21 to buy alcohol or enjoy the bar scene in the

> **"New Orleans itself never stops partying!"**

cafés and clubs that dot the French Quarter, a sophomore explains that "alcohol is accessible." Mardi Gras is such a celebration that classes are suspended for two days and students from all over the country pour in to celebrate. An annual Jazzfest in the spring also draws wide participation. Road-trip destinations include the Gulf Coast, Austin, Houston, and the Florida panhandle.

While schoolwork is taken seriously at Tulane, so are sports. Football, volleyball, and men's and women's basketball are solid, and the baseball team has a big following. The university fields 16 Green Wave teams that compete in the Division I American Athletic Conference, and many benefit from the new on-campus stadium. Club and intramural sports are big, and students can also opt for weight work, squash, or swimming, among other options, at the Reily Student Recreation Center.

While Tulane is rich in Southern tradition, it is a forward-looking school where the possibilities seem endless. And like its hometown, it is a diverse, energetic melting pot of interests and activity. Those seeking a dynamic, service-oriented education in a vibrant city need look no further. *C'est si bon!*

Overlaps

University of Miami (FL), University of Michigan, Boston University, University of Southern California, Louisiana State, Emory, Indiana University, University of Wisconsin–Madison

If You Apply To ➤

Tulane: Early decision I: Nov. 1. Early action: Nov. 15. Early decision II: Jan. 6. Regular decision: Jan. 15. Financial aid: Feb. 15. Housing: May 1. No application fee. Campus and alumni interviews: optional, evaluative. SATs or ACTs: required. Subject Tests: optional. Letters of recommendation: optional. Essay: required. Accepts the Common Application with supplement.

600 South College Avenue, Tulsa, OK 74104

Tulsa is a notch smaller than Texas Christian and Washington U, but bigger than most liberal arts colleges. The university has a technical orientation rooted in Oklahoma oil, but a much more diverse curriculum than Colorado School of Mines. Offers engineering with a personal touch. Has an innovative program allowing undergraduates to do research beginning their first semester. Modern English is an unlikely strength.

Website: www.utulsa.edu
Location: City Outskirts
Private
Total Enrollment: 4,122
Undergraduates: 3,345
Male/Female: 58/42
SAT Ranges: CR 560–700, M 570–700
ACT Ranges: 26–32
Financial Aid: 87%
Pell Grant: 15%
Expense: Pr $ $
Student Loans: 49%
Average Debt: $ $ $ $
Phi Beta Kappa: Yes
Applicants: 6,762
Accepted: 42%
Enrolled: 24%
Grad in 6 Years: 69%
Returning Freshmen: 89%
Academics: ✎ ✎ ✎
Social: ☎ ☎ ☎
Q of L: ★ ★
Admissions: (918) 631-2307
Email Address: admission@ utulsa.edu

Strong Programs:
Petroleum Engineering
Geosciences
Finance
Psychology
Nursing
Computer Science
Accounting
English Language and Literature

The University of Tulsa is a small, private liberal arts school with a growing international reputation. Known for its engineering and science programs, including petroleum engineering and geosciences, it attracts students from around the world. With an emphasis on undergraduate research, hands-on work experience, and a diverse array of course offerings, TU has found its niche. "Tulsa strives to develop well-rounded, highly intellectual individuals who are best equipped to take on the global problems of tomorrow," says a senior.

TU's 210-acre campus is just three miles from downtown Tulsa, and there's a striking view of the city's skyline from the steps of the neo-Gothic McFarlin Library. The university's more than 90 buildings run the architectural gamut from 1930s-vintage neo-Gothic to contemporary, all variations on a theme of yellow Tennessee limestone dubbed "TU stone." The Lorton Performance Center is TU's showcase facility for the musical and performance arts. The Helmerich Center for American Research opened in 2015, housing the Gilcrease Museum library and archive, which features the newly acquired, 6,000-item Bob Dylan Archive.

In accordance with the Tulsa Curriculum, the cornerstone of the school's emphasis on liberal arts, all undergraduates take two writing courses, at least one mathematics course, and one or two years of foreign language, depending on the degree. In addition, each student completes at least 25 credit hours of general curriculum classes in aesthetic inquiry and creative experience, historical and social interpretation, and scientific investigation. Freshmen participate in a weeklong orientation program prior to the start of the fall semester and are required to take an introductory First Seminar course in the spring.

In addition to its well-established and internationally recognized petroleum engineering and geosciences programs, TU offers solid majors in computer science, accounting, and English language and literature. Petroleum engineering, finance, psychology, and nursing are the most popular majors. Tulsa is one of 20 schools in the nation that train America's Cyber Corps, the first line of defense against computer hackers and terrorists. The rapidly growing English department has some impressive resources at its disposal in McFarlin Library's special collections, which boast letters, manuscripts, and other materials by 19th- and 20th-century authors; a stained necktie that once belonged to James Joyce; and more than 50,000 items representing Nobel laureate V. S. Naipaul's life and work. The new Oxley College of Health and Sciences offers a number of health-related programs, and new majors include creative writing and computer simulation and gaming.

> "The majority of [professors] have had real-world experience before teaching in the classroom."

Courses are rigorous, and students say the workload can be heavy, but, "Professors know you by name, and class sizes enable a competitive yet collaborative environment that rewards hard work," says a senior. Sixty-one percent of classes enroll fewer than 20 students. "What makes TU's quality of teaching especially outstanding is the one-on-one interaction with professors," a student says. A senior adds, "My favorite thing about our professors is that the majority of them have had real-world experience before teaching in the classroom." Students also praise the university's academic support resources, including free workshops, subsidized tutoring sessions, and grad students who serve as academic counselors, helping with goal setting, study tips, and time-management skills.

Honors students take exclusive seminars, complete a thesis or advanced project, develop portfolios, and can live together in an honors house. The Tulsa Undergraduate Research Challenge offers outstanding opportunities to conduct cutting-edge research with faculty mentors and has produced 57 of TU's total 59 Goldwater Scholarship winners, 50 of TU's total 54 National Science Foundation Graduate Fellowships, 11 Truman Scholarships, and 14 Fulbright Grants (among others). The university allows students with significant advanced placement credits in history, chemistry, or applied mathematics to complete a baccalaureate and master's program in a total of five years. Nineteen percent travel abroad for programs including global health and society in Ghana, nursing and technology in Scotland, and tropical biology in Costa Rica. "Tulsa puts a high emphasis on the vital role summer internships can play in one's academic career," says an enthusiastic senior. "I have had a high-paying internship ever since my freshman year."

The Helmerich Center for American Research features the newly acquired, 6,000-item Bob Dylan Archive.

"Tulsa puts a high emphasis on the vital role summer internships can play in one's academic career."

TU students are "dedicated, intelligent, competitive, and accepting," muses a management major. Forty-two percent of Tulsa's students are from Oklahoma; most others are from the Midwest and Southwest, with many hailing from Dallas and St. Louis. An impressive 26 percent are international. The student body is 5 percent African American, 4 percent Asian American, 5 percent Hispanic, and 3 percent American Indian. Students say all political views are represented on campus, and popular topics include environmental sustainability and gun control. "TU isn't a hotbed for political activism, though I wouldn't consider TU students uneducated or unaware," a junior says. Athletes compete for 331 scholarships in 18 sports. TU also offers merit scholarships, averaging $17,866.

The Tulsa Undergraduate Research Challenge offers opportunities to conduct cutting-edge research with faculty mentors.

At Tulsa, freshmen and sophomores are required to live on campus. "We have newly remodeled and newly built dormitories on campus, as well as our very unique on-campus apartments," says one student. Seventy-one percent of the students reside in campus housing. The single-sex dorms are quieter and more attractive to upperclassmen. The student union food court was recently renovated, and students can also choose from cafeteria and bar-and-grill options, but one junior laments, "The dining facilities are probably TU's biggest downfall." Students report that campus security is on constant patrol, and "there are three levels of security in the residence halls, so students are very safe," according to a speech-language pathology major.

The social life at TU is surprisingly robust, if not raucous, thanks to hundreds of student organizations and a healthy Greek life. "Get involved! It'll make or break the experience," advises one junior. There are scheduled events, and students enjoy simply hanging with friends at small gatherings too. The Greek organizations claim 20 percent of TU men and 22 percent of the women, and the frats host campuswide house parties, but students agree that these do not dictate the social scene. Student-initiated policies govern drinking on campus. Administrators say this self-policing has led to responsible imbibing. Campus traditions include the ringing of the college bell in the Bayless Plaza cupola by each senior after his or her last final exam. Other big events include homecoming and Springfest.

"Students *love* to be active in the community."

Nearby parks, lakes, and a huge recreational water park please outdoor enthusiasts. Downtown Tulsa offers symphony, ballet, opera, and an annual Oktoberfest. Fifty-five percent of students take active part in community service opportunities coordinated through the True Blue Neighbors program. "Students can get involved in a variety of community organizations such as churches, Habitat for Humanity, Big Brothers Big Sisters, and Tulsa's Day Center for the Homeless," says one student. "Students *love* to be active in the community," adds another. The Bricktown section of Oklahoma City and nearby casinos (for those 21 and older), along with more distant Dallas, St. Louis, and Kansas City, are popular road trips.

Here in Oklahoma, sports are important (very, *very* important!). Students get riled up when the football team is pitted against rivals Oklahoma and Oklahoma State, and when the basketball team suits up against Memphis and SMU. The Division I Golden Hurricanes compete in the American Athletic Conference in 18 intercollegiate sports. In addition to football and basketball, men's soccer, women's tennis, and men's and women's cross-country are competitive. Forty percent of undergrads participate in at least one intramural or recreational sport; the most popular by far is flag football.

TU is trying to do some things differently: be a small liberal arts school in a part of the country most known for sprawling public universities, and incorporate professional preparation with an emphasis on broad intellectual challenges. Says one senior, "The University of Tulsa genuinely cares about the lives of students, encouraging them to embrace challenges while flourishing to their highest potential."

Overlaps

University of Oklahoma, Texas Christian, Southern Methodist, Saint Louis University, Oklahoma State, Rice, University of Texas at Austin, Washington University in St. Louis

If You Apply To ➤

Tulsa: Rolling admissions. Priority deadline: Feb. 1. Early action: Nov. 2. Financial aid: Mar. 1. Housing: May 1. Application fee: $50. Campus interviews: recommended, informational. Alumni interviews: optional, informational. SATs or ACTs: required. No Subject Tests. Letters of recommendation: required. Essay: required. Accepts the Common Application with supplement.

Union College

807 Union Street, Schenectady, NY 12308

Union is split down the middle between liberal arts and engineering. That means its center of gravity is more toward the technical side than places like Lafayette, Trinity, and Tufts, but less so than Clarkson and Rensselaer. Schenectady is less than exciting, but there are outdoor getaways in all directions. Relatively anonymous because it does not fit into conventional categories.

Website: www.union.edu
Location: Small City
Private
Total Enrollment: 2,200
Undergraduates: 2,200
Male/Female: 54/46
SAT Ranges: CR 610–680, M 630–720
ACT Ranges: 29–32
Financial Aid: 77%
Pell Grant: N/A

Founded in 1795, Union College is one of the oldest nondenominational colleges in the country. Its name reflects the founders' desire to create a welcoming, unifying academic community open to the region's diverse religious and national groups. More than 220 years later, this independent liberal arts college is known for its interdisciplinary studies and its study abroad programs. At Union, engineering and the arts go hand-in-hand. Undergraduate research has deep roots at Union, starting in the 20th century when a chemistry professor began involving students in his colloid chemistry investigations. Today, "Union is constantly thinking of ways to better the students' experience," says one satisfied freshman.

Union's 100-acre campus, designed in 1813 by French architect and landscaper Joseph Jacques Ramée, sits on a hill overlooking Schenectady. Ramée's vision took shape in brownstone and redbrick, with plenty of white arches, pilasters, and lacy green trees; the campus plan also includes eight acres of formal gardens and woodlands. The 16-sided Nott Memorial, a National Historic Landmark and one of the most remarkable structures on any U.S. campus, is a meeting, study, and exhibition center—and the site of a naked run each year. Parcels of land adjacent to College Park Hall, a hotel-turned-dorm, have become soccer fields for college and community use. Butterfield Hall provides state-of-the-art bioengineering facilities, including a mechanical testing lab and a clean room.

To fulfill Union's general education requirements, students take core courses in their first and second years that promote reading, writing, and analytical skills, including a required, interdisciplinary First-Year Preceptorial. They also must take courses spread among social science, humanities, linguistic and cultural competency, quantitative and mathematical reasoning, and natural and applied science or engineering. All students must complete a senior thesis or senior seminar paper in order to graduate.

Among Union's most popular majors are economics, political science, psychology, mechanical engineering, and biology. Students also flock to geology, computer science, and history; the latter department is home to Union's most esteemed lecturer, Stephen Berk, whose course on the Holocaust and Twentieth-Century Europe is a hot ticket. Each year, about 50 incoming freshmen are named Union Scholars. The designation extends the First-Year Preceptorial to two terms from one, allows students to work on independent study projects, and gives them access to departmental honors programs and expanded study abroad options. Each spring, Union cancels classes one afternoon for the Charles Steinmetz Symposium, so that students can present scholarly projects to their peers and professors in a professional conference atmosphere.

> "Union is constantly thinking of ways to better the students' experience."

Interdisciplinary study is the norm at Union, with established programs in bioengineering, Latin American and Caribbean studies, law and public policy, Russian and Eastern European studies, and women's and gender studies, to name a few. The $22 million Wold Science and Engineering Center is home for interdisciplinary study across departments, with state-of-the-art equipment and programs in biochemistry, environmental studies, music, and electrical engineering. The educational studies program allows aspiring teachers to complete courses and fieldwork required for secondary school certification in a variety of subjects, along with a strong liberal arts grounding. The Leadership in Medicine program, a joint program with Clarkson University's Union Graduate College and Albany Medical College, gives students the opportunity to earn a bachelor's degree, an M.S. in health management or M.B.A. in health systems administration, and a medical degree in eight years.

"The workload is tough but we have a lot of support to get us through," says a sophomore. Students give the faculty high marks. "For the most part they are knowledgeable, engaging, and seem to truly care about us not just as students, but also as people," says a student. Seventy-one percent of classes have fewer than 20 students, and students can expect to see full professors at the lecterns rather than TAs. Union operates on a trimester system, which means thrice-a-year exams and a late start to summer jobs—but also the opportunity to concentrate on just three courses a term. More terms also means more opportunities for independent study and internships, either in the state capital of Albany, 20 minutes away, or in Washington, D.C. By the time graduation rolls around, 55 percent of each class has studied abroad. In addition to a number other programs, Union offers collaborative programs in Australia, Brazil, Ireland, and Vietnam in conjunction with Hobart and William Smith Colleges.

> "Union is like its own little family."

(continued)

Expense: Pr $ $ $ $
Student Loans: 67%
Average Debt: $ $ $
Phi Beta Kappa: Yes
Applicants: 5,996
Accepted: 38%
Enrolled: 25%
Grad in 6 Years: 88%
Returning Freshmen: 93%
Academics: ✍ ✍ ✍ ✍
Social: ☎ ☎ ☎
Q of L: ★ ★ ★
Admissions: (518) 388-6112
Email Address: admissions@union.edu

Strong Programs:
Economics
Political Science
Psychology
Mechanical Engineering
Biology
Geology
Computer Science
History

Each spring, students can present scholarly projects to their peers and professors at the Charles Steinmetz Symposium.

"Union is like its own little family. Everyone is very welcoming, friendly, understanding, and happy," exudes one sophomore. Sixty-one percent of Union students are New Yorkers, 7 percent are international, and most went to public high schools. Four percent of students are African American, another 7 percent are Hispanic, and 6 percent are Asian American, but the school has been working to boost these numbers. Union awards hundreds of merit scholarships averaging $9,500, and it meets the full demonstrated financial need of admitted students, but it does not offer athletic scholarships.

Eighty-nine percent of Union students live in the dorms. The Minerva house system (named after the Roman goddess of wisdom) is aimed at getting students and faculty members to contribute to Union's social, residential, and intellectual life—and, students say, at decreasing the influence of the Greek system, which draws 37 percent of the men and 42 percent of the women. Union's dorms "have singles, doubles, triples, and suites (quads)," says a student. Students recommend West, which is co-ed by room and thus very social, as well as Fox and Davidson, where freshmen and sophomores live in suites: two double bedrooms and a "huge" common room. "The housing lottery can be somewhat confusing and stressful," a freshman laments, "but otherwise it's a fair process." Dining options consist of four main eating areas and "the food is not very edible but it is slowly improving," according to one student.

"Greek life is a huge part of the social life."

"The majority of social life is on campus," says a student. "There are Minerva events and on-campus movies as well as typical fraternity parties." Campus events also include comedians, concerts, and speakers. Another student says, "Greek life is a huge part of the social life, which might make some students feel pressured to join a fraternity or sorority." The administration has established a committee of students, staff, and faculty members to oversee programming about alcohol abuse. Favorite annual traditions include the lobster bake (each student gets his or her own crustacean) and Springfest, a huge concert. An unofficial graduation requirement is to do a lap around the Nott Memorial—sans clothing.

Off campus, Schenectady is an old-line industrial city that's a decent—if not great—college town, according to a freshman. Says a sophomore, "There are essentially no college-town amenities—like bookstores—in walking distance. You need a car." What Schenectady lacks can be found in Saratoga Springs, which boasts restaurants, jazz clubs, horse racing, and Skidmore College, or in the nearby Adirondacks and Catskills. Popular road trips include Boston, Montreal, New York, and the ski slopes of nearby Vermont. And students are trying to help Schenectady rebound, through tutoring programs in local schools and work with Big Brothers Big Sisters. There's also a service project during freshman orientation. "My group had to paint one of the bridges in Schenectady," says one student. "It was actually a good time."

Union's athletic teams (the Dutchmen) compete in Division III, aside from men's and women's ice hockey, both of which are Division I. Solid teams include men's and women's swimming and soccer and women's lacrosse, basketball, softball, and volleyball. There's a full-time director of intramural sports, which include teams in everything from tennis and volleyball to broomball and lacrosse. Rugby, skiing, and ultimate Frisbee enjoy club status, and about 60 percent of students participate in intramural or club athletics.

Union's mission is constantly evolving as the college struggles to meet the needs and interests of students and faculty. It retains its commitment to a strong core liberal arts curriculum while acknowledging the increasing effect of globalization and technology. Union College has plenty to offer—a small, friendly place full of eager intellectual exchange. You just have to seek it out.

Overlaps

Rensselaer Polytechnic, Skidmore, University of Vermont, University of Rochester, Trinity College (CT), Lafayette, Hamilton, Cornell University

Ursinus College

Box 1000, Collegeville, PA 19426

Ursinus is the smallest of the cohort of eastern Pennsylvania liberal arts colleges that includes Franklin & Marshall, Lafayette, and Muhlenberg. The plus side is more attention from faculty and more emphasis on independent learning. Although Philly is within arm's reach, the setting is quiet.

Ursinus College takes its name from a 16th-century German Calvinist, Zacharias Ursinus, who directed that students should "examine all things and keep what is good." For many years, the school focused on training in practical fields ranging from business administration to sports science. Recently, though, Ursinus has reinvigorated its liberal arts roots—expanding its offerings and restructuring its core curriculum to emphasize questions of human existence and to prepare students "not just to make a living, but to make a life of purpose." What hasn't changed is the close-knit feel of the school. "Ursinus's culture is one of inquisitive learning through experimentation and discussion with peers that brings students together in a small campus atmosphere," muses a senior.

Ursinus is located in Collegeville, about 40 minutes west of Philadelphia, and 10 miles from the green, rolling hills of Valley Forge National Park. Buildings on the 170-acre campus are mostly constructed of Pennsylvania fieldstone; many have had their interiors upgraded and their exteriors preserved and restored. Actors and dancers benefit from rehearsal and exhibition space in the Kaleidoscope Performing Arts Center.

General education requirements at Ursinus fall under the college's Plan for Liberal Studies, and they are grounded in the assumption that while individuals have intrinsic value, they also live in a community. Therefore, the core includes two semesters of the Common Intellectual Experience—a course that explores topics from Plato to Buddhist scripture to Nietzsche—as well as requirements in science, culture, and history. Students also engage in at least one Independent Learning Experience—a research project, an internship, study abroad, or student teaching—before graduation, and they must complete a capstone course in their major. For honors students, the requirements are more stringent; their independent projects are evaluated by outside examiners.

> "Ursinus's culture is one of inquisitive learning through experimentation and discussion with peers."

Students choose among nearly 30 majors, with the most popular being business and economics, biology, psychology, and media and communication studies. The college also offers strong programs in neuroscience, health and exercise physiology, and politics and international relations. The academic climate is largely dependent on the course of study. "Most people are very focused on their academics, which does create a competitive environment," says a senior. "However, a lot of people are keen on working together and collaborating both in and outside of the classroom." A biology major says, "The professors want their students to succeed and really aid

Website: www.ursinus.edu
Location: Suburban
Private
Total Enrollment: 1,627
Undergraduates: 1,627
Male/Female: 47/53
SAT Ranges: CR 520–620, M 520–630
ACT Ranges: 23–30
Financial Aid: 97%
Pell Grant: 22%
Expense: Pr $ $ $
Student Loans: 74%
Average Debt: $ $ $ $
Phi Beta Kappa: Yes
Applicants: 2,634
Accepted: 83%
Enrolled: 20%
Grad in 6 Years: 78%
Returning Freshmen: 86%
Academics: ✍ ✍ ✍
Social: ☎ ☎ ☎
Q of L: ★ ★ ★
Admissions: (610) 409-3200
Email Address: admission@ursinus.edu

Strong Programs:
Business and Economics
Biology
Psychology
Media and Communication Studies
Neuroscience
Health and Exercise Physiology

in the growth of the students." Classes are small—75 percent have fewer than 20 students—and students say they are pleased with the quality of teaching, especially since there are no TAs. "The relationships I have with my professors are more personal than I could have ever expected coming into college," says a junior.

Up to 30 percent of rising seniors get fellowships from the school to fund full-time summer research projects with a faculty member. The Center for Science and the Common Good aims to unite research with "habits of reflection and judgment," offering speaker and conference series, a student fellows program, internships, and summer research opportunities. The U-Imagine Center for Integrative and Entrepreneurial Studies and the new Melrose Center for Global Civic Engagement offer similar programming. Twenty-five percent of Ursinus students study abroad each year, both in programs designed and run by the college and in programs sponsored by other institutions or consortiums. The Philadelphia Experience, newly created in 2016, places selected students in a residence hall in Philadelphia for a semester to take courses with Ursinus faculty, along with their choice of an internship, independent research project, or additional coursework offered through Drexel University.

> "The relationships I have with my professors are more personal than I could have ever expected."

Students take two semesters of the Common Intellectual Experience—a course that explores topics from Plato to Buddhist scripture to Nietzsche.

"Our students are very well known for having many different interests," says an applied economics major. "A football player may also be in the men's a cappella group. A theater star may also do honors biology research." Fifty-four percent of students are from Pennsylvania and 2 percent are from foreign countries, with most others hailing from New York, New Jersey, and other Mid-Atlantic and New England states. African Americans make up 6 percent of the student body, Asian Americans 5 percent, and Hispanics 6 percent. Social justice issues and campus diversity are frequent topics of open discussions, but a junior notes, "Most students support these issues, but they are not actively engaged." Twenty-two percent of incoming students are eligible for the Pell Grant, and there are non-need-based scholarships and grants averaging $21,020 available each year. No athletic scholarships are offered.

Ninety-six percent of students at Ursinus live in the dorms, which adds to the feeling of community. Upperclassmen quickly grab the Main Street houses, a string of Victorian-era homes across the street from campus, while freshmen are clustered in the Quad and BWC, short for Brodbeck-Wilkinson-Curtis, which have generously sized rooms. Student-run special interest housing is available too, for those who share social or academic interests. Dorms and dining are both described as "decent" but not excellent. "I think that some options could be expanded, and some hours could be adjusted, but for the most part all dietary needs are taken care of and the food is good," says one senior. A junior says, "Campus Safety is very well regarded. They are always seen around campus mingling with students and gaining their respect and trust."

> "Our students are very well known for having many different interests."

A new program places students in Philadelphia for a semester to take courses with Ursinus faculty and pursue their choice of additional learning opportunities.

"Most people find social activities on campus to occupy their time," a student reports. "The student activities board brings a bunch of performers and shows to the school. They also will have themed cuisine nights and parties for weekends." Greek life draws 19 percent of the men and 25 percent of the women, and fraternity parties are a popular weekend diversion. Registered on-campus parties are monitored by student "social hosts" who check IDs and make sure things don't get out of hand. Students appreciate the wet alcohol policy, saying that it "keeps everyone safe and on campus," according to a junior. Homecoming is a favorite tradition in the fall, and each spring, students look forward to Mayday and Airband, "a big charity lip-synching and performing event," says an English major. Sixty percent of students perform regular volunteer work.

The town of Collegeville is just 10 blocks long—and Ursinus takes up five of those. "There is very little to do off campus unless you are looking to go out to eat," grumbles one student. Still, the town offers many of the amenities that students want and need, such as a sushi restaurant, a sports bar, an ice cream and coffee shop, four pizza parlors—and, most importantly, late-night pizza delivery. Other options include the shops and restaurants of central Philadelphia, less than an hour away. Many students with cars escape to the Jersey shore during warmer months.

Ursinus students love sports, and 60 percent play on a Division III varsity or an intramural team. And for women seeking post-collegiate careers in coaching, Ursinus is a well-known stepping stone to those posts; more than 50 colleges have hired Ursinus alumnae. The Bears field hockey team is a perennial contender for the national championship, and the women's and men's lacrosse teams are also strong. Recent conference champions include field hockey, women's swimming, wrestling, and gymnastics.

Ursinus is on the rise. It may not be in the center of a big metropolitan area, and it doesn't offer big-time sports, but the college compensates for its lack of size with the feeling that students, faculty, and staff are one big family. "The special thing about Ursinus is the people," says a biology major. "Everyone—the students, professors, and staff—is so friendly and open and just wants you to succeed."

> ## Overlaps
>
> **Dickinson, Gettysburg, Goucher, Muhlenberg, Penn State, Susquehanna, Temple, University of Delaware**

If You Apply To ➤ **Ursinus:** Early action: Nov. 1. Early decision I: Dec. 1. Early decision II and regular decision: Feb. 1. Financial aid: Feb. 15. No application fee. Campus interviews: optional, informational. No alumni interviews. SATs or ACTs (with writing): optional for most students. Subject Tests: optional. Letters of recommendation: required. Essay: required. Accepts the Common Application.

University of Utah

201 South 1460 East, Room 2505, Salt Lake City, UT 84112

One of the oldest universities west of the Mississippi, the University of Utah attracts a diverse group of students drawn to the region's only major city. The majority of Utah students hail from the Salt Lake City region, and many commute from home. Science and professional programs such as business and engineering are traditional strengths.

In addition to being the flagship institution of the state's higher education system, the University of Utah is a major national scientific research center. Founded in 1850, the university is unusual in its ability to offer students the advantages of living in a city while at the same time maintaining a connection with nature. "We have the school spirit, the drive to transform the world, and the resources and connections needed for students to succeed," cheers one senior. Under a state-government-backed program called USTAR, the university has begun poaching star faculty members from other U.S. and foreign universities in fields that align with the state's existing economic strengths, such as medical devices and computer gaming.

Set in the foothills of the Wasatch Mountains near the shores of the Great Salt Lake, the university enjoys a picturesque location a half-hour drive from "the greatest snow on earth." Occupying 1,500 well-landscaped acres with nearly as many different kinds of trees as undergraduates, the campus doubles as the state's arboretum. The architectural style of the university's structures ranges

> **Website**: www.utah.edu
> **Location**: City Center
> **Public**
> **Total Enrollment**: 22,791
> **Undergraduates**: 16,787
> **Male/Female**: 56/44
> **SAT Ranges**: CR 500–640, M 510–660
> **ACT Ranges**: 21–28
> **Financial Aid**: 63%
> **Pell Grant**: 26%
> **Expense**: Pub $
> **Student Loans**: 39%
> **Average Debt**: $

Phi Beta Kappa: No
Applicants: 12,174
Accepted: 81%
Enrolled: 34%
Grad in 6 Years: 64%
Returning Freshmen: 89%
Academics: ✐ ✐ ✐
Social: ☎ ☎ ☎
Q of L: ★ ★ ★
Admissions: (801) 581-8761
Email Address: admissions@ utah.edu

Strong Programs:
Biomedical Engineering
Business Administration
Communication
Psychology
Economics
Exercise and Sport Science
Ballet and Modern Dance
Entrepreneurship

The Lassonde Entrepreneur Institute offers training to budding entrepreneurs, 400 of whom get to reside in brand-new, $45 million studios.

from 19th-century, ivy-covered buildings to state-of-the-art modern facilities. A new student center was recently completed, and a spate of new construction continues unabated.

Utah students choose from a comprehensive academic menu, including more than 100 undergraduate majors. Renowned for its research in biomedical engineering, Utah hosted the first mechanical heart transplant, and while the professional degrees in engineering and business are quite popular, the U does not skimp on general education requirements. Students must fulfill classes in writing, American institutions, math, statistics, and intellectual explorations, which includes two courses in the humanities, sciences, social sciences, or fine arts, as well as an international course requirement. Additional requirements include upper-division writing, a course in diversity, and either foreign language or quantitative courses. The most popular majors include communication, psychology, economics, and exercise and sport science. The film and media arts major offers an emphasis in entertainment arts and engineering, and programs in ballet and modern dance are also strong. The Lassonde Entrepreneur Institute offers training to budding entrepreneurs, 400 of whom get to reside in the brand-new, $45 million Lassonde Studios, featuring the sort of pods and shared spaces characteristic of high-tech workplaces.

> **"We have a very liberal campus in comparison to much of Utah and Salt Lake City."**

The academic climate can be challenging, but in general "the workload is fairly manageable," according to one sophomore. Introductory courses often enroll hundreds of students, with smaller discussion sections led by graduate student teaching assistants. Overall, 41 percent of classes have fewer than 20 students. Utah's professors generally receive high marks from the students. "Some professors are clearly more interested in their research than in teaching, but for the most part they'll still do a fair job," says a junior. The LEAP (Learning Engagement Achievement Progress) program is a learning community committed to the principles of civic awareness and service. LEAP features dedicated faculty and peer advisors who mentor new students and challenge them academically through a two-semester sequence of seminars; 13 percent of freshmen participate.

The MUSE (My Utah Signature Experience) Program seeks to provide every student with a unique experience via community engagement, global learning, innovation, leadership, internships, and research and learning communities. Eleven percent of students study abroad in more than 200 programs in more than 50 countries around the globe. The Undergraduate Research Opportunities Program offers semester grants to students who join faculty members in scholarly pursuits. The University of Utah partnered with the state of Utah to create the USTAR (Utah Science Technology and Research) initiative, which brings top research faculty and students together in developing cutting-edge technology and research, affording students the opportunity to gain real-world skills.

Utah's students are a mostly middle-class, fairly homogeneous lot; of the 71 percent of undergraduates who are from Utah, nearly all attended public schools. "We have a very liberal campus in comparison to much of Utah and Salt Lake City," a junior says. Seven percent of students come from abroad. African Americans make up 1 percent of the student population, Asian Americans 6 percent, and Hispanics 11 percent. There is an active student government and most students agree that students here are less conservative than those found at rival Brigham Young, a Mormon institution. A substantial percentage of students are Mormon, though, and, "Diversity and religion are probably the biggest issues on campus," says one student. Utah offers merit scholarships averaging $5,778 and 377 athletic scholarships in 17 sports, while 26 percent of incoming students qualify for Pell Grants.

> **"Much of the social life is recreational."**

Only 13 percent of students live on campus, but those who do seem to be pleased with the accommodations. "New facilities were built for the 2002 Olympics so our rooms are bigger, more comfortable, and well maintained throughout the year," one student reports. Students are also generally satisfied with the food, though edibility varies based on which campus eatery you choose. "There are always vegetarian options," says a senior. Students also report feeling safe on campus, thanks to emergency call boxes and a visible security presence. The university has increased the number of staff dedicated to Title IX issues and is streamlining its procedures for handling sexual assault on campus.

Social life is low-key, due in large part to the high number of commuters. Five percent of the men and 8 percent of the women go Greek. "From lectures, concerts, dance performances, and late-night Crimson Nights parties, there is something for everyone," a student says. What's more, Utah is located close to the mountains, "so much of the social life is recreational," according to one junior. Favorite road trips take students to Las Vegas, Lake Powell, and nearby ski resorts (with slopeside bus service available from the school). Salt Lake City isn't exactly a college town, but a junior says, "The nightlife in SLC downtown is great if you are over 21." Some students get very involved in community service or political activities. Adjacent to campus, the Latter Day Saints Institute of Religion sponsors dances and other social activities with a decidedly conservative bent. There are also centers for other faiths, notably Jewish and Roman Catholic. Cultural activities include the respected Utah Symphony, several dance companies, opera, and, of course, the Mormon Tabernacle Choir. For basketball fans, there's the Utah Jazz.

Utes teams compete in Division I and football and basketball bring students together in the MUSS—Mighty Utah Student Section—where cheers are loudest in games against foes such as UCLA, Arizona State, and Oregon. The football team won the 2014 and 2015 Las Vegas Bowl games. The baseball team claimed the 2016 Pac-12 Conference title, and men's basketball, women's gymnastics and softball, and men's and women's skiing make regular NCAA Tournament appearances. In addition to the university's dozens of intramurals and club sports, the Outdoor Adventure Program offers backpacking, river running, canoeing, mountain biking, and skiing trips.

Students say that diversity and academic quality are both on the rise at Utah. "The best thing about students at the U is that they are friendly to all, supportive of each other, and you can do whatever you want," says a computer animation major. It's also one of the few places where you can find nationally recognized professional programs within easy reach of nationally recognized skiing.

The USTAR initiative brings top research faculty and students together in developing cutting-edge technology and research.

Overlaps

BYU, Utah State, Utah Valley, University of Colorado–Boulder, Arizona State, University of Arizona, Weber State

If You Apply To ➤

University of Utah: Rolling admissions: Apr. 1. (Priority deadline: Dec. 1.) Financial aid: Feb. 1. Housing: May 1. Application fee: $45. No campus or alumni interviews. SATs or ACTs: required. Subject Tests: optional. No letters of recommendation. No essay (required for Honors College applicants).

Vanderbilt University

2305 West End Avenue, Nashville, TN 37240

Strongest and most selective of schools that still manage to blend Old South gentility with modern ways. Long a preferred choice for Atlanta and Birmingham elites, Vandy is becoming more diverse, geographically and otherwise. More selective than Emory but now comparable to Duke among leading schools south of the Mason–Dixon line. One of the few major universities where both academics and athletics are top-notch.

Website: www.vanderbilt.edu
Location: City Center
Private
Total Enrollment: 11,780
Undergraduates: 6,813
Male/Female: 50/50
SAT Ranges: CR 710–790, M 720–800
ACT Ranges: 32–35
Financial Aid: 64%
Pell Grant: 14%
Expense: Pr $ $ $
Student Loans: 22%
Average Debt: $
Phi Beta Kappa: Yes
Applicants: 31,464
Accepted: 12%
Enrolled: 44%
Grad in 6 Years: 93%
Returning Freshmen: 97%
Academics: ✎ ✎ ✎ ✎
Social: ☎ ☎ ☎ ☎
Q of L: ★ ★ ★ ★
Admissions: (800) 288-0432
Email Address: admissions@ vanderbilt.edu

Strong Programs:
Economics
Human and Organizational Development
Medicine, Health, and Society
Mechanical Engineering
Political Science
Education

Once a quiet, conservative school in the heart of the South, Vanderbilt University has diversified its student body and brought a more cosmopolitan atmosphere to campus. Coats, ties, and pearls may be outnumbered by Commodore fan gear at football games these days, but the university has succeeded in marrying Old South gentility with modern attitudes. The result is a relaxed, friendly culture that makes the rigorous academic environment easier to handle. "Students looking for a balance between great academics and a solid social life need to look at Vandy," says a history major.

Founded in 1873 by Cornelius Vanderbilt, the university's 330-acre tract in Nashville is a national arboretum and includes Peabody College, the central section of which is listed on the National Register of Historic Places. On the main campus, art and sculptures dot the landscape, and architectural styles range from Gothic to modern glass and brick. The 230,000-square-foot Engineering and Science Building opened in 2016. The Sarratt Student Center remains a center of student life, with a movie theater, Rand Dining Hall, a pub, and offices for the student-run newspaper, radio station, and other student organizations.

Undergraduates choose one of four schools—College of Arts and Science, School of Engineering, Blair School of Music, or Peabody College of Education and Human Development—but everyone takes their core liberal arts courses in the College of Arts and Science, where the writing program is a standout. Optional first-year Commons Seminars allow students to explore various topics in small groups with close faculty interaction; recent seminars have included everything from Strategies for Conflict Management to Classic Russian Short Novels to Introduction to Celestial Navigation. Popular majors include economics; human and organizational development; medicine, health, and society; mechanical engineering; and political science. Education majors who enroll at Vanderbilt's Peabody College are required to double major, usually in a liberal arts field. Many students interested in financial careers declare an economics major and pursue a managerial studies minor; there's also a 3–2 program with Vanderbilt's Owen Graduate School of Business, which lets talented undergraduates save a year on the path to their M.B.A.s. About 30 percent of students opt for double majors. Recently added majors include environmental sociology and biochemistry and chemical biology.

> "[Vanderbilt] provides the academic rigor I was hoping for without any of the cutthroat aspect I was afraid [of]."

"The academic climate of Vanderbilt is absolutely collaborative," an elementary education major says. "It provides the academic rigor I was hoping for without any of the cutthroat aspect I was afraid would accompany such an academically challenging school." Two-thirds of courses have fewer than 20 students, and in the classroom, Vanderbilt students are governed by the school's honor system, which dates from 1875. The system governs all aspects of academic conduct and makes it possible for professors to give unproctored exams. Students rave about the faculty. "The quality of teaching is unmatched," cheers a junior. "Many professors go out of their way to encourage students to get involved with research and internship opportunities."

Vanderbilt's study abroad program attracts 41 percent of students and offers the chance to spend a summer, a semester, or a year on one of six continents via more than 120 programs. The optional "Maymester" allows students to spend four weeks on a single project, helpful for double majors or those who'd like to spend some time in a foreign country but can't commit to being away for an entire term. Roughly half of the students, from all four undergraduate schools, participate in research, and many copublish articles. The campus is home to more than 100 interdisciplinary centers and institutes.

Ten percent of undergraduates are in-state residents, and 7 percent are international, coming from 50 countries. Asian Americans account for 12 percent of the student body, African Americans 8 percent, and Hispanics 9 percent. Politically, Vanderbilt students are divided pretty evenly between conservatives, moderates, and liberals. "I would not describe Vanderbilt as an activist campus per se, but in my two years there have been several rallies and protests that have led to tangible changes," observes an English major. Vanderbilt employs a need-blind admissions process, meets full demonstrated need, and does not include loans in financial aid packages. In addition to need-based financial aid, the university awards approximately 250 merit scholarships, complete with summer stipends, to admitted students through three signature merit scholarship programs. There are also 239 athletic scholarships awarded.

Ninety-two percent of Vanderbilt undergraduates live on campus. All first-year students live together in 10 Commons houses and take part in Vanderbilt Visions, a living/learning initiative designed to foster a sense of community among new students. Each first-year is assigned to a Visions group, which has about 18 students, a faculty advisor, and an upper-class peer mentor. In addition to meeting with their group once a week during the fall semester, students have opportunities to get to know the faculty who live in the various Commons houses. Students also compete in the Commons Cup, which, a junior explains, "is pretty much the House Cup straight out of Harry Potter, and it is a blast. You and your house compete in intramurals, sustainability, community service, and academics over the course of the whole year." Most recently, the school added the Warren and Moore Residential Colleges for upper-class students. Other options for older students include 10-person townhouses, six-room suites, theme dorms, and school-owned apartments. Seniors may move off campus but must obtain a special waiver.

Vanderbilt has more than 20 dining facilities that "always provide a delicious array of options," according to a junior, and first-years are required to buy a meal plan. The Taste of Nashville program allows students to use their meal money at two dozen local restaurants. Students report feeling safe on campus, thanks to an active security department. "Vanderbilt has its own police force and they are there solely to watch out for Vanderbilt students and keep us safe," says a student. Another adds that although there have been some recent high-profile sexual assault cases, Vanderbilt "is facing this issue head on," especially through the efforts of the Project Safe center.

Fifty-three percent of the women and 35 percent of the men join the Greek system; while many Greek parties are open to the entire campus, the effort to encourage mixing between the groups is not always successful. "Fraternities and

The campus is home to more than 100 interdisciplinary centers and institutes.

"[Professors] go out of their way to encourage students to get involved with research and internship opportunities."

Each first-year is assigned to a Visions group, which has about 18 students, a faculty advisor, and an upper-class peer mentor.

"[The Commons Cup] is pretty much the House Cup straight out of Harry Potter, and it is a blast."

sororities start the social scene," a senior says, "but certainly don't encompass all aspects of Vanderbilt's social life." The first-year Commons campus is dry, but of-age students are allowed to have alcohol elsewhere on campus, although open containers are banned in public and kegs are also taboo. As at many colleges, one student says, "underage students can find loopholes." Students get involved in more than 500 student organizations. Favorite Vanderbilt traditions are the Commodore Quake and Rites of Spring music festivals, Founders Walk, and the Anchor Dash, when all the first-years run onto the football field before the first home game.

Vanderbilt's proximity to Music City USA provides plenty to do. "Nashville is so much fun," cheers one senior. "The list of excellent restaurants, bars, shopping, and live music venues is endless." Country music fans shouldn't miss the Hall of Fame. Beyond Nashville's borders are the Great Smoky Mountains and state parks with picnic facilities, beautiful lakes, and skiing in the winter. The best road trips are to Memphis (home of Elvis!), New Orleans (for Mardi Gras), and Louisville (for the Kentucky Derby). Students also engage in the local community through a variety of service-oriented programs. "Alternative Spring Break (ASB) is a very popular program on college campuses across the country, and was actually a student-driven initiative that originated at Vanderbilt," explains an elementary education major. In fact, ASB is Vandy's largest student-run organization.

> **"Alternative Spring Break... was actually a student-driven initiative that originated at Vanderbilt."**

Vanderbilt may be the smallest—and the only private—institution in the competitive and football-crazy Division I Southeastern Conference, but there is no shortage of enthusiasm among Commodore fans. Vandy reconfigured its athletic program some years ago in an effort to cut costs. Instead of losing ground (as many feared), the programs thrived. The baseball team, a perennial powerhouse, won a national championship in 2014, as did the women's tennis team in 2015. The women's bowling team has won a national title too. The Vanderbilt Aerospace Club has won NASA's Student Launch Challenge, an eight-month-long rocketry competition, for the last four years. There are 32 club sports for weekend jocks, as well as more than 40 intramural sports.

Vanderbilt sits squarely among the top universities in the nation and has capitalized on its unique blend of Southern charm and scholarly achievement to attract students from around the country and beyond. Four years here do carry a steep before-financial-aid sticker price; witness a tongue-in-cheek campus slogan, "Vanderbilt: It Even Sounds Expensive." But for many, investing in a Vanderbilt education is money well spent.

Overlaps

Duke, Harvard, Yale, Washington University in St. Louis, Stanford, Princeton, University of Pennsylvania, Northwestern

If You Apply To ➤

Vanderbilt: Early decision I: Nov. 1. Early decision II and regular decision: Jan. 1. Financial aid: Feb. 1. Application fee: $50. Campus interviews: optional, evaluative. No alumni interviews. SATs or ACTs: required. Subject Tests: optional. Letters of recommendation: required. Essay: required. Accepts the Common Application. Apply to particular school or program.

Vassar College

Poughkeepsie, NY 12604

It is hard to imagine that Vassar once considered picking up and moving to Yale in the 1960s rather than become a co-ed institution. Half a century after admitting men, still on its ancient and picturesque campus, Vassar is a thriving, highly selective, avant-garde institution with an accent on the fine arts and humanities. At the forefront of national efforts to promote socioeconomic diversity in elite schools.

Are you a scientist who composes music in your spare time? Or perhaps an actor who also enjoys dissecting Plato and Aristotle? If so, you may feel at home at Vassar, a distinguished liberal arts college just 70 miles north of New York City. Once known as the most liberal of the Seven Sisters, and still a bastion of the left, Vassar prides itself on curricular flexibility, tolerance, and diversity. "The typical Vassar student is passionate about one of three things: their academic pursuits, their extracurriculars, or their social activism," says a senior. "There aren't many Vassar students who do things passively."

The college's 1,000-acre campus, just outside Poughkeepsie, New York, includes two lakes and plenty of trees. Daffodils bloom in the spring, and foliage is omnipresent in the fall. Encircled by a fieldstone wall, the campus also boasts an astronomical observatory with one of the largest telescopes in the Northeast, a state-of-the-art physics building, a farm with an ecological field station, and an art center with 13,500 works, from Ancient Egyptian to modern times. The architecture is predominantly neo-Gothic, with buildings also designed by notables such as Marcel Breuer, Eero Saarinen, and James Renwick. A new Integrated Science Center opened in 2016.

Vassar has no core curriculum and no general education or distribution requirements. Indeed, academic flexibility is paramount. That said, all students must take a Freshman Course, a small seminar emphasizing oral and written expression, as well as one course that requires significant quantitative analysis. Students must also demonstrate intermediate-level proficiency in a foreign language by studying one of the 20 languages taught at Vassar, or through a satisfactory score on an AP or SAT Subject test.

> **"Vassar's Career Development Office is deft at leveraging the tremendous alumni network."**

The most popular majors include economics, English, psychology, and biology. The biology building houses two electron microscopes, while music students are spoiled by a grand collection of Steinway pianos spread across the campus. Drama, film, political science, and neuroscience are also traditional strengths. Regardless of their course of study, students find the academic climate cooperative but rigorous. "At Vassar, you'll find yourself in a world where students want to actively engage in their classes and learning and to devote countless hours to their studies," a student says. Small classes and tutorials are the norm, and exams are given under an honor system. Since Vassar has no graduate students or research-only faculty, all classes are taught by professors. "Some professors are better than others, but on the whole, I feel lucky to learn from such knowledgeable and genuine individuals," a philosophy major says.

Vassar students interested in urban education benefit from the school's agreement with New York's Bank Street College. In addition, there are programs with the other 11 members of the Twelve College Exchange* and at four historically black colleges, as well as a drama program at the Eugene O'Neill Theater and a maritime

Website: www.vassar.edu
Location: Small City
Private
Total Enrollment: 2,421
Undergraduates: 2,421
Male/Female: 44/56
SAT Ranges: CR 670–750,
 M 660–740
ACT Ranges: 30–33
Financial Aid: 60%
Pell Grant: 22%
Expense: Pr $ $ $ $
Student Loans: 47%
Average Debt: $
Phi Beta Kappa: Yes
Applicants: 7,557
Accepted: 26%
Enrolled: 34%
Grad in 6 Years: 92%
Returning Freshmen: 94%
Academics: ✏ ✏ ✏ ✏ ½
Social: ☎ ☎ ☎
Q of L: ★ ★ ★ ★
Admissions: (845) 437-7300
Email Address: admissions@
 vassar.edu

Strong Programs:
Economics
English
Psychology
Biology
Drama
Film
Political Science
Neuroscience

studies program at the Mystic Seaport*, both in Connecticut. Each year, 44 percent of students study abroad via 240 programs in more than 60 countries. Vassar allows students to use their financial aid packages to support study away from campus. Also highly regarded is the college's Undergraduate Research Summer Institute, which offers stipends for students to work one-on-one with faculty members on scientific projects, either at Vassar or off campus. The Ford Scholars program offers opportunities for student/faculty collaboration in the humanities and social sciences. Most students participate in some sort of off-campus fieldwork or internship for credit during the academic year. "Vassar's Career Development Office is deft at leveraging the tremendous alumni network to educate students and find them opportunities at all grade levels," says a media studies major.

Other than the obvious chromosomal demographics, coeducation has little impact on the type of student attracted to Vassar. "Students at Vassar tend to be progressive and active," says a junior. Adds another, "Students who are not willing to have their views challenged will not do well at Vassar." Seventy-two percent of Vassar students were in the top 10th of their high school class; 24 percent are native New Yorkers and 7 percent are international. Asian Americans make up 11 percent of the student body, African Americans 5 percent, and Hispanics 11 percent. The school's ALANA Center supports and recognizes students of color and other ethnic and cultural groups. Twenty-two percent of first-year students are eligible for Pell Grants. One senior comments, "While I know Vassar is one of the most socioeconomically diverse private schools in the country, the vibe can still feel pretty rich/entitled at times." Although the college does not award merit or athletic scholarships, it does offer need-blind admissions for all first-year applicants and guarantees to meet the full demonstrated financial need of admits; it also replaces loans with grants for students whose families have annual incomes of $60,000 or less.

Housing is guaranteed for four years, and 96 percent of students live on campus, where there's an eclectic mix of nine dorms. All but one are co-ed. "Some dorms are really modern and sparkling," says a junior. "Others have a vintage college feel, with traditional wood paneling, trim, and floors." The word is that Lathrop is the best dorm for freshmen, but no halls are reserved strictly for first-year students. Juniors and seniors favor the college-owned townhouses (five-person suites) and the four-person Terrace Apartments, both with kitchens and living rooms. An on-campus nutritionist helps ensure that all dietary needs are met, and a freshman notes that with a new dining services provider lined up for fall 2017, "everyone is excited to see what changes will be made." Students report that while their open campus feels safe, administrative handling of sexual assault cases has been the focus of much student activism recently, and in response, "The school is attempting to make things more transparent and take a survivor-centered approach to sexual assault cases."

Vassar doesn't have a Greek system, so social life revolves around films, lectures, parties, concerts, and the like. "Social life primarily takes place on campus," says a junior, and the "party culture primarily happens in on-campus senior housing." Students can also party at the on-campus dance club Matthew's Mug, named for school founder Matthew Vassar. Performing arts groups provide an important social outlet too. "Between student theater, a cappella, comedy troupes, slam poetry, dance groups, and more, students can go see high-quality performances multiple times every weekend," says an economics major. The city of Poughkeepsie has undergone a renaissance in recent years and features the world's longest elevated pedestrian bridge (212 feet tall and 1.28 miles long, in case you're wondering). Restaurants and

"Students who are not willing to have their views challenged will not do well at Vassar."

"Students can go see high-quality performances multiple times every weekend."

Vassar has no core curriculum and no general education or distribution requirements.

Vassar allows students to use their financial aid packages to support study away from campus.

shops are within walking distance of campus, and malls and movie theaters aren't much farther away. In warmer weather, Mohonk State Park offers hiking and other outdoor diversions. Also close by are Franklin Roosevelt's Hyde Park (for history) and the Culinary Institute of America (for gourmet meals prepared by students). Popular road trips include New York City and Boston, both easily reached by train.

True to its heritage as one of the Seven Sisters, traditions are big at Vassar. "The year starts with Serenading—a time when the freshmen pay tribute to the seniors by singing them songs," one student explains. On Founder's Day in May, the entire community celebrates Matthew Vassar's birthday with music, carnival rides, food, and a day out on the grass. Fireworks and a movie cap off the festivities. "Founder's Day is easily the most highly anticipated day of the year," says a senior. And students can still unwind after a hard day of classes with afternoon tea in the Rose Parlor of historic Main Building.

Vassar's Division III varsity squads (the "Brewers") compete in the Liberty League, and the women's basketball team brought home the conference title recently. Other competitive teams include men's soccer, baseball, basketball, and volleyball, and women's field hockey and tennis. Intramural sports are offered at two levels, competitive and recreational, and there are also club sports; roughly half the student body participate. Teams face off in everything from basketball and soccer to rugby, rowing, kickball, and badminton.

While Vassar continues to offer a menu of high-quality liberal arts courses emphasizing interdisciplinary connections, the college has also embraced technology and diversity, helping to create an atmosphere where individual passions shine. Says one contented Brewer, "We take the time to enjoy college for what it is—a serious, but not too serious, time of life for learning and development."

Highly anticipated Founder's Day festivities include music, carnival rides, food, fireworks, and a movie.

Overlaps

Brown, Wesleyan, Yale, Princeton, Tufts, Columbia, Cornell University, Wellesley

If You Apply To ➤

Vassar: Early decision I: Nov. 15. Early decision II and regular decision: Jan. 1. Financial aid: Feb. 1. Application fee: $70. No campus interviews. Alumni interviews: optional, informational. SATs or ACTs: required. Subject Tests: optional. Letters of recommendation: required. Essay: required. "Your Space" section of application allows candidates room to show something else about themselves. Accepts the Common Application.

University of Vermont

194 South Prospect Street, Burlington, VT 05401

For an out-of-stater sizing up public universities, there could hardly be a more appealing place than UVM. The size is manageable, Burlington is a fabulous college town, and Lake Champlain and the Green Mountains are on your doorstep. UVM feels like a private university, but, alas, it is also priced like one. Attracts a mix of party animals and serious types.

With its beautiful setting, wide academic offerings, and abundance of clubs and cocurricular pursuits, the University of Vermont draws students from around the country. And, says a math major, they're not all granola types with a penchant for soy milk and snowboarding. While it's a public school, UVM's academics, research opportunities, and price tag are more akin to those of a private institution. Generous financial aid packages and growth plans are helping to ensure that Vermont remains both affordable and relevant amid increasing competition from schools of both types.

Chartered in 1791, UVM was established as the fifth college in New England. UVM's picturesque campus sits on the shores of Lake Champlain in Burlington,

Website: www.uvm.edu
Location: Small City
Public
Total Enrollment: 11,290
Undergraduates: 9,991
Male/Female: 40/60
SAT Ranges: CR 550–650, M 550–640

(continued)

ACT Ranges: 25–30
Financial Aid: 82%
Pell Grant: 20%
Expense: Pub $ $ $
Student Loans: 61%
Average Debt: $ $ $
Phi Beta Kappa: Yes
Applicants: 25,274
Accepted: 70%
Enrolled: 13%
Grad in 6 Years: 76%
Returning Freshmen: 86%
Academics: ✑ ✑ ✑ ½
Social: 🐵 🐵 🐵 🐵 🐵
Q of L: ★ ★ ★ ★ ★
Admissions: (802) 656-3370
Email Address: admissions@
   uvm.edu

Strong Programs:
Business Administration
English
Environmental Studies
Political Science
Psychology
Engineering
Preveterinary
Premed

Through the Vermont Legislative Research Service, public policy students provide state legislators with policy briefs on current issues.

virtually a stone's throw from the Canadian border. Architectural styles range from colonial to high Victorian Gothic and functional modern; the oldest structures, in the center of the campus, are recognized on the National Registry of Historic Places. Three older residence halls dubbed the "shoeboxes" have been torn down to make way for a new residence hall, and the university's newest facility is a state-of-the-art STEM complex.

The product of a merger of a private college and public university, UVM attained quasi-public status in 1862 with the passage of the Morrill Land Grant College Act. Today, the university blends the traditions of both a private and public university. UVM's seven undergraduate colleges and schools set their own curricula and general education requirements, but administrators say most students need to take courses in the arts, humanities, social sciences, languages, literature, math, sustainability, and physical sciences. Also mandatory is a credit-bearing course in Race and Culture or a course that explores race relations and ethnic diversity in the United States. All first-year students must fulfill a three-credit foundational writing and information literacy requirement.

> "Professors do an excellent job of combining curricula with a sense of purpose."

Some of the most popular majors include business administration, English, environmental studies, political science, and psychology; students also give high marks to the engineering program. Premed, nursing, and prevet students benefit from the research and teaching capabilities of Vermont's fine medical school, as well as from a seven-year program with the vet school at Tufts. A life skills program for athletes emphasizes health and wellness, academic skills, and moral and ethical reasoning. New majors in data science, biomedical engineering, and food systems have recently been added. How tough is the academic environment? "It really depends on what coursework you're following," says one student. Half of all classes enroll fewer than 20 students, and professors are said to be accessible and supportive. A junior says, "Professors do an excellent job of combining curricula with a sense of purpose. Everything we do here is worthwhile."

Special programs for first-years include the five-day TREK programs, in which students, led by upper-class mentors, go hiking or biking, do community service, or take a leadership skills development course before classes start. Students are especially enthused about the Teacher Advisory Program (TAP), in which groups of 10 to 15 first-years participate in a writing-intensive, discussion-oriented seminar taught by a professor who is also each student's advisor. Students in the Honors College are required to write a senior thesis, and an environmental studies major notes, "There are also lots of opportunities for undergraduates to get involved in professors' research because we have a relatively small population of grad students." Through the Vermont Legislative Research Service, undergraduate public policy students provide state legislators with policy briefs on current issues. Each year, 35 percent of all undergrads go abroad; UVM offers 700 programs in 50 countries.

"UVM students are laid-back and friendly. The community is very accepting of everyone and each individual has a unique place they fill within that community," says one student. Twenty-nine percent of UVM students are native Vermonters and 3 percent are international. Hispanics comprise 4 percent of the student body, Asian

> "You can drink; you can not drink; you can do whatever makes you happy."

Americans 3 percent, and African Americans 1 percent. "UVM is incredibly lacking in racial diversity," grumbles one sophomore, and social justice is said to be a hot topic of late. "UVM is definitely a campus with a conscience," observes an English major. "Students lean left of center, but it is by no means a single-minded institution." The university offers merit scholarships averaging $9,869 and 188 athletic awards in 18 sports.

"Students have to live on campus for their first two years. After that the majority of students move off campus," one junior explains; 49 percent of students reside in campus housing. "Living in the res hall is a ton of fun and it's an awesome environment to meet new people," adds an animal science major. UVM has more than a dozen dining halls, and they buy two-thirds of their food from local farmers. "There are so many options it's nuts! Vegan, vegetarian, sushi, Indian, gluten-free, and local food every day," cheers one student. Campus security measures are said to be effective, and when it comes to sexual violence on campus, one student says, "UVM students and staff alike are constantly promoting a culture of consent and reporting."

"UVM students are very social beings," says one student. "You can drink; you can not drink; you can do whatever makes you happy." Just 7 percent of UVM men and 8 percent of women join Greek groups, so when the weekend comes, college-sponsored movies, dances, karaoke nights, and coffeehouses are big draws. The Naked Bike Ride is a notable biannual tradition, according to a senior: "On the last day of classes each semester, hundreds of people gather at midnight to run or bike naked around a campus green."

Much of the fun also happens on nearby ski slopes and in Burlington itself, especially the Church Street pedestrian mall, where the music scene draws top talent and is always bustling. "You can spend your Friday night at a gourmet restaurant, an off-Broadway theater production, or bar-hopping around town, and still be atop a mountain skiing the very next morning," says a junior. Indeed, the energetic downtown boasts symphonies, art galleries, chic shopping, and lively bars and restaurants, and Lake Champlain is only five minutes away. Students are also actively engaged with the local community through volunteer opportunities. As much as they love their little city, students do look forward to getting out of town. Per Vermont law, students under 21 may not drink, so a favorite road trip is Montreal—90 minutes away—with its even bigger music scene and a drinking age of 18. The Outing Club is one of UVM's most popular student organizations, as the nearby Green Mountains, White Mountains, and Adirondacks offer prime hiking, backpacking, and rock climbing.

UVM fields a number of highly competitive Division I Catamount ("cat of the mountains") teams. Vermont's ice hockey team is the school's pride and joy, having ranked as high as second nationally. Students get access to tickets before the general public, a nice perk since games are always sold out. There is no football team, but soccer is very competitive and draws crowds in the fall; the men's team was the 2016 America East conference champion. The school has earned numerous America East Academic Cups for the best overall combined GPA among its student-athletes. The ski team is a perennial powerhouse (and 2015 conference champs) and the lacrosse team is strong too. Most students participate in at least one intramural sport, with broomball being most popular. Joystick jocks can sign up for intramural video game tournaments.

Students at UVM may be laid-back, but they're also curious, caring, open-minded, active, and willing to work hard. They view extracurricular involvement as critical to the undergraduate experience, and at UVM they find abundant opportunities to engage both inside and outside the classroom. Says one junior, "It's hard to describe the energy that ignites everything we do."

UVM has more than a dozen dining halls, and they buy two-thirds of their food from local farmers.

"It's hard to describe the energy that ignites everything we do."

Overlaps

University of Massachusetts Amherst, University of Connecticut, University of New Hampshire, University of Delaware, Syracuse, Northeastern, Boston College

If You Apply To ➤

UVM: Early action: Nov. 1. Regular decision: Jan. 15. Financial aid: Feb. 1. Application fee: $55. No campus or alumni interviews. SATs or ACTs: required. No Subject Tests. Letters of recommendation: required. Essay: required. Accepts the Common Application. Apply to individual schools or programs.

800 Lancaster Avenue, Villanova, PA 19085

Set in an upscale suburb, Villanova is becoming increasingly respected as Philadelphia's answer to Boston College. As at BC, about 80 percent of the students are Roman Catholic (compared with about half at Georgetown). The troika of business, engineering, and nursing are popular at 'Nova. Downtown Philadelphia is a quick hop away by train.

Website: www.villanova.edu
Location: Suburban
Private
Total Enrollment: 9,073
Undergraduates: 6,604
Male/Female: 48/52
SAT Ranges: CR 590–690, M 610–710
ACT Ranges: 29–32
Financial Aid: 58%
Pell Grant: 13%
Expense: Pr $ $ $
Student Loans: 55%
Average Debt: $ $ $ $
Phi Beta Kappa: Yes
Applicants: 16,206
Accepted: 48%
Enrolled: 22%
Grad in 6 Years: 89%
Returning Freshmen: 96%
Academics: ✍ ✍ ✍
Social: ☎ ☎ ☎
Q of L: ★ ★ ★
Admissions: (610) 519-4000
Email Address: gotovu@villanova.edu

Strong Programs:
Nursing
Finance
Biology
Communication
Mechanical Engineering

Villanova University takes pride in its Augustinian roots, even basing its admissions essay on one of St. Augustine's teachings about transforming "hearts and minds." The school has all the trappings of a typical Roman Catholic university, from strong academics to deeply rooted traditions and rivalries, and students firmly dedicated to their faith. Says one junior, "There are times I walk out of a class at Villanova and just have to stop for a second to take it all in and appreciate what an amazing opportunity I've been afforded."

Founded in 1842 by the community-focused Order of Saint Augustine, Villanova's lush campus of more than 260 acres is situated along Philadelphia's suburban Main Line. Ivy-covered buildings, well-kept lawns, and secluded, tree-lined walkways are a reminder of the campus's historical roots. Planning is underway for a major project that will transform 14 acres of parking lots and asphalt into a bustling area featuring new residence halls, a bistro, a performing arts center, and a pedestrian bridge.

Undergraduates may enroll in the College of Liberal Arts and Sciences, the Villanova School of Business, the College of Engineering, or the College of Nursing. General education requirements vary by school, but all first-year students take the two-semester Augustine and Culture Seminar (ACS) and are housed with their ACS classmates in learning communities in the dorms. In the first semester, students read works from the ancient, medieval, and Renaissance periods—ranging from the Greeks and Saint Augustine to the Middle Ages and Shakespeare. In the second semester, students explore works from the Early Modern, Enlightenment, Romantic, Modernist, and Contemporary eras.

"The courses are rigorous and are often discussion-oriented and reading- and writing-intensive."

Nursing, finance, and biology are especially popular at Villanova, as are the communication and mechanical engineering programs. Additional undergraduate majors include Latin American studies, gender and women's studies, and Arab and Islamic studies. Newer programs include a major and minor in public administration, and minors in global health, statistics, and creative writing. Forty-three percent of undergraduate classes have fewer than 20 students. "The courses are rigorous and are often discussion-oriented and reading- and writing-intensive," says one communication major. Another student says, "Villanova professors go the extra mile for their students through office hours, research, and personal conversations." An honors program is available to about 200 students, by invitation only. But even outside the honors program, a biology major says that in recent years, "the academics have become more demanding, and the admissions process has become more competitive." Thirty-nine percent of students study abroad each year.

"The students who attend Villanova are passionate and devoted," says a sophomore. "They care about their work, but, more importantly, they care about their community." Many are from the East Coast, and 19 percent hail from Pennsylvania; 3 percent come from foreign countries. African Americans account for 5 percent of the student body, Hispanics 8 percent, and Asian Americans 7 percent. "We're not an extremely political campus," one student muses, "although social justice issues like poverty, hunger, and homelessness are all big issues." Merit scholarships are available, averaging $14,595, as are 283 athletic scholarships in 24 sports.

Housing on campus is guaranteed for three years, and 69 percent of undergraduates call the dorms home. "Rooms are great at Villanova," says one senior. "My first and second year I had a sink in my room so I didn't have to walk down the hall to wash my face or brush my teeth. You can get all the premium channels you want and even DVR." Freshmen live primarily on the South Campus Circle, while upperclassmen take their chances in the lottery system. Most seniors move to houses and apartments in the surrounding towns. The meal plan offers more than a dozen campus eateries, which serve everything from pizza to Chinese food, wraps, and vegetarian and vegan menus. "Food at Villanova is delicious," says a student. "Tons of variety with so many options I sometimes don't know which one to choose." The university has implemented a number of measures to prevent campus sexual assault, including appointing a Title IX coordinator and developing mandatory training programs.

All first-year students take the two-semester Augustine and Culture Seminar and are housed in learning communities.

"I have never had a dull weekend at Villanova because there is always something going on. If you are looking to party, you can. If you are looking to just chill, you can do that too," a student explains. Weekend social life centers around campus events and parties, some sponsored by Greek groups, which claim 17 percent of the men and 42 percent of the women. **"Everyone works hard, plays hard, and still finds time to give back to the community."** Students get together with friends on Fridays and Saturdays at the Student Center for Late Night at Villanova events, such as comedians, bands, open-mic, and dance parties. Despite the tough courses, a senior says, "Everyone works hard, plays hard, and still finds time to give back to the community." About 400 students per semester participate in fall and spring service trips, volunteering with Habitat for Humanity or various missions. Each fall, Villanova hosts the largest student-run Special Olympics, which draws people from across campus and the local community. Juniors and seniors tend to spend evenings at bars along the local Main Line or in Philadelphia, just 12 minutes away by train. The city's entertainment and cultural opportunities include museums and pro sports, as well as events at numerous other colleges and universities, from La Salle and Temple to Drexel, Penn, and St. Joseph's.

Each fall, Villanova hosts the largest student-run Special Olympics.

When they are not out socializing, Villanova students are cheering for the men's basketball team, which rewarded their enthusiasm by bringing home the Division I national championship in 2016. Recent Big East conference champions include men's and women's indoor and outdoor track and field, men's cross-country, and women's swimming and diving. The university has also produced nearly 60 Olympians in its history, and Villanovans have participated in every Summer Olympics since 1948. Club sports, intramurals, and recreational opportunities are a big draw and popular activities include basketball, flag football, and soccer.

Despite the changes in the world around it, Villanova continues to be a Catholic university devoted to its students, community, and strong traditions, both spiritually and academically. The administration has set its sights on Villanova becoming one of the premier Roman Catholic institutions alongside Notre Dame, Georgetown, and Boston College. While the school takes pride in tradition, it recognizes that its technology improvements, continuing upgrades to facilities, and changing and improving educational programs will help its students remain competitive in the workplace and the world beyond.

Overlaps

Boston College, Fordham, University of Pennsylvania, Northeastern, Notre Dame, University of Virginia, Georgetown, Penn State

If You Apply To ➤

Villanova: Early action: Nov. 1. Regular decision and financial aid: Jan. 15. Housing: May 1. Application fee: $80. No campus or alumni interviews. SATs (with essay) or ACTs (with writing): required. Subject Tests: optional. Letters of recommendation: required. Essay: required. Accepts the Common Application with supplement. Apply to a particular school or program.

University of Virginia

P.O. Box 400160, Charlottesville, VA 22904

Is it Thomas Jefferson? The Romanesque architecture? The Charlottesville air? Whatever it is, students nationwide go ga-ga for UVA, where competition for out-of-state admission has hit the Ivy League level. Relatively small for a top-notch public flagship, UVA combines old-line conservatism with high-quality academics and a social scene that is spirited in multiple senses of the word. Charlottesville is a big small town with plenty of culture, just over two hours from D.C.

Website: www.virginia.edu
Location: Small City
Public
Total Enrollment: 21,010
Undergraduates: 15,198
Male/Female: 45/55
SAT Ranges: CR 620–720,
   M 620–730
ACT Ranges: 29–33
Financial Aid: 54%
Pell Grant: 12%
Expense: Pub $ $ $ $
Student Loans: 36%
Average Debt: $ $
Phi Beta Kappa: Yes
Applicants: 31,021
Accepted: 29%
Enrolled: 41%
Grad in 6 Years: 94%
Returning Freshmen: 97%
Academics: ✐ ✐ ✐ ✐ ✐
Social: 🐓 🐓 🐓 🐓
Q of L: ★ ★ ★ ★ ★
Admissions: (434) 982-3200
Email Address:
   undergradadmission@
   virginia.edu

Strong Programs:
Economics
Commerce
Biology
Foreign Affairs
Psychology
Sociology
Life Sciences

Easily one of the most prestigious public schools in the nation, the University of Virginia is known to all in Charlottesville as Mr. Jefferson's University. Not just any Mr. Jefferson, mind you, but *the* Mr. Jefferson, author of the Declaration of Independence. Though he passed away nearly two centuries ago, he is referred to here as if he ran down to the apothecary shop for a bit of snuff and will be back in a moment. Of all his accomplishments, Jefferson was arguably proudest of UVA—he even asked that his epitaph speak to his role in creating the university rather than his presidency of the United States.

Located just east of the Blue Ridge Mountains in central Virginia, UVA's campus (the "Grounds") is dotted with historic buildings designed by Jefferson himself and still in use today. At the core is Jefferson's "academical village," with majestic white pillars, serpentine walls, and extensive brick-work. The village rises around a rectangular terraced green, known as the Lawn, which is flanked by two rows of identical one-story rooms reserved for undergraduate student leaders. Five pavilions, each in a different style, are arranged on either side of the Lawn; all of them open onto a colonnaded walkway. Behind the buildings are public gardens, while the Rotunda, a half-scale model of the Roman Pantheon, overlooks the Lawn and stands as a symbol of Jefferson's Enlightenment belief in secularism and freedom.

> **"[University Seminars] provide somewhat of a break from your rigorous, everyday class."**

UVA isn't just an elite public school; this university holds its own against the best private schools as well. The most popular majors are economics, commerce, biology, foreign affairs, and psychology. Sociology and the life sciences draw praise as well, but students caution that math and other quantitative disciplines can be rough. Most students matriculate into the College of Arts and Sciences, but under-graduates may also enroll in the schools of Engineering, Nursing, or Architecture. After their second year, about 320 external transfer students and students from other UVA schools transfer into the McIntire School of Commerce, UVA's under-graduate business school. Not surprisingly, competition for these spots is tough. A five-year program for aspiring teachers yields a B.A. from the College of Arts and Sciences and a Master of Teaching degree from UVA's Curry School of Education. The Batten School of Leadership and Public Policy trains students for public service careers in both domestic and international arenas and offers a five-year bachelor/ master of public policy. Students who qualify for the Distinguished Majors program may pursue independent study during their third and fourth years.

"The University of Virginia fosters a collaborative, but competitive culture," says a student. Virginia requires students in the College of Arts and Sciences and the McIntire School to master a foreign language before graduation. Arts and Sciences students must also take courses in English composition, humanities and fine arts, social science, natural sciences and mathematics, non-Western studies, and com-position. Special programs for freshmen include University Seminars, designed to develop critical-thinking skills in an environment that encourages interactive learning and intensive discussion, and are limited to 20 students each. "These classes are based on interesting, current topics that provide somewhat of a break from your rigorous, everyday class," says a sociology major. They're also taught by some of the university's best faculty. "I have received a very high quality of teaching," says a student. "Many professors are experienced researchers who are enthusiastic about their research as well as excited to welcome future researchers into their labs."

Highly capable students may win admission to the Echols Scholars program, which allows about 200 top-entering freshmen the chance to pursue academic exploration without the constraints of distribution or major-field requirements. Echols students also live together for their first year. The Rodman Scholars program in the School of Engineering and Applied Science selects its members based on financial need, leadership, and scholarship. An intensive two-week January term provides additional opportunities for research seminars, interdisciplinary coursework, and study abroad. More than 1,700 students go abroad each year in UVA's 50 sponsored programs in 30 countries.

Students instituted Virginia's notable honor system in 1842 after no one owned up to shooting a professor on the Lawn. The residence halls, student council, and Judiciary Committee remain student-run to this day—and they really put the brakes on lying, cheating, or stealing. And don't take the policies lightly—breaching the codes means a swift dismissal from campus. After a number of controversial cases recently, discussions continue

> "[Many professors] are enthusiastic about their research as well as excited to welcome future researchers into their labs."

about the appropriateness of the single-sanction system. But rest assured, some form of the honor code will remain integral to the culture here. A classics major says, "Our honor code is more than just some words scribbled on paper—it's a way of life and a bond of trust between you, your peers, and faculty."

"Students are highly involved, and it sometimes feels as if extracurricular leadership and involvement is more important than academic achievement," says one junior. But students here are accustomed to overachieving: 89 percent of freshmen were ranked in the top 10th of their high school class. Sixty-eight percent of undergraduates are Virginians, and 5 percent are international. Admission for out-of-staters gets tougher every year, and many of those students come from New York, New Jersey, Pennsylvania, and Maryland. Six percent of UVA students are African American, 12 percent are Asian American, and 6 percent are Hispanic. As for raging social and political matters, "I believe racism and gender violence are big issues on campus," says a junior. UVA is one of only two public universities in the nation that practices need-blind admissions and meets 100 percent of all admitted students' demonstrated financial need (see also UNC at Chapel Hill). The school hands out hundreds of athletic scholarships each year, along with merit awards worth an average of $7,277 each. Twenty-five to 30 top achievers receive the highly prized Jefferson Scholarships, given annually by the alumni association and good for full tuition, room, and board.

Forty-one percent of students at Virginia live on campus, including 1,100 who bunk in the three residential colleges: Brown College at Monroe Hill, Hereford College, and International Residential College. Hereford's contemporary architecture has been described by the *New York Times* as "proudly, almost defiantly modern," in contrast to most of the other campus buildings. There are foreign language houses for students who want to work on their Russian, Spanish, French, or German—and one house where students can find groups of peers speaking Arabic, Chinese, Hindi-Urdu, Italian, Japanese, or Persian. Freshmen get first, and some say best, pick for housing. "UVA has been building beautiful new dorms with AC and everything else

UVA's campus (the "Grounds") is dotted with historic buildings designed by Thomas Jefferson himself and still in use today.

Students instituted Virginia's notable honor system in 1842 after no one owned up to shooting a professor on the Lawn.

you can imagine for first-year students. [We] call them McMansions since they are so nice," quips one senior. Fifty-four top students win the honor of living in spartan rooms along the lawn, and among the outer set of rooms, called the range, students can visit room #13, which was occupied for a semester by Edgar Allen Poe in 1826 before he was suspended for nonpayment of tuition. Meal plans are required for first-years and campus fare receives decent reviews. Upperclassmen either cook for themselves or take meals at the Greek houses; fraternities draw 25 percent of Virginia's men, and sororities sign up 28 percent of the women.

UVA attracted national attention in 2014 after a *Rolling Stone* article, subsequently retracted, made allegations of a gang rape at a fraternity house. The incident put UVA at the center of a broad national debate about the extent of drinking and sexual violence on college campuses, especially at fraternities. "Since then, the students and administration have rewritten the reporting and charging of sexual assault procedures to better serve the victims of assault," says one junior. A bevy of education and prevention programs, many of them student-driven, have also been implemented, such as Not On Our Grounds, Green Dot, One Less, and Hoos Got Your Back.

"There is a vibrant party life at UVA, so long as you get involved in an organization or two."

Students report feeling safe on campus. "We have campus police, Charlottesville police, and a new Ambassadors watch program all looking out for the safety of students."

Students say the UVA social scene is dynamic and varied. "There is a vibrant party life at UVA, so long as you get involved in an organization or two," says one student, who adds, "Greek life is prominent but not overpowering." Mr. Jefferson founded UVA as a place where students could come together to "drink from the cup of knowledge," and now that fraternity rush is dry and parties must have guest lists, there's a lot less quaffing of other brews going on. Still, determined Virginians haven't stopped metamorphosing into Rowdy Wahoos when the sun goes down—the nickname comes from a school cheer about a fish that can drink twice its weight. "There is not pressure to drink, though many students choose to do so," admits one junior. For nondrinkers and those under 21, the student-run University Union and more than 500 clubs and other organizations offer movies, concerts, social hours, and other booze-free options.

"Almost everything here is a tradition," says one student. Favorites include Foxfield each April, in which students dress up and host catered parties prior to attending a steeplechase horse race; jackets and ties also come out for football games, a relic of when UVA was all male and gridiron contests were an opportunity to meet women. May brings Beach Week, and streaking the lawn is a rite of passage, students say. "Any place that values streaking as much as we do has to be a fun place to spend four years," quips one English major. We would like to tell you more about the various secret societies, but we won't—they're secret, after all!

"Almost everything here is a tradition."

As for Charlottesville (population 46,000), it's "the perfect college town," says an anthropology major, and often a pleasant surprise for those coming from larger urban areas. There are restaurants; gorgeous vineyards and wineries; and plenty of bars, shops, theaters, and other cultural attractions. Students also tend to immerse themselves in community service in the area; UVA's nationally recognized Madison House coordinates the activities of a host of volunteer groups. Outdoorsy folks can hike, bike, ski, and sightsee in the nearby Blue Ridge Mountains, or simply daydream while strolling Skyline Drive. Popular road trips include Washington, D.C., Richmond, and anywhere the Cavaliers are playing football, basketball, or soccer.

While big-time Atlantic Coast Conference basketball has long been an integral part of UVA life, the Cavaliers field a number of competitive Division I teams. The men's soccer, baseball, and tennis teams were national champions in 2014, 2015, and 2016, respectively, and men's basketball and women's rowing are recent conference champs. There are also more than a dozen intramural sports leagues or tournaments, in everything from flag football to inner-tube water polo, and more than 65 club sports.

"UVA students are very driven," says a history major. "Instead of waiting for other students or administrators to solve a problem, they step up and take the initiative." The social life is as vigorous as the academics are rigorous, and the friendships that are formed here last far beyond the college years—much as Mr. Jefferson's legacy continues to be felt on campus, years after his death.

If You Apply To ➤ **UVA:** Early action: Nov. 1. Regular decision: Jan. 1. Financial aid: Mar. 1. Housing: May 1. Application fee: $60. No campus or alumni interviews. SATs or ACTs: required. Subject Tests: optional. Letters of recommendation: required. Essay: required. Accepts the Common Application.

Virginia Tech

Blacksburg, VA 24061

Offers a unique blend of high tech and Southern hospitality. Engineering has always been its calling card, but business and architecture are popular. Admission is competitive for out-of-state applicants. Blacksburg is a nice college town, but is far from the population centers near the coast. Hokie Nation loves its football team. Compare to Clemson, Georgia Tech, and Purdue.

Officially known as the Virginia Polytechnic Institute and State University, Virginia Tech is a former land grant university that now offers a slate of solid academic programs, competitive Division I athletics, and storied traditions. Engineering, business, and architecture attract top students from around the country who are proud to be part of the "Hokie Nation."

Its campus, set on a plateau in the scenic Blue Ridge Mountains, occupies 3,000 acres and comes complete with a duck pond, hiking trails, and a 200-year-old plantation that is a local landmark. Students enjoy unlimited outdoor recreation thanks to the proximity of the Jefferson National Forest, the Appalachian Trail, the scenic Blue Ridge Parkway, and the majestic old New River. The campus buildings are an attractive mix of gray limestone structures, colonial-style brick, and modern cement buildings. The campus continues to undergo renovations and additions.

Virginia Tech is best known for its first-rate technical and professional training. For undergrads with an appetite for engineering, Tech has programs for every taste, including aerospace, ocean, biological systems, civil, chemical, computer, electrical, industrial systems, materials, mechanical (the most popular), and mining. The Pamplin College of Business is also prominent, and the five-year architecture program is considered one of the nation's best. Though no longer Tech's centerpiece, the College of Agriculture and Life Sciences remains strong, especially in animal science. The university has established a new School of Neuroscience, and students in the College of Natural Resources and Environment can choose from such concentrations as environmental conservation, fisheries science, forestry, and wildlife management. They may also select a new, interdisciplinary major in water: resources, policy, and management.

> "[Professors] keep you on the edge of your seat."

Website: www.vt.edu
Location: Rural
Public
Total Enrollment: 29,766
Undergraduates: 24,800
Male/Female: 57/43
SAT Ranges: CR 540–640, M 560–680
ACT Ranges: N/A
Financial Aid: 60%
Pell Grant: N/A
Expense: Pub $ $ $
Student Loans: 53%
Average Debt: $ $ $
Phi Beta Kappa: Yes
Applicants: 22,280
Accepted: 73%
Enrolled: 39%
Grad in 6 Years: 83%
Returning Freshmen: 94%
Academics: ✍ ✍ ✍
Social: ☎ ☎ ☎
Q of L: ★ ★ ★ ★

(continued)

Admissions: (540) 231-6267
Email Address: admissions@
    vt.edu

Strong Programs:
Engineering
Business
Architecture
Animal Science
Biological Sciences
Performing Arts
Marketing
Family and Consumer Sciences

*The university
has established
a new School of
Neuroscience.*

*Students in the Corps
of Cadets choose
between a military/
ROTC track and a
citizen-leader track,
and can earn a minor
in leadership.*

Students in the sciences reap the benefits of their high-tech environment; other disciplines do not fare so well. The humanities have been hard-hit by budget cuts. In particular, "religious studies, foreign languages, and philosophy are dwindling away," says a senior. One bright spot is internationally known poet Nikki Giovanni, who teaches creative writing and advanced poetry. The university also has a tradition of excellence in the performing arts, and the school's theater group has received more awards from the American College Theater Arts Festival than any other college in the Southeast.

All students are required to take courses in English, math, humanities, and social and natural science. There is also a foreign language requirement, though high school coursework may cover this. Introductory class size tends to be large—sometimes well into the hundreds. Most of the big lecture classes are taught by full-time faculty, though discussions and grading are generally handled by TAs. Nevertheless, a communications major says professors "keep you on the edge of your seat." The 1,500 or so students who participate in the university honors program are guaranteed access to top faculty and research opportunities.

Each year, more than 1,000 students take advantage of Tech's co-op opportunities available in almost all majors. The nationally acclaimed Small Business Institute program enables faculty-led groups of business majors to work with local merchants, analyze their problems, and make suggestions on how to increase profits. The Corps of Cadets, a tradition since the university's founding in 1872, offers a unique opportunity for students who wish to combine leadership training with an academic major. The 1,000 Cadets who enroll follow a structured military lifestyle, living together in the Corps' five dedicated residence halls and wearing uniforms to class. In addition to choosing between a military/ROTC track and a citizen-leader track, Cadets can earn a minor in leadership. Two-thirds of undergrads conduct research, and for those who want to study abroad, Tech offers more than 200 programs in 60 nations around the globe.

Seventy-six percent of undergraduates call Virginia home, and 6 percent arrive from abroad. Not surprisingly, the admissions office is inundated with out-of-state applicants, which means stiff competition for the slots available to non-Virginians.

"[Blacksburg] revolves around Tech."

Tech's relative isolation from major cities is a drag on minority recruitment: African Americans represent 4 percent, Hispanics 6 percent, and Asian Americans 10 percent. Students looking at pricey Northeastern technical schools will find Tech a real bargain. The university hands out a few hundred athletic scholarships, in addition to thousands of merit scholarships averaging $3,334. The "Funds for the Future" program aims to provide additional aid to low-income undergraduates.

Tech housing is nothing to write home about, but adequate to meet the needs of most students. "Rooms are on the small side, but they provide all you need to live," says a freshman. Some 25 undergraduate dorms serve 8,400 students; 37 percent of students live on campus, though only freshmen and the Corps of Cadets are required to. Students who are committed to a healthy lifestyle can opt to reside in the WELL (Wellness Environment for Living and Learning), which will provide them with a substance-free atmosphere, includes special healthy-living courses, and is overseen by a specially trained wellness staff. Most upperclassmen live off campus in nearby apartment complexes. Dietrick's Depot, the largest dining hall on campus, was recently renovated. Three specialty lines supplement the standard dining-hall fare to create a café-style atmosphere.

Leisure-time favorites include school-sponsored plays, jazz concerts, arts and crafts fairs, and dances. The nearby Cascades National Park is an especially popular retreat, and tubing down the New River is a ritual for summer students. The most important annual events are the Ring Dance (when the juniors receive their school rings), the German Club's Midwinter's Dance, and the Corps of Cadets military ball. Fourteen percent of the men and 18 percent of the women join fraternities and sororities, which set the tone of social life. Blacksburg offers the usual city fare and one student says the town "revolves around Tech." Another adds, "Most students go downtown to shoot pool, dance, or go to a bar." For real big-city action, Washington, D.C., and Richmond are four and three hours away by car, respectively.

Virginia Tech competes in the Division I Atlantic Coast Conference, and the football team's multiple appearances in postseason bowl games have cheered alumni and hiked applications by several thousand. The annual big game pits the Hokies against the Cavaliers of the University of Virginia. Tech has one of the nation's most extensive intramural programs, with everything from football to horseshoes and underwater hockey—a recent rage—and more than 400 softball teams each spring, many of them co-ed.

Virginia Tech encourages students to "invent the future," and that's just what today's citizens of the Hokie Nation aim to do. By taking advantage of Tech's particular blend of high-tech learning and Southern hospitality, students have countless opportunities to gain industry experience, travel abroad, and spend four years with like-minded men and women.

Overlaps

George Mason, James Madison, University of Maryland, Penn State, University of Virginia

If You Apply To ➤

Tech: Early decision: Nov. 1. Regular decision and financial aid: Jan. 15. Application fee: $60. No campus or alumni interviews. SATs or ACTs: required. Subject Tests: optional. Letters of recommendation: optional. Essay: recommended. Music applicants must audition.

Wabash College

301 West Wabash, Crawfordsville, IN 47933

Wabash and Hampden–Sydney in Virginia are the last of the all-male breed. With steady enrollment and plenty of money in the bank, Wabash shows no signs of changing. Intense bonding is an important part of the Wabash experience, and few co-ed schools can match the loyalty of Wabash alumni. The Gentleman's Rule says it all.

Wabash was founded in Indiana in 1832 by transplanted Ivy Leaguers who shared the Enlightenment's optimistic view of human nature and envisioned a "classical and English high school rising into a college as soon as the wants of the country demand." Their vision proved to be on target. All-male Wabash has not only prospered but also remained true to its conservative academic and social traditions, including the Gentleman's Rule code of self-responsibility that students continue to live by. "Wabash College has a culture that has not changed for 50 years. It can be a hard school to fit into if you do not meet the status quo, but it also is a brotherhood," says a junior.

The Wabash campus is characterized by redbrick, white-columned, Georgian-style buildings (three are originals from the 1830s). Located in the heart of Crawfordsville, a small town of about 16,000, Wabash is surrounded by grass and tall trees that are part of the gorgeous Fuller Arboretum. The college completed a $24 million student housing construction project in 2016 that added six new residential buildings and renovated the flagship dorm, Martindale Hall.

The Wabash educational program has certainly proved itself over the years. This small college has amassed an impressive list of alumni: executives of major

Website: www.wabash.edu
Location: Small City
Private
Total Enrollment: 867
Undergraduates: 867
Male/Female: 100/0
SAT Ranges: CR 510–610, M 530–640
ACT Ranges: 22–28
Financial Aid: 98%
Pell Grant: 23%
Expense: Pr $ $
Student Loans: 91%
Average Debt: $ $ $ $
Phi Beta Kappa: Yes
Applicants: 1,247

(continued)

Accepted: 61%
Enrolled: 31%
Grad in 6 Years: 73%
Returning Freshmen: 85%
Academics: ✎ ✎ ✎ ½
Social: ☎ ☎
Q of L: ★ ★ ★
Admissions: (800) 345-5385
Email Address: admissions@
    wabash.edu

Strong Programs:
History
Political Science
Economics
Biology
Chemistry
Mathematics
Theater
Religion

corporations, doctors, lawyers, and a large number of Ph.D.s. Wabash alumni are typically faithful to their school in the form of generous donations. On a per-capita basis, the school's $355 million endowment makes it one of the wealthiest in the nation. This financial security enables Wabash to refuse any federal aid, with the exception of Pell Grants, which go directly to students; of the most recent freshman class, 23 percent qualify.

General education requirements include courses from a wide variety of fields— natural and behavioral sciences, literature and fine arts, mathematics, language studies, and a course on cultures and traditions. All freshmen take a tutorial in the fall that is designed to focus them on reading, writing, and class participation, followed by a colloquium titled Enduring Questions in the spring. All seniors complete comprehensive examinations in their final semester, consisting of two days of written exams in their major and an hour-long oral exam on their overall liberal arts experience.

> "Wabash College has a culture that has not changed for 50 years…but it also is a brotherhood."

History, political science, and economics draw the most majors at Wabash, and high accolades go to the biology and chemistry departments, which send many successful grads to medical school. Mathematics, theater, and religion are also traditional strengths. Many programs have been augmented with cross-cultural immersion learning courses with short-term travel components—at no extra cost to students. Those who can't satisfy their high-tech interests at Wabash can opt for a 3–2 program in engineering with Columbia University or Washington University in St. Louis, or a dual degree in engineering with Purdue University. New minors include neuroscience, black studies, and electronic music.

"The workload is tough, but anywhere you look you can find help. The resources at this college are endless," reassures a psychology major. Seventy-two percent of classes have fewer than 20 students, which students say creates a collaborative atmosphere. "Most professors prefer active involvement in the classroom and are passionate about what they are teaching," says one student. Students roundly praise the Quantitative Skills Center and the Writing Center for their assistance with classwork, as well as career services for connecting them with internships, jobs, and influential alumni.

The school's $355 million endowment makes it one of the wealthiest in the nation.

Paid, full-time research positions with faculty are a popular summertime pursuit at Wabash, particularly among students in the sciences. Juniors are encouraged to study abroad through programs in 40 countries, and 18 percent do so. Domestic study options are available through the Great Lakes College Association* as well. Wabash has recently developed a Liberal Arts Plus initiative that provides hands-on experience in four interdisciplinary fields: democracy and public discourse; global health; innovation, business, and entrepreneurship; and digital arts and human values. Participating students engage in such opportunities as academic summits, internships, consulting projects, volunteer work, and travel abroad.

Wabash students are "down-to-earth, hardworking, and respectful," according to one junior. Most come from public high schools in Indiana, but 23 percent come from other states, and 7 percent come from foreign countries. African Americans comprise 6 percent of the student body, Hispanics 7 percent, and Asian Americans 1 percent. A junior reports, "Wabash is predominantly conservative, so very little Black Lives Matter or LGBTQ protesting is present on campus," although the question of whether to admit transgender students to the college has recently sparked debate. Merit awards averaging $19,157 are available to qualified students.

> "The workload is tough, but anywhere you look you can find help."

Residential life revolves around the 10 fraternities, all but one of which have their own houses. Fifty-four percent of the students join up, and many end up living with their brothers. The college also offers five residence halls, two lodges, and two duplex-style townhomes; all told, 91 percent of students live on campus. Dorm residents must eat in the dining hall. "Nine times out of 10, the food is good, but that one time can really stand out," says a sophomore. Campus security gets mixed reviews.

The surrounding town of Crawfordsville leaves much to be desired. With few options off campus, fraternities tend to dominate the social scene. "Greek organizations *are* the social life on campus. No one else throws parties," says a sophomore. Many students say that there is a noticeable divide between fraternity brothers and "independents." Some non-Greeks may feel especially excluded when the fraternities "ship in" sorority members from Butler, DePauw, Indiana, and Purdue for parties. As for drinking on campus, students say that policies are generally loose, as long as students are behaving responsibly. Traditions are taken seriously at Wabash, from homecoming to not passing beneath certain archways on campus. Chapel Sing, where all the freshmen compete to see who can best sing the lengthy school song, is a favorite tradition, but undoubtedly the biggest is the school's long-standing rivalry with DePauw, which is capped off every year by the football game that decides who gets to keep the prized Monan Bell.

> "Greek organizations *are* the social life on campus."

That competitive spirit extends to all of the Little Giants (so named because the 1904 football team was performing above its weight) Division III athletic programs. In 2016, for the third consecutive season, the wrestling team won multiple national championship titles in individual weight classes, and the football team won the conference title. Cross-country and track and field are also competitive. About three-quarters of students participate in intramurals, which encompass 20 sports, including flag football and softball.

Traditions have not changed much since the school's founding in the 1830s and still play an important part in the lives of the men at Wabash. Some students complain about the lack of women and culture in the surrounding area, but many are happy with the college's intensive, rigorous programs and expanding opportunities for interdisciplinary study and hands-on experiences. It's a boys club and a brotherhood. Says one senior, "Wabash men have a sense of being in the trenches with one another. I would give a fellow student the shirt off my back because I have every confidence he'd do the same for me."

In 2016, the wrestling team won multiple national championship titles in individual weight classes.

Overlaps

Indiana University, Ball State, Purdue, Indiana State, Franklin, DePauw, Butler, Hanover

If You Apply To >

Wabash: Early decision: Oct. 15. Early action: Nov. 1. Regular decision: Jan. 15. Financial aid: Feb. 15. Housing: May 1. Application fee: $40. Campus and alumni interviews: optional, evaluative. SATs or ACTs: required (SAT essay and ACT writing recommended). No Subject Tests. Letters of recommendation: required. Essay: required. Accepts the Common Application.

Wake Forest University

Winston-Salem, NC 27109

Wake Forest's Baptist heritage and Winston–Salem location give it a more down-home flavor than Duke or Emory. With just over 4,800 undergraduates, Wake Forest is small compared with its Atlantic Coast Conference rivals but bigger than most liberal arts colleges. The strong Greek system dominates the social scene. Holds its own in the ACC with universities more than five times its size.

Website: www.wfu.edu
Location: Suburban
Private
Total Enrollment: 7,455
Undergraduates: 4,805
Male/Female: 47/53
SAT Ranges: CR 590–690,
   M 610–720
ACT Ranges: 27–33
Financial Aid: 55%
Pell Grant: 11%
Expense: Pr $ $ $
Student Loans: 39%
Average Debt: $ $ $ $
Phi Beta Kappa: Yes
Applicants: 13,281
Accepted: 29%
Enrolled: 33%
Grad in 6 Years: 88%
Returning Freshmen: 93%
Academics: ✐ ✐ ✐ ✐
Social: ☎ ☎ ☎
Q of L: ★ ★ ★
Admissions: (336) 758-5201
Email Address: admissions@
   wfu.edu

Strong Programs:
Politics and International
   Affairs
Finance
Communication
Biology
Business and Enterprise
   Management
Biomedical Sciences

Drawing on the strength of its graduate programs, the university now offers a B.S. in biochemistry and molecular biology.

Long one of the top private schools in the Southeast, Wake Forest has transformed its regional recognition into a national reputation. Known for basketball—at least half the student body attends every home game, one junior says—Wake Forest's solid academics are worthy of a look as well. Students work hard, hence the nickname "Work Forest," but the university's size and strong Greek system means it's also easy to establish close friendships. "Wake Forest is the best of both worlds," says a political science major. "Academics are challenging and you're surrounded by motivated and intelligent peers. At the same time, students pride themselves on being social."

Located in the Central Piedmont region of North Carolina, Wake Forest's 340-acre campus features flowers, wooded trails, and stately magnolias. There are more than 40 Georgian-style buildings constructed of old Virginia brick with granite trim. The campus is bordered by the lush, 148-acre Reynolda Gardens annex, which features a formal garden, greenhouses, and one of the first collections of Japanese cherry trees in the U.S. Construction is underway on a new first-year residence hall that will accommodate 225 freshmen.

To graduate from Wake Forest, students must complete two courses in health and exercise science, one foreign language course, a writing seminar, and a first-year seminar. In addition, students must take courses in each of five divisions: humanities, literatures, fine arts, social sciences, and math and natural sciences. Students must also satisfy a cultural diversity requirement. The most popular programs include politics and international affairs, finance, communication, and biology. The School

> **"Academics are challenging and you're surrounded by motivated and intelligent peers."**

of Business is highly regarded, although faculty members have expressed concerns about support that its BB&T Center for the Study of Capitalism has received from the free-market fundamentalist Koch brothers. Drawing on the strength of its graduate programs in biomedical sciences, the university now offers a B.S. in biochemistry and molecular biology and a concentration in medicinal chemistry and drug discovery. A new B.S. in engineering degree is available as well, with optional emphases in biomedical and materials engineering.

Students agree that courses at Wake Forest are rigorous, but a history and psychology double major says, "I have been impressed by how collaborative Wake students are." Fifty-eight percent of classes have fewer than 20 students. Faculty members get high marks; graduate assistants teach some labs and health classes, but otherwise professors are at the lectern. "I've been told by professors, department heads, and academic advisors that their first goal for me is that I learn the material and have enriching experiences while at school," says a physics major. "It's very refreshing to have faculty who put the emphasis on this rather than grades." The Office of Personal and Career Development takes a four-year approach to helping students prepare for future careers.

Fifty-nine percent of undergraduates receive academic credit for classes that require faculty-mentored research, and Richter Scholarships fund select independent study or research projects that involve travel away from campus. The Pro Humanitate Institute allows students to put their skills and knowledge to work helping the community; the center takes its name from the school's motto, which means "In Service to Humanity." Exceptionally able students may qualify for the Honors in Arts and Sciences distinction by taking three or more honors seminars during their first three years. And for those who get claustrophobic in Winston-Salem, Wake Forest's own residential study centers in London, Vienna, and on the Grand Canal in Venice beckon. Wake Forest offers more than 400 semester, summer, and year-long study abroad programs in more than 70 countries worldwide; 61 percent of the student body participates.

"Students at Wake Forest are highly driven above all else," says a senior. Seventy-nine percent of the student body hails from outside North Carolina, including 8 percent who come from foreign countries. "Students tend to be very conservative," says a sophomore, and a senior adds, "We are not a politically active school." Wake Forest's efforts to boost diversity continue; currently, African Americans make up 6 percent of the undergraduate population, Asian Americans add 5 percent, and Hispanics contribute 7 percent. Although the university meets 100 percent of admitted students' demonstrated financial need, it is not strong on socioeconomic diversity, with just 11 percent of freshmen qualifying for Pell Grants. Merit scholarships averaging $14,516 are awarded to eligible students, in addition to 168 athletic scholarships.

Seventy-seven percent of students live on campus, as they are required to do so for their first three years. "Many of the dorms are getting renovated, which is great because some of them were definitely in need," says a junior. In addition to all-gender restrooms across campus, the university now offers gender-neutral housing options and has increased the size and visibility of its LGBTQ Center. Dining options have improved recently, students say: "The dining options are quite good. There are two standard cafeterias, as well as a Starbucks, Chick-fil-A, Moe's, Subway, and other options."

The university now offers gender-neutral housing options and has increased the size and visibility of its LGBTQ Center.

"[Professors'] first goal for me is that I learn the material and have enriching experiences."

One student complains, "Campus security could be better. There is a fair amount of crime in certain areas of campus." Students say sexual assault is not a prevalent issue, but the Safe Office is an effective resource for those who need it.

Thirty-five percent of men and 57 percent of women go Greek, and Greek life dominates the social scene. Fraternities and sororities do not have houses on campus, but they throw open parties in dorm lounges or in off-campus houses. "Other organizations, such as Student Union, make a huge effort to bring other social options, such as concerts, movies, and events, to campus," says a student. The school's honor code helps to keep rowdy behavior in check; as one student says, "If you are caught with alcohol, and you are under 21, there are strict consequences." Everyone enjoys the annual homecoming festivities, and after the Demon Deacons score a victory on the basketball court, students roll the quad in toilet paper to celebrate. Other favorite events include a midnight concert by the school orchestra every Halloween, with members in full costume, and the Lilting Banshees comedy troupe, which helps students laugh off their stressful workloads. Another Wake Forest tradition is Hit the Bricks, an eight-hour relay race along the brick pathways of Hearn Plaza in honor of Brian Piccolo, a Wake Forest alumnus and Chicago Bears running back who died of cancer at age 26. Popular road trips are to the beach or the mountains; Chapel Hill, Durham, and Raleigh are each 100 miles away, and Atlanta and the Washington/Baltimore areas are about a five-hour drive.

Popular volunteer activities include Project Pumpkin, a trick-or-treat night on campus for underprivileged children.

The city of Winston-Salem is rich in culture, with a symphony, a Christmastime "Moravian love feast," and the well-known University of North Carolina School of the Arts. It's also home to the corporate headquarters of Krispy Kreme Doughnuts. "Winston is a very suburban town with a lot of young families and a Southern feel," a student says. In addition to Wake's on-campus Museum of Anthropology, a number of art museums—Reynolda House, the Museum of American Art, and Southeastern Center for Contemporary Art—are within three miles of campus. The town also has a strong music scene, with live bands playing at Ziggy's and the Garage. Popular volunteer activities include Project Pumpkin, a trick-or-treat night on campus for underprivileged children.

"We are a small school with big school spirit."

When it comes to sports, basketball is the undisputed king at Wake Forest. The men's team competes in the incredibly tough Division I Atlantic Coast Conference and is perennially strong. Other solid teams include baseball and men's and women's

golf, tennis, and soccer; men's tennis won the 2016 conference championship. Of course, virtually any contest against in-state rival UNC at Chapel Hill is guaranteed to get students excited. Intramural and club sports are also offered; the most popular intramurals include flag football, soccer, and softball, though volleyball, street hockey, bowling, and other sports are available too. "Fun supersedes talent," a senior says. "Students are rarely left out of a particular game if they express interest in participating."

That spirit of involvement and dedication to the community pervades the Wake Forest experience. Whether students are serving the less fortunate or chipping away at their heavy workloads, they benefit from motivated peers, dedicated faculty, and gorgeous surroundings. As one student says, "We are a small school with big school spirit."

If You Apply To >

Wake Forest: Early decision I: Nov. 15. Early decision II, regular decision, and financial aid: Jan. 1. Application fee: $65. Campus interviews: recommended, evaluative. No alumni interviews. SATs or ACTs: optional. Subject Tests: optional. Letters of recommendation: required. Essay: required. Accepts the Common Application with supplement.

Warren Wilson College

P.O. Box 9000, Asheville, NC 28815

Among a handful of schools where students combine academics, community service, and on-campus work that helps keep tuition down. Roots in the culture of Appalachia combine with a strong international and environmental orientation to give Warren Wilson its distinctive flavor. Setting in the mountains of western North Carolina is tough to beat. Campus atmosphere ranges from liberal to far-out alternative.

Warren Wilson is a small liberal arts college flush with engaging little quirks. It promotes global perspectives, puts many students to work on the campus farm, and makes service learning a central part of the educational experience. The school is also at the forefront of the "green" movement and has partnered with the city of Asheville to purchase offsets for 100 percent of its carbon emission. And at what other college is white-water paddling considered a leading intercollegiate sport? "We are a very expressive group," says a senior. "We wear the clothes that we want to wear, we dance and sing and play music, we talk about whatever comes to mind. This is a place where you can be whoever you want and you don't get judged for it."

Founded by the Presbyterian Church in 1894 as the Asheville Farm School, Warren Wilson College initially provided formal schooling for "mountain boys." In 1967, it transmogrified into a four-year, co-ed liberal arts college that, while still maintaining its Presbyterian heritage, welcomes students of all backgrounds. WWC is located 15 minutes from downtown Asheville in the lush Swannanoa Valley of the Blue Ridge Mountains. Its 1,132-acre campus features formal gardens, fruit and vegetable gardens, a 300-acre farm, and approximately 15 miles of hiking trails. Consistent with campus culture, the wood and stone buildings are small in scale and done in an architectural style that emphasizes natural earth tones accented by extensive stonework by traditional Appalachian stonemasons. The campus is home to one of

> **"This is a place where you can be whoever you want and you don't get judged for it."**

Website: www.warren-wilson.edu
Location: City Outskirts
Private
Total Enrollment: 796
Undergraduates: 737
Male/Female: 40/60
SAT Ranges: CR 518–650, M 470–590
ACT Ranges: 21–28
Financial Aid: 95%
Pell Grant: 41%
Expense: Pr $
Student Loans: 71%
Average Debt: $
Phi Beta Kappa: No
Applicants: 809
Accepted: 84%
Enrolled: 29%
Grad in 6 Years: 53%
Returning Freshmen: 63%

the most important Cherokee archaeological sites in the Southern Appalachian Mountains, dating from as early as 5000 B.C.

The signature feature of the WWC curriculum is its unique Triad Education Program, which combines liberal arts coursework, community service, and campus work. To graduate, students have to perform at least 100 hours of service learning through organizations such as Habitat for Humanity or environmental organizations. Warren Wilson is also one of only a half dozen four-year colleges in the nation that requires all residential students to work on campus. To fulfill their weekly 15-hour work requirement, students work on design and construction, blacksmithing, locksmithing, carpentry, and recycling projects, as well as keeping the college farm going. To meet general education requirements, WWC students take a broad range of liberal arts courses aimed at developing four core competencies: critical inquiry, effective communication, civic engagement, and self-awareness. The First-Year Experience Program lays a foundation for academic success by introducing students to the study-serve-work trinity through small, interactive group activities. All first-year students enroll in the First-Semester Seminar, which includes field experience and/or a service-learning component that takes students and faculty off campus for a day or a weekend. In addition, every undergraduate major requires a culminating capstone project.

> "Professors are really hit or miss, to be totally honest."

Students may choose from 34 majors, many of which offer concentrations, and 24 minors. The most popular majors are environmental studies, history/political science, psychology, and art. The creative writing program is highly regarded, and students give high marks to the natural sciences, especially biology, but say physics could use improvement. Dual-degree programs are available in pre-environmental management, preforestry, and applied science, and the integrative studies major allows students to develop and complete individually designed majors. The outdoor leadership major prepares students to lead outdoor adventure education programs, focusing on both technical skills like backpacking and rock climbing and interpersonal skills like leadership and counseling. Appalachian studies, a minor within the global studies program, serves as a catalyst for local cultural activities, including numerous musical groups. And where else does the music department offer you the choice of "finger-picking" or "flat-picking" guitar?

"I would say the academic environment is collaborative, but that definitely doesn't mean that it is easy or relaxed," says one student. Eighty-five percent of classes have fewer than 20 students. "Professors are really hit or miss, to be totally honest. My social work professors have been incredible, dedicated, knowledgeable, and accessible," says one student. The college offers honors programs in biology, chemistry, English, and environmental studies; 3 percent of students enroll. Internship opportunities are available in most undergraduate programs. Fifty-three percent of students study abroad during their time at WWC. Juniors take a semester-long course and then spend two to four weeks on an international "field experience"—with the cost partly built into their regular tuition—and qualified students may also study for a semester or two in countries such as Italy, China, India, Finland, and South Korea.

Typical Warren Wilson students are "drum majors for social justice," according to one sophomore. "There are smokers, artsy people, hippies, preppy people, rich and poor people, hard workers and chill workers," adds a junior. Upon graduation, most go into service professions such as teaching or working for environmental or other nongovernmental organizations. The first step for some is into the Peace Corps. Twenty-six percent of students are native North Carolinians, and 2 percent are international. African Americans and Hispanics account for 4 percent and 9 percent, respectively, while Asian Americans account for 1 percent.

> "[Students are] drum majors for social justice."

(continued)

Academics: ✐ ✐ ✐ ½
Social: ☎ ☎ ☎ ☎
Q of L: ★ ★ ★ ★ ★
Admissions: (800) 934-3536
Email Address: admit@ warren-wilson.edu

Strong Programs:
Environmental Studies
History/Political Science
Psychology
Art
Creative Writing
Outdoor Leadership
Appalachian Studies
Global Studies

Wilson requires all residential students to work on campus for 15 hours per week.

Roughly 41 percent of students are Pell-eligible. Merit scholarships averaging $9,105 are available, but not on the basis of athletic achievement.

Eighty-eight percent of students live in dorms. "Residence halls are okay," says an environmental studies major. "They're nothing fancy and sometimes have some cosmetic issues, but they get the job done." The 36-bed EcoDorm—the first building on a college campus to achieve LEED Platinum certification in the category of Existing Buildings—incorporates solar heating and natural ventilation, and is made of hardwoods milled on campus. Other theme housing options are also available. Overall, housing is plentiful and well maintained (unless the student workforce slacks off). "There are two main dining halls and two other cafés," a student explains. "All options account for vegan, vegetarian, gluten-free needs in one way or another." A junior says students feel safe on campus. "We have a Public Safety office and crew which is always responsive and helpful." The Office for Gender and Relationships provides advocacy, support, and education regarding diverse gender identities and campus sexual assault.

> *The 36-bed EcoDorm incorporates solar heating and natural ventilation, and is made of hardwoods milled on campus.*

"Most social life occurs on campus, but there are ample opportunities to get off campus and have fun in Asheville," says one student. Another adds, "Most students are not involved in the party scene, and I would say that the primary way in which people socialize is by dropping by someone else's dorm room to hang out." Despite the absence of Greek organizations, students find plenty of ways to have fun and blow off steam. The outdoor program is the largest on campus and sponsors weekly hiking, skiing, or other excursions. Students of legal drinking age are allowed to imbibe indoors, and students say it's very easy for underage students to obtain alcohol. "The unofficial policy is that if you are being respectful and responsible, no one is going to question your actions," says one student. Popular events include Warren Wilson Circus and homecoming, which features live bluegrass music, a barbecue, and dancing.

> **"Most students are not involved in the party scene."**

Asheville "has tons to offer," says an elementary education major. Museums, cafés, theaters, music clubs, and the symphony are only 15 minutes away. "The downtown scene is amazing for the relatively small size of the town," says a student. Thanks to the college's service requirement, students take an active role in the community through volunteer work. WWC sponsors short-term service projects during vacation breaks, and popular road trips include Atlanta and the beaches of South Carolina. The best excursions "are to protests and political events or camping and backpacking trips," according to a political science major.

> *Co-ed mountain biking won its first national championship in 2016.*

In a state famed for its rabid sports fans, Warren Wilson students are decidedly laid-back about athletics; there are no big sports teams or rivalries, and students say they prefer it that way. The Fighting Owls are members of the U.S. College Athletic Association and competitive sports include co-ed mountain biking, which won its first national championship in 2016, cyclocross, and men's and women's basketball, cross-country, soccer, swimming, and road cycling. Twenty percent of WWC students participate in intramural and recreational sports, which range from tennis to basketball to timbersports. The men's and women's club paddling teams are recent national champs.

Success at Warren Wilson is measured not only by grades, but by community service and a sense of stewardship. "It's a pretty self-selecting school," a junior advises. "If you aren't attracted to the ideals we hold dear here, don't come." Those who aren't afraid to get their hands dirty will see this small liberal arts college as a valuable place that combines the notion of thinking globally with acting locally.

Overlaps

UNC Asheville, Appalachian State, Green Mountain, Bennington, UNC at Chapel Hill, Guilford, Hampshire, North Carolina State

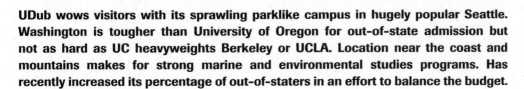

If You Apply To ➤

University of Washington

BEST BUY

1410 N.E. Campus Parkway, Seattle, WA 98195

UDub wows visitors with its sprawling parklike campus in hugely popular Seattle. Washington is tougher than University of Oregon for out-of-state admission but not as hard as UC heavyweights Berkeley or UCLA. Location near the coast and mountains makes for strong marine and environmental studies programs. Has recently increased its percentage of out-of-staters in an effort to balance the budget.

Washington has cemented its reputation as a solid research institution. Students here understand that anonymity and size are the prices that must be paid for the wealth of opportunities that await them. Those looking for an extra-personal touch might want to investigate the school's two branch campuses in Tacoma and Bothell, where class sizes average 25 students. But if the Seattle campus is your focus, one senior hints, just "learn to work the system."

Washington's Seattle campus blends Gothic architecture and the lush, green landscape of the Pacific Northwest. It features a number of distinctive landmarks. Red Square sits atop the Central Plaza parking garage and features the Broken Obelisk, a 26-foot-high steel sculpture gifted to the university by the Virginia Wright Fund. All of the university's energy comes from renewable resources (including, of course, hydropower) and, despite campus growth, UW has reduced its overall energy use.

Undergraduates in both professional and liberal arts programs must take five credits in English composition, seven credits in writing beyond composition, and one course in quantitative and symbolic reasoning. Students must also fulfill 40 credits in general education, including the arts, individuals and societies, and the natural world. Schools and colleges also have their own requirements. Freshmen are given special attention via the Freshman Interest Group (FIG) program, which offers freshmen a chance to meet, discuss, and study with other freshmen who have similar interests. Each FIG consists of 20 to 24 students who share a cluster of classes (which meet graduation requirements), and includes a weekly seminar led by a junior or senior peer advisor.

> **"The residence halls are really new and nice facilities for the most part."**

Many of Washington's diverse undergraduate strengths correspond with its excellent graduate programs. The competitive business major, for example, benefits from the university's highly regarded business school and is one of the most popular undergraduate majors, along with communication, psychology, economics, and biochemistry. Similarly, students majoring in public health, community medicine, pharmacy, and nursing profit from access to facilities and faculty at the medical school, an international leader in cancer and heart research, cell biology, and organ transplants. Drama and English are traditional strengths in the humanities. Also recommended for undergraduates are biological and life sciences and most engineering programs, especially computer science, human centered design and engineering, and bioengineering. Reflecting the focus on natural resources in Washington's

Website: www.washington.edu
Location: City Center
Public
Total Enrollment: 40,024
Undergraduates: 28,327
Male/Female: 47/53
SAT Ranges: CR 540–660, M 580–710
ACT Ranges: 26–31
Financial Aid: 43%
Pell Grant: 20%
Expense: Pub $ $
Student Loans: 40%
Average Debt: $
Phi Beta Kappa: Yes
Applicants: 36,840
Accepted: 53%
Enrolled: 35%
Grad in 6 Years: 84%
Returning Freshmen: 94%
Academics: ✐ ✐ ✐ ✐ ½
Social: ☎ ☎ ☎
Q of L: ★ ★ ★
Admissions: (206) 543-9686
Email Address: info@uwb.edu

Strong Programs:
Business
Communication
Psychology
Economics
Biochemistry
Drama

(continued)

English
Computer Science

economy, the program in fisheries is excellent, as are earth and atmospheric sciences, including oceanography.

Academics are challenging, and a common complaint about UW is that "it is too competitive, once you get in. Many majors are hard to get into and the quarter system feels rushed," says a global health major. Entry into preprofessional and STEM-related programs is particularly difficult, and students say you might want to have a backup plan. Many Washington professors are tops in their field, but students may have to be patient about seeing professors after class. Like other major state universities, UW faces budget difficulties, resulting in larger classes and limited course selection. Thirty-eight percent of undergraduate classes have fewer than 20 students. Raves one sophomore, "The faculty is top-notch. All of the teachers I've had have been passionate about the courses they teach."

Freshman Interest Groups consist of 20 to 24 students and include a weekly seminar led by a junior or senior peer advisor.

For those interested in skirting the masses, UW sports an honors program that offers small classes on interesting subjects taught by fine professors. And if students get the itch to see some different scenery, there are hundreds of study abroad programs across the globe; 7 percent of students take part. A program in experiential learning encourages students to find internships and participate in community service. This fits in with a variety of classes that give students the opportunity to volunteer as part of their coursework. "There's simply no better way to learn than by combining challenging courses with real-world experience," says a senior. "Experience adds to your learning, and it helps you remember it."

Sixty-nine percent of undergraduates are state residents, and although the university has traditionally preferred to keep its focus on the home folks, it now has a notably large proportion of international students, at 15 percent. It also has an unusually large population of students over the age of 25. The student body is 24 percent Asian American, 7 percent Hispanic, and 3 percent African American. Students say the school strives for diversity by offering Valuing Diversity workshops to foster increased awareness of and sensitivity to individual differences. Students, says a senior, "are go-getters and active in the world around them." Merit scholarships averaging $5,800 are awarded to Washington residents with good high school records and test scores. Hundreds of athletic scholarships are awarded to men and women in 20 sports. The Husky Promise covers full tuition and fees for qualifying in-state students from low-income backgrounds.

"On campus there are over 800 registered student organizations."

Entry into preprofessional and STEM-related programs is particularly difficult.

Twenty-five percent of students live in the school's eight co-ed dorms. "The residence halls are really new and nice facilities for the most part. The main drawback is that they are pretty expensive," says a junior. Hagget provides a comfortable setting for freshmen, and McMahon is recommended for those inclined to party. The rest live off campus in Seattle or other parts of King County. Each dorm has its own cafeteria and fast-food line based on a debit card system. The Husky Union Building also offers a dining hall, espresso bar (don't forget, this is Seattle!), writing center, sun deck, and lounges. In response to issues of sexual assault, a sophomore says, "I have seen an increase in discussion and education on sexual assault, with a focus on the Greek community."

Given the large number of commuters, it's no surprise that most of Washington's social life takes place away from campus, except for the Greeks. Sixteen percent of the men and 15 percent of the women join a combined total of 48 fraternities and sororities. "The dorms and fraternities seem to contain the most social activity, and what they lack is made up for by the proximity to downtown Seattle," says one student. A junior adds, "On campus there are over 800 registered student organizations, so you can pretty much guarantee that there is a group for you." Neither dormies nor Greeks are supposed to drink if they're under 21. Sooner or later most students hit "the Ave," University Way, where shops and restaurants await them. A 10-minute bus ride connects students to a full array of urban offerings in Seattle. The Seattle

Center and other venues host outstanding operas, symphonies, and touring shows, while Qwest Field houses the NFL's Seahawks and Safeco Field the MLB Mariners.

But who needs pro sports with Washington's Division I Huskies around? Husky Fever breaks out on every football weekend, and the stands are always packed for UW's team, especially when Washington State comes to town to vie for the coveted Apple Cup. Men's rowing won national championships in 2014 and 2015, and women's volleyball claimed the Pac-12 conference title in 2015; football and women's basketball have also been successful. UW offers more than 80 recreational and intramural programs, in which the majority of students compete. More than anything else, the great outdoors defines the University of Washington. The campus offers breathtaking views of Lake Washington and the Olympic Mountains. Outdoor pastimes for students include boating, hiking, camping, and skiing, all found nearby, and Canada is close enough for road trips to Vancouver. The weather is consistently temperate, and natives insist that the city's reputation for rain is undeserved. Then again, the sports stadium has an overhang to protect spectators from showers.

"UW gives you a reality check...[and then] gives you the guidance and tools to be successful."

"UW gives you a reality check and tells you that you're not as smart or as special as you think you are, and then shows you all the potential that you still have and gives you the guidance and tools to be successful," says a junior. While some students will not appreciate the occasionally impersonal academics, many students can overlook these obstacles for the big picture of the up-and-coming University of Washington—one that takes in more than just the beautiful scenery.

Overlaps

UCLA, UC–Berkeley, Washington State, University of Southern California, Boston University, UC–San Diego, University of Illinois at Urbana–Champaign, Purdue

If You Apply To ➤

Washington: Regular decision: Dec. 1. Financial aid: Feb. 28. Housing: May 1. Application fee: $70. No campus or alumni interviews. SATs or ACTs: required. No Subject Tests. No letters of recommendation. Essay: required.

Washington and Jefferson College

60 South Lincoln Street, Washington, PA 15301

Premed Central would be as good a name as any for W&J, which has one of the nation's highest proportions of students who go on to medical school. Law school and business school are also popular destinations, and undergraduates in all fields pack their bags to conduct research in far-flung locales through the innovative Magellan Project. The Greek system dominates the social life.

Wannabe doctors and lawyers would be well-advised to give Washington and Jefferson College a look. This small Pennsylvania college, founded in 1781 by Presbyterian ministers, is renowned for its preprofessional programs, and graduates are almost guaranteed acceptance into medical or health-related graduate programs. Classes remain small here and, despite the somewhat rural location, students enjoy an active social life thanks to a hearty Greek scene and the nearby city of Pittsburgh.

The campus, like the student body, is tight-knit: more than 50 buildings sit on 60 acres in a small town about 30 miles outside of Pittsburgh. W&J is the 11th-oldest college in the country and houses the eighth-oldest college building, which was built in 1793. The school got its name following the merger shortly after the Civil War of two colleges whose names you can probably guess. The prevailing architectural

Website: www.washjeff.edu
Location: Small Town
Private
Total Enrollment: 1,302
Undergraduates: 1,302
Male/Female: 52/48
SAT Ranges: CR 520–620, M 540–630
ACT Ranges: 23–28
Financial Aid: 98%

(continued)

Pell Grant: 33%

Expense: Pr $ $

Student Loans: 81%

Average Debt: N/A

Phi Beta Kappa: Yes

Applicants: 6,835

Accepted: 43%

Enrolled: 13%

Grad in 6 Years: 76%

Returning Freshmen: 83%

Academics: ✍ ✍ ✍

Social: ☎ ☎ ☎

Q of L: ★ ★

Admissions: (724) 223-6025

Email Address: admission@
washjeff.edu

Strong Programs:

Premed

Prelaw

Business Administration

Accounting

Psychology

English

Economics

Biology

style is traditional colonial/Georgian, though modern structures have been added at a rapid pace during the past two decades. The four-story Burnett Center houses the economics, business and accounting, modern languages, education, and entrepreneurial studies departments. Recently opened facilities include the Swanson Tennis Center and the Ross Family Recreation Center.

Graduation requirements call for students to complete 32 full-semester courses and two intersession courses, and distribution requirements cover a range of liberal arts and sciences fields. They must also demonstrate proficiency in writing, speaking, reading, quantitative reasoning, foreign language, and use of information technology, and satisfy language, cultural diversity, and physical education and wellness requirements. Every first-year student enrolls in a First-Year Seminar, selecting from 25 options, many of which involve college-sponsored trips to major East Coast cities and some of which are linked to living/learning communities. All graduating seniors take part in a capstone experience.

> "Most students...want to work together to help others succeed."

Business administration, accounting, psychology, English, and economics are the most popular majors, and biology, history, mathematics, and German are also strong. An entrepreneurship minor gives students the chance to interact with founders of Fortune 500 companies, and the computing and information studies major offers five emphases, in big data, computer science, digital media, interaction design, and web and mobile technologies, from which students choose to concentrate. A thematic major allows students to design their own course of study, while double majors produce such types as a biologist well versed in literature. Rare among liberal arts colleges are the 3–4 programs with the Pennsylvania Colleges of Optometry and Podiatry. More technically minded students can take advantage of the 3–2 engineering programs with Case Western Reserve, Columbia, and Washington University in St. Louis. New programs include majors in public policy and environmental science and a concentration in conflict and resolution studies.

W&J's formula for success starts with individual attention in small classes; 66 percent of classes have fewer than 20 students. Students agree that the academic climate at W&J is tough, especially for those on the premed and prelaw tracks. "Most students understand how difficult the classes are and want to work together to help others succeed," a student says. Full professors teach most classes and are, according to one junior, "phenomenal" and "the best of the best." A robust alumni mentorship program ensures that every W&J student who wants an alumni mentor and career coach will have one.

The Magellan Project provides funding for approximately 70 freshmen, sophomores, and juniors to put their liberal arts education to work each year through self-designed summer research projects or internships that involve domestic or international travel. Past projects have evaluated cancer treatment in Belize and explored women's issues in Kenya. The Washington Fellows Program is an honors program that provides participating students a bevy of special opportunities to interact with distinguished faculty, alumni, and guests. During the January intersession, students find brief apprenticeships in prospective career areas, take a short-term tour abroad, or engage in nontraditional coursework. Eleven percent of students study abroad, and the Office of Study Abroad offers 40 approved semester- and year-abroad options in 20 countries.

> "The school is very evenly divided along political lines."

W&J graduates are almost guaranteed acceptance into medical or health-related graduate programs.

"Students are truly friendly and they care," says one senior. Seventy-five percent of the students hail from Pennsylvania and many are from neighboring states in the Northeast; 3 percent are international. Five percent of students are African American, 4 percent are Hispanic, and 2 percent are Asian American. "The school is very evenly divided along political lines," says a senior. Students get something of a bargain if they win one of the several hundred academic scholarships that average $16,449, and the same aid package is promised for each of a student's four years at the college. Thirty-three percent of incoming students qualify for the Pell Grant. The college does not award athletic scholarships.

Students can live in either co-ed or single-sex dorms, and 94 percent of students live on campus. Housing is guaranteed for four years, and students say the freshman dorms are fair, but the choices get better with academic rank. On-campus apartments are available based on GPA, activities, and need. "The dorms during your upper-class years are practically like new apartments," says one student. Campus meals get a hearty thumbs-up: "I *love* the food here. We have local milk, cage-free eggs, and sometimes local produce," cheers one student. W&J has significantly revised its Title IX policy and training programs and is in the process of launching a bystander awareness program.

The Greek scene is active and draws 34 percent of the men and 39 percent of the women. A crackdown on alcohol and noise violations has somewhat dampened the school's tradition of enormous parties, but the Student Activity Board has begun filling the gap with more on-campus events, such as free movies, and a student-run coffeehouse provides another

> "Washington doesn't have much to offer in the way of entertainment."

nonfrat option. "W&J provides plenty of social options," says a junior. "We have the HUB with flat-screen televisions, Wii, Netflix, pool tables, a Ping-Pong table, and a café where students get free food and milkshakes every weekend!" A nonalcoholic pub called George & Tom's has become quite a popular diversion with comedy, musical, and novelty/variety acts. There are also numerous clubs to join, from the equestrian club to the student theater company. During the course of the year, the Spring Street Fair and Spring Concert are the most popular events.

Students can explore social opportunities at nearby colleges, most notably Penn State and the University of Pittsburgh. One of the most popular excursions is a 30-minute commute to Pittsburgh. Still, not all students share the administration's appreciation for "the unique characteristics of the western Pennsylvania milieu." Many complain that there is nothing to do in this former steel/mining town, now hit by hard times. "Washington doesn't have much to offer in the way of entertainment," says a student. "Most people just take the drive to Pittsburgh," adds another. Townies tend to be a bit resentful of dressy W&J undergrads, but students try to assuage this attitude by actively volunteering in the community.

Just about anyone has a shot at varsity sports at W&J, where the teams are known, naturally, as the Presidents. Recent conference champions include men's football, golf, and baseball and women's golf. Men's wrestling produced an individual national champion in 2015. Thirty percent of students participate in intramural and recreational sports, with flag football, volleyball, and basketball attracting the most interest. "Intramurals are huge on campus. People can get very competitive and it becomes a big deal," a student says.

With expanding academic options and the freedom to self-design experiences abroad, the leadership at W&J is opening more and more doors for students. Students praise the education and enriching opportunities they receive, and the school's close-knit environment. "My experience here is unforgettable," a senior says. "I have made lifelong friends and gained so much."

A robust alumni mentorship program ensures that every student who wants an alumni mentor and career coach will have one.

The Magellan Project provides funding for self-designed summer research projects or internships that involve travel.

Overlaps

Allegheny, Duquesne, Penn State, Robert Morris, Saint Vincent, College of Wooster, Ohio State, University of Pittsburgh

If You Apply To ➤

W&J: Early decision: Dec. 1. Early action: Jan. 15. Regular decision: Mar. 1. Financial aid: Feb. 15. Application fee: $25 (paper), free (online). Campus interviews: recommended, evaluative. No alumni interviews. SATs or ACTs: optional. No Subject Tests. Letters of recommendation: required. Essay: required. Accepts the Common Application with supplement.

Washington and Lee University

Lexington, VA 24450

The ninth oldest university in the U.S., tradition-bound W&L is the most selective small college in the South, rivaled only by Davidson. W&L supplements the liberal arts with strong programs in business and journalism. Picture-postcard campus is three hours from Washington, D.C. Diversity has a ways to go.

Website: www.wlu.edu
Location: Small City
Private
Total Enrollment: 2,157
Undergraduates: 1,843
Male/Female: 51/49
SAT Ranges: CR 650–730, M 660–740
ACT Ranges: 30–33
Financial Aid: 63%
Pell Grant: 11%
Expense: Pr $ $ $
Student Loans: 34%
Average Debt: $
Phi Beta Kappa: Yes
Applicants: 5,377
Accepted: 24%
Enrolled: 35%
Grad in 6 Years: 91%
Returning Freshmen: 96%
Academics: ✐ ✐ ✐ ✐ ½
Social: ☎ ☎ ☎
Q of L: ★ ★ ★ ★
Admissions: (540) 458-8710
Email Address: admissions@wlu.edu

Strong Programs:
Business Administration
Accounting
Economics
English
Politics
Journalism
Strategic Communication

Washington and Lee University, which shares the town of Lexington, Virginia, with the Virginia Military Institute, has always epitomized Southern gentility. The Fancy Dress Ball is a highlight of each year, the Honor System is revered, and "the Speaking Tradition," tracing its roots to Robert E. Lee, ensures at least casual communication between members of the W&L community when they pass one another on the well-manicured grounds. But this is not your grandfather's W&L. More than three decades after women were first admitted, today's atmosphere is a little less 19th century and a little more 21st century—as befits one of the South's leading liberal arts colleges. Says a senior, "Each individual walks away with a unique sense of what it means to be an honorable, thoughtful, civilized participant in a global society."

W&L's wooded campus sits atop a hill of lush green lawns, sweeping from one national landmark to another. The chapel is the burial site of Robert E. Lee. Redbrick buildings feature white Doric columns, and the prevailing architectural style is Greek Revival, although the physical face is changing. The school boasts the Elrod University Commons, which contains a dining hall, movie theater, and bookstore, and the new $13.5 million Center for Global Leaning. Renovations to the historic Colonnade are set for completion in 2017.

> **"Students are intensely focused on academics but are also gregarious."**

General education requirements account for one-third of a student's coursework. Distribution requirements at W&L include courses in literature, fine arts, history, philosophy, religion, science and math, social science, foreign language, and physical education. Students must also demonstrate proficiency in swimming. The Spring Term has been transformed into a single, four-week experience intended to offer students and faculty more innovative approaches to teaching and learning. Many use the term to study abroad; 54 percent of all students spend time abroad at some point, traveling to destinations in more than 50 countries.

Although a standard liberal arts program remains the foundation of W&L's curriculum, the university offers excellent preprofessional programs, particularly in business, accounting, and economics, through the Williams School of Commerce, Economics, and Politics. English, politics, journalism, and strategic communication are popular choices as well. The Shepherd Program for the Interdisciplinary Study of Poverty and Human Capability offers a minor in poverty that requires students to complete an eight-week summer internship with an organization focused on poverty-related issues, during which they are mandated to live on $14 per day.

> **"We need diverse students... and the support system from the university is in place to welcome them."**

"Naturally, a lot of students here want to succeed and be the best in the class, so there is competition," says a German and computer science double major. "However, whether it is collaboration with your professors or with other students, everyone just wants to see the best effort and results." Classes are small—74 percent have fewer than 20 students—and there are no teaching assistants. Says one student, "There are department heads teaching intro-level classes and senior seminars, and since these classes are small all the way through, the quality of teaching is excellent." Well-qualified students can apply for the Summer Research Scholars Program, which offers students paid fellowships for assisting professors in research or doing their own; 29 percent of undergrads conduct research. The famous Honor System lends a relaxed feeling to the otherwise rigorous academic climate. Tests and final exams are taken without faculty supervision; doors remain unlocked, laptops stay on desks, and library stacks are open 24 hours a day. Counseling and career services are highly praised. "The career counselors make an effort to get to know each student on an individual basis to position students for success," says a junior.

"Students are intensely focused on academics but are also gregarious," says a junior. Though the atmosphere is still more traditional than at most leading liberal arts colleges, the days of rock-ribbed conservatism are gone. Middle-of-the-road is perhaps the best way to describe the political leanings of today's W&L student body, which is nothing if not homogenous. African Americans account for 2 percent of the student body, Hispanics 3 percent, and Asian Americans 3 percent. Thirteen percent of students are native Virginians, and students from northeast of D.C. are well represented; international students make up 5 percent of the population. Merit-based awards averaging $33,756 are available, but athletic awards are not. The university guarantees to meet the full demonstrated financial need—without loans—of all admitted students, and for those whose families earn less than $75,000 annually, the W&L Promise program provides full-tuition scholarships. These and other scholarship programs have helped increase the proportion of Pell-eligible students to 11 percent, but the majority of students still come from wealthy backgrounds. A senior observes, "There are challenges for lower-income students due to implicit expectations, such as appearances and social expenses." Despite such challenges, a first-generation student urges, "We need diverse students at Washington and Lee, and the support system from the university is in place to welcome them."

"We have the largest percentage of Greek students in the nation."

Fifty-one percent of students currently reside on campus, but that number will grow as the university implements a new on-campus residency requirement for first-years, sophomores, and juniors. Students spend their first year in co-ed dorms, and according to one student, "The freshman dorms have all been renovated in the past year so everything is modern." Many sophomores move into Greek houses or theme houses, and apartment- and townhouse-style accommodations, including the new Village complex, are available for upperclassmen. Freshmen must purchase a meal plan, and dining options get good reviews. The Honor System and campus security personnel contribute to the students' feelings of safety on campus. The university has recently revised its sexual misconduct policies, and the AAA (Advocates for an Alternative Atmosphere) student group is working to foster a positive social and sexual climate on campus.

"We have the largest percentage of Greek students in the nation, so Greek life definitely sets the tone for the social scene," explains a junior. "Our parties are very inclusive: anyone is allowed to walk into any house on campus when there is a party happening." Seventy-eight percent of the men and 81 percent of the women take part in Greek life. Greek bashes often feature live bands, although the Fancy Dress Ball, or "$100,000 prom," also draws raves. Underage drinking is banned in the dorms, but students insist "students like to party and drink." A lot of creative energy goes into fraternity parties, and Friday Underground, a weekly coffeehouse with

"W&L has adapted while still preserving the parts of the institution that make it a beloved place."

W&L offers a minor in poverty that requires an eight-week summer internship, during which students must live on $14 per day.

The famous Honor System lends a relaxed feeling to the otherwise rigorous academic climate.

free food, coffee, and student performances, has proven to be a popular social alternative. W&L's mock political convention for the party out of power, held every four years, has predicted past presidential nominees with uncanny accuracy.

The school's scenic location in the midst of the Appalachian Mountains means an abundance of activities for nature lovers, including hunting, fishing, camping, mountain biking, skiing, and tubing on the rivers. The Outing Club, the largest student organization on campus, organizes day trips throughout the year and lengthier excursions during school breaks. Lexington, a "quiet, friendly town that has much history to offer," also offers a few bars, two movie theaters, and several restaurants. The Foxfield races near Charlottesville and the Kentucky Derby are popular road-trip destinations. Washington, D.C., Richmond, and Roanoke are easily reached by car for weekend trips.

W&L offers 24 varsity sports at the Division III level, and most teams participate in the Old Dominion Athletic Conference. During the 2015–16 season, the Generals took home conference championships in 11 sports, including men's and women's swimming, lacrosse, tennis, and cross-country, as well as men's golf, soccer, and football. The university sponsors approximately 30 club and intramural sports, ranging from disc golf and handball to skiing and polo; three-quarters of the student body participate.

"Washington and Lee is an institution with a lot of history, but per our motto, we are 'not unmindful of the future,'" says an English major. "W&L has adapted while still preserving the parts of the institution that make it a beloved place for all those who have had the pleasure to attend." A sense of history and tradition does indeed pervade the campus—as does the energy of one of the nation's ablest student bodies.

Overlaps

University of Virginia, UNC at Chapel Hill, Vanderbilt, Georgetown, Dartmouth, Princeton, UC–Berkeley, College of William and Mary

If You Apply To ➤

W&L: Early decision I: Nov. 1. Early decision II and regular decision: Jan. 1. Financial aid: Feb. 15. Housing: May 1. Application fee: $50. Campus and alumni interviews: recommended, evaluative. SATs or ACTs: required. No Subject Tests. Letters of recommendation: required. Essay: required. Accepts the Common Application with supplement.

Washington College

300 Washington Avenue, Chestertown, MD 21620

Washington College is among the oldest schools in the country. Small liberal arts college with strengths in creative writing, American history, and environmental science. The college has George Washington rather than Thomas Jefferson as its *éminence grise*. Chestertown is dullsville, so students make their own fun. Best known for the annual Sophie Kerr Prize—worth more than $65,000 to a graduating senior.

Website: www.washcoll.edu
Location: Small Town
Private
Total Enrollment: 1,380
Undergraduates: 1,380
Male/Female: 44/56
SAT Ranges: CR 530–650, M 540–640

Chartered in 1782 in the closing days of the American Revolution, Washington College was the first college to be established in the newly independent United States, and the first to adopt a thoroughly secular mission: educating citizens, patriots, and leaders for the new democracy. It takes its name from George Washington, who never slept in any of its dorms but who did make a modest founding grant of 50 guineas and serve as a trustee. His spirit looms over the campus as strongly as that of "Mr. Jefferson" at UVA. One of the first things freshmen do upon arrival is to make a pilgrimage to Mount Vernon to sign the Honor Code (WC students cannot tell lies). Under a new president, the college aims to grow considerably larger, while at the same time becoming more affordable for all students, especially those of limited financial means.

Washington College sits on 112 acres adjacent to downtown Chestertown, a quiet community of 5,200 on the Chester River on the eastern shore of Chesapeake Bay. Most buildings are redbrick, Georgian-style structures connected by old brick walkways and enhanced by large shade trees. The historic heart of the campus is the green where commencement is held and where a bronze statue of You Know Who keeps watch. The Gibson Center of the Arts, the Toll Science Center, and the Hodson Commons mix large expanses of glass with traditional redbrick. With more than $34 million in renovations and new construction recently completed, including the LEED-certified Cromwell Hall that opened in 2016, the college has another $20 million in renovations and $18 million in new facilities in the pipeline.

First-year students begin their studies with a required Global Perspectives: Research and Writing (GRW) course in which they consider problems and issues from an international perspective. There are also standard distribution requirements. In order to graduate, students must also complete a Senior Capstone Experience that, depending on their major field, can take the form of a comprehensive exam, thesis, scientific research project, theatrical production, or portfolio of writing or artwork.

While the most popular majors include business management, biology, psychology, and economics, the college's signature academic strengths are English literature and creative writing. Regardless of their disciplines, all students are expected to develop writing proficiency, and the college offers a four-year integrated approach to nurturing good writers. The school has a long-standing tradition of bringing writers such as Jane Smiley, Colum McCann, and Natasha Trethewey to campus. The Rose O'Neill Literary House is a cultural hub where students can discuss poetry and literature over a cup of tea and freshly baked cookies. Seniors from all disciplines may submit writing portfolios to vie for the Sophie Kerr Prize. Named after a popular American writer of the early 20th century, it is the largest undergraduate literary prize in the country and inevitably gives the school its annual 15 minutes of fame in the national media. The 2016 winner took home a check for $65,770.

"[The academic climate is] competitive but very inclusive, as students are encouraged to work together."

Not surprisingly, WC is a wonderful place to study history and American studies. The C.V. Starr Center for the Study of the American Experience, located in the old Custom House on the Chester River, helps students study the culture of the Native Americans who once populated the area, trace the Revolutionary War campaigns in the Chesapeake region, and explore the area's maritime heritage from aboard *Sultana*, a reproduction 18th-century schooner. The center also offers Quill & Compass Scholarships for first-year students, and invites scholars working on books or other projects to live in a restored colonial house and share their expertise with the campus community. The school's location 75 miles east of Washington, D.C., affords excellent access to internships. In recent years, WC students have interned at the National Archives, the U.S. House of Representatives, and the Smithsonian American Art Museum; on average, 65 percent of students in all disciplines complete internships.

WC also takes advantage of its rural setting and nearby waterways to offer a strong program in environmental science and studies. The Center for Environment & Society promotes interdisciplinary research and learning revolving around stewardship of the area's natural resources, including a Chesapeake Semester that offers hands-on experience in the watershed and a trip to Costa Rica for comparative study. A dual-degree program in engineering with Columbia University is now available, as is a new major in communication and media studies. Other special academic programs include the Douglass Cater Society of Junior Fellows, which offers

(continued)

ACT Ranges: 25–30
Financial Aid: 90%
Pell Grant: 15%
Expense: Pr $ $
Student Loans: 64%
Average Debt: $ $ $ $
Phi Beta Kappa: Yes
Applicants: 6,847
Accepted: 54%
Enrolled: 11%
Grad in 6 Years: 75%
Returning Freshmen: 83%
Academics: ✍ ✍ ✍
Social: ☎ ☎ ☎
Q of L: ★ ★ ★
Admissions: (410) 778-7700
Email Address:
   wc_admissions@washcoll.edu

Strong Programs:
Creative Writing
History
American Studies
Environmental Science and
   Studies
Business Management
Biology
Psychology
Economics

The Chesapeake Semester offers hands-on experience in the watershed and a trip to Costa Rica for comparative study.

competitive grants to support undergraduate research anywhere in the world to about 50 of the school's top students, and the Presidential Fellows Program, which offers special academic opportunities to the top 10 percent of entering freshmen. In addition to semester-long study abroad programs available through partner institutions in more than 30 countries, the college offers multiple short-term programs led by WC faculty. One of the most popular is a three-week trek each June through the literary landscapes of England, Ireland, and Scotland to explore what inspired the likes of Wordsworth, Coleridge, and Shelley.

With the exception of a few introductory classes, students report that all of their instruction comes from full professors, and 70 percent of classes have fewer than 20 students. "I cannot say enough about the accessibility of professors, nor is it easy to describe how much they truly do care about their students," cheers a freshman. WC operates on a four-credits-per-course basis, with three hours of classes and students expected to work on their own for the fourth. A psychology major describes the academic climate as "competitive but very inclusive, as students are encouraged to work together instead of in competition with each other." Every freshman is assigned to a Peer Mentor, an older student who is trained to help them adjust to the academic and other sides of college life.

> **"The average student at Washington College is extremely involved."**

"The average student at Washington College is extremely involved in not one or two, but four or five extracurricular and cocurricular activities," explains a student. Forty-two percent of students at Washington are from Maryland, and 10 percent hail from other countries. Minority enrollment stands at 5 percent African American, 3 percent Hispanic, and 2 percent Asian American. According to a junior, liberals and conservatives are both well represented on campus, and, "Hot-button topics center around race (with the school's recent push for diversity), women's rights, immigration, language and religion, etc." Washington College's sticker price is high, but tuition is guaranteed not to increase for incoming freshmen who graduate in four years, and merit scholarships averaging $16,766 annually are available; there are no athletic scholarships. The new George's Brigade scholarship program meets the full demonstrated need of a select group of high-achieving, high-need students from urban areas, offering them academic and social support as well.

All students are guaranteed on-campus housing for all four years, and 85 percent take up the offer. Washington offers three co-ed theme houses in the historic Hill Dorms complex—international, creative arts, and science—and language suites are available to advanced students of French, German, Japanese, and Spanish. Rooms are assigned through a lottery with numbers based on class year. A sophomore reports that "not all dorms are created equal, but none of them are completely unacceptable." The newest dorm, Corsica, is among the choicest in a cluster of dorms located on what students call the "Western Shore," overlooking the athletic fields. Students take their

> **"Not all dorms are created equal, but none of them are completely unacceptable."**

all-you-can-eat meals at the newly renovated dining hall; many complain of a lack of variety, but a senior points out that the staff accommodates for various dietary needs and "pays attention to sustainable farming, local products, and reducing waste." After-hours venues sell sandwiches and such, and the recent library makeover added a café for late-night snacks and coffee. Students give high ratings to the public safety department, and an environmental science major says, "Sexual assault is present on campus, but it is a rarity. The school does an excellent job with prevention and management techniques, including counseling services."

The sleepy nature of Chestertown means that most social life takes place on campus, much of it coordinated by the school's 100 student organizations. The Student Events Board sponsors concerts, film series, open-mic nights, silent discos,

WC operates on a four-credits-per-course basis, with three hours of classes and students expected to work on their own for the fourth.

By far the biggest social event of the year is the Birthday Ball in February in honor of You-Know-Who's birthday.

bonfires, and other entertainment. Eight percent of the men belong to fraternities and 11 percent of the women to sororities. The Crab Feast, put on by the frères of Phi Delta Theta, is popular, as is the May Day celebration, which gives students an excuse to strip to their birthday suits at midnight and scamper around the quad. By far the biggest social event of the year is the Birthday Ball in February in honor of You-

> **"[Dining staff] pays attention to sustainable farming, local products, and reducing waste."**

Know-Who's birthday. "We love our namesake," says an English major. "The ball is a formal event for students, faculty, and staff to celebrate school spirit, dress up, and have a great time." Students 21 and over are allowed to imbibe on campus, and students say alcohol policies are effective and focused on student safety; the school operates a Safe Ride service for students who want a late-night ride home. A junior says, "Chestertown is quirky and charming, with historic buildings, music, food, art, and boutique shopping," but students seeking more active nightlife head for Annapolis, Baltimore, Philadelphia, or Washington, D.C.

WC's Shoremen and Shorewomen compete in the Division III Centennial Conference. The Shoremen lacrosse team won the 2014 Centennial Conference championship and made it to the Division III championship semifinals. The men's and women's rowing and the co-ed sailing teams have recently become nationally competitive. Students turn out in huge numbers for the annual War on the Shore, when the men's lacrosse team takes on its biggest rival, Salisbury University. Sixty percent of students participate in the more than 16 intramural and club sports, with soccer being the most popular.

After being around for more than 200 years without making much of a stir beyond Chesapeake Bay, Washington College now seems bent on carving out a niche for itself in academic areas where it has a comparative advantage, especially creative writing, American history, and the environment. Students describe WC as a "small, tight-knit community" bound by the classic values of a small liberal arts college. George would probably approve.

> ## Overlaps
>
> **University of Maryland, Salisbury, St. Mary's, Goucher, Towson, McDaniel, Loyola University Maryland, American University**

If You Apply To ➤

Washington College: Early decision: Nov. 15. Early action: Dec. 1. Regular decision: Feb. 15. Financial aid: Mar. 1. Housing: Jun. 1. No application fee. Campus and alumni interviews: optional, evaluative. SATs or ACTs: recommended. Subject Tests: optional. Letters of recommendation: required. Essay: required. Accepts the Common Application with supplement.

Washington University in St. Louis

Campus Box 1089, One Brookings, St. Louis, MO 63130-4899

No longer simply a backup to the Ivies, Washington U has emerged as a nationally competitive university with a wholesome Midwestern feel. Core strength in the biological sciences, but strong across the disciplines. Maintains low acceptance rate—and higher ranking—by favoring early decision and denying top applicants who it thinks will enroll elsewhere. Not much socioeconomic diversity among students.

Though it's always been well recognized regionally, Washington U long ago established itself as a truly national institution—with a friendly, relaxed Midwestern feel that differentiates it from the high-strung Eastern Ivies. Applications have skyrocketed, and with a hefty endowment, strong preprofessional programs, and an emphasis on research, it's not hard to see why. A junior sums up the atmosphere in two

> **Website**: www.wustl.edu
> **Location**: Suburban
> **Private**
> **Total Enrollment**: 12,570

The campus adjoins Forest Park, one of the nation's three largest urban parks.

words: "'name' and 'story.' Wash U lives by these words, making it a community-wide effort to learn the story of each and every member of our university, not just their name."

The school's 169-acre campus adjoins Forest Park, one of the nation's three largest urban parks. Buildings are constructed in the collegiate Gothic style, mostly in red Missouri granite and white limestone, with plenty of climbing ivy, gargoyles, and arches. The state-of-the-art Knight and Bauer Halls are home to the Olin Business School and include 11 classrooms in tiered lecture configurations and "flat" classrooms with mobile furniture, designed to enhance student and faculty interaction. The Sumers Recreation Center opened in 2016, featuring new fitness facilities and a complete interior renovation of the historic Francis Gymnasium, site of the 1904 Olympics.

Undergraduates enroll in one or more of Washington U's five divisions—arts and sciences, architecture, art, business, or engineering. Double majors and interdisciplinary majors, such as environmental studies and philosophy-neuroscience-psychology, are encouraged and easily arranged. General education requirements vary by school and program.

> **"While it is certainly a rigorous institution…Wash U maintains an ultimately healthy and productive academic climate."**

For liberal arts students, they include courses in the humanities, natural sciences and math, social and behavioral sciences, and language and cultural diversity.

Washington U's most popular majors include engineering, social sciences, and business. The university's offerings in the natural sciences, particularly biology and chemistry, have long been notable, especially among those on the premed track. The outstanding medical school runs a faculty exchange program with the undergraduate biology department, which affords bio majors significant opportunities to conduct advanced laboratory research. The University Scholars Program in Medicine allows students to apply for both undergraduate and medical school admission before entering college. If accepted, students can begin exploring their chosen career path earlier—though they aren't obligated to attend medical school if their interests change.

The freshman FOCUS program helps balance the preprofessional bent of some of Washington U's best programs with the school's desire to provide a broad and deep educational experience and a smaller class size. In FOCUS, students use a weekly seminar to explore topics of contemporary significance, such as law and society. The program lets first-year students work closely with professors and sample offerings from various departments. Other notable options include one-, two-, and four-year interdisciplinary programs such as Text and Tradition; International Leadership Program; and Mind, Brain, and Behavior. Students also have the opportunity to study in more than 50 different countries, and roughly 40 percent do so.

Students agree that the university's collaborative atmosphere is a major factor that sets it apart from its Ivy League competitors. "While it is certainly a rigorous institution, providing its students with a comprehensive education, Wash U maintains an ultimately healthy and productive academic climate," says a computer science major. Those who are struggling will find plenty of help from teaching assistants who conduct review sessions, academic advisors, study groups, and even a 24-hour peer counseling service called Uncle Joe's. Sixty-three percent of classes have fewer than 20 students, and undergrads have remarkable access to one-on-one mentoring relationships with top faculty. "The professors are all brilliant and extremely accomplished, but they are also extremely down-to-earth and make every effort to get to know each student in their class (even in large lecture classes)," says an economics major.

> **"I'm constantly surprised by the hidden interests and talents of everyone around me."**

"One of the things I love most about the students here is how diverse everyone's interests are," says a philosophy major. "I'm constantly surprised by the hidden interests and talents of everyone around me." Eighty-three percent of undergraduates are out-of-staters, with a large contingent from Eastern states like New York and New Jersey, and another 9 percent are international. African Americans comprise 6 percent, Hispanics 6 percent, and Asian Americans 19 percent. "The recently founded Center for Diversity and Inclusion has become like a second home to me because of the great study space and the opportunities to have necessary dialogues with excellent professionals and fellow students," says a sophomore. Students are engaged in social and political issues, especially racial justice and renewable energy, and tend to be moderate but left-leaning.

Academic scholarships averaging $6,813 are awarded each year, but there are no athletic scholarships. The university meets the full demonstrated financial need of admitted students and has replaced loans with grants for students from families with incomes below $75,000. Despite being one of the wealthiest universities in the country, Washington U has been one of the nation's least socioeconomically diverse top schools. Embarrassed by this distinction, it has increased its proportion of Pell Grant recipients from 6 percent of entering freshmen in 2013 to 12 percent in 2015, with a goal to reach 13 percent by 2020—still a rather modest figure for a university with a nearly $7 billion endowment. A sophomore notes that, socially, "A person who is from a low-income background may have a difficult time fitting in due to the 'spending' culture at WU."

Seventy-eight percent of Washington U students live in the school's dormitories, known as residential colleges. "The rooms are larger than your average dorm room, and we have Tempur-Pedic mattresses," boasts a student. "If that doesn't qualify us as best housing, I don't know what would." All dorms are co-ed and air-conditioned, some have suites for six to eight students, and gender-inclusive housing is now available as an option. Freshmen and most sophomores live on the "South 40" (40 acres located just south of the main campus); freshmen are guaranteed rooms, and students who stay in the dorms after that are promised campus housing for the following year. Upperclassmen may live in university-owned apartments, and some choose true off-campus digs in the nearby neighborhoods of University City and Clayton, where apartments are reasonably priced. Dorm dwellers and others who buy the meal plan may use their credits in any of the dining centers, which students say are excellent. "Dining Services offers a wealth of options, with international cuisine, vegetarian, gluten-free, dairy-free, kosher, halal, and more available at each and every dining location," cheers a junior. The campus police department and blue-light emergency system are said to be effective, and students point to the work of student-run groups like SARAH (Sexual Assault and Rape Anonymous Hotline) and LIVE (Leaders in Interpersonal Violence Education) as helping to create a safe and supportive climate on campus.

"Social life at WashU is something that each student discovers for themselves," says a marketing major. "There is both an active on-campus and off-campus social life." Washington U students pride themselves on being able to balance work and play, and on weekends, movies, fraternity parties, and concerts tear them away from their books. Every spring, the whole campus turns out for the century-old Thurtene Carnival, the oldest student-run philanthropic festival in the country. Student groups—especially fraternities and sororities, which attract 30 percent of the men and 30 percent of the women—build booths, sell food, and put on plays; profits are donated to a children's charity. Four student-led cultural shows—Diwali, Lunar New Year Festival, Black Anthology, and Carnaval—are always well attended. Another big

The University Scholars Program in Medicine allows students to apply for both undergraduate and medical school admission.

"The recently founded Center for Diversity and Inclusion has become like a second home to me."

Washington U has increased its proportion of Pell Grant recipients to 12 percent, a rather modest figure for a university with a $7 billion endowment.

event is WILD (Walk In Lay Down), held at the beginning and end of the academic year. Everyone brings blankets and inflatable couches to the main quad, assumes a horizontal position, and listens to big-name bands. Alcohol policies emphasize safe and responsible drinking, and students say that, in that regard, they are effective.

The century-old Thurtene Carnival is the oldest student-run philanthropic festival in the country.

Washington U offers robust recreational options because of its location abutting Forest Park: a golf course, an ice-skating rink, a zoo, a lake with boat rentals, art and history museums, an outdoor theater, and a science center are all within a short walk. So too are the restaurants, bars, shops, and galleries of the Delmar Loop. The St. Louis Blues and Cardinals attract pro hockey and baseball fans, and the city is also home to the addictive Ted Drewes frozen custard. The school runs a free shuttle service to parts of St. Louis not within walking distance and offers a Metro Pass for free access to the city's bus and light-rail systems. "St. Louis is often described as the largest small town you will ever visit or the smallest big city you will ever see," says a sophomore. "I appreciate St. Louis because there is plenty to do without it being overwhelming." Community service programs such as Each One Teach One, in partnership with the city's schools, attract a sizable number of students. The best road trips include Chicago, Nashville, Memphis, and Lake of the Ozarks, as well as Columbia, Missouri—home of the University of Missouri.

The Washington U Bears compete in Division III, and the strongest intercollegiate teams include women's basketball (five-time national champs) and women's volleyball (with 10 national titles), as well as football, baseball, softball, women's golf and soccer, and men's and women's cross-country and track and field, all of

"I appreciate St. Louis because there is plenty to do without it being overwhelming."

which have won conference titles in the last two years. Three-quarters of the students play intramural sports, ranging from badminton, racquetball, and flag football to pocket billiards and ultimate Frisbee.

Word among high school guidance counselors is that no one gets admitted to selectivity-conscious Washington U through regular admissions—you are either locked in through early admissions or cherry-picked off the waitlist. But however they get there, students find Washington U both academically challenging and personally supportive. "The atmosphere is not only about learning academically, but growing as a person," says one senior. "My experiences have taught me to live life to the fullest."

Overlaps

Northwestern, Yale, Duke, Stanford, Vanderbilt, Harvard, University of Pennsylvania, Brown

If You Apply To ➢

Washington U: Early decision: Nov. 15. Regular decision: Jan. 15. Financial aid: Feb. 1. Application fee: $75. Campus and alumni interviews: optional, evaluative. SATs or ACTs: required. Subject Tests: optional. Letters of recommendation: required. Essay: required. Accepts the Common Application. Apply to one of five undergraduate schools. Applicants to College of Art must submit portfolio.

Wellesley College

Wellesley, MA 02481

There is no better recipe for popularity than first-rate academics and a postcard-perfect campus on the outskirts of Boston. That formula keeps Wellesley near the top of the women's college pecking order—along with superb programs in economics and the natural sciences. Among leading women's colleges, only Barnard accepts a lower percentage. Nearly a quarter of the students are Asian American, the highest proportion in the East.

Wellesley College is not just the best women's college in the nation—it's one of the best colleges in the nation, period. With an alumnae roster that includes Hillary Rodham Clinton, Madame Chiang Kai-shek, Madeleine Albright, and Diane Sawyer, Wellesley should be at the top of the list for high achievers who are seeking the benefits of an all-women's college. Wellesley women excel in whatever field they choose, including traditional male bastions like economics and the sciences. "Wellesley creates strong, smart, confident women," says an English major.

Nestled in a Boston suburb, the Wellesley campus, one of the most beautiful anywhere, occupies 500 rolling acres of cultivated and natural areas, including Lake Waban. Campus buildings range in architectural style from Gothic (with stone towers and brick quadrangles) to state-of-the-art science, arts, and sports facilities. A 22-acre arboretum and botanical garden features a wide variety of trees and plants. The Davis Museum houses 11 galleries, a cinema, and a café. The five campus libraries, which include an academic art library, boast more than a million volumes. Several facilities have recently been renovated under the Wellesley Campus Renewal Plan, including the student services building, the field house, and studio art and performance spaces.

Wellesley has distribution requirements that include three units drawn from language and literature and from visual arts, music, theater, film, and video; one unit from social and behavioral analysis; a unit each from two of the following: epistemology and cognition; religion, ethics, and moral philosophy; and historical studies; and three units from natural and physical science and mathematical modeling and problem solving. In addition, students must take a first-year writing class, a foreign language, and a course on multiculturalism.

> **"As a first-year, you have many opportunities to learn from professors who are amazing researchers."**

With its hefty endowment (the largest among the nation's all-female colleges and universities) and lavish facilities, Wellesley offers a top-of-the-line educational experience. The most popular majors are economics, political science, psychology, and neuroscience. Economics is known as the powerhouse; in fact, Wellesley has produced virtually all of the country's high-ranking female economists. Computer science is also strong, and students in biochemistry work with faculty on DNA research. Anything Wellesley women find lacking in their curriculum can probably be found at MIT, where they have full cross-registration privileges. Wellesley students can also take courses at Babson College, Brandeis University, and nearby Olin College of Engineering, or participate in exchange programs with Spelman College in Atlanta or Mills College in Oakland, California.

Academics are taken very seriously at Wellesley. "Wellesley has a reputation for being competitive, but I find that's not entirely true," observes a mathematics major. "Most students are open to collaboration and willing to support each other." Under the honor system, students may take their finals, unsupervised, at any time during exam week. Class sizes are almost always small (they average 18 to 23 students per class). Professors are highly respected and make themselves available through email, voicemail, office hours, and by appointment. "All faculty are required to teach intro-level classes," explains an East Asian studies major. "This means that as a first-year, you have many opportunities to learn from professors who are amazing researchers and leaders in their respective fields." First-years (as they are exclusively called here) and upperclasswomen alike have faculty advisors. In an effort to alleviate first-year students' stress about grades as they adjust to Wellesley's rigorous atmosphere, the college employs a shadow-grading policy, in which their first-semester grades do not appear on their academic transcripts.

Seventy percent of students conduct undergraduate research, and grants from private foundations have allowed Wellesley to add innovative programs, including

Website: www.wellesley.edu
Location: Suburban
Private
Total Enrollment: 2,178
Undergraduates: 2,178
Male/Female: 0/100
SAT Ranges: CR 640–740, M 650–750
ACT Ranges: 29–33
Financial Aid: 57%
Pell Grant: 19%
Expense: Pr $ $ $
Student Loans: 49%
Average Debt: $
Phi Beta Kappa: No
Applicants: 4,555
Accepted: 30%
Enrolled: 43%
Grad in 6 Years: 93%
Returning Freshmen: 95%
Academics: ✐ ✐ ✐ ✐ ✐
Social: ☎ ☎ ☎
Q of L: ★ ★ ★ ★
Admissions: (781) 283-2270
Email Address: admission@wellesley.edu

Strong Programs:
Economics
Political Science
Psychology
Neuroscience
Computer Science
Biochemistry

Wellesley has produced virtually all of the country's high-ranking female economists.

independent research tutorials for advanced science students and fellowship funding for joint student/faculty projects. Students can participate in the Twelve College Exchange*, including the National Theater Institute and the Maritime Studies Program*. Roughly 65 percent of students study abroad through 160 approved programs, including Wellesley-run programs in France and Germany. Through the Albright Institute, 40 students each year are chosen to be Albright Fellows, attending classes with both Wellesley and visiting professors, then completing a summer internship abroad; past Fellows have interned with the U.S. State Department, the European Union Chamber of Commerce, and the Human Rights Education and Monitoring Center.

"Students here are conscientious workers with a history of high achievement," says a sophomore. "They expect a lot of themselves." Only 15 percent of students are from Massachusetts, and although the Northeast is the best represented geographical area, students come from every state and more than 75 countries; 12 percent are international. Eighty percent ranked in the top 10th of their high school class.

> **"[Students] are very aware of what's going on in the world, and they're determined to change it for the better. "**

Five percent of Wellesley women are African American, 21 percent are Asian American, and 10 percent are Hispanic. Politically, the campus is liberal, and a sophomore says students "are very aware of what's going on in the world, and they're determined to change it for the better." All financial aid awards are based on need—meaning no merit scholarships—but admissions are need-blind, and Wellesley meets the full demonstrated need of all admitted students. Wellesley has also eliminated loans for families with incomes below $60,000 per year and has reduced loans for others.

Residence life at Wellesley is a step ahead of most institutions, to say the least. Virtually every student lives on campus, in rooms that are described as "immaculate." Residence halls feature high-ceilinged living rooms, hardwood floors, fireplaces, computers and laser printers, television annexes, walk-in closets, kitchenettes with microwaves, and even grand pianos. The halls are renovated every five years or so and all are well maintained, students say. There are no halls specifically for first-years—all classes live on all floors—and juniors and seniors are generally granted single rooms. Peer tutors also live in each hall. These students, called APT advisors, are trained to tutor in specific subjects, as well as in study skills and time management. Two co-ops, one with a feminist bent, present an educational housing option. Meal cards are valid in all six dining halls and at the campus snack bar, which is stocked with everything from milk and flour to Twinkies. "The meals at Wellesley are awesome," cheers a sophomore. "We have a dining hall that is vegetarian and kosher, as well as one that is nut- and peanut-free." As for campus security, a junior says, "Wellesley is a very safe campus, and Campus Police take student safety very seriously."

"Social life on campus is relatively quiet," says a psychology major. Wellesley is dry, but there is a student-run pub in the campus center. The Lulu Chow Wang Campus Center, referred to affectionately as "the Lulu," is a hub of activity day and night. Students enjoy going to the student-run

> **"We have a dining hall that is vegetarian and kosher, as well as one that is nut- and peanut-free."**

Café Hoop, the campus coffeehouse, to sip tea or share a fro-yo or a chocolate croissant. The closest thing Wellesley has to sororities are nonresidential societies, which sometimes host parties, for arts and music, literature, Shakespeare, politics, and general lectures. Service is also a key component of the Wellesley community, dating back to the college's inception. Wellesley's motto, *Non ministrari sed ministrare*, translates to "Not to be served, but to serve."

In an effort to alleviate first-year students' stress about grades, the college employs a shadow-grading policy.

Forty students each year are chosen to be Albright Fellows, attending classes then completing a summer internship abroad.

Wellesley is chock-full of traditions, but the most endearing ones include Flower Sunday, step-singing (an all-campus sing-along on the chapel steps), Spring Weekend (with a big-name band and comedian), and a hoop-rolling contest by seniors in their graduation robes. The winner of this contest will supposedly be the first in her class to achieve her goals, whatever they may be, and she gets off to a flying start when her classmates toss her in the lake. The lake is also the site of an unofficial campus event, Lake Day, where students take breaks between (or from) classes to enjoy a festival held on the lawn near the lake.

The crew team rowed its way to a national championship in 2016.

The town of Wellesley is an upper-crust Boston suburb without many amenities for students. "Be forewarned," cautions a student, "Wellesley is a snobby town of rich people." Still, when it comes to weekend fun, Wellesley is in a prime location. Not even half an hour away, Boston is the place where Wellesley women can mingle with males from Harvard and MIT. Cambridge—with Harvard Square, MIT frat parties, and lots of jazz clubs—is accessible by an hourly school shuttle that runs on weekdays and weekends. There is also a commuter rail station located a short walk from school. Cape Cod, Providence, and the Vermont and New Hampshire ski slopes are close by car.

Many students balance their academic schedule with Division III athletics and club sports. The crew team rowed its way to a national championship in 2016. Other top Blue teams include lacrosse, swimming and diving, cross-country, field hockey, and track and field. The big athletic rival is Smith College, another of the Seven Sisters group of great women's colleges. The sports center, named the

"Social life on campus is relatively quiet."

Nannerl Keohane Sports Center in honor of Wellesley's 11th president (who went on to run Duke), offers an Olympic-size pool; squash, racquetball, and tennis courts; dance studios; a weight room; and an indoor track. Harvard's Head of the Charles crew race and the Boston Marathon—Wellesley's "Scream Tunnel" is legendary among runners worldwide—share honors as the most popular spectator sports of the year.

When it comes to academics, Wellesley women are serious. Their school is competitive with all but the top three Ivies. Many of them enjoy the traditions of the school and appreciate the idyllic atmosphere for contemplation, but know they are poised to dominate whatever field they enter. As one contented senior says, "It's a wonderful place to grow as individuals, as students, and as women."

Overlaps

Brown, Columbia, Boston University, Cornell University, NYU, Harvard, Amherst, Smith

If You Apply To > **Wellesley:** Early decision I: Nov. 1. Early decision II: Jan. 1. Regular decision: Jan. 15. Financial aid: Feb. 15. No application fee. Campus and alumnae interviews: recommended, evaluative. SATs and two Subject Tests or ACTs (with writing): required. Letters of recommendation: required. Essay: required. Accepts the Common Application with supplement. Accepts applications from students who live as women and consistently identify as women. Current students participate on admissions board.

Wells College

Aurora, NY 13026

Recently passed the 10-year mark as a co-ed institution, with men now comprising about one-third of the students. A family atmosphere is the hallmark of Wells, right down to the dinner bell that calls everyone to the evening meal. Wells is big on interdisciplinary study and internships during the January term. Needs to increase enrollment to put itself on solid ground.

Seniors ride to graduation in an old Wells Fargo stagecoach.

Faced with a lingering cash crunch and declining appeal of single-sex education, Wells College opened its doors to men in 2005 for the first time since its founding in 1868. More students means more money to help fix old buildings, boost financial aid packages, and improve faculty salaries, or at least replace professors who retire. Still, the school hasn't abandoned its storied history. Whether it's riding to graduation in an old Wells Fargo stagecoach or showing off in the annual Odd-Even basketball game between freshmen and sophomores, the tradition of Wells is apparent at every turn. With only about 520 students, anonymity is nonexistent, and close relationships with professors and peers come with the territory.

Wells's 365-acre campus sits on the shores of Cayuga Lake—and on the National Register of Historic Places. Most buildings are old, massive, and covered with ivy—the way college should look, you might say. The lakeside location affords beautiful sunsets as well as boating and fishing opportunities, a welcome relief from the sometimes arduous studying that also goes on here. The Schwartz Athletic Center has received extensive renovations, and a 45,000-square-foot science facility is open for business.

Wells aims to give students a solid grounding in the liberal arts. To that end, general education requirements include two courses in a foreign language, one course in formal reasoning, three courses in the arts and humanities (with at least one in each area), three courses in the natural or social sciences (with at least one lab), and four courses in physical education, including one semester of swimming and one focused on wellness. Wells 101, a core course required for all first-years, covers the basics of college writing, speaking, and analytical thinking. Students are also required to complete a senior seminar in their major.

> **"All of my professors are highly qualified, extremely intelligent, and very caring."**

The most popular majors include psychology, English, biology, and history; students also give high marks to education and women's and gender studies. New majors in biochemistry and molecular biology, sustainability, and criminal justice have recently been added, and there's an unusual minor in bookbinding. Business majors may concentrate in entrepreneurship, social justice, art and art gallery management, or hospitality. Individualized majors are available for students whose needs are not met by established programs. There are also dual-degree programs in education with the University of Rochester; in business administration with Clarkson University; and in engineering with Clarkson, Columbia, and Cornell. For a change of pace, students may take one nonmajor course each semester on a pass/fail basis. They may also cross-register for up to four courses each at Cornell and at Ithaca College.

Regardless of major, "the courses are quite challenging and rigorous," says a junior, "but students are not competitive with each other." Eighty-two percent of classes enroll fewer than 20 students, and most are discussion-based, with the professor present to moderate and focus the conversation. "All of my professors are highly qualified, extremely intelligent, and very caring," a psychology major says. The student-run collegiate association enforces the honor system, and take-home and self-scheduled tests are the rule rather than the exception. Wells uses a semester calendar with elements of the 4–1–4 plan, with internships, research, and study abroad taking place in January. Ninety percent of Wells students participate in at least one internship; foreign study is available too, drawing 30 percent of students, and flagship programs include Italy, Spain, and France. Though the school doesn't focus on business and other professional fields, there is a corporate-affiliate program aimed at preparing women to work in the financial world through special courses and lectures, and portfolio-management experience.

Wells students "aren't afraid to be our genuine selves," says one English major. "We're all a little odd and that's OK." Seventy-seven percent of Wells students are state residents, while 2 percent are international. Asian Americans make up 2 percent of the student body, African Americans 13 percent, and Hispanics 11 percent. Courses, workshops, and a support network for new students help to educate the campus on the importance of multiculturalism. The campus is very liberal, and women's rights, feminism, and LGBTQ rights are key topics of discussion. A notably high portion—62 percent—of freshmen qualify for Pell Grants. Numerous merit scholarships, averaging $21,762, are awarded each year, but not for athletics.

All students are guaranteed college housing, and 94 percent do live in the dorms, since only seniors are permitted to move off campus. There are plenty of single rooms, though first-years are typically assigned to doubles. Aside from complaints that the heat is too high during the winter, students rave about their residences, some of which have bay windows and winding staircases, and all of which offer lake views. "Leach and Dodge tend to be more social dorms, while Weld is more of a study dorm," a senior explains. "Main and Weld both offer a healthy lifestyle floor, and GP is our all-women's dorm for upperclass-women." The food gets decidedly less stellar reviews—"OK" to "not great"—but at least it's served in a magnificent Tudor-style dining hall, with two working fireplaces. Security is "extremely reliable," says one student.

"We like to venture off campus since Aurora is so small."

Though there are no Greek organizations at Wells, the school doesn't need them, given its bevy of other traditions. For example, bells are rung every evening to announce dinner, and also to celebrate the first snowfall of the season. Additionally, tea and coffee are served every weekday afternoon. Though the long dresses and china cups have long since disappeared, tea is still a great time to hang out with friends, faculty members, and staff, as well as a welcome break from long afternoon seminars. On the last day of classes, there's a celebration around the sycamore tree, where sophomores present roses to seniors. Then, the president of the college and her staff serve breakfast to the graduating class.

"Most students stay on campus to socialize," says a sociology major. The Student Activities Club sponsors comedians, dances, movie and spa nights, guest speakers, and poetry slams. Underage students can get alcohol, and no one seems to bother them if they're drinking, as long as they're not bothering anyone else. Still, students say if you really want to party, head to Cornell or Ithaca College in the Wells van. The town of Aurora has a pizza parlor, ice cream shop, bar, and hotel—and that's about it. "It's a small village, not a college town at all," says a

"I already feel more independent having studied at Wells."

student, but the residents are friendly and on good terms with students, especially since Wells requires student clubs to participate in community service. "We like to venture off campus since Aurora is so small," a visual arts major says. Students head to Auburn and Syracuse for shopping, or to New York City and Montreal for shows and other big-city perks. Given the beautiful, hilly terrain, Wells students also enjoy camping in the warmer months, and cross-country or downhill skiing in the winter, especially with the slopes of Greek Peak less than an hour away.

Varsity teams at Wells compete in Division III, and the soccer, tennis, and field hockey squads are the strongest Express teams. Recent conference champs include field hockey, men's swimming, and men's and women's basketball. Lacrosse and softball are strong too—and since the college is so small, "everyone that I know of has been able to play," says a psychology major. A fledgling intramural program offers kickball and ultimate Frisbee. Anyone may use the golf course and the college's tennis and paddle-tennis courts, while the field house offers a pool and other exercise equipment.

Wells students aren't ones to shy away from a challenge, so odds are they'll weather the school's co-ed status. As for the men, well, they'll be hard-pressed to

Overlaps

SUNY–Geneseo, Hartwick, Le Moyne, Elmira, Ithaca, Syracuse, SUNY–Albany, Hobart and William Smith

change the "liberal, progressive, feminist, and independent" spirit of this place, but most students, male and female alike, say that suits them just fine. "I believe the classes are good, the community is wonderful, and Wells really prepares you for life," says one student. "I already feel more independent having studied at Wells."

If You Apply To ➤

Wells: Early decision and early action: Dec. 15. Regular decision: Mar. 1. Financial aid: Dec. 1. Application fee: $40. Campus interviews: recommended, evaluative. No alumni interviews. SATs or ACTs: optional. No Subject Tests. Letters of recommendation: required. Essay: required. Accepts the Common Application with supplement.

Wesleyan University

45 Wyllys Avenue, Middletown, CT 06459

Usually compared to Amherst or Williams, Wesleyan is really more like Swarthmore. The key differences: Wesleyan is twice as big and a little more streetwise. Wes students are progressive, politically minded, and fiercely independent. Exotic specialties like ethnomusicology and East Asian studies add spice to the scene. New York and Boston are both two hours away but not easily accessible on public transportation.

Website: www.wesleyan.edu
Location: Small City
Private
Total Enrollment: 2,961
Undergraduates: 2,814
Male/Female: 46/54
SAT Ranges: CR 620–730, M 630–740
ACT Ranges: 29–33
Financial Aid: 45%
Pell Grant: 22%
Expense: Pr $ $ $ $
Student Loans: 45%
Average Debt: $ $
Phi Beta Kappa: Yes
Applicants: 9,822
Accepted: 22%
Enrolled: 35%
Grad in 6 Years: 94%
Returning Freshmen: 95%
Academics: ✐ ✐ ✐ ✐ ✐
Social: ☎ ☎ ☎
Q of L: ★ ★ ★
Admissions: (860) 685-3000
Email Address: admission@ wesleyan.edu

Strong Programs:
Psychology

Whether they're engrossed in academics, debating and demonstrating over various issues, or engaged in community service, Wesleyan students seem to do things with a passion and intensity that helps set this school apart from tamer institutions. "Wes students take an in-your-face approach to life," says a government major. "There's an energy on this campus; for me, it's a spirit of creativity and political energy," a sophomore explains. In recent years, a significant number of Wesleyan alumni have gone on to make their mark in the high-tech world and the entertainment industry, most recently *Hamilton* creator Lin-Manuel Miranda.

Diversity begins with the Wesleyan campus architecture. The nucleus of this stately university is a century-old row of lovely brownstones that look out over the football field. The rest of the buildings can be described as "eclectic" and range from mod-looking dorms of the '50s and '60s to the beautiful and modern Center for the Arts. The Wesleyan-owned student residences look freshly plucked from Main Street, USA.

> **"There's an energy on this campus; for me, it's a spirit of creativity and political energy."**

The Gordon Career Center is situated in the heart of the campus and features a multi-purpose career commons with a broadcast suite. Wesleyan likes to describe itself as "a small college with university resources." The libraries have more than a million volumes, practically unheard of at a school this size. Students claim that whenever you happen to walk past the brightly lit, glass-walled study room of Sci-Li (the science library), you're apt to see numerous students huddled over their books.

Wesleyan's curriculum renewal program ensures the relevance of liberal arts education in the 21st century by offering seminars for first-year students, clustering courses to help students reach their academic goals, and requiring an electronic portfolio from each student that allows them to compile their work and set goals with their advisors. Students are expected to take a minimum of three courses in each of three areas—humanities and the arts, social and behavioral sciences, and natural sciences and mathematics. Wesleyan students have nearly 50 majors to choose from, in addition to a number of minors and certificate programs. At the end of their freshman year, students may apply to major in one of three competitive, interdisciplinary seminar colleges: the College of Letters (European literature, history, and philosophy), the College of Social Studies (history, government, political and social theory, and economics), and the Science in Society program (concerned with the humane use of scientific knowledge, à la Buckminster Fuller). Other interdisciplinary colleges offering linked majors include the College of the Environment and the College of Integrative Sciences. The College of Film and the Moving Image is first-rate and has an international reputation. Wesleyan also recently launched the College of East Asian Studies, boosting an already strong program that offers advanced language courses, study abroad, a focus on cultural fluency, and an authentic Japanese tea room.

(continued)

Economics
Neuroscience and Behavior
Government
Film Studies
East Asian Studies
English
History

Among Wesleyan's strongest departments are economics, English, history, music, astronomy, molecular biology and biochemistry, American studies, and earth and environmental sciences; the psychology, economics, neuroscience and behavior, and government majors enroll the most students. But even the smaller departments attract attention. Ethnomusicology, including African drumming and dance, is a particular specialty; students can be found reclining on the wide, carpeted bleachers at the World Music Hall or watching a dozen musicians play the Indonesian gamelan. The math department emphasizes problem solving in small groups rather than interminable lectures dedicated to theory. Undergraduates in the sciences and psychology work alongside faculty in their research laboratories and frequently earn the opportunity to publish in scientific journals. "Where many of Wesleyan's rivals attract straight-thinking, by-the-book individuals, Wesleyan students are proud to work creatively outside the box and search for less commonly explored answers," says one student. Students can also take advantage of dual-degree programs with Dartmouth, Caltech, and Columbia.

Each student completes an electronic portfolio that allows them to compile their work and set goals with their advisors.

"Wesleyan is an intense school with a heavy workload," a junior says, but "the academic climate is collaborative." Wesleyan has used its wealth to attract highly rated faculty members who are expected to be scholar-teachers: academic superstars who juggle groundbreaking research, enthusiastic lectures, and personal student attention at the same time—and they seem to pull it off. "The professors here are all extremely knowledgeable about their field and very enthusiastic to teach," says a government major. Wesleyan strives to keep its classes small, and 72 percent of the courses have fewer than 20 students. Some students

"Wesleyan students are proud to work creatively outside the box and search for less commonly explored answers."

claim they sometimes have trouble getting into the "hot" courses. "With popular classes, you have to be persistent, but you can get in," a history major says. If beseeching is not your style, studying abroad may be a temporary tonic to registration headaches. Programs are available in all areas of the world, and 42 percent of students take part. Students can also study off campus at domestic programs that include the Maritime Studies Program at Mystic Seaport*, the SEA Semester*, and the Semester in Environmental Science at Woods Hole, Massachusetts, or they may take a semester at another Twelve College Exchange* school. Internships are popular too.

Wesleyan recently launched the College of East Asian Studies, boosting a program that offers advanced language courses and study abroad.

Wesleyan's excellent reputation and strong recruiting network attract students from all over, ensuring the mash-up of viewpoints that makes it such a vital place. "Students at Wesleyan tend to be open-minded, culturally literate, and intellectually curious," says one student, but "people here are not all from the same mold." Just 8 percent of undergraduates are Connecticut natives, and 9 percent hail from foreign nations. The student body is 7 percent African American, 11 percent Hispanic, and 8 percent Asian American. "I think Wesleyan can pride itself on admitting students from all types of socioeconomic, geographic, and national backgrounds, as well as diverse identities," cheers a junior. Students are vocal about hot social and political issues, ranging from "single-sex Greek life to divestment from fossil fuels to the Black Lives Matter protests." Approximately 90 percent of freshmen are admitted on a traditional need-blind basis, with the rest admitted with an eye on their ability to pay, and 22 percent of the most recent freshman class qualified for Pell Grants. The university meets 100 percent of admitted students' demonstrated need and also has a policy of waiving any loan obligation for most families with incomes below $60,000 per year.

For housing, most freshmen are consigned to singles or doubles in the campus dorms. Popular opinion indicates that the Butterfield complex is the choice for quiet study, while Clark Hall is where the party people go. Housing is guaranteed for four years; upperclassmen who want to live off campus must apply for permission, and only 1 percent do so. Upperclassmen enjoy numerous campus housing options: townhouses for four or five students, college-owned houses and apartments, or special-interest houses organized around concerns such as ecology, feminism, art, community service, or minority student unity. "The housing system at Wesleyan is really unique. It's based on a system of progressive independence, so every year you have more freedom and more responsibility," explains a student. Campus dining gets good reviews too: "Vegetarians love Wesleyan and so do meat eaters. There is an option for everyone," one student says. Students report feeling safe on campus and say the university has taken an active role in sexual assault prevention.

"[Housing is] based on a system of progressive independence."

Greek membership is nominal, with just 10 percent of men and 3 percent of women joining up. Two former fraternities have turned into co-ed literary societies. As a result of a series of disputes with the administration over single-sex status and allegations of sexual harassment, the remaining fraternities have faced disciplinary actions. Wesleyan's enforcement of the 21-year-old drinking age is moderate compared with most schools. Consistent with the university's encouragement of independence, students bear a large part of the responsibility for policing themselves. "There is definitely a drinking/party culture, but there is absolutely no pressure to participate," says one senior. "Students are very understanding and respectful of their peers' decisions." Activities abound from comedy performances to a cappella groups, films, plays, bands, lectures, parties, and events planned by the more than 200 student groups. "Most students stay on campus for weekends and other social events," a junior says. Major events on the social calendar include Spring Fling and "the Mash" concert—two outdoor festivals—and Uncle Duke Day and Zonker Harris Day, two similar events with a more psychedelic, '60s flavor, in which students pay tribute to the infamous Doonesbury characters.

Middletown is a small city within easy driving distance of Hartford and New Haven, but it is off the beaten track of steady public transportation. It has undergone a renaissance in recent years, and students cheer the myriad ethnic restaurants available. "Middletown isn't a bad place for college," says a student. "There are bars on Main Street that cater to a college crowd. Plus, there is a diverse collection of restaurants, which is great for when the family comes to visit." Wes students contribute a great deal of time to community service and help maintain a peaceful, beneficial relationship with the town. And Wesleyan's rural surroundings afford the much-appreciated opportunity to jog through the countryside, swim at nearby Wadsworth Falls, or pick apples in the local orchards. Good road trips include New York and Boston, each two hours away, and decent ski areas and beaches just under an hour away.

"There is definitely a drinking/party culture, but there is absolutely no pressure to participate."

The Wesleyan Cardinals compete in the Division III New England Small College Athletic Conference (NESCAC) and field 29 varsity teams. Recent conference champions include men's basketball, baseball, and football, and the women's tennis and crew teams recently advanced to their respective NCAA tournaments. Annual encounters with "Little Three" rivals Williams and Amherst get even the most bookwormish student out of the library and into the heat of the action. Recreational sports are extremely popular, and more than half of the students compete in five intramural and 16 club sports. The ultimate Frisbee club (the "Nietzsch Factor," named after a former star player's dog, not a misspelling of the philosopher) almost always whips challengers. Athletics are enhanced by a complex that comes complete with a 200-meter indoor track, a fitness center, and a 50-meter pool.

The key to Wesleyan's success seems to be the fostering of an intellectual milieu where independent thinking and an appreciation of differences are omnipresent. This New England university offers more academic and extracurricular options than almost any school its size, and the Wesleyan experience means liberal learning in a climate of individual freedom. Freedom at Wesleyan requires motivated students who stay on task despite the laid-back atmosphere. Abundant opportunities are open to students willing to take advantage of them, which is precisely what these doers do.

Overlaps

Tufts, Vassar, UC–Berkeley, Brown, UCLA, NYU, Washington University in St. Louis, Middlebury

If You Apply To ➤ **Wesleyan:** Early decision I: Nov. 15. Early decision II and regular decision: Jan. 1. Financial aid: Mar. 1. Application fee: $55. Campus and alumni interviews: recommended, evaluative. SATs or ACTs: optional. Subject Tests: optional. Letters of recommendation: required. Essay: required. Accepts the Common Application with supplement.

West Virginia University

P.O. Box 6009, Morgantown, WV 26506

Surrounded by the likes of Ohio, Pennsylvania, and Virginia, West Virginia has traditionally exported its best students to other states for college. But WVU also attracts its share of out-of-staters, some drawn to its one-of-a-kind forensics program. The honors program is a must for top students, and the university has solid programs in professional fields ranging from journalism to engineering.

West Virginia University earned the right to be the state's flagship land grant college by being the only one in the state to offer research and doctoral-degree programs. WVU offers more than 350 majors, approximately 450 student organizations, and 17 intercollegiate varsity athletic programs. With strong academic programs and student groups, the school has become a solid choice for scholars, researchers, and athletes, as well as party animals.

WVU is situated in the picturesque mountains of north-central West Virginia, a few miles from the Pennsylvania border and overlooking the Monongahela River. A driverless rail system bridges the school's two campuses—the older Morgantown and the more modern Evansdale, which are a mile and a half apart. Ten of the ivy-covered Morgantown buildings, dating mainly from the 19th century, are listed on the National Register of Historic Places; many of their interiors have been restored or renovated.

> "The overall academic climate is generally laid-back."

West Virginia's degree programs span 14 colleges and schools, the best of which are engineering (particularly energy-related) and the allied health sciences (medical technology, physical therapy, nursing, and occupational therapy). The most

Website: www.wvu.edu
Location: Small City
Public
Total Enrollment: 21,919
Undergraduates: 20,532
Male/Female: 55/45
SAT Ranges: CR 460–560, M 470–580
ACT Ranges: 21–27
Financial Aid: 63%
Pell Grant: N/A
Expense: Pub $
Student Loans: 64%
Average Debt: $ $ $ $
Phi Beta Kappa: Yes
Applicants: 15,353

(continued)

Accepted: 86%
Enrolled: 36%
Grad in 6 Years: 57%
Returning Freshmen: 79%
Academics: ✍ ✍
Social: ☎ ☎ ☎ ☎
Q of L: ★ ★ ★
Admissions: (304) 293-2121
Email Address:
wvuadmissions@mail.wvu.edu

Strong Programs:
Journalism
Engineering
Allied Health Sciences
Psychology
Nursing
Criminology
Mechanical Engineering
Exercise Physiology

The First-Year Experience helps students adjust to college with New Student Orientation, dorm-based Freshman Interest Groups, and Resident Faculty Leaders.

Mountaineer Week showcases the customs of Appalachia.

popular majors are psychology, nursing, criminology, mechanical engineering, and exercise physiology. Additional programs include undergraduate majors in management information systems, business for foreign languages, art history, music, and theater. Regardless of major, students must complete the General Education Curriculum (GEC), designed to ensure all students have a foundation of skills and knowledge necessary to reason clearly, communicate effectively, and contribute to society. Graduates are expected to possess knowledge and experience in nine objective areas—communication, math and science, issues of contemporary society, history, artistic expression, the individual in society, American culture, non-Western culture, and Western culture.

Half of all undergraduate classes have fewer than 20 students. Students say the difficulty of WVU academics depends largely on the classes they take. "The overall academic climate is generally laid-back," says a senior, "but certain classes and a segment of the student population create a competitive climate." The First-Year Experience helps students adjust to college with New Student Orientation, dorm-based Freshman Interest Groups, and Resident Faculty Leaders, who live next door to the dorms and serve as mentors and friends. A one-credit course, First-Year Seminar, also helps students understand the academic, social, and emotional expectations of the college experience, covering study skills, university and community support services, goal setting, and career planning. An honors program offers small classes, special housing, and early registration to the top 5 percent of WVU students.

"Every football game is a festival in some way."

Though WVU attracts students from all U.S. states and nearly 100 countries, its appeal is primarily regional. Forty-seven percent of undergraduates are in-staters, and 6 percent are international; a sizable contingent arrives from western Pennsylvania and southern New Jersey—so many that the university has been dubbed "New Jersey University: West Virginia campus." Says one student: "WVU has a unique conglomerate of students, ranging from Appalachian natives to a lot of inner-city NYC kids and New Jersey natives." African Americans comprise 5 percent of the student body, Hispanics 4 percent, and Asian Americans 2 percent. The university offers thousands of merit scholarships, worth an average of $2,437, and nearly 250 athletic scholarships.

Fifteen percent of WVU's undergraduates live on campus, where dorms are said to be mediocre but fill up fast because of the increase in students flocking to the university. Most are co-ed; the older ones are known for their character, while the newer residential complexes on the Evansdale campus have larger rooms and luxuries like air-conditioning. Many upperclassmen opt for nearby apartments. Seven percent of the men and 6 percent of the women go Greek and may live in their respective chapter houses, which have their own cooks. Each dorm has its own cafeteria, and students may buy meal plans regardless of where they live. The campus is so large students say they need cars to get around, but have trouble finding a place to park them. Students can also ride the Morgantown Mountain Line buses, which stop at all university housing, for free.

Morgantown is a small city with a college-town feel and plenty of community service opportunities, students say. "This town revolves around the university and provides so much for the students," says a senior. The school has worked hard to curtail underage drinking, banning alcohol in the dorms and limiting each frat to three social events per semester with 300 members and guests. Students report that it's now nearly impossible for those under 21 to be served on campus and say off-campus bars have also cracked down. That said, social life is still centered on campus, often focused on the free food, movies, bands, and comedians offered Thursday through Saturday by the school-sponsored Up All Night program. Spring Fest and Fall Fest provide stress relief each semester, and Mountaineer Week showcases the customs of Appalachia. For those with cars, road trips to Columbus, Washington,

D.C., or Pittsburgh are quick and easy. Football rivalries with Syracuse, Maryland, and Pittsburgh (the "Backyard Brawl") take students farther afield.

Mountaineer football has achieved national prominence, especially with its move to the Big 12, and a senior says, "Every football game is a festival in some way." West Virginia also fields competitive Division I teams in women's soccer, riflery, gymnastics, and basketball and men's soccer, basketball, rowing, and wrestling. There are hundreds of intramural teams, the most popular being basketball, flag football, dodgeball, and indoor soccer.

As WVU grows, the university continues to be dedicated to research that will improve the lives of citizens not only in West Virginia, but across the globe. At the same time, WVU's mission is changing to be more student-centered. And the campus is forever growing and changing. "WVU is a school," says a senior, "that won't look the same for very long."

Overlaps

Fairmont, James Madison, Marshall, Penn State, Ohio State, Towson, University of Delaware, University of Maryland

If You Apply To >   **West Virginia:** Rolling admissions: Aug. 1. Financial aid: Mar. 1. Housing: May 1. Application fee: $45. No campus or alumni interviews. SATs or ACTs: required. No Subject Tests. No letters of recommendation. No essay. Accepts the Common Application.

Wheaton College (IL)

501 College Avenue, Wheaton, IL 60187

Wheaton is at the top of the academic heap in Evangelical education, rivaled only by Pepperdine (with its Malibu digs) and traditional competitors such as Gordon and Calvin. Students must not only follow Wheaton's stringent code of conduct but also affirm their personal faith in Christ. Wheaton's low tuition makes it relatively affordable. The worldly temptations of Chicago are less than an hour away.

Wheaton College combines academic rigor and Evangelical orthodoxy with a firm commitment to the liberal arts, preparing students "to help build the church and improve society worldwide For Christ and His Kingdom." It is one of only two Evangelical schools with an admissions process that requires students to be professing Christians (see also Gordon College). The Community Covenant prohibits the use of alcohol, tobacco, or drugs; professors are allowed to drink and smoke, but are discouraged from doing so, especially in front of students. Though most adolescents would chafe under such restrictions, Wheaties take it all in stride. A happy junior says, "Wheaton offers a unique balance of academic excellence, extracurricular activity, and Christian community that simply cannot be found anywhere else."

Wheaton is nondenominational and its verdant, 80-acre campus is an oasis of sorts, in the midst of one of Chicago's oldest and most established suburbs. The castle-like Blanchard Hall, completed in the last century, keeps watch over the community from atop the front campus hill; when couples get engaged, they climb to the top of the tower to share their news by ringing the bell. Nearby is the Billy Graham Center, which houses a museum and the college archives, making it a hub for research on American Evangelicalism. (Graham is a Wheaton alumnus.) An $80 million science center provides 135,000 square feet of research, teaching, and exhibit space. A new

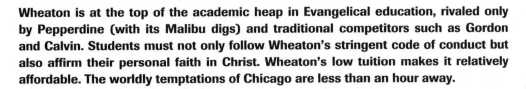
"[Professors] provide a stimulating intellectual experience in light of the Christian faith."

Website: www.wheaton.edu
Location: Suburban
Private
Total Enrollment: 2,657
Undergraduates: 2,409
Male/Female: 47/53
SAT Ranges: CR 600–710, M 600–700
ACT Ranges: 27–32
Financial Aid: 80%
Pell Grant: 20%
Expense: Pr $
Student Loans: 58%
Average Debt: $ $
Phi Beta Kappa: No
Applicants: 1,971
Accepted: 71%
Enrolled: 44%
Grad in 6 Years: 89%
Returning Freshmen: 95%

(continued)

Academics: ✎ ✎ ✎
Social: ☎ ☎ ☎
Q of L: ★ ★ ★ ★
Admissions: (800) 222-2419
Email Address: admissions@ wheaton.edu

Strong Programs:
Business
English
Applied Health Science
Biology
Communication
Theater
Digital Media

The Billy Graham Center is a hub for research on American Evangelicalism.

welcome center and Conservatory of Music building are set to open in fall 2017, with a new concert hall to follow.

Sporting the largest endowment among the nation's Evangelical schools, Wheaton offers students a generous bevy of programs and facilities. New general education requirements ("Christ at the Core") took effect in fall of 2016. In addition to a broad array of thematic coursework, the outcomes-based model includes a first-year seminar, an advanced seminar, and a core curriculum capstone experience. Business is Wheaton's most popular major, followed by English, applied health science, biology, and communication. Other signature programs include theater and digital media. Motivated students may opt for 3–2 programs that allow them to combine an undergraduate degree in the liberal arts with a master's in nursing or engineering, saving a year in the process. In the classroom, there's an emphasis on teamwork, though classes can be demanding. "Many students and professors have a genuine desire to change the world and advance Christ's Kingdom," says one sophomore. "As a consequence, that zeal and expectation can affect studying and preparation for lectures." The quality of teaching varies, but students get "the benefit of Christian professors who provide a stimulating intellectual experience in light of the Christian faith," according to one junior.

Students have the opportunity to perform research at Argonne National Laboratory, just down the road, and for those seeking a truly global experience, there's study abroad in more than 30 countries throughout Europe, East Asia, and Latin America; 47 percent of students partake. "Study abroad programs are quite common to the Wheaton experience," a student says, describing them as "superb and life-changing." Those concerned with social justice, a definite focus at Wheaton, may be interested in the Human Needs and Global Resources program, which sends students to Third World countries for six months of work on development projects such as building roads and schools. Wheaties may also spend a semester at one of the 12 other Evangelical schools that belong to the Council for Christian Colleges and Universities*. Summer study in astronomy, meteorology, biology, chemistry, geology, and environmental science is available at the Black Hills Science Station, while leadership training takes place at Honey Rock, Wheaton's campus in the Wisconsin North Woods. For incoming freshmen, the 18-day Wheaton Passage wilderness trek provides "an experience in team building, self-discovery, and physical challenge that should not be missed," says a sophomore; an urban experience is also available at Wheaton's urban studies facility in Chicago's Uptown neighborhood.

> **"Study abroad programs are quite common to the Wheaton experience."**

"The student body is extremely motivated and high achieving," says one student. "They desire to encourage their peers to pursue excellence in their God-given gifts." Twenty-six percent of Wheaton students hail from Illinois, and 3 percent come from overseas. African Americans comprise 3 percent of the student body, Hispanics make up 6 percent, and Asian Americans add 9 percent. Current events and issues find their way into campus conversation. "The biggest social and political issues would probably be issues tied to faith or race," says one student. Wheaton's Community Covenant shuns "homosexual behavior and all other sexual relations outside the bounds of marriage between a man and woman"; thus, LGBTQ issues—and students—have been controversial on campus. The number of Pell-eligible freshmen has been rising and now stands at 20 percent. Merit awards averaging $6,228 are awarded to qualified students. There are no athletic scholarships.

> **"We have a lot of fun here, but all alcohol-free fun."**

Eighty-seven percent of Wheaton students live in campus housing, and accommodations range from single-sex dorms with traditional double rooms and bathrooms down the hall to college-owned houses and apartments. "In general, housing is very good, with well-kept dorms and apartments," says one senior. Opposite-sex visitation is limited to certain hours on certain days, though "each semester, dorms are allowed two 'raids' to their opposite floor," says an education major. Everyone eats in Anderson Commons, where an outside vendor, Bon Appétit, does the cooking. "They offer such diversity—Cajun, Asian, Italian, pizza, sandwiches," says a sophomore. "Everything is made from scratch!" a senior adds. Students report feeling safe on campus: "Campus security is excellent," says a business major. "They are a phone call away."

Since Wheaton lacks fraternities and sororities, and because students agree to abstain from alcohol, drugs, and tobacco, the social life revolves around other pursuits. "We have a lot of fun here, but all alcohol-free fun," says a psychology major. "We have tons of fun events on campus and through student clubs or college union. Plus, there's always just hanging out with friends or having Nerf battles in their apartments." A commuter train near campus whisks students to downtown Chicago in 45 minutes, where restaurants, blues clubs, theaters, museums, shopping, and professional sports are in abundance. Favorite traditions include Missions in Focus week, which brings missionary organizations and Christian speakers to campus, and the individual dorm floors' own traditions, one of which includes an annual root beer kegger.

Wheaton's athletic teams (the Thunder) compete in Division III, and men's and women's soccer, basketball, and swimming are particularly competitive. Football (recent conference champs), basketball, and soccer games "are always exciting and well attended," says one student, especially if the opponent is Augustana College. The debate and chess teams are competitive too. Roughly one-third of students play intramural sports. And while it's not an athletic competition per se, juniors and seniors do get excited about decorating "the Bench," a reinforced concrete slab that is the subject of an ongoing and often rough-and-tumble game of keep-away.

Even after more than 150 years, Wheaton remains "committed to the principle that truth is revealed by God through Christ, in whom is hidden all the treasures of wisdom and knowledge." Students believe their school's dedication to Christianity only strengthens the bonds they develop with one another and their understanding of the broader world. "The Wheaton education is hard to duplicate," says one student. "Learning at Wheaton truly does prepare you for Christ and His kingdom."

The Human Needs and Global Resources program sends students to Third World countries for six months of work on development projects.

Overlaps

Taylor, Calvin, Biola, Baylor, Gordon, Northwestern, Vanderbilt, Bethel University (MN)

If You Apply To ➤   **Wheaton (IL):** Early action: Nov. 1. Regular decision: Jan. 10. Financial aid: Feb. 1. Application fee: $50. Campus interviews: optional, evaluative. No alumni interviews. SATs or ACTs: required. No Subject Tests. Letters of recommendation: required (one academic and one pastoral). Essay: required.

Wheaton College (MA)

Norton, MA 02766

Although its address says it's in Massachusetts, Wheaton is actually closer to Providence than to Boston. But getting to either by train is quick and easy. One of the few nationally known institutions in the area that is still relatively accessible. Curriculum includes interdisciplinary, hands-on, and project-based work in addition to traditional courses. Smaller than Skidmore, comparable to Connecticut College.

Website: www.wheaton
college.edu

Location: Suburban

Private

Total Enrollment: 1,567

Undergraduates: 1,567

Male/Female: 36/64

SAT Ranges: CR 550–658,
M 550–665

ACT Ranges: 25–30

Financial Aid: 88%

Pell Grant: 20%

Expense: Pr $ $ $

Student Loans: 66%

Average Debt: $ $ $

Phi Beta Kappa: Yes

Applicants: 4,322

Accepted: 64%

Enrolled: 14%

Grad in 6 Years: 79%

Returning Freshmen: 86%

Academics: ✐ ✐ ✐

Social: ☎ ☎ ☎

Q of L: ★ ★ ★ ★

Admissions: (508) 286-8251

Email Address: admission@
wheatoncollege.edu

Strong Programs:
Psychology
Business and Management
Economics
Biology
English
Fine Arts
Chemistry

*Wheaton remains
among the top 10
liberal arts colleges
for Fulbright scholars.*

Wheaton College offers students plenty of opportunities to make their academic marks. Since 2000, more than 200 Wheaton students have received national fellowships, including three Rhodes scholars and four Marshall scholars. The college remains among the top 10 liberal arts colleges for Fulbright scholars as well. Increasingly focused on experiential learning, Wheaton makes sure its students shine outside the classroom too. Says one satisfied senior, "Wheaton's commitment to supporting its students to leverage their liberal arts education and change the world permeates all aspects of life on campus."

Wheaton's rural location offers few distractions from intellectual pursuits. Its 400-acre campus blends Georgian brick buildings and modern structures set among beautiful lawns and shade trees. The two halves of the campus are separated by Peacock Pond, which probably qualifies as the only heated duck pond on any American campus.

Wheaton's curriculum shows students how to make linkages between disciplines. Rather than simply checking off required courses, all Wheaton students study across the major academic fields, developing a fully dimensional view of the world. In practical terms, this means that every student must take a series of courses on a single topic from various departments. Core classes include English, quantitative skills, foreign language, natural science, and non-Western history. Students also choose a first-year seminar from among roughly 25 sections, each focused on "controversies" that have generated debate or heralded changes in how they experience or understand the world. The curriculum links experiential learning to each department and requires a capstone senior project.

Psychology, business and management, economics, biology, and English are Wheaton's most popular majors. Programs in the arts are well recognized—impressive given the school's small size—and the chemistry department is also strong. "I would highly recommend the science departments," says a junior. "They have the most readily available opportunities for student/professor research." Students interested in interdisciplinary study can choose majors like math and economics or theater and English dramatic literature, or they may design their own majors. The major in Hispanic studies benefits from its affiliation with a study abroad program in Córdoba, and a Mellon Foundation grant supports native speakers in Spanish and other languages. Dual-degree programs with Dartmouth, George Washington University, and other institutions are available in engineering, business, communication, religion, and optometry. Wheaton students can also take classes at other schools in the Twelve College Exchange Program* or at nearby Brown University. For those tired of studying on land, Wheaton offers the Maritime Studies Program*. The Center for Global Education offers more than 70 approved study abroad programs in more than 90 different nations around the world; 45 percent of students participate.

> **"Professors at Wheaton go out of their way to make sure you are doing well."**

According to a psychology major, "Critical thinking, intensive writing, and collaborative projects are part of almost every class, which allows for in-depth exploration of concepts, themes, and lessons." Two-thirds of Wheaton's classes have fewer than 20 students, encouraging close ties between students and faculty. "Professors at Wheaton go out of their way to make sure you are doing well," a student cheers. Aside from a faculty advisor, students get a staff mentor and two peer advisors, known as preceptors. The Filene Center for Academic Advising and Career Services gets high marks from students seeking internships—and jobs after graduation. In fact, the center's Wheaton Edge program guarantees each student a $3,000 to $5,000 stipend to pursue unpaid internships, research opportunities, or service projects, ensuring that, in the words of one senior, "students never have to worry about choosing between a paycheck and a professional experience."

About a third of Wheaton's students come from Massachusetts, and 12 percent hail from foreign nations. The student body is largely white; African Americans account for 6 percent, Hispanics 7 percent, and Asian Americans 5 percent. Students are said to be friendly and open to differing views; politically, liberals and conservatives are both well represented on campus. "Wheaton's legacy as a former women's college means that people are very attuned to feminist and gender issues," explains a senior. "These are issues that students rally around." The administration has undertaken a massive capital campaign, using some of the proceeds to hire more minority scholars—and recruit more minority students. Merit awards averaging $11,878 are available, but there are no athletic awards.

As might be expected on this small, suburban campus, virtually everyone (95 percent) lives in one of Wheaton's dorms or theme houses. All students are guaranteed housing for four years; freshmen live in doubles, triples, or quads, and upperclassmen try their luck in the lottery system. "Many of the dorms are old and need improvements," says a chemistry major. The recently renovated dining halls are bright and spacious, and the biggest winners of all are the ducks, which thrive on the leftover bread students toss into Peacock Pond. "There's a big push for local, fresh, and organic produce," says a junior. Students also say they feel safe on campus and that security is visible and active. "They patrol 24 hours a day to ensure things are OK," says a sophomore. A senior adds, "Students are constantly collaborating with the administration to increase discussion, engagement, and education around the issue of sexual assault on campus."

The Wheaton Edge program guarantees each student a stipend to pursue unpaid internships, research opportunities, or service projects.

"[Wheaton Edge ensures that] students never have to worry about choosing between a paycheck and a professional experience."

Social life at Wheaton includes dances, concerts, lectures, parties on campus, and other activities organized by the more than 100 student groups. Students unwind at the college's student center, which offers a café, dance studio, and sun deck for afternoon study breaks. There are no sororities or fraternities here. Students say that, as on most campuses, "drinking and partying does occur," but they appreciate the school's "Safety Always Matters Most" policy. Students love to put on their dancing shoes—whether for the Boston Bash party on a boat in Boston Harbor, for the Valentine's Dance, or for any number of events at Rosecliff, a mansion in Newport, Rhode Island. Spring Weekend features the Head of the Peacock race, where students build vessels (no boats allowed) and race them across the pond, as well as live bands and outdoor barbecues. When it rains, students get dirty as they slide around the craters on Wheaton's lawns, an activity known as "dimple diving."

Spring Weekend features the Head of the Peacock race, where students build vessels and race them across the pond.

The town of Norton, just outside campus, draws more than half of students with services opportunities, such as a Big Brother Big Sister program, hospital visits, and academic tutoring, but there's little to do otherwise, students say. "It's a very quiet town, and most students stay on campus rather than venture off into Norton," says a student. Relatively convenient access to two

"Wheaton's legacy as a former women's college means that people are very attuned to feminist and gender issues."

state capitals livens up the social scene. "We're 20 minutes from Providence, and 40 minutes from Boston. If you can't find something to do on the weekend, you're just looking for something to complain about," a student says.

The Wheaton Lyons compete in Division III. The Lyons nickname goes back to Wheaton's days as an all-female school, and it honors Mary Lyons, the 19th-century educational pioneer who founded Mount Holyoke. The strongest teams include men's and women's soccer—both of which have won numerous championships.

Other recent conference champs include baseball, softball, women's lacrosse, and synchronized swimming. The athletic facility boasts an eight-lane swimming pool, a field house, and an 850-seat arena for basketball or volleyball. Almost 50 percent of students participate in intramural sports.

Students at Wheaton take an active role and are involved in campus planning and college operations, as well as in their community. "We don't just have coffee in the café," says a political science major. "We text with deans, have lunch with professors, coffee with advisors, a beer with our favorite professor. These kinds of relationships are the Wheaton way. They supplement the intellectual energy and debate that takes place among students." Indeed, students here take pride in their achievements inside and outside the classroom, while striving to preserve the school's friendly, small-town feel.

If You Apply To ➤ **Wheaton (MA):** Early decision I and early action: Nov. 1. Early decision II and regular decision: Jan. 1. Financial aid: Feb. 1. Application fee: $60. Campus and alumni interviews: recommended, evaluative. SATs or ACTs: optional. Subject Tests: optional. Letters of recommendation: required. Essay: required. Accepts the Common Application. Students may submit optional, supplemental academic writing sample or personal portfolio.

Whitman College

345 Boyer Avenue, Walla Walla, WA 99362

Whitman has quietly established itself as one of the West's leading liberal arts colleges. Don't bother with the umbrella: Walla Walla is in arid eastern Washington. Whitman's isolation breeds community spirit and alumni loyalty. True to its liberal arts heritage, Whitman has no business program. Combines outdoorsy camaraderie with the slower pace of life in the rural Northwest.

You don't have to own a Frisbee to succeed at Whitman, but if you've got one, bring it along—you'll find a campus full of friendly students eager to toss it back to you. Though it isn't well known outside the Pacific Northwest, Whitman offers a top-notch liberal arts education, along with plenty of fun for outdoorsy types. Students are down-to-earth and friendly and feel a deep loyalty to one another—and to their school. "The Whitman community is more supportive and inspiring than I would have thought possible," says a senior. "Here you can grow and excel to your absolute potential."

Whitman was founded in 1882 and named in honor of Marcus and Narcissa Whitman, who served the Cayuse Indians and immigrants on the Oregon Trail. Even today, everything important is within walking distance of campus, including the main drag of Walla Walla, which once won a national Best Main Street award. The 117-acre campus, where colonial buildings and modern facilities sport New England ivy, sits at the foot of the Blue Mountains, surrounded by golden wheat fields and vineyards. Beyond Walla Walla (which means "many waters" in the Cayuse Indian language) are gorgeous mountains, rivers, and forests.

All Whitman students complete the General Studies Program, which includes both a first-year core and distribution requirements in various disciplines. The first-year program revolves around a seminar called Encounters that emphasizes analytical reading of texts—such as Plato's *Symposium*, Homer's *Odyssey*, the Bible, and Mary Shelley's *Frankenstein*—as well as effective writing. Students then take at least six credits in social sciences, humanities, fine arts, and science, as well as three or more credits in quantitative analysis, and two courses that focus on alternative voices. Depending on their major, all seniors must either complete a written senior thesis and oral defense or pass comprehensive written and oral exams in their major; Whitman was the first U.S. college or university to require seniors to do so.

Biology, psychology, economics, English, and the interdisciplinary major in biochemistry, biophysics, and molecular biology are some of the best (and most popular) programs at Whitman; the school also boasts an astronomy program, unusual among small colleges. Whitman has an extensive Asian art collection, and additional coursework in Chinese language and Asian studies is offered through a summer program in China. Whitman has 3–2 or 3–3 programs in engineering and computer science (with Caltech, Columbia, Duke, the University of Washington, and Washington University in St. Louis), international studies and international business (Monterey Institute of International Studies), computer science and oceanography (University of Washington), forestry or environmental management (Duke), and law (Columbia). Students may also pursue teacher certification through partnerships with the University of Puget Sound.

"Here you can grow and excel to your absolute potential."

Seventy percent of classes have fewer than 20 students, fostering a collaborative atmosphere. "Classes are generally difficult, but in a way that encourages cooperation among students rather than a malicious competition where grades and rank are most important," says a sophomore. A freshman adds, "I bounce paper ideas off of my peers all the time and because of their collective input, I turn in much better work than I would on my own." An environmental studies major reports, "Professors are extremely knowledgeable in their fields and are excited to get to know their students." Foreign study is greatly encouraged and available through 88 approved programs in 40 countries, ranging from Japan and Sri Lanka to England, Italy, Ireland, and Egypt; 43 percent of students go abroad, and financial aid packages can be applied to all 88 programs. Students may also take urban studies terms within the U.S. in Philadelphia and Washington, D.C. "Semester in the West is the biggest up-and-coming program," explains a psychology major. "Students travel for one semester along the West Coast, learning from different professors in variable environments." During the day-long Whitman Undergraduate Conference, student scholarship and creativity are celebrated with presentations, posters, and performances.

"No matter how different they may be, most Whitties seem to absolutely love the school," a junior says. "Students are very passionate about what they study, whether it's social justice or poetry." Thirty-three percent of students are from Washington State, and many of the rest hail from the suburbs of Western cities, notably San Francisco and Portland; 6 percent arrive from overseas. Five percent are Asian American, 7 percent are Hispanic, and 1 percent are African American. The Intercultural Center and Glover Alston Center help support diversity and intercultural awareness on campus. Political issues don't dominate campus conversation. "There's a handful of super-vocal students and then a sea of apathy surrounding them," says a freshman. There are numerous merit scholarships averaging $9,595 but no athletic awards.

"Classes are generally difficult, but in a way that encourages cooperation among students."

Sixty-four percent of students live in campus housing; freshmen and sophomores are required to do so. "Dorms are very comfortable, especially compared to dorms I have seen at other schools," says one student. A freshman adds, "ResLife does a great job of matching people up with roommates, and the living options are diverse and spread out across campus." Prentiss Hall and Lyman House, both built in 1926, have received multimillion-dollar face-lifts. Theme houses are

(continued)

Social: ☎ ☎ ☎
Q of L: ★ ★ ★ ★
Admissions: (509) 527-5176
Email Address: admission@ whitman.edu

Strong Programs:
Biology
Psychology
Economics
English
Biochemistry, Biophysics, and Molecular Biology
Astronomy
Asian and Middle Eastern Studies

Whitman was the first U.S. college or university to require seniors to pass comprehensive written and oral exams in their major.

available for students interested in foreign languages, fine arts, writing, community service, Asian studies, environmental studies, multiculturalism, and the outdoors. "The food is very good, especially at the beginning of the semester, although it is hard not to get sick of it by the end," says a sophomore. Students report feeling safe on campus and "the worst problem is bike theft," according to one Spanish major.

The social life at Whitman revolves around fraternity parties—44 percent of the men and 44 percent of the women go Greek—and other on-campus events, such as theatrical productions and the spring Renaissance Faire. "Students at Whitman are very social," says one sophomore. "Most large parties take place either in one of the four fraternity houses or in off-campus houses. Smaller get-togethers and parties are also popular in personal rooms in the residence halls." The close-knit campus fosters a community vibe, but it can be a hassle too. "Dating here is insane because everyone knows everyone's business," says a freshman. Annual traditions include

"Walla Walla is small, but full of culture."

Duckfest, in which students create ducks, place them all over campus, and then design a map indicating where they are, so that peers, professors, and community members can take a walking tour—and the college president can rank the best efforts. Dragfest is a popular dance party, and the end of the year brings "the Beer Mile, where students celebrate on Ankeny Field, and the administration is thankful we're safe," says a junior.

The town of Walla Walla (population 32,000) supports a symphony, community playhouse, art galleries, two rodeos, and a hot-air balloon festival. "Walla Walla is small, but full of culture," says one student. About 70 percent of students get involved in community service opportunities. Outdoor pursuits are important in this part of the country, where autumn is gorgeous, winter sporadically snowy, and spring delightfully warm. Walla Walla is located in the center of agricultural southeastern Washington, in an arid valley. Hiking, biking, and backpacking are minutes away, and white-water rafting and rock climbing are popular on weekends. Two ski centers and other recreational areas are within an hour's drive, and Seattle (260 miles) and Portland (235 miles) offer a welcome change of scenery.

The Whitman Missionaries compete in Division III. Men's tennis brought home Northwest Conference championships in 2015 and 2016. Women's tennis and golf, men's cross-country, and men's and women's basketball and swimming are solid too. Nearly 70 percent of students play intramurals. Club lacrosse and rugby tournaments draw crowds, as does "Onionfest," the ultimate Frisbee competition, and "Anchor Smash," the spring intramural football tournament. Rock climbers can challenge themselves on two walls. The Whitman Debate Team is one of the most successful debate programs in the country.

"If you're choosing a liberal arts school in the Northwest," says a student, "choose Whitman!" Indeed, students seeking a solid liberal arts education with a healthy dose of outdoor fun would do well to heed this enthusiastic Whittie's advice. Professors here know their stuff and care about teaching and their students. Combine the college's beautiful campus with the close friendships nurtured by its small size, and it's easy to see why Whitties remain loyal to each other—and their school—long after they've left campus.

Overlaps

University of Puget Sound, Middlebury, Pomona, Willamette, University of Washington, Lewis & Clark, UC–Berkeley, Carleton

If You Apply To >

Whitman: Early decision I: Nov. 15. Early decision II: Jan. 1. Regular decision and financial aid: Jan. 15. Housing: May 1. Application fee: $50. Campus interviews: recommended, evaluative. No alumni interviews. SATs or ACTs: optional. Subject Tests: optional. Letters of recommendation: required. Essay: required. Accepts the Common Application with supplement.

13406 East Philadelphia, P.O. Box 634, Whittier, CA 90604

Whittier's Quaker heritage brings a touch of the East to suburban L.A. Less selective than Occidental and the Claremont Colleges, Whittier lures ethnically and socioeconomically diverse students with a bevy of academic scholarships. Whittier's functional campus lacks the opulence of the Claremonts and the panache of Pepperdine.

Founded in 1887 by members of the Religious Society of Friends, Whittier College is fast becoming a global training ground. Whittier students can be found all around the world, studying in 30 foreign countries. And when they return to the Whittier campus, they have access to caring faculty and a close-knit environment. "Whittier students tend to be open and friendly," says a student majoring in comparative cultures. "You aren't afraid to sit with someone you haven't met before."

Located just 18 miles away from downtown Los Angeles, the college is perched on a hill overlooking the town of Whittier, California, with the San Gabriel Mountains rising up from the horizon. The 73-acre campus is a pleasant mixture of modern buildings tucked between the red-roofed, white-walled Spanish traditionals. Its landmark building, Deihl Hall, includes a digital audio/video computer lab for languages. A four-foot-high granite monument stands on the north campus lawn honoring Whittier's most famous alum, former president Richard Nixon. The state-of-the-art Science and Learning Center opened in 2016.

Whittier offers its undergraduates two major curricular programs: the liberal education program and the Whittier Scholars Program. About 80 percent of the students take the revised liberal education track, in which they fulfill distribution requirements in writing skills, mathematics, natural sciences, global perspectives, comparative knowledge, and creative and kinesthetic performance. The emphasis of the liberal education program is on an interdisciplinary focus, globalism, and critical and quantitative thinking. These liberally educated Whittierans next choose a major from among 26 departments, the strongest and most popular of which include business administration, kinesiology and nutrition science, psychology, and English. Biology, child development, and theater are solid too. The Center for Science, Health, & Policy incorporates the humanities and social sciences into the study of science and technology to prepare future scientists, health professionals, policy makers, and teachers for real-world challenges.

> **"The quality of the teaching has been very intense, but very rewarding."**

Whittier's signature program is the Whittier Scholars Program, a path taken by 20 percent of the undergraduates, who choose to bypass the traditional liberal education program. They are relieved of most general requirements and start from square one with an "educational design" process. With the help of an academic advisor, Whittier Scholars carve their majors out of standard offerings by taking a bit of this and a bit of that. Majors have included such names as symbol systems, visual studies and business, and dynamics of politics and urban life. The program is highly regarded because of the more active role it allows students to play and the freedom it affords them in pursuing their interests.

All students, no matter which curriculum they choose, must fulfill a yearlong freshman writing requirement, choosing their preferences from a variety of seminars that focus on critical-thinking and communication skills. They are also encouraged to take an additional writing course, mathematics, and lab science during their

---

Website: www.whittier.edu
Location: Suburban
Private
Total Enrollment: 1,942
Undergraduates: 1,620
Male/Female: 44/56
SAT Ranges: CR 463–580, M 470–590
ACT Ranges: 20–26
Financial Aid: 92%
Pell Grant: 38%
Expense: Pr $ $
Student Loans: 79%
Average Debt: $ $ $ $
Phi Beta Kappa: No
Applicants: 5,192
Accepted: 63%
Enrolled: 14%
Grad in 6 Years: 66%
Returning Freshmen: 81%
Academics: ✍ ✍ ✍
Social: ☎ ☎ ☎
Q of L: ★ ★ ★ ★
Admissions: (888) 200-0369
Email Address: admission@whittier.edu

Strong Programs:
Business Administration
Kinesiology and Nutrition Science
Psychology
English
Biology
Child Development
Theater

freshman year. First-years also must attend a series of speakers who discuss topics relevant to student coursework and must take part in the Exploring Los Angeles series, which includes trips to museums and cultural events. Seniors complete a capstone requirement.

Whittier officially ended its affiliation with the Quakers in the 1940s, but the prevailing spirit of community hearkens back to their traditions. One senior says, "The academic climate is competitive and rigorous, but definitely manageable."

"The college is involved a lot with the community."

Fifty-five percent of classes have fewer than 20 students, and freshmen are taught by full professors. "For the most part, the quality of the teaching has been very intense, but very rewarding," says a student. For those looking to add global scope to their college experience, as many do, study abroad options include programs in Denmark, India, Mexico, and Asia. Short-term foreign study tours are also available during the January interim.

"We have a hippie vibe," says an international business major, and the campus is "very liberal." Three-quarters of the undergraduates come from California, and the rest are from all over the U.S. and the world—5 percent are international. While African Americans make up 5 percent of the students, Hispanic enrollment is an impressive 44 percent, and Asian Americans constitute 10 percent. An on-campus cultural center focuses on diversity programming and resources. "Tolerance is a big watchword on campus," a junior says. "You can get severely disciplined or expelled for being intolerant." Thirty-eight percent of students receive Pell Grants. In addition to need-based aid, the college awards merit scholarships averaging $21,921.

In the Whittier Scholars Program, students carve their majors out of standard offerings with the help of an academic advisor.

Half of Whittier students seek off-campus housing, but the Turner Residence Hall entices many students to stay on campus and vie for a chance to get a room with a panoramic view of Los Angeles. "The price for on-campus housing is unreasonably high," complains one student. "Dorms have old furniture and many do not have air-conditioning." Most freshmen are assigned rooms, while Whittier Scholars, athletes, and members of Whittier's social societies tend to cluster in selected dorms and houses. As part of the meal plan, all campus residents must take at least 10 meals at the Campus Inn dining hall, where the food is said to be typical college fare. "Food is diverse and edible," a sophomore says. The Spot (Whittier's popular campus coffeehouse) includes a state-of-the-art nightclub called—logically enough—the Club.

Nine social societies (they're not called fraternities or sororities here) attract 9 percent of the men and 13 percent of the women but hardly dominate the social scene. Their dances, however, which frequently feature live entertainment, are welcomed by all. For many, a favored diversion is road tripping, everywhere from Disneyland to the California beaches. Other common destinations include Las Vegas, Mexico, Joshua Tree, Hollywood,

"It's a small, friendly place where everybody knows everybody."

San Diego, and northern California. For nightlife closer to campus, Los Angeles looms large. The local community, known as Uptown Whittier, offers quaint shops, restaurants, and cobblestone sidewalks and is a spot for community-minded students to get involved. "Whittier is a friendly town," one junior says. "The college is involved a lot with the community." Indeed, the Center for Engagement with Communities provides course-based service-learning internships and research; 25 percent of students participate.

Johnny Poet is Whittier's pen-wielding mascot, inspired by the school's namesake, Quaker poet John Greenleaf Whittier.

Whittier has a fairly strict alcohol policy, and students say it's difficult for underage drinkers to get served at campus events. Popular annual events include the football game against archrival Occidental College (dubbed the Battle of the Shoes), a Spring Sing talent show, the Midnight Breakfast served by professors during second-semester finals, and Sportsfest, which is a campuswide competition in which dorms compete in a variety of athletic, intellectual, and wacky games and events. Another favorite among students is Mona Kai, a Hawaiian party put on by the Lancer Society that features tons of sand shipped in for the event. The most important campus landmark is the Rock, which sits near the front of campus and is given a fresh coat of paint by countless aspiring artists.

Johnny Poet is Whittier's pen-wielding mascot (inspired by the school's namesake, Quaker poet John Greenleaf Whittier), and Division III men's lacrosse is the school's most successful team. Men's water polo, football, and soccer and women's water polo, soccer, softball, and track are the most popular. Intramurals and club sports are a big draw too, especially the rugby, martial arts, and equestrian clubs.

The students at Whittier have created a supportive, intimate environment where people work together and celebrate their diversity. "It's a small, friendly place where everybody knows everybody," a junior says. And with the opportunity to design their own majors, students here are active in their own education.

If You Apply To ➤

Whittier: Rolling admissions. (Priority deadline: Feb. 1.) Early action: Nov. 15. Financial aid: Mar. 2. Application fee: $50. Campus interviews: recommended, evaluative. Alumni interviews: optional, evaluative. SATs or ACTs: optional (required for applicants with GPA below 3.0). No Subject Tests. Letters of recommendation: required. Essay: required. Accepts the Common Application.

Willamette University

900 State Street, Salem, OR 97301

Willamette is strategically located next door to the Oregon state capitol and 40 minutes from Portland. Bigger than Whitman, smaller than U of Puget Sound, and more civic-minded than Lewis & Clark, Willamette offers extensive study abroad enhanced by ties to Asia. Well-known in the West but has yet to develop a national reputation to equal that of competitors such as Lewis & Clark.

Willamette University, founded in 1842, was the first university in the West. Students can take advantage of their proximity to the state's legislative offices and a nearby hospital for internships, jobs, or off-campus learning experiences. A comprehensive study abroad program carries students to destinations around the globe. On campus, students find a more personal atmosphere than larger universities nearby and appreciate the low-key yet challenging academic milieu. One satisfied chemistry major says, "This is the place where you can grow as a student, leader, and person as you pursue your passions."

The 61-acre campus is home to full trees (thanks to Oregon's omnipresent rain), small wildlife, and occasionally steelhead salmon that splash around in the Mill Stream that runs between WU's redbrick academic buildings. Zena Forest is a 300-acre outdoor laboratory used by hundreds of students each term. Ford Hall is a LEED Gold–certified building featuring large, collaborative learning spaces and faculty offices. The Sparks Fitness Center was recently remodeled.

All students at Willamette (pronounced "Will-AM-it") complete the freshman College Colloquium seminar, four writing-centered courses, two courses in quantitative and analytical reasoning, study in a language other than English, and coursework in six modes of inquiry—the natural world; the arts; arguments, reasons, and values; thinking historically; interpreting texts; and understanding society. Students also take capstone senior seminars, often culminating in research or thesis projects. The most popular majors are economics, politics, exercise science, and psychology.

Website: www.willamette.edu
Location: Small City
Private
Total Enrollment: 2,549
Undergraduates: 1,905
Male/Female: 43/57
SAT Ranges: CR 550–670, M 550–660
ACT Ranges: 25–30
Financial Aid: 98%
Pell Grant: 24%
Expense: Pr $ $ $
Student Loans: 64%
Average Debt: $ $
Phi Beta Kappa: Yes
Applicants: 6,332
Accepted: 78%
Enrolled: 8%
Grad in 6 Years: 77%
Returning Freshmen: 87%

(continued)

Academics: ✍ ✍ ✍ ½
Social: ☎ ☎ ☎
Q of L: ★ ★ ★ ★
Admissions: (844) BEARCAT
Email Address: bearcat@
    willamette.edu

Strong Programs:
Economics
Politics
Exercise Science
Psychology
Biology
Theatre
Japanese Studies
History

*The management
and law schools offer
3–2 (B.A./M.B.A.)
and 3–3 (B.A./J.D.)
programs that
integrate the liberal
arts and professional
education.*

Other particularly strong programs include biology, theatre, Japanese studies, and history. The management and law schools offer 3–2 (B.A./M.B.A.) and 3–3 (B.A./J.D.) programs that integrate the liberal arts and professional education.

Academics are rigorous, but students don't compete for grades. "Students are expected to work hard, read copious amounts, and actively contribute in class," says a senior. "That being said, the climate is very collaborative." Classes are small; 56 percent have fewer than 20 students on the roster. "The professors here exemplify what it means to be dedicated to their students. All have office hours, all are accessible outside of those hours by appointment, and all are invested in their students' success," says one student. And for those seeking additional support, "Tutors are available in every subject, for free, and there is a writing center within which students can arrange appointments for help with papers or academic projects," reports a senior.

> "Willamette tends to be very involved in state and city political issues."

When students aren't reading or writing papers, numerous undergraduate research opportunities beckon. Support has more than doubled with the creation of the Carson Undergraduate Research Awards, the Science Collaborative Research Program, and a humanities center. Half of the student body participates in a robust study abroad program that sends them to nearly 40 nations, and Willamette also benefits from its proximity to the U.S. campus of Tokyo International University.

"I think Willamette students are more community-minded than a lot of other institutions. It's not just about learning the material, it's about what impact you'll make, whether that's right now in the local community or the world at large after you graduate," says one senior. Twenty-one percent of WU students are native Oregonians, and much of the remainder comes from Western states, notably California and Washington; just 1 percent are international. African Americans make up 2 percent of the student body, Hispanics 12 percent, and Asian Americans 9 percent. Social justice issues spark discussion on campus. Says a sophomore, "Willamette tends to be very involved in state and city political issues." Willamette offers talent and academic merit scholarships each year averaging $19,120; there are no athletic awards. Twenty-four percent of incoming students receive Pell Grants.

Sixty-eight percent of Willamette students live in campus housing, which is social and convenient to classes and parties; doing so is required for freshmen and sophomores. "Willamette's dorms are not remarkable, but they provide incredible experiences for fostering community," says a student. All housing is co-ed, and theme wings or floors are available, focused on community service, the outdoors, wellness, or substance-free living. The student-owned and operated Bistro offers a coffeehouse atmosphere and is a popular alternative to cafeteria fare. "All of the food is fresh, local, and made on campus by staff that students grow to know personally," explains a senior. Students report

> "Willamette's dorms are not remarkable, but they provide incredible experiences for fostering community."

that the university has taken a strong stance on responding to and educating the community about sexual assault. One survivor says, "Willamette has hired a number of staff to investigate and build support structures for survivors, and they have generally done a good job of doing so. I was sexually assaulted my freshman year and I feel safe on campus."

"The campus is the center of student social life," says one senior, whether it's free movies and lectures, open-mic nights at the Bistro, dance parties (salsa or swing), or performances by the music and theatre departments. Twenty-eight percent of the Willamette men and 25 percent of the women go Greek, but students say that Greeks don't dominate the social scene. When it comes to drinking, "Parties happen, but [students] are remarkably well behaved," a student says. The Ram Brewery draws big crowds on Thursdays. Annual social highlights include the spring Wulapalooza festival, celebrating Earth Day, art, and music (and boasting the slogan "It's actually pretty good!"), and the Hawaiian Club Luau, where students chow down on spit-roasted pig. Each fall, students from Tokyo International organize the Harvest Festival. According to a politics major, "Willamette has started a new tradition of breaking a world record every other year. Thus far, both world records have been for the largest game of Red Light/Green Light."

Downtown Salem is a short walk from campus, and while students say it's no college town, it does have movies, shopping, restaurants, and coffeehouses. Also nearby are the Cascade Mountains and rugged beaches of Lincoln City and Coos Bay (an hour's drive), skiing and snowboarding on Mount Hood or in the high desert town of Bend (three hours), and the cosmopolitan cities of Portland (40 minutes) and Seattle (about four hours north). Willamette students remain true to the school motto, "Not unto ourselves alone are we born," when they go "Into the Streets" for a day of service each fall.

The Willamette Bearcats compete in Division III, and track and field and women's volleyball are strong. The men's and women's cross-country teams have won numerous West Region Championships in recent years. The annual football game against Pacific Lutheran usually has conference championship implications, and games against Linfield are also well attended. About 65 percent of Willamette students compete in 42 intramural and club sports.

Willamette may be the best little school you've never heard of, at least if you're from outside the California-Oregon-Washington corridor. "Willamette is unabashedly itself," says one student. "Community members from all backgrounds feel very comfortable being themselves and embracing who they are." The school's close-knit community is strengthened by its emphasis on service and by warm, supportive faculty members who push students to achieve. Says a senior, "Students fall in love with learning at Willamette."

Willamette benefits from its proximity to the U.S. campus of Tokyo International University.

Overlaps

Lewis & Clark, University of Puget Sound, UC–Santa Cruz, UC–Davis, UC–Berkeley, University of Portland, UC–Santa Barbara, University of Washington

If You Apply To >

Willamette: Early decision I and early action: Nov. 15. Regular decision: Jan. 15. Financial aid: Feb. 1. Housing: May 1. Application fee: $50. Campus interviews: recommended, informational. No alumni interviews. SATs or ACTs: optional (test-optional applicants must answer supplemental essay question). No Subject Tests. Letters of recommendation: required. Essay: required. Accepts the Common Application. Applicants may select optional gender identity and sexual orientation fields.

College of William and Mary

P.O. Box 8795, Williamsburg, VA 23187

Founded in 1693 as a private university, William and Mary is the original public Ivy. History, government, and international relations are among the strongest departments. With 6,200 undergraduates, larger than Mary Washington and Richmond, and smaller but more intellectual than the University of Virginia. Williamsburg is more exciting for tourists than college students.

Traditions abound at the College of William and Mary, yet this historic university—the second oldest in the nation after Harvard—continues to evolve in its pursuit of academic excellence. "Students at William and Mary choose to attend the college for its intense academic rigor, strong sense of community, rich history, and legacy of traditions," says one senior. It has graduated three former U.S. presidents—Thomas Jefferson, James Monroe, and John Tyler. Rival UVA prides itself on being

Website: www.wm.edu
Location: Small City
Public
Total Enrollment: 7,886
Undergraduates: 6,214

Male/Female: 43/57

SAT Ranges: CR 630–730, M 630–730

ACT Ranges: 28–32

Financial Aid: 52%

Pell Grant: 9%

Expense: Pub $ $ $ $

Student Loans: 37%

Average Debt: $ $

Phi Beta Kappa: Yes

Applicants: 14,952

Accepted: 34%

Enrolled: 29%

Grad in 6 Years: 90%

Returning Freshmen: 96%

Academics: ✍ ✍ ✍ ✍ ✍

Social: ☎ ☎ ☎

Q of L: ★ ★ ★

Admissions: (757) 221-4223

Email Address: admission@wm.edu

Strong Programs:
History
International Relations
Business
Government
Biology
Psychology
English
Accounting

"Mr. Jefferson's" university, but W&M has the distinction of having educated Mr. Jefferson in the first place.

A profusion of azaleas and crape myrtle adds splashes of color to William and Mary's finely manicured campus, located about 150 miles southeast of Washington, D.C. The campus is divided into three sections and includes Lake Matoaka, the oldest human-made lake in Virginia, and a wooded wildlife preserve, which is filled with trails and widely used by the science departments. The Ancient Campus is a grouping of three colonial structures, the oldest being the Sir Christopher Wren Building, which was constructed between 1695 and 1700 and is the oldest college building, and arguably one of the loveliest, in the country still in use. The Old Campus, where the buildings date from the '20s and '30s, recently added a 330-room residence hall. New Campus, where ground was first broken in the '60s, includes a recreation center, the 95,000-square-foot Sadler Center, and a new Integrated Science Center. The W&M campus boasts one of the most romantic spots of any in the nation: Crim Dell, a wooded area with a small pond spanned by an old-style wooden bridge.

> "Students are far more likely to compete with themselves than with other students."

William and Mary, which was founded as a private college and did not go public until 1906, created Phi Beta Kappa in December of 1776. The honor code, established by Thomas Jefferson in 1779, demands much from the college's students. W&M's new graduation requirements (the College Curriculum) include proficiency in a foreign language, writing, quantitative skills, and information literacy. Students take one course each in the knowledge domains of the natural sciences and quantitative reasoning, the cultural and social sciences, and the arts and humanities, along with three courses that each integrate ideas and methods from the different knowledge domains. All freshmen take a required seminar, limited to 15 students each, choosing from 100 options that focus on critical thinking and independent learning and provide close faculty interaction. All seniors complete a capstone project. The Center for Honors and Interdisciplinary Studies allows outstanding students four semesters of intensive liberal arts seminars, with lectures by top scholars from around the country, and facilitates interdisciplinary majors like American studies, environmental science, and women's studies.

Fittingly, the history department, which cosponsors the Omohundro Institute for Early American History and Culture with Colonial Williamsburg, is a signature program at William and Mary. Business, government, biology, psychology, and English are among the most popular majors, and international relations is well regarded. The accounting program ranks in the top 20 nationwide. A 3–2 engineering program with Columbia University is available, as is a joint degree program with the University of St Andrews in Scotland—one of the few international undergraduate joint degrees available in the U.S. Although academics are rigorous, one student says, "Students are far more likely to compete with themselves than with other students." Nearly half of all classes have fewer than 20 students, although a few introductory lectures may have a couple hundred. Virtually every class is taught by a full professor, and TAs are used for grading or lab purposes only. Says a marketing and sociology major, "Professors at William and Mary are not just teachers; they are mentors, career advisors, and lifelong friends to their students."

> "[Professors] are mentors, career advisors, and lifelong friends to their students."

W&M offers summer and yearlong study abroad programs around the globe, including more than 40 faculty-designed programs and hundreds of other exchange and affiliate options. Nearly half of W&M's graduating class receive credit for studying abroad. The top 7 percent of freshmen are designated Monroe scholars and receive summer research stipends to support independent projects, typically used after their sophomore or junior year. Students cheer the Cohen Career Center, which provides workshops, on-campus recruiting opportunities, and one-on-one counseling appointments.

W&M students are "quirky, passionate, and intelligent," says one psychology major. "Everyone is passionate about something, be it a social cause, an academic discipline, or even something like Harry Potter." Because William and Mary is a state-supported university, 66 percent of its undergraduates are Virginians. Eighty-one percent

"William and Mary has three centuries' worth of traditions, legends, and mysteries."

of freshmen ranked in the top 10th of their high school class, so competition for the nonresident spots—mostly taken by students from the mid-Atlantic and farther north—is stiff. Six percent of undergrads are international. The college has made a major effort to recruit and retain more minorities; Asian Americans now account for 8 percent of the students, Hispanics 9 percent, and African Americans 7 percent. An ongoing series of programs in the residence halls addresses safety issues as well as diversity and gender communication. "As a gay man, I feel accepted by the entire student body, and I am comfortable being myself on campus," says one marketing major. Merit scholarships averaging $6,425 are doled out to qualified undergrads, and W&M has its share of eagerly recruited athletes—more than 300 athletic scholarships are offered annually. Only 9 percent of freshmen, however, are eligible to receive Pell Grants.

The history department cosponsors the Omohundro Institute for Early American History and Culture with Colonial Williamsburg.

Seventy-four percent of the undergraduates live on campus in mostly co-ed dorms that range from stately old halls with high ceilings to modern buildings equipped with air-conditioning. All freshmen are guaranteed a room on campus, but after that students try their luck with the infamous room selection process. Special-interest housing is available—there are seven language houses and an International Studies hall, Africa House, Community Scholars House, and a Mosaic House—and life in a fraternity or sorority house is also an option. All freshmen must purchase a meal plan, and though students give the three campus cafeterias less-than-stellar reviews, they can seek alternatives like cooking in the dorms and dinner plans in sorority and fraternity houses. Crime is not a big concern. "Williamsburg is a fairly safe community, but it is reassuring to know that the school is under the jurisdiction of three different police departments," says one student.

On campus, students can enjoy the soothing voices of one of the many a cappella groups, dance the night away at fraternity parties, grab a midnight snack at the Sadler Center, or watch the latest dance or theater performance at Phi Beta Kappa Theater. Twenty-six percent of the men and 34 percent of the women join Greek organizations, which host most of the on-campus

"Eventually, you don't raise an eyebrow when Colonial reenactors are behind you at the grocery store buying beer."

parties. Students also frequent off-campus house parties and the local bars. The college has strict policies against underage drinking, but students say as long as they are safe, they stay out of trouble. "Greek organizations do not set the social scene, but most groups will have events involving alcohol," a student reports.

Traditions are the stuff of which William and Mary is made, and perhaps the most cherished is the annual Yule Log Ceremony in the Wren Building, where students sing carols and hear the president, dressed in a Santa Claus outfit, read the Dr. Seuss story *How the Grinch Stole Christmas*. Grand Illumination is a great Christmas fireworks display in nearby Colonial Williamsburg, and on Charter Day, bells chime and students celebrate the distinguished history of their nearly 325-year-old institution. Each year, freshmen walk through the Wren Building for Opening Convocation, where they're greeted by cheering upperclassmen and

A joint degree program with the University of St Andrews in Scotland is one of the few international undergraduate joint degrees available in the U.S.

faculty. Four years later, as they graduate, they walk through the Wren in the other direction. Romantics will be happy to learn that any couple who kisses at the top of Crim Dell Bridge will eventually be married. The Seven Society, a secret society of students dedicated to the college, is among the most revered on campus. "William and Mary has three centuries' worth of traditions, legends, and mysteries," says one senior.

Anyone who gets restless can always step across the street to Colonial Williamsburg to picnic in the restored area, walk or jog down Duke of Gloucester Street (called "Dog Street"), or study in one of the beautiful gardens. "Eventually, you don't raise an eyebrow when Colonial reenactors are behind you at the grocery store buying beer," quips one senior. Its appeal to tourists notwithstanding, Williamsburg leaves much to be desired as a college town. Nightlife is a hit-or-miss affair (mostly miss), although volunteer opportunities abound and many students participate. Richmond and Norfolk, each an hour's drive, are top road trips; the University of Virginia, although an archrival, is also popular. Virginia Beach, a favorite springtime mecca, is a little farther away.

Each year, more than 500 Tribe athletes compete on 23 Division I teams. Recent conference champs include men's and women's cross-country and tennis, men's basketball and swimming, and women's gymnastics. Intramurals and clubs such as softball and ultimate Frisbee attract a large percentage of the student body. The recreational athletic complex serves the health and fitness needs of students and faculty.

From Thomas Jefferson to Jon Stewart, William and Mary has educated some of the nation's most famous and colorful. William and Mary's traditions stretch back to the dawn of this nation, and its grand old campus and stirring history make it a distinguished and cherished part of many students' lives. "I chose W&M for the close-knit community," says one junior. "'One tribe, one family' is not just a saying; it is truly something that can be felt the minute you step onto campus."

Overlaps

University of Virginia, Georgetown, Duke, UNC at Chapel Hill, Princeton, Virginia Tech, Cornell University, Notre Dame

If You Apply To > **William and Mary:** Early decision: Nov. 1. Regular decision: Jan. 1. Priority financial aid: Feb. 1. Housing: May 1. Application fee: $70. Campus interviews: optional, evaluative. No alumni interviews. SATs or ACTs: required. Subject Tests: optional. Letters of recommendation: recommended. Essay: required. Accepts the Common Application.

Williams College

Williamstown, MA 01267

Running neck and neck with Amherst on the selectivity chart, Williams occupies a campus of surpassing beauty in the foothills of the Berkshires. Has shaken the preppy image, but still attracts plenty of well-toned, all-around jock-intellectuals who will one day be corporate CEOs. The splendid isolation of Williamstown is either a blessing or a curse.

Website: www.williams.edu
Location: Small Town
Private
Total Enrollment: 2,117
Undergraduates: 2,065

Williams College vies with rival Amherst for possession of both the color purple— they each use it on team uniforms and in their logos—and the title of most selective liberal arts college in the United States. While both schools have large numbers of "preppy, white, rich kids," students at Williams tend to be more "athletic, well-rounded, driven, friendly, and liberal," says a junior. At this isolated hamlet in the Berkshires, school spirit abounds, and the stunning natural backdrop helps keep everyone in a good mood. When not gazing at the purple mountains' majesty, students at Williams are digging into their studies with fervor.

The college's buildings constitute a virtual *omnium-gatherum* of architectural styles, from the elegantly simple Federal design of the original West College to contemporary structures by Charles Moore and William Rawn. The brick and gray stone buildings are arranged in loosely organized quads, which are both enclosed and open to nature. Students may take advantage of WCMA (the Williams College Museum of Art), the Clark Art Institute, and MASS MoCA, a nearby center for contemporary visual, performing, and media arts. Williams recently opened a new library/media center.

> **"Professors insist on having a personal connection with the students and always help if needed."**

The Williams curriculum emphasizes interdisciplinary studies and personalized teaching. Distribution requirements include at least three courses in each of the school's three divisions: languages and arts, social studies, and sciences and mathematics; two must be completed by the end of the sophomore year. Students must also fulfill requirements in writing and in quantitative and formal reasoning, pick a major from more than 35 options, pass four quarters of phys ed, spend at least six semesters in residence, and complete four winter study projects or courses during the January Winter Study.

One of Williams's greatest strengths is in art, which benefits from one of the finest college art museums in America, and popular majors include economics, English, history, psychology, and political science. Students in the environmental science program can perform fieldwork in the 2,600-acre, college-owned Hopkins Forest. If the walls of campus threaten to close in, especially during the bitter and blustery winter, students take a term away in more than 250 programs offered through the college's study away office, including relatively inexpensive, faculty-led study tours, or through the Twelve College Exchange* or the Williams at Mystic Seaport* program. There's also an innovative yearlong program organized with Oxford's Exeter College in England. Forty-seven percent of students study abroad each year.

"Courses are rigorous and most professors are very demanding both in terms of workload and critical engagement," says one senior, "but there is little sense of competition between students." There are only two small graduate programs at Williams—in art history and in development economics—so graduate students are few and far between, and you'll never find them at the lectern. Seventy-eight percent of classes enroll fewer than 20 students. Williams has increased the number of its courses taught in the Oxford tutorial format: two students and a faculty member meet each week, with the students alternating who has to write a paper and who gets to critique it. "Professors insist on having a personal connection with the students and always help if needed," a student explains. Faculty members are quick to return email, says a sophomore, and may invite students over for informal get-togethers and home-cooked meals. The college also provides a stipend for advisors to take their charges out for a bite to eat.

The typical Williams student is bright, enthusiastic, energetic, and well-informed about current events; 93 percent graduated in the top 10th of their high school class. One student says, "I know people who can read *Harry Potter* in Latin, translate rap songs into Arabic, and sight-read 'Rocket Man' perfectly on the piano." Twelve percent of students are in-state and another 8 percent are international. African Americans make up 8 percent of the student body, while Asian Americans add 12 percent and Hispanics comprise 13 percent. Politically, Williams is mostly liberal, says a student, and "there

> **"I know people who can read *Harry Potter* in Latin, translate rap songs into Arabic, and sight-read 'Rocket Man' perfectly on the piano."**

(continued)

Male/Female: 49/51
SAT Ranges: CR 670–780, M 660–770
ACT Ranges: 31–34
Financial Aid: 49%
Pell Grant: 22%
Expense: Pr $ $ $ $
Student Loans: 43%
Average Debt: $
Phi Beta Kappa: Yes
Applicants: 6,883
Accepted: 18%
Enrolled: 45%
Grad in 6 Years: 95%
Returning Freshmen: 97%
Academics: ✏ ✏ ✏ ✏ ✏
Social: ☎ ☎ ☎
Q of L: ★ ★ ★ ★
Admissions: (413) 597-2211
Email Address: admission@williams.edu

Strong Programs:
Art
Economics
English
History
Psychology
Political Science

Forty-seven percent of students study abroad each year.

are students who are passionate about politics and social issues, but they are not a majority." Twenty-two percent of freshmen are eligible for the Pell Grant. There are no merit or athletic scholarships, but Williams guarantees to meet the full demonstrated financial need of all admitted students.

Ninety-three percent of students live on campus; most remain in the dorms for all four years because they're guaranteed a bed—and because only seniors are eligible to move out. "All the dorms at Williams are good," says one student. "You can't go wrong with any housing here." First-years live in groups of about 20 students each (known as "entries") along with junior advisors, who serve as big siblings, mentors, and sounding boards. Some freshmen luck into large single rooms. After the first year, students have an affiliation with one of four upperclassmen residential neighborhoods and enter their housing draw. Small co-ops are available for seniors who want to cook and simulate a more off-campus living experience. Campus dining receives mixed reviews: "They make a big effort, but the results are unpredictable," says one student.

> **"For the most part, the social life revolves around parties in dorms."**

Fraternities and sororities were abolished long ago, but that hasn't stopped Williams students from partying. "Social life is mostly on campus because there really isn't anything to do in Williamstown," says one student. Another adds, "The school brings in a lot of speakers, comedians, and musical groups, but for the most part, the social life revolves around parties in dorms." Drinking is a popular pastime on weekends, but most students report no pressure to imbibe. The college has taken steps to make sure that whatever drinking does go on happens safely by offering a first-year education program at the beginning of the school year, outlawing drinking games, requiring registration of parties over a certain size, mandating availability of food and nonalcoholic beverages whenever alcohol is present, and regulating tailgating. Favorite traditions include homecoming, Winter Carnival, Spring Fling, and Mountain Day, held on one of the first three Fridays in October. Which day it will be is a well-kept secret, broken only when the college president sends out an email canceling classes, and church bells begin tolling at 8 a.m. Students hike to the top of Mount Greylock, where hot cider and donuts are waiting on the summit.

The small village of Williamstown is "sort of the quintessential New England town," says a student. The main street boasts "several strange clothing stores that I've never been in, a bunch of overpriced antique shops and pharmacies, and three ethnic restaurants," says a political science major. The Clark Art Institute, within walking distance of campus, possesses one of the finest collections of Renoir and Degas in the nation, as well as a great library. The modern college music center attracts top classical musicians, and the college theater is home to the Williamstown Theatre Festival, which often features Broadway stars. When students aren't holed up in the library, nearby slopes and trails beckon, offering skiing, cycling, and backpacking. There's a Walmart 15 minutes away and a Stop and Shop grocery store even closer, and civilization—in the form of Albany, New York—is just an hour's drive. Other popular destinations include New York City (three hours by car).

> **"You feel safe here— isolated, yet shielded from the outside world."**

Sports are more like a religion here than an extracurricular activity. The Williams Ephs are a perennial winner of the Division III Directors' Cup, awarded annually to the school with the strongest overall athletic program. Any contest with archrival Amherst ensures a big crowd. After all, Amherst was founded in 1821 by a breakaway group of Williams students, along with the school's then-president. The men's and women's swim teams are nationally ranked, and the men's tennis, basketball, and track and field teams are among the many that have brought home conference

First-years live in groups of about 20 students each (known as "entries") along with junior advisors.

On Mountain Day, students hike to the top of Mount Greylock, where hot cider and donuts are waiting on the summit.

titles. Women's soccer and tennis are likewise strong, and the squash and ski teams are so good they compete in Division I.

It takes a special kind of student to be happy at Williams. Those who delight in the life of the mind, who can take or leave the creature comforts found at more urban schools, will no doubt bleed purple by the time they leave. "You feel safe here—isolated, yet shielded from the outside world," says a Chinese major. Certainly, what's warm and fuzzy for some is claustrophobic for others. Generally, though, among students who stick it out, "complaints are few and far between," reports a recent graduate. "We love it!"

If You Apply To ➤ **Williams:** Early decision: Nov. 15. Regular decision: Jan. 1. Financial aid: Jan. 15. Housing: May 1. Application fee: $65. No campus or alumni interviews. SATs or ACTs: required. Subject Tests: optional. Letters of recommendation: required. Essay: required. Accepts the Common Application with supplement.

University of Wisconsin–Madison

702 W. Johnson Street, Suite 1101, Madison, WI 53706

Madison draws a third of its students from out of state, one of the highest proportions among leading Midwestern public universities. Why brave the cold? Reasons include top programs in an array of professional fields and several innovative living/learning programs. There's also the pleasure of life in Madison, a combination state capital/college town in the mold of Austin, Texas.

For more than a century, the University of Wisconsin has been guided by the Progressive-era philosophy of the "Wisconsin Idea" that the purpose of a great state university is to seek truth and apply the resulting knowledge to the benefit of the students and society as a whole. Such a philosophy has turned Wisconsin into one of the world's leading universities—one where nearly 30,000 undergraduates take advantage of high-level academics and a rich array of resources. This tradition of excellence has recently been threatened by a series of budget cuts and overt hostility from the governor and other state leaders with no sympathy for the Wisconsin Idea. For the moment, though, Wisconsin is a place where professional and other programs are outstanding. Just bring a strong desire to learn—and a very warm coat.

Described by one Madison student as "architecturally olden with a modern touch," the mainly brick campus is distinctive. It spreads out over 936 hilly, tree-covered acres and across an isthmus between two glacial lakes, Mendota and Monona, named by Native Americans who once lived along their shores. From atop Bascom Hill, the center of campus, you look east past the statue of Lincoln and the liberal arts buildings, down to a library mall that was the scene of many a political demonstration during the '60s. Farther east you see rows of State Street pubs and restaurants and the bleached dome of the Wisconsin state capitol. On the other side of the hill, another part of campus, dedicated to the agricultural and health sciences, twists along Lake Mendota. But students from both sides of the hill congregate in the old student union, Memorial Union, where political arguments and backgammon games can rage all night. Outside on the union's veranda, students can look out at the sailboats in summer or iceboats in winter.

"It's easy to get lost in the crowd here, so you have to be fairly strong and confident."

(continued)

Email Address: onwisconsin@
admissions.wisc.edu

Strong Programs:
Economics
Biology
Political Science
Psychology
Communication Arts
Education
Agriculture
Business

*Madison boasts
70 programs
considered in the
top 10 nationally.*

Distribution requirements vary among the different schools and academic departments, but they are uniformly rigorous, with science and math courses required for B.A. students, and a foreign language for virtually everyone. All students must fulfill a three-part graduation requirement in quantitative reasoning, communication, and ethnic studies. Students who prefer the academic road less traveled can opt for the Integrated Liberal Studies certificate program, which allows them to fulfill several gen eds with a series of related, interdisciplinary courses, rather than taking electives at random.

"[Students] are continually looking for newer and better ideas."

Madison's academic climate is demanding. "There are a lot of smart people studying here," notes one student. A list of first-rate academic programs at Madison would constitute a college catalog elsewhere. There are 70 programs considered in the top 10 nationally. Some highlights include education, agriculture, communications, biological sciences, and social studies. The most popular majors are economics, biology, political science, psychology, and communication arts. Due to overcrowding, some popular fields, such as business and engineering, have more selective admissions criteria than others. Although many classes are large, 45 percent have fewer than 20 students. Professors at Madison are certainly among the nation's best, with Nobel laureates, National Academy of Science members, and Guggenheim fellows scattered liberally among the departments.

While the university's size can be daunting, harried freshmen aren't left to fend for themselves. The university offers a number of first-year programs designed to ease the transition into college life. A first-year seminar encourages students to examine learning strategies; connect with faculty, staff, and peers; and become familiar with campus resources. First-Year Interest Groups consist of 20 first-year students who may live in the same residence hall or "residential neighborhood" and who also enroll in a cluster of three classes together. Each FIG cluster of courses has a central theme; the central or "synthesizing" course integrates content from the other two classes. After freshman year, many students participate in internships, and 26 percent choose to study abroad in programs all over the world, including France, Brazil, India, Israel, and Thailand. Thirty-seven percent conduct undergraduate research.

If there is one common characteristic among Madison undergraduates, it is assertiveness. "It's easy to get lost in the crowd here, so you have to be fairly strong and confident," declares one student. "No one holds your hand." The flip side is that "anyone can fit in, you just have to find your own niche." Sixty-seven percent of undergraduates are from Wisconsin, and 8 percent are international. The school is a heartland of progressive politics, and Madison's reputation as a haven for liberals remains intact. "Students here are called liberal because they are eager and willing to change and are continually looking for newer and better ideas," explains one activist. Asian Americans make up 6 percent of the student body, Hispanics 5 percent, and African Americans less than 1 percent. Academic merit scholarships averaging $3,939 are awarded each year, and most of the sports on campus offer full scholarships. Various campus programs raise funds for need-based institutional aid for low-income undergraduates.

"Frat parties are a very popular break from the bar scene."

Twenty-six percent of undergrads reside in university housing. Dorms are either co-ed or single sex and come equipped with laundry facilities, game rooms, and lounges. Most also have a cafeteria. The student union also offers two meal plans, and there are plenty of restaurants and fast-food places nearby. The school supports a variety of services intended to keep students safe on campus, including escort services for those walking and those needing a ride, and a free shuttle system that operates seven days a week.

One old standby for social life that is still as popular as ever is the student union, which hosts bands, shows, and so forth and provides a great atmosphere in which to hang out. There are more film clubs than anyone can follow, and everyone has a favorite bar. Nine percent of the men and 8 percent of the women go Greek. "Frat parties are a very popular break from the bar scene," reports one expert on both options. Madison (a.k.a. Madtown) is an excellent college town and has been the stomping ground for many fine rock 'n' roll or blues bands on the road to fame. Volunteering is a tradition here; the university consistently tops the list for providing the Peace Corps with the most entrants of any college or university in the nation. Nature enthusiasts can lose themselves in the university's 12,000-acre nature preserve or hit nearby ski slopes.

The students at this Big Ten school show "tons of interest" in sports, especially hockey and football, and especially when the Badgers try to rout the University of Michigan's Wolverines. The Badgers have produced a number of Big Ten champions, most notably men's cross-country, men's basketball, men's indoor and outdoor track, and women's hockey. Bucky Badger apparel, emblazoned with slogans ranging from the urbane to the decidedly uncouth, is ubiquitous. However, the much-acclaimed marching band may outdo all the teams in popularity. Intramurals are another favorite pastime, with 25 sports offered at varying levels of competitiveness.

One of the best and most well-rounded state schools anywhere, Madison remains a school that students sum up as "diverse, intellectual, fashionable, and moderately hedonistic." And these are the qualities that attract bright and energetic students from everywhere. "You feel you're accepted for who you are no matter what," says one student. "It's so nice to just be yourself."

The much-acclaimed marching band may outdo all the Badger teams in popularity.

Overlaps

Boston University, University of Illinois at Urbana–Champaign, Indiana University, University of Michigan, Northwestern

If You Apply To ➤

Wisconsin: Rolling admissions: Feb. 1. Early action: Nov. 1. Financial aid: Dec. 1. Housing: May 1. Application fee: $60. No campus or alumni interviews. SATs or ACTs: required. No Subject Tests. Letters of recommendation: required. Essay: required. Accepts the Common Application with supplement. Special consideration given to students from disadvantaged backgrounds.

Wittenberg University

P.O. Box 720, Springfield, OH 45501

Wittenberg is an outpost of cozy Midwestern friendliness. Less national than Denison or Wooster, Witt has plenty of old-fashioned school spirit and powerhouse Division III athletic teams. Top students should aim for the honors program, which provides a chance for independent research. Witt doles out plenty of merit scholarships to better-than-average students.

Founded in 1845 by German Lutherans, Wittenberg University remains true to its faith by emphasizing strong student/faculty relationships—and making sure that students don't become too comfortable in the campus bubble. In fact, before granting their diplomas, Wittenberg requires students to complete 30 hours of community service in the surrounding town of Springfield (population 60,000). "The campus is beautiful, it's a great school, and it's so obvious how much everyone here loves it," gushes an education major. "It already feels like home."

The Wittenberg campus is classic Midwestern collegiate, with a mixture of 1800s and Gothic-inspired buildings on 100 rolling acres in southwestern Ohio. The red-brick Myers residence hall, with picturesque white pillars and an open-air dome

Website: www.wittenberg.edu
Location: Small City
Private
Total Enrollment: 1,760
Undergraduates: 1,760
Male/Female: 44/56
SAT Ranges: CR 490–610, M 490–610
ACT Ranges: 22–28

(continued)

Financial Aid: 95%
Pell Grant: N/A
Expense: Pr $
Student Loans: 73%
Average Debt: $ $ $ $
Phi Beta Kappa: Yes
Applicants: 6,487
Accepted: 77%
Enrolled: 10%
Grad in 6 Years: 64%
Returning Freshmen: 75%
Academics: ✍ ✍ ✍
Social: ☎ ☎ ☎
Q of L: ★ ★ ★
Admissions: (877) 206-0332
Email Address: admission@
  wittenberg.edu

Strong Programs:
Social Sciences
Business
Biology
Psychology
Education
Nursing
Sport Management
Music

First-year programs include a leadership development program, a service-learning course, and a new, required First-Year Seminar.

dating from the 19th century, stands at the center. Blair Hall, which houses the university's education department, includes more than 21,000 square feet of combined classroom and laboratory space. Edwards-Maurer Field has recently been upgraded with new turf.

Wittenberg's general education requirements emphasize a solid liberal arts background. The school's Wittenberg Plan includes 17 learning goals, ranging from experience with writing and research to exposure to the natural sciences and foreign languages. Students select courses from a variety of disciplines to meet the goals and also must fulfill requirements in religion or philosophy, non-Western cultures, and physical education. Wittenberg has comprehensive first-year programs for new students, which include a leadership development program, a service-learning course, and a new, required First-Year Seminar that helps students transition from high school to college.

> **"Witt students are proactive. We are constantly championing new causes."**

Wittenberg students give high marks to the school's education department, and the most popular majors include social sciences, business, biology, and psychology. Health-related fields, especially nursing and other prehealth professional programs, are particularly well regarded, and newer majors in exercise science and sport management are also popular. Other strong programs include music, East Asian studies, Russian and Central Eurasian studies, theater, and dance. Wittenberg also offers 3–2 engineering programs with Columbia University and Case Western Reserve. The academic climate is described as "challenging but friendly," and study groups are common, according to one junior. Professors are roundly praised for their teaching styles and willingness to make themselves available outside the classroom. "Students take advantage of having professors who are extremely knowledgeable by getting help with class problems or even career advice," one senior says. Fifty-three percent of classes have fewer than 20 students. Despite Wittenberg's small size, students say they have no trouble registering for needed courses. So long as students declare their major on time and complete all courses with a C or better, the college guarantees a degree in four years—and will pay for any additional necessary courses.

The new Compass program, designed to help students plan an individual, four-year path to success, combines nine different student support services in one collaborative space in the Thomas Library. In addition to offering academic support, Compass connects students to research, community service, and internship opportunities. A University Honors Program enrolls 13 percent of students, who conduct independent research culminating in a senior thesis, and individual departments offer ample opportunities to work on research with faculty members. Wittenberg also encourages students to take a semester or a year away from campus, either in the U.S. or abroad, and 22 percent do so. Options include the International Student Exchange Program, field study in the Bahamas, work with the National Institutes of Health in Washington, D.C., or a summer in Wittenberg's Local Government Management Internship Program.

"Witt students are proactive," says a junior. "We are constantly championing new causes, whether through community service or fund-raising. We are always on the go!" Seventy-one percent of Wittenberg students are native Ohioans and 2 percent hail from other countries. Many others are from nearby states like Indiana, Michigan, and Pennsylvania.

> **"Everyone is open to different opinions."**

African Americans comprise 9 percent of the student body, Hispanics 3 percent, and Asian Americans 1 percent. The administration looks to boost those modest numbers through changes in minority recruiting and advising, while the Diversity Center houses three student awareness organizations to help support minority populations on campus: Concerned Black Students, the American

International Association, and the Gender and Sexual Diversity Association. Students say the campus is fairly evenly split between conservatives and liberals, and both groups are vocal. "Everyone is open to different opinions," a biology major says. Wittenberg offers merit scholarships averaging $18,745 but no athletic scholarships. The Wittenberg College Access Program provides special financial aid packages to academically talented students from low-income families.

Eighty-six percent of all Wittenburg students reside on campus; freshmen and sophomores are required to do so. After that, most choose nearby houses and apartments owned by the school. "Dorms are spacious and air-conditioned," a student says, "with options for all-girl, honors, and substance-free housing." Greek groups draw 28 percent of the men and 36 percent of the women; members may live in chapter houses. For those in need of sustenance (perhaps to fuel those all-night study sessions), there is a variety of dining options, including vegetarian and low-fat items. "The food doesn't taste the best, but is acceptable," says one sophomore. In an effort to mitigate sexual assault on campus, the university is working to implement bystander awareness and response training programs.

Students at Wittenberg work hard at their studies, but they are also actively engaged in more than 120 student organizations, performing arts groups, and intramurals. When the weekend rolls around, social life centers on parties in houses, dorm rooms, and apartments on or near campus. "There is always something to do," says a junior. Greek groups, Union Board, and the Residence Hall Association bring in guest speakers, movies, comedians, and concerts. Favorite annual events include Greek Week, Homecoming ("the alumni involvement is incredible"), W Day, and Wittfest, a campus festival and concert with games, food, prizes, and socializing before finals. "It is open to the community, but all the students go," a senior says. "It resembles a carnival, and at night there's a big concert on the lawn." Springfield has movie theaters, a mall, restaurants, and a $15 million performing arts center, and students say they appreciate the campus locale. "Our proximity to quaint country living and the abundance of opportunity in the city makes for an ideal location," says a junior. Popular road trips include Dayton (30 minutes), Columbus (45 minutes), and Cincinnati (90 minutes), and for those with more time, Washington, D.C., New York City, and Chicago.

Wittenberg's athletic teams (the Tigers) are competitive in Division III, and rivalries with Allegheny, Wabash, and The College of Wooster really get students riled up. Football, women's basketball, and volleyball are recent North Coast Athletic Conference champions. Intramurals and club sports are a huge draw too, with sports such as crew, ice hockey, and rugby. Weekend warriors may take advantage of the Bill Edwards Athletic and Recreational Complex, which boasts a stadium and eight-lane track, football and soccer fields, 12 lighted tennis courts, a state-of-the-art fitness center and weight room, plus a pool and racquetball courts. Nearby state parks also offer swimming, camping, biking trails, and picnics in the warmer months, and skiing in the winter.

While not as well known as many of its bigger Midwestern brethren, Wittenberg has plenty to offer those students who decide to attend, including a solid honors program, an active Greek scene, and serious Division III athletics.

The new Compass program is designed to help students plan an individual, four-year path to success.

"Our proximity to quaint country living and the abundance of opportunity in the city makes for an ideal location."

Overlaps

Ohio State, Miami University (OH), Ohio University, University of Dayton, University of Cincinnati, Xavier, Otterbein, College of Wooster

If You Apply To ➤ | **Wittenberg:** Early decision: Nov. 15. Early action I: Dec. 1. Early action II: Jan. 15. Regular decision: Mar. 15. Financial aid: Mar. 1. Application fee: $40 (paper), free (online). Campus interviews: recommended, informational. Alumni interviews: optional, informational. SATs or ACTs: optional. No Subject Tests. Letters of recommendation: recommended. Essay: recommended. Accepts the Common Application.

Wofford College

429 North Church Street, Spartanburg, SC 29303-3663

Wofford is about half the size of Furman and somewhat larger than Presbyterian. Strong in the life sciences and study abroad. With more than a few gentleman jocks, Wofford is one of the smallest institutions to compete in Division I football. Fraternities and sororities dominate the traditional social scene.

Website: www.wofford.edu

Location: Small City

Private

Total Enrollment: 1,613

Undergraduates: 1,613

Male/Female: 50/50

SAT Ranges: CR 520–630,
    M 530–630

ACT Ranges: 23–29

Financial Aid: 92%

Pell Grant: 18%

Expense: Pr $

Student Loans: 48%

Average Debt: $ $ $

Phi Beta Kappa: Yes

Applicants: 2,795

Accepted: 72%

Enrolled: 22%

Grad in 6 Years: 82%

Returning Freshmen: 88%

Academics: ✍ ✍ ✍

Social: ☎ ☎

Q of L: ★ ★ ★

Admissions: (864) 597-4130

Email Address: admission@
    wofford.edu

Strong Programs:
Biology
Premed
Prelaw
Finance
Business Economics
Accounting
English
Environmental Studies

Wofford students take pride in the Wofford Way, combining a well-rounded curriculum built on traditional strengths in the STEM disciplines with career-related internships and study abroad. The college has taken bold steps to increase enrollment while lowering the student/faculty ratio. Students study hard under the "eyes of Old Main" and often visit their professors' homes for dinner, forming lasting friendships with peers and faculty members. Wofford "is a world of its own and it holds a special place in every student's heart," says a sophomore.

Wofford is near the heart of Spartanburg, a midsize city in the northwest corner of South Carolina. Founded in 1854, it's one of fewer than 200 existing American colleges that opened before the Civil War—and it still operates on its original campus, a National Historic District. Azaleas, magnolias, and dogwoods surround the distinctive, twin-towered Main Building and four original faculty homes on the 170-acre campus, which is also a designated arboretum. Nearly 5,000 trees have been planted since 1992. A new residential Greek village opened in 2016, and two new facilities, a center for the arts and an indoor stadium—both donated by alumnus Jerry Richardson, owner and founder of the NFL's Carolina Panthers—are due to be completed in 2017.

Wofford has added dozens of new courses and interdisciplinary course sequences to the curriculum in the past decade. Courses are required in English, fine arts, foreign languages, humanities, science, history, philosophy, cultural perspectives, math, and physical education. Wofford also boasts a unique program called the Novel Experience, part of the first-year orientation. The program consists of a common reading, which is then discussed during a meeting of all humanities classes at different restaurants throughout Spartanburg.

Traditionally, Wofford's strongest and most attractive programs have been in the life sciences, which account for more than one-third of its graduates and a large share of its Phi Beta Kappas. Nearly two dozen of the school's 325 graduates go on to graduate medical or dental programs within two years of graduation; another two dozen go on to prestigious law schools. Business programs, especially when combined with a second major in foreign languages, and English,

"Professors help students secure research positions, internships, and other opportunities."

with its emphasis on creative writing, are solid and getting better, and environmental studies is also strong. For aspiring entrepreneurs, Wofford's alumni network has clout: more than 3,200 of its 17,000 living graduates serve as heads or owners of corporations or organizations. Students in the Creative Writing Sequence end by writing a novella, the best of which is given the Benjamin Wofford Prize and is published in paperback. The most popular majors are biology, finance, business economics, and accounting. Prospective engineers may apply for 3–2 programs with Clemson or New York's Columbia University. Among the newest programs are Middle Eastern and North African studies and Asian studies. Just over half of classes enroll fewer than 20 students, and students agree that, across the board, the workload is heavy. "I would say the academic climate at Wofford is very competitive in the sense that students feel pressured to excel," says a sophomore.

"Professors get to know students on a personal level and encourage students to come visit their office about both class and personal concerns," says a psychology major. "Many help students secure research positions, internships, and other opportunities." Indeed, special enrichment opportunities abound at Wofford. The Wofford College Space to Impact is a noncredit, scholarship-based learning community that complements the curriculum, reinforcing traditional liberal arts concepts such as critical thinking and communications through intellectual explorations and experiences. Students take one exploration each fall semester and propose an independent or small-group exploration that could form the basis of team projects. The Presidential Seminar brings together 20 outstanding graduating seniors representing different majors for selected readings from classical and contemporary essays. The seminar participants and invited guests meet once a week for a three-hour class in which they discuss philosophy, politics, and the complexities of human nature. And every year, one lucky junior is chosen as the Presidential International Scholar. This student is sent around the world, all expenses paid, to study an issue of global importance for a semester. Overall, 64 percent of Wofford students participate in some form of study abroad, embarking on programs in more than 70 countries.

"Students are driven perfectionists who are known to overcommit themselves to too many different activities and organizations," says a junior. Fifty-four percent hail from South Carolina, and just 1 percent from abroad. African Americans comprise 7 percent of the student population, Asian Americans 3 percent, and Hispanics 3 percent. Conservative students from middle- to upper-class backgrounds make up the vast majority, and students note that diversity can be a source of tension on campus. "Wofford administration is a lot more liberal and encourages diversity, whereas Wofford students and alums often show distaste or frustration toward more socially liberal and inclusive endeavors," comments a student. Merit scholarships averaging $15,323 are available to qualified students, and those with the greatest financial need may be eligible for the Bonner Scholars program. There are also 110 athletic scholarships available in 19 sports.

> **"Students are driven perfectionists who are known to overcommit themselves."**

Ninety-two percent of Wofford's students live in the dorms, where first-years get doubles in Greene Hall and Marsh Hall; students report Marsh to be in poor condition (one cites issues with "snakes, flooding, bug infestations, and mold"). On the bright side, explains a biology major, "Each year that you are at Wofford, the housing situation gets better and better, culminating in the Village—a fantastic apartment community for the seniors." Eight living/learning communities are available for first-years wishing to live with classmates who share their academic interests. Students give so-so marks to the college cafeteria and point out that options for vegetarians, vegans, and other dietary restrictions are often lacking. Campus security gets mixed reviews as well. "Sexual assault is an issue on Wofford's campus because most cases go unreported," says a junior, who also credits the administration with increasing the visibility of Title IX staff and resources "so more cases will be reported."

The Greek system is a huge force in Wofford's social life, with fraternities attracting 45 percent of the men and sororities enlisting 54 percent of the women. Each fraternity has a house and most host parties every Friday and Saturday—with some kicking off the weekend on Thursday. The Student Affairs Committee offers campuswide events like comedians and music for those uninterested in the Greek system. The campus is dry, except for certain events, like Spring Weekend, where alcohol for those of age is

> *The Novel Experience consists of a common reading, which is discussed at different restaurants throughout Spartanburg.*

> *More than 3,200 of Wofford's 17,000 living graduates serve as heads or owners of corporations or organizations.*

> **"Our college has a family feel. We all come together as a community."**

allowed on Fraternity Row, a student says. "Spring Weekend is an event that is always a much anticipated time of the year at Wofford, as there are bands, cookouts, shaving-cream fights, and a beach volleyball tournament." Bid Day, when the fraternities tap their new members, is another annual tradition involving lots of mud and then a bath in the college fountain. Off campus, Spartanburg is home to Converse College and a few other schools. Students say it's not a great college town, but there are some new coffee shops and other fun hangouts. Almost every Wofford student participates in some type of volunteer work. Terrier Play Day brings kids from the community to campus for a fair with booths and games. For a change of pace, students can head to Greenville, Atlanta, and Charlotte.

The Wofford Terriers compete in the Division I Southern Conference and have produced a number of competitive teams, including men's basketball (conference champs in 2015) and men's soccer; games against rival Furman always draw crowds. The school's quiz bowl and chartered financial analyst teams are nationally competitive. Students are also active in intramural, recreational, and club sports, and some of the most popular programs include Terrier Tag, soccer, basketball, lacrosse, and ultimate Frisbee.

Wofford's former chaplain was fond of saying, "You don't come to Wofford—you join it." And students say that's true, citing the close-knit community and intimate student/faculty relationships fostered by the school's small size. "Our college has a family feel," says a freshman. "We all come together as a community and support each other through our endeavors."

Overlaps

University of South Carolina, Furman, Clemson, College of Charleston, UNC at Chapel Hill, Presbyterian, Sewanee, Wake Forest

If You Apply To ➤

Wofford: Early decision: Nov. 1. Early action: Nov. 15. Regular decision: Jan. 15. Financial aid: Jan. 1. Housing: May 1. Application fee: $35. Campus and alumni interviews: optional, evaluative. SATs or ACTs: required (essay and writing components recommended). No Subject Tests. Letters of recommendation: recommended. Essay: required. Accepts the Common Application with supplement.

The College of Wooster

Wooster, OH 44691

Though not well-known to the general public, Wooster is renowned in academic circles around the world. Access is easy, but graduating takes work, with students completing an independent study project in their last two years. More intellectually serious than competitors such as Denison. Prides itself on turning above-average students into real scholars.

Website: www.wooster.edu
Location: Small City
Private
Total Enrollment: 2,016
Undergraduates: 2,016
Male/Female: 45/55
SAT Ranges: CR 540–670, M 560–680
ACT Ranges: 25–30
Financial Aid: 75%
Pell Grant: 16%
Expense: Pr $ $ $

Instead of teaching students what to think, The College of Wooster focuses on teaching students how to do it. From the first freshman seminar to the final day when seniors hand in their theses, the college paves each student's path to independence. The emphasis here is on global perspectives, mentored research, and the heritage that stems from its origin as a college founded by Scottish Presbyterians. The one-on-one attention from faculty makes Wooster an intellectual refuge in the rural countryside of Ohio. "Mentorship and collaboration are pervasive across campus," says a history major. "Students are constantly interacting with their peers, faculty advisors, and other community members in an effort to gather diverse perspectives and motivate their learning."

Located in the city of Wooster, Ohio, COW's hilltop campus is spread over 240 acres, with many campus buildings designed in the English–collegiate Gothic style and constructed of cream-colored brick. More recent buildings are trimmed in

Indiana limestone or Ohio sandstone. The central arch and two towers of Kauke Hall (the central building in Quinby Quadrangle, the square around which the college grew) make it stand out. The Gault Library for Independent Study offers a private carrel for each senior in the humanities and social sciences. Brush Hall, a new 56-bed residence hall, opened in 2016.

What goes on behind the facades of Wooster's attractive buildings is more impressive than the structures themselves. The required First-Year Seminar in Critical Inquiry, limited to 15 students per section, introduces students to intensive writing, critical thinking, and interdisciplinary study. Recent section topics include The Drugs We Drink: Biological and Societal Perspectives;

"Mentorship and collaboration are pervasive across campus."

Heating Up the Planet: Response to a Catastrophe; and The History of the Future. In addition to the first-year seminar, three semesters of Independent Study, and six cross-discipline courses, Wooster mandates courses in writing, global and cultural perspectives, religious perspectives, and quantitative reasoning, foreign language proficiency, and seven to nine courses in the student's major.

"Classes frequently require collaborative work to complete assignments, and students often work together in a relaxed environment that focuses simultaneously on building connections as well as growing academically," says one Spanish major. The most popular majors at Wooster are history, biology, communication studies, and English. Global and international studies and geology are also strengths. The chemistry department has traditionally ranked near the top among private colleges in the number of graduates who go on to earn Ph.D.s. Only a few introductory courses have teaching assistants, who run review sessions and offer extra help. "Professor/ student relationships are rarely limited to the classroom," says one history major, and students praise faculty members for their devotion to teaching and mentoring.

Indeed, mentored undergraduate research is the heart of a Wooster education, highlighted by opportunities in the Applied Methods and Research Experience and Sophomore Research Program. The Independent Study (IS) required of all seniors lets students explore subjects they're passionate about with one-on-one faculty guidance. "The research skills you develop are second to none," affirms one student. IS has become such a part of COW that each year seniors celebrate IS Monday—the day they turn in their projects—with a campuswide parade led by bagpipers. Completion of the IS earns you a Tootsie Roll, to eat or keep for posterity next to your diploma. "It's a day all Wooster graduates will always remember!" a senior says. The college even awards nearly $100,000 each year for student research, travel, or materials to support thesis work. The APEX (Advising, Planning, and Experiential Learning) center combines several offices related to student and career services and helps coordinate opportunities for internships and study abroad, which has been expanding as students seek the world beyond rural Ohio. Students may choose from semester-long programs in more than 40 countries worldwide, or short-term TREK programs led by Wooster faculty during winter, spring, and summer breaks; 30 percent of students participate. The school's membership in the Great Lakes Colleges Association* offers additional opportunities for off-campus study.

"Students are eclectic, spirited, and incredibly down-to-earth," a student says. As the college's reputation spreads, it's becoming more selective, with acceptance rates dropping and freshman-retention rates improving. African Americans constitute 8 percent of the student body, Asian Americans 5 percent, and Hispanics 5 percent. Wooster has a notable international flavor—10 percent of students hail

"Personally, I do not leave campus very often because there are many events going on on campus."

from foreign nations. Thirty-five percent of the students are from Ohio, and 46 percent graduated in the top 10th of their high school class. Politically, Wooster "leans

(continued)

Student Loans: 62%
Average Debt: $ $ $
Phi Beta Kappa: No
Applicants: 5,748
Accepted: 55%
Enrolled: 18%
Grad in 6 Years: 82%
Returning Freshmen: 88%
Academics: ✍ ✍ ✍ ½
Social: ☎ ☎ ☎
Q of L: ★ ★ ★
Admissions: (330) 263-2322
Email Address: admissions@ wooster.edu

Strong Programs:
History
Biology
Communication Studies
English
Global and International Studies
Geology
Chemistry

An Independent Study (IS) project is required of all seniors, with one-on-one faculty guidance.

left but is not a very far left campus," reports a political science major, and a class-mate adds that "the movement to provide our hourly staff with a living wage" has been a hot topic recently. Merit awards averaging $20,958 are available, and students are admitted without regard for financial need.

All students live on Wooster's campus in 17 co-ed dorms, where rooms are small but comfortable. "Housing has vastly improved from a few years ago," says a senior. Students seriously committed to service may apply to live in one of the college's 30 residential program houses, each of which is affiliated with a community group. "Food is delicious, diverse, constantly being updated, and caters to all students regardless of dietary restrictions," a junior says. A senior notes that the college has "responded aggressively" to the national issue of sexual assault by expanding resources for survivors and increasing security measures aimed at prevention. But in general, students say that given Wooster's location "in the middle of cornfields," safety isn't an issue, and "campus security is well respected."

Despite the school's isolated location, students say they enjoy the "quaint and friendly" town of Wooster, a 10-minute walk from campus. "In recent years, the town of Wooster has really taken off, and a lot of new restaurants and shops have popped up," says a senior. Still, the vast majority of social life is campus-based. "Personally, I do not leave campus very often because there are many events going on on campus," says an economics and math major. Visiting lecturers and student performances keep students busy on weekdays, and the Wooster Activities Crew organizes events like craft and karaoke nights on weekends. One major weekend hangout is the Underground, a bar and dance club that hosts well-known bands, as well as the campus's bowling alley, pool hall, and game room. The college has no national Greek organizations, but local "sections" draw 12 percent of men and "clubs" attract 18 percent of women. Students say the party scene is low key and no one is pressured to drink alcohol.

> "Having that big [IS] project on the horizon from the day you enroll changes the way you engage with your education."

The school's Scottish heritage is on display in its bagpipe band, which naturally performs in kilts, and in its Scottish dancers, who trot on stage during the fall's Scot Spirit Day. Other annual traditions include the outdoor fall concert, Party on the Green, and the formal Winter Gala. When it snows—which it does quite often in Wooster—the student body descends upon the Kauke arch and fills it with snow, a tradition that goes back more than 100 years.

Wooster fields a number of competitive Division III teams. Fighting Scots basketball is a spectator favorite, especially when the opponent is rival Wittenberg, and men's basketball and baseball are recent conference champions. Football, swimming and diving, and track and field have also been strong in recent years. Moot Court has been successful in regional and national competition, and about 60 percent of students compete in intramural sports.

The College of Wooster is nationally recognized for its commitment to mentored research and its international focus. Wooster students are proud to be Fighting Scots and independent thinkers. And as a political science major explains, the college's distinctive Independent Study requirement actively shapes both the individual student experience and the campus atmosphere: "Having that big project on the horizon from the day you enroll changes the way you engage with your education, and I think that brings an element of intensity, dedication, and commitment to the academics at Wooster."

Overlaps

Denison, Kenyon, Ohio State, Kalamazoo, Case Western Reserve, Miami University (OH), Dickinson, St. Olaf

If You Apply To ➤

Wooster: Early decision I: Nov. 1. Early action: Nov. 15. Early decision II: Jan. 15. Regular decision and financial aid: Feb. 15. Application fee: $45 (paper), free (online). Campus and alumni interviews: recommended, evaluative. SATs or ACTs: required. No Subject Tests. Letters of recommendation: required. Essay: required. Accepts the Common Application.

Worcester Polytechnic Institute

100 Institute Road, Worcester, MA 01609-2280

Small, innovative, and undergraduate-oriented, WPI is anything but a stodgy technical institute. The WPI Plan is hands-on and project-based and takes a humanistic view of engineering. Emphasizes teamwork instead of competition. Global focus unusual for an engineering school. WPI is half the size of Rensselaer and a third as big as MIT.

As a pioneer in STEM education, Worcester Polytechnic Institute has built a solid reputation, particularly for its engineering programs. But with its ever-expanding academic curriculum, surprising devotion to music and theater, and dedication to hands-on undergraduate experiences, WPI has expanded the definition of what it means to be a techie haven. Students must complete several extensive projects, endure rigorous seven-week terms, and engage in real-world experiences. But it's WPI's humanistic approach to engineering that really sets it apart.

WPI is the third-oldest independent science and engineering school in the nation. Its compact 95-acre campus is set atop one of Worcester's "seven hills" on the residential outskirts of town and borders two parks and the historic Highland Street District, where local merchants and students come together to form the neighborhood community. Old English stone buildings complete with creeping ivy are focal points of the architecture, but modern facilities have moved in to claim their own space on the immaculately kept grounds.

The intent of WPI's unique educational philosophy is to polish social skills, build self-confidence, produce well-rounded students, and nurture young people interested in using their knowledge to improve the world. WPI focuses especially on developing teamwork. The curriculum remains remarkably flexible for a high-powered technological university. Standard course distribution requirements vary by major but include courses in engineering, math, and science. Every WPI student must also complete a humanities and arts requirement. The Interactive Qualifying Project (IQP) is a distinctive requirement that has students

> "We work together to get through the tough courses."

apply technical knowledge to one of society's problems, usually working in teams of two to four students with a faculty advisor. The Major Qualifying Project (MQP) requirement serves as a capstone in which students work on a truly professional-level problem in their major course of study. Many IQPs and MQPs involve corporate, nonprofit, or government sponsors, to whom students present their research findings and recommendations.

The most popular majors are mechanical engineering, chemical engineering, biomedical engineering, and computer science. Architectural engineering and environmental engineering are traditional strengths, as are interdisciplinary programs, such as interactive media and game development, bioinformatics and computational biology, and environmental and sustainability studies. The school launched the nation's first undergraduate robotics engineering program, which has grown to include M.S. and Ph.D. programs, making it the first university to offer all three levels. Many biomedical engineering majors do their projects at UMass Medical and Tufts Veterinary, as well as at local hospitals. WPI also offers a rare fire protection engineering B.S./M.S. program. Math and science types can pick up middle or high school teaching credentials on the way through the university's STEM education center. The theater technology major requires projects in set, lighting, or audio design, which means school shows often highlight cutting-edge production

Website: www.wpi.edu
Location: Small City
Private
Total Enrollment: 4,894
Undergraduates: 4,085
Male/Female: 67/33
SAT Ranges: CR 570–680,
   M 640–740
ACT Ranges: 27–32
Financial Aid: 97%
Pell Grant: 12%
Expense: Pr $ $ $
Student Loans: N/A
Average Debt: N/A
Phi Beta Kappa: No
Applicants: 10,172
Accepted: 49%
Enrolled: 22%
Grad in 6 Years: 85%
Returning Freshmen: 96%
Academics: ✍ ✍ ✍ ½
Social: ☎ ☎ ☎
Q of L: ★ ★ ★ ★
Admissions: (508) 831-5286
Email Address: admissions@wpi.edu

Strong Programs:
Mechanical Engineering
Chemical Engineering
Biomedical Engineering
Computer Science
Architectural Engineering
Environmental Engineering
Interactive Media and Game
   Development
Robotics Engineering

techniques. Well over 300 students participate in 22 musical and theatrical groups; WPI has one of the largest music programs among technological universities.

"At WPI, students understand that classes are hard, and instead of competing against one another, we work together to get through the tough courses," says one student. An academic year at WPI consists of four terms, each lasting seven weeks, which means classes are fast-paced and intense. When students are not completing their IQP and MQP projects, they take three courses per term. Although some introductory classes enroll more than 100 students, most classes are small—64 percent have fewer than 20 students—facilitating the university's emphasis on collaboration. Professors are praised for their availability and willingness to establish relationships. "Most of my professors have been inspiring men and women who really want to allow students to develop their interest in the subject matter," says an industrial engineering major. To further promote cooperation and cohesiveness, the only recorded grades are A, B, C, or No Record. Failing grades do not appear on transcripts, and the school does not compute GPAs or class ranks.

In light of an increasingly interdependent global economy, WPI offers a unique Global Projects Program that spans more than 45 project centers across six continents. Forty-eight percent of WPI students study abroad, primarily traveling to project centers to conduct their IQPs. Extremely motivated students can also complete Individually Sponsored Residential Projects, in which they design their own independent, off-campus study project, under the direction of a faculty member, in addition to their other project work. The co-op program enables students to take time away from the classroom to pursue paid, full-time work experience; participants can expect to add on extra time to their degree program.

"Most of my professors… really want to allow students to develop their interest in the subject matter."

"Students at WPI are passionate about learning and want to succeed in the classroom," says one junior. Thirty-seven percent of undergraduates are Massachusetts natives, and ninety-one percent ranked in the top quarter of their high school class. African Americans account for 2 percent of the students, Hispanics 8 percent, and Asian Americans 5 percent. International students comprise 14 percent of the student body. The dearth of females on campus is a typical complaint. One male freshman says, "The women at WPI tend to be very strong-willed and play an important part in keeping WPI balanced." Politics don't factor too much into campus debates, though students are aware of current events. Merit scholarships averaging $15,763 are doled out annually, but there are no athletic scholarships. The Unity Scholarship recognizes the academic achievements of African American, Latino, and American Indian students, and awards typically range from $12,500 to $25,000.

Only first-year students are guaranteed spots in the university residence halls, and upperclassmen tend to move to Greek houses or off-campus apartments; 49 percent of all undergrads live in campus housing. There are 12 co-ed halls offering traditional and suite-style options, as well as on-campus apartments and smaller houses for more homelike living. Students say they enjoy the accommodations, but "more rooms need to be built" as enrollment continues to increase, according to a freshman. Students can take their meals in a main dining hall, food court, or on-campus restaurant. The food is described as acceptable, and one student notes, "a greater variety would do some good." The university has developed a number of initiatives related to sexual assault, including student/faculty committees, peer education programs, and various training programs, which students say have been well received on campus.

"Students can stay busy and entertained for the entire year with just the events on campus," says one senior, which include student-organized coffeehouses, board game nights, laser tag, concerts, poetry readings, movies, and pub shows. Greek parties are another popular option, as 31 percent of the men join fraternities and 49 percent of the women enter sororities. A junior explains, "All fraternity parties are regulated, and a limit is placed on how many drinks an individual will be served." A notable campus tradition is the Goat's Head Rivalry, a grudge match between the freshman and sophomore classes that includes the Pennant Rush, a rope pull next to Institute Pond, and a WPI trivia competition. The prize? A 100-year-old bronze goat's head trophy (the winning class's year is engraved on it). There is also an annual festival of international culture and QuadFest, complete with carnival rides.

> **"The women at WPI tend to be very strong-willed and play an important part in keeping WPI balanced."**

Nearby colleges such as Assumption, Clark University, and Holy Cross are linked to WPI through shuttle buses, which provide even more social and academic opportunities. While not exactly scenic, Worcester does offer a large number of clubs and restaurants, an art museum, and a large multipurpose arena that hosts concerts and sporting events. "WPI is placed in a rather convenient and nice location in the city," a freshman says. Boston and Hartford are both an hour's drive, as are ski resorts and beaches.

The WPI Engineers compete in Division III sports and field a number of competitive teams. Women's basketball and softball were NEWMAC conference champions in 2016, and men's basketball made its fourth straight appearance in the NCAA championship tournament. Men's and women's swimming and diving, men's and women's track and field, and men's cross-country are also competitive. More than half of the student body participates in intramural and recreational sports, with underwater hockey being a particular favorite.

One of WPI's chants is fittingly mathematic: "E to the x, d-y, d-x, e to the x, d-x; cosine, secant, tangent, sine; 3.14159; e^i, radical, pi; fight 'em fight 'em WPI!" If you know what any of that stuff means, you'll fit right in.

Overlaps

Rensselaer Polytechnic, Northeastern, University of Massachusetts Amherst, Rochester Institute of Technology, University of Massachusetts Lowell, University of Connecticut, Boston University, Wentworth Institute of Technology

If You Apply To ➤

WPI: Early action I: Nov. 1. Early action II: Jan. 1. Regular decision and financial aid: Feb. 1. Application fee: $65. Campus interviews: optional, informational. No alumni interviews. SATs or ACTs: optional, only if applicants submit alternate materials in lieu of test scores. Subject Tests: optional. Letters of recommendation: required. Essay: required. Accepts the Common Application.

Xavier University of Louisiana

1 Drexel Drive, New Orleans, LA 70125

The only historically black college with Roman Catholic ties, Xavier is bigger than a small college but smaller than most universities. Competes with Howard, Morehouse, and Spelman. Strong in pharmacy and the physical sciences and nationally known for turning out science teachers. About a quarter of students are Catholic. Location in New Orleans is a big plus.

As the nation's only historically African American Roman Catholic college, Xavier University of Louisiana remains committed to "the promotion of a more just and humane society." This small New Orleans university prepares students for their chosen careers while providing a strong foundation in the liberal arts. With its stellar reputation for graduating a wealth of scientists,

Website: www.xula.edu
Location: City Center
Private
Total Enrollment: 2,796

Undergraduates: 2,239
Male/Female: 27/73
SAT Ranges: CR 450–550,
 M 420–560

ACT Ranges: 20–26
Financial Aid: 93%
Pell Grant: 53%
Expense: Pr $
Student Loans: 82%
Average Debt: $
Phi Beta Kappa: No
Applicants: 4,847
Accepted: 66%
Enrolled: 21%
Grad in 6 Years: 43%
Returning Freshmen: 71%
Academics: ✍ ✍ ✍
Social: ☎ ☎ ☎
Q of L: ★ ★ ★
Admissions: (504) 520-7388
Email Address:
 apply@xula.edu

Strong Programs:
Biology
Chemistry
Psychology
Business
Political Science
Education
Premed
Pharmacy

Xavier has frequently led the nation in the number of African Americans placed into medical school.

Xavier has much to offer. Says one English major: "Xavier is where future leaders are made."

The school was founded in 1915 by Katharine Drexel, a former Philadelphia socialite who devoted her life to the education of African Americans and Native Americans and who was canonized in 2000 by Pope John Paul II. Xavier is located near the heart of New Orleans in a quiet neighborhood dotted with bungalows. The focal point of the campus is the Library Resource Center, which, with its green roof and stately neo-Gothic architectural style, has become a landmark for those traveling by car from the New Orleans airport to the French Quarter. A closed campus green mutes the urban feel of the encroaching city, and yellow brick buildings have been erected among the older limestone structures. Xavier was hard-hit by Hurricane Katrina (much of the campus was under water), but since then it has gone on a $65 million renovation and building spree that includes the state-of-the-art Qatar Pharmacy Pavilion (donated by the Persian Gulf country), a fitness center, and the stunning St. Katharine Drexel Chapel designed by renowned Argentine architect Cesar Pelli.

The university maintains its reputation as one of the most effective teaching institutions anywhere; the National Science Foundation has designated it as one of only a few Model Institutions for Excellence. Nearly two-thirds of undergraduates major in a science-related field; biology and chemistry are the most popular majors, along with psychology and business. Political science is a small but good department, and the education department has been a traditional strength. The Center for the Advancement of Teaching works to improve pedagogy across the curriculum and encourages African American students to become teachers and researchers, especially in the sciences. "If you want to go into medicine, I would recommend Xavier," explains a student. "They have one of, if not the best, premed programs for minority students." Xavier has frequently led the nation in the number of African Americans placed into medical school and in the number of undergraduate physical science degrees awarded to African Americans. Xavier is also credited with educating 25 percent of all African American pharmacists nationally. In addition to the many internships available, Xavier offers cooperative education programs in all fields and study abroad programs throughout Europe; Africa; Japan; and North, Central, and South America. The university's Confucius Institute offers travel opportunities to China to learn Mandarin Chinese.

> "Xavier is where future leaders are made."

"I would describe the academic climate as competitive in terms of obtaining internships," says one student, "but collaborative as well because most students here are willing to help one another with their studies." Xavier's undergraduate curriculum is centered on the liberal arts. All students are required to take a core of prescribed courses in theology and philosophy, the arts and humanities, communications, history and the social sciences, mathematics, and the natural sciences. Freshmen also take a mandatory, two-semester seminar sequence involving a common reading and a service-learning project, to help them adjust to college life. Priests and nuns teach and help run the school, though the notably diverse faculty and staff are composed of laypeople. Forty-one percent of classes have fewer than 20 students. "The small environment means that all teachers are accessible and give personalized attention," says one senior, "especially in upper-level courses." Academic and career advising are well received, and there is a strong emphasis on community service, which is required with some on-campus organizations.

"Most of the students I know tend to be very studious, hard workers, committed to making the grade, but also balancing that studiousness with a weekend social life," says one student. For a historically African American college, Xavier's student body is quite diverse. Seventy-six percent of undergrads are African American,

10 percent are Asian American, and 4 percent are Hispanic. Xavier has achieved a national reputation for its programs to reach out to local high schools to identify and nurture talented minority students. Twenty percent of students graduated from public schools, and most come from the Deep South; 57 percent are from Louisiana, and many are second- or third-generation Xavierites. Two percent are international. A limited number of academic awards, worth an average of $13,751, are available to qualified students, as are athletic scholarships. A substantial 53 percent of incoming students are eligible for the Pell Grant.

Forty-six percent of Xavier students live in the residence halls. "The freshmen dorms are cramped and dirty. The upperclassmen dorms are much better quality because they are more recently built," says a senior. Three of the four contemporary-looking residence halls are single sex. Students report being satisfied with the campus dining options. "The dining facilities have gotten much better. The food is diverse and edible," says a junior. New Orleans is a major city with a fair share of crime, so campus security is always an issue. Although Xavier's campus security is highly visible, it "definitely needs to be tightened up," says a chemistry major.

Freshmen take a mandatory, two-semester seminar sequence involving a common reading and a service-learning project.

"The on-campus social scene is noticeably lacking," grumbles one computer science major. "Basketball and volleyball games and food and music events at Friday lunch can draw crowds, but each Friday night there is a large exodus of students heading for local bars, clubs, and house parties." Fraternities and sororities play a leading role in extracurricular and social life, though less than 1 percent of the men and 1 percent of the women go Greek. Popular events include Bayou Classic and Spring Fest. But don't get caught drinking—Xavier is a dry campus. "They do room inspections and confiscate prohibited items," explains a sophomore. When it comes to road trips, students head to Baton Rouge, Shreveport, Tallahassee, Houston, and Miami.

> **"Each Friday night there is a large exodus of students heading for local bars, clubs, and house parties."**

Varsity sports (which compete in the NAIA Division I) include men's and women's basketball, tennis, and cross-country (all recent conference champs), and the teams are enthusiastically supported, especially when the opponent is rival Dillard. Intramural sports are also offered with high participation in basketball, tennis, soccer, Ping-Pong, and flag football.

With a mind for the future, Xavier stays true to its beginnings as a historically black and Catholic university and to a mission of preparing students for a future that will "promote a more just and humane society."

Overlaps
Southeastern Louisiana, Louisiana State, Florida A&M, Howard, Spelman, Tuskegee, Southern University (LA), Northwestern Louisiana State

If You Apply To >

Xavier: Rolling admissions. Priority deadline: Mar. 1. Application fee: $25. Campus and alumni interviews: optional, informational. SATs or ACTs: required. Subject Tests: optional. Letters of recommendation: required, very important. No essay. Accepts the Common Application with supplement.

38 Hillhouse Avenue, New Haven, CT 06520

Yale is the middle-sized member of the Ivy League's big three: bigger than Princeton, smaller than Harvard. Its widely imitated residential college system helps Yale strike a balance between being a research university and an undergraduate college. New Haven isn't New York, but it has developed a lively urban scene in recent years. Plan to work hard.

Website: www.yale.edu
Location: Small City
Private
Total Enrollment: 12,179
Undergraduates: 5,508
Male/Female: 51/49
SAT Ranges: CR 720–800, M 710–800
ACT Ranges: 31–35
Financial Aid: 64%
Pell Grant: 13%
Expense: Pr $ $ $
Student Loans: 17%
Average Debt: $
Phi Beta Kappa: Yes
Applicants: 30,236
Accepted: 7%
Enrolled: 67%
Grad in 6 Years: 96%
Returning Freshmen: 99%
Academics: ✍ ✍ ✍ ✍ ✍
Social: ☎ ☎ ☎
Q of L: ★ ★ ★
Admissions: (203) 432-9300
Email Address:
   student.questions@yale.edu

Strong Programs:
Economics
Life Science
Political Science
History
Engineering
English
Architecture
Modern Languages

Founded in 1701 by Connecticut Congregationalists concerned about "backsliding" among their counterparts at a certain school in Cambridge, Massachusetts, Yale has long been recognized as one of the world's finest private universities, and one of the handful of Ivy League schools focused on undergraduates. Students here remain as focused on their studies as ever and tend to carry their achievements lightly. And thanks to Yale's residential college system, this huge research university feels like more of a home for its students. "Yale students are truly happy to be here," says a sophomore. "Everyone has a massive crush on Yale, and that makes all the difference in living and working here for four years."

Yale's campus looks like the traditional archetype—magnificent courtyards, imposing quadrangles, Gothic buildings designed by James Gamble Rogers, and Harkness Tower, a 201-foot spire once washed with acid to create its aged, stately look. All the residential colleges, most of which date back to the 1930s, have been renovated, and substantial investments have been made in basic science, engineering, and biomedical research programs on campus. The Malone Engineering Center offers state-of-the-art facilities for undergraduate research. Kroon Hall is a LEED-certified building that houses the environmental studies program. Yale is currently building two new residential colleges that will open in the fall of 2017, enabling undergraduate enrollment to grow from 5,400 to 6,200 students.

Inside Yale's wrought-iron gates, academic programs are superb across the board, with arts and humanities programs especially outstanding. With tradition ever-present on campus, the Puritan work ethic remains. Graduating from Yale requires 36 courses—nine a year—rather than the 32 courses required at most other colleges. Students agree that despite all the hard work, the academic environment is not based on competition.

"While the workload is challenging, most classes help students collaborate."

"While the workload is challenging, most classes help students collaborate by promoting study groups, facilitating discussions in small, seminar classes, and organizing class section meetings for larger lecture classes," says a senior.

Although Yale has 12 professional schools and a Graduate School of Arts and Sciences, Yale College—the undergraduate arts and sciences division—remains the university's heart. Virtually all professors teach undergraduates, and the professional schools' resources—especially architecture, fine arts, drama, and music—are available to them as well. Yale's superb economics department, replete with budding hedge fund managers and management consultants, offers the most popular undergraduate major, followed by life science, political science, history, engineering, and English. History offers one of the most demanding programs, including a mandatory 30- to 50-page senior essay. The English department is routinely at the vanguard of literary theory, while an outstanding interdisciplinary humanities major includes the study of the medieval, Renaissance, and modern periods. While some science majors grumble about the walk up Science Hill where most labs and science classrooms are located, they agree it's worth the trip. (The sciences were latecomers to all of the oldest U.S. universities and had to find space outside campus cores.) The biological science department is excellent, and its students' interests range from biomedical engineering research to preparation for medical school. Architecture and modern languages, especially French and Chinese, are first-rate, and the school's Center for the Study of Globalization is renowned as well.

Elite freshmen with a particularly strong appetite for the humanities can enroll in Directed Studies, a three-course program that examines the literature, philosophy, history, and politics of Western tradition. Prospective DSers, who must apply in May or June of their senior year in high school, should be prepared for some serious bonding with their books—they don't call it "Directed Suicide" for nothing. Ninety-five percent of science and engineering majors do research with faculty members in any of the more than 800 labs on campus; many are doing their own research as early as the summer after their freshman year. Yale's Science, Technology, and Research Scholars Program offers research and mentorship opportunities, career planning, and other specialized support for historically underrepresented students, including women, minorities, and those from economically disadvantaged backgrounds.

Despite its reverence for tradition, Yale doesn't require any specific courses for graduation, and it doesn't have a core curriculum. Instead, students must take two classes in humanities and arts, social sciences, and sciences, along with two courses that emphasize writing and another two that emphasize quantitative reasoning. Yale also mandates intermediate-level mastery of a foreign language. Instead of preregistering, students spend two weeks "shopping" at the beginning of each term, sampling morsels of the various offerings before finalizing their schedules. The university offers hundreds of study, internship, and research opportunities around the world. "Study abroad is an incredible experience that Yale wants every student to have, and Yale works hard to make it affordable for every student," says a senior political science major. "I spent a summer abroad in Siena, Italy, and, best of all, the entire experience was covered by my Yale financial aid." Each year, about 100 juniors participate in the Junior Term/Year Abroad program, while many others do so during the summer, on a leave of absence, or after graduation.

> "Yale works hard to make [study abroad] affordable for every student."

Introductory-level classes at Yale can be large lectures, accompanied by small recitation and discussion sections typically led by graduate teaching assistants, although freshman seminars are offered each year on a wide range of topics, allowing first-year students to interact with professors and peers in small groups. Upper-level seminars are small and plentiful. Of the 1,000 classes offered each semester, 74 percent have fewer than 20 students. The quality of undergraduate teaching at Yale is as high as it gets at elite schools, and "professors are extremely accessible," says one junior. Some of the most popular courses, such as John Gaddis's Cold War history class, seem more like performances, students say. Robert Shiller, winner of the 2013 Nobel Prize in Economic Sciences, teaches introductory economics. A political science major recalls a freshman seminar in which he was taught by "one of the discoverers of the entire field of nanoscience," adding, "None of us in that class are going to become nanoscientists, but he was ecstatic to teach us all about it nonetheless."

A senior engineering major says that Yale is a magnet for overachievers "who are passionate about something, whether it be research, community service, music, art, or anything else." Nevertheless, a freshman adds, "The student body is amazingly down-to-earth, especially given the insane accomplishments and talents of the students." Ninety-three percent of undergraduates are from outside of Connecticut, including many from the Northeast and 11 percent from other countries, and the

Ninety-five percent of science and engineering majors do research with faculty members in any of the more than 800 labs on campus.

Students spend two weeks "shopping" at the beginning of each term, sampling various offerings before finalizing their schedules.

student body is evenly split along gender lines. African Americans make up 7 percent of students, Hispanics 11 percent, and Asian Americans 17 percent. Yalies are far less conservative than their counterparts at Harvard and Princeton, and they aren't shy about expressing their opinions. "Yale students are incredibly active politically and socially and are very conscious of world issues," one history major says. No merit or athletic awards are available, but the university meets the full demonstrated financial need of all its undergraduate students, and students are not expected to take out loans. Yale seeks to attract more students from low-income backgrounds; families making less than $65,000 a year don't pay any portion of the cost of their child's education.

The 12 residential colleges that serve as Yale's dorms are the focal points for undergraduate social life and central to the distinct culture of Yale. "Yale's dorms are like palaces," cheers one student. Endowed by Yale graduate Edward S. Harkness (who also began the house system at Harvard) and modeled on those at Oxford and Cambridge, Yale's colleges provide intimate living/learning communities, creating the atmosphere of a small liberal arts college within a large research university. A senior says they are "similar to the house system at Hogwarts in the Harry Potter series." Each college has a library, dining hall, and special facilities such as a photography darkroom or small theater—one is even said to have an endowment used solely for whipped cream. All colleges also have their own dean and affiliated faculty members, a few of whom live in the college, who can help undergraduates struggling to adapt to the rigors of college life. Residential colleges organize social and cultural events, including teas, where prominent public figures meet with groups of students. College-sponsored seminars, along with plays, concerts, lectures, and other events, add to the cultural life of the university as a whole. The 15 dining halls serve good meals and multiple options. "Dining has been a pleasant surprise," says a student. A senior notes, "We have an iPhone app that tells you the menu in each dining hall each night. It even tells you how crowded they are in real time."

Much of each residential college's distinctive identity comes from its architecture. Some buildings are fashioned in a craggy, fortress-like Gothic style, while others are done in the more open colonial style, with redbrick and green shutters as the prevailing motif. All colleges have their own special nooks and crannies with cryptic inscriptions paying tribute to illustrious Yalies of generations past. Most freshmen live together on the Old Campus, the historic 19th-century quadrangle, before moving into their colleges

"The student body is amazingly down-to-earth, especially given the insane accomplishments and talents of the students."

as sophomores. Students generally live in suites with a living room and single or double bedrooms, but many seniors get singles. Residential colleges offer amenities such as gyms, kitchens, TV and game rooms, computer clusters, and "butteries" that sell late-night food. Some upperclassmen move into New Haven, although 84 percent choose to stay on campus all four years. Despite New Haven's urban character, students say that they feel physically safe. A female biochemistry major adds, "There have been sexual assaults on campus, and, fortunately, the school's administration has been responding swiftly and appropriately to discipline the assailant."

In addition to identifying with their colleges, many Yale students identify strongly with extracurricular groups, clubs, and organizations, spending most of their waking hours outside class at the newspaper, radio station, or computer center. Particularly clubby are the a cappella singing groups, whose members do everything from drinking together on certain weeknights to touring together during spring break. Many of Yale's mysterious secret societies, such as Skull and Bones (which counts former president George W. Bush and former secretary of state John Kerry as members), have their own mausoleum-like clubhouses and issue invitations to those with the right qualifications. There are also the Yale Anti-Gravity Society and improv comedy groups.

Though studying takes the lion's share of their time, students find ways to unwind. About 10 percent of Yalies belong to a fraternity or sorority, and Greek parties are open to all. "There is not pressure to get involved in a party culture," says a freshman. The undergraduate Yale Symphony Orchestra puts on an original show every

"Dining has been a pleasant surprise."

Halloween that fills Woolsey Hall with students in costume. "The Halloween Show has been home to some of my favorite memories at Yale," says one student. "It is an incredible production." Each year freshmen gather in the Commons for a holiday dinner that features a procession of culinary treats known as the Parade of Comestibles. The evening of the first large snowfall of the season brings the annual snowball fight on Old Campus. Each residential college mounts a spring "fun day" likely to include, in the words of a senior, "a petting zoo, free food, and bouncy castles." For the artistically inclined, there are lots of concerts every weekend and local film societies offer numerous weekend screenings. The Shubert Performing Arts Center hosts touring Broadway musicals, dance companies, musicians, and popular singers. The Tony Award-winning Yale Repertory Theater depends heavily on graduate school talent but always brings in a few top stage stars each season. For those who want more excitement, the typical Yalie refrain on New Haven—"It's halfway between New York and Boston"—tells it all. Metro North trains run almost hourly to New York, and visiting Boston is nearly as easy.

The Yale campus is in the middle of downtown New Haven, a once-gritty small city that is riding the crest of a resurgence that, in the words of a junior psych major, has made it "the perfect blend of manageable quaintness and urban opportunity." A political science major notes, "There is a movie theater, two world-renowned art galleries, a popular dance club, and countless shops and restaurants within a 10-minute walk from my dorm room." Natural history and art museums on and near campus, especially the Yale University Art Gallery and the British Art Center, are excellent. The city's long-standing theatrical tradition—it was once the place to try out plays headed for Broadway—continues at two grand old theater and concert halls a block from campus. Locals will swear that Pepe's on Wooster Street was the first (and best!) pizza parlor in the country, while Louis's Lunch was the first true hamburger joint. Once-testy relations between students and locals are improving. "The city definitely caters to students to make

"The city definitely caters to students to make them feel welcome and safe."

them feel welcome and safe," says a biochemistry major, and nearly two-thirds of Yale undergrads reciprocate by doing volunteer work in town through Dwight Hall, the largest college community service organization in the country. "Community service is part of the fabric that makes Yale what it is," says a senior. "It's a major part of student life and culture."

Yale fields a full complement of 33 athletic teams (the Bulldogs), which play in Division I. Recent Ivy League champions include men's ice hockey and basketball, women's volleyball, and co-ed sailing. The co-ed and women's sailing teams also claimed recent national titles. More than half the student body takes part in intramural competition among the residential colleges; the winning college gets the coveted Tying Cup. The annual Harvard–Yale football game—known simply as The Game—is an occasion for tailgating by thousands of blue-clad students, whether it takes place in New Haven or Cambridge. Yale's Mock Trial team won the national championship in 2016.

Yale is one of America's oldest institutions of higher learning, and students and graduates here take seriously the intonation, "For God, for country, and for Yale." For proof, just remember that among its alumni, Yale counts the presidents

The undergraduate Yale Symphony Orchestra puts on an original show every Halloween that fills Woolsey Hall with students in costume.

Overlaps

Harvard, Princeton, Stanford, Columbia, University of Pennsylvania, Brown, Cornell University, Duke

or former presidents of about 70 other colleges and universities and five U.S. presidents. As the university moves into its fourth century, its past and former students continue to make their marks on the world. "When I meet other Yalies abroad, we can immediately connect by talking about our residential colleges, and other shared Yale traditions, such as the Halloween show," says one student. Yale has found a way to pursue world-class teaching and learning with what one senior describes as "a collegial and relaxed atmosphere that makes your four years here some of the most enjoyable times of your life."

If You Apply To >

Yale: Single choice early action: Nov. 1. Regular decision: Jan. 2. Financial aid: Mar. 15. Application fee: $80. Campus interviews: optional, evaluative. Alumni interviews: recommended, evaluative. SATs (with essay) or ACTs (with writing): required. Subject Tests: recommended. Letters of recommendation: required. Essay: required. Accepts the Common Application with supplement.

Consortia

Students who feel that attending a small college might limit their college experiences should realize that many of these schools have banded together to offer unusual programs that they could not support on their own. Offerings range from exchange programs—trading places with a student on another campus—to a semester or two anywhere in the world on one of the seven continents or somewhere out at sea.

The following is a list of some of the largest and oldest of these programs, some sponsored by groups of colleges and others by independent agencies. An asterisk (*) after the name of a college indicates that the institution is the subject of a write-up in the *Fiske Guide*.

The **Associated Colleges of the Midwest** (www.acm.edu) comprises 14 institutions in five states: Colorado College* in Colorado; Lake Forest*, Knox*, and Monmouth in Illinois; Coe, Cornell*, Grinnell*, and Luther College in Iowa; Carleton*, Macalester*, and St. Olaf* in Minnesota; and Beloit*, Lawrence*, and Ripon* in Wisconsin.

The consortium offers its students semester-long programs to study art in London and Florence, humanities and culture in Florence, ecology and human origins in Tanzania, development in Southern Africa in Botswana, culture and tradition in India, liberal arts or environmental science in Brazil (Brazil programs are taught in Portuguese and restricted to ACM students), language and culture in Costa Rica, tropical field research in Costa Rica, and a semester-long program about contemporary China in Shanghai. Students can stay in Japan for either a term or an academic year with a host family. During the summer, students can also travel to Pune, India, or Mexico City, Mexico, for service learning programs.

The Arts of London and the Florence programs are the most popular with students. Language study is a component of all the ACM overseas programs. Prior language study is required for the programs in Costa Rica, Japan, and Mexico. Domestic off-campus programs include Humanities at the Newberry Library (an in-depth research project) or a semester in Chicago in the arts, business, entrepreneurship and society, urban education, or urban studies. Scientists can study at the Oak Ridge National Laboratory in Tennessee.

Living arrangements vary with the program and region. Students in Chicago programs live in apartments and residential hotels. Oak Ridge scientists live in an apartment complex. There are no comprehensive costs for any of the ACM programs, domestic or foreign, and tuition is based on the home school's standard fees. The programs are open to sophomores, juniors, and seniors majoring in all fields. The only programs that tend to be especially strict with admissions are the Oak Ridge, Newberry, and Brazil arrangements.

The **Associated Colleges of the South** (www.colleges.org), incorporated in 1991, is composed of 16 Southern schools (Birmingham–Southern College*, Centenary, Centre College*, Davidson*, Furman*, Hendrix*, Millsaps College*, Morehouse College*, Rhodes College*, the University of Richmond*, Rollins*, University of the South (Sewanee)*, Spelman College*, Southwestern University*, Trinity University*, and Washington and Lee University*). Established to strengthen liberal education in the South, the consortium focuses on academic program development (with attention to international programs) and faculty, staff, and student development. ACS has a vision for 2020 to improve its liberal arts through residential experiences and collaboration between the 16 members. Overseas courses are offered year-round. Affiliated and ACS-managed programs offer students several international opportunities: They can trace the transformation of Central Europe through study based in Hungary, explore field biology and sustainable development in Costa Rica, or participate in service learning in Honduras. Students can also study at Oxford and the University of Sydney.

The **Atlanta Regional Council for Higher Education** (www.atlantahighered.org) comprises 20 public and private colleges and universities in the Atlanta area, as well as several specialized institutions of higher education.

Members are Agnes Scott College*, Brenau University, Clark Atlanta University, Clayton State University, Columbia Theological Seminary, Emory University*, Georgia Gwinnett College, Georgia Institute of Technology*, Georgia State University, Interdenominational Theological Center, Kennesaw State University, Mercer University (Atlanta and Macon campuses), Morehouse College*, Morehouse School of Medicine, Oglethorpe University*,

Savannah College of Art and Design–Atlanta, Spelman College*, the University of Georgia*, and the University of West Georgia.

Students from member colleges and universities may register for approved courses at any of the other institutions, including those with highly specialized courses. The consortium's interlibrary lending program uses a daily truck delivery service to put more than 10 million books and other resources at students' disposal.

The **Christian College Consortium** (www.ccconsortium.org) comprises 13 of the nation's top evangelical liberal arts schools that collectively enroll 25,000 undergraduates and 7,500 graduates: Asbury University, Bethel University (MN), George Fox University, Gordon College*, Greenville College, Houghton College*, Malone University, Messiah College, Seattle Pacific University, Taylor University, Trinity International University (IL), Westmont College, and Wheaton College (IL)*.

The consortium offers a "student visitors program" whereby students can spend a semester—with little paper pushing—at any of the member schools. Each school sets the GPA requirement for its off-campus options, which include sustainable tropical agriculture in Haiti, Chinese economic development, and Christian service learning in Guatemala.

More than 100 students (not including freshmen) participate each year, and the cost is strictly the home school's regular fees. Other than a reasonably good grade average, there are no special requirements. Consortium schools share a wide array of international programs on a space-available basis.

The **Five College Consortium** (www.fivecolleges.edu) is a nonprofit organization that comprises Amherst College*, Hampshire College*, Mount Holyoke College*, Smith College*, and the University of Massachusetts Amherst* and is designed to enhance the social and cultural life of the 30,000 students attending these Pioneer Valley colleges. Established in 1965 and legally known as Five Colleges, Inc., this cooperative arrangement allows any undergraduate at the four private liberal arts colleges and UMass Amherst to take any of the 5,300 courses offered by the 2,200-member faculty for credit and use the library facilities of any of the other four schools. A free bus service shuttles students between the schools.

The consortium sponsors joint departments in dance and astronomy, as well as a number of interdisciplinary programs, including African American/black studies, East Asian languages, coastal and marine sciences, Near Eastern studies, and peace and world security studies. Certificate programs are available in Asian studies, African studies, Buddhist studies, coastal and marine sciences (not open to Amherst College), cognitive neuroscience (closed to both Amherst College and UMass Amherst), culture, health, and science, ethnomusicology (pending approval at UMass Amherst), international relations, Latin American studies, logic, Middle Eastern studies, American Indian studies, Russian studies, East European studies, and Eurasian studies. There are five college centers for American studies, East Asian studies, women's studies research, and world languages. Additionally, the consortium offers a major in film studies.

Students from the four smaller colleges benefit from the large number of course choices available at the university. The undergrads from UMass Amherst, in turn, take advantage of the small-college atmosphere as well as particularly strong departments such as art at Smith, sculpture at Mount Holyoke, and film and photography at Hampshire. There is also a Five College Orchestra and an open theater auditions policy that allows students to audition for parts in productions at any of the colleges. The social and cultural aspects of the Five College Consortium are more informal than the academic structure. The consortium puts out a calendar listing art shows, lectures, concerts, and films at the five schools, as well as the bus schedules. In addition, student-sponsored parties are advertised on all campuses, and there is a good deal of informal meeting of students from the various schools.

For those students taking courses on other campuses, one's home-school meal ticket is valid on any of the five member campuses for lunch. Dinners are available with special permission. Taking classes at other schools is encouraged, but not usually for first-semester freshmen. The consortium is a big drawing card for all schools involved.

The **Great Lakes Colleges Association** (www.glca.org) comprises 13 independent liberal arts institutions in four states. In Indiana: DePauw University*, Earlham College*, and Wabash College*. In Michigan: Albion College*, Hope College*, and Kalamazoo College*. In Ohio: Antioch College, Denison University*, Kenyon

College*, Oberlin College*, Ohio Wesleyan University*, and The College of Wooster*. And, in Pennsylvania: Allegheny College*. The GLCA offers students off-campus opportunities both in the U.S. and overseas. Domestic programs include a liberal arts urban-study semester in Philadelphia; a New York City arts program; a Newberry Library humanities program in Chicago; and scientific study at Oak Ridge National Laboratory in Tennessee (see the Associated Colleges of the Midwest description for further detail). International offerings include a Japan program based at Waseda University and the Border Studies Program, a hybrid domestic/international program focusing on immigration and other border issues in Tucson, Arizona, and Mexico. The ACM, a similar consortium, collaborates with the GLCA on the Oak Ridge Sciences, Newberry Library, and Japan Study programs. Primarily juniors participate, but the programs are open to sophomores and seniors. The domestic programs in New York and Philadelphia are popular domestic choices for American as well as international students.

The **Lehigh Valley Association of Independent Colleges** (www.lvaic.org) is a half-century old cooperative effort between six colleges in the same area of Pennsylvania: Cedar Crest College, DeSales University, Lafayette College*, Lehigh University*, Moravian College, and Muhlenberg College*.

Approximately 400 students each year cross-register at member campuses, although the bulk of the activity occurs between schools that are closest to each other. LVAIC facilitates occasional conferences at member colleges on women's studies, ecology and evolution, mathematics, social justice, and medieval studies. A Jewish studies program, headquartered at Lehigh, draws on the faculties of Lehigh, Lafayette, and Muhlenberg. Faculty members travel from college to college in order to offer students a variety of courses in this field. The association's Consortium Professors program puts faculty on two other member campuses each year to teach unusual or special-interest courses. Several members exchange courses by video conferences. Special seminars are arranged at central locations for selected students, with transportation provided. Students at each college are eligible for reduced-rate tickets to plays and other events on campuses of association schools. But the most frequently used service of the association is its interlibrary loan program, which permits students at one institution to use the research facilities of the others. Summer study abroad programs take students to the United Kingdom, Germany, Italy, and Spain.

The **Maritime Studies Program** (www.williams.edu/williamsmystic) of Williams College and Mystic Seaport Museum is an interdisciplinary semester, established in 1977, designed for about 20 undergraduates (primarily juniors, but some second-semester sophomores and seniors) who are eager to augment liberal arts education with an in-depth study of the sea. Participants take four Williams College courses (maritime history, literature of the sea, marine policy, and oceanography or marine ecology). Classes are taught with an emphasis on independent research in the setting of the Mystic Seaport Museum. Classroom lectures are enhanced by hands-on experience in celestial navigation, board building, sailing, blacksmithing, and other historic crafts. Students spend two weeks offshore in deep-sea oceanographic research aboard a traditionally rigged schooner highlighting the purpose of the program: to understand our relationship with the sea—past, present, and future.

Although students from all accredited colleges and universities can apply to the program, most participants come from 20 affiliate colleges: Amherst College*, Bates College*, Bowdoin College*, Colby College*, Colgate University*, Connecticut College*, Dartmouth College*, Hamilton College*, Middlebury College*, Mount Holyoke College*, Oberlin College*, Smith College*, Trinity College*, Tufts University*, Union College*, Vassar College*, Wellesley College*, Wesleyan University*, Wheaton College (MA)*, and Williams College*. Credit is granted through Williams College, and financial aid is transferable. Students are evenly split between scientific and humanities backgrounds, and those from all four-year liberal arts colleges are encouraged to apply.

SEA Semester (www.sea.edu, not to be confused with Semester at Sea), established in 1971, is a similar venture for water lovers, but it is designed for students geared more toward the theoretical and practical applications of the subject. Each year, two 12-week voyages are offered in both the fall and spring, as is an eight-week summer trip. Each expedition is thematic and prerequisites vary accordingly. For example, Ocean Voyages is open to students from any major, while Documenting Change in the Caribbean and Oceans and Climate are designed for students from the social sciences and sciences, respectively. Depending on the program, 25 or 48 students are in each session. All majors are considered as long as students are in good academic standing, submit transcripts and recommendations, and have an interview with an alumnus in their area.

Students spend the first half of the term living on Sea's campus in the Woods Hole area and immersing themselves in oceanography and maritime and nautical studies. Independent-study projects begun ashore are completed during the sea component aboard either a schooner or a brigantine, which cruises along the eastern seaboard and out into the Atlantic, North Atlantic, or Caribbean, depending on the season. Recent Pacific programs include San Francisco to Honolulu, Honolulu to the Midway Islands, and Mexico to Tahiti. Six weeks on the ocean is when theory becomes reality, and the usual mission consists of enough navigation, oceanographic data collection, and record keeping to keep even Columbus on the right course. Students from affiliated colleges (American University, Barnard College*, Boston University*, Carleton College*, College of Charleston*, Colgate University*, Connecticut College*, Cornell University*, University of Denver*, DePauw University*, Drexel University*, Eckerd College*, The Evergreen State College*, Franklin and Marshall College*, The George Washington University*, Hamilton College*, Hawaii Pacific University, Ithaca College*, Jacksonville University, Lafayette College*, Lawrence University*, Macalester College, University of Massachusetts Dartmouth, University of New Hampshire*, University of North Carolina at Chapel Hill*, University of Northern Colorado, Northeastern University*, Oberlin College*, Oregon State University*, University of Pennsylvania*, Purdue University*, Reed College*, University of Rhode Island*, Rice University*, Ripon College*, Rochester Institute of Technology*, Roger Williams University, University of San Diego*, Stonehill College, SUNY College of Environmental Science and Forestry, Syracuse University*, Ursinus College*, Utica College, Villanova University*, and Whitman College) receive a semester's worth of credit directly through their school. Students from other schools must receive credit through Boston University.

Semester at Sea (www.semesteratsea.com) takes qualified students from any college and whisks them around the globe on a study/cruise odyssey. Established in 1976 to promote global education and understanding, the program is sponsored by Colorado State University, and administered by the nonprofit Institute for Shipboard Education. It takes around 600 students each term (from second-semester freshmen to grads) and puts them on a ship bound for almost everywhere. The vessel itself is a college campus in its own right. Seventy-five courses are taught by 39 professors in subjects ranging from anthropology to marketing, and usually stressing the international scene as well as the sea itself. What's more, over 50 student organizations, including art, theater, music, service, journalism, and student government, can be found on board. When students aren't at sea, they're in port in any of 12 foreign countries in Europe, the Middle East, Asia, Africa, and South America, and it's not uncommon for leaders and diplomats to meet them along the way.

The program requires a cumulative GPA of 2.75 or higher. Limited financial aid is available in the form of a range of merit scholarships based on demonstrated leadership and GPA. Work-study and the usual federal grants and loans can help to defray the cost. Credits are awarded by CSU. Most colleges do recognize the Semester at Sea program and will provide participating students with a full term's worth of credits.

The **Twelve-College Exchange Program** comprises 11 selective schools in the Northeast: Amherst College*, Bowdoin College*, Connecticut College*, Dartmouth College*, Mount Holyoke College*, Smith College*, Trinity College (CT)*, Vassar College*, Wellesley College*, Wesleyan University*, and Wheaton College (MA)*. In addition, the Williams-Mystic maritime program is open to exchange students.

The program means that students enrolled in any of these schools can visit for a semester or two (usually the latter) with a minimum of red tape. Approximately 300 students utilize the opportunity each year; most of them are juniors. Placement is determined mainly by available space, but students must also display good academic standing. While the home college arranges the exchange, students must meet the fees and standards of the host school. Financial-aid holders can usually carry their packages with them. Study at the Eugene O'Neill National Theater Institute is also available through the consortium.

The **Washington Semester of American University** (www.american.edu/washingtonsemester) takes about 750 students each year from hundreds of colleges across the country (who meet the minimum academic qualification of a 2.75 GPA) and gives them unbeatable academic and political opportunities in the nation's capital. The program is the oldest of its kind in Washington.

Students take part in a semester of seminars with policymakers and lobbyists, an internship, and a choice between an elective course at the university or a self-designed, in-depth research project. Program concentrations include American politics, foreign policy, global economics and business, international law and organizations, journalism and new media, justice and law, and sustainable development. Recent seminar topics include Peace and Conflict Studies with travel to Serbia, Croatia, and Bosnia; an International Environment and Development practicum based in Ghana; and an American Politics seminar that brought notables such as Justice Scalia and Sy Hersh to campus. Students live in dorms on the campus and are guided by a staff of 21 American University professors.

Ninety percent of the students are drawn from 240 affiliated schools. Each semester, approximately 100 students from nonaffiliated schools participate. Although admissions competition depends on the home school and how many it chooses to nominate, the average GPA hovers around a 3.32. Most who participate are juniors, but second semester sophomores and seniors get equal consideration. The most common major of participating students is Political Science, however this program attracts students from all disciplines. The cost is either American University's tuition, room, board, and fees or that of the home school. Just over a third of the affiliated colleges are profiled in the *Fiske Guide*.

Index

Acknowledgments

FISKE GUIDE TO COLLEGES STAFF

Editor: Edward B. Fiske
Managing Editor: Michelle Lecuyer
Contributing Editor: Bruce G. Hammond
Production Coordinator: Julia Fiske Hogan

The *Fiske Guide to Colleges* reflects the talents, energy, and ideas of many people. Chief among them are Michelle Lecuyer, the managing editor, and Julia Fiske Hogan, the production coordinator. I am also grateful for the support of Bruce G. Hammond, my coauthor on the *Fiske Guide to Getting Into the Right College* and other books about college admissions. Thanks also to Shawn Logue, a longtime colleague, for his continuing interest in the *Fiske Guide* and his help with things technological.

One of the great joys of producing the *Fiske Guide* each year is the opportunity to work alongside the talented and dedicated members of the editorial team at Sourcebooks. They are true professionals who understand that providing college-bound students with accurate information about colleges and universities is an important mission. Among them are Dominique Raccah, Todd Stocke, Anna Michels, Alex Zimay, Chris Francis, Becca Sage, Heather Hall, and Sarah Otterness. Others who played important roles were Bob Lessard, Tina Silva, and Lin Miceli. Thanks also to Alexis Brooke Redding for her thoughtful editorial suggestions and to Joe Klunder and Matthew Simons for their research assistance.

In the final analysis, the *Fiske Guide* is dependent on the contributions of the thousands of students and college administrators who took the time to answer detailed and demanding questionnaires. Their candor and cooperation are deeply appreciated. While I, of course, accept full responsibility for the final product, the quality and usefulness of the book is a testimony to their thoughtful reflections on the colleges and universities with which they are associated.

Edward B. Fiske
Durham, NC
May 2017

EDITORIAL ADVISORY GROUP

Richard Avitabile, Westport, CT
Nancy Beane, Atlanta, GA
Sam Bigelow, Concord, MA
Eileen Blattner, Shaker Heights, OH
Lauren Cook, San Francisco, CA
Carol Gill, Mount Kisco, NY
Peggy Hoch, Santa Clara, CA
Marsha Irwin, San Francisco, CA
Gerimae Kleinman, Delray Beach, FL
Matt Lane, Ross, CA
Katrin Muir Lau, Houston, TX

Frank Leana, St. Louis Park, MN
David Miller, Pebble Beach, CA
Judy Muir, Houston, TX
Susan Moriarty Paton, New Haven, CT
Gay S. Pepper, Naples, FL
William Pruden III, Raleigh, NC
Jan Russell, Moraga, CA
Rod Skinner, Milton, MA
Geoff Smith, San Francisco, CA
Mark van Warmerdam, Danville, CA

COLLEGE COUNSELORS ADVISORY GROUP

Marilyn Albarelli, Moravian Academy (PA)

Christine Asmussen, St. Andrew's–Sewanee School (TN)

Greg Birk, American School in Switzerland, Montagnola (CH)

Francine E. Block, American College Admissions Consultants (PA)

Robin Boren, Education Consultant (CO)

John B. Boshoven, Community High School & Jewish Academy of Metro Detroit (MI)

Mimi Bradley, St. Andrew's Episcopal School (MS)

Claire Cafaro, Clear Directions (NJ)

Nancy Caine, St. Augustine H.S. (CA)

Jane M. Catanzaro, College Advising Services (CT)

Kathy Cleaver, Durham Academy (NC)

Alice Cotti, Polytechnic School (CA)

Rod Cox, St. Johns Country Day School (FL)

Kim Crockard, Crockard College Counseling (AL)

Carroll K. Davis, North Central H.S. (IN)

Lexi Eagles, Greensboro Day School (NC)

Ralph S. Figueroa, Albuquerque Academy (NM)

Emily E. FitzHugh, The Gunnery (CT)

Larry Fletcher, Salesianum School (DE)

H. Scotte Gordon, Moses Brown School (RI)

Freida Gottsegen, Education Consultant (GA)

Molly Gotwals, Suffield Academy (CT)

Kathleen Barnes Grant, The Catlin Gabel School (OR)

Mimi Grossman, St. Mary's Episcopal School (TN)

Elizabeth Hall, Education Consulting Services (TX)

Darnell Heywood, Columbus Academy (OH)

Bruce Hunter, Rowland Hall–St. Mark's School (UT)

Gerimae Kleinman, Delray Beach (FL)

Sharon Koenings, Brookfield Academy (WI)

MaryJane London, Los Angeles Center for Enriched Studies (CA)

Martha Lyman, Deerfield Academy (MA)

Brad MacGowan, Newton North H.S. (MA)

Robert S. MacLellan Jr., Hebron Academy (ME)

Susan Marrs, The Seven Hills School (OH)

Karen A. Mason, Germantown Academy (PA)

Lynne McConnell, Rumson–Fair Haven Regional H.S. (NJ)

Lisa Micele, University of Illinois Laboratory H.S. (IL)

Corky Miller-Strong, The Culver Academies (IN)

Janet Miranda, Prestonwood Christian Academy (TX)

Gunnar W. Olson, Indian Springs School (AL)

Stuart Oremus, Wellington School (OH)

Julie Rollins, Episcopal H.S. (TX)

Heidi Rose, Crystal Springs Uplands School (CA)

Bruce Scher, Chicagoland Jewish H.S. (IL)

David Schindel, Sandia Preparatory School (NM)

Barbara Simmons, Notre Dame High School (CA)

Paul M. Stoneham, The Key School (MD)

Linda Zimring, Los Angeles United School District (CA)

About the Authors

In 1980, when he was education editor of the *New York Times*, **Edward B. Fiske** sensed that college-bound students and their families needed better information on which to base their educational choices. Thus was born the *Fiske Guide to Colleges*. A graduate of Wesleyan University, Fiske did graduate work at Columbia University and assorted other bastions of higher learning. He left the *Times* in 1991 to pursue a variety of educational and journalistic interests, including a book on school reform, *Smart Schools, Smart Kids*. When not visiting colleges, he can be found hiking, sailing, or doing research on the educational problems of South Africa and other Third World countries for UNESCO and other international organizations. Fiske lives in Durham, North Carolina, near the campus of Duke University, where his wife, Helen Ladd, is a member of the faculty. They are coauthors of *When Schools Compete: A Cautionary Tale, Elusive Equity: Education Reform in Post-Apartheid South Africa*, and *Handbook of Research in Education Finance and Policy*.

© Sourcebooks, Inc.

Fiske Guide to Colleges 2018 is the seventh edition of the *Fiske Guide* that **Michelle Lecuyer** has worked on, and her first as managing editor. After serving in a range of editorial roles at Sourcebooks, Inc., the publisher of the *Fiske Guide*, she joined the *Fiske Guide to Colleges* staff as managing editor in 2016. Lecuyer also works as an independent writer and editor for a variety of print and online publishers. She earned a B.A. from Augustana College (IL) and an M.A. from Iowa State University. She lives near Chicago.

Invitation to Readers

The *Fiske Guide to Colleges* welcomes comments from readers on the write-ups contained in the guide, as well as suggestions regarding ways that we could better serve our readers. Please send your comments to:

Fiske Guide to Colleges
Tel: (603) 835-6523
Email: editor@fiskeguide.com

Thanks for your interest in the *Fiske Guide*.

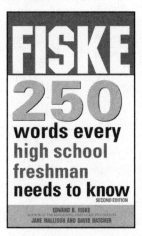

FISKE'S

College Admission Pledge
for Students

I have accepted the fact that my parents are clueless. I am serene. I will betray not a tremor when they offer opinions or advice, no matter how laughable. My soul will be light as a feather when my mother elbows her way to the front of my college tour and talks the guide's ear off. I am serene.

Going to college is a stressful time for my parents, even though they are not the ones going. I recognize that neurosis is beyond anyone's control. Each week, I will calmly reassure them that I am working on my essays, have registered for my tests, am finishing my applications, have scheduled my interviews, am aware of all deadlines, and will have everything done in plenty of time. I will smile good-naturedly as my parent asks four follow-up questions at College Night.

I will try not to say "no" simply because my parents say "yes," and I will remain open to the possibility, however improbable, that they may have a point. I may not be fully conscious of my anxieties about the college search—the fear of being judged and the fear of leaving home are both strong. I don't really want to get out of here as much as I say I do, and it is easier to put off thinking about the college search than to get it done. My parents are right about the importance of being proactive, even if they do get carried away.

Though the college search belongs to me, I will listen to my parents. They know me better than anyone else, and they are the ones who will pay most of the bills. Their ideas about what will be best for me are based on years of experience in the real world. I will seriously consider what they say as I form my own opinions.

I must take charge of the college search. If I do, the nagging will stop, and everyone's anxiety will go down. My parents have given me a remarkable gift—the ability to think and do for myself. I know I can do it with a little help from Mom and Dad.

FISKE'S
College Admission Pledge
for Parents

I am resigned to the fact that my child's college search will end in disaster. I am serene. Deadlines will be missed and scholarships will be lost as my child lounges under pulsating headphones or stares transfixed at an Xbox. I am a parent and I know nothing. I am serene.

Confronted with endless procrastination, my impulse is to take control—to register for tests, plan visits, schedule interviews, and get applications. It was I who asked those four follow-up questions at College Night—I couldn't help myself. And yet I know that everything will be fine if I can summon the fortitude to relax. My child is smart, capable, and perhaps a little too accustomed to me jumping in and fixing things. I will hold back. I will drop hints and encourage, then back off. I will facilitate rather than dominate. The college search won't happen on my schedule, but it will happen.

I will not get too high or low about any facet of the college search. By doing so, I give it more importance than it really has. My child's self-worth may already be too wrapped up in getting an acceptance letter. I will attempt to lessen the fear rather than heighten it.

I will try not to say "no" simply because my son or daughter says "yes," and I will remain open to the possibility, however improbable, that my child has the most important things under control. I understand that my anxiety comes partly from a sense of impending loss. I can feel my child slipping away. Sometimes I hold on too tightly or let social acceptability cloud the issue of what is best.

I realize that my child is almost ready to go and that a little rebellion at this time of life can be a good thing. I will respect and encourage independence, even if some of it is expressed as resentment toward me. I will make suggestions with care and try to avoid unnecessary confrontation.

Paying for college is my responsibility. I will take a major role in the search for financial aid and scholarships and speak honestly to my child about the financial realities we face.

I must help my son or daughter take charge of the college search. I will try to support without smothering, encourage without annoying, and consult without controlling. The college search is too big to be handled alone—I will be there every step of the way.

Notes

Notes

Notes